World History

Patterns of Civilization

Area Specialists

Early Civilizations — Elizabeth Carney, Clemson University, Clemson, South Carolina

Classical Civilizations — Louis Cohn-Haft, Smith College, Northampton, Massachusetts

Middle Ages — Thomas Glick, Boston University, Boston, Massachusetts

Early Modern Europe — Helen Nader, Indiana University, Bloomington, Indiana

Nineteenth-Century Europe — Charles F. Delzell, Vanderbilt University, Nashville, Tennessee

Twentieth-Century Europe — Marian Nelson, University of Nebraska, Omaha, Nebraska

Africa — Marylee Crofts Wiley, African Studies Center, Michigan State University, East Lansing, Michigan

— Burton F. Beers, North Carolina State University, Raleigh, North Carolina

Latin America — Stanley R. Ross, University of Texas, Austin, Texas

Middle East — Helen Rivlin, State University of New York, Binghamton, New York

Curriculum Advisors

Susan K. Hustleby, Byron-Bergen Central School, Bergen, New York
Aaron L. Pope, Westchester Senior High School, Houston, Texas

Teacher Reviewers

Dean Barlow, Kennedy High School, Winston-Salem, North Carolina
Dennis R. Dreher, DeVilbiss High School, Toledo, Ohio
Gloria J. Emanuel, Waco High School, Waco, Texas
Jocelyn E. Kimm, North High School, Evansville, Indiana
Ronald W. Kruse, Ygnacio Valley High School, Concord, California
Elizabeth S. Mefford, Northwest School District, Cincinnati, Ohio
Louis Pappas, Highline School District, Seattle, Washington
Charles A. Thompson, Wichita Public Schools, Wichita, Kansas

World History

Patterns of Civilization

Burton F. Beers

Professor of History
North Carolina State University

PRENTICE HALL
Englewood Cliffs, New Jersey

Burton F. Beers

Burton F. Beers is Professor of History at North Carolina State University. In the course of his career, Dr. Beers has taught European history, Asian history, and American history. He has published numerous articles in historical journals and has written several books on East Asia, including *The Far East: A History of Western Impacts and Eastern Responses* with Paul H. Clyde and *China in Old Photographs*. As a consultant to the North Carolina Department of Public Instruction for many years, Dr. Beers has developed social studies curriculum in western and nonwestern studies. He has also planned and directed numerous workshops for social studies teachers.

FOURTH EDITION

SUPPLEMENTARY MATERIALS
Annotated Teacher's Edition
Teacher's Resource Book
Computer Test Bank

ISBN 0-13-968124-8   10 9 8 7 6 5 4

PRENTICE-HALL OF AUSTRALIA, PTY. LTD., Sydney
PRENTICE-HALL CANADA INC., Toronto
PRENTICE-HALL HISPANOAMERICANA, S.A., Mexico
PRENTICE-HALL OF INDIA PRIVATE LTD., New Delhi
PRENTICE-HALL INTERNATIONAL (UK) LIMITED, London
PRENTICE-HALL OF JAPAN, INC., Tokyo
PRENTICE-HALL OF SOUTHEAST ASIA PTE. LTD., Singapore
EDITORA PRENTICE-HALL DO BRASIL LTDA., Rio de Janeiro

Prentice Hall
A Division of Simon & Schuster
Englewood Cliffs, New Jersey

Photo Consultant: Michal Heron
Photo Researcher: Roberta Guerette
Text Maps, Graphs, and Charts: Lee Ames & Zak, Ltd.
Reference Maps: R.R. Donnelley & Sons Company

About the Cover

The illustration on the cover is a bust of Menelaus, which is located in Museo Pio Clementino in the Vatican, Rome. In Greek mythology, Menelaus, the husband of Helen of Troy, was king of Sparta. A brother of Agamemnon, he appears as a character in Homer's *Iliad* and *Odyssey*.

Illustration Credits

Frequently cited sources are abbreviated as follows: AMNH, American Museum of Natural History; TBM, The British Museum; EPA, Editorial Photocolor Archives; LC, Library of Congress; NYPL, New York Public Library; UPI, United Press International.

key to position of illustrations:
b, bottom; *l,* left; *r,* right; *t,* top

Cover Scala/Art Resource **Pages ii-iii** Clockwise from top right: Lee Boltin; Lee Boltin, Collection of Laurie Platt Winfrey; Collection of Laurie Platt Winfrey; Art Resource; Lee Bolton; **v** *t* Scala/Art Resource; *b* Collection of Laurie Platt Winfrey; **vi** *t, b* Giraudon/Art Resource; **vii** *tl* The Granger Collection; *tr* Collection of Laurie Platt Winfrey; *b* The Granger Collection; **viii** *t, b* Giraudon/Art Resource; **ix** Scala/Art Resource; **x** *t* The Granger Collection; *b* Giraudon/Art Resource; **xi** *t* Scala/Art Resource; *b* TBM; **xii** *t* Chicago Historical Society; *b* Scala/Art Resource; **xiii** *t* Collection of Laurie Platt Winfrey; *b* The Granger Collection; **xiv** *t* LOC; *b* Marc & Evelyne Bernheim/Woodfin Camp & Associates; **xv** *t* Rene Burri/Magnum; *b* Steve Benbow/Woodfin Camp & Associates.

UNIT ONE **Page xx** *tl* © David Mazonovicz/Art Resource; *tr* Lee Boltin; *bl* Giraudon/Art Resource; *br* Collection of Laurie Platt Winfrey; **1** *tl* SEF/Art Resource; *tr* Newsweek Books Picture Collection; *bl, br* Scala/Art Resource; **2** The British Tourist Authority; **4** Lee Boltin; **5** EPA; **7** French Government Tourist Office; **8** John Nance/Panamin-Magnum Photos, Inc.; **10, 14** EPA/Scala; **17** Diane Shapiro; **18** EPA; **21** Maria Da Rocha; **23** EPA/E. Peter Ayala; **25** EPA/Borromeo; **26** Oriental Institute; **30** EPA/Scala; **33, 34** TBM; **39** The Granger Collection; **46** Courtesy, Museum of Fine Arts, Boston; **49** John Woollen; **49** Courtesy, Museum of Fine Arts, Boston; **52** The Cleveland Museum of Art, Gift of George P. Bickford; **56** Columbia University Libraries; **59** Freer Gallery, Smithsonian Institution.

(continued on page 828)

Contents

Unit Surveys

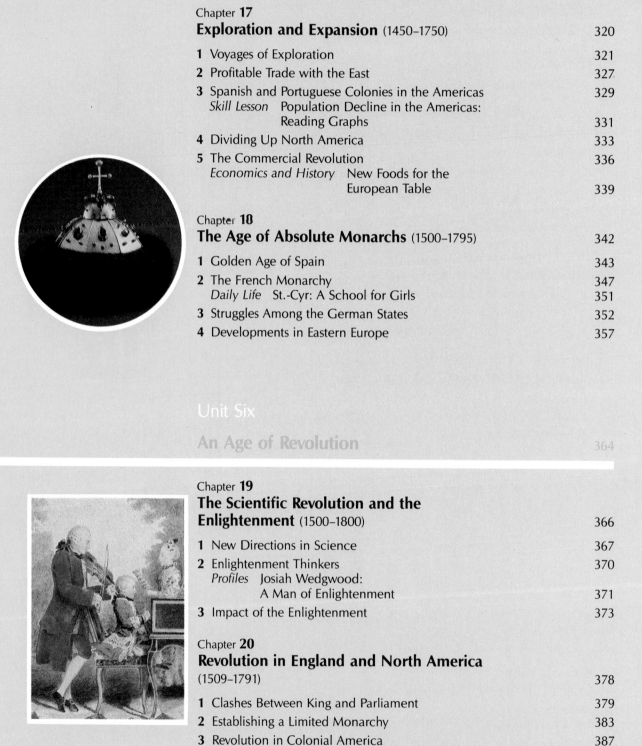

x

Unit Seven

Dawn of the Industrial Age   426

Unit Eight

The Age of Imperialism   505

Unit Nine

World War and Peace   560

Unit Ten

The World Today   666

Special Features

Skill Lessons

Maps

Charts and Graphs

To the Student

Through a study of world history, you will become familiar with the varied experiences of people throughout history as well as with common patterns of civilization. You will learn about the political, social, and economic developments that have created the world as you know it. As you study the past, you will begin to better understand the challenges of the present and the major issues of the future.

Many features have been included in this book to assist you during your course of study:

Unit Time Line Each unit begins with a colorful, illustrated time line that provides an overview of the political, economic, social, and cultural developments you will study in the unit.

Chapter Opener Each chapter opens with an outline of the chapter, an illustration, and a story or an excerpt from a primary source that tells you about a person or an event from the time period covered in the chapter.

Aids for Understanding Several features can help you read and understand the chapters. Each section of a chapter begins with **Read to Learn** statements that provide a focus for the section. Historical terms and vocabulary words are italicized and defined the first time they appear. These terms also appear in a glossary in the Reference Section. Section Reviews include questions to test your understanding.

Illustrations Maps, graphs, charts, paintings, and photographs help you understand major events and developments. They also bring history to life. Captions provide additional tidbits of information, as well as tie the illustration to what you are reading.

Special Features These features give you a close look at people and events in world history. They include profiles of individuals and extracts from primary sources, plus features about daily life, about the impact of economics on history, and about the relationship of the past to the present.

Skill Lessons Special boxed skill lessons help you understand and practice important skills such as reading maps and graphs, using visual evidence and statistics, and analyzing conflicting sources.

Chapter Review The segments included in the Chapter Review allow you to review what you have learned in the chapter. **In Perspective** summarizes the chapter. The **time line** highlights major events and developments to help you understand how they are related in time. **Recalling Facts** questions review basic facts. **Chapter Checkup** questions review key concepts. **Critical Thinking** questions ask you to apply critical thinking skills to deepen your understanding of world history. In **Relating Past to Present,** you will have an opportunity to consider history in the context of the present. In **Developing Basic Skills,** you will practice such skills as comparing, map and graph reading, researching, and analyzing source material.

Reference Section At the back of the book, you will find a section of reference material to be used throughout the course. It includes an atlas, a chronology, a glossary with pronunciation key, a list of suggested readings and an index.

Burton F. Beers

Beginnings of Ancient Civilization

Cave paintings, such as this one found in France, provide information about prehistoric peoples.

Items made from gold and precious stones, such as this pair of sandals, were created for the pharaohs of Egypt.

	3000 B.C.	2500 B.C.	2000 B.C.
POLITICS AND GOVERNMENT		**2700 B.C.** Egyptian rulers take title of pharaoh	**2500–1500 B.C.** Indus Valley civilization in India
ECONOMICS AND TECHNOLOGY	**3000 B.C.** City-states develop in Sumer		**2200 B.C.** Bronzemaking develops in China
SOCIETY AND CULTURE		**2600 B.C.** Great Pyramid of Khufu built in Egypt	**2000 B.C.** Egyptian literature flourishes

In this tomb painting, Egyptians carry offerings of food for their gods.

Bronze bird from ancient China, representing wealth and prestige.

In ancient Persia, scenes of heroic events were carved on the sides of mountains.

Phoenician statue of a woman from Baza.

1500 B.C.	1000 B.C.	500 B.C.
1600 B.C. Shang dynasty is first in China	**1000 B.C.** Kingdom of Israel flourishes under King David	**550 B.C.** Cyrus begins creation of Persian Empire
1700 B.C. Hammurabi's code is first effort to record all laws	**1000 B.C.** Phoenicians develop alphabet	**700 B.C.** Sanskrit emerges as written language in India
1500 B.C. Hittites among first to use iron for spears and battle axes	**800 B.C.** Metal coins become medium of exchange in China and Lydia	

1339 B.C. Figure of an Egyptian official, decorated with gold, found in the tomb of Tutankhamon.

720 B.C. This winged bull was found in the ruins of the temple of Sargon II, an Assyrian emperor.

1

1 Foundations of Civilization

(Prehistory–3000 B.C.)

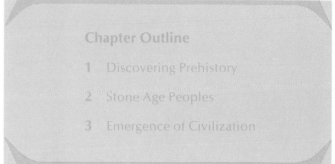

Chapter Outline

1 Discovering Prehistory

2 Stone Age Peoples

3 Emergence of Civilization

Stonehenge in southern England.

Before dawn, crowds gather at Stonehenge, an ancient monument in southern England. The sky brightens early on June 21, the longest day of the year. All eyes are fixed on the huge, heel-shaped stone beyond the great circle of stones. At dawn, the sun sweeps above the horizon. Its warm light shines directly above the heel stone and slices through an archway of stones.

The crowd of visitors is filled with awe. Like others before them, they are fascinated by the stone monument. For centuries, people have wondered who designed this massive circle of stones. When was Stonehenge built? How were the enormous blocks raised into position? Most important, what purpose did Stonehenge serve?

Scholars have offered some answers to questions about Stonehenge. They have learned, for example, that early inhabitants of England started to build Stonehenge about 3,800 years ago. Experts have discovered that the 82 enormous stones of Stonehenge were quarried from a mountain in Wales about 240 miles (386 kilometers) away. The stones were probably loaded on barges, shipped by water, and then hauled on sleds over log rollers to Stonehenge.

Yet many questions about the purpose of Stonehenge remain unanswered. Was it a temple, a palace, or a fort defended by warrior kings? Or was it, as one astronomer has suggested, an ancient calendar used to predict eclipses and other heavenly events?

Stonehenge is one of the many puzzles left by ancient peoples. Tantalizing clues about the distant past are uncovered all the time in different parts of the world. Some evidence, like that at Stonehenge, is on a grand scale. Other evidence includes only fragments of stone, pottery, or bone.

By studying the evidence, scholars have begun to answer questions about ancient peoples. For example, they have discovered that over thousands of years people have made significant advances in knowledge and skills. As you will read, these advances helped build the foundations for civilization.

1 Discovering Prehistory

Read to Learn   ■ how scientists investigate prehistory
                    ■ why some prehistory remains unknown

Historians use many sources to learn about the past. Among the most important sources are written records such as inscriptions, letters, diaries, and newspapers. But written records have existed for only 5,000 or 6,000 years.

Scholars use the term *prehistory* to describe the long period before writing was invented. To learn about prehistory, they use unwritten records such as buildings, pottery, and bone. Historians and scientists work together to unravel the prehistoric mysteries.

The Study of Prehistory

Evidence from prehistory is of special interest to *archaeologists*, scientists who find and analyze objects left by early people. These objects, called *artifacts*, include anything shaped by human beings, such as tools, pottery, and weapons. Archaeology is a branch of anthropology. *Anthropologists* use artifacts and bone fragments to study the physical characteristics of people and the ways people organize societies.

Other scientists are also interested in prehistory. For example, geologists often find *fossils*, evidence of plant or animal life preserved in rock. Fossils show the types of plants and animals that existed at a particular time.

Like detectives, archaeologists piece together what they and other scientists discover to form a picture of the past. As new evidence is uncovered, this picture changes.

Uncovering Archaeological Evidence

Archaeologists have a three-part task in their search for evidence about early people. First, they find a site, or area, where they think early people lived. Second, they excavate, or dig, at the site to uncover artifacts. Third, they analyze any artifacts and draw conclusions about the people who made them.

Although some important sites have been found by accident, more often archaeologists choose places where they think people would have lived. For example, they might pick a location because it was near water. Once a site is located, archaeologists begin to dig carefully. Even the smallest fragment of a piece of pottery can be important. The exact location of every find is noted. Then the objects are cleaned and marked for identification.

A major step in the analysis of artifacts is estimating their ages, or dating them. Scientists have developed several methods for dating an object. The carbon-14 method* can be used to date organic matter—that is, anything that was once alive, such as wood and hair. A second method of dating objects is called amino acid racemization (ras eh mih ZAY shuhn). Some scientists prefer this method since it can be used to date items that are up to one million years old. The carbon 14 method can be used to date only

_____
* When a living organism dies, the radiocarbon atoms in its cells begin to disintegrate, or decay. By measuring the rate of decay, scientists can estimate how long the organism has been dead.

The skeleton of this fish was buried thousands of years ago. By studying fossils and the rocks surrounding them, scientists have developed theories about the climate in which prehistoric plants and animals lived.

items that are up to 40,000 years old. Finally, the potassium argon method is used to calculate the age of volcanic rock and thereby the age of any objects preserved in the rock.

Unanswered Questions

Archaeologists have made impressive advances over the past 30 years. New methods of dating artifacts, aerial photography to find likely sites, and computer analysis of bone fragments are just a few of the techniques that are revealing new evidence about prehistory. But new discoveries can raise as many questions as they answer.

Many questions remain unanswered because so few artifacts survive. Over thousands of years, much evidence has been destroyed by natural elements. Excavations often produce only tiny bone fragments or a few tools. With such limited evidence, views of prehistoric life can vary.

Some evidence about prehistory has also been destroyed by human settlement. Yet much remains. Even today, construction workers discover artifacts. For example, ancient ruins were uncovered in Mexico City during the construction of subways. In a race with time, archaeologists have been able to preserve some valuable remains. As you will read later, the discoveries of archaeologists, combined with written records, have helped answer many questions about the first ancient civilizations.

SECTION REVIEW

1. Define: prehistory, archaeologist, artifact, anthropologist, fossil.
2. What evidence do anthropologists use to expand knowledge of the past?
3. What three methods are used to estimate the age of an artifact?
4. What is the main reason many questions about prehistoric people remain unanswered?

2 Stone Age Peoples

Read to Learn
- how people lived in the Old Stone Age
- what advances took place in the New Stone Age

In their search for prehistoric artifacts, archaeologists have uncovered many stone axes and arrow tips. As a result, scholars use the term "Stone Age" to describe the prehistoric period of time when people used simple stone tools. The term also describes a way of life in which people rely on such stone tools.

The Stone Age is often divided into the Old Stone Age, or Paleolithic (PAY lee uh LIHTH ihk) Age, and the New Stone Age, or Neolithic (NEE uh LIHTH ihk) Age. The Paleolithic Age may have begun as early as 500,000 B.C.* It lasted to about 10,000 B.C. The Neolithic Age lasted from about 10,000 B.C. to about 3500 B.C.

_____

* Civilizations influenced by Christianity date historical events from the birth of Christ. B.C. stands for dates before the birth of Christ. A.D. stands for "anno domini," a Latin phrase meaning "in the year of Our Lord." A.D. is used for dates after the birth of Christ. For B.C. dates, the higher number is always the earlier date.

The Old Stone Age

Archaeologists have found remains and artifacts of Paleolithic people in many parts of the world, including East Africa, China, Southeast Asia, Europe, the Middle East,* and the Americas. Based on their findings, scientists have begun to construct a picture of life in the Old Stone Age.

Paleolithic people lived by fishing, hunting, and gathering plants that grew wild. They were *nomads,* people who moved in search of food. For example, they would follow herds of animals such as the woolly mammoth. Or if wild berries and nuts became scarce in an area, they would migrate to another area where food was plentiful.

A simple social structure developed during the Old Stone Age. Groups of related families joined to form small hunting bands numbering about 30 people. They built no permanent shelters. Instead, they camped in caves or slept under lean-tos made of branches and grasses. While some people hunted, others stayed near the camp to gather wild food and care for the young.

There is evidence that during the Old Stone Age people developed spoken languages and learned how to control fire. With spoken language, hunters could organize hunts of large animals. Fire provided light and warmth, protection against wild animals, and heat for cooking food.

Paleolithic people made simple tools such as hand axes and choppers. The earliest tools were pieces of flint, a hard stone, chipped to produce a sharp cutting edge. Later, people made stone and bone tools for more specialized uses. These tools included needles, skin scrapers, harpoons, fishhooks, arrowheads, and spear points.

Some scholars suggest that during the Old Stone Age people developed basic religious beliefs. For example, they think that cave paintings made by prehistoric hunters had a religious meaning. (See page 7.) Perhaps the hunters believed that drawing the animals would help them in the hunt.

---

* The Middle East has also been called the Near East. When Europeans began visiting China and Japan in large numbers, they referred to those Asian countries as the Far East. The lands between Europe and the Far East then became known as the Near East.

Changes in the Environment

The date often used to indicate the end of the Old Stone Age, about 10,000 B.C., also marks the end of the last ice age. Scientists think the earth has experienced four ice ages over millions of years. During the last ice age, thick sheets of ice, called *glaciers,* spread out from the polar regions. In North America, glaciers stretched as far south as present-day Kentucky. Glaciers also covered much of northern Europe and parts of Asia.

According to scientific theory, much of the world's water was frozen during the last ice age. As a result, ocean levels dropped, and land areas today covered with water were exposed. A land bridge may have connected North America and Asia where the Bering Sea is today. Some scientists think that about 25,000 years ago people from Asia followed herds of wild animals across the land bridge into North America. When the glaciers melted, the level of the ocean rose. The land bridge disappeared, and the people in North America were cut off from Asia.

Stone Age peoples developed a variety of flint tools, which they used for cutting, chopping, and scraping the hides of animals. Gradually, they became more skillful at making tools. For example, the stone implement on the left has a well-shaped handle.

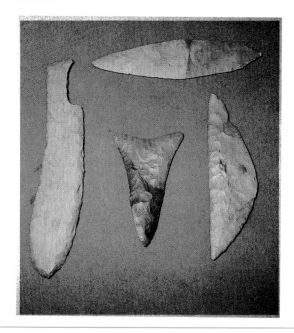

Like detectives, historians examine many different kinds of evidence for clues to the past. One valuable source of information is visual evidence, including paintings, statues, drawings, and photographs. Prehistoric people left no written records, but they did leave visual evidence in the form of colorful pictures sketched on cave walls.

Pictures and paintings are useful because they often show how people saw themselves, how they dressed, what games they played, or what events they thought were important. However, visual evidence presents only what the artist or photographer wants you to see. In order to make the best use of visual evidence, you must study each piece carefully.

The following steps will help you use visual evidence effectively. Study the picture on page 7 and then follow these steps.

1. **Identify the subject of the painting.** Sometimes when you look at a picture two or three times you see details you did not notice at first glance. Answer the following questions about the picture: (a) What figures are shown in the cave painting? (b) What do you think is happening in the painting? Explain.

2. **Evaluate the visual evidence to decide if it is a reliable source.** A picture does not always tell the full story. An artist may have painted it with a specific purpose and left out some details. You have to decide whether the picture is a reliable source of information. Answer the following questions about the cave painting: (a) What objects or figures are most prominent in the cave painting? What does this tell you about the artist's purpose in painting this picture? (b) Do you think the artist portrayed everything exactly as it was? Explain. (c) Does this painting give you a complete idea of the everyday life of prehistoric people? Explain. (d) Does the picture indicate that prehistoric people were skilled hunters? Explain.

3. **Study the visual evidence to learn about a particular people, event, or development.** Use the cave painting and your reading to answer the following questions: (a) About when was this picture painted? Where was it found? (b) What example or examples of the technology of prehistoric peoples can you find? (c) Using this painting as evidence, draw three conclusions about prehistoric people.

The end of the last ice age caused dramatic changes in local climates around the world. Deserts appeared where lush plants had grown, and warm weather brought new plants to life in formerly frigid areas. The new climate patterns contributed to a change in the way people lived—a change so profound that scholars often call it a revolution. This revolution marked the beginning of the Neolithic Age.

The New Stone Age

Between 10,000 B.C. and 3500 B.C., people in many parts of the world gradually stopped hunting and gathering food and became farmers. They domesticated, or tamed, wild animals such as dogs, sheep, and goats and began to grow grain and vegetables for food.

In the New Stone Age, agriculture developed in many places. Anthropologists have generally concluded that it began first in the Middle East. People grew crops that were suited to the local soil and climate. In the Middle East and Africa, for example, they grew wheat, barley, and oats. They grew rice and root crops such as yams in Asia. Beans, squash, and maize, or corn, were grown in Central and South America.

The agricultural revolution, or the change from hunting and gathering food to growing food, had a far-reaching effect on the way people lived. Since people no longer had to move in search of food, they formed permanent settlements, or villages. They built houses, and property became important. Even so, not everyone abandoned the nomadic way of life. Some people remained

In 1940, at Lascaux (la SKOH) in southern France, four boys were on their way home from school when their dog disappeared down a hole. The boys followed the dog into a large underground cave. Later, they returned to the cave with lights. On the ceiling and walls of the cave, they saw colorful paintings like the ones above. Archaeologists identified the paintings as the work of Stone Age hunters living sometime between 15,000 B.C. and 10,000 B.C.

hunters and gatherers. Others established a stable way of life as herders of sheep, cattle, or goats.

In farming villages, people had to cooperate in new ways. The heads of each family probably met to make decisions about planting and harvesting. As villages grew, a chieftain and a council of elders assumed the task of making decisions. Increasingly, people relied on these leaders to settle disputes over such issues as land ownership. This issue had not come up among nomadic people, who did not own land.

According to archaeologists, Neolithic farmers believed that spirits, or gods, controlled the forces of nature. Since floods and droughts meant starvation or death, farmers took care to keep the spirits happy.

Technology of the New Stone Age

The growth of a farming economy led to the development of new *technology*, that is, tools and skills people use to meet their basic needs. To turn over the soil, people fash-

ioned sturdy hoes from granite, a hard stone that could be sharpened. They also invented weaving. When they learned to make cloth from wool and flax, Neolithic people no longer had to slaughter their animals for the hides. They made baskets for storing grain, nets for fishing, and fire-hardened pottery for cooking.

Toward the end of the New Stone Age, several more developments greatly changed the way some people lived. For example, farmers began to use animals such as the ox to pull plows instead of pulling the plows themselves. As a result, farmers could plow more land and reap larger harvests, which supported a growing population.

Other important developments included the invention of the wheel and the sail and the use of metal. Wheeled carts gradually replaced wooden sleds, making land transportation easier. The invention of the potter's wheel meant that people could make better pots and other vessels. The sail improved transportation on water and made longer voyages possible. In addition, people in the late Neolithic Age began to use metal as well as stone for tools and weapons. They first used copper. Eventually they discovered that copper combined with tin formed a harder metal, called *bronze.*

By 3000 B.C., each of these inventions was being used in some part of the world. However, they were not invented everywhere at the same time. Most appeared first in the Middle East. Some were not used in other places for thousands of years. The people of Central America, for example, used the wheel on toys but did not use wheels on carts until after the arrival of Europeans in the 1500s A.D. People used the inventions of the late Neolithic Age to build more complex societies called civilizations.

SECTION REVIEW

1. Identify: Paleolithic Age, Neolithic Age, agricultural revolution.
2. Define: nomad, glacier, technology, bronze.
3. Why was learning to control fire important for Paleolithic people?
4. List two ways in which the agricultural revolution affected the way people lived.
5. What metals did late Neolithic people begin to use?

Then and Now ■ The Tasaday: A Stone Age People Today

In 1967, a discovery was made in the dense tropical forest of Mindanao, in the Philippine Islands. A local hunter came across a small band of people who apparently had never been in contact with the outside world. These people, called the Tasaday, numbered only 24 men, women, and children. Many scientists believe that the Tasaday were living as their ancestors had for thousands of years.

When anthropologists learned of the discovery, they were eager to study the Tasaday as a living example of Stone Age people. Several anthropologists went to Mindanao. They found that the Tasaday were food gatherers who depended on the forest for food and clothing. They lived in natural limestone caves in the mountainside.

Each morning, the men and women would go out to gather enough food for the day. They used tools made out of bamboo, stone, and vines to dig wild yam roots or cut bananas. The Tasaday twisted orchid leaves into cone-shaped cups, which they then filled with crabs, tadpoles, frogs, and small fish caught by hand. They wore clothing made of vines and orchid leaves.

The Tasaday knew how to control fire, an important discovery for Stone Age people. They used fire to cook food and to keep warm during damp and chilly nights. The Tasaday did not have a written language or any system of telling time or counting. Their spoken language revealed something of their way of life. For example, they had no words for anger or war.

The Tasaday told anthropologists that the band had lived in the same caves for a very long time, perhaps 1,000 years. They believed that one of their ancestors had had a dream promising good health to those who stayed in the caves and illness to those who left. Most of their religious beliefs were based on that dream.

The Tasaday thought their discovery by the outside world had been predicted by their ancestor's dream. The ancestor spoke of a "Bringer of Good Fortune" who would show the Tasaday the way out of darkness. The Philippine government has made the forest where the Tasaday live a protected area so the Tasaday can continue to live in peace.

3 Emergence of Civilization

Read to Learn ■ what changes marked the beginnings of civilization
■ how civilizations spread

In different parts of the world, simple farming settlements grew into large cities by the end of the Neolithic Age, about 3500 B.C. This development, known as the urban revolution, marked the beginning of civilization. In fact, the word "civilization" comes from the Latin root "civitas," meaning city.

The development of cities was only one characteristic of early civilizations. Other characteristics included complex religions and governments, specialized skills and occupations, social classes, and methods of recordkeeping.

Growth of Cities

The earliest cities appeared in four great river valleys. Cities may have emerged as early as 6000 B.C. in the valley of the Tigris (TĪ grihs) and Euphrates (yoo FRAY teez) rivers in western Asia. Other cities developed in the valleys of the Nile River in North Africa, the Indus River in South Asia, and the Yellow River in East Asia.* (See the map on page 11.)

Conditions in the river valleys favored the development of cities. For example, fertile soil in the valleys made a surplus of food possible. When the rivers flooded, the water left deposits of *silt*, a soil rich in minerals, which made the land especially fertile. Flood waters also brought needed moisture to the land, and people used river water for irrigation during dry periods. In addition, the rivers contained plentiful fish and attracted animals, two additional sources of food. Finally, the rivers served as transportation arteries, which allowed people to trade for goods.

With food surpluses, the populations of farming settlements increased, and villages grew into cities. The populations of the earliest cities ranged from several thousand to half a million residents. City dwellers undertook major projects such as clearing new farm land and building vast irrigation systems as well as constructing temples, palaces, and walls for defense. Because such projects required organization and leadership, they contributed to the development of governments.

Government and Religion

In the early cities, government and religion were closely related. Like the people of the New Stone Age, city dwellers were *polytheistic*—that is, they worshipped many gods. They believed that gods and goddesses controlled the forces of nature. It was, therefore, important to them to win the gods' favor in order to prevent disasters. Only priests knew the rituals to influence the gods. Thus they gained enormous power.

Priests probably headed the government as priest-kings. The form of government in which priests serve as kings is called a *theocracy*. Gradually, successful military leaders began to replace the priest-kings as rulers. Scholars theorize that these leaders emerged as a result of warfare between cities over scarce resources.

Military rulers had clear responsibilities. They shared the priests' task of keeping the gods friendly, and they were responsible for defending their cities against enemies. They acted as judges, made laws, and appointed officials to keep order. They also supervised building and irrigation projects.

To support the temple and pay for vast construction projects, city dwellers had to contribute a portion of their labor or their harvest to the government. This payment represents the earliest system of taxation by government.

---

* Early cities were not limited to river valleys. As you will read in Chapter 14, cities also grew in the highlands of the Americas.

The Economy and Society

The innovations in technology of the late Neolithic Age were important to city dwellers. Bronze came into such widespread use for vessels, tools, and weapons that historians have often called the period of early civilization the "Bronze Age." Important social and economic changes also occurred during the Bronze Age.

Specialized skills and occupations. The new technology often required special skills. As a result, specialized occupations gradually developed. Skilled workers called *artisans* hammered out plows, scythes, helmets, and swords. Jewelers shaped precious metals into charms and necklaces. Sculptors, potters, painters, priests, and government officials acquired specialized skills and knowledge.

The food surplus, an important characteristic of early civilizations, also contributed to the development of occupations. Because of the surplus, some people did not have to

In early civilizations, people spent much of their time planting, cultivating, and harvesting grain crops. Once harvested, grains such as wheat and barley had to be ground by hand. This statue shows a slave using a stone board and roller to crush the kernels of grain into flour.

farm. Rather, they could trade products or labor for the food they needed. For example, a potter might trade a clay cooking vessel to a farmer for grain. The system of exchanging one set of goods or services for another is called a *barter economy.*

Social classes. As a city grew, a more complex social structure emerged. The social structure defined a person's place in society. At the top of the structure was the priest-king or king. Below the priest-king or king was a class of priests and nobles. Nobles generally based their power and wealth on owning large amounts of land. Being a noble was hereditary—that is, the children of nobles were also nobles.

In some cities, government officials and wealthy merchants formed the class below the nobility. Artisans and small traders ranked next, followed by the largest class, made up of peasant farmers and workers. At the bottom of the social structure were slaves. Slaves were men, women, and children who had been taken captive in war or who were enslaved to pay their debts.

In early civilizations, people generally could not move from one social class to another. Children usually learned a trade from their parents and so tended to stay in the same occupation.

Recordkeeping

Some historians consider recordkeeping one of the most important characteristics of civilization. The Inca of South America kept detailed records on pieces of knotted string called quipus (KEE pooz). Most ancient peoples, however, developed writing in order to keep accurate records.

Priests were probably the first to start making the marks or drawing the pictures that eventually evolved into systems of writing. They needed precise information about how and when to perform ceremonies.

Temples became the schools of ancient civilizations. Priests taught only a select few the secrets of writing. A young man who mastered the difficult task of learning to read and write was called a *scribe.* Scribes worked

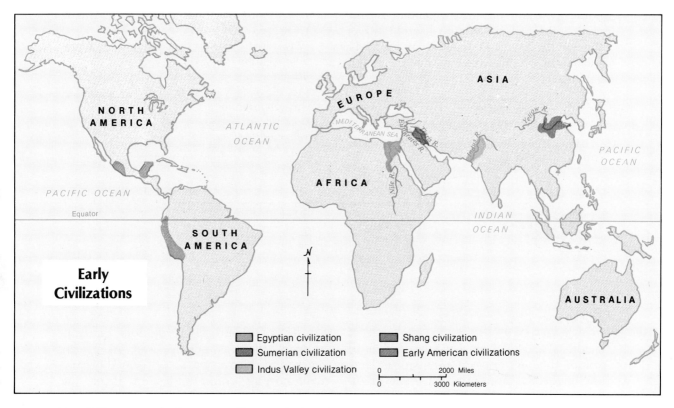

Map Skill *Name the four river valleys in which early civilizations began. Where did civilizations develop in the Americas?*

in the king's service, in the temples, or in the homes of wealthy merchants. Rulers depended on scribes to keep track of taxes, property deeds, treaties, and marriage documents. Merchants needed copies of business contracts and records of debts.

Writing was more than recordkeeping, however. It became the means of passing the wisdom and learning of one generation on to the next.

Contacts Among Early Civilizations

Although the first river valley civilizations appear to have developed independently, they did have some contact with one another. Trade, warfare, and migration helped spread ideas and products from one city to another and from one civilization to another. For example, city dwellers along the Tigris

and Euphrates rivers traded with people in other parts of the Middle East for timber, metal, and stone.

Warfare sometimes destroyed elements of a civilization, but it also helped spread ideas. When a highly civilized people conquered a region, the conquered people often absorbed ideas from the conquerors. In addition, migrating people adopted the more advanced skills of people they encountered.

In early civilizations, people absorbed or adapted only those ideas that seemed to suit their own way of life. From this process, distinct patterns of culture developed that were passed on to future generations. *Culture* is the customs, ideas, and ways of life of a group of people.

As you will read, ancient civilizations of the Middle East, Asia, and Africa developed traditions that still influence large parts of the world. The ancient civilizations of the

Middle East and the Mediterranean region greatly influenced western civilization in Europe and the Americas. In addition, the early civilizations of the Americas helped shape later cultures.

SECTION REVIEW

1. Locate: Tigris River, Euphrates River, Nile River, Indus River, Yellow River.

2. Define: silt, polytheistic, theocracy, artisan, barter economy, scribe, culture.
3. Why were farmers in river valleys able to produce a surplus of food?
4. Why were priests powerful in early cities?
5. List the major social classes that existed in early civilizations.
6. Why did the people of early civilizations develop writing?

Chapter 1 Review

In Perspective

Scientists and historians work together to explore the mysteries of prehistory. They have uncovered thousands of artifacts at ancient sites all over the world. Archaeologists have developed sophisticated techniques for analyzing and dating their finds. However, many questions about prehistoric peoples remain unanswered.

During the Paleolithic Age, people were nomadic, moving in small bands in search of food. Over thousands of years, they made important advances by learning to use language and control fire and by inventing stone and bone tools. About 10,000 B.C., when the last ice age ended, revolutionary changes ushered in the Neolithic Age.

The agricultural revolution radically changed the way people lived. As people learned to raise crops, some formed permanent farming communities. In Africa, the Middle East, Asia, and the Americas, people developed new tools and skills. The use of the plow, the wheel, the sail, and metals altered food production and transportation.

In the late Neolithic Age, farmers began producing food surpluses that could support large populations. Some farming communities grew into cities. The urban revolution helped give rise to the first ancient civilizations. Favorable geographical conditions encouraged the growth of civilizations in the Nile, Tigris-Euphrates, Indus, and Yellow river valleys.

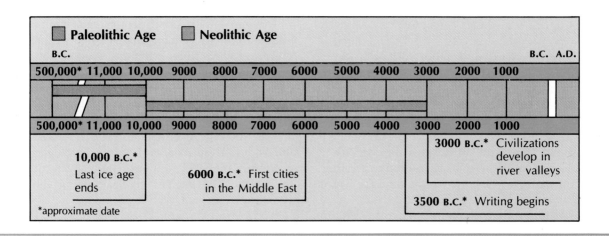

Recalling Facts

Decide if the following statements are true or false. If a statement is false, rewrite the statement to make it true.

1. Written records have existed for about 5,000 to 6,000 years.
2. Artifacts include weapons and tools.
3. Paleolithic people lived in permanent farming communities.
4. During the last ice age, Europe and North America were joined.
5. The wheel was invented in the New Stone Age.
6. Food surpluses favored population growth.
7. Early city dwellers believed in one god.
8. People in early cities had no contact with outsiders.

Chapter Checkup

1. (a) What types of evidence provide information about prehistoric peoples? (b) How is such evidence found?
2. (a) What new techniques have enabled archaeologists to make impressive advances? (b) How has much evidence about prehistoric peoples been destroyed?
3. Describe the climate change that occurred about 10,000 B.C.
4. Compare the way Paleolithic and Neolithic people lived, in terms of: (a) food; (b) shelter; (c) technology.
5. (a) What evidence suggests that Paleolithic people developed religious beliefs? (b) Why was religion important to Neolithic farmers?
6. (a) List three inventions of the late Neolithic Age. (b) How did each invention affect the way people lived?
7. (a) How were early civilizations different from Neolithic farming communities? (b) How were they similar?

Critical Thinking

1. **Analyzing** (a) Why was writing an important development? (b) How do you think it affected the way people lived?
2. **Expressing an Opinion** Reread the feature on page 8. (a) How did the Tasaday meet their basic needs of food, clothing, and shelter? (b) In your opinion, why did the Tasaday have no words for anger or warfare? (c) How do you think studying the Tasaday can help anthropologists learn about Stone Age peoples?

Relating Past to Present

1. (a) How did the end of the last ice age affect local climates? (b) What effects might these changes have had on the way people lived? (c) Do you think major climate changes today would alter the way people live? Explain your answer.
2. (a) Describe three ways in which new ideas and products were spread from one area to another. (b) What modern ideas or products have spread from one culture to another? (c) By what means were they spread?

Developing Basic Skills

1. **Using Visual Evidence** Review the steps you learned on page 6 for using visual evidence. Then answer the following questions about the picture on page 10: (a) What does the picture show? (b) Do you think the picture is a reliable source of information about early peoples? Why or why not? (c) What can you learn about the technology of early peoples from the picture?
2. **Map Reading** Study the map on page 11. Then answer the following questions: (a) On what continents did early civilizations develop? (b) What geographical features made travel between different regions difficult? (c) Which early civilizations were most likely to have had some contact with other peoples? Explain.

See page 803 for suggested readings.

2 Ancient Egypt

The sarcophagus of Tutankhamon.

Chapter Outline

1 Early Egyptian Civilization

2 Government in Ancient Egypt

3 Ancient Egyptian Society
—

On the west bank of the Nile River near Thebes is the Valley of the Kings. This rocky and narrow gorge served as the burial ground for many rulers of ancient Egypt. Egyptian kings and nobles were buried with many of their possessions to make them comfortable in the afterlife. Their tombs were mazes of corridors and chambers cut out of the rock. They were often hidden from view and tightly sealed to protect their treasures.

In the late 1800s, archaeologists began to explore the Valley of the Kings. All the tombs they found had been plundered by grave robbers. Yet a dazzling discovery was still to be made—the tomb of King Tutankhamon (TOOT ahngk AH muhn).

In 1922 after a long search, English archaeologist Howard Carter finally discovered Tutankhamon's tomb. He described his first glimpse of the interior in these words. "At first I could see nothing, the hot air escaping from the chamber causing the candle flame to flicker, but presently, as my eyes grew accustomed to the light, details of the room within emerged slowly from the mist, strange [figures of] animals, statues, and gold—everywhere the glint of gold." Carter then shone a light into the room, "the first light that had pierced the darkness of the chamber for three thousand years. . . . The effect was bewildering, overwhelming."

In the burial chamber, Carter found Tutankhamon's coffin. Carved on the lid of the coffin was a golden statue of the king, inlaid with precious jewels. On his forehead "were two emblems delicately worked in brilliant inlay—the Cobra and the Vulture—symbols of Upper and Lower Egypt, but perhaps the most touching by its human simplicity was the tiny wreath of flowers around these symbols . . . the last farewell offering of the widowed queen."

Since Carter's discovery, the riches of Tutankhamon's tomb have come to symbolize the achievements of Egyptian civilization. By the time Tutankhamon inherited the throne, in 1360 B.C., Egyptian civilization was already almost 2,000 years old. Between 3500 B.C. and 3000 B.C., people living in the Nile River valley had established the first civilization in Africa. Early Egyptians probably had some contact with Sumer, a civilization in the Tigris-Euphrates Valley of western Asia. But the life-giving Nile had far greater influence on the development of Egyptian civilization.

1 Early Egyptian Civilization

Read to Learn   ■ how the Nile influenced the development of ancient Egypt
   ■ what role religion played in ancient Egypt

About 8000 B.C., the climate of northern Africa gradually became drier, forcing Stone Age hunters in the region to move in search of food. Some hunters migrated into the Nile River valley of northeastern Africa. There they found plentiful wild game and water.

Archaeologists theorize that by 7000 B.C. the agricultural revolution had reached the Nile Valley. People living there grew barley, wheat, and vegetables. Early farmers eventually grew enough food to support permanent settlements. By 3500 B.C., many small farming villages clung to the banks of the Nile.

The people called their land Kemet, meaning rich, black soil. As farmers, they valued the fertile soil that produced good harvests. Yet fertile soil was only one geographic advantage enjoyed by the Nile villages as they grew over the next few centuries.

The Nile River: Giver of Life

The Nile River is the longest river in the world. It flows north from Lake Victoria in the mountains of central Africa to the Mediterranean Sea, 4,145 miles (6,672 kilometers) away. In ancient times, as today, the Nile was considered the source of life in Egypt. Without the Nile, which brings valuable moisture to the parched land, Egypt would be an extension of the Libyan Desert.

Until recently, the Nile overflowed its banks every July following the rainy season in central Africa. The Nile floods were predictable. Although the floods occasionally caused destruction or failed to bring enough water, Egyptians usually knew to within a few feet how high the waters would rise. The flood waters soaked deep into the soil where the next crop of grain would be planted.

In addition to moisture, the flood waters carried silt, which was deposited on the fields as the waters receded. The rich soil replenished the farmland each year.* At the mouth of the Nile, where the river empties into the Mediterranean Sea, deposits of silt have formed a *delta*, that is, a triangle-shaped area of marshy flatlands.

Throughout Egyptian history, the Nile has helped to unite the villages along its banks. It served as a major highway, connecting Upper Egypt in the south to Lower Egypt in the north. (See the map on page 16.) Trade along the river was active. The river currents carried barges loaded with grain downstream to the delta. Then with sails raised, the barges caught the prevailing winds and returned upstream.

---

* The yearly floods continued until 1970, when the Aswan High Dam was completed. The dam provides electrical power and a steady supply of water to Egypt, but it also traps silt behind its walls. Today, Egyptian farmers spread artificial fertilizers on their fields.

The Nile touched people's lives in many other ways. For example, it provided river wildlife, which Egyptians hunted for sport and food. Furthermore, Egyptians used a reed called *papyrus* (puh PĪ ruhs) that grew along the Nile's marshy shores for making paper. The ancient Egyptians recognized the importance of the Nile, as the following lines from one of their hymns show: "If the Nile smiles the earth is joyous, every stomach is full of rejoicing."

Natural Barriers

Although the Nile River dominated everyday life, other geographic features also influenced early Egyptian civilization. As you

Map Skill *During a visit to Egypt, the Greek historian Herodotus declared that the land was "wholly the gift of the Nile." Egyptian civilization developed on narrow strips of fertile land (shown in green on the map) along either side of the river. What type of land lay beyond the reach of the annual flood waters?*

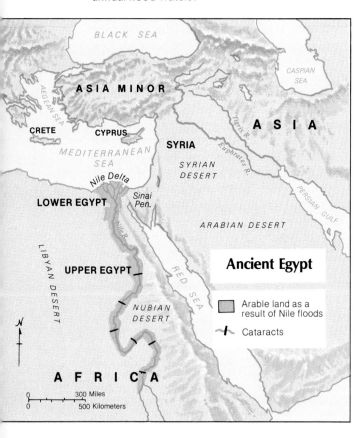

can see on the map below, the Libyan and Nubian deserts, the Mediterranean Sea, and the Red Sea form natural barriers that almost surround Egypt. These barriers protected the early Nile villages from attack by outsiders. To the south, the Nile is interrupted six times by *cataracts* (KAT uh RAKTS), or waterfalls and rapids. The cataracts and a huge swamp, where the Nile became impassable, posed obstacles to invaders from Kush, present-day Ethiopia.

Egyptians were not completely protected by natural barriers, however. Over the centuries, Egyptian rulers faced many invaders. Most reached Egypt across the Sinai Peninsula, the triangle of land that connects Egypt and western Asia. The northern Sinai also served as a path for Egyptian armies when they marched off to establish an empire in western Asia.

The natural barriers of Egypt presented obstacles to Egyptians as well as to outsiders. The land along the river was fertile, but farmers could not grow crops in the surrounding deserts. Thus, most Egyptians lived in crowded Nile villages. As the population grew, Egyptians had to overcome limitations imposed by geography. They built extensive irrigation systems to carry Nile water into the desert, and they drained the marshy swamps of the Nile delta.

Religion in Ancient Egypt

Religion was a thread deeply woven into Egyptian life. The Egyptians' religious beliefs reflected the importance of nature in their lives. Egyptians believed that different gods controlled the forces of nature, giving good harvests or causing crops to die. They thought gods had the power of life and death over everyone. Egyptians were polytheistic. People in each village worshipped a village god in addition to other gods. They also identified certain gods with animals such as cats.

Egyptian gods. The sun god Amon-Re (AH muhn RAY) was the most important Egyptian god. The east, where the sun rose, symbolized birth to the Egyptians. The west, where the sun set, represented death. Thus,

The language of ancient Egypt reflected the influence of the Nile River. The word for "travel" was either "khed," meaning "to go downstream," or "khent," meaning "to go upstream." This photograph shows Egyptians using sailboats to carry goods along the Nile today much as their ancestors did 4,000 years ago.

Egyptians always built tombs and funeral temples on the west bank of the Nile.

Egyptian farmers gave special attention to Osiris (oh SĪ rihs), god of the Nile. According to an Egyptian legend, Osiris was murdered by his brother Set, an evil god who caused harvests to wither and die. Isis (Ī sihs), the wife of Osiris, brought her husband back to life. But Osiris did not return to the world of the living. Instead, he reigned as god of the underworld and judge of the dead. Every year, Egyptians celebrated the death and rebirth of Osiris, which they identified with the rise and fall of the Nile.

Life after death. Belief in life after death was central to Egyptian religion. When a person died, friends said, "You have not gone away dead. You have gone away alive." Egyptians thought that in the afterlife people were happy, well fed, and busy with the same activities they had enjoyed in life.

They believed that the dead did not automatically go to the afterlife. Instead, they went first to the underworld, where they were judged by Osiris. Standing before Osiris, the dead declared that they were innocent of sin. To see if they spoke the truth, Osiris weighed each heart against a feather, the symbol of truth. Those who failed the test were eaten by a monster. The reward for those who had lived moral lives was entry into the afterlife, or "the Happy Field of Food."

Egyptians planned carefully for life after death. The wealthy prepared elaborate tombs, or "Houses for Eternity." Early Egyptian rulers built huge stone pyramids as tombs, which they filled with the treasures, furniture, and food they thought they would need in the afterlife. Although the poor made simpler preparations, they, too, believed in the afterlife.

Egyptians believed that they would need their bodies as a home for the soul in the afterlife. For this reason, they practiced mummification, a process that preserved the

17

Wealthy Egyptians had scenes of the journey through the underworld painted on the walls of their tombs. Here, an Egyptian nobleman and noblewoman stand before the god Osiris, who will decide if they will enter the "Happy Field of Food." The writings in the background are prayers and charms meant to help the souls of the dead pass safely through the underworld.

body of the dead. At first, only rulers and nobles were allowed to have their bodies preserved after death. Eventually, the lower classes gained the same right. The Egyptians developed remarkably effective techniques of mummification. By examining the well-preserved mummies from Egyptian tombs, present-day scientists have even been able to identify many health problems and causes of death among ancient Egyptians.

A System of Writing

The need to keep records of religious rituals and temple property probably led Egyptian priests to develop a system of writing, later known as *hieroglyphics* (HĪ er oh GLIHF ihks). The earliest hieroglyphics, dating from about 3100 B.C., were *pictograms*, or pictures of objects. In a pictogram, a picture of an ox meant an ox. Gradually, Egyptian hieroglyphics became more complex. Because a

pictogram could not express an action or an idea, such as truth or honesty, Egyptians added ideograms. An *ideogram* is a picture that symbolizes an idea or action. For example, a picture of a reclining figure meant sleep.

As writing became more important, Egyptians modified their system, adding symbols to represent sounds. An example of this in English would be using a picture of a bee and a leaf to represent the word "belief." Egyptians developed symbols for consonant sounds but not for vowel sounds.

Egyptians first wrote by carving hieroglyphics on stone or wood. Later, they flattened papyrus reeds into strips and wrote on the strips with brushes and ink. In fact, the English word "paper" comes from the word "papyrus."

The meaning of Egyptian hieroglyphics was lost until the early 1800s, when a French scholar, Jean Champollion (shahm poh

LYOHN), deciphered the Rosetta Stone. The Rosetta Stone, a slab of black rock, was found in 1799 by French soldiers in Egypt. On it was an inscription in three kinds of writing: Egyptian hieroglyphics, demotic, which was a shorthand version of hieroglyphics, and Greek. Champollion, who read Greek, spent years comparing the Greek words with the hieroglyphics. By 1822, he had translated the entire Egyptian text. After Champollion cracked the code of Egyptian hieroglyphics, scholars began translating thousands of records written on papyrus as well as elaborate inscriptions on temple and tomb walls.

2 Government in Ancient Egypt

Read to Learn ▪ how the Old and Middle Egyptian Kingdoms differed
▪ what developments occurred during the New Kingdom

Before Champollion deciphered the Rosetta Stone, most knowledge about ancient Egypt came from studying unwritten records such as temples, pyramids, tomb paintings, and mummified bodies. Since 1822, written records have revealed a great deal about government in ancient Egypt.

Uniting Upper and Lower Egypt

The villages that grew up along the Nile gradually became part of one of two kingdoms, Upper Egypt or Lower Egypt. About 3100 B.C. Menes (MEE neez), the ruler of Upper Egypt, united the two kingdoms by conquering Lower Egypt, thus greatly increasing his power. He gained both farmland and access to copper mines in the Sinai Peninsula. He then also controlled trade from Upper Egypt to the mouth of the Nile. Menes' successors wore a double crown symbolizing the unity of the two kingdoms. They built their capital at Memphis, where Upper and Lower Egypt met.

Although little is known about Menes, he probably established the first *dynasty*, or ruling family, in Egypt. In a dynasty, the right to rule passes from the ruler to one of the children of the ruler. Occasionally, a ruling family dies out or is overthrown by a powerful challenger who establishes a new dynasty.

According to a history of Egypt written about 250 B.C., there were at least 30 dynasties in Egypt between 2700 B.C. and 1090 B.C. Scholars have used this history to divide ancient Egyptian history into three major periods: the Old Kingdom (2700 B.C.–2200 B.C.), the Middle Kingdom (2050 B.C.–1800 B.C.), and the New Kingdom or Empire Age (1570 B.C.–1090 B.C.).* In the years between the three kingdoms, civil wars and invasions left Egypt without a strong dynasty.

The Old Kingdom

During the Old Kingdom, Egyptian rulers acquired extensive power. They took the title *pharaoh* (FAIR oh), meaning "great house." Egyptians believed that the pharaoh was a

---

* Since Egyptians recorded events according to which dynasty was in power, historians have no exact dates to guide them. They make educated guesses based on written and archaeological evidence, but they sometimes differ over the exact dates of the three kingdoms.

god, the son of the sun god, Amon-Re. The pharaoh had absolute control over people's lives. Not only was he the source of all law, but he also owned all land, quarries, mines, and water in Egypt. He shared these resources with the people, and they, in turn, paid taxes and obeyed his commands.

With this absolute power, pharaohs could organize a strong, centralized government. They divided the kingdom into provinces and appointed officials to supervise tax collection, building projects, and irrigation systems in each province. At first, officials were responsible to the pharaoh and could be replaced. But gradually their positions became hereditary, and the officials became part of the noble class. While the pharaohs remained strong, they controlled the officials. Late in the Old Kingdom, however, powerful nobles began to challenge royal authority.

The Old Kingdom was a period of significant achievements. Egyptians improved hieroglyphics and developed the engineering skills needed to construct more elaborate tombs for the pharaohs. The Egyptians believed that, as a god, the pharaoh needed a suitable house for his spirit in the afterlife. When the pharaoh Zoser ordered a tomb prepared, his chief minister, Imhotep (ihm HOH tehp), a brilliant engineer, designed the Step Pyramid at Sakkara (sah KAH rah). This terraced tomb, constructed about 2650 B.C., is the oldest surviving stone building.

The Old Kingdom has sometimes been called the Pyramid Age because Zoser's successors, as well as many wealthy nobles, erected pyramid tombs. Three gigantic pyramids built during that period still stand at Giza.

These massive tombs are evidence of the great wealth and power of Egyptian rulers in the Old Kingdom. Thousands of laborers had to be recruited, fed, clothed, and housed during the years it took to build a pyramid. The cost in human lives and suffering was enormous. The common people resented the nobles and pharaoh who made them work in labor gangs and who increased taxes to pay for the tombs.

Despite heavy taxes, the huge expense of building pyramids exhausted the treasury. Gradually, the power of the pharaohs weakened. By 2200 B.C., officials in the provinces seized control of their territories. Peasant revolts and civil wars disrupted trade and farming. A period of disorder lasting about 150 years marked the end of the Old Kingdom.

The Middle Kingdom

Around 2050 B.C., a new dynasty from the south restored order in Egypt and established the Middle Kingdom. Compared to earlier rulers, pharaohs of the Middle Kingdom seemed more interested in the common people. During this period, lower class Egyptians gained the right to have their bodies mummified after death. The common people believed that this privilege gave them the same access to the afterlife as nobles and pharaohs.

Pharaohs of the Middle Kingdom undertook some major projects. One project, the draining of swampland in the Nile delta, created thousands of acres of new farmland. Another undertaking, the digging of a canal to connect the Nile to the Red Sea, benefited trade and transportation. At about the same time, two huge temples were built at Luxor and Karnak near the new capital city of Thebes on the east bank of the Nile.

During the Middle Kingdom, Egypt expanded its borders and had greater contact with other civilizations. Pharaohs sent trade expeditions to Kush, Syria, Mesopotamia, and Crete. Contact with outsiders contributed to the flourishing of Egyptian literature and art. One famous story, the *Tale of Sinuhe*, described the adventures of an Egyptian traveling in foreign lands. It became the basis of the Sinbad the Sailor stories.

By 1800 B.C., a succession of weak pharaohs again left Egypt in turmoil, with strong nobles battling for power in the provinces. Divided by civil wars, the Egyptians suddenly faced another threat. The Hyksos (HIHK sohs) of western Asia streamed across the Sinai Peninsula into northern

Egypt. The newcomers used horses and war chariots, both unknown in Egypt. They easily crushed the disorganized Egyptian forces, who fought from donkey carts.

The Hyksos ruled Egypt for about 200 years. During that time, the Egyptians learned important military skills from their conquerors. They learned to ride horses and became expert charioteers. By 1570 B.C., Egyptian nobles united to expel the foreigners. The nobles established another Egyptian dynasty, which began the New Kingdom.

Economics and History ■ An Ancient Engineering Marvel

"The most curious question is how the stones were raised to so great a height," wrote the Roman statesman Livy about 77 A.D. Like others before and since, Livy wondered how the Egyptians built the Great Pyramid at Giza for the Old Kingdom pharaoh Khufu.

The builders of the Great Pyramid of Khufu left no written records. However, archaeologists and engineers have pieced together clues from smaller, unfinished pyramids and from tomb paintings that showed how Egyptian builders moved heavy stones. They learned, for example, that the Egyptians built the Great Pyramid of Khufu about 2600 B.C. without using wheels, pulleys, or iron tools, which were unknown at the time.

The first step in building the pyramid was flattening the 13-acre site so the pharaoh's tomb would not tilt. To level the rough terrain, workers had to cut through solid rock. Engineers probably used string attached to sticks and trenches filled with water to make sure that the ground was level.

Meanwhile, at quarries, stonecutters used copper chisels, wedges, and hard stone hammers to cut huge slabs of limestone and granite. They shaped each block to precise measurements. Some stonecutters carved their names onto the blocks they cut. At one pyramid site, stones bear the names of work crews: "Vigorous Gang," "North Gang," and "Enduring Gang." The average block weighed about 2.5 tons (2.3 metric tons). Stonecutters prepared more than two million stone blocks for Khufu's pyramid.

Most blocks came from quarries near Giza in Lower Egypt, but limestone blocks for the outside and granite for the king's burial chamber were brought from Upper Egypt. To move the stones, workers laid a log roadway from the quarry to the river's edge.

With ropes lashing the blocks to sleds, workers hauled the sleds to the Nile. Water, or possibly milk, was poured over the log road and the sled runners to reduce friction. The stones were loaded onto barges during the flood season, when the strong Nile current carried boats swiftly down river.

The pyramid rose level by level to a towering height equal to that of a modern 45-story building. To raise blocks to a new level, workers built ramps of earth and brick, almost like scaffolding, around the outside of the pyramid. The winding ramps formed a roadway along which the stones were dragged.

Before the ramps were finally removed, workers completed the burial chambers inside the pyramid. Along passages connecting the different chambers, priests carried the treasures that Khufu would need in the afterlife. The Grand Gallery, an enormous hallway with a 28-foot-high (8.5 meters) ceiling, led to the King's Chamber. Here, at the heart of his House of Eternity, Khufu was buried.

Maps are very important to the study of world history because they answer the question "Where did it happen?" Maps help show why certain events or developments took place. They also illustrate how geography has influenced the way people live.

Maps provide many different kinds of information. Most maps include a title, legend, scale, and direction arrow. In addition, some maps in this book also give topographical, political, or economic information.

The following steps will help you read the map on page 23 and draw conclusions about the influence of geography on ancient Egyptian civilization. You can use the steps to study other maps in this book.

1. **Decide what is shown on the map.** The *title* tells what the map is about and, usually, the date or time period covered. The *legend* explains the meaning of colors and symbols used. The *scale* allows you to translate distances on the map into distances in miles and kilometers, while the *direction arrow* shows which way is north. Answer the following questions about the map on page 23: (a) What is the title of the map? (b) What color represents the Egyptian Empire? (c) What is the approximate distance in miles from Thebes to the mouth of the Nile? In kilometers? (d) In what direction does the Nile River flow?

2. **Practice reading the information on the map.** *Topographical* maps include the physical features of a region, such as mountains, oceans, rivers, and lakes. *Political* maps show the sizes of empires or boundaries of nations. *Economic* maps give information about topics such as population, trade, and natural resources. Many maps in this book give all three kinds of information. Answer the following questions about the features of the map on page 23. (a) Name four physical features shown on the map. (b) What political information does the map give? (c) Describe the area in which the Egyptians and Hittites were most likely to come into conflict. (d) What economic information does the map show?

3. **Study the map to draw conclusions about a historical event or development.** (a) In which direction or directions did Egyptian civilization expand? (b) What geographic features limited Egyptian expansion? (c) Why did Egypt need a strong navy during the height of its empire? (d) Where was Egypt most open to invasion? Explain.

The New Kingdom

During the New Kingdom, Egyptian power reached its peak. Ambitious pharaohs established an empire stretching from Kush to the Euphrates River. (See the map on page 23.) Tribute and loot from conquered territories filled the treasury. Taxes on flourishing trade further increased Egyptian wealth. Because of political and economic expansion during the New Kingdom, this period is also called the Empire Age.

The first woman ruler known to history, Queen Hatshepsut (haht SHEHP soot), reigned during the Empire Age. For 22 years, she administered an efficient government. Hatshepsut sent a trading expedition south to the area of present-day Somalia. Mer-chants returned to Egypt with a rich cargo of ivory, incense, ebony, gold, and monkeys for private zoos. A record of this successful expedition was carved onto the walls of Hatshepsut's funeral temple near Thebes.

Hatshepsut was succeeded by her stepson, Thutmose III (thoot MOH suh). A brilliant military leader, Thutmose expanded the Egyptian Empire to its greatest size. He conquered Palestine and Syria and organized a navy to subdue cities along the eastern Mediterranean coast. Like other rulers, Thutmose raised monuments to his own greatness. On tall, pointed stone pillars, called obelisks (AHB uh lihsks), stonemasons carved hieroglyphic inscriptions describing the pharaoh's accomplishments.

A controversial pharaoh. The pharaoh Amenhotep IV (ah muhn HOH tehp) was less interested in foreign conquests than in changing some traditional religious practices. He wanted Egyptians to worship the god Aton, whose symbol was the sun disk. After ordering the priests to stop worshipping other gods and to remove these gods' names from the temples, he changed his own name from Amenhotep to Akenaton (AH kuh NAH tahn), meaning "It goes well with Aton."

During his lifetime, Akenaton's policies aroused controversy and created serious divisions in Egypt. The priests of Amon-Re bitterly opposed the pharaoh's reforms. When Akenaton neglected the defense of the empire in order to worship Aton, he lost the support of the military. The common people were afraid to abandon their old gods in favor of Aton. Today, Akenaton remains a controversial figure. Scholars are unsure if

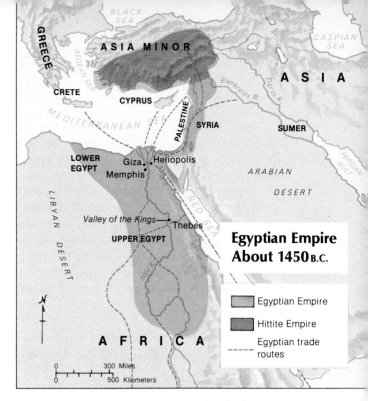

Egyptian Empire About 1450 B.C.

- Egyptian Empire
- Hittite Empire
- Egyptian trade routes

Map Skill   *The Nile River remained at the heart of Egyptian civilization even at the height of the empire, as you can see on this map. However, trade routes greatly extended Egyptian influence. Into what areas did Egyptian trade routes penetrate?*

Rulers of ancient Egypt celebrated their power by building magnificent stone monuments. At Abu Simbel on the Upper Nile, Ramses II had a temple carved into a mountainside. The two giant statues of Ramses shown here tower above the life-sized figures at the entrance to the temple.

Akenaton was trying to introduce *monotheism*, the worship of a single god, or if he just wanted to raise Aton to the highest status among the gods.

When Akenaton died in 1358 B.C., his son-in-law, a boy just eight years old, inherited the throne. The young pharaoh soon changed his name from Tutankhaton to Tutankhamon. By dropping Aton's name in favor of Amon's, Tutankhamon showed he had returned to traditional religious practices.

Decline of Egyptian power. The last great ruler of the New Kingdom was Ramses II (RAM seez). He spent most of his 67-year reign reviving the empire and fighting the Hittites (HIHT īts) of Asia Minor. In 1280 B.C., the first written treaty in history ended the costly struggle between the Hittites and the Egyptians. Ramses II raised many monuments to commemorate his victories.

Following the reign of Ramses II, Egyptian power steadily declined. By 1090 B.C., civil wars had left Egypt too weak to defeat a stream of invaders. First came raiders known as the Sea Peoples. Scholars think these people came from islands in the Aegean to attack the Nile delta.

After the Sea Peoples, the Assyrians and then the Persians conquered Egypt. In 331 B.C., the Greeks, led by Alexander the Great, occupied the Nile lands. Three hundred years later, Queen Cleopatra (KLEE oh PAT ruh), a descendant of one of Alexander's generals, tried to restore Egyptian greatness. But Cleopatra was the last pharaoh. In 31 B.C., a Roman fleet defeated Egyptian naval forces, and the next year Egypt became a province of the Roman Empire.

SECTION REVIEW

1. Locate: Memphis, Giza, Thebes.
2. Identify: Menes, Hyksos, Hatshepsut, Thutmose, Amenhotep, Tutankhamon, Ramses II.
3. Define: dynasty, pharaoh, monotheism.
4. List one important development that occurred during the (a) Old Kingdom; (b) Middle Kingdom; (c) New Kingdom.
5. (a) How did Akenaton try to change the religious practices of the Egyptians? (b) Did he succeed? Explain.
6. What events showed that Egyptian power declined after 1090 B.C.?

3 Ancient Egyptian Society

Read to Learn   ■ how Egyptian society was structured
                    ■ what contributions Egypt made to civilization

The structure of Egyptian society in the Old Kingdom barely changed for thousands of years. A person's social class and occupation were set at birth. Children of peasants farmed the same fields their parents and grandparents had. Artisans, such as weavers, taught their children their trades.

Social Classes

Egyptian social structure resembled a pyramid. The pharaoh, living in great splendor, stood at the top of society. Just below the pharaoh was a ruling class of priests and nobles. Next came a small middle class of merchants, artisans, doctors, and other skilled workers. Far below, at the base of the pyramid, were free peasants and, finally, slaves.

The ruling class. Because Egyptian life revolved around religion, priests had the highest status after the pharaoh. Egyptians believed that the gods, who controlled the universe, required constant attention. Only the priests knew how to please the gods. Priests conducted daily sacrifices to the gods, cast spells to make the land fertile, and recited prayers to help souls of the dead reach the afterlife. As guardians of this special religious knowledge, priests enjoyed great power and prestige. To support priests and temples, Egyptians paid taxes in the form of grain, linen, gold, and wine.

Nobles made up the second segment of the ruling class. Nobles often held positions as governors of provinces, court officials, or tax collectors. The chief minister, who administered the business of the country, was usually chosen from the noble class. Many nobles owned large estates with gardens and pools surrounding spacious homes.

The middle class. Egypt was mainly a civilization of farming villages, but a small middle class did develop. As the wealth of Egypt increased, the middle class settled in cities, such as Memphis and Thebes, which grew up around temples and palaces.

The middle class consisted of merchants, artisans, physicians, and skilled workers, who provided goods and services to the ruling class. Traders brought dyes, ivory, or other items, which merchants sold to nobles. Nobles paid artisans to produce goods such as pottery and glass, intricate stone and wood carvings, and linen so fine that it looked like silk.

The harvest scenes shown in this tomb painting illustrate the importance of farming to Egyptian life. Officials measure the height of the ripening grain, while peasants harvest and sift the grain. Scribes carefully record the amount of grain harvested in order to determine what taxes are owed.

Peasants and slaves. The vast majority of Egyptians were peasant farmers whose way of life changed little over thousands of years. Each year, farmers waited for the Nile floods to renew the land. When the waters receded, they planted crops of wheat and barley. Since the pharaoh owned all the land, peasants paid about three fifths of each harvest to government tax collectors. In addition to farming, peasants were often required to work on palaces and temples, clear irrigation channels, and serve in the army.

The peasants lived very simply. Their homes were low, thick-walled buildings made of sunbaked mud bricks. They fur-nished their few rooms with a bench, a bed, baskets, pots for cooking, and utensils for grinding grain.

Like peasants, slaves also worked on temples and irrigation projects. Most slaves were descendants of people brought back to Egypt as prisoners of war. Some lived like free peasants, farming plots of land. Those who served in the houses of nobles sometimes enjoyed comfortable lives or gained their freedom. On occasion, pharaohs appointed trusted slaves to high positions in the palace or in government. However, such opportunities were rare, and most slaves endured a hard existence.

The Status of Women

Compared to women in other ancient civilizations you will study, women in Egypt enjoyed a relatively high status. During the New Kingdom, women had the right to buy and sell property and to testify in court. In statues and paintings, noble women were often pictured as prominently as their husbands. Although divorce was rare, women as well as men had the right to seek divorce. Moreover, in Egyptian society, property descended through the female line.

Egyptians especially valued the woman's role as wife and mother. Women gained greater status when they had children. Yet despite the relatively high status of women, Egyptian writers often referred to wives as property of their husbands and

During the New Kingdom, women achieved a new prominence in Egyptian life. This painting shows the goddess Isis, at right, leading Queen Nefertari to the afterlife. Nefertari was the wife of the pharaoh Ramses II. In one temple that Ramses had built during his reign, Nefertari was worshipped as the chief divinity.

urged men to treat their wives with kindness. This advice suggests that women were not always well treated.

In the royal family, the queen occupied a privileged position because she was the wife of a god and the mother of the next pharaoh. At times, queens ruled jointly with their husbands. Although the pharaoh might have more than one wife, his first wife was the most important because her son would become the next pharaoh.

Education

In ancient Egypt, schools were first established to train priests. At schools attached to temples, students learned reading, writing, and arithmetic, as well as religious ceremonies and rituals. As Egyptian civilization became more complex, temple schools provided a more general education. Most students who attended temple schools were sons of the wealthy, but occasionally a poor child received an education. Girls did not attend temple schools, although they learned the skills they would need at home.

In the temple schools, students learned by dictation, copying the words of the teacher as he spoke. Most students took notes on scraps of broken pottery. Only advanced students wrote on papyrus, which was expensive. Pottery fragments unearthed by archaeologists show that school discipline was strict. One Egyptian student copied this warning: "Do not spend your time in wishing, or you will come to a bad end." After completing their studies, students either learned a trade or were apprenticed as scribes, or clerks, to priests or government officials.

Scribes performed an important function in ancient Egypt. As recordkeepers, they noted the heroic deeds of pharaohs as well as the ordinary events of daily life, such as births, marriages, and deaths. Scribes were essential to an efficient government since they kept records of taxes and expenses. A scribe who served a powerful noble or pharaoh might become rich, acquire great influence, or be appointed to an official position himself. In this way, a man from the lower class might move up in society.

The ancient Egyptians produced a large body of written literature. Many texts were prayers, hymns, or charms that people believed would help the souls of the dead reach the happy afterlife. These works were eventually collected into the Book of the Dead, *which was written on papyrus and on tomb walls. Egyptians also wrote many nonreligious biographies, histories, love songs, and poems.*

Still another kind of Egyptian literature included practical advice on how to succeed in life. The following excerpts are from the Instructions of the Vizier Ptah-hotep, *one of the oldest books in the world. Ptah-hotep, who lived about 2450 B.C., was vizier, or chief minister, to the pharaoh. In the* Instructions, *he gives advice to his son.*

From the *Instructions*

Do not let your heart be puffed-up because of your knowledge; do not be confident because you are a wise man. Take counsel with the ignorant as well as with the wise. . . .

If you, as a leader, have to decide on the conduct of a great many people, seek the most perfect manner of doing so, that your own conduct may be blameless. . . .

If you are sitting at the table of one greater than you, take what he may give when it is set before you. Let your face be cast down until he addresses you, and you should speak only when he addresses you. Laugh after he laughs, and it will be very pleasing to his heart. . . .

Be active while you live, doing more than is commanded. . . . Activity produces riches, but riches do not last when activity slackens.

If you are one to whom petition is made, be calm as you listen to the petitioner's speech. Do not rebuff him . . . before he has said what he came for. A petitioner likes attention to his words better than fulfilling of that for which he came. . . .

If a son accepts what his father says, no project of his miscarries. Train your son to be a teachable man whose wisdom is agreeable to the great.

1. What advice about leadership did the vizier give his son?
2. Would the vizier's advice be useful today? Explain.

In addition to temple schools, Egyptians established centers for higher education. The center of learning at Heliopolis, for example, was famous for teaching astronomy, the study of the planets, stars, and other bodies in space.

Scientific Accomplishments

During the Old Kingdom, the Egyptians made many practical advances in mathematics and the sciences. Egyptian farmers devised methods of land surveying out of necessity. When annual floods washed away boundary markers, farmers had to remeasure their fields. The need to survey land led to the development of mathematics, particularly geometry. Egyptians learned to measure the areas of squares and circles and to figure the volumes of cylinders and spheres.

The need to predict regular events such as Nile floods and eclipses led to advances in astronomy. Priests observed the skies and plotted the courses of stars and planets. These priest-astronomers used their knowledge to produce a calendar with a 365-day year. They divided a year into 12 months, with three seasons: the Nile flood season, the planting season, and the harvest season. They calculated that each month had 30 days, and they added five days to the last month to total 365 days. Although the Egyptians made no allowance for leap years, their calendar, as modified by the Greeks and Romans, is the basis for the modern calendar.

The Egyptians also invented techniques to build impressive stone monuments. Stoneworkers learned how to cut tall obelisks from a single rock, using hot fires and cold water to make the surrounding rocks crack. They then finished the job with hammers and crowbars. Egyptian engineering of temples and pyramids was so precise that each block fit perfectly into the next one.

27

Egyptians also made important medical discoveries. Although Egyptian doctors relied heavily on magic, they made scientific inquiries. For example, by studying the human body, doctors learned to perform surgery. Ancient papyrus texts describe successful operations to set fractured bones and treat spinal injuries. The Greeks and Romans acquired much of their medical knowledge from Egyptian sources.

SECTION REVIEW

1. Why did priests hold such a high position in Egyptian society?
2. What rights did women have in ancient Egypt?
3. Why were scribes necessary to an efficient government?
4. How did the Nile floods contribute to the development of land surveying?

Chapter 2 Review

In Perspective

In ancient Egypt, small farming villages prospered, largely because of the fertile soil and favorable geography of the Nile River valley. The importance of good harvests was reflected in Egyptian religious beliefs. Although Egyptians worshipped many gods, the two most important were Amon-Re, the sun god, and Osiris, whom the Egyptians believed controlled the life-giving waters of the Nile.

Egyptian religion stressed a belief in a happy afterlife, which people earned by living moral lives on earth. On temple and tomb walls, Egyptians wrote in hieroglyphics, recording their beliefs and the deeds of their rulers.

By 3100 B.C., powerful rulers had successfully united the Nile villages. Because Egyptians believed their rulers were gods, pharaohs enjoyed absolute power. Sharp distinctions separated the ruling class from the small middle class and the huge class of peasant farmers, whose lives were regulated by the annual Nile floods. The one way to rise in society was by getting an education at a temple school and becoming a scribe.

During three periods of political unity—the Old Kingdom, the Middle Kingdom, and the New Kingdom—Egyptians made advances in engineering, trade, literature, and art. Their discoveries not only affected their own civilization but also helped shape later civilizations.

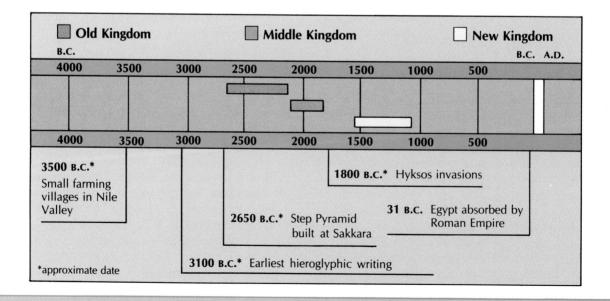

Old Kingdom   Middle Kingdom   New Kingdom

B.C.

| 4000 | 3500 | 3000 | 2500 | 2000 | 1500 | 1000 | 500 | B.C. A.D. |

| 4000 | 3500 | 3000 | 2500 | 2000 | 1500 | 1000 | 500 |

3500 B.C.* Small farming villages in Nile Valley

1800 B.C.* Hyksos invasions

2650 B.C.* Step Pyramid built at Sakkara

31 B.C. Egypt absorbed by Roman Empire

3100 B.C.* Earliest hieroglyphic writing

*approximate date

Recalling Facts

Match each name at left with the correct description at right.

1. Osiris
2. Hatshepsut
3. Lower Egypt
4. Heliopolis
5. Champollion
6. Giza
7. Akenaton
8. Sinai

a. pharaoh who tried to change traditional religious practices
b. center of learning in ancient Egypt
c. northern Egypt and the delta region
d. queen who ruled Egypt for 22 years during the New Kingdom
e. French scholar who deciphered the Rosetta Stone
f. site of three great pyramids
g. Egyptian god of the Nile
h. peninsula connecting Egypt to western Asia

Chapter Checkup

1. Describe who the Nile River affected each of the following in ancient Egypt: (a) farming; (b) trade; (c) religion.
2. (a) How did Egyptians view life after death? (b) What preparations did Egyptians believe were necessary for the afterlife?
3. Describe how the pharaohs in the Old Kingdom organized the government.
4. (a) What did the pharaohs of the Middle Kingdom do for the people of Egypt? (b) Why was the New Kingdom called the Empire Age?
5. (a) What were the main social classes in ancient Egypt? (b) How did each class contribute to Egyptian civilization?
6. Describe ancient Egyptian accomplishments in the following areas: (a) mathematics; (b) astronomy; (c) engineering; (d) medicine.

Critical Thinking

1. **Analyzing** (a) Discuss the ways in which the geographic setting of ancient Egypt both helped and hindered the Egyptians. (b) Do you think the effect of geography was mainly positive or negative? Explain.
2. **Synthesizing** (a) What is the difference between a pictogram and an ideogram? (b) How did Egyptian writing become more complex over time? (c) How did writing contribute to the development of Egyptian civilization?
3. **Applying Information** Akenaton's religious reforms created controversy in ancient Egypt. (a) What factors do you think might explain the failure of his reforms? (b) How might his reforms have been successful?

Relating Past to Present

1. (a) How did the pyramids demonstrate the wealth and power of Egyptian rulers? (b) How do buildings today indicate power and influence?

Developing Basic Skills

1. **Using Visual Evidence** Review the steps for using visual evidence given on page 6. Then study the tomb painting on page 18 and answer the following questions: (a) What does the tomb painting show? (b) Do you think the noble man and woman respect Osiris? How can you tell? (c) Do you think this tomb painting is a reliable source of information about ancient Egypt? Why or why not?
2. **Using Time Lines** A time line enables you to see the order in which events occurred. The earliest date on a horizontal time line is on the left, and the latest date is on the right. Study the time line on page 28. Then answer the following questions: (a) What is the date of the latest event shown on the time line? (b) Which lasted longer, the Old Kingdom or the Middle Kingdom? (c) Did the Hyksos invasions come before or after the New Kingdom was formed?
3. **Map Reading** Review the map reading steps given on page 22. Then study the map on page 16 and answer the following questions: (a) What information does the map provide? (b) For about how many miles on either side of the Nile were the lands flooded during the flood season? (c) Describe the route an Egyptian army might take to travel from Upper Egypt to the Euphrates River.

See page 803 for suggested readings.

3 The Ancient Middle East

(4500 B.C.–331 B.C.)

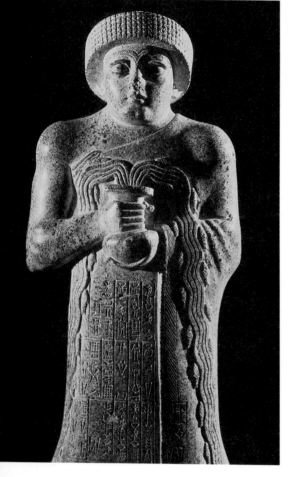

Gudea, ruler of a Sumerian city-state.

> **Chapter Outline**
>
> 1 Sumerian Civilization
>
> 2 A Blending of Cultures
>
> 3 Contributions of Smaller States

"Why do you idle about? Go to school, stand before your schoolfather [teacher], recite your assignment, open your schoolbag, write your tablet, let your big brother [assistant teacher] write your new tablet for you. After you have finished your assignment and reported to your monitor, come to me, and do not wander about in the street. Come now, do you know what I said?"

Nearly 4,000 years ago, a father wrote these words to his son. Then he made his son copy the instructions so he would not forget them. The father was a scribe in ancient Sumer. Sumerian scribes held influential positions in government. The father, who wanted his son to follow his profession, was critical of the boy's ungrateful behavior and lack of interest in school.

"I never said to you 'Follow my caravans.' I never sent you to work, to plow my field," continued the scribe. "Others like you support their parents by working. . . . Night and day am I tortured because of you. Night and day you waste in pleasures."

The clay tablet containing these words is just one of thousands of written records that have enabled scholars to learn about Sumerian civilization. The people of Sumer lived in the Tigris-Euphrates Valley in what is today Iraq. The Sumerians may have been the first people to develop a system of writing, sometime after 3500 B.C. The development of writing was significant because it enabled people to record their beliefs and traditions.

The Sumerians were the first of many peoples to contribute to the civilization of the ancient Middle East. Later peoples built on Sumerian achievements. The Sumerians and their successors were establishing their distinctive patterns of civilization at the same time the Egyptians were shaping their civilization in the Nile River valley.

Unlike Egypt, the Middle East was a battleground on which successive invaders fought for supremacy. The result of these invasions was a constant exchange of ideas and mingling of beliefs. The great palaces and temples of the ancient Middle East have long since disappeared. Yet the Middle East was a source of ideas that have influenced the world to the present day.

1 Sumerian Civilization

Read to Learn ■ how civilization developed in the Tigris-Euphrates Valley
■ how Sumerians advanced civilization

About 4500 B.C., nomadic herders began to plant crops and build permanent settlements on the delta plain at the mouths of the Tigris and Euphrates rivers. Scholars know very little about these early farmers. However, archaeological excavations indicate that between 4000 B.C. and 3500 B.C. other nomadic people, migrating from the Armenian Plateau northwest of the delta, conquered the delta region. The newcomers, the Sumerians, created the first known civilization in the ancient Middle East.

The civilization that emerged in the Tigris-Euphrates Valley differed in many ways from Egyptian civilization. The Sumerian outlook on life, their government, and their religion were unlike those in Egypt. So, too, was the geography of the area.

The Fertile Crescent: Crossroads of the World

The Tigris-Euphrates Valley lies in the eastern end of the Fertile Crescent, an area that stretches from the Persian Gulf to the Mediterranean Sea. (See the map on page 32.) The Fertile Crescent received its name from the rich soil of the region and its half-circle, or crescent, shape.

The Fertile Crescent has often been called the crossroads of the world because it commands access to three continents: Asia, Africa, and Europe. Unlike Egypt, the Fertile Crescent has few natural barriers. The Arabian and Syrian deserts offered less protection to early civilizations than the Libyan Desert did in Egypt.

The position of the region made it subject to frequent migrations and invasions. Waves of migrating peoples descended from the mountains north and west of the Tigris-Euphrates Valley. Invaders such as the Hittites swept into the Fertile Crescent from Asia Minor. Because of the migrations and invasions, the Fertile Crescent was the site of frequent warfare.

The diversity of the people living in the Fertile Crescent made if difficult to unite the area under a single ruler. Yet the continuous contact among different peoples also stimulated an exchange of ideas that led to significant achievements. For example, the wheel and writing probably originated in the Fertile Crescent.

Land Between Two Rivers

The Greeks called the Tigris-Euphrates Valley "Mesopotamia," meaning "land between two rivers." Like the Nile in Egypt, the Tigris and Euphrates rivers dominated the lives of the people in Mesopotamia. The two rivers originate in the rugged highlands of the Armenian Plateau and run parallel for over 1,000 miles (1,600 kilometers). In the spring or early summer, melting snows from the mountains sometimes cause the rivers to overflow. However, the floods of the Tigris and Euphrates, unlike those of the Nile, are unpredictable. In some years, the rivers do not rise above their banks. In others, savage floods inflict enormous damage.

In ancient times, many floods swept across lower Mesopotamia. About 4000 B.C., flood waters deposited a bed of clay eight feet (2.4 meters) thick. The flood destroyed farms, villages, and animals and drowned many people. Only a few towns, which were built on high ground, survived. In addition to floods, lower Mesopotamia suffered summer droughts and hot winds, which could turn fertile soil to dust, shrivel crops, and cause famine.

Despite the danger of flooding, however, the rivers supported the development of an advanced civilization. Trade along the rivers contributed to the wealth of Mesopotamian cities. Silt left by floods made the soil fertile. Good soil meant that the people living in Mesopotamia could rely on a stable food supply in most years.

Map Skill *The fertile soil and the wild game of the Tigris-Euphrates Valley made the area attractive for early settlers. The rivers served as arteries for trade among the cities of Mesopotamia. Why was the Fertile Crescent called the crossroads of the world?*

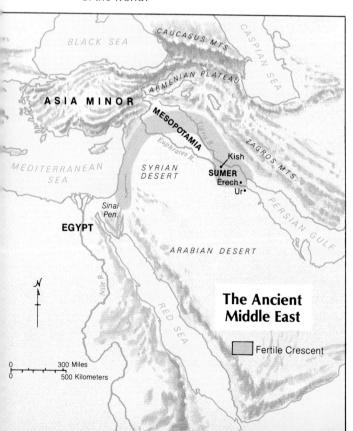

The Ancient Middle East

☐ Fertile Crescent

Silt also created a delta at the mouths of the Tigris and Euphrates rivers. Like the Nile delta, the delta in lower Mesopotamia was a maze of swamps and marshlands. To drain the swamps and channel the water to farmland, the people of Mesopotamia built an intricate network of dikes and canals. The construction and upkeep of this complex irrigation system required an elaborate, well-run government.

City-State Government

By 3000 B.C., the villages of lower Mesopotamia had grown into prosperous cities. Tens of thousands of people lived in the chief Sumerian cities of Ur, Erech, and Kish. Each city was an independent city-state with its own government and ruler. In a *city-state*, a large town or city and the surrounding countryside cooperate for mutual defense. In addition, the government of a Sumerian city-state supervised the building and maintenance of dikes and canals in the surrounding farmlands. The government also constructed strong defensive walls and stored food in case of invasion. When threatened by attack, farmers took refuge behind the city walls.

Each city-state worshipped its own god or goddess as well as other gods. The people of the city-state believed they were wholly dependent on their city's god for food and protection. The land and everything people produced belonged to the god. Farmers turned over about two thirds of each harvest to the temple.

In Mesopotamia, where a disaster such as a flood or invasion could strike suddenly, people believed that their survival depended on keeping their gods content. Priests alone knew how to appease the gods, and they acted as intermediaries between citizens and the gods. As a result, in the early city-states priests ruled in the name of the gods.

As Sumerian city-states grew, they were in constant conflict. For example, Ur fought with Erech for control of the lower Euphrates. Some scholars suggest that frequent warfare gave military leaders who could successfully defend their city-states increased power. According to this theory, military

The Sumerian city-states battled each other for control of Mesopotamia. This wooden panel is believed to be a standard carried in battle by a prince from Ur. It shows foot soldiers marching into battle and wheeled war chariots. The Sumerians were among the first people to use wheeled chariots.

leaders gradually replaced priests as rulers of the Sumerian city-states.

The Sumerians did not worship their rulers as gods. Instead, they believed their kings were the gods' representatives on earth. But as intermediaries between the gods and the people, Sumerian kings commanded absolute obedience.

Religion

The most important building in each Sumerian city-state was the *ziggurat* (ZIHG u rat), the home or temple of the god of that city. Pyramid-shaped, the ziggurat was often six to seven stories high. The Sumerians believed that gods descended to earth using the ziggurat as a ladder.

Like the Egyptians, the Sumerians were polytheistic. They worshiped other gods in addition to the god of their city-state. Sume-

rians believed that a council of gods and goddesses ruled the earth, deciding the fate of individuals and cities. Each god had a specific rank or place within this council.

Sumerians explained natural events as the results of actions by gods and goddesses. For example, they believed that winter, the season of hunger and hardship, occurred when the god Dumuzi (duh MOO zee) died and descended into the underworld. Only when the goddess Inanna (ihn AH nah) rescued her husband Dumuzi from the underworld did spring arrive, bringing new life. Every year, to ensure the return of the growing season, the story of Inanna and Dumuzi was reenacted.

In Egypt, the favorable climate of the Nile Valley allowed the people to enjoy life and see their gods as kindly forces. By contrast, fear of natural disasters and invasion probably contributed to a gloomy outlook on

33

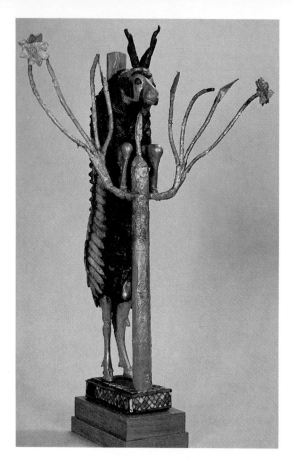

The Sumerians believed that their well-being depended on keeping the gods happy. Therefore, they made elaborate images of sacred animals such as this golden goat. The goat poised against a golden tree vividly reminded Sumerians of the different forms their gods might take on earth. This figure may have been used in religious ceremonies as an offering stand or incense holder.

life among the Sumerians. They believed that the gods punished them by sending floods or famine. The Sumerians' outlook on life colored their belief about the afterlife. At death, they expected to descend forever into a dark underworld, a huge cave filled with nothing but dust and silence.

A Written Language

The need for accurate records led to the development of writing after 3500 B.C. Sumerian writing originated as pictograms and ideograms, but scribes gradually simplified the system, using symbols to represent sounds and syllables.

Sumerians used a stylus, or sharpened reed instrument, to make symbols on tablets of wet clay. They then baked the tablets to harden the clay. Because the symbols were made up of wedge-like shapes, the writing was later called *cuneiform* (kyoo NEE uh FORM), from the Latin word "cuneus," or wedge. Traders and conquering armies helped spread cuneiform writing to other peoples of the Fertile Crescent.

As the Sumerian city-states grew, the need for scribes increased. Priests employed scribes to write down laws, treaties, and religious texts. As trade expanded, merchants hired scribes to record business deals, property holdings, and contracts.

To train scribes, priests set up schools in the temples. Only boys, usually the sons of scribes, attended temple schools. Students paid tuition fees and endured strict discipline in order to earn a privileged position as a scribe. Although no schools existed for girls, priestesses and the daughters of wealthy Sumerians probably learned to read and write from private tutors.

Legacy for Later Peoples

Sumerians were the first people known to use a wheel. They either invented it or borrowed the idea from earlier settlers in Mesopotamia. Wheeled carts and the sail, another Sumerian invention, enabled merchants to engage in long-distance trade. Sumerians also used wheels on war chariots. The use of wheeled vehicles spread slowly across the ancient world. You will recall that the Hyksos introduced war chariots to the Egyptians at the end of the Middle Kingdom.

The Sumerians made many improvements in farming. They constructed complex irrigation systems to channel water through the sun-baked plains, planted trees to serve as wind breaks, and invented a plow. They also developed an accurate twelve-month calendar to keep track of the seasons.

Like the Egyptians, the Sumerians used arithmetic and geometry to survey land and reestablish property lines after floods swept away boundary markers. The Sumerian system of arithmetic was based on the number

In long narrative poems, or epics, the peoples of Mesopotamia preserved ancient legends and passed on religious teachings, accounts of disasters, and stories of heroes. The oldest example of Mesopotamian literature is the Gilgamesh Epic, which originated in Sumer.

The Gilgamesh Epic is a rich collection of stories and myths. Different characters speak with Gilgamesh about matters of life and death. Here Enkidu describes to Gilgamesh a place he was forced to enter in a dream.

He [a lion-pawed man] seized me and led me
    down to the house of darkness, house of
    Irkalla,
the house where one who goes in never
    comes out again,
the road that, if one takes it, one never comes
    back,
the house that, if one lives there, one never
    sees light,
the place where they live on dust, their food is
    mud;
their clothes are like birds' clothes, a garment
    of wings,
and they see no light, living in blackness:

on the door and door-bolt, deeply settled
    dust.

In the house of ashes, where I entered,
I saw the mighty, their crowns fallen to the
    dirt.
I heard about crowned kings who ruled the
    lands from days of old,
worldly images of Anu and Enlil, waiting table
    with roast meats,
serving baked goods, filling glasses with water
    from cool steins.

In the house of ashes, where I entered,
there lives the funeral priest who brings to-
    gether gods and men. . . .
There sits the queen of below-earth, Ereshki-
    gal:
Belit-tseri, tablet scribe of the underworld,
    kneels before her.
She holds a tablet and reads aloud to her.
Lifting her head. Ereshkigal looked directly at
    me—me:
"Who has brought this one here . . . ?"

1. What place is Enkidu describing to Gilgamesh?
2. What does the extract show about the Sumerian view of the afterlife?

60, which led to such present-day measurements as the 60-second minute and the 60-minute hour.

Sumerian architecture influenced the civilizations of Mesopotamia for more than a thousand years. The Sumerians were the first to use arches, columns, ramps, and inclined walks. Because stone was scarce, Sumerian builders used bricks made of sun-baked clay. Later peoples built temples that rose in a series of terraces to heights of six or seven stories like the Sumerian ziggurat. The Egyptians may have adopted the idea of pyramids from the Sumerians.

About 2500 B.C., invaders conquered the city-states of Sumer. Sumerian civilization ceased to exist about 1750 B.C., but its traditions and achievements left a lasting impression on its conquerors.

SECTION REVIEW

1. Locate: Sumer, Tigris River, Euphrates River, Armenian Plateau, Arabian Desert, Syrian Desert, Ur, Erech, Kish.

2. Identify: Fertile Crescent, Mesopotamia.

3. Define: city-state, ziggurat, cuneiform.

4. List two consequences of the movement of peoples across the Fertile-Crescent.

5. Give one advantage and one disadvantage of living in the Tigris-Euphrates Valley in ancient times.

6. How did the Sumerian view of an afterlife differ from the Egyptian view?

7. (a) What role did scribes play in Sumerian city-states? (b) How were they trained?

8. List four contributions the Sumerians made to civilization.

2 A Blending of Cultures

Read to Learn ■ how ideas spread throughout the Fertile Crescent
■ what contributions Assyrians and Persians made to civilization

Many different peoples invaded the Fertile Crescent between 2500 B.C. and 500 B.C. Each group of invaders brought with them their own culture, but they also adopted some of the achievements of the people they conquered. During this period, the peoples of the Fertile Crescent advanced civilization.

The First Empire

As older Sumerian city-states declined, Akkad, a city to the north, rose to power. About 2350 B.C., Sargon, an Akkadian soldier of humble origins, established the first empire in recorded history. With an empire reaching from southern Mesopotamia to the Mediterranean Sea, Sargon proclaimed himself "Lord of the Four Quarters of the World," a title adopted by many later conquerors. A talented ruler, Sargon repaired and extended the flood control and irrigation systems of Mesopotamia. He also sent his armies to protect trade caravans.

Sumerian civilization exerted a powerful influence on the Akkadian Empire. Although the Akkadian language differed from the Sumerian, the conquerors adopted cuneiform for writing. Scribes translated Sumerian religious, scientific, and literary works into Akkadian. As a result, the Akkadians absorbed Sumerian religious beliefs and ideas about government and society.

Later Akkadian rulers lacked Sargon's abilities, and civil war resumed. For a brief time, Ur-Nammu, ruler of Ur, reunited the city-states. About 2050 B.C., Ur-Nammu compiled the first known code of laws. This code summarized Sumerian ideas of justice, emphasizing the king's duty to protect the people and correct any existing wrongs.

About 2000 B.C., groups of nomadic peoples invaded Mesopotamia, attacking the river valley cities. One group, the Amorites, built the small village of Babylon on the Euphrates River. Slowly, the small village rose from obscurity into a magnificent city-state boasting of a giant ziggurat dedicated to the chief Babylonian god, Marduk. By 1700 B.C., the king of Babylon, Hammurabi (HAH mu RAH bee), had carved out an empire in Mesopotamia. (See the map on page 37.)

The Code of Hammurabi

Hammurabi was one of the great rulers of ancient times. He was an outstanding general, an excellent administrator, and a patron of the arts. In hundreds of surviving letters, he shows concern for details such as clearing blocked river channels, punishing dishonest officials, reforming the calendar, and honoring the gods. However, he is best known for drawing up a uniform code of laws.

To achieve unity within his empire, Hammurabi appointed a committee to revise existing laws. His purpose, he declared, was "to cause justice to prevail in the land, to destroy the wicked and the evil, to prevent the strong from oppressing the weak. . . . and to further the welfare of the people."

Although the resulting system of laws relied on earlier law codes, the Code of Hammurabi represents the first effort by an empire to record all its laws. The code contained 282 laws arranged under headings such as trade, family, labor, real estate, and personal property.

The basic principle behind Hammurabi's Code was "an eye for an eye and a tooth for a tooth." A man who blinded another was punished by losing an eye. If a house collapsed and killed the owner, the builder was put to death.

Despite the severity of most punishments, Hammurabi's Code was a fundamental contribution to civilization. It distinguished between major and minor offenses, established the state as the authority that would enforce the law, and attempted to ensure social justice. Hammurabi had the laws carved on a stone column, which was placed for everyone to see. Atop the column sat

Shamash, the sun god and god of justice, handing the laws to Hammurabi. The god's image reminded Babylonians that by breaking a law they not only offended the king but also the gods.

Beginning of the Iron Age

After Hammurabi's death, rebellions and invasions weakened the Babylonian Empire. In 1600 B.C., it fell to the Kassites, who invaded from the east. About 1550 B.C., another group of invaders, the Hittites, moved into the Fertile Crescent from Asia Minor. The empire established by the Hittites eventually reached as far as the northern Euphrates Valley. Hittite rulers adopted Babylonian cuneiform and ideas about government and religion, which they carried back into Asia Minor.

The Hittites owed their military success to careful strategy, skillful diplomacy, and superior weapons. Expert metalworkers, they were among the first people to use iron for spears and battle axes. Iron weapons gave the Hittites an advantage over enemies armed with softer, bronze spears.

The Hittites carefully guarded the secret of ironworking. Even so, the new technology spread to other peoples. By 1200 B.C., iron was being used in place of bronze, ushering in the Iron Age. The Hittites soon lost their military advantage. About the same time, a new onslaught of invaders swept into Asia Minor and the Fertile Crescent, destroying the Hittite Empire and the sophisticated city-state civilizations of Mesopotamia.

The Assyrians

Among the peoples who invaded the Fertile Crescent after 1200 B.C., the most feared and hated were the Assyrians (uh SIHR ee uhnz). The Assyrians were hardy nomads who settled in the Tigris Valley, where they built a city-state named after their chief god, Assur (AH sur). Beginning about 1100 B.C., the Assyrians systematically established an empire that included the entire Fertile Crescent and Egypt. (See the map on page 40.)

The mighty Assyrian Empire depended on a highly disciplined army. Iron weapons, an excellent cavalry, and effective siege

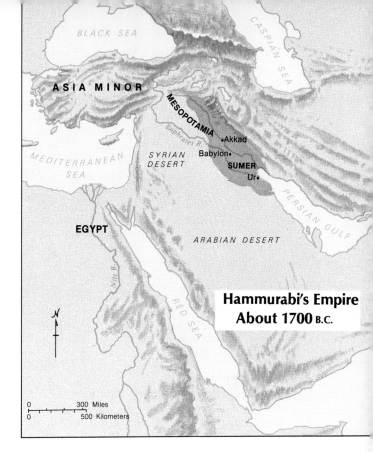

Map Skill   *The empire established by Hammurabi included most of the land that had been ruled by the Akkadians. How many miles did Hammurabi's Empire extend along the Tigris River?*

equipment, or machines used to destroy fortified cities, carried the Assyrians from one victory to the next. In addition to military strength, the Assyrians relied on terror to subdue their enemies. For example, when the Assyrians captured Babylon, about 700 B.C., they tortured and beheaded prisoners, enslaved women and children, and reduced the city to rubble.

Assyrian government was as harsh and efficient as the Assyrian army. The empire was divided into provinces, each ruled by a governor responsible to the king, who had absolute power. The Assyrians built roads to speed the movement of their army from the capital to the provinces. They deported groups of troublesome people to remote parts of the empire, where they could not organize rebellions. One side effect of these forced migrations was an exchange of ideas among the conquered peoples of the Fertile Crescent.

37

When people developed systems of writing, they created written records. Today these records provide scholars with useful information about historical events, everyday activities of people, and the values or beliefs of different societies. Historians distinguish between two types of written records: primary sources and secondary sources.

Primary sources are first-hand, or original, accounts based on the experiences of people who were involved in an event, or who lived in a particular society. For example, eyewitness accounts, official government documents, treaties, law codes, letters, and business contracts are primary sources. By contrast, *secondary sources* are second-hand accounts based on the writings or evidence of others. Textbooks and encyclopedias are secondary sources because they summarize information from primary sources and from other secondary sources.

When scholars discover a primary source, such as a clay tablet covered with cuneiform, they translate and study the document to see what it reveals about an event or a civilization. Study the following excerpts from Hammurabi's Code. Then follow the steps described below to analyze the code.

1. **Identify the document by asking what, who, when, where, and why.** Based on the document and your reading on pages 36 to 37, answer the following questions: (a) What kind of primary source is this? (b) Who wrote it? (c) About when was it written? (d) Where was it written? (e) Why was it written?

2. **Read the document to discover information about a particular event or society.** As you read each statement, analyze what it says. (a) What does law 138 say? (b) Which law or laws give information about when a woman may leave her husband's house? (c) What information about government does this document provide? (d) Which law or laws gave women certain rights? What rights did they give?

3. **Study the document to draw conclusions about a particular event or society.** To draw conclusions, you need to review all the information given and evaluate the resulting picture. Refer to the excerpts to answer the following questions: (a) Under what circumstances could a man divorce his wife in Babylonian society? Under what circumstances could a woman leave her husband? (b) Did Babylonian women have freedom to make their own decisions? Cite evidence to justify your answer. (c) Based on these laws, how would you describe the attitude toward women in Babylonian society?

Excerpts from Hammurabi's Code

133   If a free man was taken captive, but there was enough to live on in his house, his wife shall not leave her house but shall wait for his return.

134   If a free man was taken captive and there was not sufficient to live on in his house, his wife may enter the house of another man without incurring any blame.

138   If a free man wishes to divorce his wife who did not bear him children, he shall return to her the dowry which she brought from her father's house and then he may divorce her.

142   If a woman so hated her husband that she refused to stay with him, her record shall be investigated at her city council, and if she was careful and was not at fault, even though her husband has been going out and criticizing her greatly, that woman, without incurring any blame at all may take her dowry and go off to her father's house.

With war loot and taxes collected from conquered peoples, the Assyrians built a capital at Nineveh (NIHN uh vuh). The Assyrian king Assurbanipal (AH sur BAHN ih pahl) built a great library at Nineveh. In it, he stored a vast collection of over 22,000 clay tablets written in the cuneiform of Sumer and Babylon. Although the Assyrians were despised as brutal conquerors, they made a lasting contribution to civilization by organizing and preserving these invaluable records in the world's first library.

"I am Assurbanipal, King of the Universe, King of Assyria. . . . I seized . . . a fierce lion of the plain by his ears. . . . I pierced his body with my lance." Thus, the ruthless Assyrian leader celebrated his hunting skill. The lion hunt shown here was one of a series of sculptures that decorated Assurbanipal's palace at Nineveh.

Revival of Babylon

In 612 B.C., oppressed peoples within the Assyrian Empire joined the Medes and Chaldeans (kal DEE uhnz) to capture and completely destroy Nineveh. The victors divided up the Assyrian Empire. The Medes occupied the highlands north of Mesopotamia, and the Chaldeans established an empire in Mesopotamia proper. During the reign of Nebuchadnezzar (NEHB uh kuhd NEHZ uhr), the Chaldeans extended their empire over the entire Fertile Crescent.

Nebuchadnezzar rebuilt Babylon as a symbol of strength. Massive walls surrounded the city and the outlying farmlands, thereby protecting the food supply during a siege. Nebuchadnezzar's immense palace, decorated with blue glazed bricks, was rivaled in splendor by the famous hanging gardens of Babylon. According to legend, Nebuchadnezzar designed the gardens for his wife, who despised the flat plains of Mesopotamia and longed for the mountains of her Median homeland. The many terraces filled with exotic plants and trees amazed travelers, who returned home awed by this wonder of the ancient world.

Like earlier peoples of Mesopotamia, the Chaldeans advanced the study of mathematics and astronomy, largely because of their interest in astrology. They believed that the positions of the stars, planets, and comets determined the fates of individuals and empires. By charting the paths of planets, stars, and comets, Chaldean priests acquired a vast store of knowledge about eclipses and the movement of heavenly bodies. They also accurately calculated the length of a year to within a few minutes. Priests, who used their knowledge of the stars to predict the future, occupied a privileged position in Chaldean society.

After the death of Nebuchadnezzar, the Chaldean Empire, like those before it, suffered civil wars. In 539 B.C., Babylon fell to invading Persians. Unlike the Assyrians, the Persians left the city standing, and it remained a flourishing center of commerce and learning.

The Persians

The Persians rapidly became a powerful force in the ancient Middle East. In 550 B.C., Cyrus (SĪ rehs), king of Persia, led a successful revolt against the Medes. Within 20 years, he had conquered the Fertile Crescent and Asia Minor. His successors added Afghanistan, northern India, and Egypt to the Persian Empire. (See the map on page 56.) Cyrus was a remarkable military leader and a wise ruler. He treated conquered peoples with tolerance, allowed them a measure of self-government, and respected their religions and customs.

Government. Cyrus's son-in-law, Darius, completed the task of organizing the vast Persian Empire. Following the Assyrian model, he divided the empire into 20 provinces, or *satrapies* (SAY truh peez). Each satrapy was ruled by a governor, or satrap, who collected taxes and administered uniform laws. As a check on the satrap, Darius sent royal inspectors, called "the Eyes and Ears of the King," into every province.

To ensure rapid communication, the Persians improved the Assyrian road system. The main highway, the Great Royal Road, stretched from Asia Minor to Susa, one of

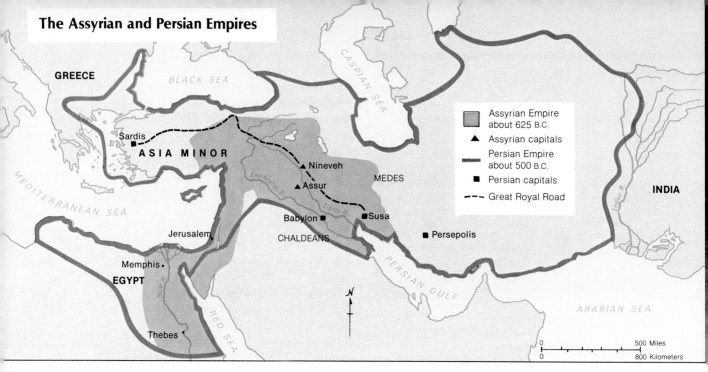

The Assyrian and Persian Empires

Map Skill   *The Assyrians and the Persians established vast empires in the ancient Middle East. Both depended on good roads to help tie their empires together. Why do you think the Persians created four separate capitals?*

the four capitals of the empire. Relay stations with fresh horses were set up along the Great Royal Road so that royal messengers could cover 1,600 miles (about 2,500 kilometers) in under ten days.

The efficient government and transportation system, as well as trade and the policy of toleration, helped draw the empire together. Yet Persian power did not go unchallenged. As you will read in Chapter 5, Darius and his heirs failed to conquer Greece, and in 331 B.C. a weakened Persian Empire fell to the armies of Alexander the Great.

Religion. The early Persians were polytheistic, but by the time of Darius they had adopted a new religion named after its founder, Zoroaster (ZOH roh AS ter). According to Zoroaster, who lived about 600 B.C., the world was a battleground for the forces of good and evil. Every individual made a choice in his or her lifetime to join Ahura Mazda (AH hu ruh   MAZ duh), god of goodness, wisdom, and truth, or to follow Ahriman (AH rih muhn), the evil spirit. Zoroaster predicted that at the end of the world Ahura Mazda would win the final battle. Those who had lived moral lives would be rewarded with eternal life in paradise. Those who had

followed Ahriman would be condemned to eternal suffering.

The sacred book of Zoroastrianism was the *Zend Avesta* (ZEHND uh VEHS tuh). This collection of hymns and religious poems contained several ideas that influenced later peoples of the Fertile Crescent. For example, Zoroastrianism emphasized ethical, or moral, conduct, a final day of judgment, and the individual's role in determining his or her salvation. Later, Hebrews and Christians stressed similar concepts.

SECTION REVIEW

1. Locate: Akkad, Babylon, Asia Minor, Nineveh, Susa.

2. Identify: Sargon, Hammurabi, Assurbanipal, Nebuchadnezzar, Great Royal Road, Zoroaster, *Zend Avesta.*

3. Define: satrapy.

4. (a) Why did Hammurabi draw up a law code? (b) What aspects of life did it cover?

5. How did the Assyrians organize their empire?

6. How did the Persian ruler Cyrus treat the peoples he conquered?

7. According to Zoroaster, what two forces were at war in the world?

3 Contributions of Smaller States

Read to Learn ◾ how the Phoenicians and Lydians left their mark on the economy of the Middle East
◾ how the Hebrews influenced religion and ethics

The great empires of the ancient Middle East contributed to civilization and spread their knowledge through conquest. Several small, independent states also made contributions. Between 1200 B.C. and 500 B.C. the Phoenicians (fuh NEESH uhnz), Lydians (LIHD ee uhnz), and Hebrews made advances in the areas of writing, trade, and religion.

Phoenicians: Carriers of Civilization

The Phoenicians built small city-states along the eastern Mediterranean coast, in the area of present-day Lebanon. They thrived on profits from trading. The Phoenicians were well known for timber from cedar trees and for a rare purple dye made from murex, a marine snail found along the Mediterranean coast. Because Phoenician purple cloth was worn mostly by kings, the color purple came to be associated with royalty.

From the bustling port cities of Tyre and Sidon, Phoenician traders crisscrossed the Mediterranean. Beginning about 1200 B.C., they established a network of colonies from Cyprus to Gibraltar. (See the map on page 42.) About 814 B.C., they settled Carthage in northern Africa. Carthage dominated trade in the western Mediterranean until 221 B.C.

The Phoenicians earned the name "carriers of civilization" for their role in spreading the culture of the ancient world. Through trade and colonization, they introduced the achievements of Mesopotamia and Egypt to the less advanced peoples of the western Mediterranean. They also made their own contribution by improving the alphabet.

The Phoenician alphabet contained 22 symbols, each of which represented a single consonant. Unlike cuneiform and the Egyptian system of writing, the new alphabet was fairly easy to learn.

Phoenician merchants and colonists helped spread the use of their alphabet. About 800 B.C., the Greeks adopted it and added vowel sounds. Later, the Romans adapted the Greek alphabet, and they passed the resulting written language on to the western world. The very word "alphabet" comes from "aleph" and "beth," the first two symbols of the Phoenician alphabet.

The Lydians: Influential Traders

Like the Phoenicians, the Lydians left their mark on history through trade rather than conquest. From their capital, Sardis, the Lydians dominated trade in Asia Minor.

The most significant contribution of the Lydians was the introduction of coined money as a medium of exchange in trade. Traditionally, people had relied on the barter system, exchanging one set of goods for another. The barter system limited the development of trade because two people could trade with one another only if each had a product the other one wanted. The use of coins eliminated that problem. Furthermore, coins could be stored and saved for later use, and they allowed merchants to establish a system of set prices. An economic system based on money rather than barter is called a *money economy.*

Through trade with the Greeks and Persians, Lydian merchants spread the idea of using coined money. Lydian coins were imprinted with the king's image as a guarantee that they were the correct weight and value. Wherever coinage came into use, a more complex economic system developed.

The Hebrews

Palestine, which was southeast of Phoenicia, was another crossroads for nomadic herders and conquering armies. (See the map on page 42.) Arameans, Hurrians, and Philistines, after whom the region was named, were among the many peoples who migrated into the Jordan River valley of Palestine after 2000 B.C. About the same time, the Hebrews were moving from Mesopotamia into northern Palestine. Although the Hebrews ruled only a small state for a relatively brief period, their religious beliefs profoundly affected later civilizations in the western world.

Early history. The Hebrews believed that God was the moving force behind everything that happened to them. To show God's role in history, they preserved their early history in a sacred text, known to many people today as the Old Testament. According to the Old Testament, God gave Canaan, or Palestine, to the Hebrews. About 1800 B.C., drought and famine forced some Hebrews to migrate to Egypt, where the pharaohs eventually enslaved them.* The Old Testament book Exodus records how a courageous man named Moses forced the pharaoh Ramses II to free the Hebrews.

The Hebrews considered Moses one of their most important leaders and their chief law giver. After leading the Hebrews out of Egypt, Moses gave them the Ten Commandments, a set of religious and moral laws. The Hebrews believed that God had revealed the

---

* Some scholars suggest that the Hebrews settled in the Nile delta region about the time of the Hyksos invasions. After the Egyptians expelled the Hyksos, the New Kingdom pharaohs began to enslave other foreign peoples, including the Hebrews.

Map Skill   *The Phoenicians established colonies along the shores of the Mediterranean Sea, as this map shows. Daring Phoenician sailors ventured into the Atlantic as far north as Britain and probably rounded southern Africa in search of gold and ivory. How did the locations of Phoenicia and Palestine make them vulnerable to invasion by other peoples?*

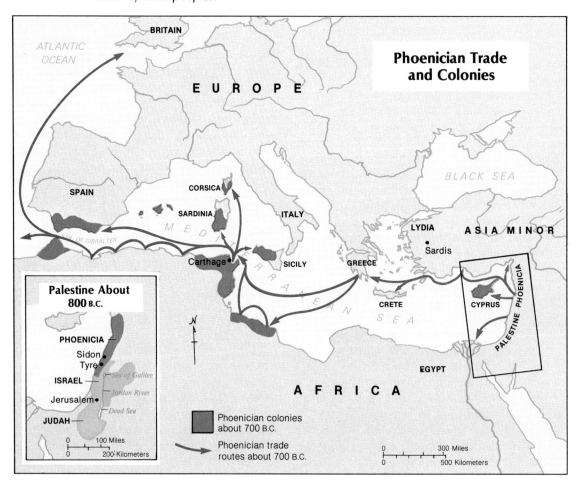

laws to Moses and had thereby made a *covenant*, or binding agreement, with them. According to that covenant, God would protect the Hebrews as the "Chosen People" if they obeyed the commandments.

Obedience to God's laws bound the Hebrews together as they wandered from Egypt, across the Sinai, into Palestine. Hardened by life in the desert, they fought the Philistines and other peoples for control of the Jordan River valley. About 1025 B.C., the Hebrews organized the kingdom of Israel in Palestine.

The kingdom of Israel. During the reigns of David and Solomon, from about 1000 to 930 B.C., the kingdom of Israel flourished. A successful general and skillful diplomat, David decisively defeated the Philistines and forged alliances with other peoples to make the Hebrews supreme in Palestine. David's son Solomon transformed the city of Jerusalem into a splendid capital. In the center of Jerusalem, he built a massive temple that symbolized the Hebrew faith.

Although Solomon won recognition as a wise ruler, his lavish spending resulted in heavy taxes, which caused popular discontent. After Solomon died, in 930 B.C., violent disagreements split the kingdom into two separate states: Israel in the north and Judah in the south. Powerful empires soon threatened the Hebrew kingdoms. In 722 B.C., the Assyrians conquered Israel and transported thousands of Hebrews to distant corners of their empire. In 586 B.C., the Chaldean king Nebuchadnezzar seized Judah, destroyed the temple in Jerusalem, and sent the Hebrews as slaves to Babylon.

The Persians later freed the Hebrews from captivity. Some of the Hebrews returned to Jerusalem and rebuilt their temple. However, Israel no longer existed as an independent state. The Persians, then the Greeks, and later the Romans ruled Palestine. Although they no longer had a separate political identity, the Hebrews preserved their religious ideas and cultural traditions because of the covenant they believed they had with God. Many of these ideas would influence two other religions that later rose in the Middle East—Christianity and Islam.

An Ethical World View

Unlike other peoples of the ancient Middle East, the Hebrews were monotheistic. They believed in one all-powerful God, called Yahweh. But their view of God changed over time. To the early Hebrews, God was a fierce, vengeful figure who inflicted harsh punishments if angered. Later, the Hebrews came to see God as wise and forgiving.

Hebrew law. The Hebrews developed an ethical world view—that is, they believed that people and their rulers should lead moral lives. This view grew out of the moral and religious laws recorded in the first five books of the Old Testament, which are called the Torah. Among the most important laws of the Torah are the Ten Commandments, which forbid lying, cheating, stealing, and murder. The commandments also counsel men and women to be just, love their neighbors, and obey their parents.

According to the Hebrews, no one was above God's law, not even a king. A Hebrew king was not considered a god or the earthly representative of gods as kings were in neighboring cultures.

Hebrew laws, as expressed in the Torah, have been compared to Hammurabi's Code since both law codes contained the principle of "an eye for an eye." However, Hammurabi's laws, which set the death penalty for many minor offenses, were more severe. Hebrew law generally held human life in greater respect, leaving the ultimate judgment and punishment to God. Furthermore, while slavery was an accepted practice in the ancient world, Hebrew law demanded that slaves be treated with kindness.

Women had few rights under Hebrew law, but respect for women was taught in the commandment "honor thy father and thy mother." In addition, the Hebrews honored certain outstanding women, such as the prophet Deborah, who, according to the Old Testament, led the Hebrews to a victory against their enemies in Palestine.

Prophets. Prophets also contributed to the Hebrew's ethical world view. The Hebrews believed that the prophets were messengers God sent to reveal His will. Prophets scolded the Hebrews for wickedness, laziness, and worshipping other gods. The prophet Isaiah (ī ZAY uh), for example, called on the king and people of Judah to "cease to do evil, learn to do good, seek justice, relieve the oppressed, judge [look after] the fatherless, plead for the widow." Out of the teachings of the prophets, the Hebrews developed strong traditions that stressed respect for the individual, concern for the poor, and obedience to God's laws.

Some Hebrew beliefs were similar to the beliefs of other peoples in the ancient Middle East. Like the Zoroastrians, for example, they believed that individuals had to make a choice between good and evil. However, the Hebrews were the first people to develop an ethical world view, which included the basic principles of belief in one God and concern for individuals.

SECTION REVIEW

1. Locate: Sidon, Tyre, Phoenicia, Carthage, Sardis, Palestine, Jordan River, Jerusalem.
2. Identify: Ten Commandments, Moses, David, Solomon, Torah.
3. Define: money economy, covenant.
4. Why were the Phoenicians called "carriers of civilization"?
5. How did Hebrew law differ from Hammurabi's code?

Chapter 3 Review

In Perspective

Sumer was the first civilization to develop in the ancient Middle East. Like Egypt, Sumer was a river valley civilization. It rose in the fertile Tigris-Euphrates Valley. But the Tigris and Euphrates rivers behaved very differently from the Nile, with its predictable floods. Despite destructive floods, the Sumerians built an advanced civilization.

The constant migrations of peoples into the Fertile Crescent helped spread Sumerian achievements across the ancient Middle East. Also, each of the peoples who conquered the Fertile Crescent left their marks on civilization in this region. For example, the Hittites introduced ironworking, and the Assyrians developed an efficient government organization. The Persians' system of government and religion had widespread influence.

Smaller trading states, such as Phoenicia and Lydia, also helped spread the civilization of the Middle East. The Phoenicians improved the alphabet, and the Lydians introduced coined money. The Hebrews developed a monotheistic religion that stressed ethical conduct.

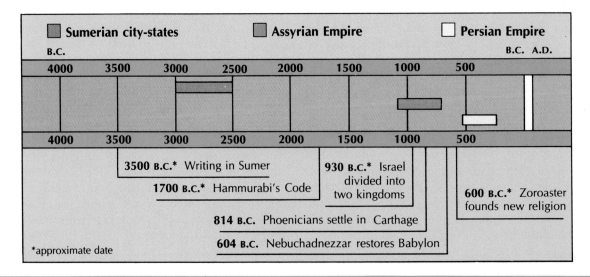

| ■ Sumerian city-states | ■ Assyrian Empire | □ Persian Empire |

B.C. | | B.C. A.D.

4000 3500 3000 2500 2000 1500 1000 500

3500 B.C.* Writing in Sumer
1700 B.C.* Hammurabi's Code
930 B.C.* Israel divided into two kingdoms
814 B.C. Phoenicians settle in Carthage
604 B.C. Nebuchadnezzar restores Babylon
600 B.C.* Zoroaster founds new religion

*approximate date

Recalling Facts

Decide if the following statements are true or false. If a statement is false, rewrite the statement to make it true.

1. The people of Mesopotamia built dikes and dug canals to control their environment.
2. The Sumerians viewed their gods as friendly and helpful.
3. Many peoples of the ancient Middle East adopted cuneiform writing.
4. Under Hammurabi's Code, the penalty for every crime was death.
5. The Assyrians destroyed the records of earlier civilizations.
6. Nebuchadnezzar rebuilt Nineveh.
7. The Persian king Darius employed inspectors to check on royal governors.
8. Zoroaster believed the forces of evil would defeat the forces of good.
9. The Phoenicians improved the alphabet by using symbols to represent sounds.
10. The Hebrews were polytheistic.

Chapter Checkup

1. How did the environment of Mesopotamia probably affect Sumerian religious beliefs?
2. (a) What was the basic principle of the Code of Hammurabi? (b) Why was Hammurabi's Code an important achievement?
3. Describe the contribution or contributions each of the following peoples made to civilization: (a) Hittites; (b) Assyrians; (c) Chaldeans.
4. Based on the map on page 40 and your reading, compare the Assyrian and Persian empires in terms of: (a) size; (b) treatment of conquered peoples; (c) government organization.
5. (a) What were the main religious beliefs of the Zoroastrians? (b) How did the teachings of Zoroaster encourage people to live good lives?
6. (a) What laws helped mold the ethical world view of the Hebrews? (b) How did the teachings of the prophets contribute to the Hebrew world view? (c) How did Hebrew religious beliefs differ from the beliefs of other peoples of the ancient Middle East?

Critical Thinking

1. **Comparing Civilizations** (a) What practical advances did the Sumerians make in writing, mathematics, and architecture? (b) How were these advances similar to Egyptian achievements? (c) How might you explain similar achievements in both civilizations?
2. **Applying Information** Rulers of the great empires of the ancient Middle East had to develop ways to unite many different peoples and control large territories. Describe the methods Sargon, Hammurabi, and Darius used to bind their empires together. Which ruler do you think developed the most effective methods of establishing unity? Explain.

Relating Past to Present

1. Which civilization of the ancient Middle East do you think had the greatest impact on the world today? Give examples to support your answer.

Developing Basic Skills

1. **Comparing** Make a chart with four columns. In column one, list the geographical advantages of Egypt. In column two, list the disadvantages. In columns three and four, list the geographical advantages and disadvantages of Sumer. (a) Which civilization had the most geographic advantages? (b) Which had the most geographic disadvantages? (c) How might geographic advantages and disadvantages have contributed to the differing outlooks of the Egyptians and Sumerians?
2. **Map Reading** Study the map and the inset map on page 42. Then answer the following questions: (a) What information do the maps provide? (b) Where did the Phoenicians establish colonies? (c) What geographic factors might have encouraged the Phoenicians to turn from agriculture to trade? (d) Based on your reading and the maps, suggest reasons why the Phoenicians were in a good position to become "carriers of civilization."

See page 803 for suggested readings.

4 Ancient India and China

(2500 B.C.–256 B.C.)

Chinese bronze statue of a boy holding jade birds.

> **Chapter Outline**
>
> 1 The First Civilization in India
>
> 2 The Aryans
>
> 3 Beginning of Chinese Civilization
>
> 4 Expansion Under the Chou Dynasty

Waiting in his chariot for the great battle to begin, Arjuna was filled with doubts. "My limbs are weakened, my mouth is parching, my body trembles, my hair stands upright," he complained to Krishna, his chariot driver. At that moment, all of India seemed to be in a vast civil war. To Arjuna, the thought of fighting friends and relatives was agonizing. Even though he knew his cause was just, Arjuna hesitated. "How could we dare spill the blood that unites us? Where is the joy in the killing of kinsmen?"

But Krishna, a god who had taken mortal form, scolded Arjuna for his weakness. Through the night, Krishna instructed the young warrior about life, death, and the right course of human action. "There is more joy in doing one's own duty badly," said Krishna, "than in doing another man's duty well." It was Arjuna's duty, Krishna explained, to destroy his enemies. "If you do not fight this just battle, you will fail in your own law and in your honor and you will incur sin." The battle raged for 18 days. In the end, Arjuna and his brothers were victorious, and they restored peace to India.

The conversation between Arjuna and Krishna appears in the "Bhagavad-Gita" (BUHG uh vuhd   GEE tuh) or "The Song of God," a religious poem of India. The "Bhagavad-Gita" is part of a long epic poem that contains legends about wars that took place in ancient India.

The Aryan (AIR ee uhn) civilization that produced the "Bhagavad-Gita" was the second civilization to develop in India. Around 2500 B.C., the earliest Indian civilization had emerged in the Indus River valley. The great cities of the Indus Valley civilization flourished for about 1,000 years but were destroyed by invading Aryans. The invaders extended their conquests from the Indus Valley across the entire northern plain of India. As Aryan civilization evolved, it created traditions that have shaped Indian culture up to the present.

Thousands of miles northeast of India, in the Yellow River valley of China, small agricultural settlements formed the basis for the first Chinese civilization. Like the Aryans in India, the Chinese established enduring traditions.

1 The First Civilization in India

Read to Learn ■ how geography influenced development in India
■ what archeologists have learned about Ancient India

In India, as in Egypt and Sumer, farming villages in a fertile river valley gave birth to the first civilization. From 2500 B.C. to 1500 B.C., the great cities of Harappa (hah RAP ah) and Mohenjo-Daro (moh HEHN joh DAHR roh) dominated a prosperous civilization in the Indus River valley. To understand the development of civilization in ancient India, one should look first at the geographic setting.

Geographic Setting

The Indian subcontinent is a large peninsula, surrounded on three sides by bodies of water—the Arabian Sea, the Indian Ocean, and the Bay of Bengal. In the north, the Himalaya (HIH muh LAY uh) Mountains separate India from the rest of Asia. The towering Himalayas form a nearly impassable barrier 1,500 miles (2,400 kilometers) long. The rugged Hindu Kush Mountains to the northwest also presented barriers to travel. (See the map on page 48.)

Geographic barriers allowed the first Indian civilization to develop mostly on its own. Yet India was not totally isolated. Determined invaders made their way through steep passes, such as the Khyber (KĪ ber) Pass through the Hindu Kush. Indian traders carried goods through the mountain passes to the Middle East and China. Furthermore, the surrounding seas served as highways for commercial and cultural contact.

Three regions of India. Diverse geography characterizes the Indian subcontinent.

There are three major geographical regions of India: the northern plain, the Deccan (DEHK uhn) Plateau, and the coastal plains. These geographic divisions have contributed to the development of diverse cultures.

Three great rivers—the Indus, Ganges (GAN jeez), and Brahmaputra (BRAH muh POO truh)—flow through the crescent-shaped northern plain. These broad, slow rivers originate in the snow-covered Himalayas. Together with their tributaries they supply water for farming and for transportation across the northern plain. The fertile soil of the river valleys supports extensive farming. For these reasons, the northern plain became the home of the first Indian civilization. Later, invaders pushed across the northwestern frontier and established powerful empires in the northern plain. The area has played a dominant role in the history of India ever since.

The Deccan Plateau is the triangular-shaped heart of the subcontinent. The Vindhya (VIHND yah) Mountains separate the plateau from the northern part of the subcontinent. The plateau is bordered on the west and east by long mountain ranges, the Western and Eastern Ghats. Because it lacks the numerous snow-fed rivers found in the north, the Deccan Plateau suffers from droughts, which make farming difficult.

Along the eastern and western coasts of India lie narrow coastal plains, which support both agriculture and fishing. Although India has a few good natural harbors, many

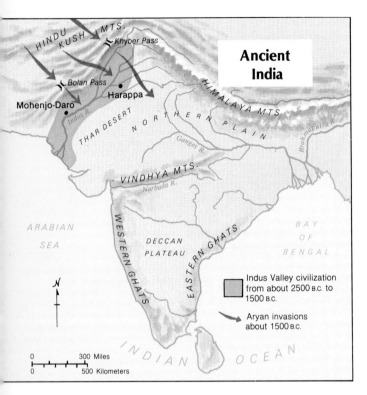

Ancient India

Indus Valley civilization from about 2500 B.C. to 1500 B.C.

Aryan invasions about 1500 B.C.

0 300 Miles
0 500 Kilometers

Map Skill *Geography played an important role in the development of civilization in India as it did elsewhere. Mountains to the north helped isolate India from other areas. How did invading Aryans find their way into India?*

coastal peoples of India were seafarers who traded with peoples in other parts of Asia, Africa, and the Middle East.

The monsoon. The chief feature of the Indian climate is the *monsoon,* a seasonal wind. The monsoon regulates Indian life much as the different seasons affect life in North America. From June until September, the summer monsoon blows from the southwest, picking up moisture over the Indian Ocean and dropping torrential rains on the coast and the northern plain of India. From October to May, the winter monsoon blows from the northeast. These hot, dry winds raise temperatures to over 100°F (38° C), shrivel crops, and make outdoor work nearly impossible.

Every year, the people of India wait anxiously for the summer monsoon to bring desperately needed moisture to the parched farmlands. When the rains come, temperatures drop and crops spring to life. If the monsoon is late, crops fail and food shortages result. Occasionally, the heavy rains cause destructive floods, especially in the lower Ganges Valley.

Discovery of the Indus Valley Civilization

In 1921, archaeologists discovered traces of an ancient civilization in the Indus River valley. Since then, excavations have revealed that this civilization developed about the same time as the early Egyptian and Sumerian civilizations. The Indus Valley civilization stretched for 950 miles (1,500 kilometers), covering an area larger than the Old Kingdom in Egypt. Each of its chief cities, Harappa and Mohenjo-Daro, was larger than any Sumerian city-state. Yet scholars know little about the Indus Valley civilization compared to what they know about ancient Egypt and Sumer.

Two factors have left scholars with many unanswered questions. First, efforts to decipher the written language of the Indus Valley people have so far been unsuccessful. Second, Harappa and Mohenjo-Daro can be only partially excavated. Because these cities lie close to rivers, deep trenches cannot be dug without the danger of flooding. Despite these handicaps, archaeologists have uncovered some valuable information about the Indus Valley civilization.

A Planned Urban Society

The ruins of Harappa and Mohenjo-Daro reveal that they were the products of the first city planning in history. Wide, straight streets divide residential areas into square city blocks. Archaeologists have uncovered houses, granaries, public halls, and shops. Both cities had extensive sewer systems. Walled fortresses with towers provided protection.

To create such well-planned cities, the people needed a knowledge of surveying and geometry. Furthermore, only a strong central government in Harappa and Mohenjo-

The large cities of the Indus Valley civilization enforced strict building regulations. This photograph shows walls uncovered at Mohenjo-Daro. Notice the regular bricks used on the left. The rough, uneven wall on the right may have been built at a later date when the city had declined and orderly architecture had given way to careless work.

Daro could have supervised the practical details of planning and construction.

Government and religion. Scholars are not certain who ruled the Indus Valley cities, but they suggest that a priest-king probably headed the government of each city. The rulers must have had considerable power because the governments exercised strict control over the cities. For example, they regulated construction of new buildings and established standards of weights and measures. Because of the tight control, writing, building styles, street plans, and even the size of bricks remained unchanged for nearly 1,000 years.

Like the Egyptians and Sumerians, the Indus Valley people were polytheistic. Stat-

ues and masks show that they worshipped a mother-goddess and a three-faced god. They also revered sacred animals such as the bull and certain sacred trees.

Economic life. The Indus Valley civilization had a thriving agricultural economy. On the lands surrounding the cities, farmers constructed dams and levees to channel water from the rivers to crops of wheat, barley, melons, and dates. Food surpluses supported the large city populations and prompted the growth of trade. Indus Valley farmers were the first people to grow cotton, and cotton cloth became an important item of trade.

Trade and commerce supported a prosperous merchant class in the cities. Merchants exported cotton cloth to Mesopotamia in exchange for precious metals. In turn, wealthy citizens hired artisans to make furniture inlaid with the precious metals. Artisans also crafted fine gold jewelry and realistic stone carvings of monkeys and birds.

Decline of the Indus Valley civilization. Archaeological evidence shows that the Indus Valley civilization began to decline many years before it ended about 1500 B.C. Builders abandoned the uniform standards

About 4,000 years ago, merchants of Mohenjo-Daro probably used carved stone seals like the one shown here to stamp their possessions. Stone seals may also have had a religious meaning. This one shows a bull, a common religious symbol, standing by an incense burner.

of earlier times, and the quality of work declined. The arts showed less creativity, and trade with Mesopotamia dwindled. These signs of decay indicate that the government had lost some of its power.

Most authorities believe that about 1500 B.C. Aryan invaders struck the final blow to the Indus Valley civilization. When the Indus Valley cities fell, the people fled to other parts of India. Thus, while the river valley civilizations of Egypt and Sumer affected later peoples, the Indus Valley civilization had little lasting impact. After 1500 B.C., it was virtually forgotten until modern times.

SECTION REVIEW

1. Locate: Arabian Sea, Indian Ocean, Bay of Bengal, Himalaya Mountains. Hindu Kush Mountains, Indus River, Ganges River, Brahmaputra River, Deccan Plateau, Harappa, Mohenjo-Daro.

2. Define: monsoon.

3. Which geographical region was the home of the first Indian civilization? Why?

4. Why is the summer monsoon important to the people of India?

5. What evidence suggests that the Indus Valley cities were the result of careful planning?

2 The Aryans

Read to Learn ▪ what effect Aryans had on Indian beliefs
▪ how Aryan society was structured

About 1500 B.C., Aryans swept into India through the passes of the Hindu Kush Mountains. These fierce nomadic herders had come originally from the region between the Black and Caspian seas north of the Caucasus Mountains.* The Aryans used horses, which were unknown in the Indus Valley, and superior weapons to overpower the people of Harappa and Mohenjo-Daro.

The Aryan Conquest

Like many nomadic people, the Aryans did not move as a single unit. Rather, they were loosely organized into tribes. A *tribe* consists of groups of related families who recognize a common ancestor, speak the same language, and share the same traditions and beliefs. In each Aryan tribe, a *rajah* (RAH juh), or elected chief, served as the leader in war. He governed the tribe with the aid of councils

made up of elders and other free men. The rajah was not worshipped as a god, nor did he have power to impose taxes. His wealth depended on gifts from the people and plunder taken in war.

Under the rajahs, Aryan tribes fought their way into the Indus Valley and destroyed villages and cities. Between 1500 B.C. and 1000 B.C., they pushed eastward, clearing the jungles of the Ganges Valley and bringing the northern plain under their control. Gradually, the Aryans gave up their nomadic way of life and settled into villages.

The chief enemies of the Aryans during the conquest of the northern plain were the Dravidians (druh VIHD ee uhnz), who were probably survivors of the Indus Valley civilization. In time, the Dravidians retreated into southern India, where their kingdoms later rivaled those of the north.

Even after the Aryans conquered the northern plain, warfare continued to dominate their life. Between 1000 B.C. and 700 B.C., local rajahs battled for control of the region. Slowly, the more successful rajahs forged strong, independent kingdoms. By 700 B.C., powerful rajahs were building large capital cities and encouraging trade with the Middle East.

---

*The Aryans were only one group of people who migrated out of that area between about 2000 B.C. and 1500 B.C. Some, such as the Hittites, invaded the Middle East. Others, such as the ancestors of the Greeks and Romans, moved into Europe. Because of the common origins of these groups, historians have called them Indo-Europeans.

Aryan Beliefs

Most information about the early Aryans comes from oral religious traditions contained in the Vedas (VAY duhz). The Vedas, composed between 1500 B.C. and 1000 B.C., include sacred hymns, prayers, and magic spells used by priests in religious ceremonies. They represent one of the world's oldest surviving religious literatures. Priests memorized the Vedas and carefully handed them on to each new generation.

According to the Vedas, the early Aryans worshipped gods of nature, the sun, sky, thunder, and fire, but Indra, the warrior god, generally led the others. Pictured as courageous, youthful, and invincible, Indra reflected the optimism and confidence of the Aryans. In return for sacrifices to the gods, the Aryans sought long life, prosperity, and healthy sons. They were more interested in day-to-day concerns than in an afterlife.

Aryan religious beliefs gradually changed. For example, the Rig Veda, the oldest of the Vedas, consists of over 1,000 hymns addressed to different gods. But later Vedic hymns suggest a growing belief in a single unifying force.

Further changes in religious beliefs appear in the Upanishads (oo PAN ih SHADZ), oral teachings composed between 800 B.C. and 600 B.C. In the Upanishads, priests sought to answer philosophical and religious questions about the meaning of life and the creation of the world. They introduced new doctrines such as the belief in *reincarnation,* or the rebirth of the soul in another bodily form.

As you will read in Chapter 9, both the Vedas and the Upanishads form part of the sacred literature of Hinduism, the religion that developed out of early Aryan beliefs.

Epic literature. The power struggles between rival Aryan kingdoms from 1000 B.C. to 700 B.C. gave rise to a new oral literature. Stories about civil wars and great heroes formed the basis of two long epic poems: the *Mahabharata* (muh HAH BAH ruh tuh) and the *Ramayana* (rah MAH yuh nuh).

Like most epics, the *Mahabharata* mixes fact and fiction and magnifies the deeds of heroes. The *Ramayana* tells the story of one hero but also contains numerous short stories that illustrate the duties and ideals of Aryan warriors. While both epics focus on worldly concerns such as success in battle, they also weave in significant religious themes. Because of their religious teachings, both epics became part of the sacred Hindu texts.

Sanskrit. By about 700 B.C., almost 1,000 years after their arrival in India, the Aryans had developed a written language called Sanskrit. Knowledge of Sanskrit belonged almost solely to priests, who used the language to record sacred texts. Despite the introduction of a written language, priests continued to memorize the ancient hymns and epics and to recite them for the people. In this way, the oral traditions were preserved.

Life in Aryan Villages

As the nomadic Aryans settled into villages, they established patterns of life that have given order and stability to Indian culture down to the present. Although a rajah ruled all the villages within a region, most villages enjoyed a measure of self-government. A headman, usually a wealthy farmer, had overall responsibility for a village. Appointed by the rajah, the headman worked with a village council to settle disputes. He also oversaw the maintenance of community irrigation ditches and canals.

Aryan villages depended on a mixed herding and farming economy in which cattle had a prominent place. Aryans had valued cattle since their nomadic days, when a major goal of Aryan warriors had been to seize cattle from their enemies. In fact, their word for war meant "the desire for cattle." In the village barter economy, cattle retained their value. People measured their wealth in terms of cattle and used them as the medium of exchange. Thus, the value of land and tools was expressed in heads of cattle. In the villages, cattle were used for food, plowing, and transportation.*

---

* In early Aryan society, cattle were killed for food. Later, the slaughter of cattle was forbidden, and people used only the milk.

51

An ancient Hindu epic, the Ramayana, has inspired artists for centuries. Its hero, Rama, hurtles from one lively adventure to the next. Rama is sent to earth by the gods to overcome the ten-headed Ravanna, the powerful king of the demons. Disguised as a monk, the evil Ravanna kidnaps Rama's beautiful wife Sita, shown in this illustration from the 1700s A.D. Aided by the monkey god, Rama eventually rescues his wife and defeats Ravanna.

The extended family. The extended family was at the heart of village life. An *extended family* includes a husband and wife, their unmarried children, their married sons, and the sons' wives and children. The several generations of an extended family generally live under the same roof. Among the Aryans, joint ownership of land and cattle encouraged strong ties within the family. Family members looked after each other and provided for the weak, the old, and even the lazy.

As head of the family, the oldest man had many responsibilities. He performed the family's religious rituals and was its spokesman in village affairs. He arranged marriages for his daughters, educated his sons, and managed the family income.

The status of women. In early Aryan society, women apparently enjoyed relatively high status. When the Aryans invaded India, women warriors fought alongside the men. Women composed hymns in the Vedas, and the Upanishads mention one learned woman who asked her teacher so many searching questions that he exclaimed, "You mustn't ask too much, or your head will drop off!"

As Aryan civilization developed, the status of women declined. At first women were active in village life and joined in public debates. Later, they were forbidden to attend public meetings, although they still were free to walk unattended in the village. Women eventually became subordinate to men. As a child, a girl obeyed her father. In her teens, she married the man chosen by her family and moved into her husband's household. A young wife owed the same obedience to her husband and his family that she once had owed to her own family.

Social Classes

The Aryan social structure gradually changed as the nomadic Aryans settled into villages. The early Aryans were loosely divided into three classes: warriors, priests, and commoners. Because the classes were not strictly defined, it was possible to rise from a lower class to a higher one. By the time powerful rajahs established united kingdoms, a new social organization had emerged.

In the new social structure, the Aryans recognized four classes: Kshatriyas (KSHAT ree uhz), or warriors; Brahmans (BRAH muhnz), or priests; Vaisyas (VĪS yuhz), or landowners, merchants and herders; and Sudras (SOO druhz), or servants and peasants tied to the land. As religious rituals grew more complex, the Brahmans strengthened their position in society and in time replaced the Kshatriyas as the highest class. This class system gradually became rigid. Birth alone determined a person's place in society.

Scholars think that the social structure became more rigid because the Aryans wanted to maintain a separate racial and cultural identity. During their conquests, some Aryans had intermarried with the Dravidians, and a few Dravidians had found a place in Aryan society. But as the new social system developed, the top three classes were reserved for Aryans, and the lowest class was comprised of non-Aryans, such as the Dravidians.

In time, the four main social classes were further divided into *castes*, or social groups based on birth. Children belonged to the same caste as their parents. As the caste system evolved, a strict set of rules emerged that prohibited marriage between members of different castes and specified the jobs caste members could hold.

The caste system grew immensely complex. Over 3,000 subcastes, or groups, eventually developed. There were also many people outside the caste system. Because they were considered to be impure, these people were called "untouchables." They had the lowest status in society. In Chapter 9, you will read how the developing caste system was closely tied to Hindu religious beliefs.

SECTION REVIEW

1. Identify: Dravidian, Vedas, Upanishads, *Mahabharata, Ramayana,* Sanskrit.
2. Define: tribe, rajah, reincarnation, extended family, caste.
3. What had some Aryan rajahs accomplished by 700 B.C.?
4. What new religious belief did the Upanishads contain?
5. (a) List the four main classes in Aryan society. (b) What occupations were identified with each class?

3 Beginning of Chinese Civilization

Read to Learn
- how geography affected culture in China
- how the Shang dynasty advanced civilization

You have read about three ancient civilizations that rose in the river valleys of the Nile, the Tigris and Euphrates, and the Indus. A fourth civilization developed in the Yellow River valley of northern China. Between 5000 B.C. and 3000 B.C., Stone Age farmers began building permanent villages in northern China. As they discovered more effective ways to produce food, they developed a more complex social and economic system, which by 1600 B.C. gave rise to the Shang civilization.

Geographic Setting

As you can see from the map on page 55, China covers an immense area. Today, as in the past, the river valleys and coastal plains of central China support most of the population because of the good farmland there. Four outlying regions—Manchuria, Mongolia, Sinkiang (sihn kyang), and Tibet—surround the heartland of China.

Imposing geographic barriers encircle China. For example, the Himalayas in Tibet are among the world's highest, coldest mountains. Barren deserts, such as the Gobi, rugged plateaus, and dense subtropical forests stretch along China's frontiers. To the east is the vast Pacific Ocean.

The Middle Kingdom. Geographic barriers and great distances limited contact between China and other early centers of civilization. As a result, the Chinese developed a civilization quite different from others. The Chinese considered themselves unique and believed that their land was at the center of the world. They called it Chung Kuo (juhng gwoh), meaning the "Middle Kingdom."

However, China's isolation was far from complete. The early farming villages of China had contact with people in the Fertile Crescent. As civilization advanced in both regions, trade and travel across western China increased. Furthermore, nomadic invaders from Manchuria and Mongolia frequently threatened China and overran the cities and villages of the north.

The Chinese adopted some ideas of outsiders, but outside influence was limited. The Chinese considered people who did not speak Chinese to be barbarians. Eventually, the Chinese called all outsiders barbarians. Newcomers, even successful conquerors, found it necessary to adopt Chinese traditions and customs. Thus, the Chinese gained a reputation for absorbing their conquerors.

The Yellow River. In the Yellow River valley, winter winds and river flood waters deposit a fine yellow soil called *loess* (LOH ehs) across the broad, flat plain. The loess is fertile and easily worked with hand hoes.

The Yellow River provides water for irrigation, fishing, and transportation. Because rainfall is not regular, the area suffers from both droughts and floods. In fact, the Chinese have called the Yellow River the "River of Sorrows" because its floods have caused much death and destruction. The early Chinese learned to dredge the river channel and construct dikes to lessen the danger of floods. They also built their villages on high ground.

Shang Civilization

As in Egypt and Sumer, busy farming villages in northern China grew into towns and cities. Local rulers fought for power until about 1600 B.C., when powerful kings established their authority over northern China and founded the Shang dynasty. The Shang dynasty, or ruling house, was the first in China. It survived until 1122 B.C. and gave its name to the earliest Chinese civilization.

In recent years, archaeologists have excavated over 130 Shang sites, including Anyang, Loyang, and Chengchow (jehng jou). The excavations have revealed much about the Shang civilization.

A Shang king ruled over his capital city and the surrounding region. Other land was governed by nobles, usually the king's relatives, who paid tribute to the king or performed military service for him. Shang rulers could raise armies to fight prolonged wars against nomadic peoples who threatened the frontier regions.

Chinese Writing

During the Shang dynasty, the Chinese developed a system of writing. Like the Egyptians and Sumerians, the early Chinese used pictograms, or drawings of objects. Later, they added ideograms, symbols that expressed ideas such as wisdom or unity. The Shang Chinese written language included over 3,000 symbols, or characters.

Chinese written characters have remained in use for over 3,500 years. Each character has two elements, one that tells its meaning and one that suggests its pronunciation. As new words were added to the language, the number of Chinese characters gradually increased to over 50,000. Until recent reforms simplified the system, a Chinese student had to learn at least 10,000 characters. For centuries, the difficulty of learning the complicated characters meant that only the wealthy had the leisure to learn to read and write.

Shang scribes drew characters with a sharp stick or brush on many types of material, including bone, bamboo, bronze, pottery, wood, jade, and silk. Scribes usually wrote on strips of bamboo or wood, which were tied together in rolled bundles. Because the strips were narrow, the characters were written in vertical columns.

Shang Religious Beliefs

The Shang people believed that many gods and spirits resided in nature. The principal god, Shang Ti, presided over heaven and the other gods. The power of the gods was awesome. They could cause floods, drought, and locust plagues.

Gods controlled all human affairs. Therefore, people tried to influence the gods by calling on the spirits of their own ancestors to act as go-betweens. The Shang believed that if they made the right sacrifices, their ancestors would bring them good fortune. Bad fortune was considered a sign of an ancestor's displeasure. Therefore, ancestor worship was an important part of Shang religion.

The Shang king, as chief priest, made daily sacrifices to ensure that his ancestors acted favorably on behalf of the kingdom. Priests assisted the king in these ceremonies. Shang priests also tried to foretell the future.

Before undertaking an important action, a person would ask a priest to consult his or her ancestors. To do this, the priest scratched a question on the shoulder bone of an ox. Then he carved notches in the bone

Map Skill *Early Chinese traders guided rafts of wood and bamboo up and down the Yellow River. This trade helped transform small farming villages into thriving cities. Cities, such as Anyang, Loyang, Chengchow, were centers of Shang civilization. Besides aiding trade, how else did the Yellow River affect life in China?*

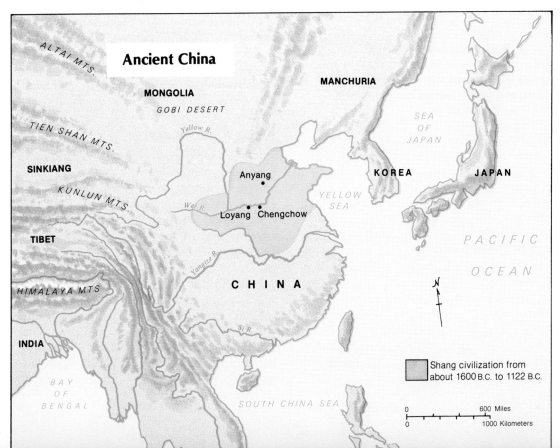

Daily Life

Shang society had a strict division of classes. The king, supported by nobles and priests, performed political and religious duties in the capital. The majority of the people were peasants living in scattered villages. They paid a portion of each harvest to the king or noble governor of the region. Sometimes peasants were drafted to serve as foot soldiers or to build royal palaces, tombs, and temples. In contrast to the luxurious dwellings of the wealthy, Shang farmers lived in tiny houses, built partially underground. The ground helped insulate the house during the hot summers and cold winters on the North China plain.

The extended family was the focus of Shang village life, as it was in Aryan villages in India. Several generations lived in the same household, headed by the oldest male. He and his wife made the necessary sacrifices to the family ancestors. Ancestor worship contributed to respect for age and duty to family.

Little is known about women in Shang China. Queens seem to have received considerable respect. Among the royal family and nobles, men often had more than one wife, but the first wife and her sons were the most important. Among peasant families, men probably married only one woman. Peasant women worked in the fields alongside men. They were also responsible for silkmaking and weaving.

Shang Achievements

Shang artisans developed new technologies, especially in bronzeworking. They invented bronze weapons, such as daggers, spears, and armor. Other inventions, including the yoke, harness, and spoked wheel, led to the development of the two-horse war chariot. These military advances gave Shang rulers an advantage over neighboring peoples who did not know about them.

The Shang also made advances in the arts and sciences. Working with a white clay, artisans manufactured fine pottery, which was the forerunner of porcelain. Silk textiles, jade ornaments, and ivory carvings attest to the skill of Shang artisans. In mathematics,

Oracle bones like the one shown here commonly were inscribed with questions such as: "Will the weather be good tomorrow?" and "Are the prospects for hunting good?" The questions usually required only a yes or no answer from a person's ancestors.

and applied a heated bronze rod to the notches. The heat caused the bone to crack. The priest interpreted the cracks to find an answer to the question. Bones used for telling the future in this way are called *oracle bones.*

Archaeologists have found thousands of oracle bones near Anyang and other Shang cities. Most were inscribed with questions addressed by kings to their ancestors. One king asked if 5,000 soldiers would be enough to defeat an enemy. Another wondered if his ancestors were responsible for his toothache. By reading the oracle bones, scholars have learned much about religious beliefs and daily life in Shang China.

the Shang developed a decimal system. Priest-astronomers devised a calendar with 12 months and 365¼ days. These advances were the foundation for later Chinese achievements.

From northern China, the Shang civilization expanded in many directions. Some people moved eastward along the Yellow River to the Pacific. Many migrated toward the south, spreading Chinese culture into the Yangtze (YANG see) River valley and eventually in the Si (shee) River valley. Others pushed into Manchuria, Mongolia, and central Asia.

SECTION REVIEW

1. Locate: China, Manchuria, Mongolia, Sinkiang, Tibet, Himalaya Mountains, Gobi Desert, Yellow River, Yangtze River, Si River.
2. Define: loess, oracle bone.
3. Give two reasons that outside influence on Chinese civilization was limited.
4. Why was the Yellow River called the "River of Sorrows"?
5. Why was Chinese writing difficult to learn?
6. Why were ancestors considered important in Shang religion?

4 Expansion Under the Chou Dynasty

Read to Learn
- how the idea of "Mandate of Heaven" developed
- how the Chinese lived under the Chou dynasty

In 1122 B.C., the Chou (joh) people, who lived on the northwestern border, invaded Shang China. According to Chinese tradition, the "Martial King," Wu Wang, captured the Shang capital at Anyang and established a new dynasty. The Chou dynasty lasted from 1122 B.C. to 256 B.C., longer than any other dynasty in history.

Earlier the Chou had adopted many features of Shang civilization, such as the war chariots and bronze weapons with which they defeated the Shang. After 1122 B.C., the Chou retained many Shang laws and customs. However, they also made their own contributions to Chinese civilization.

The Mandate of Heaven

To justify their seizure of power from the Shang, the Chou developed the idea of the "Mandate of Heaven," or a divine right to rule. According to the Chou, a dynasty enjoyed heaven's blessing only as long as it governed wisely and justly. If a ruler was lazy, cruel, or corrupt, heaven withdrew the mandate, or right, to rule.

"It was the case that the last sovereign of your Shang was luxurious to the extreme of luxury," proclaimed the Chou, "while his schemes of government showed neither purity nor progress, so that heaven sent down such ruin on him." Heaven then looked for a new ruler and found "our kings of Chou, who were able to sustain the burden of virtuous government."

The Mandate of Heaven established a ruler's responsibility to provide good government and put the well-being of the people above self-interest. The Chinese believed that natural disasters and invasions revealed a ruler's failure to please heaven.

It was not considered a crime to revolt against a ruler who had lost the Mandate of Heaven. The overthrow of the Shang by the Chou was the first of many dynastic changes in China. Historians refer to the rise and fall of Chinese dynasties as the *dynastic cycle*. (See the diagram on page 58.)

Chou Government

During the Chou dynasty, a feudal system* emerged in China. Since the Chou controlled more territory than the Shang had, Chou kings could not extend their authority over all the land. Therefore, the king ruled his

---

* In a feudal system, lords held lands that, in theory, belonged to the king. The local lords governed these lands, protected the people who farmed them, and owed military and other services to the king or other lords. In practice, local lords often became virtually independent.

The Dynastic Cycle in China

The New Dynasty

Restores peace

Appoints loyal officials

Redistributes land to peasants

Builds canals, irrigation systems, and roads

Repairs defensive walls

New dynasty claims the Mandate of Heaven.

After several generations, the new dynasty becomes an aging dynasty.

Problems

Floods, famine, earthquakes

Invasions

Armed bandits in the provinces

Peasant revolts

Aging dynasty loses the Mandate of Heaven.

The Aging Dynasty

Neglects government duties

Ignores lazy or corrupt officials

Loses control of the provinces

Imposes heavy taxes to pay for luxuries

Allows defensive walls to decay

Chart Skill *The idea of a Mandate of Heaven was an important part of the dynastic cycle in China. To the Chinese, problems like those shown on the diagram indicated that a ruler had lost the Mandate of Heaven. How did a new dynasty try to solve the problems left by an aging dynasty?*

capital and the surrounding lands, but he allowed powerful nobles to govern large parts of the kingdom. In exchange, the nobles owed loyalty, military service, and tribute to the king.

For about 250 years, Chou kings controlled the feudal nobles. They settled disputes between warring nobles and granted all titles to land. But Chou strength gradually declined as powerful nobles carved out independent states. Between 771 B.C. and 256 B.C., weak Chou rulers could not prevent warfare among hundreds of feudal states.

During these centuries of upheaval, a few nobles created large states that expanded north into Manchuria and south into the Yangtze Valley. These nobles protected their power by replacing hereditary office holders with appointed officials. In the larger states, complex government bureaucracies developed. A *bureaucracy* (byoo RAH kruh see) is a system of organizing government by departments or bureaus.

In the feudal states of Chou China, different bureaus controlled finances, the armed forces, law enforcement, and record-keeping. The state with the most efficient organization had the advantage in the power struggles of the late Chou dynasty. Government bureaucracy remained important in China for 2,500 years.

Life in Chou China

Constant feudal warfare after 771 B.C. weakened the warrior nobility. As large, well-organized states emerged, a new class of able, ambitious government officials gradually gained power. Eventually, these officials became the new ruling class in China.

By the late Chou period, a social system had evolved in China that would remain a stable force through succeeding dynasties. At the head of Chinese society were the government officials. They gained greater status by becoming landowners. Below them was the huge peasant class. Some peasants were tenant farmers on estates owned by wealthy landlords. Others farmed land allotted to them by villages. Artisans and merchants ranked below peasants because they did not work the land. Although warfare was a prominent feature of Chou China, soldiers also occupied a low position in society.

Education became increasingly important as the need for government officials grew. In the cities and at feudal courts, tutors trained boys for government service. Educated people wrote books that were later considered classics. The *Book of Odes*, for example, contained myths, legends, and love poems. Students of Chou China studied the *Book of Odes*, together with royal histories and books of court etiquette.

Economic Growth

The Chou era was a time of economic growth in China. For the first time, peasants used fertilizers and iron tools. With the help of government-sponsored irrigation projects and the newly introduced ox-drawn plow, they farmed more land and increased food production. Feudal lords offered peasants favorable terms to settle in newly conquered territories. Settlers carried Chinese culture well beyond the old borders of the Shang kingdom.

Economic growth was also evident in the expansion of trade, the growth of cities, and the beginning of a money economy. To encourage trade and maintain good communication in their growing states, feudal lords

Then and Now ■ Two Arts of Ancient China

The origins of bronzeworking and silkworm cultivation date from China's prehistoric period—perhaps as early as 2200 B.C. According to Chinese legends, an early emperor and empress introduced farming, writing, bronzeworking, and silkmaking to China. These legends demonstrate the importance of bronze and silk in ancient China.

In the Shang and Chou dynasties, bronze was a symbol of wealth and prestige. Chinese metalworkers produced magnificent bronze cups, vases, and cooking vessels. Rulers and wealthy nobles used bronze vessels to make offerings to their ancestors.

Shang artisans developed advanced techniques to manufacture the splendid bronze ritual vessels. First, they made a clay or stone mold of an object. Around the mold, they fashioned a second mold. Heated bronze was poured between the two molds. When the bronze cooled, the molds were removed and the bronze surface polished to a smooth finish.

Chinese bronzeworkers were fine artists. Elaborate decorations on Shang bronze vessels featured masks of tigers and dragons. During the Chou dynasty, decorative styles changed and intricate, abstract patterns replaced the fierce-looking animal heads.

While many ancient Chinese bronzes have been found, no examples of early Chinese silk have survived. Silk is one of the world's oldest textiles. Yet how the Chinese discovered the process of silkmaking remains a mystery. Oracle bones indicate that in Shang times, the Chinese already knew how to extract silk thread from the cocoon of the silkworm caterpillar.

In ancient China, as today, silk farmers cultivated mulberry trees because young silkworms fed on mulberry leaves. Silkworms spin cocoons to protect them while they change into moths. Silkworkers placed these cocoons in boiling water to soften them so that the delicate threads could be unwound. The Chinese designed special looms to weave the silk thread into cloth. They then dipped the cloth in brilliant dyes to give it a rich, lustrous look.

The Chinese recognized the value of the silk industry. They made every effort to prevent spies from smuggling silkworm eggs or the seeds of the mulberry tree out of China. By doing so, they managed to keep the process of gathering and weaving silk a secret for almost 3,000 years.

improved land and water transportation. Roads, rivers, and inland canals carried products from villages to towns and cities. Through trade contacts with western Asia, the Chinese learned about such animals as the mule, donkey, and camel.

The introduction of metal coins further encouraged large-scale trade. But the money economy also widened the gap between rich and poor. For example, some merchants made huge profits by buying grain and then selling it at high prices in times of famine. Peasants, on the other hand, worked small plots and paid high taxes. During famines, they were forced to borrow money or grain to survive. If a peasant could not pay back a loan, he and his family lost the right to farm the land. The problem of peasants being

forced off the land continued to face Chinese rulers for the next 3,000 years.

Warfare among the feudal states marked the end of the Chou dynasty. Yet the strong institutions and traditions that developed in the Chou period would become the cornerstone for a unified Chinese state.

SECTION REVIEW

1. Define: dynastic cycle, bureaucracy.
2. How did the concept of the Mandate of Heaven encourage good government?
3. Why did the Chou dynasty decline?
4. What group made up the ruling class in Chou China?
5. What economic problems did Chinese peasants face?

Chapter 4 Review

In Perspective

In India and China, geography helped shape the patterns of life. The first civilization in India developed near the Indus River. Excavations of its major cities reveal a well-organized society with a thriving agricultural economy and active trade.

Around 1500 B.C., the Aryans invaded India. They gradually established a new civilization in northern India. Oral religious literature and epics preserved the developing

beliefs and early history of the Aryans. Eventually, powerful rajahs established kingdoms, and a strict class system evolved.

The first civilization in China grew up along the Yellow River, where the Shang kings established a dynasty about 1600 B.C. During the Shang dynasty, the Chinese developed writing, a calendar, and advanced skills in bronzeworking as well as other artistic and scientific techniques.

Under the Chou, who followed the Shang, a feudal system of government emerged. Despite constant warfare among feudal lords, the Chou period was one of economic and political growth.

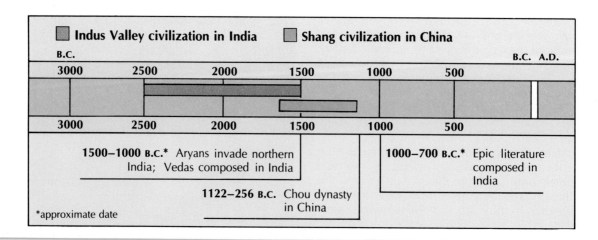

Recalling Facts

Choose the best word or phrase to complete each of the following statements.

1. The chief feature of the Indian climate is the (a) constant heat; (b) inadequate rainfall; (c) monsoon.
2. The first civilization in India developed in the (a) Indus Valley; (b) Deccan Plateau; (c) Eastern Ghats.
3. The sacred hymns and prayers of the early Aryans are called the (a) Sudras; (b) Vedas; (c) *Ramayana.*
4. In the Aryan economy, the medium of exchange was (a) gold; (b) iron tools; (c) cattle.
5. The ancient Chinese called their land (a) the Middle Kingdom; (b) the Mandate of Heaven; (c) Anyang.

Chapter Checkup

1. (a) What geographic barriers helped isolate ancient India from other parts of the world? (b) What contacts existed despite these barriers?
2. (a) Why is there less evidence of Indus Valley civilization than Egyptian or Sumerian civilization? (b) Why do scholars think Indus Valley rulers were strong?
3. Describe the following aspects of Aryan society: (a) village government; (b) economy; (c) family structure.
4. (a) Describe the class system that developed in Aryan society. (b) Why did such a rigid system develop?
5. (a) Describe the class structure of Chou China. (b) How was it different from the class structure of Shang China?

Critical Thinking

1. **Thinking in Terms of Geography** (a) How do the monsoons affect the economic life of people in India? (b) How do climate conditions affect the economic life where you live? (c) Do you think climate has more impact on the economy in India or where you live? Explain.
2. **Comparing** (a) Describe the calendars developed by the various civilizations you have studied in Chapters 2, 3, and 4. (b) How are the calendars similar? (c) How are they different? (d) Why do you think most early civilizations developed a calendar?

Relating Past to Present

1. (a) What kinds of questions did Shang priests include on oracle bones? (b) What do the questions tell you about the concerns of the people? (c) Do you see any similarities between the use of oracle bones in ancient China and the use of horoscopes today? Explain.

Developing Basic Skills

1. **Making a Review Chart** Information that is organized in a chart can be easily reviewed and compared. Make a large chart with four columns and five rows. Title the columns Egypt, Sumer, Indus, and Shang. Title the rows Location, Government, Religious Beliefs, Social Classes, and Achievements. Fill in the chart with information you learned in Chapters 2, 3, and 4. Then answer the following questions: (a) What similarities do you notice in the locations of all four civilizations? (b) Did Egyptians and Sumerians have the same kind of government? Explain. (c) How did the religious beliefs of Shang China differ from Egyptian religious beliefs? (d) What social classes existed in all four civilizations?
2. **Making Generalizations** A generalization is a broad statement based on facts. Making accurate generalizations can help you identify important patterns in history. Review what you have read about how people made a living in ancient India and China. (a) Make one generalization about how most people made a living. (b) List the facts that support your generalization. (c) Does your generalization apply to other ancient civilizations? Explain.
3. **Placing Events in Time** The time lines at the end of each chapter in your text show the relationship between events in regard to time. For B.C. dates, remember that the higher number is always the earlier date. Answer the following questions based on the time lines on pages 28, 44, and 60. (a) Was the New Kingdom in Egypt formed before or after the beginning of Indus Valley civilization? (b) Did Sumerian civilization develop before or after the Aryan invasions of India? (c) Which civilizations existed at about the same time?

See page 803 for suggested readings.

Rise of Classical Civilizations

The Buddha (563–483 B.C.) taught in India, but the religion he founded spread throughout Asia.

79 B.C. This glass jug was found in the ruins of Pompeii, a Roman city buried by a volcano.

		600 B.C.	400 B.C.	200 B.C.	0
POLITICS AND GOVERNMENT		**594 B.C.** Solon reforms government of Athens		**210 B.C.–220 A.D.** Han dynasty rules in China	
ECONOMICS AND TECHNOLOGY		**600s B.C.** Greeks found colonies around the Mediterranean		**221–210 B.C.** Great Wall built in China under the Ch'in	
SOCIETY AND CULTURE			**461–429 B.C.** Golden Age of Athens under Pericles	**70–19 B.C.** Virgil, author of *Aeneid*, lives in Rome	

Greeks used sailing ships to trade throughout the Mediterranean world.

Women in Athens were expected only to manage their homes and raise children.

Unit Outline

64 A.D. During the reign of Nero, shown on this coin, a fire nearly destroyed the city of Rome.

The Romans inherited many things from the Greeks, including theater and drama, where masks such as these were used.

0	200 A.D.	400 A.D.	600 A.D.

27 B.C.–180 A.D. Pax Romana

320 A.D. Gupta Empire founded in India

476 A.D. Fall of Rome

100s A.D. Chinese develop process for making paper

400s A.D. Ideas of zero and a decimal system developed in India

100s A.D. Buddhism reaches China

312 A.D. Roman Emperor, Constantine, converts to Christianity

During the Han dynasty, the Chinese invented the water mill to grind grain in graneries such as this one.

The fish remained a symbol of early Christians even after Christianity became the official religion of the Roman Empire in 395 A.D.

5 Ancient Greece

(2000 B.C.–371 B.C.)

The Acropolis in Athens.

> **Chapter Outline**
>
> 1 Early Civilizations in the Aegean
>
> 2 The Greek City-States
>
> 3 A Century of Wars

In 431 B.C., Pericles (PEHR uh KLEEZ), a respected and successful general, addressed the people of Athens. They had gathered to honor the soldiers who had fallen in the opening battle of the Peloponnesian Wars, which pitted Athens against Sparta. As Athenians mourned their dead relatives and friends, they listened to Pericles' Funeral Oration, in which he praised Athenian greatness.

"Our system of government is called a democracy because power is in the hands not of a minority but of the whole people. When it is a question of settling private disputes, everyone is equal before the law. When it is a question of putting one person before another in positions of public responsibility, what counts is not membership in a particular class but the actual ability which the man possesses."

Pericles had done much to make Athenian government democratic, and he reminded Athenians of the importance of public service. "Here each individual is interested not only in his own affairs but in the affairs of the state as well. . . . We do not say that a man who takes no interest in politics is a man who minds his own business; we say that he has no business here at all."

The Greek historian Thucydides (thoo SIHD uh DEEZ), who attended this ceremony, recreated Pericles' Funeral Oration from memory. Although Pericles may not have said these exact words, the Funeral Oration has come to symbolize the ideas that the Greeks developed about the individual's role in society and about government.

The systems of government that evolved in Greece differed from those of the river valley civilizations described in Unit One. Unlike the people of the river valley civilizations, the ancient Greeks were not united under a single ruler. Rather, they lived in small, independent cities constantly at war with one another. Their struggles to maintain their independence may have led the Greeks to develop a concern for the rights and responsibilities of individual citizens.

The Greeks were heir to an earlier civilization that had developed in the Aegean region. Although Greeks absorbed many ideas from other peoples, they established their own distinct civilization.

1 Early Civilizations in the Aegean

Read to Learn
■ why Greece became a trading civilization
■ why Achaean civilization declined

The first Aegean civilization developed on the island of Crete. From there, it spread to the Greek mainland. Unlike the river valley civilizations of Egypt, the Fertile Crescent, India, and China, neither the Cretans nor the Greeks created a large land empire. Instead, each became a great sea power. To understand why this happened, it is necessary to look at the geography of the Aegean islands and the nearby Greek mainland.

Geographic Setting

Greece is a mountainous peninsula that juts into the eastern Mediterranean Sea. Because of the rugged terrain, only about a quarter of the land can be cultivated. The early Greeks were both herders and farmers. Olive trees and grapevines thrived in the mild climate. But as the Greek population increased, the limited amount of usable land forced many Greeks to turn to fishing and trading for a living. The Greeks traded olive oil and wine for the wheat and grain needed to feed a growing population.

The mountains limited transportation and communication and made the country difficult to unite. Cut off from each other, Greeks developed small, separate communities. Each community valued its independence and fiercely resisted outside interference. As a result, the Greeks were frequently at war with one another.

As you can see from the map on page 66, hundreds of fingers of land poke out from the Greek coastline, forming good natural harbors. The Aegean Sea, which washes the eastern shores of Greece, is dotted with islands to shelter storm-tossed ships.

Aided by favorable winds, Greek sailors crossed to the shores of North Africa and the eastern Mediterranean. Trade introduced the Greeks to other civilizations, some more advanced than their own. As a result, the Greeks became practical about new ideas. They sifted through the achievements of other peoples, adopting some, such as the Phoenician alphabet, and rejecting others.

Minoan Civilization

Between 2000 B.C. and 1400 B.C., Minoan (mih NOH uhn) civilization* flourished on Crete. The Minoans were a great trading power in the eastern Mediterranean. Powered by sails and oars, Minoan vessels carried goods from the Black Sea to the Nile Valley and Phoenicia. The Minoans exchanged olive oil, honey, and wine for gold, precious stones, grain, and linen.

At the height of Minoan civilization, a king ruled the prosperous cities of the island from his palace-city at Knossos (NAHS uhs).

---

* Minoan civilization is named after Minos, a legendary Cretan king. Minos was credited with building a huge palace in which he kept the Minotaur, a monster that was half human and half bull.

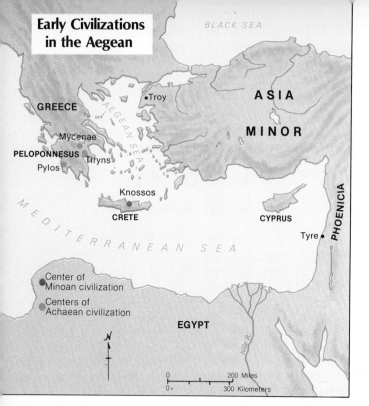

Early Civilizations in the Aegean

BLACK SEA

GREECE

Troy

ASIA MINOR

AEGEAN SEA

Mycenae

PELOPONNESUS

Tiryns

Pylos

Knossos

CRETE

CYPRUS

PHOENICIA

Tyre

MEDITERRANEAN SEA

Center of Minoan civilization

Centers of Achaean civilization

EGYPT

Nile R.

0   200 Miles

0   300 Kilometers

Map Skill *The sea was crucial to the development of early Aegean civilizations. For hundreds of years, it protected the Minoan civilization on the island of Crete. The sea also served as a highway for trading ships from Crete and the Greek mainland. Sailors traveled by day in boats equipped with sails and oars. At night, they sought the safety of harbors. What were the leading ports on the mainland?*

In 1898 A.D., British archaeologist Sir Arthur Evans excavated the site of the palace. He discovered that the palace contained over 800 rooms, including a magnificent throne room. The rooms were connected by courtyards and corridors. The complex structure served as royal residence, temple, storeroom, and government center. The palace had an elaborate drainage system. Yet it had no defensive walls. Apparently, the Cretans felt that their ships and the sea itself protected them from invaders.

The colorful *frescoes* (FREHS kohz), or wall paintings, decorating the palace at Knossos illustrate many aspects of Minoan life. Some frescoes show athletic young men and women competing in acrobatic contests. Others picture elegantly dressed women strolling in the royal gardens. Among the Minoans, women probably enjoyed nearly equal status with men.

From the palace frescoes and statues, it appears that Minoan religious beliefs centered on worship of the bull and a mother goddess. The people of Crete obviously enjoyed life. Wealthy merchants spent lavishly on their homes and on personal comforts rather than on temples and tombs as the Egyptians and Sumerians had.

The record of Minoan civilization is incomplete. The Minoans developed a writing system based on pictograms and signs made up of lines. Scholars call this writing Linear A, but they have as yet found no clue to deciphering it. Most information on the Minoans has come from Evans' excavations at Knossos.

The Minoan civilization eventually grew weak, and Crete was invaded by people from the Greek mainland. About 1400 B.C., Knossos itself was destroyed, perhaps by an earthquake, a volcano, or invaders. Like the Indus Valley civilization, this early civilization on Crete remained buried for a long time. Yet Crete directly influenced the peoples of mainland Greece.

Achaean Civilization

About 2000 B.C., the Achaeans (uh KEE uhnz), an Indo-European people like the Hittites and Aryans, invaded the Greek peninsula from the north. The Achaeans settled in one region for a few generations. Then they pushed further south. As they conquered new territory, they intermarried with the people already living in the Greek peninsula. Eventually, the Achaeans extended their conquests over the Peloponnesus (PEHL uh puh NEE suhs), the southern half of Greece.

The Achaeans expanded their empire through warfare and trade. By about 1400 B.C., they controlled the Aegean and probably occupied Knossos. They built strong fortress cities on the mainland. Each city was ruled by a warrior king. Riches from trade and war loot allowed Achaean rulers to fill their palaces and tombs with gold treasures. Outside of each walled city, traders,

The bull had an important place in Minoan religion. Crete lies in an earthquake zone, and the Minoans may have thought that earthquakes were caused by a bull rampaging beneath the ground. Minoan religious ceremonies included dances in which skilled acrobats turned somersaults over wild bulls. Both men and women participated in these dangerous rituals, as you can see in this fresco from Knossos.

merchants, artisans, and farmers lived in small villages that paid tribute to the king.

The Achaeans built on the achievements of Minoan civilization. Artisans at Mycenae (mī SEE nee) reproduced Minoan designs on their jewelry, pottery, and tools. The Achaeans also learned writing from the Minoans. Achaean writing, called Linear B, consists of signs adapted from Minoan Linear A.

The Trojan War

Around 1250 B.C., the Achaeans banded together under the leadership of the king of Mycenae to attack Troy, a rival commercial power. From the map on page 66, you can see that Troy controlled trade routes between the Aegean and Black seas. After a long and devastating war, the Achaeans emerged the victors.

Scholars first learned about the Trojan War from the *Iliad* (IHL ee uhd) and the *Odyssey* (AHD uh see), two of the best-known epic poems in the world. The poems were probably composed by Homer, a blind Greek poet, about 750 B.C., long after the fall of Troy.* Homer based his poems on stories that had been passed on by earlier generations.

According to the *Iliad*, the tragic struggle occurred because Paris, a Trojan prince, kidnapped Helen, wife of the king of Sparta. The Spartan king and his brother, King Agamemnon (AG uh MEHM nahn) of Mycenae, enlisted the help of other rulers and eventually involved all of Greece in the effort to rescue Helen. After ten years of war, the Achaeans destroyed Troy and drove the Trojans into exile. In the *Odyssey*, Homer described the wandering and adventures of the Achaean warrior Odysseus (oh DIHS ee uhs) after the fall of Troy.

Until the late 1800s, historians considered the *Iliad* and *Odyssey* to be fiction. The

---

* Some scholars question whether Homer actually existed. Others have suggested that the *Iliad* and *Odyssey* were the work of several poets. The ancient Greeks, however, believed that Homer was a real person.

Heinrich Schliemann uncovered this gold mask when he excavated a royal tomb at Mycenae. Schliemann thought it might be the death mask of King Agamemnon, a leader of the Achaeans in the Trojan War.

poems, which mixed stories of gods and goddesses with legends of human heroes, seemed to have no historical value. However, Heinrich Schliemann (SHLEE muhn), an amateur archæologist, believed otherwise. He thought Troy had really existed, and he set out to prove it.

Schliemann began to excavate a site in northwestern Asia Minor that matched Homer's description of Troy. Digging revealed the ruins of an ancient city, but Schliemann soon discovered that at least nine cities had been built at different times on the same spot.* Finally, the charred wood and destruction found on one level suggested that this was the city actually destroyed by the Achaeans. Later, Schliemann excavated the site of Mycenae, which was also described by Homer.

---

* In ancient times, as today, people often rebuilt a city that had been destroyed by war or natural disaster. The new city would be built on the ruins of the old city.

Through Their Eyes ■ The Blind Bard and the Trojan Horse

In ancient Greece, professional storytellers, or bards, sang Homer's Iliad *and* Odyssey *to attentive audiences. From an early age, children heard the thrilling tales of gods and goddesses. Citizens quoted passages from the epics to support their views. In addition, Greek poets and artists were inspired by Homer.*

The story of the Trojan horse, which follows, was told in the Odyssey *by a blind poet, who might have been modeled on Homer, himself a blind poet.*

From the Odyssey

The bard inspired of heaven took up the story at the point where some of the Greek warriors from Argos set fire to their tents and sailed away while others, hidden within the horse, were waiting with Odysseus in the Trojan place of assembly. For the Trojans themselves had drawn the horse into their fortress, and it stood there while they sat in council around it, and were in three minds as to what they should do. Some were for breaking it up then and there; others would have it dragged to the top of the rock on which the fortress stood, and then thrown down the precipice; while yet others were for letting it remain as an offering . . . for the gods. And this last way was how they settled it. . . .

But the city was doomed when it took in that horse, within which were all the bravest of the Argives waiting to bring death and destruction on the Trojans.

Then Demodocus sang how the sons of the Achaeans issued from the horse, and sacked the town, breaking out from their ambush. He sang how they overran the city hither and thither and ravaged it, and how Odysseus went raging like Ares [the god of war] . . . to the house of Deiphobus. It was there that the fight raged most furiously; nevertheless by Athena's help he was victorious.

1. Name the three ways of handling the horse that the Trojans considered.
2. What does the story reveal about ancient Greek culture?

The Dark Age

Shortly after the fall of Troy, Achaean civilization suffered a disastrous blow when Dorian (DOR ee uhn) invaders swarmed into Greece. The invaders had a military advantage because they had iron weapons and the Achaeans did not. The Dorians plundered the rich cities of the Peloponnesus and disrupted trade. Between 1100 B.C. and 750 B.C., Greece entered a troubled period. The glory of Achaean civilization vanished. Artistic skills and writing were largely forgotten. Scholars have called this period of Greek history the Dark Age.

Yet the past was not totally forgotten. During the Dorian invasions, some Greeks from the mainland had fled to the western coast of Asia Minor, where they preserved the memories of Achaean civilization. In the cities founded by the refugees, ideas and traditions emerged that would influence later Greek civilization. In fact, Homer lived in Asia Minor when he composed the *Iliad* and *Odyssey*.

During the Dark Age, the Greeks of Asia Minor benefited from trade and from travel to the centers of Middle Eastern and Egyptian civilizations. It was during this period that the Greeks adopted the Phoenician alphabet. In addition, a few Greek thinkers began to subject traditional ideas to the test of reason. From the Greek emphasis on reason and logic would come unique contributions in philosophy, history, and science, as you read in Chapter 6.

SECTION REVIEW

1. Locate: Aegean Sea, Crete, Greece, Mediterranean Sea, Knossos, Peloponnesus, Mycenae, Troy, Black Sea.
2. Identify: Linear A, Achaeans, Linear B, *Iliad*, *Odyssey*, Homer, Dorians.
3. Define: fresco.
4. Describe two ways in which geography affected the early Greeks.
5. What did the Achaeans adopt from Minoan civilization?

2 The Greek City-States

Read to Learn
- how democracy developed in Athens
- how Sparta differed from Athens

During the Dark Age, Greeks on the mainland lived in small, isolated villages. The more prosperous villages and towns gradually developed into independent city-states. A city-state or *polis* (POH lihs), consisted of a fortified hilltop and the surrounding fields. When the Greek city-states emerged from the Dark Age, they grew rapidly. Eventually, Athens and Sparta emerged as the leading city-states, but their governments and outlooks on life differed dramatically.

Early City-States

In the Greek city-state, life revolved around the *acropolis* (uh KRAHP uhl ihs), or hilltop fortress. There, the people assembled to defend the polis, to discuss the affairs of the community, and to honor the gods. During the Dark Age, a *monarchy,* or government headed by a king, ruled each Greek polis. This system of government changed about 800 B.C., when noble families who counseled the king and provided leadership in war gained power.

Eventually, *aristocracies,* or governments by a privileged minority or upper class, replaced the monarchies. The power of the aristocracies rested on land ownership. Between 750 B.C. and 500 B.C., social and economic changes spurred the development of new forms of government.

Greek colonies. After 750 B.C., thousands of Greeks left the mainland and set up colonies on distant shores. Some colonists

Greeks established colonies and traded throughout the ancient Mediterranean world. They exchanged wine, olive oil, and their finely decorated pottery for spices and purple dye from the eastern Mediterranean and grain from the Black Sea area. Greeks built battleships like the one painted on this vase to protect their farflung trade.

were involved in the growing trade of the city-states. Others were farmers who fled Greece to escape their debts. Still others were discontented citizens seeking their fortunes.

By 600 B.C., Greek settlements were thriving from the Black Sea coasts to southern Italy, North Africa, and Spain. About this time, Greeks founded the forerunners of the modern cities of Marseille (mahr SAY), Naples, and Istanbul.

The Greek colonies fostered more trade and put the Greeks in touch with other Mediterranean peoples. Contact with other peoples made Greeks aware of their common heritage. While local rivalries often divided the city-states, the Greeks had the same traditions and spoke the same language. To the Greeks, outsiders were "barbaroi," chatterers who spoke unintelligible languages. The modern word "barbarian," which has come to mean an uncivilized person, is derived from this Greek word.

Contact with other peoples also led to the sharing of new ideas. For example, the Greeks gradually adopted coins, which were introduced by the Lydians. The use of coined money and increased trade gave rise to a strong merchant class. This new class began to challenge the nobles and to demand a greater say in government.

The rise of tyranny. Another challenge to the nobles came from citizen-soldiers. Military service was the duty of every citizen in a Greek city-state. However, a change in the nature of warfare had made foot soldiers even more important than before.

War chariots driven by nobles had been the decisive force on the battlefield. By 650 B.C., war chariots were replaced by the *phalanx* (FAY langks), a massive formation of heavily armed foot soldiers. The success of the phalanx depended on long hours of training. Soldiers had to maintain their own equipment, including helmets, shields, swords, and spears. As their role in defending their city-state grew, citizen-soldiers demanded a greater voice in government.

During the sixth century B.C.,* citizen-soldiers supported revolts of the lower class that broke out in many city-states. The lower class had become discontent as a result of the practice of debt slavery. Persons who could not afford to repay loans had to sell themselves into slavery to pay off their debts. Widespread discontent resulted in the rise of *tyranny*, or government by an individual who seizes power by force.

To the ancient Greeks, the word tyranny did not have a negative meaning. A tyrant gained power as a champion of the people. He ruled for as long as he could keep their support. In order to stay in power, tyrants increased employment through public works such as building temples and defensive walls. They also supported the arts. As a result, some city-states made great cultural and economic progress under the tyrants.

In some Greek city-states, the rule of tyrants marked a transition between aristocratic government and *democracy*, or government by the citizens. Although a number of city-states became democracies, the institutions of democratic government were first developed in Athens.

Early Government of Athens

According to Greek legend, the sea god Poseidon (poh SĪ duhn) competed with the goddess Athena for control of Athens. Athena won, giving her name to the city, but Athenians still felt close to the sea. Located in Attica, a peninsula with poor, rocky soil, Athens prospered from overseas trade. The sea linked Athens to the outside world and new ideas.

Athens moved slowly toward democratic rule. As in other city-states, the land-owning aristocracy in Athens replaced the king as head of government around 800 B.C. The aristocracy governed through a council, headed by three *archons* (AHR kahnz), or officials. The nobles administered the laws in

---

* Since B.C. dates are counted backwards from zero, the span 100 B.C. to 1 B.C. represents the first century B.C. Therefore, the sixth century B.C. is the 500s B.C.

their own favor and passed measures that put their interests above the good of the polis. An assembly of citizens met to discuss government affairs, but citizens who were not nobles were almost powerless.

Resentment against the nobles by merchants, small farmers, and many noncitizens created dangerous tensions in Athens. Because of their growing wealth, merchants wanted greater political power. But the nobles excluded them from the government. At the same time, nobles were taking large amounts of land from farmers who were forced into debt by poor harvests. Some farmers became tenants on the estates of wealthy landowners. Others had to sell themselves into slavery to pay their debts.

Many Athenian residents from other parts of Greece, especially skilled artisans, resented their inability to become citizens. Like other Greeks, Athenians considered anyone born outside their city a foreigner, and foreigners could not be citizens. The discontent of these groups led to increasingly violent outbreaks.

Foundations of Democracy in Athens

In 621 B.C., the archons of Athens appointed Draco (DRAY koh), a noble, to draw up a written code of law. They felt that such a code was necessary to prevent civil war. Like Hammurabi's Code, the first Athenian law code was harsh. It ordered the death penalty for many offenses. But Draco's code made the laws public and required that judges, usually nobles, apply the laws equally to all classes.

Unfortunately, Draco's code failed to satisfy the demands of most Athenians, and violence continued to disrupt the city. In the next century, other leaders would make further changes that became the foundations for democracy in Athens.

Beginnings of reform. In 594 B.C., Athenians turned to Solon (SOH luhn), a wise, well-educated, sensitive leader, to solve Athens' problems. Solon abolished the practice of debt slavery and freed citizens previously forced into slavery. He also limited the amount of land one citizen could own and extended citizenship to some skilled artisans from other cities. To increase the food supply and keep prices down, he stopped the sale of grain abroad. However, he encouraged the export of olive oil and wine, which helped make Athens a great trade center.

Through Solon's reforms, ordinary citizens gained greater political power. The assembly of citizens obtained the right to approve government decisions. A new law code, milder than Draco's, guaranteed citizens the right to bring charges against other citizens in a law court. To check the power of those who administered the laws, Solon created new law courts in which citizens owning a certain amount of property served as jurors.

Despite Solon's reforms, unrest persisted. Land ownership was still the basis of real political power. Landless citizens could not hold many official positions, and families freed from debt slavery were left with no land. As a result, the landowning nobility continued to dominate Athenian government.

Discontent eventually paved the way for the establishment of a tyranny. In 560 B.C., Pisistratus (pī SIHS truh tuhs) seized power with the support of poor citizens. Pisistratus redistributed land, giving more to the peasants. He also reduced the privileges of the nobles and directed new building projects. Under Pisistratus, Athenian trade and commerce thrived, and Athens gained prestige throughout the Greek world.

Cleisthenes. In 508 B.C., Cleisthenes (KLĪS thuh NEEZ) moved Athens further along the road to democratic government. He made the Athenian Assembly the law-making body. All citizens, regardless of whether they owned land, participated in the Assembly. Cleisthenes also granted citizenship to some immigrants and former slaves. He established a council of 500 citizens to propose laws and to administer those laws that the Assembly approved. Members of the council were chosen by lot.

Cleisthenes tried to extend the power of citizens further by introducing the idea of ostracism. *Ostracism* (AHS trah sihzm) was the temporary exile of a citizen from the city. If citizens thought a person was a threat to Athens, they could vote to ostracize him by writing his name on a piece of pottery. Anyone receiving more than 6,000 such votes was banished from Athens for ten years.

The development of democracy in Athens continued in the fifth century B.C. It reached its height under the great statesman Pericles, as you will read in the next section.

Training for Athenian Citizenship

In general, citizenship in Athens was a privilege and responsibility reserved for free men whose parents were both free, native-born Athenians. At age 18, these men took an oath to defend the city and its gods. After two years of military training, they became citizens and took their places in the Assembly. Later they might serve as jurors or as elected officials.

Athenian education prepared young men for their place in society. Curiosity and the free discussion of ideas were encouraged. An educated slave served as tutor and companion, supervising a boy's learning between the ages of 8 and 18. Students learned grammar, music, and rhetoric—that is, the art of public speaking. The study of grammar included memorizing literature, such as the *Iliad* and *Odyssey*. From such ancient works, Athenian boys learned Greek religious beliefs and history, as well as the values of the ideal warrior.

Athenians prized a sound mind and a well-trained body. In lively public discussions, young men debated questions on art, politics, and philosophy. Sports and gymnastics occupied an equally important place in a youth's training.

Women in Athenian Society

Women in Athens had no political or legal rights. They could not attend the Assembly, hold office, own property, or conduct any legal business. A woman's nearest male relative acted as her legal guardian.

Athenian women lived in strict seclusion, attending only occasional religious festivals. When they left the house, they were always attended by slaves. Furthermore, husbands and wives lived in separate parts

In Athens, women seldom left the home. Men did the shopping, and slaves carried the food home. However, in most Greek towns and villages, getting water from the town fountain was a woman's chore. Going for water was a social occasion, as this painting on a water jug shows.

of the house. "The best reputation a woman can have," claimed the Athenian leader Pericles, "is not to be spoken of among men either for good or for evil."

Another Greek wrote that the duty of a wife was "to bear us . . . children and to be faithful guardians of our households." In this role, women managed their homes and slaves and raised children. A mother trained her daughters in domestic skills. Between the ages of 14 and 16, a daughter married a man chosen by her parents.

Sparta

Life in the city-state of Sparta differed from life in Athens. As you can see from the map on page 76, Sparta was landlocked in Laconia (luh KOH nee uh), an isolated region in the Peloponnesus. During the Dark Age, Dorian invaders settled in Sparta and enslaved the local population. The slaves, called *helots* (HEHL uhts), worked the land

for the Spartans. Because the helots outnumbered their rulers 20 to 1, the Spartans created a strong military state to prevent slave uprisings.

The Spartan government was a monarchy headed by two kings. A council of 28 elders advised the kings, and an assembly of Spartan citizens met to approve all government decisions. At such meetings, citizens showed their support by shouting loudly. Each year, the assembly elected five overseers, or *ephors* (EHF orz), to direct the daily affairs of state. The ephors supervised the helots and kept a close watch on the private lives of citizens.

The Spartan way of life. In Sparta, the desire for a strong military state dominated all other interests. To achieve such a state, the Spartans developed a strict system that governed every aspect of a citizen's life from birth to death.

State control began when a newborn infant was brought before the ephors. Weak

73

and sickly babies were placed on mountainsides to die of exposure. The Spartan state required brave warriors who displayed absolute loyalty. At the age of seven, boys left home to begin military training in barracks. Brutal discipline during military training taught Spartan youths to fend for themselves. They had no shoes and few clothes even in winter. They were expected to steal food to supplement a meager diet, but they were beaten if caught.

Spartans told a story about a boy caught stealing a fox. The boy allowed the animal to claw him to death rather than admit he had it hidden under his coat. To the Spartans, the endurance and courage displayed by the youth were admirable.

In addition to long hours of military drill, boys spent time learning to read and write. Discussion was discouraged. When asked a question, a boy was expected to answer in the fewest words possible. Today, a person who gives answers very briefly is called laconic (luh KAHN ihk), from Laconia, the region around Sparta.

At the age of 20, Spartan soldiers married, but they continued to live in barracks for another 40 years. At the age of 30, they became citizens and took their places in the assembly. The state provided each citizen with land and slaves to support his family.

Spartan women also endured strict discipline and learned to defend Sparta. They were expected to show absolute obedience first to their fathers and later their husbands. Unlike women in other Greek city-states, who lived largely in seclusion, Spartan women took part in public group exercises and military drills. They participated in gymnastics so they would be strong mothers.

Spartan women were tough minded, and they expected the same of Spartan men. Once, as Spartan soldiers were leaving for battle, a group of Spartan women called out, "Come back with your shield or on it."

Sparta and the Greek world. Art and literature had no place in Spartan education. The state discouraged new ideas and forbade travel outside Sparta. Sparta increased its isolation from other Greek city-states by prohibiting the use of coined money, which was considered a corrupting influence.

Spartan girls learned to accept the same harsh discipline as boys. They were expected to stay as physically fit as this young Spartan runner. Athenians, who thought women should remain in seclusion, considered the women of Sparta immodest.

Other Greeks respected the Spartans for their discipline and courage. To the historian Herodotus, the Spartans were "the best fighters in the world." The secret of their success, he believed, was their discipline and absolute obedience to the law: "never to retreat in battle, however great the odds, but always to stand firm, and to conquer or die."

SECTION REVIEW

1. Locate: Attica, Athens, Sparta, Laconia.
2. Identify: Draco, Solon, Pisistratus, Cleisthenes.
3. Define: polis, acropolis, monarchy, aristocracy, phalanx, tyranny, democracy, archon, ostracism, helot, ephor.
4. Describe the effects of the expansion of trade in the Greek world after 750 B.C.
5. Why were tyrants popular leaders in ancient Greece?
6. (a) What political conditions in Athens created discontent among merchants? (b) What happened to small farmers in Athens who could not pay their debts?
7. Why did the Spartans feel the need for a strong military state?

3 A Century of Wars

Read to Learn ■ how people lived during Athen's Golden Age
■ how the Peloponnesian Wars affected Greek culture

During the sixth century B.C., events took place in the Middle East that would greatly affect the Greek world. As you read in Chapter 3, around 550 B.C. Cyrus began to carve out an empire in Persia. He and his successors gradually extended the Persian Empire from the Indus Valley to the Black Sea. In 546 B.C., Cyrus conquered the Greek city-states on the coast of Asia Minor.

The Greek city-states remained largely self-governing under Persian rule, and for 50 years the peoples of the coastal cities accepted the situation. But in 499 B.C., the city-state of Miletus (mī LEET uhs) revolted. Soon the Greek world came under attack by Persia.

Beginning of the Persian Wars

Miletus led the Greek cities of Asia Minor against the powerful Persian Empire. Despite aid from Athens, the rebel cities were crushed by the Persians in 493 B.C. Herodotus wrote in his history of the Persian Wars that when the Persian king Darius learned of the Athenian intervention he swore revenge and ordered a servant to repeat every day, "Master, remember the Athenians."

In 490 B.C., Darius launched an attack across the Aegean Sea. When the main Persian force landed near the plain of Marathon, Athens asked for help. But it received little support. Nevertheless, the outnumbered Athenians won a stunning victory over the Persians. According to legend, Pheidippides (fī DIHP uh DEEZ), the best runner in the Athenian army, was chosen to carry news of the victory to Athens. He ran 26 miles (about 42 kilometers) over hilly terrain, gasped, "Rejoice, we conquer," and died. Today, a marathon is a 26-mile foot race.

Athenians regarded the battle of Marathon as their finest hour. They honored their fallen soldiers by setting up a stone in the central marketplace of Athens that read: "The valor of these men will shine as a light imperishable forever."

Even as they celebrated their victory, the Athenians realized the Persians would seek revenge. The Athenian leader Themistocles (thuh MIHS tuh KLEEZ) convinced the Assembly that Athens should build a fleet of ships. With a strong navy, Themistocles reasoned, Athens could not only defend itself against a new Persian attack but could also become dominant in trade.

Victory for the Greeks

Darius died before he could renew his attack on the Greek mainland, but his son Xerxes (ZERK seez) prepared a huge invasion force to attack by land and by sea. Xerxes sent envoys to demand the surrender of the Greek cities. Fearing Persian strength, many cities submitted. The rest formed an alliance and chose Sparta to lead them.

The Persian king Darius ruled a huge empire from the Black Sea to the Persian Gulf. An able and ambitious general, Darius dreamed of extending his empire into Europe by conquering Greece. In this council of war, Darius and his advisors plan an expedition against Greece.

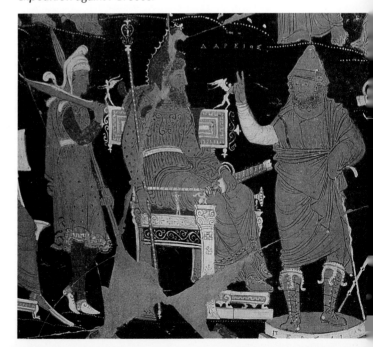

In 480 B.C., the Persians landed in Greece. A small Spartan force marched north to delay them. Led by Leonidas (lee AHN uh duhs), the Spartans and soldiers from Thespia heroically defended the narrow mountain pass at Thermopylae (ther MAHP uh lee).

A generation after the battle Herodotus wrote:

> There was a bitter struggle over the body of Leonidas. Four times the Greeks drove the enemy off, and at last by their valor succeeded in dragging it away. ... They withdrew into the narrow neck of the pass. ... Here they resisted to the last, with their swords, if they had them, and if not, with their hands and teeth, until the Persians ... finally overwhelmed them.

The stand at Thermopylae gave the Athenians time to evacuate their city and take refuge on the island of Salamis. From there, they watched the Persians burn and loot their homes and the temples on the Acropolis. At the same time, Themistocles tricked Xerxes into sending his fleet into the narrow straits of Salamis. Xerxes expected an easy Persian victory. Instead, the new Athenian navy destroyed most of the Persian fleet.

The Greek success at the battle of Salamis forced Xerxes to withdraw to Asia Minor. The following year, the Greeks soundly defeated the remaining Persian forces at the battle of Plataea (pluh TEE uh).

The resounding Greek victories marked the end of the Persian Wars and created an upsurge in Greek confidence. Persian armies never again invaded mainland Greece, although Persian rulers used bribery and intrigue to foster disunity among the city-states. For a time, the Greek cities of Asia Minor remained independent. But in 404 B.C., they were peacefully absorbed into the Persian Empire. Because of its decisive role in the Persian Wars and its superb navy, Athens emerged as the leader of Greece.

The Athenian Empire

In 477 B.C., more than 160 delegates from Greek cities met on the island of Delos. They formed a defensive alliance to guard against possible future Persian attacks. The alliance was called the Delian League. Athens, the greatest commercial and naval power, dominated the alliance from the start. The larger city-states supplied ships, and the smaller ones made annual payments. Athenians collected the tribute, commanded the league's fleet, and dictated policy. In 454 B.C., as evidence of its dominance, Athens moved the league treasury from Delos to the Acropolis.

Through its control of the Delian League, Athens established an empire. Riches from trade and tribute poured into the city. In an atmosphere of prosperity, Athenians enjoyed their greatest political freedom ever, and Greek culture bloomed. The period following the Persian Wars has often been called the "Golden Age of Athens."

The chief architect of Athenian policy during this period was Pericles. The son of a noble family, Pericles had received an excellent education and had won fame as a general, statesman, poet, and philosopher. Between 461 B.C. and 429 B.C., Pericles

Map Skill *During the Dark Age, many Greeks left the Greek mainland and settled in cities along the coast of Asia Minor. In the fifth century B.C., some of these cities became part of the Athenian Empire, as you can see on this map. How did the Athenian Empire differ geographically from other ancient empires you have studied?*

Ancient Greece

BLACK SEA

MACEDONIA
THRACE
Byzantium
SEA OF MARMARA
Mount Olympus
Troy
PERSIAN
Pergamon
EMPIRE
Thermopylae
Delphi
Plataea
Thebes
Marathon
Corinth
Athens
Sardis
Salamis
ATTICA
SAMOS
Ephesus
PELOPONNESUS
Miletus
Sparta
DELOS
LACONIA
COS
RHODES
CRETE
Knossos
MEDITERRANEAN SEA

Area settled by Greeks
Athenian Empire about 450 B.C.
Persian War battles

0   150 Miles
0   200 Kilometers

dominated Athenian political life. Because of his many achievements, he came to symbolize Athenian greatness.

Pericles undertook an ambitious building program to beautify Athens. In 480 B.C., the Persians had destroyed the city and its sacred shrines. For years, the ruined temples served as reminders of the Persian menace. But Pericles proposed to rebuild the temples as monuments to the greatness of Athens. Atop the Acropolis, Athenians built the dazzling, white marble Parthenon (PAHR thuh NAHN), a temple to Athena. Phideas (FIHD ee uhs), considered the greatest sculptor of his day, carved a huge statue of Athena that stood inside the temple. Outside, there was another statue of Athena so large that returning sailors could see it far out at sea.

In addition to building temples, Athenians strengthened the defensive walls that connected Athens to the busy port at Piraeus (pī REE uhs). These building programs employed thousands of workers and attracted stonemasons and artisans from all over Greece. At the same time, talented artists, philosophers, and poets converged on Athens, making it the center of Greek culture. Pericles called Athens the "school of Greece" for its artistic and intellectual achievements as well as for its political system.

The Height of Athenian Democracy

Democracy, which had been developing in Athens over many years, reached its peak under the leadership of Pericles. He opened all political offices to any citizen. He also arranged payment for jurors so that poor citizens as well as the wealthy could serve. Furthermore, citizens employed in the building projects no longer depended on noble families for a living and felt freer to voice opinions in the Assembly.

Athens had a *direct democracy*—that is, all citizens had the right to attend the Assembly and cast a vote. Only a minority of Athenians were citizens. Therefore, the entire citizen body could meet in open discussion, and citizens did not elect people to represent them. Pericles believed that Athenian democracy owed its success to shared values,

loyalty to the city, and a willingness to do public service.

But Athenian democracy was far from complete. Citizens had time for public service largely because they owned slaves who worked their land and ran their businesses. Most residents of Athens were not citizens and had no say in government. Furthermore, the many Greeks who flocked to Athens from other cities were considered foreigners and were usually denied citizenship. Women, too, had no political rights. Although Athenian democracy was limited, it served as the model for other Greek city-states.

The Peloponnesian Wars

Other Greek city-states resented Athenian success and power. Some of them formed an alliance called the Peloponnesian League. This alliance was headed by Sparta. In 431 B.C., a dispute between Athens and Corinth, a member of the Peloponnesian League, flared into a major conflict. War engulfed all of Greece as Athens and its allies battled the Peloponnesian League. At the outset, the Athenian navy triumphed on the seas. But a Spartan army marched north into Attica and surrounded Athens, forcing Pericles to move the people inside the city walls. The overcrowded conditions that resulted caused an outbreak of plague. Over a third of the Athenian population, including Pericles, died.

Fighting dragged on for 27 years, until the Athenian navy was destroyed and both sides were exhausted. Finally, with help from the Persian navy, Sparta blockaded Athens while Spartan armies again surrounded the city. Facing starvation, Athens surrendered in 404 B.C. Sparta's allies in the Peloponnesian League called for the destruction of Athens. However, Sparta spared the city out of respect for Athen's role in the Persian Wars.

The Peloponnesian Wars cost Athens its navy, its empire, and for a time its democratic form of government. Although Athens remained the cultural center of Greece, it never regained the power it had enjoyed during its golden age.

After the Peloponnesian Wars, the Greek city-states continued to fight among themselves, and Persia continued to encourage disunity. For over 100 years, the Greek city-states were at war, first against Persia and then among themselves. The struggles took a devastating toll in lives and sapped the resources of the cities. Yet as you will read, this period was marked by great achievements in the arts and philosophy.

SECTION REVIEW

1. Locate: Miletus, Marathon, Thermopylae, Salamis, Plataea, Delos.

2. Identify: Themistocles, Xerxes, Delian League, Pericles, Parthenon.

3. Define: direct democracy.

4. (a) What event led to the Persian Wars? (b) List two results of these wars.

5. (a) What were the democratic features of Athenian government? (b) How was Athenian democracy limited?

6. What effect did the Peloponnesian Wars have on Athens?

Chapter 5 Review

In Perspective

Between 2000 B.C. and 1400 B.C., the Minoan civilization flourished on the island of Crete. About 1400 B.C., the Achaeans invaded from the Greek mainland and captured the Minoan capital. Both the Minoans and the Achaeans prospered as a result of trade. Invaders eventually destroyed the Achaean civilization, and Greece was plunged into the Dark Age between 1100 B.C. and 750 B.C.

After 750 B.C., independent city-states began to emerge in Greece. These city-states gradually developed new forms of government in which individual citizens played an increasingly important role. In Athens, reformers such as Solon established the foundations of democratic government. In Sparta, the government maintained strict controls over the lives of the people in order to prevent slave revolts.

Victory in the Persian Wars increased the wealth and power of Athens. During its golden age, Athens dominated the Delian League. It also became a center of Greek culture and a model of democracy. Resentment of Athenian power among other Greek city-states led to the Peloponnesian Wars, which ended with the defeat of Athens in 404 B.C. The endless wars weakened the Greek city-states and left them open to conquest.

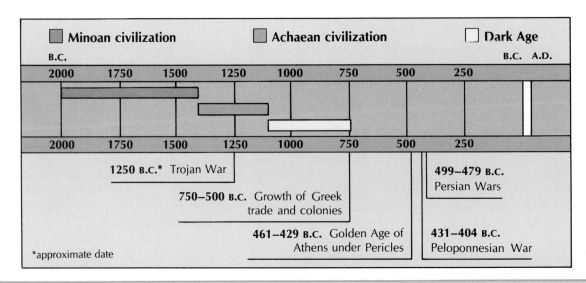

| ■ Minoan civilization | ■ Achaean civilization | □ Dark Age |

B.C.   B.C.   A.D.

| 2000 | 1750 | 1500 | 1250 | 1000 | 750 | 500 | 250 |

1250 B.C.* Trojan War

750–500 B.C. Growth of Greek trade and colonies

461–429 B.C. Golden Age of Athens under Pericles

499–479 B.C. Persian Wars

431–404 B.C. Peloponnesian War

*approximate date

Recalling Facts

Arrange the events in each of the following groups in the order in which they occurred.

1. (a) Knossos is destroyed.
   (b) Linear A is developed.
   (c) The *Iliad* is written.
2. (a) The Dorians invade Greece.
   (b) Greece undergoes the Dark Age.
   (c) The Achaeans attack Troy.
3. (a) Pisistratus becomes tyrant.
   (b) Pericles rules in Athens.
   (c) Draco draws up a law code.
4. (a) The Delian League is formed.
   (b) The Greeks defeat Persian invaders.
   (c) Athens and Sparta fight in the Peloponnesian Wars.

Chapter Checkup

1. Describe the evidence each of the following persons uncovered about early Aegean civilizations: (a) Sir Arthur Evans; (b) Heinrich Schliemann.
2. (a) How were the Minoan and Achaean civilizations similar? (b) How were they different? (c) How would you explain the similarities and differences?
3. Describe the following types of government developed by the Greeks: (a) monarchy; (b) aristocracy; (c) tyranny; (d) democracy.
4. Compare each of the following features of life in Athens with those of life in Sparta: (a) government; (b) education; (c) role of women.
5. (a) How did the Persian Wars affect the Greek city-states? (b) How did the Peloponnesian Wars affect them?

Critical Thinking

1. **Evaluating** In his Funeral Oration, Pericles stated that the government of Athens was a democracy because "power is in the hands not of a minority but of the whole people." (a) In what ways was his statement accurate? (b) In what ways was it not accurate? (c) Do you think the government of Athens was a true democracy? Why or why not?
2. **Synthesizing** The ancient Greeks memorized the *Iliad* and the *Odyssey*. (a) Why do you think epic poems were so important to ancient civilizations? (b) Do you think they give an accurate picture of what really happened in those societies? Explain.

Relating Past to Present

1. How would you compare education in Athens with education in the United States today?
2. How would you compare education in Sparta with education in the United States today?

Developing Basic Skills

1. **Identifying Immediate and Long-Range Causes** When historians investigate the causes of an event or development, they distinguish between immediate and long-range causes. An *immediate cause* is the actual incident or change that triggers an event or historical development. *Long-range causes* are the underlying reasons. (a) Based on your reading in this chapter, what was the immediate cause of the Peloponnesian Wars? (b) What long-range cause or causes can you identify? (c) What connection do you see between the immediate and long-range causes of the Peloponnesian Wars?
2. **Map Reading** Study the map on page 76 and answer the following questions: (a) Based on the map, explain why the Greek city-states became leading sea powers. (b) What geographic features help explain the existence of strongly independent city-states in Greece? (c) What geographical features help explain why Sparta did not become a great sea power?
3. **Placing Events in Time** Historians use the terms "decade" and "century" to describe specific lengths of time. A decade is 10 years. A century is 100 years. The 100 years from 200 B.C. to 101 B.C. are called the second century B.C. The years from 100 B.C. to 1 B.C. are called the first century B.C. The period from 1 A.D. to 100 A.D. is the first century A.D. Review the chapter and study the time line on page 78. Then answer the following questions: (a) What years are included in the decade before the battle of Marathon? (b) In what century was the Delian League formed? (c) Which events shown on the time line took place in the fifth century B.C.?

See page 803 for suggested readings.

6 The Greek Heritage

(750 B.C.–133 B.C.)

The Greek goddess Athena.

In the Greek play *Antigone* (an TIHG uh NEE), a courageous young woman of Thebes named Antigone must make a difficult decision. Her brother has been killed while attacking the city. Their uncle Creon, the king of Thebes, has ordered that no one may bury the traitor on pain of death. Antigone, however, refuses to leave her brother unburied, and she sprinkles dust over his body as a symbol of burial. Caught in this illegal act, she is brought before Creon. He demands to know why she has defied a law of the city. Antigone replies that she obeyed the law of the gods, which she considers a higher law than Creon's.

"For me, it was not Zeus who made that order," she tells Creon. "Nor did I think your orders were so strong that you, a mortal man, could overrule the gods' unwritten and unfailing laws."

Creon is angered by his niece's disobedience. In his opinion, Antigone has openly broken the law, and she must be punished as an example to the citizens of Thebes. He declares, "Since I have caught her in the open act, the only one in town who disobeyed, I . . . will kill her." In the end, he concludes, "the man the state has put in place must have obedient hearing to his least command when it is right or even when it is not."

Sophocles (SAHF uh KLEEZ), the author of *Antigone,* based this drama on an ancient Greek legend. But he enriched the story of Antigone and her uncle by making it into a dramatic clash between an individual and the government. To audiences who watched this play during the Golden Age of Athens, intellectual and political problems were the proper subjects for art, drama, and philosophy. More than most ancient peoples, the Greeks were concerned with defining the rights and responsibilities of the citizen. This concern contributed to the rich Greek culture of the fifth and fourth centuries B.C.

1 Patterns of Greek Life

Read to Learn ■ how religion affected Greek culture
■ how Greek art expressed Greek philosophy

Because the climate of Greece was mild, Greeks spent much time outdoors. People gathered in the marketplace to discuss the news of the day. These discussions dealt largely with the world around them since the Greeks were more interested in this life than in an afterlife. But the Greeks did not neglect their gods. They frequently assembled for daylong religious festivals, and elegant temples graced the acropolis of every Greek city-state. In Greece, religion, along with literature and the arts, helped bind the people together.

Religious Beliefs

Ancient Greek myths wove complex stories about the many Greek gods and goddesses. In these myths, the gods and goddesses often looked and behaved like ordinary humans. They differed from humans, however, because they were more powerful and had eternal life. Greeks did not fear their gods, but failure to honor the gods was considered a serious offense.

The Olympian gods. The Greeks believed that the 12 most powerful gods and goddesses met in a council on Mount Olympus, a snow-covered peak in northern Greece. The chief Olympian god, Zeus, ruled the universe and made his presence known through thunder, lightning, and earthquakes, which often shook the Greek peninsula. Poseidon, lord of the seas, and Hades, ruler of the underworld, were Zeus's brothers. Their sister Hestia was the goddess of the hearth, or home fire.

Each Olympian presided over different aspects of life. Hera, the wife of Zeus, was the goddess of marriage. Athena, the patron of Athens, embodied wisdom and protected handicrafts and agriculture. Other Olympian gods included Artemis (AHR tuh mihs), goddess of the woods; Aphrodite (AF ruh DĪT ee), goddess of love; Hermes (HER meez), the messenger of the gods; Hephaestus (hih

FEHS tuhs), god of fire and metalworkers; and Ares (EHR eez), god of war.

Apollo, god of the sun, music, and healing, was probably the most popular Olympian. Greeks flocked to his shrine at Delphi (DEHL fī), where they consulted the Delphic oracle. The oracle was thought to speak for Apollo. Because many Greeks believed the oracle could foretell the future, they followed the advice given by Apollo's priests and priestesses.

Religious festivals. Each Greek city-state held festivals to honor individual gods. Athens, for example, set aside about 60 days each year for religious celebrations. On these occasions, all citizens took part in the day's events. Many religious festivals included athletic contests dedicated to a particular god. Every four years, athletes assembled at Olympia to honor Zeus. Unlike local religious festivals, the Olympic games were open to all Greeks.

In addition to festivals honoring the Olympian gods, many Greeks participated in festivals connected with mystery religions. These religions emphasized secret rituals and promised immortality, or eternal life, to followers. Because they offered spiritual comfort to the poor, the mystery religions were very popular.

Greek Drama and Literature

In ancient Greece, religion, drama, and poetry were linked. For example, chanting verses around the altar of Dionysus (DĪuh NĪ suhs), god of wine, led to the development of dramatic poetry. According to tradition, the Athenian poet Thespis (THEHS pihs) created the first play, when he gave a person a speaking part. By the fifth century B.C., Athenian playwrights were competing for prizes at the annual festival of Dionysus.

Greek plays were performed in outdoor theaters built into hillsides. The audience sat on sloping tiers of stone seats. There was no scenery or curtain. Three male actors performed all the different parts, while an all-male chorus chanted verses to explain the play's action. Elaborate costumes and high boots set the actors apart from the chorus. The attendance was limited to men, although both rich and poor men attended.

Tragedies. The earliest Greek plays were *tragedies*, dramas that focused on the suffering of a major character and usually ended in disaster. Inspired by stories from the *Iliad* and *Odyssey* and by ancient myths, Greek playwrights posed profound questions about the behavior of the gods and the causes of human suffering. They were especially concerned with individuals who struggled to achieve excellence but failed because of fate or their own weaknesses.

Three great writers of Greek tragedy lived in Athens during the fifth century B.C.:

Performances of tragedies and comedies were well attended in ancient Greece. One theater in Athens held about 20,000 people. Because the outdoor theaters were so large, actors wore huge masks that symbolized the characters and emotions they were portraying. A funnel built into the mouth of each mask probably amplified the actor's voice. In this sculpture, a poet examines a mask to be worn in one of his plays.

Aeschylus (EHS kuh luhs), Sophocles, and Euripides (yoo RIHP uh DEEZ). Aeschylus has been called the father of Greek tragedy because his work served as a model for others. His plays were concerned with the relationships between people and the gods. He treated the themes of murder, revenge, and divine justice in *The Oresteia* (aw REHS tee ah). This series of three plays centered on the fate of the Greek hero Agamemnon and his family after the Trojan War.

The poet Sophocles wrote 123 plays. However, only 7, among them *Antigone*, have survived. In the tragedy *Oedipus the King*, he examined how destiny affected the lives of individuals. Warned by the Delphic oracle that he would commit a terrible crime, Oedipus (EHD uh puhs) left home to avoid this fate. But he could not escape it.

Euripides won fewer prizes than Sophocles in playwriting competitions because he questioned the actions of the Olympian gods and was more critical of traditional ideas. In *Medea* and *The Trojan Women*, for example, he expressed sympathy for women and the oppressed.

Comedies. Like tragedy, Greek comedy originated in Athenian celebrations honoring Dionysus. Comedies were plays in which poets ridiculed people, ideas, and social customs. In plays such as *The Birds*, *The Clouds*, and *The Frogs*, the comic playwright Aristophanes (AR uh STAHF uh NEEZ) mocked just about every figure in Greek life, from politicians and philosophers to poets and even his audience. Skilled in poking fun at pretense and self-importance, Aristophanes enjoyed great popularity and influence.

In the fourth century B.C., theaters were built throughout the Greek world. Comedies and tragedies informed and entertained Greek, and later Roman, audiences. Through the Greeks, drama and the theater became a permanent part of western civilization.

Poetry. The Greeks admired epic poetry such as the *Iliad* and *Odyssey*. They also enjoyed *lyric poems*, in which the poet expresses his or her emotions or thoughts. Lyric poems were sung by a musician playing a lyre, a small harplike instrument. Although Greeks seldom admired the accom-

In ancient Greece, athletic competitions, or games, were held to honor the gods. The games were meant to demonstrate human excellence, which the Greeks considered a worthy offering to the gods. At the games, an athlete either finished first or lost. Placing second was no better than finishing last. The poet Homer reflected the desire to win when he praised the athlete who tried "always to be first and to surpass the others."

The greatest glory for an athlete was to win in the games held every four years at Olympia, a site sacred to the god Zeus. Athletes and spectators from all over the Greek world assembled at Olympia. An Olympic victory brought fame and honor to the athlete and his city. The winner wore a wreath of olive leaves from the sacred grove at Olympia. Upon his return home, he received a hero's welcome, and poets praised his success.

Olympic contestants competed as individuals since the Greeks did not participate in team sports. A chariot race opened the Olympic games. Charioteers like the one shown here drove teams of horses around a hazardous course. The greatest event was the pentathlon (pehn TATH lahn), which included a foot race, jumping, wrestling, throwing the discus, and throwing the javelin.

Women could not compete in the Olympics or even watch the games because they were barred from the sacred site at Olympia. However, technically, women could win the horse and chariot races because the horse's owner was considered the winner. For example, Cynisca, daughter of a Spartan king, won the Olympic chariot race in 396 B.C. and again in 392 B.C. Like other winners, she made generous gifts to the temple of Zeus in honor of her victories. Women also participated in their own games, called the Heraca.

Despite frequent wars, the Greeks observed a sacred truce during the Olympic games. As the time for the Olympic games approached, city-states stopped fighting. The truce lasted for the duration of the festival and extended to athletes and spectators traveling to and from Olympia.

The ancient Olympic games, first held in 776 B.C., were abolished in 394 A.D. by a Roman emperor. Fifteen hundred years later, in 1896, the French baron Pierre de Coubertin (KOO ber TAN) revived the Olympic games in Athens.

plishments of women, Sappho (SAF oh) won fame for her lyric poetry. Another poet, Pindar (PIHN duhr), wrote *odes*, or poems honoring special occasions. In many of his odes, Pindar praised winning Olympic athletes.

The Visual Arts

The Greeks excelled in architecture, sculpture, and painting. The simple, elegant buildings they designed were a reflection of their

In the fourth century B.C., the sculptor Praxiteles (prak SIHT uh LEEZ) carved this marble statue of the god Hermes holding the infant Dionysus. The elegant, graceful pose of Hermes is an example of the Greek desire to portray the ideal. Even though Praxiteles was portraying two gods, he showed them in human form.

love of balance and beauty. No buildings were more important to them than their temples. Thus, when Pericles decided to rebuild Athens, he lavished attention on the Parthenon and other temples on the Acropolis.

The Parthenon, which still stands, is a rectangular building supported by stately marble columns. The carefully carved columns glitter in the sunlight and give the impression of lightness and height. Today, many public buildings use graceful stone columns modeled on Greek architecture.

Greek sculptors believed that perfect harmony and proportion existed in the natural world, and they sought to show this perfection in their sculptures. Sculptors portrayed the ideal rather than the real. For example, when the sculptor Polyclitus (PAHL ee KLĪT uhs) carved athletes, generals, and statesmen, he showed Greek idealism by portraying the human body in its most beautiful and graceful form.

Greek artisans produced fine pottery that was exported all over the Mediterranean. On vases and bowls, artists painted figures of legendary warriors, chariot races, or simple scenes from the marketplace. The elegant designs and beautiful proportions of such common items as water jugs are further evidence of the Greek love of beauty.

The arts of ancient Greece were widely admired and frequently copied. As a result, the achievements of Greece influenced artistic styles first in Rome and later in the rest of Western Europe.

At Home and in the Marketplace

Most Greeks were farmers who made a meager living from the rocky soil using ox-drawn plows and hand hoes. Greek farmers built very simple houses of sundried brick. At the center of every home was the hearth, which the Greeks believed was guarded by the goddess Hestia.

In Greek cities, dwellings were packed tightly along narrow streets. Since there was no sewage system, garbage and waste littered the streets. As a result, plagues like the one that terrorized Athens during the Peloponnesian Wars broke out from time to time.

City life revolved around the marketplace. Potters, weavers, and metalworkers practiced their trades in small shops. Merchants bargained for the wines, olive oil, and manufactured goods that they exported in exchange for grain and other raw materials.

Public discussions were held on street corners and in the gymnasium, a room or building in the marketplace in which young men trained for athletic contests. Through these public discussions, men exchanged ideas that helped shape the traditions of Greek politics and philosophy.

SECTION REVIEW

1. Identify: Zeus, Aeschylus, Sophocles, Euripides, Aristophanes.
2. Define: tragedy, comedy, lyric poem, ode.
3. Why did so many Greeks visit Apollo's shrine at Delphi?
4. What was the major concern of writers of tragedies?
5. How did Greek sculptors portray the ideal in their works?

2 Shaping New Views of the World

Read to Learn
- how Greek philosophy shaped the Greeks' view of the world
- about the ideas and influence of Greek thinkers

The Greeks were intensely curious about the world and the place of people in it. They believed in the individual's ability to reason and discover important truths. "Man is the measure of all things," announced the Greek thinker Protagoras. Their faith in human abilities led Greeks to ask probing questions about the nature of the universe.

Faith in Human Reason

In the seventh century B.C., a few bold thinkers began to be dissatisfied with the traditional explanation that the gods caused all natural events. The Greeks called these thinkers *philosophers,* or seekers of wisdom. Greek philosophers searched for order in nature. By studying the world in a systematic way, they made important discoveries.

According to tradition, the first Greek philosopher was Thales (THAY leez), who lived about 600 B.C. Thales observed the physical world to discover the basis of life. He concluded that water was the basis of life since moisture was necessary to make things grow. The earth was made of condensed water, he explained, and water in different forms also made up the air, sun, stars, and planets. Furthermore, he argued, the process by which water formed these substances followed a regular pattern. To Thales, the actions of the gods were not needed as an explanation of this process.

Although Thales' theory was incorrect, he and his followers made an important breakthrough. They claimed that the universe was governed by natural laws and that people could understand these laws through reason. By rejecting the belief that gods controlled the universe, they provided the basis for later scientific achievement.

A scientific approach to learning. Greek philosophers studied all branches of human knowledge, from physics and astronomy to music and art. Pythagoras (pih THAG er uhs), a musician, mathematician, and astron-

omer, is well-known to students of geometry because he found a relationship between the lengths of the sides of a right triangle. Pythagoras also developed theories about the movements of the sun, moon, and planets.

Curiosity along with reason and observation led to impressive advances in medicine. Greek physicians detailed the symptoms and stages of many diseases. From their observations, they concluded that illnesses have natural causes and are not the result of evil spirits, as most people believed.

Physicians trained on the island of Cos at a medical school associated with a great legendary doctor, Hippocrates (hih PAHK ruh TEEZ). According to tradition, Hippocrates urged physicians to maintain high moral standards. Today, doctors still take a version of the Hippocratic Oath, part of which follows:

> I will use that treatment which, according to my ability and judgment, I consider for the benefit of the sick ... I will give no deadly

An emphasis on direct observation and reasoning gave Greek medicine a scientific basis. Physicians learned to examine patients and recognize the symptoms of disease. They rejected charms, magic, and other superstitious practices that had been used in the past. Here, a physician treats one patient while others wait to be examined.

medicine to anyone if asked, nor will I suggest such a course. . . . Into whatever houses I enter, I will go for the benefit of the sick and I will avoid intentional wrong-doing and harm.

The Sophists. Toward the end of the Peloponnesian Wars, a new school of philosophy appeared in Athens. The Sophists, or "men of wisdom," as followers of this philosophy were called, were not interested in the nature of the physical world. Instead, their main concern was how to achieve political and social success.

The Sophists were professional teachers who trained rich, ambitious young men for public life. From the Sophists, Athenian youths learned rhetoric, the art of public speaking. The ability to argue clearly before the Assembly or a jury was highly prized.

Some Athenians considered the Sophists a dangerous influence on the young because the Sophists believed that success was more important than obedience to laws or respect for tradition. Other philosophers, including Socrates, disapproved of the Sophists because the Sophists were not interested in ethical standards.

Socrates: The Questioning Philosopher

The Greek philosopher and teacher Socrates lived in Athens from 469 B.C. to 399 B.C.. He was one of the most influential figures in history. Socrates championed the use of reason. He thought that individuals should be guided by reason alone in their search for knowledge and truth. Socrates left no writings of his teachings. He is known through the works of his famous pupil, Plato.

Socrates spent his days in the streets of Athens teaching those who would listen. He attracted many young students, who admired his intelligence and applauded his use of reason to challenge traditional ideas. Socrates was searching for a code of conduct for human behavior. The most important thing, he felt, was: "Know thyself." Through knowledge, Socrates believed, people discovered how to act correctly.

Socrates developed a conversational, question-and-answer technique that today is called the *Socratic method.* He asked his stu-

Today, Socrates is considered one of the greatest philosophers in history. Yet Socrates had little formal schooling. As a boy, he learned the trade of a sculptor in his father's workshop, but he neglected his chores to develop his ideas. Later in life, he haunted the streets of Athens, challenging Athenians to debate with him.

dents questions and insisted that they answer clearly. The Socratic method was designed to make people examine their beliefs using reason.

Socrates' search for truth using reason alarmed many Athenians. Stung by defeat in the Peloponnesian Wars, they looked for a scapegoat. They came to see Socrates as a dangerous troublemaker. The authorities accused him of failing to honor the gods and corrupting the youth of Athens. Socrates could have gone into exile, but he chose to stand trial and was condemned to death by an Athenian jury.

Socrates accepted the penalty, maintaining that a citizen should obey the laws of the state. "Above all," he told the jury, "I shall be able to continue my search into true and false knowledge; as in this world, so also in that, I shall find out who is wise, and who pretends to be wise and is not."

Plato and Aristotle: The Heirs of Socrates

Plato was 28 years old when Socrates died. Unlike Socrates, who was the son of a poor stonecutter, Plato was a wealthy aristocrat. Upset by his teacher's death, Plato left Athens for 12 years. On his return, he set up a school, the Academy, in a public garden outside the city. The Academy survived for nearly 900 years as an important center of learning in the ancient world.

At the Academy, Plato taught philosophy, science, and mathematics. Most of his students were men, although a few women were allowed to attend. Like Socrates, Plato examined issues such as the meaning of justice and the nature of truth and beauty. Plato raised more questions than he answered, and his questions are still being debated by philosophers today.

Plato's written works are in the form of dialogues, or conversations in which different speakers express their views. In *The Republic*, Plato explained his concept of the ideal state. He believed that the ruler of such a state should be a philosopher-king. There should be no wealth, luxury, or commerce in the state, and each citizen should do the job best suited to his or her abilities.

The most brilliant student at the Academy was Aristotle (AIR ihs TAHT'L). After the death of Plato, Aristotle left the Academy. Eventually, Philip II, king of Macedonia, invited Aristotle to teach his son Alexander. When Alexander inherited the Macedonian throne (see page 88), he gave Aristotle a generous gift of money. Aristotle used the money to establish the Lyceum (lī SEE uhm), a school in Athens. The Lyceum became the world's first scientific institute.

Aristotle believed that reason was the highest good. He also taught that people should aim for moderation in all things. To Aristotle, virtue, or moral behavior, was a balance between extremes. He praised the virtues of self-control and self-reliance.

Aristotle studied a wide range of subjects. His writings include works on logic, politics, philosophy, biology, botany, and the arts. In each of these fields, Aristotle's ideas have remained influential.

The Greek Historians

The Greeks developed a new approach to history. Unlike the Egyptians, who recorded only the deeds of the pharaohs, and the Hebrews, who wanted to show God's hand in history, the Greeks tried to understand why people acted as they did. To them, history was the study of human behavior.

Herodotus has been called the founder of history because he made the first attempt to gather and analyze historical evidence. In order to write *History of the Persian Wars*, Herodotus traveled extensively, questioned many people, and recorded the customs of the people and the geography of the places he visited. Although he did not always distinguish between fact and legend in his histories, he presented much useful information about the ancient world.

Thucydides, who wrote *History of the Peloponnesian Wars*, improved on Herodotus' methods. He tried to include only facts that he could prove. He also tried to remain impartial. For example, as an Athenian general, he was on the losing side of the war between Athens and Sparta. But he tried to present a balanced account of the events by recording the strengths and weaknesses of both Sparta and Athens. In the process, Thucydides wrote about the Peloponnesian Wars as the work of people, not the gods. He also set an example of unbiased reporting for future historians.

SECTION REVIEW

1. Identify: Thales, Pythagoras, Hippocratic Oath, Sophists, Socrates, Plato, Aristotle.

2. Define: philosopher, Socratic method.

3. Name four subjects that Greek philosophers studied.

4. What did Greek physicians contribute to medical knowledge?

5. (a) What rule did Socrates think people should live by? (b) According to Plato, who should rule the ideal state? (c) How did Aristotle define virtue?

6. (a) Why is Herodotus called the founder of history? (b) What did Thucydides contribute to the study of history?

3 The Spread of Greek Civilization

Read to Learn ■ how Greek civilization spread
■ what characteristics marked Hellenistic civilization

By 359 B.C., an endless series of wars had weakened the Greek city-states. In Macedonia, north of Greece, Philip II had inherited the throne. Philip II dreamed of uniting Greece and Macedonia into a grand alliance to fight the Persian Empire. Philip's son Alexander fulfilled this dream and spread Greek civilization across a vast empire.

Philip of Macedonia

Philip II became king of Macedonia in 359 B.C. He respected Greek military techniques and hired Greek generals to train his soldiers in the latest fighting methods. He also admired Greek culture and invited Aristotle to supervise the education of his son. The nobles of Macedonia were required to speak Greek in Philip's presence.

At the same time, Philip plotted against the Greek city-states. He wanted to expand his power and sought to divide the Greek city-states by playing on their distrust of one another. He won the support of many through bribery and threats.

The Greeks were divided in their opinions of Philip. Some favored this energetic leader. Others, especially the Athenian orator Demosthenes (dih MAHS thuh NEEZ), warned that Philip posed a serious threat to Greek independence. When Athens and Thebes finally united against Philip in 338 B.C., they were quickly defeated at the battle of Chaeronea (KEHR un NEE uh). Philip made himself master of Greece and began to plan an invasion of Persia. But at his daughter's wedding in 336 B.C., Philip was killed by an assassin.

Alexander the Great

Alexander was only 20 years old when he inherited his father's kingdom. But he was well prepared to rule. Philip had given him command of a cavalry force at the battle of Chaeronea and had sent him as an ambassador to Athens. Furthermore, Alexander had come to respect Greek culture and learning through the teaching of Aristotle.

In 334 B.C., Alexander was strong enough in Macedonia and Greece to take on the Persian Empire. He assembled an army of 30,000 foot soldiers and 5,000 cavalry troops. It was the best-organized and best-equipped fighting force in the world.

When Alexander landed in Asia Minor, he defeated a Persian army at the Granicus (gruh NĪ kuhs) River and liberated the Greek cities of Asia Minor. According to legend, while in Gordium Alexander heard a story about a knot, called the Gordian knot, that could be undone only by the man who would rule the world. Rather than untie it, Alexander simply drew his sword and cut the knot in two.

Just as swiftly, Alexander defeated the Persians at Issus and marched into Egypt. There, he founded the city of Alexandria, ideally located to link Greece with the eastern Mediterranean. Alexander and his armies then conquered the rest of the Persian Empire. At Susa, Alexander found two statues of Athena that had been stolen by Xerxes during the Persian Wars. Alexander sent them back to Greece and later burned the palace at Persepolis to avenge the destruction of Athens 150 years earlier.

Alexander made Babylon his capital but pushed eastward into India, where he faced the most bitter battles of his life. In India, his soldiers mutinied. They had marched for over 11,000 miles (18,000 kilometers) since they had left Macedonia, and they had fought many battles. Alexander was forced to return to Babylon, where he began organizing his empire. But within a year he caught a fever, and on June 13, 323 B.C., he died.

Between 334 B.C. and 323 B.C., Alexander conquered the largest empire the world had ever seen and spread Greek civilization as far east as the Indus River. (See the map on page 90.) But during his 13-year reign, Alexander spent most of his time at war. He

Alexander the Great, shown in this mosaic, was not only a brilliant military leader, but he was also an admirer of learning and culture. Shortly after Alexander became king, the Greek city-state of Thebes rebelled against the Macedonians. Alexander crushed the Theban rebels and leveled their city. But he ordered his soldiers to spare the home of Pindar, a poet whose writing he admired.

had barely begun to organize the newly conquered territories and had not chosen a successor when he died. As a result, his death left the empire in confusion. Alexander's generals and his family competed in a violent power struggle.

By 305 B.C., the huge empire was divided among three generals: Ptolemy (TAHL uh mee) in Egypt, Seleucus (suh LOO kuhs) in the Fertile Crescent and Asia Minor, and Antigonus (an TIHG uh nuhs) in Greece and Macedonia. Warfare plagued the three kingdoms until Rome eventually conquered all three regions.

Blend of East and West

Alexander's most lasting achievement was to spread Greek culture. Alexander's armies marched across the Persian Empire into northwestern India. Thousands of Greek officials, merchants, artisans, and artists followed and settled in these eastern lands. In the lands he conquered, Alexander established cities modeled on the Greek polis. As many as 70 cities named after Alexander were set up across the empire.

Alexander encouraged the mixing of Greek culture with the cultures of the ancient Middle East. For example, he married a Persian princess and arranged a huge ceremony in which thousands of his soldiers married Persian women. He hoped children from these marriages would help unite the empire. In addition, he worshipped Persian as well as Greek gods and adopted Persian customs and dress. Although Alexander thought of himself as Greek, he gained the support of his new subjects by adopting some of their practices.

After Alexander's death, a rich new culture known as Hellenistic civilization gradually developed in Greece and in the other lands he had conquered. Hellenistic civilization was a blend of eastern and western influences. Greek settlers in Persia, Egypt, and India were influenced by the cultures of these lands. In turn, the conquered peoples were influenced by Greek language, art, architecture, and traditions.

Alexandria, the city that Alexander founded at the mouth of the Nile, flourished as the center of Hellenistic civilization. Sailors, merchants, and scholars from Greece,

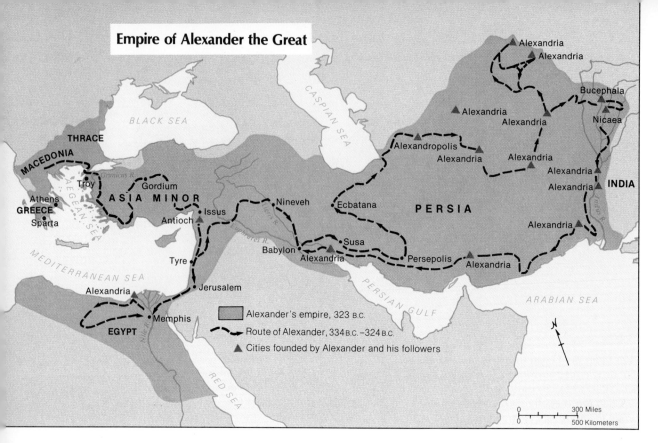

Empire of Alexander the Great

Alexandria
Alexandria
Bucephala
Nicaea
Alexandria
Alexandria
Alexandria
Alexandria
INDIA
Alexandropolis
Alexandria
Alexandria

CASPIAN SEA
BLACK SEA
THRACE
MACEDONIA
Troy
Gordium
Athens
GREECE
Sparta
ASIA MINOR
Nineveh
Ecbatana
PERSIA
AEGEAN SEA
Antioch
Issus
Susa
Babylon
Alexandria
Persepolis
Alexandria
Tyre
MEDITERRANEAN SEA
Jerusalem
Alexandria
PERSIAN GULF
ARABIAN SEA
Memphis
EGYPT
RED SEA

Alexander's empire, 323 B.C.
Route of Alexander, 334 B.C.–324 B.C.
Cities founded by Alexander and his followers

0   300 Miles
0   500 Kilometers

Map Skill *Alexander the Great's empire stretched from Greece to India. The cities he and his followers founded often served as centers of Hellenistic civilization. Many of these cities were named after Alexander. One, Bucephala, was named after Alexander's horse, Bucephalus (byoo SEHF uh luhs). Describe the relationship between the route of Alexander's armies and the extent of the empire.*

Italy, and the Middle East came to Alexandria to exchange products and ideas.

In Alexandria, Ptolemy built a museum, or temple dedicated to the Muses, the Greek goddesses of the arts and sciences. The museum contained botanical and zoological gardens, used for research, as well as art galleries, an astronomical observatory, and a paid staff of scholars. It also housed a library with more than 500,000 papyrus scrolls containing the ancient world's knowledge of science, philosophy, and literature.

Hellenistic Science

After 323 B.C., great progress was made in the sciences. Herophilus (hihr RAHF ih luhs) and other Greek physicians studied anatomy, described the human nervous system, and discovered how the blood circulated through veins and arteries. Greek physicians

living in Alexandria learned from the Egyptians how to perform surgery using anesthetics. Hellenistic medical advances were not matched in Western Europe for 1,800 years.

Greek astronomers and geographers who worked in Alexandria used ancient Egyptian and Babylonian knowledge to develop new scientific theories. Eratosthenes (EHR uh TAHS thuh NEEZ) thought that the earth was round and accurately computed its diameter. He also drew excellent maps of the ancient world. Aristarchus (AR ihs TAHR kuhs) concluded that the earth revolved around the sun, but this idea was not widely accepted. Most people believed that the earth was the center of the universe and that the sun and moon revolved around it.

Euclid (YOO klihd) advanced the study of geometry. His work *The Elements* contained a survey of mathematical learning of the ancient world. Today, nearly 2,300 years later, Euclid's work is still the basis for high school geometry courses.

Another Hellenistic scientist, Archimedes (AHR kuh MEE deez), discovered the principle of the lever. "Give me a lever long enough," Archimedes reportedly boasted, "and I will move the world." He also invented the double pulley and a catapult, a machine for hurling stones at enemy forts. But to Archimedes, such practical inventions were unimportant. He wanted to be remembered instead for his work as a mathematician.

New Currents of Thought

After the conquests of Alexander, individual Greek city-states declined in importance although Athens continued to thrive as a center of learning and culture. Two new schools of philosophy took root in Athens. These philosophies reflected the changing attitudes within the Greek world. During the Golden Age of Athens, philosophers had been concerned with the role of the citizen in society. But Hellenistic philosophers were less interested in citizenship and more interested in the individual.

The philosopher Epicurus (EHP uh KYOOR uhs) claimed that the gods took no interest in human affairs and that there was no afterlife. Therefore, he argued, the greatest good was being happy in life. He defined happiness as freedom from fear and pain.

Epicureans believed they could achieve happiness by living calm, simple, well-regulated lives. However, some Epicureans later emphasized personal enjoyment over moral conduct. As a result, "epicurean" has come to mean a person who is fond of luxury and pleasure.

Another philosopher, Zeno, founded a rival school of thought. Zeno and his followers were called Stoics.* Like Epicurus, Zeno believed that happiness was the greatest good. However, he taught that a divine lawgiver had a fixed plan for the universe, in which everything had its place. Stoics be-

---

* The name comes from the word *stoa*, or porch, since Zeno and his followers met on a porch.

lieved that happiness resulted from living in harmony with nature and accepting whatever life brought, including misfortune.

The Stoics developed several ideas that later influenced Roman and Christian thinkers. They thought all people were basically alike because they shared the power of reason. To the Stoics, the differences between Greeks and foreigners or between free people and slaves were less important than the common humanity of all individuals. The Stoics stressed self-discipline, courage and

New art styles developed during the Hellenistic period. Hellenistic sculptors stressed vigorous movement and emotion rather than the cool detachment of classical Greek works. They also brought greater realism to art. This statue of Nike, the winged goddess of victory, dates from the second century B.C. It reflects the dynamic poses preferred by Hellenistic artists.

moral conduct. Because Stoics urged people not to be upset by events, "stoic" has come to mean a person who remains calm in the face of pain or misfortune.

New currents of thought were reflected in the arts. In architecture, the simple classical style of Athenian temples gave way to grander, more elaborate buildings. In sculpture, huge heroic figures replaced the balanced, idealized portraits of generals, statesmen, and athletes. Hellenistic poets wrote more comedies than tragedies, and they dealt with lighter topics than earlier Greek poets had.

SECTION REVIEW

1. Locate: Macedonia, Granicus River, Gordium, Issus.
2. Identify: Demosthenes, Euclid, Archimedes, Epicurus, Zeno, Stoics.
3. How did Philip II of Macedonia show that he admired Greek culture?
4. How did Alexander encourage the blend of eastern and western cultures?
5. List two medical discoveries of the Hellenistic period.

Chapter 6 Review

In Perspective

Greek civilization reached its height during the fifth and fourth centuries B.C. Greek playwrights and poets produced great works of literature. Sculptors and other artists tried to reproduce the harmony and perfection they saw in nature.

Curiosity and faith in human reason affected the way the Greeks looked at the world. Philosophers studied every branch of knowledge, seeking to learn more about nature and human behavior. They rejected the belief that the gods were responsible for ev-

erything and searched for order in nature. Socrates influenced Greek thinking by emphasizing the use of reason.

The conquests of Alexander the Great brought an end to the political independence of the Greek city-states. Yet Alexander spread the Greek heritage across a huge empire. The mixing of Greek culture with eastern cultures helped create Hellenistic civilization. During the Hellenistic period, great advances took place in the sciences and mathematics. Hellenistic civilization would continue to influence the Mediterranean world for centuries.

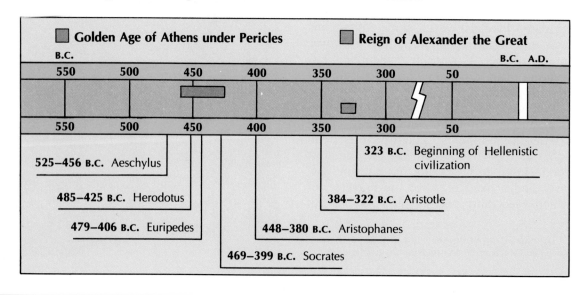

Golden Age of Athens under Pericles   Reign of Alexander the Great

B.C.   550   500   450   400   350   300   50   B.C. A.D.

550   500   450   400   350   300   50

525–456 B.C. Aeschylus

485–425 B.C. Herodotus

479–406 B.C. Euripedes

469–399 B.C. Socrates

448–380 B.C. Aristophanes

384–322 B.C. Aristotle

323 B.C. Beginning of Hellenistic civilization

Recalling Facts

Match each name at left with the correct description at right.

1. Euclid
2. Zeus
3. Epicurus
4. Sophocles
5. Plato
6. Aristophanes
7. Apollo
8. Archimedes
9. Thucydides
10. Polyclitus

a. inventor of the double pulley
b. god whose shrine was at Delphi
c. mathematician who advanced the study of geometry
d. philosopher who taught that the greatest good was being happy
e. historian who wrote *History of the Peloponnesian Wars*
f. philosopher who set up the Academy
g. sculptor who carved idealized statues of athletes and statesmen
h. comic playwright who wrote *The Frogs*
i. tragic playwright who wrote *Antigone*
j. chief Olympian god

Chapter Checkup

1. (a) How did Greek religion contribute to the invention of drama? (b) How were Greek tragedies and comedies similar? (c) How were they different?
2. How did Greek sculptors of the fifth and fourth centuries B.C. try to reflect nature?
3. Describe what each of the following contributed to knowledge about the physical world: (a) Thales; (b) Pythagoras; (c) Aristarchus.
4. (a) What method did Socrates use to try to teach people to act correctly? (b) Why did his actions alarm Athenians? (c) How did Plato and Aristotle carry on Socrates' work?
5. (a) Describe the conquests of Alexander the Great. (b) What happened to the empire after he died? Why?
6. (a) What is Hellenistic civilization? (b) Describe the scientific advances made during the Hellenistic period.

Critical Thinking

1. **Defending a Position** "Greeks were too idealistic to take any interest in practical matters." Criticize or defend this statement using specific examples to support your answer.
2. **Analyzing** (a) Describe how the Greeks emphasized the individual. (b) Why do you think the individual played an important role in Greek life?

3. **Expressing an Opinion** If Socrates were alive today, do you think his ideas would be controversial? Why or why not?

Relating Past to Present

1. (a) What purpose do you think the Hippocratic Oath served in ancient Greece? (b) Why do you think it is still used today?
2. In what occupations other than medicine do people today take an oath of office?

Developing Basic Skills

1. **Using Visual Evidence** Study the sculptures shown on page 84 and 91. Then answer the following questions: (a) What is the subject of each sculpture? (b) When was each work carved? (c) What differences in style do you see? (d) What can you learn about art in classical and Hellenistic Greece from these two sculptures?
2. **Map Reading** Study the map on page 90. Then answer the following questions: (a) Describe the boundaries of Alexander the Great's empire. (b) What ancient centers of civilization did Alexander conquer? (c) What reasons might Alexander have had for establishing so many new cities named after him?

See page 803 for suggested readings.

7 Ancient Rome: From Republic to Empire

(509 B.C.–180 A.D.)

Augustus, the first Roman emperor.

If you could have asked someone in ancient Rome how Rome began, you would probably have been told the following story of the twin brothers Romulus and Remus. About a year before the twins were born, their great-uncle had seized power from their grandfather. When the new king learned of the twins' birth, he ordered them thrown into the Tiber River, fearing that they would grow up to threaten his rule.

But the gods took pity on the infants and directed the river to place them safely on the shore. A wolf heard the babies crying and protected them. After a shepherd discovered the twins, he took them home and raised them as his own sons. When Romulus and Remus reached adulthood, they took revenge on their great-uncle and restored their grandfather to his throne. Then, on the seven hills overlooking the Tiber River, the two young men founded the city of Rome.

Years later, when Romans encountered the older, more sophisticated cultures of the eastern Mediterranean, the story of Romulus and Remus seemed pale when compared to the heroic Greek tales of the Trojan War. So the Roman poet Virgil created a new legend. In his epic poem the *Aeneid* (ih NEE uhd), he told the story of the valiant Trojan hero Aeneas, who fled from the fiery destruction of Troy, carrying his father on his back. After years of wandering and many adventures, Aeneas founded a colony in Italy, where years later Romulus and Remus were born.

Both of these legends were important to Roman culture. The story of Romulus and Remus said that strength, justice, and the favor of the gods were the best protection against danger and greed. The *Aeneid* linked Rome to the older civilizations of Greece and Asia Minor, assuring Romans that they were not mere newcomers to the Mediterranean world.

Rome was only a small town on the west coast of Italy when Athens flourished. By 323 B.C., however, when Alexander the Great had conquered his empire, Rome was emerging as a strong city-state. Between 265 B.C. and 44 B.C., Rome won control of the Mediterranean world, uniting many different peoples and regions under its rule.

1 The Roman Republic

Read to Learn   ■ how Roman culture developed
■ how people lived in ancient Rome

Around 2000 B.C., about the same time the Achaeans migrated into Greece, other Indo-Europeans invaded Italy. Among the newcomers to Italy were the Latins. The Latins grazed their herds in the lands just south of the Tiber River. By 750 B.C., the Latins had settled into a farming life and established several small villages, which gradually grew into the city of Rome.

Geographic Setting

As you can see from the map on page 96, the Italian peninsula juts out like a boot into the Mediterranean Sea. Off the toe of the boot lies the island of Sicily. The sea provided some protection for the early peoples of Italy. Later, the Romans used the sea as a highway for conquest and trade.

At the top of the boot are the Alps, which block cold winds but give only limited protection from invaders. The Po River, which is fed by melting snows from the Alps, provides water for the rich farming region of the northern plain. Another mountain range, the Apennines (AP uh NĪNZ), runs down the length of Italy. While the mountains in Greece isolated Greek city-states, the Apennines were a less serious barrier to unity in Italy.

Few people lived along the east coast of Italy, where the land was poor and there were few good harbors. Most lived in the west, where the land was fertile and the mountains were further inland. In the west, there were good harbors and long rivers that could be easily navigated by small boats.

The city of Rome enjoyed many natural advantages. It was centrally located on the fertile coastal plain halfway up Italy's west coast. From the seven hills overlooking the Tiber River, Romans could watch for enemy attacks. The Tiber provided food and transportation. Since Rome lay 15 miles (about 24 kilometers) inland, it was not exposed to raids from the sea. Romans built the port of Ostia at the mouth of the Tiber for ships too large to move up the river.

The Peoples of Italy

The Latins who founded Rome were farmers and herders. During their early history, they frequently fought with other Latins for control of the neighboring countryside. The struggle for survival helped shape a belief in duty, discipline, and patriotism. At the same time, contact with other peoples affected the development of Roman culture.

Romans adopted some ideas from the advanced civilizations of the Phoenicians and Greeks, who had established trading colonies in Sicily and Italy. For example, from the Greeks, the Romans learned to build fortified cities and to grow grapes and olives.

The Etruscans (ih TRUHS kuhnz), who had migrated into Italy from Asia Minor and settled north of the Tiber, also influenced the Romans. About 600 B.C., the Etruscans crossed the Tiber and seized Rome and the

Ancient Italy About 600 B.C.

ALPS
GAULS
APENNINES
ADRIATIC SEA
CORSICA
• Rome
LATINS
SARDINIA
MEDITERRANEAN SEA
SICILY
Carthage •
AFRICA

Greeks
Etruscans
Phoenicians

0   200 Miles
0   300 Kilometers

Map Skill *Many people influenced the development of civilization on the Italian peninsula. The Latin people who settled Rome learned much from Greek and Phoenician traders. From where did the Phoenicians come?*

surrounding lands. During the next 100 years, the Romans absorbed many ideas from their Etruscan conquerors.

The Romans adopted the Etruscan alphabet, which the Etruscans had borrowed from the Greeks. They copied Etruscan artistic styles and worshipped Etruscan gods alongside their own. They also learned Etruscan building techniques, including the

arch. In addition, the Romans learned how to drain the marshes along the Tiber, turning low-lying areas into useful farmland.

Founding the Republic

In 509 B.C., the Romans overthrew the Etruscan king and established a republic. In a *republic*, all citizens with the right to vote choose their leaders. The elected leaders represent the people and rule in their name. The Roman Republic lasted for 500 years, during which time it grew from a small city-state into a world power.

In the early Republic, Roman society was dominated by a class of wealthy landowners, or *patricians* (puh TRIHSH uhnz). The common people, including farmers, artisans, small merchants, and traders, were called *plebeians* (plih BEE uhnz). Plebeians were citizens and could own land, but they could not hold public office or marry into patrician families.

Slaves made up the lowest class in Roman society. Most slaves were prisoners of war, but some were plebeians who had been enslaved for debt. Slaves farmed patrician lands or worked as household servants. They were not citizens and had no legal rights.

The economy of the early Republic was based on agriculture. Most people were farmers who worked on small plots of land. Later, as Rome expanded, its economy grew to include manufacturing and commerce.

Early government. Patricians controlled the government of the early Republic through the Senate. The Senate, which was made up of 300 patricians who served for life, guided foreign and domestic policies. Every year, the Senate chose two *consuls*, or officials, from the patrician class to administer the laws of Rome. A popular assembly, elected by the plebeians, had to approve the choice of consuls. However, in the early Republic, the popular assembly had little power and did not challenge the Senate.

During their one-year terms, the consuls directed the government and commanded the army. The consuls had equal power, and each had the right to *veto*, or block, an action of the other. In Latin, the word "veto" means

"I forbid." After a consul completed his term in office, he became a member of the Senate.

In times of crisis, the Senate could appoint a dictator to replace the consuls. A *dictator* had absolute power but could only hold office for six months.

The Roman army. At first, only patricians served in the Roman army. But the Republic faced many enemies, including the Etruscans, neighboring Latins, and the Gauls. The Gauls had migrated to Italy from central Europe and had settled north of the Po River. When the Gauls attacked and burned Rome in 390 B.C., the Senate turned to the plebeians for help. To strengthen Roman defenses, the Senate required all citizens who owned land—plebeians and patricians—to serve in the army.

Roman soldiers trained in the use of slings, javelins, spears, and swords. Patricians and wealthy plebeians provided their own equipment and served without pay. Poorer citizens received small salaries. Roman commanders had complete authority over their troops, and they enforced strict discipline. Training, discipline, and loyalty made the Roman army effective.

The Roman army was divided into *legions* made up of about 6,000 soldiers. Each legion was further divided into smaller units that could be moved around swiftly to attack the enemy or to reinforce threatened positions. This freedom of movement gave the Roman army an advantage over the massed ranks of enemies.

Changes in Government

As you will read in the next section, Rome conducted many wars of expansion between 509 B.C. and 133 B.C. Because of its growth, Rome faced new problems of government. First, more officials were needed to supervise the expanding Republic. Second, plebeians who had fought to defend Rome demanded a greater role in government.

Roman government changed gradually to meet these needs. The Senate retained its power and prestige. However, an Assembly of Centuries and an Assembly of Tribes replaced the popular assembly. The Assembly

The Romans adopted many ideas from the Etruscans, including the art of wall painting. This wall painting once decorated a Roman house, which may have belonged to the young couple shown here. The man, who was probably a Roman official, grasps a papyrus scroll. The woman holds a stylus and wax tablets, symbols of learning. The sharpened end of a stylus was used to inscribe letters on a wax tablet. The blunt end of the stylus served as an eraser.

of Centuries was made up of the entire Roman army, which included both patricians and plebeians. This assembly passed laws and elected the consuls, formerly chosen by the Senate. It also chose other officials, including *praetors*, or judges who ruled in all legal matters, and the *censor*, who registered the population for tax and voting purposes. The censor also enforced the moral code. All government officials were patricians. They served one-year terms and then entered the Senate.

The Assembly of Tribes, which was made up of plebeians, elected ten *tribunes* to speak for their interests. At first, the tribunes had no official role in government. But when angry plebeians refused to fight for Rome, the Senate agreed to consider the tribunes' demand for a law code. It appointed a commission to record the laws of Rome.

In 451 B.C., the first written law code in Rome was carved onto 12 stone tablets that were set up in the Forum, or central marketplace. The Twelve Tables of Law maintained the strict separation between patrician and plebeian and prohibited plebeians from serving as consuls, entering the Senate, or marrying patricians. Yet by listing laws and punishments, the Twelve Tables protected all citizens from arbitrary treatment.

Over the next 200 years, the plebeians struggled successfully for more rights. The ban on marriages between patricians and plebeians and the strict laws punishing debtors were eased. Tribunes obtained veto power over any government action that threatened the rights of plebeians. The Assembly of Tribes gained the right to pass laws, at first with Senate approval and later without it. By 367 B.C., one of the two consuls was a plebeian. Eventually, plebeians won the right to hold any office. They were even allowed into the Senate.

The reforms did not ensure equality for all citizens, however. By the third century B.C., a new class of rich plebeians who had married into old patrician families dominated the government. Their wealth came from Roman wars of expansion and the resulting growth in trade and industry. They held most government positions and carefully guarded their power. Only the tribunes continued to speak for common citizens.

The Roman Family

The extended family was the basic social unit in the Roman Republic. In addition, Romans favored large families so there would be enough farmers to settle new lands and enough soldiers to fight in wars. The government rewarded parents of many children and penalized bachelors.

Under Roman law, the father headed the family and had absolute power over the entire household. Roman law gave a father the right to sell his son or daughter into slavery and to abandon an unwanted infant.

In practice, Roman fathers were generally fair-minded. They imposed strict discipline on their children but also were concerned for the family welfare. Children were taught the responsibilities of Roman citizenship at an early age. Parents stressed the virtues of hard work, courage, and loyalty.

Education. By 250 B.C., some wealthy families were importing Greek tutors to teach their children a broad range of subjects. But most fathers continued to supervise their children's education personally.

Profiles ■ Cincinnatus: A Model Patriot

Lucius Quinctius Cincinnatus (SIHN suh NAT uhs) was the most admired hero of the early Republic. Romans believed that this general embodied the Roman virtues of duty, hard work, simplicity, and unselfish public service.

In 458 B.C., enemy forces surrounded a Roman consul and his army some distance from Rome. Five Roman soldiers escaped enemy patrols to carry word to Rome of the impending disaster. The crisis led the Senate to take a drastic course of action. It chose to name a dictator with unlimited power for a period of six months.

Messengers from the Senate went to ask Cincinnatus, a patrician landowner, to become dictator. They found him plowing a field on his farm outside Rome. Cincinnatus left his plow, called for his toga, and hurried to Rome. He ordered every man of military age to report for duty.

Cincinnatus led the hastily assembled soldiers to aid the surrounded Roman army. He quickly defeated the enemy and then marched back to Rome in triumph. Sixteen days after being named dictator, Cincinnatus resigned from the powerful office and returned home to finish the plowing. Later Romans admired Cincinnatus because he chose not to keep power a minute longer than necessary.

In ancient Rome, teachers set up private schools to which Romans sent their sons and sometimes their daughters. Students like those shown here learned to write by copying well-known sayings onto wax tablets. Arithmetic was difficult with the cumbersome Roman numerals, so students learned to use an abacus, or counting board, to solve problems in mathematics.

Boys and girls from patrician or rich plebeian families attended private schools, where discipline was as strict as it was at home. Girls often received as thorough an education as boys.

Roman education emphasized history, which students recited aloud. Stories of Roman heroes gave children a sense of pride in their city. Students also learned practical skills such as reading, writing, and public speaking.

Women in Roman society. During the early Republic, Roman women had few legal rights. Although they were citizens and might be called on to testify in court, they could not vote or hold public office. Fathers usually arranged marriages for their daughters by the time girls were 14 years old.

Later, Roman women gained greater rights largely because new laws allowed them to control their own property. Women could then make wills leaving their property as they chose. Some women also owned businesses.

Roman attitudes toward women differed from Greek attitudes. Romans did not restrict women to a separate part of the house. Also, women could attend the theater and join in public festivals. Some women acquired political influence in Rome, especially if their husbands or fathers held public office. Roman women frequently shared in household decisions, and they often kept the family accounts. In addition, they supervised the children and any slaves owned by the family.

Religion

The Romans worshipped many gods in private and public ceremonies. Each household had a shrine devoted to spirits that the family believed protected the home and the fields. Everyday, family members gathered to make offerings to Vesta, goddess of the hearth. Such daily rituals taught children to respect and defend the family and its gods.

Public religious festivals and games were dedicated to individual gods and goddesses. For example, Romans worshipped Janus, the god of beginnings, at the start of each month and year. His name has survived in the English word "January." Religious festivals honoring Janus lasted several days and included street carnivals and feasts.

Romans also adopted other people's religious beliefs. Jupiter, an Etruscan god, was identified with the powerful Greek god Zeus. The Roman goddess Venus was similar to Aphrodite (AF ruh DĬT ee), the Greek goddess of love. As Rome grew stronger, its gods acquired new powers. For example, Mars, god of the fields, became god of war during the centuries of Roman conquests.

2 The Expansion of Rome

Read to Learn
- how Rome gained power in the Mediterranean
- how winning an empire affected Rome

During the early years of the Republic, Rome's well-trained army fought in many wars. Between 509 B.C. and 133 B.C., Roman legions fought first for control of Italy and then for supremacy in the Mediterranean world. Success in war transformed the small city of Rome into the rich, turbulent capital of a huge empire. It also presented Rome with the problem of how to rule its new territories and preserve order at home.

The Conquest of Italy

For 200 years after the founding of the Republic, Romans fought for control of central Italy. Gradually, they subdued other Latin cities and conquered the Samnite people to the south and the Etruscans to the north. By 290 B.C., Rome was the leading state in Italy.

When Roman expansion threatened the Greek cities of southern Italy, these cities appealed to Pyrrhus (PIHR uhs), king of Epirus, for aid. Pyrrhus raised a large army and defeated the Romans in two hard-fought battles. But his own casualties were so heavy that he reportedly complained, "Another such victory and I am lost." Today, the expression "pyrrhic victory" refers to a victory won at great cost. When Pyrrhus was unable to gain a final victory over Rome, he abandoned the Greek cities and returned home.

By 264 B.C., Rome ruled all of Italy, as you can see from the map on page 102. Roman officials had to work out ways to govern the new territories. They gave nearby Latins full citizenship, including the right to vote, thereby winning their loyalty. More distant peoples did not receive Roman citizenship, but they were allowed to control their own affairs.

New military roads such as the Appian Way connected Rome to other Italian cities. These roads permitted rapid movement of troops and also encouraged trade, which helped unify the peoples of Italy. Roman settlers also contributed to Italian unity. Roman farmers and soldiers who received land in the new territories helped spread Roman customs and the use of Latin, the Roman language. Furthermore, the conquered regions supplied soldiers to fight in the Roman legions and often carried Roman ways back home with them.

Rivalry Between Rome and Carthage

Roman expansion in Italy led to conflict with Carthage, a city-state on the coast of North Africa. As you read in Chapter 3, Phoenician traders founded Carthage about 750 B.C. Carthage had flourished, and its huge commercial empire, protected by a powerful navy, stretched across North Africa and into Spain.

When Rome conquered the Greek cities of southern Italy, it inherited the trade rivalry between those cities and Carthage. Moreover, Rome and Carthage viewed each other's power with suspicion. A struggle for control of the western Mediterranean seemed unavoidable. Between 264 B.C. and 146 B.C., Rome and Carthage fought three long, exhausting wars. These are called the Punic Wars, from the Latin word "Punicus," meaning Phoenician.

The First Punic War. In 264 B.C., a minor dispute between two cities in Sicily involved Carthage and Rome in the First Punic War. For 23 years, fighting raged across Sicily. Although Rome had excellent armies, Carthage controlled the seas. But the Romans quickly built a fleet and developed new ways of fighting at sea. For example, they used a wide plank to grasp hold of an enemy ship. Roman soldiers then boarded and seized the enemy vessel.

By 241 B.C., Rome and Carthage were exhausted. Rome had nearly won control of Sicily, and its new navy was victorious at sea. Carthage finally sued for peace, and Rome forced Carthage to pay a fine and surrender Sicily, Sardinia, and Corsica. The war made Rome an important naval power and gave the Romans their first overseas provinces. However, Carthage remained a great power.

The Second Punic War. Two generals, Hamilcar (huh MIHL kahr), who had fought Rome in the First Punic War, and his son Hannibal (HAN uh b'l) helped extend Carthaginian power during the next 20 years. Together they brought much of Spain under Carthaginian control and began to plan revenge on Rome. According to legend, Hamilcar had made his son swear on a sacred altar to remain Rome's enemy for life. After his father's death, Hannibal pushed deeper into Spain. When Rome tried to stop him, he took the offensive.

In 218 B.C., Hannibal led an army on a hazardous winter march from Spain, across the Alps, into northern Italy. Hannibal used African war elephants to carry heavy equipment across the Alps. However, in the midwinter crossing, all but one of the elephants

died. Roman legions rushed north to fight Hannibal, but Hannibal soundly defeated them. Hannibal then marched south, hoping to rally the peoples of Italy against their Roman conquerors, but most remained loyal to Rome.

The Second Punic War lasted for 15 years. During that time, Hannibal's troops roamed across Italy, destroying towns and villages. Although Roman armies constantly harrassed Hannibal, they avoided open battle. Finally, a Roman army landed in North Africa, and Hannibal was forced to leave Italy to defend Carthage.

Hannibal was decisively defeated at Zama, and he fled to Asia Minor. In 201 B.C., Carthage agreed to a peace that made Rome supreme in the western Mediterranean. Carthage was forced to pay a heavy fine and give Spain to Rome. Carthage also promised not to wage any war without Roman consent.

"Carthage must be destroyed." In 150 B.C., Carthage fought its neighbor, Numidia, without Roman consent. The violation of the peace terms enraged the Romans. The Senate rang with the words of Cato, a veteran of

Roman armies conquered an empire stretching from the Atlantic Ocean to the Euphrates River in Syria. The scenes that decorated many public buildings and monuments recalled Roman victories. These Roman legionnaires are shown in bas-relief, sculpture in which figures project slightly from the background.

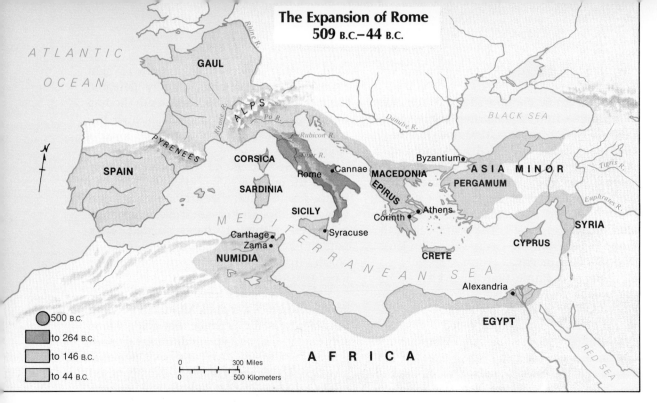

The Expansion of Rome
509 B.C.–44 B.C.

ATLANTIC OCEAN

GAUL

Rhine R.

ALPS

Po R.

Rhone R.

PYRENEES

SPAIN

CORSICA

SARDINIA

Rubicon R.

Tiber R.

Rome • Cannae

SICILY

• Syracuse

Carthage •
Zama •

NUMIDIA

MACEDONIA

EPIRUS

Corinth •

• Athens

CRETE

Danube R.

BLACK SEA

Byzantium •

ASIA MINOR

PERGAMUM

Tigris R.

Euphrates R.

SYRIA

CYPRUS

Alexandria •

EGYPT

MEDITERRANEAN SEA

AFRICA

RED SEA

N

500 B.C.
to 264 B.C.
to 146 B.C.
to 44 B.C.

0   300 Miles
0   500 Kilometers

Map Skill *Rome often expanded its empire through warfare. The Punic Wars, which ended in 146 B.C., brought large amounts of territory into the empire. Rome also acquired territory when the king of Pergamum died and left his empire in Asia Minor to Rome. During which period did Rome gain the most territory in Africa?*

the Second Punic War, "Carthage must be destroyed!"

The Third Punic War lasted only three years, from 149 B.C. to 146 B.C. A Roman army invaded North Africa, attacked Carthage, and burned the ancient city. The surviving population of Carthage was massacred or sold into slavery, and the territory around Carthage became the Roman province of Africa.

Winning an Empire

During the Punic Wars, Roman armies also won territory elsewhere. As you can see from the map above, Rome acquired parts of Spain, southern Gaul, Macedonia, and Greece. At first, Rome had allowed the city-states of Greece some independence. But when the Greeks pursued policies contrary to Roman interests, Rome intervened. In 146 B.C., Roman armies destroyed Corinth in the same brutal manner as they had Carthage.

Wars in the eastern Mediterranean brought Rome into conflict with many states

that had been part of Alexander the Great's empire. By 133 B.C., Rome controlled many of these states. Over the next 100 years, Roman conquests created a vast empire of diverse peoples.

Rome organized its foreign lands into provinces. The Senate chose former consuls or other officials to serve as provincial governors. Each Roman governor supervised tax collection, organized the defense of the province, and settled disputes between provincials and Romans. Rome did not attempt to change the customs, religion, or local governments of its foreign subjects. This tolerant policy made Roman domination more acceptable to the conquered peoples.

Yet Roman rule was a mixed blessing. Some governors built roads, developed the economy, and founded new towns. However, many Romans who served well as consuls or praetors at home abused their power in the provinces. Governors received no pay because the job was considered an honor, but many grew rich accepting bribes or keeping a portion of the taxes they collected.

Changing Economic and Social Conditions

Winning an empire brought Romans many gains. They were introduced to the advanced learning of Hellenistic civilization. Also, trade and commerce increased as wealthy Romans demanded expensive luxuries from the conquered territories. But the wars of expansion created problems for Romans at home. Three "prizes" of war had a profound effect on economic and social conditions in the capital: grain, treasure, and slaves.

Huge amounts of grain poured into Rome as *tribute*, or forced payment, from conquered areas. This influx created a surplus of grain, which lowered the price of grain. As prices dropped, many small farmers in Italy had to sell their land to pay their debts.

At the same time, a new class of Romans grew rich from captured treasure and trade in luxury goods. This new class bought up land from small farmers and created vast estates caled *latifundia* (LAT uh FUHN dee uh). Large numbers of slaves brought back as prisoners of war provided cheap labor for the latifundia. Small farmers could not compete and were forced off their land.

Landless farmers drifted to Rome, where they joined thousands of unemployed soldiers also attracted to the capital. In Rome, the poor became increasingly bitter about the luxuries enjoyed by the rich. As the numbers of the poor grew, they became a huge, restless mob easily swayed to violence by bribes and promises. The economic and social problems created by the wars of expansion were to plague Rome for years.

3 Decline of the Republic

Read to Learn ▪ why the Roman government needed reform
▪ about the rule of Julius Caesar

Between 133 B.C. and 44 B.C., bitter disputes divided Rome. The Senate had emerged from the wars of expansion as the most powerful governing body in Rome. But wealthy senators were more interested in preserving their privileges than in solving the problems of the empire. Meanwhile, popular leaders demanded reforms to help the landless poor who had crowded into Rome.

Early Attempts at Reform

In 133 B.C., Tiberius Gracchus (GRAK uhs), the son of a distinguished Roman family, was elected tribune. As spokesman for the plebeians, Tiberius campaigned for land reform:

The men who fight their country's battles enjoy nothing but the air and sunlight. . . . They fight and die to protect the wealth and luxury of others. They are called masters of the world, but they have not a foot of ground to call their own.

Tiberius called for limiting the size of large estates and redistributing land to unemployed farmers in Rome. Such measures, he argued, would strengthen the Republic because as landowners farmers could be recruited to fight in the army. But the Senate, which feared Tiberius and his supporters, strongly opposed the land reform program. To prevent his reelection as tribune, a mob of wealthy nobles murdered Tiberius and 300 of his followers.

Ten years later, in 123 B.C. Gaius Gracchus, brother of the slain Tiberius, was elected tribune. Gaius pressed for reforms that would resettle landless farmers in southern Italy and North Africa. In addition, he urged the Assembly of Tribes to make grain available at low cost to the poor and to extend Roman citizenship to all the peoples of Italy. Again the Senate, fearful of Gaius' immense popularity, responded with violence. Gaius and 3,000 of his supporters were killed.

Eventually, the Senate enacted minor land reforms and kept grain prices low. But it did nothing to prevent growing numbers of unemployed soldiers and landless farmers from swelling the mobs in Rome.

Rise of the Generals

For the next 100 years, violent upheavals shook Rome. The Senate was deeply divided between the majority of senators, who opposed reforms, and a few senators who championed plebeian demands. Abroad, serious slave revolts erupted, and Rome's allies in Italy and elsewhere rebelled. The Senate relied on Roman legions to suppress the rebellions and protect the empire while it dealt with crises at home. But the Roman army itself had changed, and Roman generals began to take a hand in politics.

In the early Republic, you will recall, only landowning citizens served in Roman legions. But in 110 B.C., Gaius Marius (MEHR ee uhs), a popular general, began recruiting soldiers from among Rome's landless poor. With promises of loot to supplement a soldier's low pay, he attracted many volunteers. He turned these volunteers into a professional army, loyal to his personal command rather than to Rome. Marius' legions fought successfully in North Africa and Gaul and helped reelect him as consul six times. Other generals, such as Lucius Cornelius Sulla, also used legions loyal to them to advance their political careers.

In 88 B.C., a bloody civil war erupted in Rome between supporters of Marius and Sulla. Thousands died. Sulla triumphed and was made dictator in 82 B.C. He then abolished the law limiting a dictator's length of rule to six months. Although the Senate retained its prestige, Sulla held the real power. From this point until the end of the Republic, Rome was ruled by a series of generals who won victories abroad and then returned to Rome to reap political rewards. Another general who hoped to follow this pattern was Gnaeus Pompey (NĪ uhs   PAHM pee).

The First Triumvirate

Between 67 B.C. and 62 B.C., Pompey and his legions cleared the Mediterranean of pirates and won new provinces in Asia Minor, Syria, and Palestine. Following his successful campaign, Pompey promised to give his soldiers land for their efforts. Then he discharged them.

Pompey returned to Rome expecting the Senate to approve his conquests. But the Senate was not interested in the eastern provinces, and it refused to approve land grants to Pompey's soldiers. Without an army to support him, Pompey had to accept the Senate's decisions while he sought allies. He found one in the talented young general Julius Caesar.

Caesar had fought successfully in Spain and won the personal loyalty of his legions. An excellent speaker, he had attracted a large following in Rome. Like Pompey, Caesar resented the Senate. In 61 B.C., he had hoped to be elected consul, but the Senate, fearful of Caesar's growing influence, blocked his bid for power.

In 60 B.C., Caesar and Pompey formed an alliance with Marcus Lucius Crassus (KRAS uhs), a wealthy general. They agreed to pool resources and rule Rome together. This alliance is known as the First Triumvirate (trī UHM ver iht), or three-man commission. As a result of their efforts, Caesar was elected consul in 59 B.C. He also became governor of Illyria (ih LIHR ee uh) in northern Greece and Gaul in southern France. Pompey took control of Italy, and Crassus was appointed governor of the eastern provinces.

The First Triumvirate did not last long. Crassus and Pompey disliked each other, and they both feared Caesar. Between 58 B.C. and 49 B.C., Caesar conquered more territory in Gaul. He also led two expeditions to Britain. In 53 B.C., Crassus died fighting in the east. Fearing Caesar's power, Pompey allied himself with the Senate. In 49 B.C., the Senate ordered Caesar to disband his armies and return to Rome. Caesar refused.

Caesar took his troops across the Rubicon River, the boundary between Gaul and Italy. In defying the Senate, Caesar had taken an irreversible step toward seizing power in Rome. Today, the expression "crossing the Rubicon" means taking a final, decisive step. Caesar led his troops against those of Pompey, and by 48 B.C. he had crushed Pompey's forces.

The Reforms of Julius Caesar

Between 49 B.C. and 44 B.C., Caesar was largely occupied with regaining control over the Roman Empire. He led successful campaigns in the Middle East, North Africa, and Spain. On his triumphant return to Rome, Caesar pardoned many of the senators who had supported Pompey. In 44 B.C., he was appointed dictator for life.

Caesar introduced reforms designed to strengthen Rome and ensure his own power. He redistributed land to the poor and allowed settlers who moved to the provinces to keep the privileges of Roman citizenship. Rome's Italian allies had already been granted citizenship in 89 B.C. But Caesar extended citizenship to people in provinces outside Italy. This action helped unite the empire by giving people in the provinces a stake in Rome.

Caesar's program included public building projects to reduce unemployment and increased pay for soldiers. He improved administration in the provinces in an effort to end corruption. He also introduced a more accurate calendar based on Hellenistic astronomy. The Julian calendar, as it was called, was used in Europe until 1582 A.D.

Although the Senate and Assembly of Tribes continued to exist, Caesar had absolute power. A few supporters urged Caesar to become king. He refused the title, but he wore purple robes, the symbol of royalty in the eastern provinces.

Opposition to Caesar grew in the Senate. Some senators denounced him as a tyrant

The Roman sculptor who carved this portrait of Julius Caesar conveyed a sense of Caesar's strength and ruthlessness. Caesar had his image stamped on Roman coins and had portraits of himself sent throughout the empire. Why do you think Caesar wanted his portrait displayed so widely?

who was destroying the Republic. Others feared his power or were jealous of his popularity. On March 15, 44 B.C., members of a conspiracy led by Gaius Cassius and Marcus Brutus stabbed Caesar to death as he entered the Senate. The conspirators claimed they wanted to restore the Republic, but in the civil war that followed, the Republic suffered a fatal blow.

The Second Triumvirate

Shortly before his death, Caesar adopted his 18-year-old grandnephew Octavian (ahk TAY vee uhn) as his son and heir. After Caesar's assassination, Octavian formed an alliance with two of Caesar's chief commanders, Mark Antony and Marcus Lepidus, to rule Rome. This alliance is called the Second Triumvirate.

The Second Triumvirate dissolved when a power struggle took place between Antony and Octavian. Antony formed an alliance with Cleopatra, queen of Egypt. (See page

24). Fearful that Antony and Cleopatra planned to seize power, Octavian declared war. At the battle of Actium in 31 B.C., he defeated them. Antony and Cleopatra fled back to Egypt. They committed suicide when they learned that Octavian and his armies had landed at Alexandria. The next year, Egypt became part of the Roman Empire.

On his return to Rome, Octavian claimed he would restore the Republic. He gave the Senate control over Italy and half the empire. He ruled the remaining provinces himself. In practice, however, Octavian had absolute authority. In 27 B.C., he offered to resign, but the Senate realized that peace depended on his leadership and his legions.

They awarded Octavian the title Augustus, or "Exalted One," a name normally reserved for the gods. After 100 years of civil war, peace was finally restored under Augustus.

SECTION REVIEW

1. Identify: Tiberius Gracchus, Marius, Sulla, Julian calendar, Octavian, Antony.
2. Why did Pompey, Caesar, and Crassus form the First Triumvirate?
3. List three ways in which Caesar tried to strengthen Rome and ensure his own power.
4. Why did the Senate award Octavian the title Augustus?

4 The Roman Empire

Read to Learn
- how Augustus brought peace to Rome
- how people lived under the Pax Romana

"May I be privileged to build firm and lasting foundations for the government of Rome," Augustus stated in 27 B.C. "May I also achieve the reward to which I aspire: that of being known as the author of the best possible government, and of carrying with me, when I die, the hope that these foundations will abide secure." Augustus achieved his goals. Under him and his successors, Rome recovered from the destructive civil wars of the preceding century and entered a period known as the Pax Romana (pahks roh MAH nah), or Roman peace, which lasted from 27 B.C. to 180 A.D.

The Age of Augustus

Under Augustus, Rome ceased to be a republic and became an empire. The Senate gave Augustus the title *imperator* (IHM puh RAHT uhr), or commander-in-chief of the Roman armies. The English word "emperor" is derived from this Latin title. Augustus retained the forms of republican government, such as the Senate, but he ruled as a monarch.

Between 27 B.C. and 14 A.D., Augustus sponsored many reforms to strengthen the empire. He reorganized the army into a highly disciplined, professional body loyal to the emperor. He encouraged former soldiers to settle in the provinces, where they could bolster local defense. He continued Caesar's policy of granting Roman citizenship to people in the provinces and extended citizenship to army veterans. Such measures ensured the loyalty of these people to Rome and spread Roman ideas.

The reforms helped restore confidence in Rome. To reduce corruption and improve local administration, Augustus created an efficient civil service. High-level jobs were open to men of talent, regardless of their social class. Also, civil servants were given salaries for their service. The emperor ordered a complete census, or population survey, so that taxes could be set fairly.

The Successors of Augustus

The first four emperors who succeeded Augustus were members of his family. Tiberius and Claudius were dedicated to peace and order and continued to make reforms. However, Caligula and Nero were notorious for their insane behavior.

In 64 A.D., a great fire largely destroyed the city of Rome. An unconfirmed rumor circulated that Nero had started it. Nero blamed Christians for the fire and killed hundreds of them. Nero's rule sank into a vicious reign of terror, and Roman soldiers in Gaul and Spain revolted. In 68 A.D., Nero committed suicide. Nero's death set off the first of many struggles over who would become emperor. The Roman Empire had no established procedure for succession. As a result, when an emperor died without naming an heir, civil wars often erupted, with ambitious generals scrambling for power.

In the second century A.D., Rome benefited from the peaceful succession of several outstanding emperors. Under Trajan, a Spaniard, the empire reached its greatest size. (See the map on page 108.) Trajan ensured a peaceful succession by adopting Hadrian as his heir.

Hadrian was an able and tireless administrator. He issued laws protecting women, children, and slaves from mistreatment. He also reorganized the army so that soldiers were recruited in each province to defend their homelands. He constructed defensive walls across northern Britain. Long stretches of Hadrian's Wall still stand.

The emperor Marcus Aurelius (aw REE lee uhs) was a well-educated man who studied the Greek Stoic philosophers. (See page 91.) He undertook the wearying, complicated task of ruling the empire with a strong sense of duty. In the *Meditations*, the emperor set out his philosophy:

> Keep yourself ... simple, good, pure, grave, unaffected, the friend of justice, religious, kind, affectionate, strong for your proper work. Wrestle to continue to be the man Philosophy wished to make you. Reverence the gods, save men.

Although Marcus Aurelius preferred his books and studies to war, he spent much of his reign from 161 A.D. to 180 A.D. fighting on the frontiers of the Roman Empire. German tribes, which you will read more about in Chapter 8, attacked along the Danube River. To restore peace, the emperor allowed many Germans to settle inside the frontiers. Before his death, Marcus Aurelius appointed his son Commodus (KAHM uh duhs), a vain, violent

man, as heir. Although no one realized it at the time, Rome entered a period of decline after 180 A.D.

Prosperity During the Pax Romana

Between 27 B.C. and 180 A.D., an efficient, stable government ensured peace and allowed the Roman Empire to grow in wealth and power. Most Romans believed the Roman Empire was the entire civilized world. They did not know much about the Persian Empire beyond the Euphrates River and the more distant civilizations of India and China. Most Romans also believed the empire was eternal, that it would exist forever. They saw the city of Rome as the symbol of Roman eternity.

Rome: The Eternal City. During the Pax Romana, Rome became an international city. Its population grew to nearly one million as people from the provinces flocked to the capital in search of education, advancement, and entertainment. People from the eastern Mediterranean brought with them the achievements of Hellenistic civilization as well as the ideas of older cultures.

Roman emperors undertook expensive projects to beautify the city. "I found Rome built of sundried brick; I leave her clothed in marble," boasted Augustus. Indeed, the face of Rome had changed. Its culture was far richer and more sophisticated than it was during the Republic.

Thanks to trade, most people enjoyed a varied diet, with meat and fish in addition to the traditional Roman menu of porridge and vegetables. A few wealthy people feasted on imported delicacies such as peacocks and ostriches.

Yet Rome was also a city of marked contrasts. On the seven hills and along the Tiber, the rich built spacious townhouses with lavish gardens and exotic fish ponds. But the poor crowded into seven-story tenements that kept narrow back streets in continual gloom.

Trade and commerce. During the Pax Romana, trade and commerce flourished across the empire. The Roman navy protected merchants and travelers on the seas, and Roman legions protected them on land.

As trade expanded, cities of the empire prospered. Coined money, issued regularly by Roman emperors, further aided trade and commerce.

In the second century A.D., a Greek traveler marveled at the "endless flow of goods" that poured into Rome. "Anyone who wants to behold all these products must either journey through the whole world to see them or else come to this city . . . Whatever cannot be seen here belongs to the category of nonexistent things." (See the map below.) Cargoes of grain from Sicily and Egypt, copper from Cyprus, and tin from Britain jammed the docks of Ostia at the mouth of the Tiber.

Social Conditions

Not everyone prospered as a result of increased trade and commerce. Sharp class divisions largely based on wealth existed everywhere in the empire. In the city of Rome, the aristocracy had declined in influence since the time of the Republic, but a small, powerful business class had emerged. Emperors appointed these wealthy citizens to high offices, confident of their support for a strong, central government to keep order. Poorer citizens worked in shops and markets or built monuments. Thousands of unemployed depended on the emperor to provide bread. If grain ran short, riots broke out.

Social conditions in provincial cities mirrored those in Rome. Officials from Rome ruled with the help of local leaders. Merchants and artisans formed an active middle class. The poor were not as numerous as in Rome, but they depended on the government to provide food, too. Outside the cities, most people were small farmers or tenants who worked on huge estates owned by rich landlords.

As you read earlier, cheap slave labor flooded Rome during the wars of expansion. Legally, slaves were considered property, not people. In practice, however, treatment of slaves varied. Romans prized household slaves, especially highly skilled or well-educated Greeks. Augustus, for example, ap-

Map Skill *Products flowed into Rome from far and wide, as you can see on this map. In turn, straight, paved roads radiating from Rome carried Roman goods and culture throughout the empire. What products came to Rome from Arabia?*

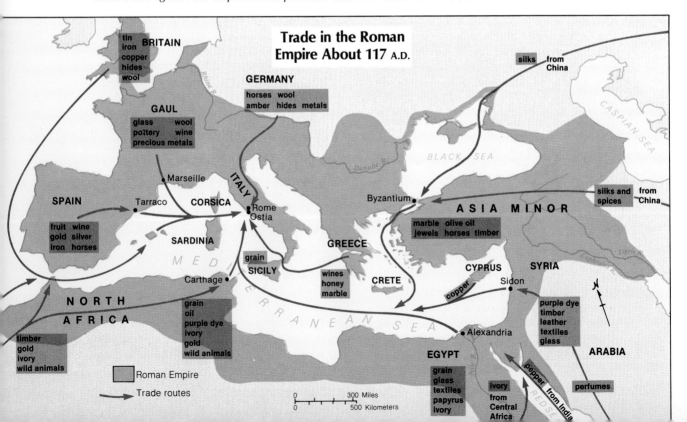

Trade in the Roman Empire About 117 A.D.

BRITAIN: tin, iron, copper, hides, wool

GERMANY: horses, wool, amber, hides, metals

GAUL: glass, wool, pottery, wine, precious metals

SPAIN: fruit, wine, gold, silver, iron, horses

ASIA MINOR: marble, olive oil, jewels, horses, timber

silks from China

silks and spices from China

SICILY: grain

CRETE: wines, honey, marble

CYPRUS: copper

SYRIA: purple dye, timber, leather, textiles, glass

NORTH AFRICA: timber, gold, ivory, wild animals; grain, oil, purple dye, ivory, gold, wild animals

EGYPT: grain, glass, textiles, papyrus, ivory

ivory from Central Africa

ARABIA: perfumes

pepper from India

Roman Empire
Trade routes

300 Miles
500 Kilometers

Shortly before dawn, crowds of men, women, and children streamed through the streets of Rome toward the Circus Maximus, the vast outdoor arena where chariot races took place. Admission to the races was free, but to get a good seat, Romans set out early. As the crowds surged toward the Circus, bets were shouted back and forth. Sometimes Romans bet on a well-known charioteer. More often, they chose a color because charioteers raced under the colors of four teams: the blues, greens, reds, or whites.

To race, charioteers stood on frail-looking, two-wheeled chariots pulled by teams of two or four horses. The reins were lashed around their waists. They held a whip in one hand and a knife in the other to slash the reins if they overturned. Charioteers were usually slaves trained by wealthy owners. Only the most skillful drivers survived the hazardous course. The greatest danger in chariot racing was the tight turn at either end of the track. Slaves and race officials stood near these spots to drag fallen charioteers and horses out of the way before they were trampled to death. Despite the danger, a few successful charioteers won as many as 3,000 races and earned fortunes for themselves and their owners.

The Circus Maximus in Rome was the largest and oldest arena in the city. It could hold up to 250,000 people. But it was not the only arena in Rome. In the Colosseum, for example, Romans could watch battles between trained fighters, called gladiators, as well as contests between wild animals and lightly armed gladiators, like the one shown here. There were also arenas in the provinces.

Chariot races and other spectacles amused the idle city crowds who might otherwise be bored and troublesome. On one occasion, the emperor had a Roman naval victory reenacted. He built an artificial lake and two fleets. He then sent costumed slaves to fight and die as enemies of Rome. Thousands of people died daily in such events. The poet Juvenal lamented that Romans only cared about free "bread and games in the circus."

pointed freed slaves to the civil service. Some slaves owned property, and a few amassed large fortunes. But most slaves suffered inhumane treatment. They worked until they were too old or weak to be profitable. Then they were abandoned.

The supply of new slaves dwindled as Rome made fewer conquests, but slavery continued to exist. The use of slaves on latifundia undermined the small farmer during the Pax Romana as it had during the Republic. The practice of slavery also destroyed many small businesses because rich people employed slaves rather than free artisans to make clothing and furniture. Furthermore, some people came to consider hard work as fit only for slaves.

Troubling Signs

The overall prosperity of the Roman Empire during the Pax Romana hid signs of trouble. Governing the empire required large amounts of money. Maintaining soldiers along the frontiers was especially expensive. When the wars of conquest ended, the government could no longer rely on loot to meet expenses, so it increased taxes. Emperors tried to lower expenses by reducing the size of the army. This reduction gradually weakened Roman defenses.

The Roman economy suffered from an unfavorable balance of trade—that is, Romans imported more goods than they exported. Money, especially gold, flowed out of

Rome to pay for imported luxuries. To increase the supply of money at home, emperors ordered new coins to be made. In the new coins, lead was added to gold. The addition of lead *devalued* the coins, or lowered their value, because their value was based on their gold content.

Since the devalued coins were worth less than older coins, merchants demanded more new coins for the same product—that is, they raised prices. Higher prices, in turn, meant that more money was needed. An increase in the money supply followed by an increase in prices is called *inflation*. Inflation became a problem during the Pax Romana, and it was to grow worse in later years, as you will read in Chapter 8. Such problems seemed to bother few Romans during the Pax Romana, as everyone scrambled for a share of the wealth.

SECTION REVIEW

1. Identify: Pax Romana, Hadrian, Marcus Aurelius.
2. Define: imperator, devalue, inflation.
3. List three reforms introduced by Augustus.
4. What conditions helped trade and commerce flourish during the Pax Romana?
5. How did Roman treatment of slaves vary?
6. Describe one economic problem the Roman Empire faced during the Pax Romana.

Chapter 7 Review

In Perspective

When the Roman Republic was founded in 509 B.C., Rome was only a small city-state. Patricians controlled the government of the early Republic. Gradually, plebeians gained more influence, and Rome developed new institutions of government.

Between 509 B.C. and 264 B.C., Rome conquered Italy. Three long, costly wars with Carthage made Rome supreme in the western Mediterranean. As they expanded, the Romans developed new ways of ruling the conquered territories and binding them together.

The wars of expansion brought economic, social, and political changes to Rome. An influx of cheap grain from newly won territories caused many small farmers to lose their land, while other Romans grew rich. Attempts at reform failed, and years of civil war between rival generals plagued Rome.

In 49 B.C., Julius Caesar seized control of Rome. He began to restore order in Rome but was killed in 44 B.C. In 27 B.C., Augustus became the first emperor. Augustus finally brought peace to Rome. During the Pax Romana, the Roman Empire prospered.

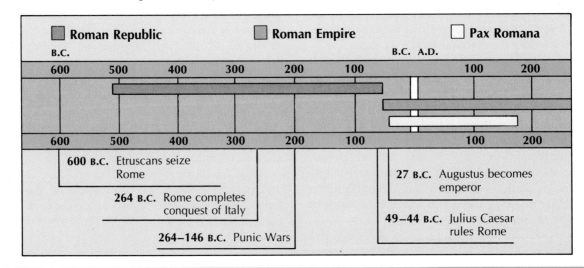

Roman Republic	Roman Empire	Pax Romana

B.C. | | | | | | B.C. A.D. | |
600 | 500 | 400 | 300 | 200 | 100 | 100 | 200

600 | 500 | 400 | 300 | 200 | 100 | 100 | 200

600 B.C. Etruscans seize Rome

264 B.C. Rome completes conquest of Italy

264–146 B.C. Punic Wars

27 B.C. Augustus becomes emperor

49–44 B.C. Julius Caesar rules Rome

Recalling Facts

Decide if the following statements are true or false. If a statement is false, rewrite the statement to make it true.

1. In the early Republic, patricians and plebeians were equal.
2. The Twelve Tables of Law was the first written law code in Rome.
3. The Punic Wars helped establish Rome as a great Mediterranean power.
4. Tiberius and Gaius Gracchus wanted to preserve the privileges of rich senators.
5. Julius Caesar was popular with the Roman Senate.
6. The Roman Empire began under Nero.

Chapter Checkup

1. Describe each of the following in the early Republic: (a) army; (b) family; (c) religion.
2. (a) Who had political power in Rome during the early Republic? (b) Why were changes in government necessary during the wars of expansion? (c) How did government change?
3. (a) How did Rome gain control of Italy? (b) What did Rome gain from each of the three Punic wars?
4. (a) How did conquering an empire affect the Roman economy? (b) What economic reforms did Tiberius and Gaius Gracchus propose? (c) Who opposed their reforms?
5. (a) How did Julius Caesar come to power in Rome? (b) What reforms did he introduce?
6. Describe how Augustus' actions affected each of the following: (a) army; (b) government.
7. (a) Why was the Pax Romana a time of prosperity? (b) What signs of trouble existed even during the Pax Romana?

Critical Thinking

1. **Comparing** (a) Compare the lives of women in Rome with the lives of women in Athens. (b) What differences existed in the legal rights of Greek and Roman women?
2. **Synthesizing** (a) Do you think that war between Rome and Carthage was inevitable?

Why or why not? (b) Why do you think Rome won all three Punic Wars?
3. **Drawing Conclusions** (a) What Roman policies contributed to the unity of the Roman Empire? Explain. (b) Do you think extending Roman citizenship to conquered peoples was a good idea? Why or why not?
4. **Understanding Economic Ideas** (a) How did Roman emperors increase the supply of money? (b) What effect did this increase have on the Roman economy? (c) What measures do you think the emperors could have taken to prevent inflation?

Relating Past to Present

1. (a) How is the government of the United States similar to that of the early Roman Republic? (b) How is it different?

Developing Basic Skills

1. **Map Reading** Study the map on page 102. Then answer the following questions: (a) What information is shown on the map? (b) During what period did Rome conquer Italy? (c) Describe the areas Rome conquered between 264 B.C. and 146 B.C. (d) During what period was Gaul conquered by Rome? (e) During what period did Rome acquire the most territory?
2. **Map Reading** Use the map reading steps you learned in Chapter 2 to study the map on page 108. Then answer the following questions: (a) What economic information is given on the map? (b) What political information is given? (c) What trade goods came to Rome from Asia Minor? (d) From which areas did Rome acquire horses? Textiles? Grain? Wool? Gold?
3. **Using Time Lines** Roman history covers both B.C. and A.D. dates. Study the time line on page 110. Then answer the following questions: (a) What is the date of the first event shown on the time line? (b) What is the date of the last event shown? (c) How many years does the time line cover? (d) Was Caesar assassinated before or after Augustus ruled?

See page 803 for suggested readings.

8 The Roman Heritage

(509 B.C.–476 A.D.)

The Apostle Andrew in a mosaic from Ravenna, Italy.

Chapter Outline

1 Greco-Roman Civilization

2 Rise of Christianity

3 Breakdown of Unity

4 Collapse of the Empire

For six years, the general Constantine had fought many rivals for control of the western part of the Roman Empire. In 312 A.D., Constantine was master of most of Italy. But he still had to capture the city of Rome, which was the stronghold of another general. As Constantine marched on Rome, he knew his forces were badly outnumbered.

Years later, Eusebius (u SEE bee uhs), a Christian bishop and friend of Constantine, described the day before the crucial battle. "About noon, when the day was already beginning to decline, Constantine saw with his own eyes . . . . a cross of light in the heavens, above the sun, bearing the inscription, 'Conquer by this.' At this sight, he was struck with amazement, and his whole army also . . . witnessed this miracle.

"And while he continued to ponder . . . its meaning, night suddenly came on; then in his sleep the Christ . . . appeared to him with the same sign . . . and commanded him to make a likeness of the sign that he had seen in the heavens and to use it as a safeguard against his enemies."

At dawn, Constantine prepared for the upcoming battle. He called in artisans and described the sign in his dream. According to Eusebius, they shaped "a long spear, overlaid with gold" into a cross. Above the cross was a "wreath of gold and precious stones," which encircled two Greek letters, the first two letters of Christ's name. Constantine ordered his soldiers to inscribe the same two letters on their shields and had the jeweled cross carried into battle.

Constantine triumphed in the battle for Rome and became the Roman emperor. A year later, in 313 A.D., he proclaimed freedom of worship for everyone in the Roman Empire, including Christians. Before his death in 337 A.D., Constantine was baptized a Christian.

The conversion of Constantine to Christianity changed the course of history. For centuries, Christians had struggled to survive in the face of severe persecution. By 313 A.D., Christianity had won many converts, but Christians were still a minority in the Roman Empire. By embracing Christianity, Constantine not only ended the persecution but also opened the way for Christianity to become the official religion of the empire.

Christianity was only part of the heritage Rome transmitted to the peoples of its empire. Through Rome, Western Europe was introduced to the advanced learning of the ancient Mediterranean world, including Greek art, science, and philosophy. In addition, Rome made its own contributions, especially in government, law, and engineering. Yet even while Roman civilization flourished, internal and external forces were weakening the ties that bound the empire together.

1 Greco-Roman Civilization

Read to Learn
■ how Greek culture influenced Rome
■ about Roman achievements in science, technology, and law

"Greece has conquered her rude conqueror," observed the Roman poet Horace early in the Pax Romana. Everywhere Horace looked, he saw evidence of Greek influence. Romans studied Greek art and architecture as well as Greek theories of government. Romans who traveled to Athens and to Alexandria in Egypt absorbed the ideas of Hellenistic civilization.

Romans preserved much of Greek culture, but they also retained their own traditions. The result was a blend of Greek and Roman traditions. Through Roman conquest, Greco-Roman civilization was carried to every corner of the empire.

Art and Architecture

When the Romans conquered Greece, they shipped home thousands of Greek statues. Roman sculptors did a brisk business copying Greek works, and talented Greek artists found rich patrons in Rome. In time, however, Roman sculptors developed their own style. Greek sculptors, you will recall, idealized the human form, using athletes as models of perfection. Romans created more realistic portraits.

Roman artists produced beautiful paintings to decorate walls of homes. Although few Roman paintings have survived, landscapes and scenes based on the *Iliad* or *Odyssey* were preserved in Pompeii (pahm PAY), a city buried by a volcano in 79 A.D. Romans also designed magnificient mosaics, pictures formed of chips of colored stone.

While Romans borrowed many ideas in architecture, they also made important advances. From the Etruscans and Greeks, they learned to use columns and arches. They improved on the arch by inventing the dome, a roof formed by rounded arches. The Romans also introduced new building materials such as concrete. New building techniques allowed architects to design massive structures. For example, the Colosseum had three stories of arches and columns.

Roman architecture was more ornate than the simple, elegant temples of classical Greece. Emperors erected solid, richly decorated monuments, such as huge public stadiums, to symbolize Roman strength.

113

Technology and Science

The Romans applied their technical knowledge to many practical concerns. They built strong bridges, supported by arches, to span turbulent rivers. Romans designed roads to last forever. They made them of heavy blocks set in layers of crushed stones and pebbles. Roman roads were still in use as recently as 100 years ago, and the stone foundations can be seen in parts of Europe today.

Romans constructed *aqueducts* (AK wuh duhkts) to carry water from reservoirs in the country to the cities. Roman aqueducts, some of which have survived, were canal-like stone structures that tunneled through mountains and spanned valleys.

The major Roman contributions to science and medicine were collections of information similar to encyclopedias. Pliny (PLIHN ee) the Elder produced the 37-volume work *Natural History*, a storehouse of information on subjects ranging from astronomy to medicine, geography, and botany. Pliny's curiosity about natural occurrences proved to be his downfall. In 79 A.D., he visited Pompeii to observe the erupting Mount Vesuvius (vuh SOO vee uhs) and was killed by the poisonous gases from the volcano.

Scientific works produced during Roman times were studied for centuries. The Greek physician Galen (GAY luhn) wrote a medical encyclopedia that was used in Europe until the 1400s. The ideas of the astronomer Ptolemy also influenced scholars for hundreds of years. Ptolemy taught that the earth was at the center of the universe and that the sun and planets revolved around it. Those theories were not disproved until the 1500s.

Roman engineers were proud of their practical achievements. Aqueducts like this one carried water from the countryside to the cities of the empire. "Who will venture to compare these mighty aqueducts with the idle pyramids or the famous but useless works of the Greeks?" boasted one Roman engineer. The Roman aqueduct in Segovia, Spain, is still used as part of the public water system.

Roman Literature

Roman writers adapted Greek literary forms such as lyric poetry and drama to the Latin language. Romans also developed new styles of writing that were influenced by Greek oratory, the art of persuading an audience.

Some statesmen, such as Caesar and Cicero, were fine writers. When Caesar was away on military campaigns, he kept his name before the public by writing the *Commentaries on the Gallic Wars*. In this work, he skillfully combined a history of the wars with reminders of his own military successes. Cicero developed a clear, logical style of writing that became a model for other writers. In essays on government, morality, and philosophy, he expressed his admiration for the Roman Republic and for the Roman idea of justice.

Poets. Under the emperor Augustus, Roman literature flourished. Augustus supported writers, especially those who praised Roman achievements. The poet Horace was famous for his odes praising Rome and the Pax Romana.

The poet Virgil admired the early Republic. When Augustus commissioned him to write a poem celebrating the rise of Rome, Virgil composed the *Aeneid*, which you read about in Chapter 7. (See page 94.) Although the *Aeneid* imitated the heroic epics of Homer, it emphasized Roman justice, practical wisdom, and power:

> You, O Roman, remember to rule the nations with might. This will be your genius—to impose the way of peace, to spare the conquered and crush the proud.

Historians. During the Pax Romana, Rome produced many historians. Livy, a contemporary of Virgil, wrote the lengthy *History of Rome*. Unlike the Greek historian Thucydides, who tried to be impartial, Livy admitted that his goal was to glorify Rome. "I do honestly believe that no country has ever been greater or purer than ours or richer in good citizens and noble deeds," he claimed.

Another well-known historian, Tacitus (TAS uh tuhs), wrote the *Annals*, a history of Rome from the death of Augustus to 70 A.D. Unlike Livy, he was critical of Roman em-

Many Roman women were well educated in history and literature. A few wrote poetry. With slaves to do the housework, well-to-do women like the one pictured here had the leisure to take an active part in the intellectual and political life of Rome.

perors. But he seemed resigned to the present. "I may regard with admiration an earlier period," wrote Tacitus, "but I accept the present, and while I pray for good emperors, I can endure whomever we may have."

Roman Law

To deal with the practical problems of government, Romans developed a system of law, today considered one of Rome's greatest achievements. Roman law established a common standard of justice for the entire empire. Under Roman law, an accused person was considered innocent until proven guilty. Judges based their decisions on evidence presented in court. They also followed standard procedures to ensure a fair hearing for both sides in a dispute.

Roman law evolved during the Republic and was suited to the needs of a simple farming society. The Twelve Tables of Law, for example, had applied only to Roman citizens. (See page 98.) As Rome expanded, two systems of law developed: civil law and the law of nations. Civil law dealt with claims of Roman citizens. The law of nations dealt with the claims of foreigners and took local customs into account. Eventually, the two codes were merged into a single law system that applied everywhere in the empire.

During the Pax Romana, punishments were less severe than they had been during the Republic. Furthermore, the law code provided some protection for slaves and women. It set limits on the absolute rights of fathers and husbands. Also, women and slaves were given the right to own property.

Roman law was the foundation for the law codes that developed in Europe and were carried to other parts of the world. Today, in some American courthouses, you can see statues of the Roman goddess of justice.

She stands holding a scale in each hand as a symbol of balanced judgment.

SECTION REVIEW

1. Identify: Pliny the Elder, Galen, Ptolemy, Virgil, Livy, Tacitus.
2. Define: aqueduct.
3. How did Roman sculpture differ from Greek sculpture?
4. What contributions did the Romans make to science and medicine?
5. What was Livy's opinion of Rome?
6. What two systems of law developed as Rome expanded?

2 Rise of Christianity

Read to Learn   ■ about Christianity and how it spread in Rome
■ why Rome persecuted Christians

During the Pax Romana, a new religion, Christianity, spread across the Greco-Roman world. At first, Christianity was just one of the many religions practiced within the Roman Empire. But by 395 A.D., it had become the official religion of the empire. The success of Christianity was due in part to the religious climate of the Roman world.

The Religious Climate

Roman emperors tolerated different religious practices. Officially, Romans were required to offer sacrifices to the emperor, who was thought to have divine power. These ceremonies had little religious meaning, however, They merely showed loyalty to Rome. As long as people made sacrifices, they could worship as they chose.

Many Romans continued to worship the old gods, such as Jupiter. Others turned to mystery religions like those in ancient Greece. (See page 81.) People who believed in mystery religions used magical signs and secret passwords hoping to win immortality. Mystery religions gave people in the huge impersonal Roman Empire a sense of belonging.

Roman Rule in Palestine

The Hebrews, or Jews, were among the peoples in the empire whose religions were tolerated. Roman officials in Palestine respected the Hebrew belief in one God and excused Jews from worshipping the emperor. For example, the face of the emperor was not imprinted on coins issued in Palestine because Hebrew law forbade Jews to worship images.

Although Rome allowed Jews to follow traditional laws, many resented foreign rule. Some Jews believed that a *messiah*, a savior chosen by God, would lead them to freedom from Roman rule. The Zealots sought political freedom through armed resistance. But Rome responded to criticism and violence with severe punishment.

In 66 A.D., the Jews in Palestine rose in revolt. Rome sent an army to destroy Jerusalem. In 70 A.D., Rome abolished the Jewish state, which had existed since ancient times. The Jews were enslaved and dispersed throughout the empire. But scattered Jewish communities survived, where Jews preserved their religion and culture.

In the New Testament, the Apostle John quotes Jesus as saying, "I am the good shepherd; the good shepherd giveth his life for the sheep." The symbol of Christ as a shepherd appears in much early Christian art. This mosaic from a church in Ravenna, Italy, shows Jesus with a flock of sheep, perhaps representing 6 of the 12 Apostles.

The Life and Teachings of Jesus

About 70 years before the Jewish uprising against Rome, Jesus, the founder of Christianity, was born in Bethlehem, a town in southern Palestine. Information about the early life of Jesus comes from accounts written by Jesus' disciples after his death. These accounts, called the Gospels, or good news, make up the first four books of the New Testament of the Bible.

According to the Gospels, Jesus grew up in Nazareth, studied with priests in the synagogue, and learned the trade of a carpenter. As a young man, Jesus began preaching to the poor. The Gospels also say that Jesus performed miracles such as healing the sick. Many people who heard Jesus or witnessed the miracles believed he was the Messiah. The Greek word for messiah was Christos. Followers of Jesus eventually became known as Christians.

The large crowds Jesus attracted when he preached worried Jewish and Roman authorities. Some Jewish officials considered him a troublemaker bent on challenging Hebrew laws. Others rejected Jesus' claim to be the Son of God. Denounced by his enemies, Jesus was arrested and taken before Pontius Pilate, a Roman official. Pilate saw Jesus as a threat to Rome's authority in Palestine. As a result, Jesus was condemned to die. He was executed according to Roman custom by crucifixion, or being nailed to a cross to die of exposure.

In his teachings, Jesus stressed love for God and compassion for other people. A person's chief duties, he said, were to "love the Lord thy God with all thy heart" and to "love thy neighbor as thyself." In *parables*, short stories with simple moral lessons, Jesus taught people how to show kindness to one another. Jesus offered his followers a loving and forgiving God. He taught that earthly

117

riches were unimportant and that people who were humble, merciful, and unselfish, would be rewarded with eternal life.

The teachings of Jesus were rooted in Hebrew religious traditions. (See page 43.) For example, Jesus preached obedience to one God, to the Ten Commandments, and to other Hebrew laws of the Old Testament. In addition, like the ancient Hebrew prophets, Jesus condemned injustice and criticized false pride. As a result, the Hebrew ethical world view became a fundamental part of Christianity.

The Apostles and Paul

According to the New Testament, Jesus chose 12 disciples as Apostles to carry on his teachings. At first, the Apostles preached to the Jews of Palestine. The Apostle Peter traveled to Rome, where he converted Jews in the capital to Christianity. But Paul, the person most responsible for spreading the message of Jesus, was not one of the original Apostles.

Paul, a Greek-speaking Jew from Asia Minor, helped establish Christian communities in the eastern cities of the Roman Empire. For 30 years, he traveled tirelessly through Palestine and Syria to Asia Minor, Macedonia, Greece, and Rome. Like the Apostles, he sought converts among the Jews. But Paul also took Christianity on a new course when he decided to preach the Gospel to Gentiles, or non-Jews.

Paul played a key role in shaping Christian thought. As part of his missionary work, he wrote hundreds of letters to different Christian communities. These letters, which explained Christian beliefs, are part of the New Testament. Paul taught that people who believed in Jesus need not fear death because Jesus promised everlasting life.

Persecution and Toleration

Unlike other religions within the Roman Empire, Christianity aroused official persecution because Christians refused to worship the emperor. Roman authorities had excused

Map Skill *Christianity gradually spread from Jerusalem throughout the Roman Empire. What areas were Christian by 200 A.D.? Why do you think these areas were the first to become Christian?*

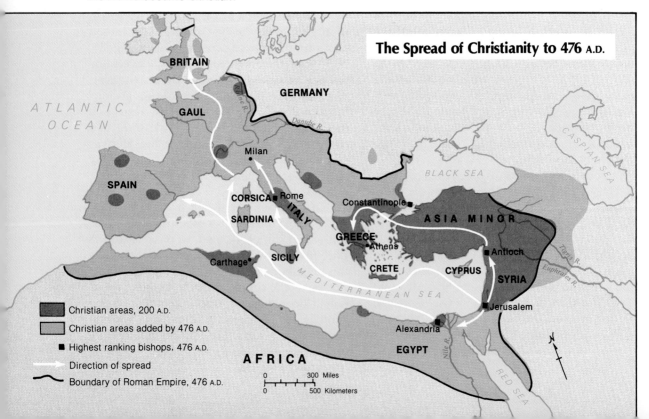

The Spread of Christianity to 476 A.D.

ATLANTIC OCEAN

BRITAIN
GERMANY
GAUL
SPAIN
Milan
CORSICA Rome
SARDINIA ITALY
SICILY
Carthage
BLACK SEA
CASPIAN SEA
Constantinople
ASIA MINOR
GREECE
Athens
CRETE
CYPRUS
Antioch
SYRIA
MEDITERRANEAN SEA
Jerusalem
Alexandria
EGYPT
AFRICA
RED SEA

- ■ Christian areas, 200 A.D.
- ☐ Christian areas added by 476 A.D.
- ■ Highest ranking bishops, 476 A.D.
- → Direction of spread
- ⌒ Boundary of Roman Empire, 476 A.D.

0   300 Miles
0   500 Kilometers

Jews from emperor worship out of respect for their ancient traditions. But Roman authorities saw Christians as dangerous troublemakers because they were winning converts throughout the empire.

Official policy alternated between brutal persecution and toleration. Emperors tended to use Christians as scapegoats, especially when political or economic conditions were bad. Both Peter and Paul perished in Rome under the persecution of the emperor Nero.

Persecution strengthened rather than weakened the new religion. During periods of intense persecution, some Christians renounced their faith. But many others became *martyrs*, people who suffer or die for their beliefs. Christians believed that martyrs received God's special favor. "The blood of the martyrs," wrote one Roman, "is the seed of the Church." Many people were impressed by a faith that inspired such devotion in its followers, and they converted in great numbers.

As you read at the beginning of this chapter, the emperor Constantine officially recognized Christianity. In 313 A.D., he introduced a policy of official toleration by the Edict of Milan. Christianity achieved its greatest triumph in 395 A.D., when it was proclaimed the official religion of the Roman Empire.

The Appeal of Christianity

From humble beginnings in Palestine, Christianity spread to the eastern cities of the Roman Empire and then throughout the entire Roman world. (See the map on page 118.) Scholars have suggested many reasons for the widespread appeal of Christianity.

The simple, direct message of Christianity appealed to many people. The poor and oppressed found hope in the God who loved people regardless of their place in society. Equality, human dignity, and, above all, the promise of eternal life were comforting teachings. Many educated people who had rejected the Roman gods and the mystery religions turned to Christianity. To them, the Christian emphasis on a life of moderation and discipline echoed Greek and Roman philosophies.

The work of dedicated missionaries such as Paul was made easier by the unity of the Roman Empire and the ease of travel between cities. In the eastern Mediterranean, the use of a common language, Greek, and the concentration of people in cities contributed to the early success of Christianity. Furthermore, many early Christians were women who brought other members of their families into the faith. In some Christian communities, women conducted worship services and enjoyed equality with men.

During the troubles of the later Roman Empire, which you will read about in the next section, the old mystery religions lost vitality. As Christianity gained in strength, more people adopted the religion. Eventually, Christians developed an efficient, dynamic church organization. The Christian Church maintained unity among its members and ensured the survival of the new faith.

Church Organization

The Christian Church developed gradually during the first few centuries A.D. At first, bishops ranked as the highest officials. Each bishop administered the churches in a territory called a see. Below the bishops were priests, who conducted worship services and taught Christian beliefs. As the Church expanded, archbishops were appointed to oversee the bishops. An archbishop's territory was called a province. The type of organization in which officials are arranged according to rank is called a *hierarchy* (HĪ uh RAHR kee).

As the Church hierarchy emerged, women lost their influence in Church government. They were not allowed to become priests or conduct the Mass, the Christian worship service. But women continued to play a prominent role in spreading Christian teachings across the Roman world.

In time, the bishop of Rome acquired a dominant position in the Church by claiming that Peter, the chief Apostle, had made Rome the center of the Christian Church. The bishop of Rome eventually took the title *pope*, or father of the Church. Bishops in the eastern Mediterranean cities such as

Constantinople, Alexandria, Jerusalem, and Antioch opposed the pope's claim to be supreme ruler of the church.

Together, the clergy, which included archbishops, bishops, and priests, helped keep Christianity alive in the early years of persecution. The clergy also maintained order and discipline in the Church. For example, bishops and archbishops met in councils to decide which ideas or practices the Church would accept. In 325 A.D., Church officials met in Nicaea (nī SEE uh) in Asia Minor, where they drew up the Nicene Creed, a statement of basic Christian beliefs.

SECTION REVIEW

1. Identify: Gospels, Peter, Paul, Gentiles, Nicene Creed.
2. Define: messiah, parable, martyr, hierarchy, pope.
3. How did Rome show respect for Hebrew religious beliefs?
4. Why did Roman authorities believe Jesus was dangerous?
5. What did Paul teach Christians?
6. List three reasons for the widespread appeal of Christianity.

3 Breakdown of Unity

Read to Learn
- why the Pax Romana failed
- how Diocletian and Constantine tried reforms

During the centuries that Christianity was struggling to survive, events were reshaping the Roman world. The death of Emperor Marcus Aurelius in 180 A.D. plunged Rome into civil wars that ended the Pax Romana.

End of the Pax Romana

The Romans had never established an effective system of succession. Often, an emperor would name his son or an adopted son as his heir, and the Senate would approve the new ruler. After the death of Marcus Aurelius, this system broke down. Civil wars plagued Rome as generals competed for the throne. Between 234 A.D. and 284 A.D., at least 26 emperors ruled. Some held power for only a few months. All but one suffered violent deaths.

During the years of turmoil, the authority of Rome weakened, and corruption reduced government efficiency. Law and order declined. The civil wars disrupted commerce in the cities, which had once produced the wealth of the empire. To raise money, emperors continued to devalue the coinage. (See page 110.) By making coins of copper with only a thin coating of gold, they could issue more coins. Because the new coins were worth less than the old ones, prices and wages rose sharply. In this unstable economic atmosphere, businesses and cities declined further.

At the same time, invaders attacked the empire. Many farmers abandoned their land or turned their land over to wealthy nobles. The small farmers, or *coloni* (kuh LOH nī), continued to work the land, but the noble landowner paid the taxes and protected the coloni. In frontier regions, powerful nobles acquired vast holdings, which they governed almost independently of Rome.

Reforms of Diocletian

In 284 A.D., legions in the east made the general Diocletian (dī uh KLEE shuhn) emperor. The new ruler introduced harsh new laws meant to strengthen the empire. Diocletian divided the Roman Empire in half and took control of the wealthier eastern provinces himself. He then appointed a co-emperor to rule the western provinces. The co-emperor was responsible to Diocletian.

To restore government efficiency, Diocletian reorganized the civil service and made officials directly responsible to the emperor. He enlarged the army and trained new cavalry units to fight invaders. New

The energetic Emperor Diocletian divided his attention between rebuilding Roman military power and strengthening the economy. But government spending on the army and new palaces caused prices to soar. From one day to the next, people had no idea what their money would buy.

In an effort to curb runaway inflation, the emperor issued the Edict on Maximum Prices. The edict set a ceiling on prices for over 1,000 items, including nearly all goods produced in the empire. In addition, it regulated wages for many services.

Unfortunately, Diocletian's edict did not reduce prices. As one Roman noted when the edict was posted, "nothing appeared on the market because of fear, and prices soared much higher." Eventually, the emperor allowed people to ignore the edict.

A closer look at some of the items on Diocletian's list reveals much about the comparative value of goods and services in the year 301 A.D. Prices are given in denarii, a common coin of the day.

Wages

Farm laborer	25d. with keep per day
Stone mason and carpenter	50d. with keep per day
Barber	2d. per customer
Scribe	20 or 25d. per 100 lines
Elementary teacher	50d. per month per boy

Prices

Wheat	11d. per litre
Salt	11d. per litre
Oil	24–80d. for one litre
Beef and goat	24d. per kilo
Ham	60d. per kilo
Cheese	24d. per kilo
Chickens	60d. a pair
Eggs	1d. each
Cabbage and lettuce	0.4 or 0.8d. each
Peaches	0.2 or 0.4d. each
Patrician shoes	150d. a pair
Soldier's boots (no nails)	100d. a pair
Hooded cloak	4500d. each

forts and roads were built to reinforce the frontier defenses. For a time, these measures ensured peace.

Diocletian also tried to solve economic problems in the empire. To slow the rapid rise in prices, he set limits on prices and wages. He also wanted to make agriculture and manufacturing more stable, so he ordered people to remain in their jobs. A shoemaker or farmer, for example, could not change occupations. Neither could their children or grandchildren.

The Reign of Constantine

When illness forced Diocletian to retire in 305 A.D., a long power struggle resulted. In 312 A.D., Constantine emerged victorious, as you read on page 112. In 324 A.D., Constantine reunited the eastern and western territories under his personal rule. Significantly, he built a new capital at Byzantium, a Greek city on the Bosporus. The new Roman capital came to be called Constantinople. Making Constantinople the capital symbolized the declining influence of the city of Rome and the growing importance of the eastern provinces of the Roman Empire.

Constantine had many reasons for building a new capital. He believed that Rome was full of its "pagan," or non-Christian, past. Constantine wanted the new capital to be a Christian city. Also, Constantinople was closer to the great commercial centers of the eastern Mediterranean. The trade and commerce of those cities supplied most of the empire's riches. Furthermore, the eastern frontier was more secure from invaders than the western frontiers.

Constantine built on the strict reforms of Diocletian. He ordered officials to enforce the harsh laws tying artisans to their trades and farmers to the land. However, this action had few positive results. Without the hope of getting ahead, people saw little reason to work hard.

The policies of Diocletian and Constantine did not halt the political and economic decay. Corruption and violence resurfaced after Constantine's death in 337 A.D. The empire was again divided. The Eastern Roman Empire flourished, but the Western Roman Empire was collapsing under internal stress and the pressure of invaders.

4 Collapse of the Empire

Read to Learn
- why German tribes invaded Rome
- what caused the decline of Rome

The emperors Diocletian and Constantine had struggled to restore Roman power. But new threats to the empire arose when invaders swept across the frontiers. These attacks shattered forever the unity of the Roman Empire.

The German Tribes

During the Pax Romana, Roman armies had often fought German tribes living north of the Rhine and Danube rivers. The Germans included many different groups of seminomadic herders and farmers who had migrated from Scandinavia, the area of present-day Norway, Sweden, and Denmark.

The Roman historian Tacitus left one of the earliest descriptions of the German tribes. Their military strength, courage, and strict morality impressed Tacitus. An elected king ruled each German tribe with the aid of a council of chiefs. Chiefs were chosen for their bravery by assemblies of free men. Each chief led a band of young warriors. In exchange for their services in battle, the chief supplied his warriors with a shield, a javelin, food, and shelter. "The chief fights for victory," Tacitus noted, while his "companions fight for their chief." Each chief administered justice in his region. Under the Germanic system, a person who was guilty of assault had to pay a fine to the injured person.

By the third century A.D., a growing population forced the Germans to seek new land. Attracted by the wealth and the warmer climate of southern Europe, some crossed into the Roman Empire. Weakened by civil wars, frontier legions were hard pressed to withstand the pressure of the German migrations. Then, around the middle of the fourth century A.D., the Huns, a fierce nomadic people from Central Asia, attacked the German tribes of Eastern Europe.

Invasions of the Roman Empire

Historians do not know why the Huns burst out of Asia into Europe. Huns were superb riders and warriors who easily defeated the Ostrogoths, a German tribe that lived north of the Black Sea.

Fearing a similar fate, a neighboring German tribe, the Visigoths, sought protection inside the Roman Empire. In 376 A.D., they received permission to cross the Danube river. Two years later, the Romans regretted their decision and sent an army against the Visigoths. But at the battle of

Adrianople, the Visigoths crushed the Roman legions. The Roman defeat signaled to all that Rome was no longer unbeatable.

After Adrianople, Germans flooded into the empire seeking safety from the Huns. But they also looted Roman cities as they came. In 410 A.D., the Visigoth general Alaric (AL uh rihk) invaded Italy and sacked Rome. Roman officials bought peace by granting Alaric much of southern Gaul and Spain.

Meanwhile, the Huns conquered Eastern Europe, including the areas of present-day Romania, Hungary, Poland, and Czechoslovakia. Under their leader Attila, whom Christians called the "Scourge of God," they poured across the Rhine. Rome formed a hasty alliance with some German tribes. At the battle of Troyes (twah) in 451 A.D., Rome and its allies stopped the Hun advance. Attila was not defeated, but he withdrew his forces. When he died not long after this battle, the Hun empire collapsed.

Other invaders continued to threaten Rome. A German tribe, the Vandals, moved through Gaul into Spain before settling in northern Africa. From Carthage, the Vandals raided Italy. In 455 A.D., they sacked Rome.* As Roman legions were withdrawn from the

---

* The English word "vandalism," meaning the malicious destruction of property, came from the name of this German tribe.

Map Skill *Diocletian hoped to strengthen the Roman Empire by dividing it into the Western Roman Empire and the Eastern Roman Empire. What was the actual result of his action? Which tribes reached Rome?*

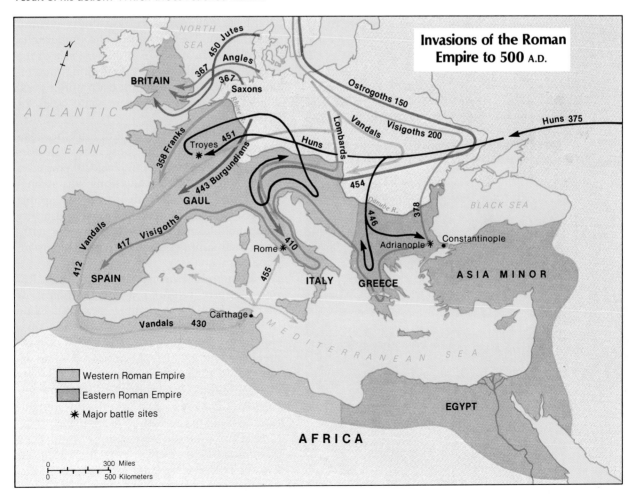

frontiers to defend cities in Italy, the Burgundians, the Franks, and later the Lombards moved into the western empire.

The "Fall of Rome"

In 476 A.D., a minor German chief, Odoacer (OH doh AY suhr), captured Rome and forced the emperor to give up the throne. Odoacer then proclaimed himself king of Italy. Many historians refer to this incident as the "fall of Rome." Yet Rome did not collapse suddenly.

As you have read, the Roman Empire had faced severe problems for centuries. Moreover, Roman civilization did not disappear after 476 A.D. Although German tribes conquered the western empire, the people of Gaul, for example, still considered themselves Romans. People continued to enforce Roman laws, and they spoke Latin, although local dialects developed. However, after 476 A.D., there was no emperor in the west. Without an emperor to serve as a rallying point, the unity of the Western Roman Empire ended.

The Eastern Roman Empire survived for 1,000 years after the fall of Rome. From Constantinople, emperors played one German ruler off against another, hoping to dominate affairs in the west. Thriving commerce and a strong civil service in the eastern empire enabled it to preserve Greco-Roman civilization. In Chapter 13, you will read more about the Byzantine Empire, as the Eastern Roman Empire was later called.

Causes of the Decline

Why did Rome decline? Most scholars agree that no single problem caused the decline of Rome. Instead, they think that numerous political, economic, and social problems gradually destroyed the strength of the Roman Empire.

Political causes. Roman citizens gradually lost feelings of responsibility toward government. They expected the emperor to look after their needs. But the vast size of the empire and widespread corruption made efficient government difficult even under good rulers. And many emperors were weak or evil rulers.

The division of the empire hurt the western empire because the best administrators and generals served the eastern emperor. Just when the tide of invasions was strongest, Rome suffered from a lack of capable leaders. Furthermore, as Roman authority weakened, some wealthy landowners withdrew their support from Rome and set up independent states.

Economic causes. Governing the Roman Empire required a huge amount of money. Much of the empire's wealth came from the eastern provinces. Thus, the division of the empire deprived Rome of desperately needed revenues. Moreover, Roman armies were no longer bringing in loot from newly conquered territories. Civil wars and German invasions hurt trade and agriculture, making tax collection more difficult. Attempts to increase the money supply by devaluing the currency only increased inflation. The resulting high prices were a burden to most Romans.

The German tribes that invaded the Roman Empire had their own artistic traditions. Although their art was less sophisticated than that of Greco-Roman civilization, German artisans produced fine animal figures in metal. The horse and rider shown here may have been part of a pendant or brooch.

As you read earlier, historians use primary sources to learn about events or developments that took place in the past. (Review "Analyzing a Primary Source," page 38.) Some primary sources are eyewitness accounts written by individuals for a particular purpose. Therefore, the writer might not give a completely objective or accurate account. Thus, when using a primary source, it is important to identify the writer's point of view.

The following excerpts were taken from the *Histories* of Ammianus Marcellinus (AHM ih AY nuhs   MAHR seh LĪ nuhs), written about 378 A.D. As a soldier in the emperor's bodyguard, Ammianus had paid visits to Rome and seen how Romans lived. Read the excerpts from the *Histories*. Then use these steps to identify the writer's point of view.

1. **Determine what information is being given.** You can do this by asking what the source is describing. Answer the following questions about the excerpts: (a) What aspects of Roman life does the writer describe? (b) What does the writer say about the clothing worn by Romans? (c) According to Ammianus, how did poor Romans spend their time?

2. **Distinguish between fact and opinion.** A *fact* is something that has actually happened. A fact can be proven or observed. An *opinion* is a judgment that reflects a person's feelings or beliefs. Use the following questions to identify the facts and opinions in the source: (a) What three facts about life in Rome can you identify in this excerpt? (b) What is the writer's opinion of the amusements of Romans? (c) How does the writer show his opinion of Roman banquets?

3. **Evaluate the reliability of the source.** Answer the following questions to see if the writer is presenting a complete, accurate picture: (a) How could the fact that Ammianus was a visitor to Rome have affected his view of the capital? (b) In what way

could his occupation as a soldier have influenced his view of Rome? (c) What aspects of Roman life does Ammianus seem to ignore? (d) Would you consider this a reliable description of life in Rome? Why or why not?

4. **Use the source to draw conclusions about a historical event or development.** (a) What conclusions would you draw about conditions in Rome in the late 300s A.D. based on this source? (b) What generalizations about the decline of Rome can be made from this source?

From the *Histories* by Ammianus Marcellinus

Rome is still looked on as the queen of the earth, and the name of the Roman people is respected. But the magnificence of Rome is defaced by the thoughtless conduct of a few, who ... fall away into error and vice. Some men think that they can gain immortality by means of statues ... as if they would obtain a higher reward from bronze figures unendowed with sense than from a consciousness of upright and honorable actions; and they are even anxious to have them plated over with gold!

Others place greater importance on having a couch higher than usual, or splendid clothing. They toil and sweat under a vast burden of cloaks which are fastened to their necks by many clasps. ...

The whirlpool of banquets and other luxuries I shall pass over lest I go too far. Many people drive their horses recklessly ... over the flint-paved city streets. They drag behind them huge numbers of slaves, like bands of robbers.

As for the lower and poorer classes, some spend the whole night in the wine shops. Some lie concealed in the shady arcades of the theaters. They play at dice so eagerly as to quarrel over them. ... Such pursuits as these prevent anything worth mentioning from being done in Rome.

In the cities, heavy taxes and high unemployment contributed to declining prosperity. The idleness of the wealthy and the expense of providing free grain to the poor further drained Roman resources.

Social causes. As contemporary historians suggested, the loyalty and civic pride that once unified Rome had gradually decayed. Because citizens evaded military service, for example, soldiers were increasingly recruited from people who had little loyalty to Rome. These soldiers lacked the discipline and patriotism of the armies that had conquered the Mediterranean world. As a result, they were no match for the well-trained Germans, who were inspired by loyalty to their chiefs.

Many people no longer felt they had a stake in the empire. They did not care whether the ruler was Roman or German. Devastating epidemics that swept through the western provinces in the fourth century A.D. increased the sense of hopelessness.

Despite these formidable pressures, the breakup of the Western Roman Empire was a slow process. The remarkable feature of the empire was that it endured for so long.

SECTION REVIEW

1. Locate: Adrianople, Troyes.
2. Identify: Huns, Visigoths, Vandals.
3. What role did the chief play in the German tribes?
4. List two reasons why Germans moved into the Roman Empire.
5. What event marks the "fall of Rome" according to many historians?
6. Describe one way in which the division of the Roman Empire hurt the western provinces.

Chapter 8 Review

In Perspective

The Romans adapted many ideas from other cultures of the ancient Mediterranean world. They built on Greek achievements in art and architecture. And one of their most lasting contributions was the Roman system of law.

During the early centuries A.D., Christianity developed in the eastern Mediterranean. Paul carried the teachings of Jesus to many parts of the empire. Persecution by Roman officials only seemed to strengthen the new religion. Finally, Constantine ended the persecutions. By 395 A.D., Christianity was the official religion of the empire.

After 180 A.D., civil wars disrupted the economy of the empire. Attempts by Diocletian and Constantine to revive Roman authority failed.

In the fourth and fifth centuries A.D., German and Hun invaders crippled the Western Roman Empire. The capture of the city of Rome in 476 A.D. marked the end of political unity in the west. Yet the Roman heritage survived in both Western Europe and the Eastern Roman Empire.

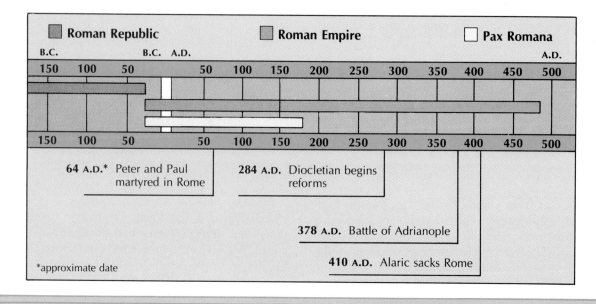

| ■ Roman Republic | ■ Roman Empire | □ Pax Romana |

| B.C. | | | B.C. | A.D. | | | | | | | | | A.D. |
| 150 | 100 | 50 | | 50 | 100 | 150 | 200 | 250 | 300 | 350 | 400 | 450 | 500 |

| 150 | 100 | 50 | 50 | 100 | 150 | 200 | 250 | 300 | 350 | 400 | 450 | 500 |

64 A.D.* Peter and Paul martyred in Rome

284 A.D. Diocletian begins reforms

378 A.D. Battle of Adrianople

410 A.D. Alaric sacks Rome

*approximate date

Recalling Facts

Arrange the events in each of the following groups in the order in which they occurred

1. (a) The Pax Romana ends.
   (b) Odoacer captures Rome.
   (c) The Roman Empire is divided into an eastern and a western empire.
2. (a) Diocletian introduces government and economic reforms.
   (b) Constantine builds a new capital in the east.
   (c) Christianity becomes the official religion of the Roman Empire.
3. (a) Roman armies destroy Jerusalem.
   (b) Nicene Creed adopted.
   (c) Jesus is born in Bethlehem.
4. (a) Huns attack German tribes in Eastern Europe.
   (b) Visigoths defeat Romans at the battle of Adrianople.
   (c) Vandals sack Rome.

Chapter Checkup

1. (a) How did Greek culture influence Roman civilization? (b) In what fields did Rome make its own contributions?
2. (a) What were the main themes emphasized by Roman writers? (b) How did Livy's writing of history differ from that of the Greek historian Thucydides?
3. Describe the system of law that developed under the Roman Empire.
4. (a) In general, what was the Roman attitude toward the many different religions in the empire? (b) Why did Roman authorities persecute Christians?
5. Explain how each of the following contributed to the spread of Christianity: (a) Paul; (b) Roman persecution; (c) the message of Christianity; (d) unity of the Roman Empire.
6. (a) Describe the reforms of Diocletian and Constantine. (b) In what ways were they successful? (c) In what ways were they unsuccessful?

Critical Thinking

1. **Analyzing** Many people have admired Romans for their practical achievements. (a) What were these achievements? (b) How do you think the Roman emphasis on practical matters helped unify the empire?
2. **Comparing** (a) How is law in the United States today similar to law in the Roman Empire? (b) How is it different? (c) How might you explain the similarities and differences?

Relating Past to Present

1. (a) In your opinion, why did Rome borrow so much from Greek civilization? (b) What present-day example can you give of one culture strongly influencing another?

Developing Basic Skills

1. **Using Visual Evidence** Study the sculpture on page 105 and answer the following questions: (a) What is the subject of the sculpture? (b) What features does it emphasize? (c) In what ways does it show Greek influence? (d) How is it different from the Greek statue on page 84?
2. **Analyzing a Primary Source** Review the feature on page 121. Then answer the following questions: (a) What type of source is this? (b) What was the purpose of Diocletian's Edict on Maximum Prices? (c) What items of food were most expensive? (d) What items of food were least expensive? (e) What conclusions could you draw about what poorer Romans ate?
3. **Map Reading** Use the map on page 123 and your reading in this chapter to answer the following questions: (a) Which of the invaders of Rome came from Asia? (b) Describe the route taken by the Vandals through the Roman empire. (c) Which part of the Roman Empire suffered most from the invasions? Which suffered the least? (d) How do the routes taken by the invaders help explain the fall of the Western Roman Empire?
4. **Classifying** Make a chart with three columns. In column one, list political causes for Rome's decline. In column two, list economic causes. In column three, list social causes. Then answer the following questions: (a) What connections do you see between political and economic causes? (b) How did economic problems contribute to social problems? (c) What do you think was the most important cause of Rome's decline? Explain.

See page 804 for suggested readings.

9 The Heritage of India and China

(600 B.C.–550 A.D.)

A Chinese statue of the Buddha.

In 399 A.D., a Chinese traveler, Fa-hsien (FAH shee ehn), set out on foot for India. He walked from China into Afghanistan and crossed the Hindu Kush to the northern plain of India. The journey took him six years. Fa-hsien, a Buddhist monk, made this difficult journey because India was the birthplace of Buddhism, one of the world's major religions. He even learned Sanskrit so he could read the sacred Buddhist texts.

Fa-hsien was impressed by what he saw in India. "The people are numerous and happy," he reported. "The king governs without beheading or other corporal punishments." Fa-hsien noted in his journal other customs and practices that he saw in India. For example, he wrote:

"Throughout the whole country, the people do not kill any living creature, nor drink intoxicating liquor, nor eat onions or garlic. The only exception is the untouchable caste who are held to be wicked people and live apart from others. . . . Only the untouchables are fishermen and hunters and sell flesh meat.

"In the cities and towns of this country . . . the inhabitants are rich and prosperous. . . . In the cities, certain families establish houses for dispensing charity and medicines. The poor and destitute, orphans, widowers . . . and all who are diseased go to those houses and are provided with every kind of help. Doctors examine their diseases. They get the food and medicines which their cases require, and are made to feel at ease. . . ."

Fa-hsien visited India at the height of the Gupta (GUP tuh) Empire. At the same time that Greco-Roman civilization flourished in the Mediterranean world, the civilizations of India and China also reached high levels of development. Between 600 B.C. and 550 A.D., India experienced great economic growth and made impressive advances in the arts and technology. Indian culture spread to other parts of Asia. During the same period, China achieved political unity and also influenced its Asian neighbors.

Perhaps the most significant development in both India and China was the emergence of strong religious and philosophical traditions. In the sixth and fifth centuries B.C., great philosophers in India and China developed ideas about the goals of life and the individual's place in society. This was the same time that Socrates, the Hebrew prophets, and Zoroaster were developing their ideas in other parts of the world.

Like Rome, both India and China suffered from civil wars and invasions. Yet their societies were not subject to the drastic upheavals that led to the collapse of Rome. As a result, the civilizations in India and China continued to thrive at a time when people in Western Europe were building the foundations for a new civilization.

1 Two Influential Religions

Read to Learn ■ about the beliefs and impact of Hinduism
■ about the beliefs of Buddhism and its spread

Two major religions helped shape the civilization of India. First, ancient Aryan beliefs and practices evolved into Hinduism. In turn, Hindu traditions influenced Buddhism, which emerged in India about 500 B.C. Both religions still have many followers.

Hinduism

Hinduism cannot be traced to one person's ideas. Instead, it blended ancient Aryan traditions with the religious beliefs of peoples the Aryans conquered. Over the centuries, Aryan priests preserved religious beliefs in sacred texts, including the Vedas and the Upanishads. (See page 51.) To Hindus, these writings reveal basic truths about life and the place of the individual in the universe.

Hindus believe in *brahma*, a single, supreme force uniting everything in the universe. Hindus worship many gods, each symbolizing a different aspect of brahma. Thus, the three main gods in Hinduism—Brahma, Vishnu, and Shiva—are part of the same universal spirit. The god Brahma is seen as the creator of the world, Vishnu as the preserver, and Shiva as the destroyer.

The Hindu belief in the unity of all life is reflected in the idea of soul. Hinduism teaches that every individual has a soul, which is part of a larger universal soul, called *atman*. However, most individuals pursue imperfect goals such as material riches and personal pleasures. Hindus believe that the pursuit of these goals brings suffering and pain and keeps the soul separate from the universal soul. The goal of life, according to Hinduism, is to free the soul from its individual existence through reunion with atman.

The process of reunion with atman takes more than one lifetime. Thus, Hindus believe that the soul passes through a series of rebirths. When the body dies, the soul is reincarnated, or reborn, in another person or in an animal. During each life, an individual can move closer to the goal of oneness with atman. According to Hinduism, the cycle of reincarnation continues until the individual soul has reached the highest level of spiritual

Shiva, one of the most popular gods in Hinduism, appears in many roles. In this statue, he is shown as lord of the cosmic dance. The dwarf under his feet represents the illusions that Shiva dispels. Shiva holds a drum, symbol of creation, in one hand and a flame, symbol of destruction, in another hand.

understanding and is reunited with the universal soul.

Hinduism provides a guide for correct conduct. It encourages virtues such as truth, respect for all life, and detachment from this world.

Hinduism and the Caste System

Hinduism has profoundly influenced Indian culture because its teachings were closely connected to the caste system. In early Aryan society, you will recall, there were four major classes that were eventually divided into numerous castes and subcastes. (See page 53.) Hindus believe that the law of karma determines whether a person is born into a high or low caste. *Karma* includes all the actions in a person's life that affect his or her fate in the next life.

At birth, a person has a set of social and religious duties that include obedience to caste rules as well as to moral laws. People acquire good karma by obeying caste regulations about diet, work, and social behavior. For example, if a person in the Sudra caste were a faithful servant and followed caste rules, his or her soul would be reincarnated in a higher caste in the next life. However, those who ignore their duties could be reborn in a lower caste or as an animal.

By 600 B.C., Brahmans, or priests, had emerged as the highest caste because they were thought to be closest to reunion with the universal soul. As guardians of the sacred Hindu texts, they alone could perform the rituals that guided the soul to this reunion. Because most people believed that their current positions were due to actions in previous lives, they felt they had no choice but to obey the strict caste rules.

However, a few people criticized the power of the Brahmans and called for reform. They rejected the idea that only complicated rituals performed by Brahmans could open the way to salvation. Some, like the Jainists, believed that self-discipline and meditation would lead to higher spiritual understanding. Yoga grew out of this tradition. One influential reformer was Siddhartha Gautama (GOWT uh muh), whose ideas gave rise to a new religion, Buddhism.

Siddhartha Gautama: Founder of Buddhism

Siddhartha Gautama was born in the foothills of the Himalayas about 563 B.C. As the son of a wealthy rajah, he was a member of the warrior class. Scholars know little about Gautama's early life, although he apparently grew up in luxury, protected from the world outside the palace walls. Gautama married and had one son. According to legend, one day when Gautama was 29 he met first an old man, then a sick man, and finally he saw a corpse. The experience haunted him, and he began to see the world as being full of misery and decay.

Shortly afterwards, Gautama left his family. He exchanged the silks and jewels he wore for beggar's rags and set out to discover the causes of human suffering. First, he studied the sacred Hindu texts, but he failed to find a satisfactory answer. Then he tried self-denial, disciplining his body to near starvation. But this also yielded no results.

After six years of wandering, Gautama sat meditating one day under a sacred tree. Suddenly, he felt he had found the knowledge he sought. In that moment, he is said to have attained enlightenment. Thereafter, Gautama was called the Buddha, or "the Enlightened One."

During his lifetime, the Buddha taught the way to salvation that he had discovered. He attracted many followers. He organized them into religious communities of monks and nuns. Buddhist monks and nuns abandoned their families and possessions for a life devoted to poverty and self-discipline.

According to Buddhist tradition, Gautama died in 483 B.C., while visiting a poor blacksmith. The Buddha ate the spoiled food set before him rather than embarrass the poor family. As he lay dying, he advised his disciples: "Decay is inherent [inborn] in all things. Work out your own salvation with diligence."

The Teachings of Buddhism

The "Four Noble Truths" the Buddha discovered while he sat under the sacred tree form the heart of Buddhist teachings. The first truth was that suffering and misery were universal. The Buddha believed that people everywhere were subject to pain, sickness, and death. The second truth was that the cause of suffering was desire. Happiness, riches, and other pleasures caused pain, said the Buddha, because they could not last.

The third truth was that the way to end suffering was to overcome desire. The ultimate goal of life was release, or escape from desire, in nirvana. *Nirvana* was the condition of wanting nothing. The fourth truth was that the way to escape pain and suffering was to follow the Middle Way.

The Middle Way offered practical guidelines known as the Eightfold Path. These guidelines stressed virtuous conduct as well as compassion for all living things. They also stressed right knowledge, intentions, speech, conduct, livelihood, effort, mindfulness, and meditation. To the Buddha, the Middle Way was a path that avoided the extremes between the worldly aspects of Hinduism and the excessive self-discipline of other groups.

The Buddha had set out to reform Hinduism. He did not plan to establish a new religion. Therefore, Buddhism reflected many Hindu traditions. For example, although the Buddha did not believe in a permanent soul, he believed in karma and a cycle of rebirth. Both religions viewed the world as a place of sadness and suffering from which people wished to escape.

Yet Buddhism differed from Hinduism in several important ways. The Buddha denied the existence of any gods. He believed that all people, no matter what their social class, could achieve nirvana through the Middle Way. Furthermore, he rejected the caste system and the Hindu view that priests were more worthy than other people.

The Spread of Buddhism

In the years after the Buddha's death, missionaries carried the new religion to the people of India. (See the map on page 132.) The Buddha's disciples collected Buddhist teachings into sacred texts called the *Three Baskets of Wisdom.*

Gradually, two sects, or schools, developed within Buddhism. At first, most Buddhists belonged to the Theravada (THER uh VAH duh) sect. They studied the original sayings of the Buddha and believed that people must seek nirvana through proper ethical conduct. Theravada Buddhism spread from India to Ceylon and all through Southeast Asia.

A second school, Mahayana (MAH huh YAH nuh) Buddhism, gave new direction to Buddhist teachings. For example, Mahayana

131

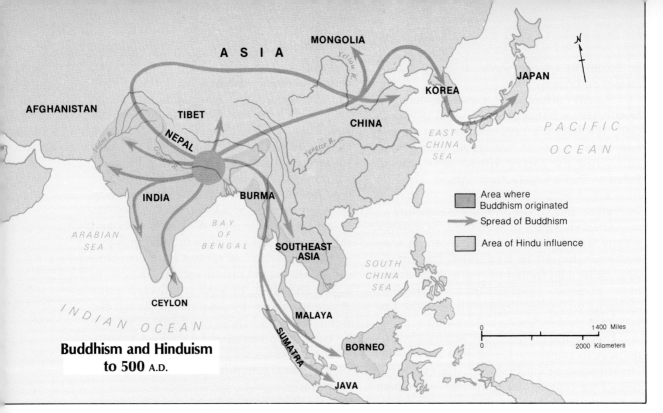

Buddhism and Hinduism to 500 A.D.

ASIA

MONGOLIA

KOREA

JAPAN

AFGHANISTAN

TIBET

NEPAL

CHINA

PACIFIC OCEAN

EAST CHINA SEA

INDIA

BURMA

BAY OF BENGAL

ARABIAN SEA

SOUTHEAST ASIA

SOUTH CHINA SEA

CEYLON

MALAYA

INDIAN OCEAN

SUMATRA

BORNEO

JAVA

Area where Buddhism originated
Spread of Buddhism
Area of Hindu influence

0   1400 Miles
0   2000 Kilometers

Map Skill   *From its birthplace, Buddhism spread to other parts of Asia. Although it was absorbed back into Hinduism in India, Buddhism has remained a vital force in other parts of Asia. In which major directions did Buddhism spread?*

Buddhists worshipped the Buddha as a god. But they believed there were other buddhas, people who had reached enlightenment. Missionaries carried Mahayana Buddhism into China, Korea, Tibet, and Japan.

In India, Buddhism and Hinduism coexisted for centuries. Gradually, Hinduism absorbed many Buddhist beliefs, and Buddha was worshipped as a Hindu god. Eventually, Buddhism merged back into Hinduism.

SECTION REVIEW

1. Identify: Brahma, Vishnu, Shiva, Four Noble Truths, Middle Way, Eightfold Path.
2. Define: brahma, atman, karma, nirvana.
3. According to Hindu beliefs, what should be the goal of life?
4. Describe the sects that developed in Buddhism.

2 Great Empires in India

Read to Learn   ■ why the Maurya dynasty succeeded in India
■ what the Gupta empire achieved

By around 512 B.C., the Persians controlled the Indus Valley region. In northeast India, however, Magadha, a strong Aryan kingdom, formed alliances with its neighbors to rebuff the Persians. Magadha eventually extended its power as far as the Ganges region, creating a large state.

Magadha was the first of several strong empires to rule northern India between 600 B.C. and 500 A.D. But all Indian rulers faced serious obstacles in uniting the many Aryan kingdoms, in part because invaders regularly penetrated northern India seeking new conquests.

Founding the Maurya Empire

By 334 B.C., the Magadhan state had declined in strength. In 321 B.C., Chandragupta Maurya (CHUHN druh GUP tuh MAWR yah) ousted the last ruler of Magadha and established the Maurya dynasty. Chandragupta founded the largest empire yet seen in ancient India. The empire included the whole of northern India from the Bay of Bengal to the Hindu Kush Mountains. To Chandragupta's court at Pataliputra (PAH tah lih POO trah) came ambassadors from all over the world. One Greek envoy reported that the entire city was surrounded by a wide moat and wooden walls. He counted 570 watchtowers along the walls.

The emperor lived in a splendid wooden palace and was attended by servants dressed in gold-embroidered robes. It appears that women took an active role at court. A Greek envoy reported that armed women guarded the emperor and hunted with him. Because he feared assassination, the emperor seldom left the safety of the palace. However, he established the basis for efficient government.

Maurya rulers after Chandragupta divided the vast empire into provinces. Governors sent out from the capital oversaw tax collecting, justice, and defense. The emperor had absolute power, but he was advised by a council of ministers. Government spies traveled in disguise through the empire, reporting on the honesty of officials. These paid informers used homing pigeons to send messages to the capital. To improve communications, Maurya emperors built roads and made local governors responsible for repair of the roads.

Under the Maurya dynasty, trade flourished. Indian merchants exported elephants, silk, cotton, perfumes, and precious stones to China and to the Hellenistic cities of western Asia. Chandragupta's son traded with the Seleucid kings, heirs to Alexander the Great's eastern conquests. (See page 89.) Once he wrote to the Seleucid ruler Antiochus requesting a sample of Greek wines, raisins, and a Sophist philosopher. Antiochus sent the first two items but politely replied that the Greeks did not export philosophers.

Asoka

The best known Maurya emperor is Asoka (uh SOH kuh), who ruled from about 269 B.C. to 232 B.C. Under Asoka, the empire reached its greatest size. (See the map below.) After a brutal campaign to subdue Kalinga, a state in southern India, Asoka learned that more than 100,000 people had been slaughtered. Stricken with remorse, he renounced violence and warfare. Soon after, he converted to Buddhism because it rejected hatred and killing.

Map Skill *Maurya emperors extended their rule over much of India. The Maurya Empire, shown here, reached its greatest extent under the emperor Asoka. Why was Maurya expansion probably limited to the north?*

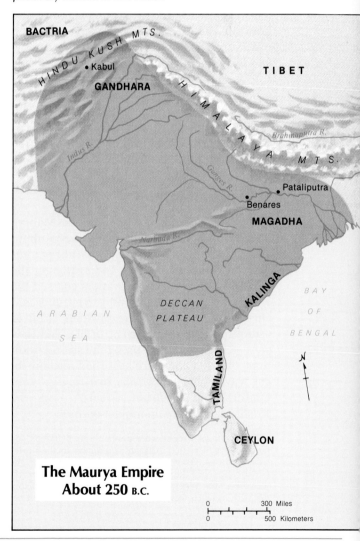

The Maurya Empire About 250 B.C.

Following his conversion to Buddhism, Asoka set out to rule by example instead of by force. He relaxed the harsh justice of earlier rulers. Government officials traveled across the empire teaching the importance of good works, nonviolence, and religious toleration. Asoka himself journeyed through the empire, urging people to live in peace with one another. Asoka's edicts were inscribed onto stone pillars set along the roads for all to see. "It is good to give," proclaimed one edict, "but there is no gift, no service, like the gift of Righteousness."

During Asoka's reign, Buddhism became a strong influence in daily life. The emperor built many *stupas* (STOOP uhs), large, domelike structures that contained the remains of saintly monks. He encouraged pilgrimages, or journeys to religious shrines. To make travel easier, he repaired roads and built rest houses. Wells were dug and fruit trees were planted to provide water, shade, and food for weary pilgrims.

Asoka also helped spread Buddhism by sending missionaries to Ceylon, Burma, and the rest of Southeast Asia. Along with Buddhist beliefs, missionaries introduced other aspects of Indian civilization to the peoples of Southeast Asia.

An Age of Invasions

Civil war shattered the unity of the Maurya Empire after Asoka's death. Between about 180 B.C. and 300 A.D., many small kingdoms rose and fell in northern India. During the same period, numerous invaders crossed the Hindu Kush Mountains into the Indus and Ganges river valleys. The invaders tried to establish their own patterns of life. But they were generally caught up by the strong traditions of India and were absorbed into the local way of life. However, two foreign conquerors, the Bactrian Greeks* and the Kushans, did have an impact on India.

---

*The Bactrian Greeks were descendants of Greek soldiers who had settled in Bactria, a region to the northwest of India. As you will recall, after Alexander the Great conquered the Persian Empire, he invaded northwestern India. When his weary army mutinied, Alexander withdrew. However, some of his soldiers stayed behind.

Major Events in India 500 B.C.–500 A.D.	
500 B.C.*	Magadha rulers unite Aryan kingdoms
326 B.C.	Alexander the Great invades India
321–183 B.C.	Maurya Empire
269–232 B.C.	Asoka rules Maurya Empire
250–150 B.C.*	Bactrian kingdoms flourish
78*–227 A.D.	Kushan Kingdom
320–467 A.D.	Gupta Empire
450 A.D.*	Hun invasions begin

*Approximate dates

In the second century B.C., the Bactrian king Demetrius pushed deep into northwestern India. Like Alexander the Great, Demetrius encouraged the blending of east and west. For example, Bactrian coins carried both Greek and Indian inscriptions. Demetrius transformed his capital at Gandhara into a Hellenistic city. Greek sculpture influenced Indian stonemasons, and Indian scholars studied Hellenistic medicine, astronomy, and astrology. Like other invaders, however, the Bactrian Greeks were eventually absorbed into Indian culture. Finally, around 30 B.C., a new wave of invaders swept into India and defeated the Bactrians.

Among the newcomers were the Kushans, who conquered the northern plain in the first century A.D. During the Kushan kingdom, which survived for about 200 years, Indian civilization flourished. An able Kushan ruler, Kanishka (kuh NIHSH kuh), supported the arts and medical studies and encouraged building.

Like Asoka, Kanishka converted to Buddhism. He greatly influenced its development by convening a council of 500 monks to regulate Buddhist teachings. Out of these meetings came the Mahayana school of Buddhism. (See page 131.) Furthermore, Kushan rulers opened India to greater trade with China. The increased contacts helped spread Mahayana Buddhism along caravan routes into Central Asia and China.

The Gupta Empire

The third century A.D. was a time of upheaval in India. However, out of the confusion rose a powerful new empire ruled by the Gupta dynasty. The rule of the Guptas, from 320 A.D. to about 535 A.D. is considered a golden age because India enjoyed peace and made advances in the arts and sciences. During the same period, the Western Roman Empire was collapsing.

The founder of the new dynasty, Chandra Gupta I (CHUHN druh GUP tuh), successfully reunited the warring states of northern India. Through marriage, Chandra Gupta gained control of the Ganges River, the main trade route across the northern plain. At the height of Gupta power, the empire reached to the Narbada (ner BUHD uh) River. (See the map at right.)

The greatest achievement of the Guptas was the renewal of peace and prosperity. According to Fa-hsien, the Chinese Buddhist monk who visited India about 400 A.D., serious crime was rare. Fa-hsien reported that in the years he traveled about India he was never attacked.

Hinduism was the dominant religion under the Guptas. Buddhist influences remained, but during the Gupta Empire Buddhism in India lost its separate identity and was gradually absorbed into Hinduism.

In the late 400s A.D., the Gupta Empire became weak. About the same time, Huns invaded from Central Asia and dealt the final blow to the empire. For about 1,000 years after the breakup of the Gupta Empire, small, independent kingdoms ruled in India.

Central and Southern India

In central and southern India, fighting among many small kingdoms prevented unity. Kingdoms in the Deccan Plateau occa-

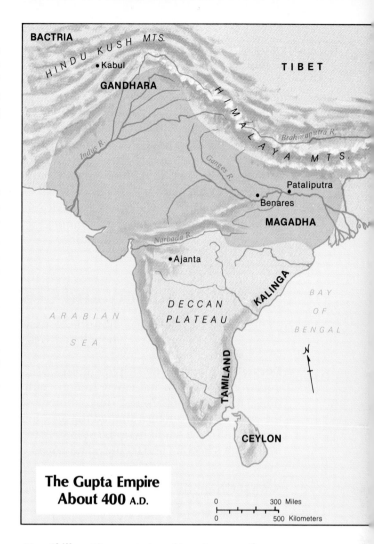

The Gupta Empire About 400 A.D.

0 — 300 Miles
0 — 500 Kilometers

Map Skill *After centuries of invasions, northern India was reunited by the Gupta dynasty, who revived the old Maurya capital at Pataliputra. What territories included in the Maurya Empire (see page 133) were not included in the Gupta Empire?*

sionally came under the control of northern kingdoms. But the Dravidians, who had established kingdoms further south in Tamiland, were never conquered by northerners.

The traditions of the ancient kingdoms of the south were different from the traditions of the Aryan north. For example, the Dravidians spoke a language called Tamil. Despite the variety of cultures in central and southern India, Hinduism spread steadily into these regions. Hinduism absorbed the gods and religious practices of the southern

135

peoples. For this reason, Hinduism became a diverse religion with many different gods.

Trade was important to the Tamil kingdoms of the south. Tamil sailors crossed the Indian Ocean with cargoes of silks, spices, and wild animals, which were highly prized in the Roman Empire. During the reign of Augustus, Tamil merchants traveled to Rome—a trip that took four years. Tamil rulers upgraded harbors and built wharves to attract the profitable overseas trade. As the Roman Empire declined, the Tamil kingdoms increased their trade with China.

3 Indian Society and Culture

Read to Learn
- how the caste system affected Indian life
- how Indian religion influenced art

During the Maurya and Gupta empires, Hinduism continued to influence Indian traditions. Religious beliefs not only influenced the caste system but also shaped the arts and literature. In the same period, Indians made important scientific and technical advances.

Social Changes

Under the Maurya and Gupta dynasties, a growing concern for religious purity led to a more restrictive caste system. Many new subcastes emerged, and caste rules became more complex. People of different castes were prohibited from speaking together or eating at the same table. By the time of the Gupta Empire, contact with "untouchables," or outcasts, was severely restricted. Untouchables had to strike a piece of wood as they entered a town so that people could hear them and avoid them. Marriage outside a person's caste became almost impossible.

Changes in Indian society also affected the status of women. Under Hindu laws, women could own a certain amount of money, jewelry, and clothing, but they had fewer rights than in earlier Aryan society. Increasingly, women married in their very early teens. As a wife, a woman's first duty was to obey her husband and his family, with whom she and her husband lived. If a man died before his wife, she stayed with his family but was expected to devote herself to her husband's memory.

Because a widow was considered unlucky, she was isolated and generally ignored by her husband's family. As a result, in some parts of India, widows threw themselves on their husband's funeral fires rather than endure isolation. A widow who died in this manner was known as a sati, or "virtuous woman." Some Hindus believed that such an action removed the sins of both the woman and her husband. A widow of a high caste was more likely to feel family pressure to become a sati than a woman of a low caste.

Caste also influenced other family practices. For example, high caste women were more secluded than women who had to earn a living outside the home. The practice of having more than one wife was more common in wealthy families than among the lower classes. A first wife was in charge of the household. Her dominant position was assured if she gave birth to sons.

In Indian families, sons were valued much more than daughters. Only a son could perform the proper sacrifices at his father's funeral, which enabled a man's soul to pass into the next life. Furthermore, a son carried on the family line.

Art

Most ancient Indian art reflected religious themes. For example, giant stupas were raised to honor the Buddha. Although the Buddha had forbidden his followers to worship statues or idols, this teaching was later ignored. As a result, sculptors decorated Buddhist stupas with elaborate carvings showing gods and animals as well as scenes from the life of the Buddha.

During the Kushan kingdom, a new style of sculpture flourished. Gandharan art, as it is called today, reflected Greco-Roman influences. The most typical subject of Gandharan sculptors was the Buddha. They portrayed him as a graceful figure. The half-closed eyes and suggestion of a smile were meant to convey the compassion the Buddha had shown toward all living things.

During the Gupta Empire, artists produced some of India's finest paintings and sculptures. The best-preserved examples of Gupta art were found in the cave temples at Ajanta (uh JUHN tuh). Centuries before the Guptas, monks had excavated these caves to use as temples and monasteries. Gupta artists decorated the walls of the Ajanta caves with brilliantly colored murals.

Literature

During the Gupta Empire, many fine writers added to the rich literature of India. The greatest figure in Indian literature during this period was Kalidasa (KAH lee DAH sah), who wrote poems and plays in the fifth century A.D. Kalidasa drew on ancient legends to write about the gods, nature, and love.

In one poem, "The Birth of the War-God," Kalidasa dramatically pictured a battle between an army of demons and a god. Before the demons go into battle, they see a fearful sight foretelling the future:

> The sun put on a ghastly robe
> of great and terrible snakes, curling together,
> as if to mark his joy
> at the death of the enemy demon.

While poets such as Kalidasa were writing in Sanskrit in northern India, the Tamil-speaking kingdoms of the south produced

At Ajanta in western India, artists painted murals on the walls of cave temples. Most of the Ajanta paintings illustrate the life of Buddha, but this scene, painted during the Gupta Empire, shows different castes and ethnic groups living in India.

their own fine literature. The lives of ordinary people, the grim results of famine, and the fierceness of warfare were featured prominently in Tamil writings. Among the earliest known Tamil poets was a woman named Avvaiyar (AH vay YAHR). In the following excerpt, Avvaiyar praises the conduct of her king:

> My king, when rich, freely gives food away,
> when poor he eats with his men.
> He is the head of the family of the poor,
> yet great is he, with his sharp-pointed spear.

Science and Technology

Science and technology flourished during the Gupta Empire. Scholars gathered in cities, where they taught young men from the upper class. Early universities and monasteries became important centers of learning in ancient India.

Indians made a major breakthrough in mathematics that influenced the rest of the world. They developed the concept of zero and developed a symbol for it. They also devised a decimal system, with symbols for the numerals 1 through 9. Today, these symbols are known as Arabic numerals because Western Europeans learned them from the Arabs. The Arabs had adopted the Indian decimal system around 700 A.D. At the time,

137

Europeans were using the cumbersome Roman numerals.

Indian physicians made important medical advances. They made medicines from animal, plant, and mineral sources. They knew the importance of keeping wounds clean, invented the scalpel for use in surgery, and were skilled in setting broken bones. In addition, they developed plastic surgery to a high degree. A thousand years later, Europeans learned this art from the Indians.

About 100 A.D., a great Indian doctor, Caraka (kah RAH kah), established a code of ethics to be taught to all medical students. Like the Hippocratic Oath of ancient Greece, this code governed medical behavior.

Indians demonstrated great technological skills in several areas, especially metalworking. For example, Indian metalworkers made excellent steel for weapons and armor. They also produced a very high grade of iron. The Iron Pillar of Delhi, a solid iron column 23 feet (7 meters) tall, was erected during the Gupta age. Despite the annual monsoon rains, the iron in that column has never rusted. In addition, Indians produced many textiles and dyes that were in great demand as export items.

SECTION REVIEW

1. Identify: Ajanta, Kalidasa, Avvaiyar, Caraka, Iron Pillar of Delhi.
2. (a) List two ways in which the caste system became more restrictive during the Maurya and Gupta ages. (b) How did the status of women change?
3. Why were sons valued in Indian families?
4. What was the main subject of Indian art?
5. Describe two contributions Indians made to mathematics.

4 The Shaping of Chinese Traditions

Read to Learn
- how Confucianism affected Chinese life
- how Taoism shaped Chinese traditions

In China, as in India, thinkers puzzled over perplexing questions of human nature and the place of the individual in society and in the universe. Unlike Hindus or Buddhists, who wanted to free the individual soul from its cycle of rebirth, Chinese philosophers were concerned with this world. They sought ways of establishing a stable, orderly society.

Between 500 B.C. and 200 B.C., three significant schools of thought emerged in China: Confucianism (kuhn FYOO shuhn izm), Taoism (DOW izm), and Legalism. Each proposed a different route for achieving good government. Each viewed the individual in society in a different way. Yet all three philosophies profoundly influenced China for over 2,000 years.

Confucius: A Great Teacher

Confucius, the most influential Chinese philosopher, was born around 551 B.C. He was a scholar who held a minor government position. Confucius tried to gain higher office but was unsuccessful. Eventually, he became a teacher to the sons of noble families. Although Confucius always regretted his failure to achieve high political office, his teachings had enormous impact on Chinese civilization.

Confucius lived during the late Chou dynasty. As you read in Chapter 4, this period saw frequent warfare among feudal lords. The violence and the moral decay of Chou China troubled Confucius. To return to the harmony of the past, he suggested a code of conduct based on high moral ideas. For years, Confucius traveled about China, seeking to convert warring rulers to his way of thinking. But none of the rival feudal lords would follow his ideas.

Confucius spent his last years teaching students in the hope that they would continue his campaign to encourage high ethical

Through Their Eyes ■ The Sayings of Confucius

Confucius learned about government first-hand during the years he traveled to different feudal courts seeking political appointments. He gained a reputation for wisdom and acquired a devoted following of students. At the time, few rulers were willing to follow his advice, but later his teachings became the foundations for Chinese government.

Confucius did not record his teachings. However, his students often inscribed his answers to questions. They would write: "K'ung Fu-Tze says." In China, K'ung was a family name; Tze meant master or philosopher. Thus, they wrote: "The Master K'ung says." When European visitors to China first heard of the great philosopher and teacher, K'ung Fu-Tze, they pronounced the name "Confucius." The following excerpts from the Analects include some answers Confucius gave to people who sought advice on government and the right way to act.

From the *Analects*

Tzu Chang asked Confucius about humanity. Confucius said: "To be able to practice five virtues everywhere in the world constitutes humanity. These virtues are courtesy, magnanimity, good faith, diligence, and kindness. He who is courteous is not humiliated; he who is magnanimous wins the multitude; he who is of good faith is trusted by the people; he who is kind can get service from the people. . . .

If a ruler himself is upright, all will go well without orders. But if he himself is not upright, even though he gives orders they will not be obeyed. . . .

Lead the people by laws and regulate them by penalties, and the people will try to keep out of jail, but will have no sense of shame. Lead the people by virtue and restrain them by the rules of decorum [good taste], and the people will have a sense of shame, and moreover will become good. . . ."

Tzu Kung asked about government. Confucius said: "The essentials are sufficient food, sufficient troops, and the confidence of the people. If you are forced to give up one of these three, you should first let go of the troops. If you are forced to give up one of the

two remaining, you should let go of food. For from of old, death has been the lot of all men, but a people without faith cannot survive. . . ."

When Confucius was travelling to Wei, Jan Yu drove him. Confucius observed: "When there is a dense population, people having grown numerous, enrich them. And when one has enriched them, what should be done next is to educate them."

1. According to Confucius, what are the five virtues?
2. Which essential of government does Confucius say is the most important? Do you agree?

standards. In the years after his death in 479 B.C., his ideas slowly won acceptance. Eventually, they became the official philosophy of China.

The Confucian Code of Conduct

Confucius was interested in ways to organize a good society. To him, a good society was one that preserved peace and order among individuals and between people and their government. As a result, Confucianism, or the teachings of Confucius, was a practical philosophy. It offered a code of conduct for individuals to follow in their social and political relationships. Confucius did not write books, but his followers collected his teachings into the *Analects*.

The Confucian code of conduct stressed virtues such as loyalty, courtesy, hard work, and kindness. If people practiced these virtues, Confucius believed, the result would be social harmony. Confucius set out five basic relationships that defined everyone's place in society. These were the relationships between ruler and subject, parent and child, husband and wife, older brother and younger brother, and friend and friend.

The five relationships determined how society should be organized. In each relationship, each individual had responsibilities, or duties, toward the other. Confucius reasoned that if everyone obeyed his or her duty, an orderly, balanced society was possible. For example, the ruler had the responsibility to provide good government. At the same time, the subject owed loyalty and respect to the ruler. He also felt that a ruler could achieve more by setting a good example than by passing laws.

Because the family was the basic unit of Chinese society, Confucius emphasized family relationships. He felt that the virtues of loyalty and respect for authority were essential to the family. Thus, he stressed *filial piety*, respect for one's parents and elders. A child was expected to show filial piety to both parents as well as to other relatives. Although women were considered inferior to men, sons and daughters learned to honor their mothers.

The Impact of Confucianism

Unlike Hinduism or Buddhism, Confucianism was not a religion. Confucius accepted traditional Chinese religious practices. He believed in the power of heaven, where the gods and the ancestors' spirits lived. But his teachings were mainly concerned with life on earth. The goal of Confucianism was not the soul's salvation but order in society.

Over the centuries, Confucian ideals shaped Chinese society. Chinese law was based on Confucian principles, and the idea of filial piety shaped family life. Emperors ordered temples honoring Confucius to be established in every province. Furthermore, Confucian scholars became the main force in government. Every candidate for government office had to memorize the *Five Classics* and the *Four Books*, which contained the teachings of Confucius and his followers.

Yet Chinese rulers sometimes strayed from Confucian ideals. Emperors occasionally used Confucius' name to demand obedience from their subjects without providing the good government that was required of them. Even so, Confucian ideals remained at the heart of Chinese civilization.

Taoism: Following "The Way"

Taoism was another philosophy that shaped Chinese traditions. Little is known about its founder, Lao-tse (low dzoo). However, his teachings have survived in the *Tao Te Ching*, or *The Way and Its Power*. Like Confucius, Lao-tse was concerned with how to achieve a good society, but he totally rejected the rules of behavior and duties laid down by Confucius.

Lao-tse taught that the goal of life was to become attuned to the tao. The *tao* was a universal force that could not be defined but could only be felt. The tao also meant the way or the road a person followed to reach that goal. Lao-tse believed a person reached harmony with nature not by using reason but through contemplation. Unlike Confucius, who demanded social involvement, Lao-tse cautioned against doing anything.

To the Taoists, the best government was the one that governed the least. "The more laws and edicts are imposed," began one Taoist saying, "the more thieves and bandits there will be."

Taoism was both a religion and a philosophy. Taoism was concerned with ways of improving a person's life in this world, rather than with salvation. The Chinese believed that spirits and ghosts were everywhere and had to be appeased. Taoist priests provided charms and magic that could influence the spirits. As a result, Taoism became immensely popular among the common people. Taoist philosophy stressed simplicity, meditation, and a closeness with nature.

The Taoist emphasis on nature shaped Chinese science and technology. Taoists recorded the movement of the planets, thereby increasing knowledge of astronomy. Taoists also studied and recorded their observations in chemistry and botany. Taoist priests may have invented gunpowder for use in firecrackers to frighten ghosts. Taoists may also have developed the magnetic compass to determine the most favorable position for graves. Later, the magnetic compass would make long ocean voyages possible.

The Strict Code of Legalism

Legalism was the third major Chinese philosophy. Among its chief supporters was Han Fei Tzu (hahn fay dzoo), who died in 233 B.C. Unlike Confucius, Han Fei Tzu was not interested in ethical conduct. He also op-

posed the Taoist emphasis on meditation. He felt that the way to create a stable society was through efficient government. And he believed that the ruler should have absolute power to make the system work.

Legalism was an authoritarian philosophy—that is, it taught unquestioning obedience to authority. Han Fei Tzu said that people were easily swayed by greed or fear. Only the ruler knew how to look after their best interest. Therefore, the ruler should make laws as needed, enforcing them with rich rewards for obedience and severe punishment for disobedience.

To the Legalists, rule by law was far superior to the Confucian idea of rule by good example. Legalists had such a low opinion of human nature that they did not believe people were capable of loyalty, honesty, or trust. Only the threat of harsh punishment, they argued, would ensure order and stability in society. As you will read in the next section, China's first emperor adopted Legalist ideas as he set about unifying the country.

SECTION REVIEW

1. Identify: Confucius, Lao-tse, Han Fei Tzu.
2. Define: filial piety, tao.
3. What were the five basic relationships according to Confucius?
4. What kind of government did the Taoists favor?
5. According to Han Fei Tzu, how could a stable society be created?

5 Unification of China

Read to Learn ■ how the Ch'in dynasty reorganized China
■ how the Han built a powerful empire

Confucius, Lao-tse, and Han Fei Tzu all lived at the end of the Chou dynasty, when civil wars disrupted Chinese political life. During this period, ambitious feudal lords created powerful states. In the third century B.C., at the same time that Rome was conquering

Italy, the feudal state of Ch'in was defeating its rivals in China. By 246 B.C., the Chou dynasty had come to an end, and the Ch'in had centralized power. Although the Ch'in Empire was shortlived, a unified China was the goal of all succeeding dynasties.

141

First Emperor of China

In 221 B.C., the victorious ruler of Ch'in emerged as master of China. He founded the Ch'in dynasty* and adopted a new title: Shih Huang Ti (shee hwahng dee), meaning "First Emperor."

Shih Huang Ti was determined to centralize power in his own hands. To do this, he reorganized the old feudal states into provinces and appointed provincial officials responsible to him. His policies were guided by the ruthless principles of Legalism.

With iron discipline and constant watchfulness, Shih Huang Ti imposed unity on China. He eliminated all opponents, by execution if necessary. Some ancient Chinese sources claim that he forced 120,000 noble families to resettle in his capital so he could watch over their activities. Wearing disguises, he would spy on his own officials.

The emperor also tried to control ideas and prevent the teaching of different points of view. He ordered the burning of almost all books. Only practical works, he said, were worth saving.

---

*Some scholars suggest that the name China came from the Ch'in dynasty.

Like Roman rulers, the Chinese emperor issued coins, dug new canals, and built a highway system that radiated out from the capital to distant regions. The improvements in transportation helped to bind the empire together. Yet these impressive achievements took a terrible toll of human lives. The Ch'in government forced millions of peasant laborers to work on roads and canals. Many died of starvation or overwork.

The emperor's most spectacular achievement was the construction of a long defensive wall known today as the Great Wall of China. The Great Wall connected many smaller walls that had been built to prevent nomadic tribes from raiding northern China. It stretched for 1,400 miles (2200 kilometers), from the Yellow Sea to the interior of China. Although the Great Wall did not always hold back invading armies, it established a clear boundary between China and "barbarian" foreigners.

Shih Huang Ti set out to create an empire that would last forever. Yet it collapsed within a few years of his death in 210 B.C. After eight years of turmoil, a general seized power and established the Han dynasty, which lasted for over 400 years.

During the reign of Shih Huang Ti, tens of thousands of laborers worked on the Great Wall. The huge stone wall stretches across the mountains and valleys of northern China. It was completed, some said, at the cost of one life for every stone put in place. Chinese emperors posted guards all along the Great Wall to defend northern China from barbarian invaders.

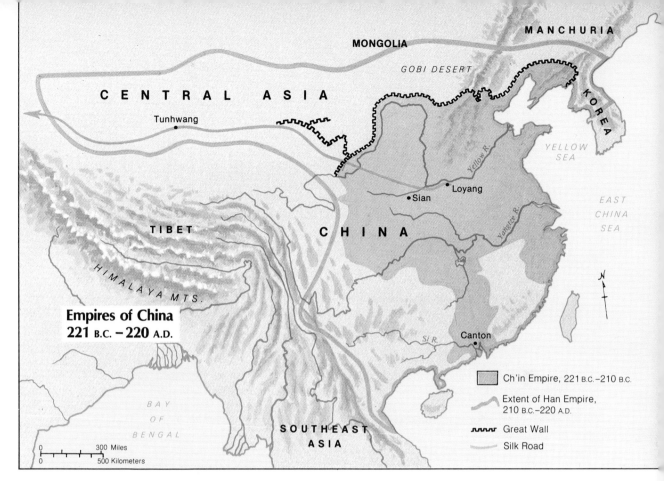

MONGOLIA

MANCHURIA

GOBI DESERT

CENTRAL ASIA

Tunhwang

KOREA

YELLOW SEA

TIBET

CHINA

Sian Loyang

Yellow R.

Yangtze R.

EAST CHINA SEA

HIMALAYA MTS.

**Empires of China
221 B.C. – 220 A.D.**

BAY OF BENGAL

Si R. Canton

SOUTHEAST ASIA

N

☐ Ch'in Empire, 221 B.C.–210 B.C.

Extent of Han Empire,
210 B.C.–220 A.D.

〰〰〰 Great Wall

Silk Road

0   300 Miles
0   500 Kilometers

Map Skill   *Ch'in and Han rulers greatly expanded the borders of China and spread Chinese civilization over a wide area. Like the Roman Empire to the west, the Han Empire enjoyed two centuries of peace and prosperity. Why do you think Han rulers extended the Great Wall westward?*

Founding the Han Dynasty

During the Han dynasty, China enjoyed one of its most brilliant periods. Han emperors restored the unity achieved by Shih Huang Ti and expanded the borders of China. They also adopted Confucianism and spread Chinese culture over much of East Asia.

The best known Han ruler was Wu Ti (woo dee), the "Warrior Emperor." When Wu Ti ascended the throne in 140 B.C., the Huns were threatening China in the north and west. These nomadic people were ancestors of the Huns who would invade Europe in the fourth century A.D. Wu Ti drove the Huns back and extended the Han Empire over Central Asia, southern China, and parts of Southeast Asia.

An energetic and ambitious ruler, Wu Ti believed that the Han Empire included all lands under heaven. By the time Wu Ti died

in 87 B.C., he had established peace that was to last for about 200 years. Soldiers patrolled the Han Empire from the Yellow Sea to Central Asia and protected thriving trade along the caravan routes.

An Efficient Civil Service

When Han rulers centralized power, they needed well-trained officials to administer the government. They encouraged education to provide these officials.

Education for service. The system of education that developed under the Han dynasty influenced Chinese culture for 2,000 years. The Han thought government officials should be thoroughly familiar with the teachings of Confucius. As a result, students memorized the Confucian classics. They also learned Chinese history and law.

143

The teachings of Confucius influenced education for women as well as for men. Women at court, for example, learned the correct behavior for every occasion. This painting on silk shows an imperial governess and two of her students. The governess is writing instructions on proper conduct at court, which the young women must memorize.

The requirements of Chinese education were rigorous. Learning to read the complex Chinese language was a life-long task. Scholars were also expected to perfect their skills in calligraphy, the art of fine writing. Furthermore, they had to memorize an immense amount of material. For example, the Chinese code of law consisted of 960 scrolls. Only science and mathematics were missing from the demanding course of studies. Chinese scholars did not consider these subjects to be essential.

The civil service examination. The Han developed a system of testing candidates for government service. In theory, the civil service examination, as it was called, was open to anyone. But usually only the sons of nobles or government officials could afford the years of study needed to pass the rigorous tests.

The civil service examination involved extensive tests that were given on the local, provincial, and national levels. The provincial examinations alone lasted for three days. During these three days, students were walled up in cells, where they ate, slept, and wrote their examinations. The fortunate few who reached the highest level took their final examinations before the emperor.

In order to pass the exams, a candidate had to have a thorough knowledge of the Confucian classics. This requirement increased the influence of Confucianism on the government. Although most people could not afford to prepare for the exams, a few people were able to move up in society by passing the examinations and becoming government officials. This examination system contributed to social and political stability through many succeeding dynasties.

Chinese Advances in Art and Science

During the Han dynasty, the Chinese made significant advances in learning. The Ch'in emperor had introduced a uniform writing system.* By 100 A.D., scholars had compiled a dictionary of 10,000 Chinese characters. About the same time, the Chinese invented paper. Gradually, they began to write on paper instead of bamboo, wood, and silk.

---

*This official writing style remained largely unchanged until 1949. Although the Chinese spoke different dialects, they could all read the same written language.

During the Han period, many written histories appeared. Like the Greek historian Herodotus, Ssu-ma Ch'ien (soo mah chih YEHN) traveled extensively before writing. He claimed that his work, *Memoirs of a Historian*, was entirely factual and contained no fanciful creations. Chinese rulers studied histories such as this to learn what policies had succeeded or failed in the past.

The Chinese also made advances in science. Like the Greeks, they based their ideas on observation. They also tried to discover natural laws. "Eclipses are regular occurrences," wrote the philosopher Wang Ch'ung, "and are not caused by political action." Chinese astronomers observed sunspots that were not described by Europeans until the 1600s A.D. Timekeepers invented sundials and waterclocks superior to any instruments known elsewhere. Under the Han dynasty, an accurate calendar was developed. It remained in use until 1912.

Practical inventions improved the lives of the common people. For example, the wheelbarrow made it easier for peasants to carry heavy loads, and the water mill reduced the time needed to grind grain. The development of the harness made farming more efficient because animals could be used to pull plows. Weavers developed better looms, which increased silk production.

Trade and Travel

Han emperors encouraged commerce between China and western Asia and Europe. The silk industry in China expanded rapidly. Silk was light and easy to carry, and it commanded high prices in foreign markets such as Rome. In addition to silk, the Chinese traded jade, bronze, and lacquerware for horses, rugs, and Roman glass.

New trade routes meant more contacts between China and other parts of the world. Camel caravans laden with exports traveled from Chinese cities to Central Asia and the Middle East. So much silk was carried on this route to the west that the route became known as the Silk Road. (See the map on page 143.) Sea routes between Southeast Asia and India also opened up.

Traveling merchants helped introduce new products. For example, envoys of the emperor Wu Ti who had visited Bactria introduced grapes and alfalfa into China. Among the most important effects of the increased trade and travel, however, was the spread of Buddhism.

The Chinese developed a process for making paper about 100 A.D. They used bark from mulberry trees, rags, and fishing nets. These materials were beaten into a pulp, which was then stiffened with starch. Next, papermakers rolled the pulpy mixture into sheets and dyed them to an even color. In this paper shop, the paper hangs on racks so that customers can select the sheets they want to buy.

Buddhism in China

The first Buddhist missionaries to China were apparently well received, although their ideas spread slowly. To many Chinese, the new religion, which taught respect for all life and rejected worldly desires, seemed to be an offshoot of Taoism. Yet Buddhism differed from both Taoism and Confucianism. For example, Buddhist monks and nuns left their families for a life of poverty and seclusion. This practice ran against the Chinese devotion to the family. Buddhism was also unlike Chinese philosophies because it was mainly concerned with an afterlife.

Nevertheless, Buddhism appealed to many Chinese. Intellectuals were interested

145

in the ideas contained in Buddhist literature. Peasants found spiritual comfort in the Buddha, who recognized the pain and suffering of this world and offered hope.

Buddhism attracted many new converts after the downfall of the Han dynasty in 220 A.D. Like Rome, the Han Empire had been unable to defend its borders against invaders. Weak leadership and economic problems hastened its collapse. The fall of the Han dynasty plunged China into civil wars.

After 220 A.D., contact between China and the Mediterranean world declined. However, China and India maintained a steady flow of trade and travel. The Chinese Buddhist monk Fa-hsien, you will recall, vis-

ited India about 400 A.D. Visitors returning from India brought back Indian ideas in such fields as medicine, science, and art.

SECTION REVIEW

1. Locate: Great Wall, Silk Road.
2. Identify: Shih Huang Ti, Wu Ti.
3. Why did Shih Huang Ti build the Great Wall?
4. (a) Why did Han rulers encourage education? (b) What areas of study were considered most important?
5. (a) List two practical inventions of the Chinese during the Han dynasty. (b) How did each make life easier?
6. Why did Buddhism appeal to some Chinese?

Chapter 9 Review

In Perspective

By 600 B.C., Hinduism had developed from Aryan religious beliefs. Hindu beliefs were closely tied to the caste system, which defined everyone's role in society. Eventually Buddhism grew out of Hinduism. Both religions influenced Indian civilization. Buddhism also spread to other parts of Asia.

In the fourth century B.C., the Maurya dynasty established an empire across north-

ern and central India. The emperor Asoka converted to Buddhism and brought peace to India. Later, during the Gupta Empire, India enjoyed a golden age.

In China, philosophers looked for ways to establish order in society. Confucius taught that people should follow an ethical code of conduct. Taoists believed people should find harmony with nature. Legalists emphasized the importance of strict laws.

The Ch'in emperor followed Legalist ideas in unifying China. Later, Han leaders followed Confucian thought. They built a powerful empire that lasted 400 years.

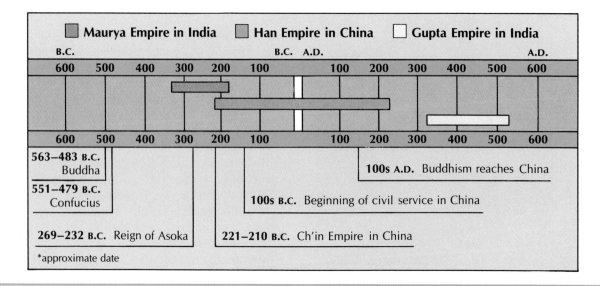

Recalling Facts

The following statements describe beliefs or practices in Hinduism, Buddhism, Confucianism, Taoism, or Legalism. Identify the religion or philosophy each statement describes.

1. Strict laws and harsh punishment will ensure good government.
2. The goal of life should be freeing the soul so it can achieve reunion with atman.
3. Nirvana can be found through the Middle Way.
4. Both a ruler and the people should follow an ethical code of conduct.
5. The Four Noble Truths explain the cause of suffering.
6. People acquire good karma by obeying caste rules.
7. Filial piety should govern behavior within the family.
8. The best government is the one that governs least.

Chapter Checkup

1. Explain how Hinduism supported the caste system in India.
2. (a) How were Hinduism and Buddhism similar? (b) How were they different? (c) What happened to Buddhist beliefs in India during the Gupta Empire?
3. (a) What problems did rulers face in uniting India? (b) How did the Bactrian Greeks influence Indian civilization? (c) What contributions did the Kushans make?
4. Describe Indian achievements in each of the following areas: (a) art; (b) medicine; (c) technology.
5. How did Confucianism affect each of the following aspects of Chinese society: (a) family life; (b) education; (c) government.
6. (a) How did the First Emperor centralize power in China? (b) How did the Han dynasty build on the First Emperor's achievements? (c) What new policies did the Han introduce?

Critical Thinking

1. **Expressing an Opinion** Do you think Confucianism, Taoism, or Legalism was most likely to produce a peaceful, orderly society? Explain your choice.
2. **Comparing Civilizations** (a) In what ways was the Han Empire like the Roman Empire? (b) How was it different?
3. **Comparing Ideas** (a) What were the main beliefs of Hinduism? (b) What were the main ideas of Confucianism? (c) How might the ideas of Hinduism and Confucianism contribute to different outlooks on life?

Relating Past to Present

1. (a) How did the Chinese civil service examination ensure that qualified people were chosen for government? (b) What subjects or skills do you think civil service exams in the United States today should test? Explain your answer.

Developing Basic Skills

1. **Map Reading** Study the map on page 143. Then answer the following questions: (a) What information does the map provide? (b) What part of China did the Great Wall protect? (c) In what directions did the Han Empire expand? (d) What relationship do you see between the Han expansion and Chinese trade with other parts of the world?
2. **Analyzing a Primary Source** Use the steps you learned on page 38 to analyze the excerpts from the *Analects* of Confucius on page 139. Then answer the following questions: (a) What is the nature of the document? (b) What did Confucius say were the essentials of good government? Was this fact or opinion? (c) What evidence suggests that Confucius thought education was important? (d) According to Confucius, how should a ruler behave? (e) Do you think such behavior would ensure good government? Explain.

See page 804 for suggested readings.

Middle Ages in Western Europe

800 Gifts of foreign kings being offered to Emperor Charlemagne.

900s Feudal knights had to provide their own armor, weapons, and horses.

	800	900	1000	1100
POLITICS AND GOVERNMENT	**800** Charlemagne crowned emperor	**900s** Vikings invade Europe		**1096** Crusades to reclaim Holy Land begin
ECONOMICS AND TECHNOLOGY	**800s** Three-field system of farming develops			**1100s** Trade fairs held at Champagne
SOCIETY AND CULTURE	**800s** Charlemagne orders monasteries to set up schools	**900s** Feudalism develops in response to invasions and warfare		

800 This illustration is from the Book of Kells, an early illuminated manuscript.

Farming in the Middle Ages changed dramatically because of new methods and inventions.

1492 Ferdinand and Isabella of Spain are shown here entering Granada after the defeat of the Muslims.

Scribes, who were often monks, laboriously made copies of manuscripts by hand.

1200	1300	1400	1500

1215 King John of England signs the Magna Carta

1337 Hundred Years' War begins

1492 Ferdinand and Isabella complete reconquest of Spain

1290 Eye glasses are invented

1400s Longbow invented during Hundred Years' War

1321 Dante completes *The Divine Comedy*

1386 Chaucer writes *The Canterbury Tales*

1189 Family and friends gather to see off knights as they leave on the Third Crusade.

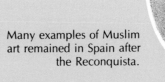

Many examples of Muslim art remained in Spain after the Reconquista.

149

Charlemagne.

10 Foundations of Medieval Europe

(500–1050)

Late in the year 800, Charlemagne (SHAR luh MAYN), ruler of the German kingdom of the Franks, traveled south to Rome. He went there to help Pope Leo III, who had been attacked by rebellious Romans. Charlemagne restored order in Rome, and on Christmas Day he attended Mass at St. Peter's Basilica. Years later, a Frankish writer described the events of that day:

"As the king rose from praying . . . before the tomb of the blessed apostle Peter, Pope Leo placed a crown on his head and all the Roman people cried out, 'To Charles Augustus, crowned by God, great and peace-giving emperor of the Romans, life and victory.' And after [that] he was called emperor and Augustus."

The coronation of Charlemagne was symbolic of changes in Europe after the fall of the Western Roman Empire. In the heart of the old Roman Empire, the head of the Christian Church crowned a German king emperor. By this action, the pope revived the ideal of a unified empire like that of ancient Rome. Roman traditions were just one of the forces that would shape a new civilization during the Middle Ages. This new civilization, known as medieval civilization, blended Roman, Christian, and German traditions.

Western Europe in 500 seemed an unlikely place to build a new civilization. As you read in Chapter 8, Roman political power in Western Europe had collapsed in the fifth century. Trade slowed to a trickle, Roman cities dwindled in size, and some fell into ruins. During the German invasions of the fifth and sixth centuries, trade, travel, and learning declined further. The knowledge of the ancient world as well as practical skills such as road building were largely forgotten. Crude wooden buildings replaced massive Roman structures. Roman roads and aqueducts fell into disrepair.

Despite the disorder and decay, Western Europe was a place of great potential. It had fertile land and other resources, such as timber, furs, and tin. In the early Middle Ages, from about 500 to 1050, a new political system emerged and restored a measure of order.

1 The German Kingdoms

Read to Learn ■ how German kingdoms developed
■ why Charlemagne's empire fell

During the early Middle Ages, different German tribes set up small kingdoms in Italy, Gaul, Spain, Britain, and North Africa. The different kingdoms were constantly at war with each other. Gradually, however, the Kingdom of the Franks established control over much of the Western Roman Empire.

Roman Influence on Government

The governments of the German tribes were simple compared to the complex system Rome had developed to rule its vast empire. Whereas Roman emperors depended on an organized government, German rulers depended on the loyalty of their warriors. German tribes had few government officials and few taxes. Free men gave unpaid military service to their rulers, so taxation was largely unnecessary. The Romans had written law codes to settle disputes among their many peoples. German laws were based on custom and were designed mainly to prevent feuds between families.

As German kings extended their rule over parts of the Western Roman Empire, some adapted ideas of Roman government. For example, when Theodoric (thee AHD uhr ihk) established the Kingdom of Ostrogoths in Italy, he issued a simplified version of Roman law.

In other areas, however, Roman influence was weaker. The Angles, Saxons, and Jutes moved into Britain after Roman legions had withdrawn. These peoples kept their German customs and languages, which eventually evolved into modern English.

The Christian Church helped preserve Roman traditions in the German kingdoms. For example, when the Roman monk Augustine converted the Anglo-Saxons in England, he set up new Christian communities along Roman lines. Furthermore, German kings relied heavily on the clergy, who were almost the only educated people in Western Europe.

The Kingdom of the Franks

The strongest kingdom to emerge in the early Middle Ages was that of the Franks, a small German tribe who lived in the areas of present-day Germany and Belgium. The Franks rose to power in the late 400s under the brilliant but ruthless leadership of King Clovis. Through cunning and treachery, Clovis conquered lands from the Pyrenees Mountains to central Europe.

Clovis's reign reached a turning point when he became a Christian. His wife, who was a Christian, urged her husband to convert, but political interests may also have encouraged him. Clovis thought that the support of the Church in Rome would make him more powerful than neighboring German kings. These kings were also Christian, but they belonged to the Arian sect, which had developed in the early years of Christianity. The Church in Rome, now calling itself the Roman Catholic Church, regarded the Arians as *heretics*, or untrue Christians. Thus, as the only Roman Catholic king in Gaul, Clovis won the Church's support.

When Clovis died in 511, his lands were divided among his four sons, according to German custom. Although Clovis's family ruled until 751, its power had declined by the mid 600s, and the real ruler of the Frankish kingdom was the chief court official, the Mayor of the Palace.

Invasion by the Muslims

In the 700s, the German kingdoms of Western Europe faced invasion by Muslim armies. Muslims believed in the teachings of Islam, a religion founded in the Middle East during the seventh century. (You will read more about Islam in Chapter 13.) Muslims won many converts around the southern rim of the Mediterranean. Then they pushed into Europe through Spain.

The German kingdoms of Spain fell before the advancing Muslim armies, and by 732, Muslim forces were spilling into France. Charles Martel, the Frankish Mayor of the Palace, rallied Christians against the invaders. At a battle near Tours, Christian armies defeated the Muslims and stopped the spread of Islam into Western Europe.

Yet during the Middle Ages, Islamic civilization continued to affect Europe. For centuries, Muslims ruled Spain, Sicily, and parts of southern Italy. From these areas, the advanced learning of Islam reached the people of Europe.

The Age of Charlemagne

After the defeat of the Muslims, Charles Martel founded the Carolingian (KAR uh LIHN jee uhn) dynasty in the Frankish kingdom and began to organize a strong central government. His son Pepin was elected king by the Frankish nobles. Pepin then had his election approved by the pope. This action symbolized the strong ties between the king and the Church. Later popes would use this incident to justify their claims of authority over political rulers.

After Pepin's death, his son Charles continued to build a strong central government. During his long reign, from 768 to 814, he so impressed his contemporaries that he was called Charlemagne, or Charles the Great.

An able general, Charlemagne conquered an empire that reunited large areas of the Western Roman Empire. (See the map on page 153.) He defeated the Lombards who had occupied Italy. In a hard fought campaign, he won land in northern Spain back from the Muslims. In an effort to spread Christianity, he battled the non-Christian Saxons in the north. In the west, he defeated the Avars and occupied their land.

In 800, Charlemagne journeyed to Rome. As you read at the beginning of the chapter, Pope Leo III crowned him "Emperor of the Romans." The pope's action reaffirmed the Roman goal of a universal empire.

Charlemagne was an efficient, energetic ruler. From his court at Aachen (AH kuhn), he kept firm control over the empire. He recruited talented officials to carry out his policies, designed to improve government and unify the empire. Royal officials, called *missi dominici* (MIH see   DOHM ih NEE kee), or lord's messengers, checked on local nobles who were responsible for justice and defense in their own lands. Charlemagne issued regulations, which helped establish uniform laws, and appointed local judges to uphold the laws.

Charlemagne promoted Christianity throughout the empire. He strongly supported the work of Christian missionaries to convert the Saxons. He also encouraged the efforts of the Church to organize *parishes*, or rural districts, each with its own priest. To support the parishes, Charlemagne required all Christians to pay a *tithe*, 10 percent of their income, to the Church.

A Revival of Learning

To encourage education, Charlemagne invited scholars from all over Europe to his court. Alcuin (AL kwihn), a learned Anglo-

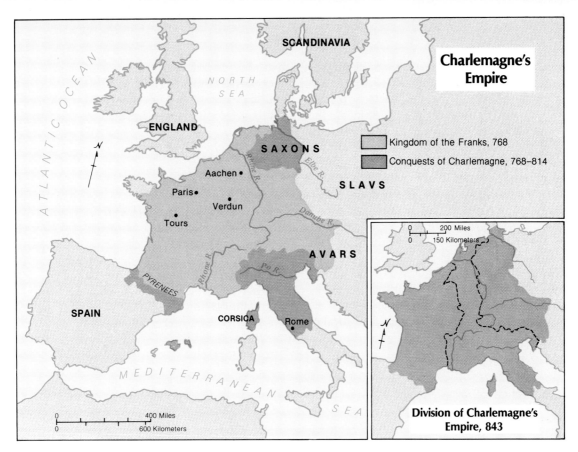

Map Skill *Charlemagne had a reputation as "the most able and noble-spirited" ruler of his time in part because he was successful in warfare. Notice the areas he added to Frankish lands. After Charlemagne's death, his empire was divided by the Treaty of Verdun. What geographic factors made it difficult for the empire to remain united?*

Saxon monk, set up a palace school to teach Charlemagne's sons and daughters as well as the children of Frankish nobles. Charlemagne himself could read, but he did not know how to write. Yet he is reported to have slept with pen, ink, and paper under his pillow.

Charlemagne issued rules for the education of the clergy. He also ordered monasteries to establish schools and libraries. In monastery schools, students learned Latin, which became the language of the Church.

Monks made copies of the Bible and of the few surviving ancient Greek and Roman texts. They also developed the art of illumination. *Illumination* involved decorating the first letter of a paragraph and the margins of a page with brilliant designs. In addition, monks invented a clear written script known as the Carolingian minuscule. Romans had written only in capital letters. Carolingian minuscule used both capital and lower case letters, the form of writing still used today.

By encouraging scholarship throughout the empire, Charlemagne strengthened the foundations of medieval civilization. During his reign, the distinctions between Roman and German traditions blurred, and a new European culture began to emerge.

A New Wave of Invasions

The heirs of Charlemagne lacked his wisdom and forceful character. They weakened the empire by fighting among themselves. In 843, Charlemagne's grandsons drew up the Treaty of Verdun. This treaty divided the

153

empire into three kingdoms. (See the map on page 153.) Despite the Treaty of Verdun, rulers in the western and eastern regions fought for control of the middle region. These struggles would shape events in Europe for over 1,000 years.

The division of Charlemagne's empire occurred just when a new wave of invaders battered Europe. In the ninth century, the Magyars, or Hungarians, a nomadic people from Asia, drove the Slavs from their lands in Eastern Europe. Soon, both Slavs and Magyars were attacking Western Europe. About the same time, Muslims gained ground in Italy. But the most longlasting invasions were those of the Vikings.

The Vikings were farmers and traders from Scandinavia, the area of present-day Norway, Sweden, and Denmark. A growing population may have forced these expert sailors to seek land in other parts of Europe. Sailing from northern harbors in long boats, the Vikings burned and looted towns, castles, churches, and monasteries in Western Europe.

In 911, the king of the Franks gave part of northern France to some Viking raiders. This region acquired its name, Normandy, from the French word "Norman," meaning "men from the north." Vikings from Sweden explored, raided, and traded along the rivers of Eastern Europe and Russia. Other Vikings settled in Iceland and Greenland. About 1000, the Viking Leif Ericson spent a winter in Newfoundland on the eastern coast of North America.

Map Skill   *During the 800s and 900s, Western Europe was battered by Viking, Magyar, and Muslim invaders. The Viking raids lasted the longest. Which areas did the Vikings attack? Why might they have been able to cover such distances?*

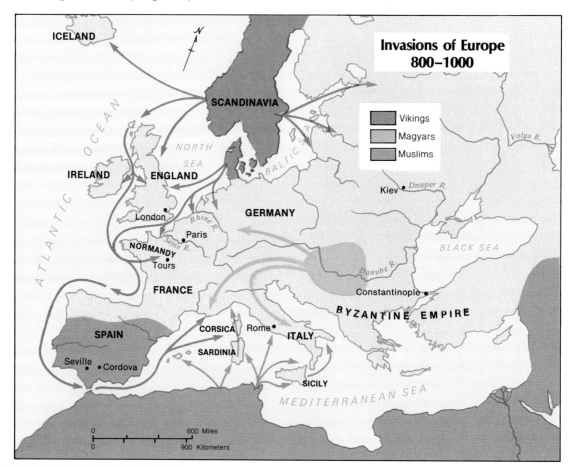

In the ninth century, the Vikings, whom the English called Danes, occupied part of England. The area they took became known as the Danelaw because the Danes lived there under their own laws. Anglo-Saxons resisted the Danish invasions, however, and eventually won back the lost territories.

The Viking invasions seriously disrupted life in Western Europe, but they did not completely destroy the work of Charlemagne. The Church sent missionaries to convert the Vikings. In addition, under strong local leaders, the people of Western Europe resisted the invaders.

SECTION REVIEW

1. Locate: Pyrenees Mountains, Tours, Aachen.
2. Identify: Clovis, Charles Martel, Charlemagne, Alcuin, Treaty of Verdun, Danelaw.
3. Define: heretic, missi dominici, parish, tithe, illumination.
4. Contrast government under the Germans with that under the Romans.
5. How did Charlemagne improve education?
6. What groups invaded Western Europe in the eighth and ninth centuries?

2 Feudal Society

Read to Learn
- what conditions furthered the development of feudalism
- how feudal society was structured

From the death of Charlemagne until about 1000, invasions and warfare disrupted life in Western Europe. Because kings were often too weak to resist the invaders, powerful nobles defended their own lands and maintained order. While remaining loyal to the king, they usually acted independently. The system of rule by local lords who were bound to a king by ties of loyalty is today called *feudalism*. Feudalism brought order out of chaos during the Middle Ages. It also helped produce a new way of life.

The Emergence of Feudalism

Feudalism grew out of German customs. In German tribes, warriors swore an oath of loyalty to their chief. Warriors fought for their leader, and in turn he provided for their needs. Nobles in the German kingdoms carried on this tradition. Lesser nobles would serve as *knights*, or mounted warriors, for a *lord*, or greater noble.

In the eighth century, new technology furthered the development of feudalism. The stirrup changed the nature of warfare. The stirrup supported the knight while he was on horseback. Thus, he could wear heavy protective armor and carry heavier weapons.

But armor and horses were costly, and, to be effective, a knight had to be well trained. Most knights did not have the money to buy armor and horses or the time for training.

Charles Martel realized the value of heavily armed knights in his campaigns against the Muslims. Since he had no money to pay his knights, he granted them rights to land. With the land, a knight could support himself and his family while he served the king. In the next few centuries, the practice of granting land in exchange for military service spread across Western Europe.

During the Viking invasions, powerful lords took control of large tracts of land, which they divided among lesser lords called *vassals*. A lesser lord, in turn, might divide his land among his own vassals. The process could continue down to the lowest knight, who had no vassals. He had only enough land for himself and his family. (See the diagram on page 157.) The relationship between lord and vassal was central to feudalism.

An Unwritten Arrangement

Feudalism was based on a mutual exchange of rights and obligations between nobles. As feudalism developed, a set of unwritten rules

155

evolved to govern the relationship between a lord and his vassal. The rules, which became known as the *feudal contract*, grew out of customs and traditional practices. Eventually, some of these rules were written down.

Under the feudal contract, a lord provided his vassal with a *fief*, or estate. A fief ranged in size from a few acres to hundreds of square miles, depending on the importance of the vassal. The fief included the peasants who worked the land as well as any houses or villages on the estate. The lord still owned the land, but his vassal had the right to use it and pass it on to his heirs. The lord also protected his vassals. He provided a court of justice to settle disputes between vassals, and he acted as a guardian for young children if a vassal died.

In exchange for his fief, a vassal gave his lord military service, usually about 40 days a year. In addition, he agreed to serve his lord on certain holidays and special occasions. A vassal took part in the lord's court of justice, giving advice or participating in legal decisions. A vassal also had financial obligations to his lord. These included payment of an annual fee, called a relief; payment of ransom money if his lord was captured in battle; and payment of a fee when the lord's eldest daughter was married or when his eldest son was knighted.

At a public ceremony, the lord and his vassal confirmed the feudal contract. The vassal knelt before his lord. Placing his hands between the hands of his lord, he swore allegiance to the lord and promised to be loyal. The lord then gave the vassal the rights to his fief. Often, the lord gave his vassal a handful of earth or a blade of grass as a symbol of the fief. The ceremony took place whenever a new fief was granted or when a son inherited his father's fief.

A Complex System

In theory, everyone in feudal society had a lord except the king. The king owned all the land and granted fiefs to his chief nobles. As vassals of the king, the chief nobles owed him loyalty and military service. They, in turn, were lords to numerous vassals. Even commoners such as peasants and townspeople were part of the social structure because they had obligations to the lord on whose land they lived.

In reality, feudal kings had very limited power. They could not collect taxes or enforce laws outside their own estates. As feudal lords, they could summon their vassals to fight. But their chief vassals also ruled large fiefs. These vassals could challenge the king's authority and call on their own knights to support them. Despite a king's limited power, however, people still thought of him as the highest noble in the land.

As feudalism developed, it became more complex because of the practice of subdividing fiefs. With each new generation, fiefs changed hands. Vassals gained land through inheritance, marriage, and war. A powerful lord might inherit a fief that would make him a vassal to a weaker lord. Or a vassal might have several fiefs, each from a different lord. The vassal owed loyalty to each of his lords even if the lords were fighting each other. This practice created a web of conflicting loyalties, which fragmented power.

This detail from an illuminated manuscript shows a king knighting a kneeling warrior. The knighting ceremony began as a fairly simple act. Often, it took place on the battlefield, where a king or lord rewarded a squire's bravery by buckling on his armor, thereby making him a knight.

Feudalism was never a single, unified system. Nor did it emerge everywhere at the same time. It developed first in northern France during the 700s and 800s. It reached the Netherlands, England, and western Germany in the eleventh century. Feudalism was weaker in frontier areas such as eastern Germany, Poland, Russia, and Spain. In Italy, too, it never fully developed.

The Importance of Warfare

Feudalism emerged as a result of invasions. But even when the threat of invasions lessened, warfare continued. Powerful lords competed with one another for power. Nobles fought over boundaries and over inheritance rights. Greed, honor, and family feuds fueled small local wars. When a conflict arose over the rights or obligations of a vassal, the issue was often resolved by warfare.

In the Middle Ages, most battles were small, involving only a few hundred or a few thousand knights. Knights were more likely to be captured than killed because hostages could be held for ransom. But fighting in medieval battles involved tough hand-to-hand combat. Knights wore cumbersome suits of iron armor. A full suit of armor, which weighed up to 30 pounds, was hot and uncomfortable. A knight's horse also had armor to protect its head and flanks. A knight carried heavy weapons such as lances, swords, axes, and maces.

Among feudal nobles, warfare was a way of life. "It gives me great joy to see, drawn up on the field, knights and horses in battle array," wrote one noble. For the peasants who farmed the land, however, warfare was disastrous. An attacking army would destroy their crops, seize their animals, and burn their homes.

Feudal lords built strong stone castles or fortified homes for protection. When attacked, the lord, his family, his vassals, and the peasants from his estate took refuge behind the thick stone walls. Castles were built on top of hills or near rivers for added protection. A heavy iron gate as well as an encircling river or moat helped people defend the castle.

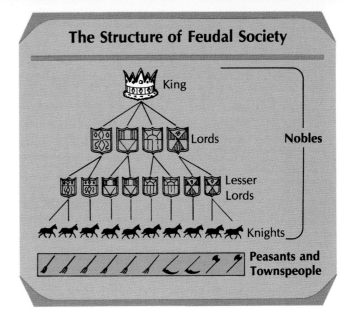

The Structure of Feudal Society

Diagram Skill *Everyone had a well-defined place in feudal society. Nobles could be powerful lords or simply knights. The common people, peasants and townspeople, made up 90 percent of the population. What term could be used to describe feudal society?*

Although castles provided protection, they were unpleasant places to live. They were dark, damp, and drafty and had no windows. Narrow openings high in the walls provided the only light. But the openings also let in cold air, rain, and snow. Banquets were held in a large central hall, where a huge fireplace offered a hint of warmth. Only in the late Middle Ages did homes of nobles become luxurious or even comfortable places to live.

Feudal warfare declined gradually in the eleventh and twelfth centuries. This was partly the result of efforts by the Church to reduce the fighting among nobles. In addition, some feudal lords built large, powerful states and were able to control the fighting among their vassals.

Chivalry: A Code of Conduct for Knights

Beginning in the eleventh century, feudal nobles developed a code of conduct called *chivalry*. The code of chivalry combined Christian values and the virtues of being a warrior. A knight was expected to be brave, generous, and loyal. He was supposed to respect and protect noblewomen and to defend his family's honor.

Chivalry also dictated rules of warfare. For example, armor was so hot that knights wore it only during a battle. According to the code of chivalry, it was disgraceful to attack a knight before he had put on his armor. Chivalry promoted ideals of behavior for knights that reduced the brutality of a fighting age. But few knights followed all the rules. Furthermore, the code of chivalry did not govern a knight's behavior toward peasants and other common people.

Noblewomen in Feudal Society

In early feudal society, warfare dominated life. Since noblemen were the warriors, they dominated society, and noblewomen had few rights. A woman could inherit a fief, but she was not allowed to rule it. Her father, husband, or eldest son acted as her legal guardian. However, some women did gain influence either through their husbands or when their husbands were off fighting. When a lord was absent, his wife could command his vassals and servants.

Among nobles, a woman's father or guardian arranged her marriage. A married woman's main duty was to raise a large family. She also supervised the household and entertained her husband's guests. Because travel was often difficult and dangerous, guests stayed for long visits. A woman had to see that they were well-fed and entertained.

Education for women focused on practical skills. Girls learned to spin, weave, and cook. Women also learned medical remedies, since they usually cared for the sick and wounded. In early feudal society, few men or women could read or write. But later, when women acquired these skills, they would teach their children to read and write.

In the 1100s, the treatment of noblewomen improved. The code of chivalry placed them on a pedestal as objects to be cherished and protected. Wandering poets, or *troubadours* (TROO buh DORS), who entertained at feudal castles did much to further this view. In their songs and poems, they glorified women, praising their beauty, wisdom, and kindness.

The poets' idealistic image of noblewomen was far from reality. Noblewomen, as well as peasant women, worked extremely hard. They gave birth to many children and endured the dangers of disease and warfare.

The lives of most women in the Middle Ages revolved around their homes and families. The life of Christine de Pisan, shown here at her writing table, was an exception to this rule. Christine de Pisan became a professional writer. Born to a wealthy family in Venice, she received an excellent education, which enabled her to write knowledgeably about many subjects.

SECTION REVIEW

1. Define: feudalism, knight, lord, vassal, feudal contract, fief, chivalry, troubadour.
2. How did the stirrup affect the nature of warfare?
3. (a) What duties did a vassal have? (b) What were the responsibilities of a lord?
4. (a) Where did feudalism develop first? (b) Where was feudalism weakest?
5. List three causes of feudal warfare.
6. How did the treatment of women change in the 1100s?

3 Life on the Manor

Read to Learn
■ how people lived under the manorial system
■ how justice functioned during the Middle Ages

During the ninth and tenth centuries, a new economic system, closely tied to feudalism, evolved in Western Europe. Because nobles were busy fighting or training for battle, they depended on peasants to farm their lands.

In early feudal society, most peasants barely produced enough crops to support the nobles and themselves. But by about 1050, advances in agriculture resulted in crop surpluses.

Peasants and Lords

At the heart of the medieval economy was the *manor*, administered by a lord. A manor might include a village or several villages and the surrounding lands. Like feudalism, the manorial system grew out of earlier traditions. Under the Roman Empire, coloni, or peasant farmers, had worked the estates of great landowners. (See page 120.) In exchange for their labor, the coloni had received cottages and small plots of land. The coloni were not slaves, but they could not leave the estate without permission. When German nobles replaced Roman landowners, they retained the coloni system.

During the turbulent years of the early Middle Ages, many free peasants gave their land to powerful lords in exchange for protection. Eventually, they, too, became tied to the lord's land. Peasants who were tied to the land were called *serfs*. By the 1100s, most peasants were considered part of the fief that a lord gave to his vassal. A few peasants could move away if they wanted to.

The relationship between a lord and his serfs involved duties and obligations on both sides. The arrangement was somewhat similar to the one between a lord and his vassals. A lord divided most of the manor land among his serfs, but he reserved a portion, called the *demesne*, (dih MAYN), for his own use. In theory, at least, the lord could not

Chart Skill   On a typical medieval manor such as this one, each peasant family had its own cottage and farmed strips of land in different fields. Peasants also worked on the lord's demesne. What purposes might the meadows, pastures, and woodlands have served? Why do you think the mill was placed so close to the river?

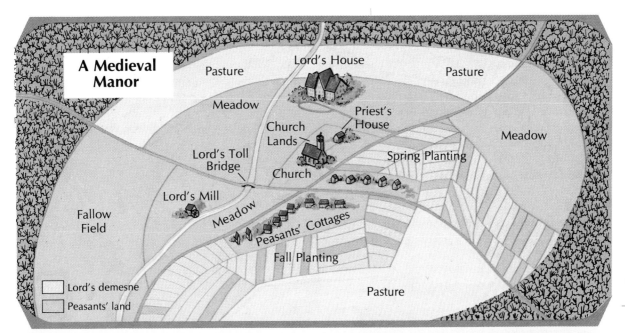

A Medieval Manor

Pasture · Lord's House · Pasture · Meadow · Priest's House · Church Lands · Spring Planting · Meadow · Lord's Toll Bridge · Church · Lord's Mill · Meadow · Fallow Field · Peasants' Cottages · Fall Planting · Pasture

☐ Lord's demesne
☐ Peasants' land

How did a peasant family live in the early Middle Ages? Historian Eileen Power studied many different sources to construct a picture of peasant life. The following description of a typical peasant family is based on her research.

The peasant Bodo and his wife Ermentrude lived during the reign of Charlemagne. Bodo farmed the land on a manor near Paris. Every day, the family rose at dawn. Bodo and his son Wido plowed the fields, tended their small flock of sheep, or worked in their vineyard. Often they joined neighboring peasants to do heavy work such as carting wood and harvesting crops.

Three times a week, Bodo and his neighbors left their own lands to work for the lord of the manor. In this way, they paid rent since the lord owned the land that the peasants farmed. The peasants also paid other fees. Three times a year, Ermentrude walked up to the lord's house to deliver the chicken rent—a fine plump chicken and some fresh eggs.

While Bodo and Wido farmed the land, Ermentrude worked at home. She watched their two smallest children, sheared the sheep, spun the wool, and sewed the garments that would keep her family warm. Some days she worked in the vineyard. She also prepared the breads and puddings that the family ate. Occasionally, they had pork, but meat was a luxury seldom enjoyed by peasant families.

On Sundays and holidays, the family took a break from their daily routine. At the urging of the Church, Charlemagne had forbidden "tending vines, plowing fields, reaping corn and mowing hay, setting up hedges or fencing woods, cutting trees, or working in quarries or building houses" on holy days. Instead, peasants attended Church or celebrated the feast days of saints. After church, they sang, danced, and joked in the churchyard.

Every year on October 9, Bodo and his family would walk to the great fair of St. Denys held just outside the gates of Paris. Merchants from all over Europe came to display their wares at the month-long fair. Even though they had no money to buy the exotic foods, clothes, and jewelry that the merchants offered, peasants enjoyed looking.

Once a year, Charlemagne sent two traveling justices to Paris to check on the local lords. If Bodo had been cheated or injured by anyone, he could take his case before the justices. Even if he had no complaints, he might attend the hearings just to listen. These activities provided brief diversions for the hardworking peasant family.

---

seize peasant land unless the peasants did not fulfill their obligations. The lord was supposed to protect his peasants in time of war and provide justice through the manor court.

Serfs owed their lords certain payments. Peasants had to spend about three days a week working for the lord. They farmed the lord's demesne, repaired his castle, and dug his moat. Each peasant family had to pay rent for the land they farmed themselves. They also had to pay fees to use the mill for grinding grain and the ovens for baking bread. When the head of a peasant family died, his heirs paid a fee for the right to continue farming the land. Because coined money had largely disappeared in the early Middle Ages, peasants might pay their fees with grain, woven cloth, chickens, or eggs.

A Self-Sufficient Community

During most of the Middle Ages, the manor was a small, self-sufficient world. Peasants grew grain for food and raised sheep for wool, which was spun into cloth. In the village, a blacksmith made tools and weapons. Since towns were small and scattered, there was little traffic or trade between the manor and towns. Only a few items such as salt and iron came from outside the manor. The manor had its own court and usually its own church and priest. If a lord owned several manors, a *bailiff*, or agent, managed his smaller estates.

Manors varied in size and physical layout. However, most had certain features in common. (See the diagram on page 159.) Set on the highest land was the manor house.

Depending on the lord's wealth and power, the manor house could be simply a large, fortified wooden house or a huge, stone castle. Below the manor house were peasant cottages clustered in a small village, the church, the lord's mill, and village workshops. Fields and forest lands surrounded the village and manor house.

Peasant life was controlled by the cycle of planting and harvesting. Occasionally, a local fair enlivened the year, and there were important religious festivals, such as Christmas and Easter, to celebrate. But the hazards of warfare, disease, flood, drought, and other natural disasters overshadowed daily life.

Improvements in Agriculture

In the early Middle Ages, farming methods were primitive and inefficient. At planting time, peasants tossed seeds onto plowed fields, where grateful birds greedily ate their fill. Few plants grew, and yields were low. However, people gradually adopted new methods and technology. As a result, the manor economy of Western Europe developed an efficient farming system.

Improvements in agriculture began in the 700s and 800s and became widespread after 1000. One important advance was the three-field system, a method of crop rotation. On the manor, there were usually several large fields. Each autumn, peasants planted one field with a winter crop such as wheat or rye. In the spring, they planted a second field with a summer crop such as oats, peas, beans, and barley. They left the third field fallow, or uncultivated, to allow the soil to rest. The following year, the crops were rotated, and a different field was left fallow.

The three-field system was more efficient than earlier farming systems. It spread planting and harvesting over the year, and it did not wear out the soil. New crops, especially peas, helped improve the peasant diet. In addition, by planting different crops, peasants reduced the risk of starvation if disease wiped out one crop.

Advances in agriculture helped peasants produce food surpluses. In this scene, a plowman directs a team of horses that are probably shod with iron horseshoes. The speed of horses made them much more efficient for plowing than oxen. Notice the man shooting the birds that are eating the newly sown seed.

New inventions also increased food production. The heavy plow could turn the dense, moist soils of northern Europe. The invention of the horseshoe and a better harness meant that horses could be used for plowing. Because horses plowed faster than oxen, peasants could cultivate more land and produce more food. The watermill and windmill provided new sources of energy for grinding grain and powering forges. Moreover, in northern France and England, miners began producing large quantities of iron, which was used for farm implements as well as weapons.

The advances in agriculture were especially significant in northern Europe. Peasants produced food surpluses, which supported a growing population. Gradually, as the population increased in the north, the

161

center of western civilization shifted from the Mediterranean northward.

From the mid-eleventh to the thirteenth century, agriculture continued to improve. Lords cleared large areas of forest and drained swamps for farmland. The "Great Clearing" helped some serfs gain their freedom. Work on clearing projects was not one of the serfs' traditional obligations to the lord. Therefore, lords sometimes offered freedom to serfs who would work on clearing new land. Peasants would then live on the new land and pay rent rather than the feudal duties they had owed in the past.

Feudal Justice

During the Middle Ages, lords preserved order on a local, limited basis. They were supposed to provide justice both for their vassals and peasants. Feudal justice was based largely on custom since there were few written laws. One custom recognized the right of an individual to be tried by his peers, or equals. Another prevented a lord from taking away a vassal's fief unless the vassal's peers agreed that the action was just.

A feudal lord administered two courts: one for his vassals, another for the peasants on his manor. Many disputes between a lord and his vassal were settled by war, but some were decided in the court. On such an occasion, a lord would summon all his vassals to meet as a court and decide the issue. Although all free men and women had the right to be tried by their peers, the feudal lord could override a court's decision. The lord or his bailiff presided over the manor court, which settled disputes between peasants. Peasants were also protected to some extent by customs, which had the weight of law.

Most cases in either court were routine trials. In cases of serious crime, however, the accused had two choices. He or she might admit guilt and receive a sentence, probably a fine. Or the accused might deny any guilt. The accused then faced trial by ordeal or, if he were a knight, trial by combat. In trial by combat, another knight challenged the accused to battle. If the accused won, he was considered innocent. If he lost, he was considered guilty.

Trial by ordeal involved a physical test. For example, the accused might have to carry a burning hot iron over a certain distance. If "blood be found [on the iron] the accused shall be judged guilty. But if, however, he shall go forth uninjured, praise shall be rendered to God." Thus, the people believed God decided guilt or innocence of the accused.

SECTION REVIEW

1. Identify: three-field system, trial by combat, trial by ordeal.
2. Define: manor, serf, demesne, bailiff.
3. (a) List two duties a lord had toward his peasants. (b) List three obligations a peasant owed the lord.
4. How did the three-field system make farming more efficient?

---

4 The Medieval Church

Read to Learn ▪ how Christianity extended its influence
▪ how the Church served as a force for civilization

During the Middle Ages, faith in God was an accepted fact of life. A church with its spire pointed toward heaven was a prominent feature in the medieval village. But the Church was more than a place of worship. It became a powerful institution, with its own government, laws, courts, and system of taxation. Furthermore, Christian teachings influenced everyone in feudal society from king to peasant.

Growing Influence of the Church

In the early Middle Ages, the Church faced two difficult tasks in Europe. One was converting non-Christians. The other was adjusting the Church organization to new conditions. Missionaries preached the gospel in northern and eastern Europe. Monks, such as Patrick in Ireland and Augustine in England, won many new converts. In the eighth century, the Anglo-Saxon monk Boniface carried Christian teachings to the German peoples in Saxony. Later, other dedicated men and women converted the Slavs, Magyars, and Vikings. (See the map at right.)

Under the Roman Empire, Christianity had flourished in the cities. Yet in the early Middle Ages, most Christians lived in scattered rural villages. As you read, Charlemagne helped the Church develop a system of rural parishes. A priest was appointed in each parish, which was often a single manor.

Several parishes made up a see or diocese, the district ruled by a bishop. In turn, an archbishop administered several dioceses. In the Middle Ages, bishops and archbishops were usually nobles. Parish priests generally were commoners. The pope in Rome was the spiritual leader of Christendom, as Christians in Western Europe called their world. He also ruled the Papal States, lands in central Italy owned by the Church.

For most Christians, the parish priest was the only contact with the Church. The priest celebrated the Mass in the manor church. He helped care for the sick and poor. He also collected the tithe, or tax paid each year to the Church. If he could read and write, he served as the only teacher in the village. Yet many parish priests were poorly educated. Few priests understood the Latin phrases they recited during the Mass. Charlemagne had been so shocked at their ignorance that he introduced reforms to make sure that parish priests could read and write Latin.

The Church and Feudalism

The Church became an essential part of feudal society. During much of the Middle Ages, kings and great feudal lords depended on educated clergy to fill positions in their courts. The clergy thus gained great influence in political affairs. Furthermore, churches and monasteries controlled huge tracts of land in Western Europe. High

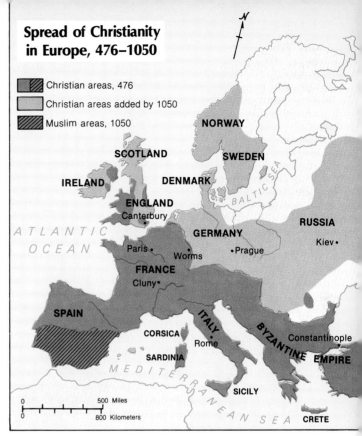

Map Skill *The Christian Church played a central role in shaping the civilization of Western Europe during the early Middle Ages. In the centuries after the fall of Rome, into which areas did missionaries carry Christianity?*

church officials were feudal lords with their own fiefs and vassals. Some Church officials were also vassals to a king or other lord. As churchmen, they were not required to fight in battle. But they often had to decide between loyalty to a feudal lord and loyalty to the Church.

The Church influenced every aspect of feudal life. Church officials gave blessings at ceremonies for knighthood. Documents such as marriage contracts between two noble families were sworn before a member of the clergy. Knights waged war in the name of Christian ideals. They frequently carried a holy relic, or sacred object, embedded in their sword belts.

In the eleventh century, the Church used its authority to reduce feudal warfare. It tried to enforce periods of peace known as the "Peace of God." The Church also demanded that warring nobles avoid harming noncombatants and clergy "so that those who travel and those who remain at home may enjoy security and peace." When nobles ignored such restrictions, the Church declared that fighting must stop between Friday and Sunday each week and during religious holidays. These efforts may have contributed to the decline of feudal warfare in the 1100s.

Importance of Salvation

Faced with the hardships of everyday life, people found comfort in Christian teachings. As you read in Chapter 8, Christians believed that life on earth was less important than salvation and everlasting life in heaven. The route to salvation was through the *sacraments*, the seven sacred rites, which were administered by the Church through the parish priest.

The Church taught that the alternative to salvation was eternal suffering. Those who wavered in their faith were thought to be doomed to this fate. Since the Church believed that its mission was to save souls, it used harsh measures to enforce discipline.

Christians who disobeyed the Church faced the threat of *excommunication.* People who were excommunicated could not receive the sacraments. They lost their property and were treated as outcasts. A king who defied the Church could also be excommunicated. The pope could release the king's subjects from their feudal obligations.

In the twelfth century, the Church established a special court, the Inquisition, to try people accused of heresy, or holding beliefs that differed from those of the Church. If convicted, the guilty person was usually burned at the stake. If a heretic admitted guilt and asked forgiveness, the Church court then decided whether to show mercy. As you will read in Chapter 12, the Church used such measures more often in the late Middle Ages.

Religious Orders

In the early centuries A.D., some Christian men and women believed that the best way to serve God and achieve salvation was to withdraw from the world. This tradition gave rise to religious orders, groups of monks and nuns who dedicated their lives to God. During the Middle Ages, monasteries and convents dotted the European landscape. Some religious orders became rich, powerful landowners. Their land, like other feudal manors, was farmed by serfs and free peasants.

In the sixth century, St. Benedict established a monastery at Monte Cassino in Italy. To ensure strict discipline among the monks, he drew up a set of rules. According to the Rule of St. Benedict, a monk "shall not have anything of his own ... neither a book, nor tablets, nor a pen." In addition to poverty, monks took vows of chastity, or purity, and of absolute obedience to the abbot, the head of the monastery. The Rule of St. Benedict served as a guideline for other religious orders.

Although the Church barred women from becoming priests, women were allowed to become nuns. Some nuns, like the Abbess Hilda in England, achieved lasting fame. "So great was her prudence," wrote an Anglo-Saxon monk after Hilda's death, "that not only ordinary folk, but kings and princes used to ask her advice ... and take it."

Life in a monastery or convent revolved around prayer and hard work. A bell summoned monks or nuns to prayer at dawn and at set hours during the day. Each monk or nun also had assigned duties such as working on the monastery land, copying manuscripts, studying, and teaching.

Some religious orders helped improve medieval life. Monastery farms often experimented with new agricultural techniques. Some orders were famous for their herb gardens and medical knowledge. Charitable religious orders cared for the sick, orphans, and the homeless. Since inns were rare, monasteries and convents welcomed travelers. They also established schools, usually for the children of nobles.

Later in the Middle Ages, two teaching orders became prominent. In the thirteenth century, a wealthy young man, Francis of Assisi, decided to dedicate his life to poverty and service. He founded the Franciscan order of monks. The Franciscans owned no property or worldly goods. They survived on

During the Middle Ages, religious orders helped preserve and pass along the knowledge of earlier times. Monks and nuns copied ancient manuscripts and established schools to spread learning beyond their own orders. This picture shows several monks preparing illuminated manuscripts while others ring the monastery bells to call people to prayer.

charity and worked to help the poor. About the same time, a Spanish priest, Dominic, founded a new order of monks. The Dominicans were teachers who set up schools in the new towns that were springing up in the 1200s.

A Force for Civilization

Parish priests, religious orders, and Church officials helped to make Christian values part of everyday life in Western Europe. The medieval Church also helped preserve ancient learning. In the ninth century, Charlemagne had ordered monks to copy classical Greek and Latin texts. But at the time, education was in such a poor state that the monks, who were supposed to know Greek and Latin, often wrote in the margins of manuscripts: "Greek, it can't be read." The situation slowly improved as clergy became better educated.

Generally, only a few scholars studied the ancient works, and they rejected any portions that were contrary to Christian faith. However, by carefully copying Greek and Roman works, they preserved the traditions of the ancient world for future generations.

Eventually, great monasteries and convents flowered as centers of learning and the arts. On the island of Iona, for example, Irish monks produced beautiful illuminated manuscripts such as the *Book of Kells*. Like other religious works, this beautifully decorated masterpiece was designed to glorify the Christian faith. Outstanding religious music was also composed in many medieval monasteries.

Challenges to Church Authority

Despite its strength, the Church faced challenges to its authority. One problem it faced was control of the clergy. Influential churchmen often ignored vows of poverty and obedience. They dressed in expensive clothes and lavishly entertained kings and nobles. Corruption and immorality among the clergy led to demands for reform.

By the tenth century, some monasteries had grown extremely rich and careless in their standards. A reform movement begun by the monastery of Cluny in France swept across Europe. The abbot of Cluny banned *simony*, the buying and selling of religious offices. He also stressed the virtues of hard work and service to God. The Cluny reforms helped restore discipline among the clergy.

The Church also waged a constant campaign against people who disagreed with its teachings. Some heretics denied the value of the sacraments in achieving salvation.

Others, like the Albigensians (AL buh JEHN see uhnz) in southern France, condemned the Church for its worldliness. They wanted the Church to return to what they saw as the simple ways of early Christianity. In the 1200s, the Church launched a holy war to destroy the Albigensians, whom they saw as a dangerous sect.

The Church also met opposition when it competed with kings and feudal lords for political power. As you will read in Chapter 12, when kings began to centralize their power, they considered the Church an obstacle. In the late Middle Ages, bitter disputes erupted between popes and kings.

SECTION REVIEW

1. Identify: Peace of God, Inquisition, Rule of St. Benedict, Hilda, Francis of Assisi, Dominic, Book of Kells, Albigensians.
2. Define: sacrament, excommunication, simony.
3. What two tasks faced the Church in the early Middle Ages?
4. Describe two ways in which the Church influenced feudal society.
5. Why did Christians believe the sacraments were important?
6. How did religious orders improve life?
7. How did the Cluny reforms affect the Church?

Chapter 10 Review

In Perspective

After 500, Europe adjusted to the conditions that resulted from the collapse of the Roman Empire in the west. For centuries, small German kingdoms competed for power. Under Clovis, the kingdom of the Franks emerged as the strongest. About 800, Charlemagne united a large empire that covered much of Western Europe. The revival of learning under Charlemagne became the foundation for medieval civilization.

Civil wars and invasions devastated Europe in the century after Charlemagne's death. During this time, feudalism took firm root. Local lords established order over their own lands. In feudal society, vassals and lords had mutual duties and obligations.

A new economic system based on the manor ruled the lives of peasants. Most peasants were serfs tied to their lord's land. Important technological progress eventually improved medieval life. Peasants cleared new lands and produced food surpluses.

In the early Middle Ages, the Church extended its influence across Europe by converting people to Christianity and organizing rural parishes. It also helped shape the values of feudal society. Through the educated clergy, the Church preserved some learning from the ancient world.

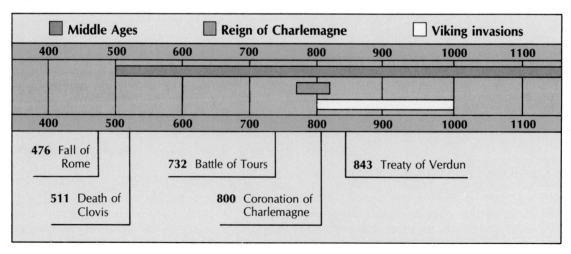

■ Middle Ages	■ Reign of Charlemagne	□ Viking invasions

| 400 | 500 | 600 | 700 | 800 | 900 | 1000 | 1100 |

476 Fall of Rome	732 Battle of Tours	843 Treaty of Verdun
511 Death of Clovis	800 Coronation of Charlemagne	

Recalling Facts

Choose the word or phrase that best completes each of the following statements.

1. The battle of Tours was important because it (a) stopped the Muslim advance into Europe; (b) ended Roman rule in the west; (c) showed the strength of the Church.

2. Charlemagne sent out missi dominici to (a) collect taxes; (b) teach people to read and write; (c) check on the administration of justice and defense.

3. After Charlemagne's death, his empire was (a) conquered by Muslims; (b) attacked by Vikings; (c) ruled by the Danes.

4. A vassal's chief duty to his lord was (a) military service; (b) paying ransom; (c) advice in legal matters.

5. Under the manorial system, a peasant owed his lord (a) a tithe; (b) about three days work each week; (c) free use of the village mill.

6. One way the Church disciplined its critics was by (a) demesne; (b) excommunication; (c) simony.

Chapter Checkup

1. (a) What steps did Charlemagne take to improve government and unify the empire? (b) How did he help revive learning?

2. What happened to Charlemagne's empire after his death?

3. (a) Why did feudalism develop in Western Europe? (b) How did feudalism become more complex?

4. (a) What rights did noblewomen have in feudal society? (b) What were their main duties? (c) How did the lives of noblewomen and peasant women differ? How were they similar?

5. (a) Describe a medieval manor. (b) In what ways was it self-sufficient?

6. (a) How did changes in methods and technology improve agriculture? (b) What effect did the "Great Clearing" have?

7. Describe how each of the following influenced life in the Middle Ages: (a) parish priests; (b) "Peace of God"; (c) religious orders.

Critical Thinking

1. **Expressing an Opinion** Do you think feudalism was an effective system for enforcing law and order? Why or why not?

2. **Taking a Stand** In the fifteenth century, some people referred to the early Middle Ages as the "Dark Ages" because they thought civilization had disappeared after the fall of Rome. Do you agree or disagree? Explain.

3. **Applying Information** The medieval Church has often been described as the heir of the Roman Empire. What evidence supports this view?

Relating Past to Present

1. (a) Why was the code of chivalry important in medieval society? (b) Are there any modern rules of conduct that might be considered a code of chivalry? Explain.

Developing Basic Skills

1. **Map Reading** Study the map on page 153. Then answer the following questions: (a) What information does the map provide? (b) Describe the territories Charlemagne added to his empire. (c) What do you think prevented further expansion? (d) How did the Treaty of Verdun affect Charlemagne's empire?

2. **Using Diagrams** The diagram on page 159 illustrates many common features of medieval manors. Study it carefully and answer the following questions: (a) What major buildings were located on a manor? (b) How was manor land used? (c) Why do you think peasants were given strips of land in different fields? (d) How does the diagram show that the manor was self-sufficient?

3. **Making Generalizations** Reread the feature on page 160 and the discussion of life on the manor on pages 159–161. Then answer the following questions to make generalizations about peasant life: (a) What three facts support the generalization that peasants worked very hard? (b) Make a generalization about payments peasants owed their lord. (c) What generalization can you make about peasants' leisure time?

See page 804 for suggested readings.

11 The Height of Medieval Civilization

(1050–1350)

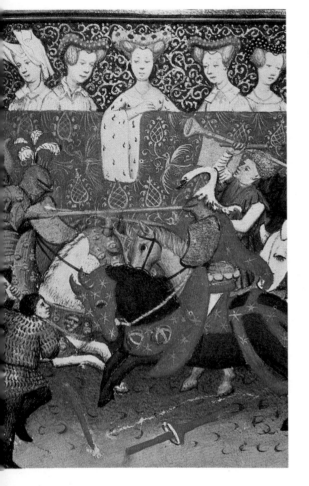

Two knights joust in a tournament.

Tournaments, or contests between knights in armor, were a lively feature of the late Middle Ages. Tournaments were sometimes held to celebrate religious occasions or simply for entertainment. Only the wealthiest nobles could afford to sponsor tournaments and entertain the throngs of knights and their followers who gathered for the event. Even peasants could attend the exciting contests since the tournaments were held out of doors.

In the 1300s, an eyewitness described a tournament: "Sir John Holland and Sir Reginald de Roye armed themselves, and rode into the spacious enclosure . . . where the tilts [contests] were to be performed. There were stands for the ladies, the king, the duke and the many English lords who came to witness this combat. The two knights were so well armed that they lacked nothing. Their spears, battle-axes, and swords were brought to them. Each was mounted on the best of horses. They placed themselves about a bow-shot distance apart, and at times they pranced about on their horses; for they knew that every eye was upon them.

"They viewed each other through the visors of their helmets, then they spurred their horses, spear in hand. Though they allowed their horses to gallop as they pleased, they advanced on as straight a line as if it had been drawn with a cord; and hit each other on their visors with such force that Sir Reginald's lance was shivered into four pieces. . . . All present thought this had been gallantly done."

The knights took up new lances and galloped at each other two more times. Then, they fought "three rounds with swords, battle-axes, and daggers, without either of them being wounded." Not all tournaments ended so well. Sometimes, groups of mounted knights charged each other on horseback, and the event quickly became a violent brawl.

Tournaments kept knights in training for war, but they also served to channel the energies of knights into mock battles rather than real ones. Thus, tournaments may have helped reduce the fighting that had plagued Europe in the early Middle Ages.

The knight in armor has become a symbol of the late Middle Ages, from about 1050 to 1350. During these centuries, medieval civilization reached its height. While the pace of change was slow, a stable feudal society did emerge. Feudalism, the manor economy, and the Church provided the solid foundations for that society.

1 Economic Patterns

Read to Learn ■ why trade revived in the late Middle Ages
■ how medieval towns developed

In the eleventh and twelfth centuries, warfare declined in many parts of Western Europe. The manor economy became more productive, and the population expanded. Trade revived and towns grew. Slowly, peasants and nobles became aware of a larger world outside the isolated, self-sufficient manor.

The Revival of Trade

Trade and towns had declined dramatically during the early Middle Ages, but they had never completely disappeared. Viking traders carried honey, furs, and rough woolen cloth from Scandinavia to the towns of Antwerp and Bruges (broozh) in Flanders. (See the map on page 170.) In France and England, some trade continued along ancient Roman roads. In northern Italy, cities such as Genoa, Pisa, and Venice traded with the cities of the Byzantine Empire.

Constant feudal warfare had limited trade. But as warfare declined in Western Europe, trade revived. Wool was the basis for much of that early trade. Sheep farming was widespread in Flanders and England. Weavers in Antwerp and Bruges produced a fine woolen cloth that was prized all over Europe. The Italian towns of Milan and Florence also prospered from the wool trade.

In the eleventh and twelfth centuries, newly built fleets from the coastal cities of northern Italy regained control of the Mediterranean from the Muslims, who had dominated it for centuries. During the Crusades, which you will read about later in the chapter, these Italian cities extended their trade to the eastern Mediterranean.

Gradually, some obstacles to trade were overcome. Crumbling roads of the Roman Empire were slowly repaired and traffic increased. Even so, both river traffic and overland travel were expensive because each feudal lord charged tolls to cross his territory. The gradual reappearance of a money economy also simplified trade.

Trade Fairs and the Hanseatic League

Annual trade fairs held in centrally located areas were an early sign of economic revival. The fairs of Champagne in northern France became the bustling marketplaces of Europe. Traders from northern and southern Europe met in Troyes and other towns to exchange goods. During the 1100s, nobles of Champagne actively encouraged trade fairs. They provided protection for people traveling to the fairs. They also rented booths to merchants and hired money changers to

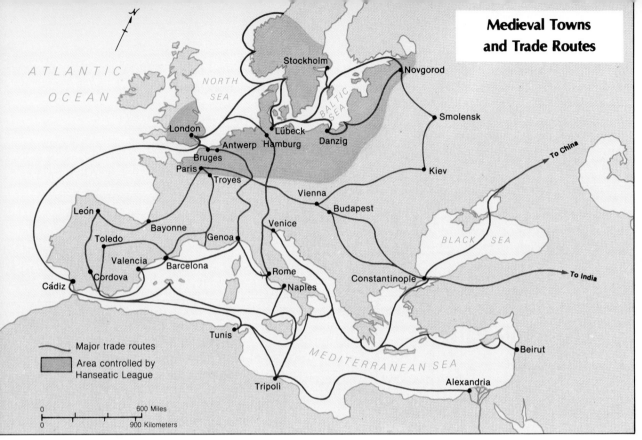

Map Skill   *Italian city-states and cities of the Hanseatic League dominated trade in Western Europe during the late Middle Ages. Merchants from Venice and Genoa brought silks and spices from the eastern Mediterranean to markets in Bruges and Antwerp. There, they met merchants who traded in furs, fish, and textiles. What other towns and cities of northern Europe were becoming important centers of trade?*

evaluate coins from different regions. The nobles profited from fees and a sales tax imposed on all transactions.

At the Champagne fairs, Italian traders bought raw wool, furs from Russia, and hides. Northern merchants and feudal lords bought luxuries from the eastern Mediterranean as well as weapons, armor, and horses. The trading lasted for weeks or months. By the late 1100s, at least one fair was usually in progress at any time in the year.

The trade fairs became elaborate events. They introduced people to the languages, customs, and goods of other places. Peasants as well as nobles and townspeople attended. Peasants gazed at exotic cloaks made of peacock feathers and marveled at monkeys imported from Asia.

In the late 1200s, the Champagne trade fairs declined in part because rents and

taxes became too high. Competition from the Hanseatic League also hurt the fairs. The Hanseatic League was an association of about 80 large towns and cities in northern Germany that banded together for protection and trade purposes. Most of these cities bordered the North or Baltic seas.

Members of the Hanseatic League had large shipping fleets because their economies had originally been based on the herring industry. They used their fleets to enter the profitable wool trade, carrying wool between England and Flanders. Eventually, the league dominated the shipping lanes of northern Europe. League fleets cleared the northern seas of pirates so that its ships could safely transport rich cargoes of furs, timber, and fish. The league also gained control of the overland trade through Germany and Italy.

Member cities had immense power. They coined their own money, negotiated treaties, and maintained their own armies and warships. They were even strong enough to wage war on rulers who threatened their interests.

Growth of Towns

As trade increased, merchants established permanent headquarters in ancient Roman towns along the trade routes and at important river crossings. Some merchants and traders stayed year-round at the site of trade fairs. Gradually, these headquarters grew into towns with inns to shelter travelers. Artisans such as shoemakers, bakers, carpenters, and tailors also moved to towns, where they found customers for their goods and services.

The growth of towns stimulated local economies. Peasants sold food grown on the manor to townspeople. With the money they earned, peasants could buy products in town. Local industries, such as the manufacturing of wool cloth in Flanders, expanded. In time, Flanders became a great commercial center. Elsewhere, towns specialized in other industries, such as lacemaking or leatherworking. As townspeople prospered, they demanded imported products. These demands further stimulated trade.

Chartering a town. Most medieval towns were located on lands owned by feudal lords or monasteries. Townspeople paid fees to the local lord or abbot. But often their obligations were unclear or disputed. As towns grew, townspeople began to ask for *charters,* written documents that guaranteed their rights.

Although charters varied, most gave towns limited control over their own affairs. Town charters usually allowed townspeople to pay the lord a fixed money rent instead of many separate fees. Some charters prevented the lord from seizing the property of townspeople. Others permitted towns to set up special courts for commercial cases. An important provision in many charters granted freedom to serfs who spent a year and a day in a town. "Town air makes a person free" was a common medieval saying.

Some feudal lords resisted the efforts of townspeople to win charters, but many came to realize that towns were a valuable source of money. Fees from town courts and taxes on trade helped feudal lords pay for the luxuries they wanted. Furthermore, towns trained their own militias. These militias fought for the lord in wartime.

A middle class. Even though medieval towns were under the control of feudal lords, townspeople were neither peasants nor nobles. They were part of a new, middle class between nobles and peasants. In France, townspeople were called the bourgeoisie (boor zhwah ZEE); in England, they were called the burgesses; and in Germany, the burghers.

Some townspeople were runaway serfs. Others were peasants who had bought their freedom. Still others were merchants or artisans. Like everyone else in medieval society, townspeople developed a social hierarchy. However, in towns, wealth rather than hereditary titles or land ownership usually determined a person's status. A person's status was also related to the guild system that developed in many towns.

Medieval Guilds

In the charters of many early towns, people were given the right to form a *guild,* an association of merchants and artisans that governed the town. The first guilds, called merchant guilds, governed prices and wages in the towns. A merchant guild also maintained standards of quality on goods produced and sold in town. In addition, it restricted the activities of foreign merchants and settled disputes among guild members in its own courts.

Craft guilds. Because merchants dominated the early guilds, artisans set up craft guilds. Like merchant guilds, craft guilds protected their members and imposed standards of quality to protect the public. Only members of a guild for a particular trade could practice that trade in town. Guilds of shoemakers, weavers, wool dyers, and goldsmiths set prices and wages, regulated work hours, and supervised the standards of goods produced. Craft guilds also provided money to needy members. They sponsored entertainment on religious feast days and contributed to the building and repair of the local church.

Craft guilds established what was considered a just price for their goods. According to the Church, it was immoral to make money at the expense of other people. Pricing goods according to what people would pay was considered sinful. Therefore, a *just price* included the cost of materials plus a reasonable profit. Once the guild set a just price for a product, the price was expected to remain unchanged.

Training for membership. By the late 1200s, craft guilds had begun restricting membership, in part to prevent an oversupply of goods. Only a man who completed a long, rigorous training could become a guild member. At the age of seven or eight, a boy could become an apprentice. An *apprentice* learned the trade from a master crafts-

man who was a guild member. The apprentice earned no wages but was housed, fed, and clothed by the master craftsman.

After an apprenticeship that lasted from 3 to 12 years, the apprentice became a journeyman. A *journeyman* earned wages by working for a master craftsman while he perfected his skills. Eventually, the journeyman submitted a "masterpiece," or sample of his work, to the guild masters. If they decided that his masterpiece met guild standards and that his character was worthy, the journeyman became a master craftsman. Only then could he open his own shop.

Guilds protected their members by preventing competition. Membership in a guild often passed from father to son. Most guilds excluded women, although women worked in many crafts, especially in textiles. However, if a master craftsman died, his wife often kept the business going with his apprentices and journeymen.

Shops of every kind lined the narrow, crowded streets of medieval towns. In this picture, a tailor and a spice merchant sell their wares. In the background, a barber shaves a customer.

Town Life

Most medieval towns had only a few thousand residents. A typical town was surrounded by thick defensive walls. As the town grew, people settled outside the walls, but they retreated inside if the town were attacked. The church, the homes of the wealthiest citizens, and an open square stood in the center of town. Narrow streets radiated out from the central square. Closely packed houses five or six stories high blocked out most of the daylight along these streets.

Medieval towns were always crowded. People walked with care along the streets, where pigs and dogs scavenged in the garbage. Towns seldom had any sanitation system. Waste was simply flung out a window with a warning cry to passersby. Members of the most powerful guilds enjoyed the privilege of walking close to building walls, where they were better protected from debris.

Each craft had its own district within a town. For example, hatmakers and everyone connected with hatmaking would have their shops along the same street. In the medieval economy, this system worked well because suppliers of raw materials, wholesalers, and consumers could all meet in the same place.

Town life had its dangers. Most buildings were wooden. Once fires started, they raged out of control. Thieves and pickpockets haunted the streets. Some towns had night patrols, but assaults could occur at any hour. The greatest danger, however, was the terrible epidemics of smallpox and typhoid, which were made worse by overcrowding.

Yet towns offered many attractions. There were wrestling contests and visiting jugglers. On feast days, guilds produced elaborate plays based on Biblical stories or on the lives of saints. In the late Middle Ages, comedies with clowns and buffoons became popular. But perhaps the main attraction of town life was the opportunity to make money and to rise in society.

As towns grew, they began to play a greater role in medieval life. The great towns of Flanders and northern Italy became bustling centers of commerce and industry. The wealth of these towns contributed to the growth of medieval culture.

SECTION REVIEW

1. Locate: Antwerp, Bruges, Genoa, Naples, Venice.
2. Identify: Hanseatic League.
3. Define: charter, guild, just price, apprentice, journeyman.
4. Where were the main trade centers during the early Middle Ages?
5. List three rights town charters usually gave townspeople.
6. (a) What economic role did the guilds play in the towns? (b) What social role did they play?

2 Medieval Culture

Read to Learn
- how the Church influenced medieval art
- how science and technology advanced in the Middle Ages

In the 1100s, towns became the centers of cultural activity. Trade and commerce expanded peoples' horizons. The reappearance of coined money gave rise to a wealthy class who could afford to educate their children and support the work of artists. However, as the dominant force in society, the Church inspired and supported the flowering of medieval culture.

Art and Architecture

Medieval art and architecture reflected the power and influence of the Church. During the prosperous twelfth and thirteenth centuries, hundreds of churches and monasteries were built of wood and stone. But the greatest efforts were poured into the cathedrals.

The Church, kings, nobles, and townspeople provided the money to build new cathedrals. Construction of a single cathedral could last for 30 years or more. Architects, stonemasons, carpenters, and sculptors might spend their entire lives working on a cathedral that would be completed by their children or grandchildren.

During the Middle Ages, two distinct styles of church architecture developed: Romanesque and Gothic.* The Romanesque style flourished between about 1000 and 1150. The massive churches and monasteries built in this style showed the influence of Roman architecture in the rounded arches and the domed roof. To support the immense weight of the domed roof, the outside

---

*People in the 1500s made fun of the Middle Ages. They called the great medieval cathedrals the work of "barbarians" or Goths. The word Gothic has remained as the name of one style of medieval architecture.

walls were made very thick. Since windows would weaken the walls, only a few narrow slits were included to let in light. The darkness, bare stone walls, and solid arches of Romanesque churches created a sense of the austere, orderly world of the Middle Ages.

In the mid-1100s, French architects overcame great technical difficulties and began to build cathedrals that were tall, light, and airy. The new Gothic architecture depended on inventions such as the flying buttress. The *flying buttress* was a graceful stone arm that leaned against the outside wall to help support the weight of the roof. With this support, architects could make the walls thinner and higher. Gothic cathedrals had tall pointed arches and large windows that lighted the interior. Between 1150 and 1300, townspeople all over Europe rushed to build new cathedrals in the Gothic style.

During the Middle Ages, people saw cathedrals as monuments "to the greater glory of God." The soaring heights and brightly colored stained glass windows of Gothic cathedrals were designed to remind worshippers of the power of God. The Cathedral of Notre Dame (NOH truh   DAHM), shown here, was built in Paris between 1163 and 1200. It is one of the finest examples of Gothic architecture. Notice the flying buttresses at the back of the cathedral.

Painters and sculptors decorated the new cathedrals. Artists created colorful stained glass windows with scenes of Old and New Testament stories. At the cathedral entrance, statues of Christ, the Apostles, or saints reminded worshippers of Christian teachings. In an age when few people could read and write, stained glass and stone sculpture were used to illustrate the Bible.

Literature

In the twelfth and thirteenth centuries, a new style of literature emerged in Europe. The new literature was written in the *vernacular*, the everyday language of the people. Throughout the Middle Ages, scholars wrote in Latin, the language of the Church. Monks wrote histories in Latin, and documents such as town charters were written in Latin. But most people did not speak or understand Latin, and languages varied from region to region.

The vernacular languages that developed in France, Spain, Italy, and Portugal were strongly influenced by Latin. Today, these languages are called Romance languages—from the language of Rome. In Germany, Scandinavia, and England, the vernacular languages were based on German. Today, the languages of these regions are called Germanic languages.

Troubadours wandering from court to court helped spread the use of vernacular languages. They sang love songs and recounted the deeds of legendary warriors in the vernacular. Each region of Europe had its own heroes, although the stories usually focused on the same themes of love and war. Eventually, these tales were written down.

A popular form of vernacular literature was the chanson de geste (SHAN sohn duh JEHST). This long, narrative poem portrayed the ideals of chivalry. One famous chanson de geste, the *Song of Roland*, described the heroic death of Roland, a knight in Charlemagne's army. During Charlemagne's campaign against the Muslims in Spain, Roland and his men were cut off from the main Christian forces. Courageous and loyal to the end, Roland displayed the vir-

tues of a Christian knight. In Germany, Spain, and England, epic poems celebrated heroes such as Siegfried, El Cid, and Beowulf.

The chansons de geste and troubadour poems of love influenced the manners of the nobles by encouraging chivalry and courtesy. However, troubadour poetry had little appeal for the new middle class. Among townspeople, fables were more popular. These short, humorous poems mocked nobles, the clergy, and even the townspeople. In *Reynard the Fox*, for example, animals behaved like humans with such weaknesses as greed and pride.

Perhaps the most famous medieval poet was Dante (DAHN tay), who lived in Florence from 1265 to 1321. In typical medieval fashion, the *Divine Comedy* combined poetry, theology, and history. In the poem, Dante, guided by the Roman poet Virgil, visits souls in hell, purgatory, and heaven. On the journey, Dante and Virgil talk to great historical figures such as Homer and Plato. Although Dante wrote brilliantly in Latin, he composed his masterpiece, the *Divine Comedy*, in Italian. This work was so widely read that it helped establish the Italian vernacular.

Like Dante, the English poet Geoffrey Chaucer influenced vernacular literature. Chaucer's work shows the influence of the town life that developed in the late Middle Ages. In *The Canterbury Tales*, Chaucer wrote about the lives of everyday people rather than legendary heroes.

Centers of Learning

The towns of the late Middle Ages attracted many scholars. In some towns, scholars established centers of learning that grew into universities. The first universities were associations of students and teachers. Before long, universities came under the control of the Church. Universities obtained official charters, just as the towns had, which gave them rights to self-government. However, university officials were members of the clergy and therefore answerable to the Church.

Through Their Eyes ■ Chaucer's *The Canterbury Tales*

Geoffrey Chaucer's poem The Canterbury Tales *is one of the best-known works in English literature. Chaucer started to write it in 1386, but he also had a varied career as a soldier and diplomat.*

*The Canterbury Tales *is a collection of stories told by pilgrims on their way to Canterbury, a popular shrine in southern England. To pass the time, they tell each other about their lives. In the following excerpts, Chaucer sketches the character of several pilgrims.*

From *The Canterbury Tales*

There was a *Knight,* a most distinguished man,
Who from the day on which he first began
To ride abroad had followed chivalry,
Truth, honour, generousness and courtesy.
He had done nobly in his sovereign's war
And ridden into battle, no man more,
As well in Christian as in heathen places
And ever honoured for his noble graces.

A *Monk* there was, one of the finest sort
Who rode the country;
        hunting was his sport. . . .
The Rule of good St. Benet or St. Maur
As old and strict he tended to ignore;
He let go by the things of yesterday
And took the modern world's
        more spacious way.

There was a *Merchant* with a forking beard
And motley dress; high on his horse he sat,
Upon his head a Flemish beaver hat
And on his feet daintily buckled boots.
He told of his opinions and pursuits
In solemn tones, he harped on his increase
Of capital; there should be sea-police
(He thought) upon
        the Harwich-Holland ranges;
He was expert at dabbling in exchanges.
This estimable Merchant so had set
His wits to work,
        none knew he was in debt. . . .

A worthy *woman* from beside *Bath city*
Was with us, somewhat deaf,
        which was a pity.
In making cloth she showed so great a bent
She bettered those of Ypres and of Ghent. . . .
And she had thrice been to Jerusalem,
Seen many strange rivers
        and passed over them;
She'd been to Rome and also to Boulogne,
St. James of Compostella and Cologne. . . .

1. What values of chivalry does Chaucer's knight express?
2. How do *The Canterbury Tales* reflect the expanding horizons of the Middle Ages?

Universities were similar to guilds. They protected the interests of students and teachers, established courses of study, and set standards. Like many guilds, universities excluded women.

University students trained for high positions in the Church or in government. They studied the seven liberal arts: grammar, rhetoric, logic, geometry, arithmetic, astronomy, and music. After completing the basic curriculum, a student took an examination to become a bachelor of arts. After additional study, he submitted a written masterpiece to become a master of arts. With this degree, a student could then join the guild of teachers.

The medieval university offered few comforts. Students sat for two or three hours on hard benches in an unheated room, taking notes while a scholar lectured. Manuscript books were scarce and very expensive. The teacher's life was not easy either. He was responsible for the instruction of his students. He also had to find them housing, supervise their behavior outside the classroom, and collect tuition.

Despite the discomforts, universities thrived throughout Western Europe. Oxford University was founded by English students who had to leave Paris when France and England were at war. Later, some Oxford students formed a new university at Cambridge. Some universities earned reputations for excellence in a particular field. The University of Salerno in Italy was known for medicine. Bologna was famous for teaching Church and Roman law, and the University of Paris specialized in theology and law.

The Challenge of the New Learning

In the eleventh century, scholars from Bologna, Italy, traveled to Constantinople to bring back manuscripts of Roman law. About the same time, new translations of Aristotle's works reached scholars in Western Europe from Muslim Spain. When scholars began studying these new translations, serious debates broke out in the universities. Aristotle's system of knowledge relied on reason, and it required people to examine all sides of an issue. Yet medieval thinkers accepted ideas on faith. They believed that Church teachings were the final authority on all questions.

During the late Middle Ages, the most brilliant scholars worked to resolve apparent differences between faith and reason. Eventually, they developed a school of thought

"Why does he speak of the sayings and deeds of the ancients?" complained a student over 600 years ago. "We have inside information; our youth is self-taught." As this picture suggests, the student may have been struggling to stay awake during a three-hour lecture. Although medieval classrooms were cold and uncomfortable, most students were willing to endure these hardships for the sake of an education.

called scholasticism. *Scholasticism* used reason and logic to support Christian beliefs.

The most famous medieval scholastic thinker was Thomas Aquinas (uh KWĪ nuhs). Aquinas taught that there was no conflict between faith and reason. He explained that the ability to reason was the gift of God. Faith, too, came from God. When differences arose between faith and reason, the problem was caused by mistaken reasoning.

In his work *Summa Theologica*, Aquinas set out to explain all Christian beliefs in the light of reason. Aquinas wrote that rulers should obey the law of God and protect human lives through just laws. He stressed the virtues of wisdom and moderation and the importance of the sacraments for achieving salvation. The teachings of Aquinas have influenced Christian thought to the present.

Science and Technology

The scientific knowledge of the ancient world was largely lost or forgotten in the early Middle Ages. In science, as in all other areas of learning, the Church was the unquestioned authority. Its teachings about the universe were generally based on a few surviving classical works. Yet those works often contained errors. For example, the Church accepted the views of the ancient astronomer Ptolemy who taught that the sun revolved around the earth.

Despite the lack of scientific observation and experiment in the early Middle Ages, scholars made important advances. In the ninth century, Europeans learned Arabic numerals through the Muslims in Spain. The use of Arabic numerals opened the way to new developments in mathematics. For example, although scholars mistakenly believed that the earth was the center of the universe, they did prove that the earth was round.

Great advances were made in technology throughout the Middle Ages. As you read in Chapter 10, the heavy plow, the waterwheel, and the windmill increased food production. Later inventions included the flying buttress, clocks, lenses for glasses, and glass for windows and mirrors. About 1000,

People in the Middle Ages were fascinated by machines. Many medieval inventors tried to build perpetual motion machines, which would never stop. Their efforts led to the invention of the clock. To the medieval clockmaker in this picture, the intricate wheels and gears of his invention did more than simply keep time. They symbolized the order, complexity, and energy of the universe.

an English monk designed and built a glider that flew about 600 feet (180 meters). Three hundred years later, Guido da Vigevano, an Italian physician, sketched plans for an automobile engine and a submarine.

In the late Middle Ages, scientists began to draw conclusions from experiments. Experiments had long been used by *alchemists*, who combined philosophy, magical beliefs, and chemistry in an attempt to change worthless metals into gold. Alchemists' workshops resembled some present-day laboratories, with containers of bubbling liquids and smoky furnaces. Although alchemists did not find a way to change other metals into gold, they did establish methods of study that led to the development of laboratory experiments.

In the thirteenth century, Roger Bacon, a prominent philosopher and scientist, noted the importance of experiments.

Experimental science controls all other sciences. It reveals truths which reasoning from general principles would never have discovered. . . . It starts us on the way to marvelous inventions that will change the face of the world.

Bacon conducted many experiments in optics, the branch of physics that studies light and vision. He predicted the invention of cars, flying machines, and fast ships powered by engines. Today, Bacon is known as the founder of experimental science.

Medieval Medicine

At the universities of Salerno and Montpellier, physicians received fine training and made some advances in medicine. Most people, however, could not use trained physicians. They relied on folk medicine, which combined traditional remedies, superstition, and Christian beliefs.

Cures for minor illnesses were usually herbal medicines. "For toothache, mix vinegar, oil, and sulphur and put it in the mouth of the sufferer," read one prescription. Another suggested: "For headache, take root of peony mixed with oil of roses. Soak linen with the mixture and apply to where the pain is." Although many of these remedies did little good, some worked.

Many people believed that illness was the work of evil spirits or the devil. Surgery was sometimes performed to release evil spirits. People also prayed to the saints for cures. In cases of serious illnesses, some people made pilgrimages to holy shrines, where they prayed for a miraculous cure.

SECTION REVIEW

1. Identify: chanson de geste, Dante, Geoffrey Chaucer, Thomas Aquinas, Roger Bacon.
2. Define: vernacular, scholasticism, alchemist.
3. (a) How did Romanesque architecture show Roman influence? (b) How did the flying buttress make Gothic architecture possible?
4. What two kinds of vernacular literature developed in the late Middle Ages?
5. List three inventions of the late Middle Ages.

3 Expanding Horizons

Read to Learn
- why the Crusades took place
- how the Crusades changed feudal society

During the Middle Ages, Europe was politically divided, but the Church was a powerful unifying force. The Church benefited from the economic growth of the late Middle Ages, and its power increased. In the eleventh century, the Church used its enormous influence to send thousands of Christians on holy missions beyond the borders of Europe.

The Holy Land

During the Middle Ages, Christians thought of Palestine and other places connected with the life of Jesus as the Holy Land. Beginning in the third century, many Christians from Western Europe made long, difficult pilgrimages* to Jerusalem. In the seventh century, Muslim Arabs conquered Palestine. The new rulers generally tolerated Christian pilgrims. Christians and Jews living in Palestine were allowed to worship as they pleased, although they had to pay a special tax.

In the eleventh century, the Seljuk Turks, a warlike people who had recently converted to Islam, invaded Arab lands. When the Seljuk Turks took Palestine in 1071, conditions worsened for non-Muslims. Returning pilgrims reported that the Turks were torturing Christians who traveled to sacred shrines in Palestine.

_____
* A pilgrimage is a journey that is taken for a specific purpose, such as visiting a holy place.

Turkish armies also threatened the Byzantine Empire. In 1095, the Byzantine emperor asked Pope Urban II for some knights to help fight the Muslim Turks. However, relations between Christians in the Byzantine Empire and in Western Europe were far from friendly. In 1054, the Christian Church had split into two churches: the Eastern, or Orthodox, Church in the Byzantine Empire and the Roman Catholic Church in Western Europe. You will read about the causes of this split in Chapter 13. Despite the split in the Church, Urban responded quickly to the emperor's plea.

The Crusades Begin

At the Council of Clermont in southern France, Urban preached a *crusade*, a military expedition against enemies of the Church. In stirring words, he urged Christian knights to rescue the Holy Land from the Muslims. He promised that those who died on a crusade would gain salvation. "Undertake this journey for the remission [forgiveness] of your sins," the pope declared, "with the assurance of everlasting glory in the kingdom of Heaven." Moved by the pope's appeal, the assembled nobles and clergy roared, "God wills it."

Urban had several reasons for turning the request for a few hundred knights into a great crusade. He hoped a crusade would help reunite the Christian Church. Also, a successful crusade would increase the prestige of the Church. Furthermore, the pope saw a crusade as a way to reduce feudal warfare. Instead of fighting in Europe, knights could use their energies in the Holy Land.

Urban's speech ignited an immediate response. Thousands of peasants and knights sewed crosses to their clothes. They were called crusaders, people who take up the cross. Many crusaders earnestly believed

Map Skill *"Jerusalem is the center of the earth; the land is fruitful above all others, like another paradise of delights," proclaimed Pope Urban II in 1095. At the pope's urging, many Christians set out on crusades to free Jerusalem from Muslim control. During which crusade did the crusaders travel the longest distance?*

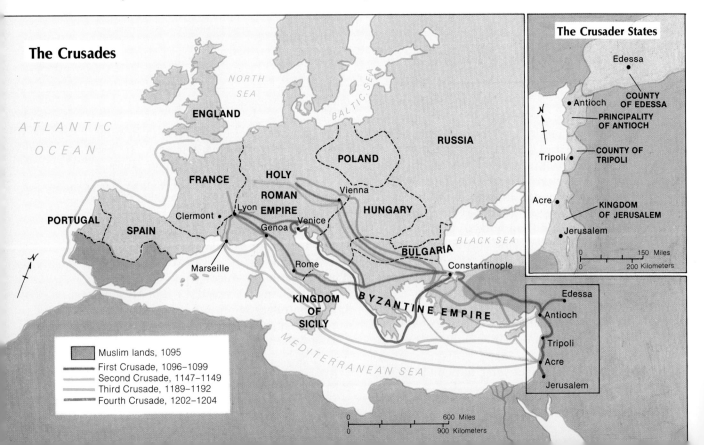

During June and July 1099, crusaders besieged the city of Jerusalem in the heart of the Holy Land. Their attacks were fiercely resisted by Muslim defenders, who also saw Jerusalem as a holy city. Finally, on July 15, Jerusalem fell to the Christians. In this painting, Christian knights surge through gaps in the walls, killing the last Muslim defenders.

they were obeying God's command. They wanted only to win salvation. However, some crusaders were more interested in rumors that Palestine was a land of fabulous riches. Others dreamed of carving out kingdoms in the Holy Land. A crusade offered them a chance to fight for the worthiest of all causes—the glory of God. In addition, the pope excused crusaders from certain taxes and debts while they were away fighting.

Before the pope could organize an army of knights for the long trip to Palestine, thousands of poor, unarmed peasants from France and Germany set off for the Holy Land. Most believed that a barefoot preacher named Peter the Hermit was leading them to heaven. Without food or money, the disorganized peasant bands looted the towns of Eastern Europe and attacked non-Christian communities along the way. When they reached Constantinople, the Byzantine emperor quickly sent them into Asia Minor

where most of them were killed by the Turks.

In 1096, the first official crusade crossed from Constantinople into Asia Minor. The crusaders fought bravely, winning victories there and in Syria. In 1099, they took Jerusalem. When they entered Jerusalem, the crusading knights slaughtered Muslim and Jewish men, women, and children. "Men rode in blood up to their knees," observed one knight. He justified the massacre because those killed were not Christians.

The crusaders set up four feudal states in Palestine and Syria: Edessa, Antioch, Tripoli, and Jerusalem. (See the map on page 180.) Although the crusader states lasted for nearly 200 years, they depended for survival on Italian merchants who ferried supplies and knights from Europe. Some crusaders who stayed in Palestine adopted local customs and grew more tolerant of their Muslim and Jewish neighbors.

Later Crusades

The intense religious enthusiasm of the First Crusade prompted later generations of Christians to take up the cross. For 200 years, a steady stream of pilgrims, merchants, and knights traveled back and forth across the Mediterranean. When Edessa fell to the Turks in 1144, a French monk, Bernard of Clairvaux (klehr VOH), called for a second crusade. The armies of the Second Crusade, however, failed to recapture Edessa.

In 1187, Muslim armies commanded by the able general Saladin (SAL uh dihn) captured Jerusalem. Saladin offered to negotiate with the Christian kings of Europe, but they refused. In the Third Crusade, which lasted from 1189 to 1192, King Richard of England reconquered some land but could not win back Jerusalem. He finally accepted a truce that guaranteed protection for Christians who visited Jerusalem.

The Fourth Crusade assembled in Venice. Venetian merchants convinced the crusaders to attack Constantinople, the Venetians' chief trade rival. In 1204, crusaders captured Constantinople, looted its rich Christian churches, and established a kingdom in Greece.

The Fourth Crusade seriously weakened the Byzantine Empire, which had served as a buffer between the Turks and Western Europe. Also, the attack on Constantinople diverted attention from the Holy Land. In addition, the Fourth Crusade showed that the high ideals of the early crusades had largely given way to greed and political ambition.

Yet strong religious faith continued to spark new crusades. In 1212, about 20,000 French and German children set out for the Holy Land in what became known as the Children's Crusade. The young crusaders expected the Mediterranean Sea to part miraculously and open a path to Jerusalem. Instead, corrupt merchants at the port of Marseille sold the children into slavery.

Despite several more military crusades, Muslim forces slowly regained lands captured by Europeans. In 1291, they seized Acre, the last Christian stronghold in the Holy Land. After 200 years of bitter fighting, the Holy Land was again under Muslim rule.

Results of the Crusades

At first, the spirit of the Crusades increased the power and prestige of the Church. As a result, the pope launched crusades against Muslims in Spain and against heretics in other parts of Europe. However, the misguided action of the Fourth Crusade tarnished the image of the Church as the leader of Christendom.

The Crusades began just as Europe was emerging from the isolation of the early Middle Ages. They helped to quicken the pace of changes already under way. Crusaders needed ships to carry them to Palestine so shipbuilders in the towns of northern Italy constructed large fleets. Italian merchants increased their trade with the Middle East. In Palestine, they bought Indian and Chinese goods that Arab traders had brought from Asia. They then carried the cotton cloth, silks, and spices to Venice, Genoa, and Pisa. From these cities, the goods were taken into other parts of Europe.

Increased trade and travel influenced the way Europeans saw the world. Pilgrims and merchants discovered that Muslims were not the monsters rumors described. People in Western Europe grew curious about even more distant regions. In the 1270s, Marco Polo, an Italian merchant, traveled overland to China. Few people believed his description of Chinese wealth and splendor. (See page 242.) Yet within a few centuries, adventuresome explorers would use a Chinese invention, the compass, to sail into unknown seas.

New Attitudes Toward Wealth

The increase in trade led to other economic changes. During the 1200s, the use of coined money became more widespread in Europe. The reappearance of a money economy affected peoples' attitudes toward wealth. In the growing towns and cities, making money was no longer seen as cheating the customer. Merchants charged whatever price they could get for a product, and they were not ashamed to make huge profits.

Some merchants also began to lend money for interest. This practice was called *usury*. The Church had banned usury during the early Middle Ages. But by the 1200s, wealthy merchants sought more profitable ways to invest their money. They began to lend money for profit. They avoided the Church ban on usury by charging money to carry the loan to the borrower rather than charging interest. Eventually, the Church decided that a reasonable interest charge based on the risk involved was not immoral.

By the 1300s, wealthy Italian families who made loans to merchants, kings, and popes had become Europe's first bankers. They provided useful banking services such as bills of exchange. *Bills of exchange* allowed merchants to pay for goods in distant cities without actually carrying gold coins. A merchant could deposit money with a banker in Venice, receive a bill of exchange, and travel to London. There he visited another Venetian banker and received the cash he needed to buy goods in England. Banks charged fees for such services, but the service helped make foreign trade easier.

Economic Change and Feudal Society

The increased trade and the development of a money economy made the manor less self-sufficient. Feudal lords no longer wore rough wool clothes made by their serfs or fought in armor made by the village blacksmith. Instead, they bought silks from town merchants and fine steel weapons imported from Syria. Peasants also began to buy goods in towns or at trade fairs.

Between about 1050 and 1350, other changes took place on the manor. Feudal lords needed money to buy trade goods. Therefore, they allowed peasants to pay rents in money rather than in grain or labor. In addition, they were willing to grant their serfs freedom in exchange for a large sum of money. The freed serfs could then work as hired laborers, usually on the lord's land. Some free peasants left the manor to try their luck in the towns.

The relationship between feudal lords and the townspeople was often strained. Lords looked down on townspeople who seemed more interested in wealth than warfare and the knightly code of chivalry. They

In the late Middle Ages, wealthy merchants and freed serfs lived side by side in the bustling towns and cities of Western Europe. This illustration shows daily activities in Paris. Merchants sold their wares from rented stalls. Farmers from the countryside brought livestock, fruit, and vegetables for the townspeople.

also resented the wealthy class of merchants and bankers who often lived in greater luxury than nobles.

Yet the most powerful feudal lords benefited from the money economy. They acquired wealth from the towns on their land. Furthermore, they were no longer dependent on their vassals for military or other services because they could hire people to fight for them.

Jewish Communities in Europe

The religious fervor and economic changes of the late Middle Ages affected the Jewish people in Europe. In the early Middle Ages, Christian kings and lords willingly granted town charters to Jewish communities. The charters gave Jews some self-government in exchange for tax payments. Jews followed many trades, farmed, and engaged in commerce. In towns and cities, Jewish academies of learning flourished.

During the Crusades, however, religious feeling ran strongly against Jews. Fanatical preachers accused Jews of killing Christian children. Christian mobs attacked Jewish communities. New laws forbade Jews to own land. The guilds forced Jewish artisans out of most trades.

Increasingly, the one occupation left for Jews was money-lending. Feudal lords would allow Jews to live on their land and lend money for interest. They would then tax the Jews at a high rate. As Christian lords, they were obeying the Church ban on usury, but they profited from money-lending. Although the Church reluctantly approved the large-scale banking practices of Christian merchants, it loudly condemned the Jews who were generally restricted to lending small sums of money.

In the late Middle Ages, popular resentment led to laws expelling Jews from many parts of Western Europe. Some Jews settled in Eastern Europe and Spain, where local rulers granted them special protection. Despite persecution, Jewish communities maintained their faith and ancient traditions.

SECTION REVIEW

1. Locate: Clermont, Edessa, Antioch, Tripoli, Jerusalem, Marseilles, Acre.
2. Identify: Seljuk Turks, Urban II, Saladin.
3. Define: crusade, usury, bill of exchange.
4. What were two results of the Fourth Crusade?
5. How did wealthy merchants avoid the Church's ban on usury?
6. How did the Crusades affect Jewish communities in Europe?

Chapter 11 Review

In Perspective

In the late Middle Ages, important economic developments transformed Europe. As the Church and feudal lords restored order, trade revived, and towns grew. A new middle class with its own interests emerged in towns. The expansion of commerce and growth of towns contributed to the flowering of medieval civilization. The influence of the Church was reflected in the soaring cathedrals built in many cities of Europe.

Along with religious faith, people in the late Middle Ages acknowledged worldly interests. Literature reflected the concerns of townspeople as well as of nobles. Scholars studied new translations of Greek and Roman works and tried to prove that Christian beliefs could pass the test of reason.

In the late 1000s, an upsurge in religious feeling led to the Crusades. Christian knights returned home with a new view of the world beyond Europe. The Crusades quickened the pace of changes already underway.

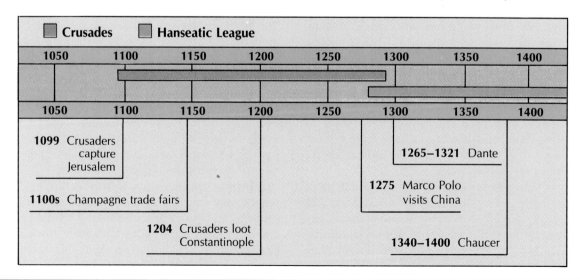

Crusades   Hanseatic League

| 1050 | 1100 | 1150 | 1200 | 1250 | 1300 | 1350 | 1400 |

1099 Crusaders capture Jerusalem

1100s Champagne trade fairs

1204 Crusaders loot Constantinople

1265–1321 Dante

1275 Marco Polo visits China

1340–1400 Chaucer

Recalling Facts

Decide if the following statements are true or false. If a statement is false, rewrite the statement to make it true.

1. The Hanseatic League was a group of Italian cities.

2. Medieval towns obtained charters to protect the rights of townspeople.

3. An association of artisans was called a craft guild.

4. In the Middle Ages, a just price meant charging whatever customers would pay.

5. Gothic cathedrals were dark and gloomy buildings.

6. Physicians received advanced medical training at some medieval universities.

7. The Fourth Crusade recaptured the Holy Land.

8. Italian merchants became the first bankers in Europe.

Chapter Checkup

1. Describe how each of the following contributed to an economic revival in Europe during the late Middle Ages: (a) decline of warfare; (b) trade fairs; (c) Hanseatic League; (d) growth of towns.

2. (a) Why did townspeople want charters? (b) How did the growth of towns affect the medieval social structure?

3. (a) What was the purpose of merchant and craft guilds? (b) Describe the steps by which a young man became a guild member.

4. (a) How did Aristotle's work influence medieval scholars? (b) How did Thomas Aquinas resolve differences between faith and reason?

5. (a) What contribution did Roger Bacon make to science? (b) What advances in technology were made during the Middle Ages?

6. (a) Why did people go on crusades? (b) Which crusade was most successful for the Christians? Why?

7. (a) What effect did the Crusades have on the Church? (b) How did the Crusades contribute to increased trade and travel?

Critical Thinking

1. **Analyzing a Quotation** Victor Hugo, a French writer of the 1800s, observed: "In the Middle Ages, men had no great thought which they did not write down in stone." Why do you think people lavished so much time, money, and hard work on stone architecture?

2. **Understanding Economic Ideas** (a) How did the reappearance of coined money contribute to the economic revival in the late Middle Ages? (b) Why do you think the idea of a just price became less important in the late Middle Ages? (c) Why do you think the Church relaxed its ban on usury in the 1300s?

3. **Expressing an Opinion** Some people today consider the Middle Ages an "age of faith". Do you agree? Explain.

Relating Past to Present

1. (a) How were medieval towns similar to modern towns and cities? (b) How were they different?

Developing Basic Skills

1. **Map Reading** Study the map on page 170. Then answer the following questions: (a) What information does the map show? (b) In what region or regions did the Hanseatic League dominate trade? (c) Where did the Italian cities probably dominate trade? (d) How did trade contribute to the expanded horizons of Europeans?

2. **Researching** Find out more about the hero of one of the epic poems mentioned on page 175. Then answer the following questions: (a) Who was the hero of the poem? (b) What goal or goals did the hero pursue? (c) Did the hero succeed? Explain. (d) How did the hero represent the ideals of chivalry?

3. **Identifying Immediate and Long-Range Causes** Review the discussion of the Crusades on pages 179–182. Then answer the following questions: (a) What was the immediate cause of the First Crusade? (b) What were the long-range causes of the Crusades? (c) How did the Crusades reflect the growing strength of medieval Europe?

See page 804 for suggested readings.

12 Building National Monarchies

(1000–1500)

Detail from a painting showing a monarch and church officials.

In the stifling summer heat of 1137, hundreds of the richest, most respected nobles in France set out from Paris. They made an impressive escort for Louis, heir to the French throne. It took a month for the expedition to reach Bordeaux in the south. At Bordeaux, they witnessed the marriage of Louis to Eleanor, Duchess of Aquitaine and Countess of Poitou (pwah TOO).

The French considered Eleanor a great prize. When her father had died earlier that year, 15-year-old Eleanor had inherited the rich, fertile fiefs of Aquitaine and Poitou. With these lands, she ruled more territory than the king of France.

For almost 70 years, Eleanor played a central role in medieval Europe. She negotiated with popes, kings, and emperors. She traveled across much of Europe and went on a crusade to Jerusalem. When Louis of France divorced her, she married Henry, heir to the English throne. Her vast lands thus passed into English hands. England's possession of Aquitaine fueled a bitter rivalry with France that lasted for over 300 years. Two of Eleanor's sons later became kings of England.

In Poitiers, Eleanor presided over the most brilliant court in Western Europe. Troubadours and scholarly philosophers flocked to her court, where learning and culture flourished. Towards the end of her life, a contemporary described her in these words: "Queen Eleanor, a matchless woman, beautiful and chaste, powerful and modest, meek and eloquent . . . [who had] two husbands and two sons crowned kings . . . whose power was the admiration of her age. . . ."

Eleanor of Aquitaine was one of many dynamic figures who shaped political life in the late Middle Ages. In the early Middle Ages, feudal monarchs were often pawns of their chief vassals. But in the late Middle Ages, the situation changed dramatically as ambitious rulers extended royal authority.

All medieval monarchs faced similar challenges. They had to establish control over their lands and limit the power of feudal nobles and the Church. Between 1000 and 1500, monarchs formed powerful alliances with the middle class, enriched the royal treasury, and built strong standing armies. They also created new political institutions and established the foundations for the present-day nations of Europe.

1 Growth of Royal Power in England and France

Read and Learn
- why England developed a strong monarchy
- how French kings expanded royal power

In 1000, Western Europe was divided into many small, independent states, each ruled by a feudal lord. Although feudal lords were, in theory, vassals of a king, kings had little real power. Between 1000 and 1500, however, kings in England and France increased their power and unified their territories. As monarchs grew stronger, people transferred their loyalty from feudal lords to a king.

Foundations for Unity

During the Middle Ages, political power was fragmented. Feudal nobles ruled vast lands, presided over their own courts, and coined their own money. Because they had their own vassals, these nobles could raise armies and make war. The Church was also a center of political power. Churches and monasteries owned a huge amount of land in Western Europe. Church officials heard all cases involving the clergy in Church courts. Like feudal nobles, the Church could raise armies and coin money.

In the early Middle Ages, the feudal system had worked well. People looked to the local lord for protection and order. However, in the late Middle Ages, monarchs took advantage of political, economic, and social changes to centralize power.

Townspeople usually supported the king. Because feudal warfare disrupted trade and commerce, townspeople preferred a powerful king who could keep the peace. Kings encouraged trade by issuing uniform coins. They also reduced the number of tolls and taxes along roads. Furthermore, kings established royal courts, which townspeople preferred because these courts administered uniform laws throughout the country.

A king benefited from increased trade. A money economy allowed him to tax rich towns and use the income to raise an army of paid soldiers. As a result, the king became less dependent on the military service of feudal lords. With a strong, professional army, a king could suppress rebellious nobles.

Royal power in Western Europe grew slowly over hundreds of years. Monarchs in nations such as England and France faced different conditions, however. As a result, different types of governments developed.

The Norman Conquest of England

Unlike the rest of Western Europe, England had not become a feudal society during the Viking invasions. Instead, Anglo-Saxon kings kept some authority over the country and united the people against the Danes. In 1066,

The Normans recorded their successful conquest of England on the 200-foot-long Bayeux tapestry. The tapestry, embroidered a few decades after William invaded England, also traces events leading up to the Norman conquest. In this scene, the Saxon leader Harold embarks on a friendly visit to William of Normandy a few years before the invasion. The two men became enemies after Harold was made king of England. William defeated Harold at the battle of Hastings in 1066.

England was conquered by William, Duke of Normandy, later known as William the Conqueror. Although William introduced some elements of feudalism to England, he carefully safeguarded his own power.

William divided Anglo-Saxon lands among the Norman lords, or barons, who had helped in the conquest. To ensure his control over the barons, William made them swear allegiance to him as the sole ruler of England. He declared that everyone, peasant and lord, owed loyalty first to the king, not to another feudal lord. He ordered his barons to build castles as symbols of Norman power. But he forbade them to build any new castles on their fiefs without his permission.

William established the foundations for a strong central government in England. He sent out officials to gather accurate information about all property in the kingdom. These officials asked a group of men in each village to swear under oath to the value of nearby estates. The group was called a jury, from the French word "jure," meaning "sworn under oath." The king's officials then compiled their information into a huge survey called the *Domesday Book*. The king used this survey to decide what taxes people owed. The *Domesday Book* has given scholars much useful information about medieval England.

Extending Royal Power in England

William's successors made royal government even more effective. His son Henry I replaced hereditary officeholders with paid royal officials. Because they owed their jobs to the king, royal officials were more likely to be loyal to the king than hereditary ones. Henry also increased royal income. He allowed vassals to make money payments instead of providing military service. Then he organized a central treasury called the *exchequer*. By keeping accurate tax records, the exchequer added to the king's authority.

In the twelfth century, Henry II, grandson of Henry I, further strengthened royal government. He expanded the power of royal courts by sending circuit judges into the countryside. In each town, a circuit judge ordered juries to report on crimes and disputes. These early juries also heard cases. No witnesses appeared, and no evidence was presented. The jurors, who were local people, made their decisions based on whatever facts were generally known. Eventually, two types of juries developed: the *grand jury*, which decided what cases would be brought to trial, and the *trial jury*, which gave verdicts on the cases.

Any free man could bring a case before a royal court. The decisions of royal courts were recorded, and they became the basis for *common law*. Under common law, accepted legal principles were applied to everyone throughout England. People usually preferred royal courts and common law to manor courts and trial by ordeal. Thus, royal courts increased the king's power. They also helped the royal treasury, which received the fines and fees imposed by the courts.

The Magna Carta

The expansion of royal power in England did not go unopposed. Henry II's efforts to control Church courts resulted in a tragic conflict. Henry had his friend Thomas Becket appointed Archbishop of Canterbury. Once in power, Becket opposed the king's policy toward the Church courts, and the two men became enemies. When four of the king's knights murdered the archbishop, Henry was blamed.* The king had to do heavy penance to avoid excommunication.

Henry's son John battled unsuccessfully with both the Church and his barons. In 1209, the powerful Pope Innocent III excommunicated John. To regain the pope's favor, John agreed to make England a papal fief and to pay an annual fee to Rome.

Meanwhile, John levied heavy taxes on his barons to support wars in France. When he lost land in northern France that England had held since 1066, the barons became angry. They resented the taxes and were outraged at England's loss of prestige. In 1215, they forced John to sign a charter that spelled out their rights. This document be-

---

*According to tradition, Henry exclaimed before his knights, "Who will free me of this turbulent priest?" Becket was murdered in 1170 in the cathedral at Canterbury. Two years later, the Church declared him a saint, and Canterbury soon became a popular shrine. As you read in Chapter 11, Chaucer wrote about pilgrims traveling to Canterbury.

came known as the Magna Carta, or Great Charter.

To John's barons, the Magna Carta was simply a written guarantee of their traditional rights and privileges. However, the Magna Carta was of lasting importance for several reasons. First, the rights given to nobles were later extended to all classes. Second, certain clauses were later used to limit the power of the monarch. For example, in one clause, the king agreed to consult the Great Council before imposing any new feudal taxes. The Great Council was made up of high officials, nobles, and bishops. Eventually, this clause was interpreted to mean that a representative body had to approve all taxes. Finally, the Magna Carta established the idea that the king had to respect the law. (See page 190.)

Origins of the English Parliament

Power struggles between the king and his nobles continued in the 1200s. Both sides recognized the growing importance of the towns. Some meetings of the Great Council began to include lesser knights and representatives from the towns. These meetings came to be known as Parliament, from the French word "parler," meaning "to talk."

In 1295, King Edward I needed money to pay for wars in France. Edward wanted wide support for the new taxes, so he summoned a meeting of Parliament. The meeting was to include the great nobles and bishops, two knights from each county, and two citizens from each town. The Parliament of 1295 has been called the Model Parliament because later Parliaments included similar representatives.

When Parliament first met, the great nobles and clergy made the decisions. The lesser knights and commoners from the towns stood at one end of the room and listened. They expressed their opinions only when asked to do so. Later the two groups met separately. This division eventually resulted in two houses of Parliament: the House of Lords, made up of representatives of great nobles and bishops, and the House

On June 15, 1215, King John of England made peace with rebellious barons by putting his seal on the Magna Carta. This document contained the barons' demands for reform. Although many clauses were soon forgotten, the principle that the king had to obey the law of the land was established. The charter eventually became the basis for democratic government in England. Following are some of its provisions.

From the Magna Carta

John, by the grace of God, king of England, lord of Ireland, duke of Normandy and Aquitaine, count of Anjou; to the archbishops, bishops, abbots, earls, barons, justiciars, foresters, sheriffs, reeves, servants, and all bailiffs and his faithful people greeting. . . .

1. In the first place we have granted to God and by this our present charter confirmed . . . that the English church shall be free, and shall hold its rights entire. . . .

We have granted moreover to all free men of our kingdom for us and our heirs forever all the liberties written below, to be held by them and their heirs from us and our heirs. . . .

12. No scutage [a tax paid instead of military service] or aid [tax] shall be imposed in our kingdom except by the common council.

14. And for holding a common council of the kingdom concerning the assessment of an aid . . . we shall cause to be summoned the archbishops, bishops, abbots, earls, and greater barons. . . . [In addition], we shall cause to be summoned by our sheriffs and bailiffs all [our other vassals] . . . for a certain day . . . and for a certain place. . . .

39. No free man shall be taken, or imprisoned, or dispossessed, or outlawed, or banished, or in any way destroyed, except by the legal judgment of his peers or by the law of the land.

1. Who was to serve on the common council?
2. How did the Magna Carta affect the common people?

of Commons, made up of representatives of lesser knights and townspeople.

Over the centuries, Parliament gradually increased its financial and legislative powers. For example, before voting new taxes needed by the king, Parliament would demand other rights. In this way, Parliament exercised some control over the monarchy. A government where a monarch does not have absolute power is called a *limited monarchy.*

Building the French Monarchy

William the Conquerer had swiftly established royal power in England, but French kings struggled for centuries to unite their kingdom and gain control over feudal lords. In 843, the Treaty of Verdun had divided Charlemagne's empire into three parts. (See page 153.) The western part, which is present-day France, suffered greatly during the Viking invasions. Because French kings were too weak to resist the Vikings, powerful feudal lords set up their own independent states.

The process of building the French monarchy began in 987 when the feudal lords elected Hugh Capet, Count of Paris, as king. Over the next 350 years, the Capetian dynasty slowly increased the power and prestige of French rulers. First, they made the crown hereditary within their family. Then they used diplomacy, marriage, and war to add to royal lands.

The first Capetian kings ruled only a narrow strip of north-central France. The Norman kings of England controlled large parts of northwestern France. Gradually, French kings such as Philip II reduced the English holdings. By defeating King John of England, Philip II won Normandy, Anjou, and Poitou. In the thirteenth century, the Church launched a crusade against the Albigensians, a group of heretics in southern France. The French king then seized the lands of nobles who had sided with the heretics. By 1328, the French king ruled most of central and southern France. (See the map at right.)

A Strong Central Government

As they added to their lands, French monarchs set up an efficient royal bureaucracy, a group of officials who govern through departments. The king appointed educated clergy, lesser knights, and townspeople to administer the districts of France. Royal officials were chosen for their ability and were paid a salary. These officials upheld royal policies and added to the power of the French king.

As in England, monarchs in France increased their power through the royal courts. However, the king did not encourage the growth of a common law. Instead, he ordered his officials to respect local customs and traditions if they did not interfere with royal justice. The highest royal court was the Parlement of Paris. Because this court had greater authority than any feudal court, people came to see the king as the source of justice.

Good government ensured the king of his subjects' loyalty. In the late Middle Ages, this loyalty helped French kings in their conflicts with the Church. In 1302, Philip IV clashed with Pope Boniface VIII because the king wanted to tax the clergy and appoint bishops. To show he had the support of the French people, Philip summoned an assembly that represented the three estates, or classes, in France. The first estate was the clergy; the second was the nobility; and the third was the bourgeoisie, or townspeople. The Estates General, as this assembly was called, supported the king against the pope.

The Estates General did not become as powerful as the English Parliament in part because it did not have power over taxation. Instead, the royal bureaucracy grew in strength. Since the king controlled the bureaucracy, he gained great power.

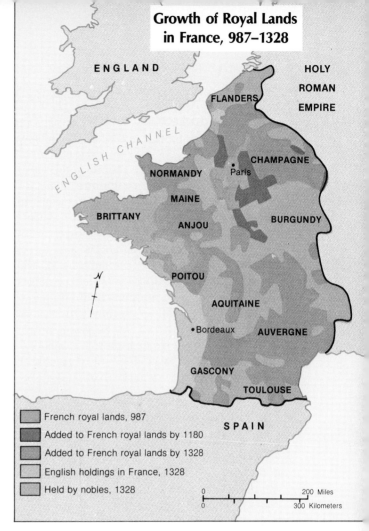

Growth of Royal Lands in France, 987–1328

ENGLAND

HOLY ROMAN EMPIRE

FLANDERS

ENGLISH CHANNEL

CHAMPAGNE

NORMANDY   Paris

MAINE

BRITTANY

ANJOU

BURGUNDY

POITOU

AQUITAINE

•Bordeaux   AUVERGNE

GASCONY

TOULOUSE

SPAIN

- French royal lands, 987
- Added to French royal lands by 1180
- Added to French royal lands by 1328
- English holdings in France, 1328
- Held by nobles, 1328

0   200 Miles
0   300 Kilometers

Map Skill *When Hugh Capet was elected King of France in 987, he ruled only the lands around Paris, shown here in purple. During the next 350 years, much of France was brought under royal control. Which regions were held by England in 1328?*

SECTION REVIEW

1. Identify: William the Conquerer, *Domesday Book*, Magna Carta, Model Parliament, Hugh Capet, Estates General.

2. Define: exchequer, grand jury, trial jury, common law, limited monarchy.

3. How did William keep control over feudal lords in England?

4. What economic power did Parliament acquire in England?

5. What methods did French kings use to increase their landholdings?

6. Why did Philip IV call the Estates General?

191

2 The Struggle Between Popes and Emperors

Read to Learn ■ how German emperors became involved in Italian affairs
■ what conflicts existed between popes and emperors

While French kings were reuniting the western part of Charlemagne's empire, the eastern and central regions fell into turmoil. In the eastern region, which is present-day Germany, Charlemagne's heirs lost power to local lords called dukes. When the last Carolingian died, the dukes elected one of the dukes as king. The king was able to rule his own lands but could not control the dukes.

In 936, the Duke of Saxony, Otto I, was chosen king. He soon tried to gain control over the other German dukes. He also extended his power over the central region of Charlemagne's empire in northern Italy.

The Holy Roman Empire

In order to centralize power in Germany, Otto I developed close ties with the Church. He appointed clergy as advisors, and he supported missionary work. In exchange, Otto gained the right to appoint German bishops and archbishops who would support him against the dukes. His ties with the Church led Otto to invade Italy to protect the pope from Roman nobles. In addition, Otto claimed northern Italy through his marriage to Adelaide, widow of an Italian King.

In 962, the pope crowned Otto "Emperor of the Romans." Otto claimed to be the successor of Charlemagne and leader of Christendom. The lands ruled by Otto and his heirs became known as the Holy Roman Empire.

Otto's coronation had long-lasting consequences. In the next 250 years, German emperors became deeply involved in Italian affairs. At first, they supported reforms in the Church, which had fallen under corrupt influences. They often intervened to ensure the election of able popes. But as the Church gained greater power in the eleventh and twelfth centuries, popes and emperors clashed in a great power struggle.

Sources of Conflict

As you read in Chapter 10, a religious reform movement beginning at Cluny swept across Europe in the eleventh century. Many of the reforms were designed to reduce the influence that political rulers had over the Church. For example, the Holy Roman Emperor appointed many high Church officials. In a solemn ceremony, the emperor invested, or gave, a new bishop the symbols of his office—usually a ring and a staff. This practice was known as *lay investiture*.

The investiture controversy. In 1073, the monk Hildebrand was elected Pope Gregory VII. Hildebrand was an outspoken and able reformer. The new pope worked to end such abuses as the sale of Church offices. He also banned the practice of lay investiture.

Gregory's ban on lay investiture brought an angry response from the Holy Roman emperor Henry IV. Henry wanted to appoint Church officials as support against the German dukes. In a bitter letter, addressed to "Hildebrand, now no longer pope, but false monk," the emperor refused to obey the pope's order.

In answer to Henry's challenge, Gregory excommunicated the emperor. He then encouraged the German dukes to elect another emperor. Desperate to save his throne, Henry crossed the Alps into Italy. He found the pope at the castle of Canossa in northern Italy. He is reported to have stood in the snow outside the castle for three days. Barefoot and wearing the rough garments of a repentant sinner, Henry begged the pope's forgiveness. Gregory undoubtedly knew that the emperor only wanted to save his throne, but he obeyed his priestly duty to forgive Henry and readmit him to the Church.

Concordat of Worms. Henry returned to Germany and continued to appoint bishops. When he was excommunicated a second

In the winter of 1077, the Holy Roman emperor Henry IV crossed the Alps to find Pope Gregory VII at Canossa. Henry, seen kneeling in the center of this illustration, begged the pope to readmit him into the Church. Pope Gregory had gone to Canossa to consult with one of his most powerful allies, Countess Matilda of Tuscany, shown on the right. According to tradition, Matilda helped reconcile the pope and the emperor, who had quarreled over the investiture issue.

time, he marched on Rome and drove Gregory into exile. The battle over lay investiture continued until 1122 when a compromise known as the Concordat of Worms (vohrms) was reached. By this agreement, Church officials elected bishops and abbots. The emperor kept the privilege of granting any lands and secular powers that accompanied the Church office.

Although the Concordat of Worms gave the Church final authority over its officials, it did not end the struggle between emperors and popes. The investiture controversy had centered on two issues: the Church's spiritual authority, such as its right to choose bishops, and its political authority, such as its power over secular rulers. The Concordat of Worms settled the first issue. The second issue remained a source of conflict, especially in Italy.

The Struggle for Italy

In 1152, Frederick I, who was nicknamed Barbarossa, or "red beard," became Holy Roman Emperor. He was determined to rule both Italy and Germany. Frederick spent years fighting to win control of the wealthy towns of northern Italy. By marrying his son to the king of Sicily's daughter, he also secured southern Italy.

The pope saw Frederick's actions as a threat to the Papal States in central Italy. He therefore encouraged the northern Italian towns to unite against the emperor. The struggle for control of Italy involved both pope and emperor in endless wars and intrigue.

The long struggle between popes and emperors had a lasting effect on the Holy Roman Empire. In England and France, rulers were establishing the foundations for unified nations, but German emperors spent their energies fighting in Italy. As a result, they could not win control over the powerful feudal lords of Germany. German dukes continued to rule their lands as independent kingdoms, largely ignoring the emperor.

Italy, too, suffered from the constant warfare on its soil. Northern towns formed leagues to fight the emperor or the pope, but they were never united under a single ruler. It was not until the 1800s that the many small states of Germany and Italy were finally united into two independent nations.

Church Power at its Height

Despite the conflict with the Holy Roman emperors, the Church reached its peak of power in the late 1100s. The reforms of the previous century had given it control over the clergy. The success of the early Crusades also added greatly to its prestige. Even kings who challenged the Church in their own lands supported the Crusades. For example, Frederick Barbarossa led his army on a crusade to the Holy Land.

Between 1198 and 1216, Pope Innocent III came close to making the Church supreme in both spiritual and worldly affairs. He kept strict control over the bishops, who in turn watched the lower clergy. He successfully asserted his authority over secular rulers. In 1209, you will recall, Innocent III excommunicated King John. He lifted the ban only when the English king became his vassal. Innocent also deposed one German emperor and intervened to ensure the election of another who promised not to threaten papal power in Italy.

Before his death, Innocent was the unquestioned leader of Christendom. Yet his success hid important problems. The pope had involved the Church in power struggles with many feudal rulers. Critics attacked the Church for being too concerned with political power and for ignoring its spiritual duties. Furthermore, medieval rulers increasingly saw the Church as an obstacle to national unity. In the late Middle Ages, they renewed their efforts to limit Church power.

SECTION REVIEW

1. Identify: Holy Roman Empire, Gregory VII, Concordat of Worms, Innocent III.
2. Define: lay investiture.
3. What ties did Otto I have with the Church?
4. Why did Gregory VII excommunicate Emperor Henry IV?
5. What actions by Frederick I threatened the pope?

3 Strong Monarchies in Spain and Scandinavia

Read to Learn
- how Spain developed a strong monarchy
- how the Scandinavian nations united

During the late Middle Ages, monarchs in Spain and Scandinavia established the foundations for strong central governments. Various cultures had influenced both regions. Muslims ruled parts of Spain for over 700 years. In Scandinavia, the people had become Christians by 1100, but German traditions often prevailed.

Muslim Spain

In the 700s, Muslim armies conquered most of Spain. Only a few small Christian kingdoms survived in the north. In the early Middle Ages, commerce did not decline in Muslim Spain as it had in other parts of Western Europe. Towns prospered. Jewish communities especially benefited from the tolerant policies of the Muslims.

In large cities such as Cordova and Granada, merchants sold products from all over the world. Markets displayed handmade goods from the eastern Mediterranean and Asia as well as agricultural products such as dates, lemons, and peaches. In the tenth century, traders began to carry these goods into the Christian areas of Europe.

Cordova, capital of Spain, was the most prosperous city in Western Europe. Christian visitors marveled at its graceful gardens, splendid mansions, and busy marketplaces. Cordova had police and sanitation services when London was merely a town.

Spain was also a thriving center of Islamic civilization.* Peaceful contacts took place between Muslim and Christian scholars. Muslim scholars had preserved Greek and Roman texts, many of which were unknown in Western Europe. Christian scholars translated these works and thus rediscovered the learning of the ancient world.

---

* You will read more about Islamic civilization in Chapter 13.

During most of the Middle Ages, Spain was a center of Islamic civilization. Many examples of Islamic architecture survive. This picture shows the Court of Lions at the Alhambra Palace in Granada, Spain. The elegant, sun-filled buildings of Muslim Spain contrasted sharply with the stern, stone palaces and cathedrals of northern Europe.

The Reconquest

Despite peaceful exchanges among scholars and traders, Christian kingdoms in the north of Spain had fought to expel the Muslims since the 800s. In the 1100s and 1200s, while crusaders battled in Palestine, Spanish knights launched a crusade in Spain. They called their crusade the *reconquista*, or reconquest.

By 1250, Muslims held only the kingdom of Granada in southern Spain. Three Christian kingdoms controlled the rest of the peninsula. In the west, Portugal had become an independent state with its own language and a strong interest in overseas trade. The kingdom of Castile dominated central Spain. The kingdom of Aragon controlled the northeast. (See the map on page 196.)

During the reconquest, local nobles acquired great power. Most continued the Islamic policy of religious toleration. They allowed both Muslims and Jews to follow their own beliefs. Towns, which had large populations of Muslims and Jews, remained prosperous.

Isabella and Ferdinand. In 1469, Queen Isabella of Castile married Ferdinand, heir to the Kingdom of Aragon. Their marriage united most of Spain. The new rulers soon acted to centralize power. They joined forces with the townspeople against the nobles. They limited the power of the Cortes (KOR tehz), an assembly similar to the Estates General in France. Unlike English and French rulers who had fought bitter battles with the Church, Ferdinand and Isabella made the Church a powerful ally. Isabella worked hard to reform the clergy and won the right to appoint high Church officials in Spain.

In 1492, a Christian army captured Granada, the last Muslim outpost in Spain. This event ended the centuries of crusades in

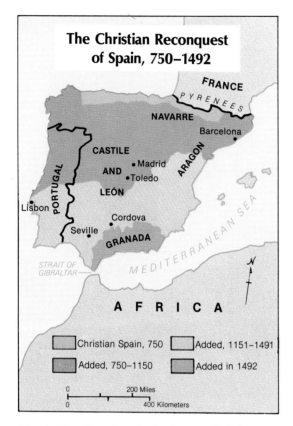

The Christian Reconquest of Spain, 750–1492

FRANCE

PYRENEES

NAVARRE

Barcelona

CASTILE

AND

Madrid

Toledo

LEÓN

ARAGON

PORTUGAL

Lisbon

Cordova

Seville

GRANADA

MEDITERRANEAN SEA

STRAIT OF GIBRALTAR

A F R I C A

N

Christian Spain, 750

Added, 1151–1491

Added, 750–1150

Added in 1492

0   200 Miles

0   400 Kilometers

Map Skill *Over hundreds of years, Christian knights slowly pushed Muslim forces further south in Spain. What area was the last Muslim outpost to fall to the Christian armies?*

Spain. It also ignited strong national feeling among Christians in Spain, who united behind Ferdinand and Isabella. While Spain celebrated its victory, an Italian navigator, Christopher Columbus, received permission from Queen Isabella to sail on a voyage of discovery. You will read about the outcome of this voyage in Chapter 17.

Religious policy. Ferdinand and Isabella were determined to bring religious as well as political unity to Spain. Thus, they ended the policy of religious toleration. They ordered Jews and Muslims to convert or leave Spain. A few converted to Christianity. Many others were expelled. Religious unity came at a high price. Among the Jews and Muslims expelled were many doctors, merchants, scholars, and other leaders of Spanish economic and cultural life.

Spanish rulers used the Inquisition to increase their power and enforce their reli-

gious policy. As you will recall, the Inquisition was a special Church court set up to try people accused of heresy. Jews and Muslims who had converted were often accused of practicing their original religions in secret. They were brought before the Inquisition, and their property was seized. If they were condemned as heretics, they were usually burned at the stake.

For centuries, the Inquisition created an atmosphere of suspicion and intolerance in Spain. Later Spanish monarchs followed the example of Ferdinand and Isabella. They allowed no one to challenge their absolute power.

Nations of Scandinavia

As you read in Chapter 10, beginning about 800, Viking invaders from Norway, Sweden, and Denmark had terrorized Europe. During the Viking invasions, missionaries worked among the peoples of Scandinavia to convert them to Christianity. Christian missionaries introduced a system of writing as well as other aspects of medieval civilization. By about 1000, the Viking raids ended. However, Viking traders continued to have widespread contacts with Eastern and Western Europe.

In Scandinavia, as elsewhere in medieval Europe, great lords competed with kings for power. In Sweden, for example, the leading nobles elected the king, according to German custom. Once they chose a king, however, they prevented him from acquiring further power.

Although close ties bound the ruling families of Denmark, Norway, and Sweden, trade rivalries and clashes over boundaries led to frequent warfare. At different times, various strong rulers united the peoples of Scandinavia. In 1017, the Danish king Canute (kuh NOOT) conquered a northern empire that included England, Norway, and parts of Sweden. However, his successors could not hold onto the empire.

In the late Middle Ages, Queen Margrete of Denmark was able to unite Denmark, Norway, and Sweden peacefully. She outlived both her husband and son, and in 1387, she became Queen of Denmark. The same year, Norway introduced the system of electing a monarch. The nobles chose Margrete. A year later, Swedish nobles deposed their king and asked Margrete to take the throne of Sweden.

While Margrete lived, the union worked well. After her death, however, rivalries resurfaced. In the fifteenth century, commerce and industry made Sweden one of the strongest states in Europe. In 1523, it broke away from the union. Denmark and Norway remained united until 1814.

SECTION REVIEW

1. Locate: Cordova, Granada, Portugal, Aragon, Castile.
2. Identify: Ferdinand, Isabella, Margrete.
3. Define: reconquista.
4. What attitude did Muslims in Spain take toward Jewish communities?
5. How did the marriage of Ferdinand and Isabella help unify Spain?
6. What led to frequent warfare among Scandinavian nations?

4 Decline of Medieval Society

Read to Learn ▪ how the Black Death affected Europe
▪ how the Hundred Years' War affected Western Europe

The late Middle Ages was an unsettled time in Western Europe because changing political and economic conditions undermined the foundations of medieval society. In the early 1300s, poor harvests resulted in terrible famines. Agriculture, trade, and commerce declined. Added to these problems was an outbreak of a disastrous epidemic of bubonic plague, often called the Black Death.

The Black Death and Its Aftermath

In 1348, the bubonic plague, a disease carried by fleas on rats, struck Western Europe.* The plague, which broke out first in Asia, spread rapidly along the trade routes. It inflicted enormous casualties because no one knew how to treat it. Panic and fear led to desperate measures. In some towns, the first people to show symptoms of the disease were walled up inside their homes to keep the plague from spreading.

As the disease swept through Europe, it destroyed entire communities. Some towns lost more than half their population. In all, the Black Death killed about a third of the people of Western Europe.

_____
* The bubonic plague had broken out from time to time in the ancient world. It also caused many deaths in Western Europe during the 500s and 600s A.D.

The huge population loss had a profound effect on the economy. Farms were abandoned. The busy commerce of the twelfth and thirteenth centuries, which had spurred the growth of cities, collapsed. Outbreaks of plague continued in the late 1300s, and Western Europe did not fully recover for over 100 years.

Attack on the Church

During the social and economic turmoil of the 1300s and 1400s, the leadership of the Church weakened. At the same time, monarchs and reformers challenged its authority. As you read, popes had resisted attempts by kings to increase their power. In the process, the Church had gained great political power.

Medieval monarchs opposed the Church's political power for several reasons. The Church owned large amounts of land. The clergy and monasteries did not pay royal taxes on their land, but they did pay Church taxes. Thus, money was sent to Rome rather than to the royal treasury. Rulers also resented Church courts, which they felt competed with royal courts. Finally, monarchs became angry when Church officials interfered in political matters. By the early 1300s, monarchs were becoming more successful

Statistics provide factual information in number form. Historians often use statistics to draw conclusions about historical events or developments. Historical statistics can range from population figures to the size of grain harvests or the number of ships built.

Statistics must be used with care. Sometimes statistics are estimates because exact figures are not available. For example, the figures in the following table are estimates of the population in medieval Europe. These estimates are based on the few records that exist for the period. Furthermore, statistics present only a partial picture. The table gives numbers, but it does not give the reasons for population growth or decline. Therefore, statistics must be interpreted using other information.

Use the following steps to read and interpret the statistics in the table.

1. **Identify the type of information given in the table.** The title of the table as well as the titles of the columns and rows show you what information is provided. Answer the following questions about the table: (a) What is the title? (b) What time period is covered? (c) For how many different years are population figures given? (d) For how many regions are population statistics given?

2. **Practice reading the statistics.** Statistics often involve numbers in the millions. When they do, the zeros are usually left off and the table notes "in millions," which means you add six zeros to the numbers listed. Answer the following questions about the table: (a) What was the population of Italy in 500? (b) What was the population of Spain in 1000? (c) When did the population of France and the Low Countries reach 19 million? (d) When did the total population of Europe reach the highest figure?

3. **Study the table to find relationships among the numbers.** You can use the table to compare the population in different parts of Europe at a specific time period. You can also use the table to study the changes in population in one region during the Middle Ages. Answer the following questions based on the table: (a) How did the population of Italy change between 500 and 650? (b) How did the population of Spain change between 650 and 1000? (c) In what region did the population grow the most between 1000 and 1340? In what region did it grow the least? (d) How does the population of Europe in 1340 compare to the population of Europe in 1450?

4. **Use the statistics to draw conclusions about a historical event or development.** Use your reading in the textbook and the table to draw conclusions about population changes in Western Europe during the Middle Ages. Answer the following questions: (a) Describe in your own words the population changes in Western Europe between 500 and 1500. (b) What generalization can you make about population changes between 500 and 650 and between 1340 and 1450? (c) What might explain the population change between 1340 and 1450?

Population of Western Europe, 500–1500

(estimated figures, in millions)

	500	650	1000	1340	1450	1500
Italy	4.0	2.5	5.0	10.0	7.5	11.0
Spain	4.0	3.5	7.0	9.0	7.0	9.0
France, Belgium, Holland	5.0	3.0	6.0	19.0	12.0	18.0
British Isles	0.5	0.5	2.0	5.0	3.0	5.0
Germany, Scandinavia	3.5	2.0	4.0	11.5	7.5	13.0
Total	17.0	11.5	24.0	54.5	37.0	56.0

Sources: Carlo M. Cipolla, ed., *The Fontana Economic History of Europe: The Middle Ages.*
Carlo M. Cipolla, *Before the Industrial Revolution: European Society and Economy, 1000–1700.*

in their efforts to dispute Church claims to political power.

The Babylonian Captivity. In 1294, King Philip IV of France tried to tax the clergy. The pope ordered the French clergy not to pay the tax. To show that he had the support of the French people in his struggle with the pope, Philip called the first Estates General. (See page 191.) When the dispute continued, Philip kidnapped the pope. Later, he engineered the election of a French pope. The new pope moved the papacy to Avignon (ah vee NYOHN) in southern France. From 1309 to 1378, popes lived in Avignon. During this period, which became known as the Babylonian Captivity, popes were pawns of the French kings.

In 1378, the Church suffered another humiliation when two competing popes were elected: one in Avignon and the other in Rome. The Great Schism, as the new crisis was called, lasted until 1417. Finally, a Church council ended the crisis. It elected an Italian pope to rule from Rome and convinced the French king to accept the new pope.

During these scandals, the Church lost much of its political power. In France, kings assumed the right to tax the clergy. In England, Edward I declared that his country was no longer a papal fief. The Great Schism also hurt the religious authority of the Church. Many Christians were outraged at the spectacle of two popes, each claiming supreme spiritual authority.

Demands for reform. In the late 1300s, reformers attacked the Church for its wealth and the worldly concerns of the clergy. They accused the clergy of corruption and failure to perform their religious duties. One outspoken critic was John Wycliffe, a teacher of theology at Oxford University. Wycliffe questioned the spiritual authority of the Church. He claimed that the sacraments and the priests who administered them were not necessary for salvation. He encouraged his followers to translate the Bible into English so people could read it themselves. Wycliffe's ideas spread across Europe. The Church persecuted Wycliffe's supporters as heretics.

In Bohemia, part of what is today Czechoslovakia, John Huss preached against corruption in the Church. Huss was accused of heresy and burned at the stake. For years afterwards, the Church waged a crusade against the Hussites, as his followers were called. Despite severe punishments, heresies multiplied during the late Middle Ages.

The Hundred Years' War

Medieval monarchs competed with the Church and with one another as they centralized power. The efforts of the English and French kings to build strong central governments involved them in a long struggle. The fighting, known as the Hundred Years' War, lasted from 1337 to 1453.

Outbreak of war. In 1337, the English held many lands in France. As you read at the beginning of this chapter, the marriage of Eleanor of Aquitaine and Henry II had brought her vast lands under English control. Economic as well as political rivalries led to bitterness between England and France. When Edward III of England claimed the French throne, war broke out.

In the first phase of the Hundred Years' War, England won stunning victories. At the battles of Crécy and Poitiers, English armies easily dispersed the poorly led French knights.

The English victories were due in part to new weapons: the longbow and gunpowder. English archers used the longbow with deadly accuracy against heavily armed, mounted knights. Gunpowder was a Chinese invention that was probably brought to Europe by the Muslims. During the Hundred Years' War, gunpowder was used in cannons. The first cannons were not very effective. But when they were improved, cannons could destroy the walls of fortified castles and towns.

The English victories took a heavy toll on France. The French not only lost territory to the English, but also after each victory, English soldiers plundered the French countryside. To pay for the war, the French king increased taxes. The combination of war, famine, and heavy taxes led French peasants to revolt. Adding to the confusion, bitter quarrels divided the French royal family. Just when England seemed on the point of

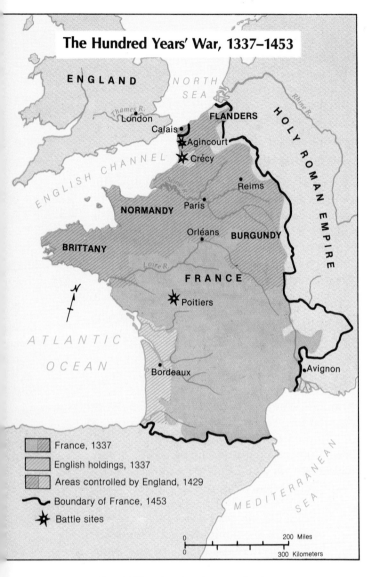

The Hundred Years' War, 1337–1453

ENGLAND

NORTH SEA

Thames R.

London

Calais

FLANDERS

★ Agincourt

★ Crécy

Rhine R.

HOLY ROMAN EMPIRE

ENGLISH CHANNEL

Reims

NORMANDY

Paris

Loire R.

Orléans

BURGUNDY

BRITTANY

F R A N C E

★ Poitiers

ATLANTIC OCEAN

Bordeaux

Avignon

MEDITERRANEAN SEA

N

France, 1337

English holdings, 1337

Areas controlled by England, 1429

Boundary of France, 1453

★ Battle sites

0   200 Miles

0   300 Kilometers

Map Skill *During the Hundred Years' War, French and English armies battled for control of France. Joan of Arc helped oust the English from Orléans and Reims, the ancient cathedral city where kings of France were crowned. What was the last city the English held?*

complete victory, the French rallied behind an uneducated peasant girl named Joan of Arc.

Joan of Arc. In 1429, Joan of Arc made her way to Charles VII, the uncrowned king of France. She claimed that heavenly voices had told her to lead the French forces. Charles reluctantly agreed to give Joan command of his armies. Under her leadership,

the French forced the English to retreat from Orléans. Joan's absolute faith and intense patriotism soon inspired the French to new victories.

In 1429, at the Cathedral of Reims, Charles was crowned King of France. Joan stood at his side. Shortly afterward, Joan was captured by the Burgundians, allies of the English. The Burgundians sold Joan to the English, who tried her for heresy. In 1431, she was burned at the stake.

Even after her death, Joan continued to inspire the French. Her martyrdom fueled a strong national feeling. Slowly but steadily, the French expelled the English from their lands. In 1453, after almost 120 years of war, the English held only Calais.

Effects of the Hundred Years' War

The people of France emerged from the Hundred Years' War with a growing sense of national pride. The French had also developed strong loyalty to their king. During the war, the king gained the power to raise taxes. Therefore, he could keep a standing army rather than depend on his vassals.

With the English gone, the king ruled most of France. Only Burgundy and Brittany remained outside royal control. The crafty French king Louis XI worked cautiously against the powerful Duke of Burgundy to bring that province under French rule. Brittany came into royal hands when Louis XI's son married Anne, the Duchess of Brittany.

Before his death in 1483, Louis XI established the basis for the absolute power of later French kings. He ruled an efficient government bureaucracy that collected taxes and administered justice. He improved the quality of the standing army and restored economic prosperity. Louis also limited the power of feudal lords. At a meeting in 1469, the Estates General asked Louis to rule without consulting it.

Although the English had lost their French lands, both the English king and Parliament emerged from the Hundred Years' War in stronger positions. Because they were no longer distracted by their fiefs in France, English kings could devote their full atten-

According to legend, when a 17-year-old peasant girl, Joan of Arc, appeared at the French court claiming that the saints had told her to save France, the king decided to test her story. He had another man sit on his throne and pretend to be king while he stood among his nobles. Although Joan had never seen the king before, she ignored the impostor on the throne and curtsied to the real king. Thus, the king took her claims seriously and gave her command of his armies.

tion to England. Parliament benefited from the king's need for money during the war. It bargained for additional rights in exchange for approving new taxes.

Soon after the Hundred Years' War ended, a civil war broke out in England. This war was known as the War of the Roses because each side supposedly used a rose as its symbol. During this 30-year struggle, most of England's feudal nobles were killed. When the war ended in 1485, a new king, Henry VII, established the strong Tudor dynasty.

In England, as in France, loyalty to the nation and the monarch replaced old feudal loyalties. But in England, monarchs did not have absolute power. They had to obey the law and learn to deal with Parliament.

Decline of Feudalism

By the late Middle Ages, the world of feudalism had changed. As strong rulers emerged to protect the people and provide good government, the need for a warrior class disappeared. The growth of towns and a money economy hurt feudal nobles. In addition, many nobles had died in battle during the Hundred Years' War.

The changing nature of warfare made mounted, armored knights almost useless. Arrows shot from the longbow knocked knights off their horses. Heavy armor prevented a fallen knight from being an effective fighter on foot. The use of cannons meant that feudal lords could no longer take refuge behind castle walls. With money from taxes, kings established standing armies. The professional soldiers in these armies were often recruited among townspeople or peasants. However, nobles did not disappear. Instead, they tended to gather at increasingly splendid royal courts.

New weapons used during the Hundred Years' War helped change the nature of warfare in the late Middle Ages. At Crécy, English foot soldiers, at the right in this picture, used the new longbow to inflict heavy casualties on the French, armed with cumbersome crossbows. The longbow gave foot soldiers new importance because they could use it to repel charges of mounted knights.

SECTION REVIEW

1. Locate: Avignon, Aquitaine, Crécy, Poitiers, Orléans, Reims, Calais.
2. Identify: Black Death, John Wycliffe, John Huss, Hundred Years' War, Joan of Arc.
3. Describe one effect of the Black Death in Western Europe.
4. What led Philip IV of France to kidnap the pope?
5. Why did the Church lose prestige and power during the late Middle Ages?
6. How did new technology help the English in the Hundred Years' War?
7. List one result of the Hundred Years' War: (a) in France; (b) in England.

Chapter 12 Review

In Perspective

During the Middle Ages, rulers in England and France established the foundations for strong central governments. In England, William the Conqueror and his successors increased royal power by establishing courts and securing a steady income from taxes. However, the Magna Carta established the principle that the English king was not above the law. In France, kings added to their landholdings and built an efficient royal bureaucracy.

For centuries, popes and Holy Roman emperors struggled for power in Italy and Germany. When the emperor Henry IV refused to obey the pope's ban on lay investiture, he was excommunicated. While emperors were distracted in Italy, feudal dukes in Germany gained power.

In Spain, Christian crusaders fought to expel the Muslims. In 1492, Ferdinand and Isabella finally won control over the entire country. In close alliance with the Church, they established absolute royal power. In Scandinavia, after the Viking raids subsided, Norway, Sweden and Denmark took steps to become unified nations.

In the 1300s and 1400s, the foundations of medieval society weakened. The Black Death had a devastating impact on Western Europe. Both France and England emerged from the Hundred Years' War with strong kings. But the war also contributed to the decline of feudalism.

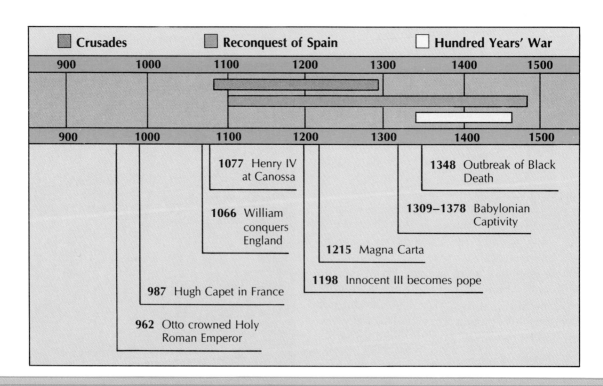

Recalling Facts

Indicate whether the following events occurred in England, France, the Holy Roman Empire, or Spain.

1. King John signed the Magna Carta.
2. Crusading knights fought to expel Muslims.
3. Philip IV called the first Estates General.
4. The jury system developed.
5. Rulers clashed with the pope over lay investiture.
6. Rulers used the Inquisition to enforce religious unity.
7. A strong bureaucracy supported the king's power.
8. Rulers tried to govern both Germany and Italy.

Chapter Checkup

1. Describe how each of the following affected royal power in England: (a) the exchequer; (b) royal courts; (c) common law; (d) the Magna Carta.
2. (a) Why were William the Conqueror's heirs able to unite England more easily than French rulers were able to unite France? (b) How did French rulers increase royal power?
3. (a) Why was there conflict between the Church and Holy Roman emperors in the 1000s and 1100s? (b) How did the conflict affect the political developments in Germany and Italy?
4. (a) Describe the Church at the height of its power under Innocent III. (b) What types of attacks were made on the Church in the 1300s and 1400s?
5. (a) Describe the reconquest of Spain. (b) How did the unification of Spain affect Muslim and Jewish residents?
6. (a) How did the Hundred Years' War affect royal power in France? (b) How did it affect royal power in England?

Critical Thinking

1. **Comparing** (a) How did the relationship between the monarch and the Church differ in England, France, Spain, and the Holy Roman Empire? (b) How would you explain the differences?

2. **Expressing an Opinion** (a) Describe the investiture controversy. (b) Do you think Gregory VII should have forgiven Henry IV and readmitted him to the Church? Explain.
3. **Analyzing a Quotation** An English soldier who saw Joan of Arc burned at the stake exclaimed: "We are lost; we have burned a saint." How did the death of Joan of Arc help the French in the Hundred Years' War?

Relating Past to Present

1. New technology often affects the outcome of battles. (a) Explain how this was true during the Hundred Years' War. (b) What new technology had affected warfare in the early Middle Ages? (c) What technological developments today will change the way war is fought?

Developing Basic Skills

1. **Map Reading** Study the map on page 200. Then answer the following questions: (a) What information is shown on the map? (b) What lands did English kings hold in France in 1429? (c) How did these holdings change between 1429 and 1453? (d) How did these changes probably affect royal power in France?
2. **Using a Primary Source** Reread the excerpts from the Magna Carta on page 190. Then answer the following questions: (a) What type of document is it? (b) What does the document say about the king's right to tax? (c) Who met in the "common council"? (d) What rights does the Magna Carta protect? (e) What do you think were the main concerns of the English barons?
3. **Making a Review Chart** Make a chart with two columns and five rows. Title the columns Early Middle Ages and Late Middle Ages. Title the rows Government, Law, Warfare, Economy, and Social Classes. Use what you learned about the Middle Ages in Chapters 10, 11, and 12 to complete the chart. Then answer the following questions: (a) How did government change during the Middle Ages? (b) How did these changes affect law? (c) What changes occurred in warfare? (d) How did changing economic conditions influence social classes in the late Middle Ages?

See page 804 for suggested readings.

Golden Ages Outside Europe

Porcelain figures manufactured during the T'ang dynasty in China.

Christian themes were important in Byzantine art. This medal from the 1100s shows Saint George.

	500	700	900	1100
POLITICS AND GOVERNMENT	**529** Justinian's Code summarizes Roman law	**800** Ghana rises to power in Africa	**960** Sung restore order in China	
ECONOMICS AND TECHNOLOGY		**800s** Gold-salt trade grows in West Africa	**1000s** Avicenna writes medical books	
SOCIETY AND CULTURE	**622** Muhammad journeys to Medina	**800s** Cyril and Methodius create Slavic alphabet	**1050** Movable type developed in China	

630 When Muhammad returned to Mecca from the hejira, he destroyed the idols in the Kaaba.

Golden figures such as this one reveal the skill of African artists and the wealth of early African kingdoms.

Muslim mosques such as this one from Persia were decorated with elaborate designs.

Samurai warriors developed a code of chivalry in feudal Japan.

1100	1300	1500	1700

1206 Muslims set up Delhi sultanate in India

1450 Inca create empire in the Andes

1603 Tokugawa shogun unites Japan

1405 Chinese begin trading expeditions

1543 Portuguese trading ships first arrive in Japan

1325 Aztec build capital of Tenochtitlán

1623 Muslim ruler of India builds Taj Mahal

Red grasshopper carved by an Aztec artist.

Hindu traditions, reflected in this painting, remained strong in India even after the Muslim conquest.

13 Byzantine and Islamic Civilizations

(330–1453)

Mosaic of the Byzantine empress Theodora.

> **Chapter Outline**
>
> 1 The Byzantine Empire
>
> 2 Eastern Europe: Heir to Byzantine Civilization
>
> 3 Emergence of Islam
>
> 4 Islamic Civilization

In the twelfth century, crusaders and other travelers from Western Europe passed through Constantinople on their way to Palestine. They marveled at the splendor of the city. One visitor, Benjamin of Tudela, noted: "Great stir and bustle prevails at Constantinople because of the many merchants who travel there, both by land and by sea, from all parts of the world for purposes of trade. . . ."

The visitor was dazzled by the riches of the emperor's palace. "The pillars and walls are covered with pure gold," he exclaimed, "and all the wars of the ancients, as well as [later] wars, are represented in pictures. The throne in this palace is of gold, and ornamented with precious stones. . . ." The source of this great wealth was "the tribute which is brought to Constantinople every year from all parts of Greece, consisting of silks, purple cloths, and gold." Such riches, he claimed, were unmatched anywhere in the world.

In fact, Constantinople was the richest city in Europe in the twelfth century. In 330, you will recall, Constantine had moved the capital of the Roman Empire to the Greek town of Byzantium, which was soon renamed Constantinople. When the empire was divided in 395, Constantinople became the capital of the Eastern Roman Empire. Unlike the Western Roman Empire, which collapsed in the fifth century, the Eastern Roman Empire survived until 1453. It was called the Byzantine Empire from the original name of the Greek town.

During the Middle Ages, when Western Europe was politically weak and divided, the Byzantine Empire flourished. For centuries, it absorbed the shock waves of invasions from further east and served as a buffer for Western

Europe. Eventually, Byzantine civilization passed its heritage on to the peoples of Eastern Europe.

In the seventh century, the religion of Islam took root in the Middle East. Islam spread rapidly to many regions of the world, and Muslim armies conquered parts of the Byzantine Empire. Islam gave birth to a new civilization that built on many ancient traditions.

1 The Byzantine Empire

Read to Learn
- what the strengths of the Byzantine Empire were
- why the Byzantine Empire declined

While medieval civilization was developing in Western Europe, the Byzantine Empire dominated the eastern Mediterranean. Although both Western Europe and the Byzantine Empire inherited Roman traditions, each developed its own distinctive civilization.

Building and Defending the Empire

Justinian, who ruled the Byzantine Empire from 527 to 565, dreamed of restoring a united Roman Empire. He spent most of his reign fighting to recover the western parts of the Roman Empire from German invaders. His armies defeated the Vandals and seized southern Spain and parts of northern Africa. In another long and costly war, the Byzantines retook the Italian peninsula from the Ostrogoths. (See the map on page 208.) But these victories were short-lived. Within a few years after Justinian's death, the Lombards drove the Byzantines out of Italy.

Byzantine armies also fought in the east. In the fifth century, the empire absorbed the worst of the Hun invasions. Later, the Slavs, Bulgars, and Magyars swept out of Eastern Europe but were held at bay. In addition, the Byzantine Empire was locked in a long struggle with the large and powerful Persian Empire. Then, in the seventh century, the armies of Islam attacked the Byzantine Empire. Muslims reached the walls of Constantinople before they were driven back.

To survive, Byzantine emperors became skillful diplomats. A network of spies fed them with information. Byzantine rulers acquired a reputation for intrigue because they often used bribery or other means to play one enemy off against another. They also bought peace by marrying their daughters to potential rivals. When all else failed, emperors depended on military strength.

Strengths of the Empire

The Byzantine Empire lasted over 1,000 years, from 395 to 1453. During this period, the will of the emperors was law. An efficient civil service administered the daily business of government. A loyal, well-trained army and a strong economy also helped the empire survive periods of instability and invasion.

The emperor had complete control over the Byzantine economy. He set wages and prices and established a monopoly, or exclusive control, over manufacturing. For example, in the sixth century, silkworms were smuggled out of China and brought to Constantinople. The emperor made the manufacture of silk a state monopoly. Profits from that thriving industry helped fill the imperial treasury. The emperor also benefited from taxes on trade.

At a time when political chaos brought trade to a near standstill in Western Europe, the towns and cities of the Byzantine Empire prospered. Byzantine coins were accepted as the most stable currency in the Mediterranean world. Merchants from the Middle East and Viking traders from the north brought goods to the busy markets of cities such as Constantinople.

Constantinople itself became a center of world commerce. It overlooked the Bosporus, the narrow straits that separate Europe from Asia. The city, which had about one million inhabitants, reflected extremes of wealth and poverty. The officials and nobles of the court spent fabulous sums on clothing, jewelry, and entertainment. But the masses of men and women struggled for survival. Riots were common. On occasion, rioters tried to overthrow the emperor.

A Split Between East and West

Religious disputes and economic competition strained relations between the Byzantine Empire and Western Europe. The Byzantine emperor did not recognize the pope as leader of the Christian Church. As an absolute ruler, the emperor headed the Church within his lands. Thus, the Church did not become a rival center of political power in the Byzantine Empire, as it had in Western Europe.

In the Byzantine Empire, the clergy were considered state officials and were responsible to the emperor. The emperor appointed *patriarchs*, the bishops of the major cities. The emperor also interfered in religious disputes and made decisions on matters of faith.

Religion was very important to Christians in both Western Europe and the Byzantine Empire. However, Christian churches in the two areas developed different practices and forms of worship. Greek rather than Latin was the language of the Church in the Byzantine Empire. Unlike clergy in Western Europe, Byzantine priests could marry. Furthermore, the Byzantine Church was tolerant of non-Christian religions such as Islam.

In the eighth century, a bitter dispute arose between the emperor and the pope over the use of sacred images called icons. This conflict set the stage for the final split in the Christian Church. In an effort to reform

Map Skill *The Byzantine Empire, which reached its greatest size under Justinian, was constantly threatened by invaders. Parts of the empire fell to the Lombards, the Persians, and other armies. Why did the location of Constantinople help it withstand attacks? What parts of the empire remained by 1000?*

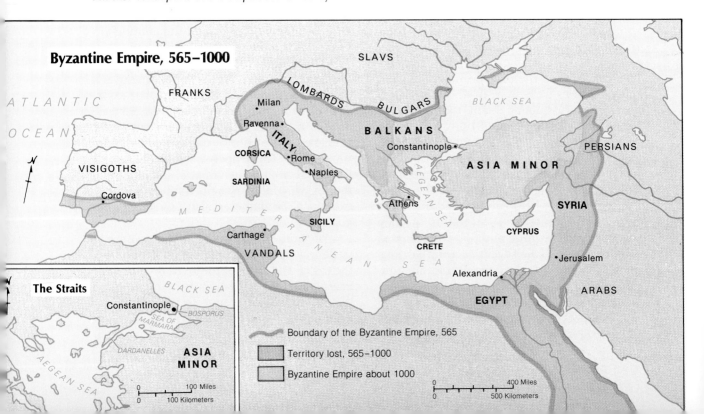

the Church, one Byzantine emperor banned the worship of icons. However, the pope thought icons, which portrayed Christian saints, helped people understand Church teachings. Therefore, he excommunicated the emperor.

Although Byzantine churches eventually restored the use of icons, later popes and emperors regularly excommunicated each other. In 1054, a schism, or split, left the Christian Church divided into the Roman Catholic Church and the Eastern Orthodox Church.

As trade revived in Western Europe, economic rivalry worsened relations between the two regions. In 1204, Venetian merchants bribed crusaders to attack Constantinople. (See page 182.) For centuries, the Greeks of the Byzantine Empire kept alive bitter memories of Christian knights looting their city and burning their churches.

The Byzantine Heritage

As the center of Byzantine civilization, Constantinople reflected a blend of Roman, Christian, Greek, and Middle Eastern influences. This mixed heritage was evident in Byzantine art and architecture.

The Church of Santa Sophia built by the emperor Justinian reflected these varied traditions. It was designed on a grand scale like the monuments of ancient Rome. Beneath the huge domed roof was a magnificent interior. Elaborate mosaics illustrated Christian stories. Byzantine artists copied ancient Greek and Roman styles in picturing lifelike figures of saints. Persian and other Middle Eastern styles were reflected in the brilliant colors and detail of the mosaics.

Byzantine emperors such as Justinian made significant contributions to civilization because they helped preserve the Greco-Roman heritage. They collected classical works on science, mathematics, and philosophy and stored them in libraries.

Preserving Roman Law

By preserving Roman traditions, the Byzantine Empire had a lasting impact on ideas about law and justice. The emperor Justinian ordered scholars to summarize all exist-

Byzantine architects created a monument of lasting beauty in the Church of Santa Sophia. It was built in Constantinople in 537. The church is crowned by a huge dome. Its walls were decorated with glittering mosaics. Architects in Western Europe later copied Byzantine building techniques. This photograph shows how light from many windows illuminates the interior of Santa Sophia.

ing Roman law. They produced a huge work later known as Justinian's Code.

The code kept Roman legal traditions alive in the Byzantine Empire. It also became the chief source of Roman law in Western Europe. During the early Middle Ages, Roman law was largely forgotten in the west. But when scholars from universities in Italy and France visited Constantinople, they eagerly copied Justinian's Code.

The code contained basic principles that helped shape the legal systems of Western Europe and, later, of the Americas. For example, it listed rules of evidence: "The person who accuses someone must prove that his charge is true. This is not the obligation of the person denying the charge." This principle developed into the idea that an accused person is innocent until proven guilty.

Decline of the Empire

Internal and external pressures led to the decline of the Byzantine Empire. As in ancient Rome, civil wars over succession to the throne weakened the government. External threats came from the east and the west. In the late 1000s, the Seljuk Turks conquered the Middle East, including Byzantine lands in Asia Minor. As you read, Christian crusaders attacked the Byzantine Empire in 1204. The empire recovered, but it then faced a new Turkish threat in Asia Minor when the Ottoman dynasty came to power.

The Ottomans built a strong Turkish state with disciplined, able officials. In the 1400s, the Ottoman Turks bypassed Constantinople and advanced into the Balkans. The Byzantine emperor appealed to rulers in Western Europe for help but received none.

In 1453, the Ottomans took Constantinople. They changed the name of the city to Istanbul and made it the capital of the Ottoman Empire. You will read more about the Ottoman Empire in Chapter 18.

The fall of Constantinople signaled the end of the Byzantine Empire. However, Byzantine traditions continued to influence Western Europe and Eastern Europe.

SECTION REVIEW

1. Locate Constantinople, Bosporus, Balkans.
2. Identify: Justinian, Eastern Orthodox Church, Santa Sophia, Justinian's Code, Ottoman Turks.
3. Define: patriarch.
4. List the areas Justinian added to the Byzantine Empire.
5. Describe two factors that caused strained relations between the Byzantine Empire and Western Europe.
6. Describe one way in which the Byzantine Empire preserved the Greco-Roman heritage.

2 Eastern Europe: Heir to Byzantine Civilization

Read to Learn
- how Byzantine civilization influenced Europe
- how Russia developed under the first czars

For many centuries before it collapsed, the Byzantine Empire influenced the Slavic peoples of Eastern Europe. Religion was the chief means by which the Byzantines transmitted their heritage to the Slavs.

The Peoples of Eastern Europe

Eastern Europe stretches from the Ural Mountains in the east to the Oder River in the west. It includes the lands lying between the Baltic Sea in the north and the Adriatic Sea in the south.

The Slavs were an Indo-European people who lived in the region around Kiev in Russia. Between 200 A.D. and 400 A.D. some Slavs migrated from Kiev into the Balkans. They settled in what is today Yugoslavia and Bulgaria. Others moved further west into Poland and Czechoslovakia.

The Slavs organized states in Eastern Europe similar to those set up by the early Germans in Western Europe. The Slavs who settled in the Balkans soon came under the influence of Byzantine civilization. In the ninth century, Cyril and Methodius, two Greek monks, converted many Slavs to Christianity. For their work, they became known as "Apostles to the Slavs."

Cyril and Methodius were successful in part because they spoke the Slavic language. The Slavs had no written language, so the monks devised an alphabet. They used mostly Greek letters, but they also included some Hebrew letters. The Slavic alphabet is called the *Cyrillic alphabet* (suh RIHL ihk) after Cyril. With the new alphabet, people could translate the Bible and other Christian works into the Slavic vernacular.

Kievan Russia

In the 800s and 900s, Kiev emerged as the center of a prosperous Slavic state, known as Kievan Russia. Byzantine civilization had a great impact on the developing Russian culture. Kiev was linked to Constantinople by the Dnieper (NEE puhr) River, which flows into the Black Sea.

Russians first converted to Christianity because of contacts with the Byzantines. When the Russian prince Vladimir decided to abandon the old Slavic gods, he debated whether to choose Islam, Judaism, or Christianity. He rejected Islam and Judaism because these religions forbade eating certain foods. He then sent envoys to Rome and Constantinople to help him decide which form of Christianity to follow. The envoys to Rome reported that Christians in the west observed periods of fasting.* Vladimir then chose the Byzantine Church.

Vladimir had other reasons for being attracted to Byzantine Christianity. His envoys to Constantinople had described the magnificent Byzantine civilization. Upon seeing Byzantine churches, they exclaimed, "We knew not whether we were in heaven or on earth, for on earth there is no such splendor or beauty." In addition, the Byzantine Church allowed the Slavs to use their own language whereas the pope would have insisted on Latin. Finally, in the Byzantine Empire, the secular ruler, not the pope, headed the Church.

After they converted to Byzantine Christianity, Russians came into even closer contact with Byzantine culture. Princes of the towns and cities of Kievan Russia imitated Byzantine emperors. For example, the prince of Kiev built his own Church of Saint Sophia, which reflected the Byzantine style of architecture. In addition, the Christian clergy became an important class in Kievan society. They established schools and taught the Cyrillic alphabet.

After about 1050, Kievan Russia declined because of civil wars among the rul-

Greek monks carried Christianity to the peoples of Eastern Europe and Russia. When Slavic artists created religious works of art, they often imitated Byzantine styles. This icon from Eastern Europe shows St. Dimiter slaying a dragon. Byzantine influence is evident in the frozen positions of the figures as well as in the domed building and gold background.

ing princes. In the 1200s, the Russian cities were too weak to withstand the fierce Mongol armies that burst out of central Asia.

Mongol Invasions

The Mongols were originally nomadic herders, but in the thirteenth century, they conquered an empire extending from China to Eastern Europe.† In 1240, one group of Mongols captured and destroyed Kiev. The "Golden Horde," as the invaders were called, ruled Russia for nearly 250 years.

---

*On certain holy days, Christians fasted in memory of saints or events in the life of Jesus. During fasts, they ate little or no food.

---

†You will read about Mongol rulers in India and China in Chapter 15.

The Mongols demanded heavy tribute from the Russians. Russian princes collected and delivered the yearly payments. As long as the Russians paid their tribute, the Mongols did not interfere with Russian daily life. However, Mongol rule affected Russian life in many ways. Some Russian princes adopted the manners and practices of Mongol rulers. Furthermore, taxes to raise the tribute money burdened the peasants, who sometimes revolted. Local princes quickly crushed such revolts.

Most important, Mongol rule cut Russia off from contacts with Western Europe. Commerce and industry, which had prospered in early Kievan Russia, largely disappeared. Between 1240 and 1500, Russians were scarcely aware of the ideas that were shaping the civilization of Western Europe.

Princes of Moscow

In the 1300s, the princes of Moscow, a city in northern Russia, gained power at the same time as Mongol strength declined. They grew rich by keeping part of the tribute collected for the Mongols. Eventually, a prince of Moscow took the title "Grand Prince of All Russia." He persuaded the Eastern Orthodox Church to move its center to Moscow.

During the 1400s, Moscow became the center of a unified Russian state. Ivan III, a prince of Moscow who ruled from 1462 to 1505, has been called the founder of modern Russia. In 1480, Ivan announced that he would no longer pay tribute to the Mongols. He made alliances with other Russian princes and finally ended Mongol rule. Ivan III also expelled German nobles from the lands they had seized in western Russia.

Ivan freed Russia from foreign rule and established a strong government. The new Russian state reflected Byzantine traditions. Ivan married Sophia Paleologus (pay lee OHL oo guhs), niece of the last Byzantine emperor. He then took the title "czar," the Russian word for Caesar.

Ivan called Moscow the "third Rome," the successor to ancient Rome and Constantinople, the second Rome. Russian rulers adopted the double-headed eagle, symbol of Byzantine emperors, as their own symbol. Like Byzantine rulers, the czars gained absolute power over both the government and the Church.

Ivan IV, who ruled from 1533 to 1584, exercised this absolute power. He claimed his power came directly from God and had hundreds of *boyars*, powerful nobles, killed because they opposed his will. He estab-

Map Skill *Over many years, the princes of Moscow gradually took control of a great deal of territory. By 1584, Ivan IV ruled a large Russian state. However, Russian power and foreign trade were limited by the location of Russia. What geographical factors cut Russia off from contacts with western nations?*

Growth of Russia, 1300–1584

SWEDEN
Novgorod
Moscow
LITHUANIA
Warsaw
POLAND
Kiev
KAZAN
URAL MTS
Ob R.
Ural R.
Volga R.
CAUCASUS MTS
BLACK SEA
CASPIAN SEA
BALTIC SEA
Danube R.
Dnieper R.
Constantinople

Extent of Mongol conquest, 1300
Moscow, 1300
Territory added, 1300–1462
Territory added, 1462–1533
Territory added, 1533–1584

0   800 Miles
0   1000 Kilometers

lished a secret police force that brutally enforced his authority. He was called Ivan the Terrible for his cruelty and madness.

In the 1500s, Russian rulers renewed their contacts with Western Europe. Yet Russia continued to develop differently from Western European nations. A form of feudalism evolved in Russia just when feudalism was declining in Western Europe. Ivan IV gave fiefs to nobles who agreed to perform military service. But he kept strict control over the nobles. He also issued laws that tied peasants to the land. Thus, many Russian peasants lost their freedom and became serfs at a time when serfs were winning their freedom in Western Europe.

SECTION REVIEW

1. Locate: Ural Mountains, Baltic Sea, Kiev, Dnieper River, Moscow.
2. Identify: Golden Horde, Ivan III, Ivan IV.
3. Define: Cyrillic alphabet, boyar.
4. What factor helped Cyril and Methodius convert the Slavs to Christianity?
5. List two reasons why Vladimir converted to Byzantine Christianity rather than Roman Christianity.
6. What was the major effect of the Mongol invasion of Russia?
7. Give one example of how the rulers of Moscow were influenced by the Byzantine Empire.

3 Emergence of Islam

Read to Learn
■ how Islam emerged in the Middle East
■ why Islam spread throughout the Mediterranean world

During the seventh century, the religion of Islam rose in the Middle East. Like Judaism and Christianity, Islam had a profound impact on history. Within 100 years after Islam was founded, its followers had built an empire that was larger than the Roman Empire at its height.

Geographic Setting

Arabia, the birthplace of Islam, is the largest peninsula in the world. It is a hilly, arid land dotted with occasional oases, fertile areas with enough water to support trees and plants. As great civilizations rose and fell in the Fertile Crescent to the north, the Arabs developed a way of life well adapted to desert conditions.

Most Arabs were nomads who herded goats and camels. They were loosely organized into tribes with strong codes of honor. Their poets praised the fierce independence of their warriors. This independence led to frequent feuds that prevented unity among the different Arab tribes.

Arabia was a vital link between the Mediterranean world, Asia, and the east coast of Africa. Some Arabs, who lived in towns along the Red Sea, traded with the Greco-Roman world as well as with India, China, and Africa.

Mecca, a town near the Red Sea, prospered as a trading and religious center. Pilgrims traveled to Mecca to worship at the Kaaba, a sacred shrine that housed images of all the Arab gods. The Kaaba also housed a black stone—probably a meteorite—that the Arabs believed was sent from heaven.

Muhammad: Founder of Islam

Muhammad was born in Mecca about 570. His parents died when he was still a child, and he was raised by relatives who belonged to a poor but prominent Arab family. Little else is known about Muhammad's early life.

At age 25, Muhammad married Khadija (kah DEE jah), a wealthy widow who ran her late husband's business. With Khadija's help, Muhammad became a successful merchant. Yet he was troubled by the violence and treachery he saw in the world. He often went into the desert to pray. When he prayed, Muhammad believed that the angel

Gabriel spoke to him, saying that God had chosen Muhammad to be his prophet. Muhammad's duty was to proclaim that Allah, or God, was the one and only God.

At first, only Khadija and a few friends believed Muhammad. The merchants and innkeepers of Mecca opposed him. They thought that his teaching about one God would destroy their income from Arab pilgrims. Threatened with death, Muhammad and his followers fled Mecca in 622. They were welcomed at Yathrib, a rival commercial town on the Red Sea. Yathrib, later renamed Medina, became known as the City of the Prophet.

Muslims call Muhammad's journey from Mecca to Medina the *hejira* (hih JĪ ruh), or departure. The year 622 was made the first year of the Muslim calendar. The hejira marked a turning point in Muhammad's life. In Medina, he gained power as both a religious and political leader.

In 630, Muhammad returned to Mecca at the head of an army and captured the city. He went directly to the Kaaba, where he proclaimed, "There is but one God, and Allah is his name." He then destroyed the hundreds of idols inside the Kaaba. Muhammad left the Black Stone untouched because he believed it had come from God. Thus Arabs continued to make pilgrimages to Mecca, which remained the holy city it had been in the past. Before Muhammad died in 632, he worked to unite the Arabs. After his death, his followers carried the message of Islam in many directions.

Teachings of Islam

The word Islam means "submission." Muslims believe that they must submit their will to God. The Five Pillars of Islam refer to the essential duties of every faithful Muslim. First, and most important, is the belief in one God. The Muslim call to prayer repeats this basic belief: "There is no God but Allah, and Muhammad is the prophet of God." Muslims do not worship Muhammad as a god. He is considered a human who was the messenger of God.

The second duty is prayer. Five times a day, faithful Muslims turn to face the holy city of Mecca and pray. Islam teaches concern for the poor, so giving alms, an act of charity, is the third duty. The fourth duty is fasting during the holy month of Ramadan (RAM uh DAHN). Finally, all Muslims are supposed to make a pilgrimage to Mecca at least once in their lives. The act of worshipping together at the Kaaba has helped to unify Muslims from all over the world.

Islam has no formal church or clergy. All worshippers are considered equal. They may pray alone or assemble at a *mosque*, the Muslim meeting place. At the mosque, an imam (ih MAHM) leads the worshippers in prayer.

The Koran. Muslims rely on the Koran, their holy book, for guidance in all matters. They believe the Koran contains the word of God as it was revealed to his prophet Muhammad. "Let the Koran always be your guide," said Muhammad. "Do what it commands . . . shun what it forbids." The Koran became the basis for government and law in the Islamic world.

The Koran was written in Arabic. As a result, Arabic became the universal language among Muslims from many different cultures. Arabic continues to be used for religious purposes even among Muslims who are not Arabs.

People of the Book. Muhammad accepted the Old and New Testaments as God's word. He called Jews and Christians "People of the Book" because they believed in God's revelations in the Bible. Muslims recognized a close relationship with the People of the Book and, therefore, protected Jews and Christians—in theory if not always in practice.

Some teachings of Islam are similar to those of Judaism and Christianity. Muslims share with Jews and Christians the belief in one God. Like Jews and Christians, Muslims believe in a last judgment day, when people will be rewarded or punished, depending on how they conducted their lives. They also believe that Abraham, Moses, and Jesus were great prophets. But Muhammad, as God's final messenger, has the highest authority.

Because Muslims believed that the Koran is the sacred word of God, they reproduced it with special care. Pages from the Koran, such as the one shown here, were decorated with elaborate calligraphy, or writing, and patterned borders.

Like other influential teachers and philosophers, Muhammad established rules for ethical behavior. Individuals, he said, were responsible for their own actions. They should behave with charity, humility, and mercy.

Effect of Islam on the Status of Women

The Koran gave women a legal and economic status they had not previously enjoyed in Arabia. Before Muhammad, Arab women had no property rights. They were entirely at the mercy of their fathers or husbands. Islamic law gave women inheritance rights and control over their own property. Although the Koran permitted a man to divorce his wife, he was required to return her dowry, that is, the property she had brought to their marriage. In addition, the Koran strictly forbade the killing of unwanted baby girls, a common practice in many ancient societies.

In early Islamic society, women enjoyed considerable freedom. Women artists, physicians, and religious scholars had influence in society and government. However, gradually, restrictions were placed on them. Women were excluded from public places and were secluded within the home. Yet a woman was always protected. If she were divorced, her family took care of her. If her husband died, her sons looked after her. An unmarried woman could rely on her father or brothers to protect her.

A woman's duties were to obey her husband, care for the children, and manage the household. As head of the household, the man enjoyed complete authority. But within her home, a woman could, and often did, exercise considerable influence.

Expansion of Islam

Between 622 and 732, Islam spread with amazing speed. The Arabs carried their religion to the peoples of Palestine and Syria and across North Africa into Spain. By 732, Muslim forces had crossed the Pyrenees Mountains into southern France, where they were stopped by Charles Martel. (See page 152.) Just as swiftly, Islam won converts from the Fertile Crescent east to the Indus Valley. (See the map on page 216.)

There were many reasons for the rapid spread of Islam. Its message was clear and simple. Muslims believed in one God and the equality of all believers. They did not need a church or clergy in order to practice their faith. Furthermore, Muhammad and his successors united the Arabs for the first time and gave them a strong sense of purpose—to spread the message of Islam. Inspired by loyalty to Islam, Arab soldiers believed that if they died fighting for the faith they would immediately enter paradise.

The weakness of the neighboring Byzantine and Persian empires also contributed to the success of Islam. Centuries of warfare had exhausted these empires. Many people were dissatisfied with Byzantine or Persian rule, and they did not fight the Arabs effectively. Some people welcomed the armies of Islam as liberators. Islam brought stable, orderly government in place of corruption.

When Muslim armies conquered parts of the Byzantine Empire, some Christians, Jews, and Zoroastrians were ready to accept the teachings of Islam. Yet Muslims did not force people to convert. They required non-Muslims to pay a special tax, but otherwise non-Muslims could worship as they chose. In fact, Muslim conquerors often were not anxious to convert people because this would lower tax revenues.

Ruling an Empire

When Muhammad died, he left no heir to lead Islam. A close friend, Abu Bakr, was elected *caliph* (KAY lihf), or successor to the prophet. The caliph acted as both religious and political leader. He used the law of the Koran as the basis for ruling the empire.

Power struggles surrounded the elections of the first four caliphs. Then, in 661, a leading family of Mecca established the Umayyad (oo MĪ ad) dynasty. For a century, the Umayyads presided over the expansion of Islam. The Umayyad dynasty made Damascus in Syria the capital of the Islamic Empire. Mecca remained the spiritual center of Islam. Under the Umayyads, the Arabs absorbed ideas from Hellenistic and Byzantine civilizations.

Despite the enormous success of the Umayyad armies, problems appeared within the Islamic Empire. Some of the people who had been absorbed into the empire began to assert their independence. In addition, two competing branches developed within Islam, the Sunnite (SOON īt) and Shiite (SHEE īt).

The two branches differed over who was the rightful successor to Muhammad. The more numerous Sunnites supported the Umayyad caliph. The Shiites were loyal to a

Map Skill *Islam spread rapidly in the century after the death of Muhammad. By 750, Muslims controlled much of the trade of the Mediterranean world. Under which caliphs did Islam reach the limits of its expansion? In what years?*

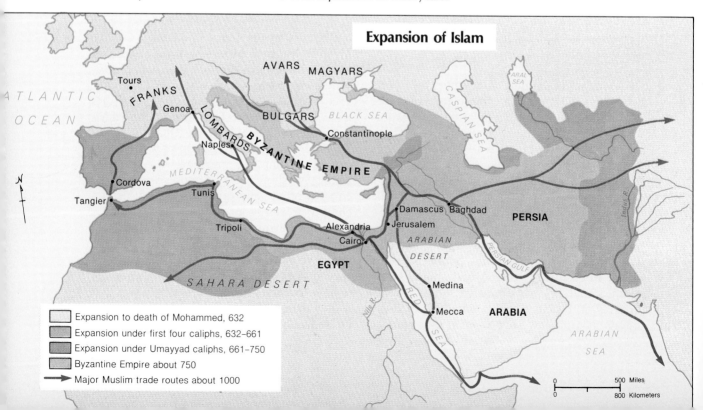

Expansion of Islam

Expansion to death of Mohammed, 632
Expansion under first four caliphs, 632–661
Expansion under Umayyad caliphs, 661–750
Byzantine Empire about 750
Major Muslim trade routes about 1000

religious leader who traced his family back to Ali, Muhammad's son-in-law. Shiites broke into many sects. Those groups rallied support among people who were discontent with the established rule.

In 750, discontent erupted into violence. A new dynasty, the Abbasids (uh BAS ihds), overthrew the Umayyads. However, in Spain, a member of the Umayyad dynasty became caliph and ruled outside of Abbasid control. North Africa also remained outside.

The early Abbasid rulers were effective leaders. They built a splendid new capital in Baghdad. In the late 700s, under Harun al-Rashid, the Islamic Empire enjoyed a golden age. Later Abbasid rulers left the business of government to corrupt officials, and after 1000, the empire became fragmented.

In the eleventh century, the Seljuk Turks invaded the Islamic Empire. Although they converted to Islam, their traditions differed from those of the Arabs. The rule of the Seljuks in Palestine, you will recall, brought the first wave of crusaders to the Holy Land. (See page 179.) Later, the Islamic Empire faced other invaders. In 1258, the Mongols destroyed Baghdad and ended Abbasid rule. Eventually, the Ottoman Turks reunited Egypt, Syria, Iraq, and Arabia into an Islamic state that lasted until 1918.

(See page 179.)

SECTION REVIEW

1. Locate: Arabia, Mecca, Medina, Damascus, Baghdad.
2. Identify: Kaaba, Muhammad, Koran, People of the Book, Sunnite, Shiite.
3. Define: hejira, mosque, caliph.
4. Describe the Five Pillars of Islam.
5. List two reasons for the rapid spread of Islam.
6. When did the Islamic Empire enjoy its golden age?

---

4 Islamic Civilization

Read to Learn
- why the Islamic world became prosperous
- what Muslims contributed to art and science

Islamic civilization drew on the rich heritages of Greek, Roman, Byzantine, Persian, and Indian cultures. Muslims blended these traditions to create their own distinct civilization. In addition, Muslims played a significant role in shaping civilization in Western Europe because they transmitted many ideas to the peoples of Europe.

Economic Prosperity

From its center in the Middle East, the Islamic Empire commanded the vital trade routes of the world. Muslim merchants handled the products of three continents—Africa, Asia, and Europe. During much of the Middle Ages, Muslim fleets patrolled the Mediterranean.

Cities and commerce thrived in the Islamic world at a time when most people in Western Europe lived on small, isolated manors. The spectacular wealth and luxury of cities such as Baghdad were unknown in Western Europe. The Abbasid capital boasted hospitals, libraries, palaces, public gardens, and even street lighting.

The Arabs developed commercial practices that made trade easier. They introduced the use of letters of credit in place of cash. They issued receipts for payment and bills of lading that listed all goods in a shipment. Merchants and bankers in Western Europe later adopted these practices from the Arabs.

Within the empire, manufacturing flourished. Steel used in swords and textiles such as cotton, gauze, and satin were the most important industries. In addition, improvements in agriculture helped farmers produce more food to feed large city populations.

Traditions of Learning

Islam had an impact on many fields of learning. Muhammad taught that "the ink of the scholar is holier than the blood of the martyr." Encouraged by this idea, scholars flocked to the centers of learning that grew up in the cities of the Islamic Empire.

The Koran was the focus of much Muslim scholarship. Legal experts wrote many texts in which they interpreted the Koran. Their writings became part of the Islamic law code. Islamic law, along with common religious beliefs and the use of Arabic, helped unite Muslims on three continents.

Yet Muslim scholars did not limit their studies to the Koran. They translated ancient Greek works on philosophy and science. At centers of learning such as the House of Wisdom in Baghdad, scholars also studied Roman, Jewish, Persian, and Indian texts. In this way, the Arabs preserved much ancient learning.

Achievements in Medicine, Mathematics, and the Sciences

Muslim scholars made original contributions in medicine, mathematics, and other sciences. Guided by ancient Greek texts, Muslim doctors perfected techniques for diagnosing and treating diseases. In the ninth century, Muhammad al-Razi (RAY zee), known to Europeans as Rhazes, published a huge medical encyclopedia called the *Comprehensive Work in Medicine.* In it, he detailed the symptoms of such contagious diseases as smallpox and measles.

Muslims also set up an advanced system of medical training, which included a qualifying examination for doctors and pharmacists. Medical schools in Europe later drew on Muslim medical research and practices.

Muslim mathematicians studied the works of ancient scholars such as Euclid. They also adopted the decimal system and the system of numerals from India.* With the decimal system, Muslims made advances

in algebra and trigonometry. In fact, the word "algebra" is based on an Arabic term.

Like the Greeks, Muslim scientists were interested in all aspects of the natural world. Geographers described their travels from China to Spain. In their search for precious metals, Muslim alchemists advanced the science of chemistry. They invented equipment such as beakers and crystallizing dishes still used in laboratories today.

Other Muslim scientists made significant discoveries. One scholar proposed that the earth was round and accurately estimated its circumference. He also suggested that the earth rotated on its axis. Muslims used the magnetic needle, invented by the Chinese, to produce the mariner's compass.

The astronomers shown here are at work in the Istanbul Observatory. Muslim astronomers studied the theories of Ptolemy and discovered that his theories did not fit their own findings. Through careful observation and new methods of calculation, they made startling discoveries that influenced scientific thinking everywhere.

---

*As you read earlier, people in Western Europe later called this system "Arabic numerals."

Muslims translated many ancient Greek and Persian works into Arabic and also made their own contributions to the world's knowledge. One of the most brilliant Muslim thinkers was Ibn Sina, known to Europeans as Avicenna (AV ih SEHN uh).

Avicenna was born in 980 near Bukkara, a center of Islamic culture in Persia. As a boy, he quickly learned the Koran and mastered geometry, logic, law, and Arabic literature. Soon, he knew more than his teachers. When the Muslim ruler of Persia heard of young Avicenna's genius, he invited the boy to study in his library. There, Avicenna taught himself physics, theology, mathematics, astronomy, philosophy, and medicine.

Avicenna put his learning to good use. At age 16, he was a successful physician. He treated Persian nobles and later served as chief minister and personal physician to several rulers.

His life at court was full of adventures. From time to time, he fell into official disfavor and was thrown into prison. Once, he escaped from prison disguised as a religious beggar. During his lifetime, he traveled widely in Persia practicing medicine. It was said that he studied wherever he was, even while on horseback or in prison.

Avicenna wrote over 100 books on subjects ranging from astronomy, music, and philosophy to medicine and poetry. His books on philosophy, which reflected the teachings of Aristotle and Plato, influenced Christian scholars in the late Middle Ages. His major work was the *Canon of Medicine,* a summary of what the Greeks, the Arabs, and Avicenna knew about the diagnosis and treatment of disease. The *Canon* was translated into Latin in the 1100s. It remained the leading medical textbook among Muslims and Christians for about 600 years.

Avicenna was not only a brilliant scholar and physician but also a dedicated medical researcher and pharmacist. For example, he explained how disease could be spread by water from a polluted well or river. On his travels, he collected a great deal of information about medicines and herbs. He studied over 750 medical remedies and published the first handbook that told physicians the remedies for different diseases.

The mariner's compass and the astrolabe, another Muslim invention, enabled sailors to find their position at sea. These inventions would have a great impact on European explorers, as you will read in Chapter 17.

The Arts and Literature

Muslims adapted ideas in architecture from the many peoples within the Islamic Empire. Mosques reflected a blend of Roman, Byzantine, and Persian styles. Graceful Roman arches made up arcades, which were decorated with Persian designs. Columns supported domed roofs similar to those of Byzantine churches. Outside the mosque, architects designed slender towers called *minarets.*

To Muslims, the Koran was the greatest written work in Arabic because they believed it was the revealed word of God. Muslim philosophers frequently wrote about religious questions. For example, the philosopher Averroës (uh VEHR oh EEZ), a Spanish Muslim, tried to reconcile the teachings of Aristotle with Islam. Through careful logic, he tried to prove that there was no conflict between faith and reason. His writings later influenced Christian scholastics like Thomas Aquinas. (See page 194.)

Poets held an honored place in the Islamic world. Romantic themes often inspired poetry. In his long poem *The Rubaiyat*, the Persian poet Omar Khayyám wrote about nature and love. In another well-known work, *A Thousand and One Nights*, Muslims collected stories, from all over the world. These stories, which include "Aladdin

and His Magic Lamp," have been translated into almost every known language.

SECTION REVIEW

1. Identify: Muhammad al-Razi, Averroës, Omar Khayyám.

2. Define: minaret.

3. What commercial practices did the Arabs develop?

4. How did the Arabs preserve much ancient learning?

5. Describe one contribution Muslims made to medicine.

Chapter 13 Review

In Perspective

During the Middle Ages, the Eastern Roman Empire continued to exist as the Byzantine Empire. The Byzantine Empire reached its greatest size under Justinian. A strong economy helped it withstand many enemies until it fell to the Ottoman Turks in 1453.

The Byzantines preserved Greek learning and Roman law. They also influenced the Slavic peoples of Eastern Europe. Many Slavs, including those in Russia, converted

to the Eastern Orthodox Church. In the 1200s, the Mongol invasions cut Russia off from Western Europe. Later, the princes of Moscow fought to expel the Mongols.

In 622, Muhammad founded the religion of Islam in Arabia. Muslims believe that there is only one God and that Muhammad is God's messenger. Islam spread rapidly. For centuries, caliphs presided over the rich and powerful Islamic Empire.

Muslims made important original contributions in medicine, mathematics, science, and philosophy. Much of this knowledge was transmitted to Western Europe.

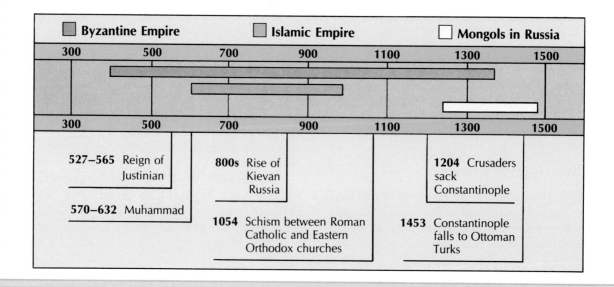

■ Byzantine Empire		■ Islamic Empire		□ Mongols in Russia		
300	500	700	900	1100	1300	1500
300	500	700	900	1100	1300	1500

527–565 Reign of Justinian

570–632 Muhammad

800s Rise of Kievan Russia

1054 Schism between Roman Catholic and Eastern Orthodox churches

1204 Crusaders sack Constantinople

1453 Constantinople falls to Ottoman Turks

Recalling Facts

Choose the word or phrase that best completes each of the following statements.

1. Constantinople was the capital of the (a) Holy Land; (b) Byzantine Empire; (c) Persian Empire.
2. The head of the Eastern Orthodox Church was the (a) pope; (b) emperor; (c) patriarch.
3. Cyril and Methodius converted many Slavs to Christianity because they (a) spoke the Slavic language; (b) ruled the Balkan peninsula; (c) were successful merchants.
4. The most important pillar of Islam is (a) giving alms; (b) prayer; (c) belief in one God.
5. Muslims tolerated Christians and Jews because they (a) were People of the Book; (b) worshipped at the Kaaba; (c) were converts to Islam.
6. Islamic law was based on (a) the Koran; (b) Justinian's Code; (c) the work of al-Razi.

Chapter Checkup

1. (a) Why was the Byzantine Empire able to survive for over 1,000 years? (b) Why did it eventually decline?
2. (a) Describe Justinian's law code. (b) How did it influence the people of Western Europe?
3. (a) How did Byzantine civilization influence Kievan Russia? (b) How did it influence princes of Moscow such as Ivan III?
4. (a) Why did Muhammad become a prophet? (b) How did the people of Mecca respond to his teachings at first? (c) What areas did Islam share with Judaism and Christianity?
5. (a) What effect did Islam initially have on the status of Arab women? (b) How did the status of women change?
6. (a) Why did many people welcome Muslim armies? (b) How did Muslims treat non-Muslims within the Islamic Empire?
7. How did Islamic civilization influence the peoples of Western Europe?

Critical Thinking

1. **Analyzing** The Byzantine Empire and Western Europe shared the heritage of Rome. Yet during the Middle Ages, they drifted further apart. (a) What aspects of the Roman heritage did they share? (b) What do you think was the main reason they drifted apart? Explain.

2. **Applying Information** (a) Why did Russian rulers prefer Byzantine Christianity to the Christianity of Rome? (b) Why do you think this choice was significant? (c) In what other ways did Russia develop differently from Western Europe?

Relating Past to Present

1. Islam has remained a powerful force in many parts of the world since the time of Muhammad. Describe how each of the following contributed to the unity of Islam: (a) Arabic language; (b) Koran; (c) Islamic law.

Developing Basic Skills

1. **Map Reading** Study the map on page 208. Then answer the following questions: (a) What information does the map provide? (b) How far west did the Byzantine Empire extend at its height? (c) Describe the territories the Byzantine Empire lost between 565 and 1000. (d) Why was the early Byzantine Empire in an excellent position to prosper from trade?
2. **Map Reading** One map can give you useful information about a specific place and historical period. By comparing maps, however, you can make generalizations about changes that took place in a particular region of the world. Compare the maps on page 208 and 216. Then answer the following questions: (a) What territories in Europe did Islam win from the Byzantine Empire? (b) What other lands did Islam win from the Byzantine Empire? (c) After 661, where would the armies of Islam and the Byzantine Empire be most likely to clash? (d) What areas of the Islamic Empire were probably influenced by Byzantine civilization?
3. **Making a Review Chart** Draw a large chart with five columns and five rows. Title the columns Hinduism, Buddhism, Judaism, Christianity, and Islam. Title the rows Founder, Original Location, Areas of Influence, Main Teachings, and Sacred Book. Use what you have learned about the five world religions discussed in Chapters 3, 8, 9, and 13 to complete the chart. Then answer the following questions: (a) Which religion or religions were founded by a single leader? (b) Which religions began in the same area? (c) Which were monotheistic? (d) Which have teachings in common? Can you suggest reasons for this?

See page 804 for suggested readings.

14 Africa and the Americas

(3000 B.C.–1532 A.D.)

Bronze sculpture of a Benin woman.

Chapter Outline

1 Africa: The Land and Early Peoples

2 African Empires and Trading States

3 Patterns of Daily Life in Africa

4 The First Americans

5 Early Civilizations in the Americas

The Bushongo lived in the forest lands of West Africa. Like many other African peoples, they preserved a careful oral record of their history. In the early 1900s, a European traveler, Emil Torday, visited the Bushongo. He interviewed Bushongo leaders, who described 121 kings who had ruled their people. Torday anxiously waited for his hosts to mention a date, any date, so he could fit their history into a familiar time frame.

Torday recalled later, "As the elders were talking of the great events of various reigns, and we came to the 98th chief, Bo Kama Bomanchala, they said that nothing remarkable had happened during his reign except that one day at noon the sun went out, and there was absolute darkness for a short time.

"When I heard this I lost all self-control. I jumped up and wanted to do something desperate. The elders thought that I had been stung by a scorpion. . . ." Torday was delighted because he knew the Bushongo were referring to an eclipse of the sun. By studying other records, he learned that a total eclipse that occurred on March 13, 1680, would have been seen in the Bushongo lands. Torday finally had the date he needed.

In many West African societies, specially trained men and women called griots preserved the oral traditions of their people. Griots memorized important events and the names and deeds of rulers going back for hundreds of years. Oral traditions were one way in which the peoples of Africa preserved records of their achievements.

Advanced civilizations developed in both Africa and the Americas. As elsewhere, people built large cities, organized complex governments, and developed technical skills. They had well-defined religious beliefs and systems of recordkeeping. Different social classes emerged, with some people learning specialized skills.

The many different societies that emerged in Africa and the Americas were largely isolated from the European and Asian civilizations you have studied. Yet within each continent, societies had frequent contact with one another. Through these contacts, people learned about advances in farming, science, and technology.

1 Africa: The Land and Early Peoples

Read to Learn
■ how geography influenced development in Africa
■ how early peoples lived in Africa

Africa is a huge continent, more than three times the size of the continental United States. Within Africa, different peoples have developed their own distinct patterns of civilization. The variety of African cultures is reflected in the 800 to 1,000 African languages identified by scholars.

As in other parts of the world, geography has helped shape the civilizations of Africa. The varied climates and terrain of Africa contributed to the growth of many different traditions and civilizations.

Geographic Setting

Most of Africa lies in the tropics, that is, the area between the Tropic of Cancer and the Tropic of Capricorn. As a result, much of the continent has warm temperatures. However, the amount of rainfall varies greatly. Four main climate zones stretch in belts across Africa: rain forest, savanna, desert, and Mediterranean. (See the maps on page 224.)

Climate zones. The rain forest zone is located along the Equator, where the heaviest rainfall occurs. The ample moisture and warm temperatures of the zone support rich plant growth, including the dense forests. About eight percent of Africa is covered by rain forests. Some farming is possible in the rain forest zone, but the heavy rains in certain areas wash out soil nutrients and leave the land infertile.

The damp climate provides favorable conditions for disease-carrying insects. For example, certain mosquitoes are carriers of malaria and yellow fever. The tsetse fly carries sleeping sickness, which can infect both people and animals. Therefore, people living in the rain forest zone do not raise cattle or use animals for plowing or transportation. Today, sleeping sickness has been brought under control in many areas.

The second climate zone, the savanna, stretches across Africa north and south of the rain forests. *Savannas,* or grasslands dotted with trees, cover about half the continent. Rainfall can be unreliable in the savanna climate zone. On the average, enough rain falls to support farming and herding. But the amount of rainfall varies from one year to the next. As a result, severe floods or drought can destroy crops and herds.

Deserts make up a third climate zone, which covers 40 percent of Africa. Hardy grasses and shrubs grow in many parts of the African deserts. Some people who live in desert regions dig wells at oases and grow a few vegetable crops. Others are herders.

Travel across the giant Sahara Desert in the north has always been difficult. However, even in ancient times, traders made

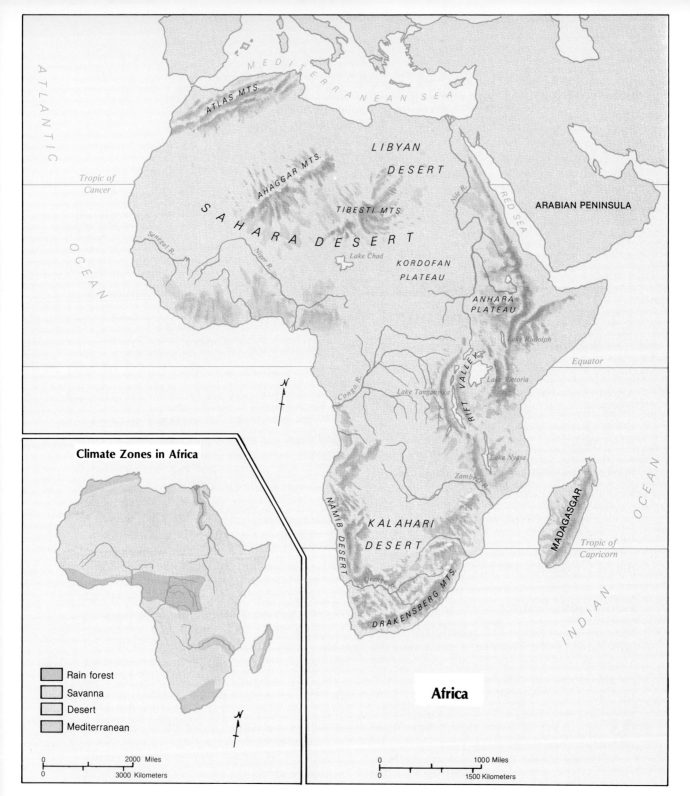

Africa

Climate Zones in Africa

Rain forest
Savanna
Desert
Mediterranean

2000 Miles
3000 Kilometers

1000 Miles
1500 Kilometers

Map Skill *Africa is a vast continent with varied climates and terrains, as these maps show. People in Africa, as in other parts of the world, adapted their ways of life to local geographic conditions. Which type of terrain occupies the largest territory? Where might most people live?*

their way across it. After 400 A.D. when the camel was introduced from Arabia, camel caravans carried goods on the long, hazardous journey across the Sahara. The Kalahari and Namib deserts in southern Africa are much drier than the Sahara. Only a few skilled hunters and food gatherers adjusted to the harsh life there.

A mild Mediterranean climate zone lies at the northern and southern tips of Africa. In northern Africa, farmers grow crops similar to those in southern Europe. The people of northern Africa had continuous contact with other parts of the Mediterranean world. As you read earlier, Romans, and later Muslims, extended their empires across North Africa. But the southern tip of Africa was sparsely populated, and people there had almost no contact with outsiders until the 1500s.

Physical features. Much of Africa is a high plateau that drops sharply into narrow coastal plains. Rivers that originate in the interior descend steeply from the plateau through a series of cataracts, waterfalls, and rapids. These obstacles protected the interior from outsiders. However, the same rivers provided excellent transportation in the interior. The Nile, Niger, Congo, and Zambezi rivers have carved out wide valleys. Silt from seasonal floods renews the soil and makes the river valleys fertile farming regions.

Another distinctive feature of the African terrain is the Rift Valley in East Africa. The valley was formed by movements in the earth's crust in prehistoric times. The shifting earth pushed up highlands and mountains that tower above deep canyons. As a result, the region has a variety of climates. The peak of Mt. Kilimanjaro is ice-capped, while the lowlands are warm.

Early Peoples of Africa

In recent years, archaeologists have begun to excavate prehistoric sites in Africa. They have found what they believe is the earliest evidence of human life in East Africa. Yet the record is incomplete. Archaeologists are still searching for evidence that might show a direct connection between the earliest humans and the Stone Age cultures that emerged thousands of years later.

During the Stone Age in Africa, as elsewhere, hunters and food gatherers followed herds of wild game and collected edible roots and berries. Between 8000 B.C. and 2000 B.C., Stone Age people in the Sahara painted a record of their lives. They drew pictures of their cattle, sheep, and goat herds on rock cliffs. Other paintings showed scenes of women tending children. Still others showed hunters stalking wild game.

The Sahara was covered with grasses and trees when these pictures were drawn. It had rivers and lakes filled with fish. However, the climate of the Sahara gradually grew drier, and Stone Age hunters migrated. Some probably settled in the Nile River valley, and others moved south into the river valleys of West Africa.

When the agricultural revolution began in Africa, some hunters and food gatherers gave up their nomadic way of life. Early farmers tamed animals and developed crops suited to the local climate. In the Nile Valley, for example, they grew wheat and barley. In West Africa, farmers planted sorghum, millet, and rice, which grew better in the savanna climate.

With the agricultural revolution, populations expanded, and people spread out across many regions of Africa. By 3000 B.C., the first African civilizations were taking shape in Egypt and in Nubia and Kush to the south.

SECTION REVIEW

1. Locate: Tropic of Cancer, Tropic of Capricorn, Equator, Sahara Desert, Kalahari Desert, Namib Desert, Nile River, Niger River, Congo River, Zambezi River, Rift Valley.
2. Define: savanna.
3. Describe the four main climate zones of Africa.
4. What features of many African rivers protected the interior from outsiders?
5. What did Stone Age hunters do when the climate of the Sahara became drier?

2 African Empires and Trading States

Read to Learn
- how trade affected growth in West Africa
- how East African states became prosperous

Between 3000 B.C. and 1600 A.D., powerful empires and trading states flourished in widely separated areas of Africa. They reflected the diversity of African geography, peoples, and cultures.

The Kingdoms of Kush and Axum

At a bend in the upper Nile, the Kingdom of Kush developed at the same time as ancient Egypt. An active trade grew up between the two kingdoms. The merchants of Kush traded ivory, gold, ebony wood, and perfumes for products of Egypt and the Mediterranean world. They also traded extensively across the Indian Ocean. Kings and queens of Kush used riches from trade to build large walled palaces, a huge temple to the sun, and burial pyramids.

In 750 B.C., King Kasha led his armies north and conquered Egypt. For about 80 years, Kasha's successors ruled an empire stretching from the Mediterranean to what is today Ethiopia. They retreated back to the south when the Assyrians, who were armed with weapons made of iron, invaded Egypt.

The value of iron was not lost on the people of Kush, and they soon learned how to make it. The plentiful supply of iron ore in Kush supported a large iron industry in the capital of Meroë (MEHR oh EE). Huge mounds of black slag, the waste product of iron making, still lie in the ruins of Meroë.*

Kush declined about 200 A.D. At the same time, its southern neighbor Axum grew in power. Like Kush, Axum carried on a thriving trade with the Mediterranean world and with Asia. Traders brought gold, ivory, and animal hides from the interior of Africa to ports on the Red Sea. Arabs who took part in this trade settled alongside farmers and merchants of Axum. As a result, the civilization of Axum blended Arab and African cultures.

In 324 A.D., King Ezana of Axum converted to Christianity, as did many of his people. In the seventh century, the spread of Islam across North Africa broke the connection between the Christian world and Axum. But Christianity survived in Axum. Today, the people of Ethiopia trace their Christianity back to the civilization of Axum.

Growth of Trade in West Africa

During the Middle Ages in Europe, a complex system of trade developed in West Africa. They key to this trade was the exchange of gold and salt.

Parts of West Africa had large supplies of gold but little salt. Yet people living in the warm climate of this region needed salt in their diet. Several hundred miles to the north, there were large natural salt deposits in the Sahara. At Taghaza, salt was so plentiful that people built their houses out of it. Camel caravans loaded up with salt at Taghaza and made the long desert trip to the West African savanna, where salt was said to be worth its weight in gold.

In the gold mining district of Wangara near the Senegal River, gold and salt were exchanged in a silent trade. The gold miners of Wangara refused to meet openly with outsiders who might want to seize their gold fields. Therefore, traders left salt and other goods and then withdrew to a safe distance. The miners examined the offerings and set out payment in gold. When the traders returned, they either accepted the price, taking the gold back north, or they withdrew to wait for a larger payment.

As the gold-salt trade grew, powerful rulers emerged in West Africa. They sought to control the caravan routes and established strong states to protect trade markets.

---

*The use of iron began to spread across Africa about 500 B.C. Iron plows enabled farmers to increase food production. People who had iron weapons had an advantage over those who did not.

The Kingdom of Ghana

Ghana was the first major trading state of West Africa. The gold-salt trade route passed through Ghana, which was located in the Niger Valley.* (See the map below.) About 400 A.D., the rulers of Ghana began to acquire a large empire. They extended their power over neighboring peoples and demanded tribute from them.

Although most people were farmers, the power and prosperity of Ghana depended on gold. In fact, the word "ghana" came to mean gold. The king of Ghana controlled all the gold in his empire. The Arab writer al-Bakri (ahl bahk REE) reported that if the king did not regulate the gold trade, gold would be so plentiful that it would lose its value.

In the seventh century, Muslim merchants from North Africa traveled south along the caravan routes. The king of Ghana did not convert to Islam, but he employed Muslims as interpreters and advisors. Soon, Arab geographers and scholars learned of the wealthy West African kingdom.

Ghana reached the height of its power in the tenth century. Tribute and taxes from trade filled the royal treasury. Whenever the king appeared in public, he wore splendid clothes and a rich gold headdress. His pages carried gold-mounted swords. The royal court was guarded by dogs with gold and silver collars.

The kingdom of Ghana suffered a severe blow in the eleventh century. The Almoravids (ahl MOH rah vihdz), devout Muslims from North Africa, launched a holy war against the non-Muslims of Ghana. When the Almoravids occupied Ghana, states that had been paying tribute broke away. Although Ghana soon ousted the invaders, it never recovered its former strength.

The Empire of Mali

After Ghana's decline, the Mandingo people to the southeast formed the powerful empire of Mali. A resourceful young leader named

*Present-day Ghana is about 500 miles (800 kilometers) to the southeast of the ancient kingdom of Ghana.

Sundiata Keita (suhn dee AH tuh KĪ tuh) defeated his rivals and absorbed the remains of the kingdom of Ghana. By 1240, Mali had won control of the profitable gold-salt trade. During the next century, Mali controlled both the gold mining regions of West Africa and the salt deposits of Taghaza. (See the map below.) Although Mali thrived on commerce, most Mandingo were cattle herders and farmers.

The rulers of Mali converted to Islam in the eleventh century. In 1324, Mali's ruler,

Map Skill *Advanced civilizations emerged in several regions of Africa, as this map shows. Where did the earliest African civilizations develop? Why do you think they grew up there?*

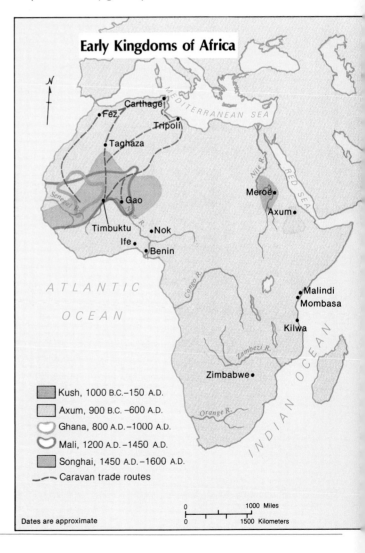

Early Kingdoms of Africa

Kush, 1000 B.C.–150 A.D.
Axum, 900 B.C.–600 A.D.
Ghana, 800 A.D.–1000 A.D.
Mali, 1200 A.D.–1450 A.D.
Songhai, 1450 A.D.–1600 A.D.
— Caravan trade routes

Dates are approximate

0   1000 Miles
0   1500 Kilometers

Mansa Musa, left his capital at Timbuktu to make a pilgrimage to Mecca. He passed through Cairo with hundreds of servants and camels loaded with gold. His wealth created a vivid impression in the busy Egyptian city. "This man," observed one Egyptian, "spread upon Cairo the flood of his generosity. There was no person or holder of any office who did not receive a sum of gold from him."

Mansa Musa and his successors respected local traditions within the empire and established a peaceful, orderly government. Ibn Battuta (IHB uhn bah TOO tah), an Arab visitor to Mali, noted the peace and safety of Mali. Battuta described the Mandingo as faithful Muslims, careful in prayer and in their study of the Koran. Yet he observed how the Mandingo blended Islam

News of the wealth of Mali reached Europe after Mansa Musa's pilgrimage to Mecca. This Spanish map of West Africa was drawn about 1375. It shows Mansa Musa in the lower right, holding a scepter and a gold nugget. The mapmaker noted: "So abundant is the gold which is found in his country that he is the richest and most noble king in all the land."

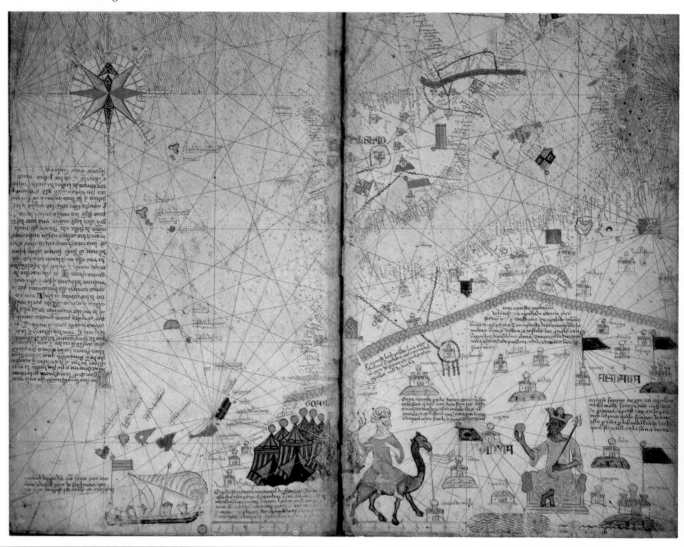

with their own traditions. For example, women enjoyed greater freedom than in other Muslim countries. They were not secluded at home, and they could talk to whomever they chose.

In the late 1300s, civil war weakened Mali. Over the next century, the kingdom of Songhai (SAWNG hī) replaced Mali as the most powerful state in West Africa.

The Rise of Songhai

From their capital at Gao, the rulers of Songhai controlled the gold-salt trade. About 1464, Sonni Ali, an able but ruthless leader, came to the throne. Before his death in 1492, Sonni Ali had conquered the largest empire yet seen in West Africa. (See the map on page 227.)

Ali created an efficient government. He divided the empire into provinces and appointed trusted officials to regulate commerce, agriculture, and justice. Inspectors toured local markets to see that merchants used only official weights and measures.

Under Askia Mohammed, Ali's successor, Timbuktu became a great center of learning. Askia Mohammed welcomed Muslim scholars, doctors, and judges to Songhai. The university at Timbuktu produced many scholars, including Ahmad Baba, who gained fame throughout the Muslim world for his works on Islamic law.

In 1590, the ruler of Morocco in northern Africa sent an army across the Sahara to seize the gold mining regions of Songhai. Only about 2,000 soldiers survived the long desert march. But armed with cannon and muskets, which were unknown in Songhai, the invaders defeated the Songhai forces. The Songhai Empire then broke up into small, independent states. Trade continued, but the political unity of the West Africa trading empires had ended.

City-States of East Africa

Along the coast of East Africa, scattered farming villages grew into independent city-states during the Middle Ages. Trade became as important in East Africa as it was in West Africa. However, East African commerce centered on the sea, not on desert caravans.

The coastal cities made large profits by taxing all goods passing through their markets. Traders brought gold, ivory, and iron from inland states to such cities as Mombasa and Malindi. The goods were then shipped across the Indian Ocean to India and China, where they were sold at high prices. Merchants brought back Indian and Chinese goods to exchange for more gold from the interior.

As in Axum to the northeast, many Arab traders settled in the East African coastal cities. The newcomers brought their own culture, which blended with African traditions. For example, Arabs introduced Islam to East Africa.

As trade across the Indian Ocean increased, Indian civilization also influenced the cities of East Africa. Swahili (swah HEE lee), the language of the coastal people, included Arab and Indian words. Today, Swahili is the most important language of East Africa.

In the 1100s and 1200s, the growth of a money economy in medieval Europe increased the demand for gold. Arab merchants bought gold in Africa and sold it in Europe for use in coins. The cities of East Africa flourished until the early 1500s. By that time, Portuguese sailors had reached East Africa. Not long after their arrival, the Portuguese destroyed the coastal cities.

Zimbabwe: A Powerful Inland State

Zimbabwe (zihm BAH bweh) was the most powerful inland state to export gold to the coastal cities of East Africa. (See the map on page 227.) Around 1000 A.D., migrating farmers and herders settled in the lands between the Zambezi and Limpopo rivers. These pioneers discovered gold in their new homeland. With the wealth from gold, they established a large trading empire. In the ruins of Zimbabwe, archaeologists have found Chinese and Indian goods, which the rulers of

Zimbabwe had bought with profits from the gold trade.

About the time that Europeans embarked on the Crusades, the rulers of Zimbabwe built a large walled capital. Highly skilled masons constructed a vast complex of palaces, stone houses, and temples.

Zimbabwe reached its height in the fifteenth century. In the 1500s, Portuguese traders in East Africa heard rumors of Zimbabwe's great wealth. They looked for Zimbabwe but did not find it. However, when the Portuguese destroyed the coastal cities, Zimbabwe declined because trade was cut off. About the same time, weak rulers, shortages of salt, and soil exhaustion left the land open to invaders.

SECTION REVIEW

1. Locate: Kush, Axum, Taghaza, Ghana, Mali, Timbuktu, Songhai, Mombasa, Malindi, Zimbabwe.
2. Identify: Kasha, Ezana, Mansa Musa, Sonni Ali.
3. What event showed the people of Kush the value of iron?
4. What were the two main trading items of the West African kingdoms?
5. What steps did the Songhai ruler Sonni Ali take to make his government efficient?
6. What factors helped make the East African city-states prosperous?
7. What role did Zimbabwe play in African trade?

3 Patterns of Daily Life in Africa

Read to Learn
- how societies functioned in Africa
- how religion influenced African civilization

People in Africa organized their lives in a variety of ways, and different political and social institutions emerged. However, respect for the family, law, and religion helped ensure stable societies.

Importance of Family

Family organization in Africa varied according to the needs of individual cultures. People in hunting and food-gathering societies lived in small nuclear families. A *nuclear family* consists of parents, children, and occasionally grandparents. Several nuclear families made up a hunting band.

In farming and herding societies, the extended family was the basic unit of society. In farming areas, the family used the land that its ancestors had cleared and settled. Generally, each family member cultivated a different portion of the land. But they worked together on projects such as building houses and clearing new land. In herding societies, family members shared the duties of tending the family's cattle.

Members of extended families lived in separate houses that surrounded a common living area. In some African societies, men had more than one wife. Each wife had her own house where she lived with her children.

In addition to the family, an individual's place in society depended on a system of age grades. An *age grade* included all boys or girls born in the same year. Children of each age grade had privileges and responsibilities particular to that age grade. Children in older age grades took part in certain village activities, which helped create ties beyond the family.

The Status of Women

The status of women varied in different African societies. Women were respected because marriage and children were basic to family life. However, as in many other cultures, a girl's marriage was arranged by her family when she was in her early teens. If a woman had a child, she won a place in her husband's family. If she had no children, she might be sent back to her family.

In some societies, women had legal rights such as the right to own property. They also might have religious and political responsibilities. In the Wolof kingdom of West Africa, for example, a woman could become head of state.

In farming cultures, men and women had clearly defined roles. Men cleared and plowed the land. Women planted and harvested the crops. In West Africa, women often controlled the granary, the food storage area. Women also sold surplus crops they had harvested in local and regional markets.

In some parts of Africa, families were *matrilineal*—that is, children traced their ancestors through their mother. In these societies, a boy inherited wealth or land from his mother's brother. Many other African societies, however, were *patrilineal*—that is, children traced their family line through their father.

Government and Law

In the large trading states of West Africa, the king was often considered divine, and he exercised considerable power. Kings depended on local officials to maintain order so they usually did not interfere with local village government. Villages were normally governed by a council of elders. The elders were men who had acquired influence because of their age and experience.

In much of Africa, there was no central government. Instead, people lived in self-sufficient villages and regulated their affairs by mutual agreement or compromise. For example, the Tiv, a people who lived in what is today Nigeria, numbered nearly one million people, but they had no appointed officials. Yet Tiv farming villages enjoyed peace and stability. The Tiv depended on kinship, or family ties, which bound people to respect the compromises reached by the community.

Compromise was a central feature of village government. When the community faced an important decision, the elders gathered to discuss all sides of the issue. Discussions would last for days if necessary, until an agreement was reached.

In some African societies, when boys reached a certain age they underwent training to become hunters and warriors. Not every boy completed this rigorous training successfully. This bronze plaque portrays a warrior dressed for battle. He wears an elaborately decorated helmet and breastplate and carries a shield.

Legal questions were settled in a similar way. Courts were more like community meetings than formal hearings. Both parties in a dispute would explain their positions. Then, the judges would help the two sides reach a compromise acceptable to both.

Religious Beliefs

Religious beliefs were part of everyday life in Africa, just as they were in other regions of the world. Although religious rituals varied, many African societies had similar beliefs.

Most African religions were monotheistic. People believed in a Supreme Spirit who had created the universe and everything in it. But people saw the Supreme Spirit as a remote power. They thought that the creator of the universe was too great to be concerned with the details of individual human beings. Therefore, they sought divine help from intermediaries such as their ancestors and "spirit helpers" who would make their prayers known to the Supreme Spirit.

In many societies, people considered their ancestors part of the family. Death only changed the position of the family member. People believed ancestors were closer to the Supreme Spirit and could help the family. They therefore showed respect for their ancestors by performing special ceremonies and offering sacrifices.

Many African peoples believed that spirits resided in natural objects such as water and soil. They respected nature because they believed the Supreme Spirit had created all things. For example, a woodcarver in East Africa once explained that he prayed when he cut down a tree because he was changing the Supreme Spirit's creation. He did not believe the wood was a spirit, but he saw it as a part of the natural world that the Supreme Spirit had created.

In some African religions, diviners played a central role. If disasters such as illness or a crop failure struck, people consulted diviners to discover whether a neglected ancestor or spirit had caused the trouble. The diviner revealed the cause and then prescribed a course of action to solve the problem. Diviners had years of training and were well-versed in herbal medicine.

The Arts

In African societies, the arts were an important part of daily life. Musicians and dancers performed at funerals, weddings, naming ceremonies, or just for entertainment. Musicians also accompanied villagers when they undertook major projects such as building a wall or clearing forest land. Africans developed a wide range of musical instruments. They played horns, xylophones, bells, drums, and stringed instruments.

Africans passed on their history through oral literature. Storytellers taught their au-

diences songs and responses so that people could participate in the dramatic tales. Many tales ended with a moral that taught correct behavior.

A variety of art styles developed among the different peoples of Africa. Some of the earliest West African sculpture has been dis-

Benin sculptors created striking bronze figures such as this musician by a process known as the "lost wax" technique. The artist molded a clay figure and then coated it—first with a layer of wax and then with a layer of clay. An opening was left at the base. Next, the figure was baked so the wax melted and was "lost." Melted bronze was poured into the opening in the base of the figure. After the bronze cooled and hardened, the clay shell was removed, revealing the bronze figure.

covered in present-day Nigeria. Between about 900 B.C. and 200 A.D., the Nok culture flourished in this forest region. Working with terra cotta clay, Nok artists fashioned nearly life-sized human figures. The work of Nok artists probably influenced later sculptors of Ife and Benin.

About 1000 A.D., the Ife made splendid glazed pottery figures. They also produced bronze portraits that rank among the world's finest sculptures. In the 1300s, bronze workers in Benin created decorative plaques showing scenes of court life. The royal family and wealthy citizens hung the plaques on their palace walls. The art of early Africa has influenced some art today.

SECTION REVIEW

1. Identify: Tiv, Nok, Ife.
2. Define: nuclear family, age grade, matrilineal, patrilineal.
3. How did family members in farming societies divide their work?
4. Why were women respected in many African societies?
5. How did the village council of elders make decisions?
6. According to African religious beliefs, how could an ancestor help the family?
7. How did many people in Africa pass on their history?

4 The First Americans

Read to Learn
- how the changing climate affected the Americas
- how geography influenced early American cultures

Like Africa, the Americas were vast continents with varied climates and physical features. Early Americans developed diverse cultures. Scholars have identified over 30 Native American languages and more than 2,000 dialects.

Geographic Setting

North and South America are lands of great contrast. In the far north, the land is covered permanently with ice and snow. Hot deserts can be found in the southwestern part of North America and along the western coast of South America. Southern Mexico, Central America, and the vast Amazon Basin contain thick rain forests.

The high, rugged Rocky Mountains begin in Alaska and continue into Mexico, where they become the Sierra Madres. In South America, the Andes Mountains stretch from the north to the southern tip of the continent.

The center of North America is a relatively flat, open plain, where the summers are hot and the winters cold. Thick forests and fertile soils dominate the eastern part of North America. The highlands of the Mexi-

can Plateau also offer rich land for farming, as does the pampas, or grasslands, of Argentina.

The different environments led to a variety of cultures developing in the Americas. Early people adapted their way of life to different climates and sources of food. Some people hunted or gathered food. Others combined hunting with farming. Still others developed advanced farming civilizations.

Path to the Americas

According to scientific theory, much ocean water was frozen into glaciers during the last ice age. Sea levels dropped, exposing new land areas. Between 100,000 and 10,000 years ago, a land bridge connected Asia and the Americas where the Bering Strait is today. Mammoths, bison, camels, and horses wandered across the bridge. Stone Age hunters followed the animals into North America.

When the climate gradually grew warm again, the melting ice raised sea levels. The sea flooded the land bridge, leaving hunters and their prey cut off in the Americas. The climate change resulted in vast changes in local environments. However, Stone Age hunters adjusted to the new environment and slowly populated the two continents.

As scholars uncover more evidence, they revise their theories about prehistoric life in the Americas. Many scholars suggest that hunters crossed the land bridge in successive waves, but they are uncertain exactly when the first Americans arrived. Recent discoveries indicate that people were living in southern California as early as 70,000 years ago. Most scholars agree that by 7000 B.C. migrating people had reached Cape Horn at the southern tip of South America.

Map Skill   *After Stone Age hunters crossed into North America, they slowly fanned out across two continents. A rich variety of Native American cultures developed in the Americas. What were the major cultural regions of North America? Which empires were established in Mexico and Central and South America?*

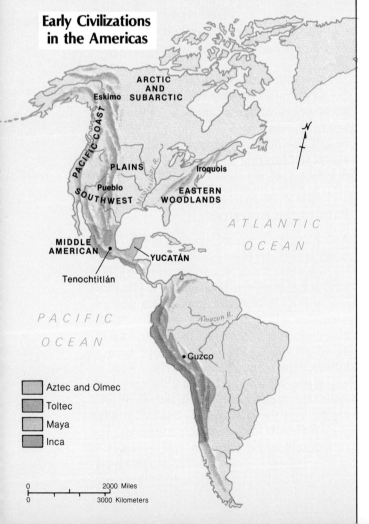

Early Civilizations in the Americas

ARCTIC AND SUBARCTIC
Eskimo
PACIFIC COAST
PLAINS
Iroquois
Pueblo
SOUTHWEST
EASTERN WOODLANDS
Mississippi R.
ATLANTIC OCEAN
MIDDLE AMERICAN
YUCATÁN
Tenochtitlán
PACIFIC OCEAN
Amazon R.
Cuzco

- Aztec and Olmec
- Toltec
- Maya
- Inca

0   2000 Miles
0   3000 Kilometers

Peoples of North America

The first Americans were organized into many different tribes. Each tribe developed its own religious beliefs, technology, and government. In the Americas, as elsewhere, geography affected the way people lived.

Anthropologists have identified many cultural regions, as you can see on the map below. Within each region, people often had similar traditions. Among the major cultural regions in North America are the far north, the Pacific coast, the Great Plains, the eastern woodlands, and the southwest.

The far north. Some experts suggest that after the land bridge was flooded, a few more people crossed the narrow Bering Strait from Asia by boat. According to this theory, the newcomers were the Eskimos. Like other peoples of the far north, the Eskimos lived by hunting and fishing. But since they lived in the arctic region, the Eskimos had to adjust to one of the harshest environments on earth.

The Eskimos made maximum use of limited local resources. They carved harpoons and knives from bone. Using bone needles, they sewed animal skins into clothing, kayaks, and snowshoes. They built temporary shelters out of ice and made permanent homes from driftwood, sod, or stone. As in hunting bands elsewhere, family members cooperated to ensure the group's survival. Among the Eskimos, hospitality and the sharing of food were unwritten laws. Their religion reflected the belief that people should work with nature and not fight against it.

Pacific coast. The peoples of the Pacific coast lived in a much milder climate. They developed a fishing economy. Some netted salmon along rivers such as the Columbia. Others fished the ocean in huge canoes built from cedar and redwood trees. They supplemented the fish of their diet by gathering acorns and seeds or hunting deer.

Communities on the Pacific coast ranged in size from a few families to over 1,000 people. Some families acquired great wealth, which increased their status in the community. To prove their high social position, wealthy families gave feasts called *potlatches* (PAHT latch ehz). The family giving a potlatch served its guests lavishly and gave away valuable possessions.

The southwest. In what is today the southwestern United States and northern Mexico, people developed advanced farming civilizations. In the dry, semi-desert climate, the Pueblo cultivated beans, squash, and maize, or corn. They built houses several stories high out of *adobe*, sun-dried brick. Each *pueblo*, or group of dwellings, was self-contained. It had its own government, elected officials, and council of elders who acted as advisors.

The Pueblo were a peaceful people. Whenever possible, they avoided war. Returning warriors went through purifying rituals to cure them of the "madness of war."

Although men performed the main religious and political duties, Pueblo society was matrilineal. After marriage, a husband moved in with his wife's family.

Great Plains. A wide stretch of grasslands, known as the Great Plains, stretches from the Rocky Mountains to the Mississippi River. People on the Great Plains combined farming and hunting. They lived in villages, usually near rivers to ensure a steady water supply. Women did most of the farming. They raised maize, beans, and squash.

During the summer, men left the villages to hunt buffalo. They planned their hunts carefully. They would stampede the buffalo into a narrow space, where they could then kill many animals. People relied on buffalo for food and used buffalo skins for clothing and for movable tents, or teepees.

Eastern woodlands. In the eastern woodlands, a region stretching from Quebec to the Gulf of Mexico, people hunted a variety of animals, including deer, squirrels, and turkeys. Along the coast and inland rivers, they fished or gathered mussels and snails.

Some woodlands people, such as the Iroquois (IHR uh kwoi), combined farming with hunting and fishing. The Iroquois lived in loosely organized bands. They built large, bark-covered homes called longhouses, well-suited to the cold, snowy winters and warm summers of the northeast.

In the late 1400s, the Iroquois formed a league to end warfare among five Iroquois tribes. A council of 50 *sachems*, or chiefs, settled disputes among league members.

Iroquois women enjoyed considerable influence and had a voice in selecting the sachems. The importance of women was recognized in Iroquois law. Anyone found guilty of murdering a woman owed the dead woman's family 20 strings of wampum, the Iroquois money. For a murdered man, the fine was only 10 strings of wampum.

SECTION REVIEW

1. Define: potlatch, adobe, pueblo, sachem.
2. How did the end of the last ice age affect people living in the Americas?
3. List five major cultural regions of North America.
4. Describe two ways the Eskimo made use of natural resources.
5. What political influence did Iroquois women have?

5 Early Civilizations in the Americas

Read to Learn
- what advances the Olmecs and Mayans made
- about the Aztec and Inca empires

About 6000 B.C., early Americans began to cultivate maize, which grew wild in the dry valleys of southern Mexico. Within a few thousand years, farming spread to other parts of the Americas. As in the river valleys of Africa, the Middle East, and Asia, some farming villages in America established the foundations for great civilizations.

The civilizations of the Olmec, Maya, Aztec, and Inca had features in common, such as great cities and complex governments. But each developed its own pattern of life.

Legacy of the Olmec

In the swampy lowlands of southern Mexico, the Olmec built one of the earliest civilizations in the Americas. By 1200 B.C., the Olmec had established large planned cities. Olmec cities were mainly religious centers. A huge, pyramid-shaped, stone temple towered above each city. There, priests performed religious ceremonies. Near the temple, Olmec sculptors carved enormous grim-faced stone heads that may have represented rain gods.

Archaeologists have only recently learned about the Olmec. They have concluded that a highly organized government was needed to supervise the building projects. Thousands of people had to drag huge stone blocks from distant mountains to the building sites.

The Olmec made several important advances. They invented hieroglyphic writing and a counting system that led to practical discoveries in mathematics. They also developed a calendar. The Olmec spread their influence over a wide area through trade.

In the first century A.D., the Olmec suddenly abandoned their cities. They smashed or buried the giant stone heads. Scholars have not yet discovered why the Olmec did this. However, many think that the Olmec migrated into other parts of Mexico and Central America, taking their advanced knowledge with them.

Maya Civilization

The Olmec may have influenced the Maya, another farming people, who lived in the tropical highlands of what is today Guatemala. While Rome was winning control of the Mediterranean world, the Maya cleared dense rain forests, built elaborate irrigation systems, and organized independent city-states. Maya civilization slowly expanded into much of Central America and southern Mexico. (See the map on page 234.) Between

---

Daily Life ■ Pok-a-tok: An Ancient Game of the Americas

Amid the jungle ruins of every great Maya city stands a large, rectangular stone court. The Maya used the court in playing a ball game known as pok-a-tok. People started playing pok-a-tok about 500 B.C. The game was popular in many parts of the Americas for more than 2,000 years.

Scholars know little about how pok-a-tok was played, but they have pieced together some information. The pok-a-tok court was usually larger than a modern-day football field. Tall stone walls bordered the two long sides of the court. High in the middle of each wall was a stone ring. Unlike the basketball hoops of today, which are mounted horizontally, the stone rings were mounted vertically.

The goal of pok-a-tok was to knock a ball through the vertical stone ring. The ball, made of solid rubber, was about six inches (15 centimeters) in diameter. Scholars wonder how players ever scored a point, except by luck, because the rings were often mounted as high as 30 feet (10 meters) above the stone floor. Moreover, players could not touch the ball with their hands or feet. They had to knock the ball with their elbows, wrists, or hips. To protect themselves against the hard rubber ball, they wore gloves and hip pads made of wood and leather.

Spectators sat on stone benches above the walls and bet wildly on who would win. Whenever a player scored a point, he could demand the spectators' clothing and jewelry. So, the moment a ball shot through the ring, the spectators would race for the gates. The scoring player's friends dashed to catch them. Luckily for the spectators, few points were scored.

Pok-a-tok was probably more than a game to early Americans. Among the Maya, for example, it was also a religious and patriotic event. Rulers and priests attended the games on the eve of important battles. Each game ended with religious and magical ceremonies. The walls of the court and players' padding were elaborately decorated with heads of animals such as toads and snakes. The animals may have symbolized different gods.

The Maya covered the walls of their temples with murals of scenes from daily life. Few Maya murals have survived. This scene was copied by artist Antonio Tejeda from an 1,100-year-old Maya temple. It portrays priests preparing to make sacrifices to the gods.

300 A.D. and 900 A.D., during the early Middle Ages in Europe, the Maya created the most advanced civilization yet seen in the Americas.

Cities. Like the Olmec cities, Maya cities were chiefly religious centers. An immense pyramid temple stood at the heart of each city. On the edge of the city were cleared fields, and just beyond was the dense tropical forest. The Maya cities were linked to one another by trade and a common language.

Priests and warrior nobles made up a powerful ruling class. Priests supervised religious ceremonies, but they may also have influenced government decisions.

The majority of Maya were artisans, peasants, or slaves. Artisans produced fine jewelry and jade ornaments. Sculptors carved huge stone figures and pillars that still stand on Maya sites.

Peasants lived in thatched wooden houses in the maize fields. In addition to farming, peasants worked on temple buildings and constructed long, rectangular courts where ritual ball games were played. Slaves did the heaviest and most dangerous work. The Maya had no draft animals, such as oxen and horses, so slaves carried trade goods long distances from the highlands to the coast.

Influence of religion. Religion was central to Maya life. The Maya were polytheistic. They worshipped many gods, but they had special respect for the storm god because without rain their crops would die.

Maya priests were fascinated by time, in part because they had to decide which days were best for hunting, planting, and offering sacrifices to the gods. They used a hieroglyphic writing to keep historical records. Priest-astronomers developed a precise calendar. This calendar was more accurate than any used in Western Europe until the 1700s.

Maya priests also made advances in mathematics. They invented a numbering system that included zero. Using this system, they made accurate measurements of days and years.

About 900 A.D., the Maya stopped building cities and their civilization declined. No one knows why. Some scholars suggest that overpopulation, disease, or drought disrupted Maya life. Others think that peasants revolted against the priests and nobles. Despite the decline, the Maya continued to live in the Yucatán Peninsula.

The Aztec Empire

As the Maya civilization weakened, other people such as the Zapotec and Toltec fought for control of southern Mexico. Like the Maya, they were farmers whose chief crop was maize. They also built large cities and pyramid temples. Then in the 1200s A.D., the Aztec pushed their way into the Valley of Mexico.

The Aztec were a warlike people. In 1325, they established a capital, Tenochtitlán (tay NOHCH tee TLAHN), on an island in the middle of Lake Texcoco. They then conquered neighboring towns and cities. The Aztec forced the conquered peoples to pay tribute in the form of food, feathers of tropical birds, gold, cotton, or slaves. The Aztec Empire reached its height under Montezuma II (MAHN tuh ZOO muh). During his reign, from 1502 to 1521, the Aztec collected tribute from 371 states.

Government and society. The Aztec emperor had supreme power in his own lands. He appointed officials to administer justice and regulate trade. Although the emperor allowed the conquered peoples to govern themselves, he could demand more tribute from them or take prisoners.

Like the Romans, the Aztec built military roads to link distant outposts to the capital. Soldiers were stationed at strategic spots along the roads to protect travelers such as merchants, who carried on a brisk trade.

In the 1500s, Tenochtitlán was a bustling city with about 100,000 inhabitants, including priests, nobles, peasants, and slaves. As the population of the city grew, the Aztec enlarged their island capital. Engineers built causeways, roads made of packed earth, to connect the island to the mainland. Farmers filled in parts of the lake and dug drainage canals to create more farmland. They also anchored reed baskets filled with earth in the shallow lake. They then planted crops in the baskets, which became floating gardens.

A huge pyramid temple and the emperor's palace dominated Tenochtitlán. The palace served as a storehouse for tribute. It also housed the royal family, thousands of servants and officials, a zoo, and a library full of history books and accounting records. Like the Romans, the Aztec adapted ideas from the peoples they conquered. Aztec

Art and religion were closely linked in all ancient civilizations. This double-headed snake is made of turquoise and shell and probably decorated the armor of an Aztec warrior. The snake had religious significance to the Aztec because it was a symbol of life. The Aztec god of art and learning, Quetzalcóatl (keht SAHL koh AH tuhl), was sometimes represented as a snake.

priests used the knowledge of astronomy and mathematics from other cultures to develop a calendar and counting system.

Religion. The Aztec calendar was like a religious text. The Aztec worshiped many gods, including gods of corn, rain, sun, and war. The Aztec calendar told the people which month was sacred to each god and goddess. A large class of priests performed the complicated ceremonies that were meant to ensure the goodwill of the gods.

Aztec religious practices included human sacrifices. The people believed that the sun god, Huitzilopochtli (WEE tsee loh POHCH tlee), required human sacrifices. The victims in these sacrifices were prisoners of war.

Early in the 1500s, priests predicted that dreadful events were about to happen. They said the gods needed even more sacrifices. When the conquered people fought demands for more tribute, the Aztec put down the revolts and took new captives. This created even greater discontent, as you will read in Chapter 17.

Thus, by the 1500s, the Aztec had built a major empire. They had also made many outstanding accomplishments in architecture, agriculture, education, and the arts.

The Inca Empire

On the Pacific coast of South America, people began farming about 2000 B.C. In the high Andes Mountains, they grew potatoes. Along the coastal lowlands, they planted maize. Early empires expanded along the coast and fought with each other for control of vital food resources. About 1450 A.D., the Inca created the last great empire in the Andes region.

The Inca Empire stretched for about 2,500 miles (about 4,000 kilometers) from what is today Ecuador through Peru, Bolivia, Chile, and Argentina. (See the map on page 234.) The Inca ruled as many as 12 million people, who lived in coastal villages, in the rugged Andes, and in the rain forests along the Amazon River.

Government and religion. The Inca developed an efficient system to govern their huge empire. The emperor was an absolute ruler. He divided the empire into provinces and appointed nobles as governors. Governors were responsible for taking a census so people could be taxed.

The Inca government regulated the activities of the entire population. People were divided into groups of ten. Each group was responsible to a local official, who collected a portion of their harvest as tax and assigned them to work on public building projects. The government also cared for the aged, sick, and poor.

Religion was central to Inca life. The Inca worshiped many gods and depended on priests to tell them the will of the gods. The chief god was Inti, the sun god. The Inca believed the emperor was Inti's son, and they called themselves "children of the sun." In the capital of Cuzco, priests and priestesses performed outdoor ceremonies in the Great Sun Temple.

Achievements. The Inca developed advanced technology in many practical areas. They diverted rivers and streams to mine for gold, which artisans then made into fine ornaments. They invented the crowbar and a system of measurement. Inca priests had enough medical knowledge to perform successful brain surgery. They also learned to treat victims of malaria with quinine. Europeans did not understand the value of quinine until the 1800s.

As builders, the Inca outshone even the Romans. Early peoples in the Americas did not use the wheel. Even without the wheel the Inca were able to haul huge stone blocks to build temples and palaces. They shaped the stones to fit perfectly without cement. During the violent earthquakes that occasionally rock the Andes, Inca stone walls sway, but they do not crumble as do many modern buildings.

The Inca constructed a road system that linked distant provinces to Cuzco. Roads snaked across the Andes Mountains, and bridges spanned deep gorges. Inca building skills also aided agriculture. Farmers built terraces, or walls, on steep mountainsides to create level areas of land that could be farmed.

The Inca had no system of writing. However, they kept detailed records. Certain people memorized Inca history and taught it to the next generation. In addition, the government recorded census data, the size of harvests, and historical events on the quipu, a cord with many knotted strings.

In the early 1500s, the Inca Empire reached its greatest size. When the emperor died in 1526, two of his sons fought for control of the empire. Finally, in 1532, the younger son, Atahualpa (AH tah WAHL pah), defeated his brother and ended the bloody and bitter conflict. That same year Spanish soldiers arrived on the coast of Peru.

SECTION REVIEW

1. Locate: Yucatán, Tenochtitlán, Amazon River, Cuzco.
2. Identify: Montezuma, Huitzilopochtli, Inti, Atahualpa.
3. List two achievements of the Olmec.
4. (a) What was the main purpose of Maya cities? (b) How were the cities linked to one another?
5. How did the Aztec enlarge their capital?
6. List two ways in which the Inca government was involved in people's lives.

Chapter 14 Review

In Perspective

In Africa, people adapted to a variety of climates and terrains. The earliest African civilizations rose along the Nile River. In West Africa, several powerful trading states profited from trade in gold and salt. In East Africa, city-states became thriving marketplaces where gold and ivory from Central Africa were exchanged for goods from India, China, and the Middle East. African peoples organized their societies around family, religion, and local government.

Early Americans also developed many different patterns of life. In North America, people adjusted to environments ranging from the arctic cold of Alaska to the semidesert of the southwest. Farming began in Mexico and spread to other areas. The Maya built large cities and worshipped their gods in pyramid temples. The civilizations of the Aztec and Inca reached their heights about the time that Europe was emerging from the Middle Ages.

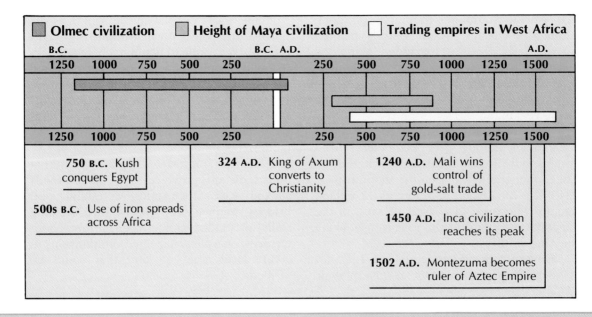

Recalling Facts

Match each name at left with the correct description at right.

1. Zimbabwe
2. Kush
3. Aztec
4. Timbuktu
5. Maya
6. Inca

a. important center of learning in West Africa
b. South American people who built terraces in the mountains to add to the farm land
c. Central African kingdom that exported gold to the cities of East Africa
d. early American civilization that flourished between 300 A.D. and 900 A.D.
e. warlike people who conquered much of Mexico in the 1300s
f. ancient African kingdom on the Nile that traded with Egypt

Chapter Checkup

1. (a) Why did powerful trading empires emerge in West Africa? (b) How did Islam influence these kingdoms?

2. (a) How did the city-states of East Africa differ from the West African trading kingdoms? (b) How did events in Europe affect the African gold trade?

3. (a) What types of family organization were found in early African societies? (b) Describe the age-grade system.

4. Describe one way in which early Americans in each of the following regions adapted to their environments: (a) far north; (b) Pacific coast; (c) southwest; (d) Great Plains; (e) eastern woodlands.

5. (a) What achievements did the Olmec probably pass on to other peoples of Central America and Mexico? (b) What advances did the Maya make? (c) What ideas did the Aztec adapt from the peoples they conquered? (d) Describe the main achievements of the Inca.

Critical Thinking

1. **Understanding Geographic Ideas** (a) Which geographic features in Africa do you think had the greatest impact on peoples' lives? (b) Which geographic features in the Americas do you think had the greatest impact on peoples' lives?

2. **Expressing an Opinion** (a) How was music a part of everyday life in Africa? (b) Do you think music has a similar role in the United States today? Explain.

Relating Past to Present

1. (a) Describe how self-sufficient African villages ruled themselves. (b) How is this system similar to local government in the United States today? (c) How is it different?

Developing Basic Skills

1. **Map Reading** Study the map on page 227. Then answer the following questions: (a) What information does the map provide? (b) Which West African kingdom controlled the largest territory? (c) Why do you think strong kingdoms rose in West Africa?

2. **Placing Events in Time** Draw a vertical time line on a blank sheet of paper. Make one end of the line 400 A.D. and the other 1500 A.D. Mark off 100-year intervals. Label the right side of the time line Africa and the left side Europe. Use the time line on page 240 and the text to identify the major events in Africa. Write them on the right side of the time line. Review Unit Three. Then list on the left side of the line the major events that took place in Europe. Then answer the following questions: (a) What was the first West African trading kingdom? (b) What was happening in Europe when Mali reached its height? (c) When did the city-states of East Africa flourish? (d) What was happening in Europe then? (e) Why do you think Europeans and Africans were generally unaware of events taking place on each other's continent?

See page 804 for suggested readings.

15 India, China, and Japan

(550–1650)

The wedding of Ghazan Khan, son of Mongol emperor Kublai Khan.

In 1271, Marco Polo traveled across half the world from Venice, Italy, to Peking, China. The trip took four years and involved great hazards. For nearly 20 years after his arrival, Polo worked for Kublai Khan, the Mongol emperor who had recently conquered China. When he returned to Venice, Polo published an account of his travels entitled *Description of the World*. His account was translated into many languages and was read throughout Western Europe. Although Polo was not the first European to visit China, his account was the first to be widely circulated.

"To this city [Peking] are brought more precious and costly goods than to any other city in the world," Marco Polo recalled. "People of every description and from every region bring things including precious stones, pearls, and spices from India. . . . every day over 1,000 cartloads of silk enter the city from which quantities of silk and gold cloth are woven. . . ."

Polo also praised Kublai Khan's palace, with its countless rooms adorned in gold and silver and a magnificent hall large enough to hold 6,000 guests. He reported that the Chinese used "a sort of black stone which is dug out of veins in the hillsides and burns like logs." The black stones were as cheap as wood, and they were plentiful enough to heat thousands of bathhouses "since there is no one who does not go to a bathhouse at least three times a week . . . and in winter every day, if he can manage it."

To Europeans in the late Middle Ages, the splendors of China were unimaginable. The black stones Polo described were coal, which was unknown in Europe. Furthermore, people in Europe seldom bathed. Because Polo's stories seemed so unbelievable, people called him the "prince of liars."

Compared to the small kingdoms of Western Europe during the Middle Ages, China was a wealthy, unified nation. By the thirteenth century, China had already experienced several golden ages, each marked by long periods of peace and prosperity.

Indian civilization also advanced during the European Middle Ages. Foreign invasions, weak rulers, and regional differences posed constant challenges to Indian rulers. But strong Hindu traditions preserved the underlying unity of Indian culture.

Between 550 and 1650, the Japanese were shaping a society that would figure prominently among the world's civilizations. Thus, when European sailors began venturing into Asian waters in the 1500s, they discovered advanced civilizations in India, China, and Japan.

1 A Meeting of Cultures in India

Read to Learn   ■ what caused hostility between Hindus and Muslims
                   ■ how the Moguls governed India

In the fifth century, the Huns attacked the powerful Gupta Empire in India. When the Gupta Empire collapsed, the northern plain of India became a battleground for rival rulers. Repeated invasions over hundreds of years disrupted Indian life. But just as Christianity helped shape medieval Europe, a common cultural tradition based on Hinduism helped shape Indian society.

Hindu Traditions

During the Gupta Empire, Hindu traditions spread throughout India, in part because Hinduism tolerated a wide range of beliefs and practices. As you read in Chapter 9, Hinduism had slowly absorbed Buddhism. In addition, many Hindu sects developed in different parts of India, influencing basic patterns of life.

The caste system and the power of the Brahmans helped ensure a stable society. Caste rules established what occupations people could follow, whom they could marry, and where they could live. In farming villages, a council of elders made the decisions, but the local Brahman priest often influenced the council. Brahmans also enjoyed great prestige in the palaces of Hindu princes because Brahmans were the educated class and the preservers of ancient traditions.

Despite these strong social and religious traditions, India had no single ruler. Between the fifth and tenth centuries, warring Hindu princes fought for control of the northern plain. The frequent warfare had relatively little effect on most people. They paid tribute to whichever ruler was in power. Yet because India lacked a strong, unified government, it was unable to resist determined invaders, who brought with them powerful traditions of their own.

Muslim Expansion into India

As you have read, Islam expanded westward across North Africa and eastward across the Fertile Crescent. In the tenth century, Muslim Turks and Afghans from Central Asia conquered the Indus Valley. They then moved farther east. By 1206, Muslim rulers, known as *sultans*, had established a capital at Delhi. Eventually, an empire called the Delhi sultanate included most of India.

The Muslim invaders had several advantages over Hindu forces. Muslim armies were highly mobile. Their archers rode horses while the Hindu cavalry rode slow-moving war elephants. Muslim troops were extremely well-disciplined. They believed that they were fighting a holy war against "pagan" Hindus. They were also motivated by a desire for loot. The Hindu princes fought bravely, but personal rivalries prevented them from organizing a truly united defense.

The Delhi sultans. The Delhi sultans organized a government that resembled those of the Maurya and Gupta empires. They divided the empire into provinces, each with a governor responsible for collecting taxes and maintaining order. The sultans also appointed a council of ministers to oversee government departments.

The Delhi sultans created a lavish court, paid for by heavy taxes on all non-Muslims. Persian styles strongly influenced the Delhi court. Under the sultan Firuz Shah Tughlak (fee ROOZ SHAH tuhg LAK), India enjoyed a period of peace and economic prosperity. Between 1351 and 1388, he built new irrigation systems, colleges, towns, and dozens of hospitals. A devout Muslim, he persuaded many Hindus to convert to Islam.

Tamerlane. After the death of Firuz Shah Tughlak, civil war weakened the Delhi sultanate. In 1398, Mongols from Central Asia overran northern India. Their leader, Tamerlane, was an ambitious general who was determined to conquer the world. He led his armies into Persia, Syria, and Asia Minor as well as India.

Mongol armies looted and destroyed Indian cities in their path. When they reached Delhi, they killed or enslaved the entire population and reduced the buildings to rubble. One witness reported that not a bird on the wing moved for two months. Only artisans were spared. They were sent to build Tamerlane's new capital at Samarkand in what is now the Soviet Union. Intent on further conquests, the Mongols left India. The Muslim Delhi sultanate was restored, but it had been weakened by the conquest.

Impact of Islam

Unlike earlier conquerors of northern India, Muslims were not absorbed into Hindu society. They remained a separate and powerful force that was hostile to Hindu traditions. The Muslims who founded the Delhi sultanate were determined to convert nonbelievers. Hindus who did not accept Islam had to pay a heavy tax. Some sultans also persecuted Hindus.

Differing beliefs caused hostility between Hindus and Muslims. Since the first pillar of Islam was the belief in one God, Muslims were horrified by Hindu temples filled with images of many gods and goddesses. As a result, Muslim armies often destroyed Hindu places of worship. Furthermore, Muslims preached the equality of all believers before God, while Hindus believed in a caste system based on inequality. In addition, Islam required strict obedience to the laws of the Koran, while Hinduism tolerated many different beliefs.

Conflicts between Islamic and Hindu beliefs affected daily life. To Hindus, the cow was a sacred animal that could not be killed. Muslims regarded cattle as a source of food. Also, music was an important part of Hindu festivals, but Muslims considered music an offense to God.

In parts of northern India where the Delhi sultans were strongest, many Hindus converted to Islam. Some converted to avoid paying the nonbeliever tax. Others sought to escape from the Hindu caste system. Still others converted in order to obtain a government position or to marry a Muslim. In the Deccan Plateau, far from Delhi, few Hindus converted, and Hindu traditions remained strong.

Tensions between Muslims and Hindus sometimes flared into violence, but the two cultures also borrowed ideas from each other. For example, a new language, Urdu, emerged. Urdu was a combination of Persian and Hindi and was written in Arabic script. Muslim mosques were often designed and built by Hindu architects, and Hindu artists painted works that illustrated Persian stories. *Purdah*, the practice of secluding women, probably originated in northern India. After the Muslim conquest of northern India, purdah was introduced in other Islamic lands.

The Mogul Empire

The Mongols swept into India again in 1526, and the Delhi sultanate collapsed. The invaders were led by Babur, who claimed to be descended from Tamerlane and Genghis Khan (GEHNG gihs KAHN), another Mongol conqueror. Although Babur disliked Indian customs and traditions, he established the Mogul* Empire in India. (See the map at right.)

The Mogul Empire lasted for over 300 years, but its golden age occurred during the reign of Akbar, Babur's grandson. Akbar ruled from 1556 to 1605. He tried to provide efficient, honest government. For example, he ordered a land survey to determine soil fertility and crop yields in each region. Officials used these findings to establish a fair tax system.

Akbar hoped to unify the empire by following a policy of religious toleration. Although a Muslim himself, he appointed qualified Hindus to high office. He forbade the destruction of Hindu temples, and he lifted the nonbeliever tax. He also married a Hindu princess. Toward the end of his reign, Akbar supported a religion that blended Hindu and Muslim beliefs.

The blending of Islamic and Hindu cultures reached its peak under the early Mogul emperors. Wealthy Moguls built splendid palaces and mosques with elaborate landscaped gardens. The Taj Mahal in Agra is probably the most famous example of Mogul architecture. (See page 288.)

Although Akbar's successors continued to support the arts, they ended his policy of religious toleration. They closed Hindu schools, destroyed temples, and reimposed the nonbeliever tax. Such actions sparked fierce resistance among Hindus, who struggled to overthrow the Moguls. At the same time, civil wars among Muslim princes weakened Mogul power.

Trade with Western Europeans

The Portuguese sailor Vasco da Gama† reached India in 1498, a few years before the Mogul Empire was established. His voyage led to direct contacts between Western Europe and India. Previously, Arab merchants

*Mogul was the Persian word for Mongol.
†You will read about Vasco da Gama and the Portuguese voyages of exploration in Chapter 17.

Mogul Empire 1526–1707

Mogul Empire, 1526
Added by 1605
Added by 1707

Map Skill *Mogul emperors established a strong government that ruled most of the Indian subcontinent. The emperor Akbar conquered part of the Deccan Plateau. His successors completed the conquest, but their reigns were often marred by revolts. During which period was the largest amount of territory added to the Mogul Empire?*

had carried spices and other products from India to Mediterranean ports. As a result of da Gama's voyage, the Portuguese were the first Europeans to gain commercial privileges in India. They arranged treaties with local rulers on the west coast and made Goa their headquarters.

Goa also became a center for Christian missionaries who followed the Portuguese merchants to India. In the 1500s, the efforts of Christian missionaries to convert Hindus and Muslims angered the Mogul emperor. He sent his armies to end their activities.

245

Mogul rulers ordered the construction of many new buildings, which blended Indian and Persian architectural styles. In this bustling scene, the emperor Akbar supervises construction of the Red Fort in Agra.

However, on the whole, the Moguls did not feel threatened by the Europeans. They regarded the Europeans as somewhat backward because they did not have the silks, spices, or wealth of India.

The Portuguese soon had to compete with merchants from other Western European nations. In 1600, English merchants established the East India Company to finance trading ventures. As you will read in Chapter 28, the English East India Company would play a central role in Indian affairs as Mogul power declined.

SECTION REVIEW

1. Identify: Delhi sultanate, Tamerlane, Urdu, Babur, Akbar, Taj Mahal, Vasco da Gama.

2. Define: sultan, purdah.

3. Describe two advantages Muslim invaders had over Hindu forces.

4. List three differences between Hinduism and Islam.

5. What attitude did Akbar take toward Hindus?

6. How did the Mogul emperor react to the activities of Christian missionaries?

2 Flowering of Chinese Civilization

Read to Learn ■ how Chinese civilization achieved its golden ages
■ how the Chinese lived under the T'ang and Sung dynasties

During the period of the Middle Ages in Europe, Chinese civilization reached great heights. Like the Western Roman Empire, the Han Empire fell under internal and external pressures. However, in China, strong rulers eventually restored unity.

Two Golden Ages

After the Han Empire collapsed in 220 A.D., several dynasties rose and fell. Some lasted for hundreds of years. During the T'ang and Sung dynasties, China enjoyed two long golden ages. The economy expanded, the population grew, and the arts flourished.

The T'ang dynasty lasted from 618 to 907. T'ang rulers united an empire that reached from the Pacific Ocean to the borders of India and Persia. Under the T'ang, Chinese influence spread into Korea, Japan, and parts of Southeast Asia.

Peasant revolts ended T'ang rule, but the Sung dynasty eventually restored order. The Sung ruled China for about 300 years, from 960 to 1279. Under the Sung, China became a truly unified state, a goal not reached by Western European nations until the 1400s.

Chinese Government

During the T'ang and Sung dynasties, an efficient civil service system provided good government. As you read in Chapter 9, Han emperors had begun recruiting Confucian

Profiles ■ Wu Chao: China's Woman Emperor

During the reign of the emperor T'ai Tsung, founder of the T'ang dynasty, the planet Venus was visible during the day for several days in a row. Court astrologers declared that this was a sign that the throne would soon be occupied by a woman. Such a prediction was astounding because in China women were regarded as inferior to men. However, the prediction came true less than 50 years later when Wu Chao (woo chow) became Emperor of China.

At age 13, Wu Chao entered the T'ang court in a low-ranking position. On the day she left home, her mother wept because her daughter's future looked so bleak. However, Wu Chao scolded her tearful mother, saying: "To be admitted to the presence of the Son of Heaven—how can you tell that means unhappiness? Why are you crying like a little girl?"

Wu Chao's confidence and optimism were apparently well placed. She used her wit, intelligence, and beauty to gain power and influence at court. Eventually, the emperor Kao Tsung (gah oh dzoong) made her empress. When Kao Tsung suffered a serious stroke, the empress Wu took control of the government.

After her husband's death, she took the title of emperor and ruled on her own.

The empress was a brilliant administrator. She reorganized the army and oversaw the conquest of Korea. By reducing taxes and encouraging silk production and agriculture, she prevented the peasant uprisings that had plagued other Chinese rulers.

A strong-willed ruler, she ruthlessly eliminated those who threatened her power. But she was generous toward people in the lower ranks of society. For example, she promoted talented men regardless of their social class. She also used the civil service examination to recruit loyal new officials.

Empress Wu encouraged the growth of Buddhism in China. During her reign, Buddhism reached its height. The empress asked scholars to translate important Buddhist texts.

In 705, the aging empress was too ill to prevent a group of generals from seizing the palace. They forced the 83-year-old ruler to give up the throne in favor of her son. Wu Chao died soon after. Yet her successful administrative and social policies had paved the way for one of the most glorious periods of Chinese history.

247

scholars to carry out government policy. T'ang and Sung rulers expanded the civil service system.

Scholars who served as government officials had the highest status in Chinese society. In theory, a man from any class could qualify for the civil service. In practice, however, few peasants could afford the expensive education needed to pass the examinations. Generally, only the sons of officials and wealthy merchants attended the private schools that were set up across China.

At its best, the civil service attracted educated, loyal officials. Because they had been trained as Confucian scholars, government officials helped spread Confucian values and Chinese culture across the huge empire.

Important Inventions

Chinese inventions during the T'ang and Sung dynasties had far-reaching effects. In the eighth century, the Chinese invented printing. Earlier Chinese inventions such as paper and the use of seals to stamp documents had paved the way for printing.

Buddhist monks probably developed block printing to reproduce sacred texts and prayers. They carved characters onto wooden blocks that were inked and pressed onto paper. The earliest known printed work is a Buddhist text called the *Diamond Sutra*, produced in 868. It was printed on six large sheets that were then attached to form a 16 foot-long (5 meter) scroll.

About 1050, the Chinese began to use movable type, pieces of metal containing Chinese characters that could be combined to form sentences. The pieces could be used again and again. Both block printing and movable type enabled the Chinese to produce many more books than before.

The people of Korea and Japan soon learned about printing from the Chinese. However, Chinese inventions such as paper and printing did not reach Western Europe until much later. The Arabs brought Chinese papermaking techniques to Europe, but paper was not widely used in Europe until the 1400s.

During the T'ang and Sung dynasties, the Chinese made other practical advances. They used the waterwheel to power forges and blast furnaces. T'ang mapmakers drew the most advanced maps of the day. The Chinese also developed a magnetic compass and built large ships equipped with several masts. By 1000, the Chinese had begun to use gunpowder in weapons such as mines, hand grenades, and explosive rockets.

The Arts

During the centuries of peace and prosperity under the T'ang and Sung, the arts flourished in China. Wealthy people flocked to the cities, especially the T'ang capital of Chang-an. They bought books, paintings, and other fine works of art to decorate their homes and tombs.

T'ang potters captured the rich variety of Chinese city life in brightly glazed ceramics. They often portrayed foreigners, such as this bearded Middle Eastern wine merchant. Trade brought new products and ideas to China, enlivening the highly sophisticated culture of Chinese cities.

T'ang artisans perfected the manufacture of porcelain, a hard, shiny pottery. They created lively porcelain figures of musicians and dancers who entertained at court. They also made porcelain horses, camels, and even bearded foreigners, all of which showed the importance of foreign trade in China.

In T'ang China, literature, especially poetry, was important. Poets wrote about human emotions, nature, and the individual's place in the universe. One of China's greatest poets was Li Po (lee boh). A Taoist, Li Po wrote about his feelings for nature in the following lines:

> My friend is lodging in the Eastern Range,
> Dearly loving the beauty of valleys and
>   hills. . . .
> A pine-tree wind dusts his sleeves and coat;
> A pebbly stream cleans his heart and ears.
> I envy you who far from strife and talk
> Are high-propped on a pillow of grey mist.

Landscape painting reached a high point in China during the Sung Empire. Sung painters were influenced by Taoist respect for nature and the natural scenery of China. Artists would meditate for days on a landscape, trying to capture the mood of the scene. Then they would paint the scene without looking at it again. Most paintings were done with brushes and ink on silk. Artists captured the sense of rugged mountains and rushing rivers with simple lines in black and shades of gray. Sung styles of painting influenced Chinese artists for hundreds of years.

Patterns of Life

Between about 600 and 1000, the Chinese economy expanded dramatically. New seeds and better farming methods helped increase food production. The resulting food surpluses enabled some Chinese to leave the farms and move to the cities, where they worked as artisans, shopkeepers, servants, or actors. However, most Chinese were still farmers.

Trade and commerce also increased in this period. Cities bustled with activity as camel caravans, loaded with porcelains,

Time seems to stand still in Chinese landscape paintings. This painting shows the emperor Kuang Wu crossing a river, but the human figures are less important than the mountains, trees, mist, and river.

249

silks, and other luxuries left for the Silk Road and the Middle East.

Contacts with the world. The Chinese were open to outside ideas during T'ang and Sung times. For example, the T'ang government officially tolerated Buddhism, which thrived. Many Chinese, both rich and poor, became Buddhist monks or nuns. Chinese Buddhists traveled to India and Southeast Asia and returned home with new knowledge of history, geography, and the sciences.

Trade and travel exposed the Chinese to many new products. They learned about new foods such as peppers and dates. Furthermore, the Chinese learned about new seeds and farming methods from their contacts with the foreigners.

Enduring traditions. Under the Sung, China became one of the largest and wealthiest empires in the world. At the same time, Chinese society remained firmly rooted in Confucian ideas. (See page 140.)

Confucius had emphasized the importance of harmony in human relationships. The Chinese believed that harmony would result from a well-ordered society where individuals accepted their roles. They did not accept the idea that all people were equal.

Throughout China's long history, the silk trade linked China to the rest of the world. The manufacture of silk, a major industry in China, was largely the work of women. This twelfth century painting shows women pounding newly woven silk fabric before it was ironed.

Instead, they thought that educated people were superior to uneducated people. They also believed that farmers, who produced food, were superior to merchants, who merely exchanged goods.

Confucian ideals led the Chinese to stress a person's duties rather than his or her rights. For example, the people had a duty to obey the emperor. The emperor, in turn, had a duty to provide good government.

Women in China. China was a society of unequals in which women were thought to be inferior to men. When a girl married, she joined her husband's family. As a wife, she was expected to obey her husband.

During the Sung dynasty, the custom of footbinding was introduced at court. This custom involved binding a girl's feet at birth so they would remain small and delicate. Court dancers were the first to have their feet bound. But soon almost all Chinese women were affected by the custom.

Footbinding severely limited a woman's freedom of movement. She had to take tiny steps, which were considered beautiful and feminine. A woman with unbound feet was considered ugly and was unlikely to marry. Rather than risk such a fate for their daughters, peasants as well as upper class parents adopted the custom of footbinding. For centuries, Chinese women suffered from this painful and often crippling custom.

SECTION REVIEW

1. Identify: *Diamond Sutra*, Li Po.
2. (a) In theory, who could qualify for the Chinese civil service? (b) In practice, who usually entered the civil service?
3. (a) Describe block printing. (b) Who probably developed block printing? Why?
4. What subjects interested T'ang and Sung poets and artists?
5. How did footbinding affect Chinese women?

---

3 Mongol and Ming Empires in China

Read to Learn ■ how the Mongol invasion changed China
■ what the Ming dynasty accomplished

In the twelfth century, the Sung dynasty faced ruthless Mongol armies led by Genghis Khan. Genghis Khan was a merciless warrior. "The greatest joy," he declared, "is to conquer one's enemies, to pursue them, to seize their property, to see their families in tears." In 1215, Mongol armies annihilated the Chinese defenders of Peking. The Sung emperor fled south. Genghis Khan did not conquer the rest of China, but he won other victories across Asia and set up the Mongol Empire.

A Foreign Dynasty

Under Genghis Khan's sons and grandsons, the Mongol Empire extended from the Pacific Ocean to the Danube River. The huge empire was later divided among several rulers. (See the map on page 252.) In 1279, Kublai Khan, a grandson of Genghis Khan, completed the conquest of China and established the first foreign dynasty in China.

Aware of China's reputation for absorbing its conquerors, Kublai Khan tried to limit Chinese influence on the Mongols. He set up a separate law code for Mongols and allowed only Mongol nobles and foreigners to serve in high positions at court. However, the Mongols used Chinese officials at the local level. Even Kublai Khan was influenced by Chinese culture. He rebuilt Peking, making it his capital. He also adopted a Chinese name for his dynasty, the Yuan (yoo AHN).

The Mongols built great highways across their empire. As a result, trade and travel increased, and China was in constant contact with other lands. Arabs, Italians, Russians, and many others went to China. They helped spread knowledge of Chinese inventions across Europe and Asia. As you

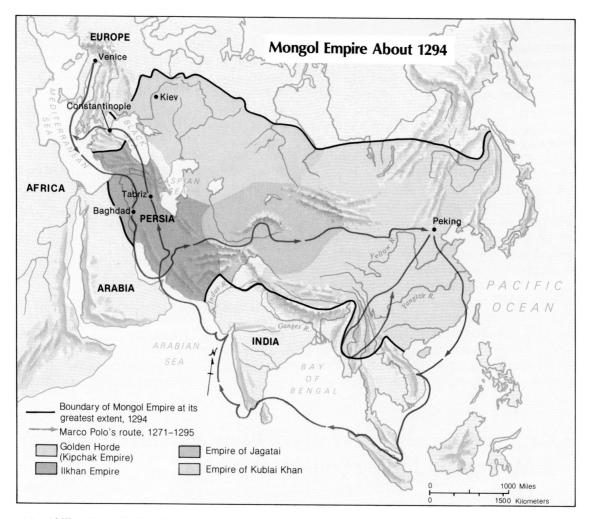

Map Skill *Genghis Khan led nomadic peoples of Central Asia on a ruthless course of world conquest. Mongol armies swept westward into Russia and eastward into China. At one time, the Mongols dominated almost all of Asia. What parts of the Mongol Empire did Marco Polo visit?*

read earlier, Marco Polo was one of the foreigners who visited China and stayed to serve Kublai Khan.

The Yuan dynasty declined under Kublai Khan's sucesssors. To meet the expenses of their courts, emperors printed more and more paper money. Inflation combined with Chinese resentment against the foreign dynasty resulted in revolt. A Buddhist monk organized rebel armies and drove out the Mongols. He then founded the Ming dynasty, which ruled China from 1368 to 1644.

Restoring Chinese Rule

Ming emperors were determined to erase all traces of foreign rule. They modeled their government on the T'ang and Sung empires.

They revived the civil service system, and Confucian scholars regained their influence at court. Under the Ming, the Chinese felt confident that their culture was second to none.

Between 1405 and 1433, the Ming outfitted seven huge fleets, which sailed on voyages of exploration. For the first voyage, the capable Chinese admiral Cheng Ho assembled 63 ships, which carried over 27,000 sailors, soldiers, and civilians.* Ming fleets visited Southeast Asia, India, Arabia, and East Africa. They traded, collected tribute, and gathered information about sea routes.

---

*Some Chinese ships weighed up to 1500 tons each. In contrast, 60 years later, the largest of the first European vessels that sailed to India weighed only about 300 tons.

In 1433, the voyages suddenly stopped. No one knows why. Court officials may have been jealous of the fleet admirals and may have convinced the emperor that the expeditions were too costly. Or the Chinese may have decided that they did not need to look beyond their borders because they believed they had everything the people needed.

China was probably the most technologically advanced nation in the world when the Ming emperor ended the voyages of exploration. However, the Chinese cut themselves off from the world just as people in Western Europe were expanding their horizons. While Europeans were experimenting with new ideas, the Chinese were content with the institutions and values that had served them so well in the past.

Restrictions on Trade and Travel

In addition to ending the voyages of exploration, the Ming emperor also brought foreign travel and trade under close regulation. In 1514, when Portuguese trading ships sailed up the coast of China, Ming officials refused to let them land. Instead, the Portuguese had to sell their cargoes to Chinese traders who came out to their ships. As soon as the goods were unloaded, the foreigners had to leave. Later on, the Portuguese gained the right to settle in Macao, but they were kept under close Chinese supervision.

In the 1600s, other Europeans tried to win trading rights from the Ming emperor. The Chinese restricted all foreign merchants to one city, Canton. Every summer, foreigners went to Canton to do their trading. They were not allowed to bring their families, carry firearms, or learn Chinese. All business was conducted through Chinese agents.

For 250 years, Chinese officials enforced the laws limiting the activities of foreigners. As you will read, it was only during the decline of a later dynasty that foreigners successfully challenged Chinese power.

SECTION REVIEW

1. Identify: Kublai Khan, Marco Polo, Cheng Ho.
2. How did Kublai Khan try to keep the Mongols from being absorbed by Chinese culture?
3. What effect did the building of roads have on China?
4. Describe the Ming sea voyages.
5. What restrictions did the Ming put on Portuguese traders?

4 Foundations of Japanese Civilization

Read to Learn ■ how geography affected Japanese life
■ how Chinese culture influenced the Japanese

In his *Description of the World*, Marco Polo reported that a remarkable people lived in a land east of China. He was referring to the Japanese, who occupied a chain of islands on the rim of Asia.

In prehistoric times, the Ainu, a hunting and fishing people, crossed to Japan from the Asian mainland. Later immigrants from the mainland brought a knowledge of rice farming as well as bronze and ironworking. By the early centuries A.D., the Japanese had developed their own culture. The Japanese later adopted ideas from the Chinese. But they were never overwhelmed by outside influences, in part because of their location.

Geographic Setting

Japan is an *archipelago* (AHR kuh PEHL uh GOH), a chain of islands, off the northeast coast of Asia. (See the map on page 254.) The four main islands of Japan are Hokkaido (hoh KĪ doh), Honshu (hahn shoo), Shikoku (SHEE koh KOO), and Kyushu (khoo shoo).

Japan has a mild climate, abundant rainfall, and fertile soil. Farmers grow crops such as rice, barley, and soy beans. However, because Japan is mountainous, only about 20 percent of the land is suitable for farming. The Japanese learned to terrace hillsides in order to create more farmland.

Map Skill *The four main islands of Japan, which are shown on this map, are the highest peaks of a large underwater mountain chain. Hundreds of other islands, which dot the ocean south of Kyushu are also part of Japan. About how far does Japan extend from north to south?*

The sea strongly influenced early Japanese life. The Japanese fished in the waters surrounding their islands. The Sea of Japan to the west was a barrier to invaders from the Asian mainland and thereby allowed the Japanese to develop largely on their own. Yet the sea also served as a highway for the Japanese, linking the islands to one another and to the mainland.

Early Japanese Society

The early Japanese were organized into *clans,* family groups who traced their origins to a common ancestor. A clan was headed by a hereditary chief who was both a military and religious leader. Within the clan, people lived in extended families. Each family's position in society was inherited. A family inherited the right to be farmers, weavers, potters, or warriors—the highest group in society.

Japanese religious beliefs centered on respect for nature. People did not fear nature. Rather, they were in awe of its unseen forces. They worshipped *kami,* or spirits, which they believed controlled the forces of nature.

Ancient Japanese religious traditions were later called Shinto, the way of the gods. Shinto is a religion of festivals and rituals. At shrines dotting the land, people offered gifts to the kami to ensure good harvests. Unlike Christianity, Islam, and Buddhism, Shinto has no sacred texts.

About 400 A.D., the Yamato emerged as the strongest clan in Japan. They established the first and only Japanese dynasty. The present Japanese emperor traces his origins to the Yamato clan. According to legend, the sun goddess Amaterasu created Japan, and one of her descendants became the first emperor. The Yamato traced their ancestors back to that first emperor. By claiming divine descent, Japanese emperors gained the respect and support of the people.

Selective Borrowing

Between the fifth and ninth centuries, the Japanese borrowed many ideas from China. They adapted Chinese writing to their own language, and that opened the way for further borrowing. However, the Japanese kept only the ideas that fitted their own social, political, and religious traditions.

In 552, the Yamato ruler welcomed Chinese Buddhist missionaries who came to Japan by way of Korea. In doing so, he set

Japan on a new path. Just as Christianity transmitted the Greco-Roman heritage to the people of Western Europe, Buddhism became the vehicle for spreading Chinese culture to Japan. Japanese rulers accepted many Buddhist beliefs. Yet they also kept their traditional role as chief priests in Shinto. Buddhist monks also introduced Confucian ideas about the family and ancestor worship. Because these ideas reinforced Japanese traditions, they were easily absorbed.

Prince Shotoku, a scholar and member of the Yamato ruling family, was fascinated by Chinese civilization. Under his leadership, the pace of borrowing from China increased. In 607, he sent representatives to China to study its government, history, and philosophy as well as its arts and sciences. The Japanese returned with dazzling reports of Chinese achievements.

In a wave of enthusiasm, Japanese rulers set out to remodel their society along Chinese lines. The court eagerly adopted Chinese styles in art and literature. Nobles studied Confucian and Taoist philosophy. When the Japanese built a new capital at Nara in the 700s, they modeled it on the splendid T'ang capital in China. Palaces and Buddhist temples reflected Chinese styles of architecture. Even Japanese clothing and furniture showed the impact of Chinese culture.

Japanese rulers tried to reform the government based on Chinese ideas. They set up a government bureaucracy and introduced the civil service system. But the Japanese eventually dropped the civil service system because it did not fit in with the Japanese tradition that a person's position in society was inherited. For the same reason, the Japanese could not accept the Confucian idea of opening offices to all social classes. As a result, hereditary nobles rather than scholars held official positions in Japan.

The Court at Heian

In 794, the emperor moved his capital to Heian (hay ahn), present-day Kyoto. At Heian, Chinese ideas were blended with Japanese traditions. But as the T'ang dynasty declined in China during the 800s, Japanese fascination with China decreased. Japanese visitors no longer flocked to the mainland. Trade and travel continued, but on a reduced scale.

The role of the emperor changed during the 800s. In theory, the emperor remained supreme. In practice, he became a figurehead whose chief duties were religious. Noble families at court ran the government.

One family, the Fujiwara, acquired their power in the government through marriage. The Fujiwara arranged for their daughters to marry the heirs to the Japanese throne. In this way, the Fujiwara gained influence over the emperor. Outwardly, the Fujiwara supported the tradition of respect for the emperor. But in practice, they held the actual power.

The Fujiwara appointed their followers to government positions. With few government responsibilities, other nobles at court turned to the arts, literature, and music. Noblewomen were especially influential in developing a distinctly Japanese literature. Unlike Japanese men, who wrote in Chinese, Japanese women wrote in their own language. Many court women kept diaries and composed poetry. *The Tale of Genji*, written by Lady Murasaki Shikibu, is a great masterpiece of Japanese literature. The work was one of the world's first novels. (See the Skill Lesson on page 256.)

SECTION REVIEW

1. Locate: Hokkaido, Honshu, Shikoku, Kyushu, Sea of Japan, Heian.
2. Identify: Shinto, Yamato, Lady Murasaki.
3. Define: archipelago, clan, kami.
4. Describe one advantage and one disadvantage of the geography of Japan.
5. Why did the Yamato rulers have the respect of the people?
6. (a) List three aspects of Chinese culture the Japanese borrowed. (b) List one Chinese idea the Japanese rejected.
7. How did women contribute to the development of Japanese literature?

255

5 From Feudalism to Unified Nation

Read to Learn ■ how feudal society took shape in Japan
■ what the Tokugawa shoguns accomplished

The court at Heian was the center of an elegant world. However, by the 1100s, the noble court families had lost power to strong rural lords. The system of government then emerging in Japan resembled the feudalism of Western Europe.

Japanese Feudalism

Feudalism in Japan developed out of several centuries of warfare. In the early feudal period, warrior knights called *samurai* battled for control of the land. Samurai were nobles descended from early clan chiefs.

Skill Lesson   The Japanese Court: Analyzing Fiction as Historical Evidence

Fictional works of literature, such as novels, short stories, and plays, can be valuable historical evidence. They sometimes provide useful information about the ideas and customs of people from another culture or from another time. You need to analyze a fictional work carefully before using it as historical evidence. The work might present only a limited picture of a historical period or event.

The excerpt that follows is taken from *The Tale of Genji,* a novel by Lady Murasaki. Lady Murasaki was a noble who lived at the Japanese court of Heian. As lady-in-waiting to the empress, she took part in the elegant court rituals and ceremonies. She probably wrote her novel about 1004. The long story describes the many adventures of a legendary Prince Genji, the young son of a Japanese emperor.

Read the excerpt. Then use the following steps to analyze it as historical evidence.

1. **Identify the nature of the document.** Ask yourself the following questions: (a) What type of document is it? (b) Who wrote it? (c) What connection, if any, did the author have with the events described? (d) When was the document written?

2. **Study the content of the document.** Answer the following questions about the excerpt: (a) What preparations for Genji's initiation does the author describe? (b) What does the author say about Genji's appearance? (c) What does the author say about the emperor's role in the preparations?

3. **Analyze the document as a historical source.** Answer the following questions

about the excerpt: (a) What can you learn about Japanese court life from this excerpt? (b) In what ways is the excerpt of limited use as historical evidence? (c) Would you use this document to learn how all Japanese lived in the 1000s? Explain.

From *The Tale of Genji*

Though it seemed a shame to put so lovely a child into man's dress, he was now twelve years old and the time for his Initiation was come. The Emperor directed the preparations with tireless zeal and insisted upon a magnificence beyond what was prescribed.... The ceremony took place in the eastern wing of the Emperor's own apartments, and the Throne was placed facing toward the east, with the seats of the Initiate-to-be and his Sponsor (the Minister of the Left) in front.

Genji arrived at the hour of the Monkey [3 p.m.] He looked very handsome with his long childish locks, and the Sponsor, whose duty it had just been to bind them with the purple ribbon, was sorry to think that all this would soon be changed and even the Clerk of the Treasury seemed reluctant to sever those lovely tresses with the ritual knife....

Duly crowned, Genji went to his chamber and changing into man's dress went down into the courtyard and performed the Dance of Homage, which he did with such grace that tears stood in every eye. ... It had been feared that his delicate features would show to less advantage when he had put aside his childish dress; but on the contrary he looked handsomer than ever....

In 1192, a powerful samurai leader, Yoritomo Minamoto, obtained the title of *shogun,* or chief general, from the emperor. Feudal society took shape under Yoritomo and his successors. The emperor remained at the head of society, but he had no political power and performed only religious duties. The shogun was the actual ruler of Japan. He controlled taxes, issued laws, and commanded the samurai who had pledged to serve him.

Below the shogun were the *daimyo* (DĪ myoh), the strongest samurai. Daimyo carved out huge estates. Like feudal lords in Western Europe, they gave some of their land to lesser samurai in exchange for military service and personal loyalty. With their samurai armies, the daimyo fought among themselves and were largely independent of the shogun. (See the diagram at right.)

Far below the samurai were peasants, artisans, and merchants. Peasants were the backbone of feudal society in Japan. Peasant families farmed the estates of samurai. Some peasants also became foot soldiers. On rare occasions, an able peasant soldier would rise into the ranks of the samurai. Merchants ranked below the peasants.

The way of the warrior. The samurai developed a code of conduct that resembled the European code of chivalry. (See page 157.) The samurai code was called *bushido,* meaning the way of the warrior. Bushido stressed loyalty and unquestioning obedience to one's lord. It also emphasized simplicity, courage, and honor. A samurai who violated the code was thought to have disgraced himself and his family. In order to remove this disgrace, he was expected to commit seppuku, a ritual suicide.

Under feudalism, Japanese women had less freedom than they had enjoyed in the past. In Western Europe, the code of chivalry put noblewomen on a pedestal. In contrast, samurai wives were expected to endure hardships without complaint.

Signs of change. In the 1400s and 1500s, the number of daimyo decreased as stronger lords absorbed the estates of weaker ones. Furthermore, lower-ranking samurai became so numerous that they lost prestige.

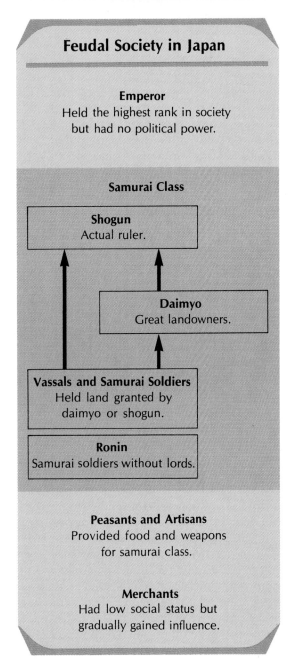

Feudal Society in Japan

Emperor
Held the highest rank in society but had no political power.

Samurai Class

Shogun
Actual ruler.

Daimyo
Great landowners.

Vassals and Samurai Soldiers
Held land granted by daimyo or shogun.

Ronin
Samurai soldiers without lords.

Peasants and Artisans
Provided food and weapons for samurai class.

Merchants
Had low social status but gradually gained influence.

Diagram Skill *Samurai dominated feudal society in Japan, as this diagram shows. Why do you think the emperor had less power than the shogun?*

Many samurai who had no lord to serve were considered outcasts. Bands of homeless samurai roamed the country, attacking travelers, and raiding peasant villages.

Despite the constant feudal warfare, the Japanese economy grew. Foreign trade stimulated economic growth. Merchants developed a busy trade with China and other

257

parts of East Asia. Japanese artisans improved the methods of papermaking, metalworking, and weaving that had been introduced from China. By the 1500s, Japanese swords, folding fans, and screens were in great demand in China. Shipbuilding and manufacturing industries expanded to keep pace with demand.

Creating a Unified Nation

In the late 1500s, a powerful general, Hideyoshi (HEE day YOH shee), established the foundations for a unified nation. He subdued the warring daimyo and brought all of Japan under his control. Upon Hideyoshi's death, Tokugawa Ieyasu (toh koo GOW wah ee YAH soo) seized power. In 1603, he established the Tokugawa shogunate, which lasted until 1868.

Under the Tokugawa shoguns, Japan enjoyed peace and stability. Like European monarchs in the late Middle Ages, the Tokugawa shoguns created a strong central government. They put an end to feudal warfare and organized a government bureaucracy to supervise taxation, finance, and justice. Although in Europe the rise of strong monarchs led to the decline of feudalism, this did not happen in Japan. The Tokugawa shoguns preserved the traditional feudal order.

To stay in power, the Tokugawa shoguns imposed a new system of government known as centralized feudalism. The daimyo were allowed to keep their lands, but the shogun limited their power. The daimyo had to spend every other year in the Tokugawa capital of Edo, present-day Tokyo. Their wives and families had to stay in Edo all year round to discourage the daimyo from organizing revolts. Furthermore, a daimyo needed official approval before he could repair his castle, arrange his daughter's marriage, or sign any contract. The emperor continued to live in Kyoto and conduct religious ceremonies.

The Japanese economy benefited from peace and national unity. The shogun abolished local feudal fees in many cities. Merchants could then expand their activities and develop trade on a national scale. Money replaced rice and grain as the means of exchange, and the merchant class thrived.

Cities, especially Edo, grew rapidly. The daimyo built splendid homes for their families in the capital. They spent lavishly on their trips back and forth to Edo. They traveled with hundreds of servants and wagons loaded with household goods. Innkeepers and shopowners set up businesses along the way, and new roads were built. As a result, travel became easier and safer.

Cultural Traditions

During the long feudal period, samurai values influenced Japanese culture. Short stories and paintings glorified warfare and the samurai code of honor.

Buddhism also shaped Japanese culture. As you read in Chapter 9, Buddhism spread from India to China, where it underwent many changes. In Japan, Buddhism developed in still other directions.

Zen, a Buddhist sect that originated in China, strongly influenced Japanese traditions. Zen monks taught the unity of nature, which complemented the Shinto idea of respect for the forces of nature. Because Zen Buddhism emphasized physical and mental discipline, it appealed to the samurai. Zen also influenced Japanese theater. The first Japanese dramas were Noh plays, which incorporated dances and poetry that taught Zen ideas.

Buddhist monasteries were centers of learning and the arts. For example, Zen monks created fine landscape paintings. Monks also taught upper class men and women to express the Zen devotion to nature in such activities as flower arranging and landscape gardening. Both men and women learned the tea ceremony, which was meant to reflect peace, simplicity, and love of beauty.

Under the Tokugawa shoguns, merchants became important supporters of the arts. They enjoyed lively entertainments such as Kabuki theater. Unlike the slow-paced Noh plays, Kabuki dramas were violent and emotional. In towns, people flocked to see puppet plays and sumo wrestling.

A new kind of poetry, haiku, also became popular. A *haiku* is a short poem with only 17 syllables. In a few words, a haiku poet sketches a mood or scene that suggests many meanings. In the following haiku, the poet shows his regard for nature:

> All night the ragged
> clouds and wind
> had only one
> companion . . . the moon

Japan and the World

During the feudal period, Japan traded with China, Korea, and Southeast Asia. In 1543, the first Portuguese ships arrived in Japanese waters. Christian missionaries followed the traders. Led by the Jesuit priest Francis Xavier, the missionaries won many converts.

By the early 1600s, there were about 300,000 Japanese Christians.

However, the shoguns became suspicious of the missionaries. They disliked the fact that Japanese Christians pledged obedience to the pope, whom they saw as a foreign ruler. The fierce competition that developed among European traders further increased their concern. When Spain conquered the Philippines, the Japanese feared the Europeans might try to seize Japan. Eventually, the shogun outlawed Christian missionaries and persecuted Japanese Christians.

In 1639, the shogun expelled all Europeans and forbade contacts between Japanese and foreigners. He banned foreign trade and travel and stopped the building of ocean-going ships. Only the port of Nagasaki

The Japanese greeted the Portuguese, their first European visitors, with interest and curiosity. Europeans set up trading posts at which they conducted business with Japanese merchants. Yet the Japanese considered their European visitors less civilized than they. For example, the Japanese, who bathed frequently, were shocked that Europeans seldom bathed. The Japanese referred to Europeans as the "southern barbarians" and "garlic eaters."

remained open to the world. At Nagasaki, Chinese and a few Dutch merchants were allowed to trade under close supervision. Like the Ming emperors in China, the Tokugawa shoguns strictly enforced their decision. For over 200 years, Japan shut itself off from the world.

SECTION REVIEW

1. Identify: Hideyoshi, Tokugawa Ieyasu, Zen, Noh, Kabuki.

2. Define: samurai, shogun, daimyo, bushido, haiku.

3. (a) What was the highest class in Japanese feudal society? (b) What was the lowest class?

4. What values did the samurai code emphasize?

5. Give one example of how the Tokugawa shoguns limited the power of the daimyo.

6. What two cultural traditions influenced the arts in Japan?

Chapter 15 Review

In Perspective

During the period of the Middle Ages in Europe, the civilizations of India, China, and Japan made impressive advances. In the 1200s, Muslims invaded India and set up the Delhi sultanate. Despite the influence of Islam, Hindu traditions survived. In the sixteenth century, most of India was united under the Mogul Empire. The Mogul emperor Akbar practiced religious toleration and made many reforms in government.

Under the T'ang and Sung dynasties, the Chinese experienced two golden ages. They perfected the civil service system and expanded economically. The Chinese also made practical advances and produced outstanding works of art. In the 1200s, the Mongols conquered China, but they were eventually ousted by the Ming. The Ming dynasty financed voyages of exploration, but in the 1500s, the Ming imposed strict isolation.

The Japanese developed their own culture, but they borrowed selectively from the Chinese. For example, the Japanese adapted Buddhist and Confucian teachings to their own needs. Japan developed a feudal society in the 1100s, and for centuries warfare was a way of life. But by 1600, the Tokugawa shoguns had successfully transformed Japan into a strong, centralized nation.

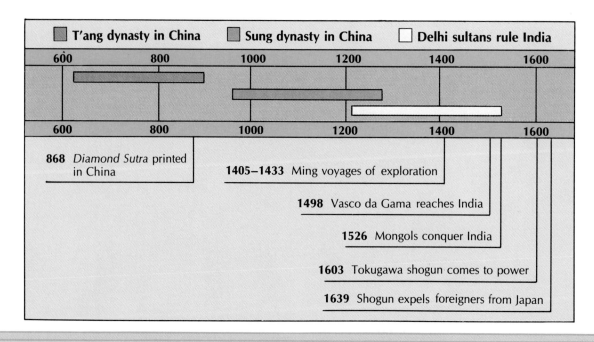

Recalling Facts

Arrange the events in each of the following groups in the order in which they occurred.
1. (a) Delhi sultanate established.
   (b) Hindu princes compete for control of the northern plain.
   (c) The Mogul Empire enjoys a golden age under Akbar.
2. (a) Marco Polo travels across Kublai Khan's empire.
   (b) China restricts all foreign traders to Canton.
   (c) China enjoys a golden age under the T'ang dynasty.
3. (a) Tokugawa shoguns expel all foreigners.
   (b) Yamato clan wins control of Japan.
   (c) Japanese adapt ideas from China.

Chapter Checkup

1. (a) How did Hinduism influence life in India? (b) What effect did Muslim rule have on India?
2. (a) How did Akbar try to unify the Mogul Empire? (b) How did his successors change his policies? (c) What happened as a result of these changes?
3. Describe Chinese achievements in each of the following areas: (a) government; (b) technology; (c) art.
4. (a) How did foreign trade affect China during the T'ang and Sung empires? (b) Why did trade become even more extensive under the Mongols? (c) What attitude did the Chinese take toward foreign trade by the 1500s?
5. (a) How did Chinese culture influence the Japanese? (b) Why did the Japanese borrow some Chinese ideas and not others?
6. (a) What type of government did the Tokugawa shoguns establish in Japan? (b) How did they limit the power of the daimyo?
7. (a) How were Buddhist teachings brought to Japan? (b) How did Buddhism affect Japanese society?

Critical Thinking

1. **Analyzing** (a) How did differences in religious beliefs contribute to clashes between Hindus and Muslims in India? (b) In what ways was there a peaceful blending of the two cultures?
2. **Applying Information** (a) How did Chinese and Japanese attitudes toward foreigners change in the 1500s and 1600s? (b) Why do you think their views of foreigners changed?
3. **Analyzing a Quotation** A Japanese saying states: "The rice that Hideyoshi cooked was eaten by Tokugawa Ieyasu." Do you think this saying accurately described what happened in Japan after the late 1500s? Explain.
4. **Comparing** (a) Describe the structure of Japanese feudal society. (b) How was Japanese feudalism similar to feudalism in Western Europe? (c) How was it different?

Relating Past to Present

1. Chinese art flourished during the T'ang and Sung dynasties. (a) Why was this so? (b) What conditions would encourage a "golden age" in art to develop today?

Developing Basic Skills

1. **Using Visual Evidence** Study the painting on page 249. Does the painting express the same feelings about nature as Li Po's poem? Explain.
2. **Map Reading** Study the map on page 252 and the maps on pages 787–788. Then answer the following questions: (a) What was the extent of the Mongol Empire? (b) What countries today are located in the lands once ruled by the Mongols? (c) Why do you think Genghis Khan divided his empire among his sons and grandsons?
3. **Using Diagrams** Study the diagram of feudal society in Japan on page 257. Then answer the following questions: (a) Who held the highest status in Japanese society? (b) Who had the lowest status? (c) Why do you think the daimyo had so much power and influence? (d) What does the diagram tell you about the structure of Japanese society?

See page 805 for suggested readings.

Ancient civilizations come to life in the art that has survived throughout the ages. This wheeled cart made of iron symbolizes the creative spirit that spurred early civilizations to new achievements.

Unit One
A BRIEF SURVEY

Beginnings of Ancient Civilization

(Prehistory—256 B.C.)

Unit Survey

About noon on a spring day in 1300 B.C., the Egyptian ruler Ramses II was camped with his army near the city of Kadesh in Syria. Ramses was planning a surprise attack on the Hittites. Like the Egyptians, the Hittites had conquered a vast empire and were determined to expand their power.

While Ramses waited for his forces to assemble, Hittite chariots suddenly appeared out of nowhere. They sliced through the camp, creating panic. The Egyptians fled, leaving their ruler to face the enemy alone. Later, Ramses had scenes of the battle carved on temple walls all over Egypt.

According to these temple carvings, he called on Amon, the chief Egyptian god. "I call to thee, my father, Amon. I am in the midst of foes whom I know not," Ramses prayed. "My soldiers and charioteers have forsaken me . . . but I call and find that Amon is worth more to me than millions of foot soldiers and hundreds of thousands of chariots."

The temple carvings show that Ramses rallied his forces and defeated the Hittites. However, recent discoveries of Hittite texts tell that the Egyptians suffered a setback at the battle of Kadesh. Eventually, after several campaigns in Syria, Ramses II and the Hittites signed a treaty in 1284 B.C. that set the borders of the two empires. This treaty, in Egyptian and Hittite writing, is the oldest complete treaty in existence.

At the time of the battle, over 3,000 years ago, powerful civilizations had emerged in several parts of the world. In the fertile river valleys of Egypt, the Middle East, India, and China, people had learned to farm, producing enough food to support large cities and strong governments. These early civilizations had basic features in common, but each also had its own distinctive patterns that shaped its religion, government, and society.

1 Foundations of Civilization

Read to Learn
- how scientists investigate prehistory
- how civilizations developed in the Old and New Stone Ages

From written records, art, architecture, and other remains, scholars have pieced together the evidence about how early civilizations emerged. They have learned that the first civilizations were built on the achievements of still earlier people. Finding evidence about these people, however, has often proved difficult.

Stone Age People

Scholars use the term *prehistory* to refer to the long period of time before the invention of writing. By analyzing *artifacts*, objects such as tools and weapons left behind by early people, scientists have learned about the lives of these ancient people.

Because the earliest tools and weapons were made of stone, scholars have called the long period from about 500,000 B.C. to 3500 B.C. the Stone Age. During the Old Stone Age, from about 500,000 B.C. to about 10,000 B.C., people were *nomads*, living in small bands, always on the move hunting and gathering food. They invented simple tools and learned to control fire. They probably also developed spoken languages.

About 10,000 B.C., people in different parts of the world learned to grow grain and plant vegetables. The development of agriculture ushered in the New Stone Age. The change from hunting and food gathering to farming had profound effects on the way people lived. They began to build permanent settlements and develop new ways to cooperate with one another. In villages, a form of government emerged with a chief and a council of elders who made decisions about planting and harvesting. Religion, too, developed formal rituals as farming people prayed to spirits for good harvests.

In the New Stone Age, people made important advances in *technology*, that is, the tools and skills that people use to meet their basic needs. They made farm tools, learned to use animals to pull plows, and invented the wheel, the sail, and weaving.

Emergence of Civilization

In some places, simple farming communities gradually expanded into cities. As the cities grew, complex religions and well-organized governments developed. People acquired specialized skills and specialized occupations. Soon social classes appeared, and people began to keep records.

The first cities developed in river valleys in North Africa, the Middle East, and Asia. (See the map on page 11.) Fertile soils and moisture from the rivers allowed farmers to produce surplus food that supported large populations. In the early cities, government and religion were closely related. People were *polytheistic*, that is, they worshipped many gods. Powerful priest-kings combined the tasks of keeping the gods friendly by performing the proper rituals and defending the cities against enemies. These early rulers also organized the people to clear the land and build the irrigation systems that were essential to farming.

With the growth of cities, other patterns emerged. As people learned skills such as weaving or bronze making, different occupations appeared. Most people remained farmers, but some became merchants, traders, or artisans. In the social classes that developed, a person's place in society became well defined and usually determined by birth.

A major achievement of early civilizations was the development of recordkeeping. *Scribes,* or people who could read and write, were trained in the temples. Their records of harvests and taxes preserved important information for future generations.

SECTION REVIEW

1. Identify: Stone Age.
2. Define: prehistory, artifact, nomad, technology, polytheistic, scribe.
3. List two advances made in the Old Stone Age and two in the New Stone Age.
4. How were religion and government related in the early cities?

2 Ancient Egypt

Read to Learn
  - how the Nile influenced the development of Egypt
  - what contributions Egypt made to civilization

Scholars believe that farming had begun by 7000 B.C. in the Nile River valley. In time, the farmers of the Nile Valley produced enough food to support a thriving civilization.

Geographic Setting

Geography favored the growth of Egyptian civilization. In ancient times, the Nile River was seen as the "giver of life." Once a year, the Nile flooded, bringing rich soil to the farmlands along its banks. The river provided moisture to the surrounding lands and served as a highway that helped to unite Upper Egypt in the south and Lower Egypt in the north. During its early history, the surrounding natural barriers of seas and deserts protected Egypt from invasion.

Religion in Ancient Egypt

The religious beliefs of the ancient Egyptians reflected the importance of the Nile and other forces of nature. Like other ancient peoples, the Egyptians were polytheistic. Through prayer and religious rituals, they called on the gods to give good harvests.

Among their most important gods were Amon-Re, the sun god, and Osiris, god of the Nile.

The Egyptians believed in a life after death. This concern with the afterlife affected their daily lives. They believed, for example, that only those people who lived moral lives would enjoy a happy afterlife. To prepare for the afterlife, Egyptians built elaborate tombs and developed the process of mummification to preserve the body after death. *Hieroglyphics,* the Egyptian system of writing, was also connected to religion. Priests probably developed hieroglyphics to keep records of religious rituals and temple property.

Growth of Unified Government

In its long history, Egypt was ruled by at least 30 *dynasties,* or ruling families. Historians have divided these dynasties into three periods: the Old Kingdom (2700 B.C.–2200 B.C.), the Middle Kingdom (2050 B.C.–1800 B.C.), and the New Kingdom (1570 B.C.–1090 B.C.). At the beginning of each period, strong rulers united the land. Toward the end of each, civil wars, peasant revolts, and invasions occurred.

During the Old Kingdom, Egyptian rulers took the title pharaoh, meaning "great house." To the Egyptians, the pharaoh was a god who ruled with absolute power. The pharaohs set up a strong central government. They appointed officials to supervise the collection of taxes and the building of irrigation systems. The power and importance of the Old Kingdom pharaohs was shown in the building of vast pyramid tombs. Pyramids required the efforts of thousands of workers and cost huge amounts.

During the Middle and New kingdoms, Egypt expanded its borders. Through trade and conquest, it increased contacts with other lands. The first woman ruler known to history, Hatshepsut, reigned for 22 years during the New Kingdom. Another noted pharaoh of the New Kingdom was Akenaton. He tried to change the traditional religious practices, replacing the worship of Amon-Re with the worship of Aton. But Tutankhamon, his successor, restored traditional religious practices.

Wealthy Egyptians had scenes of the journey through the underworld painted on the walls of their tombs. The god Osiris, shown here, decided who would enter the "Happy Field of Food."

Egyptian Society

During the Old Kingdom, Egypt developed a social order that remained relatively unchanged for thousands of years. At the top was the pharaoh, who lived in luxury and splendor. Below him was the ruling class of priests and nobles. Priests enjoyed great power and influence because only they knew the correct ceremonies to please the gods. Nobles served as government officials.

A small middle class came next, which included artisans, merchants, physicians, and skilled workers who provided services to the ruling class. At the bottom were the majority of people—peasants and slaves. They worked the land, built the irrigation systems, and constructed the palaces, temples, and tombs of the pharaohs.

Achievements of Egyptian Civilization

The Egyptians made remarkable advances in engineering, science, mathematics, the arts, and literature. Many achievements grew out of practical needs. To the Egyptians, building and decorating temples and pyramids were necessary to ensure the goodwill of the gods or to protect individuals in the afterlife.

Egyptians also developed methods of surveying and measuring to divide up their fields and set boundaries. Priests studied the skies to know the change of seasons and predict eclipses. Their observations led to the development of a 365-day calendar that became the basis for the calendar used today.

SECTION REVIEW

1. Identify: Amon-Re, Osiris, Hatshepsut, Akenaton.
2. Define: hieroglyphics, dynasty.
3. List three ways in which geography helped the ancient Egyptians.
4. How did religion affect different aspects of life in Egypt?

3 The Ancient Middle East

Read to Learn ■ how cultures blended in the ancient Middle East
■ how smaller Middle Eastern nations left cultural legacies

While the Egyptians were shaping their civilization in the Nile River valley, other people were building the foundations of civilizations in the ancient Middle East.

Geographic Setting

The civilizations of the ancient Middle East developed in the Fertile Crescent, an area of fertile farmland that stretched in an arc from the Persian Gulf to the Mediterranean Sea. The Fertile Crescent had no natural barriers. Thus, it became the "crossroads of the world" as many different people migrated, invaded, or settled in the area. The diversity of people made the region difficult to unite, but it also encouraged a vital exchange of ideas.

The earliest civilization developed in the valley of the Tigris and Euphrates rivers. It was called Mesopotamia, which means the land between two rivers. Like the Nile, the Tigris and Euphrates were central to the lives of the people. The rivers provided water, brought fertile soil, and served as a means of transportation. However, unlike the Nile, whose annual flood was predictable, the Tigris and Euphrates sometimes overflowed their banks with unexpected ferocity, causing widespread destruction.

Sumerian Civilization

The need to control the flooding and to clear land for farming led to the development of Sumerian civilization in lower Mesopotamia. As small villages expanded, they set up independent city-states. In each *city-state*, a town and the surrounding countryside cooperated for mutual defense. Although rival city-states often fought for power, trade among the Sumerian cities helped bring wealth to the region.

As in Egypt, religion played an important role in the lives of the Sumerians. However, the Sumerians had a gloomy outlook on life and did not believe in a happy afterlife. They believed that natural disasters such as floods and famine were punishments sent by the gods. Priests held great power because, here again, they were believed to be the only people who knew how to satisfy the gods.

Over the years the Sumerians made many achievements on which later people built. They developed a system of writing, called *cuneiform*. They were the first people to use the wheel, and they invented the sail. Like the Egyptians, they developed mathematics to survey land and set boundaries. The Sumerian system of counting, based on the number 60, led to such measurements as

Map Skill   *The fertile soil and the wild game of the Tigris-Euphrates Valley made the area attractive for early settlers. The rivers also served as arteries for trade. Why was the Fertile Crescent called the crossroads of the world?*

BLACK SEA
CAUCASUS MTS.
CASPIAN SEA
ARMENIAN PLATEAU
ASIA MINOR
MESOPOTAMIA
Tigris R.
Euphrates R.
ZAGROS MTS.
Kish
SUMER
Erech
Ur
PERSIAN GULF
MEDITERRANEAN SEA
SYRIAN DESERT
Sinai Pen.
EGYPT
Nile R.
ARABIAN DESERT
RED SEA

The Ancient Middle East

☐ Fertile Crescent

0   300 Miles
0   500 Kilometers

the 60-second minute and the 60-minute hour.

Blending of Cultures

As the Sumerian city-states declined, other peoples conquered Mesopotamia. Some built strong empires that lasted for centuries. Among the most powerful rulers of Mesopotamia was Hammurabi. To achieve unity in his empire, Hammurabi had a code drawn up of all existing laws. The Code of Hammurabi was a landmark achievement because it set up a unified system of justice. It distinguished between major and minor crimes and spelled out the punishment for each crime.

As conquerors swept across Mesopotamia, they helped blend many cultures. When the Hittites invaded from Asia Minor, they introduced their knowledge of ironmaking. Then they carried back to Asia Minor cuneiform and Mesopotamian ideas of government. Later, the Assyrians conquered the Fertile Crescent, destroying their enemies with ruthless brutality. One Assyrian ruler, however, collected a huge library of cuneiform tablets that preserved much of the knowledge of ancient Mesopotamia. By 500 B.C., the Persians had conquered a large empire stretching from the Indus River in Asia to the Mediterranean Sea. They set up an efficient system of government that became a model for many later peoples.

Contributions of Smaller States

Several small states made important contributions to the civilizations of the ancient Middle East. The Phoenicians were merchants and traders who lived in port cities along the Mediterranean coast. They earned the name "carriers of civilization" because they spread the learning and culture of ancient Mesopotamia to colonies they set up throughout the Mediterranean world.

The Hebrews made a lasting impact on the world through their *monotheism*, the worship of one all-powerful god. They also advanced an ethical world view—that is, the belief that all people should lead moral lives. Hebrew prophets taught their people to do good, respect other individuals, look after the poor, and obey God's laws. Many of these ideas of Judaism would later become a part of two other world religions—Christianity and Islam.

SECTION REVIEW

1. Identify: Fertile Crescent, Mesopotamia, Code of Hammurabi.
2. Define: city-state, cuneiform, monotheism.
3. List two ways in which the geography of the Fertile Crescent differed from that of the Nile River valley.
4. Describe one contribution of each of the following people: (a) Persians; (b) Phoenicians; (c) Hebrews.

4 Ancient India and China

Read to Learn   ■ how geography influenced early civilizations in India and China
■ how the Chinese lived under the Shang and Chou dynasties

In India and China, ancient civilizations likewise developed in fertile river valleys. The people in each region, however, developed their own distinct patterns of civilization.

Indus Valley Civilization

In India, as elsewhere, geography influenced the emergence of early civilization. Natural barriers such as the towering Hindu Kush and Himalaya mountains limited contact between the Indian subcontinent and the rest of Asia. However, the mountains did not completely protect India. On many occasions, invaders forced their way through steep passes in the Hindu Kush to descend onto the fertile plains of northern India.

It is thought that the first Indian civilization rose about 2500 B.C. in the Indus River valley. Little is known about the Indus Valley civilization, in part because scholars have not yet deciphered its form of writing. However, the remains of two well-planned cities—Harappa and Mohenjo-Daro—have revealed that a powerful government ruled the Indus Valley for more than 1,000 years.

Aryan Conquest

About 1500 B.C., the Aryans, nomadic herders, crossed the Hindu Kush and conquered the Indus Valley civilization. The Aryans brought their own traditions and beliefs to India, gradually creating a new culture whose patterns have shaped India to the present day.

The Aryans originally worshipped many gods, but in time they came to believe in a single unifying force. They also developed a belief in *reincarnation*, the rebirth of the soul in another body. These beliefs formed the foundations of Hinduism, the major religion of India today.

The Aryans developed a written language, called Sanskrit, but maintained a rich oral literature. During their conquest of India, a social structure emerged that gradually evolved into a rigid *caste* system. The four main castes, or social groups, were the warriors, priests, landowners and merchants, and peasants. A person's caste was determined by birth alone.

Early Chinese Civilization

Like India, China was surrounded by imposing geographic barriers that limited contact with outsiders. High mountain ranges, rugged plateaus, deserts, and the Pacific Ocean protected China. As a result, the Chinese came to see their land as the Middle Kingdom—the center of the universe.

The first Chinese civilization developed in the Yellow River valley. There, fertile soil, called *loess*, was easily worked. However, this region of China suffers from droughts and floods, and the Yellow River earned the title "River of Sorrows" for the death and destruction brought by its flooding.

The Shang dynasty. As in Egypt and Sumer, powerful rulers extended control over the farming villages of the river valley. The Shang dynasty was the first of many

Bronzemaking was an important art of ancient China. This bronze statue shows a boy holding jade birds.

families to rule China. Many traditions and beliefs that emerged in Shang times shaped Chinese civilization for thousands of years.

The Chinese believed that the gods controlled the forces of nature. They also believed that their ancestors could influence the gods. Shang kings acted as priests, performing daily ceremonies to ask their ancestors for the favor of the gods. The Shang invented a system of writing that used pictograms, or pictures of objects and ideograms, as symbols that expressed ideas or actions. In time, the Chinese writing system became so complicated that only years of education could enable a person to read and write. The Shang also developed skills in bronze working and silk weaving and invented an accurate calendar that was passed on to later civilizations.

The Chou dynasty. The Chou dynasty, which overthrew the Shang, built on these early achievements. The Chou claimed to have won the "Mandate of Heaven," or divine right to rule. According to this belief, only a just ruler who provided good government was entitled to rule.

The Chou ruler divided his land among powerful nobles who then owed loyalty, military service, and tribute to the king. These feudal lords expanded the borders of China, often setting up their own independent states. As their states expanded, they developed complex bureaucracies. A *bureaucracy* was a system of organizing government into departments with appointed officials. In Chou China, government officials gained an important place in society. Despite frequent warfare among rival feudal states, the Chou era was a time of economic growth.

SECTION REVIEW

1. Identify: Harappa, Aryans, Shang dynasty, Mandate of Heaven.
2. Define: reincarnation, caste, loess, bureaucracy.
3. What religious beliefs did the Aryans have?
4. How did Chou rulers govern China?

Review

Survey Checkup

1. Describe the major differences between the Old Stone Age and the New Stone Age.
2. List five basic characteristics of early civilizations.
3. Why were scribes important to early civilizations?
4. How were the religious beliefs of ancient Egypt tied to natural forces?
5. What were the major achievements of the ancient Egyptians?
6. Why has the Fertile Crescent been called the "crossroads of the world"?
7. (a) What was the first civilization in India? (b) Why do scholars know little about it?
8. What religious and social ideas shaped early Aryan civilization?
9. Describe two achievements of the Shang dynasty that shaped later Chinese civilization.

Critical Thinking

1. **Applying Information** (a) How do scholars learn about ancient civilizations? (b) What problems do they face when they study those civilizations?
2. **Analyzing the Importance of Geography** (a) Why was the Nile River known as the "giver of life"? (b) Why was the Yellow River known as the "River of Sorrows"? (c) Why did rivers play such an important part in the development of early civilizations?
3. **Comparing Civilizations** Why do you think early civilizations developed different forms of government and different religious beliefs?

Developing Basic Skills

1. **Using Visual Evidence** Read the Skill Lesson on page 6 called "Cave Paintings: Using Visual Evidence." Then study the picture on page 33. (a) What does the picture show? (b) About when was it made? (c) What conclusion can you draw about Sumerian life?
2. **Map Reading** Read the Skill Lesson on page 22 called "Egyptian Empire About 1450 B.C.: Reading Maps." Then study the map on page 11 and answer the questions that follow. (a) What does this map show? (b) What geographic features does it include? (c) In which direction would an Egyptian travel to reach the Fertile Crescent?
3. **Analyzing a Primary Source** Read the Skill Lesson on page 38 called "Hammurabi's Code: Analyzing a Primary Source." Then read Ramses II's prayer to Amon at the beginning of this survey. (a) What was the purpose of this prayer? (b) Where was it recorded? (c) Is it a primary source? Why or why not?

The Romans adopted many ideas from the ancient Greeks, including drama. In this Roman mosaic, the actor at right dons his costume, which includes the mask on the table.

TWO

Unit Two
A BRIEF SURVEY

Rise of Classical Civilizations
(2000 B.C.–550 A.D.)

In 399 B.C., the great philosopher Socrates sat in a prison cell under a death sentence. He had been convicted by the citizens of Athens for failing to honor the gods and for corrupting the youth of the city. According to Plato, a young man who admired Socrates, the philosopher could have avoided a trial and escaped the death sentence.

In *Crito,* Plato reported how a young Athenian tried to persuade Socrates to escape. Socrates listened to the plan but then carefully reasoned with Crito to show him why escape would be wrong.

Socrates: Are we to say that we are never intentionally to do wrong . . . [and] . . . that injustice is always an evil and dishonor to him who acts unjustly?
Crito: Yes. . . .
Socrates: . . . Ought a man to do what he admits to be right, or ought he to betray the right?
Crito: He ought to do what he thinks right.
Socrates: But if this is true, what is the application? In leaving the prison

against the will of the Athenians, . . . do I not wrong those whom I ought least to wrong? Do I not desert the principles which we acknowledge to be just?

More than 2,400 years ago, Socrates was one of many thinkers who was concerned with important moral issues. He carefully distinguished between personal convictions of right and wrong and the individual's duty to obey the laws of the state.

Socrates lived at the height of ancient Greek civilization. Later, Rome built on Greek achievements in the arts, literature, and learning. The civilizations of Greece and Rome became known as "classical civilizations" because they established standards of excellence against which later civilizations were judged.

In India and China, too, this period saw the emergence of strong religious and philosophical traditions that had a lasting impact. The advanced civilizations of India and China achieved high levels of development and created strong empires that preserved the unique heritage of each.

1 Ancient Greece

Read to Learn
- how geography influenced Greek civilization
- how Athens and Sparta differed

Unlike the river valley civilizations of Egypt, Mesopotamia, India, and China, the civilization that emerged in ancient Greece was built on small, independent cities that were often at war with each other. Although the Greeks did not conquer a vast empire, their civilization has had a lasting impact on the Western world.

Geographic Setting

Several forces helped shape the civilization of ancient Greece. The Greek mainland is a mountainous peninsula. The rugged terrain limited transportation and communication and led the Greeks to develop small, separate communities. Each community valued its freedom and fiercely resisted any outside interference.

The Greek coastline has excellent harbors, and the nearby Aegean Sea is dotted with islands. As a result, the early Greeks turned to the sea. They built a thriving trade, building colonies and carrying goods to and from many parts of the Mediterranean. Because of their frequent contact with other civilizations, they developed a practical attitude toward new ideas and adopted any that suited their needs.

Government in the Greek City-States

The Greek city-states developed different forms of government. At first, a *monarchy*, or government headed by a king, ruled each city-state. Gradually, *aristocracies*, or governments by a small, privileged upper class, replaced the monarchies. As city-states grew and prospered, other classes demanded the right to participate in government, which led to the formation of democracies.

Growth of democracy in Athens. Like the other Greek city-states, Athens was ruled first by a monarch and then by a landowning aristocracy. By the sixth century B.C., however, many ordinary citizens were discontent with the rule by nobles. Over the next 200 years, Athenian leaders introduced a series of reforms that became the basis for Athenian *democracy*, or government by the citizens.

Athens reached the peak of its power under Pericles, in the fifth century B.C. The government was a *direct democracy* in which all citizens had the right to vote in the Assembly. Although resident aliens, slaves, and women had no political rights, the example of Athenian public service and free exchange of ideas inspired the growth of democracy in other Greek city-states.

Military government in Sparta. Athens' rival for power was the landlocked city-state of Sparta. Spartan life differed greatly from that of Athens. The Spartans created a strong military government headed by a monarch. The government kept a close watch on the lives of its citizens and the thousands of *helots*, or slaves, who worked the land. The Spartans valued strict discipline, obedience, and endurance, qualities that made them highly respected fighters in the Greek world.

Rivalry between Athens, Sparta, and other city-states led to frequent warfare. For a brief time in the fifth century B.C., the Greeks united to defeat the expanding power of the Persian Empire. However, the emergence of Athens as the dominant Greek city-state led to renewed fighting. The Peloponnesian Wars, from 431 B.C. to 404 B.C., finally ended with Sparta's defeat of Athens.

SECTION REVIEW

1. Identify: Pericles, Peloponnesian Wars.
2. Define: monarchy, aristocracy, democracy, direct democracy, helot.
3. Describe one way in which geography affected the ancient Greeks.
4. How did Sparta differ from Athens?

2 The Greek Heritage

Read to Learn
- how Greek philosophy influenced religion and art
- what characteristics marked Hellenistic civilization

Greek culture reached its height in the fifth and fourth centuries B.C. The influence of this culture, however, stretched well beyond the shores of Greece and has enriched the world to the present day.

Drama and the Arts

The Greeks built temples and held festivals to honor their gods. Out of the festivals honoring Dionysus, the god of wine, came the first of the Greek dramas. The early Greek dramas were *tragedies*, plays that focused on the suffering of a major character and usually ended in disaster. In later comedies, the Greek writers poked fun at human weaknesses.

In art and architecture, the Greeks expressed their love of beauty and harmony. The graceful columns of the Parthenon, the temple of Athena in Athens, show the Greek respect for simple elegance. Greek sculptors always emphasized the ideal, or perfect form, whether they were carving statues of humans or their gods.

Philosophy

The Greeks developed ways of looking at the world that differed from those of earlier people. They questioned the traditional view that the gods were the cause of all natural events. Greek philosophers believed that

Athena was the Greek goddess of wisdom, purity, and reason.

through observation and the use of reason they could discover natural laws to explain the universe. Curiosity and logical reasoning led the Greeks to make important advances in science and medicine.

In pursuit of truth, the philosopher Socrates developed a question and answer technique, called the *Socratic method*. By persistent questioning he tried to make people examine their beliefs using reason. Like Socrates, the philosopher Plato raised many questions about the meaning of justice and the nature of beauty and truth.

Hellenistic Civilization

In the fourth century B.C., Alexander the Great of Macedonia emerged as a world conqueror. In just a few years, he won an empire stretching from Greece to the Indus River. Alexander's greatest achievement was not his short-lived empire but his creation of a new culture, known as Hellenistic civilization. The new civilization represented a blend of Greek, Persian, and other ancient civilizations.

Alexandria, a city in Egypt, came to symbolize the vitality of Hellenistic civilization. There, thinkers from Greece, Egypt, and Persia exchanged ideas and produced outstanding works in science, mathematics, medicine, astronomy, and philosophy.

SECTION REVIEW

1. Identify: Dionysus, Parthenon, Socrates, Plato.
2. Define: tragedy, Socratic method.
3. How did Greek philosophers try to learn about the universe?
4. What cultures were blended in Hellenistic civilization?

3 Ancient Rome: From Republic to Empire

Read to Learn
- how the Roman Republic developed
- how winning an empire changed Rome

While Greek civilization was flourishing, the small city-state of Rome was building the foundations for a strong government. From small beginnings on the Italian peninsula, Rome grew to become a powerful empire that brought many lands and people under its control.

The Roman Republic

In 509 B.C., the Romans overthrew their Etruscan rulers and set up their own form of government. They established a *republic*, a government in which citizens with the right to vote chose their leaders. In the early Roman Republic, *patricians*, or wealthy landowners, controlled the government. *Plebeians*, the common people, were also citizens, but they had to struggle for 200 years before they gained a voice in government.

The early Romans had to battle to survive against powerful neighbors. These early struggles shaped their belief in duty, discipline, and patriotism. Yet the Romans also benefited from the more advanced civilizations with which they came in contact. From the Greeks, Phoenicians, and Etruscans they acquired the alphabet, learned skills in building and engineering, and adapted religious ideas.

Expansion of Rome. Between 509 B.C. and 133 B.C., well-trained Roman armies fought many wars of expansion. First, they won control of the Italian peninsula. In the three Punic Wars, Rome defeated Carthage, its rival for power in the western Mediterranean, and gained new territories. Roman armies also won lands in the eastern Mediterranean.

As the wars of expansion changed Rome from a small republic into a large empire, they brought social and economic changes. Cheap grain, paid as tribute by the conquered lands, caused hardships for Roman

273

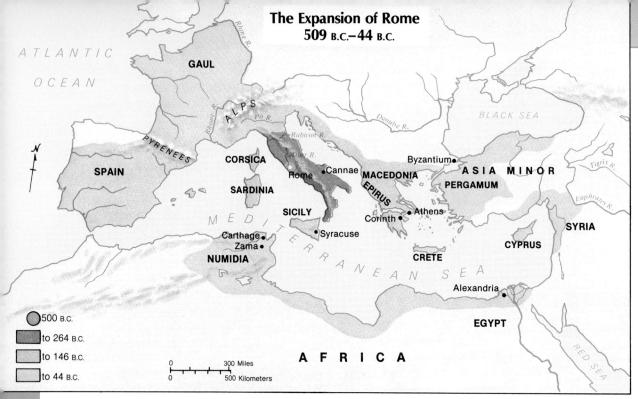

The Expansion of Rome
509 B.C.–44 B.C.

ATLANTIC OCEAN

GAUL

ALPS

Rhône R.

Rhine R.

Po R.

Danube R.

BLACK SEA

Rubicon R.

Tiber R.

CORSICA

Rome

Cannae

Byzantium

ASIA MINOR

Tigris R.

SPAIN

PYRENEES

MACEDONIA

PERGAMUM

SARDINIA

EPIRUS

Euphrates R.

SICILY

Corinth

Athens

SYRIA

MEDITERRANEAN SEA

Carthage

Syracuse

CYPRUS

Zama

CRETE

NUMIDIA

Alexandria

AFRICA

EGYPT

RED SEA

500 B.C.
to 264 B.C.
to 146 B.C.
to 44 B.C.

0   300 Miles
0   500 Kilometers

Map Skill *Rome often expanded its empire through warfare. The Punic Wars, which ended in 146 B.C., brought large amounts of territory into the empire. Rome also acquired territory when the king of Pergamum died and left his empire in Asia Minor to Rome. During which period did Rome gain the most territory in Africa?*

farmers. Many were forced to leave their farms. They swelled the population of landless poor in the city. At the same time, treasure from booty made other Romans rich.

Decline of the Republic. When attempts at reform failed, Romans turned to military leaders. For years, civil war raged as rival generals battled for power. In 49 B.C., Julius Caesar seized control of Rome and restored order. He made reforms, extended Roman citizenship to many people, and redistributed land to the poor. With Caesar's assassination in 44 B.C., however, the Roman Republic ended.

The Roman Empire

Caesar's heir, Augustus, took the title *imperator,* a Latin word meaning commander-in-chief. The rule of Augustus marked the beginning of the Roman Empire. Augustus set up a strong, stable government that united the vast Roman Empire. For nearly 200 years, Rome enjoyed the Pax Romana, a period of peace, commerce, and prosperity.

Rome divided its empire into provinces, connected by excellent roads. It administered its government with an efficient civil service.

Despite the prosperity, Rome faced serious social and economic problems. The cost of maintaining the empire was enormous. Prices rose as Rome was forced to *devalue,* or lower the value, of its coins. Also, many Romans looked down on hard work and duty as fit only for slaves. These attitudes undermined the strength of the Roman Empire.

SECTION REVIEW

1. Identify: Punic Wars, Julius Caesar, Augustus, Pax Romana.
2. Define: republic, patrician, plebeian, imperator, devalue.
3. What qualities did the early Roman's emphasize?
4. What benefits did Roman government bring to the Empire?

4 The Roman Heritage

Read to Learn ■ what Roman civilization contributed to the world
■ how Christianity arose and spread in Rome

Roman settlers, soldiers, and officials spread Roman ideas from Spain to Mesopotamia. Through Rome, the knowledge and achievements of the ancient world were gathered, preserved, and handed on to the peoples of Western Europe.

Greco-Roman Civilization

The Romans recognized the achievements of civilizations they conquered, and blended them with their own. "Greece has conquered her rude conquerors," observed the Roman poet Horace, who saw evidence of Greek influence everywhere in Rome. This blend of traditions is known as Greco-Roman civilization.

The Romans emphasized practical concerns, developing technical skills and knowledge in building and engineering. They in-vented the dome, learned to mix concrete, and built strong roads and bridges. Their *aqueducts* carried water from rural reservoirs to the cities.

To solve the practical problems of government, the Romans developed one of their major achievements: a system of law and justice for the empire. They introduced the principle that the accused is innocent until proven guilty. They also allowed the use of evidence in the courtroom and set up procedures to ensure a fair trial. Roman law became the basis for later law systems in Western Europe.

Rise of Christianity

During the Pax Romana, Christianity was founded in Palestine. The new religion was based on the teachings of Jesus, whose mes-

In the New Testament, the Apostle John quotes Jesus as saying, "I am the good shepherd; the good shepherd giveth his life for the sheep." The symbol of Christ as a shepherd appears in much early Christian art. This mosaic from a church in Ravenna, Italy, shows Jesus with a flock of sheep, perhaps representing 6 of the 12 Apostles.

sage was rooted in Hebrew traditions. He stressed love for God, compassion for other people, and the hope of eternal life. Despite persecution, the followers of Jesus spread this message across the Greco-Roman world. In 395 A.D., Christianity was made the official religion of the Roman Empire.

In time, Christians developed a strong church organization. At the head of the Church was the pope in Rome. Below him were other members of the clergy, including archbishops, bishops, and priests. The clergy maintained order and discipline in the Church.

Decline of Rome

Christianity was growing in strength at a time when the Roman Empire was weakening. Struggles for power over who would succeed each emperor led to frequent civil wars. The fighting disrupted trade, and the economy of the empire declined. Occasionally, a strong ruler rose to stem the tide of decay. Diocletian, for example, introduced reforms to restore order and solve basic economic problems. To govern better, he divided the empire into an eastern and western part. The emperor Constantine continued Diocletian's policies and moved the capital to Constantinople, closer to the rich cities of the eastern Roman Empire. But these attempts at reform failed to halt the decline.

In addition to internal problems, the empire faced external threats from German and Hun invaders. Roman legions were withdrawn from the frontiers to protect the towns and cities. As Roman government disappeared, the economy fell into disorder. Under constant pressure from invaders, the Western Roman Empire fell in the fifth century. Yet the Roman heritage survived in Western Europe and in the Eastern Roman Empire.

SECTION REVIEW

1. Identify: Greco-Roman civilization, Jesus, Diocletian, Constantine.
2. Define: aqueduct.
3. Describe two practical achievements of the Romans.
4. What external problems did the Roman Empire face?

5 The Heritage of India and China

Read to Learn
■ about the impact of Hinduism and Buddhism in India
■ how religions shaped Chinese traditions

While Greco-Roman civilization flourished in the Mediterranean world, the civilizations of India and China were developing their own lasting traditions. In both regions, strong empires were created, and important advances were made in government, learning, and the arts.

Two Religions of India

India was the birthplace of two major world religions—Hinduism and Buddhism. Hinduism grew out of early Aryan beliefs. Although Hindus worship many gods, they believe that these gods are part of *brahma*, the supreme force that unites everything in the universe. To Hindus, the ultimate goal of life is to free the soul from its individual existence and achieve reunion with a larger universal soul. Hindus believe this process takes more than one lifetime.

Hinduism supported the caste system. People were taught to obey caste rules so that they might be reincarnated, or reborn, into a higher caste in the next lifetime. By the sixth century B.C., some Hindus were critical of the power of priests, the highest caste. One critic was Siddhartha Gautama.

the Maurya Empire (321 B.C.–183 B.C.) and the Gupta Empire (320 A.D.–467 A.D.) left their mark on India. Asoka, the best known Maurya ruler, extended his rule over much of India. After he converted to Buddhism, he set out to establish a government based on nonviolence and religious toleration.

By the time of the Gupta Empire, Buddhism had been reabsorbed into Hinduism, although its influence remained strong in other parts of Asia. The caste system became

Map Skill *Maurya emperors extended their rule over much of India. The Maurya Empire, shown here, reached its greatest extent under the emperor Asoka, who added new territories, including Kalinga, in the south.*

Shiva, one of the most popular gods in Hinduism, appears in many roles. In this statue, he is shown as lord of the cosmic dance. The dwarf under his feet represents the illusions that Shiva dispels. Shiva holds a drum, symbol of creation, in one hand and a flame, symbol of destruction, in another hand.

He set out to reform Hinduism, but his teachings became the basis for a new religion, Buddhism.

After a long search for the meaning of life, Gautama discovered certain basic truths. He taught that the only way to salvation was to overcome desire. Desire was the cause of pain and suffering. Buddhism offered guidelines to achieve *nirvana*, the condition of wanting nothing. From India, Buddhism spread to China, Korea, Japan, and Southeast Asia.

Great Empires

Throughout India's long history, the northern plain was a battleground for rival rulers. Some built strong empires. Among these,

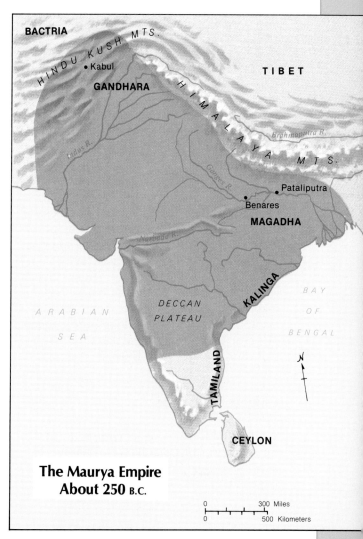

BACTRIA
HINDU KUSH MTS.
• Kabul
GANDHARA
TIBET
HIMALAYA MTS.
Indus R.
Brahmaputra R.
Ganges R.
• Pataliputra
Benares •
MAGADHA
ARABIAN SEA
DECCAN PLATEAU
Narbada R.
KALINGA
BAY OF BENGAL
TAMILAND
N
CEYLON

**The Maurya Empire
About 250 B.C.**

0   300 Miles
0   500 Kilometers

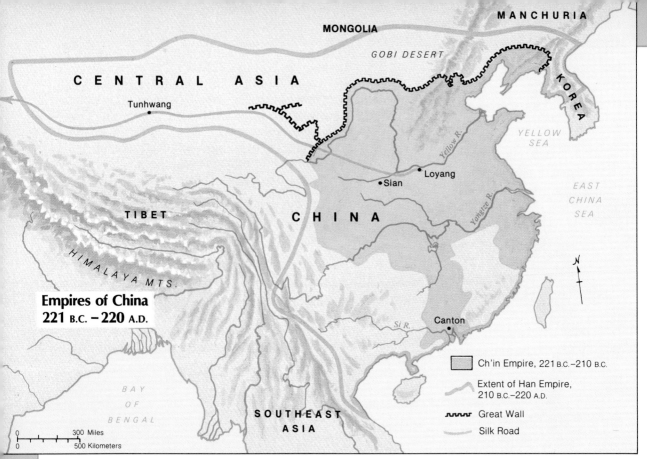

**Empires of China
221 B.C. – 220 A.D.**

MONGOLIA

MANCHURIA

GOBI DESERT

CENTRAL ASIA

Tunhwang

KOREA

YELLOW
SEA

Loyang
Sian

EAST
CHINA
SEA

TIBET

CHINA

HIMALAYA MTS.

Yellow R.

Yangtze R.

Si R.

Canton

Ch'in Empire, 221 B.C.–210 B.C.

Extent of Han Empire,
210 B.C.–220 A.D.

Great Wall

Silk Road

BAY
OF
BENGAL

SOUTHEAST
ASIA

0   300 Miles
0   500 Kilometers

Map Skill *Ch'in and Han rulers greatly expanded the borders of China and spread Chinese civilization over a wide area. Like the Roman Empire to the west, the Han Empire enjoyed two centuries of peace and prosperity. Why do you think Han rulers extended the Great Wall westward?*

more restrictive, and many new subcastes emerged. Strict rules forbade people of different castes from speaking to one another.

During the Gupta period, artists and writers produced some of India's finest works. In science and technology, Indians made important advances. They devised a decimal system and developed the concept of zero, ideas that would later be carried from India to Western Europe.

Chinese Traditions

While Buddhism was emerging in India, three schools of thought were shaping Chinese traditions: Confucianism, Taoism, and Legalism. Confucius, who was born about 551 B.C., was China's most influential philosopher. He was concerned with how to establish a stable, orderly society. Confucius taught that each person had a place in society, and each individual had responsibilities and duties toward others. He urged the ruler to set a good example. Confucius emphasized *filial piety,* or respect for one's parents and elders, and loyalty, courtesy, and hard work.

Taoism was both a religion and philosophy. Taoists were more concerned with contemplation and achieving harmony with nature than with a proper code of conduct. The third school of thought, Legalism, claimed that the only way to achieve a stable society was through strict government control and rigid obedience to authority.

Unification of China

Legalist principles dominated the government of Shih Huang Ti, a powerful leader of the feudal state of Ch'in, who united China in 221 B.C. After the years of civil war that ended the Chou dynasty, Shih Huang Ti was determined to build a strong, central government. He appointed officials loyal to him and improved the transportation system to ensure his control of the empire. His most spectacular achievement was the building of the Great Wall to protect northern China from invaders.

Although the Ch'in Empire was short-lived, its successor, the Han Empire (210 B.C.–220 A.D.), was one of the most brilliant periods in Chinese history. Han rulers extended the borders of China and established efficient government based on a civil service open to men of talent. During Han rule, the arts, sciences, and learning advanced. As trade increased, new ideas, including Buddhism, entered China.

SECTION REVIEW

1. Identify: Siddhartha Gautama, Asoka, Confucius, Shih Huang Ti, Great Wall of China.
2. Define: brahma, nirvana, filial piety.
3. How did Hinduism support the caste system?
4. What was the major concern of each of the following: Confucianism, Taoism, and Legalism?

Review

Survey Checkup

1. How did Athenians participate in their government?
2. (a) What was Hellenistic civilization? (b) Why was it important?
3. What social classes existed in the Roman Republic?
4. What legal concepts did the Romans develop?
5. Explain the main teachings of (a) Hinduism and (b) Buddhism.
6. How did Confucianism differ from Taoism?

Critical Thinking

1. **Analyzing a Quotation** The great Athenian statesman Pericles once said: "We do not say that a man who takes no interest in politics is a man who minds his own business; we say that he has no business here at all." (a) What do you think Pericles meant by this statement? (b) How are his ideas important for democratic government?

2. **Drawing Conclusions** (a) What did Confucious believe was the way to establish a stable, orderly society? (b) Why do you think Chinese rulers after Confucius adopted his ideas?

Developing Basic Skills

1. **Map Reading** Study the map on page 274. Then answer the questions that follow. (a) What political information is given on the map? (b) During which period did Rome conquer Spain? (c) During which period did Rome make the most conquests?

2. **Using Time Lines** Make a time line for this unit survey. At the far left, write the earliest date B.C. mentioned in this survey. At the far right, put the latest date A.D. in this survey. Remember that historians used the term century to describe a 100-year time period. The 100 years from 500 B.C. to 401 B.C. are called the fifth century B.C. the 100 years from 400 A.D. to 499 A.D. are called the fifth century A.D. (a) What is the earliest date on your time line? (b) What is the latest date? (c) What event or events occurred in the sixth century B.C.?

Most people in medieval Europe were peasants whose lives were ruled by the cycle of planting and harvesting. By the late Middle Ages, however, a few wealthy nobles and merchants enjoyed the comfort and elegance shown in the scene above.

Middle Ages in Western Europe (500–1500)

Early in the summer of 1083, a council of clergy met in Cologne. Among other matters, the clergy discussed the need to end the constant warfare that threatened their land. To secure the peace, they issued a declaration called the Truce of God. In it, they announced that "peace shall be observed" on certain days.

"Let no one, however irritated by wrong, presume to carry arms, shield, sword, or lance, or any kind of armor, from the Advent of our Lord to the eighth day after Epiphany, and from Septuagesima to the eighth day after Pentecost. On the remaining days, indeed, namely on Sundays, Fridays, apostles' days . . . and on every day set aside . . . for fasts or feasts, arms may be carried, but on this condition, that no injury shall be done in any way to any one."

The efforts of the clergy of Cologne were similar to those of clergy elsewhere in Europe. To enforce their decree, the clergy of Cologne declared that "if any one attempt to oppose this pious institution and is unwilling to promise peace to God . . . no priest in our diocese shall presume to say a mass for him or shall take any care for his salvation."

The Church's attempts to impose order were partly successful. With the collapse of the Roman Empire in the West, Europe entered a period known as the Middle Ages. During the early Middle Ages, from about 500 to 1050, the remains of Greco-Roman civilization decayed as Europe suffered from repeated invasions. Despite the disorder, Europeans slowly built the foundations for a new civilization dominated by the Christian Church.

During the late Middle Ages from about 1050 to 1350, a stable, orderly society emerged. Farming methods improved, trade revived, and towns grew. Strong monarchs centralized royal power. As conditions grew better, Europeans began to take a broader view of the world.

1 Foundations of Medieval Europe

Read to Learn ■ what conditions furthered the development of feudalism
■ how the Church served as a force for civilization

As the Western Roman Empire collapsed in the fourth and fifth centuries, Europe became a battleground for many German tribes. During this time, trade and travel became difficult. Learning declined, and much of the knowledge of the ancient world was lost.

The Kingdom of the Franks

During the early Middle Ages, the kingdom of the Franks emerged as the strongest power in Western Europe. Under Charlemagne, who ruled from 768 to 814, the Frankish kingdom enjoyed a golden age. An able general, Charlemagne extended the borders of his kingdom. He fought the Muslims in Spain, the Saxons in northern Europe, and the Avars in the East. He set up an efficient government and encouraged learning throughout his vast empire. The revival of learning helped set the stage for later medieval civilization.

Emergence of Feudalism

For two hundred years after the death of Charlemagne, Western Europe was battered by invasions. The Muslims attacked southern France and Italy. The Magyars and Slavs invaded from the east, and the Vikings raided towns and villages from England to Russia.

During this time, feudalism emerged in Western Europe. *Feudalism* was a system of rule by local lords who were bound to a king by ties of loyalty. Feudalism produced a way of life that governed the political, social, and economic order.

In the feudal society, everyone had his or her place. In theory, the king ruled the land as a *fief*, or estate, which he divided among his great nobles. In fact, these powerful lords often acted independently of the king. They divided their vast lands among *vassals*, or lesser lords, who in turn subdivided their fiefs among *knights*, or mounted warriors. Each knight or vassal owed loyalty and service to his lord.

During the early Middle Ages, warfare was constant as lords battled for power. To protect their lands, they built fortified castles where lords and peasants took refuge from invasions. In the later Middle Ages, feudal warfare declined, and *chivalry*, a code of conduct for knights, emerged. Chivalry emphasized Christian virtues, generosity, loyalty, and respect for noblewomen.

Life on the Manor

The economic system that supported feudal society was based on the medieval manor. The *manor* included a village and the land administered by a lord. During the invasions of the ninth and tenth centuries, each manor became a self-sufficient unit. It produced almost everything that was needed to survive.

During the Middle Ages, most people were peasants who worked on the manor. The majority were *serfs*, who were tied to the lord's land. Serfs owed their lords certain services, such as farming their lord's land and giving their lord a portion of their own

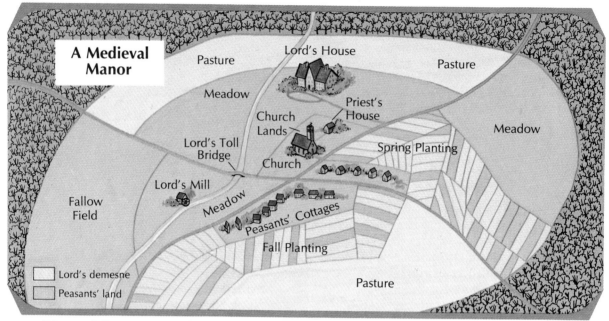

A Medieval Manor

Pasture

Lord's House

Pasture

Meadow

Priest's House

Church Lands

Church

Meadow

Spring Planting

Lord's Toll Bridge

Lord's Mill

Meadow

Fallow Field

Peasants' Cottages

Fall Planting

Pasture

☐ Lord's demesne
☐ Peasants' land

Diagram Skill   *On a typical medieval manor such as this one, each peasant family had its own cottage. The family farmed strips of land in different fields. Peasants also worked on the lord's demesne. What purposes might the meadows, pastures, and woodlands have served? Why do you think the mill was placed so close to the river?*

harvests. In turn, the lord was supposed to protect his peasants and provide justice.

During the early Middle Ages, peasants barely produced enough to survive. By about 1000, however, peasants were using new technologies such as crop rotation, the heavy plow, windmills, and watermills that increased output. As a result, peasants began to produce food surpluses to support a growing population.

The Medieval Church

The Church played a central role in shaping and unifying medieval Europe. It had its own government, laws, courts, and system of taxation. During the early Middle Ages, the Church expanded its influence by converting non-Christians in eastern Europe to Christianity.

The Church was closely tied to feudalism. It controlled huge amounts of land, and high church officials were often feudal lords. Also, kings and feudal lords depended on the educated clergy to fill important roles in their courts.

To peasants and nobles alike, the Church offered the only hope of salvation.

The Church controlled the *sacraments*, the seven sacred rites that offered the only route to eternal life. Only priests could administer the sacraments and save the souls of the faithful from eternal suffering.

The Church served as a force for civilization. In the local parish churches, priests taught Christian virtues that helped shape medieval Europe. In monasteries, a few educated clergy carefully copied and studied ancient manuscripts. Although much knowledge was lost during this period, the foundations were built for a new civilization.

SECTION REVIEW

1. Identify: Kingdom of the Franks, Charlemagne.
2. Define: feudalism, fief, vassal, knight, chivalry, manor, serfs, sacrament.
3. How did Charlemagne establish order in his kingdom?
4. What was the relationship between a lord and his vassal?
5. How did the Church influence life in medieval society?

282

2 The Height of Medieval Civilization

Read to Learn   ■ how trade changed civilization in the late Middle Ages
   ■ how the Church influenced medieval culture

In the late Middle Ages, medieval civilization gradually flowered. By the eleventh and twelfth centuries, feudal warfare had declined, and the manor economy was producing surpluses. The narrow world of the manor was slowly expanding.

Economic Patterns

The decline in warfare encouraged the growth of trade and travel. Some feudal lords and kings made efforts to repair roads and bridges. Also, a money economy slowly reappeared. At annual trade fairs, merchants and traders from different parts of Europe gathered to exchange goods.

The increase of trade led to the growth of towns. Merchants set up permanent headquarters in old Roman towns, while new towns grew up at important crossroads. Towns negotiated with local feudal lords for *charters,* written documents that guaranteed their rights. In medieval society, a new class of townspeople emerged.

Economic activities within the towns was regulated by *guilds,* associations of merchants or artisans that governed the town. Guilds governed prices, wages, and the quality of goods. They prevented competition and regulated who might become a master craftsman.

Medieval Culture

Towns served not only as centers of new economic activity but also of medieval culture. The middle class townspeople had money to educate their children and support the work of artists. Although worldly interests emerged, the Church still dominated medieval life. Nowhere was the influence of the Church more evident than in the towering Gothic cathedrals built by wealthy towns in the twelfth and thirteenth centuries. The new churches had tall pointed arches. Their paintings, sculptures, and large stained glass windows told the stories of the Old and New Testaments.

Medieval culture represented a blend of spiritual and worldly concerns. The literature of the late Middle Ages was written in the *vernacular,* the everyday language of the people. In Florence, the poet Dante wrote in the Italian vernacular. In the *Divine Comedy,* Dante combined medieval poetry, theology, and history. The English poet Chaucer used the vernacular in *The Canterbury Tales,* in which he had ordinary people on a pilgrimage tell stories about their lives.

During the late Middle Ages, associations of students and teachers evolved into the first universities. In these new centers of learning, scholars pored over the works of ancient writers. The writings of Aristotle and others whose works emphasized reason and logic caused medieval thinkers to reexamine ideas that they had taken on faith. A new school of thought, *scholasticism,* flourished. Scholastics, such as Thomas Aquinas, believed that reason and logic could be used to support Christian faith.

Expanding Horizons

Late in the eleventh century, the pope called for a *crusade,* a military expedition against the enemies of the Church. Rallying to the cry "God wills it," Christians from all over Europe traveled to Palestine to capture the Holy Land from the Muslims. Various motives contributed to the enthusiasm with which Christians undertook the Crusades. Many people believed that they were obeying God's will and wanted to achieve salvation. Others wanted to carve out kingdoms of their own. Still others saw the Crusades as a way to avoid taxes and debts at home.

Effects of the Crusades. During the early Crusades, Christian forces won lands in Syria and Palestine. They divided the conquered territory into four crusader states. In time, however, all four states were retaken by Muslim forces. Yet the Crusades helped to quicken the pace of changes already underway in Europe.

For 200 years, Christian knights, pilgrims, and merchants traveled to the eastern Mediterranean. They brought home new ideas as well as tastes for the goods of Asia and the Middle East. Merchants in the cities of northern Italy built large fleets to carry the crusaders and benefited from the growth in trade with the eastern Mediterranean. Also, the increased trade and travel introduced the people of Western Europe to other civilizations.

Other changes. Other social and economic changes occurred in the late Middle Ages. As a money economy slowly replaced the barter system, a few wealthy families set up banks, making loans to kings, nobles, and popes. With the growth in trade and travel, the manor became less isolated. Peasants and feudal lords bought goods from merchants and no longer had to make everything they needed.

Feudal lords were at a disadvantage in the new money economy. Because their wealth was in land, they lacked money to buy the luxury goods they wanted. As a result, they allowed peasants to pay rents in money. Some lords even permitted serfs to buy their freedom.

Despite the changes, however, the basic structure of medieval society remained the same. The Church dominated the medieval world, and the majority of people worked the land on feudal estates.

SECTION REVIEW

1. Identify: Dante, Chaucer, Thomas Aquinas.
2. Define: charter, guild, vernacular, scholasticism, crusade.
3. Describe two economic changes that took place in the late Middle Ages.
4. How did the approach to learning of the ancient philosophers differ from that of medieval thinkers?
5. Why did Christians go on the Crusades?

Map Skill *"Jerusalem is the center of the earth; the land is fruitful above all others, like another paradise of delights,"* proclaimed Pope Urban II in 1095. At the pope's urging, many Christians set out on Crusades to free Jerusalem from Muslim control. During which Crusade did the crusaders travel the longest distance?

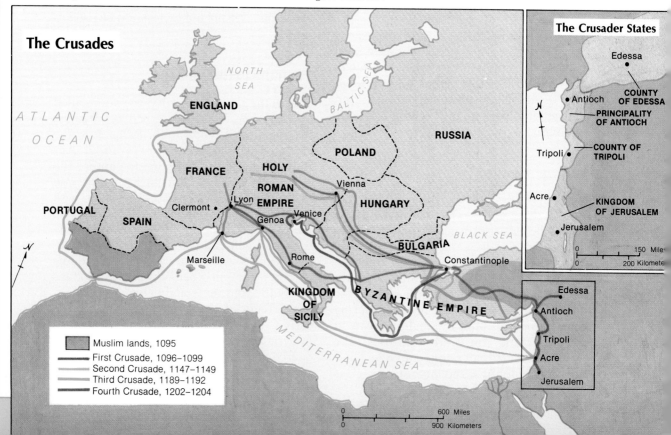

The Crusades

Muslim lands, 1095
First Crusade, 1096–1099
Second Crusade, 1147–1149
Third Crusade, 1189–1192
Fourth Crusade, 1202–1204

The Crusader States

3 Building National Monarchies

Read to Learn
- how English, French, and Spanish monarchs centralized their power
- what forces caused medieval society to decline

In the early Middle Ages, Western Europe was divided into many small states ruled by feudal lords. During the late Middle Ages, the situation changed as powerful monarchs centralized power. As royal power grew, people transferred their loyalty from local lords to national monarchs.

Growth of Royal Power in England

In 1066, William of Normandy conquered England and set up the foundations for royal power. He made all feudal lords swear allegiance to him. He limited the number of fortified castles built in England and had a survey, known as the *Domesday Book*, made of all property that could be taxed.

William's successors further strengthened royal power. They established a royal bureaucracy made up of officials loyal to the king. They set up the *exchequer*, or central treasury, and improved justice in the royal courts. The decisions of royal courts became part of the *common law*, the accepted legal principles that applied to everyone throughout the land.

Challenges to royal power came from the Church and feudal lords. King John I, for example, battled both unsuccessfully. In 1215, John's barons forced him to sign the Magna Carta, or Great Charter, a written guarantee of their rights. In time, the Magna Carta came to be seen as a significant document because the rights given to nobles were gradually extended to other people. Also, it established the principle that the king must obey the law.

In the late thirteenth century, the power of the king was further limited by a Parliament, or great council made up of officials, nobles, and bishops. Parliament grew into an assembly of two houses. The House of Lords was made up of great nobles and bishops. The House of Commons was made up of representatives of lesser knights and townspeople. Eventually, it helped establish a limited monarchy.

Growth of the French Monarchy

In France, rulers faced a difficult task. By 1000, French kings ruled only a small strip of north-central France. Over the next 300 years, they gradually extended their control over most of France. They set up effective royal government, employing educated clergy and townspeople in the royal bureaucracy. They established royal courts that had more power than local feudal courts. As a result, people gradually turned to the king as a source of justice.

As French kings increased their power, they came into conflict with the Church. To show that they had the support of the people, they summoned the Estates General, a representative assembly. It was made up of representatives from three estates, or classes, the clergy, nobles, and bourgeoisie, as the townspeople were called.

The Holy Roman Empire and the Church

In the eastern and central parts of what had once been Charlemagne's empire, a number of powerful dukes ruled over separate states. In 962, Otto, the duke of Saxony, gained the title of Holy Roman emperor and began extending his power over neighboring German lands and northern Italy. Otto and his successors developed close ties with the Church. These ties involved the German emperors deeply in Italian affairs. During this period, the Church also increased its political power. The result was a great struggle between the German emperors and the Church.

In the 1100s and 1200s, German emperors were determined to extend their rule over both Italy and Germany. In fact, they neglected their German lands to wage an endless series of wars in Italy. During these struggles, feudal lords in Germany continued to rule their lands as independent kingdoms. Italy, too, remained divided. Thus, unlike England and France, where national monarchs were building a basis for royal power, neither Germany nor Italy was united under a strong ruler.

Emergence of Christian Spain

During the late Middle Ages, Spain emerged as a strong, unified state. In the 700s, Muslims had conquered Spain and for centuries had presided over a prosperous center of Islamic civilization. During the 1100s and 1200s, however, Christians in northern Spain launched a series of crusades, known as the *reconquista*, to free Spain from Muslim control. Christian knights slowly pushed the Muslims back to the southern tip of Spain. Several Christian kingdoms emerged, including Portugal in the west, Castile in the center, and Aragon in the northeast.

In 1469, Queen Isabella of Castile and Ferdinand, heir to Aragon, married, thereby uniting their kingdoms. The two rulers then embarked on a policy to consolidate royal power. They made the Church an ally in this battle. Ousting the Muslims from their last stronghold in Granada, they imposed religious unity on Spain. They forced Muslims and Jews to convert to Christianity or leave the country. Although Isabella and Ferdinand established religious and national unity, they paid a high price by losing many productive citizens to exile.

Decline of Medieval Society

In the late Middle Ages, the foundations of medieval society weakened. The 1300s and 1400s were a difficult time for the people of Western Europe. In 1348, bubonic plague, the Black Death, a disease carried by rats, struck with terrifying consequences. About a third of the population of Western Europe was killed. In the resulting chaos, land was abandoned, commerce declined, and cities shrank in size.

During this time, the Church came under frequent attack. Medieval monarchs in-

Advances in agriculture helped peasants produce food surpluses. In this scene, a plowman directs a team of horses that are probably shod with iron horseshoes. The speed of horses made them much more efficient for plowing than oxen. Notice the man shooting the birds that are eating the newly sown seed.

creasingly challenged Church power. They tried to tax the clergy and limit the influence of Church courts. In 1305, the French king Philip IV managed to have the papacy moved from Rome to Avignon in France. For the next 70 years, the French controlled the papacy. Another crisis further weakened the Church when it split into two groups, each electing its own pope. Even after unity was restored, the Church came under attack from reformers who then criticized its wealth and worldliness.

As monarchs in England and France increased their power, they became involved in a struggle that lasted from 1337 to 1453, known as the Hundred Years' War. For centuries, English kings had ruled lands in France. However, during the Hundred

Years' War, the French ousted the English from France. The war gave the French a strong feeling of national pride and increased their loyalty to the king. In England, the war gave Parliament the opportunity to increase its power, in exchange for approving the king's taxes.

By the mid-1400s, feudalism was declining. Many feudal nobles were killed in the Hundred Years' War. The nature of warfare, too, was changing. With the invention of the longbow and the use of cannons, armored knights and fortified castles were becoming outdated. Nobles remained powerful, however. Instead of engaging in frequent battles as in the past, they took their place in the splendid royal courts that were set up by strong monarchs.

SECTION REVIEW

1. Identify: *Domesday Book*, Parliament, Estates General, Otto, Black Death, Hundred Years' War.
2. Define: exchequer, common law, reconquista.
3. Which groups challenged the growth of royal power?
4. Describe two results of the Hundred Years' War.

Review

Survey Checkup

1. Describe the structure of medieval society.
2. How did technology influence peasant life around the year 1000?
3. Why did economic conditions change in the later Middle Ages?
4. How did towns influence medieval culture?
5. (a) What was the purpose of the Crusades? (b) Did they succeed or fail? Explain.
6. Explain the importance of each of the following: (a) *Domesday Book*; (b) Magna Carta.
7. Why did Germany remain divided at a time when England and France were becoming united?
8. Describe three developments that contributed to the decline of medieval society.

Critical Thinking

1. **Analyzing a Quotation** A French bishop summed up the medieval social order in these words: "God's house is threefold. Some pray in it, some fight in it, and some work in it." (a) To what three classes in medieval society do you think he was referring? (b) Which class did he think was most important?

2. **Applying Information** Why do you think the Crusades have often been called a successful failure?
3. **Comparing** Compare life in the early Middle Ages with that in the late Middle Ages.

Developing Basic Skills

1. **Map Reading** Study the map on page 284. Then answer the following questions. (a) What information is shown on the map? (b) Which Crusade included armies from England, France, and the Holy Roman Empire? (c) Which Crusade went only as far as Constantinople? (d) During which Crusade were Edessa, Antioch, and Jerusalem taken? (e) Why do you think the Crusades expanded the horizons of Europeans?

2. **Using Statistics** Read the Skill Lesson on page 198 called "Population Changes in the Middle Ages: Using Statistics." Then answer the following questions. (a) What happened to the population of most parts of Europe between 500 and 650? between 650 and 1000? between 1000 and 1340? (b) Which part of Europe lost the largest number of people in the 100 years after the Black Death? (c) Which part lost almost half its population? (d) About how long did the population of Europe take to regain the size it had before the Black Death?

287

The Taj Mahal was built by a Muslim ruler of India, the Shah Jahan in the 1600s. The gleaming white marble walls are decorated with carved quotations from the Koran, the sacred book of Islam.

Unit Four
A BRIEF SURVEY

Golden Ages Outside Europe

(330–1650)

In the mid-fourteenth century, an Arab traveler named Ibn Battuta journeyed across Africa. About 1355, he reached the West African kingdom of Mali and commented on the peacefulness of the empire. "The Negroes possess some admirable qualities," he reported. "They are seldom unjust and have a greater abhorrence of injustice than any other people. Their sultan [ruler] shows no mercy to any one guilty of the least act of injustice. There is complete security in their country. Neither traveler nor inhabitant has anything to fear from robbers or men of violence."

Ibn Battuta was one of many travelers whose accounts have preserved the record of civilizations that grew and flourished outside Europe during the Middle Ages. His visit to the thriving kingdom of Mali highlighted several key developments. Earlier in the seventh century, the Arabs had erupted out of their desert homeland and started to carry a new religion, Islam, across much of the world from Spain to India and to Africa. Through trade and travel, the people of the Islamic world shared ideas and learned about each other.

Other important changes had also taken place around the world. The Western Roman Empire collapsed in the fifth century, but the Eastern Roman Empire,

known as the Byzantine Empire, flourished. Islam, at the same time, created a dynamic new civilization that blended traditions of the ancient Greeks and Romans with those of the peoples it conquered. As Islam swept into India, it made a lasting impact on the subcontinent.

Between 500 and 1500, China enjoyed several golden ages under strong dynasties. Farther east, Japan drew on Chinese achievements to develop its own distinct civilization. In the Americas, too, advanced civilizations were making remarkable achievements at a time when Europeans were struggling to build the foundations of medieval society.

1 Byzantine and Islamic Civilizations

Read to Learn ■ what contributions the Byzantine Empire made to civilization
■ why Islam spread rapidly throughout the Mediterranean world

After the fall of the Roman Empire in the West, the Eastern Roman Empire flourished for another 1000 years. Eventually, its civilization passed on to the peoples of Eastern Europe. Farther east, another civilization, based on the religion of Islam, emerged in the seventh and eighth centuries.

The Byzantine Empire

The emperor Constantine, you will recall, made the city of Constantinople the capital of the Eastern Roman Empire. While the Roman Empire in the West collapsed under the pressure of invasions, the Eastern Roman Empire managed to survive. For centuries, the Byzantine Empire, as the Eastern Roman Empire came to be called, served as a buffer. It absorbed the attacks of many invading people from the East who might have otherwise overrun Western Europe.

Absolute rulers. Byzantine rulers exercised absolute power over their empire. They created an efficient civil service, kept a strong army, and controlled all aspects of the economy. Their capital, Constantinople, was the wealthy center of a flourishing world trade.

Byzantine emperors acted as head of the Christian Church. When these eastern emperors refused to recognize the authority of the pope in Rome, a schism, or split, within

Christianity eventually took place. The pope continued to rule the Roman Catholic Church in the west, but the Eastern Orthodox Church fell under the rule of the Byzantine emperor.

In the 1200s and 1300s, the Byzantine Empire declined. By the 1400s, it was unable to withstand the invasions of the Ottoman Turks. In 1453, the Ottomans captured Constantinople, signaling the end of the Byzantine Empire.

The Byzantine heritage. Arts and learning had flourished in the rich cities of the Byzantine Empire. At a time when education was barely kept alive in the monasteries of Western Europe, Byzantine scholars actively studied and preserved manuscripts from Rome and Greece. Under the emperor Justinian, scholars summarized all existing Roman law into a vast work known as Justinian's Code. This code contained many principles of justice that later helped shape legal systems in Western Europe and the Americas.

The Christians of Eastern Europe who had been converted by Byzantine missionaries carried on the Byzantine heritage. Vladimir, the prince of Kiev, in the 1100s, for example, chose Byzantine Christianity over the Roman Catholic Church. He then supported the conversion of the Russian people, thus ensuring close ties between Russia and the Byzantine Empire.

After the fall of Constantinople, the rulers of Moscow claimed to be the heirs of the Roman and Byzantine emperors. The Russian ruler, Ivan III, took the title "czar," the Russian word for Caesar. Russian czars then modeled their government on the absolute rule of the Byzantine emperors.

Rise of Islam

In 622, Muhammad founded the religion of Islam in Arabia. The Five Pillars of Islam taught the basic duties of all Muslims. They included the belief in one God, Allah; prayer five times each day; almsgiving to the poor; fasting during the month of Ramadan; and a pilgrimage to Mecca at least once in a lifetime. The Koran, the holy book of Islam, contains the word of God as revealed to the prophet Muhammad.

The teachings of Islam were rooted in traditional Arab beliefs as well as those of Judaism and Christianity. Muhammad recognized his debt to these two religions. He called Jews and Christians the People of the Book because they believed in God's revelations in the Bible. In theory, if not always in practice, Muslims were tolerant of the People of the Book.

Spread of Islam. Between 622 and 732, Islam spread rapidly from Arabia to Spain in the west and to India in the east. Many people accepted Islam because its teachings were simple and clear. Islam did not require a clergy or a church. Also, Arab soldiers were inspired to fight for Islam. They believed that by dying in its cause they would enter paradise.

As Islam expanded, a government was set up to rule the vast empire. The government was headed by a *caliph*, as the successor to Muhammad was called. The caliph was both the religious and political leader of Islam. The Koran served as the source of law for the Islamic Empire.

In the years after Muhammad's death, a division developed within Islam between the Sunnites and Shiites over who was the rightful heir to Muhammad. Islam also faced other problems over the next centuries. It was attacked by invaders such as the Seljuk and Ottoman Turks and the Mongols. Al-

Map Skill *Islam spread rapidly in the century after the death of Muhammad. By 750, Muslims controlled much of the trade of the Mediterranean world. Under which caliphs did Islam reach the limits of its expansion? In what years?*

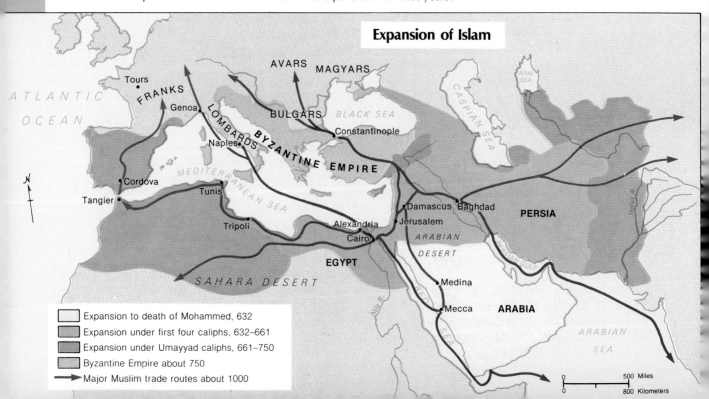

Expansion of Islam

Expansion to death of Mohammed, 632
Expansion under first four caliphs, 632–661
Expansion under Umayyad caliphs, 661–750
Byzantine Empire about 750
Major Muslim trade routes about 1000

though the invaders converted to Islam, their traditions differed from those of the Arabs.

Islamic civilization. During the expansion of Islam, a new civilization emerged. It blended Arab, Greek, Roman, Byzantine, Persian, and Indian traditions. The new Islamic civilization benefited from the thriving trade and agriculture within the empire.

Islamic teachings encouraged learning. Throughout the empire, scholars studied the Koran as well as Roman, Jewish, Persian, and Indian texts. By examining ancient Greek texts, Muslim doctors perfected ways to diagnose and treat disease. In mathematics, Muslims adopted the decimal system from India and made advances in algebra and trigonometry.

In philosophy, Muslim thinkers were influenced by the logic of Aristotle. Even before the development of scholasticism in western Europe, philosophers like Averroës struggled to prove that there was no conflict between Islamic faith and reason. Later, these and other ideas made their way into Western Europe.

SECTION REVIEW

1. Identify: Eastern Orthodox Church, Ottoman Turks, Justinian's Code, Ivan III, Muhammad, Five Pillars of Islam, Koran, People of the Book, Averroës.
2. Define: caliph.
3. How did the Byzantine Empire differ from Western Europe in the early Middle Ages?
4. What are the central teachings of Islam?

2 Africa and the Americas

Read to Learn
- how powerful trading kingdoms arose in Africa
- how religion dominated early American civilization

While advanced civilizations flourished in Europe and Asia, people in different parts of Africa and the Americas produced their own civilizations. As elsewhere, the people of these civilizations built large cities, organized complex governments, developed technical skills, and invented systems of recordkeeping.

The Kingdoms of Kush and Axum

Africa is a vast continent with a variety of climates and terrains. As people adapted to these varied conditions, they developed many distinct cultural patterns. The powerful kingdom of Kush flourished at the same time as ancient Egypt and engaged in a thriving trade with its northern neighbor along the Nile.

After Kush declined about 200 A.D., the neighboring state of Axum carried on a lively trade with the Mediterranean world and Asia. In the fourth century, the ruler of Axum converted to Christianity. Today, the Christian culture of Ethiopia has its roots in the civilization of Axum.

Rise of Trading States

During the Middle Ages in Europe, several strong trading kingdoms rose in West Africa. Camel caravans from North Africa made the long desert crossing to exchange salt and other goods for gold mined in West Africa. About 400 A.D., the kingdom of Ghana began to extend its control over the gold-producing regions of West Africa. In the seventh century, traders from North Africa brought Islam to West Africa. Although the king of Ghana did not convert, the new religion had a lasting impact on West Africa.

After the decline of Ghana, two other trading states—Mali and later Songhai—gained control of the profitable gold-salt trade. The rulers of Mali converted to Islam. In 1324, Mansa Musa of Mali made a pilgrimage to Mecca. The wealth displayed by this West African king made a great impression on the people he met in the Middle East.

Trade also contributed to the rise of independent city-states in East Africa. There, goods were brought by sea rather than by desert caravans. The coastal cities taxed all goods that passed through their markets, gaining great wealth. Many Arab traders settled in the cities of East Africa. They helped create a new culture that blended African and Islamic traditions.

Patterns of Daily Life

People in different parts of Africa organized their lives in a variety of ways. As elsewhere,

Benin sculptors created striking bronze figures such as this musician by a process known as the "lost wax" technique. The artist molded a clay figure and then coated it—first with a layer of wax and then with a layer of clay. An opening was left at the base. Next, the figure was baked so the wax melted and was "lost." Melted bronze was poured into the opening in the base of the figure. After the bronze cooled and hardened, the clay shell was removed, revealing the bronze figure.

however, people built their societies around respect for family, law, and religion. Family organization varied according to the needs of individual cultures. In farming and herding societies, for example, the basic unit was the *extended family*, where several generations lived and worked together.

Religion was part of everyday life. Although religious practices varied, many African people had similar beliefs. Most Africans believed in a single Supreme Spirit, the creator of the universe. They saw everything in nature as part of this Supreme Spirit and called on ancestors and "spirit helpers" to make their prayers known to the Supreme Spirit.

Peoples of the Americas

Like Africa, the Americas are vast continents where many different peoples have developed their own distinct cultures. The first Americans are thought to have crossed a land bridge that connected Siberia and Alaska more than 10,000 years ago. Bands of Stone Age hunters slowly migrated south, adapting to different climates and terrains.

Because the people within each geographic region tended to have similar traditions, scholars have divided the peoples of North America into cultural regions. Among these regions are the far north, Pacific coast, Great Plains, eastern woodlands, and southwest. In the far north, for example, the people adjusted to a harsh climate, living by hunting and fishing. They used local resources such as bone for harpoons and knives. Farther south, warmer climates allowed people to develop agriculture. The people of the southwest, for example, cultivated crops such as beans, squash, and maize.

Civilizations of the Americas

Farming began in the Americas about 6000 B.C. As elsewhere, agriculture led to the growth of early civilizations, such as that of the Olmec in southern Mexico. By 1200 B.C., the Olmec lived in large cities whose central focus was a huge, pyramid-shaped, stone temple. The Olmec developed a form of hieroglyphic writing, a system of counting, and a calendar.

Scholars think that the Olmec may have influenced the Maya civilization that grew up later in Central America and southern Mexico. Like the Olmec, the Maya built cities that were largely religious centers. Priests and warriors made up a powerful ruling class. Maya priests were fascinated by time and developed a precise calendar. They also made advances in mathematics and invented a numbering system that included the concept of zero.

Two other civilizations flourished in the Americas. In the 1300s and 1400s, the Aztec conquered a large empire in Mexico. From the Aztec capital at Tenochtitlán, a bustling city of about 100,000 people, the Aztec emperor ruled over many different peoples.

The Inca built an even larger empire in the Andes region of South America. They developed an efficient system of government and built an excellent system of roads so that news could be relayed across their vast empire. The Inca built huge stone temples and palaces that withstood centuries of earthquakes.

SECTION REVIEW

1. Identify: Kush, Axum, Ghana, Mansa Musa, Olmec, Maya, Aztec, Inca.
2. Define: extended family.
3. How did Ghana, Mali, and Songhai gain power?
4. What were some achievements of the Olmec?

3 India, China, and Japan

Read to Learn ■ how Hindu and Muslim cultures clashed in India
■ what cultural traditions emerged in China and Japan

During the Middle Ages in Europe, three major civilizations in Asia were making important advances. In India, Hindu traditions helped preserve unity during centuries of invasion. China was a unified nation that enjoyed several golden ages between the seventh and sixteenth centuries. Farther east, Japan was shaping its distinct civilization.

A Meeting of Cultures in India

By the sixth century, Hindu traditions were deeply rooted in Indian society. The caste system and the power of the Brahmans, or priestly caste, helped ensure a stable social order at a time when warfare among Hindu princes prevented political unity.

Expansion of Islam. In the tenth century, the forces of Islam advanced into northern India. During the next 300 years, Muslim rulers, known as *sultans,* extended their control over much of the subcontinent. From their capital at Delhi, sultans set up a strong government.

Unlike earlier conquerors of India, the Muslims were not absorbed into Hindu society. They remained a powerful, separate force that was strongly hostile to Hindu beliefs. To Muslims, who believed in one God, Allah, the Hindu worship of many gods was a terrible evil.

Among the many points of conflict was the Muslim belief in the equality of all believers that clashed with Hindu belief in the caste system. Also, Muslims insisted upon strict obedience to the Koran, while Hindus were tolerant of many religious beliefs. Despite the frequent clashes, some blending occurred between Hindu and Muslim cultures, especially in the arts and learning.

The Mogul Empire. In the sixteenth century, Mongol invaders swept into India, creating the Mogul Empire that lasted for over 300 years. The greatest Mogul ruler was Akbar. Although he was a Muslim, he followed a policy of religious toleration. Akbar's successors, however, did not continue this policy. As a result, they faced the constant threat of rebellion from Hindu princes. In the 1500s and 1600s, Europeans began to set up trading posts to profit from the silks, spices, and wealth of Mogul India.

Flowering of Chinese Civilization

During the Middle Ages in Europe, China benefited from two long periods of peace and good government. Under the T'ang dynasty (618–917) and Sung dynasty (960–1279), Chinese civilization spread. Its far-reaching influence ranged from Korea and Japan in the east to Southeast Asia and the borders of India.

The Chinese produced remarkable works of art and technology. They invented paper and a process for printing, developed the magnetic compass, and began to use gunpowder. As the economy expanded, the Chinese came in contact with ideas and new products from other parts of the world.

Despite these advances, Chinese society remained largely unchanged. Confucian ideals remained the basis of government and family life. The Chinese accepted the idea that each person had his or her place in society and that an inferior owed loyalty and respect to a superior.

In the thirteenth century, the Mongols overran China and set up their own government. During the rule of the Mongol emperor Kublai Khan, the Venetian traveler Marco Polo visited China. When he returned home, he published a book describing the advanced civilization he had seen. But Europeans refused to believe his reports.

In the fourteenth century, the Chinese drove out the foreign rulers and established the Ming dynasty. The early Ming rulers launched several voyages of exploration. Chinese fleets traveled to Southeast Asia, India, and East Africa. Then, suddenly, in 1433, the voyages stopped, and the Ming imposed restrictions on trade and foreign travel. In the 1400s, China was probably the most technologically advanced civilization in the world. But it slowly fell behind at a time when Western Europeans were beginning to expand their horizons.

Emergence of Japan

To the east of China lies the Japanese *archipelago*, a chain of islands. The sea strongly influenced Japan, providing a source of food and a barrier to invaders. By 400 A.D., the Yamato family had established the first and only Japanese dynasty.

Between the fifth and ninth centuries, the Japanese borrowed many ideas from China. They adapted Chinese writing to their own language and welcomed Buddhist missionaries. They studied Taoist texts and adopted Confucian ideas about family and ancestor worship. At the same time, they kept their traditional religious beliefs, called Shinto.

By the 1100s, strong lords had gained power in the countryside. As *samurai*, or warrior knights, battled for power, feudalism emerged in Japan. As in Western Europe, everyone had a place in feudal society. Although the emperor held the highest rank, he had no political power. The *shogun*, or chief general, was the actual ruler. Below him were the *daimyo*, powerful samurai lords who owned large estates, and the lesser

T'ang potters captured the rich variety of Chinese city life in brightly glazed ceramics. They often portrayed foreigners, such as this bearded Middle Eastern wine merchant. Trade brought new products and ideas to China, enlivening the highly sophisticated culture of Chinese cities.

samurai. Peasants worked the land and sometimes fought alongside their lords.

In the 1600s, the Tokugawa shoguns imposed a form of centralized feudalism on Japan. They limited the power of the daimyo and ended the constant warfare. As a result, trade and commerce improved. To stop the growing influence of Christian missionaries and traders who had reached Japan in the 1500s, the Tokugawa shoguns banned all foreign trade and travel. This self-imposed isolation lasted for 200 years.

During the feudal period, the Japanese developed strong traditions. Bushido, the samurai code of honor, emphasized simplicity, courage, and honor. Zen, a form of Buddhism, became deeply rooted. Zen emphasized physical and mental discipline. It also taught the unity of nature that complemented the Shinto idea of respect for the forces of nature.

SECTION REVIEW

1. Identify: Mogul Empire, Akbar, Kublai Khan, Marco Polo, Shinto, Tokugawa shoguns.
2. Define: sultan, archipelago, samurai, shogun, daimyo.
3. Explain two differences between Hinduism and Islam.
4. Describe three ideas that the Japanese borrowed from the Chinese.

Review

Survey Checkup

1. (a) Why did a division develop within Christianity? (b) Which people followed the Eastern Orthodox Church?

2. (a) To what parts of the world did Islam spread after the death of Muhammad? (b) Why did many people accept its teachings?

3. Describe two reasons why learning flourished in the Islamic Empire.

4. How did the gold-salt trade influence West Africa?

5. How did the first people reach the Americas?

6. (a) What was the Aztec empire like in the 1400s? (b) How did the Inca control their huge empire?

7. Why were Muslims hostile to Hindus in India?

8. What practical inventions did the Chinese make during the T'ang and Sung dynasties?

9. How did centralized feudalism of the Tokugawa shoguns affect Japan?

Critical Thinking

1. **Comparing Civilizations**   Compare the early civilizations of the Americas to those you read about in ancient Egypt, Sumer, India, and China. (a) How were they similar? (b) How were they different?

2. **Analyzing**   Why do you think Chinese society remained stable throughout many centuries of political and economic change?

Developing Basic Skills

1. **Map Reading**   Study the map on page 290. Then answer the following questions. (a) What does the map show? (b) What political information is shown? (c) With what parts of the world did Muslim merchants trade? (d) What do you think were the results of this vast trading network?

2. **Comparing Diagrams**   Study the diagrams "The Structure of Feudal Society" on page 157, and "Feudal Society in Japan" on page 257. Then answer the following questions. (a) How was feudal society similar in both Japan and Western Europe? (b) How was it different?

Europe in Transition

Renaissance artists, such as
Botticelli, emphasized realism
in their paintings.

1534 Henry VIII broke with Rome and
became head of the Church of
England.

	1300	1400	1500
POLITICS AND GOVERNMENT	**1300s** Italian city-states grow wealthy and powerful	**1453** Constantinople falls to Turks	**1513** Machiavelli writes *The Prince*
ECONOMICS AND TECHNOLOGY		**1397** Medici bank founded in Florence	**1455** Gutenberg Bible printed with movable type
SOCIETY AND CULTURE		**1348** *Decameron* is first prose written in Italian language	**1508** Michelangelo begins painting in Sistine Chapel

1517 Martin Luther's protest
of church practices led
to the Protestant
Reformation.

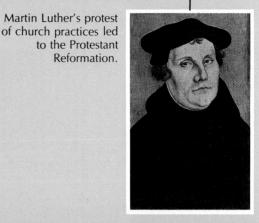

By the late Middle Ages, trade and commerce revived.
Entrepreneurs opened new businesses such as this tailor's shop.

1588 The defeat of the Spanish
Armada marked the end of
Spain's dominance in Europe.

1682 This hat of sable, gold,
and jewels symbolized
the wealth and power
of Peter the Great of
Russia.

1600   1700   1800

1588 British sink   **1643** Louis XIV rules France   **1762** Catherine the Great
Spanish Armada   becomes ruler of Russia

1578 Sir Francis Drake   **1682** La Salle reaches mouth
begins trip around the world   of the Mississippi River

1605 *Don Quixote*   **1698** Peter the Great begins
published   modernizing Russia

Leonardo da Vinci conducted many scientific
experiments. This helicopter model is based
on one of his drawings.

New tools of navigation
increased trade and
exploration as this Chinese
watercolor of a Jesuit
missionary shows.

16 The Renaissance and Reformation

(1350–1600)

Chapter Outline

1 Spirit of the Renaissance

2 Art and Literature of the Renaissance

3 Changing Patterns of Life

4 Beginnings of the Protestant Reformation

5 Further Challenges to the Catholic Church

A procession of the Medici, the leading family of Renaissance Florence, with their servants and followers.

In Florence, Italy, the Guasconti family was sitting down to dinner when a young man burst into the room. He drew a knife and threw himself at one of the startled diners, crying: "Traitors, this is the day on which I mean to murder you all!" When none of the terror-stricken family dared offer battle, the man changed his mind. He ran down the stairs, only to find a dozen other members of the Guasconti household, armed with shovels, iron pipes, and clubs.

Later, the young man recalled, "When I got among them, raging like a mad bull, I flung four or five to the earth, and fell down with them myself, continually aiming my dagger now at one and now at another." Incredibly, when the dust settled, no one was hurt, and the man ran off down the street.

The young fighter was Benvenuto Cellini (chehl LEE nee), a talented goldsmith and sculptor who lived from 1500 to 1571. Cellini led an amazingly turbulent and full life, which he described in his *Autobiography*. He explained in the book that he had fought with the Guasconti because they questioned his skill as a goldsmith.

Cellini was proud of his many talents. He played the flute, wrote elegant poetry, and was a clever diplomat. His drive and determination knew no bounds. When Rome was beseiged by a neighboring city-state, Cellini stood at a crucial castle post, firing artillery at the advancing enemy. In his *Autobiography*, he boasted, "It was I who saved the castle."

Cellini was just one of many gifted personalities whose bold achievements proclaimed a new age. These individuals left a lasting mark on the European scene during the period from 1350 to 1600, known as the Renaissance.

Renaissance is a French word meaning rebirth. During the Renaissance, scholars reacted against what they saw as the "dark ages" of medieval Europe and revived the learning of ancient Greece and Rome. They thought they were bringing about the rebirth of civilization.

The Renaissance was both a worldly and a religious age. Great achievements in the arts and sciences were combined with deep religious concerns. In fact, during the Renaissance, fierce debates over questions of faith and salvation sparked the Reformation, a movement that divided Christians in Europe into many different groups. By 1600, Europeans had left behind the world of the Middle Ages and had established the foundations for modern Europe.

1 Spirit of the Renaissance

Read to Learn ■ how the Renaissance began in Italy and then spread
■ what ideas were stressed in the Renaissance

During the 1300s, economic distress, war, and the Black Death had swept across Western Europe. As Western Europe recovered from these disasters, a new creative spirit emerged. This spirit was at the heart of the Renaissance. The Renaissance began first in the city-states of northern Italy. Later, it spread to northern Europe.

The Italian City-States

The political and economic situation in northern Italy provided fertile ground for the Renaissance. During the Middle Ages, many Italian towns had expanded into city-states. Each city-state governed itself and the surrounding countryside. Such independence left the rulers of the city-states free to experiment in the larger world of ideas.

By the late Middle Ages, Italian city-states had grown wealthy from trade and industry. Merchants from Venice, Genoa, and Pisa controlled trade to the eastern Mediterranean. Other cities, such as Florence, thrived on the sale of manufactured goods, especially wool cloth. In addition, Italian bankers made large profits by financing commercial ventures and making loans to princes and popes. The wealth of the city-states supported the Renaissance.

Merchants and bankers made up a powerful middle class in the Italian city-states.

Map Skill *The Renaissance spirit flourished in the northern Italian city-states. The major city-states are shown on this map, but there were dozens of smaller city-states. Which state was most likely to have used the sea in building its economy?*

Renaissance Italy About 1494

- Duchy of Milan
- Duchy of Savoy
- Republic of Genoa
- Republic of Florence
- Papal States
- Venetian Republic
- Kingdom of the Two Sicilies
- Republic of Siena
- Other city-states

FRANCE · Avignon · Milan · Genoa · Venice · OTTOMAN EMPIRE · Pisa · Florence · CORSICA · Rome · ADRIATIC SEA · TYRRHENIAN SEA · SARDINIA · Naples · SICILY · IONIAN ISLANDS · MEDITERRANEAN SEA

0   200 Miles
0   300 Kilometers

Political and economic leadership fell to this class rather than to landowning nobles because feudalism had never fully developed in northern Italy.

The concerns of the wealthy middle class helped shape the Renaissance in Italy. For example, the Renaissance reflected their concern for education and individual achievement. Furthermore, they had the time and money to become patrons, or supporters, of the arts.

Florence was typical of the Italian city-states in some ways. During the 1400s, a single powerful family, the Medici (MEHD ih chee), ruled Florence. Giovanni de' Medici had organized a bank in Florence in 1397. Over the next 30 years, the bank flourished, and the family opened offices as far away as London. Giovanni's son, Cosimo, and then his great-grandson, Lorenzo, controlled the government of Florence. The Medici and their supporters frequently clashed with other leading families in an atmosphere of intrigue and treachery. Yet under the Medici, Florence came to symbolize the creative spirit of the Renaissance.

Like many Renaissance rulers, the Medici were well-educated and had many interests. For example, Lorenzo, known as "the Magnificent," was a skilled architect. The Medici were proud of Florence and wanted all citizens to share their pride. They used part of the Medici fortune to hire local painters, sculptors, architects, and silversmiths to create works of art to beautify Florence. Many artists felt that as true artists they should be actively involved in the life of their city, not withdrawn from the everyday world.

Study of the Humanities

People in the Italian city-states developed a renewed interest in education, especially in the learning of ancient Greece and Rome. At the universities, theology, law, and medicine were traditionally the most highly respected subjects. However, during the Renaissance, scholars also stressed the studia humanitatis, the study of the humanities. The humanities included the subjects taught in ancient Greek and Roman schools—grammar, rhetoric, poetry, and history. Renaissance scholars who studied those subjects were called humanists.

Renaissance humanists were practical people. They wanted to learn more about the world. By reading ancient texts, they rediscovered knowledge that had been lost or for-

In the Italian city-states, rulers lived in great luxury. At the courts of these Renaissance rulers, good manners, loyalty, wit, and piety were considered essential. This painting shows a wedding procession in Florence. Notice the rich clothes of the people attending the wedding.

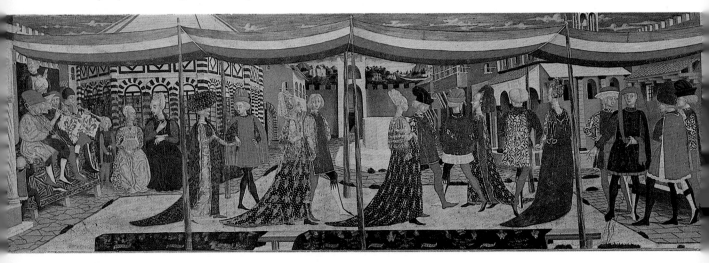

gotten during the Middle Ages. Many were closely involved in the political and economic life of their age. Many Renaissance humanists were also devout Christians. They felt that the study of the humanities enriched their lives as Christians because it went beyond the dry, abstract works of medieval scholars.

Renaissance scholars thought education was the way to become a well-rounded individual. Only with a proper education, they argued, could a person enjoy a full, rewarding life. One scholar advised a student:

> I beg you, take care. Add a little every day and gather things in. Remember that these studies promise you enormous prizes both in the conduct of your life and the fame and glory of your name.... acquaint yourself with what pertains to life and manners—those things that are called humane studies because they perfect and adorn man.

This philosophy reflected the Renaissance confidence in individual abilities.

Recovering the Classics

Francesco Petrarch (PEE trahrk) was an early Renaissance humanist from Florence who lived from 1304 to 1374. Petrarch traveled about Europe in search of old manuscripts. He especially prized the works of the Roman statesman Cicero and the early Christian writer St. Augustine. Medieval scholars had studied the writings of both men, but Petrarch uncovered new evidence about the times when Cicero and St. Augustine had lived. During his research, Petrarch began to realize how much of the classical heritage had been lost.

Petrarch's work encouraged others to try to recover writings of the classical world. They searched for ancient manuscripts in monastery libraries. Often, the conditions they found shocked them. A visitor to one monastery library discovered that only the walls remained standing. There was no door or roof. A thick layer of dust covered everything, and grass grew on the window sills. The manuscripts lay in disorganized piles.

While searching for classical texts, Renaissance humanists rescued many hidden treasures. They wanted to restore the classics they found to their original form. Therefore, they compared copies of the same work to discover where mistakes had been made when it was recopied.

Scholars also tried to learn when ancient manuscripts were written. To do so, they developed sophisticated techniques for analyzing historical documents. One scholar, Lorenzo Valla, examined the Donation of Constantine, a document in which the emperor Constantine supposedly gave the pope control over Rome and the Western Roman Empire. By careful analysis, Valla exposed the document as a forgery. For example, he pointed out that it contained the term "fief," which was unknown in Constantine's time. This search for knowledge carried Renaissance thinkers such as Valla into dangerous areas because their work questioned long-held assumptions about the accuracy of ancient writings.

Handbooks for Proper Behavior

Renaissance writers often prepared manuals that told individuals how to behave. One well-known manual was *The Prince* by Niccolò Machiavelli (MAHK ee uh VEHL ee). Machiavelli wrote *The Prince* as a handbook for rulers of the Italian city-states, who often faced unstable political conditions. Within a city, different factions, or groups, constantly struggled for power. In addition, city-states were frequently at war with one another.

In *The Prince*, Machiavelli recommended that a ruler adopt a realistic course of action in order to stay in power. If a ruler could afford to be benevolent, that was fine. But Machiavelli cautioned, "It is much safer to be feared than to be loved, if one must choose." He taught that "the end justifies the means"—that is, a ruler should employ any methods to achieve his goal. He advised rulers to use a mixture of cunning, diplomacy, and ruthlessness.

Another influential manual was *The Book of the Courtier* by Baldassare Castiglione (KAHS tee LYOH neh). Castiglione described the qualities that a courtier, or refined, educated aristocrat, should possess.

Niccolò Machiavelli, a diplomat and government official in Florence, dedicated The Prince *to Lorenzo de' Medici. The advice Machiavelli gave on how a ruler can stay in power is often considered ruthless and cynical. A typical piece of advice was: "If all men were good, this advice would not be good, but since men are wicked and do not keep their promises to you, you likewise do not have to keep yours to them."*

the arts. Renaissance ideas spread slowly northward.

In northern Europe and Spain, the Renaissance took a different form. For one thing, feudalism, with its traditions of knighthood and chivalry, was stronger in northern Europe than in Italy. Therefore, kings, queens, and nobles, rather than merchants and bankers, were the chief patrons of the arts.

Furthermore, Renaissance scholars in northern Europe and Spain took a more traditional approach to religion than some Italian humanists. They studied classical works, but they were more likely to study the writings of early Christians than of Greeks and Romans. Northern European humanists devoted their time to uncovering what they believed was the simpler, purer faith of the early Christians.

Despite differences between the Renaissance in Italy and the Renaissance in the rest of Europe, Renaissance artists, writers, and scholars pursued similar goals. They stressed individual achievement and classical learning. Furthermore, they stimulated a vigorous creative spirit that revolutionized thinking in Western Europe. Compared to people in the Middle Ages, people during the Renaissance were more concerned with achieving worldly success. Yet they maintained a strong faith in Christianity.

He praised the study of the humanities and urged courtiers to cultivate their talents. They should learn to appreciate music and play a variety of instruments. They should also be able to speak gracefully and provide rulers with witty, pleasant company. In short, Castiglione drew a picture of what he considered an ideal Renaissance person, someone who had a broad education in many different areas.

The Renaissance in Northern Europe

The Renaissance blossomed first in the Italian city-states, where commerce and a wealthy middle class supported learning and

SECTION REVIEW

1. Identify: Lorenzo de' Medici, Francesco Petrarch, Niccolò Machiavelli, Baldassare Castiglione.
2. How did the wealth of the Italian city-states encourage the Renaissance spirit?
3. (a) What subjects made up the humanities? (b) According to Renaissance scholars, what was the purpose of education?
4. How did scholars try to find errors in ancient manuscripts?
5. What advice did Machiavelli give to rulers?
6. According to Castiglione, what was the ideal Renaissance person?
7. Describe one way in which the Renaissance in northern Europe differed from the Renaissance in Italy.

2 Art and Literature of the Renaissance

Read to Learn ▪ how the Renaissance affected the arts
▪ how the Renaissance differed in Italy and northern Europe

The Renaissance spirit came vividly to life in literature and the arts. Writers produced a huge outpouring of literature, which both shaped and reflected Renaissance ideas. Artists, especially, found an important place in the Renaissance world.

During the Middle Ages, painters and sculptors decorated many churches and cathedrals, but they received little individual recognition. The names of only a few medieval artists are known today. In contrast, dozens of Renaissance artists are well known today. Popes, rulers, merchants, and bankers competed for their services. Renaissance artists proudly accepted the fame that their creative genius brought.

Classical Influence

During the Renaissance, artists returned to the classical principles of Greek and Roman art. The Greeks, you will recall, stressed harmony and balance in nature, and the Romans emphasized realism.

Renaissance artists in Italy found inspiration in ancient Roman buildings scattered across the land. In the early 1400s, the sculptor Donatello (DAHN uh TEHL oh) and the architect Filippo Brunelleschi (BROO nehl LEHS kee) traveled from Florence to Rome. There, they sketched the ruins of ancient buildings as well as ancient marble and bronze statutes.

The visit to Rome produced dramatic results. When Donatello returned to Florence, he created a statue of David, a king of the ancient Hebrews. The statue was unlike medieval sculptures, in which individual figures appeared as part of a larger work on tombs or cathedral walls. Like ancient Greek and Roman statues, Donatello's David stood alone, free to be admired from all sides. Furthermore, it portrayed David with realism and grace.

Brunelleschi and other Renaissance architects rejected medieval Gothic architecture and revived classical styles. They designed elegant buildings, using columns and domes. Brunelleschi created a sensation when he proposed to top the unfinished cathedral of Florence with a vast dome. Many people thought the building would collapse. But Brunelleschi had studied ancient Roman buildings, and he overcame the technical problems involved in raising the dome.

Years later, when the artist and architect Michelangelo Buonarroti (MĪ k'l AHN juh LOH BWOH nahr ROH tee) designed Saint Peter's Cathedral in Rome, he designed the dome using the engineering principles developed by Brunelleschi.

New Techniques in Art

Many Renaissance artists tried to show the world realistically, as it actually existed. Early in the Renaissance, the Florentine artist Gioto (JAHT oh) used shadings of dark and light to add a feeling of space to his paintings. Later, the painter Tommaso Masaccio (mah SAHT choh) and Brunelleschi developed rules of perspective, enabling artists to paint scenes that appeared to be three dimensional. For example, to give a sense of depth or distance in a scene, figures closer to the viewer were drawn larger. Those further off were drawn smaller.

Artists in Flanders* made significant contributions to Renaissance art by improving paints. Medieval artists had worked with tempera paints. In tempera paints, the pigments, or colors, were mixed with watered-down egg yolk. Tempera paints dried quickly, so artists could not make changes

---

* Flanders included parts of what is today Belgium and the Netherlands. People from Flanders were called Flemish.

once they had applied the color. Further-more, tempera paints did not blend easily.

Flemish artists experimented with paints that had an oil base. The new oil paints dried more slowly and were easier to blend. Therefore, artists could create subtle new shades.

Great Italian Artists

During the opening decades of the 1500s, three artists dominated the world of Italian art: Leonardo da Vinci, Michelangelo, and Raphael Santi. Together with many other Renaissance artists, these artists have in-fluenced painting and sculpture until the present.

Leonardo da Vinci. Leonardo da Vinci achieved the Renaissance goal of doing many things and excelling in all. He was

Michelangelo's David symbolizes the spirit of the Renaissance, proud, fierce, and confident. The statue still stands in the heart of Florence. To the people of Florence, the Biblical hero David represented independence and liberty.

Leonardo da Vinci's Mona Lisa *is one of the most famous works of art in the world. Most people remember the haunting smile of the woman in this painting. The portrait is of Lisa della Giaconda, wife of a Florentine merchant.*

curious about everything. He continually ob-served the world around him and recorded his findings in dozens of notebooks. Because he was fascinated by flight, he observed birds on the wing. In his notebooks, he showed how he thought humans might use wings to fly. In order to understand the anat-omy of the human body, he dissected corpses. He then used his knowledge to paint more realistic figures.

Sadly, much of Leonardo's work has been lost. Only 15 of his paintings survive, in-cluding such masterpieces as the *Last Supper* and the *Mona Lisa*.

Michelangelo. Like Leonardo, Michelan-gelo had many talents. He considered him-self first and foremost a sculptor, but he was also an accomplished musician, poet, painter, and architect. Like other Renais-sance sculptors, Michelangelo carefully stud-ied the human figure. Yet Michelangelo's fig-ures do not exhibit the relaxed poses of other sculptures, such as Donatello's David. Instead, Michelangelo's statues of David and Moses convey a sense of tension.

In 1508, Pope Julius II asked Michelan-gelo to paint the ceiling of the Sistine Chapel in the Vatican, the pope's palace in Rome. Michelangelo devoted four years to the task. For hours each day, he lay on his back atop a high scaffold and painted scenes from the Bible, such as God creating the world, Noah and the flood, and Christ's crucifixion.

Raphael. Raphael Santi was a skillful painter whose work was influenced by both Leonardo and Michelangelo. Born in Umbria, Raphael favored the bright colors traditionally used by painters from that region of Italy. He often painted the Madonna, or mother of Jesus, and the infant Jesus. Unfortunately, Raphael's promising career was cut short by his death at age 37.

Artists of Northern Europe

In the 1400s and 1500s, northern European painters also created splendid masterpieces. Because ancient Roman ruins lay beyond the Alps, northern artists were less influenced by classical styles than their contemporaries in Italy. However, rules of perspective and the new oil-based paints did affect their work and marked a break with medieval painting.

Flanders was the artistic center of northern Europe. Flemish artists such as Jan van Eyck (van ĪK) were interested in painting the world realistically. To do this, van Eyck gave careful attention to detail. When he painted a satin robe, every fold was drawn exactly. Similarly, every jewel in a royal crown sparkled. Van Eyck's paintings often had a religious message. Each object had a symbolic meaning that reinforced the message of the painting.

Another Flemish painter, Pieter Bruegel (BROI guhl), found inspiration in everyday scenes of peasants working and in country landscapes. Although Bruegel showed the lives of common people in his paintings, he sometimes used symbolic figures, as van Eyck had, to express deeper meanings. Bruegel influenced later Flemish and Dutch painters, who painted scenes of daily life rather than religious or classical themes.

Many German artists painted realistic portraits. For example, Hans Holbein the Younger painted portraits of nobles and rulers, as well as of philosophers and com-

Northern Renaissance artists often painted realistic scenes of everyday life. This painting by Jan van Eyck shows the artist's friend Giovanni Arnolfini with his wife Jeanne Cenami. Many details of home life can be seen in the painting. Certain details have a symbolic meaning. The little dog is a symbol of faithfulness. The single lighted candle in the chandelier represents the presence of Christ. The writing above the mirror reads: "Jan van Eyck was here."

moners. Another German artist, Albrecht Dürer (DYOO ruhr), traveled to Italy to study the techniques of the Italian masters. Dürer helped spread their ideas across northern Europe.

Renaissance Writers

Like painting and sculpture, literature expressed the attitudes of the Renaissance. In towns and cities, the middle class formed a demanding new audience, especially for popular literature such as dramatic tales and comedies.

Popular literature was often written in the vernacular although many Renaissance writers continued to use Latin. (See page 175.) The Italian writer Petrarch, for example, felt comfortable writing in either Latin or Italian. His works included poetry and polished essays written in the form of letters. Petrarch perfected the sonnet, a 14-line poem that expresses a complete thought.

Another Italian writer, Giovanni Boccaccio (boh KAH chee OH), also contributed to Renaissance literature. Boccaccio's best known work is the *Decameron*, 100 stories told by seven men and three women who had fled from a plague in Florence. The *Decameron* was the first prose work written in Italian. Its clear narrative style served as a model for later writers.

The French writer Francois Rabelais (RAB uh LAY) fit the ideal of a Renaissance person. He began his career as a monk. Later, he studied the classics and trained in medicine. Rabelais exhibited immense curiosity, which he summed up in these words: "Abandon yourself to Nature's truths, and let nothing in this world be unknown to you."

Rabelais expressed his view of the world through two famous characters he created: the giant Gargantua (gahr GAN choo wuh) and his son Pantagruel (pan TAG roo WEHL). Gargantua wanted his son to study everything in the arts and sciences. He also advised Pantagruel to learn Arabic, Latin, Greek, and Hebrew. Rabelais' writing contained witty discussions of philosophy and politics.

Miguel de Cervantes (suhr VAN teez) was a leading Renaissance writer in Spain. An adventurer, Cervantes served in the Spanish army. He was captured by pirates and held as a slave in North Africa for five years. Later, he turned to writing.

In his novel *Don Quixote* (DAHN kee HOHT ee), Cervantes gently mocked the medieval ideals of chivalry. The hero, a knight named Don Quixote, believed so strongly in chivalry that he kept imagining himself in the middle of dangerous adventures. Sancho Panza, Don Quixote's servant, tried without success to convince the knight that the "castles" he saw were only lowly inns and the "jousting knights" were simply windmills.

Poet and playwright William Shakespeare is one of the finest writers in the English language. He wrote tragedies, comedies, and historical dramas, which were performed at the Globe Theater in London. In London, as in other European cities, both well-to-do and poorer people attended the theater. At the theater, they found entertainment, but they also learned about the ideas of their times.

A Call for Reform

Renaissance writers emphasized religious as well as worldly themes. In the early 1500s, some Christian scholars who had made a

"If anyone has not seen Erasmus, this portrait, drawn skillfully from life, gives his image." So wrote Hans Holbein the Younger, the German artist who painted this portrait of Erasmus. An influential Renaissance figure, Erasmus was called "the Scholar of Europe."

study of the Bible and early Christian writings urged reform of the Church. They wanted the Church to return to its early traditions based on the teachings of Jesus.

In northern Europe, the Dutch scholar and priest Desiderius Erasmus (ee RAZ muhs) led the Christian humanists. Erasmus knew Greek so he could study early copies of the New Testament, which were written in Greek. In *Praise of Folly* and other works, Erasmus used witty dialogues to point out the ignorance of some clergy. He also criticized the church for emphasizing pomp and ritual rather than the teachings of Jesus.

Despite his criticism of Church practices, Erasmus accepted its teachings. He remained in the Church even when other reformers rejected its authority and established their own churches.

A friend of Erasmus who shared his concerns was the English scholar and statesman Sir Thomas More. More thought that literature should serve Christian goals. In his book *Utopia*, More described an ideal society in which people lived at peace with one another.* He created an imaginary kingdom to show how such a society should be organized. Later writers used More's method to express their own ideas about society.

---

* Today, the word utopia is used to mean a perfect place or situation.

SECTION REVIEW

1. Identify: Donatello, Brunelleschi, Leonardo da Vinci, Michelangelo, Raphael, Jan van Eyck, Pieter Bruegel, Albrecht Dürer, Boccaccio, Rabelais, Cervantes, Shakespeare, Erasmus, Sir Thomas More.
2. How was Donatello's David different from medieval sculpture?
3. Describe two new techniques that affected Renaissance art.
4. (a) Why did Erasmus criticize the Church? (b) What did he think the Church should emphasize?

3 Changing Patterns of Life

Read to Learn
- how Renaissance technology advanced learning
- how society changed during the Renaissance

During the Renaissance, only a relatively few people were directly affected by the outpouring of creative genius in literature and the arts. The wealthy filled their palaces with artistic masterpieces. They also had the leisure time to read widely and expand their knowledge of the world. However, in later years, advances in technology gradually helped spread the new learning to a wider audience. As a result, Renaissance learning slowly filtered into the lives of ordinary people.

The Introduction of Printing

The invention of printing in the 1400s dramatically affected the production of books. Before this time, few books were reproduced because each one had to be copied by hand. A good copier could complete only about two books a year. Furthermore, books were costly because they were written on parchment made from the skin of a sheep or a goat.

Both problems were gradually overcome. In the 1300s, Europeans learned from the Arabs how to make paper from rag and wood pulp. The Arabs had learned about papermaking from the Chinese.

The technique of printing also grew out of earlier developments. In the 1300s, engravers experimented with printing books from wood blocks. They carved a page on the block, which was then inked and pressed on paper. By the 1400s, German engravers had developed movable type. Movable type consisted of tiny pieces of metal engraved with a letter. The pieces of metal could be combined to form words and then sentences. Also, the pieces of metal could be used again and again.

The final step in the development of printing was probably taken by Johann Gutenberg in Mainz, Germany. Gutenberg invented a metal alloy that could be used to make movable type. He developed a printing press that used this alloy. In 1455, he used his invention to print a complete edition of the Bible. With the Gutenberg Bible, as it was called, the era of printed books began.

Printing spread rapidly. By 1500, there were over 250 presses in Europe turning out books. As printing methods improved, the cost of producing books fell. Because prices were reasonable, people who could never have afforded hand-copied books now bought printed books.

The use of paper and the development of printing had a revolutionary impact on the world of learning. Books could be produced more quickly and less expensively than before. Ideas spread rapidly through the printed word. Many of the newly printed books were religious works such as the Bible and biographies of saints. Others dealt with subjects ranging from mining and medicine to philosophy and politics. The availability of books on the sciences and technology would greatly affect the Scientific Revolution, which you will read about in Chapter 19.

Everyday Life

For people in Renaissance Europe, life was much as it had been for their parents and grandparents. However, social and economic changes were slowly taking place.

In medieval Europe, most people lived in an extended family. On the manor, for example, the extended family was an important economic unit because many people were needed to work the land. During the Renaissance, the nuclear family gradually began to emerge, especially in the towns and cities. In a nuclear family, only parents and their children live in a household.

The impact of printing was enormous because books, especially the Bible, became more readily available. This picture shows different phases of early printing. At left, typesetters select pieces of movable type from trays. At right, a printer operates the press. The first printing presses were fairly simple machines adapted from wine presses.

The Flemish painter Pieter Brueghel was nicknamed "peasant Bruegel" because of paintings such as this Peasant Wedding. *This painting offers a realistic view of everyday life. The young peasant bride is seated against the dark background. How is this wedding scene different from the one on page 300?*

Another change affected the way businesses were run. Most businesses in the Middle Ages were small and were managed by a single family. During the Renaissance, some people formed business partnerships with people outside the family. Two or more families might pool their resources in order to expand business activities.

Some changes in agriculture and industry were the result of the continuing effects of the Black Death. (See page 197.) The Black Death had greatly reduced the population of Europe. Thus, the demand for wheat and other grains fell. Farmers began producing new types of food, which they hoped would be more profitable. The new foods included meat, fruit, and dairy prod-

ucts such as cheese and butter. As these products gradually became more plentiful, people's diets changed.

As a result of the Black Death, the demand for manufactured goods such as wool cloth also fell. In Florence, for example, half the population had died of the plague, and wool production dropped drastically. The demand for wool cloth increased when the population throughout Europe began to grow again. Wool workers then found their skills in much demand, and they asked for higher wages. When employers tried to keep wages low, the workers revolted. Although worker revolts were brutally suppressed, the wages of city workers did rise during the Renaissance.

At the height of the Renaissance, Isabella d'Este ruled over Mantua, one of the most brilliant courts in Italy. She so impressed her contemporaries with her knowledge, lively wit, and political skill that they called her "la prima donna del mondo"—"first lady of the world."

Isabella d'Este began life with many advantages. Her family, the Este, ruled Ferrara, a wealthy city-state in the Po River valley. At the time of Isabella's birth in 1474, the Este court sparkled as a center of Renaissance culture.

During the Renaissance, noble families like the Este often gave their daughters as well as their sons a thorough education. As a child, Isabella studied the humanities, including Latin and Greek. A fast learner, she astonished visitors when she quoted the verses of Virgil

from memory or translated the letters of Cicero.

Isabella also learned to sing, play the lute, dance, and embroider. With her lively intelligence and fine education, she was able to talk easily with the scholars and artists who visited her father's court. By the time she was married, at age 16, Isabella fit the Renaissance ideal of a cultivated individual with many skills and talents.

Isabella married Francesco Gonzaga, heir to the ruler of Mantua, a small but wealthy Italian city-state. In addition to being a wife and mother of nine children, Isabella devoted herself to Mantua.

The Italian city-states were nests of intrigue. Rivalries among the cities and the ambitions of French and Spanish kings caused frequent fighting. A skillful diplomat, Isabella helped her husband preserve the safety of Mantua. When the Venetians captured Francesco, Isabella ruled in his absence. Despite threats of invasion, she kept the people of Mantua calm and eventually secured her husband's release.

In Mantua, Isabella set the artistic fashions and standards of her day. Writers, artists, and poets gathered around her. She was a generous but demanding patron of the arts. She collected the finest paintings as well as marble and bronze statues, crystal, jewels, and clocks. Poets wrote songs in her honor, and books printed in Venice were sent to Mantua for her approval.

During her lifetime, Isabella wrote more than 2,000 letters, which show the wide range of her interests. In them, she commented on everything from art and politics to war and family matters. She knew the leading figures of the Renaissance, from Michelangelo and Leonardo da Vinci, who sketched this portrait of her, to the pope and the most powerful kings of Europe.

Women in the Renaissance

Women's occupations changed little during the Renaissance. Their main responsibilities remained in the home, where they raised the children and took care of the family. At sowing and harvesting time, farm women and children worked in the fields alongside the men.

However, women also worked outside the home. Some women were employed as servants in households of wealthy farmers, merchants, or nobles. Many women also earned money as spinners and weavers, although most workers in the cloth industry were men. Women in the merchant class helped manage family businesses. In addition, many farm and city women ran their own small businesses, selling handwork or garden produce at local markets.

A few women played central roles in governing city-states or nations. Queen Isabella of Spain, for example, was a forceful and effective ruler. (See page 195.) At different times during the Renaissance, queens ruled Naples, Scotland, and England. In France, Catherine de Medici, the widow of King Henry II, acted as regent* for her young sons until they were old enough to rule.

Some Renaissance scholars argued that women as well as men would benefit from

---

* A regent governs in place of a monarch who is too young or is otherwise unable to rule.

studying the classics. As the number of schools increased, more women learned to read and write. For example, Isabella d'Este received an excellent education that enabled her to translate Greek and Latin writings and take part in the learned discussions of her day.

SECTION REVIEW

1. Identify: Johann Gutenberg.
2. How did the introduction of printing affect the spread of ideas?
3. Describe one way in which the Black Death affected farming.
4. Give three examples of work some women did outside the home.

4 Beginnings of the Protestant Reformation

Read to Learn
- why the demand for Church reform grew
- what Martin Luther accomplished

During the Middle Ages, various reform movements had restored the vigor of the Roman Catholic Church. However, during the Renaissance, many pious Christians again clamored for reform. Unlike earlier reform efforts, which had strengthened the Church, these efforts shattered forever the medieval ideal of the unity of Christendom.

Need for Reform

In the 1300s and 1400s, many Christians lost confidence in the Church's ability to provide religious leadership. The Babylonian Captivity and the Great Schism had seriously hurt the power and prestige of the Church. (See page 199.) To many, the Church seemed overly concerned with worldly affairs. The pope and clergy tried to preserve Church privileges as powerful monarchs chipped away at its power. Rulers of France, Spain, and Germany often interfered in Italian affairs, forcing the pope into long, costly wars to protect the Papal States.

The worldliness of the Church was evident in the splendor of the papal court. For example, in 1506, Pope Julius II decided to rebuild St. Peter's Cathedral in Rome. He hired architects and artists such as Michelangelo to design and decorate the new church.

To finance such projects and pay for their wars, Renaissance popes increased the fees that Christians paid for baptism, marriage, and funerals. They also permitted the sale of indulgences. An *indulgence* was the reduction of the punishment a sinner would suffer in purgatory after death.

Indulgences were first granted during the Crusades, when the pope agreed to cancel penalties for any sins that a crusader committed. Eventually, popes granted indulgences not only for a specific service, but also for money contributions to the Church. By the 1500s, people could buy indulgences to cancel the punishments dead relatives might be suffering in purgatory.

Many faithful Christians protested such practices. They also objected to the worldliness of the Church. As you read in Chapter 12, reformers such as Wycliffe and Huss had gained many followers for their teachings, which emphasized the Bible and the simple lives led by early Christians.

In the 1490s, an outspoken monk, Girolamo Savonarola (SAV oh nuh ROH luh), preached reform in Florence. He attacked the Church and condemned immorality. He inspired his audiences to reject their worldly possessions. Eventually, Savonarola was executed for heresy. Elsewhere, Christian scholars such as Erasmus also urged reform. Their suggestions for reform were soon taken up by others who introduced revolutionary changes.

Luther's Challenge

In 1517, the written protests of a German monk, Martin Luther, sparked a reform movement that split the Roman Catholic Church. The son of a wealthy peasant, Martin Luther studied law. In 1505, during a summer storm, Luther was knocked to the ground by a bolt of lightning. "St. Anne, help me!" he cried out in terror. "I will become a monk."

True to his word, Luther entered a monastery and later taught Bible studies at the University of Wittenberg in Saxony. He tried to lead a holy life. However, he became convinced that good works such as fasting and prayer did not ensure salvation because a person could not buy God's favor. He believed that God would grant salvation regardless of whether or not a person did good works.

The 95 theses. Luther's beliefs led him to denounce the practice of granting indulgences. In 1517, the monk Johann Tetzel was actively selling indulgences near Luther's home at the University of Wittenberg. Tetzel was quoted as saying, "As soon as the coin in the coffer rings, the soul from purgatory springs." Tetzel was collecting huge sums of money to be sent to Rome.

Luther was outraged at Tetzel's activities. He posted 95 theses, or questions for debate, on the door of the Wittenberg castle church. In the 95 theses, he condemned the selling of indulgences. He argued that indulgences could neither release a soul from purgatory nor cancel a person's sins.

Within weeks after Luther's attack, his message had been printed and spread across Europe. Forced to defend his statements, Luther expanded his criticism of the Church. Soon he was denying Church authority in other matters. He claimed that the authority of the Bible and a person's own conscience outweighed the pope's authority.

Pope Leo X became alarmed at the activities of the "wild boar," as he called Luther. In 1520, he excommunicated Luther. The next year, the Holy Roman emperor Charles V questioned Luther before the Imperial Diet, or assembly, then meeting at Worms. Luther refused to withdraw his criticisms of the Church. Instead, he declared: "I cannot . . . go against my conscience. Here I stand. I cannot do otherwise. God help me." Luther's stand established him as the leader of reform-minded churches in the Holy Roman Empire.

Luther's teachings. Three ideas were at the core of Luther's reforms. First, he taught that individuals could not achieve salvation by their own efforts, such as by performing good works. A person's only hope of salvation was faith in God's mercy. The watchwords of Luther's teaching were "faith alone."

Second, Luther established the Bible as the only guide for Christians. He rejected many Church ceremonies as well as the authority of the pope because he said the Bible made no mention of them.

Finally, Luther emphasized the role of the individual. "The pope is no judge of matters pertaining to God's word and faith," he said. "But the Christian man must examine and judge for himself." He claimed that the individual did not need a priest to interpret the Bible. Like Wycliffe and Huss, he urged Christians to read the Bible themselves. Luther translated the Bible into the German vernacular and conducted services in German, instead of Latin, so that people could understand what was being said.

Luther also made other changes. For example, he simplified religious services and rituals. He allowed priests to marry because the Bible had not forbidden it. Such changes were adopted by the Lutheran churches organized by Luther's followers.

In 1521, Martin Luther was called before Charles V, the Holy Roman emperor, at the Diet of Worms. Luther, standing in the center of this picture, expected to be allowed to explain his views. Instead, the emperor asked him to renounce his heresy. When Luther refused, Charles V declared him an outlaw. Luther found refuge in Saxony, where he translated the New Testament into German in just 11 weeks.

Impact of Luther's Reforms

Luther's ideas won widespread support in Germany. Among the clergy, many sympathized with his criticism of Church abuses. In the towns, some people applauded Luther's reforms because they resented paying Church taxes, which were sent to Rome. Some townspeople echoed Luther's warning that any messenger from Rome seeking money "should receive a strict command either to keep his distance, or else to jump into the Rhine or the nearest river, and take ... a cold bath." Many town governments eagerly took over Church property, and they soon established independent churches.

Some German princes supported Luther and his followers. They wanted to assert their independence of the Holy Roman emperor. Like townspeople, princes seized Church lands and stopped the flow of Church taxes to Rome. When the emperor tried to force the German princes to remain loyal to the pope, they protested. They became known as Protestants. Later, the movement to reform the Church was called the Protestant Reformation.

Luther's reforms also appealed to the peasants, who bore a heavy burden of Church taxes. Peasants eagerly accepted the idea that the individual Christian was free to interpret the Bible. Moreover, they took the idea of freedom a step further and began to voice other complaints against the Church and noble landlords. In 1524, the Peasants' Revolt broke out in Germany. Peasants demanded the right to read the Bible and choose their own ministers. They also wanted to end serfdom and feudal rent payments, which were still required.

At first, Luther supported the peasants' demands. Later, he drew back in horror when he heard reports of peasants burning, looting, and killing. He bitterly criticized their actions and sided with the nobles, who stamped out the revolt. From this time on, Luther and his followers rejected political revolution. Many peasants felt betrayed by Luther and eventually returned to the Catholic Church. By Luther's death in 1546, about half the princes within the Holy Roman Empire had adopted the new Protestant faith.

In response to the success of the Protestants, the Holy Roman emperor Charles V launched a military campaign in 1547 to force the Lutheran princes back into the Catholic Church. When neither side could win the war, Charles accepted a compromise. In 1555, at the Diet of Augsburg, he agreed that each prince could choose whether his territory would be Catholic or Lutheran. By allowing individual rulers to determine the religion of a territory, the Peace of Augsburg officially recognized the split within Christendom.

By 1555, most princes in northern Germany were Lutheran, while most princes in southern Germany were Catholic. Lutheran ideas had also spread to Scandinavia. However, the Peace of Augsburg did not end the dispute between Catholics and Protestants. Other reformers were also winning followers across Europe.

SECTION REVIEW

1. Identify: Martin Luther, Johann Tetzel, Protestant Reformation, Peace of Augsburg.
2. Define: indulgence.
3. How was the Church affected by the actions of European monarchs?
4. (a) What Church practice did Luther attack in his 95 theses? (b) Describe two major teachings of Luther.
5. Give one reason why German princes supported Luther.

5 Further Challenges to the Catholic Church

Read to Learn
■ how Protestant ideas spread
■ how the Catholic Church countered Protestantism

From Germany, Protestant ideas spread to other parts of Europe as reformers challenged the authority of the pope. In England, King Henry VIII challenged the pope, not on questions of religious faith, but on more worldly matters. As new Protestant movements sprang to life, the Catholic Church took steps to stop them and to revive its spiritual leadership of the Christian world.

The Spread of Protestant Ideas

Switzerland emerged as a center of the Protestant Reformation. Ulrich Zwingli, a priest and admirer of Erasmus, taught in the Swiss city of Zurich during the same years that Luther was launching the Reformation in Germany. Like Luther, Zwingli had no use for elaborate church rituals. In his church, he abolished the Catholic Mass, confessions, and indulgences. He also allowed priests to marry.

Zwingli believed that a good pastor, or minister, and a strong sense of discipline among church members would help Christians lead a spiritual life. He held services in undecorated buildings and read sermons based on the Bible. By 1529, Zwingli's ideas had spread to many parts of Switzerland.

John Calvin. In the Swiss cities of Basel and Geneva, John Calvin led one of the best-organized Protestant movements. Born in France, Calvin studied law at the University of Paris before he decided to devote his life to religion. As part of his studies, Calvin read the works of Erasmus and Luther. In 1536, he published the *Institutes of the Christian Religion*, in which he outlined his beliefs in a clear, orderly way.

Like Luther, Calvin rejected the idea that good works would ensure salvation. However, Lutheran and Calvinist teachings differed in emphasis. Luther taught that people could work toward their own salvation through faith in God. Calvin stressed the all-powerfulness of God. God alone, Calvin said, decided whether an individual received eternal life.

Calvin believed in *predestination*, the idea that God had chosen who would be saved and who would be condemned. Calvin's critics warned that predestination would lead people to act irresponsibly. Why should individuals lead a good life, they asked, if God had already determined their fate? But Calvin answered that people should lead good lives in order to show that God had chosen them for salvation.

Calvin established a church with strong, disciplined leadership. Calvinists practiced the strict morality taught in the Old Testament. With the *Institutes* as a guide, the new faith spread rapidly.

Calvinists won many converts in commercial centers such as the Netherlands. There, as elsewhere, middle class townspeople were attracted to Calvinism because it reflected their belief that people should live simply and work hard. Moreover, Calvinism answered many people's criticisms of the Catholic Church. French Calvinists, called Huguenots (HYOO guh NAHTS), were powerful in southern France. During the 1550s, John Knox took the new faith to Scotland. Followers also established churches in England, where they eventually became known as Puritans.

Other Protestant groups. A number of Protestant sects sprang up all across Europe. Some clashed violently with each other and with Catholics. Each group saw itself as God's agent and viewed all others as the devil's workers. Many years would pass before Europeans accepted the idea that two or more religions could coexist.

Protestant sects developed their own beliefs based on reading and interpreting the Bible. For example, Anabaptists—later called Baptists—argued that infants could not be baptized as members of a church because they were too young to understand the Christian faith. They restricted baptism and church membership to adults. Anabaptists in Germany were vigorously persecuted by other Protestants and Catholics alike. Yet their ideas continued to influence Protestant thinking in many countries.

Henry VIII's Quarrel with Rome

Throughout his life, Henry VIII of England considered himself a faithful Catholic. In 1521, Henry published a stinging attack on the teachings of Martin Luther. The attack delighted the pope, who awarded Henry the title "Defender of the Faith." However, a few years later, the king was at odds with the Catholic Church over the issue of marriage.

After 18 years of marriage to Catherine of Aragon, Henry had no son to inherit the English throne. Catherine had given birth to many children, including several boys, but only one child, Mary Tudor, survived infancy. When Henry asked Pope Clement VII to grant him an annulment* so he could remarry, the pope refused. A strong-willed man, Henry would not accept defeat. Instead, he built up English sentiment against the pope.

Between 1529 and 1536, Henry took the English church from under the pope's control and placed it under the king's. In 1533, the Archbishop of Canterbury, Thomas Cranmer, annulled Henry's marriage to Catherine of Aragon. Henry then married Anne Boleyn. Parliament recognized the king as the supreme head of the Church of England by the Act of Supremacy of 1534.

English Protestants applauded the steps taken by the king and Parliament to break away from Rome. However, other English reformers, such as Sir Thomas More, wanted change to come from within the Catholic Church. Henry feared his opponents would disrupt the peace so he ordered the execution of More and others who would not accept the Act of Supremacy.

Before long, Henry took further steps against the Catholic Church. When he heard reports that many monasteries were corrupt, the king promptly closed them. About 10,000

---

*An annulment is an official statement declaring a marriage invalid.

English monks and nuns were forced to seek other homes. Because he needed money, the king then seized monastery lands, which he sold to nobles, wealthy farmers, and merchants. In the years ahead, those who bought monastery lands would resist any effort to restore land or power to the Catholic Church.

Despite the break with Rome, Henry did not want to change Catholic beliefs. In fact, Henry proclaimed that the Anglican Church, as the Church of England was called, would preserve traditional Catholic practices. However, he did allow priests to use an English translation of the Bible, and he permitted them to marry.

A Protestant Nation

Henry VIII died in 1547 after a turbulent life that included six marriages. After his death, the official religion of England swung back and forth between Protestant and Catholic. Henry's son, Edward VI, inherited the throne at age ten. During Edward's reign, Protestant bishops issued the *Book of Common Prayer*, which outlined the official rituals and prayers for the Anglican services. The *Book of Common Prayer* combined both Protestant and Catholic ideas.

When Edward died in 1553, Henry VIII's daughter, Mary Tudor, inherited the throne. Raised as a Catholic, Mary was determined to make England truly Catholic again. She persecuted Anglican bishops who would not accept the authority of the pope. Mary angered many subjects when she married Philip II, the Catholic king of Spain. When Mary died in 1558, her Protestant half-sister, Elizabeth I, became queen.

Queen Elizabeth adopted a skillful policy of religious compromise. She moved cautiously at first but gradually enforced reforms that she felt moderate Catholics and Protestants could accept. However, Elizabeth persecuted both Catholics and Protestants who opposed her policies. Elizabeth firmly established England as a Protestant nation. Yet she took England along a middle road and preserved many traditional Catholic beliefs.

Elizabeth I, Protestant Queen of England, did not personally feel strongly about religion. But she wanted to restore unity to a nation divided over religious questions. Therefore, Elizabeth I reaffirmed the role of the monarch as head of the Anglican church and completed the seizure of church lands that her father had begun.

The Catholic Reformation

During the Protestant Reformation, many loyal Catholics worked to revive the spiritual leadership of the Catholic Church. In addition, they fought against Protestants, who they regarded as heretics. The movement to reform the Catholic Church and fight Protestants became known as the Catholic Reformation. Some historians have also called it the "Counter Reformation."

Paul III, who was pope from 1534 to 1549, led the reform of the Catholic Church. Paul appointed able scholars and reformers to high church offices. He also summoned many officials to a church council at Trent to discuss reforms.

The Council of Trent was in session from 1545 to 1563. In response to Protestant attacks, the council reaffirmed traditional Catholic doctrines. The council also reformed church finances and administration and called for better training of priests. As a result of the Council of Trent, the Catholic Church ended many abuses that Luther and other Protestant reformers had criticized. Catholic rulers in Spain, France, and Italy strongly supported the reforms.

New religious orders helped strengthen the Catholic Church. In Spain, Ignatius of Loyola formed the Society of Jesus, a group of dedicated missionaries. As a young knight, Loyola had been wounded in battle. While recovering from the injury, he spent hours reading about the saints and thinking about religious questions. Loyola then wrote *Spiritual Exercises*, a manual that taught strict religious discipline.

In 1540, Pope Paul III officially recognized the Society of Jesus. The Jesuits, as Loyola's followers were called, swore absolute obedience to the pope. They traveled to the new lands that Europeans were exploring and won many converts. In addition,

they brought many Protestants in Germany and Eastern Europe back into the Catholic Church.

The Catholic Church also took other steps to stop the spread of Protestant ideas. For example, it revived the Inquisition. As you read earlier, the Inquisition was the church court that had tried to root out heresies during the Middle Ages. The Inquisition was most active in Spain, Portugal, and Italy. In addition, the Catholic Church published the *Index*, a list of forbidden books. By limiting what books Catholics could read, the church hoped to prevent the spread of the Protestant ideas.

After the Catholic Reformation, Protestants made few new gains. By 1600, the lines between Catholic and Protestant areas in Europe were sharply drawn. They have remained largely unchanged to the present. Lutherans, Calvinists, and other Protestant sects flourished in England, Scotland, Scandinavia, and northern Germany. Under

Map Skill   *The Protestant Reformation shattered the unity of Christendom, as you can see on this map. Anglicans, Lutherans, and Calvinists, as well as other Protestant groups, such as the Anabaptists, established churches. Which parts of Europe were most affected by the Protestant Reformation?*

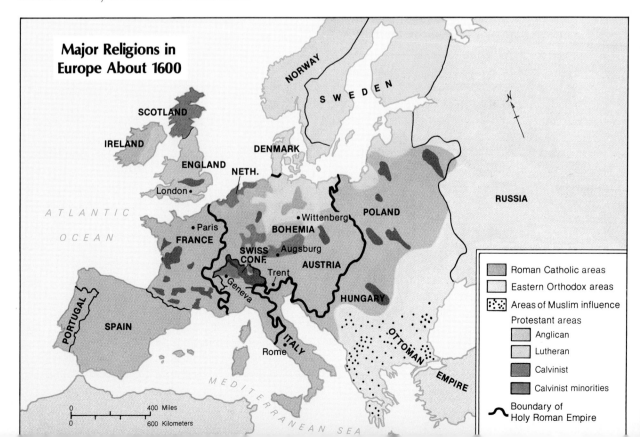

the banner of the Council of Trent, Catholics remained strong in Italy, France, Spain, and southern Germany. (See the map on page 317.) These religious divisions contributed to bitter wars, as you will read in Chapter 18.

SECTION REVIEW

1. Identify: Ulrich Zwingli, John Calvin, Huguenot, John Knox, Anabaptist, *Book of Common Prayer*, Ignatius Loyola, Jesuits, *Index*.
2. Define: predestination.
3. (a) Why did Calvin believe people should lead good lives? (b) To what parts of Europe did Calvinism spread?
4. (a) Why did Henry VIII of England quarrel with the pope? (b) What religious policy did Elizabeth I follow?
5. Describe one action of the Council of Trent.
6. (a) By 1600, what parts of Europe were mainly Protestant? (b) What areas remained mainly Catholic?

Chapter 16 Review

In Perspective

In the 1300s, the Renaissance spirit emerged among the wealthy city-states of northern Italy and spread slowly to other parts of Europe. Renaissance scholars studied the classics in order to expand their knowledge of the world.

During the Renaissance, the arts flourished. Leonardo da Vinci and Michelangelo added new dimensions to painting and sculpture. In northern Europe, some painters emphasized realism by painting scenes of peasant life. Renaissance writers produced many outstanding works. The invention of the printing press helped spread new ideas.

Many scholars studied the writings of early Church leaders. They called on the pope and clergy to reform the Church. By the 1500s, reformers such as Martin Luther and John Calvin had begun to reject the authority of the pope and establish their own churches. The Catholic Church eventually launched a counterattack against Protestant groups and reformed itself. However, Europe remained divided between Protestants and Catholics.

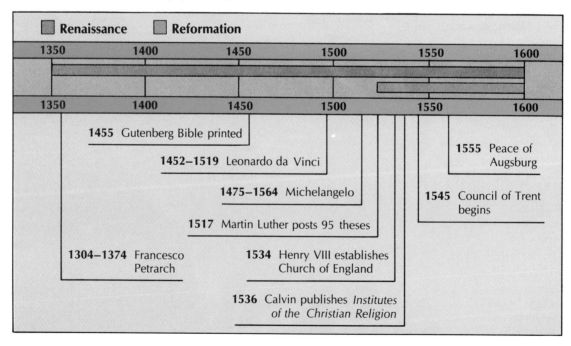

Renaissance	Reformation					
1350	1400	1450	1500	1550	1600	

| 1350 | 1400 | 1450 | 1500 | 1550 | 1600 |

1455 Gutenberg Bible printed

1452–1519 Leonardo da Vinci

1555 Peace of Augsburg

1475–1564 Michelangelo

1545 Council of Trent begins

1517 Martin Luther posts 95 theses

1304–1374 Francesco Petrarch

1534 Henry VIII establishes Church of England

1536 Calvin publishes *Institutes of the Christian Religion*

Recalling Facts

Match each name at left with the correct description at right.

1. Niccolò Machiavelli
2. William Shakespeare
3. Ignatius Loyola
4. John Calvin
5. Leonardo da Vinci
6. Johann Gutenberg
7. Pieter Bruegel
8. Michelangelo
9. Miguel de Cervantes
10. Lorenzo de' Medici

a. author of *Don Quixote*
b. founder of the Society of Jesus
c. inventor of a movable type
d. English poet and playwright
e. ruler of Florence and patron of the arts
f. Protestant reformer who believed in predestination
g. author of *The Prince*, a handbook for rulers
h. northern European painter of peasant life
i. artist who painted the *Mona Lisa*
j. artist who painted the Sistine Chapel

Chapter Checkup

1. (a) Why did the Renaissance begin in Italy? (b) How did the Medici influence the Renaissance in Florence?

2. (a) What were the main interests of Renaissance scholars? (b) How did the work of Petrarch influence Renaissance scholars?

3. Describe the contributions Renaissance artists made in each of the following areas: (a) sculpture; (b) architecture; (c) painting.

4. (a) What were Luther's main teachings? (b) How did Calvinist beliefs differ from Lutheran beliefs? (c) How was the Protestant Reformation in England accomplished?

5. (a) What reforms did the Catholic Church introduce in the mid-1500s? (b) What methods did the Catholic Church use to fight the Protestants? (c) What evidence indicates that the Catholic Reformation succeeded?

Critical Thinking

1. **Synthesizing** After a visit to Italy in the early 1500s, a scholar from northern Europe exclaimed: "Immortal God, what a day I see dawning!" What do you think the scholar might have seen or heard that could have led to this remark?

2. **Analyzing** The Renaissance is often considered a time when people were mostly concerned with worldly matters. Yet the Reformation occurred during the Renaissance. How do you think the Renaissance spirit encouraged the Reformation? Explain.

Relating Past to Present

1. Today, someone who is knowledgeable in many areas is called a "Renaissance person." (a) What ideas might a "Renaissance person" today have in common with a Renaissance figure such as Leonardo da Vinci? (b) How might their ideas differ?

Developing Basic Skills

1. **Using Visual Evidence** Study the painting on page 305. Then answer the following questions: (a) What is shown in the painting? (b) How does the painting reflect Renaissance ideas?

2. **Researching** Choose one of the men or women who wrote, painted, or ruled during the Renaissance. Research the person's background in order to answer the following questions: (a) Where was the person born and raised? (b) What were the person's main contributions to the Renaissance? (c) Do you think he or she fit Castiglione's ideal of a Renaissance person?

3. **Ranking** Review the causes of the Protestant Reformation. Then rank them according to their importance in causing a split within the Christian world. Explain your ranking.

See page 805 for suggested readings.

17 Exploration and Expansion

(1450–1750)

Departure of Columbus in 1492 on his voyage in search of a western route to Asia.

In August 1519, five ships sailed out of Seville harbor in Spain. Crowds on the shore watched as guns thundered a salute to the departing sailors. On board the ships, the 268 sailors under the command of Ferdinand Magellan had great hopes for the expedition. They expected to discover a route around South America that would lead them to the East Indies, the center of the rich spice trade.

Among Magellan's crew was a Venetian noble, Antonio Pigafetta. He kept a journal in which he recorded both the successes and the incredible hardships of the long voyage. By November 1520, the ships had battled through the stormy straits at the southern tip of South America. Late that month, Magellan and his crew became the first Europeans to sail into the Pacific Ocean.

Pigafetta described the voyage across the Pacific in these words: "We remained 3 months and 20 days without taking on any food or other refreshments. We ate only old biscuit reduced to powder and full of grubs . . . and we drank water that was yellow and stinking." In desperation, the sailors cooked pieces of leather that "were so hard they required being soaked four or five days in the sea. After this, we boiled them to eat."

Many sailors died from disease. Wrote Pigafetta, "Had not God and His blessed mother given us so good weather, we would have died of hunger in that exceeding vast sea . . . I believe no such voyage will ever be made again." After 80 days in the Pacific, Magellan finally reached land, the island of Guam. But he did not live to complete the voyage. In the Philippine Islands, he quarrelled with local peoples and was killed in a battle. However, in 1522, Pigafetta and 17 surviving sailors returned to Spain. They were the first Europeans to sail around the world.

Magellan's voyage symbolizes the many daring exploits of sailors during the Renaissance. While scholars were rediscovering the classics and artists were experimenting with new techniques, other individuals were exploring lands beyond the world then known to Europeans.

The period from about 1450 to 1750 has been called the "Age of Exploration." In the 1400s, Portuguese and Spanish sailors led the way across the oceans of the world. Soon, England, France, the Netherlands, and Sweden outfitted ships for voyages of exploration. The voyages were important for several reasons. First, Europeans learned how to use the oceans as highways. Second, they discovered a vast continent in the Western Hemisphere. Third, the discovery of new ocean routes and new lands resulted in a race to establish profitable trading empires in Asia and the Americas. Finally, increased trade altered the economic life of Europe.

1 Voyages of Exploration

Read to Learn
- how technology contributed to exploration
- why Portugal and Spain led in exploration

In the 1300s, the busy commerce of the Italian city-states depended largely on trade with other European cities. Merchant ships plied the Mediterranean and Atlantic coasts. During the 1400s, however, this situation changed. Two European nations, Portugal and Spain, began searching for new trade routes. As a result, they sponsored many voyages of discovery.

Expanding Horizons in Europe

Advances in technology helped make the European voyages of exploration possible. Using travelers' reports such as those of Marco Polo and information from Arab geographers, mapmakers drew more accurate land and sea maps. On charts of the oceans, they began to include lines of *latitude*, which showed distance north and south of the equator. Mapmakers also showed the direction of ocean currents.

Navigators developed better ways to chart courses at sea. Sailors could calculate the ship's latitude using the *astrolabe*, an instrument that measured the positions of stars. They had no instruments to measure

Navigators used astrolabes like the one shown here to find their latitude at sea. However, in rough seas errors of hundreds of miles were common.

With the development of better instruments, maps became more accurate, and navigators could confidently chart courses across thousands of miles of ocean. In this picture, a geographer prepares a map. Notice the lodestone floating in a vessel of water in the foreground. The magnetized lodestone was an early form of compass.

longitude, the distance east or west of a certain point, but they could estimate longitude. Europeans improved the magnetic compass, a Chinese invention that the Arabs had acquired and passed on to Europe in the 1200s. With it, sailors could determine their location even when they were out of sight of land.

Shipbuilders designed sailing vessels that were suited to ocean voyages. For example, the Portuguese developed the three-masted caravel. The caravel could carry more sail than earlier ships, and it had more space for cargo and food supplies. Europeans also used the lateen, or triangular sail, borrowed from the Arabs. The lateen sail and another improvement, the stern rudder, allowed ships to sail closely into the wind.

Building and outfitting of ocean-going ships was an expensive undertaking. Although Italian city-states such as Venice and Genoa organized some early voyages, individual city-states lacked the resources for large undertakings. Therefore, emerging national monarchies sponsored the great expeditions of the 1400s and 1500s. Through exploration, monarchs hoped to increase trade and build empires.

Individual Europeans had several reasons for participating in the voyages of exploration. Some people were curious about the unknown. Others sought adventure and wealth. Devout Christians wished to carry their faith to other peoples. Often, several such motives sent people into unexplored waters.

Portuguese Explorations

Portugal led the way in the voyages of exploration. The Portuguese had been at a disadvantage in trade with Asia because Portugal faced the Atlantic Ocean rather than the Mediterranean Sea. Most spices and other goods from India and China were brought overland by Arab merchants to ports in the eastern Mediterranean. From there, Italian ships carried goods across the Mediterranean to Europe.

During the 1400s, Portugal was ruled by several practical, ambitious monarchs who wanted to increase their nation's wealth. They supported voyages in search of gold. They also saw that the only way to gain a share in the rich spice trade was to bypass the Italian and Muslim traders who controlled the Mediterranean markets.

Early voyages. Prince Henry, known as Prince Henry the Navigator, encouraged the early Portuguese explorations. Henry, who lived from 1394 to 1460, established an informal school for sailors at Sagres on the southern tip of Portugal. There, he brought together astronomers, geographers, and mathematicians to share their learning with Portuguese sea captains and pilots.

At first, the Portuguese tried to open new trade routes by conquering coastal cities in North Africa. But the Sahara caravans that had brought gold to North Africa from the West African kingdoms no longer operated.* The Portuguese then decided to seek the source of gold itself, and they began to explore the west coast of Africa.

The sea route along the African coast had been unpopular because ocean currents and winds off Cape Bojador (boh huh DOHR) often drove ships onto the rocky coast and wrecked them. To avoid this, the Portuguese charted a new route. They sailed west, where they discovered two groups of islands in the Atlantic—Madeira and the Azores. From these islands, they picked up favorable winds and currents that carried them safely south along the African coast.

---

* As you read in Chapter 14, gold from West Africa had been exchanged for salt from the Sahara. Much of this gold eventually reached Europe, where it was made into the gold coins that were used in the Middle Ages.

As the Portuguese moved south, they searched for gold wherever African rivers ran into the Atlantic. However, they could not travel far inland along the rivers because of waterfalls and rapids. (See page 225.)

The Portuguese established trading stations along the African coast. Portuguese traders bought gold and ivory from people living nearby. In fact, the area became known to Europeans as the "Gold Coast." In 1441, traders also began buying slaves. As you will read in Chapter 27, the slave trade expanded over the next few centuries and ruined many African kingdoms.

Rounding the Cape of Good Hope. After Prince Henry's death in 1460, Portuguese exploration lagged. In 1481, an energetic ruler, King John II, launched new efforts. John dreamed of a rich trading empire in Asia. He knew he had to find an all-water route around Africa that would allow Portugal to trade directly with India and China. The king urged Portuguese sea captains to explore farther and farther south along the African coast.

In 1488, Bartholomeu Dias rounded the southern tip of Africa. Dias named it the Cape of Storms because his ship had been buffeted so violently there. But John II renamed it the Cape of Good Hope because he realized Dias had found the passage around Africa to India.

King John then decided to send an expedition to India. In July 1497, after much preparation, Vasco da Gama set out from Portugal with four ships. Da Gama quickly rounded the Cape of Good Hope and visited the cities along the East African coast. At one port, he picked up an Arab pilot who helped the Portuguese sail on to India. Da Gama reached the Indian port of Calicut in May 1498. His voyage took Portugal a step closer to realizing King John's vision of a trading empire in Asia.

A Westward Voyage

Spain watched the success of neighboring Portugal with envy. In the 1400s, you will recall, Christian monarchs in Spain devoted their energies to conquering the last Muslim stronghold of Granada. When Ferdinand and Isabella completed this task in 1492, they were ready to pursue other goals.

Like Portugal, Spain wanted to share in the profitable spice trade of Asia. Even more important to the pious Queen Isabella was the hope of forming an alliance with rulers in India and China against the Muslims. She believed Christopher Columbus, a capable sea captain from Genoa, might help Spain achieve those goals.

For years, Columbus had tried to convince first Portugal, and then Spain, to spon-

sor a voyage to Asia westward across the Atlantic. Columbus believed that by sailing westward, a ship could reach Asia within two months.

In the 1400s, people held conflicting views about the size of the earth. Some people, such as Columbus, based their estimates on the work of Ptolemy. However, Ptolemy had underestimated the size of the earth. Scholars at the University of Salamanca in Spain had calculated correctly that the earth was much larger. They argued that it would take four months to reach Asia, and

Map Skill   *During the Age of Exploration, a few daring sailors charted the oceans of the world. Which European nations were chiefly involved in exploration? Why were monarchs willing to support such risky ventures?*

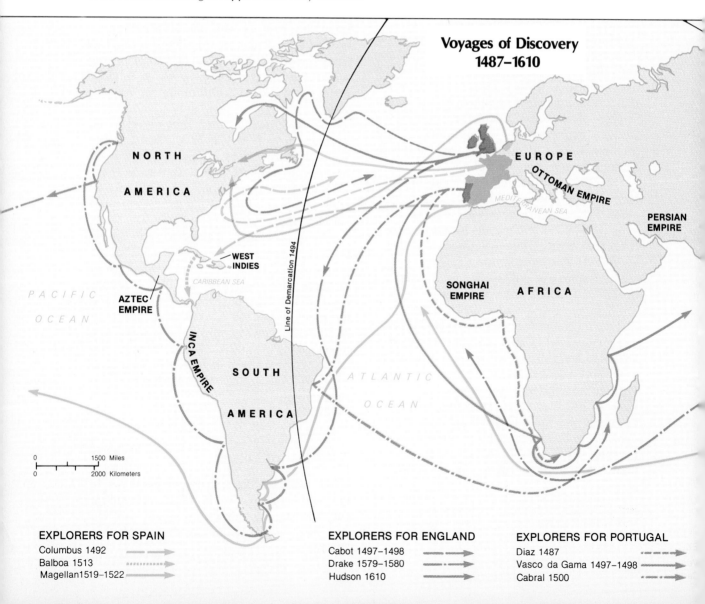

Voyages of Discovery 1487–1610

EXPLORERS FOR SPAIN
Columbus 1492
Balboa 1513
Magellan 1519–1522

EXPLORERS FOR ENGLAND
Cabot 1497–1498
Drake 1579–1580
Hudson 1610

EXPLORERS FOR PORTUGAL
Diaz 1487
Vasco da Gama 1497–1498
Cabral 1500

ships could not store enough food and fresh water for the trip. What neither the scholars nor Columbus knew was that a continent lay just where a two-month supply of food would run out.

Queen Isabella accepted Columbus' argument and agreed to sponsor his voyage. On August 3, 1492, three small ships carrying 90 sailors left Palos, Spain. Despite good sailing westward, the crews grew anxious as provisions ran low and they had still not sighted land. Finally, on October 12, they were rewarded with their first sight of land.

Convinced that he had reached the East Indies, Columbus called the local people "Indians" and happily accepted the gold objects they gave him. In fact, Columbus had reached a group of islands later called the West Indies.

In three more voyages, Columbus explored the Caribbean islands of Cuba and Hispaniola, present-day Haiti and the Dominican Republic. He claimed the new lands for Spain and established settlements. Columbus did not realize that he had not reached the East Indies, but his explorations opened the way for the Spanish to colonize a vast new continent.

The Treaty of Tordesillas

Columbus' voyages fueled the rivalry between Spain and Portugal. John II of Portugal rejected Spanish claims to the Caribbean islands. Each country disputed the right of the other to explore the new lands. To keep peace, the pope arranged a settlement.

After long negotiations, Spain and Portugal signed the Treaty of Tordesillas (tor day SEE yahs) in 1494. The treaty drew a Line of Demarcation that ran north and south about 1,100 miles (1,770 kilometers) west of the Azores Islands in the Atlantic. The treaty gave all newly discovered lands west of the line to Spain. Portugal received the right to colonize and trade with any lands that lay east of the line.*

The treaty gave Spain the right to claim most of North and South America, although no one realized the extent of these lands. In 1500, the Portuguese explorer Pedro Cabral was blown off course during a storm. He landed in Brazil. Because Brazil lay east of the Line of Demarcation, Portugal claimed this part of South America.

A Continent in the Path to India

Further voyages revealed that Columbus had not reached the East Indies but had discovered a huge continent. Amerigo Vespucci (ah

ASIA

MING EMPIRE

MOGUL EMPIRE

Line of Demarcation 1494

PACIFIC OCEAN

INDIAN OCEAN

EAST INDIES

AUSTRALIA

EXPLORERS FOR FRANCE

Verrazano 1524

Cartier 1534–1536

EXPLORERS FOR THE NETHERLANDS

Hudson 1609

---

* The Line of Demarcation was eventually extended around the globe. (See the map at left.) Thus, the Portuguese claimed trading rights in India, China, and the East Indies.

may REE goh veh SPOO chee), an Italian who represented the Medici bank in Spain, undertook several voyages for Spain. He charted the coastline of Central America and described the continent as the "Mundus Novus," a Latin phrase meaning "New World." In 1507, a German mapmaker labeled the continent America in recognition of Amerigo Vespucci.

Spanish explorers soon fanned out across the Caribbean Sea. Their discoveries became the basis for a Spanish empire in the Americas. In 1513, Juan Ponce de León set out to find the legendary fountain of youth, whose waters supposedly made people young. Ponce de León never found the fountain, but he did discover Florida.

That same year, Vasco de Balboa pushed through the steaming jungles of Central America and sighted a vast body of water. Balboa named it the South Sea, thinking it lay to the south of Asia. In fact, he had discovered the Pacific Ocean.

Six years later, a Spanish sailing expedition led by Ferdinand Magellan entered the vast Pacific Ocean. As you read at the beginning of the chapter, Magellan set out in 1519 to find a western sea route to Asia. He sailed south along the coast of South America and into the Pacific through the narrow straits that still bear his name.

In 1578, the English sea captain Sir Francis Drake rounded the tip of South America. He raided Spanish settlements on the west coast. Then he continued around the world, returning to England in 1580.

Seeking a Northwest Passage

Spain and Portugal were the first nations to sail across the Atlantic, but other nations soon followed. The Treaty of Tordesillas excluded the claims of these nations to new lands, but England, the Dutch Netherlands, and France ignored the treaty. During the 1500s and early 1600s, these countries sent explorers to chart the coast of North America. Because the southern passage around Cape Horn was so difficult to navigate, they hoped to find a northwest passage to India.

In 1497, John Cabot, an Italian sea captain, agreed to sail for England. In two voyages, he explored the coast of North America from what is today Delaware to Newfoundland. English exploration then lagged until 1576, when Martin Frobisher searched for a northwest passage. Frobisher reached the Hudson Strait, returning home with a cargo of what he claimed was gold ore. The ore proved to be worthless, however, and the English temporarily gave up the search for a northern sea route to Asia.

In 1524, France financed a voyage by the Italian explorer Giovanni da Verrazano (VEHR rah TSAH noh). He explored the coast of North America from what is today the Carolinas to Nova Scotia. A few years later, Jacques Cartier (kahr tee YAY) sailed up the broad St. Lawrence River, hoping it would lead to the Pacific. Although he heard many tales of gold, Cartier found neither gold nor a sea route to India.

Like the Portuguese, the Dutch were sailing around Africa to reach Asia. But they also hired an English sailor, Henry Hudson, to look for a passage through the Americas. In 1609, Hudson explored the river that bears his name. He sailed as far north as Albany, New York, but realized it was not a route to India.

Although these explorers did not find a northern passage to Asia, they added greatly to European knowledge of the world. Furthermore, their voyages led to settlement of new lands, and this would have far-reaching consequences.

SECTION REVIEW

1. Locate: East Indies, West Indies, Line of Demarcation.

2. Identify: Prince Henry the Navigator, Bartholomeu Dias, Christopher Columbus, Treaty of Tordesillas, Amerigo Vespucci, Ferdinand Magellan.

3. Define: latitude, astrolabe, longitude.

4. List three technical advances that helped make the voyages of exploration possible.

5. (a) Why were the discoveries of Ponce de León and Balboa important to Spain? (b) What did Magellan set out to find?

6. (a) What countries sent explorers to seek a northwest passage to Asia? (b) What areas were explored as a result?

2 Profitable Trade with the East

Read to Learn ■ how Portugal built a trading empire
■ how Europeans competed for Asian trade

After Vasco da Gama's voyage around the southern tip of Africa, the Portuguese moved quickly to build trade with Asia. They could now avoid Arab and Italian middlemen and buy spices directly. Therefore, they could sell spices at a quarter of the earlier price and still make a good profit. Soon, they dominated the spice trade in Europe.

The Portuguese Trading Empire

When da Gama reached India, local rulers asked him why he had come. His reply was "Christians and spices." Christian missionaries accompanied Portuguese traders wherever they established trading posts. But the traders were mainly interested in spices, which Europeans used to preserve meat. Portuguese ships carried cargoes of pepper from India, cinnamon from Ceylon, and cloves and nutmeg from the East Indies.

Arab merchants, who had traded in India for centuries, resisted the Portuguese efforts to win trading privileges from local Hindu and Muslim princes. Because the Arab traders were Muslims, the Portuguese saw the competition for control of the spice trade as a Christian crusade. They burned Arab ships and wharves, ransacked the Muslim cities of East Africa, and tortured prisoners.

In 1509, the Portuguese appointed Affonso de Albuquerque (AHL boo KEHR kuh) governor of their trading posts. Over the next six years, Albuquerque pursued a ruthless policy that created the basis of a Portuguese trading empire. From his headquarters at Goa on the west coast of India, he seized key points along the trade routes. For example, he captured Ormuz at the entrance of the Persian Gulf, which gave Portugal control of the Indian Ocean.

Most important, Albuquerque seized the narrow Strait of Malacca, the gateway to the Moluccas, which Europeans called the Spice Islands. By controlling the Strait of Malacca, Portugal hoped to prevent other Europeans from gaining a foothold in the East Indies.

Fierce Competition

By the late 1500s, Portugal faced stiff competition for the spice trade from France, England, and the Netherlands. The northern European countries knew that by conquering or bypassing a few key ports, they could break Portuguese control of the spice trade.

The Dutch acted first. In 1595, they sent a fleet to explore the East Indies. Seven years later, they formed the Dutch East India Company, which financed many trading expeditions. The Dutch were as ruthless as the Portuguese in gaining their ends. They attacked Portuguese ships and raided Portuguese trading stations. During the 1600s, the Dutch replaced the Portuguese as the dominant power in the spice trade. (See the map on page 328.)

England and France also equipped trading expeditions to Asia. Because the Dutch position was so strong in the East Indies, English and French merchants concentrated on India. The English and French established small outposts along the southern coasts of India. They were able to win trading privileges in these areas in part because the Mogul Empire in India was weak in the south. In addition, some Hindu princes made alliances with Europeans against their Muslim rulers.

Trade with China and Japan

The first Portuguese traders met Chinese merchants at Malacca. Tempted by Chinese silks, satins, and porcelain, the Portuguese sailed east into Chinese waters. As you read in Chapter 15, the Ming Chinese permitted

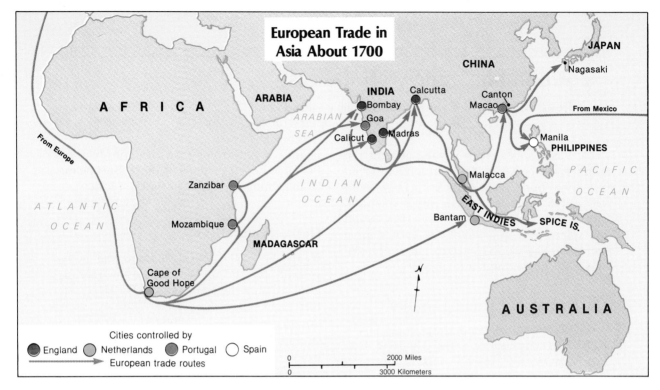

European Trade in Asia About 1700

Map Skill *European nations competed for control of the rich spice trade of the east. Although the Portuguese were first to reach India, the Dutch, English, and Spanish soon followed, as this map shows. Which nation held the Strait of Malacca? Why was this strait important?*

only limited trade. By 1535, the Portuguese had to confine their trading activities in China to Macao. Other Europeans were restricted to Canton.

In 1542, a storm blew a Portuguese ship off course. The battered vessel found refuge in the Japanese islands, and a new source of trade was opened. At first, the Japanese welcomed trade with Portugal. Soon, Spanish vessels also visited Japan. They sailed west from the Americas, carrying potatoes, watermelons, and pumpkins.

Despite the growing trade, both the Chinese and Japanese regarded Europeans as barbarians. Aside from guns, Europeans had few goods they wanted. Furthermore, the Chinese and Japanese distrusted Europeans. They heard stories about the Portuguese and Dutch seizing land in the East Indies.

The activities of Jesuit missionaries also strained relations. At first, the Chinese and Japanese tolerated Christians. Later, however, Chinese and Japanese rulers suspected that the Christian missionaries were allies of the foreign traders who were taking land at gunpoint.

In Japan, Protestant merchants from England and the Netherlands encouraged the shogun's suspicion of Portuguese and Spanish Catholics. However, their interference did them little good. As you read in Chapter 15, by 1639, the Japanese had decided to expel all foreigners. Only the Dutch were allowed to send one ship a year to trade at the port of Nagasaki.

SECTION REVIEW

1. Locate: Goa, Malacca, Spice Islands, Macao, Canton, Nagasaki.

2. Identify: Affonso de Albuquerque.

3. (a) What were the main products Europeans wanted from Asia? (b) What nations competed for trading rights in Asia?

4. (a) What attitude did the rulers of China and Japan have toward European traders? (b) What policy did China and Japan eventually follow toward foreigners?

3 Spanish and Portuguese Colonies in the Americas

Read to Learn ■ what Spanish goals were in the Americas
■ how the Spanish empire developed

In the 1500s and 1600s, Europeans set up a few scattered trading outposts in Asia. But Asian rulers often dictated the terms of trade and limited the movements of Europeans. In the Americas, however, Europeans established colonies, settlements that they ruled. The Spanish and Portuguese were the first Europeans to carve out colonial empires in the Americas during the early 1500s.

Conquests in the Americas

By the Treaty of Tordesillas, Spain claimed the right to most of the New World. Spanish explorers, hearing of wealthy kingdoms in the Americas, set out on new expeditions.

Instead of financing expeditions directly, Spanish rulers granted *conquistadores* (kohn KEES tah DOH rehs), or conquerors, the right to establish outposts in America. In exchange, conquistadores agreed to give the crown one fifth of any treasure they discovered. Thus, the Spanish rulers launched expeditions at little risk or cost to themselves. If a conquistador failed, he lost his own fortune. If he succeeded, both he and Spain won fame and riches.

The conquistadores were successors to the crusading knights who had fought the Muslims in Spain. When Ferdinand and Isabella completed the Reconquista in 1492, many knights looked for other ventures, in the Americas. One conquistador summed up his reasons for going to the Americas in these words: "We came here to serve God and the king, and also to get rich."

Cortés. In 1519, the conquistador Hernando Cortés, a shrewd fighter and skillful diplomat, landed on the coast of Mexico in search of gold. He soon heard about the powerful Aztec Empire, which demanded heavy tribute from peoples it conquered. Cortés made alliances with various Indian tribes who hated their Aztec rulers. He then marched his small army of 400 soldiers and 16 horses into the crowded Aztec capital of Tenochtitlán. There, he began to negotiate with the Aztec ruler, Montezuma.

After a tense game of diplomacy that lasted for months, Montezuma finally agreed to become a subject of the Spanish king. In 1520, the Aztecs revolted against the Spanish. Corteés and his army barely escaped with their lives. However, with the help of his allies, in 1521 Cortés surrounded and destroyed Tenochtitlán. Within a few years, the Aztec Empire crumbled.

Pizarro. Nine years later, the conquistador Francisco Pizarro and 180 Spanish soldiers landed on the Pacific coast of South America. Pizarro learned that the Inca were in the midst of a civil war. Taking advantage of divisions among the Inca, Pizarro captured their ruler Atahualpa and executed

This picture drawn by an Aztec artist records a meeting between Cortés and the emperor Montezuma, seated at left. Standing behind Cortés is Doña Marina, a Native American who acted as translator. Donã Marina knew several Indian languages as well as Spanish. She helped Cortés negotiate alliances with peoples who opposed Aztec rule, and she kept track of Aztec spies.

many Inca officials. The Inca were accustomed to obeying commands from their rulers. Without this leadership, they were unable to fight effectively. By 1535, Pizarro controlled most of the huge Inca Empire, including the rich capital of Cuzco.

Within 15 years, the two most powerful empires in the Americas had fallen to the conquistadores. Historians have suggested a number of reasons why Cortés and Pizarro, with the help of a few Spanish soldiers, were able to conquer the Aztec and Inca. For one thing, the Spanish had better weapons. They used guns and cannons, which were unknown in the Americas. Furthermore, the Aztec and Inca had never seen horses before they saw Spanish soldiers riding them. Some were terrified by the animals. Some believed that the conquistadores riding the horses were gods.

Disease also played an important role in the Spanish victories. Native Americans had no immunity to many diseases carried by Europeans. Epidemics of smallpox, chicken pox, and measles destroyed entire villages. The death of so many people did much to weaken Aztec and Inca resistance. Finally, many Indian tribes hated their Aztec and Inca rulers, and these tribes helped the Spanish conquistadores.

Organizing the Spanish Empire

Once the conquistadores had overthrown the Native American empires, Spain stepped in to rule the new lands. Spanish rulers set up a strong, centralized government in the Americas just as they had done at home. As a result, their empire in the Americas would last for nearly 300 years.

The new lands were divided into five provinces. The wealthiest and most important provinces were New Spain, or Mexico, and Peru. The Spanish king appointed a viceroy as his representative in each province. The viceroy enforced royal policy in the New World. The king also established a Council of the Indies. The council met in Spain and made laws for the colonies.

In theory, the viceroys and the Council of the Indies worked together to rule the em-

pire. In practice, they were often at odds. Because the viceroy lived in his province, he was often in a better position to make decisions. But the Council of the Indies wanted to preserve the king's power in the New World, and it regulated even the most minor matters. It made laws, for instance, about how long a city block must be and in which direction village streets should run. Between 1524 and 1630, the Council issued over 400,000 orders.

Spain also supervised local governments in the Americas. In each town or city, the king appointed members of the *cabildo* (cah BEEL doh), or city council. The cabildo had extensive powers, which it used to preserve order and spread Spanish civilization. Local governments supervised the building of towns and cities. By the 1550s, Mexico City, the capital of New Spain, had a public water system, paved and lighted streets, printing presses, and its own university.

Spanish Policy Toward Native Americans

In the early 1500s, conquistadores, settlers, and Christian missionaries flocked to the Spanish colonies. The Spanish government granted settlers *encomiendas* (ehn koh mee EHN dahs), the rights to demand taxes or labor from Indians living on the land. In theory, the encomienda protected the Indians' land rights. In practice, it developed into a system of forced labor, which bound Indians to the land.

The discovery of rich silver deposits in Peru and Mexico resulted in further mistreatment of the Indian population. The Spanish used forced Indian labor to work the mines. Mining involved exhausting, dangerous work in deep shafts. Cave-ins killed many Indian miners. Others died from malnutrition, overwork, and disease.

Spanish missionaries condemned the cruel treatment of the Indians. One outspoken critic was the Dominican priest Bartolomé de Las Casas (lahs KAH sahs). He described the abuses he saw in the New World to the authorities in Madrid and pleaded for strict laws to protect the Indians.

As you learned in Chapter 12, statistics can provide valuable information about a historical event or development. (See page 198.) Historians often use graphs to present statistics visually. Graphs can be used to show data about such things as population, trade, and government expenses.

Three kinds of graphs are frequently used: line graphs, bar graphs, and circle graphs. Line graphs and bar graphs can illustrate changes that take place over a period of time. They are often used to show large numbers in the thousands or millions. In a circle graph, a circle is divided into parts. The graph shows how each part relates to the whole circle.

The following steps will help you read the graphs in this book. Use these steps to answer the questions about the line graph that follows.

1. **Identify the type of information shown on the graph.** The title of the graph and the labels on the vertical axis and horizontal axis will tell you the subject of the graph. Study the line graph and answer the following questions: (a) What is the title of the graph? (b) What do the numbers on the vertical axis show? (c) What do the numbers on the horizontal axis show?

2. **Practice reading the data shown on the graph.** Use the following questions to practice reading this line graph: (a) What was the approximate Native American population of central Mexico in 1520? (b) What was the approximate population of this area in 1540? (c) About how much did the population decline between 1520 and 1600? (d) During what period did the population decline the most?

3. **Use the information shown on the graph to draw conclusions about an event or development.** Answer the following questions using information from the line graph and your reading in this chapter: (a) In your own words, describe what happened to the Native American population of central Mexico between 1520 and 1600. (b) What factors help explain the population change? (c) Why do you think so many Indians died at the beginning of this period? (d) Do you think other areas such as the West Indies and Peru experienced a similar population decline? Why? (e) What effect do you think the population decline might have had on the Indian cultures of the Americas?

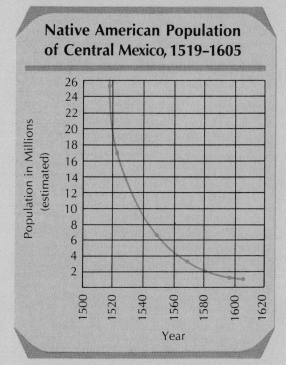

Native American Population of Central Mexico, 1519–1605

Source: Nicolas Sanchez-Albornoz, *The Population of Latin America*.

The Spanish government took its responsibility toward the Indians seriously. It believed the Spanish had a duty to convert the Indians to Christianity. Furthermore, it looked on Indians as loyal subjects. In answer to Las Casas' plea, the government passed the New Laws of 1542. The New Laws forbade making Indians slaves and gave Indians the right to own cattle and raise crops. Although the laws were not always enforced, the Spanish government did try to correct the worst abuses.

The Plantation System

Some settlers in the Americas made fortunes by exporting crops and raw materials to Spain. From Central and South America, they sent gold and silver, as well as cacao, coffee, and lumber. In the West Indies, tobacco and sugar cane were the main exports. Sugar cane became enormously profitable because it could be refined into sugar, molasses, and rum.

To profit from sugar, settlers in the West Indies developed the plantation system. A *plantation* was a large estate operated by the owner or an overseer and farmed by workers living on it. Many laborers were needed to grow and harvest a sugar crop. At first, the Spanish used Indians to work their plantations. But in the West Indies, as elsewhere in the Americas, cruel labor practices and European diseases killed off the local population.

In his effort to help the Indians, Bartolomé de Las Casas had suggested that the Spanish replace Indian workers with slaves from Africa. He thought that Africans were better able to withstand hard labor in the hot climate. Although Las Casas later regretted his misguided advice, Spain began importing thousands of Africans to the West Indies.

The Slave Trade

As you read, Portuguese sailors explored the west coast of Africa in the 1400s. Along with gold, they took a few black slaves back to Europe. In the 1500s, both Spain and Portugal brought ever increasing numbers of African slaves to their colonies in the Americas. European traders bought men, women, and children from Africans along the coast.

The newly enslaved Africans suffered brutal hardships on the Middle Passage, as the voyage across the Atlantic was called. Chained together and packed below the ship's deck, they had no room to move. Some captains took so many slaves on board that their ships could carry very little food and fresh water. When the decks above were sealed, the heat below caused many captives to die of suffocation. During the two-month voyage, many more died from disease or as a result of attempted revolts.

Those who survived the Middle Passage were sold to plantation owners. On sugar plantations in the West Indies, African slaves worked long hours. During the harvest of sugar crops, for example, they worked through the night.

As profits from sugar, molasses, and rum increased, the slave trade increased. By the late 1500s, the plantation system and slavery were an essential part of the economy of Spanish and Portuguese colonies. The products of the plantations of the West Indies along with the gold and silver of the New World made Spain the richest, most powerful nation in Europe.

A Portuguese Empire in Brazil

The Portuguese established their own system of settlement in Brazil. The king appointed a captain general to oversee the entire colony. He then gave loyal subjects large parcels of

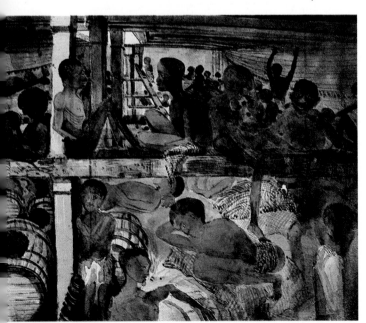

Slave ships brought millions of Africans to the Americas in chains. Captains packed as many men, women, and children as they could carry into the holds of their ships. This painting by a British naval officer is the only existing picture painted from life of the inhuman conditions aboard slave ships.

land. The *donatario*, or land owner, governed the territory he received. He enlisted settlers to farm or trade on his land.

By 1580, Brazil was a thriving colony. Like the Spanish in the West Indies, the Portuguese in Brazil imported thousands of slaves to work on sugar plantations. In the late 1600s, the Portuguese discovered deposits of diamonds and emeralds. Thousands of new settlers streamed to the colony.

In the 1500s, both Spain and Portugal established colonial empires in the Americas. They looked on their colonies as resources to be exploited. In the 1600s, other European nations would rush to establish colonies, hoping to win a share of the riches.

SECTION REVIEW

1. Identify: Hernando Cortés, Francisco Pizarro, Council of the Indies, Bartolomé de Las Casas, Middle Passage.
2. Define: conquistador, cabildo, encomienda, plantation, donatario.
3. What three motives brought the conquistadores to the Americas?
4. List two reasons the Spanish were able to defeat the Aztec and Inca empires with so few soldiers.
5. How did the New Laws of 1542 protect the Indians?
6. Why did Spain begin bringing slaves to the Americas?

4 Dividing Up North America

Read to Learn
- what French interests were in North America
- about English goals in North America

For almost 100 years, Spain and Portugal were the only European powers with colonies in the Americas. Political troubles and religious wars in Europe distracted other nations. However, during the 1500s, Dutch, French, and English sea captains raided Spanish treasure ships sailing from the Caribbean to Spain. They also intruded on Spanish and Portuguese trade in the Caribbean and seized islands in the West Indies.

In the 1600s, the Netherlands, France, and England began to explore and settle North America, where neither Spain nor Portugal had a strong foothold.

The First European Settlements

Spanish conquistadores undertook the earliest explorations in North America. In the 1520s and 1530s, they led expeditions into the southern part of the continent, searching for gold. But explorers hunted in vain for the seven cities of gold described by Indian legend.

During the same period, Spanish captains explored as far north as present-day California, charting the Pacific coast of North America. Wherever the Spanish explored, they claimed the lands for Spain. A few Christian missionaries set up churches in North America, and some settlers filtered into the new territories, but Spain paid more attention to its colonies to the south. The West Indies, Mexico, and South America provided the silver, gold, and sugar that made Spain wealthy.

In the late 1500s, the Dutch made the Netherlands into a powerful commercial nation. The Dutch fought a long war to win independence from Spain. (See page 344.) Then they outfitted trading expeditions to challenge Portugal in the East Indies. They also organized the Dutch West India Company to investigate trade opportunities in the New World.

By the early 1600s, the Dutch were establishing settlements along the Hudson River as far north as present-day Albany, New York. Peter Minuit (MIHN yoo wiht) became the first governor of New Netherland, as the Dutch colony was called. In 1626, Minuit bought Manhattan Island from local Indians for cloth and beads. About 200 Dutch settlers built a village on the island, which they named New Amsterdam.

In order to attract more people to New Netherland, Minuit granted large estates to *patroons*, or wealthy landowners. The patroons then brought over farmers and other laborers to work as tenants on their estates. Patroons ruled their land like feudal lords. They had their own law courts and settled all local disputes.

When the Dutch West India Company criticized Minuit for allowing the patroons to exercise too much power, Minuit left New Netherland. At the request of the Swedish government, he then helped Swedish settlers found a colony on the Delaware River, near what is today Wilmington, Delaware. The Dutch resented the nearby Swedish settlement. During the 1640s and 1650s, Dutch and Swedish colonists raided each other's villages. Finally, in 1655, the Dutch seized the Swedish colony, adding it to New Netherland.

French Fishing and Fur Trading

To the north of the Dutch and Swedish colonies, the French explored along the St. Lawrence River and built settlements in what is today Canada. Since the early 1500s, French fishing vessels had sailed regularly to the waters off Newfoundland to catch cod. After Cartier explored the St. Lawrence in 1535, the French discovered that furs bought from the Indians sold in Europe for big profits.

Distracted by political and religious turmoil at home, French monarchs took little interest in North America and did little to encourage settlement. For example, many Huguenots, French Protestants, wanted to move to Canada to escape persecution at home. But the French government forbade them to settle in New France, as the French colony was called. As a result, the population remained small.

However, a group of traders obtained exclusive rights to the fur trade. In 1608, the group sent Samuel de Champlain (sham PLAYN) to establish a permanent settlement in Quebec. From Quebec, the French moved into other parts of Canada, where they built trading posts to collect furs gathered by Indian and French trappers. By 1665, French traders had reached Lake Superior. They set up a string of forts across the Great Lakes and along the St. Lawrence to protect the fur trade. Missionaries joined the fur traders on the long, difficult journeys by canoe and on foot. They sought to gain converts among the Indian peoples of North America.

In the late 1600s, the French king Louis XIV took more interest in North America. Louis limited the privileges of the fur trading companies and appointed his own governor, the Comte de Frontenac (FRAHN tuh nak), to rule New France.

Frontenac strongly supported new explorations that helped spread French influence across North America. In 1673, Louis Joliet, a fur trader, and Jacques Marquette, a Jesuit priest, mapped a route from Lake Michigan down the Wisconsin River into the Mississippi River. Like other explorers, Marquette and Joliet sought precious metals as well as a water passage to the Pacific Ocean. When they realized that the Mississippi flowed into the Gulf of Mexico and not into the Pacific Ocean, they returned north.

In 1682, another French explorer, Robert Cavelier, Sieur de la Salle, reached the mouth of the Mississippi. He claimed the lands for France and named the region Louisiana after Louis XIV. (See the map on page 335.)

The English Colonies

During the 1600s, the English settled in North America from Newfoundland and Nova Scotia south to what is today Georgia. The English eventually founded 13 colonies. Some colonies, such as Massachusetts and Virginia, were established by trading companies that received charters from the English government. Others were *proprietary colonies*—that is, they were owned by individuals, usually friends of the king.

Each English colony had an elected assembly that passed local laws. The English government appointed a royal governor in each colony to carry out its policies. Although a governor was responsible to Parliament, he also needed the cooperation of the colonial assembly. For example, the assembly had to approve the governor's salary and consent to laws he issued. Thus, the colonists had some control over their own affairs.

Unlike the French government, the English government encouraged people to settle in its New World colonies. Between 1630 and about 1700, the population of the English colonies grew from 900 to 200,000. Eventually, the English colonies would have greater influence on events in North America than the Spanish, Dutch, or French.

People crossed the Atlantic to the English colonies for many reasons. Some sought religious freedom. For example, the Puritans, who were persecuted in England for their strict Calvinist beliefs, founded the colonies of Massachusetts, Rhode Island, and Connecticut. The Quakers, another group seeking religious freedom, settled in Pennsylvania. English Catholics led by Lord Baltimore emigrated to Maryland. In addition to seeking religious freedom, many settlers hoped to improve their economic and social positions. In the colonies, they had the opportunity to become independent farmers, merchants, fur traders, and artisans.

Small farms dominated the northern and middle colonies as well as parts of the south. However, in Virginia, the Carolinas, and Georgia, a plantation system developed. Like Spanish settlers in the West Indies, large landowners in the southern colonies imported African slaves to work on their tobacco and rice plantations.

French traders had lived in relative peace with the Indians. In the English colonies, however, the large numbers of settlers soon displaced the Indian population. Settlers sometimes signed treaties with the Indians to purchase land. Just as often, however, they moved onto Indian lands without a treaty. Determined to protect their way of life, Indians attacked and destroyed many English frontier settlements. The English fought back with equal determination. The fierce competition for land would continue until the 1800s.

European Rivalries

During the 1600s, Spain, France, the Netherlands, and England competed for land in North America. As the colonies of each nation grew, they clashed over rival land

Map Skill *In the 1500s and 1600s, Europeans planted settlements across America. By 1700, the English colonies were well established on the eastern seaboard of North America. Which areas were claimed by Spain? Which countries were rivals in North America? Which countries claimed territory in South America?*

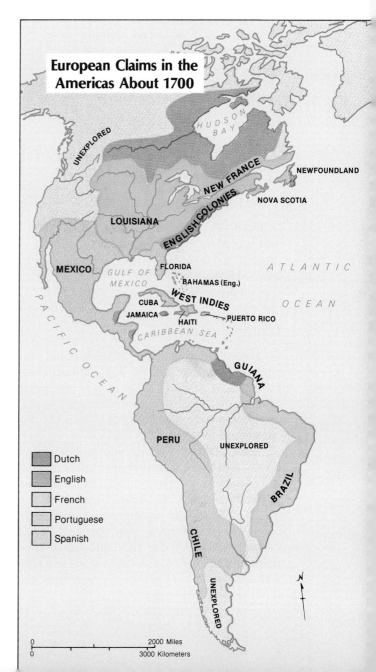

European Claims in the Americas About 1700

claims. In the 1700s, wars fought in Europe affected relations among the colonies.

During these struggles, some European powers sought help from Native Americans. Because the French were interested in the fur trade, they formed an alliance with the Algonquin, their chief trading partner. At the same time, the Dutch formed an alliance with the Iroquois. Fighting between the French and Dutch led to clashes between the two Indian nations.

In 1664, England ousted the Dutch from New Netherland and renamed the colony New York. During the next 100 years, the chief rivals in eastern North America were England and France. Although Spain still held Florida, it could not expand north because of the English in Georgia and the French in Louisiana. Throughout the 1700s, England and France battled for control of Canada and the lands west of the Appalachian Mountains. As you will read in Chapter 18, this conflict was part of a larger struggle fought on battlefields in Europe and India.

SECTION REVIEW

1. Locate: Newfoundland, New France, Louisiana, English colonies.
2. Identify: Peter Minuit, Samuel de Champlain, Louis Joliet, Jacques Marquette.
3. Define: patroon, proprietary colonies.
4. Why did Spain show little interest in its northern territory?
5. What was the economic basis of New France?
6. What motives led people to move to the English colonies?
7. Which two nations were the main rivals in North America in the 1700s?

5 The Commercial Revolution

Read to Learn
■ why the commercial revolution began
■ how mercantilism developed

In the 1500s and 1600s, European explorers and traders opened up vast new worlds. Expansion overseas helped bring about a commercial revolution that transformed European economic life.

Economic Recovery

As you read in Chapter 12, the economic growth of the late Middle Ages ended when the Black Death wiped out almost one third of the population of Western Europe. As the population grew in the 1400s, however, the economy began to revive.

The demand for clothing and food increased. More workers were needed to produce cloth, and many people moved from the countryside to the cities to work in the textile industries. Growing city populations needed food, so farm workers became highly valued. To keep them from moving to the cities, landowners had to pay more to farm workers and permit some to rent land on more favorable terms.

As the economy recovered, merchants again carried manufactured goods between cities by road and sea. Some merchants carried goods to the countryside, where they bought grain to sell in the cities. Other merchants operated on an international scale. For example, they bought raw wool in sheep-grazing countries such as Spain and England and sold it to cloth manufacturers in the Netherlands and Italy. Finally, they purchased the finished cloth to sell to the Spanish and English.

During the Renaissance, growing trade increased the importance of merchants. Some merchants became so wealthy that they lived like princes. Powerful merchants such as the Medici of Florence dominated the politics of their cities.

The Entrepreneur

The hope of high profits lured many merchants into overseas ventures. They imported spices, sugar, silks, and other valuable cargoes. However, overseas trade was both risky and expensive. A merchant had to outfit a ship and hire a crew for a long, dangerous voyage. The merchant also had to buy large quantities of goods before knowing what prices their customers in Europe would pay.

Merchants who were willing to take such risks in the hope of high profits were known as *entrepreneurs*. They expanded commerce by pursuing trade opportunities around the world. In doing so, they slowly turned the economy of Europe from a local system into a complex national and international system.

Entrepreneurs developed new ways of doing business to reduce financial risks. Both land and sea commerce were dangerous. Merchants faced highway robbers, pirates, floods, and shipwreck. The loss of a single shipment could bankrupt a merchant. To cover losses, entrepreneurs developed a system of insurance. For a small payment, a merchant would insure his shipment. If the goods arrived safely, the merchant lost only the small insurance payment and still made a good profit. If the shipment was destroyed or lost, the merchant collected most of its value from the insurers.

Another way to reduce business risks was to spread the risk among more people. Italian entrepreneurs often formed partnerships with two or three others so that if the shipment was lost, they would share the loss.

Entrepreneurs further reduced risks by investing their money in several different types of business. A wool manufacturer, for example, might also buy and sell grain, own buildings in the city, and invest in several partnerships. If one type of investment suffered because of bad weather, a shipwreck, or a poor market, the others were likely to provide a steady income.

Financing New Ventures

Merchants needed *capital,* or large sums of money, to invest in businesses and trading ventures. Monarchs in Spain, Portugal, and France also needed capital to pay for wars and finance overseas exploration. Increasingly, both merchants and monarchs turned

Gold and silver brought from the Americas enabled Europeans to make and use more coins. Nations, individual cities, nobles, and bishops minted their own coins. Money changers like the couple shown here charged a fee for exchanging coins. They assessed the metal content of the different coins to determine their values. Some money changers became bankers, making loans for interest. The banking business grew during the commercial revolution.

to a few extremely wealthy merchant families who became the bankers of Europe. The Medici bank in Florence, for example, made loans to entrepreneurs and monarchs in Spain, England, and Germany.

In the late 1300s, Johann Fugger (FOO ger) founded another influential banking firm in Germany. Like the Medici, Fugger was a merchant before he became a banker. In the 1370s, Fugger began importing cotton from Egypt to make fustian, a cloth superior to the linens and wools most Europeans wore. Soon Fugger branched out into other activities, such as importing spices and silks. With the fortune he made in commerce, Fugger became a banker and lent money for interest to other merchants. By the 1500s, the Fugger family was one of the richest in Europe.

Merchants also developed the joint stock company to finance new ventures. A *joint-stock company* was a private trading company that sold shares to investors. If a

337

small partnership could not raise enough capital, a group of merchants would pool their resources to form a trading company. They then sold shares of stock in the company to other investors. Once a joint-stock company raised enough capital, it outfitted a voyage. If the ships returned with their cargo safe, each investor received a share of the profits. Investors also shared any loss if the ship went down.

A European monarch sometimes granted a charter to a trading company. A charter gave the company the exclusive right to trade in a particular area. The Dutch East India Company was formed in this fashion. In the late 1500s, several joint-stock companies sent fleets to the East Indies. The competition was so fierce among them that it threatened to disrupt the spice trade. As a result, in 1602, the Dutch government gave the Dutch East India Company exclusive trading rights in the East Indies.

The Dutch East India Company had wide powers. It could negotiate treaties, enlist soldiers, and wage war on enemies of the Netherlands. Princes, nobles, and merchants eagerly invested in the company. Stockholders could hope to recover as much as 30 times their investment on a single successful voyage.

The Search for Gold and Silver

Increased commercial activity created a need for a larger money supply. The more people bought and sold, the more money they needed to carry on their business. Europeans did not use paper money. Instead, money consisted of gold, silver, and copper coins. But Europe had limited gold and silver resources. As a result, when business increased, there was a shortage of money.

The situation worsened when Europeans began buying costly spices and silks in Asia. Asian merchants insisted on payment in gold and silver, so these metals were being taken out of circulation in Europe. As you read, the search for gold had led Prince Henry the Navigator to explore the coast of Africa. He hoped to find the source of the gold that had formerly been carried across the Sahara from West Africa.

The need for gold had also driven the Spanish, Dutch, French, and English to explore new lands. The Spanish were the most successful. They found valuable gold and silver deposits in Mexico and Peru. The Spanish minted coins and used their new wealth to become the most powerful country in Europe in the sixteenth century.

Mercantilism

European monarchs recognized that their political power rested on economic strength. During the 1500s, they believed that the key to economic strength was precious metals. They reasoned that a nation should collect and keep as much gold and silver as possible. However, it was not possible for a nation to merely hoard gold. In Spain, for example, gold from the New World was used to buy goods such as cannons, guns, timber, and silk. Because Spain imported more goods than it exported, its gold treasure rapidly disappeared into the hands of other nations. Thus, European rulers came to see that trade was as important as gold.

In the 1600s, a new economic philosophy called *mercantilism* developed. According to mercantilist ideas, a nation's economic strength depended on keeping and increasing its gold supplies by exporting more goods than it imported.

Mercantilists stressed that there was more profit to be made in selling manufactured goods than in selling raw materials. For example, the person who sold shirts made from woven wool cloth made a greater profit than the sheep farmer who produced the wool in the first place. So mercantilists encouraged nations to manufacture finished goods for export.

Furthermore, mercantilists thought rulers should regulate trade and commerce to make a nation self-sufficient. They also said rulers should support industries such as shipbuilding since new ships were needed to carry the increased trade.

Colonies fit into the mercantilist theory because colonies could supply raw materials to the industries of the country. The colonies could also serve as markets for manufactured goods from the parent country.

Changing Patterns

The expansion of trade and mercantilist practices helped cause a commercial revolution that affected ways of doing business at every level of society. For example, the guilds declined in importance in part because they regulated production too tightly. Therefore, they could not meet the needs of a growing population.

Instead of relying on guilds, entrepreneurs developed a system of having work done in the countryside. The arrangement, known as the *domestic system*, bypassed guild regulations. Entrepreneurs provided farm women and men with raw wool. The peasants earned money by spinning the wool or weaving the cloth in their own cottages.

Some new industries required large amounts of money from the start. For example, the printing industry expanded rapidly in the 1500s and 1600s. But to set up shop, a printer had to buy expensive equipment, including a printing press, paper, and movable type. A printer would, therefore, turn to *capitalists*, or individuals with money to invest in business to make a profit. Capitalists financed many new industries, especially mining and shipbuilding, which were popular with mercantilists.

Another development was the great wealth acquired by the upper classes during this period. Nobles, merchants, and bankers made fortunes from investments in joint stock companies and other ventures. They built huge palaces and decorated them with the finest works of art. They dressed in silks from China and exotic furs from Canada. They also developed a taste for the new foods of the East Indies and the Americas.

The Age of Exploration and growth of commerce changed the way Europeans saw the world. Most Europeans thought their way of life was superior to the civilizations they were encountering in Asia, Africa, and the Americas. Yet they sometimes adopted ideas and customs of other civilizations. Two centuries of expansion made Europeans confident and optimistic. They believed the world was meant to be explored, conquered,

---

Economics and History ■ New Foods for the European Table

During their voyages of exploration, Europeans encountered many new foods, which eventually became part of their everyday diets. Cinnamon and black pepper imported from the East Indies allowed Europeans to add zesty flavors to their foods. From the Americas, explorers brought home new plants such as corn, potatoes, tomatoes, and several kinds of beans. New foods from the Americas, including chocolate, made from cacao beans, affected European customs and eating habits.

In 1502, Columbus carried the first cacao beans to Spain from the Caribbean. But it was not until 1519 that the conquistadores tasted a drink that the Aztec made from cacao beans. The Aztec called this drink xocoatl (CHOH koh ahtl), meaning "bitter water." Europeans called it chocolate.

From the Aztec, the Spanish learned to make chocolate. The Aztec dried, shelled, and roasted cacao beans. They then ground the beans into a paste, which they cooked over a fire. After adding vanilla and spices to the paste, they divided it into small cakes. To make the chocolate drink, they combined the paste with water and shook the mixture vigorously. The chocolate drink delighted the Spaniards, although they preferred to sweeten the bitter taste by adding sugar.

For nearly 100 years, Spain controlled the production and consumption of chocolate. It tried to protect its monopoly over this new food. However, by the early 1600s, the recipe for chocolate had reached Italy and Flanders.

Chocolate became immensely popular wherever it was introduced. People claimed great health benefits from it. As one observer noted, people downed the drink "in one swallow with admirable pleasure and satisfaction." He added that "it gives strength, nourishment, and vigor."

In the late 1600s, enterprising business people opened chocolate houses. In London and Paris, people lingered over a cup of hot chocolate while they discussed the news of the day. Drinking hot chocolate became a fashionable pastime. However, chocolate candy was not manufactured until the 1800s.

and civilized by them. For better or worse, Europe had outgrown the narrow boundaries of the Middle Ages.

SECTION REVIEW

1. Define: entrepreneur, capital, joint-stock company, mercantilism, domestic system, capitalist.
2. What led to economic recovery in the 1400s?
3. (a) What risks did entrepeneurs face? (b) Describe one way in which they reduced these risks.
4. Why did the Dutch government give the Dutch East India Company exclusive trading rights in the East Indies?
5. How did growing trade with Asia lead to a shortage of gold and silver in Europe?
6. What economic role did mercantilists think colonies should play?
7. Why did guilds become less important?

Chapter 17 Review

In Perspective

In the 1400s and 1500s, Europeans explored many parts of the world. The Portuguese led the way by sailing around Africa to India. Later, Columbus sailed west, hoping to find another route to India. Instead, his voyages led to exploration of the Americas. The Portuguese profited from the Asian trade. Other European nations wanted a share, but the Chinese and Japanese restricted foreign trade.

In the Americas, Europeans staked out huge empires. Spanish conquistadores captured the Aztec and Inca empires, and Spanish settlers established colonies. In the 1600s, the French developed a profitable fur trade in Canada. English settlers founded colonies along the eastern seacoast.

The expansion of overseas trade contributed to a commercial revolution in Europe. Entrepreneurs developed new ways of doing business. The growing economic strength of European rulers would have a far-reaching impact.

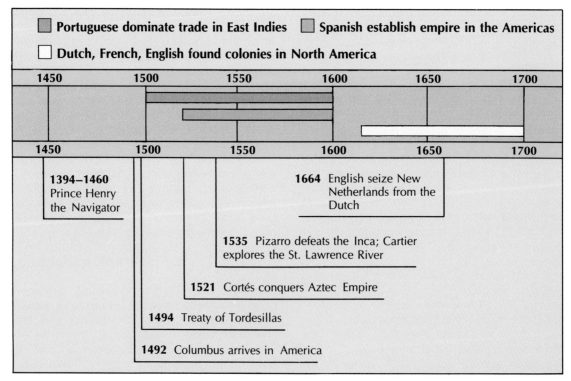

■ **Portuguese dominate trade in East Indies**   ■ **Spanish establish empire in the Americas**

□ **Dutch, French, English found colonies in North America**

| 1450 | 1500 | 1550 | 1600 | 1650 | 1700 |

1394–1460 Prince Henry the Navigator

1664 English seize New Netherlands from the Dutch

1535 Pizarro defeats the Inca; Cartier explores the St. Lawrence River

1521 Cortés conquers Aztec Empire

1494 Treaty of Tordesillas

1492 Columbus arrives in America

Recalling Facts

Decide if the following statements are true or false. If a statement is false, rewrite the statement to make it true.

1. The astrolabe was a three-masted ship that could sail on long voyages.

2. The first European nation to explore the coast of West Africa was Portugal.

3. Columbus believed he had reached the East Indies when he landed in the Americas.

4. The Council of the Indies was the Aztec ruling assembly.

5. Las Casas believed Spain should pass laws to protect Indians.

6. Each English colony had its own elected assembly.

7. The commercial revolution benefited the merchant class.

Chapter Checkup

1. (a) Why did Portugal take the lead in exploring a sea route to Asia? (b) Why did Spain want to find a route to Asia? (c) Why did other countries seek a northwest passage?

2. (a) How did the Portuguese establish a trading empire in Asia? (b) Why were the Portuguese unable to hold on to their empire?

3. (a) How did Spain organize its empire in the Americas? (b) What policy did the Spanish government take toward Indians?

4. (a) Why did the Spanish and Portuguese develop the plantation system? (b) How did they supply the plantations with workers?

5. (a) Describe French exploration in North America. (b) Why did the French undertake these explorations? (c) What did they achieve?

6. (a) Describe government in the English colonies. (b) How were economic activities in the English colonies different from economic activities in New France?

7. Describe how each of the following contributed to the development of overseas trade and expansion: (a) bankers; (b) insurance; (c) joint stock-company.

8. (a) What were the chief goals of mercantilists? (b) How did they think governments should make a nation self-sufficient?

Critical Thinking

1. **Comparing** (a) How did the experience of Europeans in Asia differ from their experience in the Americas? (b) How might you explain these differences?

2. **Analyzing** Bartolomé de Las Casas later referred to his suggestion to replace Indian workers with African slaves as a "misguided proposal." In your opinion, what did he mean by this statement?

3. **Understanding Economic Ideas** (a) What impact did the commercial revolution have on Europeans? (b) Which people in Europe do you think benefited most from the economic changes? Why?

Relating Past to Present

1. (a) In your opinion, why were entrepreneurs important to economic expansion during the Age of Exploration? (b) What kinds of businesses might be started by entrepreneurs today?

Developing Basic Skills

1. **Making a Review Chart** Make a chart with three columns and five rows. Title the columns Explorer, Purpose of Exploration, and Result. Title the rows Portugal, Spain, Netherlands, France, and England. Use what you learned in reading the chapter to fill in the chart. Then answer the following questions: (a) What similarities do you see in the purposes of exploration? (b) What differences do you see? (c) What were the main results of the voyages of exploration?

2. **Map Reading** Study the map on page 328 and review your reading. Then answer the following questions: (a) What nations were trading in Asia in 1700? (b) What cities did Portugal control? (c) Why was control of Malacca important? (d) How would you describe the relationships among European nations trading in Asia?

3. **Map Reading** Study the map on page 335 and review your reading. Then answer the following questions: (a) What nations claimed lands in North America? (b) What areas did each claim? (c) In your opinion, where were conflicts between rival European powers most likely to occur?

See page 805 for suggested readings.

18 The Age of Absolute Monarchs

(1500–1795)

Portrait of Louis XIV by Hyacinthe Rigaud.

Chapter Outline

1 Golden Age of Spain

2 The French Monarchy

3 Struggles Among the German States

4 Developments in Eastern Europe

By 1682, Louis XIV had been king of France for almost 40 years. In this year, Louis moved his court from Paris to his new palace at Versailles (ver SĪ). The king surrounded himself with splendor at Versailles. He created a daily routine in which the most ordinary aspects of life were transformed into impressive rituals.

The king's day began at 8 A.M. In the royal chamber, the first valet stood outside the curtained four-poster bed with its canopy of rich red velvet embroidered with gold. "Sire, it is time," he said to the king. Just beyond the royal bedchamber, about 200 courtiers were already assembled. They were dressed in expensive silks and wore their finest jewels and wigs. Each hoped for the honor of a word or nod from the king.

Members of the royal family were the first to enter the king's chamber after the king awoke. A few minutes later, court officials were admitted. A doctor and surgeon tended the king, changed his shirt, and washed his hands with wine. The king's priest then led a short prayer service. Afterward, the royal barber gave the king his morning wig. A duke handed Louis his slippers, and a prince offered him the royal dressing gown.

The ceremonies continued with practiced ease. Certain privileged nobles helped the king remove his nightcap, shave, and dress. It was considered a high honor to hand the king an article of clothing, whether it was his breeches, silk stockings, or diamond buckled shoes. Once the king was dressed, he led a procession from the royal apartments to the chapel. After Mass, the king met with his advisors or held an audience. As the day unfolded, the king moved from one ceremony to the next.

With precise attention to detail, Louis XIV controlled the lives of his courtiers just as he dominated all France. The daily rituals kept the nobles of France occupied. They also symbolized the absolute power of the French king.

From the 1500s to the 1700s, monarchs such as Louis XIV gained enormous power. They developed strong armies to replace the private armies of the nobles, and they enlarged their territories. With their greater resources, they expanded royal government and exercised strict control over the lives of their people.

During this period, powerful monarchs built the foundations for the nations of present-day Europe. As strong monarchies emerged, sharp rivalries developed. Older powers such as Spain, France, England, and the Holy Roman Empire were joined by newer states, including the Dutch Netherlands, Prussia, and Russia.

1 Golden Age of Spain

Read to Learn ■ how Spain became a wealthy world power
■ about the Golden Age of Spain

Between 1520 and 1550, the conquistadores gave Spain a colonial empire and spectacular wealth. At the same time, Spain was swept into the center of European politics when the powerful Hapsburg dynasty inherited the Spanish throne.

The Hapsburg Empire

The first Hapsburgs were dukes of Austria. Through carefully arranged marriages, they gradually acquired an empire larger than any since the days of ancient Rome. A favorite Hapsburg saying took note of their policy: "Others shall wage war; you, O happy Austria, shall marry!"

The Hapsburg Empire reached its greatest size under Charles V, who ruled from 1516 to 1556. Charles inherited Spain and its empire in the Americas through his grandparents Ferdinand and Isabella. From his other grandparents, he inherited Austria and the Netherlands.

In 1519, the German princes elected Charles Holy Roman Emperor. The title added to his prestige. However, because the emperor was an elected ruler, he had limited power over the many small kingdoms and independent cities of the Holy Roman Empire.

Ruling the many Hapsburg lands proved to be difficult. Early in the reign of Charles V, the Protestant Reformation began in Germany. A devout Catholic, Charles tried to force the German princes to respect the pope's authority. But the princes and independent cities resisted his attempts to restore religious unity. As you read in Chapter 16, Charles V eventually accepted the Peace of Augsburg in 1555. It allowed each German prince to determine the official religion within his territory.

In Spain, Charles V gained the respect of his subjects through diplomacy and a shrewd use of power. Yet he had to spend the riches of Spain to finance wars in France, Italy, and Germany. Charles battled the French for control of Italy, Burgundy, and Flanders. He also had to defend his Austrian lands against the Turks.

The Ottoman Turks, who had captured Constantinople in 1453, expanded into Eastern Europe in the 1500s. Led by Suleiman (soo lay MAHN), the Turks invaded Hungary and advanced up the Danube River to Vienna, in the heart of Austria. Charles V and his brother, King Ferdinand of Hungary, finally arranged a truce that left the Turks in control of most of Hungary.

By 1556, Charles was an exhausted man. He abdicated and divided his empire between his brother and son. Then he retired to a monastery. Charles divided the empire because he believed it was too vast for any one person to rule. He left Austria to his brother Ferdinand, who was then elected Holy Roman Emperor. He gave Spain, the Spanish empire in the Americas, the Netherlands, Naples, and Milan to his son, who ruled as Philip II.

A Hardworking Monarch

Philip II ruled Spain from 1556 to 1598. During his reign, Spain was the most powerful nation in Europe. Spanish fleets carried treasure from the New World to Seville. Spanish armies, navies, diplomats, priests, and missionaries fanned out across Europe and the Americas. Behind these Spanish forces stood Philip II.

Philip centralized royal power in Spain and governed as an absolute monarch. An *absolute monarch* is a ruler who has complete authority over the government and over the lives of the people. Philip trusted no one, so he watched over everything. He spent hours studying reports and making both minor and major decisions.

An intensely religious person, Philip believed that his right to rule came from God. As a result, he governed with a high sense of duty, and he worked hard to ensure justice. In a legal case in which he stood to lose much, Philip once instructed an official to "inform the Council, that in cases of doubt the verdict must always be given against me."

Nowhere was Philip's character and style of ruling more evident than in the Escorial (ehs KOHR ee uhl), the somber palace he built outside Madrid. The Escorial served as royal residence, office, monastery, and burial vault. In the palace, Philip kept the coffins of his dead father, brother, wives, and children to remind him of his own mortality. From his bedroom window, he could see the main altar of the monastery. Behind the high palace walls, Philip devoted himself day and night to governing his large empire.

Philip believed that his mission in life was to fight heretics and restore the unity of the Catholic Church. He led the Catholic Reformation in Spain. He also sent Jesuit priests to convert Protestants all across Europe. In the end, his efforts helped bring parts of Germany, Eastern Europe, and the Netherlands back under the pope's authority.

Like his father, Philip was drawn into many wars. He continued the Hapsburg rivalry with the French over control of Italy. As part of his crusade to revive Christendom, Philip attacked Turkish strongholds in the Mediterranean. In 1571 at the battle of Lepanto, his fleet decisively defeated the Turkish navy. However, the Turks soon rebuilt their navy, and Philip did not achieve his goal of driving them from the Mediterranean.

Revolt in the Netherlands

Philip's attempts to centralize royal power led to a long, bitter struggle with his subjects in the Netherlands. Since the Middle Ages, the Netherlands had flourished as a center of trade and commerce. The wool industry made the cities of Bruges and Ghent prosperous, and Antwerp and Amsterdam were busy trading ports. Although the Netherlands was divided into 17 provinces, the people had common economic concerns. Many resented the fact that Philip put the interests of Spain above the interests of the Netherlands.

Religious differences also contributed to Dutch discontent. By the middle 1500s, Calvinist preachers had won many converts among the Dutch. In 1566, when Philip ordered officials to enforce laws against Protestants, the Dutch revolted. Many Dutch Catholics joined the Protestants because they resented Spanish rule.

The struggle was bitter. Protestant townspeople broke stained-glass windows and destroyed statues of saints in Catholic churches. Philip responded by sending 20,000 Spanish troops. The Spanish commander boasted that in a six-year period his troops killed almost 18,000 people. The

This painting of the battle of Lepanto gives some idea of the huge number of ships that took part. Lepanto was the largest naval battle up to that time. It pitted ships from many Christian European states against the fleet of the Muslim Turks. Ships were identified by their flags. For example, the Turks fought under crescent flags.

Spanish seized Dutch property and imposed punishing taxes that hindered trade.

In 1581, the seven northern provinces, which were mostly Protestant, declared their independence from Spain. They then became known as the Dutch Netherlands. The ten southern provinces, with their largely Catholic populations, remained the Spanish Netherlands.* The war dragged on into the 1600s, but Spain did not regain its lost provinces in the north.

The Dutch Netherlands emerged from the war with Spain as a leading commercial power. With more ships than any other nation, the Dutch dominated seaborne trade in Europe and overseas. As you read in Chapter 17, they successfully competed with the Portuguese in the East Indies. They also seized islands in the Spanish West Indies and sent settlers to North America.

The Mighty Armada

During the Dutch rebellion, the English watched Philip's activities with keen interest. The Protestant Queen Elizabeth feared that if Philip crushed the Dutch he would invade England. Therefore, she cautiously sup-

ported the Dutch. She also allowed English captains known as Sea Dogs, a polite name for pirates, to wage an undeclared naval war on Spain.

The English Sea Dogs attacked Spanish ports in America and captured Spanish ships. The most famous Sea Dog, Sir Francis Drake, made several voyages to the West Indies to seize Spanish treasure. Philip wanted Queen Elizabeth to punish Drake as a pirate. Instead, she made Drake a knight, which infuriated the Spanish king.

In 1588, Philip finally moved against the English. He assembled a huge armada, or armed fleet, to carry an army to England. As the mighty Spanish Armada sailed up the English Channel, it engaged the English fleet in a great naval battle. The smaller, quicker English ships badly mauled the heavy Spanish ships and forced them to sail into the North Sea. Violent storms in the North Sea destroyed many ships and scattered the rest. The storms were later nicknamed the "Protestant Wind" by the English.

The victory over the Spanish gave the English a feeling of confidence. With the help of the Protestant Wind, they had ended the threat of the Spanish Armada. Yet the defeat did not seriously weaken Spain's powerful position in Europe.

---

* In 1830, the Spanish Netherlands became the nation of Belgium.

345

A Century of Spanish Genius

Under Philip II, Spanish culture blossomed. His reign marked the beginning of what is called the "Century of Gold." From about 1550 to 1650, Spanish writers, philosophers, and artists created great masterpieces that marked a high point in Spanish culture.

As you have read, Cervantes wrote *Don Quixote* during this period. (See page 306.) Another writer, Lope de Vega, a contemporary of Shakespeare, wrote at least 700 plays and greatly influenced drama. His works, which included comedies, religious dramas, and histories, focused on God, the king, and romance. Jesuit writers such as Francisco Suárez wrote about the relationship between faith and reason and influenced religion and philosophy.

During the Century of Gold, Spanish art also flourished. The painter El Greco expressed intense religious feelings in his portraits of saints. Born in Crete, El Greco received his nickname "The Greek" when he moved to Spain. El Greco drew long, distorted faces and bodies that produced a dramatic effect. Another Spanish artist, Diego Velázquez (vuh LAHS kehs), gained fame as a court painter at Madrid. His portraits of the Hapsburgs captured the personalities of the royal family.

A Troubled Economy

Before the Century of Gold ended, Spain had lost its position as the most powerful nation in Europe. Although Spain still ruled a vast empire in the Americas, it suffered severe economic problems. In fact, ruling the vast New World empire contributed to Spain's economic problems.

The Spanish government depended almost entirely on gold and silver from the Americas. Every year, the treasure fleet sailed to Spain with gold and silver from mines in Mexico and Peru. In the 1500s, the value of these shipments increased dramatically. (See the graph at right.) However, Spanish rulers quickly drained the treasury to pay for wars. They even had to borrow money from German and Italian bankers.

Much of the money spent on maintaining the Spanish army and navy went to businesspeople and foreign bankers. This increased the number of gold and silver coins in circulation and contributed to inflation. As the money supply increased, people tended to charge more for their goods and services. Prices rose all over Europe. However, the steepest rise in prices occurred in Spain.

Inflation hurt Spanish industry because higher prices meant that it cost more to produce goods in Spain than elsewhere. Other nations shunned costly Spanish goods. Even in Spain, foreign goods were cheaper than locally produced goods. As a result, Spanish businesses failed.

The religious policies of Philip II and his successors also contributed to the economic

Graph Skill *Gold and silver treasure from the Americas flowed into Spain, as you can see on this bar graph. The treasure was a mixed blessing because it contributed to steep inflation in Spain. During which period did Spanish income from the colonies begin to decline? Why?*

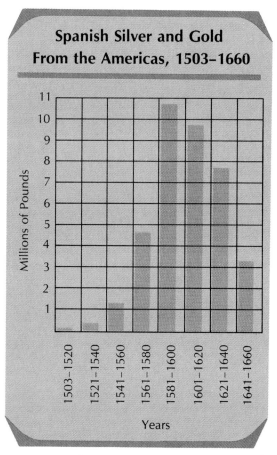

Source: Earle J. Hamilton, *American Treasure and the Price Revolution in Spain, 1501–1650.*

decline. Like Ferdinand and Isabella, later Spanish rulers allowed the Inquisition to persecute the Moriscoes (muh RIHS koos), Spanish Muslims who had converted to Christianity. Moriscoes were accused of secretly practicing their old religion. In the early 1600s, hundreds of thousands of Moriscoes were driven from Spain.

By 1660, the amount of treasure being brought from the Americas had dwindled. Spanish industry and agriculture had also declined. Old rivalries between different regions of Spain resurfaced, and weak rulers were unable to impose unity as Philip II had done. Although the Hapsburgs in Austria would continue to play a leading role in Eu-

ropean affairs, the Spanish Hapsburgs no longer dominated events on the continent.

SECTION REVIEW

1. Identify: battle of Lepanto, Spanish Armada, Lope de Vega, El Greco, Diego Valázquez.
2. Define: absolute monarch.
3. What lands did Charles V govern?
4. What role did Philip II play in the Catholic Reformation?
5. (a) List two reasons the Dutch rebelled against Spain. (b) How did Queen Elizabeth react to the Dutch rebellion?
6. Describe the Spanish Century of Gold.

---

2 The French Monarchy

Read to Learn
■ how French rulers became absolute monarchs
■ how the wars of Louis XIV affected France

In the late 1500s, Spain was able to dominate Europe, in part because its chief rival, France, was weakened by civil wars. Since the Middle Ages, provinces in France had enjoyed special privileges. When French kings tried to exert their authority over local affairs, powerful nobles in the provinces rebelled. Religious divisions between Catholics and Huguenots also led to civil wars.

Wars of Religion

In 1559, King Henry II of France was accidentally killed during a jousting tournament. Henry II left three young sons, but none of them proved to be a strong ruler. Their mother, Catherine de Medici, tried to keep peace between Catholic and Protestant nobles at court. However, in the provinces, Huguenot townspeople and nobles took the opportunity to resist royal authority.

Fighting between Protestant and Catholic nobles plunged France into chaos, and royal power melted away. The Huguenots sought outside help from English, Dutch, and German Protestants, and the Catholics found an ally in Philip II of Spain.

Wars of religion raged on and off in France between 1562 and 1598. Fanatics on both sides committed savage acts. For example, on August 24, 1572, the eve of St. Bartholomew's Day, Catherine de Medici allowed her Catholic supporters to kill Huguenot leaders who had come to Paris for a royal wedding. That night, mobs of Parisians roamed the streets, killing thousands of Huguenots. Soon, the slaughter spread beyond Paris. Outraged Huguenots responded to the so-called St. Bartholomew's Day Massacre with their own attacks.

In 1589, Henry of Navarre inherited the French throne as Henry IV. Henry was a Huguenot, but he saw clearly that the only way to restore peace was to put the interests of France before those of religion. Because Paris, the French capital, was strongly Catholic, Henry IV converted to Catholicism. He reportedly remarked, "Paris is well worth a Mass." Still, the fighting continued.

Finally, in 1598, Henry issued the Edict of Nantes to reassure the Huguenots that their interests would be protected. The edict gave Huguenots freedom of worship and the right to establish churches in certain places.

It also gave them the same civil rights as Catholics and the right to have Protestant troops defend over 100 fortified towns in Huguenot areas.

Foundations of Royal Power

Henry IV worked hard to restore order to his war-torn nation. He revived royal authority by rebuilding the bureaucracy, collecting taxes to pay for a strong army, and overseeing justice. In addition, he had roads repaired and encouraged new business ventures. However, in 1610, Henry IV was assassinated, and his ten-year old son Louis XIII inherited the throne.

Early in Louis XIII's reign, French nobles tried to reestablish their influence. In 1614, they forced the king to call the Estates-General. (See page 191.) But when the Estates met, the nobles could not agree among themselves. The assembly was dismissed in 1615 without much protest. The Estates-General did not meet again for 175 years. During this time, the French kings gained absolute power over the government.

Louis XIII's advisor, Cardinal Richelieu (RIHSH uh LOO), was chiefly responsible for increasing the power and prestige of the French monarchy. Richelieu wanted to prevent the Huguenots from challenging royal power. He realized that he could not destroy the Huguenots without provoking another civil war. Therefore, he permitted the Huguenots religious freedom but forced them to give up the right to fortify their towns.

To further reduce the risk of civil war, Richelieu ordered the destruction of all private fortresses belonging to provincial nobles. He also outlawed dueling because feuding among nobles was a frequent cause of civil war.

Richelieu was a mercantilist, and he believed that successful trade would strengthen the monarchy. To promote commerce, he encouraged nobles to participate in such ventures as overseas trading companies. He rewarded successful merchants who contributed to French prosperity. For example, he allowed them to buy titles of nobility. Since the new nobles were strongly

This portrait of Richelieu suggests the many-sided nature of the man—French duke, cardinal of the Catholic Church, and virtual ruler of France during the reign of Louis XIII. Richelieu was a skillful diplomat and tough-minded politician. He put the interests of France above those of the Catholic Church and crushed opponents of royal power.

loyal to the king, Richelieu often appointed them to official positions.

The Sun King

When Louis XIII died in 1643, his son Louis XIV was a child of four. As a result, Louis XIV's mother, Anne of Austria, and Cardinal Mazarin, Richelieu's successor, ruled in the boy's name. They continued Richelieu's policy of centralizing power.

When Cardinal Mazarin died in 1661, Louis XIV was 23 years old. The king immediately summoned his advisors and announced he would rule on his own.

For the next 54 years, Louis XIV ruled France with a skill and power unmatched by any other ruler in Europe. During his long reign, France dominated Europe as Spain had in the late 1500s. Louis XIV's motto was "none his equal." His symbol was the sun, which suggested that just as the earth depended on the sun for its existence so the people of France depended on the Sun King for their well-being.

"I am the state." Louis XIV believed that as king he had a divine right to rule with absolute power because kings were representatives of God's power on earth. Louis XIV summed up his idea of absolute monarchy when he said: "L'etat, c'est moi." ("I am the state.")

Louis XIV continued the policy of imposing royal authority on local sources of power. For example, until Louis XIV's reign, French armies were similar to feudal armies. Soldiers were recruited, trained, and paid by local nobles, and each noble commanded his own troops.

Under Louis XIV, the French army was reorganized. All French soldiers were to fight for the king. For the first time, they were given uniforms and assigned ranks. Furthermore, Louis XIV increased the standing army from 100,000 to 400,000 soldiers. With a strong, loyal army, the king could suppress local uprisings as well as assert French power in Europe.

Louis XIV also closely directed government administration. He appointed *intendants*, or royal agents, to rule the provinces. Intendants collected taxes, recruited soldiers, and administered royal policy. Local parlements were supposed to approve the laws. However, if they tried to resist the king's edicts, Louis would make a grand appearance and leave them speechless.

Louis was a staunch Catholic and was determined to make France a unified Catholic country again. In 1685, he cancelled the Edict of Nantes, which had guaranteed freedom of worship to the Huguenots. During the persecution that resulted, many Huguenots fled to England, the Dutch Netherlands, and the Americas.

The palace of Versailles. Louis XIV built a spectacular new palace at Versailles, 12 miles (19 kilometers) west of Paris. The palace of Versailles, which took more than 27 years to complete, symbolized the splendor and power of the Sun King. The palace faced 20,000 acres of formal gardens and woods. Inside the palace were the royal apartments as well as rooms for hundreds of nobles and servants. On formal occasions, the Hall of Mirrors, a long gallery, was lit with 4,000 candles, mounted in silver and crystal chandeliers.

Versailles served many purposes. Louis made it the center of government, in part because it was a safe distance from Paris, where disturbances had occurred in the past. He encouraged nobles to live there so he could keep close watch on their activities.

Versailles became a center of French culture. The king invited playwrights, poets, and artists to the palace. From Versailles, French influence spread throughout Europe. Other rulers modeled their governments on the absolute monarchy of Louis XIV. People adopted French manners and fashions in clothing and art, and French became the language of European diplomats.

Colbert: Architect of French Economic Policies

Louis XIV needed money to maintain the pomp and splendor of court life. The palace itself cost a fortune to build. Louis XIV's programs for government and the army were also expensive. During much of Louis's

The palace at Versailles and its magnificent gardens were commissioned by Louis XIV. The royal family lived in the palace along with many nobles, who felt privileged to have even a small, damp room there. Construction of the palace required 35,000 workers and took 27 years. Louis XIV destroyed the bills so no one would know how much it had cost to build. Maintaining the court at Versailles cost more than half the taxes collected in France.

reign, Jean Baptiste Colbert (kohl BEHR) successfully managed the royal finances.

Colbert was a mercantilist who was determined to increase royal power by strengthening the economy. He developed a two-part strategy for increasing royal revenues. First, he reformed the existing system of collecting taxes. Local tax collectors were often corrupt. Because tax money passed through many hands before it reached Paris, the royal treasury seldom received what was due. Colbert introduced a strict system of accounting for all taxes that were collected. The new system ended much of the corruption.

Second, Colbert introduced higher taxes. This was difficult to do because nobles and even some bourgeoisie, or middle class, did not have to pay taxes. Louis XIV and Colbert knew that the nobles would never

agree to being taxed unless they had some say in how the money was spent. However, as an absolute monarch, Louis had no wish to share power. Thus, Colbert could not tax nobles. Instead, he decided to follow the mercantilist policy of promoting trade and commerce. This would make the country more prosperous. Then the lower classes would earn more and be able to pay higher taxes.

Under Colbert's direction, the French economy prospered. He encouraged new industry and commerce by excusing investors from taxes for a few years. Once new businesses were thriving, they would be taxed. Colbert also encouraged the building of ships, roads, and canals, which would improve transportation and trade. To further encourage trade within France, Colbert eliminated some local tariffs that provinces charged for goods coming from other parts of France. However, he imposed high tariffs on foreign imports to protect French industries. In addition, he supported the growth of colonies such as New France.

The Wars of Louis XIV

Louis XIV spent much of the money Colbert raised on foreign wars. He dreamed of extending France to what he called its "natural frontiers." In the south, France had already reached the Pyrenees, a natural frontier. But Louis believed that the frontier in the east should stretch from the Alps, north along the Rhine River, to the North Sea or English Channel.

French ambitions threatened nearly every other European power. For 30 years of Louis XIV's 54-year reign, France was at war. At one time or another, the French fought the Dutch Netherlands, Sweden, England, Spain, and the Holy Roman Empire.

The bitterest struggle was Louis's last war, known as the War of the Spanish Succession. It began in 1701, when the grandson of Louis XIV inherited Spain and all its possessions. French forces occupied the Spanish Netherlands. Then other European powers formed an alliance to prevent Louis from uniting Spain and France. Years of fighting followed between the allies on one side and France and Spain on the other.

The allies finally got their way. At the Peace of Utrecht in 1713, Louis XIV agreed that the French and Spanish crowns would never be united. Louis's grandson was recognized by the allies as Philip V of Spain, but it was agreed that Philip could never become king of France. Spain kept its American colonies, but its Italian lands, including Milan, Naples, and Sicily, went to the Austrian

Daily Life ■ St.-Cyr: A School for Girls

In the 1600s, few girls in France received an education. Girls of wealthy noble families might learn to read and write at convent schools or from tutors hired to teach their brothers. However, many nobles did not think it was worthwhile to educate their daughters because the girls were expected to marry or become nuns. A noblewoman at the court of Louis XIV once remarked: "I wish that someone had taught me something when I was a girl."

Madame de Maintenon, Louis XIV's second wife, did much to improve education for girls. In 1686, she founded a boarding school for girls at St.-Cyr (san SEER), near Versailles. The daughter of a poor noble family, Madame de Maintenon was determined that St.-Cyr should provide girls from such families with a first-class education.

Together with the king, she decided on the curriculum and chose the 250 girls who would make up the first classes. At St.-Cyr, students learned reading and writing, poetry, letter writing, conversation, and needlework. Religion was also an essential part of the curriculum from the start. Madame de Maintenon later added courses in arithmetic and geography.

Girls entered St.-Cyr at age 7 and left at age 20. Their day began at 6 A.M., when they rose and dressed for Mass. They then attended classes until noon. After a midday dinner, they returned to their studies until 6 P.M. Their 15-hour day ended at 9 P.M. with prayers and bed. Despite the school's rigorous schedule, hundreds of girls applied for admission.

St.-Cyr soon came to symbolize excellence in education. Convent schools all over France were reformed along the lines of St.-Cyr. New academies for girls opened, and they patterned their classes after St.-Cyr. Because graduates of St.-Cyr were seen as the best-educated women in France, they could easily get positions as teachers or headmistresses at the new schools.

For most of the 1700s, St.-Cyr was the foremost girls' school in France. Moreover, Madame de Maintenon's idea of providing girls from poor families with a good education spread from France to other parts of Europe.

Hapsburgs. For its part in the war, England received Newfoundland and Nova Scotia in America from France as well as Gibraltar and Minorca in the Mediterranean from Spain.

Louis's wars left France deeply in debt, a problem his successors would never solve. Louis himself lost popularity in his last years. But Louis XIV had demonstrated what a monarch at the head of a strong, centralized state could do. He ruled his people with absolute power, and his ambitious foreign policy affected all of Europe. During the 1700s, Louis XIV's heirs would try to live up to the brilliant traditions of the Sun King.

SECTION REVIEW

1. Identify: Edict of Nantes, Jean Baptiste Colbert, War of the Spanish Succession, Peace of Utrecht.
2. Define: intendant.
3. Why did Henry IV become a Catholic?
4. Give two examples of how Cardinal Richelieu increased royal power.
5. How did the French army change under Louis XIV?
6. Describe Colbert's two-part plan for increasing royal revenues.
7. What was Louis XIV's goal in his foreign wars?

3 Struggles Among the German States

Read to Learn
- what the Peace of Westphalia accomplished
- why a balance of power prevailed in Europe

While powerful rulers created an absolute monarchy in France, the Austrian Hapsburgs failed to establish their authority over the Holy Roman Empire. Instead, the German states that made up the empire engaged in a conflict known as the Thirty Years' War.

The Thirty Years' War

As you read in Chapter 12, the German people lived in hundreds of small, independent states. In theory, these states were under the authority of the Holy Roman emperor. In practice, the emperor had little power over them, and the princes who ruled each state were often bitter rivals.

Whenever a Holy Roman emperor died, seven leading German princes, called electors, met to choose a new emperor. From the 1400s on, the electors always chose a Hapsburg, because as ruler of Austria, Bohemia, and Hungary he was the most powerful prince. Although other princes accepted the Hapsburg emperor, they did not recognize his right to rule them. As a result, there was constant friction between the German princes and the Holy Roman emperor.

Political divisions within the empire deepened during the Reformation. Under the Peace of Augsburg, each German prince had the power to decide whether his lands would be Catholic or Lutheran. German Catholics, however, became increasingly upset when one prince after another became Protestant. In their eyes, the problem grew even more serious when some princes converted to Calvinism, which had not even been recognized by the Peace of Hapsburg.

Protestants, in turn, were concerned because the Catholic Reformation, under the forceful leadership of the Hapsburgs, began to bring many Protestant princes back into the Catholic Church.

In 1618, the Hapsburg emperor Ferdinand II tried to restore the Catholic Church in Bohemia, where many nobles were Protestant. When the Protestants resisted, the emperor decided to crush them. The crisis in Bohemia then exploded into a general war.

The struggle lasted for 30 years. In the early years of the war, religious issues fueled the fighting. Protestant princes sought help from Denmark, Sweden, and the Dutch Netherlands. Ferdinand was aided by the strongly Catholic Spanish Hapsburgs. However, as the war dragged on, political and territorial issues became more important than religion. Ferdinand tried to establish Hapsburg control over all the German states. To prevent the Hapsburgs from becoming too powerful, the Catholic Cardinal Richelieu of France supported the German Protestants.

During the Thirty Years' War, invading armies devastated the German states, burning and looting towns and cities. Peasants suffered terribly. In some regions, entire villages were wiped out. Farming became difficult or impossible. Famine and plague broke out, causing great misery. Some historians estimate that the population of the Holy Roman Empire dropped from 21 million people in 1618 to about 13.5 million in 1648.

Peace of Westphalia

Neither side could gain a lasting victory in the war. Finally, in 1648, the nations of Europe sent representatives to Westphalia, where they negotiated a peace settlement.

The Peace of Westphalia ended the Hapsburg dream of creating a strong central government to rule the Holy Roman Empire. The Hapsburgs still held their family lands in Austria, Bohemia, and Hungary, and they remained the most powerful of the German rulers. But they had little power over the other princes.

The peace settlement guaranteed the independence of about 300 small German states. Each prince had the right to declare war and negotiate treaties. The princes would continue to meet in the Imperial Diet, or assembly, and they had to approve any request from the emperor for taxes. Each prince could choose the religious faith of his territory. The settlement recognized Calvinists along with Lutherans and Catholics, but other Protestant groups still suffered persecution.*

The Peace of Westphalia also acknowledged territorial and political changes that

---

* To escape persecution, many German Protestants emigrated to the Americas, where quite a few of them settled in the English colony of Pennsylvania.

This painting records the signing of the Treaty of Munster between Spain and the Dutch Netherlands. The Treaty of Munster was part of the Peace of Westphalia. The Dutch delegates swear an oath with their hands upraised, while the Spanish delegates place their hands on a Bible. The Peace of Westphalia was the first international peace conference at which diplomats gathered to settle a war.

Europe After the Peace of Westphalia, 1648

NORWAY
SCOTLAND
IRELAND
ENGLAND
London
DENMARK
NORTH SEA
SWEDEN
RUSSIA
Moscow
BALTIC SEA
PRUSSIA
POLAND
DUTCH NETH.
BRANDENBURG
Berlin
SAXONY
SILESIA
Prague
WESTPHALIA
BOHEMIA
SPANISH NETH.
LORRAINE
Paris
ALSACE
Rhine R.
BAVARIA
Vienna
AUSTRIA
HUNGARY
FRANCHE-COMPTÉ
SWISS CONF.
FRANCE
MILAN
ATLANTIC OCEAN
PORTUGAL
SPAIN
BALEARIC ISLANDS
CORSICA
SARDINIA
PAPAL STATES
Rome
NAPLES
Danube R.
OTTOMAN EMPIRE
Constantinople
BLACK SEA
MEDITERRANEAN SEA
SICILY
CRETE

Legend:
- Spanish Hapsburgs
- Austrian Hapsburgs
- Brandenburg–Prussia
- Italian city-states
- Sweden
- Boundary of Holy Roman Empire

400 Miles
600 Kilometers

Map Skill   *The Holy Roman Empire was more fragmented after the Peace of Westphalia than before. Brandenburg-Prussia gained lands that would form the basis for a strong Prussian state in the 1600s and 1700s. Who controlled the largest empire in Central Europe?*

had taken place in the preceding 50 years. European rulers recognized the Dutch Netherlands and the Swiss Confederation as independent states. During the war, King Gustavus Adolphus of Sweden had conquered and then lost large parts of German territory. The treaty left Sweden in control of some German lands along the Baltic and North seas. In addition, France gained parts of Alsace and Lorraine. The boundaries established by the peace remained almost unchanged for 150 years.

Rise of Prussia

One German prince gained more than most from the Peace of Westphalia. He was Frederick William, Elector of Brandenburg. His family, the Hohenzollerns (HOH uhn TSAHL ernz), had ruled Brandenburg since the 1400s. During the Reformation, they became Lutherans. In 1618, the Hohenzollerns inherited Prussia in northeastern Germany. By the Peace of Westphalia, they acquired other scattered German lands.

Brandenburg was invaded several times during the Thirty Years' War. Invaders devastated the main town of Berlin as well as the countryside. After the war, Frederick William, later called the Great Elector, was determined to establish strong rule over his scattered lands. To achieve this goal, he decided to build a strong army. He told his son, "A ruler is treated with no consideration if he does not have troops and means of his own."

However, an army cost money. When the Great Elector tried to raise money through taxes, noble landlords, known as Junkers (YOON kerz), refused to grant him the right to impose taxes. Eventually, by force and compromise, he won the right to collect taxes for the army, but the Junkers themselves did not have to pay any. With a strong army at their command, the Hohenzollerns used every opportunity to expand their power.

In 1701, during the War of the Spanish Succession, the Holy Roman emperor asked Brandenburg for help against Louis XIV. The elector at the time was the son of the Great Elector. He agreed, with one condition: He wanted the emperor to recognize his title as king of Prussia. The emperor agreed to the request. At the Peace of Utrecht in 1713, other European rulers also recognized the new title.

Building a Strong Prussian State

During the 1700s, the Hohenzollerns established an absolute monarchy and transformed Prussia from a small kingdom into a major European power. The Great Elector's grandson, King Frederick William I, dedicated his life to strengthening the Prussian army. Between 1713 and 1740, he doubled its size to 80,000 soldiers. He recruited officers from the Junker class and set up universities where they would be trained. In addition, peasants were drafted to serve as soldiers. The army helped unify Prussia because soldiers and officers shared a common loyalty to the king.

Frederick William I was a tireless worker who believed in obedience and discipline. In public, he always wore a military uniform. He cared nothing for luxury. On occasion, he would patrol the streets of Berlin lecturing citizens for wearing frivolous clothes or living in too much luxury. His tight-fisted financial policies were necessary to support his large standing army. But he cleverly avoided going to war because that would have put a greater strain on the economy.

Frederick William I also moved to strengthen the Prussian economy. Because the Prussian population was small, he encouraged Protestants from France and other Catholic areas to settle in his lands. The newcomers included farmers, artisans, and merchants, who contributed to the country's prosperity. When a famine, flood, or war occurred elsewhere in Europe, the king would send agents to recruit new settlers. The agents promised land to peasants and offered loans to merchants so they could reopen their businesses in Prussia.

To Frederick William I, his son Frederick seemed an unlikely successor, because the boy loved to read books and play the flute. The king thought such pastimes were useless, and he harshly disciplined his son. Yet when Frederick became King Frederick II in 1740, he proved to be a more vigorous leader than his father. Frederick still enjoyed reading literature and philosophy, but he ruled Prussia with a firm hand. He eventually became known as Frederick the Great.

Forceful Rulers in Austria

While Prussia was emerging as a new power in Germany, the Austrian Hapsburgs tried to establish tighter control over their empire, which included Austria, Bohemia, and Hungary. However, each region had a separate heritage. Austria was for the most part German-speaking. Bohemians were descended from the Slavs, and Hungary was the homeland of the Magyars.

Between 1648 and 1740, the Hapsburgs worked hard to reduce the power of local nobles and make the Austrian Empire a Catholic stronghold. For example, in Bohemia, they took land from Protestant nobles and gave it to other nobles who would be loyal to the emperor. Despite such efforts, the unity of Hapsburg lands remained fragile. This was especially apparent to Charles VI, emperor from 1711 to 1740.

The Pragmatic Sanction. Charles VI had no son to inherit his throne. He feared that the German princes and nobles in the Hapsburg lands might not recognize his daughter Maria Theresa as ruler of Austria. Therefore, he persuaded them to sign the Pragmatic Sanction.

The Pragmatic Sanction guaranteed that the Hapsburg lands would not be divided, and it recognized Maria Theresa's right to inherit the Austrian throne. Charles convinced other European nations to accept the agreement. However, when the emperor died in 1740, Frederick the Great of Prussia ignored the agreement and seized the Austrian province of Silesia. Silesia was considered a valuable prize because of its iron ore and a strong textile industry. Maria Theresa had to move quickly.

War of the Austrian Succession. Maria Theresa was only 23 years old when she became queen of Austria, but she proved to be a capable and decisive leader. Shortly after she gave birth to her first son, Maria Theresa traveled to Hungary to seek help against Prussia. The Hungarian nobles were usually hostile toward Austria, but Maria Theresa made a dramatic appeal to them. She promised to safeguard their traditional rights and showed them her infant son, the future ruler of Austria. The Hungarian nobles responded by sending 100,000 troops to fight the Prussians.

While Maria Theresa mustered her forces, the fighting quickly widened into a general European war, known as the War of the Austrian Succession. Spain and France, a longtime rival of the Hapsburgs, joined Prussia. Great Britain* and the Dutch Netherlands sided with Austria, but they sent only money and few troops.

The war in Europe grew into a worldwide conflict between France and Britain. The French won victories in Europe, but the

---

* In 1707, the crowns of England and Scotland were joined into the United Kingdom of Great Britain. After 1707, the country became known as Great Britain or Britain.

Soon after Maria Theresa inherited the Hapsburg throne, Austria was attacked by other European countries. When enemy forces approached Vienna, Maria Theresa fled to Hungary to seek help from the Hungarian nobles. In this picture, she stands before the Hungarian Parliament with her infant son in her arms. According to one story, the nobles rose, drew their swords, and shouted: "Our lives and blood for your Majesty! We will die for our king, Maria Theresa!"

British attacked French possessions in Canada and the West Indies. Finally, in 1748, the European nations signed a peace treaty at Aix-la-Chapelle. Only Frederick the Great benefited from the war because he was allowed to keep Silesia. Otherwise, the treaty provided that all territories should be returned to the nations that held them before the war.

The European Balance of Power

By the mid-1700s, two German states—Austria and Prussia—were among the major powers in Europe. Like France, they had strong central governments led by absolute monarchs, and they had well-trained standing armies. Two other strong nations, Russia, which you will read about later in this chapter, and Britain, also played important roles in European affairs. Diplomats scurried about Europe negotiating alliances to maintain a balance of power. To them, the balance of power meant that no single nation was strong enough to dominate Europe.

Competition between the major European powers was keen. For example, Britain and France competed for trade and territory in India and North America. These rivalries made them enemies in any European conflict. In Europe, Austria was determined to recover Silesia and take revenge on Prussia. Meanwhile, both Prussia and Russia were eager to expand their territories.

Conflicting interests soon led to the Seven Years' War, which was fought on three continents: Europe, Asia, and North America. In North America, the war was called the French and Indian War.

In 1756, Frederick the Great invaded Saxony, a German state west of Silesia. Prussia proved to be a strong military power, but it soon faced the combined forces of France, Austria, and Russia. Only Russia's leaving the alliance saved the outnumbered Prussians from disaster.

The French and British fought each other in North America and India. The fighting began in North America in 1754. During the war, British troops and soldiers from the colonies captured Quebec, which in effect gave them control of New France. In India, the British drove the French from their trading outposts.

At the Peace of Paris in 1763, Britain received Canada and all French lands east of the Mississippi River. Spain acquired the French territory of Louisiana. France, however, recovered its trading stations in India. It also recovered two profitable sugar-producing islands in the West Indies that the British had captured.

The rivalry between Britain and France would continue for decades. Also, the Seven Years' War left both nations deeply in debt. The policies each nation developed to reduce the debts would profoundly influence the British colonies in North America and the absolute monarchy in France.

SECTION REVIEW

1. Locate: Austria, Bohemia, Hungary, Brandenburg, Prussia, Silesia, Saxony.
2. Identify: Hohenzollerns, Junker, Maria Theresa, Pragmatic Sanction.
3. (a) Describe one cause of the Thirty Years' War. (b) How did the Peace of Westphalia affect the Hapsburgs?
4. (a) Why did the Great Elector build up the Prussian army? (b) Give two examples of how King Frederick William I tried to strengthen Prussia.
5. What different peoples lived in the Austrian Empire?

4 Developments in Eastern Europe

Read to Learn ■ what Suleiman achieved in Turkey
■ how Peter the Great and Catherine the Great changed Russia

In Eastern Europe, the Ottoman Empire, Russia, and Poland ruled over large territories. Each state had customs and traditions that differed from those of Western Europe. However, between 1500 and 1795, all three became more involved in developments in Western Europe.

The Ottoman Empire

In the 1500s, the Ottoman Empire extended from Eastern Europe across Asia Minor into the Middle East and Egypt. (See the map on page 358.) As you read in Chapter 13, Constantinople fell to the Turks in 1453. The Turks renamed the city Istanbul, converted churches into mosques, and restored its earlier splendor.

The Ottoman Empire included peoples who practiced many different religions. The Turks were far more tolerant of religious differences than Europeans were at that time. Islamic law recognized Christians and Jews living in the empire as "People of the Book." (See page 214.) As a result, they were allowed to follow their own faiths.

The Ottoman Empire reached its height under Suleiman, who ruled from 1520 to 1566. Suleiman had absolute control over the government and the army. However, like all Turkish rulers he had to obey Islamic law.

Suleiman sponsored the building of mosques, schools, hospitals, bridges, and public baths. An effective police force in Istanbul made the city safer than any European city at that time.

Suleiman also led Turkish armies on successful military campaigns. The Turks captured Belgrade in what is today Yugoslavia. They then moved up the Danube, taking Hungary. In 1529, Suleiman advanced on Vienna with 100,000 troops and almost broke through the city walls before he was beaten back.

After Suleiman's death, the Ottoman Empire began a long, slow decline. Weak sultans ignored their duties and failed to control corrupt officials. Local governors, or pashas, ruled Turkish provinces in Europe and Afrca. As long as they paid tribute to the sultan, they were free to rule as they pleased. Despite the decline, the Ottoman Empire survived until 1918. Although largely isolated from cultural developments in Europe, the empire continued to influence events in Eastern Europe.

Map Skill   *Under Suleiman the Magnificent, the Ottoman Turks advanced deep into Europe, as you can see on this map. In what other areas did the Ottoman Empire gain substantial territory during his rule?*

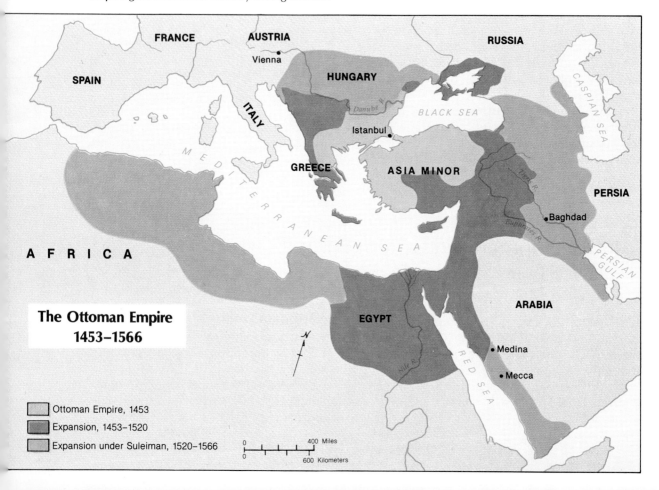

The Ottoman Empire 1453–1566

Ottoman Empire, 1453
Expansion, 1453–1520
Expansion under Suleiman, 1520–1566

0   400 Miles
0   600 Kilometers

The Romanov Dynasty in Russia

During the 1400s and 1500s, Russia emerged as a powerful state in Eastern Europe. As you read in Chapter 13, Ivan III and Ivan IV brought lands around Moscow under their control. As czars, they claimed absolute power. However, for many years after the death of Ivan IV in 1584, Russia had no strong leader.

During the Time of Troubles, from 1604 to 1613, nobles schemed to put their own candidates on the throne. As soon as a new czar was installed, a rival would murder him. Finally, in 1613, the nobles elected 17-year-old Michael Romanov as czar. Once established, the Romanov dynasty ruled Russia until 1917.

Michael Romanov realized that being an elected monarch would limit his power. Therefore, he and his heirs worked to end the practice of electing monarchs and tried to bring the nobles under their control. To win the support of the nobles, the Romanovs gave them absolute control over their peasants and enacted strict laws to prevent peasants from running away.

Russian peasants were increasingly reduced to serfdom during the 1600s. Unlike serfs elsewhere, Russian serfs were treated like slaves. They were not only forced to give unpaid labor but could also be bought and sold. Harsh treatment of serfs led to many peasant uprisings. But such uprisings were quickly suppressed.

During the 1600s, the Romanovs expanded their territory eastward. Russian traders and trappers had crossed the Ural Mountains during the 1500s and discovered that Siberia had valuable iron, timber, and fur resources. Russian explorers pushed as far as the Bering Straits. In 1689, Russia signed a treaty with China that recognized Russian claims to lands north of Manchuria. By the end of the century, Russia had acquired an empire stretching to the Pacific Ocean.

Peter the Great

Under the Romanovs, Russia also began to expand in the west. As you have read, Russia had been isolated from the west for centuries. During this time, the nations of Western Europe had developed military and technical skills that the Russians lacked. Peter I became czar in 1682, when just a child. By 1689, he was a czar in fact as well as name. He was determined to make Russia a powerful nation by introducing western technology and customs. Between 1689 and 1725, his reforms transformed Russia and earned him the title of Peter the Great.

Peter was a towering figure—almost seven feet tall. He possessed a sharp, inquiring mind. As a boy, he spent much time talking to German and Dutch merchants who lived in Moscow. From them, he learned about developments in the rest of Europe.

In 1696, Peter visited Western Europe. As he traveled through Holland, England, and Germany, he realized how much Russia had to learn from the west. Peter acted more like an apprentice than an absolute monarch during his travels. He worked in a Dutch shipyard and learned about guns and cannons. He toured hospitals and visited printing shops. He met with government officials, merchants, and sea captains, always eager to learn. Although he traveled in disguise, he was often recognized because of his great height.

Peter's reforms. On his return to Russia in 1698, Peter was determined to westernize his nation. He hired over 700 European engineers, shipbuilders, and mathematicians. He paid them high salaries to teach their skills to the Russians. Peter also ordered scholars to simplify the Russian alphabet.

The czar allowed nothing to stop his efforts to impose a new way of life on his people. He forced Russian nobles to give up customs that he considered backward. For example, he ordered noblemen to shave off their long beards, and he fined those who refused. Noblewomen in Russia had lived in seclusion. Peter insisted that they appear in public and dress in French fashions.

Peter modeled his government after the government of Louis XIV. He replaced the Duma, a council of nobles, with a Senate that would follow his will in all matters. He established a government bureaucracy and promoted talented commoners to office. He

Peter the Great saw the long beards worn by Russian men as an example of his country's backwardness and ordered nobles to shave their beards. Many men objected because they believed that God had a beard and that man was made in God's image. Eventually, Peter allowed men to keep their beards if they paid a special tax. This cartoon shows Peter the Great, at right, clipping the beard of a protesting noble.

required nobles to serve either in the army or as government officials, and he sent sons of nobles abroad to study.

Foreign policy. Like earlier czars, Peter wanted to expand Russian borders. His main goal was to gain a warm-water port that would allow Russia to trade directly with Western Europe all year around. He hoped to win such a "window on the west" on the Baltic and Black seas.

In 1700, he fought Sweden, which controlled the Baltic coastline. The brilliant Swedish king Charles XII defeated a Russian force of 40,000 with only 8,000 Swedish troops. Undaunted, Peter rebuilt his army on the western model. In 1709, he overwhelmed the Swedes at the battle of Poltava. The war dragged on, but Peter won his window on the west. Russia did not reach the Black Sea, however, until later in the century.

A new capital. Soon after his victory over the Swedes, Peter decided to build a new capital on the icy, swampy shores of the Baltic. The city, named St. Petersburg, was built by thousands of peasant laborers, who were forced to work under terrible conditions. Often they dug only with sticks and carried dirt away in their coats.

Just as Versailles symbolized the reign of Louis XIV, St. Petersburg stood as a monument to Peter the Great's power. Peter ordered nobles and merchants to live in his new capital. Unlike Moscow, St. Petersburg was a seaport. Through it, the Russians could keep in touch with developments in Western Europe.

Before his death in 1725, Peter had achieved his dream of making Russia a more modern and more powerful nation. From the 1700s on, Russia would be increasingly involved in European affairs.

Catherine the Great

Peter had demanded the right to choose his successor, but on his deathbed he scribbled only the phrase, "I leave all..." No one knew whom he meant to choose as his heir. Power struggles among various Romanovs left Russia without a strong czar until 1762. In that year, Czar Peter III died and his wife Catherine became czarina, or empress, of Russia.

For 34 years, Catherine directed the Russian government with a firm hand. Although she was a German princess by birth, Catherine had learned Russian and converted to the Eastern Orthodox faith when she married. She won the support of the Russian nobles by giving them a charter of their rights. It exempted them from taxes and excused them from the service to the state that Peter the Great had required.

After Catherine gave the nobles their charter, peasants expected their own charter of rights from noble landlords. When it did not come, they rebelled. The peasant rebellion was the largest in Russian history, but it failed. Furthermore, it convinced Catherine to take stiff measures against the peasants. During Catherine's reign, conditions for peasants grew worse, and more were forced into serfdom. According to one estimate, 34 million Russians were serfs out of a total population of 36 million.

Catherine earned the title "the Great" for her aggressive foreign policy. Like Peter the Great, she ruthlessly tried to expand Russian borders. She won a warm-water port on the Black Sea by defeating the Ottoman Empire. Russia might have carved up the declining Ottoman Empire, but Austria and Prussia rushed to prevent Russia from becoming too powerful in Eastern Europe. Frederick the Great of Prussia persuaded Catherine to give up her ambitions in the south in return for a slice of Poland in the west.

The Partitions of Poland

In 1772, the first of three partitions of Poland took place. Catherine took part of eastern Poland, where many Russians and Ukrai-

nians lived. Frederick eagerly took West Prussia, which finally united the scattered lands of Brandenburg and Prussia. Maria Theresa of Austria took Galicia, although she protested the idea of dividing up Poland. Prussia, Russia, and Austria knew that Poland was too weak to resist.

During the 1400s and 1500s, Poland had been a large and powerful nation. It stretched across Eastern Europe from the Oder River to the Dnieper River. However, during the 1600s and 1700s, Polish nobles became increasingly independent of the king. They ruled their own lands with a free hand, acting like feudal lords. As a result, government in Poland was chaotic.

Nobles met in the Diet, or legislature, to pass laws, but the Diet was ineffective. All laws had to be approved by all nobles. Each noble had a right known as the "liberum veto," or free veto. By saying he was totally opposed to a proposed law, a noble could

Map Skill *Russia acquired new lands in Europe during the 1600s and 1700s. Which nations benefited from the partitions of Poland?*

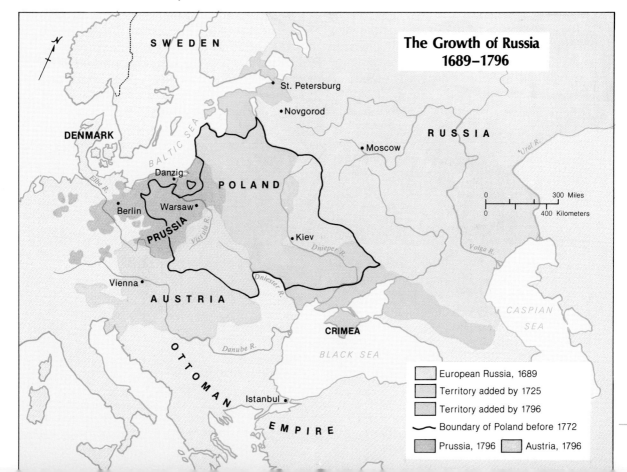

The Growth of Russia
1689–1796

	European Russia, 1689
	Territory added by 1725
	Territory added by 1796
—	Boundary of Poland before 1772
	Prussia, 1796		Austria, 1796

force the Diet to disband and wipe out all laws the Diet had already passed. Such an action was known as "exploding" the Diet. Between 1652 and 1754, nobles "exploded" 48 of the 55 Diets that met. Poland's weakness left it at the mercy of its neighbors.

After the first partition, the Poles united behind their king, but it was too late. In 1793, Russia and Prussia each took another slice of Poland. Then, in 1795, Russia, Prussia, and Austria carried out the third and final partition. Poland ceased to exist as an independent nation until 1919.

SECTION REVIEW

1. Locate: Istanbul, St. Petersburg.
2. Identify: Suleiman, Time of Troubles, Michael Romanov.
3. What was the Turkish attitude toward non-Muslims in their empire?
4. Describe the treatment of serfs in Russia.
5. How did Catherine the Great gain a warm-water port for Russia?
6. What nations participated in the partition of Poland?

Chapter 18 Review

In Perspective

During the 1500s and 1600s, monarchs in Europe created strong national governments. They limited the rights of nobles and ruled with absolute power. Under the rule of Philip II, Spain enjoyed a golden age in the 1500s. Philip used the treasure of the New World to make Spain the dominant power in Europe. But in the 1600s, a weak economy contributed to Spain's decline. France suffered through wars of religion in the 1500s, but it replaced Spain as the leader of Europe in the 1600s. Louis XIV centralized power and claimed "I am the state."

In Germany, religious differences led to the Thirty Years' War. The years of fighting left Germany physically devastated, and the Peace of Westphalia recognized the independence of hundreds of small German states. However, in the 1700s, Prussia and Austria emerged as the two leading German states.

The Ottoman Empire and Poland were powerful nations in Eastern Europe in the 1500s, but they declined in the next century. In Russia, Peter the Great introduced western ideas and technology. Both Peter and Catherine the Great made Russia a major force in European affairs.

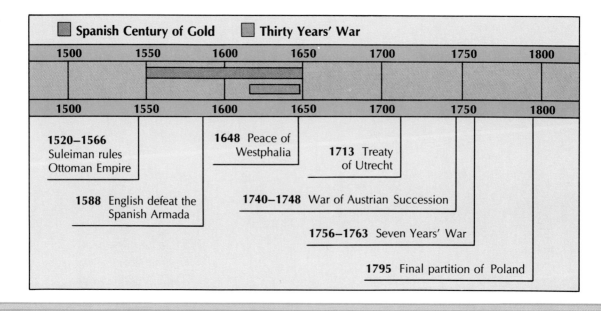

Recalling Facts

Review the time line on page 362 and your reading in this chapter. Then choose the letter of the correct time period for each of the following events.

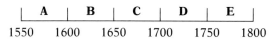

A	B	C	D	E
1550	1600	1650	1700	1750	1800

1. Louis XIV cancels the Edict of Nantes.
2. Suleiman rules the Ottoman Empire.
3. The Dutch revolt against Spanish rule.
4. Peter the Great wins a "window on the west."
5. Spain launches the Armada against England.
6. King Frederick William I strengthens the Prussian army.
7. Maria Theresa inherits the Austrian throne.
8. Final partition of Poland occurs.
9. The Seven Years' War is fought.
10. The Thirty Years' War devastates Germany.

Chapter Checkup

1. (a) How did Philip II help make Spain the most powerful nation in Europe? (b) Why did Spanish power decline during the 1600s?
2. Explain how each of the following individuals helped make France an absolute monarchy: (a) Henry IV; (b) Cardinal Richelieu; (c) Louis XIV.
3. (a) How did Colbert's policies strengthen the French economy? (b) Why were his policies important for Louis XIV's foreign policy?
4. What events and developments prevented the creation of a centralized German state in the 1600s?
5. Explain how each of the following rulers helped make Prussia a powerful nation: (a) the Great Elector; (b) Frederick William I; (c) Frederick the Great.
6. (a) Describe the Ottoman Empire under Suleiman. (b) Why did the empire decline after his death?
7. (a) How did Peter the Great bring Russia into closer contact with Western Europe? (b) What actions by Catherine the Great showed that Russia was a major European power?

Critical Thinking

1. **Understanding Economic Ideas** (a) What effect did the increase in gold and silver from the Americas have on Spain? (b) Why did much of Spain's wealth leave the country? (c) In the long run, did Spain benefit from the wealth of the New World? Explain.
2. **Analyzing a Quotation** Bishop Bossuet, tutor to Louis XIV's son, defended the idea of absolute monarchy with these words: "The royal throne is not the throne of a man, but the throne of God himself." (a) Explain the meaning of the quotation in your own words. (b) What monarchs discussed in this chapter do you think would have agreed with Bossuet? Explain.

Relating Past to Present

1. (a) What did Europeans mean by the balance of power? (b) What country or countries might have upset the balance of power in Europe in the 1700s? (c) Do you think nations are still concerned about the balance of power today? Explain.

Developing Basic Skills

1. **Graph Reading** Review the graph-reading steps you learned on page 331 to study the graph on page 346. Then answer the following questions: (a) How many millions of pounds of gold and silver did Spain import from the Americas from 1541 to 1560? (b) During what period did Spain import the most gold and silver? (c) In your own words, describe what happened to gold and silver imports during the 1500s and 1600s. (d) What effect do you think New World treasure had on Spain?
2. **Classifying** Make a chart with two columns. In column one, write Philip II, Louis XIV, and Peter I. In column two, list the ways each monarch increased royal power in his own country. (a) What similarities do you see? (b) What differences do you see? (c) What do you think was the most important achievement of each monarch?
3. **Map Reading** Study the map on page 358. Then answer the following questions: (a) Describe the boundaries of the Ottoman Empire in 1453. (b) What areas did Suleiman add to the Ottoman Empire? (c) What European states were most directly affected by the expansion of the Ottoman Empire?

See page 805 for suggested readings.

An Age of Revolution

1649 Oliver Cromwell was head of the English republic which lasted until 1660.

Mozart, at the piano, began composing music before the age of five.

	1600	1650	1700
POLITICS AND GOVERNMENT		**1642** English civil war begins	**1660** Charles II restored to throne	**1715** Louis XIV of France dies
ECONOMICS AND TECHNOLOGY	**1609** Kepler notes elliptical orbit of planets		**1687** Newton publishes book of mathematical proofs
SOCIETY AND CULTURE		**1645** Levellers demand abolition of noble titles in England	**1690** John Locke publishes *Two Treatises on Government*

This painted fan shows the opulence of the nobles in France under the Old Regime.

1671 Model of a telescope developed by Sir Isaac Newton.

During the French Revolution, many French people demanded "liberty," symbolized here by a statue.

1804 Napoleon, who had become First Consul in 1799, proclaimed himself emperor in 1804.

1750	1800	1850

1776 American colonies declare independence

1789 French Revolution begins

1848 Nationalist revolutions break out in Europe

Mid-1700s Wedgewood develops new methods of pottery making

1770s Economic crisis grows in France

1848 National workshops set up for the unemployed in France

1748 Montesquieu publishes *The Spirit of Laws*

1819 Carlsbad Decrees suppress freedom of speech

Jean Jacques Rousseau believed in equality and the will of the majority.

1775 The Battle of Bunker Hill took place before Americans had declared their independence from Britain.

365

The Alchemist, by
Giovanni Stradano.

19 The Scientific Revolution and the Enlightenment

(1500–1800)

One day in 1671, Anton van Leeuwenhoek (LAY vuhn HOOK), a Dutch cloth merchant, took a glass lens used to examine the weave of different fabrics and mounted it between two metal plates. He then constructed a specimen holder and attached it to his simple magnifying glass. With this primitive microscope, Leeuwenhoek began to study such everyday objects as bits of pepper and plant seeds as well as his own skin.

Eventually, Leeuwenhoek put a drop of water on the specimen holder and peered through his microscope. He was amazed to find what he called little "wretched beasties" swimming around in the droplet of water. He described these creatures as "moving about very nimbly" because they had "incredibly thin feet!" What Leeuwenhoek saw were single-cell living organisms such as bacteria.

Leeuwenhoek's startling discovery created a stir among scholars because it opened up a whole new world of study. As Leeuwenhoek and other scientists pursued their investigations using the microscope, they discovered hundreds of previously unknown organisms. As they learned more about the life cycles of these tiny organisms, they had to discard long-held ideas about biology.

During the 1500s and 1600s, inventions such as the microscope and numerous other discoveries transformed the natural sciences and medicine. New technology and improved methods of research led to an explosion in knowledge that became known as the Scientific Revolution.

Discoveries about the physical world affected philosophers. They applied scientific principles to the study of government and society. During the first half of the 1700s, philosophers emphasized the use of reason. They thought that people should use reason to free themselves from ignorance and superstition and thereby become enlightened. They were convinced that enlightened people could perfect themselves and society. Thus, the eighteenth century is known as the Enlightenment.

Together, the Scientific Revolution and the Enlightenment would change the way people saw the world and help shape the attitudes that made the scientific advances of the modern world possible.

1 New Directions in Science

Read to Learn
- about scientific discoveries during the Renaissance
- how inventions contributed to the Scientific Revolution

During the Renaissance, a spirit of curiosity encouraged a few people to study the natural world. For example, the painter and sculptor Leonardo da Vinci kept detailed notebooks in which he described his scientific observations. He drew plans for fantastic inventions including a flying machine and a device that looked like a bicycle. By the late Renaissance, scholars had greatly expanded scientific knowledge and developed a new approach to scientific studies.

The Scientific Method

The ancient Greek philosopher Aristotle created a system of thought based on observation and a process of reasoning called logic. During the Middle Ages, the teachings of Aristotle dominated scientific thinking.

Between 1200 and 1700, scholars began questioning the views of ancient philosophers. Some scholars made observations and conducted experiments that disproved accepted theories. At the same time, the increased use of Arabic numerals led to advances in mathematics that revealed errors in Aristotle's logic.

Slowly, this new approach developed as the *scientific method*. The scientific method is a threefold approach to scientific study. First, careful experiments and observations are made. Second, reason is used to interpret the results of the experiments and observa-

tions. Third, mathematics rather than logic, or reasoning from principles, is used to prove scientific theories.

Copernicus

Nicolaus Copernicus (koh PUR nih kuhs), a Polish mathematician and astronomer, played a central role in developing the scientific method. In 1543, he published *On the Revolutions of the Heavenly Bodies*. His work challenged Ptolemy's view of the universe. As you read in Chapter 6, Ptolemy taught that the earth was the center of the universe.

Copernicus used mathematical calculations to show that Ptolemy was wrong on two crucial points. First, Copernicus said that the earth was not stationary but that it turned on its axis once a day. Second, he declared that the earth was not the center of the universe. He argued that the earth and the planets revolved around the sun in perfect circles. Although Copernicus' theories were partly correct, he could not provide enough convincing evidence to prove that Ptolemy was wrong. As a result, many educated people rejected his views.

Many scholars argued that Ptolemy and the other ancient philosophers could not have been wrong. In Western Europe, all scientific knowledge and many religious teachings were based on the logical arguments developed by the ancient philosophers. The scholars thought that if their reasoning about the planets was wrong, then the whole of human knowledge would become uncertain.

Although Copernicus' ideas were not readily accepted, they had far-reaching consequences because they affected the method of testing ideas. After Copernicus, scientists increasingly backed up observation of nature with mathematical calculations.

Further Discoveries

In the late 1500s, Danish astronomer Tycho Brahe built an observatory to study the planets and stars. He carefully recorded what he saw, and his assistant, Johannes Kepler, used this information to prove Copernicus' theories.

Like Copernicus, Kepler thought that the earth and other planets traveled around the sun. Kepler performed thousands of hours of calculations based on Brahe's observations. His calculations supported the idea that the planets revolve around the sun but not that they revolve in perfect circles as Copernicus had thought. In 1609, Kepler announced that the planets move in another kind of orbit, called an ellipse.

In Italy, the astronomer Galileo Galilei used a new magnifying instrument, the telescope, to observe the planets and stars. His observations led to further discoveries about the universe. Since ancient times, astronomers had believed that the moon, planets, and stars were all perfect, unchanging bodies.

Through the telescope, Galileo saw that the moon had a rough surface broken by jagged mountains. He discovered that the planet Jupiter had four moons, which no one had seen before. The sun was seen to be imperfect because it had dark, changeable spots on its surface. Galileo's discoveries showed that the universe was very different from what ancient philosophers had taught.

Galileo on Trial

When Galileo announced his discoveries in the early 1600s, the conflict between traditional thinking and the new science broke into the open. Galileo offended many scien-

The telescope made possible more detailed observation of the sky than ever before. This painting shows two Italians examining the moon's surface through a telescope made by Galileo. Through his telescope, Galileo observed that the moon had a rough surface. He also discovered that the Milky Way, once thought to be a kind of heavenly mist, was in fact a vast belt of stars.

tists by declaring that the heavenly bodies were imperfect and changing. An outspoken man, he did not hesitate to defend his views. He made powerful enemies when he humiliated his critics in public.

These enemies convinced the Catholic Church to condemn the teachings of Copernicus and to forbid Galileo from defending the new ideas. When Galileo refused to obey, church officials called him before the Inquisition. They demanded that he publicly admit his error. In order to avoid being condemned as a heretic and face death, Galileo declared at the trial that the earth stood motionless at the center of the universe. But as he left the court after the trial, Galileo whispered softly under his breath, "And yet it moves."

Newton and Natural Laws

An English mathematician, Sir Isaac Newton, built on the work of many earlier scientists. In 1687, Newton published *The Mathematical Principles of Natural Philosophy*. In this book, he provided mathematical proofs of what people such as Kepler and Galileo had observed. Newton invented calculus, a method of calculation, which he used to prove his theories.

Among Newton's most important contributions to science was the law of gravity, which he wrote as a mathematical formula. Newton's *law of gravity* states that there is a force of attraction between objects that increases as objects move closer together. Newton's law explains mathematically how the moon's gravity causes tides on the earth and how the sun's gravity keeps the planets within their orbits. Newton is said to have developed the law of gravity after he saw an apple fall. He wondered why it fell to the ground and did not fly into space. His law explains that an apple falls to the ground because it is attracted by the earth's gravity.

Newton's work helped to develop a new view of the universe. Newton saw the universe as a huge, well-regulated machine that worked according to definite laws of nature, such as the law of gravity.

Newton's work had many effects. Navigators and mapmakers used his mathematics to make more precise charts. Calculus was used to improve weapons such as guns and cannons. Later, inventors improved on Newton's ideas and developed such practical devices as the steam engine.

Improvements in Medicine

During the 1500s and 1600s, scientists made significant advances in medicine. Some challenged the theories of Galen, a Greek physician whose work had dominated medicine in the Middle Ages.

In the early 1500s, a Swiss physician known as Paracelsus (PAR uh SEHL suhs) experimented with chemistry. He disproved Galen's idea that chemical changes, such as transforming one substance into another, were impossible. He produced distilled liquids that he used as medicine.

At the University of Padua in Italy, scholars studied the human body. In 1543, Andreas Vesalius (vih SAY lee uhs), a professor of anatomy, wrote *On the Structure of the Human Body*. He made accurate drawings of the human anatomy that corrected some of Galen's errors.

A French physician, Ambroise Paré (pah RAY), studied Vesalius' textbook and soon made his own contributions to medicine. Traditionally, doctors had tried to prevent infection in wounds by pouring boiling oil into the wound, an extremely painful remedy. Paré developed an ointment that could be applied instead. Later, Paré also developed a technique for closing wounds with stitches.

In the early 1600s, an Englishman, William Harvey, studied the circulation of the blood through the body and showed that the heart acted as a pump to circulate blood through arteries and veins. Traditionally, doctors had thought that blood remained stationary.

The work of these physicians and others resulted in further medical breakthroughs. In the 1700s, for example, doctors learned how to produce a vaccine that could be used to prevent smallpox. As medical and scientific knowledge increased, scholars formed scientific societies to exchange information.

SECTION REVIEW

1. Identify: Nicolaus Copernicus, Tycho Brahe, Johannes Kepler, Galileo Galilei.
2. Define: scientific method, law of gravity.
3. Why was mathematics important to the scientific method?
4. Give two reasons why scholars challenged the ideas of Copernicus.
5. What did Galileo's observations through the telescope reveal?
6. How did Newton think the universe worked?
7. Describe one way each of the following contributed to medical knowledge: (a) Paracelsus, (b) Andreas Vesalius, (c) Ambroise Paré, (d) William Harvey.

2 Enlightenment Thinkers

Read to Learn   ■ how the philosophes influenced government and society
■ why the physiocrats favored a free market over mercantilism

In the late 1600s and the 1700s, philosophers reexamined society using the scientific method. During the Enlightenment, philosophers felt confident that they could use reason to discover natural laws that governed human behavior. As a result, this period is also called the Age of Reason.

Hobbes and Locke

The ideas of two English philosophers, Thomas Hobbes and John Locke, affected how people viewed the individual's role in society. During the 1640s, Hobbes witnessed the upheavals of a civil war in England.* Hobbes became convinced that if people were left alone they would constantly fight among themselves. In 1651, he published his ideas in *Leviathan*. In this work, he described a state of nature in which people had no laws or government. Hobbes claimed that such a life would be "nasty, brutish, and short."

According to Hobbes, to escape the chaos of their natural state, people entered into a contract in which they agreed to give up their freedom to a ruler who ensured peace and order. The best government, Hobbes said, was one in which the ruler had absolute power. Furthermore, Hobbes insisted, once people entered into such a contract, they could not rebel, even if they thought the ruler was a tyrant. Hobbes' ideas, therefore, supported the rule of absolute monarchs.

In 1690, John Locke published *Two Treatises on Government*. Locke agreed with Hobbes that the purpose of government was to establish order in society. He also saw government as a contract between the ruler and the ruled. However, Locke's other ideas about government differed greatly from those of Hobbes.

Locke had a more optimistic view of human nature than Hobbes. He thought people

---

* You will read about the civil war in England in Chapter 20.

were basically reasonable and would cooperate with each other. Moreover, Locke argued that rulers could stay in power only as long as they had the consent of those they governed. If a ruler were a tyrant, he or she had broken the contract, and the people had the right to rebel.

Locke presented some very important ideas. He believed people had natural rights, including the right to life, liberty, and property. Government was responsible for protecting these rights, but its power should be limited. After Locke's death, his ideas became popular in France and in North America, as you will read in later chapters.

Social and Economic Ideas

Many writers and thinkers, especially in France, expanded on Locke's idea of natural rights. They became known as *philosophes*, a French word meaning philosophers. The philosophes had great confidence that the use of science and reason would lead to continued human progress.

Many philosophes gathered in Paris, where they helped to make Enlightenment ideas popular. Often, they were middle class, well-educated men who valued clear thinking as well as wit and humor.

The philosophes were concerned about many social issues. They urged religious toleration and condemned wars of religion. They claimed people had the right to believe as they wished. The philosophes called for freedom of speech and the press, and they criticized the strict censorship that most governments imposed. They believed censorship was harmful because it prevented people from learning about new ideas. They encouraged education as the way to end ignorance, prejudice, and superstition.

The philosophes denounced slavery because it deprived people of their most basic rights. They spoke out against torture and cruel punishments for crimes. Some philosophes campaigned for more humane treatment of the mentally ill.

One group of philosophes, known as *physiocrats*, searched for natural laws to explain economics. As you read in Chapter 17, mercantilism influenced the economic policies of most governments at the time. Physiocrats opposed mercantilism. They argued that land was the true source of national wealth, not hoards of gold and silver. They urged rulers to encourage farming.

Furthermore, physiocrats believed that restrictions on trade should be removed so farmers could sell their products wherever there was a market. They favored a *free market*, that is, a market in which all goods can be bought and sold without restraint. They argued that the resulting increase in trade would mean greater wealth for everyone.

Profiles ■ Josiah Wedgwood: A Practical Man of the Enlightenment

During the Enlightenment, middle class businesspeople, lawyers, and scientists tried to apply the scientific method and the principles of reason to everyday life. One such person was Josiah Wedgwood, who lived in England from 1730 to 1795. Wedgwood is best known for producing Wedgwood pottery, which is still sold all over the world.

Wedgwood was no ordinary potter. He combined science and art as few in his field had done before. He taught himself chemistry so he could understand the chemical changes that took place when clay was heated. He invented special thermometers to measure the high temperatures required for glazing clay. An experimenter, he frequently tried new materials and designed new ovens to improve the quality of his products.

Like many artists of this period, Wedgwood admired the simple, elegant designs of classical Greece and Rome. As a result, his pottery often carried Greek or Roman figures.

As his pottery business prospered, Wedgwood pursued other interests. He joined the Lunar Society, a group of businesspeople and scientists who met to discuss scientific developments. Among Wedgwood's friends in the Lunar Society was Joseph Priestley, the scientist who discovered oxygen. Wedgwood helped support Priestley's work financially. He also invented special laboratory equipment for Priestley.

Wedgwood used his pottery to spread ideas about social justice. Like many Enlightenment thinkers, he campaigned vigorously against the slave trade. Wedgwood designed and produced thousands of anti-slavery medallions like the one shown here. The slave in chains utters the words: "Am I not a man and a brother?" Wedgwood distributed the medallions in Britain and shipped many across the Atlantic to the American colonies. Fashionable people wore the medallions or put them on display at home, thereby expressing their support for the antislavery cause. In his own way, Wedgwood helped to channel Enlightenment ideas into the homes of many people.

Three Influential Views on Government

Among the most influential Enlightenment thinkers were Montesquieu (MAHN tuhs kyoo), Voltaire, and Rousseau (roo SOH). Each formed his own ideas about the best way to organize governments. Yet all three shared the basic beliefs of the philosophes.

Montesquieu. Born to a noble family, the Baron de Montesquieu was a keen student of government. He read the works of Newton and Locke. In *The Spirit of Laws,* he discussed various forms of government.

Montesquieu was especially impressed with the system of government that had developed in England by the mid-1700s. He believed that English government preserved the liberty of the people by the separation of power among three branches of government: the legislature, executive, and judiciary. Montesquieu thought that in England Parliament, as the legislature, made the laws; the king, as the executive, enforced the laws; and the courts, as the judiciary, interpreted the laws if disputes arose. The English system did not work that way in reality, but Montesquieu's ideas were widely discussed.

Montesquieu also thought that the power of each branch of government should be carefully defined to provide a system of checks and balances. That way no branch of government could dominate another. Montesquieu's ideas on checks and balances and the separation of powers would later influence the men who wrote the Constitution of the United States.

Voltaire. Probably the best known philosophe was François Marie Arouet, who used the pen name Voltaire. Voltaire came from a French middle class family. He traveled widely and became popular for his witty plays and novels as well as for his pamphlets attacking evils in society.

Voltaire spent much of his life arguing for religious toleration and freedom of thought. He is credited with saying, "I do not agree with a word you say but I will defend to the death your right to say it."

Voltaire praised English liberties and the works of Newton and Locke. He favored the idea of a strong monarch. To Voltaire, the best ruler was an "enlightened monarch." By that he meant a monarch who studied the science of government and protected the basic rights of the people.

Rousseau. The Swiss philosophe Jean Jacques Rousseau came from a poor and unhappy family. When he went to Paris, he always felt out of place among the sophisticated intellectuals who gathered there. A complainer and constant critic of others, Rousseau quarreled with many philosophes. Yet his political and social ideas were an important part of Enlightenment thought.

Rousseau believed that human nature was basically good. In his opinion, society corrupted people. He also argued that all people were equal and that all titles of rank and nobility should be abolished. "Man is born free," he wrote, "and everywhere is in chains."

Rousseau admired what he called the "noble savage," who lived in a natural state, free from the influences of civilization. How-

The French honored their greatest writers, including Voltaire and Rousseau, by electing them to the French Academy. Members of the French Academy were called "the immortals." This picture shows a winged spirit conducting Rousseau, on the left, and Voltaire, on the right, to the temple of glory and immortality. The writings of Rousseau and Voltaire shaped Enlightenment thinking in France and elsewhere.

ever, Rousseau realized that people could not return to the natural state.

In *The Social Contract*, Rousseau described an ideal society. In this society, people would form a community and make a contract with each other, not with a ruler. People would give up some of their freedom in favor of the "general will," or the decisions of the majority. The community would vote on all decisions, and everyone would accept the community decision.

Rousseau's beliefs in equality and in the will of the majority made him a spokesman for the common people. Revolutionaries in many countries would later adopt his ideas.

SECTION REVIEW

1. Identify: Thomas Hobbes, John Locke, Montesquieu, Voltaire, Jean Jacques Rousseau.
2. Define: philosophe, physiocrat, free market.
3. (a) What kind of government did Hobbes support? (b) According to Locke, when did people have a right to rebel?
4. Describe three concerns of the philosophes.
5. Why did Montesquieu support a government system with checks and balances?
6. (a) Who did Voltaire think should govern? (b) What did Rousseau mean by the "general will"?

3 Impact of the Enlightenment

Read to Learn
■ how Enlightenment ideas spread
■ about the impact of the Enlightenment on government and art

During the mid-1700s, as philosophes traveled and wrote, enlightenment ideas spread across Europe. One of the most successful spokesmen of the Enlightenment was Denis Diderot (DEE duh ROH), a French philosophe who supervised the publication of a huge encyclopedia that summarized human knowledge of that time.

Spread of New Ideas

Like many philosophes, Diderot moved to Paris as a young man, where he met the best thinkers of the day. A daring man, Diderot convinced a French bookseller to agree to publish the *Encyclopedia, or Classified Dictionary of the Sciences, Arts, and Occupations*. Between 1751 and 1772, Diderot assembled the 35-volume *Encyclopedia*.

Diderot hoped the *Encyclopedia* would bring about "a revolution in the minds of men to free them from prejudice." Voltaire, Montesquieu, Rousseau, and many others contributed articles on philosophy, religion, the arts, literature, and government. Other people wrote about lands in Africa and Asia, where Europeans had begun to explore. But the *Encyclopedia* devoted the most space to articles on science and technology. Diderot included diagrams that showed the latest advances in printing, spinning, medicine, and other fields.

In France, the Catholic Church and government censors banned the *Encyclopedia*. They considered it antireligious because some articles criticized religious persecution. However, censorship could not prevent it from becoming a popular work read by educated people all over Europe.

Enlightenment ideas also spread in other ways. As the number of people who could read and write increased in the 1700s, more newspapers and journals were published. Learned societies informed people of the new ideas through public lectures and published reports. In addition, middle class men met in coffee houses to discuss the latest news in science or politics. In working class neighborhoods, popular songs and political pamphlets spread new ideas.

Women's Contribution to the Enlightenment

Women played an important role in spreading Enlightenment ideas. In Paris, and elsewhere in France, wealthy women held *salons*, or informal gatherings, at which

The first English coffee house opened around 1650. London coffee houses, like the one shown here, became gathering places for writers, scientists, businessmen, and politicians. At these coffee houses, men discussed politics and the new ideas of the Enlightenment.

writers, musicians, painters, and philosophes presented their works and exchanged ideas. The salon originated in the 1600s, when a group of noblewomen in Paris began inviting a few friends to poetry readings. Only people who were considered witty, intelligent, and well-read were invited to the salons.

During the 1700s, women from the middle class such as Madame de Geoffrin began forming salons. Voltaire and other leading philosophes gathered at Madame de Geoffrin's salon at least once a week. Through their salons, women helped shape the taste and manners of the Enlightenment.

Some women acted as patrons for artists and writers. For example, Louise de Warens supported Rousseau and his family so he could devote his full time to writing. In addition, many women produced their own poetry and novels, which they circulated among their friends in the salons. A few women managed to get an education in the sciences. For example, Émilie du Châtelet became a noted physicist and mathematician and translated Newton's work from Latin into French.

Enlightened Monarchs

Many European rulers were impressed by the ideas of the Enlightenment. Some adopted policies that they hoped would improve social and economic conditions in their countries. They considered themselves "enlightened monarchs." However, they also used the new ideas to centralize their power by reducing the privileges of nobles.

In Austria, Maria Theresa and her son, Joseph II, tried to implement policies that reflected Enlightenment principles. Maria Theresa passed laws to limit serfdom by regulating the amount of unpaid work required from peasants. Joseph took her policies a step further and abolished serfdom.

He also permitted freedom of the press, banned the use of torture, and ended religious persecution. He gave equal rights to Jews and limited the power of the Catholic Church. However, after his death in 1790, his successors reversed his reforms.

Other enlightened monarchs studied the new ideas but made few major changes. Catherine the Great of Russia invited Diderot to visit Russia, and she corresponded with Voltaire. She made some effort to limit torture and introduce religious toleration, but she did nothing to end serfdom.

Frederick the Great of Prussia was so impressed with the French philosophes that he invited Voltaire to his court. Frederick codified Prussian laws, allowed religious freedom, and encouraged elementary education for Prussian children. However, like most enlightened monarchs, he did not change the social structure, which was based on inequality and serfdom.

The Arts During the Enlightenment

During the Enlightenment, artists tried to find laws that would give order to their work. Painters thought their subjects should look natural but at the same time beautiful. They were strongly influenced by classical Greek art, which had represented figures in their most ideal and graceful forms.

Classical styles also influenced European architecture. In the 1600s, buildings had become ornate and elaborate. But in the 1700s, architects returned to the simple elegance of ancient Greece.

Many talented individuals made lasting contributions to music. In the late 1600s and early 1700s, musicians, like architects, favored an ornate style in their work. Two German composers, Johann Sebastian Bach and George Frederick Handel, are among the most important composers of this period. Bach wrote many types of music, but he is

In salons, men and women enjoyed intelligent, informed conversation on many subjects. "We polish one another, and rub off our corners and rough sides by a sort of amicable [friendly] collision," wrote one man who visited salons in Paris and London. The Paris salon of Madame de Geoffrin, which is shown here, influenced art, literature, and politics in the mid-1700s.

perhaps best known for his religious music. Handel eventually settled in England, where his operas became very popular.

In the mid-1700s, music began to reflect the simplicity and elegance expressed by artists and architects of the time. In the late 1700s, this style of music was brought to its height by Franz Joseph Haydn and Wolfgang Amadeus Mozart. Haydn is best known for his symphonies.

Mozart is especially remembered as a child genius who began composing before he was five years old. At age six, Mozart played for the empress Maria Theresa. Later, his father took him and his talented sister to perform in the salons of Paris. Although he was only 35 when he died, Mozart had already written more than 600 musical works, including symphonies, operas, and church music.

SECTION REVIEW

1. Identify: Denis Diderot, Joseph II, Johann Sebastian Bach, Wolfgang Amadeus Mozart.
2. Define: salon.
3. What subjects did Diderot's *Encyclopedia* emphasize the most?
4. Describe three reforms introduced by enlightened monarchs.

Chapter 19 Review

In Perspective

During the 1500s and 1600s, the Scientific Revolution changed the way Europeans viewed the world. Scholars developed a new method to study the natural world. Mathematics played a central role in the scientific method, as did experiments and careful observation. The work of Copernicus and Galileo challenged traditional views of the universe. Although the new theories aroused fierce opposition, they were gradually accepted.

Just as Newton stated laws that he thought regulated the universe, philosophers tried to discover natural laws to explain human behavior. Hobbes and Locke had differing views of human nature, but both influenced the French philosophes.

During the Enlightenment, people felt confident that science and reason could solve the major problems facing society. Absolute monarchs believed they could use Enlightenment ideas to govern their nations.

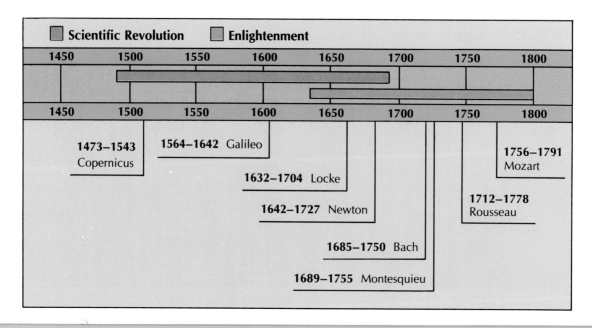

Recalling Facts

Match each name at left with the correct description at right.

1. Denis Diderot
2. John Locke
3. William Harvey
4. Sir Isaac Newton
5. Nicolaus Copernicus
6. Wolfgang Amadeus Mozart
7. Jean Jacques Rousseau
8. Galileo Galilei

a. Polish astronomer who said the earth revolved around the sun
b. English mathematician who developed law of gravity
c. English philosopher who believed people had natural rights to life, liberty, and property
d. philosopher who edited the *Encyclopedia*
e. astronomer who used a telescope to observe sunspots and the moons of Jupiter
f. physician who studied the circulation of the blood
g. composer who began writing music before age five
h. philosopher who thought society corrupted people

Chapter Checkup

1. (a) What was the basis of scientific thought during the Middle Ages? (b) Why did scholars begin to question traditional scientific views after 1200? (c) How did Copernicus help develop the scientific method?
2. (a) How did Galileo make so many enemies? (b) How did they get their revenge? (c) Why did Galileo give in to the Inquisition?
3. (a) How did Newton's work help change people's view of the universe? (b) What other effects did his work have?
4. (a) How were the ideas of Hobbes and Locke similar? (b) How were they different?
5. (a) What social and economic changes did the philosophes want? (b) Did they achieve any of their goals during the 1700s? Explain.

Critical Thinking

1. **Analyzing a Quotation** Leonardo da Vinci wrote, "No human investigation can be called true science without passing through mathematical tests." (a) How was this view reflected in the Scientific Revolution? (b) Why do you think scholars such as Newton had such confidence in mathematics?
2. **Expressing an Opinion** The philosophes were confident of human progress. They believed that life could be improved. (a) What events and developments of the time do you think contributed to this attitude? (b) Do you think people today still believe in progress? Explain.
3. **Applying Information** Joseph II was an enlightened monarch and an absolute ruler. Yet he could not greatly improve the lives of his people. Why do you think this was true?

Relating Past to Present

1. List three developments of the Scientific Revolution. What have been the long-term consequences of each?

Developing Basic Skills

1. **Classifying** Make a chart with three columns. In the first column, list Hobbes, Locke, Montesquieu, Voltaire, and Rousseau. In the second column, describe the government each philosopher thought was best. In the third column, explain why each thought his system was the best. Then answer the following questions: (a) Which philosopher's ideas were most democratic? Why? (b) Whose ideas were least democratic? Why? (c) Who was concerned with individual rights? (d) Which system do you think is most like the government of the United States today? Explain.
2. **Researching** Choose one individual who made a contribution to the Scientific Revolution of the Enlightenment. Research his or her background in order to answer the following questions: (a) To what social class did the person belong? (b) What training or education did the person receive? (c) What was the individual's contribution to the Scientific Revolution or the Enlightenment? (d) Why was the person's contribution important?

See page 805 for suggested readings.

20 Revolution in England and North America

(1509-1791)

During the 1770s, the British government angered its 13 American colonies by introducing new tax laws. In January 1776, a pamphlet entitled *Common Sense* created a great stir in the colonies. The author, an Englishman named Thomas Paine, had settled in Pennsylvania less than two years earlier. An outspoken critic of Great Britain, Paine argued that the American colonists should solve their dispute with Britain by declaring independence.

Between January and July 1776, 500,000 copies of *Common Sense* were printed and circulated throughout the colonies. Paine challenged those who wanted compromise "to show a single advantage that this continent can reap, by being connected with Great Britain." America's connection with Britain, Paine declared, only brought disadvantages to the colonies. In addition, he reasoned that for Britain to rule America was contrary to the laws of nature.

"There is something very absurd in supposing a continent to be perpetually governed by an island. In no instance has nature made the satellite larger than its primary planet; and as England and America, with respect to each other, reverse the common order of nature, it is evident that they belong to different systems—England to Europe, America to itself. . . ."

Paine helped convince many colonists to support the Declaration of Independence. After winning their independence, the colonists had to decide who should govern them and how. Ironically, 100 years earlier, the people of England had debated the same questions.

Like the European nations that you read about in Chapter 18, England had developed a strong, centralized government during the 1600s and 1700s. But

Signing the American Declaration of Independence.

the government of England had gradually evolved into a limited monarchy rather than an absolute monarchy. The English accepted many of John Locke's ideas. They believed that government should protect certain basic liberties. They also felt that the power to govern came from the consent of the governed. The ideas and institutions that emerged in England would become the basis for more democratic forms of government in both England and North America.

1 Clashes Between King and Parliament

Read to Learn   ■ how the Tudors and Stuarts dealt with Parliament
■ how Parliament tried to limit royal power

Unlike other European monarchs, English kings and queens had limits on their power. They were obliged to respect the tradition that the ruler must obey the law, and they had to deal with Parliament.

A Balance With Parliament

By the 1500s, the English Parliament had won several important rights. Parliament approved new taxes, passed laws proposed by the monarch, and advised monarchs. However, monarchs had more power than Parliament. They named officials and judges, summoned and dismissed Parliament, and conducted foreign policy. After 1534, monarchs also headed the Church of England.

The Tudor rulers, Henry VIII and his daughter Elizabeth I, were forceful personalities, but they both recognized the value of good relations with Parliament. Henry, you will recall, sought and obtained Parliament's approval to establish the Church of England.

Elizabeth followed a cautious policy in her dealings with Parliament. She lived simply so she would not have to ask for money too often. But she also clearly established her rights as monarch. She sometimes scolded Parliament for interfering in matters that she felt did not concern it. However, she also knew when to keep quiet and not to offend Parliament. During most of her reign, Elizabeth was a popular queen, and she managed to maintain a balance between exercising her power and deferring to Parliament. In this way, she preserved unity and stability.

In 1603, Elizabeth died without any direct heir. The English throne passed to the Stuarts, the ruling family of Scotland. When James VI of Scotland traveled south to London to be crowned James I of England, he knew little about English politics.

James I and the Divine Right of Kings

James I was a well-meaning ruler and a scholar. He supervised a new translation of the Bible, known as the King James version. He also wrote a book called *The True Law of Free Monarchies*. In it, he presented his belief that kings ruled by divine right. "Kings are called gods," he declared "because they sit upon God's throne on earth." Furthermore, he argued that the king should have no restraints on his power so that he could rule for the good of all his people. James's belief in his divine right to rule soon led to conflict with Parliament.

Parliament was made up of two houses: the House of Lords, in which nobles served for life, and the House of Commons, whose members were elected.* Most representatives in the House of Commons were wealthy landowners, called gentry. Many of the gentry had bought monastery lands that Henry VIII had seized from the church and sold. The gentry raised sheep for wool,

---

* Only a small number of property owners had the right to vote for members of the House of Commons.

James I was a well-educated monarch. He published articles on such subjects as witchcraft, the dangers of smoking tobacco, and rules for writing Scottish poetry. Unfortunately, he had little skill as a statesman. James was once described as "the most learned fool in Christendom."

which helped build a prosperous textile industry. The growing merchant class in England also had some representatives in the House of Commons.

James I and Parliament quarreled over three main issues: religion, money, and foreign policy. A major religious issue involved the demands of the Puritans. Puritans wanted to see the Anglican Church "purified" of Catholic rituals and ceremonies. They also demanded that local congregations be allowed to rule themselves rather than be ruled by bishops and archbishops appointed by the king. Among the Puritans were many powerful merchants, some of whom served as members of Parliament.

The House of Commons sympathized with the Puritans' demands. However, the king refused to make any changes in the church organization. Whereas Elizabeth had tolerated most Puritans, James vowed to "harry them out of the land." His per-

secution of Puritans forced some of them to leave England.

James was constantly in need of money. He spent lavishly on his court and gave generous gifts to his friends. In addition, England owed many debts to bankers for its wars against Catholic Spain. When the king summoned Parliament to approve new taxes, Parliament often refused unless he would accept its wishes on religious matters. James would angrily lecture Parliament on the divine right of kings and send the representatives home.

James would then have to bolster his income in other ways. He revived feudal fines and raised customs duties, which went directly to the crown. Although such moves were technically legal, James's actions angered Parliament.

Parliament criticized the king's foreign policy, especially when he made peace with Spain and tried to arrange a marriage between his son and a Spanish princess. Furthermore, many people in England felt that James did not give enough help to Protestants in Europe during the wars of religion there.

Charles I and Parliament

James's son Charles I inherited the throne in 1625. Like his father, Charles believed in the divine right of kings. When Parliament refused to give him enough money, Charles dismissed it and demanded loans from individual people. He imprisoned anyone who refused to pay the forced loans.

By 1628, Charles had to summon Parliament because he needed funds desperately. Parliament refused his financial demands until he signed the Petition of Right. In the petition, Charles promised not to collect forced loans or levy taxes without the consent of Parliament. He also agreed not to imprison a person without cause or house soldiers in private homes without the owner's consent. Through the Petition of Right, Parliament hoped to end the king's arbitrary actions.

However, once Parliament approved the funds he needed, Charles dissolved it. For the next 11 years, he ruled without calling another Parliament. He ignored the Petition of Right and returned to the policies of James I.

During the 1630s, Charles made many enemies because of his arbitrary rule. He appointed unpopular officials, such as William Laud to be Archbishop of Canterbury. Laud persecuted Puritans and other dissenters, Protestants who would not accept Anglican practices. Charles and his advisors also used special courts such as the Court of High Commission and the Court of Star Chamber to suppress opposition. These courts did not have to follow common law or use juries.

The gulf between the king and the country grew wider. A revolt in Scotland finally brought matters to a head. In 1638, Charles tried to impose the Anglican Church on Scotland, where the official religion was Presbyterian. The Scots resisted and invaded England. Because Charles needed money to equip and pay an army, he summoned Parliament in 1640.

The Long Parliament

The Parliament that was called in 1640 would meet in one form or another until 1660. Known as the Long Parliament, it would eventually lead a revolution against the monarchy. But in 1640, Parliament was chiefly concerned with limiting the king's power and removing unpopular officials.

Before granting Charles's request for money, Parliament demanded the trial of Charles's chief ministers, Archbishop Laud and the Earl of Strafford, for abusing their power. Both men were found guilty and executed.

Parliament abolished the Court of High Commission and the Court of Star Chamber. It also passed the Triennial Act, which stated that the king must call a parliament at least once every three years. As the Long Parliament continued to meet, critics of the king grew more outspoken. Eventually they pushed through a bill condemning Charles as a tyrant.

Charles struck back by leading a band of armed supporters into Parliament and arresting five outspoken members. The king's use of force made compromise impossible. In 1642, the king and Parliament raised their own armies, and civil war began.

The English Civil War

The civil war lasted from 1642 to 1649. People of all classes fought on both sides. In general, the king rallied to his side nobles and people in rural areas, especially in northwestern England. The king's supporters were called Cavaliers because the aristocratic leaders were mounted horsemen, or cavalry.

Parliament recruited its troops mostly from the middle class, especially from towns in southeastern England. Many Puritans fought for Parliament. Supporters of Parliament were called Roundheads because they cut their hair close to their heads to show that they rejected the aristocratic style of long hair.

In 1645, Oliver Cromwell, a strong-minded Puritan officer, reorganized Parliament's army as the New Model Army. Under his energetic leadership, the New Model Army became a well-disciplined force, and it defeated the Cavaliers and captured Charles I.

The Long Parliament, which had continued to meet during the civil war, decided the

This contemporary political cartoon reflects the views of royalists, who supported the monarchy and despised Cromwell, shown at left. Cromwell's supporters are cutting down the "Royall Oake," the source of English law and institutions.

During the English civil war, Cromwell purged the House of Commons of the king's supporters. After Charles I was captured by Cromwell, the remaining members of the House of Commons met as a court to try the king. At the trial, shown here, Charles, seated in the center, refused to recognize the authority of the court. He claimed "a king cannot be tried by any superior jurisdiction on earth." Nevertheless, he was condemned to die.

king should be put on trial. In January 1649, a court ordered the execution of Charles I. The House of Commons then voted to abolish the monarchy and the House of Lords and proclaimed England a republic. Thus, the civil war resulted in a revolution in English government.

The Commonwealth under Cromwell

Oliver Cromwell was chosen to head the English republic, which became known as the Commonwealth. Cromwell was a man with high moral principles. He supported a policy of religious toleration for all Protestants but not for Catholics. He hoped that he could restore peace with the help of Parliament.

Yet the civil war had left England bitterly divided. Presbyterians, Anglicans, and Puritans had differing views about the kind of government England should have. In addition, some extreme reformers wanted to push the revolution further. One group, the Levellers, led by John Lilburne, demanded an end to all titles of nobility. They also thought all English men should have the right to vote, a startling idea at a time when only a small number of property owners could vote.

Parliament itself was so seriously divided that Cromwell dissolved it in 1653. He then took the title Lord Protector and ruled England as a dictator until his death in 1658. As Lord Protector, Cromwell depended on the army to govern the country. Army officials imposed strict Puritan rule. They closed theaters, banned newspapers and dancing, and enforced laws against other forms of popular entertainment.

Cromwell tried to bring Scotland and Ireland under tighter English control, but he met strong resistance. Therefore, he crushed the Scots and brutally suppressed Catholic rebels in Ireland. He then encouraged Protestants to settle in Ireland, replacing Catholic landlords.*

Cromwell's rule became increasingly unpopular, and people began to long for the restoration of the monarchy. After Cromwell's death, the Long Parliament reconvened. It asked the son of Charles I, who was living in France, to return to England and be crowned Charles II.

Although the monarchy was thus restored, the civil war and the Commonwealth had lasting effects. The new king would be

___

* Both Henry VIII and Elizabeth I had given Protestants lands taken from Catholics in Ireland. Cromwell and later English rulers continued this policy.

careful in his dealings with Parliament. Moreover, Parliament took steps to prevent Charles II and future rulers from exercising power arbitrarily.

___

SECTION REVIEW

1. Identify: William Laud, Long Parliament, Cavalier, Roundhead, Oliver Cromwell, Commonwealth.
2. How did Elizabeth I deal with Parliament?
3. Describe one of the issues that created conflict between James I and Parliament.
4. What limits did the Petition of Right put on the king's power?
5. Describe two actions taken by the Long Parliament.
6. What problems did Cromwell face in trying to rule England?

___

2 Establishing a Limited Monarchy

Read to Learn
- what policies Charles II pursued
- how Britain became a limited constitutional monarchy

Charles II received a warm welcome upon his return to England in 1660. In contrast to Cromwell's stern Puritan policies, Charles, a lively man, reopened theaters and encouraged many entertainments that the Puritans had forbidden.

The Restoration Under Charles II

Charles II had spent his years in exile at the French court. Although he admired the absolute power enjoyed by Louis XIV, he knew he must accept limits on his own power. Before taking the throne, Charles agreed to respect the Magna Carta and the Petition of Right. He dealt cautiously with Parliament and generally had its support.

Meanwhile, members of Parliament protected their own interests. Most were landowners, and they passed laws abolishing the feudal dues that landowners paid to the king. In place of the feudal dues, Parliament

granted the king income from taxes.[†]

Charles II secretly preferred the Catholic Church to the Anglican Church, but he knew Parliament would not accept a return to Catholicism. Thus, he urged toleration of all religions. However, the English were not ready to accept religious toleration. In 1673, Parliament passed the Test Act, which required any person holding public office to belong to the Anglican Church. The Test Act also excluded Protestant dissenters and Catholics from the army, the navy, and universities.

In foreign policy, Charles cooperated with France. He entered into a secret treaty with Louis XIV, in part because he needed money. In return for Louis's financial support, Charles pledged to restore Catholicism in England as soon as it was practical. He

___

[†] In England, unlike other parts of Europe, nobles as well as commoners paid taxes.

383

also agreed to join France in a war against the Dutch. Under Charles, the English seized the Dutch colony of New Netherland.

Emergence of Political Parties

During Charles's reign, two political parties emerged in England: the Tories and the Whigs. The Tories generally supported the king and the Anglican Church, while the Whigs wanted to strengthen Parliament.

The Whigs tended to favor toleration of all Protestants, but they were fiercely anti-Catholic. As a result, they worried that when Charles died, his brother James would inherit the throne. Unlike Charles, who hid his religious opinions, James openly admitted to being Catholic. To prevent James from inheriting the throne, the Whigs tried to pass the Exclusion Act.

In 1679, the Tories were able to defeat the Exclusion Act, but only by accepting another piece of legislation, the Habeas Corpus Act. The Habeas Corpus Act is still considered one of the most basic guarantees of individual rights because it protects a citizen from arbitrary arrest. The act provided that if a person were arrested, a judge would issue a "writ of habeas corpus." The "writ" was an order to bring the prisoner before a judge and state the charges against the person. The judge would then decide whether or not the person should be held for trial.

The Habeas Corpus Act thus made it illegal for an individual to be held in prison without a trial. It also decreed that a person could not be imprisoned twice for the same crime. Later, the Constitution of the United States would include the right of habeas corpus.

James II and the Glorious Revolution

In 1685, James II inherited the throne. James was determined to make Parliament grant tolerance for Catholics. Ignoring the Test Act, James placed Catholics in high government posts and in the army. Parliament protested. However, it did not move against the king because it believed James eventually would be succeeded by one of his Protestant daughters. Then in 1688, James's second wife, a Catholic, gave birth to a son. The boy became heir to the throne, but Parliament feared that he would be raised a Catholic.

Parliament acted swiftly. It invited Mary, James's oldest daughter, and her husband, Prince William of Orange, to take the throne. When James realized he had no support in England, he fled the country.

William and Mary agreed to become joint rulers of England. In 1689, Parliament had the new monarchs sign a Bill of Rights to ensure its power and protect English liberties. The signing of the Bill of Rights marked the end of the bloodless revolution that the English call the Glorious Revolution.

The English Bill of Rights

The Bill of Rights included several provisions making Parliament stronger than the monarch. It stated that the monarchs could not suspend any laws without the consent of Parliament. Monarchs also needed the approval of Parliament to raise taxes and maintain an army. Furthermore, the king and queen had to summon Parliament frequently and could not interfere in its elections.

In addition to making Parliament supreme, the Bill of Rights protected the rights of individuals. It guaranteed the right of trial by jury for anyone accused of a crime. It also outlawed cruel and unusual punishments and limited the amount of bail that could be imposed on a person being held for trial.

Despite the limits Parliament placed on the power of the monarch, English government and society were not democratic. Few people had the right to vote. Members of Parliament were not paid, so only the wealthy could afford to run for office. Religious tolerance also remained limited. In 1689, Parliament passed the Act of Toleration. It assured all Protestants freedom of worship, but it did not give the same right to Catholics.

British Isles, 1707

Map Skill *The Act of Union joined Scotland and England in 1707. Ireland remained a separate nation, but it was ruled by England. What other nation had united with England earlier?*

Ireland and Scotland

Even after the Glorious Revolution, Parliament worried that James II or his heirs might reclaim the throne. This concern influenced relations between England and Ireland.

In 1689, James II led a rebellion in Ireland, hoping to regain the English throne. But he was defeated at the battle of the Boyne. In an effort to prevent James or any other Catholic from claiming the throne, Parliament passed the Act of Settlement in 1701. It stated that only an Anglican could inherit the English throne.

To prevent any future rebellion, the English Parliament imposed harsh penalties on Catholics in Ireland. English policies in Ireland bred a deep-seated resentment among the Catholic Irish. Even though the Catholics were a majority in Ireland, they could not buy or inherit land from Protestants. Furthermore, Catholics could not be elected to the Irish Parliament, making it easy for the Protestant minority to rule.

Since James II had also been king of Scotland, Parliament also worried that he or his heirs might reclaim the Scottish throne. To prevent this from happening, Parliament negotiated the Act of Union, which the Scots reluctantly accepted in 1707. The Act of Union joined the kingdoms of England and Scotland into the United Kingdom of Great Britain.

Although James and his heirs hatched plots to seize the throne, their efforts failed. After the deaths of William and Mary, Anne, James's other Protestant daughter, ruled Britain. The Act of Settlement provided that on Queen Anne's death the throne should pass to the nearest Protestant relative. Thus, in 1714, George, the German Elector of Hanover, became King George I of Britain. The peaceful transition from the Stuart to the Hanover dynasty was evidence that the Glorious Revolution had created stable government in Britain.

Growth of Constitutional Government

The English civil war and the Glorious Revolution established Britain as a limited constitutional monarchy—that is, the power of the monarchy was limited by laws and traditions. The British did not have a formal written constitution. Instead, the British constitution was composed of all acts of Parliament and documents such as the Magna Carta, the Petition of Right, and the Bill of Rights. It also included traditions and customs. The relationship between the monarch and Parliament, for example, was based largely on tradition.

In the late 1600s and throughout the 1700s, three developments affected constitutional government in England. First,

Major Events in England 1603–1701

1603	James I inherits the throne
1628	Charles I signs the Petition of Right
1642	English civil war begins
1649	Parliament declares England a republic; Charles I executed
1660	Restoration of the monarchy; Charles II agrees to respect the Magna Carta and Petition of Right
1679	Habeas Corpus Act passed
1688–1689	Glorious Revolution; William and Mary sign the Bill of Rights
1701	Act of Settlement passed

political parties acquired a more well-defined role in Parliament. Second, a cabinet system evolved. Third, the office of prime minister came into existence.

Political parties. As you read earlier in this section, the Whigs and Tories had begun to emerge as political parties after the restoration of Charles II. By the late 1600s, the differences between the two parties had become more distinct.

During the Glorious Revolution, the Whigs supported laws that limited royal power. Most Whigs were wealthy landowners who thought their power would increase as the monarch's power declined. Some Whigs were successful merchants. They favored policies, such as a strong navy, that would help promote British trade.

The Tories usually defended royal power against challenges by Parliament. Although most Tories were landowners, they usually owned less land than Whigs.

The cabinet. During the late 1600s, King William I chose his chief ministers, or advisers, from both political parties in Parliament.

But he soon realized that Whig and Tory ministers did not get along. As a result, he began to appoint ministers from the party that held the majority of seats in Parliament. The practice of appointing ministers from the majority party eventually led to the cabinet system of government.

The cabinet was made up of the ministers appointed by the king. Each cabinet member was responsible for a department of government, such as the navy or finance. Cabinet members remained members of Parliament. Therefore, they could vote for their own policies and try to convince others to do the same.

Eventually, a cabinet would stay in power as long as Parliament approved its policies. If Parliament rejected government policies, the king would call for new elections to Parliament. The new majority party would then form the next cabinet.

The prime minister. The cabinet acquired much of its power during the reign of George I in the early 1700s. Born and raised in Hanover, the king spoke only German and did not understand English politics. Therefore, he relied heavily on his English advisers. Sir Robert Walpole, an able and powerful Whig member of Parliament, became the king's chief adviser. Although Walpole did not use the title, he is usually considered the first *prime minister*, or head of the cabinet.

Between 1721 and 1742, Walpole skillfully steered legislation through Parliament. He gradually took over from the king the job of appointing many government officials, including other cabinet members. He managed government finances well, avoided costly wars, and supported laws that encouraged trade and industry. He allowed the English colonies in North America to develop on their own and avoided taking a stand on controversial issues. In fact, Walpole's motto was "Let sleeping dogs lie."

Personal Rule of George III

When George III came to the throne in 1760, he felt that the cabinet and Parliament under the Whigs had taken too much power from the king. Many small landowners agreed with the king, and they supported his efforts to regain control of the government.

From 1770 to 1782, George III supervised the government and appointed ministers. Lord North, George's prime minister, rallied a group in Parliament known as "the king's friends" to support George's policies. As you will read, some of the king's policies angered the American colonists, who declared their independence in 1776.

During the American Revolution, George lost support at home, and Parliament reasserted its power. It eventually forced the king to accept a new cabinet that would make peace with the United States. Parlia-

ment also passed a reform bill that limited the king's right to appoint officials.

3 Revolution in Colonial America

Read to Learn ■ what the complaints of the English colonists were
■ how the colonies established their independence

Events in England and Enlightenment ideas greatly influenced people in the 13 American colonies. The colonists believed they should have the same rights that people in England had won during the Glorious Revolution. When the British government appeared to violate these rights, the American colonists raised a storm of protest.

Governing the Colonies

Between 1700 and 1763, the American colonies expanded rapidly along the eastern seaboard. Busy with wars in Europe, Britain allowed the colonies to develop largely on their own. In most colonies, royal governors appointed by the king controlled trade and appointed judges and other officials. Each colony also had its own elected assembly.* Colonial assemblies had the right to approve laws related to local affairs. They also approved salaries for officials, including the

governor, and levied taxes to meet local government expenses.

Although colonists controlled local affairs, Britain regulated colonial trade. During the 1600s, Parliament had passed the Navigation Acts, which reflected mercantilist ideas. For example, one act required colonial merchants to ship goods only on colonial or English vessels.

Other Navigation Acts forbade the colonies to import goods from Europe unless these goods first went to England, where a customs duty was paid to the crown. In addition, certain colonial products, such as sugar, cotton, tobacco, and naval supplies, could be shipped only to England.

In general, the Navigation Acts benefited the colonies as well as England. The colonies developed their own shipbuilding industries to carry goods to England. In addition, freedom from foreign competition helped colonial merchants build their businesses.

Some New England merchants, however, did not like the Navigation Acts. These merchants relied heavily on sugar and molasses imported from the West Indies.

---

* As in European countries, voting in the colonies was usually limited to men who owned property or paid taxes. However, land was more plentiful in North America, so more people were landowners. Therefore, a much larger percentage of the male population in the colonies could vote than in any European nation.

According to the acts, they could buy sugar and molasses only from the British West Indies. In practice, they ignored the law and smuggled sugar and molasses from the French West Indies.

The Road to Revolution

When the Seven Years War ended in 1763 (see page 357), British policy toward the American colonies changed. The war had been expensive and left Britain deeply in debt. Furthermore, the British had to keep troops in North America to defend the vast territories it acquired from France. George III and his ministers felt that the American colonies should help pay the costs of their own defense. Therefore, the king urged Parliament to pass a series of laws to raise revenue from the colonies. One of these was the Stamp Act, passed by Parliament in 1765.

The Stamp Act taxed a variety of items, from newspapers, deeds, and wills to dice and playing cards. People in Britain and in other parts of Europe had been paying such taxes for centuries. But in the American colonies, the Stamp Act caused an angry reaction.

Delegates from 9 of the 13 colonies met in New York to protest the Stamp Act. They claimed that the colonists had the same rights as other British subjects, including the right to consent to any taxes. They argued that Parliament did not have the right to tax them because they did not send representatives to Parliament. Only colonial assemblies, they declared, had the right to impose taxes on the colonies.

When the British government tried to enforce the Stamp Act, riots erupted in the major colonial cities. For months, the colonists successfully boycotted British goods, fi-

On March 5, 1770, a crowd of angry Bostonians gathered at the Boston customs house. The crowd jeered and threw snowballs at the British soldiers guarding the building. A shot was heard, causing the British to open fire on the crowd. Five colonists were killed in the "Boston Massacre." This engraving of the scene was made by Boston silversmith and patriot Paul Revere. It was widely circulated in the colonies and stirred resentment against the British.

nally forcing Parliament to repeal the unpopular act. However, Parliament still insisted that it had the right to tax the colonies.

Between 1765 and 1775, relations between Britain and its American colonies worsened as Parliament imposed new taxes and tried to reassert British control over the colonies. In 1773, a group of Bostonians openly expressed their contempt for British policies. Disguised as Indians, they dumped a shipment of tea into Boston harbor. Many colonists cheered when they heard of the "Boston Tea Party," as the event was called. The British government was outraged by what it saw as an act of rebellion.

In 1774, to punish the colonists, Parliament passed a series of laws that the colonists called the "Intolerable Acts." Parliament closed the port of Boston, forbade the Massachusetts assembly from holding regular sessions, and imposed military rule on the colony. Parliament also passed the Quebec Act, which provided a government for the territories Britain had acquired from France. The act extended the boundaries of Quebec south to the Ohio River. The colonists saw the Quebec Act as an effort to prevent them from moving westward.

In reaction to these acts, delegates from all the colonies except Georgia met at a Continental Congress in Philadelphia. They urged residents of Boston to ignore the Intolerable Acts, and they voted to boycott all British goods. The delegates agreed to meet in a second Continental Congress in the spring of 1775. However, by that time, fighting had broken out between the colonists and British soldiers.

In April 1775, some British troops from Boston were sent to Concord to search for illegal weapons said to be stored there. At Lexington, they met armed colonists, and the first shots of the American Revolution were fired.

The Declaration of Independence

A month later, in May 1775, the Second Continental Congress met in Philadelphia. Some delegates still hoped to reach a compromise with Britain. The more radical delegates argued for independence. Finally on July 4, 1776, the delegates agreed on a Declaration of Independence that explained the reasons for their separation from Britain.

The Declaration of Independence was drafted largely by Thomas Jefferson, a patriot from Virginia. A scholar, Jefferson was familiar with the ideas of Newton, Locke, and the French philosophes.

Like Locke, Jefferson wrote that people had certain natural rights, including "life, liberty and the pursuit of happiness." Jefferson also argued that government arose from an agreement between the ruler and the ruled. A ruler had power only as long as he or she had the consent of the governed. While people could not overthrow their rulers for minor reasons, the Declaration of Independence stated that Britain had consistently and deliberately oppressed the colonists. Therefore, the colonists had the right to rebel.

An American Victory

The American Revolution lasted from 1776 to 1783. At first, the British appeared to have the military advantage. They had well-trained troops, and their armies occupied the major American cities. The Americans had few trained officers and little military equipment when the war began. Moreover, individual colonies did not always cooperate with one another, and some colonists did not support the revolution.

Yet the Americans enjoyed several important advantages. They were patriots, fighting on their own territory for their families and homes. The British, in contrast, were thousands of miles from home, and it took weeks or even months for supplies to arrive from England. Furthermore, although the British held the cities, the colonists could retreat into the countryside and then reappear to ambush the British.

Finally, the Americans found a brilliant military leader in George Washington, a Virginia landowner. Washington was able to unite the colonies in their common cause. At first, Washington suffered defeats, but he learned quickly. He successfully reorganized the colonial forces, which won important victories at Trenton and Princeton in December 1776.

The winter of 1777–1778 marked a turning point in the war. Armed with weapons secretly supplied by France, an American army defeated the British at Saratoga in October 1777. This victory convinced France to give the colonies its official support. In February 1778, France recognized the colonies' independence and signed an alliance with them. France then declared war on its old enemy, Britain, and sent money and troops to the Americans.

In 1781, with the help of the French navy, Washington captured a British army at Yorktown, Virginia. Although George III wanted to continue the war, Parliament forced him to negotiate a peace treaty that recognized the independence of the United States.

Framing a Constitution

The newly independent nation faced many challenges. It had to form a government that would preserve the liberties the people had just won. Between 1781 and 1789, the United States operated under a constitution called the Articles of Confederation. The Articles created a congress that had limited powers. For example, it could not collect taxes. Most of the political power remained with the individual states.

Washington and other leaders warned that the nation faced great dangers if the states did not cooperate. For example, Britain refused to withdraw its troops from several military posts. In 1787, leaders met in Philadelphia to revise the Articles of Confederation. They soon decided to draft a new constitution. In 1788, after much debate and compromise, the individual states ratified the Constitution of the United States.

Profiles ■ Benjamin Franklin: An American in Paris

In September 1776, the Continental Congress named Benjamin Franklin minister to France. His mission was to secure French loans and arms for the revolutionary army. With help from France, the most powerful nation in Europe, the Americans felt sure they could achieve victory in their war against Britain.

In choosing Franklin, the Americans selected a successful diplomat and experienced statesman. Between 1757 and 1775, Franklin had spent almost 18 years in London. During those years, Franklin's reputation for intelligence and humor had spread throughout Europe.

Thus, when the 70-year-old Franklin reached Paris in 1776, he was already well-known. The French had heard about his experiments with electricity, and they knew about his inventions, including bifocal lenses and the Franklin stove. Described by a French noble as "the sage whom two worlds claimed as their own," Franklin received a warm welcome wherever he went.

In the salons of Paris, where people were eager to meet the famous Dr. Franklin, the American negotiator cut an unusual figure. Amid the French, in their curled and powdered wigs, Franklin wore his own hair long and straight under an unfashionable fur cap. He dressed in a plain brown cloth coat, a somber contrast to the colorful silks and satins favored by wealthy Parisians. Yet the French were charmed by his appearance. To them, he was an American frontiersman.

Franklin owed his popularity in Paris as much to his courteous, diplomatic manner as to his style of dress. However, it took more than personality and style to secure French aid. During months of patient negotiations, Franklin urged the French king Louis XVI to make loans to the Americans. Finally, in February 1778, after the battle of Saratoga, Franklin signed the first treaty of alliance between the United States and France.

After the war ended, Franklin remained as the American minister to France until 1785. When Thomas Jefferson arrived to take his place, the French asked, "Is it you, sir, who replaces Dr. Franklin?" Jefferson replied, "No one can replace him. I am only his successor."

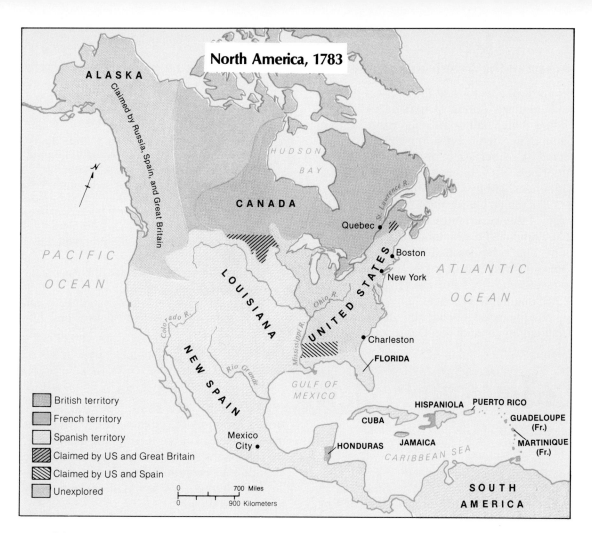

North America, 1783

ALASKA

Claimed by Russia, Spain, and Great Britain

HUDSON BAY

CANADA

Quebec

St. Lawrence R.

Boston

New York

PACIFIC OCEAN

ATLANTIC OCEAN

LOUISIANA

Ohio R.

UNITED STATES

Colorado R.

Mississippi R.

Charleston

NEW SPAIN

Rio Grande

FLORIDA

GULF OF MEXICO

Mexico City

CUBA

HISPANIOLA   PUERTO RICO

GUADELOUPE (Fr.)

JAMAICA

MARTINIQUE (Fr.)

HONDURAS

CARIBBEAN SEA

SOUTH AMERICA

British territory
French territory
Spanish territory
Claimed by US and Great Britain
Claimed by US and Spain
Unexplored

0   700 Miles
0   900 Kilometers

Map Skill   *In November 1782, the British and the Americans signed the Treaty of Paris, which ended the American Revolutionary War. The American Congress ratified the treaty in April 1783. According to the treaty, the British recognized the independence of the United States. What areas were disputed between the United States and other nations? Which nations claimed Alaska?*

The men who wrote the Constitution were inspired by the works of Locke and Montesquieu. Both philosophers had suggested that the separation of powers would prevent tyranny in government. The Constitution therefore established three separate branches of government: a legislature, the Congress made up of the House of Representatives and the Senate; an executive, the President; and a judiciary, the system of national courts.

In *The Spirit of Laws,* Montesquieu had proposed that no one branch of government should have more power than the others. Therefore, the framers of the Constitution established a system of checks and balances.

For example, the President was given the power to appoint officials and negotiate treaties, but the Senate had to approve these actions. Before a bill could become law, it had to be passed by both houses of Congress and signed by the President. The Supreme Court had the power to decide if a law was constitutional.

When the Constitution was sent to the states for approval, several states asked for a bill of rights to guarantee the personal liberties of citizens. In 1791, the Bill of Rights was added as the first ten amendments to the Constitution. The Bill of Rights protected such basic rights as freedom of speech, press, and religion.

Impact of the American Revolution

When the states ratified the Constitution, the revolutionary era in America ended. The United States had established itself as an independent, democratic republic that protected the liberties of its citizens. But the American Revolution would have consequences far beyond the United States.

To many people in Europe and other parts of the world, the events in North America symbolized a dramatic struggle for freedom. The colonists had broken away from their powerful British rulers and had created a government that put the ideas of the Enlightenment into practice.

In the years ahead, the Declaration of Independence and the Constitution of the United States would be used as models by other peoples of the world.

SECTION REVIEW

1. Identify: Stamp Act, Boston Tea Party, Intolerable Acts, Thomas Jefferson, George Washington, Articles of Confederation.
2. (a) How did the Navigation Acts help the colonies? (b) What effect did they have on New England merchants who imported molasses from the West Indies?
3. Why did the colonists object to paying taxes to Britain?
4. List three factors that helped the Americans defeat the British.
5. Why did the framers of the Constitution establish a system of checks and balances?

Chapter 20 Review

In Perspective

In the early 1600s, the Stuart kings of England clashed with Parliament over religious and financial issues as well as over the Stuarts' belief in the divine right of kings. By 1642, the dispute resulted in the English civil war. Under Oliver Cromwell, Parliamentary forces captured, tried, and executed Charles I. Cromwell governed England during the Commonwealth.

On Cromwell's death, the English restored the monarchy. However, Parliament made Charles II accept limits on his power. By 1688, King James II and Parliament were at odds over religion. When James fled England, Parliament invited William and Mary to take the throne.

After the Seven Years' War, Parliament started taxing its American colonies to help pay for their own defense. The colonists rejected Parliament's authority to tax them and declared their independence. The newly independent United States established a constitution that became a model for other peoples.

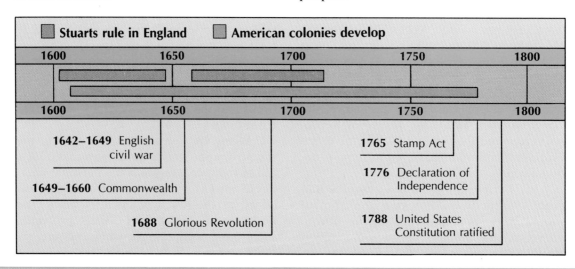

■ Stuarts rule in England	■ American colonies develop

| 1600 | 1650 | 1700 | 1750 | 1800 |

1642–1649 English civil war	1765 Stamp Act
1649–1660 Commonwealth	1776 Declaration of Independence
1688 Glorious Revolution	1788 United States Constitution ratified

Recalling Facts

Choose the word or phrase that best completes each of the following statements.

1. Elizabeth I was a popular queen in part because she (a) restored the Catholic Church; (b) kept on good terms with Parliament; (c) reconquered English lands in France.

2. In 1628, Parliament granted money to Charles I only after he signed the (a) Petition of Right; (b) Triennial Act; (c) Test Act.

3. During the Commonwealth, England was a (a) monarchy; (b) republic; (c) democracy.

4. The English Bill of Rights signed in 1688 limited the power of (a) Parliament; (b) the monarchy; (c) the prime minister.

5. The first British prime minister was (a) Lord North; (b) Archbishop Laud; (c) Robert Walpole.

6. The framers of the United States Constitution adopted the idea of checks and balances that had been proposed by (a) Montesquieu; (b) Hobbes; (c) Newton.

7. The Stamp Act angered many American colonists because it (a) limited their trade with other countries; (b) taxed them without their consent; (c) prevented them from moving westward.

Chapter Checkup

1. (a) Describe James I's views on the power of kings. (b) How did his views contribute to conflict with Parliament?

2. (a) What policies of Charles I angered Parliament? (b) What steps did Parliament take to limit the king's power? (c) How did Charles I respond to the actions of Parliament?

3. (a) What was the outcome of the English Civil War? (b) Describe English government during the Commonwealth.

4. (a) Describe the political parties that emerged in Parliament during the Restoration. (b) Which party wanted to prevent James II from becoming king? (c) Did it succeed? Explain.

5. (a) What events led to the Glorious Revolution in England? (b) What was the outcome of the Glorious Revolution?

6. Describe the role of each of the following in British government during the 1700s: (a) political parties; (b) the cabinet; (c) prime minister.

7. (a) In what ways were the American colonies relatively free from British control before 1763? (b) Why did British policy toward the colonies change after 1763? (c) How did the colonists react to the change?

8. Describe the Enlightenment ideas included in the Constitution of the United States.

Critical Thinking

1. **Expressing an Opinion** In the 1600s, the Stuart rulers in England admired the absolute power of monarchs in France. Yet when they tried to rule as absolute monarchs they failed. In your opinion, why did England become a limited monarchy?

2. **Evaluating** (a) Which English monarchs that you read about in this chapter dealt most successfully with Parliament? Why? (b) Which were least successful? Why? (c) What characteristics do you think would have helped a ruler get along with Parliament?

3. **Applying Information** (a) What ideas about government do you think English settlers brought with them to America? (b) How might these ideas have contributed to the American Revolution?

Relating Past to Present

1. How do you think the success of the American Revolution might still affect people in the world today?

Developing Basic Skills

1. **Ranking** List the events and acts of Parliament that led to the establishment of a limited constitutional monarchy in England. Then rank them according to which you think was most important in limiting the power of the monarch. Explain why you ranked them in that order.

2. **Comparing** Make a chart with three columns and three rows. Label the columns English Civil War, Glorious Revolution, and American Revolution. Label the rows Date, Causes, Results. Use what you read in this chapter to complete the chart. Then answer the following questions: (a) How were the causes of each struggle similar? (b) How were they different? (c) How were the results of the Glorious Revolution and the American Revolution similar? (d) How were they different?

See page 805 for suggested readings.

21 The French Revolution and Napoleon

(1789–1815)

The storming of the Bastille on July 14, 1789.

In the early summer of 1789, bread and other foods were scarce all over Paris. Talk of revolution filled the air. At Versailles, representatives of all classes had been meeting since May to find solutions to the economic problems that troubled France. But in Paris, many poor citizens focused their anger toward the government on the Bastille, where they believed hundreds of French citizens had been unjustly imprisoned.

On July 14, 1789, Louis de Flue was expecting trouble. De Flue was an officer in the Swiss guards who protected the Bastille, a huge prison fortress in Paris. By 3 P.M. that day, a large mob had surrounded the Bastille, demanding its surrender.

Still, Louis de Flue was not worried. He knew that the Bastille could be defended until reinforcements arrived. But to de Flue's surprise, as the mob grew, the commander of the Bastille, the Marquis de Launay, did not defend the outer drawbridge. Instead, de Launay offered to surrender the fortress if his troops were allowed to leave peacefully. But the crowd replied, "No surrender! Lower the bridge!"

Louis de Flue watched helplessly as the second drawbridge was lowered, and the mob swarmed into the courtyard. Armed with axes, the crowd ran to the prison cells and freed the astonished inmates. The mob found only seven prisoners in the entire fortress.

Louis de Flue was led roughly along the streets of Paris while angry citizens called for his death. "Swords, bayonets, and pistols were being continually pressed against me. . . . I felt that my last moment had come." Fortunately for de Flue, the guards held back the crowd. But de Launay and many others died that night.

To the common people in Paris, the Bastille symbolized the tyranny of the absolute monarchy in France. The fall of the Bastille signaled the central role that the people of Paris would take in the French Revolution. The French Revolution went through many stages and had far-reaching effects, not only on France but on all of Europe.

1 The French Monarchy in Crisis

Read to Learn
- how the Old Regime in France was structured
- why political and economic reforms were needed in France

When the Sun King Louis XIV died in 1715, France was the richest nation in Europe. It remained so throughout the 1700s. The French army was the most powerful in Europe, and its navy was rivaled only by that of Britain. French philosophers led the Enlightenment, and Europeans followed French fashions in clothes, art, and even cooking.

At the same time, France suffered from a growing economic crisis that would eventually shake the foundations of the French monarchy. Attempts to solve the problems of the country were hampered by the traditional political and social system of France, which historians call the Old Regime.

Structure of the Old Regime

Under the Old Regime, the king was an absolute monarch. Louis XIV had centralized power in the royal bureaucracy, the government departments which administered his policies. Louis's successors lacked his abilities to govern. Nevertheless, they worked to preserve royal authority and maintained the rigid social structure of the Old Regime.

As you read earlier, the people of France were divided by law into three estates: clergy, nobility, and commoners. (See page 191.) The first two estates enjoyed many privileges. In general, they opposed any reforms that would threaten their privileges. The Third Estate, however, had many grievances against the Old Regime.

The First and Second Estates. The First Estate included the higher clergy, who were nobles, as well as the parish priests, who were commoners. Some of the higher clergy lived in luxury. Parish priests usually lived a simple, hardworking life. Many criticized social injustices and resented the privileges enjoyed by the higher clergy.

The clergy administered the church, ran schools, kept birth and death records, and cared for the poor. To support these activities, the clergy collected the tithe, a tax on income. The church owned vast amounts of property on which it paid no taxes.

The Second Estate, or nobility, made up less than 2 percent of the French population. (See the graphs on page 396.) Many nobles enjoyed great wealth and privileges. Only nobles could become officers in the army or fill high offices of the church. In addition, nobles were exempt from most taxes.

Not all French nobles were wealthy. Some lived in near poverty in the country. However, they firmly defended their traditional privileges. When rising prices reduced their income, they made peasants on their estates pay long forgotten feudal dues.

After Louis XIV's death, French nobles tried to regain the political power they had lost during his reign. Leading the effort were the wealthy and influential "nobles of the robe," who had received noble status for their service to the royal government. Many were judges in the parlements, or high courts. The parlements had to register, or approve, the king's orders in order for them to become laws. Nobles of the robe sometimes exercised this power and refused to approve the king's orders if the orders limited their power.

The Third Estate. The vast majority of French people were commoners belonging to the Third Estate. The Third Estate included the bourgeoisie, or middle class, peasants, and city workers.

The bourgeoisie was small in numbers, but it was the wealthiest, most outspoken group within the Third Estate. The bourgeoisie included successful merchants and manufacturers, educated lawyers and doctors, as well as small storekeepers and artisans. They resented the privileges enjoyed by nobles. Many criticized the Old Regime because they believed in the Enlightenment ideas of equality and social justice. The bourgeoisie called for extensive reform of

the tax system because the Third Estate carried the burden of paying most taxes.

Peasants made up the largest group within the Third Estate. In general, French peasants were better off than peasants in other parts of Europe. Serfdom had largely disappeared in France, although French peasants still paid many feudal dues dating back to the Middle Ages. French peasants also had to perform unpaid services for their landlords and the king. For example, if peasants lived near a royal road, they had to spend as much as a month every year repairing the road.

Peasants were burdened by heavy taxes, the tithe to the church, and rents to their landlords. The privileges of nobles further added to the peasants' troubles. For example, only nobles could hunt. Peasants were forbidden to kill rabbits and birds that ate their crops. Nobles also damaged crops by galloping across fields during a hunt.

Graph Skill   *These graphs clearly show the unequal distribution of land in France. Moreover, within the Third Estate, a small number of bourgeoisie owned much of the land. Thus, peasants ended up with only 45 percent of the land. Which estate owned the largest percentage of land per member?*

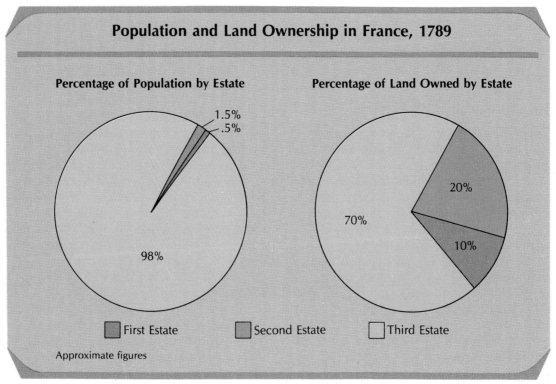

Population and Land Ownership in France, 1789

Percentage of Population by Estate

1.5%
.5%
98%

Percentage of Land Owned by Estate

70%
20%
10%

First Estate   Second Estate   Third Estate

Approximate figures

Source: Alfred Cobban, *A History of Modern France.* Vol. 1.

Another group within the Third Estate was city workers. In the towns and cities of France, thousands of men and women earned wages as servants, apprentices, and day laborers. Workers suffered when inflation hit because food prices rose faster than their wages. Like the bourgeoisie and peasants, city workers resented the privileges enjoyed by the First and Second Estates.

The Growing Economic Crisis

During much of the 1700s, the French economy prospered. The population grew from about 18 million people in 1715 to about 25 million in 1789. Farmers produced food surpluses that fed the growing population and supported economic expansion. Mercantilist policies helped manufacturers in the textile and mining industries.

In the 1770s, however, economic activity slowed. Poor harvests hurt the economy. In addition, regulations surviving from the Middle Ages hampered any further expansion of trade and manufacturing. For example, a merchant who shipped a wagonload of wine from the upper Loire Valley to Paris had to pay 11 separate customs duties and 12 different tolls. Furthermore, the guilds still had monopolies over the production of certain goods. As a result, entrepreneurs could not set up their own businesses.

However, the most serious economic problem facing the French government during the 1770s and 1780s was the huge debt it owed to bankers. The government had borrowed large amounts of money to pay for the wars of Louis XIV. Louis XV and Louis XVI continued to borrow money to support the court at Versailles and to fight wars to maintain French power in Europe and overseas. French support of the American Revolution alone nearly doubled the government's debt.

Attempts at Reform

When Louis XVI came to the throne in 1774, he recognized the need for economic reform. But Louis was not a very determined

This cartoon illustrates some of the burdens of the Third Estate. The clergyman and nobleman represent the First and Second Estates. They are riding on the back of an aged peasant, representing the Third Estate.

or able ruler. He preferred to spend his days hunting or tinkering with puzzles rather than coping with economic problems. Moreover, Louis lacked the strength of will to back his ministers when they pressed for reforms.

Louis's first finance minister, Robert Turgot (ter GOH), eased the financial crisis for a time by controlling government spending and reducing expenses at Versailles. He also removed some internal customs duties on food and tried to limit the power of the guilds. But he had little success when he proposed a major reform—taxing the nobles.

The king could not tax the nobles unless the parlements approved new tax laws. But these law courts were controlled by the nobles of the robe, and they stubbornly rejected Turgot's suggestion that they should be taxed. As one noble said, "All public financial burdens should be borne by the lower classes."

When Turgot came under attack, the king dismissed him. As he left office in 1776, Turgot ominously warned the king, "Remember, sire, that it was weakness which brought the head of Charles I to the block."

For a time, the government limped along on new bank loans. Then, in 1786, as the government debts mounted, bankers refused to lend more money to the French treasury. In 1787 and 1788, poor harvests caused bread shortages all over France. The economic situation worsened, and Louis XVI went before the Parlement of Paris to try to make it register a new tax law. "Sire, this is illegal!" one member exclaimed. "It is legal," countered Louis XVI, "because I wish it!" But even royal wishes could not prevail.

The desperate economic crisis and the opposition of the privileged classes to any reform convinced the king to take a bold action. In the fall of 1788, he summoned the Estates General to meet the following May.

SECTION REVIEW

1. Identify: Old Regime, Robert Turgot.
2. (a) What groups made up each of the three estates in France? (b) What privileges did the First and Second Estates enjoy?
3. List three factors that contributed to the French economic crisis of the 1770s and 1780s.
4. (a) What major reform did Turgot recommend? (b) Was he able to make the reform? Why or why not?

---

2 A Moderate Start to the Revolution

Read to Learn
- what reforms were made under Louis XVI
- how the French reacted to the reforms of Louis XVI

When Louis XVI summoned the Estates General, he hoped to win support for reforms that would restore economic stability. The Estates General had not met since 1614, and no one could predict what would happen when deputies representing the three estates met at Versailles.

From Estates General to National Assembly

Each estate elected its own deputies to the Estates General. Within the Third Estate, almost all adult men had the right to vote for representatives to local assemblies. These assemblies, in turn, elected the deputies to the Estates General.

When the Estates General met in May 1789, deputies from the Third Estate demanded that the three estates meet together, with each deputy having an equal vote. In the past, the three estates had met separately. Each estate voted as a group and had one vote. That way the First and Second Estates could outvote the Third Estate two to one. Deputies from the Third Estate hoped that if the estates met together and deputies voted individually, sympathizers among the clergy and nobles would give the Third Estate a majority.

When the king insisted that the estates meet separately, deputies from the Third Estate declared themselves the National Assembly. They claimed the right to write a constitution for France. Louis XVI promptly banished the rebellious deputies from their meeting hall.

Joined by many of the lower clergy and some reform-minded nobles, delegates of the Third Estate gathered at a nearby tennis court. There, they swore an oath, known as the Tennis Court Oath, promising not to disband until they had written a constitution. Louis XVI hesitated, but then he ordered the other two estates to join the Third Estate in the National Assembly. The Third Estate had taken a peaceful first step in a revolution that would eventually transform France.

Although the three estates met as one body, there were deep divisions among the estates and within each one. Many clergy and nobles sought to protect their privileges. However, some nobles and lower clergy, along with many commoners, wanted to establish a limited, constitutional monarchy like the one in Britain. A few radical reformers demanded equality for all classes

The leading artist of the French Revolution, Jacques Louis David, painted this work,
The Tennis Court Oath. *The actual scene was even more chaotic. Members of the
Third Estate along with some clergy and nobles pledged "never to separate but to
meet in any place that circumstances may require, until the constitution of the
kingdom is established on firm foundations."*

before the law. They wanted to abolish titles
of nobility and all feudal obligations. They
distrusted the king and opposed any constitution that would leave him with significant powers.

Popular Uprisings

The National Assembly had scarcely begun
work on a constitution in July 1789 when the
people of Paris and peasants in the countryside took the French Revolution along a
new, more radical course. Peasants and
workers had expected quick relief from
taxes and poverty when the Estates General
met. But little had happened. Instead, they
still faced inflation, unemployment, and food
shortages. Reports that the king was concen-
trating troops around Paris added to unrest
in the capital.

When Louis brought troops to Versailles, many citizens feared that he planned
to dissolve the National Assembly and crush
the revolution. In reaction, on July 14, 1789,
a Paris crowd stormed the Bastille, as you
read at the beginning of the chapter. They
saw the attack on the Bastille as an attack on
the injustice and inequality of the Old Regime. (Today, the French celebrate July 14 as
their national holiday.)

Disturbances soon broke out in the
countryside. During the summer of 1789,
peasants were caught up in what was called
the "Great Fear." Rumors passed from village to village that brigands, or robbers, were
destroying crops and homes all over France.
Peasants took up arms to defend themselves.

When no brigands appeared, the frightened peasants turned on their landlords.
They raided grain storehouses, destroyed tax
records, and swore never again to pay ancient feudal dues. Like the people of Paris,
the peasants were conducting their own revolution against the Old Regime.

Reforms of the National Assembly

The events in Paris and the countryside
forced the National Assembly into action.
During a long session on the night of August
4, many delegates rose to make impassioned
speeches in support of reform. One noble
urged that nobles be taxed. Another proposed that nobles give up their hunting
rights. The clergy promised to end its tithes.

By the end of the evening, the Assembly
had abolished most feudal customs. It ended
serfdom and the tax exempt privileges of the
nobles. It also made all male citizens eligible
for government and church positions. "Just

like our Frenchmen," commented the Comte de Mirabeau, a moderate leader. "They spend an entire month wrangling over syllables, and in a night overturn the whole of the ancient order of the kingdom!"

Before the end of August, the National Assembly adopted the Declaration of the Rights of Man. (See below.) The Declaration stated the democratic principles that would be the basis for French government. It called for equality for all citizens under the law and protection of personal property. However, the task of turning these ideals into a constitution remained.

While lawyers debated the wording of a constitution, angry Paris crowds rioted, forcing the National Assembly to take note of their demands. Many rioters were middle class shopkeepers and artisans.

The march on Versailles. In October 1789, a Paris crowd led by thousands of women marched in the rain to Versailles. The women were angry about high food prices. They also suspected that the king and the queen, Marie Antoinette, were plotting against the National Assembly. They demanded that Louis XVI and his family return with them to Paris, where they could watch over the king's activities. To prevent violence, the king agreed.

The return to Paris presented a striking scene. The king rode on horseback, escorted by a cheering crowd. He wore the tricolor, the red, white, and blue ribbon that the revolutionaries had adopted as their symbol. By forcing the king to wear the tricolor, the people proved that they were directing events in France. A few days later, the National Assembly also moved to Paris and resumed its work under the watchful eye of revolutionaries in the capital.

Religious reforms. All over France, the revolution swept away ancient customs and privileges. The National Assembly declared freedom of worship and abolished the special privileges of the Catholic Church. In 1790, it passed the Civil Constitution of the Clergy, which gave the French government control of the church and allowed citizens to elect bishops and priests. To raise badly needed money, the government began selling church lands. This action caused many Catholics who had supported the revolution up to this point to condemn it.

Through Their Eyes ■ The Declaration of the Rights of Man

On August 26, 1789, the National Assembly adopted the Declaration of the Rights of Man. The Declaration echoed many ideas of the philosophes. It also showed the influence of the English Bill of Rights and the American Declaration of Independence.

From the *Declaration*

The representatives of the French people, organized as a national assembly, believing that the ignorance, neglect or contempt of the rights of man are the sole causes of public misfortunes and the corruption of governments, have determined to set forth in a solemn declaration, the natural, inalienable and sacred rights of man. . . .

The aim of all political association is the preservation of the natural . . . rights of man. These rights are liberty, property, security, and resistance to oppression.

Liberty consists of being able to do everything which injures no one else. . . .

Law can only prohibit such actions as are hurtful to society. . . .

Law is expression of the general will. Every citizen has a right to participate personally or through his representative in its formation.

No person shall be accused, arrested or imprisoned except in the cases and according to the forms prescribed by law. . . .

As all persons are held innocent until they shall have been declared guilty. . . .

The free communication of ideas and opinions is one of the most precious of the rights of man. Every citizen may, accordingly, speak, write and print with freedom, being responsible, however, for such abuses of this freedom as shall be defined by law.

1. What does the declaration state is the cause of corruption of government?
2. According to the declaration, what is law?

Women played a major role in the French Revolution. This picture shows the women's march on Versailles. On October 5, 1789, a rumor that the king had worn the white symbol of the Bourbons rather than the revolutionary tricolor sent Parisian women hurrying to Versailles. Faced with the crowd of angry women, Louis XVI agreed to accompany them back to Paris.

The Constitution of 1791. In 1791, the National Assembly finally gave France its first constitution. The Constitution of 1791 made France a limited monarchy and established a system of separation of powers. At the head of the executive branch was the king. A legislature made the laws. The king could veto laws, but the legislature could override his veto. A new system of courts was set up as the judicial branch. The constitution also divided France into 83 departments, or regions, and replaced the old provincial governments with locally elected officials.

Under the constitution, the old distinctions between clergy, nobles, and commoners disappeared. "The feudal system is forever abolished in France," it declared. The constitution guaranteed equal rights under the law to all citizens.

Responses to the First Stage of the Revolution

Few people were satisfied with the new constitutional monarchy. Radical revolutionaries wanted a republic rather than a monarchy. For many nobles, the Constitution of 1791 went too far. Frightened by angry crowds in Paris and in the countryside, a growing number of nobles fled France. These *émigrés*, or political exiles, urged European rulers to oppose the revolutionaries in France.

Louis XVI grew increasingly alarmed at the actions of the National Assembly. He sought outside help, and Marie Antoinette appealed to her brother, the emperor of Austria, for support. In June 1791, the royal family decided to flee the country. When they fled toward the border, however, the king was recognized. The National Assembly sent officers to arrest the royal family and bring them back to the capital. A virtual prisoner of the Assembly, the king reluctantly accepted the new constitution in September.

In October 1791, the Legislative Assembly, elected under the new constitution, met for the first time. The seating arrangements in the Assembly reflected divisions among the revolutionaries. Moderate revolutionaries sat on the right side of the meeting hall, and radical revolutionaries sat on the left side.*

---

* The seating arrangement in the Assembly led to the use of "right" and "left" to describe political views. The right came to refer to people who wanted to preserve tradition. The left came to refer to people who supported far-reaching changes. People with views between the right and left were called the center.

The king's attempt to flee the country had deepened the divisions among the revolutionaries. Moderates were embarrassed, but they still wanted to preserve the constitutional monarchy. Radicals distrusted the king and demanded a republic.

However, the radicals themselves were further split. The most radical group, the Jacobins, demanded a true democracy in which all male citizens had the right to vote. As the French Revolution unfolded, the Jacobins and their leader, Maximilien Robespierre (ROHBS pyehr), would gain the upper hand.

SECTION REVIEW

1. Identify: Tennis Court Oath, National Assembly, Declaration of the Rights of Man, Civil Constitution of the Clergy.

2. Define: émigré.

3. Why did the Third Estate want the Estates General to meet as a single body?

4. (a) What conditions led to unrest among workers and peasants in the summer of 1789? (b) How did the National Assembly react to that unrest?

5. What two groups were dissatisfied with the Constitution of 1791? Why?

3 The Revolution Deepens

Read to Learn
- how European nations responded to French reforms
- what steps the National Convention took

Revolutionary ideas spread from France to other parts of Europe. Faced with unrest at home and abroad, European monarchs felt they had to take steps to turn back the tide of revolution. French émigrés urged Austria and Prussia to invade France and restore Louis XVI to full power. At the same time, many revolutionary leaders in France wanted war because they thought it would unite the people in defense of their homeland.

France at War

France declared war on Austria in April 1792. At first, the war went badly for France. French armies were disorganized and poorly led. Many army officers, who were nobles, had left France. Revolutionary ideas also caused some problems. For example, in the heat of battle, one regiment demanded to vote on whether or not to attack the enemy.

By August 1792, Austrian and Prussian armies were advancing on Paris. The Prussian commander, the Duke of Brunswick, issued a declaration, known as the Brunswick Manifesto. He warned that if Paris did not surrender peacefully Austrian and Prussian troops would burn the city and put its leaders to the "tortures which they have deserved."

Far from being frightened by the duke's message, the people of Paris angrily declared that no émigrés or foreign troops would crush the revolution. All over France, people rallied to defend the revolution and chanted the slogan: "Liberty, Equality, and Fraternity." Soldiers from Marseille hurried to Paris singing a patriotic marching song, the "Marseillaise," which was adopted as the national anthem of France. In September, the French defeated the Duke of Brunswick at Valmy. In the months that followed, revolutionary armies forced the invaders to retreat from France.

The war against Austria and Prussia caused high prices and desperate food shortages in France. Even while foreign troops threatened Paris, angry Parisians and sympathetic troops from the provinces joined in an uprising that has been called the second French Revolution.

Early in the morning of August 10, revolutionaries took over the Paris city government and established a new administration, the Commune. A large force of revolutionary troops marched on the Tuileries (TWEE ler eez), where the king and his family lived. The troops attacked the palace, killing many of the king's Swiss guards.

The king and queen fled to the Legislative Assembly, hoping for protection. But the radicals also seized control of the Assembly. They removed the king from office and voted to imprison the royal family. They then called for a national convention to write a new constitution.

The National Convention

The elections for delegates to the National Convention took place in a tense atmosphere. Austrian and Prussian troops were not far from Paris. In early September, mobs of poor working people roamed the streets of the capital, killing anyone they suspected of being an enemy of France. The Convention delegates elected in such an atmosphere were far more radical than the population in general.

The National Convention met in late September. As its first act, the Convention voted to abolish the monarchy and make France a republic. The Convention then had to decide what to do with the king. The radical Jacobins demanded that Louis be tried for treason. More moderate revolutionaries thought he should be imprisoned until the war ended.

In November, the Convention discovered a trunk containing letters written by the king. The letters showed that Louis was plotting with émigrés to crush the revolution. The damaging evidence sealed the king's fate. The Convention tried and convicted Louis XVI of treason. By a majority of one vote, the delegates sentenced him to death. On January 21, 1793, Louis mounted the steps of the guillotine. "People, I die innocent!" were the king's last words to the watching crowd. (See page 404.)

Attacks on the Revolution

News of Louis XVI's execution sent waves of shock and horror through the capitals of Europe. Monarchs had every reason to fear the spread of the revolution. By 1793, French armies seemed to be fighting effectively. They had captured the Austrian Netherlands and were threatening the Dutch Netherlands and Prussia. Moreover, the National Convention issued a proclamation promising to aid "all peoples wishing to recover their liberty."

In March 1793, Great Britain, the Dutch Netherlands, and Spain joined Prussia and Austria in the war against France. With five nations fighting them, the French were hard pressed. The Prussians and Dutch pushed the French back across the Rhine. Spain sent troops into southern France, and British forces captured the port of Toulon.

Trouble at home also threatened the revolution. The war caused starvation and

Map Skill *The armies of revolutionary France had expanded French territory by 1793, as you can see on this map. At the same time, the revolutionary government had to contend with uprisings in the province of Vendée and in several cities, including Marseille. Which countries sent armies to fight the French?*

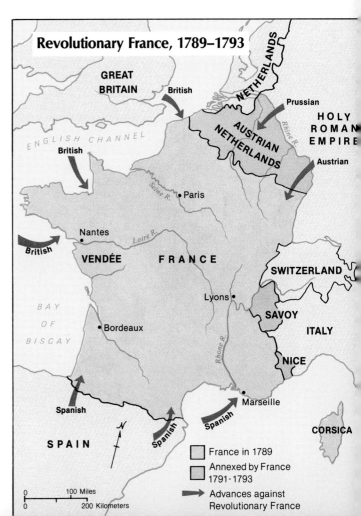

As you read earlier, primary sources provide useful information about historical events or developments. (Review "Analyzing a Primary Source," page 38, and "Identifying a Point of View," page 125.) However, primary sources, such as eyewitness accounts and official documents, can give conflicting views of an event or development.

Two descriptions of the execution of Louis XVI follow. The first is an official announcement published by the National Convention on January 23, 1793. The second is a letter written on January 23 by a noble living in Paris to a friend in England. Read both sources. Then use the following steps to analyze their value as historical sources.

1. **Read the sources to find out what information is given.** Answer the following questions about each of the sources: (a) What does each source say about the attitude of the French people toward the king's execution? (b) What does each source say about conditions in France in 1793? (c) According to each source, what was the outcome of the king's execution?

2. **Compare the two sources.** Answer the following questions: (a) Do the sources agree on any points about the execution of Louis XVI? Explain. (b) On what points do the sources disagree?

3. **Evaluate the reliability of each source.** Review the steps you used to analyze a primary source. Then answer the following questions: (a) How might the fact that the National Convention voted for Louis XVI's execution affect its proclamation? (b) How might the noble's background affect his view of the king's execution? (c) Which source do you think is more reliable? Why?

4. **Use the sources to draw conclusions about a historical event or development.** (a) Based on the sources and what you read in this chapter, what conclusions would you draw about reaction to the execution of Louis XVI? (b) How do the differences between the sources reflect divisions in France during the revolution?

Proclamation of the National Convention

Citizens, the tyrant is no more. For a long time, the cries of the victims, whom war and domestic discord have spread over France and Europe, loudly protested his existence. He has paid his penalty, and only approval for the Republic and for liberty have been heard from the people.

We have had to combat deep-seated prejudices, and the superstition of centuries concerning monarchy. Uncertainties and disturbances always accompany great changes and revolutions as profound as ours. . . . [But] respect for liberty of opinion must cause these disturbances to be forgotten; only the good which they have produced through the death of the tyrant and of tyranny now remains . . . The National Convention and the French people are now to have only one mind, only one sentiment, that of liberty and fraternity.

Now above all we need peace in the Republic, and the most active surveillance of the domestic enemies of liberty. . . . Let us unite to avert the shame that domestic discord [civil war], would bring upon our newborn republic.

A Noble's Report on the Death of the King

Monsieur . . . the frightful event of the 21st has spread dismay everywhere, and it is worth noting that even the most zealous supporters of the revolution found this measure both excessive and dangerous. It will not save us from the untold ills which threaten us, the reality and length of which are now all the more sure. We must make up our minds to sacrifice peace, security, and fortune . . . I very much fear that civil war will come as a finishing touch to the horrible crimes and all the misfortunes which now assail us. I doubt, moreover, whether this crime, added to so many others, has the universal approval of France. Even if we thought that the king were guilty, we would not wish for his death, especially after he has endured such a long and sorrowful captivity . . . Meanwhile, prudence must silence criticism because under the empire of secret accusations, of inquisition, or even more, of tyranny, it is dangerous to speak one's thoughts.

economic hardships. In many parts of France, people felt the revolution had gone too far. Counterrevolutionaries, people who oppose revolution, led uprisings in the region of the Vendée and in the cities of Marseille, Bordeaux, and Lyon.

The Reign of Terror

In the face of domestic and foreign threats, the National Convention took drastic action. It set aside a constitution that had been approved in 1793 and created a Committee of Public Safety. The Committee of Public Safety had almost dictatorial powers. It waged a brutal campaign against people it considered enemies of France. This campaign, known as the Reign of Terror, lasted from July 1793 to July 1794.

Maximilien Robespierre led the Committee of Public Safety during the Reign of Terror. He was determined to create a "Republic of Virtue," in which "our country assures the welfare of each individual and where each individual enjoys with pride the prosperity and the glory of our country . . ."

Robespierre was utterly honest and dedicated to his ideals, but he was also inflexible and narrowminded. He believed the state must be ruthless against its enemies.

The Committee of Public Safety sent agents across France to help local revolutionary committees uncover traitors. A Law of Suspects declared that people suspected of being counterrevolutionaries could be arrested for "their conduct, their relations, their remarks, or their writings." Such a vague law allowed revolutionary courts to imprison and condemn citizens on very little evidence.

During the Reign of Terror, trials were held almost daily throughout France. Between 20,000 and 40,000 men, women, and children were condemned to the guillotine. The former queen, Marie Antoinette, was one victim. Many nobles and clergy also went to the guillotine. But most victims were commoners, including peasants, laborers, shopkeepers, and merchants. The ruthlessness of the Terror had its effect, and the revolts subsided.

The Committee of Public Safety dealt with the threat of foreign invasion by organizing the nation for war. New French armies were raised, drilled, and equipped. A national draft law made every French man, whatever his age or occupation, eligible to be drafted into the army.

The Committee set strict limits on prices and wages, rationed food, and outlawed the use of scarce white flour. Citizens were asked to use whole wheat flour to make "equality bread."

By the spring of 1794, the total national effort had paid off. French forces were again victorious on the battlefield. However, even supporters of the revolution were beginning to question the need for constant executions at home. In July 1794, the National Convention ordered Robespierre's arrest. He was quickly tried and executed. With his death, the Reign of Terror ended.

This sketch shows a dignified Marie Antoinette on her way to the guillotine. Before the Revolution, the queen had been known for her beauty and grace. To many, however, she symbolized the extravagance of the French court and its indifference to the needs of the people. During the Reign of Terror, she was accused of plotting with Austria against France. She was executed in October 1793.

Impact of the Revolution on Daily Life

Between 1789 and 1794, French life had been transformed. The monarchy was gone, and the king was dead. French society had become more democratic. In place of the privileged estates of the Old Regime, the revolution had declared equality of all people. The National Convention had abolished all remaining feudal dues and customs and ended slavery in the French colonies. In addition, it had confiscated the land of émigrés.

Styles in fashion and art changed. Among the wealthy, simple dresses and long trousers replaced the elaborate gowns and knee breeches of the Old Regime. Playwrights and painters produced patriotic works that supported the revolution.

Revolutionary leaders established a uniform system of weights and measures, known as the metric system. They also called for free public schools so all citizens could receive an education. However, the schools were never set up.

After Robespierre's death in July 1794, a tide of reaction swept across France. The radical phase of the revolution had ended.

SECTION REVIEW

1. Locate: Vendée, Marseille, Bordeaux, Lyon.
2. Identify: Brunswick Manifesto, Committee of Public Safety, Robespierre, Republic of Virtue.
3. What two nations invaded France in 1792?
4. What were the National Convention's first actions in September 1792?
5. What events and developments increased the fear of revolution among European monarchs early in 1793?
6. Why did the Committee of Public Safety begin the Reign of Terror?

4 The Rise of Napoleon Bonaparte

Read to Learn
- how Napoleon came to power in France
- what reforms Napoleon made while consolidating his power

During the summer of 1794, the people of France reacted against the excesses of the Reign of Terror. They hunted down and executed many leaders of the Terror. In 1795, the National Convention wrote yet another constitution that reflected the more conservative mood of the country.

The Directory

The Constitution of 1795 established a new government, the Directory, which included an elected legislature and an executive branch with five directors. Only men who could read and who owned a certain amount of property could vote. As a result, the middle class and wealthy landowners gained influence in the new government.

The Directory, which lasted from 1795 to 1799, faced many problems. The five-man executive did not function efficiently, and corrupt deputies in the legislature bargained for political favors. Furthermore, when the government removed the controls on prices imposed during the Terror, prices rose sharply. As bread prices rose, poor workers rioted in the streets of Paris.

Despite economic problems and discontent, the Directory pursued an aggressive foreign policy. During the revolution, France had built the largest army in Europe. This army continued to fight for "liberty, equality, and fraternity." The military successes of one young officer, Napoleon Bonaparte, won the admiration of the French public.

"I am no ordinary man."

Born on the island of Corsica in 1769, Napoleon Bonaparte was the son of a minor noble family. He trained to become an army officer at a French military academy. Napoleon rose quickly in the army during the revolution because so many officers fled France.

In 1793, Napoleon commanded the French troops that ousted the British from Toulon. Two years later, he broke up a Paris mob by ordering his troops to fire a "whiff of grapeshot," small pellets shot from cannons. This action brought Napoleon to the attention of the Directory. His marriage to Joséphine de Beauharnais (boh ahr NEH) also helped him because his wife had influential friends among the directors. By age 27, Napoleon was a general.

The young general soon received command of a French army for an invasion of Italy. He won several brilliant victories over the Austrians who ruled northern Italy. Napoleon's successes forced Austria to withdraw from the war in 1797 and left Britain the only country still fighting France.

In 1798, Napoleon invaded Egypt because it was a vital lifeline to British outposts in India. Napoleon quickly defeated the Egyptian army.* However, he suffered a disastrous setback at sea. The British fleet, under Admiral Horatio Nelson, destroyed the French fleet in the battle of the Nile. The loss of their fleet meant the French could not supply their troops in Egypt or take them home.

Leaving the army in Egypt, Napoleon returned to Paris. The French people were not fully aware of the losses in Egypt, and they welcomed him as a hero.

In Paris, Napoleon found that many people were dissatisfied with the Directory. With the help of troops loyal to him, he and two directors overthrew the government in 1799. They drew up another constitution, the fourth since the revolution had begun. Under the new government, Napoleon was named First Consul.

"I am no ordinary man," Napoleon once boasted. He certainly was a person who could command the attention of friends as well as enemies, and he was admired by soldiers all over Europe. Napoleon had a sharp mind. He quickly sized up a situation and decided on a course of action. He thought and spoke so fast that he could dictate let-

---

* Napoleon asked French archaeologists and scientists to study the ancient monuments of Egypt. Among their discoveries was the Rosetta Stone, which held the clue to Egyptian hieroglyphics. (See page 19.)

Major Events of the French Revolution, 1789–1799	
1789	Estates General meets; Tennis Court Oath; fall of the Bastille; Declaration of the Rights of Man
1790	Civil Constitution of the Clergy
1791	Royal family tries to leave France; Louis XVI accepts the Constitution of 1791; Legislative Assembly meets
1792	France declares war on Austria; Brunswick Manifesto issued; royal family imprisoned; National Convention meets
1793	Louis XVI executed; European allies invade France; Reign of Terror begins
1794	Robespierre executed; Reign of Terror ends
1795	Directory established
1799	Napoleon overthrows the Directory

ters to four secretaries on four separate topics, all at the same time. Personal qualities and military talent helped Napoleon win widespread popular support. At age 30, Napoleon was the virtual dictator of France.

Napoleon's Domestic Policy

Between 1799 and 1804, Napoleon centralized power in his own hands. In 1802, he had himself made First Consul for life. A plebiscite, or popular vote, overwhelmingly approved this move. Two years later, Napoleon Bonaparte proclaimed himself "Emperor of the French." Once again, the majority of French voters endorsed his actions.

By 1804, Napoleon had gained almost absolute power. He knew the French would never stand for a return to the Old Regime. Therefore, he continued many reforms of the revolution. But at the same time, he kept firm personal control of the government. For

In 1804, Napoleon became "Emperor of the French." Jacques Louis David painted this picture of Napoleon's coronation. Pope Pius VII officiated at the ceremony, which took place in the Cathedral of Notre Dame. As the pope prepared to crown the emperor, Napoleon took the crown and placed it on his head himself. By this gesture, Napoleon showed that he did not bow to any authority.

example, he kept the system of dividing France into departments. But, he appointed local officials to replace the elected councils that had ruled during the revolution. He also allowed many émigrés to return home, but they had to agree not to demand the privileges they had enjoyed before the revolution.

The Napoleonic Code. Napoleon's greatest achievement in government was the Napoleonic Code, which has influenced French law to the present. This law code brought together many reforms of the revolution into a single, unified legal system. It recognized that all men were equal before the law and guaranteed freedom of religion as well as a person's right to work in any occupation.

The code did not always preserve the ideals of the revolution, however. It put the interests of the state above those of individual citizens. In addition, it dropped laws passed during the revolution that had protected the rights of women and children. The Napoleonic code reflected ancient Roman law and made the man absolute head of the household with control over all family property.

Other reforms. To strengthen the French economy, Napoleon enforced a law requiring all citizens to pay taxes. He also created the national Bank of France, in which the tax money was deposited. The bank, in turn, issued paper money and made loans to businesses. Napoleon's economic policies gradually brought inflation under control.

To fill the need for educated, loyal government officials, Napoleon set up *lycées* (lee SAYZ), government-run schools. The lycées encouraged extreme patriotism, and the same courses were taught at each school. Usually, only the children of wealthy parents attended the lycées because of the tuition costs. However, some students received scholarships. Thus, the lycées represented a first step toward a system of public education—a long-standing goal of Enlightenment thinkers and the French revolutionary leaders.

In dealing with religion, Napoleon shrewdly combined reform and tradition. He realized that most French people were strongly Roman Catholic and despised the

Civil Constitution of the Clergy. (See page 400.) In the Concordat of 1801, an agreement between the French government and the pope, Napoleon ended the election of bishops. Under this agreement, the French government appointed Catholic bishops and paid the clergy, but the pope had authority over them. The Concordat also stated that the Catholic Church would not demand the return of church property seized during the revolution. Thus, Napoleon did not lose the support of people who had acquired church lands.

SECTION REVIEW

1. Identify: Horatio Nelson, Concordat of 1801.
2. Define: lycée.
3. What problems did the Directory face?
4. Describe the results of each of the following: (a) Napoleon's invasion of Italy; (b) Napoleon's invasion of Egypt.
5. (a) Give one example of how the Napoleonic Code reflected the ideas of the French Revolution. (b) Give one example of how it reflected older traditions.

5 Napoleon in Triumph and Defeat

Read to Learn
- how Napoleon created an empire
- how the French Revolution and Napoleon affected Europe

Between 1792 and 1815, France was almost constantly at war. At first, French armies fought to keep a coalition of European monarchs from crushing the revolution. Then, under Napoleon, France fought several wars of conquest. Napoleon created an empire that spanned the continent of Europe.

The Empire of Napoleon

In the early 1800s, France fought all the major European powers, including Austria, Prussia, Britain, and Russia. A skilled military leader, Napoleon moved his troops in unexpected ways. For example, in 1805, he massed his troops against the Austrian army at Ulm. The Austrians expected Napoleon to attack head-on, but instead he attacked the Austrians from the rear, cutting off any retreat. A few months later, Napoleon defeated Austria and Russia at Austerlitz. Both countries then made peace on Napoleon's terms.

Through shrewd diplomacy, Napoleon usually kept the European powers divided so they could not unite against him. Thus, he managed to keep Prussia neutral during his war with Austria and Russia. But Napoleon's victories made the Prussians fearful of French power. They became even more anxious when Napoleon dissolved the Holy Roman Empire and reorganized the German states into the Confederation of the Rhine.

Finally, in 1806, Prussia declared war on France. Napoleon defeated the poorly led Prussian army and occupied Berlin.

Europe under French rule. From 1807 to 1812, Napoleon was at the height of his power. His empire stretched from France to the borders of Russia. (See the map on page 410.) He governed France and the Netherlands directly as emperor. Other nations, such as Spain and Italy, and the Confederation of the Rhine, were satellite states—that is, their rulers followed Napoleon's policies. In Spain, Napoleon made his brother, Joseph, king. In addition, he tied Austria and Prussia to France as allies.

While ruling this vast empire, Napoleon helped spread the ideas of the French Revolution across Europe. Throughout the empire, Napoleon introduced religious toleration, abolished serfdom, and reduced the power of the Catholic Church. He also made the Napoleonic Code the basis of law in many countries.

At first, some people welcomed the French emperor as a liberator. However, Napoleon lost much support when he imposed high taxes to finance his continuing conflict with Britain.

The Continental System. Although Napoleon defeated the major powers on the continent, he was unable to bring Britain to its knees. In 1805, he readied a fleet to invade Britain. But Admiral Nelson dashed Napoleon's plans by sinking most of the French fleet at Cape Trafalgar, near Spain. Napoleon then decided to blockade British ports and thereby cut off its vital trade.

Under the blockade, which was called the Continental System, Napoleon ordered all European nations to stop trade with Britain. The British responded swiftly. They declared that any ship bound for France had to stop first at a British port and pay a tax. Napoleon countered with a threat to seize any ship paying the British tax.

Unfortunately for France, the Continental System backfired. Britain did lose trade, but France suffered more. The powerful British navy was able to cut off overseas imports to France and the rest of the continent.* This weakened the French economy. It also increased opposition to Napoleon among neutral nations who blamed him for their loss of trade.

Stirrings of Nationalism

Opposition to Napoleon also grew among the conquered and allied peoples of Europe, who were developing a sense of *nationalism*,

---

* During the war with Napoleon, the British interfered with American shipping to Europe and seized American sailors, forcing them to serve on British warships. These disputes were partly responsible for the War of 1812 between the United States and Britain.

Map Skill *By 1812, Napoleon controlled nearly all of Europe. The Netherlands and parts of Italy had been annexed by France. Some areas, shown in blue on this map, were satellites of France; other areas were allies. What nations were beyond Napoleon's influence in 1812?*

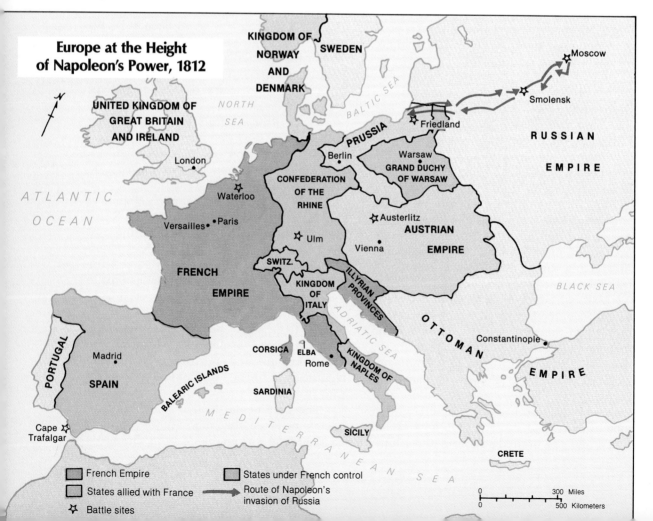

or pride and devotion to one's own country. They resented paying taxes to France and sending soldiers to serve in Napoleon's armies. They wanted to restore their own governments, customs, and traditions. As nationalist feelings grew, revolts broke out all over Europe.

Trouble came first in Spain with an uprising against Napoleon's brother. Spaniards were loyal to their former king and to the Catholic Church. They despised the French, who they considered atheists and invaders. Bands of patriotic Spaniards ambushed French troops in hit-and-run attacks that became known as guerrilla warfare. ("Guerrilla" is a Spanish word meaning "little war.") In 1808, Britain sent troops to help the Spanish and the Portuguese, who also fought against French rule. By 1812, Spanish and Portuguese nationalists had ousted the French from their nations. Each nation then set up a limited monarchy with a written constitution.

In Prussia, nationalist leaders reorganized the government to make it more efficient. They urged the king to create greater loyalty among the middle and lower classes by giving them more political freedom. Prussia also quietly rebuilt its army. The new army rewarded talent and hard work. By 1811, Prussia had an army capable of renewing the struggle against France. It only needed an opportunity to strike. The opportunity arose in 1812 when Napoleon undertook an ill-fated invasion of Russia.

The Emperor's Downfall

In 1807, Czar Alexander I of Russia agreed to abide by the Continental System, but the trade blockade hurt the Russian economy. When Alexander resumed trade with Britain in 1812, Napoleon decided to invade Russia. Napoleon assembled an army of over 500,000 soldiers, and in May 1812, he led this Grand Army into Russia.

Napoleon planned to defeat the Russians in a quick, decisive battle. To his surprise, the Russians refused to stand and fight. Instead, they retreated, burning their crops and homes as they went. They forced Napoleon to lead his army deeper into Rus-

sia. The Russians finally engaged the French near Moscow, 500 miles (800 kilometers) inside Russia. The French won, but when Napoleon entered Moscow, he found the Russian capital in flames. Napoleon soon realized he could not feed and house his army in Moscow. Thus, in October 1812, he ordered a retreat.

During the retreat, the bitterly cold Russian winter turned the French victory into a disastrous defeat. Thousands of Napoleon's soldiers starved or froze to death. The Russian army attacked the stragglers. Fewer than 100,000 escaped from Russia.

A powerful alliance made up of Britain, Austria, Russia, and Prussia pounced on the weakened French army as it limped out of Russia. Napoleon rushed home to raise a new army, but his efforts failed. In March 1814, the allies captured Paris. Napoleon abdicated and went into exile on the island of Elba, off the coast of Italy. The allies installed the brother of the executed Louis XVI as Louis XVIII.

Although the monarchy was restored, the new king did not revive the Old Regime. In 1814, Louis XVIII issued a constitution that provided for equality under the law for all citizens, an elected legislature, and religious freedom. He also kept the Napoleonic Code.

When Louis XVIII became king, many émigrés returned to France and demanded revenge on supporters of the French Revolution. Napoleon took advantage of the resulting disturbances to return to Paris. In March 1815, he again proclaimed himself emperor. Discontented soldiers rallied to his side. For 100 days, he worked to rebuild the French army. But the European allies acted swiftly. In June 1815, a joint British and Prussian army led by the Duke of Wellington defeated the French at Waterloo. Napoleon was exiled to the island of St. Helena in the Atlantic, where he died in 1821.

Legacy of the French Revolution and Napoleon

The era of the French Revolution and Napoleon had a lasting impact on France and the rest of Europe. In France, the revolution ended feudalism, with its special privileges for clergy and nobles. Although the monarchy was eventually restored in France, a written constitution limited the king's authority. In the years ahead, French citizens would continue to struggle for the ideals of "liberty, equality, and fraternity."

Under Napoleon, the revolutionary ideals of political and social justice spread throughout Europe. Through his wars and alliances, Napoleon altered European political boundaries. Both the French Revolution and Napoleon contributed to the growing spirit of nationalism in Europe.

Finally, 23 years of warfare had drained French resources. By 1815, France was no longer the strongest and richest nation in Europe. Great Britain had forged ahead in commerce and industry as you will read in Chapter 23.

SECTION REVIEW

1. Locate: Ulm, Austerlitz, Berlin, Cape Trafalgar, Moscow, Elba, Waterloo.
2. Identify: Confederation of the Rhine, Continental System.
3. Define: nationalism.
4. What reforms did Napoleon introduce in Europe?
5. What effect did the Continental System have on France?
6. What event led to Napoleon's invasion of Russia?

Chapter 21 Review

In Perspective

In the late 1780s, Louis XVI faced a severe economic crisis. When all efforts at reform failed, the king summoned a meeting of the Estates General. The French Revolution began when representatives from the three estates declared themselves the National Assembly. Between 1789 and 1794, the French Revolution became increasingly radical.

French armies defended the revolution at home and spread its ideas abroad. During the Reign of Terror, thousands of French were executed. By 1795, reaction to excesses of the Reign of Terror led to the establishment of the Directory. However, Napoleon Bonaparte overthrew the Directory in 1799 and eventually crowned himself emperor.

Napoleon consolidated many reforms of the revolution. He also led French armies to victory all over Europe. Controlling his empire proved difficult, however. Nationalist movements and the ongoing struggle with Britain drained French resources. In 1812, Napoleon undertook a disastrous invasion of Russia. In 1814, Napoleon's enemies invaded France, and the emperor abdicated. The revolutionary era ended when the monarchy was restored in France.

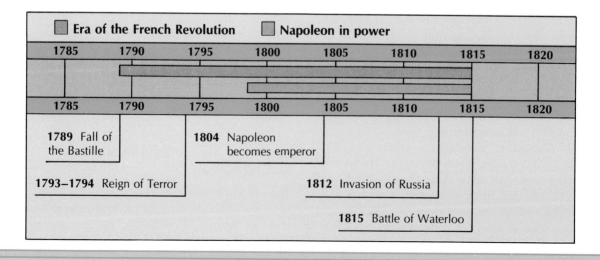

Era of the French Revolution   Napoleon in power

| 1785 | 1790 | 1795 | 1800 | 1805 | 1810 | 1815 | 1820 |

1789 Fall of the Bastille

1804 Napoleon becomes emperor

1793–1794 Reign of Terror

1812 Invasion of Russia

1815 Battle of Waterloo

Recalling Facts

Arrange the events in each of the following groups in the order in which they occurred.

1. (a) Paris mob attacks the Bastille.
   (b) Louis XVI is executed.
   (c) The Estates General meets.
2. (a) The National Assembly issues the Declaration of the Rights of Man.
   (b) Foreign invaders issue the Brunswick Manifesto.
   (c) Deputies at the Estates General take the Tennis Court Oath.
3. (a) France is ruled by the Directory.
   (b) National Assembly writes the first French constitution.
   (c) Thousands die during the Reign of Terror.
4. (a) Allied armies defeat Napoleon at Waterloo.
   (b) Napoleon invades Russia.
   (c) Napoleon overthrows the Directory.

Chapter Checkup

1. (a) Describe the economic crisis France faced in the 1780s. (b) How did Louis XVI and his ministers try to solve the crisis? (c) How did the existence of the Old Regime hamper their efforts?
2. Describe the major reforms introduced by the National Assembly.
3. Explain how each of the following responded to developments in France between 1789 and 1791: (a) French nobles; (b) Louis XVI; (c) other European monarchs.
4. (a) How did war in 1792 help unite the French people? (b) Why did the war lead to an uprising in Paris? (c) What was the result of the uprising?
5. (a) What actions by the National Convention show that it was more radical than the National Assembly? (b) How did other European monarchs react to the Convention's actions?
6. (a) What steps did the Committee of Public Safety take against counterrevolutionaries? (b) How did it defend France against foreign invaders?
7. (a) How did Napoleon gain popularity? (b) Why was he able to overthrow the Directory so easily? (c) How did he become emperor?

Critical Thinking

1. **Analyzing** Describe how each of the following developments led the French Revolution on a more radical course: (a) the fall of the Bastille; (b) Louis XVI's attempted flight from France; (c) the threat of foreign invasion.
2. **Analyzing a Quotation** Robespierre justified the Reign of Terror in these words, "To establish and consolidate democracy, to achieve the peaceful rule of constitutional laws, we must first finish the war of liberty against tyranny. . . . We must annihilate the enemies of the republic at home and abroad, or else we shall perish." (a) Who did the revolutionaries consider the "enemies of the republic at home"? (b) Do you agree with Robespierre that the Reign of Terror was necessary to save the revolution? Explain.
3. **Expressing an Opinion** In your opinion, which of the changes that occurred during the French Revolution had the greatest impact on the lives of French citizens? Why?

Relating Past to Present

1. (a) How did the French Revolution contribute to the growth of nationalism in Europe? (b) Do you think nationalism is a major force today? Explain.

Developing Basic Skills

1. **Graph Reading** Study the graphs on page 396. Then answer the following questions: (a) What percentage of the population made up the First and Second Estates? (b) What percentage of the land did these two estates own? (c) What percentage of the population made up the Third Estate? (d) What percentage of the land did it own? (e) How did the distribution of land contribute to the problems of the Old Regime?
2. **Analyzing a Primary Source** Reread the Declaration of the Rights of Man on page 400. Then answer the following questions: (a) What Enlightenment ideas appear in the document? (b) How is it similar to the American Declaration of Independence? (c) How can you use this document to learn about the French Revolution?
3. **Map Reading** Study the map on page 410. Then answer the following questions: (a) What lands did Napoleon rule directly? (b) What lands did he control by other means? (c) What problems do you think Napoleon faced in ruling his empire?

See page 805 for suggested readings.

22 Revolutions and Reaction

(1815–1848)

Street fighting in Paris, 1848.

In the fall of 1814, nine kings, dozens of princes, and hundreds of diplomats converged on Vienna, the capital of the Austrian Empire. For ten months, these imposing figures attended the Congress of Vienna, an international peace conference. "There is literally a royal mob here," wrote one visitor to Vienna. "I have worn [my hat] out in taking it off to sovereigns whom I meet at the corner of every street."

After more than 20 years of war, Europe was at peace. Napoleon was in exile on Elba, and Louis XVIII was on the throne of France. The peace was temporarily shattered in March 1815, when Napoleon returned to Paris from Elba. But by June, word reached Vienna of the final victory over Napoleon at Waterloo.

During the Congress of Vienna, the Austrian emperor bore the burden of entertaining his eminent guests. He organized elaborate banquets, hunting parties, and firework displays. In the evenings, the dignitaries dressed for fancy balls that continued far into the night. "The Congress dances," one observer noted, "but accomplishes nothing." However, the festivities served a purpose. They diverted the attention of the less powerful diplomats while the leaders of the great powers negotiated important issues. They wanted to turn the clock back to 1789 and rebuild the balance of power in Europe.

Representatives of Austria, Britain, Russia, and Prussia finally hammered out a treaty. However, the new international order created by the Congress of Vienna could not erase the ideas of political and social justice that the Enlightenment and the French Revolution had planted throughout Europe. The actions of the Congress of Vienna set the stage for unrest and revolt in many countries during the first half of the 1800s.

1 Restoring Peace

Read to Learn
- how the Congress of Vienna changed Europe
- what the Concert of Europe achieved

When delegates to the Congress of Vienna gathered in 1814, Europe was in chaos. In the preceding 20 years, some monarchs had been overthrown, and many nations had been invaded by revolutionary armies. Many people demanded written constitutions to limit the power of the remaining monarchs. The national leaders who met at Vienna were determined to restore the traditions that had existed before the French Revolution. However, they faced new forces that threatened to undermine those traditions.

Old and New Forces

During the 1800s, the philosophies of liberalism and conservatism influenced the way many people thought about government and society. To people at the time, *liberalism* was a philosophy that supported guarantees for individual freedom, political change, and social reform. *Conservatism* supported the traditional political and social order and resisted changes that threatened that way of life.

Liberals accepted the ideas of the Enlightenment and the French Revolution. They supported freedom of speech, press, and religion. To safeguard these rights, they called for written constitutions. As heirs to the Enlightenment, liberals stressed reason, progress, and education. They believed that governments should be reformed so that educated, responsible citizens, like themselves, could participate. Few liberals thought that poor and uneducated people should take part in government.

The ideas of conservatives were expressed by Edmund Burke, an English statesman, in *Reflections on the Revolution in France*. Burke condemned the French Revolution because it brought about radical changes that destroyed traditional institutions such as the monarchy and the nobility. While most conservatives accepted the idea of gradual change, they emphasized respect for custom and tradition. They believed that only the wisest, most talented people should run the government. To many conservative nobles, this meant that they alone should hold positions of power.

In the early 1800s, conservatives were in firm control of governments throughout Europe. However, support for liberalism was growing, especially among educated members of the middle class.

Another powerful force shaping Europe in the 1800s was nationalism. As it spread, it came to mean not only love of country but also pride in a common cultural heritage regardless of political boundaries. Nationalism became both a positive and a negative force. For example, it could unite people behind a common cause, such as political independence, or lead them to persecute those with different cultural traditions.

Liberals and conservatives reacted differently to nationalism. Liberals often supported nationalist leaders who wanted to free their countries from foreign control. Conservatives feared nationalism, in part because it threatened to upset the traditional political order.

The Congress of Vienna

Conservatives dominated the Congress of Vienna. The most influential leaders were Czar Alexander I of Russia; King Frederick William III of Prussia; Lord Castlereagh, the British Foreign Minister; and Prince Klemens von Metternich, the Austrian Foreign Minister. The French delegate, Charles Maurice de Talleyrand, also played a major role at the Congress.

Metternich presided over the Congress. He was guided by two general principles: legitimacy and balance of power. By *legitimacy*, he meant restoring to power the royal families that had lost their thrones when

Napoleon conquered Europe. The Congress of Vienna recognized Louis XVIII as the legitimate king of France. It also restored royal families in Spain, Portugal, and Sardinia.

To rebuild the balance of power in Europe and prevent future French aggression, the Congress reduced France to its 1790 frontiers and strengthened the countries on the borders of France. To the north of France, the Dutch and Austrian Netherlands were united into a single country, called the Netherlands, which was ruled by the Dutch king. To the east, 39 German states were loosely joined into the German Confederation, headed by Austria. The Congress recognized Switzerland as an independent nation. In addition, it strengthened the kingdom of Sardinia in northern Italy by giving it Piedmont and Genoa. (See the map on page 417.)

The Congress also made other territorial changes. In return for giving up the Austrian Netherlands, Austria received Lombardy and Venetia in Italy. With these lands, Austria became the strongest power in northern Italy. In southern Italy, the Congress established a Spanish Bourbon as ruler of the kingdom of the Two Sicilies.

In Eastern Europe, the fate of Poland became a thorny issue. Early in the Congress, Czar Alexander had pointed to Poland on a map and announced, "This belongs to me." The king of Prussia then claimed the German state of Saxony. Russia and Prussia supported each other's demands. Metternich, Castlereagh, and Talleyrand objected to these demands because they feared the expansion of Russian power. Eventually, Russia and Prussia settled for smaller portions of the land they wanted, but both still increased their territory.

The Congress of Vienna granted Britain handsome rewards for its long struggle against Napoleon. Great Britain acquired Malta, Ceylon, and islands in the East and West Indies, as well as part of Guiana in South America. It also received the Cape Colony in South Africa.

Delegates to the Congress of Vienna redrew the map of Europe after Napoleon's downfall. Seated at the far left is the Duke of Wellington, who defeated Napoleon at the battle of Waterloo. The Austrian statesman Metternich, standing at left, is introducing Wellington to the other delegates. At right, with his arm resting on the table, is the chief French delegate Talleyrand.

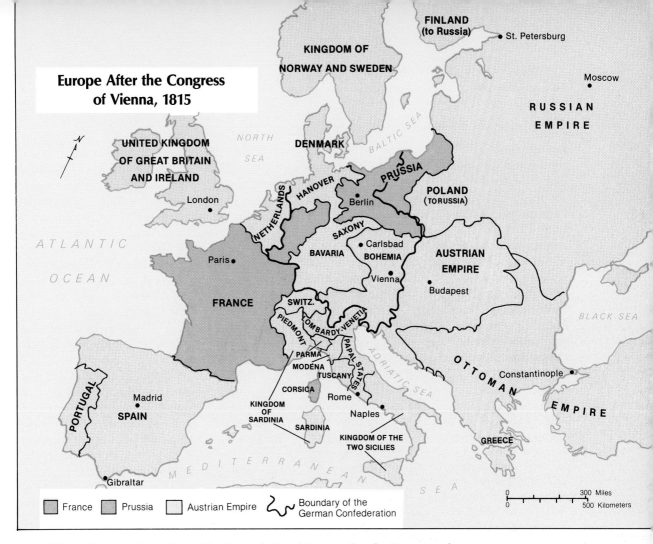

Europe After the Congress of Vienna, 1815

FINLAND (to Russia)
• St. Petersburg

KINGDOM OF NORWAY AND SWEDEN

• Moscow

RUSSIAN EMPIRE

NORTH SEA

DENMARK

BALTIC SEA

PRUSSIA

POLAND (TO RUSSIA)

UNITED KINGDOM OF GREAT BRITAIN AND IRELAND

• London

HANOVER

NETHERLANDS

• Berlin

SAXONY

• Carlsbad

BOHEMIA

AUSTRIAN EMPIRE

BAVARIA

ATLANTIC OCEAN

• Paris

FRANCE

SWITZ.

• Vienna

• Budapest

BLACK SEA

PIEDMONT

LOMBARDY-VENETIA

PARMA

MODENA

PAPAL STATES

TUSCANY

ADRIATIC SEA

OTTOMAN EMPIRE

• Constantinople

PORTUGAL

SPAIN

• Madrid

CORSICA

KINGDOM OF SARDINIA

• Rome

Naples

SARDINIA

KINGDOM OF THE TWO SICILIES

GREECE

MEDITERRANEAN SEA

• Gibraltar

☐ France   ☐ Prussia   ☐ Austrian Empire   〜 Boundary of the German Confederation

0   300 Miles
0   500 Kilometers

Map Skill *This map shows the political boundaries of Europe after the Congress of Vienna. Nations that had fought against Napoleon won new territory, and France lost territory it had conquered. Compare this map with the map on page 410. Which nations gained land from France?*

Delegates to the Congress generally ignored feelings of nationalism when they rearranged boundaries. The Congress did not consult the people living in the areas they handed over to Austria, Spain, Russia, Prussia, or Britain.

The Concert of Europe

To protect the peace settlement reached at Vienna, Britain, Austria, Prussia, and Russia formed the Quadruple Alliance in November 1815. Three years later, France was admitted to the alliance. These great powers held periodic meetings to deal with any threat to the peace and stability of Europe.

Although Czar Alexander signed the Quadruple Alliance, he had grander visions. The Czar proposed a Holy Alliance that would bind all rulers to govern according to Christian principles. Castlereagh dismissed the idea as a "piece of sublime mysticism and nonsense." Nevertheless, many European rulers eventually joined the Holy Alliance.

The two alliances encouraged nations to act together to preserve the peace. The system of meeting to settle international problems became known as the Concert of Europe. During most of the 1800s, the Concert of Europe enforced the settlement arranged at Vienna. It preserved the balance of power

417

and prevented local conflicts from flaring into a major European conflict.

The Metternich System

For more than 30 years, Prince Metternich dominated European politics. His main goal was to defend the work of the Congress of Vienna. Metternich opposed liberalism and nationalism, and he defended the *status quo*, that is, the existing state of affairs. His policies were known as the Metternich System.

Despite Metternich's efforts, there soon were challenges to the status quo. Students in German universities agitated for liberal reform and unification of the German people. Metternich responded by persuading representatives from the German states to pass the Carlsbad Decrees in 1819. These laws imposed press censorship and suppressed freedom of speech.

Austrian foreign minister Metternich dominated European politics for 30 years after the Congress of Vienna. His enormous self-confidence was expressed in these words: "I say to myself 20 times a day, how right I am and how wrong others are. And yet," he added, "it is so easy to be right."

The Carlsbad Decrees ended student agitation in Germany for nearly a generation. But challenges to the status quo arose in other areas. In 1820, liberal reformers forced the kings of Naples and Spain to grant constitutions. Metternich pressured members of the Quadruple Alliance to intervene in those countries to prevent the spread of liberalism. Britain opposed intervention and broke from the alliance. In 1821, an Austrian army marched into Naples and restored the king to power. In 1823, a French army helped the king of Spain suppress Spanish liberals.

Despite the restoration of royal power in Spain, the Spanish colonies in Latin America successfully revolted against Spanish control during the 1820s. You will read about the wars of independence in Latin America in Chapter 29.

The Greeks also fought a successful war for independence. Greece had been part of the Ottoman Empire for nearly 400 years. In 1821, Greek nationalists revolted against Turkish rule. Metternich tried to prevent other European countries from aiding the rebellion. But the British and the French admired ancient Greek civilization and eventually rallied to the Greek cause. In 1829, the Ottoman Empire was forced to recognize Greek independence.

SECTION REVIEW

1. Identify: Edmund Burke, German Confederation, Concert of Europe, Carlsbad Decrees.
2. Define: liberalism, conservatism, legitimacy, status quo.
3. (a) What political ideas did liberals support? (b) What political ideas did conservatives support?
4. (a) Which nations had the most influence at the Congress of Vienna? (b) What leaders represented each of those nations?
5. How did liberals and conservatives react to nationalism?
6. How did the Congress of Vienna try to prevent future French aggression?
7. What challenges to the Metternich System were successful in the 1820s?

2 A New Era of Revolution in France

Read to Learn ■ how the restored monarchy ruled France
■ what reforms the Second Republic achieved

The success of the Greek revolt gave new hope to many liberals and nationalists. The ideals of the French Revolution also continued to inspire demands for reform, especially in France. Middle class liberals and workers in France joined forces in 1830 and 1848 to upset the status quo created at the Congress of Vienna.

The July Revolution

As you read, the Congress of Vienna had recognized Louis XVIII as king of France. During his reign, Louis sought a compromise between conservatives and liberals. Louis knew he could not restore an absolute monarchy. Thus, he accepted the constitution of 1814, which guaranteed individual rights and provided for an elected legislature.

Louis's efforts at compromise satisfied few people, however. Liberals criticized the 1814 constitution because it limited the right to vote to wealthy people. Extreme conservatives, led by the king's brother, wanted a return to the Old Regime. On Louis's death in 1824, his brother inherited the throne as Charles X.

A tactless, stubborn man, Charles set about increasing royal power. He warned that the constitution "cannot possibly prevent me from having my way." Supported by the clergy and the nobles, Charles pressured the legislature to pass a law to pay nobles for the lands they had lost during the French Revolution. However, when the legislature refused to approve laws that restricted individual freedom, Charles dissolved it and called for a new election.

The elections of July 1830 surprised the king because voters chose liberal legislators who opposed his policies. Unable to control the newly elected legislature, Charles issued the July Ordinances. These laws dissolved the legislature, ended freedom of the press, and put new restrictions on the right to vote.

French newspapers urged citizens to resist the king's arbitrary rule. On July 28, riots broke out in Paris. Workers, university students, and middle class liberals built barricades in the streets. When soldiers refused to fire on the rebels and began to join them, Charles X abdicated and fled to England.

The July Revolution, as it was called, ended quickly. Many people had hoped to create a republic. But the middle class leaders of the revolution feared that if France became a republic, foreign powers might intervene. Therefore, they established a constitutional monarchy. They chose Louis Philippe, a cousin of Charles X, as king.

The Bourgeois Monarchy

Under Louis Philippe, the 1814 constitution was amended to give more members of the middle class the right to vote. Because the middle class, or bourgeoisie, controlled the legislature and supported the king, Louis Philippe was called the "bourgeois monarch." In keeping with this image, Louis Philippe was the first European monarch to adopt middle class dress. Wearing a top hat, frock coat, and trousers, he often walked through the streets of Paris, greeting citizens.

Although France prospered during most of Louis Philippe's reign, many French people were discontented with his government. The king's policies favored the wealthy, and many citizens felt betrayed by the July Revolution because they had not won the right to vote. Republicans and some liberals organized secret societies to work for an end to the monarchy.

Socialist demands. Changing social and economic conditions added to tensions in France. In the early 1800s, new factories in the cities attracted workers looking for jobs. Because of poor conditions in the factories and low pay, many workers listened eagerly to reformers who promised improvements.

In July 1830, workers and middle class liberals set up barricades in the streets of Paris. The streets echoed with the cry: "Down with the Bourbons." Street barricades made it difficult for government troops to move. As this picture shows, people showered troops with furniture, flowerpots, washtubs, and shovels.

One reformer was Louis Blanc. He believed in an economic and political theory called *socialism.* Under socialism, society as a whole rather than private individuals would own all property and operate all businesses. Blanc argued that a socialist government representing society as a whole would be able to protect the interests of the working class and guarantee all of them jobs.

Louis Philippe rejected the demands for reform from socialists as well as those from liberals and republicans. "There will be no reform," he said in 1847, "I do not wish it."

The revolution of 1848. On February 22, 1848, Francois Guizot (gee ZOH), the king's chief minister, cancelled a huge public banquet in Paris because he feared it would lead to demonstrations and disorder. Hearing that the banquet was cancelled, thousands of workers poured into the streets shouting: "Down with Guizot." To restore order, Louis Philippe dismissed his chief minister, but

demonstrations continued over the next few days. When troops opened fire and killed some demonstrators, the people of Paris erected barricades as they had in 1830.

The revolution of 1848 ended quickly. When crowds marched on the king's palace, Louis Philippe abdicated and fled in disguise to England. The mob swarmed into the palace. Finding the table set for lunch, they sat down to enjoy the royal meal. Meanwhile, leaders of the revolution proclaimed the Second Republic.

The Second Republic

While Paris was in turmoil, the revolutionaries quickly set up a provisional, or temporary, government, which included the socialist leader Louis Blanc. In response to socialist demands, the government created national workshops that would provide jobs for unemployed workers. Nearly 120,000 workers flocked to Paris to register at the national workshops. Because jobs could not be found for all of them, many received government aid in the form of relief payments.

To pay for the national workshops, the government imposed a heavy tax on property. The increased taxes angered the middle class as well as peasants who owned land. They blamed the socialists. Consequently, when elections were held for a National Assembly, moderate delegates who represented middle class interests won a majority.

In June 1848, the National Assembly abolished the national workshops. Paris workers immediately revolted. During the days that followed, clashes between workers and troops left more than 10,000 people killed or wounded. After the revolt was crushed, the National Assembly issued a new constitution. It guaranteed liberty and established an elected legislature and president. In addition, it provided for *universal male suffrage*—that is, all adult men were given the right to vote. However, the fighting left bitter memories and sharp divisions between the middle class and workers.

The first elections under the new constitution were held in December 1848. By a huge majority, voters chose Louis Napoleon, nephew of Napoleon Bonaparte, to be president of the Second Republic. Few people knew much about Louis Napoleon, but they associated his name with order, security, and the glorious victories of French armies.

As president, Louis Napoleon tried to please everyone. He promised jobs to workers, encouraged trade, defended property rights, and supported the Roman Catholic Church. Thus, he met little resistance when he set up a virtual dictatorship in December 1851. A year later, he assumed the title Napoleon III, Emperor of the French. Like his uncle, he won approval for this move in a popular vote. Thus, the short-lived Second Republic ended with the creation of the Second Empire.

SECTION REVIEW

1. Identify: July Ordinances, Louis Blanc, Second Republic.
2. Define: socialism, universal male suffrage.
3. Why did the French revolt against Charles X?
4. Why was Louis Philippe known as the bourgeois monarch?
5. What was the purpose of the national workshops?
6. Why did the French support Louis Napoleon?

3 Revolts in Other Parts of Europe

Read to Learn ■ why revolutions took place in 1830 and 1848
■ how governments responded to the revolutions

A wave of revolutions swept across Europe in 1830 and 1848. Inspired by events in France, liberals and nationalists in many parts of Europe fought against the old order restored by the Congress of Vienna. As Metternich observed, "When France sneezes, Europe catches cold."

The Revolutions of 1830

At the Congress of Vienna, the Dutch and Austrian Netherlands had been united under the Dutch king. However, the Belgians, who lived in the south of the new country, despised the arrangement. They spoke a different language from the Dutch, and they were largely Roman Catholic, whereas most of the Dutch were Protestants.

These cultural and religious differences sparked a Belgian nationalist movement. In August 1830, riots erupted in Brussels. The Belgians defeated a Dutch army and won the support of Britain and France for their cause. Although Austria, Prussia, and Russia at first were opposed, they eventually signed a treaty establishing Belgium as an independent nation.

The July Revolution in France and the nationalist revolt in Belgium succeeded in part because each had the support of a strong middle class. Elsewhere, however, the revolutions of 1830 failed.

For example, Polish nationalists tried to win their independence from Russia in 1830. But the Poles were divided themselves. Moreover, Britain and France did not provide help, as the Poles had hoped. A Russian army crushed the rebels, executed many leaders, and imposed a harsh rule on Poland.

Revolts also flared in Italy and Germany. Austria quickly sent troops to suppress nationalists in Italy, and Metternich persuaded the German states to renew the Carlsbad Decrees, which silenced the unrest in Germany. "The dam has broken in Europe," wrote Metternich in 1830. However, he managed to hold back the flood of liberalism and nationalism until 1848.

Revolts in the Austrian Empire

In March 1848, news of the overthrow of Louis Philippe in France led to an uprising in Vienna. University students joined by workers and middle class liberals poured into the streets. They demanded an end to feudalism, a constitution, and the removal of Metternich. Frightened by the demonstrations, the Austrian emperor promised reform. To show his good faith, he dismissed Metternich.

During the uprising in Vienna, revolts erupted among various nationalities in other parts of the Austrian Empire. In Hungary, the Magyars, led by the fiery nationalist Louis Kossuth (kah SOOTH), demanded a constitution and a separate Hungarian government. In Bohemia, the Czechs issued similar demands. In northern Italy, nationalists in Lombardy and Venetia also revolted against Austria. They were supported by the kingdom of Sardinia and other Italian states.

Overwhelmed by these events, the Austrian government granted the demands of the Magyars and the Czechs and withdrew its armies from northern Italy. Within three months, however, the tide of revolution turned. Germans who lived in Bohemia resented being under Czech control, and they helped an Austrian army occupy Prague. By June 1848, Austria had regained control of Bohemia. In October, government troops bombarded Vienna and crushed the revolution there.

The reconquest of Hungary took longer. To weaken the Magyar cause, the Austrian government took advantage of the cultural differences between the Magyars and the Croatians, a Slavic people who lived in Hungary. The Austrians supplied arms to a Croatian army, which stormed Budapest in September 1848. The Magyars successfully repelled the attack under the leadership of Kossuth. In the spring of 1849, Kossuth proclaimed Hungary a republic.

The Russian czar was anxious to see order restored in Eastern Europe, however, so he offered to help Austria. In August 1849, a Russian army invaded Hungary and suppressed the Magyar revolt.

Uprisings in Italy

The revolts in Lombardy and Venetia against the Austrians were among several uprisings in Italy in 1848. In January, revolutionaries in Sicily had overthrown their king. In other Italian states, people forced their rulers to grant liberal constitutions.

Italian nationalists in Rome tried to win the pope's support for a united Italy. However, the pope refused to give his support because he did not want to offend Austria, the main Catholic nation in Europe. Rebels then took over the city, and the pope fled into exile. Led by Giuseppe Mazzini, nationalists established the Roman Republic in February 1849.

By this time, however, the Austrians had restored order in Vienna and had begun to reestablish their control in northern Italy. Furthermore, Louis Napoleon, who wanted to win favor with the pope, sent French troops to Rome. French troops occupied the city and restored the pope to power.

Although the Italian uprisings were crushed, liberals and nationalists preserved their dreams of a unified Italy. In the years ahead, they looked to the kingdom of Sardinia for leadership because only Sardinia had managed to keep the liberal constitution won in 1848.

The German States

The revolution of 1848 in France inspired German liberals to demand reform. In many German states, rulers promised constitutions and other reforms. However, events took a different course in Prussia.

Prussia. In March 1848, a demonstration in Berlin turned into a riot when police opened fire on the crowd. Workers and middle class liberals set up barricades. When told of the revolt, the Prussian king Frederick William IV was amazed. "It cannot be," he said, "my people love me." To avoid further bloodshed, he withdrew his troops from the city and promised reform.

The Prussians elected a National Assembly to draft a constitution, but a split soon developed between moderates of the middle class and radical workers. Moreover, the king was encouraged by the Austrian success in suppressing revolts. In November, Frederick William dissolved the National Assembly and sent troops back to Berlin. Once he was in full control, the king issued his own constitution for Prussia. The constitution provided for universal male suffrage and an elected legislature.

Attempt to unify Germany. In 1848, German nationalists tried to unite the people of Germany. In May, delegates from the German states met in Frankfurt as a national parliament. They agreed to work peacefully for German unity.

Profiles ■ Carl Schurz: Memories of the Revolution of 1848

Carl Schurz was a student at the German University of Bonn when the revolutions of 1848 altered the course of his life. Until this time, Schurz's goal had been to become a professor of history. But in the revolutionary spirit of the times, the 19-year-old student embraced the cause of democratic reform. He became a student leader and ardently supported demands for German unity and a constitution. Later in life, Schurz recalled his early involvement in the events of 1848:

"One morning toward the end of February 1848, I sat quietly in my attic chamber, working hard at the tragedy of *Ulrich von Hutten*, when suddenly a friend rushed breathlessly into the room, exclaiming: 'What, you sitting here! Do you not know what has happened?'

'No, what?'

'The French have driven away Louis Philippe and proclaimed the Republic.'

"I threw down my pen—and that was the end of *Ulrich von Hutten*. I never touched the manuscript again. We tore down the stairs, into the street, to the market-square, the accustomed meeting-place for all the student societies after their midday dinner. Although it was still forenoon, the market was already crowded with young men talking excitedly. ... In these conversations ... certain ideas and catchwords worked themselves to the surface, which expressed more or less the feelings of the people. Now had arrived in Germany the day for the establishment of 'German Unity' and the founding of a great, powerful national German Empire."

Schurz fought bravely in the revolutionary army. He defended one fortress until its surrender and barely escaped a firing squad by clambering through an unused sewer. Although he found a safe refuge in Switzerland, Schurz risked his freedom to return to Germany when he learned that an old friend, a professor whom he greatly admired, had been imprisoned for life. Schurz became a hero of the revolution of 1848 by spiriting the professor safely out of Germany.

Even as an exile, Schurz did not give up his political ideals. He championed the cause of German unity in speeches in France and England. Then, like many other exiles from the political upheavals of 1848, Schurz set sail for the United States. Schurz dedicated himself to his adopted homeland and eventually was elected to the United States Senate.

In April 1849, the parliament issued a constitution for Germany. It then offered the crown of a united Germany to Frederick William IV. To their dismay, the Prussian king refused the crown because it was offered by the people and not by the German princes. He then sent an army to disband the Frankfurt Parliament, thereby ending this early attempt at unification.

Impact of the Revolutions of 1830 and 1848

Some political conditions changed as a result of the revolutions of 1830 and 1848. Greece and Belgium won their independence. Furthermore, in France and Prussia, all adult men were given the right to vote.

For the most part, however, the revolutions of 1830 and 1848 failed. Many revolutionary movements suffered from a lack of unity and clear policies. By 1848, deep divisions had emerged between middle class liberals who wanted moderate reforms and workers who demanded radical changes. In addition, conservatives were strong enough in most of Europe to defeat the rebels.

During the 1850s, conservative governments tried to suppress revolutionary ideas. Faced with political persecution, some liberals fled their homelands and found refuge in the United States. But as you will read in the next unit, liberalism, nationalism, and socialism would continue to shape events in Europe in the late 1800s.

SECTION REVIEW

1. Locate: Poland, Vienna, Lombardy, Venetia, Budapest.
2. Identify: Louis Kossuth, Guiseppe Mazzini.
3. Where did revolutions occur in 1830?
4. What was the result of the revolution of 1848 in Rome?
5. How did Frederick William IV react to the offer of the crown of a united Germany?

Chapter 22 Review

In Perspective

In 1814, the Congress of Vienna met to restore peace and stability to Europe. The victorious powers redrew political boundaries and restored monarchs to the thrones lost during the Napoleonic wars. However, the forces of liberalism and nationalism challenged the Metternich System.

In 1830 and again in 1848, a series of revolutions struck Europe. France became a republic but the Second French Republic survived for only three years. Then Louis Napoleon created the Second Empire. Elsewhere in Europe, the revolts were largely unsuccessful.

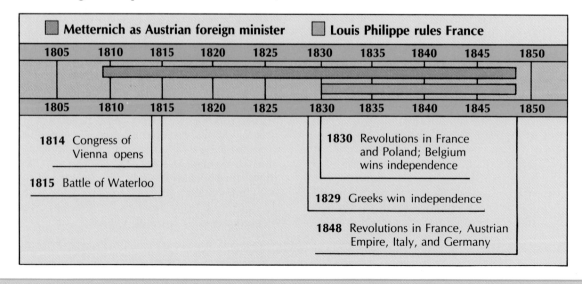

| ■ Metternich as Austrian foreign minister | ■ Louis Philippe rules France |

| 1805 | 1810 | 1815 | 1820 | 1825 | 1830 | 1835 | 1840 | 1845 | 1850 |

1814 Congress of Vienna opens

1815 Battle of Waterloo

1830 Revolutions in France and Poland; Belgium wins independence

1829 Greeks win independence

1848 Revolutions in France, Austrian Empire, Italy, and Germany

Recalling Facts

Decide if the following statements are true or false. If a statement is false, rewrite the statement to make it true.

1. During the 1800s, liberals wanted written constitutions.
2. The Congress of Vienna was dominated by conservatives.
3. Metternich encouraged nationalist revolts.
4. The Carlsbad Decrees gave German students the right to vote.
5. Greece won independence from Austria in 1829.
6. French liberals supported the July Ordinances.
7. Louis Philippe was a constitutional monarch.
8. Louis Kossuth led the nationalist movement in Hungary.

Chapter Checkup

1. Describe the main concerns of each of the following groups in the early 1800s: (a) liberals; (b) conservatives; (c) nationalists.
2. (a) What steps did the Congress of Vienna take to restore stability in Europe? (b) How did the great powers propose to keep the peace after the Congress?
3. (a) Describe the early challenges to the Metternich System. (b) How did Metternich respond to each challenge?
4. (a) Describe the revolution of 1848 in France. (b) What was the outcome of that revolution? (c) What effect did the revolution in France have on the rest of Europe?
5. (a) How were the revolutions of 1830 in Belgium and Poland similar? (b) How were they different?
6. (a) What factors contributed to the revolutions of 1848 in the Austrian Empire? (b) What actions did the Austrian government eventually take in response to the revolutionaries?

Critical Thinking

1. **Synthesizing** (a) Why did diplomats at the Congress of Vienna want to restore the old order in Europe? (b) Why did they find it so difficult to turn the clock back? (c) Under what circumstances might they have succeeded?

2. **Expressing an Opinion** (a) Why did Metternich want the Quadruple Alliance to intervene in Italy and Spain in 1820? (b) In your opinion, did the Quadruple Alliance have a legitimate reason to intervene? Explain.
3. **Analyzing** Louis Philippe's title was "king of the French by the will of the people." Earlier French kings had been called "king by the grace of God." (a) Do you think Louis Philippe's title was accurate? Why or why not? (b) How does the change in title reflect developments in France since 1789?

Relating Past to Present

1. In 1830 and 1848, revolts by liberals and nationalists took place throughout Europe. (a) What revolutionary movements have taken place within the last few years? (b) Compare the reactions of governments today with the response of those in the 1800s.

Developing Basic Skills

1. **Map Reading** Compare the maps on page 410 and 417. Then answer the following questions: (a) How did the borders of France change between 1812 and 1815? (b) How does the map on page 417 show that the great powers wanted to limit French power? (c) What nation or nations gained new territory in Europe in 1815?
2. **Researching** Choose one of the leaders at the Congress of Vienna. Research his personal background in order to answer the following questions: (a) What was the person's official title in 1814? (b) How did he gain power in his own country? (c) What were his ideas about government? (d) In your opinion, how did his background and position influence these ideas?
3. **Comparing** Make a chart with two rows and two columns. Title the rows Italy and Germany and the two columns Attempts at Unification and Result. Use what you read about the revolutions of 1848 in Italy and Germany to complete the chart. Then answer the following questions: (a) How were the attempts at unification similar in Italy and Germany? (b) How were they different? (c) Based on your reading in this chapter and earlier chapters, explain what factors made unification in each area difficult.

See page 806 for suggested readings.

Dawn of the Industrial Age

1825 Nicholas I gave the Russian secret police almost unlimited power. He is shown here leading a parade.

During the reign of Queen Victoria, 1837–1901, government in Britain became more democratic.

		1800	1820	1840	1860
POLITICS AND GOVERNMENT			**1815** Corn Laws raise the price of bread in Britain	**1831** Mazzini founds Young Italy to work for unification	
ECONOMICS AND TECHNOLOGY		**1800** Volta builds first electric battery		**1850s** Bessemer improves method of steel production	
SOCIETY AND CULTURE		**1800** Robert Owen sets up a "utopian" community in Scotland		**1834** Victor Hugo publishes *The Hunchback of Notre Dame*	

The earliest steam powered trains carried passengers and freight.

1851 Crowds flocked to the Crystal Palace in London to see the first international industrial exhibition.

By the late 1800s, reform had become a major theme in American political campaigns.

Peter Carl Fabergé designed exquisite decorative items of gold, enamel, and jewels. This box was made for Czar Nicholas II and his wife Alexandra.

1860	1880	1900	1920

1871 German Empire founded after defeat of France

1905 Revolution breaks out in Russia after Bloody Sunday

1876 Alexander Graham Bell invents telephone

1903 Wright brothers make first flight at Kitty Hawk

1871 Verdi writes the opera *Aida*

1880s British factory workers begin to play soccer

1918 Women over 30 win right to vote in Britain

This painting shows the luxurious life at the court of the Hapsburgs. Emperor Francis Joseph is the center of attention.

Thomas Hardy, a realist author, often set his novels in the countryside.

427

23 The Industrial Revolution

(1750–1914)

To one British author, Charles Dickens, whose novel *Hard Times* was published in 1854, a typical factory town was "a town of machinery and tall chimneys, out of which interminable serpents of smoke trailed themselves for ever and ever, and never got uncoiled. It had a black canal in it, and a river that ran purple with ill-smelling dye, and vast piles of buildings full of windows where there was a rattling and trembling all day long, and where the piston of the steam engine worked monotonously up and down, like the head of an elephant in a state of melancholy madness."

To Dickens, the people of the town shared the same "melancholy madness." They were "equally like one another. . . . all went in and out at the same hours, with the same sound upon the same pavement, to do the same work and to whom every day was the same as yesterday and tomorrow, and every year the counterpart of last and the next."

The conditions Dickens described were the result of the Industrial Revolution. The Industrial Revolution was neither sudden nor swift. It was a long, slow process in which production shifted from hand tools to machines and in which new sources of power such as steam and electricity replaced human and animal power.

The Industrial Revolution had two distinct stages. During the first stage, from about 1750 to 1850, Great Britain took the lead in shifting to new methods of production. During the second stage, from the mid-1800s to about 1914, the nations of Western Europe and the United States developed into modern industrial powers. The Industrial Revolution was to completely transform the patterns of life in these nations.

Detail from St. Lazare Station, *by Claude Monet.*

1 Beginnings of the Industrial Revolution in Britain

Read to Learn
- why the Agricultural Revolution occurred in England
- how inventions sparked the Industrial Revolution

By the mid-1700s, new methods of productions were being developed in Great Britain and France. Many of them were outgrowths of inventions made during the Enlightenment, a time when people began to apply scientific principles to practical problems. (See page 371.) During the late 1700s, the French Revolution disrupted the political and economic life of France. This was one reason that Britain emerged as the leader of the Industrial Revolution.

The Agricultural Revolution

One key to the beginning of the Industrial Revolution in Britain was a revolution in agriculture that greatly increased the amount and variety of food produced. During the 1700s, farmers began growing new crops, such as potatoes and corn, that had been introduced from the Americas. They also developed new ways of using the land that made it more productive.

Since the Middle Ages, farmers had planted the same crop in a given field year after year. Every third year, they left the field fallow to prevent the soil from wearing out. In the 1730s, Charles Townshend discovered that fields did not have to be left fallow if farmers would rotate the crops they planted in a field. He suggested that farmers grow wheat or barley in a field for one or two years and then plant clover or turnips in the field for one or two years.

Townshend's ideas helped revolutionize agriculture. Crops such as clover and turnips replenished the soil with the nutrients that wheat and barley used. Also, clover and turnips provided excellent feed for animals. Thus, farmers could raise cattle and sheep. As meat became available at lower cost, people could add more protein to their diet.

The invention of machines also increased food production. Jethro Tull found a method of planting seeds that was better than the random scattering, which made fields a tangle of crops and weeds. Tull developed a seed drill that planted the seeds in straight rows. The seed drill reduced the amount of seed used in planting. It also allowed farmers to weed around the straight rows of growing crops.

During the 1700s, iron plows replaced less-efficient, wooden plows. In the 1800s, mechanical reapers and threshers began to replace hand methods of harvesting crops. This further increased farm production.

Changing patterns of land ownership in Britain also contributed to the Agricultural Revolution. Since the Middle Ages, farmers had worked small strips of land in scattered fields. They grazed their animals and gathered timber on common, or public, lands. In the 1500s, wealthy landowners began claiming the right to these common lands. The *enclosure movement*, fencing off of public lands by individual landowners, spread rapidly in the 1700s.

The enclosure movement made agriculture more efficient because wealthy landowners farmed larger amounts of land and experimented with new crops. However, it forced many small farmers off land they had worked for years. Some became tenant farmers on land owned by others. Others drifted to the towns in search of work.

The Agricultural Revolution helped set the stage for the Industrial Revolution. Increased food production improved people's diet and health, which contributed to rapid population growth. As the population increased, the demand for manufactured goods, such as clothing, grew. Furthermore, more efficient methods of farming meant that fewer people were needed to work the land. Unemployed farmers, including those forced off the land by the enclosure movement, formed a large new labor force.

Changes in the Textile Industry

While improvements in agriculture released many workers from farming, inventions—especially in the British textile industry—created new demands for laborers. During the 1500s and 1600s, entrepreneurs developed the domestic system for manufacturing wool cloth. (See page 339.) Entrepreneurs supplied rural families with raw wool and cotton. In their own cottages, family members cleaned and spun the wool or cotton into thread. They then used hand looms to weave the thread into cloth.

The domestic system could not keep up with a steadily rising demand for cloth, especially cotton cloth. In the 1700s, practical-minded individuals developed ways to improve the manufacture of cloth. Each invention triggered others, revolutionizing the whole textile industry.

Mechanical inventions. In 1733, the clockmaker John Kay invented the flying shuttle, which replaced the hand-held

The Industrial Revolution began in the textile industry. By the early 1800s, large spinning mills like this one were operating all over England. Steam-powered looms required constant tending. Notice the worker at right who is cleaning debris from under the threads. The air inside the mills was kept hot and humid because threads broke less often under such conditions.

shuttle used in weaving. This invention greatly speeded up the weaving process. Weavers were soon using thread faster than spinners could produce it.

In 1764, James Hargreaves, a carpenter, developed a way to speed up spinning. He attached several spindles to a single spinning wheel. Using this spinning jenny, as it was called, a person could spin several threads at once. In 1769, Richard Arkwright devised a machine that could hold up to 100 spindles. Arkwright's invention was too heavy to be operated by hand, so he used water power to turn it. Thus, the machine was called the water frame. Ten years later, Samuel Crompton developed the spinning mule, which used features of Hargreaves' spinning jenny and Arkwright's water frame. Once again, the production of cotton thread was increased.

With more thread now available, the need arose for faster looms. In 1785, Edward Cartwright built a loom in which the weaving action was powered by water. Using this power loom, a worker could produce 200 times more cloth in a day than had previously been possible.

In 1793, the American Eli Whitney gave the British cotton industry a further boost. Before cotton fibers could be spun into cloth, workers had to remove sticky seeds, an extremely slow process. Whitney invented the cotton gin, a machine that tore the fibers from the seeds, thus speeding up the process of cleaning cotton fibers. The invention of the cotton gin helped the British cotton industry because it increased the production of raw cotton and made it cheaper. By the 1830s, Britain was importing 280 million pounds of raw cotton every year and had become the cotton manufacturing center of the world.

The factory system. The new spinning and weaving machines were expensive. They also had to be set up near rivers, where running water was available to power them.* Inventors such as Arkwright built spinning mills and started hiring hundreds of workers to run the new machines.

---

* Water flowing down a stream or river turned a water wheel that produced power to run the machines.

Coal fueled the early Industrial Revolution. In this 1814 print, a coal miner stands in front of a steam engine that is pulling a load of coal. The print is the first English picture of a steam-powered vehicle. Despite the use of steam engines, work in the coal mines remained largely dependent on the backbreaking labor of men, women, and children.

The early textile mills were examples of the factory system, which gradually replaced the domestic system of production. The *factory system* brought workers and machines together in one place to manufacture goods. Everyone had to work a set number of hours each day, and workers were paid daily or weekly wages.

Development of the Steam Engine

Many early inventions in the textile industry were powered by running water, but soon steam became the major source of energy. The idea of a steam-powered engine had existed for a long time. In 1698, Thomas Savery constructed a steam-driven pump to remove water from flooded coal mines. Unfortunately, Savery's pump often exploded because of the intense pressure of the steam.

In the early 1700s, Thomas Newcomen developed a safer steam-powered pump. But Newcomen's engine broke down frequently and required a lot of coal to fuel it. Finally, in the 1760s, James Watt, who had repaired several Newcomen engines, developed ways of improving the engine. Watt's steam engine got four times more power than Newcomen's engine from the same amount of coal.

The British found many uses for steam power. Steam engines were used in the growing textile industry. They also became important in coal mining.

Development of the Iron and Coal Industries

Producing and operating the new machines, including the steam engine, required large quantities of iron and coal. Fortunately, Britain had extensive deposits of both. During the Industrial Revolution, the iron and coal industries benefited from improved production techniques.

Iron was produced by a smelting process. Iron ore, which contains only small amounts of iron, was heated to high temperatures to burn off impurities. Then the molten iron was poured off. Charcoal, a fuel made by partially burning hard woods, was used to heat the ore. But hard woods were

431

becoming scarce in Britain. Ironworkers experimented with using coal instead of charcoal. However, coal had many gases that mixed with the molten iron, making the iron hard to work. In the early 1700s, Abraham Darby helped solve this problem. He developed a way to use coke, or coal with the gases burned off, in place of charcoal.

Iron making was further improved in the 1780s, when Henry Cort developed a puddling process in which molten iron was stirred with a long rod to allow impurities to burn off. Iron produced in this manner was stronger than iron produced in other ways and less likely to crack under pressure. Cort also developed a technique to run molten iron through rollers to produce sheets of iron.

Improved production methods enabled Britain to quadruple iron production between 1788 and 1806. In addition, the demand for coal, both for making iron and for powering steam engines, triggered a boom in coal mining.

In the 1850s, the iron industry received another boost when Henry Bessemer developed a procedure that made the production of steel, an alloy of iron and other materials, cheaper and easier. In the *Bessemer process*, blasts of cold air were blown through heated iron to remove impurities. The result was stronger, more workable steel. As steel became readily available, it triggered the growth of other industries.

Advances in Transportation and Communication

Industry requires a good transportation system to bring raw materials to factories and distribute finished goods. In the 1700s, the need for rapid, inexpensive transportation led to a boom in canal building in Britain. In 1759, the Duke of Bridgewater built a canal to connect his coal mines and his factories. Soon, canals were being built all over the country.

The 1700s were also a time of road building in Britain. The Scottish engineer John McAdam invented a road surface made of crushed stone. This surface made roads usable in all weather. By the 1800s, road travel in England had become almost as fast as it had been in Roman times.

The need for good transportation led to the development of the railroad industry. For years, mine carts had been pulled along iron rails by workers or donkeys. In 1829, George Stephenson, a mining engineer, developed the Rocket, the first steam-powered locomotive. The Rocket could barrel along iron rails at 36 miles (58 kilometers) per hour, an astounding speed at the time.

Between 1840 and 1850, the British built over 5,000 miles (8,000 kilometers) of railway tracks. As steel rails replaced iron rails, trains reached speeds of 60 miles (96 kilometers) an hour. Railroads brought raw materials, factories, and markets closer together than ever before. They also increased the demand for coal and steel.

In the 1800s, Britain led the way in railroad building and shipbuilding. However, it was an American engineer, Robert Fulton, who developed a way to use steam power for ships. In 1807, Fulton successfully tested the *Clermont*, a paddle-wheeled steamship, on the Hudson River. Other inventors improved the steamship. By 1850, steamships regularly crossed the oceans.

The railroad and the steamship improved communications within nations and across the world. Britain introduced an inexpensive postal system, which further improved communication. In 1837, Samuel F.B. Morse, an American, devised the telegraph, which sent messages by electrical impulses. Messages that once would have taken days to arrive now took minutes or seconds. In 1851, the first underwater telegraph cable was installed under the English Channel. It made rapid communication between Britain and the continent possible.

Why Britain Led the Industrial Revolution

Britain enjoyed many advantages that helped it take an early lead in the Industrial Revolution. As you have read, with the Agri-

The Industrial Revolution: Reading Thematic Maps

Maps provide much useful information about how geography can influence historical events and developments. Many of the maps you have studied in this text have shown topographical features, such as rivers and mountains, as well as political boundaries. Some have also given information about trade routes.

However, there are other kinds of maps that give valuable information about population, natural resources, rainfall, and crop production. Maps that provide this kind of specialized information are called thematic maps. Practice reading thematic maps by studying the map at right. Then follow these steps.

1. **Decide what is shown on the map.** On a thematic map, the legend tells you what the symbols mean. Answer the following questions about the map: (a) What is the topic of the map? (b) What do the areas shaded orange represent? (c) What do the purple squares represent? (d) What other information is given on the map?

2. **Read the information on the map.** Answer the following questions about the map: (a) Name two cities on the map with populations of 300,000 or over. (b) Name two cities with populations of 100,000 to 300,000. (c) Which cities with populations over 300,000 were located near iron and coal resources? (d) Which large cities were probably ports?

3. **Draw conclusions about a historical event or development.** (a) What relationship does the map show between areas with coal and iron resources and those with large cities? (b) What areas of Britain were

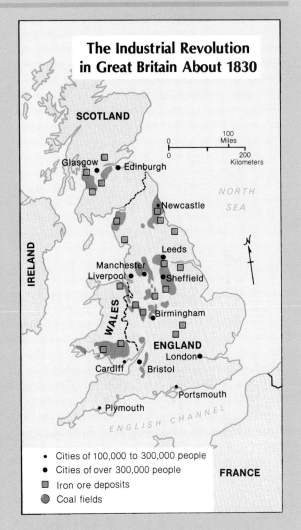

The Industrial Revolution in Great Britain About 1830

- • Cities of 100,000 to 300,000 people
- • Cities of over 300,000 people
- ▢ Iron ore deposits
- ⬤ Coal fields

probably the most industrialized? Explain. (c) What areas were probably the least industrialized? Explain.

cultural Revolution came increased food production, freeing many laborers to work in industry. Moreover, Britain had plentiful iron and coal resources, and it developed an excellent transportation system to speed the flow of goods.

Britain was also the leading commercial power in Europe. Since the 1500s and 1600s, British merchants had made huge profits from the international trade in tobacco, sugar, tea, and slaves. As a result, British entrepreneurs had the financial resources to invest in industries such as textiles, mines, railroads, and shipbuilding. Britain also had a large colonial empire that supplied raw materials to its factories. In addition, people in the colonies bought finished goods produced by British indusry.

The British government adopted policies that encouraged industrial growth. It lifted restrictions on trade. It encouraged road- and canal-building schemes and maintained a strong navy to protect British merchant ships all over the world.

The intellectual and social climate in Britain also encouraged industrialization. Although a clear class structure existed in British society, individuals could improve their social standing. The British accepted the idea that poor people did not have to stay poor forever but through talent and hard work could improve themselves.

SECTION REVIEW

1. Identify: Charles Townshend, John Kay, James Hargreaves, Richard Arkwright, Edward Cartwright, James Watt, Abraham Darby, George Stephenson, Samuel Morse.
2. Define: enclosure movement, factory system, Bessemer process.
3. List two factors that led to the Agricultural Revolution in Britain.
4. How did the factory system differ from the domestic system?
5. Describe how each of the following improvements was important to the iron industry: (a) puddling process; (b) Bessemer process.

2 The Rise of Modern Industry

Read to Learn
- how industrialization spread
- what scientific advances spurred industrialization

After the 1850s, the pace of industrialization quickened, and the Industrial Revolution entered its second stage. Between 1850 and 1914, industry grew rapidly in the nations of Western Europe, including Belgium, France, and Germany. At the same time, the United States began to industrialize and soon rivaled Britain in many fields. Japan also joined the ranks of industrialized nations, as you will read in Chapter 28.

The Spread of Industrialization

During the second half of the 1800s, other nations began to challenge British leadership in the Industrial Revolution. Belgium was one of the first nations on the continent to industrialize. Like Britain, Belgium had large deposits of coal and iron. Belgium also had a long manufacturing tradition, especially in textiles. Thus, it had a skilled labor force willing to work in industry. Moreover, Belgian entrepreneurs had the capital needed to invest in factories and machinery.

France, too, built a strong textile industry with a number of inventions. In the early 1800s, Joseph Marie Jacquard developed the first power loom that could be used to weave complex patterns. The Jacquard loom had a punched card system that controlled the intricate pattern.* Textiles produced on Jacquard looms commanded high prices among the fashion-conscious upper classes in Europe.

The French government encouraged the textile industry at home by imposing high tariffs on cloth imported from other nations. Because imported cloth was thus more expensive, people bought French textiles. The French government also supported projects to improve transportation, especially the building of railroads.

Across the Atlantic, the United States had considerable natural resources. Aided by large investments of capital from Europe, Americans began to exploit these resources. Railroad building fostered rapid economic growth in the United States. In 1869, the first railroad spanned the continent. In the 1870s,

---

* The punched cards used in early computers were based on Jacquard's idea.

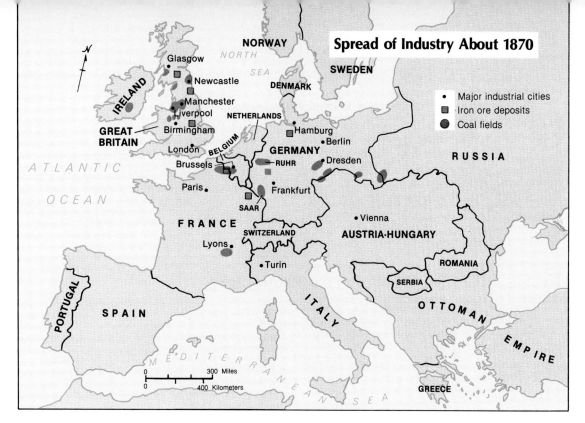

Map Skill *During the second half of the 1800s, the Industrial Revolution spread beyond Britain to other European countries. Iron and coal were essential to the growth of industry on the continent, as they had been in Britain. Some of the major iron deposits and coal fields are shown on this map. Which industrial cities in Germany, Belgium, and France were located near these resources?*

American iron and steel production was well on the way to outstripping that of Britain. In the next decade, the United States surpassed Britain as the leading industrial nation.

In the 1850s and 1860s, German industry suffered from a lack of political unity among the German states. After Germany achieved national unity, it rivaled the United States and Britain as a leading industrial power, as you will read in Chapter 26.

The nations of southern and eastern Europe remained largely agricultural during the 1800s. In Spain, Italy, Austria, and Russia, governments did little to encourage industrial growth.

Advances in Science and Technology

During the early Industrial Revolution, most inventors were people looking for ways to repair tools or improve machinery. After 1850, however, people turned to science not only to solve problems of manufacturing but also to discover new products to manufacture. Scientific research soon resulted in many inventions as well as extraordinary advances in technology. Knowledge of new technology spread quickly from one nation to another.

The results of scientific research brought sweeping changes to various industries. For example, the English chemist William Perkins discovered a brilliant dye that could be made cheaply from coal. German chemists also discovered ways to make dyes cheaply. The textile industry quickly adopted the new dyes to replace more costly natural dyes such as indigo. Other discoveries led to the development and widespread use of chemical fertilizers, which radically increased food production.

The work of physicists also stimulated new technology. In 1800, Alessandro Volta, an Italian physicist, used his knowledge of electricity to build one of the first electric batteries. The work of Michael Faraday, an English scientist, led to the construction of

435

electric generators, which eventually replaced steam engines in many factories.

Discoveries in the field of electricity also improved communications. In 1866, the first underwater telegraph cable across the Atlantic Ocean was successfully installed. Ten years later, Alexander Graham Bell invented the telephone. By the end of the century, Italian physicist Guglielmo Marconi had developed a way to send electric signals without wire or cable. His invention was called the wireless in England and the radio in America.

During this period, Thomas Alva Edison produced a stunning array of inventions in his New Jersey workshop. Among Edison's inventions were the phonograph and the incandescent light bulb. He also designed an electric generating plant that provided power to light the streets of New York City.

Then and Now ■ The Invention of Photography

On a summer afternoon in 1839, people crowded into an auditorium in Paris. They had gathered to learn about a new method of producing pictures of great clarity and detail. The method had recently been perfected by the painter Louis Daguerre (duh GEHR), shown here. These pictures, soon called daguerreotypes, were early photographs.

The audience listened intently while Daguerre's process was described. Daguerre had placed a polished silver plate coated with light-sensitive silver iodide in the camera and exposed it to light for several minutes. When the plate was removed from the camera, it appeared to be blank. But when it was treated with mercury fumes, an image appeared on the surface. The plate was then washed to remove the chemicals and coated with everyday table salt to keep the image from fading.

Many people in the audience were excited about the new invention. "[I] ran straight off to buy iodine," reported one listener. "I hated to see the sun go down, for it forced me to put off my experiments until the next day. A few days later, cameras were focused on buildings everywhere. Everyone wanted to take the view from his window, and anyone who got at the first attempt a silhouette of rooftops against the sky was in luck ... the technique was so novel and seemed so marvelous that even the poorest result gave indescribable joy."

News of Daguerre's technique traveled swiftly. But there was one drawback to this early form of photography. It was hard to produce more than one print of a daguerreotype. A British inventor, William Fox Talbot, discovered a way to produce paper negatives that allowed photographers to make as many prints as they wanted. Talbot's method, which was also announced in 1839, became the basis for modern photography.

In the following decades, inventors discovered how to make clearer prints. They also reduced the amount of time needed for exposure and experimented with ways to produce color prints.

The use of photography spread rapidly during the last half of the nineteenth century. During the American Civil War, Mathew Brady photographed battle scenes and developed prints in a horse-drawn darkroom. Newspapers and magazines began publishing photographs of events, recording them for future generations.

436

Thomas Edison called his research laboratory in Menlo Park, New Jersey, the "invention factory." There, he invented the incandescent light, storage battery, sound-synchronized motion pictures, mimeograph machine, and ore separator. This photograph of Edison was taken after he had just worked 72 hours straight improving the wax cylinder phonograph on the table.

A Revolution in Transportation

Dramatic advances were made in transportation in the late 1800s. Perhaps the most significant advance was the development of the internal combustion engine. The internal combustion engine had a number of advantages over the steam engine. For example, it could be started and stopped more easily.

In 1886, the German scientist Gottlieb Daimler devised an internal combustion engine that was fueled by gasoline and could power a small vehicle. Daimler used his engine to build one of the first automobiles. A few years later, another German engineer, Rudolf Diesel, developed an internal combustion engine that could power larger vehicles such as trucks, ships, and locomotives. This diesel engine, as it became known, used petroleum oil for fuel.

The development of the internal combustion engine would eventually revolutionize the transportation industry. By the 1920s, automobiles were a familiar sight in the United States and Europe. The growth of this industry triggered booms in industries necessary to the production of automobiles, including petroleum, steel, and rubber.

New Methods of Production

New machines and technology improved worker productivity, the amount of goods a worker could turn out in a specific time. Early in the Industrial Revolution, Eli Whitney introduced the idea of *interchangeable parts*, identical component parts that can be used in place of one another in manufacturing.

Whitney owned a factory in which guns were made. Before Whitney, parts for guns were handmade, and each similar part was slightly different. Whitney manufactured large numbers of identical parts. When guns were made of these parts, a broken part could be easily replaced. The use of interchangeable parts spread to other industries, where it improved efficiency.

Another improvement in production was the assembly line, introduced by Henry Ford in 1914. On an *assembly line*, the complex job of assembling many parts into a finished product was broken down into a series of small tasks. Each worker performed only one or two tasks. Ford, who owned an automobile factory in Highland Park, Michigan, used an assembly line to speed up production. Workers stood along a conveyor belt. As the auto body moved past, they each added their part to it.

The efficiency of the assembly line allowed manufacturers to reduce costs and lower prices. As more people were able to afford goods such as automobiles, the demand for these products rose. To meet the demand, manufacturers introduced *mass production*, turning out large quantities of identical goods.

Financing Industrial Growth

As machinery grew more complex and more expensive, new ways of financing industry developed. During the 1800s, the corporation slowly became the dominant form of business organization in industry. A *corporation* is a business owned by many investors, each of whom has bought a share in the corporation. Investors have limited liability for the debts of the corporation. They risk only the amount of their investment.

After 1870, giant corporations often bought up many small companies. Often, a corporation would establish a *monopoly,* or total control over the market for a particular product. In the United States, the Standard Oil Company, organized by John D. Rockefeller, acquired a virtual monopoly in the oil industry.

To gain this position, Standard Oil bought into the many industries connected with oil production. It owned railroads, barrel companies, pipelines, and refineries. This form of business, in which a corporation controls the industries that contribute to its final product, is known as *vertical integration.* In both Europe and the United States, large corporations used vertical integration as a means of eliminating competition.

Banks played a prominent role in financing industry. People deposited money in banks. Banks, in turn, invested this money in businesses, which grew as a result. The House of Rothschild in Paris was one of the world's leading investment banks. During the 1840s, it helped finance the building of the French railway system.

By the late 1800s, industrial growth had resulted in a complex international econ-

Through Their Eyes ■ The Flight at Kitty Hawk

For as long as people have watched the birds, they have dreamed of finding a way to fly. Orville and Wilbur Wright, two bicycle repairmen from Dayton, Ohio, became interested in flying experiments. They built and flew a glider in 1900, developing a method for guiding its flight. Then they began work on the next step: attaching a motor to the craft.

Because existing gasoline engines were too heavy for flight, they built one of their own. They attached the engine to a pair of 8-foot wooden propellers and mounted it on their craft, which they christened Flyer. *The Wright brothers took the* Flyer *to Kitty Hawk, North Carolina, for a test flight. Ten years later, Orville Wright recalled the event:*

Orville Wright

During the night of December 16, 1903, a strong cold wind blew from the north. When we arose on the morning of the 17th, the puddles of water which had been standing about camp since the recent rains were covered with ice. ... We thought that by facing the flyer into a strong wind, there ought to be no trouble in launching it from the level ground about camp. We realized the difficulties of flying in so high a wind, but estimated that the added dangers in flight would be partly compensated for by the slower speed in landing. ...

After running the motor a few minutes to heat it up, I released the wire that held the machine to the track, and the machine started forward into the wind. Wilbur ran at the side of the machine, holding the wing to balance it on the track. ... Wilbur was able to stay with it till it lifted from the track after a 40-foot run. ...

The course of the flight up and down was exceedingly erratic, partly due to the irregularity of the air and partly to lack of experience in handling this machine. ... A sudden dart when a little over 100 feet from the end of the track, or a little over 120 feet from the point at which it rose into the air, ended the flight. ... This flight lasted only 12 seconds, but it was nevertheless the first in the history of the world in which a machine carrying a man had raised itself by its own power into the air in full flight, had sailed forward without reduction of speed, and had finally landed at a point as high as that from which it started.

1. What effect did weather have on the flight of the *Flyer?*
2. How might the Wright brothers' experience as bicycle repairmen have contributed to their success?

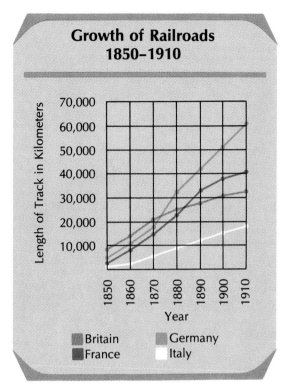

Growth of Railroads 1850–1910

Length of Track in Kilometers

70,000
60,000
50,000
40,000
30,000
20,000
10,000

Year: 1850 1860 1870 1880 1890 1900 1910

■ Britain ■ Germany
■ France   ▢ Italy

Source: B.R. Mitchell, *European Historical Statistics.*

Graph Skill *The building of railroads stimulated industrial growth in many countries. Because large amounts of iron and coal were needed to build railroads, the iron and coal industries grew. Where were railroads growing most rapidly between 1850 and 1910?*

omy. Trade expanded to meet the demands for raw materials and markets. Goods, services, and money flowed across the world. Regions distant from each other became dependent on one another as suppliers or consumers of goods. Investors in one country often organized companies in another. Many corporations and banks in Europe and the United States sought new opportunities in overseas business ventures such as building railroads in Asia and Africa. As a result, governments became increasingly involved in protecting the international markets and investments of their citizens.

SECTION REVIEW

1. Identify: Alessandro Volta, Michael Faraday, Alexander Graham Bell, Guglielmo Marconi, Thomas Edison, Gottlieb Daimler.
2. Define: interchangeable parts, assembly line, mass production, corporation, monopoly, vertical integration.
3. (a) · Which European nations industrialized rapidly after 1850? (b) Which European nations remained largely agricultural?
4. Give one example of how scientific research affected industry.
5. Describe one result of the development of the assembly line.

3 Effects of Industrialization

Read to Learn ■ how industrialization changed life in cities
■ how industrialization affected society

Before 1800, most people in Europe and North America farmed the land. They lived and worked in the country or in small towns, owned their tools, and were generally self-employed. The Industrial Revolution radically changed these patterns of life. By 1900, between one third and one half of the people in the industrialized countries of Western Europe and the United States lived in cities. Most were employed as wage earners in industry rather than in agriculture. Fewer were self-employed workers and artisans.

The Population Explosion

The beginning of the Industrial Revolution was marked by a population explosion that was to have far-reaching effects. Between 1750 and 1914, the population of Europe more than tripled. It had grown from 140 million people to 463 million.

The Agricultural Revolution improved the diets of many people, so the people were healthier. The Industrial Revolution also contributed to the population growth. Medi-

439

Populations of Six European Nations, 1750–1910

(in thousands)

	1750	1800	1850	1880	1910
Belgium	2,150	2,960	4,426	5,520	7,422
Britain	10,012	14,997	27,201	34,623	44,915
France	24,600	27,800	35,630	37,450	39,528
Germany	12,770	17,200	35,310	45,093	64,568
Italy	13,150	16,900	*	28,211	34,377
Russia	*	31,000	60,000	85,200	142,500

*Not available

Source: Witt Bowden, *et al. An Economic History of Europe Since 1750.*

Chart Skill *The population of European nations grew dramatically between 1750 and 1910, as you can see from this chart. Between which years did the population of Germany increase the most?*

cal discoveries and public sanitation reduced the numbers of deaths caused by disease. Furthermore, in the 1800s, European nations fought no major wars. Industry provided jobs as well as goods for the growing population.

Problems of Growing Cities

Until the 1800s, cities, which were often located along land or water trade routes, served mainly as marketplaces. But the Industrial Revolution changed the nature of cities. Cities seemed to spring up almost overnight as people flocked to mill and factory sites. When people poured into these fast-growing cities in search of jobs, living conditions rapidly grew worse.

The city of Manchester, England, provides an example of what often happened. In 1750, Manchester was a fairly quiet market town with 16,000 residents, but there were iron and coal deposits nearby. Soon textile manufacturers built factories there. By 1855, Manchester was the center of the British cotton industry, and its population had grown to 455,000.

The rapid growth of Manchester brought severe problems. Thousands of factory workers crowded into poorly built houses. A family of six or ten might live in a single dark, airless room. The city had an inadequate water system and almost no sanitation system. Slums became the breeding grounds for disease. Sewage was simply flung into open trenches along the streets. In many cities, pigs roaming the streets were the only "garbage collectors." Manchester was not even chartered as a city so it could not tax citizens to raise money for improving living conditions. Nor could it pass laws to ensure that housing met minimum standards of safety or sanitation.

Living conditions in rural areas had often been difficult, but in the country, people usually could count on help from their neighbors. During the early Industrial Revolution, one writer described the plight of city people who sat "in their little cells; divided by partitions of brick and board, they sit strangers. . . . They do not work together, but scramble against each other."

Working in a Factory

Most of the new city residents found themselves working in factories, where working conditions were as miserable as living conditions outside the factory. The supply of unskilled workers was large, so wages were very low. Often a whole family worked to survive. Women and children—some of whom started to work at age five—were in great demand because they worked for even lower wages than men.

Work days lasted from 12 to 16 hours, or from sunrise to sunset. Men, women, and children worked six days a week. There were no paid holidays, vacations, or sick leaves. Factories were often unhealthy, dangerous places to work. Fumes from machines combined with poor ventilation made the air foul. The loud, monotonous noise of machines assaulted the ear. Lighting was poor, and machines were not equipped with safety devices, so accidents occurred frequently. A worker injured on the job received no compensation. If an injured worker could no longer do the job, he or she was thrown out of work.

A New Social Structure

The Industrial Revolution transformed the social structure of Europe. Before industrialization, the wealthy, landowning aristocracy occupied the highest social position. Below the aristocracy was a relatively small middle class, which included merchants, lawyers, and the clergy. Next came skilled workers such as shoemakers, potters, and silversmiths. Finally, the vast majority of the people were small farmers or farm workers.

During the 1800s, the middle class expanded and challenged the landowning aristocracy in wealth and power. The wealthiest and most powerful members of the new middle class were factory and mine owners, bankers, financiers, and merchants. The middle class also included managers and the

The French artist Gustave Doré made this engraving, called Over London By Rail, in 1872. The artist conveys the bleak, overpowering sameness of a London working class neighborhood. In the smoke-filled industrial cities of Europe, most working class families lived in just one room. Crowded conditions, open sewers, polluted rivers, and filthy streets bred crime and disease.

441

The Industrial Revolution forced many women to seek jobs outside the home. Employers often exploited women workers by paying them lower wages than men. In this printing shop, The Victoria Press in London, women work as compositors, setting type for books and newspapers.

owners of small businesses. They were joined by professional people such as doctors and lawyers. Farther down the scale, artisans and business clerks also entered the ranks of the middle class.

Wealthy members of the middle class tried to adopt the customs of aristocrats. They bought magnificent country estates, which they decorated luxuriously. They took up aristocratic sports such as horseracing and sailing. Other members of the middle class lived comfortably but on a less lavish scale. Most middle class families were very conscious of their social position. They were constantly striving to live what they considered to be polite, respectable lives.

The Industrial Revolution produced a new social class of industrial workers. Largely unskilled, they occupied the lowest rank in society. Industrial workers were very much aware that they belonged to a separate social class. They saw themselves as people with little political or economic power. By mid-century, workers began banding together to change their working and living conditions, as you will read.

Changing Roles for Women

Traditionally, most women had either helped farm the land or worked in the home earning money through the domestic system.

Some women also worked as servants in the homes of the wealthy. The Agricultural Revolution and new farm machinery reduced the need for both men and women on the farms. As the Industrial Revolution got underway, the factory system replaced the domestic system.

To help support their families in the industrial economy, many women went to work in the factories or the mines. Often, the entire family worked in the same place. In mines, for example, men often dug the coal, women dragged coal trucks through low tunnels, and children sorted coal.

Working in a factory added greatly to a woman's responsibilities. She worked outside her home for 12 to 16 hours a day. Yet, she still had to cook, clean, and sew for her family. A woman's role was made even more difficult by the squalid living conditions in the factory towns and cities.

By the late 1800s, however, other developments affected the role of women in industrialized nations. As you will read in the next section, the standard of living and wages of workers began to improve. Thus, it became possible for many working class families to live on the income of only one person. As a result, a new pattern of family life emerged. Husbands tended to be the sole wage earners, and women remained at home.

At the same time, the demand for domestic servants in the cities was growing. Middle class families could afford to hire domestic servants to work as cooks, maids, and nurses for children. Many women, especially single women, left their homes to take these jobs. In Britain in the late 1800s, about one third of all women working outside the home were employed as domestic servants.

Few middle class women worked outside their homes because the social attitudes of the time encouraged women to marry and stay at home to raise their children. During the 1800s, a comfortable home became the ideal of many families as popular songs about "Home, sweet home" and mottoes such as "East, west, home's best" demonstrate.

SECTION REVIEW

1. Give two reasons why the population of Europe increased in the 1800s.
2. What problems did factory workers face in industrial cities such as Manchester?
3. Why were factories often dangerous places in which to work?
4. How did the makeup of the middle class change during the Industrial Revolution?
5. Why did women take jobs in factories early in the Industrial Revolution?

4 Responses to the Industrial Revolution

Read to Learn
- what conditions caused the rise of labor unions
- how the lives of industrial workers improved

During the early Industrial Revolution, many members of the middle class were indifferent to the suffering of workers. Factory owners, for example, had little sympathy for workers. They had invested their entire capital in risky undertakings, and they wanted to ensure survival of their businesses. As industrialization continued, however, some people began to call for reforms.

Demands for Change in Britain

Because the Industrial Revolution began in Britain, workers there were the first to feel its effects. Suffering from low wages, dangerous working conditions, and frequent unemployment, they protested against conditions, sometimes violently.

Between 1811 and 1816, workers in many parts of Britain smashed the machines that they considered the cause of their suffering. In 1819, a demonstration in Manchester was attended by about 80,000 workers who demanded economic and political reforms. Nervous soldiers fired on the orderly crowd, killing 11 men and women and wounding about 400. Initially, the British Parliament had little sympathy for the workers, and it applauded the actions of the soldiers. However, worker discontent continued to erupt in violence both in Britain and on the continent.*

Parliament investigates. Eventually, in 1831, Parliament began a series of investigations of factory and mine conditions. Middle class liberals opposed reforms because they believed the government should not interfere in business. However, conservatives sometimes attacked the conditions in factories and mines. As aristocratic landowners, they despised the way industrialization was changing life. But the findings of investigators shocked even opponents of reform.

One cotton mill worker told investigators that the workday of his entire family lasted "from six in the morning till half-past eight at night." His children were worn out at the end of the long day. He and his wife "cried often when we have given them the little food we had to give them; we had to shake them, [or] they would have fallen asleep with the food in their mouths many a time."

---

* As you read in Chapter 22, workers in Paris helped overthrow the French monarchy in the revolutions of 1830 and 1848.

Child labor was one of the worst abuses of the early Industrial Revolution. Many parents needed what little money their children could earn. As a result, they put their sons and daughters to work as soon as they could walk. Here, a young girl changes empty bobbins in a textile mill.

A 17-year-old girl described her work in a coal mine. She spent her days on her hands and knees hauling carts loaded with coal through narrow mine shafts. She dragged the carts "a mile or more underground and back. I never went to day-school," reported the girl. "I go to Sunday-school, but I cannot read or write; I go to the pit at five o'clock in the morning and come out at five in the evening."

While Parliament pursued its official investigations, the cause of reform received a boost from a few reform-minded journalists and writers. They described in vivid detail the deplorable conditions they saw in the factories and mines. Journalists awakened thousands of middle class readers to the appalling poverty among workers. Novelists also helped create a climate for reform. Charles Dickens, for example, attacked the evils of child labor in his novels *Oliver Twist* and *David Copperfield*.

Reforms begin. Prodded by its own findings and the growing public concern, Parliament took action. It passed the Factory Act of 1833, which limited the working day for children. Between the ages of 9 and 13, boys and girls could work no more than 8 hours a day. For children aged 14 to 18, the limit was 12 hours a day.

In 1842, Parliament passed the Mines Act. This law barred employers from hiring women to work in mines and made 13 the minimum age for hiring boys. A few years later, the Ten Hours Act limited the workday for women and children under 18 years of age to 10 hours. Finally in 1874, the 10-hour day was extended to all workers.

Rise of Labor Unions

Early in the Industrial Revolution, factory workers began forming associations to gain better wages, hours, and working conditions. These early worker associations later developed into labor unions.

Labor unions developed first in Britain, and from the start they met with strong opposition. The government saw labor unions as dangerous organizations. Moreover, employers argued that the shorter hours and higher wages demanded by unions would add to the cost of goods, reduce profits, and hurt business. Parliament passed the Combination Acts in 1799 and 1800 to outlaw labor unions. On the continent, similar laws were passed. A French banker summed up the attitude of many employers and government officials to worker efforts to win better treatment: "The workers must realize that their only salvation lies in patient resignation to their lot."

Yet workers refused to accept "their lot." In Britain, they struggled to have the Combination Laws repealed. They won this battle in the 1820s, although workers were still barred from striking or picketing. In the following decades, skilled workers in Britain formed trade unions based on a craft or trade such as cabinetmaking and hatmaking. Because the workers had skills that were valuable to employers, the trade unions were able to bargain with employers.

Slowly, local trade unions formed larger associations to support both political and economic goals. They struggled for the right to vote, the 10-hour workday, and the right to strike. By 1868, over 100,000 workers belonged to trade unions. In the 1870s, British unions won the right to strike and picket peacefully.

The success of the trade unions encouraged unskilled workers to form their own unions in the 1880s. They organized on the basis of their industries, forming unions of coal miners and dock workers. By 1889, London dock workers were organized well enough to mount a strike in support of their demands for higher wages. The London dock strike effectively shut down one of the world's busiest ports. From this point on, the strike was a common tool of labor unions. By the end of the century, union membership was growing rapidly in Britain, the rest of Western Europe, and the United States.

Gains for Workers

Between 1870 and 1914, the lot of industrial workers improved dramatically. Wages rose significantly. In Britain and France, wages nearly doubled in the last half of the 1800s, and workers could buy twice as much as they had before. In addition, thanks to more efficient methods of production, goods such as clothing were often cheaper than before.

Gradually, employers came to believe that workers would be more productive in a safe, healthy environment. They installed proper ventilation in factories, equipped machines with safety devices, and switched to new electric lighting. When some employers refused to make improvements, governments passed laws to ensure better conditions. Britain, Germany, and France led the way in establishing factory codes that set up minimum standards for safety and sanitary conditions.

Governments took other steps to satisfy the demands of workers. In the new industrial society, workers frequently faced financial disaster because of unemployment, accident, sickness, or old age. To protect workers from such disasters, governments in many industrial nations passed laws setting up insurance funds. These funds would help workers who could not earn a living because of sickness or accident. Some governments also established old age pension funds as well as systems of unemployment insurance for workers who lost their jobs as a result of business failure or economic slowdown.

By 1914, workers enjoyed a better standard of living than workers had 100 years earlier. They could also look forward to a better future for their children. By then, free public schools had been set up in all the industrial nations. Moreover, living conditions in cities had improved.

Improving City Life

As you have read, living conditions in early industrial cities were deplorable. As cities continued to grow, the need for reform became urgent. In Britain and France, city governments began programs to provide adequate water and sewage systems. City governments also passed building codes that set up minimum standards for housing.

Between 1850 and 1870, the city of Paris was almost completely rebuilt. Narrow, crooked streets were replaced by straight, wide boulevards. New and better houses were constructed, and large parks were opened for people to spend their leisure time. In London, a reform-minded member of Parliament, Sir Robert Peel, helped establish the first police force in that city. Londoners referred to members of the new police force as Bobbies or Peelers.

Cities became safer with the installation of gas, and later electric, lights that lit the

Fire posed a hazard to city dwellers. Some cities had voluntary bucket brigades. But steam-powered water pumps introduced in the late 1800s proved to be far more effective. Fire hydrants were set up along city streets. Professional firefighters gradually replaced volunteers. This 1866 print shows a horse-drawn wagon with a steam pump rushing to a New York fire.

streets at night. Use of electric power also led to improvements in transportation. In the 1890s, many European cities adopted an American invention, the electric streetcar. Electric streetcars were much cheaper and cleaner than horse-drawn streetcars. The new streetcars encouraged growth, enabling people to live on the outskirts of the city and travel to work. Cities such as London, New York, and Berlin also built subway systems.

By the 1900s, cities had become increasingly attractive places to live. Pockets of poverty and slums still existed, but in general even the poor had money to spend on the products of the new industrial society.

SECTION REVIEW

1. Identify: Factory Act of 1833, Mines Act.
2. (a) What was the attitude of the British government toward labor unions in the early 1800s? (b) How did this attitude change by the 1800s?
3. (a) What type of labor union developed first? (b) Why were these unions able to bargain successfully?
4. List three ways in which the lives of workers had improved by the late 1800s.
5. How did city governments improve living conditions?

Chapter 23 Review

In Perspective

The Industrial Revolution began in Great Britain in the mid-1700s. Inventions revolutionized the textile industry by introducing machines to do work once done by hand. Machines and workers were soon brought together in the factory system. As the Industrial Revolution unfolded, new sources of power were found.

Between 1850 and 1914, the nations of Western Europe and the United States industrialized. Scientific research led to the development of many new technologies. The factory system became more efficient as new methods of production were introduced. Powerful corporations and banks raised the money needed to finance new industries.

Industrialization contributed to population growth, the rise of large cities, and the development of a new social structure. Early in the Industrial Revolution, workers lived under terrible conditions, working long hours for low pay. However, the demands for change from reformers and labor unions eventually brought about improvements.

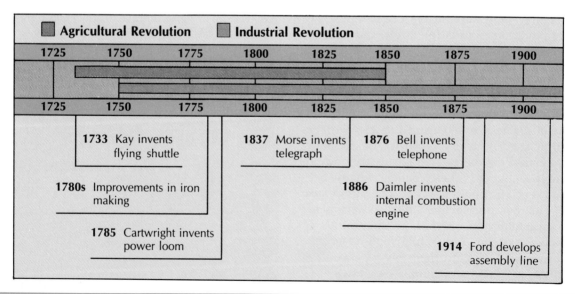

Recalling Facts

Match each inventor listed at left with the appropriate invention at right.

1. Henry Bessemer
2. Jethro Tull
3. Thomas Alva Edison
4. Eli Whitney
5. Robert Fulton
6. James Watt
7. John Kay
8. Guglielmo Marconi
9. George Stephenson
10. Samuel Morse

a. paddle-wheeled steamship
b. flying shuttle
c. radio
d. phonograph
e. steam engine
f. telegraph
g. steam-powered locomotive
h. new process of making steel
i. cotton gin
j. seed drill

Chapter Checkup

1. (a) Describe the Agricultural Revolution in Britain. (b) How did the Agricultural Revolution help make the Industrial Revolution possible?

2. (a) How did inventions revolutionize the textile industry? (b) How did new technology trigger the rise of new industries?

3. (a) Why did Britain take the lead in the Industrial Revolution? (b) Why was Belgium one of the first nations on the continent to industrialize?

4. (a) What improvements were made in communications during the Industrial Revolution? (b) What improvements were made in transportation? (c) How did these improvements contribute to a further growth in industry?

5. Describe how the Industrial Revolution affected each of the following: (a) population; (b) cities; (c) the way people worked; (d) the social structure in European countries.

6. (a) What groups in Britain supported reform to improve conditions for workers? (b) What groups opposed reform? (c) What types of reforms did governments institute? (d) What other factors contributed to improved conditions for workers?

Critical Thinking

1. **Comparing** (a) How were women's roles during the 1800s similar to women's roles before industrialization? (b) How were they different?

2. **Expressing an Opinion** Do you think the positive results of the Industrial Revolution outweighed the negative results? Give reasons to support your answer.

3. **Understanding Economic Ideas** (a) What role did corporations play in the Industrial Revolution? (b) Why do you think corporations replaced individual entrepreneurs?

4. **Synthesizing** One historian has suggested that the Industrial Revolution was "the greatest transformation in human history since the remote times when men invented agriculture, . . . writing, the city and the state." What evidence can you use to support this idea?

Relating Past to Present

1. (a) How is the way of life that developed in industrial nations during the 1800s similar to life in the United States today? (b) How is it different?

Developing Basic Skills

1. **Graph Reading** Study the graph on page 439 and then answer the following questions: (a) What is the topic of the graph? (b) How many kilometers of railroad track did Britain have in 1850? (c) How many kilometers of track did Germany have in 1900? (d) Which nation had the most track in 1910? (e) Why do you think Italy had the fewest kilometers of railroad track in 1910?

2. **Ranking** Make a list of what you consider the five most important inventions of the Industrial Revolution. Rank them in order of importance. Then explain why you ranked them in this order.

3. **Researching** Read about the life of one of the inventors discussed in this chapter. Then write a report in which you explain why you think he became an inventor.

See page 806 for suggested readings.

24 Currents of Thought

(1800–1914)

Detail from Hove Beach, *by John Constable.*

"I started from my sleep with horror; a cold dew covered my forehead, my teeth chattered, and every limb became convulsed; when, by the dim and yellow light of the moon, as it forced its way through the window shutters, I beheld the wretch—the miserable monster whom I had created. He held up the curtain of the bed; and his opened eyes, if eyes they may be called, were fixed on me. His jaws opened, and he muttered some inarticulated sounds while a grin wrinkled his cheeks. He might have spoken, but I did not hear; one hand stretched out, seemingly to detain me . . . ."

This scene is from the novel *Frankenstein,* written by Mary Shelley in 1818. It describes a nightmarish encounter between a young scientist, Frankenstein, and the grotesque monster he created. *Frankenstein* weaves together two of the major influences on thought during the 1800s: a growing interest in science and the belief that imagination and emotion were as important as reason. In the newly industrialized societies of Europe and the United States, many people had great faith in science. Scientific research, they thought, could solve the problems facing society.

The Industrial Revolution and the profound changes it caused were reflected in the work of many philosophers and artists during the 1800s. Philosophers sought to explain the changes they saw, often proposing solutions to problems created by early industrialization. Early in the century, some artists rejected industrial society and sought comfort in a simpler, more rural way of life. By mid-century, however, many writers and painters had come to accept industrialized society, and they portrayed it realistically. The feelings of nationalism unleashed by the French Revolution and Napoleon's conquests also influenced currents of thought in Europe during the 1800s.

1 New Ideas About Organizing Society

Read to Learn   ■ how laissez faire philosophers explained eonomics
■ how different reformers proposed to change society

The Industrial Revolution brought about wide-ranging social changes, as you read in Chapter 23. It changed the way people worked, the way businesses were organized, and where people lived. As philosophers became aware of the problems created by industrialization, they began to consider ways of dealing with those problems. Some proposed new ways of organizing society. Some built on the work of the physiocrats, philosophers who had foreseen some of the important developments of the 1800s.

Laissez Faire Economics

During the Enlightenment, the physiocrats had formulated natural laws that they thought explained the economy. (See page 371.) They believed that if these natural laws were allowed to operate, everyone would benefit. Consequently, the physiocrats opposed any attempt by government to interfere with the natural laws of economics. The economic system described by the physiocrats is called *laissez faire* (LEHS ay FEHR), meaning let people do as they choose.

The ideas of the physiocrats were summarized in the late 1700s by the Scottish professor Adam Smith in his book *The Wealth of Nations.* Smith contended that if individuals acted in their own self-interest, society as a whole would benefit. Profits made by industrialists paid the salaries of workers and contributed to the wealth of the nation. Therefore, the government should not try to restrict the actions of industrialists.

In England, Thomas Malthus and David Ricardo also supported laissez faire economics. In his *Essay on Population,* Malthus stated that the human population grew much faster than food production. Only forces such as disease, natural disaster, and famine kept the population from outdistancing food supplies. Malthus believed that this was a law of nature and that interfering with the process would make conditions worse. He argued

that if the government tried to correct social problems, the population would increase more rapidly. This would put even greater strains on the food supply and increase the number of workers competing for jobs. Wages would then go down, and workers would be even more miserable.

David Ricardo agreed with Malthus' analysis. His ideas gave rise to what was called the Iron Law of Wages. According to this law, population and wages go through inevitable cycles. High wages encourage workers to have more children, ultimately leading to a surplus of workers and lower wages. Lower wages meant workers would have fewer children. Thus, there would be a shortage of workers and employers would have to pay higher wages. Once wages went up, the cycle would begin again.

Malthus and Ricardo presented a gloomy picture of economics. They claimed that the economic cycle condemned workers to recurring periods of low wages and misery. Thus, economics as they described it came to be called the "dismal science."

Laissez faire theories remained influential throughout the 1800s. Industrialists supported these theories because they wanted to run their businesses as they saw fit. They warned that attempts to interfere by labor unions or governments would violate the natural laws of economics and create even more misery.

Calls for Reform

Not all observers of the effects of early industrialization accepted the conclusion that poverty was natural or inevitable. Some, such as English philosophers Jeremy Bentham and John Stuart Mill, thought efforts should be made to improve living and working conditions.

Like the laissez faire economists, Jeremy Bentham believed that it would be best if the government did not become involved

The teeming streets of early industrial cities revealed some of the problems caused by rapid population growth. This print by Gustave Doré shows the crowds and chaos of London streets in the 1800s. Many reformers looked for ways to improve living conditions in cities.

in the way people ran their businesses. However, he argued that the government should intervene if the actions of a few individuals brought misery to many.

John Stuart Mill supported active reform to correct the problems created by industrialization. He thought workers should act through labor unions or other organizations to improve working conditions. He believed that the government should take action, when necessary, to protect workers. Mill also thought both men and women should have the right to vote and the right to a good education.

Both Bentham and Mill supported the capitalist system, in which private investors own and control the means of production.* They thought industry should remain in pri-

---

* The means of production include land, machines, and factories, which are used to produce food and manufactured goods.

450

vate hands, and they advocated government action only to correct abuses of the system. Another group of reformers, the socialists, challenged the whole idea of capitalism.

Socialists argued that the capitalist system rewarded only the industrialists and not the workers whose labor supported it. Many socialists thought that the capitalist system should be replaced by a system in which the workers owned and controlled the means of production. Others favored a system of government ownership. But all believed that the means of production should be operated for the benefit of all the people.

Utopian Socialists

A group of early socialists called utopian socialists dreamed of reorganizing industry so that a new kind of society could grow out of it. This would be a utopia, or an ideal society. This utopia would have no poverty. Workers would truly share in the fruits of their labor, and all people would be treated fairly.

One of the early utopian socialists was Robert Owen. As a ten-year-old textile worker in Manchester, England, he personally experienced industrial abuses. But by age 23, Owen had become a successful cotton manufacturer himself, and he had time to think about how industry should best operate. He believed that people would work better if they lived in a healthy environment.

In 1800, Owen established an industrial community in New Lanark, Scotland, to test his ideas. Owen did not give the textile workers at New Lanark control of the factory, but he did improve their living and working conditions. He paid high wages, built comfortable and sanitary housing, provided schools, and set up stores where goods were sold at low prices.

Owen's experiment succeeded. The textile mill was profitable, and the workers prospered. From 1805 to 1825, New Lanark became a showplace for Owen's ideas, and thousands of visitors came to marvel at it.

In France, Charles Fourier (foo ree AY) was shocked by the conditions he saw in factories. Like Owen, Fourier believed that poverty would end if workers were given the chance to work together in their own best interests.

Fourier drew up plans to establish small model communities of 500 to 2,000 people. In each of these communities, called phalansteries, people would do the jobs for which they were best suited and would share the profits. Several phalansteries modeled after Fourier's plans were set up in France. Two were established in the United States—one at Brook Farm in Massachusetts and a second near Red Bank, New Jersey. All these experiments failed, but many ideas of the utopian socialists lived on.

In the mid-1800s, Louis Blanc, a French journalist, proposed that workers set up cooperative workshops with financial support from the government. As you read in Chapter 22, national workshops were set up briefly in France during the revolution of 1848 when Blanc was a member of the government. Blanc's guiding principle was "from each according to ability, to each according to need."

Karl Marx and Scientific Socialism

Two German philosophers, Karl Marx and Friedrich Engels, were formulating a different type of socialism. Karl Marx was a journalist who had been exiled from Germany for his political and religious views. Marx moved to Paris. There he met Friedrich Engels, whose father owned a textile mill in Manchester, England. Their meeting marked the beginning of a lifelong friendship and working partnership.

Both men were horrified by the working conditions in factories. They blamed the system of industrial capitalism for the terrible conditions. In 1848, Marx and Engels published their theories in *The Communist Manifesto*. In this work, they described a form of complete socialism in which there would be public ownership of all land and all other means of production. Today, such a system is called *communism*.

Marx's theories. Marx thought utopian socialists were impractical dreamers whose ideas would never work. He claimed that his theories of socialism were based on a scientific study of history, and he called his theories "scientific socialism."

Marx believed that history followed scientific laws just as nature did. He claimed the course of history was determined by economics. Marx concluded that the way goods are produced shapes the social and political structure of a society. The people who control the means of production have all the power and wealth and thus control society.

According to Marx, throughout history societies had been divided into two classes—the "haves" and the "have nots." As examples, he cited the masters and slaves of ancient Greece, the patricians and plebeians of ancient Rome, and the lords and serfs of the Middle Ages. He contended that the "haves" and "have nots" have always struggled with each other.

In industrialized societies, the bourgeoisie were the "haves" and the *proletariat*,

In this print, German artist Käthe Kollwitz pictures the bleak lives of workers. The miserable conditions of the early Industrial Revolution led to worker protests and demands that governments correct abuses. Socialists, such as Karl Marx, blamed the entire capitalist system for the abuses. Marx believed that workers would overthrow capitalism in an international revolution.

or working class, were the "have nots." Just as earlier ruling classes had been replaced, Marx argued, the bourgeoisie led by industrial capitalists would be replaced. He predicted that the proletariat would rise up to take control of the means of production. Once this revolution was won, the proletariat would destroy the capitalists and rid themselves of the ruling class. Then a classless society would emerge, and everyone would share wealth and power.

Weaknesses of Marxism. Marx thought a revolution by the proletariat was inevitable. But history did not follow the course Marx predicted. For example, Marx thought that capitalism would drag more and more people into poverty until, in desperation, they rebelled. But this did not happen. As you read, the standard of living rose in industrialized countries.

Furthermore, many abuses common early in the Industrial Revolution disappeared. Governments initiated reforms that improved working conditions, public health, and public education. Labor unions gradually won higher wages and shorter working hours. Health and accident insurance, unemployment insurance, and paid vacations also improved the lives of workers. As workers made gains under the capitalist system, they were not eager to overthrow it.

In addition, Marx had not understood the attitude of workers toward their countries. He believed that all workers, regardless of nationality, would unite against their common enemy, the capitalists. However, most workers had strong feelings of nationalism. They did not see themselves as members of an international community of workers, striving to establish a socialist state.

Nevertheless, Marx's idea of a classless society in which all would share equally appealed to many people. During the late 1800s and early 1900s, socialist parties were formed in many countries to work toward the goals Marx described. These parties have had a significant impact on historical developments, as you will read later in chapters.

SECTION REVIEW

1. Identify: Adam Smith, Iron Law of Wages, utopian socialists.
2. Define: laissez faire, communism, proletariat.
3. Why was economics, as described by Malthus and Ricardo, called the "dismal science"?
4. Under what conditions did Bentham and Mill think the government should interfere in the way people ran their businesses?
5. Describe Robert Owen's utopian community in New Lanark, Scotland.
6. (a) According to Karl Marx, what two classes were struggling against one another during the 1800s? (b) What did he think the outcome of the struggle would be?

2 An Age of Science

Read to Learn
■ how people responded to Darwin's theory
■ how science advanced knowledge in the 1800s

During the 1800s, scientific discoveries revolutionized life. Developments in transportation, communication, and manufacturing advanced industry, as you read in the last chapter. Important developments also occurred in biology, chemistry, physics, and the new social sciences—sociology and psychology. Many of these developments improved people's lives and contributed to future advances. Some created great controversy.

Charles Darwin

The work of British biologist Charles Darwin sparked a controversy that has lasted for well over 100 years. In his works *The Origin of the Species* and *The Descent of Man*, Darwin presented a theory of evolution. According to Darwin's theory, all forms of life evolve, or change, over a long period of time. Simpler forms of life evolve into more complex forms, and new forms evolve out of older ones.

Darwin based his theory on the work of earlier scientists and on observations he made during an expedition to South America. Starting in 1831, Darwin had spent five years sailing along the coast of South America and to the Galapagos Islands aboard the *Beagle*. He made a detailed study of the forms of life he saw. Upon his return to England, he began working out a theory of how and why forms of life change over time.

Darwin based his theory in part on Malthus' theory that living things tended to multiply faster than the food supply. Darwin concluded that when food grew scarce living things competed with each other for food. The strongest living things would survive to reproduce, and their offspring would inherit the biological characteristics that had helped them survive. Thus, certain characteristics would survive and others would not. Darwin called this process natural selection or *survival of the fittest* because nature weeded out weak characteristics.

Reaction to Darwin's Theory

When Darwin first published his ideas in 1859, he was greeted with a storm of protest. Darwin proposed that all life had evolved from one original organism. Some scientists accused Darwin of saying that human beings were descended from apes.

A bitter controversy. Religious leaders such as Samuel Wilberforce, a bishop in the Church of England, said Darwin's theory of evolution contradicted the Bible, ignored the human soul, and failed to explain why humans were supreme on earth. Wilberforce claimed that Darwin's theory denied God's role in creation. Many Roman Catholics and fundamentalist Protestants, who believe that the words of the Bible must be interpreted literally, also condemned Darwin's theory.

In time, many religious people concluded that the theory of evolution did not necessarily deny God's role in creation. They believed that God was still the creator of life, but that the Biblical account of creation was a symbolic rather than a literal one. Others continued to believe that Darwin's theory was in error. Scientific study of Darwin's the-

At age 22, Charles Darwin signed on as a member of a British scientific expedition to South America. Its mission was to chart the coastline of South America and study the plant and animal life. The expedition sailed on H.M.S. Beagle, shown here at anchor off Rio de Janeiro, Brazil. During the voyage, Darwin observed many species of plants and animals he had never seen before. In Brazil, for example, he counted over 60 different varieties of beetles.

ory of evolution has continued to the present.

Social Darwinism. Some people applied Darwin's ideas to the social, economic, and political issues of the 1800s. For example, the English philosopher Herbert Spencer translated Darwin's biological theory into a social theory. All human life, Spencer argued, is a struggle for existence, and in this struggle only the fittest survive. The theories of people like Spencer are called Social Darwinism.

Many industrialists eagerly adopted Social Darwinism because they saw economic competition as a struggle for survival in which strong competitors drove out weaker ones. They believed their success in business proved they were fit to survive.

Extreme nationalists also used Darwin's ideas. Nations are in a permanent struggle for existence, they argued. Strong nations who defeated weaker nations in war were superior and therefore fit to survive. Rudyard Kipling, a popular writer of the time, summarized the main idea of Social Darwinism in these words: "They should take who have the power. And they should keep who can."

Advances in Biology and Medicine

Darwin had proposed that living things passed their biological characteristics on to their offspring, but scientists did not know how they did this. During the 1870s, German biologist August Weismann studied this question. He based his work on an earlier theory that all living things are made up of tiny cells. As a result of his research, Weismann concluded that there were two kinds of cells: reproductive cells that transmit biological characteristics to the next generation and body cells that die when the living thing dies.

At about the same time, Gregor Mendel, an Austrian monk, was also investigating how living things pass on biological characteristics. By crossing different strains of garden peas, he was able to change their characteristics over successive generations. This result led him to formulate a series of laws to explain how heredity worked. Mendel's work became the basis for the scientific breeding of plants and animals.

The work of other scientists led to significant advances in medicine. The French chemist Louis Pasteur proved that tiny organisms called bacteria caused beer and wine to turn sour. He also found that bacteria could be killed by heat. Pasteur then applied this knowledge to the problem of milk spoilage. He developed a process called pasteurization in which milk was heated enough to kill most bacteria and then cooled to slow the growth of remaining bacteria.

French scientist Louis Pasteur made important breakthroughs in the study of bacteria and immunity. He won great fame when he successfully prevented a nine-year-old boy who had been bitten by a rabid dog from contracting rabies.

The German scientist Robert Koch showed that bacteria cause many diseases. He also found the specific bacteria that cause anthrax, an animal disease, tuberculosis, and cholera. Pasteur then proved that animals can be protected against diseases caused by bacteria. When he injected a weakened strain of anthrax bacteria into sheep, the sheep developed a resistance to anthrax. Later, he used the same method, called vaccination, to prevent the viral disease rabies. As other bacteria were isolated, scientists found ways to immunize people against many diseases.

The English surgeon Joseph Lister applied the findings of Koch and Pasteur to the problem of infection after surgery. Lister developed ways to kill bacteria on surgeons' hands and surgical instruments so bacteria would not be introduced into a patient's body during surgery. As Lister's methods were adopted, deaths due to post operative infection declined dramatically. Such advances in medicine led to an increase in the human life span. (See the graph below.)

Discoveries in Chemistry and Physics

The study of chemistry was revolutionized in the early 1800s by the work of John Dalton, an English schoolteacher. Earlier scientists had suggested that everything is made up of tiny, indivisible particles called atoms. Dalton concluded that all the atoms of a particular element were identical and unlike the atoms of any other element. An element is a substance that cannot be broken down chemically into different substances.

Years later, the Russian chemist Dmitri Mendeleev (MEHN duh LAY uhf) found that the properties of elements are based on their atomic makeup and that elements with similar atomic makeups have similar properties. He then drew up a periodic table in which he listed elements according to their atomic structures. Chemists used Mendeleev's discoveries to predict the properties of combinations of elements. This knowledge led to the development of alloys and synthetics used in industry.

The revolution in chemistry was accompanied by a revolution in physics. The Scottish physicist James Clerk Maxwell predicted that electric and magnetic energy move in waves. In 1895, the German physicist Wilhelm Roentgen discovered energy waves that could penetrate solid matter. He called these waves x-rays. X-rays were soon put to work in the field of medicine.

At about the same time, in France, Henri Becquerel discovered that the element uranium had unusual properties. Marie and Pierre Curie determined that these properties were due to uranium's atomic structure. They found two new elements—radium and polonium—that had similar properties.

In 1910 and 1911, the British scientist Ernest Rutherford conducted experiments based on the work of Joseph J. Thomson. He found that the atom is actually made of separate particles, a nucleus and electrons.

The work of these physicists ushered in the era of modern physics. In the early 1900s, the German-born scientist Albert Einstein used their work to develop new laws of physics. Einstein rejected the idea that matter and energy were separate things. He proposed that energy and matter were interchangeable.

Einstein also argued that since all matter is in constant motion, there is no fixed point from which to measure motion. The motion of one object can be measured only by comparing it to the motion of another. All measurements are therefore relative. This theory is called the theory of relativity. It represented a radical departure from Newtonian physics, which assumed no relative motion.

Graph Skill *An increase in the average life expectancy contributed to population growth during the 1800s and early 1900s. The average life expectancy is the average number of years people born in a given year could be expected to live. What was the average life expectancy of people born in 1860? Between which years did it increase the most?*

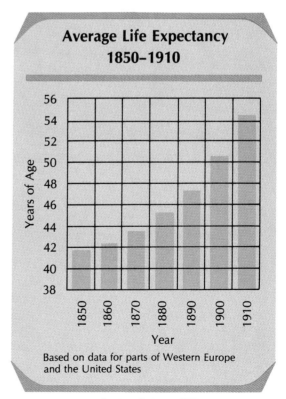

Average Life Expectancy 1850–1910

Based on data for parts of Western Europe and the United States

Source: E.A. Wrigley, *Population and History.*

455

In the late 1800s, the University of Paris attracted many scientists, including Pierre Curie and Marie Sklodowska. The two were married in 1895, and together they pioneered in a new field of study—radioactivity.

In 1896, a professor at the University of Paris, Henri Becquerel, discovered that uranium emitted something that could darken a photographic plate from a distance. Soon after Becquerel's discovery, Marie Curie began studying pitchblende, the ore in which uranium is found. She found that pitchblende was more radioactive than uranium alone. She concluded that there were other radioactive substances, as yet unknown, in the pitchblende.

Pierre Curie stopped his own research to work with his wife in her study of pitchblende. The Curies worked in the kitchen of their home trying to break the pitchblende down into its basic components. During their research, they boiled over eight tons of ore on their castiron stove. When the smell became unbearable, they moved their equipment into a small shed in their backyard.

The work was heavy and difficult. Marie wrote, "I came to treat as many as 20 kilograms [44 pounds] of matter at a time, which had the effect of filling the shed with great jars. . . . It was killing work to carry the receivers, to pour off the liquids, and to stir, for hours at a stretch, the boiling matter in a smelting basin."

In 1898, the Curies finally met with success. They discovered two new elements in the pitchblende: polonium, which Marie Curie named after her native Poland, and radium, which was a hundred times more radioactive than uranium. In 1903, the Curies and Henri Becquerel received the Nobel Prize in Physics for their work on radioactivity. In 1911, Marie Curie won a second Nobel prize, this time in chemistry, for her study of the chemical properties of radium.

New Fields of Study

Enthusiasm for science during the 1800s prompted a renewed interest in using scientific methods to study human behavior. This led to the development of two new social sciences—*sociology*, the study of society, and *psychology*, the study of behavior. Sociologists study how people act in groups. Psychologists study the behavior of individuals.

The French philosopher Auguste Comte was one of the founders of sociology. Comte argued that society, like nature, operated according to certain laws. He thought that once these laws were discovered, there would be a scientific basis for social organization and action. Comte stressed that sociologists, like other scientists, had to follow strict guidelines in their research. Only if they measured and reported what they found accurately and objectively would they arrive at valid findings.

Russian scientist Ivan Pavlov was an early psychologist. He began his work by studying the behavior of dogs. Pavlov set up an experiment in which he always rang a bell before he gave food to a dog. Food caused the dog to salivate. Eventually, the dog would salivate as soon as it heard the bell.

Pavlov concluded that the dog had been "conditioned" to respond even when the original stimulus, the food, was no longer there. Pavlov thought that people also were conditioned to respond automatically to a given stimulus. Therefore, some human behavior is based on unconscious responses rather than on conscious thought.

Sigmund Freud of Austria based his work on the idea that an unconscious part of the mind governs much human behavior. He argued that motives for a person's actions are sometimes hidden in the unconscious. Freud developed psychoanalysis, a method of trying to discover those motives. Freud's

ideas and methods still influence the study of psychology.

SECTION REVIEW

1. Identify: Social Darwinism, Gregor Mendel, Louis Pasteur, Wilhelm Roentgen, Marie and Pierre Curie, Auguste Comte, Ivan Pavlov, Sigmund Freud.
2. Define: survival of the fittest, sociology, psychology.
3. (a) Explain Darwin's theory of evolution. (b), Why did some religious leaders object to it?
4. How did Pasteur's work with bacteria help make surgery less dangerous?
5. Why did Albert Einstein conclude that all measurements are relative?

---

3 Changing Patterns in the Arts

Read to Learn
- what the romantic movement in the arts expressed
- why some artists of the 1800s were realists

The work of artists during the 1800s reflected the social and economic conditions of the time. Nationalism, advances in science, industrialization, and the growth of cities all affected artists' views of the world. As a result, new forms, styles, and themes emerged.

At the same time, a growing middle class provided a new audience for the arts. More people than ever had the education and leisure time to appreciate the arts. They also had money to buy books and paintings and to attend concerts. Thus, artists no longer had to depend on wealthy patrons as they had since the Middle Ages, and they had greater freedom to express their ideas.

The Rise of Romanticism in Literature

Late in the 1700s, many writers began to reject the Enlightenment faith in reason. They thought people should be ruled by their hearts, not their heads. They believed that

emotion, imagination, and intuition were more important than intellect and reason. This school of thought is called romanticism.

Romantics glorified the individual. They thought people should be free from confining rules so they could develop individually. Many romantics also expressed feelings of nationalism. The English poet Lord Byron combined the romantic ideal of nationalism and the yearning for individual liberty. In his poetry and his private life, he rejected the accepted rules of society. In the 1820s when the Greeks fought for independence from the Turks, Byron rushed off to Greece to help the Greek cause. He became a hero to many romantics when he died at the age of 36 while fighting there.

Perhaps in rebellion against the ugliness of industrialization, romantics glorified beauty, especially the beauty of nature. Poets such as Percy Bysshe Shelley and John Keats urged a return to a simple life, close to nature. William Wordsworth expressed this idea in his poem *The Tables Turned*. In this poem, he proclaimed that nature

> May teach you more of man,
> Of moral evil and of good,
> Than all the sages can.

The romantics looked longingly back to the past. They considered the Middle Ages a time of adventure and romance. The French romantic writer Victor Hugo set his novel *The Hunchback of Notre Dame* in the Middle Ages. Many romantic writers also reflected the upsurge in nationalism. The Russian poet Alexander Pushkin, for example, based many works on traditional Russian folk tales.

The Turn Toward Realism in Literature

By the 1800s, many writers began to rebel against romanticism. They thought that writers should present a realistic view of life, including the ugly parts. Literature, especially fiction, was deeply affected by the turn toward realism. The French writer Honoré de Balzac produced a massive work, containing about 90 novels and short stories, which he called *The Human Comedy*. In this work, Balzac realistically portrayed many aspects of French life during the 1800s. With great clarity, and sometimes wit, he described the crudeness and greed of the

French artist Jean François Millet painted the everyday lives of peasants and workers. In his work The Gleaners, *he shows poor peasants gathering the few remaining stalks of grain from the fields after reaping was finished.*

During the late 1800s, the middle and working classes had more leisure time than ever before. People in Europe and the United States discovered new ways to fill their leisure time. Their interests and tastes helped shape the pastimes of future generations.

The growth of public education in the 1800s greatly increased the number of people who could read. Publishers churned out popular novels of romance, mystery, and adventure. Booksellers peddled thousands of copies of "penny dreadfuls," inexpensive magazines that featured bloodcurdling stories. The invention of motion pictures in the early 1900s brought millions of people into theaters for the first time.

Perhaps the fastest growing form of entertainment was sports. During the late 1800s, many sports emerged in the forms that are familiar today. For example, soccer—known to Europeans as football—began as a game played by boys in private schools. Each school had its own rules for the game. At most schools, players kicked the ball with their feet but were not allowed to touch it with their hands. But at the Rugby School in England, players were allowed to carry the ball in their hands. Rugby football became the basis for football as it is played in the United States today.

In the 1880s, British factory workers began playing soccer, forming their own soccer clubs or teams. These clubs standardized rules so that teams from different places could play one another. By the early 1900s, Britain had over 10,000 soccer teams. In 1901, the British national soccer playoff drew 110,000 spectators. When the top soccer teams played, they charged admission to their games. Soon, athletes were paid for playing, and sports became a business.

Women also took an interest in sports. They joined gymnastic societies and played golf, tennis, and field hockey. Sports influenced women's fashions. Women who rode bicycles daringly raised their skirts above the ankle. Women also exchanged layers of skirts and petticoats for simpler clothes. Gradually, the new sporting fashions were accepted for everyday wear.

middle class. In contrast to romantics, Balzac found beauty in cities and factories.

Other novelists who presented realistic views of life include the Russians Feodor Dostoevski, author of *Crime and Punishment*, and Leo Tolstoy, author of *War and Peace*. The English author Charles Dickens was also highly realistic in his portrayal of life in British cities, as you read at the beginning of Chapter 23. Thomas Hardy, another English author, frequently used rural settings for his novels, but he too presented a realistic picture of life. Hardy portrayed nature as an impersonal force against which people had to struggle. This force was not the beautiful one described by romantics.

Painting

In the early 1800s, romanticism appealed to many painters who wanted to throw off the rules of the formal and rather cold classical painting of the 1700s. Romantic painters developed dramatic and emotional styles of art. They also explored new subjects, such as imagination, nature, and the past.

Eugène Delacroix (duh lah KWAH), an early French romantic painter, believed that the purpose of art was "not to imitate nature but to strike the imagination." Delacroix portrayed actual events, but he painted them with brighter colors and more sweeping strokes than earlier painters had used.

In England, the romantics' love of nature sent John Constable and J.M.W. Turner out-of-doors for the subjects of their paintings. They were not content to simply paint what they saw. They revolutionized landscape painting with their new use of color and their attempt to express their own emotions. In his painting *Hove Beach*, Constable caught the romantic's sense of the loneliness of the individual faced with the awesome power of nature. (See page 448.)

By the mid-1800s, realism began creeping into painting, just as it had into literature. French painters such as Gustave Courbet and Honoré Daumier wanted to show everyday life as it really was. They made no attempt to beautify life but instead reported it objectively.

In the late 1800s, other trends in painting emerged. One group of artists turned away from both romantic and realistic ideas. They concentrated on depicting fleeting impressions of what they saw rather than static forms. Thus, their school of painting is called impressionism.

Impressionists such as Pierre Renoir, Edgar Degas, and Claude Monet were intrigued by color and light. They experimented with placing colors side by side on the canvas rather than blending them to achieve a sense of brilliance. Monet painted the cathedral at Rouen, France, dozens of times to show it at different times of day. He wanted to capture his impression of how the cathedral looked in different lights.

Several artists, including Paul Cézanne and Paul Gauguin (goh GAN) from France and Vincent van Gogh from the Netherlands, thought that impressionist paintings lacked solidity. They experimented with new ways to show form. Their school of art is called post-impressionism.

Cézanne concentrated on the shapes of objects. By the way he arranged shapes in a painting, he tried to depict a mood or express an emotion. For example, in his painting *The Card Players*, he conveys a feeling of isolation.

Claude Monet is among the best known impressionist painters. In The Artist's Garden at Vetheuil, *shown here, he created shimmering effects by placing bands of different colors next to each other. Thus, the viewer's eye rather than the artist mixed the colors.*

Architecture

The romantic spirit and new technology changed the face of architecture during the 1800s. In the early 1800s, architecture was still dominated by the classical style of the 1700s. Buildings reflected the balanced style of Greek and Roman architecture. Thomas Jefferson designed several buildings that followed the classical style: his home at Monticello, the Virginia statehouse, and the buildings of the University of Virginia.

As the century wore on, many architects were swept up by the romantic's fascination with the past, especially the Middle Ages. They began using medieval Gothic cathedrals as their models. (See page 174.) The Gothic style became so popular that when the British Houses of Parliament burned down in 1834 they were replaced with Gothic buildings.

During the late 1800s, steel became an important building material. Steel was both strong and lightweight. Therefore, architects could design taller buildings of steel than they could of stone. The results were the first skyscrapers.

An early architect of skyscrapers was the American Louis Sullivan. He departed from classical and Gothic styles to design steel buildings with simple, clean lines. Sullivan's pupil Frank Lloyd Wright shared his enthusiasm for new materials and clean design. Wright's buildings, which include skyscrapers, homes, and museums, reflect his belief that "form follows function." By this, he meant that the design of a building should be determined by how it is to be used.

Music of the 1800s

The romantic spirit was also reflected in music. Romantic composers reacted against what they saw as the cold formalism of music in the late 1700s. They sought a freer expression of emotion.

The composer Ludwig van Beethoven was the musical heir to Haydn and Mozart. Nevertheless, his music often anticipated the romantic style and themes. His Third Symphony, the *Eroica*, was written as an expression of freedom and liberty. The beauty of nature was the theme of his Sixth Symphony, the *Pastoral*.

Early romantic composers concentrated on the expression of emotion rather than on form. In particular, they tried to write beautiful melodies. Composers such as Franz Schubert and Robert Schumann wrote warmly melodic symphonies, songs, and other works. Later romantic composers wanted to express even more powerful emotions. They wrote long, lush works that required large orchestras. Feelings of nationalism are apparent in the works of many romantic composers.

The 1800s also saw the flowering of opera. Giuseppe Verdi brought the art of Italian opera to a peak in such operas as *Rigoletto* and *Aida*. The German composer Richard Wagner wrote powerful nationalis-

The post-impressionist painter Vincent Van Gogh used short, heavy brush strokes and startlingly bright colors to convey intense energy. Van Gogh was pleased with this work, Road With Cypress and Stars. *He described it in a letter to a friend, the painter Paul Gauguin: "I still have . . . from down there, a last attempt—a night sky with a moon without brilliance . . . a star with exaggerated radiance . . . a very tall cypress, very straight, very somber."*

tic operas. His *Ring of the Nibelungen*, a cycle of four operas, was based on a heroic German epic from the Middle Ages.

Toward the end of the century, some composers began to rebel against the emotionalism of the romantics. For example, French composer Claude Debussy created the same effect in his music that impressionist painters created in their works. He concentrated on creating a subtle mood rather than on stirring emotions.

461

SECTION REVIEW

1. Identify: Lord Byron, Honoré de Balzac, Thomas Hardy, Eugène Delacroix, Claude Monet, Paul Cézanne, Louis Sullivan, Ludwig van Beethoven, Richard Wagner, Claude Debussy.

2. Describe three ideas shared by most romantic writers and artists.

3. How did realism differ from romanticism?

4. (a) What did romantic painters want to show in their landscapes? (b) What did impressionistic painters want to show in their works?

5. How did architecture change during the late 1800s?

6. How did romanticism affect music in the 1800s?

Chapter 24 Review

In Perspective

During the 1800s, philosophers reacted in different ways to the effects of the Industrial Revolution. Laissez faire economists thought that governments should not interfere in the economy because it was ruled by natural laws. Other economists thought reforms were needed. Utopian socialists and Marxist socialists argued that the capitalist economic system needed to be replaced.

While reformers tried to solve the problems of industrialization, scientists carried on research that had long-lasting effects. Charles Darwin's theory of evolution sparked a continuing controversy among scientists and religious leaders. Research about the causes of disease helped improve the lives of people. Discoveries in chemistry and physics laid the groundwork for major developments in the 1900s. The fields of sociology and psychology were born when scientists began to study society and human behavior.

Reaction to the Industrial Revolution was a major theme of the arts during the 1800s. Romantics often rejected life in industrial society while realists tried to portray what that life was really like. Much painting and music of the period reflected feelings of nationalism, and advances in science and technology were reflected in skyscrapers that appeared on urban skylines.

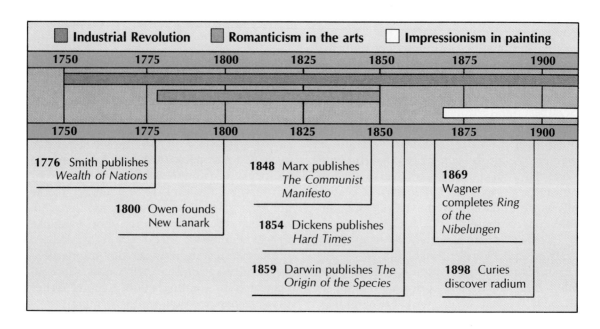

■ Industrial Revolution	■ Romanticism in the arts	□ Impressionism in painting

| 1750 | 1775 | 1800 | 1825 | 1850 | 1875 | 1900 |

| 1750 | 1775 | 1800 | 1825 | 1850 | 1875 | 1900 |

1776 Smith publishes *Wealth of Nations*

1800 Owen founds New Lanark

1848 Marx publishes *The Communist Manifesto*

1854 Dickens publishes *Hard Times*

1859 Darwin publishes *The Origin of the Species*

1869 Wagner completes *Ring of the Nibelungen*

1898 Curies discover radium

Recalling Facts

Decide if the following statements are true or false. If a statement is false, rewrite the statement to make it true.

1. Adam Smith thought governments should correct problems created by industrialists.
2. The Iron Law of Wages stated that a surplus of workers would lead to lower wages.
3. Industrialists opposed the ideas of laissez faire economics.
4. Robert Owen's utopian community at New Lanark, Scotland, was successful.
5. Darwin's ideas on evolution were met with much criticism.
6. Gregor Mendel discovered that bacteria caused disease.
7. Ernest Rutherford proved that the atom was the smallest particle of matter.
8. Psychology is the study of behavior.
9. Romantic painters most often painted scenes of factory life.
10. *The Human Comedy* is an example of realism in literature.

Chapter Checkup

1. Explain how the ideas of each of the following people contributed to the laissez faire theory of economics: (a) Adam Smith; (b) Thomas Malthus; (c) David Ricardo.
2. (a) What was the goal of the utopian socialists? (b) Why did Marx think his economic theories were more scientific than the theories of the utopian socialists?
3. What were the weaknesses of Marx's socialist theories?
4. (a) How were Darwin's ideas applied to social, political, and economic issues? (b) How did his ideas contribute to further discoveries in biology?
5. Describe how the work of each of the following scientists helped improve human health: (a) Louis Pasteur; (b) Robert Koch; (c) Joseph Lister.
6. (a) How was romanticism related to feelings of nationalism in the 1800s? (b) What developments in literature and architecture reflected the impact of industrialization?

Critical Thinking

1. **Expressing an Opinion** Adam Smith thought that government had only three duties: "First, the duty of protecting the society from . . . invasion; secondly, . . . the duty of establishing an exact administration of justice; and thirdly, the duty of erecting and maintaining certain public institutions." Do you agree that these are the only duties a government should have? Why?
2. **Synthesizing** Review what you learned in Chapter 23 about the development of labor unions in Great Britain. Which of the following people do you think would have approved of this development: Karl Marx, Adam Smith, John Stuart Mill, David Ricardo? Explain.

Relating Past to Present

1. Which of the scientific discoveries discussed in this chapter do you think has had the most direct effect on your life? Why?

Developing Basic Skills

1. **Graph Reading** Study the graph on page 419. Then answer the following questions: (a) What is the topic of the graph? (b) What was the average life expectancy in 1850? (c) What was the average life expectancy in 1880? (d) How did the average life expectancy change between 1850 and 1910? (e) What developments help explain this change?
2. **Using Visual Evidence** Study the paintings on pages 460 and 461. Then answer the following questions: (a) Which work represents the impressionist school of painting? (b) What characteristics of this work indicate that it was done by an impressionist painter? (c) What school of painting does the work on page 458 probably represent? How can you tell? (d) How do the paintings in this chapter help you understand the history of the 1800s?

See page 806 for suggested readings.

25 The Growth of Democracy

(1815–1914)

Detail from A Summer Day in Hyde Park, *by John Ritchie.*

On June 21, 1887, Queen Victoria celebrated her diamond jubilee. She had ruled Britain for 50 years. The queen described the day in her diary:

"The morning was beautiful and bright with a fresh air. Troops began passing early with bands playing, and one heard constant cheering.... At half-past eleven we left the Palace, I driving in a handsomely gilt landau drawn by six of the Creams, with dear Vicky and Alix, [two of her daughters].... Just in front of my carriage rode my three sons, five sons-in-law, nine grandsons, and grandsons-in-law. Then came the carriage containing my three other daughters, three daughters-in-law, granddaughters, one granddaughter-in-law, and some of the suite.... The crowds from the Palace gates up to the Abbey were enormous, and there was such an extraordinary outburst of enthusiasm as I had hardly seen in London before....

"Dinner was again in the Supper-room. I wore a dress with the rose, thistle, and shamrock embroidered in silver on it.... The noise of the crowd, which began yesterday, went on till late.... this never-to-be forgotten day will always leave the most gratifying and heart-stirring memories behind."

The celebrations surrounding Queen Victoria's diamond jubilee showed the respect and admiration the British people felt for their queen as well as their pride in their nation and its achievements. During the 1800s, Great Britain was the leading industrial and commercial power in the world. Victoria reigned for 63 years and became the symbol of the nineteenth century, which has often been called the Victorian Age. Although a monarch symbolized the age, this was a time of growing democracy in Britain, France, and the United States.

1 Reforms in Great Britain

Read to Learn   ■ how Great Britain extended democracy in the 1800s
■ about social reforms passed by Parliament

Victoria was queen of a nation that was stable, patriotic, and proud of being a world power. However, by the 1800s, the political power of the British monarchy had been limited. The power of Parliament had grown during the 1600s and 1700s. Yet, in the early 1800s, Parliament was far from being a democratic body. In addition, the British faced the harsh social and economic conditions accompanying the Industrial Revolution. As a result, there were many voices demanding political and social reform.

Early Attempts at Reform

Great Britain, unlike other European nations, had had a parliamentary system of government for hundreds of years. However, in the early 1800s, a small number of people dominated the British Parliament. Members of the House of Lords inherited their positions. Only 6 percent of British men could vote for members of the House of Commons. Few middle class men and no rural or urban workers had voting rights.

Also, election districts, set up originally in 1688, did not reflect population changes. Rural districts with small populations, called "rotten boroughs," were well represented in the House of Commons. But growing industrial centers, such as Birmingham and Manchester, had little representation.

The middle class demanded the vote and greater representation in parliament. Workers supported these demands. They hoped to eventually win the vote themselves. In 1832, a major political reform bill was passed by Parliament.*

The Reform Bill of 1832 gave industrial areas more representation in Parliament,

and it extended the *franchise*, or right to vote, to virtually all middle class men. After passage of the bill, 20 percent of adult men were qualified to vote. Since voters were still required to own a certain amount of property, however, neither urban nor rural workers qualified.

Disappointed with the Reform Bill of 1832, reformers continued to demand the vote for workers. In 1838, they drew up a document called the People's Charter. The Chartists, as these reformers were called, demanded the secret ballot and universal male suffrage, or the vote for all adult men. They also thought members of Parliament should receive a salary so poor people could afford to serve. The Chartist movement died out in the 1850s, but most of its demands eventually became law.

Another complaint of urban workers was the Corn Laws. In 1815, Parliament had passed the Corn Laws, which put a tariff, or tax, on imported grain. Landlords and farmers favored the Corn Laws because the tariff kept the price of grain high. However, city dwellers despised the Corn Laws because high prices for grain meant high prices for bread, the staple of the working-class diet.

Demands for repeal of the Corn Laws finally met with success in 1846. Because of crop failures in the early 1840s, the British had to import grain. Therefore, Parliament repealed the unpopular Corn Laws. Cheap grain flowed in from outside Britain, and the price of bread went down.

Extending Democracy

In the 1700s, both British political parties had represented wealthy landowners. (See page 386.) As more middle class men won the right to vote in the 1800s, both the Whig party, which became known as the Liberal party, and the Tory party, which became

---

* Britain had escaped the revolutions that erupted on the continent in 1820 and 1830. But there was scattered violence. Rioting in Bristol in 1832, for example, helped convince the House of Lords to approve the reform bill.

known as the Conservative party, tried to win the support of the new voters. They also responded to continuing demands to extend the franchise. Two capable politicians led the parties in this direction—the Conserva-tive Benjamin Disraeli (dihz RAY lee) and the Liberal William Gladstone.

Benjamin Disraeli thought that the Conservative party should support reforms that would improve the country. He considered

Profiles ■ Emmeline Pankhurst and Votes for Women

In the mid-1800s, women in Britain began demanding the right to vote. At first, their demands received little support, although Parliament had extended voting rights to all adult men by 1885. But in the early 1900s, a strong-minded woman, Emmeline Pankhurst, set out "to wake up England to the justice of women's suffrage."

Emmeline Pankhurst and her two daughters, Christabel and Sylvia, founded the Women's Social and Political Union (WSPU) in 1903. The WSPU urged Parliament to give women the right to vote. When the government failed to act, the Pankhursts and their supporters took direct action. WSPU members distributed leaflets and organized marches. Women who demonstrated for the right to vote were called suffragettes. Mounted police often broke up suffragette marches by charging into the crowds of demonstrators.

The WSPU responded with more militant actions. WSPU supporters broke into cabinet meetings. Women chained themselves to the visitors gallery in the House of Commons. They threw stones at cars of government officials, broke street lamps, and painted the slogan "Votes for Women" on sidewalks and walls. In 1908, Emmeline and Christabel Pankhurst were arrested and sent to prison for distributing leaflets urging people to "Rush the House of Commons."

The Pankhursts continued their campaign from prison. They refused to obey prison regulations. When punished with solitary confinement, they went on hunger strikes, risking death by starvation. The government responded to the hunger strikes by ordering prison authorities to force-feed the imprisoned suffragettes.

Many people were horrified by the forced feedings. Because Parliament was afraid of making the hunger strikers into martyrs, it passed the Prisoners Act of 1913. The law allowed hunger strikers to be released from prison, but they could be rearrested at a later date to complete their prison terms. Under this act, suffragettes who participated in prison hunger strikes were released and rearrested several times.

In 1918, British women over 30 years of age were granted the right to vote. Weakened by hunger strikes and many prison terms, Emmeline Pankhurst died in 1928, one week before Parliament passed a bill finally giving all women over 21 years of age the right to vote.

himself "a conservative to preserve all that is good in our constitution and a radical to remove all that is bad." William Gladstone began his career as a Conservative, but he became a staunch Liberal. These two men served alternately as prime minister from the mid-1860s to the early 1880s. Both played a key role in passing political and social reform measures during this period.

In 1866, Gladstone introduced a bill to extend the vote to working men in cities. The bill did not pass, but Disraeli introduced a similar bill the next year. In his opinion, the reform was inevitable, so he hoped the Conservatives could get credit for it and thereby win the votes of urban workers. The Reform Bill of 1867 passed with both Liberal and Conservative support. It nearly doubled the number of eligible voters.

Five years later, Parliament passed a bill introducing the secret ballot. In 1884 and 1885, other reform bills gave the vote to rural working men. Thus, by 1885, most adult men in Britain had the right to vote. In 1911, Parliament passed a bill that ended the right of the House of Lords to veto measures. The House of Lords resisted this bill. But it gave in when the king threatened to appoint new lords who would vote for the bill.

Throughout the late 1800s, the Conservatives and Liberals competed for support from the new working-class voters. Social reforms were passed, but many workers felt that the existing political parties did not do enough on their behalf. In 1900, they founded the Labour party,* headed by Ramsay MacDonald.

Other Reforms

Throughout most of the 1800s, social reform accompanied political reform in Britain. During the 1820s, Parliament lifted restrictions on the political activity of Catholics and Protestants who did not belong to the Church of England. Parliament also repealed the ban on the organization of workers, and it reformed the criminal code, reducing the

number of crimes punishable by death. The slave trade had been outlawed in 1807, and in 1833 slavery itself was abolished throughout the British Empire.

The Factory Acts of the early 1800s were followed by additional labor and social legislation. By the end of the century, Parliament had passed laws that regulated the number of hours a person worked and protected working women and children. David Lloyd George, a leader of the Liberal party, summed up the need for such laws. "Four spectres haunt the poor," he said, "old age, accident, sickness, and unemployment." He vowed to rid the country of them.

In 1912, Parliament passed a law establishing minimum wages. Parliament also extended workers' compensation to cover more workers in case of sickness or accident on the job. In 1909, it passed an old age pension bill that offered benefits to every British subject "of good character." Labor exchanges were set up to help find jobs for the unemployed. In 1911, the National Insurance Act provided health and unemployment insurance.

By the late 1800s, both Liberals and Conservatives recognized the need for better educated voters. In the 1860s, education was not compulsory, and students usually left school by age 11. The Education Act passed in 1870 allowed local school boards to require attendance. It also extended government aid to more schools. Later acts made education free and compulsory.

SECTION REVIEW

1. Locate: Manchester, Birmingham.
2. Identify: People's Charter, Benjamin Disraeli, William Gladstone, David Lloyd George.
3. Define: franchise.
4. What groups of people won the right to vote by the Reform Bill of 1832?
5. (a) Why did city dwellers oppose the Corn Laws? (b) What effect did the repeal of the Corn Laws have on urban workers?
6. What groups won the right to vote between 1832 and 1885?
7. Describe three social reforms passed by Parliament in the 1800s.

* "Labour" is the British spelling of "labor."

2 Moving Away From British Rule

Read to Learn ■ why the Irish and the Canadians resisted British rule
■ why Australia and New Zealand demanded self-government

As Britain moved toward more democratic government at home, it also faced demands for greater freedom from parts of the British Empire. The United States had won its independence in 1783. During the 1800s, Canada, Australia, and New Zealand tried to win self-rule within the empire. The Irish struggled for home rule, the right to rule themselves.

The Question of Ireland

Since the time of Henry VIII, English rulers had encouraged Protestants from England and Scotland to settle in Ireland. Many moved into the northern Irish province of Ulster, although Protestants owned large tracts of land throughout Ireland. During the 1600s and 1700s, the Protestant minority

Irish peasants suffered great hardships in the 1800s. Irish tenants rented small plots from British landlords. They raised grain and livestock to sell for cash in order to make rent payments. But their own families ate mainly potatoes. This scene, in which a tenant family is evicted for not paying rent, was a common sight in Ireland.

gained political economic control over Ireland. They passed laws limiting the rights of the majority of Irish, who were Catholic.

Irish Catholics constantly protested their lack of political and economic freedom. In 1801, the British tried to ease tensions in Ireland by formally joining Ireland and Great Britain and giving Ireland representation in the British Parliament. Parliament also repealed the law that forbade Catholics from being elected to office in Ireland. Many British political reforms, such as the Reform Bill of 1832, also applied to Ireland.

However, these moves did not satisfy Irish Catholics. Their anger had deep religious and economic roots. They resented the taxes they had to pay to the Anglican Church and the high rents that Irish Catholic peasants had to pay to Protestant landlords. They were especially bitter because the land had originally belonged to the Irish.

Irish hatred of Britain increased as a result of a disastrous famine in the 1840s. The potato was the mainstay of the Irish diet. When a blight caused potato crops to fail, there was a terrible famine. The British government did little to help. Over 20,000 Irish died of starvation. About one million died of disease because they were weak from hunger. Millions more left Ireland, many immigrating to the United States.

The famine fanned a revolutionary movement in Ireland, which grew during the late 1800s and early 1900s. The revolutionaries demanded home rule for Ireland. For years, Parliament resisted this idea. Many members wanted to protect the Protestants in Ulster. If Ireland were given home rule, the Protestants would lose their political power since Catholics were a majority.

Under Gladstone's leadership, Parliament did grant some concessions to the Irish, however. In 1869, an act was passed to free Catholics from paying taxes to support the Anglican Church. Two land acts passed in 1870 and 1881 protected Irish peasants from sudden eviction from their land, made rents fairer, and made it possible for them to buy land.

Gladstone also introduced a home rule bill for Ireland, but it was defeated each time he proposed it. Finally, in 1912, Parliament passed a home rule bill, but it never went into effect. The Protestant minority in Ulster was determined to prevent home rule, and they organized an army of 100,000 volunteers to resist it. In 1914, Parliament passed another home rule bill that did not apply to Ulster. But the outbreak of war in August of that year postponed any attempt to give southern Ireland home rule.

Demands for Self-Rule in Canada

Canada had originally been settled by the French, but the English gained the territory in 1763 as a result of their victory in the French and Indian War. To win the loyalty of its French subjects, who lived mainly in Quebec, Britain passed the Quebec Act in 1774. This act gave French Canadians who were Catholic the right to practice their religion. It also allowed them to continue living under traditional French laws and customs.

As early as the 1600s, some English-speaking settlers had begun moving to Canada. Among them were Scottish settlers who came to Nova Scotia, or New Scotland. English settlers also arrived to fish the waters off Newfoundland and establish fur-trading posts in the Hudson's Bay territory. During the American Revolution and afterward, many English-speaking settlers arrived in Canada. They settled mainly in the Maritime Provinces—Nova Scotia, New Brunswick, and Prince Edward Island—and in the area north of the Great Lakes in what is today Ontario.

From the start, there were disagreements between the French Canadians and the English Canadians. In an effort to govern the two groups separately, the British Parliament passed the Canada Act of 1791. This act divided Canada into three provinces—Upper Canada (present-day Ontario), Lower Canada (present-day Quebec), and the Maritime Provinces. Each province had a governor appointed by the crown, a royal council, and an elected assembly.

Neither the English Canadians nor the French Canadians were satisfied with this arrangement, and discontent with British rule grew. After an uprising in 1837, the British sent a special commissioner, Lord Durham, to be governor of Canada. In a report to Parliament in 1839, Durham recommended that Upper and Lower Canada be united and that the Canadians be given control over their domestic affairs. He proposed that the British government involve itself only in Canada's foreign affairs. The Durham Report was well received by the British government, and it became the basis for Canadian self-rule.

The Dominion of Canada

The Union Act of 1840 united Upper and Lower Canada. In 1849, Canada was granted the right to self-government, and in 1867 Nova Scotia and New Brunswick were joined with Ontario and Quebec to create the Dominion of Canada. In the next few decades, Prince Edward Island, Manitoba, Alberta, Saskatchewan, and British Columbia would join the Dominion.

The government of the Dominion of Canada was modeled on the British government. A governor general represented the British monarch, but his role was mainly ceremonial. The Canadian parliament had two houses, one appointed and one elected. The government was led by a prime minister.

Britain retained some power over Canadian foreign affairs until 1931, when the Statute of Westminster was passed. This statute created the British Commonwealth of Nations, which made Canada, as well as other former British colonies, equal partners with Britain. It declared all members of the Commonwealth "equal in status, in no way subordinate to each other," but it still bound members to the British crown.

Following the creation of the Dominion in 1867, Canada set out to build a united nation. A transcontinental railroad helped unite the sprawling country. The nation's rich natural resources attracted industries.

The Canadian government sought immigrants to work in these industries and farm the vast western prairies. In the 20 years before 1914, more than 3 million immigrants went to Canada. They brought the population to over 7 million—3 times what it had been 1850.

Self-Government for Australia and New Zealand

During the second half of the 1800s, Australia and New Zealand also moved toward self-government. The first European settlers in Australia were convicted criminals who had been exiled from Great Britain. Some of these exiles later fled Australia and settled in New Zealand.

Both Australia and New Zealand were rich in mineral deposits and in land suitable for raising wheat and grazing sheep. As a result, both attracted new settlers in the 1700s and 1800s. As the populations grew, people demanded that Britain stop exiling convicted criminals to Australia. In 1840, the British government stopped this practice.

Independent and proud of their progress, the people of Australia and New Zealand did not want to be governed by faraway Britain. They agitated for self-government. Australia won self-government in 1850, and New Zealand won self-government in 1852. Like Canada, Australia and New Zealand became "equal partners" in the British Commonwealth of Nations in 1931.

Democratic reforms made early headway in Australia and New Zealand. Australia introduced the secret ballot nearly 20 years before Great Britain did. In fact, the secret ballot is sometimes called the Australian ballot. In 1893, women won the right to vote in New Zealand. Australian women won the same right nine years later. Women in Britain had to wait many years for this right.

SECTION REVIEW

1. Locate: Canada.
2. How did the potato blight of the 1840s contribute to Irish hatred of Britain?
3. Describe two concessions Parliament made to the Irish after 1869.
4. What group resisted home rule in Ireland? Why?
5. What did Lord Durham recommend should be done about Canadian discontent with British rule?
6. What democratic reforms were introduced in Australia and New Zealand before they were in Britain?

3 From Empire to Republic in France

Read to Learn
- about the successes and failures of Napoleon III
- what problems the Third Republic faced

As you read in Chapter 22, Louis Napoleon proclaimed himself Napoleon III, Emperor of the French, in 1852. Napoleon's action was approved by popular vote. But he did not have the support of all French citizens, many of whom wanted a democratic republic. Others supported a return to a monarchy under either the House of Bourbon, the heirs of Louis XVIII, or the House of Orléans, the heirs of Louis Philippe. Republicans and monarchists would struggle for power during Napoleon III's reign and after it.

Napoleon III

When Napoleon III came to power, many French people looked to him to restore order after the chaos of 1848. He responded by instituting a harsh authoritarian regime. The emperor discouraged criticism by enforcing strict censorship and maintaining a powerful secret police. The empire had a constitution and an elected assembly, but the assembly could only discuss issues brought to it by the emperor. Power was actually in the hands of Napoleon and his ministers.

Despite the repressive nature of the early years of his reign, Napoleon III considered himself a great reformer. He promised to use strong government to improve the life of the people and bring peace to France. "The Empire is peace," he proclaimed.

Napoleon III sponsored legislation to improve working conditions and to provide public housing. He also supported public works, both to beautify French cities and towns and to provide employment. The broad boulevards of present-day Paris, for example, were built during the Second Empire. The wide new streets also served a political purpose. It would be much more difficult for revolutionaries to build barricades across the new streets than it was to build them across the narrow winding streets they replaced. The wide streets also allowed easy movement of government troops if an uprising began.

During Napoleon's reign, the government encouraged the growth of industry in France. It aided construction of railroads and improvement of roads and harbors. It also sponsored credit agencies to increase business investment. By 1870, France was a major industrial power, although it would eventually be surpassed by Germany and other nations. French industrial growth slowed in part because the French preferred traditional ways of doing business. Nevertheless, the growth of industry during the Second Empire led to general prosperity.

Despite economic prosperity, opposition to Napoleon grew during the late 1850s and the 1860s. His rule satisfied neither the republicans nor the monarchists. Furthermore, many French were unhappy with Napoleon's foreign policy, as you will read.

In an attempt to revive his popularity, Napoleon began to make his government less repressive and more democratic. He ended press censorship and allowed the elected assembly a greater role in government. By 1869, the assembly had the right to vote on the budget and propose laws.

The effort to create a "Liberal Empire" only increased discontent. Once opponents of the regime could openly criticize it, more

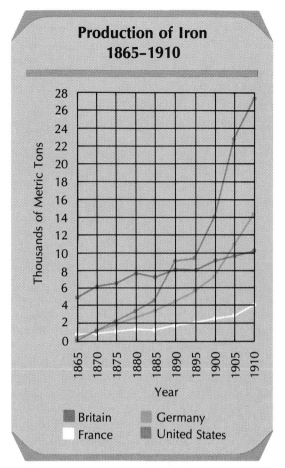

Production of Iron 1865–1910

Britain
France
Germany
United States

Source: Witt Bowden, *et. al. An Economic History of Europe Since 1750.*

Graph Skill   *In 1870, iron production in France was about the same as iron production in Germany and the United States. In what year did German iron production surpass that of Britain? When did the United States outdistance the other nations?*

of them were elected to the assembly. Strikes also increased dramatically when the ban on unions and strikes was lifted. However, it was a setback in foreign policy that brought the Second Empire down.

Adventures in Foreign Policy

French foreign policy during the 1850s seemed successful. France had begun to create a colonial empire in parts of Africa and Asia. Its participation in the Crimean War

471

was popular with the people, and the French hosted the peace conference ending the war. However, French Catholics bitterly resented their nation's role in the unification of Italy. As a result of this unification, the papacy lost extensive territory. (You will read about the unification of Italy in Chapter 26.)

Another damaging foreign policy adventure was Napoleon III's attempt to gain influence in Mexico. In 1861, Napoleon sent 40,000 French troops to Mexico. He justified this action on the grounds that the Mexican government had refused to pay debts owed to European countries. The French declared Mexico "the Empire of Mexico." They installed as emperor Maximilian, brother of Francis Joseph, the Austrian emperor.

Maximilian's reign was a disaster from the start. Only the presence of French troops kept him on the throne. The United States considered Napoleon's actions a threat to the Western Hemisphere, but the Civil War that began in 1861 prevented it from taking any action. After the Civil War ended in 1865, the United States pressured Napoleon to withdraw his troops. Napoleon, who needed his troops in Europe, gradually withdrew them. Stripped of his military protection, Maximilian was captured by Mexican soldiers in 1867 and executed. The disaster in Mexico dealt a severe blow to Napoleon III's prestige and popularity.

A Bitter Defeat

The crowning blow for Napoleon was his defeat and capture in the Franco-Prussian War in 1870. As you will read in Chapter 26, the war broke out in 1870 over the question of who would become king of Spain. The Prussians surrounded the French army at Sedan and captured the emperor. Napoleon's surrender completely humiliated the French people. Within a few days, a group of republicans in Paris proclaimed the end of the Second Empire and the beginning of the Third Republic.

After the French surrender, a National Assembly was elected. Its first duty was to negotiate a peace treaty with Germany. By the provisions of the treaty, France was forced to give Germany Alsace-Lorraine, which included the province of Alsace and part of the province of Lorraine. It also had to pay Germany a one million dollar indemnity, or repayment for damages. The Germans would occupy France until the indemnity was paid. The harshness of the treaty angered the French. For many years, they harbored a deep hatred of Germany and a desire for revenge for the loss of Alsace-Lorraine.

Radicals in Paris were furious over the National Assembly's acceptance of the peace treaty. They also feared the revival of a monarchy in France because a majority of the assembly was monarchist. In March 1871, they rose in revolt and set up a government called the Paris Commune.

Leaders of the Paris Commune demanded reforms such as lower prices, higher wages, and better working conditions. These demands were fairly moderate, and there were few socialists among the leaders of the Commune. However, many French feared a new revolution. The National Assembly sent troops that crushed the Commune. In a week-long battle, over 20,000 French men and women died. The uprising and its suppression left bitter divisions between monarchists and republicans—divisions that threatened the stability of the Third Republic.

The Third Republic

Monarchists dominated the National Assembly, but they themselves were divided between supporters of the House of Bourbon and supporters of the House of Orléans. This division gave the republicans a chance to gain strength. In 1875, by a margin of one vote, the Assembly adopted a constitution.

According to the constitution of 1875, the National Assembly, which was composed of a Chamber of Deputies and a Senate, passed the laws. All adult males elected representatives to the Chamber of Deputies. Officials of local governments elected members of the Senate. The National Assembly elected the president of France. Real governmental power rested in a cabinet of min-

French artist Honoré Daumier painted scenes of social protest. In The Uprising, *shown here, he expresses sympathy for poor city workers. Workers like these supported the Paris Commune in 1871.*

istries that was responsible to the National Assembly.

The Third Republic got off to a shaky start. It had enemies among the many monarchists and among many Catholics, who were afraid the republicans would weaken the Catholic Church in France. As many as 12 political parties were represented in the National Assembly so governments had to be based on broad *coalitions,* or temporary alliances of parties. These coalitions often broke down. The Third Republic was also beset by political scandals and official corruption.

A serious crisis revolved around General Georges Boulanger (boo lahn ZHAY), who crushed the Paris Commune in 1871. In 1886, Boulanger became minister of war. Deeply anti-republican, he won the support of many French citizens by playing on their desire for revenge against Germany. In 1889, it appeared that Boulanger might overthrow the Third Republic. The government ordered Boulanger's arrest for treason, but he fled to Belgium.

A financial scandal concerning the building of the Panama Canal also shook the Third Republic. The French company formed to build a canal across Panama was in danger of bankruptcy. In the early 1890s, the public learned that several Assembly members and government ministers had accepted bribes from the faltering company. A storm of public protest resulted. The Third Republic was able to weather the storm, but it soon faced an even more serious crisis.

The Dreyfus Affair

In 1894, Captain Alfred Dreyfus, the first Jewish officer to be named to the general staff of the French army, was accused of giving French military secrets to the Germans. Although Dreyfus proclaimed his innocence, he was convicted of treason and sent to the French penal colony on Devil's Island, off the coast of South America. The trial touched off a wave of anti-Semitism, or hostility toward Jews, in France.

It soon came to light that Major Ferdinand Esterhazy, a Catholic monarchist, was the real traitor. But the French army command refused to reopen the case. Their action reflected a deep-seated anti-Semitism shared by many French army officers as well as a desire to protect the reputation of the army. The case was kept before the public, however, especially when the French author Émile Zola published a letter accusing the army command of persecuting an innocent man.

The Dreyfus case deepened the divisions in France. On one side were Catholics, monarchists, and the military, who saw the demand to reopen the case as an effort to undermine authority in France. On the other side were the republicans and leftists, such as the socialists, who thought the injustice suffered by Dreyfus threatened democratic government as well as individual rights.

In 1899, five years after his conviction, Captain Dreyfus was finally pardoned by the president of France. The republicans considered this a victory, and they moved to further strengthen the republic.

During the Third Republic, Paris was a magnet for artists. French impressionist painters, such as Auguste Renoir, recorded scenes of Paris life. In this painting, Renoir captures the carefree mood of young couples dancing at a famous cafe, Le Moulin de la Galette—The Pancake Mill.

Reform in the Third Republic

Partly as a result of the Dreyfus Affair, republicans in the National Assembly passed a series of laws that weakened the power of the Catholic Church in France. The government stopped paying the salaries of clergy. Catholic teaching orders were broken up, and thousands of Catholic schools were forced to close. These laws effectively separated church and state in France.

Like other European governments, the government of the Third Republic passed laws to deal with problems brought on by industrialization. For example, it approved a 12-hour workday and forbade the employment of children under 13 years of age. However, France was slower to introduce social reform than Britain and Germany. Fur-thermore, it did not institute unemployment or health insurance. Such reforms seemed less important in France since it remained largely a nation of small farms and small family-run businesses.

SECTION REVIEW

1. Identify: Napoleon III, Paris Commune, Georges Boulanger, Alfred Dreyfus.
2. Define: coalition.
3. Describe two ways in which Napoleon III tried to create a "Liberal Empire" in the 1860s.
4. How did Napoleon III interfere in Mexico?
5. How did the National Assembly react to the Paris Commune?
6. Describe one of the crises that threatened the Third Republic during the late 1800s.

4 Expansion of the United States

Read to Learn
- how the United States grew and developed in the 1800s
- why the North and South fought the Civil War

In the United States, as in Britain and France, the 1800s were a period of growth—in population, agriculture, industry, and democracy. The United States also grew dramatically in size during this period.

Several factors contributed to this phenomenal growth. One was the existence of sparsely settled land stretching to the Pacific Ocean. Another was the confidence of Americans in the right and ability to expand and develop their nation.

New Territories

In 1803, President Thomas Jefferson doubled the size of the United States when he purchased Louisiana from France. Napoleon Bonaparte, in desperate need of money to fight wars in Europe, sold the vast Louisiana Territory to the United States for $15 million. In 1804 and 1805, Meriwether Lewis and William Clarke led an expedition to explore the Louisiana Purchase. Settlers soon followed.

Since they had won their independence, Americans had been moving westward across the Appalachian Mountains toward the Mississippi River. As a result of the Louisiana Purchase, the American frontier was moved west to the Rocky Mountains. Gradually, Americans came to believe that it was their destiny to extend the United States across the entire continent. In 1845, a newspaper editor labeled this idea "Manifest Destiny," and Americans quickly took up the phrase.

Even before Manifest Destiny became popular, the United States expanded. In 1819, Spain ceded Florida to it. In 1845, the United States, by treaty, annexed the Republic of Texas. Texas had originally been part of Mexico. But in 1836, settlers from the United States had proclaimed Texas an independent republic and won a war for independence against Mexico.

In 1846, a dispute over the Texas border sparked a war between Mexico and the United States. The United States was victorious in the Mexican War, and, as a result, it acquired California and the New Mexico territory in 1848. Two years earlier, the American government had gained title to the Oregon Country as a result of a treaty with Great Britain. It arranged the Gadsden Purchase from Mexico in 1853 and bought Alaska from Russia in 1867, thereby extending the nation to its present-day continental borders. (See the map on page 476.)

The Right to Vote

As the nation expanded westward, democracy also expanded. In most of the 13 colonies, only white men with property could vote. In some colonies, voters also had to meet religious requirements. After gaining independence, many states retained property qualifications for voters, and some required payment of a poll tax in order to vote. However, by 1850, most states had dropped these restrictions and had established white male suffrage, voting by all white men.

As in Europe, women in the United States had no political rights. Nor did most black Americans. A few states had allowed blacks to vote after the colonies won independence, but the right was withdrawn in some of these states during the early 1800s.

A Split Between North and South

Slavery became a major issue between northern and southern states after 1820. As new territories in the west were added to the country, disputes arose over whether slavery should be allowed in new states that were seeking admission to the union.

Support for the extension of slavery was usually found in the South, where slavery was an important part of the plantation

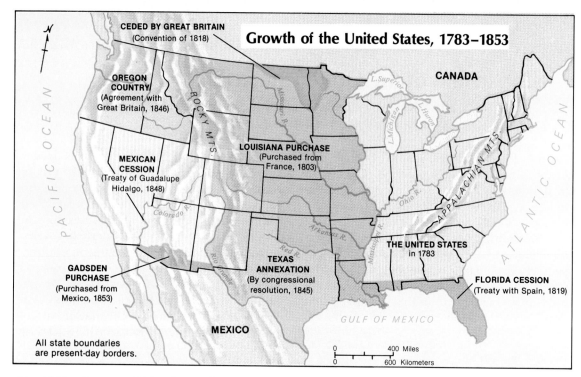

Growth of the United States, 1783–1853

CEDED BY GREAT BRITAIN
(Convention of 1818)

CANADA

OREGON
COUNTRY
(Agreement with
Great Britain, 1846)

ROCKY MTS.

Missouri R.

L. Superior

L. Michigan

L. Huron

MEXICAN
CESSION
(Treaty of Guadalupe
Hidalgo, 1848)

LOUISIANA PURCHASE
(Purchased from
France, 1803)

Ohio R.

APPALACHIAN MTS.

Colorado R.

Arkansas R.

Red R.

Mississippi R.

THE UNITED STATES
in 1783

GADSDEN
PURCHASE
(Purchased from
Mexico, 1853)

Rio Grande

TEXAS
ANNEXATION
(By congressional
resolution, 1845)

FLORIDA CESSION
(Treaty with Spain, 1819)

PACIFIC OCEAN

ATLANTIC OCEAN

MEXICO

GULF OF MEXICO

All state boundaries
are present-day borders.

0   400 Miles
0   600 Kilometers

Map Skill   *Between 1803 and 1853, the United States expanded from the Mississippi River to the Pacific Ocean. Present-day state boundaries are shown on this map. Which areas became part of the United States after 1840?*

economy. Also, many southerners hoped that new states allowing slavery would support the South in Congress. Many northerners resisted the admission of new states that permitted slavery because they were afraid of losing power in Congress. Other people opposed the extension of slavery in the west because they believed that slavery should be abolished throughout the country.

For a while, Congress maintained a balance between slave states and free states. For each state that was admitted as a slave state, another was admitted as a free state. But the tension between the North and the South continued to grow.

Differences over economic issues contributed to the tension. The North was becoming industrialized, so northerners favored high tariffs on imported goods to protect new American industries from foreign competition. But the South remained mostly agricultural, with cotton as the major crop. Southerners objected to high tariffs on imported goods. They had to buy many products from foreign countries, and they felt that the tariffs penalized them by raising prices on these products.

Civil War and Reconstruction

By 1860, tensions between the North and the South had brought them to the breaking point. Many southerners were convinced that the southern states should secede, or withdraw, from the Union. The election of Abraham Lincoln as President in 1860 finally pushed the South into secession. Lincoln was an outspoken opponent of slavery in new territories. First South Carolina and then 10 other southern states seceded from the Union. They proclaimed themselves an independent nation—the Confederate States of America.

President Lincoln wanted to preserve the Union, and he hoped it could be done without war. In his inaugural address in March 1861, he addressed the Confederate States: "The issue of war is in your hands, my dissatisfied countrymen, not mine. The government will not attack you. You can have no conflict unless you begin it." The next month, Confederate troops attacked Union-held Fort Sumter in the harbor of Charleston, South Carolina. A civil war had begun.

For four years, civil war raged. The North had a larger population than the South, more factories to arm and supply its soldiers, and more railroads to transport soldiers and supplies. The superior military ability of southern generals could not withstand these advantages. On April 9, 1865, General Robert E. Lee, the southern commander, surrendered to General Ulysses S. Grant, the northern commander.

During the course of the war, President Lincoln had issued the Emancipation Proclamation, freeing slaves in states controlled by the Confederacy. The Thirteenth Amendment to the United States Constitution abolishing all slavery was ratified in December 1865.

Most of the fighting in the war had taken place on southern soil, leaving the South in a desperate economic condition. Its agriculture was destroyed, and major cities, such as Atlanta and Richmond, lay in ruins. Many white southerners were now impoverished, as were the newly freed slaves.

In the 12 years following the war, federal troops were stationed in much of the South, a lingering reminder of bitter defeat. During this period, known as the Reconstruction, the occupying forces tried to enforce laws guaranteeing equality for blacks. But gradually northerners, who had once wanted to punish the South for the war, seemed to lose interest. By 1877, all federal troops had been removed.

Slowly, the South recovered from the war. Cities were rebuilt, and new industries were started. By the early 1900s, a "New South" was emerging, one that was more economically diverse than the "Old South," which had relied on agriculture.

Economic Expansion

The period following the Civil War was one of great economic growth for all parts of the nation. The United States industrialized rapidly. By 1914, it had outpaced Great Britain, the early industrial leader. In 1914, the value of goods manufactured by factories in the Northeast and Middle West was 12 times greater than it had been in 1860.

Map Skill   *Railroads helped tie distant parts of the United States together. Which part of the country had the most north-south branches? Why was this so?*

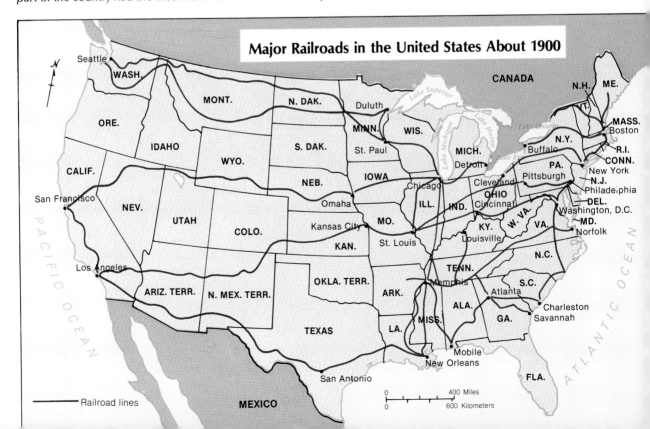

In the West, mining boomed. Huge deposits of gold, silver, and copper were discovered in Nevada, Colorado, and the Dakotas. Cattle-ranching became big business, especially in Texas. When a metal plow was developed that could cut through the tough sod of Kansas and Nebraska, farmers flocked to these states. The Great Plains eventually became one of the greatest grain-producing areas of the world.

The construction of railroads contributed to economic expansion in the United States as it did in Europe. The first transcontinental railroad was completed in 1869. The number of miles of railroad tracks crisscrossing the country increased by seven times by the end of the century. Manufactured goods flowed westward from eastern factories. Texas cattle were shipped to meat-packing plants in Chicago and St. Louis. The grain harvested on the Great Plains was sent by railroad to eastern markets and to seaports from which it was shipped overseas. (See the map on page 477.)

Money from European investors had financed much early industry in the United States. However, American profits and investments grew rapidly. By the early 1900s, Americans were investing millions of dollars in Europe.

During the last years of the 1800s, business in the United States truly became "big business." Giant corporations such as United States Steel and Standard Oil established virtual monopolies over the production and sale of certain products. Corporations also joined together to form trusts that controlled entire industries. Because trusts could produce goods at low cost, they could reduce prices and drive competitors out of business.

American Workers

The ever-expanding economy demanded large numbers of workers. One source of workers was immigrants. Between 1860 and 1910, about 23 million immigrants from Europe, Asia, and other parts of the world

Between 1860 and 1910, about 23 million immigrants arrived in the United States. Passage to the United States often cost a person the savings of a lifetime. Most immigrants traveled in the cheapest way possible—on the steerage deck of crowded steamships like the S.S. Permland shown here. The steady flow of immigrants helped transform the country into a great industrial power.

poured into the United States. Many came in search of political freedom. All hoped to find a better life. The native-born population of the United States also increased rapidly during the late 1800s.

As a result, American cities grew at a phenomenal rate. Boston and Philadelphia doubled in size; New York and Pittsburgh tripled. The population of Cleveland and Detroit grew by six times, and the population of Chicago grew by seven times. For the first time, as many Americans lived in cities as lived in rural areas.

Rapid industrialization and the growth of cities in the United States resulted in many of the same problems found in Europe. Factory workers often faced long hours, low wages, dangerous working conditions, and deplorable living conditions. Labor unions developed in response to these problems.

The path to labor organization in the United States was a rocky one. Opposition to labor unions came from different quarters. Employers objected to unions because they felt that unions hampered their freedom to run their businesses as they saw fit. Some Americans objected to labor unions because they thought organized workers' groups denied traditional American values such as "rugged individualism." Many Americans were suspicious of labor unions because many immigrants joined them. As a result, unions were often considered un-American.

Nevertheless, efforts to organize labor continued, although they were often marked by violence between employers and workers. In 1881, the American Federation of Labor (AFL) was founded. The AFL was a "union of unions" made up of hundreds of smaller, self-governing unions that joined together to gain greater strength. By 1914, AFL membership had grown to over 2 million workers.

SECTION REVIEW

1. Locate: Louisiana Purchase, Mississippi River, Rocky Mountains, Oregon Country, Gadsden Purchase.

2. Identify: Thomas Jefferson, Manifest Destiny, Abraham Lincoln, Emancipation Proclamation, AFL.

3. From which nations did the United States acquire territory between 1819 and 1867?

4. In the early 1800s, what groups did not have the right to vote in the United States?

5. What two issues caused tension between the North and South after 1820?

6. (a) How were the slaves freed in the Confederate states? (b) How were they freed in the rest of the nation?

7. How did railroads contribute to economic growth in the United States?

5 Reform in the United States

Read to Learn
- what the progressives accomplished
- how the United States became a world power

The growth of labor unions was only one sign of a growing desire for reform in the United States. By the end of the 1800s, many Americans thought that reform was needed to solve problems in government, cities, and industry.

An Age of Reform

Among the leaders of the reform movement in the early 1900s were the progressives. Progressives were reformers who believed that progress was possible, and they intended to work for it. They attacked widespread corruption in government, pointing to corrupt city officials who stole city funds and accepted bribes. They also criticized the attempts by big business to eliminate competition. Trusts were a special target of the progressives.

Between 1900 and 1914, progressives met with much success in their efforts to reform state and local governments. Several notoriously corrupt mayors lost elections to reform-minded candidates. A number of states adopted measures, including the direct primary and recall, that gave voters more direct control of government. In a *direct primary*, voters select candidates for office. Previously, candidates for office had been chosen by a few party bosses. A *recall* is a vote that allows voters to remove elected officials from office if they are considered incompetent.

Progressive reforms also began to limit the power of big business. President Theodore Roosevelt, who came into office in 1901, was a leader in this effort. Roosevelt encouraged government prosecution of several large trusts. He also supported laws that allowed the government to regulate businesses to protect the public. For example, the Pure Food and Drug Act, passed in 1906, forbade the use of harmful additives in food.

Improving the Quality of Life

The progressives were appalled by the squalid living conditions in most of the rapidly growing industrial cities. They encouraged city governments to establish building

Social critic Jacob Riis took many photographs that recorded city life in the United States. In this photograph, immigrant schoolchildren salute the American flag. Public education helped many immigrants rise out of poverty. They learned English and developed strong patriotism for their new country.

codes that set minimum standards for space, light, sanitation, and fire safety. Reformers such as Jane Addams and Lillian Wald organized settlement houses in city slums to improve the life of the poor. For example, Addams' Hull House in Chicago offered English lessons to immigrants and set up nursery schools for children of working mothers.

Education helped many people rise out of poverty. The number of American school children more than doubled between 1870 and 1910. By the early 1900s, most Americans believed that children had a right to a free public education.

Progressives and other reformers fought for improvements in the lives of factory workers. Some states passed labor legislation such as accident insurance. The federal government set limits on working hours for some occupations. However, the type of wide-ranging labor reforms found in Britain and Germany were not instituted in the United States.

Some labor legislation that did pass was aimed at protecting women who worked outside the home. Women had worked in American factories and mills since the 1700s. Inventions such as the telephone and the typewriter opened up new professions, which many women entered. As a result, the number of women in the business world grew dramatically. As women became more economically independent, they demanded equal political rights—especially the right to vote. By 1915, most states allowed women to vote, but a federal constitutional amendment guaranteeing the right to vote to all women in the United States was not approved until 1920.

Black Americans also sought political equality. The Fourteenth Amendment to the Constitution had guaranteed blacks all the rights of citizenship, and the Fifteenth Amendment had guaranteed black men the right to vote. However, in the late 1800s, southern states passed laws that made it difficult or impossible for blacks to vote. One such law, for example, stated that a man could vote only if his father or grandfather had been eligible to vote in 1867, three years before the Fifteenth Amendment was ratified.

Higher education was crucial to black Americans in their struggle to overcome discrimination. This photograph shows the chemistry laboratory at Tuskegee Institute in Alabama. Under the leadership of Booker T. Washington, Tuskegee flourished as a center of black education.

In other parts of the nation, black men kept their right to vote, but they faced economic and social discrimination. Some people violently opposed the demands of black Americans for equality, and anti-black riots resulted in a number of communities. In 1909, after a riot in Springfield, Illinois, a group of black and white reformers formed the National Association for the Advancement of Colored People (NAACP). The NAACP set out to end discrimination against black Americans. It fought for laws to protect the rights of blacks, and it defended these rights in the courts.

A New World Role

For most of the 1800s, the United States had followed George Washington's advice and had avoided close involvement in European affairs. As the United States became a large industrialized nation, however, its contacts with other parts of the world increased. American industries needed raw materials

from around the world. They also needed foreign markets in which to sell their goods.

In 1898, Albert J. Beveridge, a senator from Indiana, described the American position: "American factories are making more than the American people can use. American soil is producing more than they can [eat]. . . . The trade of the world must and shall be ours."

In part, to protect the nation's growing international trade, the government began to build up the navy. By 1900, the United States had become the third greatest naval power in the world. At the time, the size of a nation's navy was widely recognized as an indication of its power.

In addition to trade, Americans began taking a more active interest in political developments throughout the world. Some Americans believed that the United States had a mission to carry democracy to other peoples and to enforce peace, especially in the Western Hemisphere. These attitudes made the United States more willing than before to take a direct hand in the affairs of other nations. The United States would also acquire overseas territories in the late 1800s, as you will read in Chapters 28 and 29.

SECTION REVIEW

1. Identify: progressives, Jane Addams, NAACP.
2. Define: direct primary, recall.
3. How did President Theodore Roosevelt try to limit the power of big business?
4. What types of service did settlement houses such as Hull House provide?
5. Which constitutional amendment granted black men the right to vote?
6. How did industrialization increase American involvement in world affairs?

Chapter 25 Review

In Perspective

During the second half of the 1800s, governments became more democratic in Great Britain, France, and the United States. In Britain, first middle class men and then working class men won the right to vote. As the right to vote was extended, Parliament passed social and economic legislation to protect workers from some of the hardships of industrialization. Democracy also grew in parts of the British Empire.

The French did not achieve democratic government as smoothly as the British. The Second Empire under Napoleon III began as a repressive regime, although Napoleon eventually allowed an elected assembly to exercise some power. Adventures in foreign policy brought the Second Empire down, and the Third Republic was proclaimed. However, bitter political disputes marred the early years.

Democracy grew in the United States as did the nation itself. However, divisions between the North and the South led to a Civil War that devastated half the nation. After the Civil War, the American economy expanded dramatically, and the United States became an industrial leader. As in Europe, rapid industrialization caused political, social, and economic problems, which reformers such as the progressives tried to solve. The United States took a more active role in world affairs by the end of the 1800s.

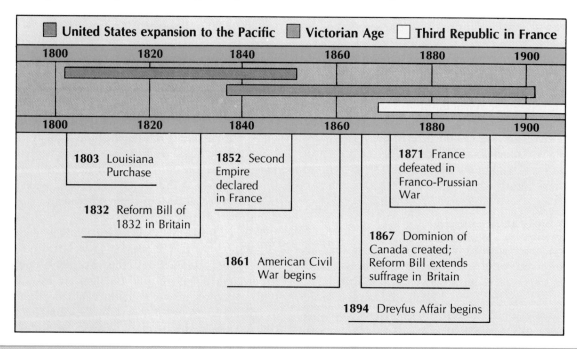

■ United States expansion to the Pacific   ■ Victorian Age   □ Third Republic in France

| 1800 | 1820 | 1840 | 1860 | 1880 | 1900 |

1803 Louisiana Purchase

1832 Reform Bill of 1832 in Britain

1852 Second Empire declared in France

1861 American Civil War begins

1871 France defeated in Franco-Prussian War

1867 Dominion of Canada created; Reform Bill extends suffrage in Britain

1894 Dreyfus Affair begins

Recalling Facts

Choose the word or phrase that best completes each of the following statements.

1. The Corn Laws were repealed because of (a) the Reform Bill of 1832; (b) crop failures; (c) the efforts of wealthy landowners.

2. The Reform Bill of 1867 extended the vote to (a) urban working men; (b) middle class men; (c) rural working men.

3. Home rule for Ireland was a demand of (a) Protestants in Ulster; (b) Scottish landlords; (c) Irish Catholics.

4. Napoleon III installed Maximilian as emperor of (a) France; (b) Mexico; (c) Prussia.

5. Real political power in the French Third Republic was in the hands of (a) the cabinet of ministries; (b) the Catholic Church; (c) the president.

6. In 1845, the United States annexed (a) Florida; (b) California; (c) Texas.

7. Progressives supported (a) the direct primary; (b) trusts; (c) monopolies.

Chapter Checkup

1. (a) How did the selection of members of the British Parliament become more democratic during the 1800s? (b) Which political parties supported the growth of democracy? Why? (c) How was the power of the House of Lords limited in the early 1900s?

2. (a) How did Irish Catholics react to Protestant political and economic control of Ireland during the 1800s? (b) What was the response of the British government to Irish demands?

3. (a) Why did Napoleon III try to create a "Liberal Empire" in France? (b) Was he successful? Explain.

4. (a) How was the Third Republic created in France? (b) Why did the circumstances surrounding its creation threaten its existence? (c) What crises did it face during the late 1800s?

5. (a) Describe the expansion of the United States between 1803 and 1853. (b) How did this expansion contribute to tensions between the North and the South? (c) How did the election of Abraham Lincoln lead to a split in the Union?

6. (a) What were the sources of labor for American industry during the late 1800s? (b) How did rapid industrialization affect American workers?

7. (a) How did progressive political reforms make American government more democratic? (b) What steps did reformers take to improve the quality of life in American cities?

Critical Thinking

1. **Analyzing** (a) Describe how Canada gained its independence from Great Britain. (b) How does it compare with the way the United States gained its independence? (c) How might you explain the difference?

2. **Expressing an Opinion** Reread the special feature on page 466. Then answer the following questions: (a) What militant actions did the Pankhursts take to win the right to vote for women? (b) Why did they feel such actions were necessary? (c) Do you think their actions were justified? Explain.

3. **Synthesizing** Review the growth of democracy in Great Britain and France. Why do you think instituting democratic reforms was more difficult in France than in Britain?

Relating Past to Present

1. (a) What rights and benefits did workers in Great Britain win in the late 1800s and early 1900s? (b) Which of those rights and benefits do American workers have today?

Developing Basic Skills

1. **Map Reading** Study the map on page 476 and then answer the following questions: (a) What does the map show? (b) What territory did the United States acquire in 1819? In 1848? (c) By what methods did the United States acquire territory between 1819 and 1853? (d) By which method did the United States acquire the most territory?

2. **Graph Reading** Study the graph on page 471 and then answer the following questions: (a) What is the subject of the graph? (b) About how much iron did France produce in 1895? (c) About how much iron did the United States produce in 1900? (d) Which country was the largest producer of iron in 1885? In 1910? (e) What conclusions about industrial development in these four countries can you draw from this graph?

See page 806 for suggested readings.

26 The Triumph of Nationalism

(1848–1914)

Arrival of King Victor Emmanuel in Parma, Italy, May 1860.

Trouble flared in Milan, the capital of Lombardy, over of all things, Austrian cigars. Cigars were a major source of revenue for the Austrians who ruled Lombardy. To protest foreign control of their province, the residents of Milan refused to smoke cigars.

On January 3, 1848, Austrian authorities responded to this defiance by issuing cigars to their soldiers and telling them to smoke the cigars in the streets of Milan. That afternoon, enraged Italians attacked the cigar-smoking soldiers with angry words, flying fists, and rocks. The Austrian troops answered with drawn swords. By the end of the day, Milan's hospitals were filled with injured and dying Italian patriots. The tense city edged toward rebellion. Overnight, the cigar became a symbol of Italian nationalism.

In the next month, news of uprisings in France reached Milan, making the mood of Italian patriots even uglier. The moment to throw off the yoke of Austrian rule and create a democratic Italy seemed at hand. On March 17, a large crowd gathered outside the Austrian government headquarters. Nervous at the sight, Austrian soldiers fired a blank volley to disperse the crowd. Shouting "Viva Italia" ("Long live Italy"), a boy of sixteen fired his pistol at the troops. The mob rushed forward, quickly overpowering the guards.

The Austrians were able to crush the uprising in Milan, but their victory was short-lived. The citizens of Milan were driven by nationalism, one of the most powerful forces during the 1800s. Between 1848 and 1914, nationalism played a key role in events in Central and Eastern Europe. In some areas, it led to the unification of national groups. In other areas, nationalism threatened the stability of large, diverse empires.

1 The Unification of Italy

Read to Learn ■ how Italy became unified
■ what problems Italy faced after unification

In 1815, Prince Metternich of Austria called Italy "a geographic expression." But to many people living on the Italian peninsula, it was much more than that. They looked back to the glorious days of the Roman Empire and to the days when Italian city-states were at the center of the Renaissance. Nationalists yearned for a unified Italy and a return to past glories.

Nationalism in Italy

Italian nationalism had roots in the French Revolution, with its ideals of liberty, equality, and fraternity. Furthermore, Napoleon Bonaparte had combined small Italian states into larger kingdoms. (See the map on page 410.) This gave Italians a taste of unity.

After the Congress of Vienna, however, most of Italy was under foreign rule. Austria ruled Venetia and Lombardy directly, and Austrian princes ruled in Parma, Lucca, Modena, and Tuscany. The Congress of Vienna had set up the Spanish Bourbon family as rulers of the kingdom of the Two Sicilies.

Italian nationalists struggled for independence and unity throughout the 1830s and 1840s. In 1831, one nationalist leader, Giuseppe Mazzini (mah ZEE nee), founded a secret society called Young Italy to work for unification. Mazzini wanted Italy to be a republic. "I give my name to Young Italy," he proclaimed, "and swear to dedicate myself to [making] Italy one free . . . republican nation."

Other nationalists favored a unified Italy led by the kingdom of Sardinia.* Count Camillo Cavour led this group. He edited a newspaper called *Il Risorgimento* (ree SOHR jee MEHN toh), meaning the resurgence or revival. Eventually, the entire movement for Italian unity was called the Risorgimento.

Nationalist attempts to rid Italy of foreign rule in 1848 failed, as you read in Chapter 22. However, Sardinia emerged from the revolutions of 1848 as leader of the struggle for unification. Furthermore, Victor Emmanuel II, who became king of Sardinia in 1849, was a staunch supporter of Risorgimento.

The First Steps

Victor Emmanuel gave the cause of Italian unification an enormous boost when he named Count Cavour his prime minister in 1852. Cavour, a skillful politician, wanted Sardinia to be a model for Italian unification. Therefore, he instituted road- and canal-building projects, land reforms, and new tariff policies. This resulted in rapid economic growth. Sardinia was soon recognized as an emerging power.

The Crimean War. Cavour also believed that tough, practical international diplomacy was essential to unification. He saw the Crimean War, which broke out in 1854, as a chance to win the allies he needed to drive Austria out of Italy.

France and Britain had declared war on Russia to prevent Russia from gaining too much influence over the weak Ottoman Empire. Sardinia entered this war on the side of France and Britain, who emerged victorious in 1856. Sardinia's participation had two important results. First, Sardinia participated in the peace conference. Cavour used the conference as a stage from which to publicize the demand for Italian unification. Second, Cavour won the support of Napoleon III of France in his effort to end Austrian influence in Italy.

War with Austria. In 1858, Cavour met secretly with Napoleon III to plot a strategy against Austria. Their plan was to trick Austria into declaring war on Sardinia. Then France would send troops to help Sardinians. In return, Sardinia agreed to give Savoy and Nice to France.

---

* As you can see from the map on page 487, the kingdom of Sardinia included the island of Sardinia plus Piedmont, Nice, and Savoy on the mainland. The capital, Turin, was located in Piedmont.

The following year the plan went into action. By encouraging nationalist revolts in the Austrian provinces of Lombardy and Venetia, Cavour provoked Austria into declaring war. As promised, the French sent troops. Following bloody battles at Magenta and Solferino, the French and Sardinians drove Austria from Lombardy.

At this point, Napoleon III suddenly withdrew his support because he thought a completely unified Italy might be a threat to France. Therefore, he negotiated a separate peace treaty with Austria. According to this treaty, Sardinia won Lombardy, but Venetia remained under Austrian control. The status of other states in northern Italy remained unchanged. Soon, however, the people of these states took action themselves. Several states held plebiscites, or popular votes, demanding unification with Sardinia. In this way, Tuscany, Modena, Parma, and the papal province of Romagna joined Sardinia.

Unification Completed

Meanwhile, in southern Italy, the nationalist movement was growing under the leadership of Giuseppe Garibaldi, a dashing military commander. Garibaldi, who had belonged to Young Italy, wanted nothing less than a completely unified Italy with a republican form of government.

In 1860, with the unofficial approval of Sardinia, Garibaldi formed a volunteer army of over 1,000 "Red Shirts," so-named for the color of their uniforms. Their objective was

Garibaldi and his Red Shirts helped free Sicily and all of southern Italy from foreign control. On May 11, 1860, Garibaldi and his forces landed in western Sicily. As they marched inland, recruits flocked to the cause. Four days after landing, Garibaldi's Red Shirts won the battle at Calatafimi, pictured here. Within two weeks, Garibaldi had taken the city of Palermo and set up a provisional government in Sicily.

to attack the kingdom of the Two Sicilies and drive out the Bourbon rulers. "To arms," Garibaldi urged Italian patriots. "Let me put an end, once and for all, to the miseries of so many centuries. Prove to the world that it is no lie that Roman generations inhabited this land."

Garibaldi and his Red Shirts landed on the island of Sicily and conquered it in a daring, brief military campaign. Then they sailed to the mainland, where once again they were victorious. The Bourbon forces fled before the Red Shirts, and Garibaldi triumphantly entered Naples.

Next, Garibaldi turned his attention toward Rome and the Papal States, which were under French protection. At this point, Cavour stepped in. He was afraid an attack on Rome would offend Italians as well as the French government. Cavour sent a Sardinian army to Naples to block Garibaldi. Cavour convinced Garibaldi to turn over Sicily and Naples to Victor Emmanuel. By the end of 1860, Sardinia had annexed Sicily, Naples, and two outlying papal provinces.

In March 1861, a parliament representing all of Italy except Venetia and Rome and its surrounding lands met in Turin. The parliament proclaimed the kingdom of Italy with Victor Emmanuel as king. Three months later, just as the unification of Italy neared completion, Cavour died.

In 1866, Italy joined Prussia in a brief war against Austria. When Prussia won, Italy acquired Venetia from Austria. Four years later, Prussia and France went to war, and France was forced to withdraw its troops from Rome. Italian troops entered the city in September 1870, and the people of Rome voted for annexation to the kingdom of Italy. Nine years after the death of Cavour, his dream of unifying the entire Italian peninsula had at last come true.

Problems of a Unified Italy

Unfortunately, unification created problems for Italy. Pope Pius IX was angry at losing control of Rome and the Papal States. He withdrew into the Vatican and urged Italian Catholics not to cooperate with their new

The Unification of Italy, 1858–1870

Map Skill   *Italy was united between 1858 and 1870. By 1860, most Italian states had united with Sardinia. In 1861, they declared themselves the kingdom of Italy. What area was added to Italy in 1866? In 1870?*

government. This action strained relations between the Catholic Church and the Italian state. It also put pressure on those people who wanted to be loyal both to Italy and the Catholic Church.

Unification increased antagonism between people living in the north and the south. Southern Italians resented the fact that Sardinians dominated the government. Economic differences contributed to the differences between north and south. While the north began to industrialize, the south remained rural and poor.

487

This cartoon illustrates Garibaldi's contribution to Italian unification. Garibaldi is fitting the boot of Italy onto the foot of Victor Emmanuel, advising him: "If it won't go on Sire, try a little more powder."

Ardent republicans such as Garibaldi disliked the government of the new nation. Although Italy had a constitution that limited the power of the king and an elected parliament, only a few men had the right to vote. Of 20 million people, only about 600,000—fewer than 1 in 30—could vote.

Some Italian nationalists were unhappy with unification because they thought it was not complete. They agitated for the addition of Trentino, Trieste, and Dalmatia, still controlled by Austria, as well as for Savoy and Nice, which France ruled. Nationalists called these areas, "Italia irredenta," which means "Italy still unredeemed." The "Italia irredenta," like the other problems of unified Italy, would contribute to unrest and instability in the future.

SECTION REVIEW

1. Locate: Venetia, Lombardy, kingdom of the Two Sicilies, kingdom of Sardinia, Savoy, Nice.

2. Identify: Young Italy, Count Camillo Cavour, Risorgimento, Victor Emmanuel, Giuseppe Garibaldi, Red Shirts, "Italia irredenta."

3. How did the French Revolution affect Italian nationalism?

4. Why did Sardinia become involved in the Crimean War?

5. (a) How did Sardinia gain Lombardy? (b) How did it gain other states in northern Italy?

6. List three problems Italy faced after unification.

2 The Unification of Germany

Read to Learn
■ why Prussia led the effort to unify Germany
■ how Bismarck unified Germany

Like the Italians, the Germans were divided into many separate states in 1815. The German Confederation, created by the Congress of Vienna, included 39 loosely grouped independent nations. But many Germans wanted a unified nation. Attempts by nationalists and liberals to unite Germany in 1848 failed, as you read in Chapter 22. During the following years, there continued to be serious obstacles to German unity.

Obstacles to Unity

The presence of Austria in the German Confederation was one of the most serious obstacles to German unity. Austria opposed attempts to unify Germany, fearing it would lose influence among the German states, especially those that bordered Austria in the south. In addition, Austria feared competition if a powerful German nation were created in Central Europe. For the same reason, other countries, especially France and Russia, did not want to see the German states united.

Many smaller German states also opposed unification. They feared Prussian control of a united Germany. Catholic states in southern Germany were especially concerned about domination by Protestant Prussia. Also, smaller German states wanted to protect their own customs and traditions. They did not want to be absorbed into a large nation.

Prussian Leadership

During the 1850s, Prussia emerged as the leader in the effort to unify Germany. Prussia had many advantages over other German states. Since the early 1700s, absolute rulers had made Prussia a strong and powerful state with a large disciplined army.

In the 1800s, the king and Junkers, or aristocratic landowners, controlled the Prussian government. Most government officials and army officers were Junkers. The constitution approved by the king in 1850 contained a provision for a parliament. But the Prussian parliament was dominated by wealthy Junkers, although a new class of industrial capitalists was gaining political influence.

The Industrial Revolution added greatly to Prussian economic strength. The Ruhr Valley in western Prussia contained the largest coal deposits in Europe. During the 1850s, this coal fueled the start of a prosperous Prussian iron and steel industry. Iron and steel production contributed to economic growth and allowed the government to construct an efficient system of railroads. In planning the railroads, the government worked closely with the military.

Government reforms in the first half of the 1800s helped strengthen the Prussian state. Although the constitution left power in the hands of the king and the Junkers, its very existence gave the Prussians a reputation for being somewhat progressive. The abolition of serfdom and the creation of a system of public education added to this reputation. However, these reforms did not mean that Prussia was either liberal or democratic. In fact, it was an authoritarian state that rigorously supported *militarism*, the glorification of the military and a readiness for war.

King William I, who came to the throne in 1861, wanted to make sure Prussia would remain both authoritarian and militaristic. To help him, the king appointed Count Otto von Bismarck as prime minister and minister of foreign affairs.

Bismarck's "Blood and Iron"

Bismarck came from a conservative Junker family. A former military officer, he believed firmly in royal power. Although Bismarck had served in the Prussian parliament, he had no respect for representative government or for liberals. "Germany does not look to Prussia's liberalism," he said, "but to her power."

Bismarck and William I shared the goal of uniting Germany under Prussian control. They wanted a unified Germany to be the most powerful nation in Europe. These goals, Bismarck insisted, would be achieved "not with speeches and majority decisions . . . but with blood and iron."

By "blood and iron," Bismarck meant warfare and the military. Once in office, he began to carry out the king's plan to expand the army. However, the lower house of parliament had to approve the budget to pay for the expansion, and it refused. Bismarck would not let parliament stand in his way. He simply claimed that the government did not need parliament's approval. According to the constitution, Bismarck was wrong, but he ignored the constitution and collected taxes to pay military expenses anyway.

In this matter as in all others, Bismarck followed a policy of "Realpolitik," a German word meaning realism. He took whatever political action he thought necessary, whether or not it was legal or ethical. He freely applied the policy of Realpolitik in the process of creating a united Germany.

First Steps

Bismarck's first step toward unification was to weaken Austria. Ironically, he began his campaign against Austria by forming a military alliance with it.

War over Schleswig-Holstein. In 1864, Prussia and Austria joined forces to seize the provinces of Schleswig and Holstein, which were ruled by the king of Denmark. (See the map on page 491.) Despite fierce resistance from the Danish army, the Austrians and Prussians quickly overran the provinces. According to the treaty that ended the war, Austria would administer Holstein, and Prussia would administer Schleswig.

Bismarck was pleased with the outcome of the war. First, it expanded Prussian influence. Second, the division of the spoils of war soon created trouble between Prussia and Austria. This gave Bismarck an excuse to go to war with Austria.

War with Austria. Before going to war with Austria, Bismarck wanted to make certain that other nations would not support Austria. He made vague promises of ceding territory to France to make sure the French stayed out of any conflict. The Russians also promised neutrality after Bismarck reminded them that Prussia had helped suppress an anti-Russian uprising in Poland in 1863. By promising Venetia to Italy if Austria were defeated, he won Italian support.

In 1866, Bismarck used a dispute over Holstein to provoke Austria into war. Prussian troops marched into Holstein, and Austria declared war. Austrian forces were no match for the highly disciplined Prussian army under brilliant military leadership. The Prussians moved troops rapidly by railroad. They also used new rapid-firing weapons such as a needle gun that fired five rounds per minute. In just seven weeks, the war was over. Observers were stunned at the speed with which the Prussians defeated the Austrians in the Seven Weeks' War.

Bismarck did nothing to humiliate Austria after the Seven Weeks' War. "We had to avoid leaving behind in her any . . . desire for revenge," he wrote later. He followed a fairly lenient policy. Austria lost Venetia to Italy and was forced out of the German Confederation, which was then disbanded. Several states, including Schleswig and Holstein, were annexed by Prussia. One year later, the 21 German states north of the Main River joined a North German Confederation led by Prussia. (See the map on page 491.)

The Franco-Prussian War

After the war with Austria, only the Catholic states of southern Germany remained outside Prussian control. Suspicion of Prussia was strong in these states. They valued their independence and did not want to be dominated by a Protestant nation. But people in the southern states also feared control by France. Bismarck decided to play on these fears. He convinced the southern German states to form a military alliance with Prussia for protection against France. Such a military alliance, he hoped, would eventually lead to political unity. Moreover, he believed that war with France would guarantee this result.

France also seemed to want war. France had suffered several disastrous foreign adventures, and Napoleon III faced growing domestic problems. (See page 471.) Napoleon was alarmed at the growing power of Prussia and hoped that a successful war would save his failing regime.

A minor dispute over who would assume the throne of Spain led to war between Prussia and France. In 1868, the Spanish government had offered the throne to Leopold of Hohenzollern, a cousin of William I. This angered the French, who did not want to see a Hohenzollern as king of Spain. A French ambassador visited William I at his vacation retreat at Ems and demanded that the Prussian king promise that no Hohenzollern would ever accept the Spanish throne. William refused. Then he sent a telegram to Bismarck describing the meeting.

The crafty Bismarck saw his chance. He edited the Ems telegram so that it seemed that the Prussian king and the French ambassador had been rude to one another. Then Bismarck released the telegram to the

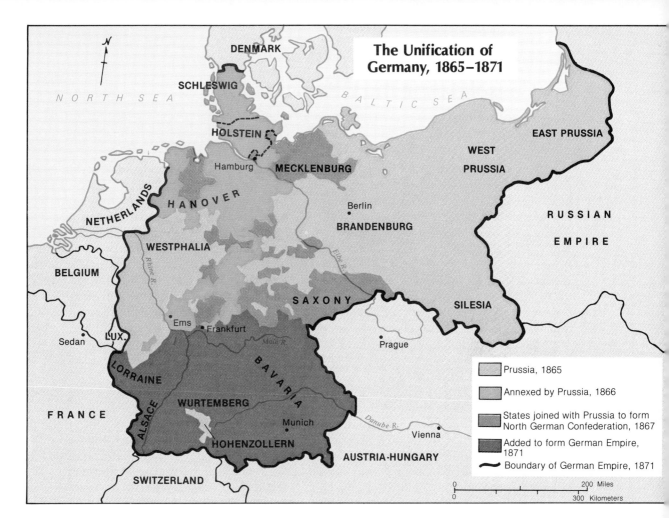

The Unification of
Germany, 1865–1871

Prussia, 1865

Annexed by Prussia, 1866

States joined with Prussia to form
North German Confederation, 1867

Added to form German Empire,
1871

Boundary of German Empire, 1871

Map Skill *Over a six-year period, Bismarck created a united Germany. Which areas were added to Germany in 1871? What long-time enemy was made as a result?*

press. People in both France and Prussia felt their nations had been insulted, and they clamored for war. On July 15, 1870, France declared war.

Once again, the Prussians could not be stopped. In September, they defeated the French army and took Napoleon III prisoner. By January 1871, all French resistance was crushed. The French had to sign a treaty giving up Alsace and part of Lorraine.

On January 18, 1871, at Versailles, William I was proclaimed kaiser, or emperor, of Germany. The new German Empire included all the members of the North German Confederation, the southern German states, and Alsace-Lorraine. German unification was complete, but the Germans had created a lasting enemy in France.

SECTION REVIEW

1. Locate: Schleswig, Holstein, Main River, Ems, Alsace, Lorraine.

2. Identify: William I, Otto von Bismarck, Real-politik, Seven Weeks' War.

3. Define: militarism.

4. What states opposed the unification of Germany under Prussian leadership?

5. Describe two reasons why Prussia led the effort to unify Germany.

6. What did Bismarck gain by going to war with Denmark?

7. What did Austria lose as a result of its defeat by Prussia in 1866?

8. (a) Why did Bismarck want war with France? (b) Why did Napoleon III want war with Prussia?

491

3 Consolidating the German Empire

Read to Learn ■ how Bismarck influenced the German Empire
■ what policies William II introduced

Following the Prussian victory over France, Bismarck needed to bind the German Empire together. Prussian Junkers were uncomfortable in the new German Empire because they feared losing their traditional privileges. Many Catholics distrusted the Protestant Prussians. Liberals and socialists disliked Bismarck's conservatism. Indeed, the forces of disunity were so great that some observers predicted a quick break-up of the German Empire. But these observers underestimated the political skills of Bismarck.

The New German Empire

The new German Empire was called the Second Reich.* The constitution of the Second Reich established a federation, a union of 25 states, each governed by its own hereditary king, prince, archduke, or duke. Each ruler appointed representatives to the upper house of a parliament called the Bundesrat (BOON duhs RAHT). The lower house, called the Reichstag (RĪKS tahg), was elected by male citizens over the age of 25.

The constitution appeared to create a representative government, but the appearance was deceiving. The Bundesrat could veto any decision made by the Reichstag. The emperor and his chancellor, or chief minister, controlled enough votes in the Bundesrat to determine its decisions. Thus, political power rested firmly in the hands of the emperor and the chancellor.

From the start, Prussia dominated the Second Reich. William I was king of Prussia as well as emperor, and he appointed Bismarck chancellor. Prussians were appointed to most top positions in the government of the empire. The Prussian tradition of compulsory military service was extended throughout the empire, with Prussian officers in charge of the army. These devel-

---

* "Reich" is the German word for empire. This empire was considered the Second Reich because Germans considered the Holy Roman Empire the First Reich.

opments won the support of Prussian Junkers for the Second Reich.

During the early years of the empire, Bismarck created a smooth-running empire. The legal systems of the different states were made uniform. The coining of money came under the control of one imperial bank, the Reichsbank. In addition, the railroad, mail, and telegraph systems of individual states were coordinated throughout the empire. Bismarck administered with a firm hand, earning the title Iron Chancellor.

Conflict Over Religion

Conflict soon developed between the strong central government and Catholics in Germany. Bismarck considered the Catholic Church a threat to government power. Catholics were a large minority in Germany, and their political party, the Center party, was the second strongest party in the Reichstag. In 1872, Bismarck launched an all-out attack on the Catholic Church. He called this attack the "Kulturkampf," meaning "struggle for civilization." Parliament passed laws expelling the Jesuit order from Germany. Members of the clergy were forbidden to criticize the government, and schools run by Catholic orders were closed.

But Bismarck soon realized that the Kulturkampf was a failure. Rather than weakening the Catholic Church, it united Catholics and strengthened the Center party. In 1878, Bismarck showed his political flexibility, and most of the anti-Catholic laws were repealed. Bismarck needed the support of the Center party because he faced a serious challenge from socialists.

Demands for Political and Social Reform

German liberals had initially been unhappy with the government of the Second Reich. They wanted a more democratic government with a truly representative parliament. Many admired the British constitutional monarchy. However, gradually, many German liberals came to support Bismarck. A major reason for this change was economic prosperity. Once Germany was unified, it experienced a period of rapid industrialization and economic growth that benefited the middle class and the industrial capitalists. Liberal feelings were strongest among these groups. But many liberals were willing to support Bismarck's government in return for economic well-being.

German workers were less enthusiastic about Bismarck and his programs. As in other nations, rapid industrialization in Germany resulted in poor living and working conditions for workers. In the 1870s, many workers supported the German Social Democratic party. The Social Democratic party, founded in 1869, promoted the ideas of Marxist socialism. (See page 451.) But many German Social Democrats were probably more interested in social and economic reform than in the violent revolution that Marx had predicted.

Bismarck hated and feared socialism, and he was determined to destroy it in Germany. In 1878, he pressured the Reichstag to pass laws restricting the Social Democrats. The laws forbade publication of socialist books and pamphlets. It also gave the police the right to break up socialist meetings and imprison socialist leaders. However, this repression only strengthened the socialists.

Bismarck then changed his tactics. He decided to defeat the Social Democratic party by introducing reforms to win the workers' support for the government. During the 1880s, the government introduced accident, health, and old age insurance for German workers. The German worker thus won a basic social security program from one of Europe's most conservative regimes. Despite Bismarck's plan, however, the Social Democrats continued to win election to the Reichstag.

A New Emperor

In 1888, the 29-year-old grandson of William I inherited the German throne as William II. (William II's father had died after a brief reign.) The new emperor believed firmly in the divine right of his family to govern Germany. He shared with Bismarck a belief that a strong Germany rested on a powerful monarchy as well as on a powerful army. At first, he kept the Iron Chancellor as his chief minister. But William II was an impulsive, self-centered man, and he resented Bismarck's domination. The young emperor was determined to be his own chief minister. In 1890, he forced Bismarck to resign after 28 years of service.

William II sought to win the support of all Germans, including the working class. He allowed the anti-socialist laws to lapse and

As a young man, William II admired Bismarck. But after he became kaiser, he often clashed with the Iron Chancellor. This cartoon compares William II's dismissal of Bismarck to a ship's captain putting the pilot ashore after a difficult voyage.

493

In 1811, Friedrich Krupp set up a small iron foundry in Essen, a town in the Ruhr Valley. Krupp employed four workers and experimented with making steel. In succeeding generations, the Krupp family expanded its iron works. By 1914, the Krupp works was the largest manufacturer of artillery, steel, and machinery in Germany, and the Krupp name was known throughout the world.

The growth of the Krupp works paralleled the growth of German industry in the 1800s. The Ruhr Valley was an area rich in iron and coal, minerals essential to the manufacture of steel. Alfred Krupp, son of the firm's founder, developed a process of manufacturing giant rolls of steel from which inexpensive seamless tableware could be made. He also discovered how to make seamless wheels for railroad cars.

In the 1840s, Alfred Krupp launched new ventures. He began manufacturing armaments, including muskets, rifles, and cannons. In 1849, the Prussian army tested the Krupp steel cannon. Krupp showed Prussian generals the benefits of his cannon, which was loaded through an opening in the side of the barrel. Krupp's cannon could be loaded more quickly and safely than the commonly used front loader. But Prussian generals distrusted the new steel barrel, and they did not order any Krupp cannons.

In 1860, the new Prussian king, William I, was impressed by the Krupp cannon, and he made the Prussian army Krupp's best cus-tomer. William's faith in Krupp was tested when Prussia declared war on Austria in 1866 and again during the Franco-Prussian war of 1870. By 1870, more than 500 Krupp cannons were in the Prussian arsenal. The power of these weapons helped assure Prussian victories.

After 1870, the success of Krupp was tied to the growing strength of the German nation and the rapid expansion of the German economy. From the blast furnaces of the Krupp works in Essen came weapons not only for Germany but also for armies all over the world.

extended the social insurance programs. No longer subject to repression, the Social Democratic party won widespread support and became the single largest party in the Reichstag. While it continued to demand more democracy, it became less revolutionary in outlook.

Under William II's personal, and often erratic, leadership, Germany set a new course in foreign policy. The ambitious ruler proposed to win Germany "a place in the sun" among great world powers such as Britain, France, and Russia. He wanted Germany to be a major commercial, colonial, and military power. He competed for colonies in Asia, Africa, and the Pacific.

Between 1892 and 1913, William II almost doubled the size of the army. He also devoted much attention to building a large navy that would rival the British navy. Both the army and navy benefited from increased German steel production. By 1900, Germany produced more steel than Britain. Only the United States produced more.

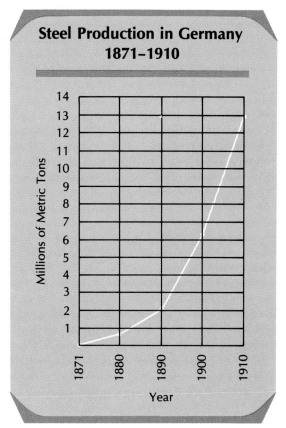

Steel Production in Germany 1871–1910

Millions of Metric Tons

14
13
12
11
10
9
8
7
6
5
4
3
2
1

1871 1880 1890 1900 1910

Year

Source: B.R. Mitchell, *European Historical Statistics.*

Graph Skill *Rising steel production was evidence of rapid economic growth in the German Empire. How does German steel production shown in this graph compare with German railroad construction and iron production shown on the graphs on pages 439 and 471?*

A National Spirit

During the late 1800s, Germans developed a strong sense of national pride. German military victories and economic progress con-tributed to this pride. By the turn of the century, Germany was the leading industrial nation in Europe.

Germans were also proud of their cultural heritage. They took special pride in renowned composers such as Beethoven and Wagner. Another source of national pride was the German educational system, which was considered the best in Europe by 1900. Students from all over the world flocked to German universities, which had a reputation for offering the most advanced scientific and technical education.

In many ways, Prussia still dominated German national life. Prussian respect and admiration for the military is one example of this dominance. As Germany became a major world power, the spirit of militarism increased. One writer summed up German attitudes toward the military in these words:

> After God the Father comes the cavalry officer, then his mount, then nothing, nothing, still nothing, then the infantry officer. Very far behind come the civilians: first the reserve officers and at last. . . . the remainder.

SECTION REVIEW

1. Identify: Second Reich, Bundesrat, Reichstag, William II.
2. Describe three ways in which Prussia dominated the Second Reich.
3. Was Bismarck's Kulturkampf successful? Why or why not?
4. What two tactics did Bismarck use in his effort to destroy socialism in Germany?
5. What were William II's foreign policy goals?

4 Repression and Reform in Russia

Read to Learn ■ how people lived under the Russian autocracy
■ what reformers demanded of the czars

By the mid-1800s, the Russian Empire sprawled from Europe to the Pacific Ocean. The economy and political system had changed little since the days of Peter the Great. The Russian czars and most aristocrats wanted to preserve the traditional or-der, but forces of change were at work in Russia as they were in other parts of Europe.

Russia in the Early 1800s

The agricultural economy of the Russian Empire was based on serfdom, as it had been for hundreds of years. Serfdom had been abolished in most of Europe by the mid-1800s, but in Russia 40 million serfs lived much as they had during the Middle Ages. Permanently attached to the land, serfs could be sold along with the land or used as domestic servants. Owners could force them to work in factories and take their wages. Runaway serfs could be brutally punished.

The system of serfdom was inefficient. Poor, ignorant serfs made reluctant workers. At the same time, many landowners were poor managers. As long as they had serfs to do the work, they did not want to introduce new farming techniques. As a result, Russian agriculture suffered.

The Russian Empire was an *autocracy*, that is, a government in which the ruler has unlimited power. However, it was difficult for the czar to extend autocratic rule over the vast empire, and laws were often enforced with highly repressive measures.

Strengthening the Autocracy

Alexander I, who became czar in 1801, was influenced by Enlightenment thinkers early in his reign. But when he realized that reform would weaken his power, he abandoned Enlightenment ideas. At the Congress of Vienna in 1815, Alexander was a strong defender of the traditional order.

The war against Napoleon had a lasting effect on Russians. Many of the officers who fought in Western Europe were impressed with what they saw there. Upon their return to Russia, some formed secret societies to discuss and spread ideas for reform. When Alexander I died in 1825, a group of army officers staged an uprising, called the Decembrist Revolt because it took place on December 26. The Decembrists demanded a constitutional monarchy. Quickly crushed, the revolt made a strong impression on the mind of Alexander I's successor, Nicholas I.

Nicholas I was determined to strengthen the autocracy during his reign. He did everything he could to stamp out opposition to the government. He gave secret police almost unlimited power over Russian life. People suspected of treason could be arrested, imprisoned, and deported without trial. The police censored newspapers and other written material to suppress subversive ideas. Universities were a special target because Nicholas was afraid students would adopt dangerous foreign ideas. The outbreak of the 1848 revolutions in other parts of Europe confirmed the czar's conviction that strict control was necessary in Russia.

A Period of Reform

Despite the efforts of Nicholas I to prevent change in Russia, demands for reform grew. Some Russians reacted against the years of repressive rule. Others began to realize that serfdom was inefficient. As Russia began to industrialize, factory owners could not find enough free workers because so many people were serfs. In addition, the number of serf revolts had increased.

When Russia was defeated in the Crimean War, many Russians blamed the defeat on the weaknesses of serfdom and the autocratic political system. Nicholas I died in the midst of the Crimean War and was succeeded by his son Alexander II. The new czar, like his father, believed firmly in the autocracy, but he thought that some reforms were needed to prevent revolution.

In 1861, Alexander II issued the Emancipation Edict freeing the serfs. The czar declared: "It is better to abolish serfdom from above than to wait until it is abolished from below." Serfs were given personal freedom, but they received no free land as many had hoped they would. Instead, the government paid landowners handsomely for their land. Then it parceled the land out to village communities, called *mirs*. The peasants who lived in the mirs had to pay the government for the land over a period of 49 years. Therefore, peasants were heavily in debt and seldom had enough land to farm efficiently. Consequently, Russian agriculture improved little.

The czar introduced other reforms. He relaxed censorship and restrictions on universities. The jury system was introduced, and regulations governing soldiers were

Before 1861, Russian nobles owned huge estates on which serfs lived and worked in virtual slavery. Nobles often led idle lives. They wasted time and money gambling and attending lavish parties. In this cartoon by French artist Gustave Doré, Russian nobles use bundles of serfs as bets in a card game.

made less harsh. The government also created local elected assemblies called *zemstvos.* Many zemstvos established schools and improved health care. In addition, through the zemstvos, some Russians gained experience in government.

The reforms of Alexander II encouraged revolutionary activity in Russia. During the 1870s, thousands of educated young people left the cities. They went into the countryside to convince peasants to support revolutionary goals. These populists, as they were called, had little success organizing the peasants. A few populists eventually formed political parties to work for revolution. The most radical populists formed a group called the People's Will. Its goal was the assassination of the czar. After several attempts, they finally succeeded in assassinating Alexander II in 1881.

A Return to Repression

Alexander III, who succeeded his father, moved quickly to crush revolutionaries and end reform. He reduced the powers of the zemstvos, restored strict censorship, and directed the secret police to seek out critics of the government.

Because of its vast size, the Russian Empire contained many ethnic minorities, including Ukrainians, Finns, Poles, and Jews. Many of these people opposed Russian rule. Alexander III wanted to strengthen the autocracy through a policy called Russification. The czar tried to force all people in the empire to use the Russian language and to adopt the Russian Orthodox religion.

The Jews were a special target of Russification. They were forbidden to own land and were forced to live in certain areas of the country. Government troops took part in *pogroms,* murderous raids on Jewish communities. This persecution drove hundreds of thousands of Jews out of Russia. Many immigrated to the United States.

In 1894, Nicholas II succeeded his father and continued his father's repressive policies. Nicholas II faced new unrest as Russia began to industrialize more rapidly. By 1900, Russia was the fourth largest iron producer in the world, and the number of industrial workers reached 2 million. Like workers in other countries, Russian workers labored long hours for little pay. Labor unions were illegal in Russia, but labor unrest led to numerous strikes, many of them violent.

The Revolution of 1905

As the new century dawned, Nicholas II sat uneasily on the throne. In addition to labor unrest, the government faced opposition from landless peasants, national minorities, and middle class liberals, who demanded a constitutional government. In addition, assassination of government officials by revolutionaries had become commonplace.

In 1904, war broke out between Russia and Japan. The two nations had been competing for influence in Manchuria and Korea. Nicholas II hoped that a Russian victory would ease discontent at home. But the Russians were soundly defeated by Japan. This humiliating defeat further increased tensions at home.

On January 22, 1905, a peaceful parade of workers approached the czar's palace in St. Petersburg. The workers wanted to present Nicholas II with a petition for better working conditions, greater personal liberties, and an elected national legislature. Some carried large pictures of the czar as a sign of their loyalty. They believed that only the czar could help improve their lot. But Nicholas saw the parade as a threat to his power. He hurriedly left the palace. But before he left, he ordered the soldiers to fire on the crowd. About 1,000 workers were killed on the day that became known as Bloody Sunday.

After Bloody Sunday, the discontent that had been building for years exploded.

The Russian people's faith in the czar was badly shaken by the events of Bloody Sunday. The massacre of unarmed demonstrators led to further protests and bloodshed in the Revolution of 1905. This painting shows mounted Russian soldiers charging a crowd and scattering them by using whips.

Russia was quickly engulfed in revolution. Riots and strikes swept industrial centers. Bands of peasants roamed the countryside, pillaging and burning mansions of nobles.

By October 1905, the clamor for more freedom and a democratic government was so loud that the czar reluctantly promised "freedom of person, conscience, assembly, and union." He approved the creation of a national assembly called the Duma. This and other concessions, he hoped, would end the violence. For a time, they did. The Revolution of 1905 came to an end. However, Nicholas never gave the Duma any real power. In 1906, he simply dismissed the first Duma when it would not cooperate with him.

The czar emerged from the Revolution of 1905 with his power largely intact. New Dumas were elected, but they were dominated by supporters of the autocracy. Nevertheless, between 1906 and 1911, the government introduced some reform. For example, the czar's chief minister, Peter Stolypin (stoh LEE puhn), began a program to help peasants buy their own land. But Stolypin was assassinated in 1911, and the government again became repressive. The problems left unsolved by the Revolution of 1905 remained as seeds for a future revolution.

SECTION REVIEW

1. Identify: Decembrist Revolt, Nicholas I, Alexander II, Alexander III, Russification, Nicholas II, Peter Stolypin.
2. Define: autocracy, mir, zemstvo, pogrom.
3. How was the system of serfdom inefficient?
4. Why did Nicholas I think he had to strengthen the autocracy?
5. What helped convince Alexander II to free the serfs?
6. How did Nicholas II respond to the Revolution of 1905?

5 Nationalism in Eastern Europe

Read to Learn   ■ how nationalism disrupted the Austrian Empire
■ why the Ottoman Empire declined

At the start of the 1800s, much of Eastern Europe was divided between the Austrian Empire and the Ottoman Empire. Nationalism, which helped create unity in Italy and Germany, threatened the unity of the Austrian and Ottoman empires. Each empire contained many different ethnic and religious groups. Between 1848 and 1914, nationalities in Eastern Europe agitated for self-rule or independence from the Austrians and the Ottomans. This situation contributed to tensions within the empires and throughout Europe.

The Austrian Empire

The Austrian Empire included more than 12 different nationalities. The Germans of Austria and the Magyars of Hungary were the two largest groups, but neither made up a majority in the empire. Other major nationalities included Poles, Czechs, Croatians, Slovaks, and Romanians. (See the map on page 500.)

The national groups within the Austrian Empire had a strong sense of pride in their own languages and customs. Most resented domination by the Austrians. As you read earlier, the Hapsburg rulers of Austria successfully crushed the nationalist revolts of 1848. (See page 422.) But this defeat did not end the agitation by nationalist groups for greater control of their own affairs.

Francis Joseph became emperor of Austria in 1848 at the age of 18. Throughout his long reign, which lasted until 1916, he sought ways to keep his diverse empire together. During the 1850s, he tried to end all nationalist agitation. However, setbacks in foreign policy forced him to consider a new policy.

In 1859, Austria lost Lombardy to Italy. In 1866, as a result of its rapid defeat by

Prussia, Austria lost its influence among the German states. (See page 490.) Although Francis Joseph continued to oppose nationalism, he realized that Austrians had to strengthen the empire at home. He decided to compromise with the Magyars.

Creation of the Dual Monarchy

The Magyars had long demanded greater *autonomy*, or self-government, within the Austrian Empire. Even though the Austrians had ignored these demands, the Magyars fought loyally with them in the war with Prussia. The Hungarian leader Francis Deák (DEH ahk) thought the time was right to win concessions from the emperor. Deák wanted Hungary to be recognized as a separate kingdom with its own territory and its own constitution.

Map Skill *Many different nationalities lived in Austria-Hungary, the Russian Empire, and the Ottoman Empire. Some major nationalities are shown on this map. Which nationalities lived in more than one country?*

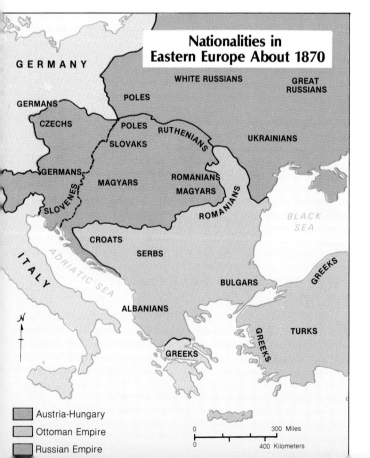

Nationalities in Eastern Europe About 1870

Austria-Hungary
Ottoman Empire
Russian Empire

0   300 Miles
0   400 Kilometers

In 1867, Francis Joseph agreed to the creation of a dual monarchy. The old Austrian Empire was divided into two parts: the empire of Austria and the kingdom of Hungary.

The Dual Monarchy of Austria-Hungary was united by a single ruler, the Hapsburg emperor, who would be the emperor of Austria and king of Hungary. Austria and Hungary shared ministries of war, finance, and foreign affairs, but in other areas they were independent of each other. Each had its own constitution and its own parliament.

The creation of the Dual Monarchy satisfied the Magyars, but other nationalities in Austria-Hungary remained dissatisfied. Austrians were a minority in Austria, and Magyars were a minority in Hungary. The Austrian government made minor concessions to other nationalities. But the Magyars tried to force everyone in Hungary to give up their own ethnic identity and become Magyars. The Romanians and the Slavs in Hungary felt especially oppressed by Magyar rule. The unrest among the nationalities in Austria-Hungary continued to threaten the unity of the empire and the peace in Europe.

Life in Austria-Hungary

In both Austria and Hungary, a small noble class dominated the political, economic, and social life. Nobles owned huge estates, while peasants had only small plots. For example, in 1895, fewer than 200 noble families owned over half the farmland in Austria-Hungary. At the same time, over 1 million peasants subsisted on seven acres or less per person.

Democracy made little headway in Austria-Hungary. For the most part, government remained in the hands of the wealthy nobles. Universal male suffrage was introduced in Austria in 1907. However, the elected parliament was paralyzed by division among the nationalities. Debates were sometimes accompanied by violent clashes between deputies, who threw inkwells at one another. In Hungary, voting was limited to 6 percent of the population. This prevented any effective challenge to the Magyar ruling class.

The economy of Austria-Hungary remained mainly agricultural during the 1800s.

Late in the century, Austria began to industrialize slowly, and Hungary followed behind.

The Ottoman Empire and the Balkans

The Ottoman Empire reached the height of its power in the 1500s, as you read in Chapter 18. But since that time it had steadily declined. Corruption in the wealthy ruling class was common.

The Ottoman Empire contained many nationalities who sought freedom from Ottoman rule. Gradually, portions of the empire had broken away. By 1850, Egypt and Arabia had gained autonomy within the empire, and Algeria was controlled by France. In the Balkans, Greece won independence in 1830, and Serbia and Montenegro gained autonomy.

In 1844, Czar Nicholas I called the Ottoman Empire "the sick man of Europe." Throughout the 1800s, many diplomats expected it to collapse, as one national group after another fought for independence. However, Britain and France worked to prevent a collapse. They considered the Ottoman Empire a block against the expansion of Russia or Austria-Hungary into the Balkan region. Therefore, in 1854, Britain and France entered the Crimean War on the side of the Ottoman Empire. They wanted to prevent the Russians from gaining control of Constantinople and the Dardanelles.

Although Russia was defeated in the Crimean War, the Ottoman Empire continued to decline. Rumania gained autonomy in 1859. In 1875, revolts against the Turks broke out in the Balkans. The Turks moved to suppress the revolts, but the Russians came to the aid of the Slavic peoples in the Balkans. In 1877, the Russians defeated the Turks and forced them to sign the Treaty of San Stefano. It gave the Russians the right to occupy a large, independent Bulgarian state.

Other European powers, fearing increased Russian influence in the Balkans, objected to the treaty. They pressured the Russians to attend an international congress at Berlin in 1878. The Congress of Berlin created a much smaller Bulgarian state, which was to be autonomous within the Ottoman Empire. Serbia, Romania, and Montenegro

Map Skill *In the 1800s, independent states were created in the Balkans. Compare this map to the one on page 358. Which states had been part of the Ottoman Empire?*

gained complete independence. Britain received Cyprus from the Ottoman Empire, and Austria-Hungary won the right to administer the areas of Bosnia and Herzegovina. (See the map above.)

The Congress of Berlin recognized new states in the Balkans, which pleased nationalists. However, it also caused much bitterness and left unfulfilled hopes. The Russians thought they had been cheated. Furthermore, the new states did not include all members of a nationality. For example, many Serbs lived in Hungary, while fellow Serbs had an independent nation across the border. The Balkans would continue to be a source of unrest and conflict.

A New International Order

The results of the Congress of Berlin reflected the new international order that had developed in Europe by the late 1800s. The emergence of new nations such as Germany and Italy and the decline of old empires upset the balance of power worked out at the Congress of Vienna in 1815. During the first half of the 1800s, the Austrian Empire under Metternich had been the dominant force in Europe. During the second half, Germany under Bismarck took the lead.

The international order was further affected by the Industrial Revolution, which had fueled economic growth in all parts of Europe, especially in Britain and Germany. Developments in technology led to new military weapons, which increased the capacity for war. Disputes over territory in Europe and the scramble for empires would cause conflict and war, as you will read.

SECTION REVIEW

1. Locate: Greece, Serbia, Montenegro, Bulgaria, Bosnia and Herzegovina.
2. Identify: Francis Joseph, Francis Deák.
3. Define: autonomy.
4. What two events led the Austrians to agree to the creation of the Dual Monarchy?
5. How were Austria and Hungary independent of each other in the Dual Monarchy?
6. Why did Britain and France want to preserve the Ottoman Empire?

Chapter 26 Review

In Perspective

Nationalism was a major force in Europe during the second half of the 1800s. Italian nationalists led a successful struggle for the unification of Italy. Once united, however, Italy still faced economic problems. Bismarck realized the goal of German unification through a series of wars with Denmark, Austria, and France. He tied the German states together into a powerful, prosperous empire.

In Russia, the czars tried to maintain their autocratic rule, but they found that some reform was necessary. Repressive political control, however, led to a revolution in 1905. The reforms carried out after the Revolution of 1905 had a limited effect.

Nationalism created problems for the Austrian and Ottoman empires. The Austrians created the Dual Monarchy but other nationalities continued to demand greater autonomy. Throughout the 1800s, parts of the Ottoman Empire broke away.

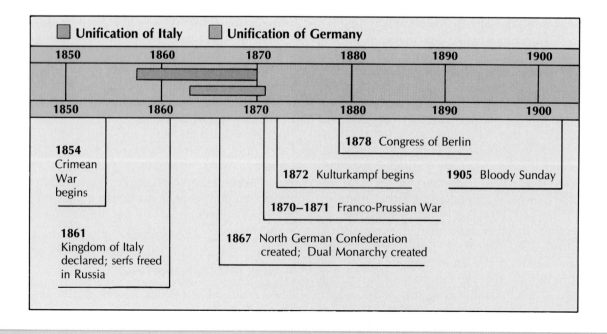

Unification of Italy   Unification of Germany

| 1850 | 1860 | 1870 | 1880 | 1890 | 1900 |

| 1850 | 1860 | 1870 | 1880 | 1890 | 1900 |

1854 Crimean War begins

1861 Kingdom of Italy declared; serfs freed in Russia

1878 Congress of Berlin

1872 Kulturkampf begins   **1905** Bloody Sunday

1870–1871 Franco-Prussian War

1867 North German Confederation created; Dual Monarchy created

Recalling Facts

Review the time line on page 502 and your reading in this chapter. Then choose the letter of the correct time period for each of the following events.

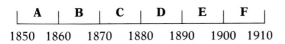

| A | B | C | D | E | F |
| 1850 | 1860 | 1870 | 1880 | 1890 | 1900 | 1910 |

1. Bismarck begins the Kulturkampf.
2. Serfs freed in Russia.
3. Crimean War breaks out.
4. Bloody Sunday takes place.
5. Austria-Hungary created.
6. Kingdom of Italy declared.
7. Cavour becomes prime minister of Sardinia.
8. Franco-Prussian War begins.

Chapter Checkup

1. (a) How did the goals of Young Italy and Cavour differ? (b) Which goal was achieved by 1870? (c) What groups were unhappy with the unification that was achieved? Why?

2. (a) What obstacles stood in the way of German unification? (b) How did Bismarck overcome these obstacles?

3. (a) In what ways was the government of the German Empire representative? (b) In what ways was it not representative?

4. (a) How did Bismarck try to strengthen the government of the German Empire? (b) How did William II try to win public support?

5. (a) Describe the system of serfdom in Russia. (b) How did the existence of serfdom affect agriculture? (c) What effect did emancipation have on the serfs?

6. Describe how each of the following tried to strengthen the autocracy in Russia: (a) Nicholas I; (b) Alexander III; (c) Nicholas II.

7. (a) How did nationalism threaten the existence of the Austrian Empire? (b) How did Austria deal with its national minorities? (c) How did Hungary deal with its national minorities?

8. What evidence convinced many diplomats that the Ottoman Empire was going to collapse during the 1800s?

Critical Thinking

1. **Comparing** Compare the ways in which Italy and Germany were unified. (a) What role did warfare play in the unification of each nation? (b) What role did international diplomacy play? (c) In which nation do you think a strong national leader was more important? Why?

2. **Analyzing** Otto von Bismarck believed that the key to German unity and power was "blood and iron." Which national leaders discussed in this chapter do you think would have agreed with Bismarck's philosophy? Explain.

Relating Past to Present

1. (a) Do any nations today have problems with national minorities? (b) How are these problems similar to problems faced by the Austrians? (c) How are they different?

Developing Basic Skills

1. **Analyzing Political Cartoons** Political cartoons can be valuable historical evidence. By analyzing political cartoons, you can learn how people at the time viewed public issues. Study the cartoon on page 488 and then answer the following questions: (a) What is the main topic of the cartoon? (b) What political figures are shown? (c) What does the boot represent? (d) Do you think the cartoonist approved of the events taking place in Italy? Explain.

2. **Map Reading** Study the map on page 491 and then answer the following questions: (a) What is the topic of the map? (b) Describe the area of Prussia in 1865. (c) What territory was added to Prussia in 1866? (d) Why do you think Austrian influence was greater among the southern German states than among the northern German states?

3. **Graph Reading** Study the graph on page 495 and then answer the following questions: (a) What information is shown on the graph? (b) How much steel did Germany produce in 1880? (c) How did German steel production change between 1871 and 1910? (d) How do you think steel production in Germany during this period probably affected economic development?

See page 806 for suggested readings.

The Age of Imperialism

The slave trade continued even after most European nations abolished it. In 1839, Cinque, the son of a Mendi chief from Sierra Leone, and a group of fellow captives seized control of a slave ship off the coast of Cuba.

During the Meiji period, Japanese art became known all over the world.

	1800	1825	1850
POLITICS AND GOVERNMENT		**1821** Mexico wins independence from Spain	**1850** In Taiping Rebellion, Chinese peasants demand land
ECONOMICS AND TECHNOLOGY		**1840** Opium War begins	**1853** Japanese trade isolation ends
SOCIETY AND CULTURE	**Early 1800s** Islam revives in West Africa		**1857** Hindu and Muslim soldiers revolt against British

1816 Officers like this one led the fight for Argentina's independence.

Before Japan was opened to trade, foreign ships could only dock in Nagasaki harbor.

Mexico and other Latin American nations inherited a rigid social structure from their days as Spanish colonies.

The French expected people in their African colonies to give up their traditions and become French. Here they are recruiting people from Madagascar for the French army.

1875	1900	1925
1868 Last shogun in Japan resigns	**1896** Ethiopians defeat Italians at Adowa	**1911** Manchu dynasty in China is overthrown
1869 Suez Canal completed	**1880s** Rinderpest leads to famine in East Africa	**1914** Panama Canal completed
1872 Japan introduces universal military service	**1898** Manchu emperor tries to reform schools	

Fine silk made by Chinese artisans, like those shown here, was in demand all over the world.

505

27 Africa in the Age of Imperialism

(1700–1914)

A European view of Africa about 1500.

In the late 1800s, Europeans entered a new era of overseas expansion. They explored and rapidly colonized much of the globe. In Africa, European expansion upset traditional patterns of life. In the novel *Things Fall Apart*, Nigerian writer Chinua Achebe (ah CHEE bee) writes about what happened in a village when Europeans arrived. The following excerpt is a conversation between a villager named Okonkwo and his friend.

" 'What has happened to that piece of land in dispute?' asked Okonkwo.

" 'The white man's court has decided that it should belong to Nnama's family, who had given much money to the white man's interpreter and messengers.'

" 'Does the white man understand our customs about land?'

" 'How can he when he does not even speak our tongue? But he says that our customs are bad; and our brothers who have taken up his religion also say that our customs are bad. How do you think we can fight when our brothers have turned against us? The white man is very clever. He came quietly and peaceably with his religion. We were amused at his foolishness and allowed him to stay. Now he has put a knife on things that held us together and we have fallen apart.' "

During the Age of Exploration, Europeans built a few trading posts on the coast of Africa, but for centuries they had little direct influence on the lives of most Africans. In the 1800s, a dramatic change occurred. The Industrial Revolution and the growth of nationalism strengthened European nations. In the 1870s, they were seeking new resources and markets. They found these resources and outlets in many parts of the world, including Africa.

1 A New Era of European Expansion

Read to Learn
- why imperialism developed in Europe
- how the scramble for Africa began

In the late 1800s, the industrial nations of Europe competed with one another for world empires. Within a few decades, European powers extended their control over much of the world. Africa, which had been largely unknown to Europeans, suddenly became the focus of attention.

Scramble for Africa

Until the 1870s, Europeans had little interest in Africa. In the 1600s and 1700s, the Portuguese and Dutch had established forts and trading posts along the African coast. The British and French had also acquired outposts. However, they used these posts only for trade, not as bases for conquest.

Between 1870 and 1914, a dramatic change occurred. With the exception of Liberia and Ethiopia, the entire African continent came under European rule. First, King Leopold II of Belgium acquired the Congo, today called Zaire. Then, the French moved into the interior of West Africa, and the British extended their control across much of the continent. Germany, Spain, Portugal, and Italy also entered the race for African territory.

The "scramble for Africa" brought European powers to the brink of war. To settle their disagreements, they held a conference in Berlin in 1884–1885. There they drew boundary lines on a map of Africa, dividing up the continent among themselves. (See the map on page 508.) They then proceeded to establish control over these regions.

The Age of Imperialism

The partitioning of Africa is just one example of European expansion in the late 1800s. As you will read in Chapters 28 and 29, the nations of Western Europe along with the United States gained influence or won control of land in Asia and Latin America as well. The period from about 1870 to 1914 is often called the Age of Imperialism. *Imperialism* is the domination by a country of the political, economic, or cultural life of another country or region.

European nations exerted their control over other parts of the world in many ways. The most common forms of imperial rule were colonies, spheres of influence, and protectorates. A *colony* is a possession that the imperial power controls directly. A *sphere of influence* is a region in which the imperial power claims exclusive investment or trading privileges. The local government usually controls all other matters. A *protectorate* is a country that has its own government but whose policies are guided by the imperial power.

A variety of motives stimulated European expansion in the Age of Imperialism. Nationalism played a major role in sending Europeans overseas. A nation increased its prestige and power by winning an overseas empire. Political rivalries and military strategy also contributed to imperialism. One nation might seize a territory to prevent a rival from expanding into that region.

The desire to expand economically was also a strong motive. Industrialists urged their governments to acquire new markets for their products. In addition, they wanted to control the supply of raw materials. Individuals, too, sought personal wealth.

Humanitarian and religious concerns often motivated individuals and their governments. Some Europeans wanted to end the slave trade in Africa. Christian missionaries were convinced that the peoples of Africa and Asia would become "civilized" only if they converted to Christianity and adopted European ways. Many Europeans believed in the superiority of the white race. They spoke of the "white man's burden" of carrying the benefits of western civilization to other parts of the world.

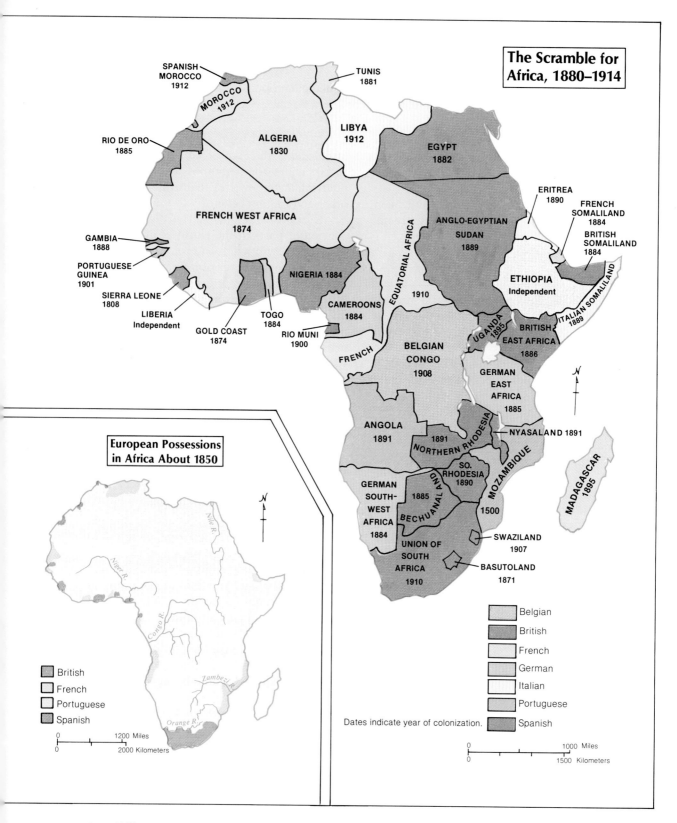

The Scramble for Africa, 1880–1914

SPANISH MOROCCO 1912

TUNIS 1881

MOROCCO 1912

RIO DE ORO 1885

ALGERIA 1830

LIBYA 1912

EGYPT 1882

ERITREA 1890

FRENCH WEST AFRICA 1874

ANGLO-EGYPTIAN SUDAN 1889

FRENCH SOMALILAND 1884

BRITISH SOMALILAND 1884

GAMBIA 1888

PORTUGUESE GUINEA 1901

SIERRA LEONE 1808

LIBERIA Independent

GOLD COAST 1874

TOGO 1884

NIGERIA 1884

CAMEROONS 1884

RIO MUNI 1900

EQUATORIAL AFRICA 1910

ETHIOPIA Independent

ITALIAN SOMALILAND 1889

FRENCH

BELGIAN CONGO 1908

UGANDA 1895

BRITISH EAST AFRICA 1886

GERMAN EAST AFRICA 1885

ANGOLA 1891

NORTHERN RHODESIA 1891

NYASALAND 1891

MOZAMBIQUE 1500

MADAGASCAR 1895

GERMAN SOUTH-WEST AFRICA 1884

BECHUANALAND 1885

SO. RHODESIA 1890

SWAZILAND 1907

UNION OF SOUTH AFRICA 1910

BASUTOLAND 1871

Belgian
British
French
German
Italian
Portuguese
Spanish

Dates indicate year of colonization.

0   1000 Miles
0   1500 Kilometers

European Possessions in Africa About 1850

Nile R.

Niger R.

Congo R.

Zambezi R.

Orange R.

British
French
Portuguese
Spanish

0   1200 Miles
0   2000 Kilometers

Map Skill   *In the late 1800s, European nations scrambled to claim territory in Africa. By 1914, almost the entire continent had been partitioned, as you can see above. Which nations remained independent?*

The philosophy of Social Darwinism was used to justify imperialism. As you read in Chapter 24, Social Darwinists argued that in nature only the strongest survived. They applied this idea to political affairs, arguing that it was natural for strong nations to conquer weaker states.

Exploring the Interior

Until the 1800s, Europeans had very little knowledge of the interior of Africa. African and Arab merchants on the coast knew the best routes into the interior, but few Europeans bothered to ask them for information. Instead, Europeans and Americans financed dozens of expeditions to explore the African continent.

Perhaps the best known explorer was David Livingstone, a British physician and missionary. Livingstone spent many years setting up Christian missions in Central Africa. He wrote detailed reports that made the British public aware of opportunities in Africa for businesspeople as well as missionaries.

Exploration along African rivers was the first step toward opening the continent to European expansion. In the 1830s, Sir George Goldie charted the Niger River. Dozens of other Europeans explored the various regions of Africa. In the 1870s, Henry Stanley trekked inland from the East African coast, discovered the source of the Congo River, and sailed down to the Atlantic Ocean.

New Technology

Despite the expeditions into the African interior, disease and resistance by Africans prevented much European expansion beyond the coastal areas before 1870.

As European interest in Africa grew, doctors searched for the causes and treatment of diseases such as malaria and yellow fever, which claimed many European lives in Africa. By the 1880s, they had learned that mosquitoes carried malaria and yellow fever. They also found that quinine, made from the bark of a certain tree, prevented people from catching malaria. Such medical discoveries made it easier for Europeans to move into the interior of Africa.

The development of new weapons gave Europeans a military advantage over Africans. These weapons included rifles and the Maxim gun, the earliest machine gun. Africans armed with weapons such as muskets had little success against Europeans using the new weapons.

SECTION REVIEW

1. Locate: Liberia, Ethiopia, Niger River, Congo River.
2. Identify: Berlin Conference, David Livingstone, George Goldie, Henry Stanley.
3. Define: imperialism, colony, sphere of influence, protectorate.
4. Describe three motives behind European imperialism.

---

2 North Africa

Read to Learn
- about imperialism in Egypt
- how Europeans gained control of North Africa

The people of North Africa had had contacts with other parts of the world since ancient times. During the Middle Ages, North Africa was an important part of the Islamic Empire, and Islamic culture helped shape the political and social life. In the early 1500s, the Ottoman Turks conquered North Africa. As the Ottoman Empire weakened in the late 1700s, four North African States—Algiers, Tunis, Tripoli, and Egypt—gained virtual independence. A fifth state, Morocco, was outside Ottoman control.

The Egyptian Empire

When Napoleon invaded Egypt in 1798, Egyptians broke away from Ottoman rule. The French invasion sparked a long civil war. Muhammad Ali, who had led Egyptian resistance to the French invasion, seized control of the country in 1805.

Ali ruthlessly suppressed his opponents and embarked on an ambitious program of reform to make Egypt a strong power. He began by introducing more efficient agricultural techniques. He had dykes and irrigation canals built so that arid land could be cultivated. He then sent peasant farmers to grow cash crops on the new lands. *Cash crops* are crops such as cotton, sugar, and tobacco that can be sold for money on the world market. Egypt soon became a major exporter of cotton to industrial nations such as Great Britain.

Income from cash crops helped pay for Ali's other projects. He established schools and sent thousands of Egyptians to study in Europe. He brought European experts to Egypt to help set up textile mills, iron works, and shipyards. He also invited French military officers to reorganize, train, and equip the Egyptian army. With a strong modern army to support him, Ali built an empire. During the 1820s and 1830s, Egyptian armies seized territory along the Red Sea coast and moved up the Nile River into the Sudan.

Growing European Interest in Egypt

Ali's programs were expensive. To finance them, he borrowed money from European banks. Under Ali's successors, Egyptian debts increased. Gradually, European creditors gained political and economic influence in Egypt. They pressured Egyptian leaders to follow policies that favored their financial interests.

The Suez Canal. Europeans had relatively little interest in Egypt until 1859, when the French began building the Suez Canal. Ali had opposed construction of a canal to link the Mediterranean Sea and the Red Sea. He feared that such a canal would increase European interest in Egypt because it would cut thousands of miles off the trip from Europe to Asia. However, his successors approved the project.

Between 1859 and 1869, a French company headed by Ferdinand de Lesseps built the Suez Canal. At first, Egyptians controlled the canal. But as British influence in India grew, Britain came to see the Suez Canal as the "lifeline of the British Empire."*

------
* You will read about British rule in India in Chapter 28.

A combination of engineering skill, steam-powered machinery, and a huge investment of money made possible the construction of the Suez Canal. Ferdinand de Lesseps, a successful promoter and engineer, oversaw the project. He predicted that the canal "will open the world to all people." When the 100-mile canal was completed in 1869, it cut in half the length of the journey between Europe and Asia.

British occupation of Egypt. In the 1870s, Britain acquired partial control over the Suez Canal by buying shares of stock from Egyptian ruler Ismail. Ismail sold the stock because the Egyptian government faced a severe financial crisis. The chaotic state of Egyptian finances eventually provided the British with an excuse to intervene militarily in Egypt. Claiming that it wanted to protect European loans and investments and reorganize the Egyptian treasury, Britain sent troops to occupy Egypt in 1882. The British then made Egypt a protectorate.

Under British control, Egypt paid off its foreign debts and built a dam at Aswan on the upper Nile. The dam improved agricultural production by supplying water for irrigation. However, Egyptian nationalists resented foreign control. They criticized the British for not encouraging education or helping Egyptian industries.

The Fashoda incident. British occupation of Egypt led to an explosive confrontation with France. The British thought their control of Egypt and the Suez Canal would only be assured if they also possessed the headwaters of the Nile in the Sudan. For 16 years, Sudanese nationalists resisted attempts to occupy their land. Finally, in 1898, a combined force of British and Egyptians conquered the Sudan. Meanwhile, a French army had reached the Sudan from bases in West Africa. British and French forces faced each other at Fashoda. For weeks, the two European powers seemed on the brink of war.

In the end, the domestic crisis over the Dreyfus Affair forced the French to withdraw. (See page 473.) Britain and Egypt then established joint control over the Sudan. The Fashoda incident reminded Europeans of the very real possibility that overseas rivalries could drag them into war.

French and Italian Expansion

While Britain was establishing control over Egypt and the Sudan, France extended its rule over other parts of North Africa. Between 1830 and 1912, France conquered Algiers, Tunis, and Morocco.* By 1861, most of Italy had been united. It began to challenge France in North Africa.

Algeria. In 1830, the French king Charles X launched an expedition against the ruler of Algiers, in part to avenge an insult to a French diplomat. Charles was also in serious political trouble at home. He hoped that a victory in Algeria would divert the attention of the French people. However, although Charles gained a foothold in Algeria, he was toppled by the revolution of 1830. (See page 419.)

During the following decades, the French government encouraged Europeans to settle in Algeria. Colonists took lands, especially along the fertile Mediterranean coast, and established successful farming and business communities.

The Algerians resisted French expansion into their land for 40 years. So many Algerians were killed in the fighting that France became even more eager to attract European settlers to Algeria. In all, almost 1 million Europeans settled in Algeria during the 1800s.

France took little interest in other North African lands until the 1880s. Then, as Britain moved into Egypt, the French rapidly occupied Tunisia. French expansion along the Mediterranean worried the Italians, whose interest in North Africa was growing.

Ethiopia and Libya. Both France and Italy sought control of the horn of Africa, present-day Somalia and Ethiopia. Aware of the European threat, the Ethiopian emperor Menelik II bought rifles and other new weapons and trained his army to use them. Thus, when the Italians invaded Ethiopia in 1896, they were defeated by strong, well-armed Ethiopian forces.

Italy had to be content with establishing protectorates over Eritrea and part of Somaliland. In 1912, the Italians occupied Tripoli, which they set up as the colony of Libya. By controlling Libya, the Italians prevented further French expansion eastward across North Africa.

---

* Algiers and Tunis are called Algeria and Tunisia today.

511

During the Age of Imperialism, Ethiopia preserved its independence largely because of the enlightened policies of its emperor Menelik II. Menelik was descended from a dynasty that had ruled Ethiopia since the 1200s. When he came to the throne in 1889, he faced many difficulties. Ethiopia was only loosely united, and local rulers showed little loyalty to the emperor. In addition, both Italy and France were acquiring colonies on the borders of Ethiopia.

Menelik moved quickly to consolidate power. He brought local rulers under his control and built a new capital at Addis Ababa, where he set up a strong central government. He asked European advisors to help him establish a modern system of education, and he promoted talented individuals. Gradually, his policies helped create a sense of national unity among the people of Ethiopia.

Menelik displayed a shrewd diplomatic ability in his dealings with European powers. He warned Britain, France, Italy, Germany, and Russia: "If powers at a distance come forward to partition Africa between them, I do not intend to be an indifferent spectator." Menelik backed up this declaration by skillfully playing off one European power against another. He acquired arms from both Italy and France, who were eager to gain influence with the Ethiopian emperor.

Menelik used his new armed forces in a showdown with Italy. In 1893, Menelik renounced a treaty he had signed with the Italians. Two years later, Italian troops seized several Ethiopian towns. Menelik stalled the Italian advance by calling for negotiations. In the meantime, he allowed inaccurate maps of his country to fall into Italian hands and sent

spies to give the Italians misleading information.

On March 1, 1896, the armies of the two nations met at Adowa. Menelik's forces routed the Italians, who were greatly outnumbered. The painting above, by an Ethiopian artist, shows the Ethiopians in triumph over their enemies. This victory ensured the independence of Ethiopia and the success of Menelik's program of strengthening his nation.

Crisis Over Morocco

Morocco, at the northwestern tip of Africa, remained largely outside European control until the 1880s. Learning from the Egyptian example, the Moroccan ruler avoided building up large debts in Europe. Despite his efforts, European nations used Morocco as a pawn in their political maneuverings.

For years, Britain and France had quarreled over Egypt. In 1904, they finally reached an agreement. France would recognize British interests in Egypt, and Britain would let France establish a sphere of influence in Morocco and not protest any French efforts to take over Morocco directly.

The agreement between Britain and France alarmed the German emperor William II. He considered it a threat to German power. Thus, in 1905, he visited Morocco and boldly announced that Germany would support an independent Morocco. William II's actions, however, only brought France and Britain closer together. In 1906, an international conference of European powers recognized French influence in Morocco.

SECTION REVIEW

1. Locate: Sudan, Algeria, Tunisia, Morocco, Ethiopia, Somaliland, Libya.
2. Identify: Muhammad Ali, Ferdinand de Lesseps, Menelik II.
3. Define: cash crop.
4. Describe three reforms Muhammad Ali introduced in Egypt.
5. How did Britain gain partial control over the Suez Canal?
6. (a) Describe the Fashoda incident. (b) Why was it significant?

3 West and Central Africa

Read to Learn
- how the slave trade affected African societies
- how European nations gained power in West and Central Africa

As you read in Chapter 17, Portuguese sailors explored the west coast of Africa in the late 1400s. Over the next 350 years, Portugal and other European nations set up small trading posts and forts along the coast. By the 1600s, these outposts had become the center of a profitable slave trade across the Atlantic to the Americas. Until the 1800s, most European interest in West Africa revolved around this transatlantic slave trade.

The Transatlantic Slave Trade

Slavery had existed in Africa since ancient times, as it had in many parts of the world. In Africa, many slaves were captives taken in war. Others were people who sold themselves into slavery for food and shelter during drought or famine. Sometimes a society took slaves in order to increase its population. Slaves were often gradually absorbed into their new societies.

The transatlantic slave trade was very different from African slavery. Africans were forced to leave their traditional societies and were transported thousands of miles across the Atlantic. In the Americas, they encountered a completely unfamiliar culture. White slave owners looked on black Africans as inferior beings whose only value was their labor.

The transatlantic slave trade involved large numbers of people. Experts now estimate that between 1451 and 1870 about 9.5 million slaves were sent to the Americas. As you read in Chapter 17, thousands died during the brutal Middle Passage.

Slaves were captured in the interior of Africa and led in chains to the coast. There, they awaited shipment across the Atlantic, as this drawing shows. In the mid-1700s, about 100,000 Africans were shipped to the Americas each year.

A SLAVE-SHED.

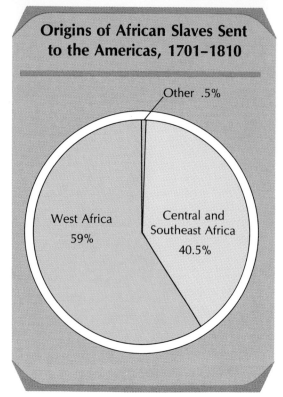

Origins of African Slaves Sent to the Americas, 1701–1810

Other .5%

West Africa 59%

Central and Southeast Africa 40.5%

Source: Philip D. Curtin, *The Atlantic Slave Trade.*

Graph Skill *Over a period of three centuries, more than 9 million Africans were sent to the Americas as slaves. Why do you think the majority of these Africans came from West Africa?*

Europeans relied on African rulers and merchants to bring slaves to trading posts on the coast. The Africans exchanged slaves for guns, ammunition, and manufactured goods. They used the guns to raid villages and capture more slaves. This exchange between Africans and Europeans has often been called the slave-gun cycle.

The demand for slaves caused several changes among West African societies. New states rose whose wealth and power were based on the slave-gun cycle. For example, in the 1700s and early 1800s, rulers of the Dahomey and Ashanti kingdoms used muskets acquired through the slave trade to conquer large areas. Raids to capture slaves created tensions among West African societies.

A Century of Change

In the century before 1870, two developments changed conditions in West Africa. First, European nations abolished the slave trade. Second, there was a revival of Islam in several West African states.

Abolition of the slave trade. During the Enlightenment, some Europeans called for an end to the slave trade and slavery. By the early 1800s, this humanitarian concern was having an effect. Britain outlawed the slave trade in 1807. Britain also convinced other nations at the Congress of Vienna to condemn the slave trade. But Portugal, Spain, and France did not end their slave trade until 1820.*

Soon after Britain abolished the slave trade, it established the West African Patrol, a naval force with orders to prevent slave ships from leaving West African ports. When the patrol captured ships with slaves on board, it carried the Africans to Freetown in the British colony of Sierra Leone. The British had established Freetown in the late 1700s for slaves they freed during the American Revolution. In the 1800s, Sierra Leone became a haven for other freed slaves. Christian missionaries worked among the African settlers there, encouraging them to adopt European ways.

In 1822, a group of free black Americans established another refuge for former slaves in West Africa. The new settlement was called Liberia. In the 1830s and 1840s, hundreds of former slaves in the United States emigrated to Liberia. By 1850, Liberia had become an independent nation.

The abolition of the slave trade undermined the economic strength of the West African states that had supplied slaves to the Europeans. Some states, such as Dahomey, declined rapidly. As the demand for slaves declined, West African societies had to find other items to trade for European manufactured goods. They began to plant cash crops, including cotton and cacao beans, which were introduced from the Americas. As a result, West African economies remained closely tied to European demand for these products.

---

* Although these European nations officially abolished the slave trade, many people still participated in it illegally. Moreover, European nations did not abolish slavery itself until later. Britain abolished slavery in all its territories in the 1830s. Other European nations ended slavery by the 1860s.

Revival of Islam. The most important development in West Africa during this period was the revival of Islam. As you read in Chapter 14, Arab traders had introduced Islam into West Africa in the 800s. However, generally only rulers and their officials converted to Islam. Most people in West Africa either continued to believe in their traditional religions or mixed Muslim beliefs with their own faiths. Devout Muslims detested the mixing of Islam with other faiths.

In the early 1800s, Muslim religious leaders called for a jihad, or holy war, to restore the purity of Islam. Muslims believe that a Muslim killed in a jihad is assured a place in heaven. With armies inspired by this belief, several Islamic states in West Africa conquered large empires.

Among the best known of these Islamic empires was the Hausa-Fulani Empire located in what is today northern Nigeria. In 1804, Usuman dan Fodio, a Muslim scholar, unified the nomadic Fulani people. The next year, he led them in a jihad against the Hausa people because he thought the Hausa had corrupted Muslim practices. Usuman's forces seized control of the Hausa cities.

Usuman then organized the new lands into a strong Islamic state.

European Conquests

As you read earlier, new technology and European exploration sparked European expansion into West and Central Africa. The scramble for colonies began in the 1870s when Belgium concluded treaties with African rulers along the Congo River. As you read, Henry Stanley explored the Congo River basin. He also negotiated treaties with local rulers for the right to exploit the mineral wealth of the region. Stanley hoped that Britain would send settlers to the Congo, but Britain was not interested. Thus, Stanley turned to King Leopold II of Belgium, who agreed to set up Belgian settlements there. Belgium thereby gained control of the region, which became known as the Congo Free State.

The brutal treatment of the local people in the Congo Free State has come to symbolize the worst aspects of European imperialism in Africa. King Leopold II ruled the

In 1815, an Italian artist painted this picture of a village at the mouth of the Congo River. Europeans established an outpost here, but village life remained largely unchanged until the Age of Imperialism. In the late 1800s, Europeans in the Congo uprooted Africans from their homes and their traditional ways of life and forced them to work on rubber plantations and in copper mines.

Congo Free State as his own private possession. The area was rich in rubber and copper and other minerals. Leopold granted monopolies to European companies and earned handsome profits for himself.

The European companies ruthlessly exploited both the land and the people in the Congo Free State. To ensure maximum profit, company managers forced Africans to work long hours and punished them brutally if they did not produce enough. They also imprisoned African women to make their husbands work harder. Workers had their hands or ears cut off if they protested.

When Christian missionaries in the Congo revealed these atrocities, the Belgian government investigated. Eventually, in 1908, the government took over the administration of the Congo Free State, which then became known as the Belgian Congo.

France, too, began taking a greater interest in Africa in the 1870s. In 1879, the French built a railroad from Dakar, on the coast, into the interior. Britain felt threatened by French expansion into West Africa and took control of Nigeria and the Gold Coast, present-day Ghana. Germany, Portugal, and Spain also annexed territory. However, France acquired the largest part of West Africa.

African Resistance

Europeans used persuasion, force, and bribery to convince individual African rulers to sign agreements giving them economic and political rights. Once they established a foothold, Europeans often ignored the agreements and simply took what they wanted. If African rulers resisted, well-armed troops were sent in to crush them. Still, many African rulers vigorously opposed European expansion.

Samori Touré, ruler of an empire in what is today Senegal, signed an agreement with the French in the 1890s. When the French broke the agreement and tried to seize control of his land, Touré fought back. For seven years, he led his army against the French. Finally, in 1898, the French captured Touré and exiled him to Gabon.

In Dahomey, King Behanzin battled the French until 1894, when he was captured and exiled to Algeria. The Ashanti, who had established a powerful state in the forest region of what is today Ghana, stubbornly resisted the British. However, not all West and Central African people fought the Europeans. Some accepted agreements that gave them minimal levels of self-rule. Others did not fight because resistance against European weapons appeared to be hopeless.

SECTION REVIEW

1. Locate: Sierra Leone, Liberia, Nigeria, Belgian Congo.
2. Identify: West African Patrol, Usuman dan Fodio, Leopold II, Samori Touré.
3. (a) Why did the British found the colony of Sierra Leone? (b) Who established Liberia?
4. Why did Muslim leaders call for holy wars in west Africa?
5. What resources did the Congo Free State have?

---

4 Southern and Eastern Africa

Read to Learn   ■ why the Boer War took place
■ why East Africa fell to the Europeans

In 1652, the Dutch founded Cape Town at the southern tip of Africa. The settlers supplied water, fresh meat, and vegetables to Dutch ships traveling to the East Indies. In the Cape area, the Dutch came in contact with local African herders. The Dutch gradually enslaved some of these people and forced others into the desert region to the north. However, by the early 1800s, the migration of other African peoples into southern Africa radically changed conditions there.

Settlers in Southern Africa

For almost 1,000 years before 1800, groups of Africans had been migrating into eastern and southern Africa. These peoples are known as Bantu-speaking peoples because they spoke languages that were related. However, their cultures were different.

Zulu expansion. The Zulu were one of the Bantu-speaking peoples migrating into southern Africa. By the early 1800s, the Zulu king Shaka had built a strong military empire northeast of the Orange River. Shaka introduced new fighting methods among the Zulu. He replaced the long throwing spears they had been using with short, stabbing swords. He reorganized the Zulu army into a powerful fighting force that expanded the Zulu empire.

The Zulu expansion created turmoil in southern Africa. The people defeated by the Zulu left their traditional homelands and retreated across southern and central Africa. They displaced other African groups, who then migrated northward.

The Boer republics. At about the same time as the Zulu were expanding their empire, the Boers, descendants of the Dutch who had founded Cape Town, were migrating north from the Cape Colony. The Boers were on the move because the British had gained control of the Cape Colony in 1814.

The Boers resented British rule because they felt that the British threatened their way of life. The British made English the official language of the colony and abolished slavery, which the Boers believed God had ordained. To preserve their way of life, about 10,000 Boers left the Cape Colony in the 1830s. They headed north in a vast migration of covered wagons, called the Great Trek. In the interior of southern Africa, the Boers set up two independent republics, the Transvaal and the Orange Free State. (See the map at right.)

The Boers soon came into conflict with the Zulu. For years the two groups fought for control of the land. Neither side was able to win a decisive victory. Finally, in 1879, the British became involved in these wars with the Zulu. The Zulu defeated the British in several battles, but the superior weapons and numbers of the British eventually led to the destruction of the Zulu empire.

The Boer War

The British officially recognized the independence of the Boer republics in 1852. But continued British interest in southern Africa worried the Boers. In the 1880s, gold and diamonds were discovered in the Transvaal and the Orange Free State. British adventurers flocked north from the Cape Colony to seek their fortunes in the mines.

By the end of the century, the British decided that control of all of South Africa was vital to their empire because South Africa was on the sea route to India. Moreover, Cecil Rhodes, the prime minister of the Cape Colony, had a grand plan to build a "Cape to Cairo" railroad, linking these British outposts in Africa.

Map Skill   *The movement of peoples into South Africa led to conflict after 1830. The Zulu, who had created a large empire, clashed with the Boers. Where did the Boers migrate after the British gained control of Cape Colony?*

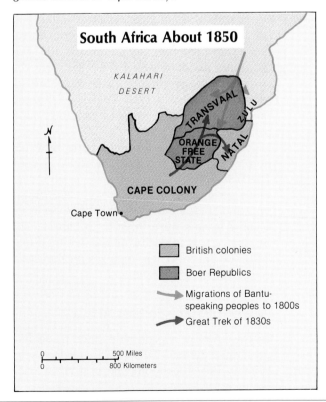

South Africa About 1850

KALAHARI
DESERT

TRANSVAAL

ZULU

ORANGE FREE STATE

NATAL

CAPE COLONY

Cape Town

☐ British colonies

■ Boer Republics

➤ Migrations of Bantu-speaking peoples to 1800s

➤ Great Trek of 1830s

0   500 Miles
0   800 Kilometers

The discovery of diamonds at Kimberley in 1871 sent thousands of fortune hunters to South Africa. Kimberley soon grew into a sprawling mining town of 50,000 people. This print shows open-shaft mining at Kimberley. The diamond mines of South Africa were a source of wealth for European investors. But African mine workers were harshly treated, as you can see in this picture.

Finally, in 1899, tension between the British and the Boers exploded into war. The Boer War lasted for nearly three years before the Boers surrendered. The war left the Boers with bitter memories because the British placed thousands of Boers in concentration camps, where many died. After the war, the Boers had to accept British rule, but the British promised them self-government as soon as possible. In 1910, The British united their South African colonies into the Union of South Africa.

Under the constitution of the new nation, only white men had the right to vote. The British felt that the Africans might eventually be given the right to vote. The Boers opposed such a move because they believed black Africans were inferior to whites. The Boers were a majority of the white population of South Africa. As a result, they won control of the government.

Powerful States in East Africa

In East Africa, a profitable slave trade had developed by the 1700s. Arab traders who lived in the cities along the east coast used slaves to carry ivory and gold from Central Africa to the coast. As the slave trade expanded, the Arabs extended their control to include the inland trade routes.

In the 1800s, several African rulers challenged Arab authority over these trade routes and the growing slave trade. Mirambo, leader of the Nyamezi people, carved out an empire in part of what is today Tanzania. Because he controlled a vital trade route, Mirambo demanded large sums of money from traders to assure safe passage. He used this wealth to buy weapons and further increase his power. However, Mirambo's empire was based on his personal leadership, and it collapsed soon after his death.

Another African leader, Tippu Tib, created a strong state in what is today eastern Zaire. Like Mirambo, Tippu Tib controlled a vital trade route from the interior to the east coast. He built a strong army and conquered new lands. But Tippu Tib's empire, too, was based on personal leadership, and it crumbled after his death.

The rise of empires such as Mirambo's and Tippu Tib's disrupted the traditional way of life in East Africa and in some ways made European expansion in the late 1800s easier. The slave trade weakened many African societies and made African peoples suspicious of each other. When Europeans arrived in East Africa, they often gained support of Africans who wanted protection from the slave-trading states.

European Rivalries in East Africa

European trade along the East African coast increased in the early 1800s. After the American Revolution, ships from Boston and Salem carried cotton cloth to East African ports. The word for cotton cloth in East Africa is still "merikani" because of that trade. German, French, and British merchants also sought trading rights from local rulers.

By the 1870s, Britain and Germany were the chief rivals in East Africa. A latecomer to the scramble for colonies, Germany wanted what it called "a place in the sun." It wanted to win colonies in East Africa, the only part of the continent that was still largely unclaimed by other European powers. At the same time, British imperialists felt that control of East Africa was vital if Britain were to extend its empire from South Africa to Egypt. Also, both Portugal and Belgium claimed parts of East Africa in an effort to extend their colonial empires across the continent from the Atlantic Ocean to the Indian Ocean.

At the Berlin Conference, European nations settled their rival claims in East Africa. They recognized British and German rule over large parts of East Africa. Mozambique became a Portuguese colony, and Belgium took two small states in the interior. (See the map on page 508.) No Africans were consulted about these arrangements.

Fighting Colonial Rule

Many Africans resisted European colonization in East Africa. The Shana and Matabele in what is today Zimbabwe fought two major wars against the British. The Germans suppressed rebellions in their colony, but at considerable cost. The Uhehe (yoo HEE hee) won fame by successfully fighting the Germans for seven years. Like so many other African people, the Uhehe were defeated by European cannons and machine guns.

Two factors, however, limited African resistance in East Africa. First, as you read, the slave states had disrupted many African societies and made some Africans sympathetic to European expansion. Second, the outbreak of rinderpest, a cattle disease, caused a disastrous famine that affected people's ability to fight the invaders.

Rinderpest was brought into Africa accidentally in the late 1880s. Cattle infected with the disease were imported from southern Europe to feed Italian troops in Somaliland. Because East African cattle had no previous exposure to rinderpest, they had no resistance to the disease. In some areas, 95 percent of all cattle died.

The epidemic spread south with terrible consequences because most East African people were cattle herders. Almost overnight their wealth and way of life were destroyed. Many people died of starvation. Others suffered severe malnutrition. Malnutrition made people vulnerable to diseases such as smallpox and malaria. Crushed by this disaster, many people lacked the resources and the will to fight the foreigners who took their lands.

SECTION REVIEW

1. Locate: Cape Town, Transvaal, Orange Free State, Uganda.
2. Identify: Zulu, Boers, Shaka, Great Trek, Cecil Rhodes, Union of South Africa, Tippu Tib.
3. (a) Why did the Boers move inland from the Cape Colony? (b) Who did they fight for control of the land?
4. Give two reasons why the British took a greater interest in South Africa in the late 1800s.
5. How did Mirambo build a strong state in East Africa?
6. What European countries claimed land in East Africa?
7. How did rinderpest affect the cattle-herding peoples of East Africa?

5 European Rule in Africa

Read to Learn ■ how colonial governments ruled Africans
■ how colonial rule affected African societies

European imperialism in Africa lasted about 100 years, from the 1870s to the 1970s. Compared to Africa's long history, this period was short. However, the impact of colonial rule on Africa was immense.

Colonial Governments

Once European nations had carved up Africa, they faced the question of how to rule their new colonies. They developed two types of colonial government: direct rule, practiced by France, Germany, Belgium, and Portugal; and indirect rule, used by Great Britain.

Direct rule. Through direct rule, the European nation controlled government at all levels in its colony. It appointed its own officials to replace African leaders and cast aside traditional African ways of governing.

Direct rule reflected the European belief that Africans were incapable of ruling themselves. Europeans used this belief to justify *paternalism*, the system of governing their colonies as parents would guide their children. Europeans thought they had to teach their African subjects the "proper" way to live, by which they meant the European way.

The form direct rule took varied among the different European colonies. France practiced a policy of *assimilation*, under which the colonies would be absorbed politically and culturally into the parent nation. Africans in the French colonies were expected to exchange their own heritage for French culture. Only when the colonies became truly French would they be made provinces of France, not just overseas territories.

To achieve assimilation, colonial schools, businesses, and law courts were patterned after those in France. Some Africans were sent to school in France and eventually gained minor government positions in the French colonies.

Portugal also followed a policy of assimilation, but it exerted rigid control over its colonies. It wanted the Africans in its colonies to become Portuguese Christians. Although some Africans converted to Christianity, very few were allowed to become Portuguese citizens.

Paternalism was the main characteristic of direct rule by Germany and Belgium. Germany looked on its African colonies as a source of wealth and labor. It exercised strict control over its colonial subjects, claiming that Africans could never learn to rule themselves. Belgium wanted to make Europeans forget the atrocities committed in the Congo during Leopold's rule. Therefore, it tried to make the Congo a model colony. The Belgians claimed to protect the interests of their African subjects by making all decisions for them.

Indirect rule. Britain was the only colonial power to rely on indirect rule. Under the system of indirect rule, a British governor and council of advisors made laws for each colony. But local rulers loyal to the governor retained some of their traditional authority. Thus, indirect rule differed from direct rule because it did not replace traditional rulers with European officials. Yet local rulers had only limited power and did not influence government decisions.

The British had practical reasons for using indirect rule. Even before the European scramble for Africa, Britain had more colonies than any other European nation. During the late 1800s, it acquired one third of the African continent, with 64 million people to rule. A small nation, Britain did not have enough officials or soldiers to control its huge empire without the help of local leaders.

Making Colonies Profitable

Although the European nations developed different methods of governing their colonies, their policies had a common goal. They all believed their colonies should be self-

As you have read, eyewitness accounts are not always completely objective or accurate. Often, the writer has a point of view that influences his or her description of an event or development. (Review "Identifying a Point of View," page 125.) Eyewitness accounts are also affected by *cultural bias,* or the way the writer's culture shapes his or her attitude toward an event.

During the Age of Imperialism, Europeans who visited Africa judged the diverse peoples and cultures they saw in terms of European civilization. The following excerpt is from *The Lake Regions of Central Africa,* the journal British explorer Sir Richard Burton kept as he traveled through East Africa in 1858. Read the excerpt. Then use the following steps to identify the writer's cultural bias.

1. **Identify the nature of the document.** Ask yourself the following questions: (a) What type of document is it? (b) Who wrote it? (c) When was the document written? (d) Under what circumstances was it written?

2. **Review the contents of the document.** Answer the following questions about the excerpt: (a) What does the writer say about the early morning activities of people in the African village? (b) What does the writer say about the way the people spend the rest of the day? (c) What does the writer say about the activities of women and girls?

3. **Study the source to discover the writer's cultural bias.** You can do this by looking at the words the writer uses and the tone of the excerpt. (a) What word does the writer use to describe the dwellings in which the people live? (b) What word is used to describe the chief occupation of the people? (c) What seems to be the writer's attitude toward the people he is describing? (d) How might this attitude have affected his description of the village?

4. **Evaluate the document as a historical source.** Answer the following questions about the excerpt: (a) What parts of the description are most likely to be accurate? (b) What parts of the description reflect the writer's cultural bias? (c) Would you use this document as evidence about life in East Africa? Why or why not?

From Richard Burton's Travel Journal

The African rises with the dawn from his couch of cowhide. The hut is cool and comfortable during the day, but the barred door impeding ventilation at night causes it to be close and disagreeable. The hour before sunrise being the coldest time, he usually kindles a fire and addresses himself to his constant companion, the pipe. When the sun becomes sufficiently powerful, he removes the reed screen from the entrance and issues forth to bask in the morning beams. The villages are populous, and the houses touching one another enable the occupants, when squatting outside . . . to chat and chatter without moving. About 7 A.M., when the dew has partially disappeared from the grass, the elder boys drive the flocks and herds to pasture with loud shouts. . . . At 8 A.M., those who have provisions at home enter the hut to eat porridge; those who have not, join a friend.

After breaking his fast, the African repairs, pipe in hand, to the *iwanza* [the village inn], where he will spend the greater part of the day talking and laughing, smoking, or torpid [sluggish] with sleep. . . .

After eating, the East African invariably indulges in a long fit of torpidity, from which he awakes to pass the afternoon as he did the forenoon. . . . Toward sunset, all issue forth to enjoy the coolness: the men sit outside the *iwanza,* whilst the women and the girls, after fetching water . . . from the well, collecting in a group upon their little stools, indulge in the pleasures of gossip. . . . As the hours of darkness draw nigh, the village doors are carefully closed, and after milking his cows each peasant retires to his hut or passes his time with his friends in the *iwanza.*

---

sufficient. That is, each colony should pay all its own expenses, including salaries for government officials and the military and the costs of building roads, railroads, and schools. These expenses were immense, and most African societies could not pay for them. But European powers found ways to make their colonies both self-sufficient and

Europeans were fascinated by African wildlife, as this painting by artist Thomas Baines shows. Baines accompanied David Livingstone on his expedition up the Zambezi River. Paintings such as this one and written accounts of Europeans who traveled in Africa often emphasized the aspects of African life that differed the most from life in Europe.

profitable. They tapped the mineral and agricultural resources of their colonies, built up trade by exporting these resources, and developed internal transportation networks.

In some colonies, Europeans found valuable mineral resources, including copper in the Belgian Congo and gold in South Africa. Where mineral resources were lacking, Europeans developed cash crops such as rubber, palm oil, and peanuts.

Colonial governments also imposed taxes on Africans, which had to be paid in cash. The only way Africans could earn cash was to work for individual Europeans or for the colonial government. Thus, many Africans had to work on large plantations or in factories and mines owned by Europeans.

Europeans made their colonies more profitable by encouraging investment in enterprises such as railroad building. Investors put up the money to build railroads and received profits from the fees people paid to use the trains.

Railroads served both political and economic goals. Politically, they helped colonial governments impose their authority by providing a reliable transportation system. Economically, they gave Europeans a relatively cheap means of moving cash crops and other products to ports for shipment overseas. In Uganda, for example, many British farmers established cotton plantations in the interior. They depended on the railroad to send the cotton to the coast so it could be shipped to factories in Britain. Because investors were interested in high profits, they built railroads only in those areas where Europeans had settled or had businesses.

The Impact of Colonial Rule

Colonial rule profoundly affected the political, economic, and social structure of African societies. Europeans believed Africans were primitive people. They generally refused to recognize the customs and traditions that had shaped African societies. Furthermore, impressed by European wealth and power, many Africans rejected their traditional rulers and accepted European paternalism.

Breakdown of traditional culture. During the Age of Imperialism, many African economic and social traditions were destroyed. As colonial cities grew, some families moved to the cities, hoping to improve their positions. Others were forced to seek jobs in European-owned factories or businesses in order to pay taxes. Still others became migrant workers, leaving their villages for long periods to work in distant mines and plantations. As a result, the close-knit village, once the center of African life, declined. People no longer had the same concern for helping each other as they had in the past.

Christian missionaries actively tried to convert Africans to Christianity. As some Africans became Christians, however, conflicts developed within communities. Christian converts rejected the religious practices and beliefs of their families and neighbors.

Education contributed further to the breakdown of traditional African cultures. Colonial schools were run by Europeans. They presented a negative view of African cultures. African children were taught that their parents' beliefs and traditions were backward. In school, children studied European, not African, history.

Educated Africans who became successful under the colonial governments continued to be affected by European paternalism. Europeans held the most important positions and made all the major decisions. Africans found they had to conform to European ways to succeed. For example, if they wore their traditional flowing robes to work, they would lose their jobs. Only European clothes were considered correct.

The benefits. Although colonial governments helped destroy traditional patterns of life in Africa, some people argue that colonial rule brought important benefits. Europeans exploited the rich natural resources of Africa. They used the wealth they obtained from mining diamonds, gold, copper, and iron ore to develop their colonies economically. They built roads, railroads, and harbors. This economic development created jobs in which Africans acquired new skills.

Europeans increased literacy, the ability to read and write, among Africans, although there were literate societies in Africa before the Age of Imperialism. Christian missionaries were particularly active in setting up schools and developing written alphabets for some African languages.

Colonial governments and missionaries also introduced improved medical care and better methods of sanitation. New crops, tools, and farming methods helped increase food production. In addition, colonial rulers ended the local warfare among Africans, which had grown out of the slave trade.

A New Generation of African Leaders

By 1914, many Africans had graduated from colonial schools. Some had completed their education at European universities. At first, some educated Africans imitated everything European and denied their African traditions. After a time, however, a new generation of educated Africans emerged. They accepted some of the benefits of European civilization. However, they also recognized the importance of their own heritage.

These Africans came to appreciate their own culture, in part because of their experiences in Europe. There, they discovered more about their colonial rulers. In Africa, they had been taught that Europeans were superior and did not work with their hands. As a result, many Africans who went to

By the early 1900s, Europeans had established schools and colleges in their African colonies. This photograph shows an African medical school in Uganda, a British colony.

Paris, London, and Berlin were shocked to see Europeans employed as street cleaners and factory workers. In addition, in European universities, Africans studied the ideas of self-government expressed by philosophers such as John Locke and Thomas Jefferson.

On their return to Africa, these western-educated Africans experienced a sense of frustration. Colonial governments continued to treat them as inferiors. They realized that Europeans would never view them as equals no matter how westernized they became. In the early 1900s, this new generation of African leaders began to organize nationalist movements aimed at ending colonial rule.

SECTION REVIEW

1. Define: paternalism, assimilation.
2. (a) Describe two features of direct rule. (b) What European nations used direct rule in Africa?
3. (a) How did indirect rule differ from direct rule? (b) What nation governed through indirect rule? Why?
4. How did colonial governments try to make their colonies self-sufficient?
5. How did colonial rule affect traditional African culture?
6. Why did educated Africans organize nationalist movements?

Chapter 27 Review

In Perspective

Between 1870 and 1914, European nations carved up most of Africa. A variety of motives, including nationalism, economic rivalries, and humanitarian concerns, sent Europeans to Africa in ever-increasing numbers.

Europeans turned their attention to Africa just when important internal changes were taking place there. The end of the slave trade and the revival of Islam altered the relationships among the peoples of West Africa. In East Africa, new states had emerged under the leadership of strong individuals. People in many parts of Africa resisted European expansion. Yet their resistance failed, in part because Europeans were better armed.

Rivalries over Africa brought various European powers to the brink of war. However, they generally settled their differences peacefully. European powers ruled their colonies differently. But they shared similar attitudes and believed their colonies should provide economic benefits.

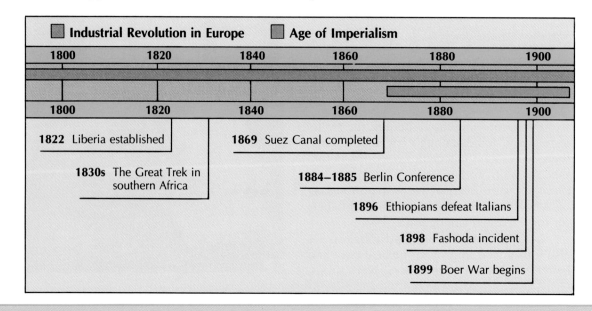

Industrial Revolution in Europe		Age of Imperialism			
1800	1820	1840	1860	1880	1900
1800	1820	1840	1860	1880	1900

1822 Liberia established

1830s The Great Trek in southern Africa

1869 Suez Canal completed

1884–1885 Berlin Conference

1896 Ethiopians defeat Italians

1898 Fashoda incident

1899 Boer War begins

Recalling Facts

Decide if the following statements are true or false. If a statement is false, rewrite the statement to make it true.

1. European nations divided up Africa at the Berlin Conference.
2. Christian missionaries wanted to preserve traditional African culture.
3. David Livingstone helped open up Central Africa to Europeans.
4. Under Muhammed Ali, Egypt increased its exports of cotton.
5. The Suez Canal was built by a German company.
6. The Congo Free State was owned by the king of France.
7. The Boers set out on the Great Trek to escape British control.
8. Britain established direct rule in its African colonies.

Chapter Checkup

1. (a) Describe the major causes of European imperialism in the 1800s. (b) How did exploration lead to increased interest in Africa? (c) What advantages did Europeans have over the people they conquered?

2. (a) How did Muhammed Ali strengthen Egypt? (b) Why did his policies eventually result in greater European influence in Egypt?

3. (a) How did Ethiopia prepare its defense against European imperialism? (b) Was it successful? Explain.

4. (a) Describe the slave-gun cycle. (b) How did the increased demand for slaves affect West Africa? (c) What effect did the abolition of the slave trade have on West Africa?

5. Explain how the expansion of each of the following groups in South Africa led to conflict: (a) Zulu; (b) Boers; (c) British.

6. (a) What powerful leaders ruled in East Africa in the 1800s? (b) How did they gain power? (c) Why were their empires short-lived?

7. (a) What attitude did most Europeans have toward the African peoples they ruled? (b) How did this view affect the kinds of government Europeans established in their colonies?

8. Explain how colonial rule affected each of the following areas of African life: (a) government; (b) farming; (c) village life; (d) religion.

Critical Thinking

1. **Analyzing a Quotation**   A British poet, Rudyard Kipling, wrote the following lines in 1899:

   Take up the white man's burden—
   Send out the best ye breed—
   Go bind your sons to exile,
   To serve your captives' need;
   To wait in heavy harness,
   On fluttered folk and wild—
   Your new-caught sullen peoples,
   Half devil and half child.

   How do these lines express European paternalism in the Age of Imperialism?

2. **Synthesizing**   (a) Describe three ways in which Africans responded to European imperialism. (b) Why were Africans generally unable to prevent European expansion?

Relating Past to Present

1. (a) Why did the British want control over the Suez Canal? (b) Do you think the Suez Canal is as important today as it was in the late 1800s? Explain.

Developing Basic Skills

1. **Making a Review Chart**   Make a chart with two columns and six rows. Title the columns Areas Claimed in Africa and European Rival. Title the rows France, Italy, Britain, Germany, Portugal, Belgium. Fill in the chart with information from your reading and the map on page 508. Then answer the following questions: (a) Which countries claimed land in North Africa? (b) What areas of Africa did Germany claim? (c) How do you think the scramble for Africa affected relationships among European nations?

2. **Classifying**   Make a chart with two columns. In the first column, describe the benefits of European imperialism for African societies. In the second column, describe the disadvantages of European imperialism for African societies. After completing the chart, answer the following questions: (a) What economic benefits resulted from imperialism? (b) What economic problems were caused by imperialism? (c) How did imperialism affect African cultures? (d) In your opinion, which were greater—the benefits or the disadvantages of imperialism? Explain.

See page 806 for suggested readings.

28 Asia and the West

(1650–1920)

In 1793, King George III of Britain sent an ambassador to the Chinese emperor, seeking an exchange of diplomats and expansion of trade with China. Although Britain was one of the most powerful nations in Europe, the Chinese emperor, Ch'ien-lung, considered it a weak, uncivilized nation. Ch'ien-lung therefore replied to George III in these words:

"You, O King, have yearned from afar after the blessings of our civilization, and in your eagerness to come into touch with our converting influence have sent an Embassy across the sea bearing a memorial [diplomatic request]. I have already taken note of your re-

A Chinese emperor granting an audience.

spectful spirit of submission and have treated your mission with extreme favor and loaded it with gifts. . . .

"Yesterday, your Ambassador petitioned my Ministers . . . regarding your trade with China, but his proposal is contrary to the usage [custom] of our dynasty and cannot be entertained. Hitherto, all European nations, including your own country's barbarian merchants, have carried on trade with our Celestial Empire at Canton. Such has been the procedure for many centuries, although our Celestial Empire possesses all things in prolific abundance and lacks no product within its own borders. There was, therefore, no need to import the manufactures of outside barbarians in exchange for your own product."

The emperor's refusal to treat Britain as an equal was due in part to the Chinese belief that no nation could match Chinese achievements. In 1793, Emperor Ch'ien-lung did not foresee that Britain and other western nations would soon challenge China. In the late 1700s, European powers were already advancing into Asia. During the Age of Imperialism, India, China, Japan, and Southeast Asia would all feel the impact of foreign expansion.

1 India Under British Rule

Read to Learn   ■ how the British established control in India
   ■ how the British changed Indian life

Following Vasco da Gama's voyage in 1498, English, French, Portuguese, and Dutch merchants established trade with India. As you read in Chapter 15, Europeans at first posed no threat to Indian rulers because the Mogul Empire was at the height of its power. In the mid-1700s, however, the Mogul Empire was collapsing.

An Empire in Decline

For almost 200 years, from 1526 to about 1712, able Mogul emperors ruled a powerful empire. But during the 1700s, the empire suffered from a lack of strong rulers. Government efficiency declined, and provincial governors became increasingly independent.

In the early days of the Mogul Empire, both Hindus and Muslims had rallied behind the emperor. As the emperor's prestige faded, however, war broke out between the two religious groups. In addition, a growing number of people saw the Mogul government as extravagant and oppressive. In the mid-1700s, rival Indian princes competed for power. Europeans took advantage of these internal struggles to advance into India.

The English East India Company

As the Mogul Empire collapsed, French and British trading companies battled for control of trade with India. During the 1700s, the English East India Company successfully promoted its interests on the subcontinent. The East India Company had been founded in 1600 to make money by selling Indian products such as cotton cloth, silk, sugar, and jute in world markets. However, as rivalry with France and the turmoil in the Mogul Empire threatened its profits, the East India Company became increasingly involved in political and military affairs.

In 1756 at the outbreak of the Seven Years War in Europe, Robert Clive, an employee of the East India Company, raised an army and ousted the French. He then used his army to ensure that a government favorable to the East India Company ruled the Indian state of Bengal. Clive and his successors continued to interfere in local Indian affairs until the East India Company became the most powerful authority in India.

The East India Company practiced *commercial colonialism*—that is, it controlled India's foreign trade and used its army to keep friendly local rulers in power. To protect its interests, the company built forts and maintained an army of *sepoys*, Indian soldiers who served in European armies. During the late 1700s and early 1800s, the East India Company gained direct political control over some parts of India.

Establishing British Rule

Though regulated by the British government, the East India Company had a fairly free hand in India until the mid-1800s. By this time, many members of Parliament felt that the British government should assume responsibility for India. In 1857, an uprising known as the Sepoy Rebellion gave Parliament the excuse it needed to end the rule of the East India Company in India.

The Sepoy Rebellion. The immediate cause of the Sepoy Rebellion was rumors that bullet cartridges used by sepoys were greased with beef or pork fat. These rumors angered both Hindu and Muslim soldiers. Hindus were forbidden to touch beef, and Muslims were forbidden to touch pork. The sepoys also resented British efforts to make them adopt Christianity and European customs. The rebellion among the sepoys spread across India.

Hindu and Muslim princes supported the Sepoy Rebellion because they saw the British as a threat to their power. Peasants joined the uprising in protest against the severe hardships of their lives. British troops suppressed the rebellion, and in 1858 the

British Parliament took control of India from the East India Company.

Colonial government. After 1858, the British government established full colonial rule in India. A cabinet minister in London was responsible for Indian affairs. A British viceroy in India carried out government policies. British governors ruled about two-thirds of India, including the parts that the East India Company had controlled directly. Local Indian princes stayed on as rulers in the rest of the country. But British officials called residents closely supervised these Indian rulers. In 1877, British Prime Minister Benjamin Disraeli had Queen Victoria recognized as Empress of India.

In 1890, about 1,000 British officials ran a colonial government that ruled some 280 million Indians. During the Age of Imperialism, the British had a clear idea of what they thought India should become. Unlike the East India Company, which had encouraged its officers to learn Indian languages and observe local customs, the British colonial government tried to impose British culture on India. British officials encouraged the Indian people to abandon their traditions and learn to speak, dress, and live like Europeans. These colonial officials believed that by adopting European ways, Indians would improve their lives.

Impact of British Rule

British rule affected Indian life in various ways. In countless Indian villages, the coming of the British had little direct impact. Farmers tilled their fields as they had for centuries. The caste system dominated village life, and the people observed traditional religious practices. However, British colonial policies opened the door to major economic and social changes.

Economic changes. The Industrial Revolution in Britain influenced British economic policies toward India. The East India Company had sold Indian-made luxury items abroad, but the British government saw India as a source of cheap raw materials for British factories. It also felt that India, which had a large population, would serve as a market for British manufactured goods. Britain, therefore, tied the Indian economy closely to its own.

The British discouraged local Indian industries. They encouraged Indian farmers to shift from growing food crops to raising cotton. Factories in Britain then used the Indian cotton to produce finished goods, some of which were sent back to India to be sold. Although this policy benefited British manufacturers, it hurt local industries in India. Village artisans could not compete with the cheaper, mass-produced British imports.

Moreover, British efforts to encourage the production of export crops, such as cotton, reduced the amount of food that was grown. As a result of reduced food supplies, famines killed millions of Indians during the 1800s.

British rule in India led to better communication and increased trade. By building

Map Skill *Britain controlled all of India after 1858. In the areas colored blue and purple on this map, British officials ruled directly over the Indian people. In the areas colored pink, they governed through local Indian rulers. Why do you think Bengal was ruled directly?*

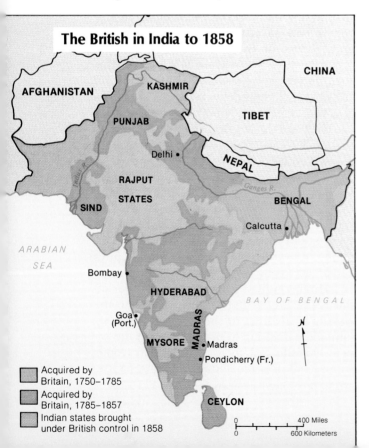

The British in India to 1858

AFGHANISTAN
KASHMIR
CHINA
PUNJAB
TIBET
Delhi
NEPAL
RAJPUT STATES
Ganges R.
SIND
BENGAL
Calcutta
ARABIAN SEA
Bombay
HYDERABAD
BAY OF BENGAL
Goa (Port.)
MADRAS
MYSORE
Madras
Pondicherry (Fr.)
CEYLON

Acquired by Britain, 1750–1785
Acquired by Britain, 1785–1857
Indian states brought under British control in 1858

0   400 Miles
0   600 Kilometers

This 1870 Indian woodcut shows one of the effects of British rule—the building of thousands of miles of railroads. Notice that the last car, known as the "purdah carriage," was reserved for women and children.

new canals, roads, and railways, the British opened up India's vast interior to trade. The opening of the Suez Canal in 1869 made trade faster and easier between Europe and India as well as between Europe and the rest of Asia. Telegraph lines also made communications easier between Britain and India. These developments resulted in a tremendous increase in exports from India.

Social changes. The British sponsored programs to improve health care and control epidemics, which occurred frequently. They built hospitals and trained doctors to work in the countryside. Improved medical care contributed to a rapid growth of the Indian population. In some regions, population growth combined with inadequate food supplies resulted in famine. At the same time, the building of railroads helped reduce the effect of famine since food could be transported quickly from one region to another.

India's growing population made Indian cities among the largest in the world. British determination to introduce their own culture in India was especially evident in the cities. There, British rule created a class of British-educated professionals and businesspeople.

Young Indians, mainly from higher-caste families, attended British-run schools and colleges. They studied the same courses in science, mathematics, history, literature, and philosophy as students in Britain. These doctors, lawyers, professors, civil servants, and businesspeople became a new upper

class in India. British officials depended on them to carry out colonial policies. By the late 1800s, however, some members of the new upper class began voicing discontent with British rule.

Indian Nationalism

Opposition to British rule was not new in India. Economic hardships in the countryside had touched off periodic uprisings. On occasion, British troops faced thousands of enraged peasants. However, these revolts did not threaten British control. The peasants were too poorly armed and organized to defeat the British.

In 1885, a group of well-educated, middle-class Indians formed a political party called the Indian National Congress. Known as the Congress, this party led the nationalist movement in India. At first, the Congress did not seek independence from Britain. It campaigned for reforms such as free compulsory education for boys and girls and greater Indian representation in local government.

In the early 1900s, Indian nationalists began calling for an end to British rule. They urged Indians to boycott, or stop buying, British goods. At the same time, Indian writers published books that restored people's pride in India's ancient heritage.

The best known nationalist leader was Mohandas Gandhi, born into the Vaisya, or merchant, caste. Gandhi rallied widespread popular support for the independence movement. India should be free, he said, so that Indians could restore their village life and live according to their ancient traditions. As you will read in Chapter 31, Gandhi eventually united the Hindu population behind the call for Indian independence.

At first the British leaders did not take the independence movement seriously. They knew that Hindus and Muslims were so deeply divided that they would not cooperate against the British. Therefore, Britain refused to give in to the demands of Indian nationalists.

SECTION REVIEW

1. Identify: Robert Clive, Sepoy Rebellion, Indian National Congress, Mohandas Gandhi.
2. Define: commercial colonialism, sepoy.
3. Give one reason why the Mogul Empire declined in the 1700s.
4. What Indian goods did the English East India Company sell?
5. List three ways in which British rule affected India.
6. (a) What reforms did the early Indian nationalists want? (b) How did their demands change in the early 1900s?

2 Conflict Between China and the West

Read to Learn
- how Europeans gained influence in China
- how the Chinese tried to regain power

In 1793 when the emperor Ch'ien-lung wrote the letter at the beginning of this chapter, China was probably the wealthiest, most powerful country in the world. A strong central government was successfully administering a vast empire. Yet within 100 years, this prosperous empire would be torn apart by internal rebellion and the growing influence of western nations* in Asia.

The Manchu Dynasty

In the early 1600s, invaders from Manchuria swept into China and overwhelmed the Ming dynasty, which had ruled China since the 1300s. (See page 252.) The victorious Manchu, as the invaders were called, established their capital at Peking. They adopted the customs and traditions of the Chinese and won the support of the Confucian official class. The Manchu, claiming they had received the Mandate of Heaven, founded a new dynasty. The Manchu dynasty ruled China from 1644 to 1911.

The Manchu presided over a powerful and prosperous empire. Western merchants reaching China in the 1600s and 1700s were amazed at the splendor of Chinese civilization. They began arriving in ever greater numbers to buy Chinese tea, silk, and porcelain.

As you read in Chapter 17, the Chinese had restricted foreigners to trading at Canton. Europeans had to pay for Chinese products with gold and silver because they had few European manufactured goods that the Chinese wanted. If foreign merchants did not observe Chinese customs, the Chinese expelled them. Although the restrictions irritated foreign merchants, they accepted the restrictions because huge profits could be made selling Chinese goods in Europe and the United States.

In the 1800s, domestic turmoil disrupted life in Manchu China. This turmoil had several sources. Under the Manchu, the Chinese population had grown to about 300 million people. Such large numbers strained food resources. A flood or drought could cause mass starvation. During times of famine, peasants in many parts of China rebelled against the government.

---

* The term "western" refers to the nations of Western Europe and the United States.

Chinese porcelain was highly prized by westerners who went to China to trade. Gradually, all glazed pottery—no matter where it originated—became known as chinaware or simply china. In this Chinese print from the 1800s, skilled artisans are shown making pottery in a shed. Outside the shed, pots are set out to dry on long tables.

Furthermore, like earlier dynasties, the Manchu eventually became corrupt. Even during the reign of the powerful emperor Ch'ien-lung, official corruption undermined Chinese strength. For 30 years, a court official and friend of the emperor, Ho-shen, ran wild with government money. It is estimated that Ho-shen skimmed a personal fortune equal to about $1 billion from taxes. Throughout the empire, officials enriched themselves with public funds. To offset the loss of these revenues, officials raised the taxes peasants had to pay. Unbearable taxes led to more peasant uprisings.

Beginning of European Imperialism

While the Manchu government struggled to suppress these uprisings, Europeans were pressuring China to end its trade restrictions. European governments also demanded that China receive their diplomats and treat them as equals. The Chinese saw their land as the center of civilization, and they thought China should receive only "tribute bearers" from states they considered inferior.

The Opium War. Tensions between China and European powers increased until they flared into violence over the opium trade. In the early 1800s, British merchants discovered that they could make huge profits trading opium from India and Turkey for Chinese goods. While the opium trade enriched many foreign and Chinese merchants, the Chinese government was outraged as opium smoking spread throughout China. Not only was opium harmful to the Chinese people, but the opium trade drained China of silver, which was used to pay foreign merchants who imported the drug.

The Chinese decided to end the opium trade. In 1839, the government destroyed $6 million worth of opium that the British had brought to Canton. To China's surprise, the British responded with military force. In 1840, the British seized Canton and attacked Chinese forces along the coast. In this conflict, often called the Opium War, the British used their navy and superior weapons to defeat the Chinese.

The unequal treaties. In 1842, the Chinese were forced to accept humiliating terms in the Treaty of Nanking. Under this treaty, China had to accept foreign diplomats and open more ports to foreign trade. Britain won the island of Hong Kong and received compensation for the opium destroyed by the Chinese.

Other provisions limited China's ability to govern itself even more seriously. For example, China agreed to let Britain determine its tariffs, or taxes on imports. The Chinese also granted the British the right of *extraterritoriality*—that is, the British would be protected by the laws of their own nation, not the laws of China. Extraterritoriality meant that China would have little authority over foreigners.

The Treaty of Nanking was the first of the "unequal treaties" that China was forced to make with foreign powers. Other nations soon demanded and received most of the rights that the British had won in the Treaty of Nanking. In later struggles with western powers and Japan, China gave up still more rights.

China was unable to defend itself against these demands in part because its military technology had fallen behind that of the foreign powers. For centuries, the Chinese had believed in the superiority of their civilization. However, by the 1800s, European advances in science and technology had, for the first time, made European nations more powerful than China.

The Taiping Rebellion

Internal unrest continued to weaken the Manchu dynasty. In 1850, discontent with Manchu rule erupted into a widespread peasant uprising known as the Taiping Rebellion. The rebels were inspired by a mixture of ancient Chinese traditions and ideas learned from Christian missionaries. Their leaders promised reforms such as the redistribution of land to poor peasants, an end to high taxes, and equality for men and women.

The rebels seized the central region of China and nearly toppled the government. They sought the aid of European nations by claiming to be Christians. But in the end, the Europeans helped the Manchu emperor since they had already signed favorable treaties with him. After 14 years of fighting, the government finally defeated the Taiping rebels. However, the rebellion weakened the Manchu dynasty further and created a strong wish for reform within China.

During the Taiping Rebellion, European powers forced China to grant them more concessions. The Chinese government had to open additional ports to foreign trade and make the opium trade legal. It also had to allow foreign diplomats to live in Peking.

Spheres of Influence

In 1860, the Russians seized a large stretch of land on China's northern border and built the port of Vladivostok on the Pacific coast. Japan, too, took advantage of Chinese weakness to increase its influence in Korea, a country that China had dominated. In 1894, China tried to stop the Japanese advance in Korea, and war broke out. Japan quickly defeated China. China was forced to recognize Korean independence, and Japan won several islands from China, including Formosa, present-day Taiwan.

Toward the end of the century, China lost still more power. Russia, Germany, France, and Britain each acquired a sphere of influence in China. (See the map on page 533.) Each nation won special economic privileges in its sphere of influence, including the right to invest in mines, railways, and factories. These four European powers also forced China to lease them land so they could build naval bases to protect their spheres of influence.

The United States did not acquire a sphere of influence in China, but the American government insisted that it receive the same commercial rights as other foreign powers. It demanded equal access to trade in China for all nations. This Open Door Policy, as it was called, was meant to prevent foreign powers from carving China up into colonies. In letters addressed to the foreign powers in China, the United States called on these countries to allow free trade in their spheres of influence and to maintain Chinese political unity. The American policy did help preserve an open door to trade in China, but it did little to keep China from foreign domination.

Chinese Efforts at Reform

Chinese leaders were outraged at the sad condition of their country. As early as the 1860s, after the defeat of the Taiping rebels, the government had adopted a policy known as "self-strengthening." It hoped to reestablish government control over both the Chinese and the foreigners living in China.

This "self-strengthening" policy involved finding ways to modernize China while retaining Confucian traditions. The government tried to introduce modern weapons and began construction of telegraph and railroad lines. Chinese students were sent abroad to study western ideas. The government also tried to weed out corrupt officials. Many officials opposed these reforms, however, so the policy had little success.

Hundred days of reform. In 1898, as foreign interference increased, a young and idealistic Manchu emperor made another attempt to save China. On the advice of reformers at court, he decided to send diplomats and other officials abroad to study. He issued decrees to reform schools, add practical subjects to the curriculum, and translate foreign books into Chinese.

Known as the "hundred days of reform," this program introduced many changes that challenged the traditional Confucian order. Conservatives at the imperial court turned to the dowager empress Tz'u-hsi (tsoo shee) for help. Tz'u-hsi strongly opposed the new reforms. In 1898, she ousted the reformers from power and had the emperor imprisoned. For the next ten years, Tz'u-hsi ruled China and prevented any major reforms.

The Boxer Rebellion. The dowager empress faced two serious problems: foreign

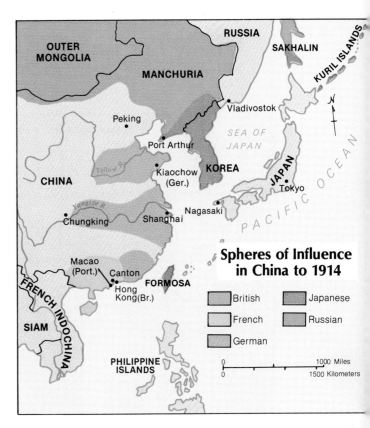

Map Skill *By the early 1900s, several European nations and Japan had acquired spheres of influence in China. Within its sphere of influence, each nation claimed exclusive trading rights. What relationship do you see between the spheres of influence and the rivers in China?*

imperialism and a growing Chinese belief that the Manchu dynasty had lost the Mandate of Heaven. In 1899, a group of Chinese founded a secret society called the "Fists of Righteous Harmony" or "Boxers." The Boxers wanted to expel the Manchu and all foreigners from China. But Tz'u-hsi negotiated with the Boxers and agreed to aid them secretly against foreigners.

In 1900, the Boxers moved through northern China attacking foreigners. They then besieged foreign diplomats in Peking. The foreigners responded by organizing an international army to march on Peking and rescue the diplomats. The army defeated the Boxers and forced Tz'u-hsi to grant them concessions. China agreed to allow foreign

533

The battle cry of the Boxers was: "Overthrow the Manchu; destroy the foreigners."
The Boxers attacked Chinese who had adopted foreign ideas such as Christianity. In
June 1900, they surrounded foreign areas in Peking. This painting shows an
international force of American, Japanese, and British troops attacking the Boxers in
an attempt to rescue the trapped foreigners.

troops to be stationed on Chinese soil and to allow foreign naval vessels to patrol Chinese rivers and coastal waters.

The Revolution of 1911

In 1908, Tz'u-hsi died. She had named a two-year-old prince to succeed her. Three years later, revolutionaries overthrew the young Manchu emperor and proclaimed a republic.

The leading figure in the Revolution of 1911 was Dr. Sun Yat-sen. Sun had led revolutionaries in earlier uprisings against the Manchu. However, he was living in the United States when the revolution broke out in 1911. Sun returned to China at once and was named the first president of the Chinese Republic. He also helped found the Kuomintang (KWOH mihn TANG), or Nationalist party.

The new republic faced civil war in the provinces. Military leaders known as warlords fought each other and looted the countryside. Amid this confusion, Sun worked to build a united, powerful, and independent China. He set out a revolutionary program called "Three Principles of the People." The principles were political unity, democracy, and a basic living for all Chinese.

Sun was influenced by his travels in the United States and Western Europe. He wanted China to have the same high standard of living he saw in these nations. Sun believed that China should be thoroughly reorganized in order to achieve this goal. In the years ahead, Sun and the Kuomintang would struggle to make China a powerful modern nation.

SECTION REVIEW

1. Locate: Manchuria, Canton, Vladivostok, Formosa.
2. Identify: Manchu, Treaty of Nanking, Taiping Rebellion, Open Door Policy, Tz'u-hsi, Boxer Rebellion, Sun Yat-sen, Kuomintang.
3. Define: extraterritoriality.
4. Give two reasons for the decline of the Manchu dynasty.
5. (a) What was the immediate cause of the Opium War? (b) What was the outcome of the war?
6. What rights did foreigners gain in the "unequal treaties"?
7. (a) Which nations had spheres of influence in China? (b) What privileges did each nation acquire in its sphere of influence?
8. What were the Three Principles of the People proposed by Sun Yat-sen?

Sun Yat-sen despised the corrupt Manchu dynasty that ruled China. In the early 1900s, he wrote: "Today we are the poorest and weakest nation in the world and occupy the lowest position in international affairs. Other men are the carving knife and serving dish; we are the fish and the meat." Sun Yat-sen led the Chinese nationalist movement after the overthrow of the last Manchu emperor.

3 Modernizing Japan

Read to Learn
■ how foreigners gained access to Japan
■ how modernization transformed Japanese society

In the 1600s, Japanese rulers expelled Europeans from their land and forbade Japanese to leave the country. Only one Dutch ship was allowed to visit Nagasaki each year. For 200 years, the Tokugawa shoguns were strong enough to enforce this policy of isolation. However, in the mid-1800s, they encountered serious domestic and international challenges.

Tokugawa Japan

As you read in Chapter 15, the Tokugawa shoguns created a strong unified government in Japan. They established a system of centralized feudalism that rested on a rigidly controlled economic and social order. The samurai were the highest class. Below them were the peasants. The lowest social class was the merchant class. (See page 257.)

During 200 years of peace under the Tokugawa shoguns, commerce and trade within Japan expanded. As a result, Japanese merchants often acquired more wealth than the samurai. Increasingly, wealthy merchants resented their low social status.

At the same time, some samurai organized revolts against the Tokugawa shogun. They were encouraged by scholars who argued that the shogun had unlawfully seized power from the true ruler, the emperor. In the 1800s, these opposition forces became a serious threat to the Tokugawa government. The movement against the government was strengthened in the 1850s when foreigners reappeared in Japan.

An End to Isolation

In 1853, the United States government sent a naval mission to Japan under the command of Commodore Matthew C. Perry. The United States wanted to negotiate a treaty to protect American sailors shipwrecked in Japanese waters, to open Japanese ports so American ships could take on food and water, and to grant the United States the right to trade with Japan. Fully aware of the Japanese attitude toward foreigners, the United States decided to back up its request with a show of force. Therefore, Commodore Perry arrived in Tokyo Bay with a fleet of steam-powered warships.

The Japanese did not want to negotiate a treaty with the Americans, but they remembered China's defeat in the Opium War. Fearing a similar fate, Tokugawa officials argued:

> If we try to drive them away, they will immediately commence hostilities, and then we shall be obliged to fight.... In time, the country would be put to an immense expense, and the people be plunged into misery. Rather than allow this, as we are not the equals of foreigners in the mechanical arts, let us have relations with foreign countries, learn their drills and tactics ... and it will not be too late then to declare war.

Thus, in 1854, Japan signed the Treaty of Kanagawa with the United States. The treaty opened up two Japanese ports to foreign trade and met the other American demands.

This treaty marked the end of Japanese isolation. Japan, like China, soon had to grant further concessions to foreign powers. In the 1850s and 1860s, the Tokugawa government signed "unequal treaties" with the United States and the major European powers. The treaties gave these foreign countries control over Japanese tariffs, extensive trading rights in Japan, and the right of extraterritoriality.

The Meiji Period

The treaties granting privileges to foreigners aroused fierce opposition to the shogun among the Japanese. In southern Japan, samurai leaders bitterly denounced the for-

During the Meiji period, the Japanese sent many people to study western governments and technology. In 1871, Prince Iwakura, shown here, sailed from Yokohama at the head of the first diplomatic mission to the West. Iwakura's main purpose was to revise the "unequal treaties" with western nations. He failed to achieve this goal. But he did bring back detailed information about the Industrial Revolution taking place in the West.

eigners, who were arriving in growing numbers. The samurai rallied around the emperor in Kyoto and proclaimed that they had restored imperial rule.

In 1868, the last Tokugawa shogun resigned, and the emperor, who was only 15 years old, moved his capital from Kyoto to Tokyo. He took the name Meiji (may jee), meaning "enlightened government." During the Meiji period, from 1868 to 1912, the Japanese government embarked on a course that transformed the country from a feudal state into a modern industrialized nation.

Abolition of feudalism. Leaders of the Meiji government were determined to save Japan from foreign domination by building up its political, military, and economic strength. The government decided to abandon the centralized feudalism of the Tokugawa period. The abolition of feudalism affected the political and social structure of Japan. Large landowners were persuaded to turn their fiefs, or vast estates, over to the emperor. In return, they received financial compensation and high level positions in government.

Other changes introduced at this time affected all classes in Japan. The samurai class lost power and prestige because the Meiji government made all classes equal before the law. Moreover, in 1872, Japan introduced a system of universal military service. This meant peasants and merchants as well as samurai might serve in the armed forces. Their exclusive military service had been a major source of power and prestige for the samurai.

Constitutional government. In 1884, the emperor asked Ito Hirobumi, a Japanese official, to draft a constitution for Japan. Ito visited the United States and several European nations to study their constitutional governments. He met with Bismarck and was especially impressed with the constitutional system of government in Germany. On his return to Japan, Ito drafted a constitution based in part on the German model.

In 1889, the emperor presented the constitution to the Japanese people. The Meiji constitution established a two-house diet, or parliament. But the diet had limited power because the emperor had the greatest authority. He could issue laws, veto laws passed by the diet, and declare war. In practice, however, ministers appointed by the emperor did the actual governing.

Daily Life ■ A Japanese View of Europe

Yukichi Fukuzawa, a Japanese scholar, made many trips to Europe and the United States during the late 1800s. Fukuzawa enthusiastically supported modernization in Japan. In these excerpts from his autobiography, he expresses his interest in western ideas.

From Fukuzawa's Autobiography

During this mission in Europe, I tried to learn some of the most commonplace details of foreign culture. I did not care to study scientific or technical subjects while on the journey, because I could study them as well from books after I had returned home. But I felt that I had to learn the more common matters of daily life directly from the people because the Europeans would not describe them in books as being too obvious. Yet to us those common matters were the most difficult to comprehend.

For instance, when I saw a hospital, I wanted to know how it was run—who paid the running expenses; when I visited a bank, I wished to learn how the money was deposited and paid out. By similar firsthand queries [questions], I learned something of the postal system and the military conscription [draft] then in force in France but not in England. A perplexing institution was representative government.

When I asked a gentleman what the "election law" was and what kind of an institution the Parliament really was, he simply replied with a smile, meaning, I suppose, that no intelligent person was expected to ask such a question. But these were the things most difficult of all for me to understand. In this connection, I learned that there were different political parties—the Liberal and the Conservative—who were always "fighting" against each other in the government.

For some time it was beyond my comprehension to understand what they were "fighting" for, and what was meant, anyway, by "fighting" in peace time. "This man and that man are 'enemies' in the House," they would tell me. But these "enemies" were to be seen at the same table, eating and drinking with each other. I felt as if I could not make much out of this. It took me a long time, with some tedious thinking, before I could gather a general notion of these . . . mysterious facts.

537

Economic and Social Changes

During the Meiji period, Japan moved rapidly to strengthen its economy. In the late 1800s, the government led the effort to modernize Japan by sponsoring new industries. Once again, the Meiji government borrowed ideas from abroad. Japanese visited factories in Europe and the United States. The government hired thousands of foreign engineers to teach their skills in Japan.

The government built defense industries such as shipyards and munitions plants. It also encouraged mining of coal and iron and developed a modern communication system by building railroads and stringing telegraph lines. Finally, it sponsored consumer industries such as textile manufacturing.

In the 1880s, the Meiji government decided to sell some of its factories and mills to private businesspeople. A few wealthy families, known as *zaibatsu* (ZĪ baht SOO), bought the chief industries and thereby came to dominate the Japanese economy. Families such as the Mitsubishi and Mitsui owned many large companies and controlled whole industries.

In Japan, cooperation among companies was more important than competition, so companies were often merged to increase efficiency. By 1914, the combination of government support and private initiative had made Japan a powerful industrial nation.

Industrialization transformed Japanese society. Millions of people abandoned farming and moved to the cities to work in factories. Because the samurai no longer enjoyed their old privileges, many of them became officers in the Japanese army and navy. Others went into business or government.

As part of its program of modernization, the government created a new educational system. By 1900, almost all children were enrolled in elementary schools. Some students continued their education in middle schools and high schools. The government also organized commercial and technical schools. At the top of the system were prestigious imperial universities, which admitted only a small number of outstanding students.

Japanese Expansion in the Pacific

By 1900, Japan was reaping the benefits of modernization. It negotiated new treaties with western nations. It also withdrew privi-

Under Meiji rulers, Japan modernized rapidly. It financed the building of modern factories. It also imported textile machinery and other western inventions. This 1883 print shows people stopping to watch the first electric street lamps being lighted in Tokyo.

leges such as extraterritoriality. In addition, Japan regained full control over its own tariffs.

As Japan gained strength, it participated in imperialist ventures. As you read, Japanese expansion in Korea led to war with China in 1894. After defeating China, Japan acquired Taiwan and the same trading privileges enjoyed by western powers in China.

Ten years later, Japan surprised people in the West by winning a stunning victory over Russia. The Russo-Japanese War broke out in 1904 over rival Russian and Japanese claims in Manchuria. The Japanese army forced the Russians to retreat from Manchuria, and the Japanese navy defeated two Russian fleets.

In 1905, President Theodore Roosevelt invited Japanese and Russian diplomats to meet in Portsmouth, New Hampshire, where they worked out a treaty ending the war. Japan acquired Port Arthur and concessions in southern Manchuria from Russia. Japan thus gained a foothold for an empire on the Asian mainland. Furthermore, the Russo-Japanese War showed the world that an Asian power could defeat a major European nation.

SECTION REVIEW

1. Identify: Matthew C. Perry, Treaty of Kanagawa, Ito Hirobumi, Russo-Japanese War.
2. Define: zaibatsu.
3. (a) Which groups in Japanese society opposed the Tokugawa shogun in the 1800s? (b) Why?
4. Why did the United States want a treaty with Japan in 1853?
5. List two results of the Russo-Japanese War.

4 Imperialism in Southeast Asia and the Pacific

Read to Learn
- how European powers gained colonies in Southeast Asia
- how imperialism affected Southeast Asian nations

Southeast Asia was another area of interest to western powers during the Age of Imperialism. As you read in Chapter 17, during the 1500s, several European nations competed for control of the spice trade in the East Indies. Later, European nations extended their influence over most of Southeast Asia.

Peoples of Southeast Asia

Southeast Asia includes the area of the Asian mainland south of China. This area stretches from present-day Bangladesh in the west to present-day Vietnam in the east. Southeast Asia also includes the Philippine Islands, the East Indies, and Indonesia. (See the map on page 789.)

Southeast Asia is home to peoples with different languages, customs, and political systems. Geography has influenced the peoples of Southeast Asia. The language and customs of people in a mountainous region usually differ from those of nearby people in a lowland area.

The early civilizations of India and China also influenced the peoples of Southeast Asia. Traders and Buddhist missionaries from India helped spread both Hindu and Buddhist beliefs. Indian culture had its greatest impact on the area that today includes Burma, Thailand, Laos, Kampuchea, and the southern part of Vietnam. During the T'ang dynasty, China began extending its influence into the northern part of Vietnam. In the 1200s, Arab and Indian Muslims carried Islam to Indonesia.

The political diversity among the peoples of Southeast Asia was evident to Europeans when they first arrived. In some areas, powerful monarchs united the people. Today, the ruins of Angkor Wat, an enormous temple built in the 1100s, recall the splendor of the Khmer Empire in Kampuchea. In other parts of Southeast Asia, there was no strong central authority. For example, when the Spanish reached the Philippines in the 1500s, they found only minor local rulers.

In the 1500s, when Europeans entered the spice trade, there were many separate states with their own cultural, social, and political traditions in Southeast Asia. Geography, trade rivalries, and religious differences further divided the peoples of the region, so they did not respond in a united fashion to the coming of the Europeans.

The Spice Trade

The early spice trade had little direct impact on the peoples of Southeast Asia. Portuguese, Spanish, and Dutch traders tried to drive Arab, Indian, and Chinese merchants out of the spice trade. They also competed fiercely with each other. They established trading posts along the coasts but did not extend their influence inland.

Only in the Philippines did Europeans have an immediate impact. In 1571, the Spanish conquered the Philippine Islands and sent a Spanish governor-general to rule the colony. For the first time, the Philippines were united under a single government. Catholic missionaries entered the islands with Spanish officials and converted many of the people to Christianity.

The Spanish seized the Philippines because they wanted to establish a direct trade route between Asia and their empire in the Americas. Spanish ships carried silver from the New World to the Philippines. They then sailed to China to buy porcelains and silk or to the Spice Islands to buy spices.

Scramble for Colonies in Southeast Asia

In the 1700s, European interest in Southeast Asia shifted from spices to crops such as sugar, coffee, and rice. To ensure production of these crops, Europeans took control of large parts of the region and set up huge plantations. As European nations industrialized, they also looked to Southeast Asia as a source of raw materials such as tin, rubber, and oil.

During the 1800s, the Dutch converted their trading outposts in Southeast Asia into a colony called the Dutch East Indies. By this time, however, Britain and France had become the chief European rivals in the region. It was the fierce competition between these two nations that led to a scramble for colonies on the mainland of Southeast Asia.

To protect the eastern frontier of India, Britain acquired Burma piece by piece between 1820 and 1890. Britain also established control over Malaya and the island of Singapore, which commands an important sea route to China. While Britain extended its influence in these regions, France established the colony of French Indochina. Both the British and the French hoped to use their

Map Skill *The spice trade originally attracted Europeans to Southeast Asia in the 1500s. In the 1800s, Europeans were more interested in cash crops such as sugar and rice and in natural resources such as oil and rubber. Which European nations claimed territory on the mainland?*

colonies as stepping stones to southern China.

During the scramble for colonies, only Siam, today called Thailand, escaped European domination. During the 1800s, Siamese rulers imported western technology to modernize their country. They also encouraged trade with western nations. Furthermore, the Siamese skillfully exploited the rivalry between Britain and France. By establishing their kingdom as a neutral buffer between the British in Burma and the French in Indochina, the Siamese guaranteed their freedom from foreign control.

Western Expansion in the Pacific

Several western powers seized control of various Pacific islands before the Age of Imperialism began. Spain conquered the Philippines, and Britain established colonies in Australia and New Zealand. In the late 1800s, Britain, Germany, and the United States seized other islands.

United States expansion in the Pacific region began after the Civil War as more and more American merchant ships began trading with China and Japan. American ships needed friendly ports where they could stop and take on fuel. In addition, the United States navy wanted bases to protect American trade. Thus, the United States began to take control of islands scattered through the Pacific. American interest in Southeast Asia and the Pacific grew as a result of a war the United States fought to free Cuba from Spain.*

The Spanish-American War began in 1898. The first American target in the war was a Spanish fleet in Manila Bay, the chief harbor in the Philippines. The American fleet commanded by Commodore George Dewey destroyed the Spanish ships and paved the way for American victory in the war. As part of the peace settlement, the United States acquired the Philippine Islands and Guam. In 1898, the United States also annexed Hawaii, where American mer-

---

* You will read more about the causes of the Spanish-American War in Chapter 29.

Many westerners had a romantic view of life on the islands of the South Pacific. They believed the people of these islands led simple lives, unspoiled by the Industrial Revolution. In 1891, Paul Gauguin, a leading French painter, went to live in Tahiti. Gauguin painted Tahitian people in their natural setting. This painting is entitled Two Tahitian Women on the Beach.

chants and sugar growers had extensive interests.

Southeast Asia Under Colonial Rule

Western imperialism greatly affected Southeast Asia. Almost everywhere, local leaders were replaced by foreign administrators. The economic structure of the region also changed. Colonial powers emphasized the production of cash crops and the export of raw materials. As a result, the people of Southeast Asia became dependent on international markets, where prices could rise and fall sharply.

A few independence movements developed in Southeast Asia. The first nationalist revolution began in the 1880s in the Philippines. In fact, Filipinos who were rebelling against Spanish rule helped American forces in the Spanish-American War. After the war, Filipino nationalists were bitterly disappointed when the United States refused to grant them independence at once. They then turned their struggle against the United States. Other colonial powers faced rebellions in Southeast Asia. However, western powers were confident that they could continue to rule their colonies indefinitely.

SECTION REVIEW

1. Locate: Philippine Islands, Burma, Malaya, Indochina, Siam.

2. What different civilizations influenced the peoples of Southeast Asia?

3. Why did Spain seize the Philippine Islands in the late 1500s?

4. (a) What products did Europeans want from Southeast Asia during the Age of Imperialism? (b) What countries established colonies in Southeast Asia?

5. How did the United States acquire the Philippine Islands?

6. Describe two effects of colonial rule in Southeast Asia.

Chapter 28 Review

In Perspective

Between the 1500s and the 1800s, European merchants and missionaries established some contacts with the civilizations of Asia. But rulers in India, China, and Japan set the terms for dealings with Europeans. In the 1800s, however, the Industrial Revolution and the decline of powerful governments in Asia allowed Europeans to change the terms.

As the Mogul Empire in India collapsed, the English East India Company gained a growing role in Indian affairs. In 1858, the British government took control of India as a colony. China suffered from internal rebellions and was humiliated by western powers in the 1800s. The weakness of the Manchu dynasty led to the overthrow of the emperor in 1911.

In 1853, Japanese isolation ended. Under the Meiji, the Japanese made their nation into a modern industrial power. Soon, they were competing with western powers for a colonial empire in Asia. Western powers controlled much of Southeast Asia. By 1900, however, nationalists in many parts of Asia were beginning to resist foreign domination of their lands.

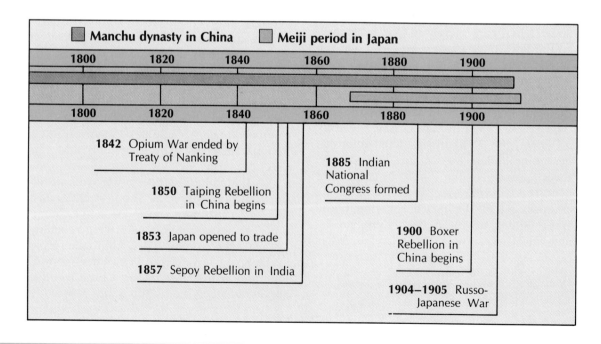

■ Manchu dynasty in China	■ Meiji period in Japan

| 1800 | 1820 | 1840 | 1860 | 1880 | 1900 |

| 1800 | 1820 | 1840 | 1860 | 1880 | 1900 |

1842 Opium War ended by Treaty of Nanking

1850 Taiping Rebellion in China begins

1853 Japan opened to trade

1857 Sepoy Rebellion in India

1885 Indian National Congress formed

1900 Boxer Rebellion in China begins

1904–1905 Russo-Japanese War

Recalling Facts

Indicate whether each of the following statements refers to India, China, Japan, or Southeast Asia.

1. Meiji leaders introduced a program for modernization.
2. Grievances against the British touched off the Sepoy Rebellion.
3. The Opium War resulted in the first of the "unequal treaties."
4. Boxers attempted to expel foreigners from their land.
5. A strong army and navy were used to defeat Russia in 1905.
6. Sun Yat-sen worked to build a unified country.
7. Britain encouraged farmers to grow cotton for its factories.
8. Europeans sought tin, rubber, and oil.

Chapter Checkup

1. (a) Why did the British government end the East India Company's control of India? (b) How did the policies of the British government differ from those of the East India Company?
2. Describe the impact of British rule on each of the following aspects of Indian life: (a) political; (b) economic; (c) social.
3. (a) What attitude did the Manchu dynasty take toward European merchants in the 1600s and 1700s? (b) How did the Opium War affect relations between China and western powers?
4. Describe how each of the following affected the Manchu dynasty: (a) Taiping Rebellion; (b) Open Door Policy; (c) Revolution of 1911.
5. How did the Chinese try to end western imperialism?
6. (a) What was Commodore Perry's purpose in visiting Japan? (b) What effect did his visit have on Japan?
7. What steps did the Japanese take to modernize their nation?
8. (a) Which European nations were the main competitors in Southeast Asia during the 1800s? (b) Why did they want to control this region?

Critical Thinking

1. **Analyzing** Benjamin Disraeli called India "the brightest jewel in the British Crown." (a) What do you think he meant by this statement? (b) Why do you think he felt that India was important to Britain?
2. **Evaluating** (a) Why did Indian nationalists want to end British rule? (b) Why did the British want to stay in India? (c) Do you think British rule was good for India? Explain.
3. **Synthesizing** In the 1700s, China was the richest and strongest nation in the world. Yet within less than 100 years it was carved into spheres of influence. How did this happen? Give specific reasons to explain your answer.
4. **Comparing** (a) How were the Chinese and Japanese responses to Europeans and Americans similar? (b) How were they different? (c) What might explain the similarities and differences?

Relating Past to Present

1. (a) Why do you think Japan was able to industrialize so quickly in the 1800s? (b) How do you think the Japanese policy of selective borrowing from other nations affected its rapid industrialization? (c) What present-day examples of Japanese success in industry can you cite?

Developing Basic Skills

1. **Analyzing a Primary Source** Reread the special feature on page 537. Then answer the following questions: (a) What is the nature of the document included in the feature? (b) Who is the author? (c) What type of information did the author want to learn on his trip to Europe? (d) What did he find most perplexing during his trip? Why? (e) Do you think the document is a good source of information about Japanese attitudes toward Europe in the late 1800s? Why or why not?
2. **Map Reading** Compare the maps on pages 533 and 540. Then answer the following questions: (a) What nation's sphere of influence included Korea? (b) What three nations possessed New Guinea? (c) What nations had spheres of influence in China? (d) Which of these nations had possessions in Southeast Asia? (e) Based on both maps, which nation do you think was most powerful in eastern Asia? Explain your answer.

See page 806 for suggested readings.

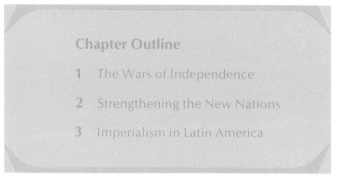

29 Revolution and Independence in Latin America

(1750–1917)

Chapter Outline

1 The Wars of Independence

2 Strengthening the New Nations

3 Imperialism in Latin America

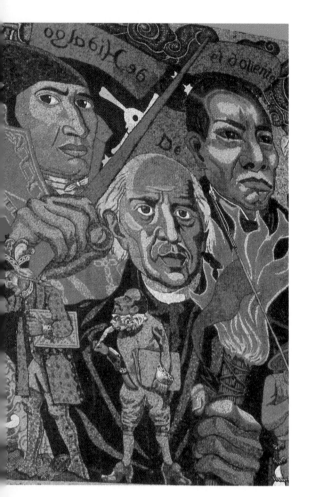

Leaders in the Mexican war of independence.

In 1806, Francisco Miranda, son of an aristocratic Venezuelan family, recruited 200 fighting men and hurried them on board the sloop *Leander* and two smaller ships. In February, James Biggs, an American aboard the *Leander,* wrote home: "Generally, I can say that we are engaged in an expedition to some part of the Spanish dominions, probably South America, with a view of assisting the inhabitants in throwing off the oppressive yoke of the parent country and establishing a government for themselves."

Biggs added ominously, "We may be plucking a thousand daggers on our heads, but we presume our Conductor [Miranda] knows what he is doing and will lead us to great exploits and splendid fortunes." Although Biggs and most of the others on this daring expedition were only interested in "splendid fortunes," Miranda had another goal. For 30 years, Miranda had been scheming to free the Spanish colonies in South America. This expedition, he hoped, would spark a revolt against Spain.

Miranda had badly miscalculated, however. When he arrived off the coast of Venezuela, he found that the Spanish had been forewarned of his attack. No general uprising occurred, and Miranda and his forces barely escaped with their lives. Nevertheless, Miranda was not to be deterred. Four years later, he returned to Venezuela, as you will read in this chapter.

Miranda has often been called "the Morning Star of Independence" for his work in the cause of freedom for South America. In Latin America, as in Europe, nationalism and liberalism were threatening the old order during the 1800s. The success of the American Revolution made a great impression on the people of Latin America. It gave people hope that they, too, might win freedom from colonial rule.

1 The Wars of Independence

Read to Learn ■ why Latin Americans revolted against Spanish rule
■ how Latin American nations won independence

Like the 13 colonies in North America, colonies elsewhere in the Americas had many grievances against their European rulers. In the late 1700s, dissatisfaction increased, fostered by the works of Enlightenment writers such as Locke, Voltaire, and Rousseau. The success of the American and French revolutions encouraged the peoples of Latin America* in their own struggles for independence. In Mexico, Central and South America, and the West Indies, colonists began trying to gain control over their own affairs.

Sources of Discontent

As you read in Chapter 17, Spain established a colonial empire in the Americas during the 1500s. Over the next 300 years the rigid social structure that emerged caused much discontent. At the top of colonial society was a small, privileged class of peninsulares. *Peninsulares* were officials who had been sent from Spain to rule the colonies. (The term peninsular referred to the Iberian Peninsula on which Spain and Portugal are located.) Only peninsulares could hold high offices in government or in the Catholic Church, a powerful force in the colonies. The Spanish king often granted peninsulares huge estates in the colonies, enabling them to become extremely wealthy.

Below the peninsulares were the *creoles* (KREE ohls), descendants of Spanish settlers who were born in the Americas. In theory, creoles were equal to the peninsulares, but in practice they were barred from the highest official positions. Nevertheless, many creoles became wealthy land or mine owners, and others were active in commerce and industry.

After the creoles came the *mestizos* (mehs TEE zohs), people of mixed European and Indian heritage. Mestizos held many different jobs in the colonial economy, from day laborers and farmers to lawyers. During the 1600s and 1700s, the mestizo population grew rapidly. At the lowest level of colonial society were Indians and African slaves. African slaves were brought to the Americas to work on the plantations and in the mines.

Except for the peninsulares, each group had reason to resent colonial rule. Creoles objected to colonial rule because it gave European-born peninsulares superior social, political, and economic positions. Furthermore, many creoles had been educated in Europe, where they had absorbed Enlightenment ideas about liberty. On their return home, they helped spread these ideas. Eventually, Spain banned the writings of Rousseau and Voltaire in its colonies because they were considered a threat to Spanish rule.

Mestizos disliked colonial rule because they were treated as third-class citizens by the Spanish and the creoles. In theory, Indians were free, but many were forced to work for Europeans. Both Indians and African slaves were ready to fight to gain freedom.

Early Revolts

During the late 1700s and early 1800s, uprisings occurred in several areas of Latin America. In 1781, the Indian leader Tupac Amaru II led a revolt against Spanish rule in Peru. The Indian army was poorly armed, and it was rapidly defeated by the Spanish troops. In the 1780s, nearly 20,000 mestizos and Indians marched on Bogotá, in what is today Colombia, to protest excessive taxes imposed by Spain. The Spanish eventually crushed this revolt and executed the rebel leaders.

As you read at the beginning of the chapter, Francisco Miranda, a creole leader, tried unsuccessfully to organize an uprising against Spanish rule in 1806. Miranda returned to Venezuela in 1810. This time, he

---

* Latin America is the term used to describe the part of the Western Hemisphere south of the United States, where the Latin languages Spanish, French, and Portuguese are spoken.

had the support of the people of Caracas. With other rebel leaders, he ousted the Spanish and set up the first Venezuelan Republic. However, jealousies among the revolutionary leaders enabled the Spanish to regain control of the colony. They captured Miranda and sent him to Spain, where he died in 1816. Although the revolution led by Miranda failed, the Spanish colonies would soon wage successful wars for independence.

Independence for Haiti

While Spanish subjects in the Americas were plotting against their colonial rulers, a successful uprising took place in the French

Toussaint L'Ouverture led the people of Haiti in a successful revolution against French rule. Although Toussaint was taken prisoner by the French, he warned before his death: "In overthrowing me, the French have only felled the tree of black liberty in Saint Domingue [Haiti]. It will shoot up again for it is deeply rooted and its roots are many."

West Indies. The French ruled Haiti, the western half of the island of Hispaniola. In the 1700s, a few French families owned huge sugar plantations worked by nearly one half million African slaves. Overseers brutally mistreated the slaves.

When the French Revolution broke out in 1789, the people of Haiti quickly adopted the ideals of "liberty, equality, and fraternity" proclaimed by the revolutionaries in Paris. When their hopes for freedom were disappointed, thousands of slaves revolted in 1791. They murdered their masters and destroyed many plantations. For the next 13 years, Haiti was the scene of violent struggles as former slaves fought the French for freedom.

The leading figure in this struggle was Toussaint L'Ouverture (too SAN loo vehr TYOOR). By 1801, Toussaint had driven the French from Haiti and conquered the Spanish-held eastern half of Hispaniola. He declared the entire island free from foreign control. In France, Napoleon was outraged by the loss of Haiti, which had been the source of valuable profits from the sugar trade. He decided to restore French rule in Haiti. He sent his brother-in-law, General Charles Leclerc, and 20,000 soldiers to carry out his plan.

The French soldiers suffered heavy casualties at the hands of the Haitians. Moreover, an unanticipated enemy—yellow fever—killed hundreds of French troops each week. Leclerc finally tricked Toussaint by agreeing to peace and then luring him to a dinner party at which the Haitian leader was taken prisoner. Later, Toussaint was sent to France, where he died in prison in 1803.

Two other Haitian leaders, Jean Jacques Dessalines and Henri Christophe, took up Toussaint's struggle. The fighting took a terrible toll. Finally, on January 1, 1804, Dessalines declared Haiti independent, making it the first independent nation in Latin America.

Elsewhere in Latin America, people watched events in Haiti with mixed feelings. Creole landowners, for example, were horrified by the slave revolt. But they were also encouraged by seeing that a strong European power could be defeated by local revolutionaries.

The Revolutionary Spirit Spreads

Spanish colonists were inspired by the revolutionary ideals spreading across Europe. During the early 1800s, events in Europe set off a series of successful revolts in Latin America.

In 1808, Napoleon conquered Spain and ousted the Spanish king Ferdinand VII. He then put his brother Joseph Bonaparte on the Spanish throne. The Spanish colonies in Latin America refused to recognize Joseph Bonaparte as king and began setting up their own governments.

After Napoleon's defeat in 1815, the European powers restored Ferdinand VII to his throne. Ferdinand set out to reestablish control over Spanish colonies in Latin America. However, by 1815, several revolutionary leaders had emerged in Latin America. They resisted the return of Spanish rule.

Simón Bolívar. Perhaps the best known revolutionary leader was Simón Bolívar, often called "the Liberator" for his role in the Latin American wars of independence. Bolívar was born to a wealthy creole family in Caracas, Venezuela. He was educated in Spain and traveled in Europe during the French Revolution. Deeply moved by revolutionary ideals, Bolívar became a firm believer in Latin American independence. He once vowed: "I will never allow my hands to be idle nor my soul to rest until I have broken the shackles which chain us to Spain."

Bolívar also visited the United States and studied the republican form of government there. In 1810, he returned to Venezuela and fought alongside Miranda. Over the next decade, Bolívar continued to lead rebel armies in a seesaw battle against Spain.

In August 1819, Bolívar led an army on a daring march from Venezuela, over the ice-capped Andes, into Colombia. In Colombia, he won a stunning victory over the Spanish. In December, he became president of the independent Republic of Great Colombia, which included what is today Venezuela, Colombia, Ecuador, and Panama. (See the map on page 549.)

Simón Bolívar led the fight for freedom from Spanish rule in much of South America. Like other revolutionary leaders, he was inspired by the ideas of the Enlightenment. True to these ideas, Bolívar freed his slaves and spent his personal fortune to finance wars for independence.

José de San Martín. While Bolívar was leading revolutionary forces in Colombia, another creole, José de San Martín, helped organize a rebel army in Argentina. In 1812, San Martín had returned from Europe, where he had been educated, to join Argentina's struggle for independence. Argentina won its freedom in 1816.

A few years later, San Martín and General Bernardo O'Higgins of Chile endured terrible hardships when they led their troops across the southern Andes into Chile. The Spanish, who never dreamed such a march was possible, were caught off guard and were forced to withdraw from Chile. By 1818, Chile had declared its independence. In the early 1820s, San Martín joined forces with Bolívar to help liberate Peru and Ecuador from Spanish rule.

Independence for Mexico and Central America

During the early 1800s, the people of Mexico also fought to win independence from Spain. In 1810, Miguel Hidalgo (hih DAL goh), a creole priest, organized a large army of Indians who were dissatisfied with Spanish rule. Hidalgo captured several Mexican provinces. He then established a government that reflected the ideals of the French Revolution. For example, he abolished slavery and returned land to the Indians. However, in 1811, Hidalgo was captured by troops that were loyal to Spain, and he was executed.

Another creole priest, José Morelos, took up the cause of Mexican independence. Like Hidalgo, Morelos was successful at first. He announced his goal of liberal reforms, including equal rights for all races and redistribution of land to poor peasants. Morelos' program angered the peninsulares and creoles. They helped Spanish troops suppress the revolt. In 1815, Morelos was captured and shot.

The Mexican war of independence dragged on. Eventually, both liberal and conservative groups united against Spain. In 1821, Agustín de Iturbide, a conservative who had once fought for Spain, declared Mexico an independent state. Because Spain had few remaining supporters, it was forced to recognize Mexican independence.

Iturbide proclaimed himself Emperor of Mexico, but his unpopular rule was short-lived. In 1823, he was forced to abdicate, and a convention met to draw up a constitution. The constitution established Mexico as a republic with a president and a two-house congress.

Emboldened by Mexico's example, creoles in Central America declared their independence from Spain in 1821. Two years later, they created the United Provinces of Central America, including what is today Nicaragua, Costa Rica, El Salvador, Honduras, and Guatemala. (See the map on page 549.)

Brazil Gains Independence

Creoles also led the struggle for independence in Brazil. However, Brazil won its independence more easily than its neighbors in Spanish America had. In 1808, when Napoleon invaded Portugal, the Portuguese royal family fled to safety in Brazil. After the defeat of Napoleon, the Portuguese king returned home. But he left his son Prince Pedro in charge of Brazil. The creoles asked Prince Pedro to end Portuguese rule by declaring Brazil independent. They offered to make him ruler of the new nation.

Pedro, who had lived in Brazil since he was 10, accepted the offer. In 1822, he was proclaimed Pedro I, Emperor of Brazil. However, he agreed to accept a constitution that provided for freedom of the press and religion as well as an elected legislature.

By 1825, most colonies in Latin America had thrown off European rule. (See the map on page 549.) Ahead, the newly independent nations faced the difficult task of establishing stable governments.

SECTION REVIEW

1. Locate: Peru, Bogotá, Colombia, Haiti, Caracas, Venezuela, Chile, United Provinces of Central America.
2. Identify: Tupac Amaru II, Francisco Miranda, Toussaint L'Ouverture, Simón Bolívar, José de San Martín, Miguel Hidalgo, José Morelos, Prince Pedro.
3. Define: peninsulare, creole, mestizo.
4. (a) What European country ruled Haiti? (b) Which group of people in Haiti revolted against foreign rule?
5. How did Napoleon's conquest of Spain affect the Spanish colonies in America?
6. What reforms did Morelos want to introduce in Mexico?

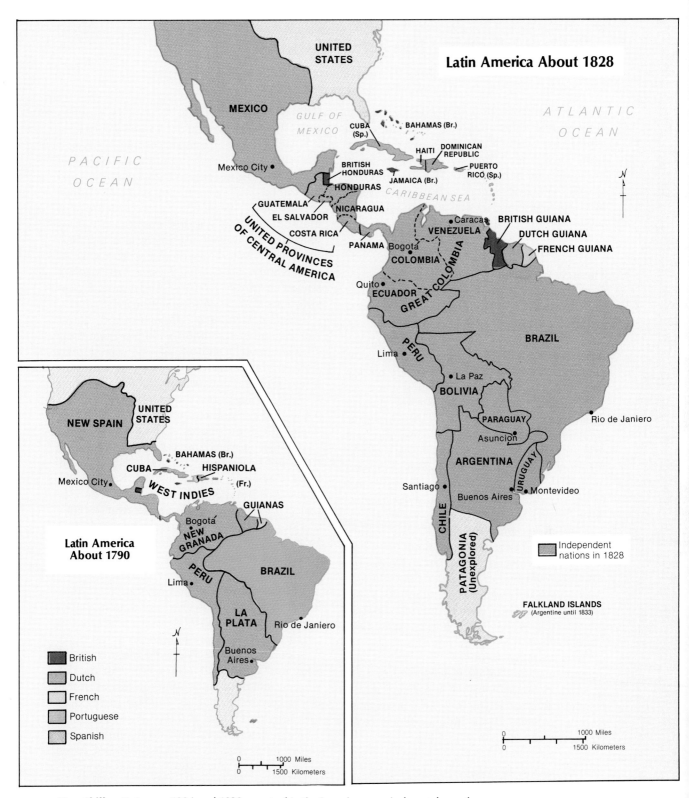

Latin America About 1828

UNITED STATES

GULF OF MEXICO

MEXICO

PACIFIC OCEAN

Mexico City •

CUBA (Sp.)

BAHAMAS (Br.)

ATLANTIC OCEAN

HAITI

DOMINICAN REPUBLIC

PUERTO RICO (Sp.)

BRITISH HONDURAS

JAMAICA (Br.)

CARIBBEAN SEA

HONDURAS

GUATEMALA

EL SALVADOR

NICARAGUA

COSTA RICA

UNITED PROVINCES OF CENTRAL AMERICA

PANAMA

Bogota •

• Caracas

VENEZUELA

BRITISH GUIANA

DUTCH GUIANA

FRENCH GUIANA

COLOMBIA

GREAT COLOMBIA

Quito •

ECUADOR

Lima •

PERU

BRAZIL

• La Paz

BOLIVIA

PARAGUAY

Rio de Janiero •

Asuncion •

ARGENTINA

URUGUAY

Santiago •

CHILE

Buenos Aires •

• Montevideo

PATAGONIA (Unexplored)

☐ Independent nations in 1828

FALKLAND ISLANDS (Argentine until 1833)

0 — 1000 Miles
0 — 1500 Kilometers

Latin America About 1790

NEW SPAIN

UNITED STATES

BAHAMAS (Br.)

CUBA

HISPANIOLA

(Fr.)

WEST INDIES

Mexico City •

GUIANAS

Bogota •

NEW GRANADA

PERU

BRAZIL

Lima •

LA PLATA

Rio de Janiero •

Buenos Aires •

☐ British
☐ Dutch
☐ French
☐ Portuguese
☐ Spanish

0 — 1000 Miles
0 — 1500 Kilometers

Map Skill   *Between 1804 and 1828, most of Latin America won independence from European rule. Which of the nations that won independence in this period were part of the Spanish territory of La Plata in 1790?*

2 Strengthening the New Nations

Read to Learn ▪ about the problems faced by Latin American nations
▪ how Mexico struggled to achieve democracy

During the wars of independence, Simón Bolívar and other nationalists dreamed of uniting the Spanish colonies into a single nation. They hoped that a common political and religious heritage would help unite the peoples of Latin America. But in the years after independence, the dream of unity faded as bitter rivalries surfaced.

Barriers to Unity

The new nations of Latin America faced numerous problems that prevented unity. During the wars of independence, different groups had united against Spain. However, after independence, these groups disagreed over what kind of government should be organized. Power struggles broke out among rival leaders, triggering violent civil wars.

Another barrier to unity was the diverse geography of Central and South America. Rugged mountains, high plateaus, the arid Atacama Desert, and the rainforests of the Amazon region limited contact between people. Rough terrain made trade and transportation difficult and encouraged *regionalism*, loyalty to a small geographic area.

Differing interests led to the establishment of 18 separate nations in Latin America. The Republic of Great Colombia, which Bolívar had organized, splintered into three separate countries: Colombia, Venezuela, and Ecuador. South America was further divided when Peru, Bolivia, Argentina, Chile, Paraguay, Uruguay, and Brazil also set up their own governments. After gaining independence, the United Provinces of Central America broke up into five separate nations. On the island of Hispaniola, the Dominican Republic declared its independence from Haiti. (See the map on page 549.)

The Colonial Heritage

The newly independent nations of Latin America became republics and adopted constitutions modeled on the Constitution of the United States. Putting these constitutions into effect, however, proved to be difficult.

Unlike the 13 British colonies in North America, the Spanish colonies had no experience with representative government. During the colonial period, they had been under the absolute rule of the Spanish viceroy. In many of the new nations, ambitious leaders won the backing of the army and installed themselves as military dictators. These dictators, known as *caudillos* (kaw DEE yohs), stayed in power by force and ignored constitutions that called for elections.

Social structure. The nations of Latin America inherited other problems from their colonial past. Rigid social and racial divisions created a stumbling block to representative government. Many creoles who had led the struggle for independence did not want to share political power once they had ousted the peninsulares.

Mestizos were angry at being excluded from political power, as were Indians and blacks. Slavery was abolished, but neither blacks nor Indians had many rights. The majority of mestizos, Indians, and blacks worked on plantations and in mines owned by wealthy creoles. They deeply resented the social and political system that kept them in poverty.

Role of the Catholic Church. The Catholic Church was a powerful political and economic force in Latin America during the colonial period. It remained so after independence. The church owned huge tracts of land and controlled education. During the wars of independence, some members of the clergy, including Father Hidalgo in Mexico, had fought for liberal ideas. However, high church officials often favored the interests of creole landowners over other classes. After independence, the church was generally a conservative force.

Economic problems. Economic conditions remained relatively unchanged after independence. Although Latin America was rich in natural resources, the wealth was controlled by a handful of people. The church and a few powerful families owned most of the land. The majority of the people were landless and poor.

The economies of most Latin American nations remained closely tied to Europe. They supplied raw materials to Europe and were a market for European manufactured goods.

Many nations became dependent on the export of one or two products. Haiti, for example, relied mainly on the export of sugar. Chile exported silver and copper. When these products sold for high prices on world markets, the nations benefited. But when world demand dropped, as it often did, they suffered. Thus, Latin American nations had little control over their own economies.

Changing Economic and Social Conditions

Despite many problems, some nations, including Argentina, Brazil, Chile, Uruguay, and Costa Rica, made progress toward achieving stable governments in the 1800s. In these nations, governments worked to improve economic conditions. Chile, for example, diversified its economy by growing a broad range of agricultural products, developing new exports such as nitrates, and building its own industries. Brazil increased its foreign trade by establishing coffee and

Exporting sugar was the basis of the economies of many Caribbean nations. Single-crop economies left these countries at the mercy of the world demand for sugar. This picture shows men and women bringing sugar cane to the mill. At the mill, rollers crushed the cane and squeezed out the juice. The juice was then made into sugar.

Gauchos were the cowboys of Argentina. They lived on the pampas, open grassy plains, and made a living selling the hides of wild cattle and horses. Gauchos were daring and skillful horsemen. They rode in swift pursuit of cattle and horses using a boleadora—three stones or iron balls lashed together with a long leather thong—to entangle the legs of the animals.

Life on the pampas was scarcely glamorous. Gauchos lived in one-room mud huts that were shingled with grass mats. They slept on heaps of hides. Their traditional costume was a pair of wide-legged trousers, high boots, and a long woolen poncho that protected them from the cold and rain.

The introduction of barbed-wire fencing and refrigerated ships marked the end of the gaucho's way of life. Refrigerated ships allowed people to raise cattle for meat instead of hides. Soon, cattle were fed in stalls rather than on the pampas. Barbed-wire fencing allowed farmers to settle on the pampas and turn the open spaces into wheat and alfalfa fields.

As the gauchos gave way to the farmers, their way of life passed into folklore. Payadors, guitar-playing cowboys, composed songs praising the adventurous deeds of the gauchos. One of the most popular figures in Argentine literature is the fictional gaucho hero Martin Fierro. His life was summed up in these lines:

A son am I of the rolling plain,
A gaucho born and bred;
For me the whole great world is small,
Believe me, my heart can hold it all,
The snake strikes not at my passing foot,
The sun burns not my head.

rubber plantations. Argentina attracted many European immigrants who raised cattle and wheat.

Economic development led to urban growth and some social change. Rio de Janeiro, Buenos Aires, and Santiago became major cities. Although the class system remained fairly rigid, new economic opportunities favored the growth of a middle class. In Argentina, Brazil, Chile, and Mexico, the middle class accounted for about 10 percent of the population. Elsewhere, it remained smaller.

A Century of Change in Mexico

Mexico, you will recall, won its independence in 1821. During the next century, it struggled to achieve political, economic, and social stability. These struggles were similar in some ways to those that occurred in many other Latin American countries during the 1800s.

Clashes between conservatives and liberals shaped political developments in Mexico. Conservatives wanted to maintain the traditional social and economic structure. Liberals favored greater democracy. They supported such goals as reducing the size of large estates and redistributing land to small farmers. They also wanted to curb the power of the army and church.

During the power struggles between conservatives and liberals, several strong leaders emerged. In the 1830s and 1840s, General Antonio Santa Anna was in and out of power many times. At first, he supported liberal reforms. Later, he won the backing of conservatives and ruled as a military dictator.

War with the United States. During this troubled time, Mexico became involved in a war with the United States. Many people from the United States had settled in Texas, an area that belonged to Mexico. In 1836, these settlers defeated Santa Anna's forces and declared Texas an independent republic. In 1845, Texas, by treaty, became part of the United States. Soon after, disputes along the Texas-Mexico border led to war between the United States and Mexico. The war, which lasted from 1846 to 1848, ended in defeat for Mexico. It lost almost half its territory to the United States, including what is today California, Nevada, and Utah as well as parts of Arizona and Colorado.

An era of reform. In the following decades, Mexico introduced liberal reforms under the leadership of Benito Juárez. Born to a poor Indian family, Juárez earned a reputation as a brilliant lawyer and was elected president. Juárez extended political power to more people, thereby reducing the influence of the creoles. During the 1860s, he reduced the power of the Catholic Church by selling its lands. He also established a system of public education and made the state, not the church, responsible for marriage laws.

Soon after the death of Juárez, Porfirio Díaz was elected president. Although Díaz promised to continue the reforms of Juárez, he gradually became more conservative. He rigged elections so that he remained in power for 35 years. During this time, Mexico made important economic progress. Landowners and businesspeople reaped huge

Profiles ■ Women in the Mexican Revolution

In 1910, Mexico was plunged into an era of revolution and social change that uprooted the old class structure and improved living conditions for the vast majority of Mexicans. Women took an active part in the revolution, although it was unusual for women to be involved in politics at all.

Women in Mexico, as elsewhere in Latin America, were expected to remain at home and raise large families. They were taught to be subordinate to men and to obey their fathers or husbands in all matters. By the early 1900s, however, some Mexican women were working in factories. Some upper class women had become teachers and journalists. Women journalists were often outspoken in their opposition to the dictator Porfirio Díaz.

Juana Belen Gutiérrez de Mendoza began her career as a teacher. She become increasingly concerned with educating poor Indian children and gaining rights for farm and factory workers. Gutiérrez sold a few goats she owned in order to buy a printing press and founded the newspaper *Vesper*. Eventually, she was jailed for criticizing Díaz in her newspaper. In prison, Gutiérrez met other women who shared her hopes for reform. She even managed to direct the publication of another newspaper while in prison. Later, Gutiérrez joined the rebel forces of Emiliano Zapata during the Mexican Revolution and earned the rank of colonel.

Other women also gained distinction in the Mexican Revolution. Carmen Alanis commanded 300 troops that helped capture Ciudad Juárez. Ramona Flores, a wealthy widow, used her inheritance to buy arms for rebel troops and later became chief-of-staff to a rebel general. Many women also served as soldiers. They trained and fought alongside

men. In 1911, *The New York Times* reported to its readers that "women have taken a spectacular part in the revolution." In addition to fighting, women served as train dispatchers, telegraph operators, nurses, and spies.

By the time the Mexican Revolution was over, women's place in Mexican life had changed permanently. The Constitution of 1917 guaranteed women basic legal rights, free education, and access to all professions. It also provided for maternity leave and equal pay for equal work. However, the Constitution did not grant women suffrage. Although some Mexican states gave women the vote in the 1920s, women did not win that right nationally until 1953.

profits from mining and the building of railroads. But the poor gained little, and large landowners took control of many Indian lands.

The Constitution of 1917. In 1910, a revolution broke out against Díaz. The Mexican Revolution plunged the nation into years of chaos and swept away most of the traditional order. Finally, in 1917, a new constitution was adopted. It passed into law many reforms that people had been demanding for decades.

Under the Constitution of 1917, large estates were broken up and sold to peasants. Over half the farmland in Mexico changed hands in this way. The new constitution reduced the creoles' power and enabled the mestizos and Indians to participate fully in government. It ensured the separation of church and state and set up a labor code dealing with hours and wages. Although many provisions of the constitution were not carried out right away, the constitution gave Mexico a stable government and enabled the country to achieve economic growth.

SECTION REVIEW

1. Locate: Ecuador, Bolivia, Argentina, Paraguay, Uruguay.
2. Identify: Santa Anna, Benito Juárez, Porfirio Díaz.
3. Define: regionalism, caudillo.
4. How did geography contribute to disunity in Latin America?
5. (a) What group or groups had the most political power in Latin American nations after independence? (b) What group or groups had little political power?
6. How did stable governments in some countries improve economic conditions?
7. Describe three reforms included in the Mexican Constitution of 1917.

3 Imperialism in Latin America

Read to Learn
- about United States and European policy toward Latin America
- how the United States implemented its Latin American policy

After winning independence, the nations of Latin America faced many internal problems as well as external threats. In the 1820s, Spain asked its allies in Europe to help it reconquer its former colonies. Although Prince Metternich of Austria was willing to support Spain, both Britain and the United States opposed any intervention in Latin America.

The Monroe Doctrine and the British Navy

Both Britain and the United States had reasons for opposing intervention. Britain wanted to bolster its trade with the new nations. A return of Spanish rule would prevent new commercial ties. The United States wanted to prevent European countries from regaining influence in the Western Hemisphere.

In 1823, the British asked the United States to make a joint declaration against European intervention in Latin America. Instead, President James Monroe decided to make a statement of his own. In his annual message to Congress in December 1823, Monroe announced United States policy toward Latin America.

"The American continents," Monroe declared, "are henceforth not to be considered as subjects for future colonization by any European powers." His policy, which became known as the Monroe Doctrine, further stated, "With the governments who have declared their independence and maintained it, we would consider any European intervention the manifestation of an unfriendly disposition [attitude] toward the United States. . . ."

The United States lacked the military strength to enforce this policy. However, Britain, which agreed in principle with the Monroe Doctrine, let other European powers know that it was prepared to use its strong navy to prevent foreign intervention in Latin

America. Thus, the Monroe Doctrine, backed up by British seapower, freed the nations of Latin America from the threat of reconquest.

Foreign Interests in Latin America

Britain and the United States were determined to prevent other powers from establishing colonies in Latin America, but they did not oppose foreign investment. During the 1800s, the United States and the industrial nations of Europe turned to Latin America as a source of raw materials and a market for their manufactured goods. Moreover, they invested heavily in building mines, railroads, bridges, and ports in Latin America.

By the early 1900s, Britain had invested $5 billion in Latin America. The United States and France each had investments of over $1 billion, and Germany was close behind. Although the nations of Latin America remained technically independent, extensive foreign investment gave European nations and the United States widespread economic and political influence. This type of influence is known as economic imperialism.

Some foreign investments were in the form of loans to governments for building railroads and ports. A corrupt dictator might use the money for his own enrichment instead of for the building project. If the dictator were overthrown, the new government might default, or refuse to repay the loan. In 1862, France used the excuse that Mexico had defaulted on foreign loans to send its army in support of Maximilian. (See page 472.)

Similar situations arose frequently in the 1800s. When investors thought their loans were in danger, they appealed to their governments to protect their investments. Foreign warships would arrive and foreign governments would force their demands on the Latin American government.

Nevertheless, foreign investments did lead to economic growth in some Latin American nations. In politically stable nations, loans were used to develop new industries. For example, in Argentina, the number of industrial businesses grew from 41 to nearly 50,000 between 1869 and 1914.

In addition to investing, many Europeans settled in parts of Latin America. In the 1800s, about 3 million immigrants poured into Argentina, Brazil, and Chile.

The United States and Latin America

In 1783, a Spanish official made the following prediction about the United States:

> We have just recognized a new power in a great region where there exists no other to challenge its growth. ... The day will come when it grows and becomes a giant and even a colossus [a gigantic power] in those regions. Within a few years we will regard the existence of this colossus with real sorrow.

A century later, people in many Latin American nations were convinced that this prediction had come true. They called the United States "the Colossus of the North."

Relations between the United States and the nations of Latin America began on a friendly note with the Monroe Doctrine. But Latin American governments came to believe that the United States was using the Monroe Doctrine to dominate the Western Hemisphere.

In 1895 during a dispute between Venezuela and Britain, American Secretary of State Richard Olney invoked the Monroe Doctrine. Olney informed Britain that the United States "was sovereign on this continent," by which he meant the Western Hemisphere. His words disturbed many people in Latin America.

The Spanish-American War

Three years later, the United States fought a war with Spain that involved it even more deeply in Latin America. In 1898, Cuba and Puerto Rico were still Spanish colonies. However, Cuban rebels were fighting for independence. Journalists in the United States whipped up public sympathy for the Cuban cause. The United States sent the battleship *Maine* to Havana to protect American citizens and property in Cuba. When the *Maine* was destoyed in a mysterious explosion, people in the United States clamored for war with Spain.

555

In April 1898, the United States recognized Cuban independence, and Spain declared war. During the Spanish-American War, the United States won quick victories in the Caribbean and the Pacific. (See page 541.) In December, Spain agreed to a peace treaty, giving the United States control of Puerto Rico as well as the Philippines and Guam in the Pacific. The United States ruled Puerto Rico directly through an American governor and an American-appointed executive council.

Cuba became an independent nation. When Cubans drafted a constitution in 1900, however, the United States forced them to add a document known as the Platt Amendment. The Platt Amendment gave the United States the right to intervene in Cuban affairs to protect American lives and property. It put limits on Cuba's right to borrow from foreign powers, and it allowed the United States to establish two naval stations in Cuba.

Many Latin American nations looked on the expansion of the United States into the Caribbean with alarm. They feared that the United States had imperialist ambitions that would threaten their independence.

Roosevelt Corollary to the Monroe Doctrine

In the early 1900s, Venezuela and the Dominican Republic defaulted on loans from Britain, Germany, and Italy. Once again, Eu-

Map Skill *In the early 1900s, some Caribbean areas were still under foreign rule, as this map shows. In addition, foreign governments often intervened when Caribbean nations were unable to pay their debts. Why would Cuba have been geographically important to the United States?*

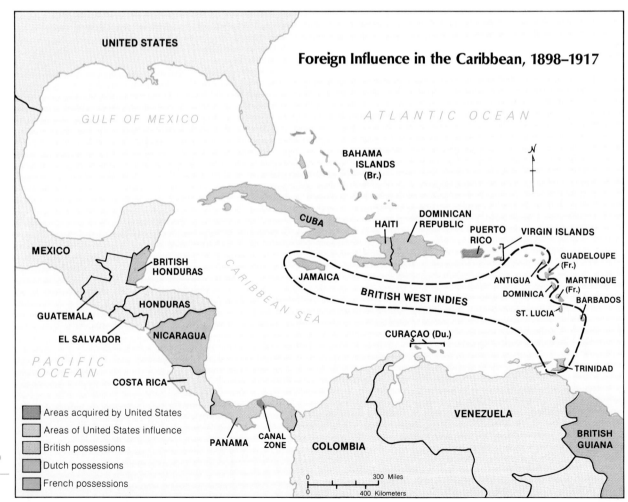

Foreign Influence in the Caribbean, 1898–1917

- Areas acquired by United States
- Areas of United States influence
- British possessions
- Dutch possessions
- French possessions

President Theodore Roosevelt was fond of quoting a West African proverb: "Speak softly and carry a big stick; you will go far." Roosevelt used a "big stick" in the form of American economic and military strength in his dealings with Latin America. In this cartoon, Roosevelt, once police commissioner of New York City, is portrayed as the world's policeman.

ropean warships menaced Latin American nations. President Theodore Roosevelt invoked the Monroe Doctrine and sent American battleships to force the Europeans to withdraw their ships. The European nations protested. They insisted that if they could not send warships to make nations pay their debts the United States must take that responsibility.

To satisfy this demand, Roosevelt announced the Roosevelt Corollary to the Monroe Doctrine in 1904. In this policy statement, Roosevelt declared that the United States would exercise "international police power" to get Latin American nations to honor their financial commitments.

Over the next 20 years, several American presidents used this police power. President William Howard Taft sent troops to Nicaragua and Honduras in order to guarantee repayment of foreign debts. On other occasions, United States troops occupied parts of Latin American nations to protect American and European investments.

The Panama Canal

During the Age of Imperialism, the United States competed with the industrial nations of Europe for international markets. As the United States expanded its interest in the Pacific, it wanted to be able to move its fleet easily from the Atlantic Ocean to the Pacific Ocean without making the voyage around South America. President Roosevelt proposed building a canal across the narrow Isthmus of Panama, an area that belonged to Colombia.

Colombia was reluctant to grant the United States the right to build a canal, fearing it would lose control of the region. In 1903, however, the United States encouraged the people in Panama to revolt against Colombian rule. The rebels quickly won independence for Panama. Three weeks later, they signed an agreement allowing the United States to build a canal.

Construction on the Panama Canal began in 1904. First, workers drained swamps

557

and marshes, the breeding grounds of mosquitos that carried yellow fever. Next, they moved millions of tons of earth to create the "big ditch." Finally, in 1914, the first ship traveled through the Panama Canal.

The United States was in a position to benefit most from the Panama Canal, although the new sea route helped the trade of many nations. Despite the advantages of the canal, many Latin American nations remained bitter about what they saw as United States imperialism in the region.

SECTION REVIEW

1. Locate: Cuba, Puerto Rico, Panama.
2. Identify: Monroe Doctrine, Colossus of the North, Spanish-American War, *Maine*, Platt Amendment, Roosevelt Corollary.
3. Why did the United States announce the Monroe Doctrine?
4. Which industrialized nations invested heavily in Latin America?
5. Why were Latin American nations suspicious of the Monroe Doctrine?

Chapter 29 Review

In Perspective

In the late 1700s, ideas of the Enlightenment as well as the examples of the American and French revolutions contributed to unrest in Latin America. Many people resented foreign rule and the rigid social structure that had developed in the colonies.

Revolutionary struggles broke out all over Latin America in the early 1800s. The first successful revolt took place in Haiti. By 1825, most of Latin America had thrown off colonial rule. The newly independent nations faced many problems. They had little experience in self-government. Strong rulers often seized power and set themselves up as military dictators.

Latin American nations were often threatened by foreign intervention during the Age of Imperialism. In the Monroe Doctrine, the United States warned European nations not to intervene in Latin America. But both the United States and the industrial nations of Europe invested in Latin America, and they were willing to use force to protect their investments. The United States gained influence in the Caribbean during the Spanish-American War, and it later acquired rights to build the Panama Canal.

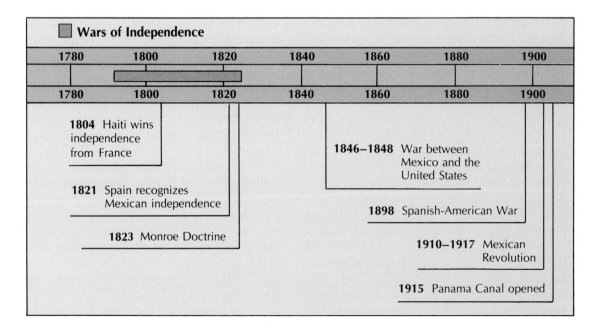

Wars of Independence

| 1780 | 1800 | 1820 | 1840 | 1860 | 1880 | 1900 |

1804 Haiti wins independence from France

1821 Spain recognizes Mexican independence

1823 Monroe Doctrine

1846–1848 War between Mexico and the United States

1898 Spanish-American War

1910–1917 Mexican Revolution

1915 Panama Canal opened

Recalling Facts

Choose the word or phrase that best completes each of the following statements.

1. The highest class in Spanish colonial society was the (a) creoles; (b) peninsulares; (c) mestizos.
2. Haiti won its independence from (a) Britain; (b) France; (c) Spain.
3. Spanish colonists were encouraged to fight for independence by the ideas of (a) the French Revolution; (b) Metternich; (c) Ferdinand VII.
4. After independence, many Latin American nations were ruled by (a) mestizos; (b) caudillos; (c) church officials.
5. One problem facing the new nations of Latin America was (a) lack of natural resources; (b) unequal land ownership; (c) revival of slavery.
6. As a result of war with the United States in the 1840s, Mexico (a) became a united country; (b) introduced liberal reforms; (c) lost half of its territory.
7. The power of the Catholic Church in Mexico was limited by (a) Antonio Santa Anna; (b) Benito Juárez; (c) Porfirio Díaz.

Chapter Checkup

1. Describe why each of the following groups was dissatisfied with Spanish rule: (a) creoles; (b) mestizos; (c) Indians; (d) slaves.
2. (a) How did the French Revolution affect Haiti? (b) Why did Napoleon try to reconquer Haiti? (c) What was the result of the French invasion of Haiti?
3. Describe the role each of the following leaders played in the Latin American wars of independence: (a) Simón Bolívar; (b) José de San Martín; (c) Miguel Hidalgo.
4. (a) How did Brazil gain its independence? (b) How was Brazil's road to independence different from those of other Latin American nations?
5. (a) Why were the Spanish colonies poorly prepared for self-government? (b) What social problems did they face after independence?
6. (a) What kind of economic growth occurred in Argentina, Brazil, and Chile? (b) How did economic growth affect society in these nations?
7. (a) Why did Britain oppose foreign intervention in Latin America in the 1800s? (b) Why did the United States oppose it? (c) What steps did each nation take to prevent intervention by other nations?

8. (a) Why did industrial nations invest in Latin America? (b) What projects did they support? (c) How did foreign loans lead to economic imperialism in Latin America?

Critical Thinking

1. **Comparing** (a) How was the experience of the United States during its war of independence and after independence similar to those of the nations of Latin America? (b) How was it different?
2. **Understanding Economic Ideas** (a) Describe the economic ties between Latin America and Europe after Latin Americans won independence. (b) Why did most Latin American nations have little control over their own economies?
3. **Analyzing a Quotation** Thomas Jefferson once said, "America, North and South, has a set of interests distinct from those of Europe, and peculiarly her own. She should therefore have a system of her own, separate and apart from that of Europe." (a) What do you think Jefferson meant by "a set of interests . . . peculiarly her own"? (b) How could Jefferson's statement be used to support the Monroe Doctrine?

Relating Past to Present

1. Many people in Latin America still refer to the United States as the Colossus of the North. (a) What actions of the United States in the 1800s contributed to this view? (b) Why do you think this image of the United States still exists?

Developing Basic Skills

1. **Ranking** Review the problems that the newly independent nations of Latin America faced. Then rank them according to the impact they had on developments in Latin America. Explain why you ranked them in this order.
2. **Researching** Choose one of the leaders of Mexico in the 1800s. Research his personal background in order to answer the following questions: (a) How did he become involved in Mexican politics? (b) What political ideas did he support? (c) How might his background have influenced his political ideas?

See page 807 for suggested readings.

World War and Peace

1918 The signing of the armistice ending World War I was greeted with great celebration.

Soviet art of the 1920s reflected the struggle to establish a socialist state.

	1914	1920	1926	1932
POLITICS AND GOVERNMENT	**1914** World War I breaks out in Europe	**1922** Mussolini marches on Rome and takes power		**1930** Japanese invade Manchuria
ECONOMICS AND TECHNOLOGY	**1916** Tank developed for use in World War I		**1929** U.S. stock crash leads to world-wide depression	
SOCIETY AND CULTURE	Danish woman elected to national post	**1924**	**1929** *All Quiet on the Western Front* is best seller	

In World War I, airplane gunners armed with machine guns had "dog fights" in the skies over Europe.

Some political parties used the fear of communist revolution to win support, as shown in this German poster from the 1920s.

1936 This poster appeals for support for the republicans in the Spanish Civil War.

During World War II, the Allies tried to build support among their people with posters such as this.

1932	1938	1944	1950

1933 Hitler comes to power in Germany

1939 World War II begins when Germany invades Poland

1947 Marshall Plan proposed to help rebuild Western Europe

1930s Passenger airlines become common

1940 Radar used in Battle of Britain

1945 Atomic bombs dropped on two Japanese cities

1935 Nuremburg Laws deprive German Jews of citizenship

1942 Japanese slogan, "Asia for the Asians" builds on anticolonial feelings

The Nazi Party in Germany encouraged young people to join the Hitler Youth.

After World War II, the Soviets set up satellite governments in much of Eastern Europe. Stalin is shown here with his "puppets."

30 World War I

(1914–1919)

British recruiting poster from World War I.

In August 1914, war erupted in Europe. In the novel *All Quiet on the Western Front,* Erich Maria Remarque (ruh MAHRK) described the terrifying ordeal endured by tens of thousands of soldiers in this war.

"We wake up in the middle of the night. The earth booms. Heavy fire is falling on us. We crouch into corners. We distinguish shells of every caliber. . . . The dug-out heaves, the night roars and flashes." After this fearful bombardment ended, the exhausted German soldiers had to leave their shelters and confront the enemy. "We seize the hand grenades, pitch them out in front of the dug-out and jump after them. . . . No one would believe that in this howling waste there could still be men; but steel helmets now appear on all sides of the trench."

Remarque, a German soldier in this war, then described the advance of enemy troops through the barbed wire. "We recognize the distorted faces, the smooth helmets: They are French. . . . The moment we are about to retreat three faces rise up from the ground in front of us. Under one of the helmets a dark pointed beard and two eyes that are fastened on me. I raise my hand but I cannot throw into those strange eyes; for one mad moment the whole slaughter whirls like a circus around me, and these two eyes that are alone motionless; then the head rises up, a hand, a movement, and my hand grenade flies through the air and into him."

The scene of this "howling waste" is northern France. Similar encounters occurred between French and German soldiers almost daily during the world war that lasted from 1914 to 1918. At the time, the war was called the Great

War. After 1939, when a second global conflict broke out, the earlier war was called World War I.

In the early 1900s, people in Western Europe and the United States had great confidence in western civilization. During the past few decades, they had carried their ideas and traditions to every corner of the globe. Many people believed that through international treaties and law western civilization had at last discovered how to keep peace. But in 1914, the peace was shattered. Europeans suffered through the most devastating war they had ever known. The war profoundly changed not only Europe but also other parts of the world.

1 Sources of Tension

Read to Learn
- how colonialism and nationalism set the stage for World War I
- how militarism and alliances hastened the onset of World War I

After the fall of Napoleon in 1814, delegates to the Congress of Vienna worked out a peace settlement for Europe that lasted 100 years. Brief local conflicts, such as the Crimean and Franco-Prussian wars, had occurred, but no long general war. The relative peacefulness of the 1800s lulled many Europeans into believing that another general war simply could not happen.

As the century closed, however, prospects for continued peace dimmed. The nations of Europe were increasingly troubled by deep-seated rivalries that sparked mistrust and even outright hatred.

Nationalism

At the source of much of the rivalry was the growth of nationalism. As you have read, nationalism became a strong force in Europe during the 1800s. Nationalism increased among people who had been politically united for centuries, such as the British. It also affected people who still sought an independent political identity, such as the ethnic groups in Austria-Hungary and the Ottoman Empire.

Nationalism created tensions between France and Germany. The French bitterly resented their defeat in the Franco-Prussian War and were anxious for revenge. Moreover, they were determined to regain Alsace-Lorraine. Germany was equally determined to keep its conquests.

Nationalist feelings were especially strong in Italy. Although Italy had become a united country in 1871, a million Italians still lived in territories controlled by Austria-Hungary. Italian nationalists agitated to have these regions united with Italy. Elsewhere, peoples living under foreign rule sought self-government or independence.

Colonial Rivalries

Events outside Europe contributed to growing tensions in the early 1900s. During the scramble for colonies in Africa and Asia in the search for raw materials, new markets, and status, European nations reached the brink of war more than once.

In North Africa, France and Germany narrowly averted war over Morocco in 1905. (See page 513.) A second Moroccan crisis developed in 1911 when the French used riots in Morocco as an excuse to send in troops to protect Europeans. In response to the French move, Germany sent a warship to the Moroccan port of Agadir. Germany then demanded the French Congo in exchange for German recognition of French claims in Morocco. Many Europeans expected that the crisis would lead to war. Only swift efforts by Britain to mediate the crisis prevented the

563

outbreak of a war. But in France and Britain, anti-German feeling increased.

There were many other trouble spots. In the Middle East, Britain and Russia vied for control of Iran. As you have read, Europeans carved out competing spheres of influence in China, while Russia and Japan fought a war over Manchuria.

Military Buildup

In this climate of heightened tensions, the nations of Europe took steps to prepare for war. Military expenditures across the continent jumped 300 percent between 1870 and 1914. Some nations embraced militarism, giving military officers a strong hand in government.

The military buildup in Europe was especially evident in the naval rivalry between Britain and Germany. For most of the 1800s, Britain had maintained a "two-power standard,"—that is, its navy was more powerful than those of any other two countries combined. In 1898, Germany began an ambitious program of naval expansion that Britain saw as a threat to its naval supremacy. Between 1900 and 1914, Germany tripled its spending on warships and became the second strongest naval power. Britain responded by in-

Colonial wars were commonplace in the early 1900s. This picture shows French troops fighting in Morocco in 1907. In the scramble for colonies in Asia and Africa, colonial powers often came into conflict. Their differences were usually resolved without war. But frequent colonial crises increased tension in Europe.

creasing its own naval spending. This naval race contributed to the growing tensions between these two countries.

European nations also competed for power and prestige by enlarging their armies. In 1913, France increased the size of its army by extending required military service from two to three years. Russia almost doubled spending on its army between 1900 and 1914. As the military buildup continued, many people believed that war was inevitable. Early in 1914, an American official wrote home from Europe: "The situation is extraordinary. It is militarism run stark mad .... There is too much hatred, too many jealousies." All that was needed, he said, was "a spark to set the whole thing off."

The Triple Alliance

In the late 1800s, the major European powers not only built up their military power but also sought allies who would support them in case a war broke out. The German chancellor Bismarck arranged several alliances with other great powers. His chief goal was to isolate France so it could not take revenge on Germany.

In 1879, Bismarck negotiated a military alliance between Germany and Austria-Hungary. Two years later, he arranged the "Three Emperors' League," a secret agreement among the emperors of Germany, Austria-Hungary, and Russia. In 1882, Bismarck masterminded the Triple Alliance, which brought Italy into the earlier alliance between Germany and Austria-Hungary. The Italians had tried unsuccessfully to block French influence in Tunisia. Unhappy with their defeat in this effort, the Italians willingly joined Germany and Austria-Hungary.

Bismarck's alliance system threatened to collapse when rivalry between Russia and Austria-Hungary in the Balkans caused the breakup of the Three Emperors' League. But the Iron Chancellor quickly reached out for Russian friendship in an agreement called the Reinsurance Treaty of 1887. Bismarck thereby succeeded in his aim of isolating France.

This German political cartoon comments on the competition for empire among the world's major industrial powers. The "dogs of war" are whipped into action by a bearded figure labeled Krieg, the German word for war. The dogs representing various European countries and Japan devour China. The dog representing the United States looks on from the sidelines. The caption reads, "After China is devoured, who will be next?"

The Triple Entente

The diplomatic isolation of France, however, did not last. When William II became kaiser, or German emperor, he wanted to conduct foreign policy on his own. In 1890, William II forced Bismarck to resign. Soon after, William allowed the Reinsurance Treaty with Russia to lapse. France seized this opportunity to ally itself with Russia. Russia accepted the French offer of friendship because it was at odds with Austria-Hungary and worried by German power. France and Russia signed

565

The Alliance System, 1907

NORTH SEA

ATLANTIC OCEAN

IRELAND
GREAT BRITAIN
SWEDEN
DENMARK
NETH.
BELGIUM
LUX.
GERMANY
RUSSIA
FRANCE
SWITZ.
ITALY
AUSTRIA-HUNGARY
BOSNIA
MONTENEGRO
SERBIA
ROMANIA
BULGARIA
BLACK SEA
PORTUGAL
SPAIN
GREECE
ALBANIA
OTTOMAN EMPIRE
MEDITERRANEAN SEA

☐ Triple Entente
☐ Triple Alliance

0   500 Miles
0   800 Kilometers

Map Skill *Between 1879 and 1907, the major European powers formed two rival alliances. Other European nations remained outside the alliance system but looked to one of the major powers for protection. What geographical advantage did the Triple Entente have?*

a military agreement in 1894. This agreement provided that if either nation were attacked by any member of the Triple Alliance the other would come to its aid.

Britain remained outside the alliance system that was dividing the continent of Europe into rival blocks. Britain had long prided itself on its "splendid isolation," its independence from alliances. But the growing power of Germany, especially its program of naval construction, worried the British. In

addition, during the Boer War, Germany had denounced British imperialism in Africa.

Thus, Britain began looking for allies. In 1904, Britain and France signed an *entente cordiale* (ahn TAHNT kor DYAHL), or "friendly understanding." The agreement only settled some colonial issues between the two nations and did not contain pledges of mutual protection. But France regarded the agreement as a major triumph because it now had agreements with Russia and Britain. The signing of an Anglo-Russian agreement in 1907 completed the Triple Entente, a loose coalition of Britain, Russia, and France.

The alliance system worked out between 1879 and 1907 heightened international tensions because any crisis involving one of the great powers would also affect the nation's allies. The alliance system also raised the possibility that a minor incident could lead to a general war.

SECTION REVIEW

1. Identify: Three Emperors' League, Triple Alliance, Triple Entente.
2. Give two examples of how nationalism contributed to tensions in Europe.
3. (a) What European nations were involved in the second Moroccan crisis? (b) How did the crisis contribute to growing tension in Europe?
4. What evidence existed of increasing militarism in Europe during the late 1800s and early 1900s?

2 On the Brink

Read to Learn ■ how hostility among Balkan states sparked World War I
■ how World War I enveloped Europe

As you read in Chapter 26, nationalism was contributing to the breakup of the Ottoman Empire and the weakening of Austria-Hungary in the early 1900s. The Balkan Peninsula was the focus of these nationalist movements. Increasingly, turmoil in the Balkans brought Europe closer to war.

The Balkan Powder Keg

In the early 1900s, the Ottoman Empire ruled only a small part of the Balkans. The Greeks had won independence in 1829. The Slavs had established the independent nations of Bulgaria, Serbia, and Montenegro in the late 1800s. However, at the Congress of Berlin in 1878, Austria-Hungary had been given the right to administer* Bosnia and Herzegovina on the western border of Serbia. Thousands of Slavs lived in Bosnia and Herzegovina. In 1908, Austria-Hungary annexed these areas outright.

This action infuriated the Serbs, who had hoped to absorb all the southern Slavs into their nation. Russia also denounced the Austro-Hungarian move. The Russians, who wanted to increase their influence in the Balkans, were motivated both by feelings of kinship with fellow Slavs and by their desire for warm-water ports. However, Russia was too weak to risk a war. Reluctantly, it pressured Serbia into accepting the situation. Although the crisis passed, both Serbia and Russia remained bitter toward Austria-Hungary.

Three years later, in 1912, trouble again broke out in the Balkans. This time, Serbia, in alliance with Bulgaria and Greece, attacked the Ottoman Empire and took most of its remaining European possessions. One result of this First Balkan War was the creation of the independent nation of Albania. However, the three victors soon quarreled over the spoils of war. A Second Balkan War erupted in 1913. Bulgaria attacked its former partners, Serbia and Greece, but was defeated. An uneasy peace followed these two wars. Many people saw the Balkans as "the powder keg of Europe."

Assassination in Sarajevo

On June 28, 1914, Archduke Francis Ferdinand, heir to the throne of Austria-Hungary, paid a state visit to Sarajevo (sar uh YAY voh), capital of Bosnia. As he and his wife were driven through the streets in an open car, a Bosnian revolutionary, Gavrilo Princip, stepped from the curb and fatally shot them both.

Princip belonged to the Black Hand, a Serbian nationalist organization that wanted to unite Bosnia and Herzegovina with Serbia. The Black Hand was not a tool of the Serbian government though some Serbian

*A nation that administers another country or region directs the government of that country or region.

officials were sympathetic to it and even knew of the assassination plot. However, Austria-Hungary believed that Serbia was deeply involved in the murder plot.

In a letter to the German emperor, Francis Joseph of Austria-Hungary declared that "the Sarajevo affair was . . . the result of a well-organized conspiracy, the threads of which can be traced to Belgrade [the capital of Serbia]." In reply, the German emperor promised to "faithfully stand by Austria-Hungary, as is required by the obligations of his alliance." Austria-Hungary interpreted this response to mean that it had received a "blank check" from Germany—that is, the Germans would back any action it took against Serbia.

Diplomatic Crisis

Tensions mounted in the month after the assassination. On July 23, Austria-Hungary issued Serbia an *ultimatum*, a final set of demands. The ultimatum required Serbia to

Archduke Francis Ferdinand and his wife, Sophie, are shown here on a visit to Sarajevo, Bosnia, on June 28, 1914. Five minutes after this photograph was taken, they were assassinated.

suppress all anti-Austrian activities and dismiss all officials hostile to Austria-Hungary. Serbia was also required to allow officials from Austria-Hungary to enter Serbia to investigate the archduke's murder. The Austrians insisted on an answer within 48 hours.

Serbia faced a difficult choice. Refusal to meet the Austrian demands would undoubtedly mean war. But allowing Austrian officials into Serbia would be a violation of Serbian independence. Serbia, therefore, accepted all the Austrian demands except this last one.

The Serbian response did not satisfy Austria-Hungary. It was determined to take a strong stand and punish Serbia in order to discourage nationalist movements threatening its empire. The German emperor now advised moderation. Austria-Hungary ignored his caution and began to mobilize its armed forces. *Mobilization* is usually a lengthy process that involves calling troops into active service. It does not necessarily mean war, but it is generally viewed as a move toward war.

The other European powers were horrified by the murder of the archduke. They condemned the violence but expected the crisis between Austria-Hungary and Serbia to pass. However, the threatening moves on the part of Austria-Hungary alarmed Russia and France. Russia was prepared to aid Serbia if Austria-Hungary declared war, so it ordered a partial mobilization of its forces. As the crisis deepened, France assured Russia of its support.

Diplomats scurried across Europe seeking a solution to the crisis. Britain proposed a great-power conference to settle the dispute between Austria-Hungary and Serbia. Germany and Austria-Hungary rejected this British proposal, however. They claimed that the issue involved the national honor of Austria-Hungary and should not become the subject of international debate.

The Outbreak of War

On July 28, 1914, Austria-Hungary declared war on Serbia. Over the next few days, the alliance system began to operate. On July 29, the Russian czar Nicholas II ordered a general mobilization of his armed forces. Germany asked Russia to cancel the mobilization order. It stated that failure to cancel the order would result in war. When Russia did not reply, Germany declared war on Russia on August 1. Convinced that France would sooner or later come to the aid of its Russian ally, Germany declared war on France on August 3.

Germany had long foreseen the possibility of having to fight on two fronts at the same time: in the east against Russia and in the west against France. To avoid this, Germany had adopted the Schlieffen Plan. It called for German troops to crush France quickly before the slower Russian war machine could be geared up to full readiness.

The Schlieffen Plan called for German troops to bypass the heavily defended eastern border of France by pushing through Belgium into northern France. Thus, on August 3, German troops marched into the neutral nation of Belgium. This German move brought Britain into the war because in 1830 Britain had pledged to uphold Belgian neutrality. On August 4, Britain declared war on Germany.

What had begun on June 28 as a local incident had grown into a major war involving the five greatest powers of Europe. Today, people still debate the question of war guilt—which nation or nations were responsible for the outbreak of war. Most people agree that no one power was responsible. Years of tensions in Europe and overseas had contributed to the climate of war. When war came, many people welcomed it. Others, however, feared what war might bring.

SECTION REVIEW

1. Locate: Serbia, Bosnia, Sarajevo.
2. Identify: Archduke Francis Ferdinand, Gavrilo Princip, Black Hand, Schlieffen Plan.
3. Define: ultimatum, mobilization.
4. Why did Serbia resent Austria-Hungary?
5. (a) Why did Austria-Hungary take a strong stand against Serbia? (b) How did Serbia respond to the Austro-Hungarian ultimatum?
6. What efforts were made to prevent war in 1914?

As you read earlier, primary sources sometimes offer differing accounts of an event or development. (Review "Analyzing Conflicting Sources," page 404.) When historians study these primary sources, they often develop different interpretations. Their interpretations may be shaped by the mood of the times or the place in which they live. Thus, a historian's environment influences his or her *frame of reference*, the way one views an event or development.

The causes of World War I have been the subject of debate among historians since 1914. The following excerpts give the views of two historians. The first excerpt was written by Emil Ludwig in 1929. The second was written by Raymond Aron in 1954. Use the following steps to analyze their interpretations of the causes of World War I.

1. **Identify the interpretations.** Answer the following questions about the two excerpts: (a) What does Ludwig suggest was the main cause of World War I? (b) What does Aron suggest was the main cause of World War I?

2. **Study the source to decide how a historian's frame of reference affects his or her interpretation.** To do this, you need to know about the mood of the times in which the historian lived. In the 1920s, many European historians rejected the wartime view of the Allies that Germany alone was responsible for the war. They hoped to learn a lesson from the war that would prevent another world conflict. In the 1950s, the world seemed to be divided into two parts: the "free world," led by the United States, and the "communist world," led by the Soviet Union. Both sides built up large arsenals of weapons. Use this background information to answer the following questions: (a) How does Ludwig think World War I might have been avoided? (b) How does this view show the influence of the 1920s on Ludwig's interpretation of the causes of World War I? (c) How might the tensions in the 1950s have affected Aron's interpretation?

3. **Evaluate the reliability of the interpretation.** Use what you have learned about the causes of World War I to answer the following questions: (a) What role do you think individual government leaders could have played in preventing the outbreak of war? (b) In your opinion, how important was the division of Europe into two armed camps in causing World War I? (c) Based on your reading about Europe and the world in the 1800s and early 1900s, what other factors do you think may have contributed to the outbreak of World War I?

Emil Ludwig

The war-guilt belongs to all Europe... Germany's exclusive guilt or Germany's innocence are fairy-tales for children on both sides of the Rhine.... This book is a study of the stupidity of the men who in 1914 were all-powerful.... Economic crises, questions of competition, and colonies had, indeed, complicated the European situation; yet war had been averted time and again, and three capable statesmen could once more have achieved what the great majority desired.... The picture of July 1914 shows a continent in which the nations trusted and obeyed their leaders, while those leaders in their turn were responsible to no central authority. The absence of any control over the individual Governments had brought about European anarchy.... Hurry, carelessness, surprise, and, above all, mutual fear... finally brought about a war which a sound League of Nations could have prevented.

Raymond Aron

In their study of the First World War, historians were deeply interested in the immediate causes.... Before the assassination of the Archduke Francis Ferdinand, Europe was living in a state of preparedness, but no one expected an outbreak from one day to the next. Following the assassination..., chancelleries [governments] and populations alike felt the dread of approaching disaster.... The rise of Germany, whose hegemony [supremacy] France dreaded and whose navy menaced England, had created an opposition that claimed to be defensive but was denounced by German propaganda as an attempt at encirclement. The two camps alarmed each other, and each tried to soothe its own fears by piling up defensive armaments. The atmosphere grew heavy with multiplied incidents, which spread the conviction of approaching disaster.

3 The War Years

Read to Learn ■ how World War I was fought on the western front
■ what events took place on the eastern front

When war broke out in August 1914, people thought it would be a short one. "The boys will be home by Christmas," Europeans on both sides declared confidently. But instead the war dragged on for four years. It was fought on a larger scale than any war before.

On one side were the Central Powers: Germany, Austria-Hungary, and the Ottoman Empire. Italy declared its neutrality. On the other side were the Allied Powers: Britain, France, and Russia. Eventually, 20 other nations, including Japan and the United States, joined the Allies.

Map Skill *Fighting on the western front was limited to a relatively small area. But the number of dead and wounded was huge. In the battle of the Somme in the summer of 1916, the Allies gained 125 square miles of land at the cost of 600,000 dead and wounded. What battles were fought at the farthest points of German advance?*

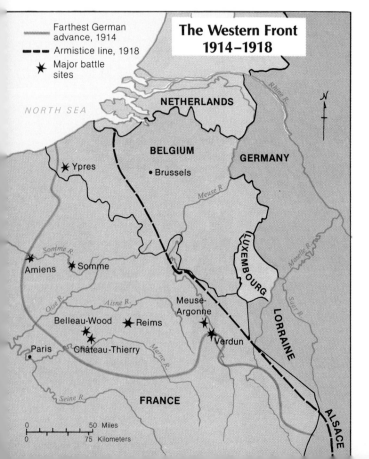

Stalemate on the Western Front

World War I was fought all over the globe. During the early months of the war, much attention was focused on the western front—southern Belgium and northern France. Within three weeks after invading Belgium, the Germans overran that small country and were fighting their way toward Paris. However, the German offensive stalled in early September 1914, when French and British troops took a stand along the Marne River and pushed the Germans back. The battle of the Marne ended the German hope for a quick victory in the west.

During the autumn of 1914, the British and French fought the Germans in a series of battles known as the "race to the sea." At Ypres (EE preh), the British stopped a German attack. The western front then stabilized along a wide arc stretching from the North Sea to the Swiss border.

By November 1914, it was clear that neither side could deal a final blow to the other, so the opposing armies dug trenches protected by mines and barbed wire. For the next three years, fighting on the western front only preserved the stalemate. There was almost no change in the position of either side.

In the maze of trenches on the western front, a new way of life emerged. Thousands of soldiers spent weeks at a time in the muddy, rat-infested trenches. Some trenches were simple shelters. Others were elaborate tunnels that served as headquarters and first-aid stations. Between the front-line trenches of the opposing sides lay "no man's land," a wasteland of barbed wire and land mines.

Trench warfare consisted of days of shelling the enemy's defenses. Then front line troops would be ordered "over the top" of their trenches to race across no man's land and attack the enemy lines. Most offensives resulted in huge casualties and little

A British sentry keeps watch in the trenches. His companions have fallen asleep from exhaustion. One huddles against the earth embankment, while others sleep wherever they find a bit of space.

gain of territory. During the six-month battle of Verdun in 1916, the Germans lost 330,000 men trying to overrun the French lines. The French lost at least that many soldiers defending their position.

New Weapons

The staggering toll of dead and wounded was due in part to the use of deadly new weapons. During World War I, the machine gun was used with tragic results. Its rapid fire mowed down waves of soldiers in seconds as they raced across no man's land.

Early in 1915, the Germans introduced poison gas that blinded and choked its victims. Later that year, the Allies began using poison gas, too. Although the effects of poison gas could be fatal, it was an uncertain weapon. Shifting winds could blow the gas

back on the side that had launched it. Eventually, the use of gas masks helped soldiers in the trenches survive these attacks.

In 1916, the British introduced the tank, a weapon they hoped would protect soldiers against machine-gun fire. The first tanks moved slowly and broke down often, but they terrified the German soldiers. By the end of the war, both sides were using tanks.

Both sides also used aircraft. At first, planes simply observed enemy troop movements. In 1915, Germany used zeppelins, gas-filled balloons, to bomb the English coast. Later, German and Allied planes were equipped with machine guns, and they battled in the skies. Although these "dogfights" were spectacular, they had little effect on the course of the war.

Another weapon, the submarine, was used on a large scale for the first time. Germany made especially effective use of its submarine fleet. When the war began, Britain blockaded the North Sea coast of Germany. The German surface navy was no match for the large British navy, which patrolled the North Sea and confiscated the cargoes of neutral ships bound for Germany. However, German submarines roamed the Atlantic and inflicted enormous damage on merchant ships carrying vital supplies to the British Isles. To counteract submarine warfare, the Allies organized convoys, or groups of merchant ships protected by warships.

The Eastern Front

While British, French, and German forces were fighting on the western front, huge armies fought a seesaw battle on the eastern front. This front was much larger than the western front. It extended from the Baltic Sea to the Black Sea. (See the map on page 573.) The Russians and Serbs battled Germans, Austrians, and Turks. Russia had the largest reserves of manpower in Europe. But its armies often suffered from an appalling lack of supplies and poor leadership. In some engagements, a quarter of the Russian army went into battle without weapons. Soldiers in the rear were expected to pick up the weapons of the dead and wounded.

In August 1914, Russian commanders threw their armies against the Germans at Tannenburg. German commanders skillfully trapped the Russians, inflicting heavy losses. The Russians were more successful against Austrian troops in Galicia, although a combined German-Austrian offensive in 1915 drove the Russians back. In the fall of 1915, Bulgaria joined the Central Powers and, with German aid, overran Serbia.

As in the west, fighting in the east killed and wounded millions but produced few decisive results. In mid-1916, the Russians launched a massive assault in the Ukraine and captured over half a million Austrian prisoners. But the Russians lost one million of their own men trying to hold their line and failed to advance further.

Revolution in Russia. In 1915, Czar Nicholas II took personal command of the Russian armies. Devastating losses at the front and poor management at home increased existing discontent with the czar. Finally, in March 1917, bread riots in St. Petersburg—renamed Petrograd early in the war—led to a revolution in Russia and the downfall of the czar.*

A provisional, or temporary, government vowed to continue the war. Allied leaders hoped that the new government would strengthen the Russian will to fight. But morale among Russian forces remained low. Many soldiers left the front and returned to their villages. According to an official report in October 1917, the army was "an immense, desperate, and weary crowd of … men united by their common desire for peace."

The Treaty of Brest-Litovsk. Popular support for the Provisional Government faded as the war continued. Radical revolutionaries led by Vladimir Ilyich Lenin promised peace if they won power. In November 1917, Lenin staged a second revolution. He seized the reins of government and negotiated a peace treaty with Germany. The Treaty of Brest-Litovsk, signed in March 1918, was harsh. Russia lost about 25 percent of its land and population. But the new Russian government was willing to pay this heavy price for peace.

Russian withdrawal from the war caused grave concern among the Allies. With the collapse of the eastern front, Germany could shift its resources to the west.

---

*You will read more about the Russian Revolution in Chapter 32.

SECTION REVIEW

1. Locate: Marne River, Ypres, Verdun, Tannenburg, Galicia.
2. Identify: Central Powers, Allied Powers, no man's land, Vladimir Ilyich Lenin, Treaty of Brest-Litovsk.
3. (a) What nations were fighting on the western front? (b) What nations were fighting on the eastern front?
4. Describe three new weapons that were widely used in World War I.
5. What problems did the Russian army face?
6. (a) What promise did Lenin make to the Russians? (b) Did he keep his promise? Explain.

4 An End to the Stalemate

Read to Learn ■ how World War I was fought on other fronts
■ why the United States entered the war

As the stalemate and slaughter of the war continued, both sides threw all their resources into a drive for victory. The Allies hoped to win by attacking the Central Powers on several fronts in Europe. The war was also fought in overseas territories.

Fighting on Other Fronts

During World War I, the Allied and Central Powers fought to a standstill on several fronts other than those in France and Russia. A new front was opened in May 1915

Map Skill   *World War I was fought on many fronts. What special problems did the Russian front present to the Central Powers?*

The War in Europe, 1914–1918

when Italy joined the Allies and declared war on Austria-Hungary and later on Germany. Italy had signed a secret treaty with the Allies. The treaty promised Italy Austrian lands in which many Italians lived.

Italian forces pinned down 200,000 Austrian troops along a southern front, the border region between Italy and Austria. In October 1917, the Austrians, reinforced by German troops, launched a major offensive against the Italian position at Caporetto. The Italians were overwhelmed and retreated in confusion. A month later, British and French forces helped Italy stop the Austro-German advance about 20 miles north of Venice.

In 1915, the British devised a plan to capture the Dardanelles, the vital straits connecting the Black Sea and the Mediterranean Sea. The Dardanelles were controlled by the Ottoman Empire. The British believed a victory there would enable them to take Istanbul, improve links with Russia, and liberate the Balkans, which were occupied by the Central Powers. British troops landed on the Gallipoli (guh LIP uh lee) Peninsula, where they met stiff Turkish resistance. After almost a year of fighting, with huge casualties, the British had to withdraw from Gallipoli.

The Allies were more successful in Africa, the Middle East, and Asia. Britain and France seized most of German East Africa. In the Middle East, the British colonel T.E. Lawrence—later known as Lawrence of Arabia—organized Arab nationalists who had revolted against Ottoman rule. He led guerrilla raids against the Turks. Eventually, the Turks lost a great deal of territory to the Arabs, including the key cities of Baghdad and Jerusalem. In Asia, Japan seized Germany's sphere of influence in China and German islands in the Pacific.

On the Home Front

World War I was a total war, involving civilian populations more directly than any previous conflict. In other wars, cities, villages, and farms had been damaged or destroyed by the fighting. But this time the damage and destruction were on a much larger scale.

During World War I, the power of governments increased everywhere as fighting nations struggled to meet the demands for more soldiers and more weapons. Governments drafted men into the armed forces. Germany set up a system of forced civilian labor as well.

Governments turned to planned economies in order to further the war effort. Central planning boards regulated factory production, established wage and price controls, and monitored foreign trade. As one German leader put it, victory was possible only "if all the treasures of our soil that agriculture and industry can produce are used exclusively for the conduct of the war." As naval blockades contributed to shortages, most countries rationed food and other necessities.

On the home fronts, war transformed the lives of many women. Thousands of women went to work outside the home for the first time. They took jobs in munitions factories, as bus drivers, and in offices.

Governments encouraged popular support for the war through propaganda. *Propaganda* is the spreading of ideas or beliefs that further a particular cause or damage an opposing cause. As the war dragged on, and its terrible casualties sapped civilian morale, every effort was made to build confidence in victory and hatred of the enemy. Journalists on both sides publicized, and even invented, reports of atrocities to make the enemy seem inhuman. Governments also manipulated public opinion by controlling the news. The British government censored newspapers and imprisoned critics of the war. German reporters were barred from the front. They were often given misleading and optimistic "news" stories of the fighting.

Entry of the United States Into the War

Both sides aimed a strong propaganda campaign at the United States. When war broke out in August 1914, President Woodrow Wilson proclaimed American neutrality and urged Americans to be "impartial in thought as well as in action." Most Americans be-

Daily Life ■ Mobilizing for Total War

The ordeal of total war involved everyone on the home fronts as well as soldiers in the trenches. Early in September 1914, during the battle of the Marne, German troops seemed ready to break through French lines and advance on Paris. In a desperate attempt to reinforce its front lines, the French government ordered that all the taxis in Paris be used to drive reserve troops to the battle.

Paris was saved. But Paris during the war was very different from prewar Paris. From time to time, it was shelled by German guns. Once filled with the sounds of its nightlife, Paris became filled with the sounds of factory machinery and passing troop trains.

Throughout Europe, men of all ages were expected to join in the war effort. In Germany, a law required all men from ages 17 to 60 to work wherever they were needed. In Britain, women gave white feathers to young, apparently able-bodied men who were not in uniform. The white feather was a sign of cowardice.

Meanwhile, millions of women did their part. They performed jobs once considered unsuitable for women. They became bus drivers, bank tellers, and mail carriers. Many women worked in munitions factories, steel mills, and mines. Others nursed the wounded in hospitals at the front. Growing food was essential to the war effort. On farms across Europe, women often planted and harvested crops alone, because their husbands, sons, and brothers were away fighting.

People on the home fronts had to deal with the problem of shortages of key supplies. German submarine attacks on Allied shipping left Britain with desperate food shortages. Sugar and butter were almost unavailable. In February 1917, the British accepted a voluntary sys-

tem of food rationing. To encourage rationing, British posters showed families eating a full meal and asked, "Are you helping the Kaiser?"

In Germany, scientists invented synthetic substitutes for imported raw materials such as rubber and nitrates, which were scarce. People also experimented with producing substitute foods. For example, they brewed acorns to make a substitute for coffee.

Children everywhere joined in the effort to make use of every available resource. They collected kitchen wastes, coffee grounds, fruit seeds, and pine cones, all of which could be recycled into substitute foods and other products. They helped tend "victory gardens" planted to combat the food shortages. Victory in a total war, people realized, meant a total effort.

lieved that the war in Europe did not directly affect them. But as the war progressed, they were drawn into the conflict on the Allied side.

Americans were swayed in part by British propaganda, which portrayed German soldiers as barbarians torturing the people of occupied Belgium. However, German submarine warfare played a more important part in bringing the United States into the war. In May 1915, the Germans torpedoed an American tanker. The next week, they sank the British passenger liner *Lusitania*. Over 1,000 people on the *Lusitania* died, including 128 Americans. President Wilson protested angrily. Germany feared that continued submarine attacks might bring the United States into the war. Therefore, it limited its use of submarine warfare for a time.

In December 1916, however, Germany decided to break the stalemate in the war by cutting Britain off from the rest of the world and starving it into submission. It announced a policy of unrestricted submarine warfare. It declared that its submarines would sink any ship in waters near enemy coasts. German leaders knew that unrestricted submarine warfare might bring the United States into the conflict. But they took this risk. They hoped to defeat Britain before the United States could mobilize its forces for war.

Early in 1917, after German submarines had attacked American merchant ships, President Wilson broke off diplomatic relations with Germany. He hoped that Germany would abandon unrestricted submarine warfare as it had in 1915. Wilson soon learned, however, that Germany would not back down.

American public opinion was outraged when newspapers published the Zimmermann telegram, a secret message from the German foreign secretary, Alfred Zimmermann, to Mexico. The British had intercepted this telegram. In it, Zimmermann suggested Mexico could "retain lost territory in New Mexico, Texas, and Arizona" if it became a German ally.

On April 2, 1917, President Wilson asked Congress to declare war on Germany. Wilson claimed that the United States had no selfish interests in entering the war. He maintained that Americans would fight "to make the world safe for democracy." Congress voted for war, and the nation prepared to send its fighting forces overseas.

Final Offensives

During the spring and summer of 1917, while American forces were still mobilizing, the Allies launched a series of offensives on the

When the United States entered the war, the American people united behind the war effort. This poster encourages Americans to lend the government money by buying Liberty Bonds. The government raised over $18 billion through the sale of Liberty Bonds.

western front. They gained little territory. By late 1917, however, 50,000 American troops were landing in Europe each month. Their arrival boosted the morale of soldiers who had been fighting for over three years.

Germany, meanwhile, was suffering terribly from the naval blockade of its ports. German leaders realized they had to win quickly or face defeat. Early in 1918, they mounted an ambitious final offensive on the western front. The Allies, reinforced by American troops, withstood the assaults and then counterattacked. An Allied tank offensive pierced the German lines on August 8, 1918, and steadily pushed the German army back. In Germany, morale collapsed and troops deserted.

By autumn, the other Central Powers were crumbling, too. Austria-Hungary was badly defeated on the southern front. The empire began to break apart when Czechoslovakia, Hungary, and Poland declared their independence. In September, Bulgaria surrendered to the Allies. The next month, the Ottoman Empire also accepted defeat. By November 1918, Germany stood alone.

While German leaders tried to negotiate an *armistice*, an end to the fighting, a revolt broke out against the government. On November 9, a German republic was proclaimed. The next day, William II fled to the Netherlands. At 11 A.M. on November 11, the Allies and Germany signed an armistice agreement. The Great War had ended. The Allies now faced the difficult task of establishing peace in a world transformed by war.

SECTION REVIEW

1. Locate: Caporetto, Gallipoli.
2. Identify: *Lusitania*, unrestricted submarine warfare, Zimmermann telegram.
3. Define: propaganda, armistice.
4. Why did the British want to take the Dardanelles?
5. Describe two ways in which the power of governments increased during the war.
6. Why did the United States enter the war on the Allied side?

5 The Peace Settlements

Read to Learn
- how the Allies hammered out the Treaty of Versailles
- how the peace treaties changed the map of Europe

World War I was the costliest war fought up to that time. In lives, the toll was staggering: almost 10 million soldiers dead, 20 million wounded, and about 1 million civilian casualties. The war had also cost the fighting powers over $350 billion. Early in 1919, the victorious Allies gathered in Paris to hammer out a peace settlement.

Wilson's Fourteen Points

Woodrow Wilson traveled to Paris for the peace conference, the first American President to visit Europe while in office. He was greeted everywhere by enthusiastic crowds. Ordinary people saw him, more than any other Allied leader, as offering hope for the future. Admiration for Wilson was due not only to the American role in ending the war but also to the President's Fourteen Points, his goals for a postwar settlement.

Wilson had issued his Fourteen Points in January 1918, almost a year before the war ended. The Fourteen Points offered a framework for a just peace. Wilson hoped his plan would prevent future international tensions such as those that had led to war in 1914.

The first point called for "open covenants [treaties] of peace, openly arrived at," because Wilson believed secret diplomacy had led to the war. Points two through five called for freedom of the seas, free trade, reduction of armaments, and the peaceful adjustment of all colonial claims. Points six through thirteen concerned the readjustment of borders and territorial settlements in Europe "along clearly recognizable lines of nationality." The fourteenth point proposed the creation of a "general association of nations" to guarantee the "political independence" and territorial integrity of great and small nations alike. Wilson firmly believed that such a league of nations could prevent war by settling disputes peacefully.

In 1918, the European Allies accepted Wilson's Fourteen Points as the basis for conducting peace negotiations. However, once the peace conference began, the European Allies became impatient with Wilson's idealism.

Crosscurrents at the Peace Conference

During the war, President Wilson had spoken of a "peace without victory"—a "just peace" that would not involve seeking revenge on the defeated powers. Many Allied leaders who gathered in Paris did not share this goal for the peace. Moreover, only the victors met in Paris. The Central Powers were not allowed to attend the peace conference.

All nations on the Allied side sent representatives except Russia, which was torn apart by revolution. The chief architects of the peace were the "Big Four": Woodrow Wilson of the United States, David Lloyd George of Britain, Georges Clemenceau (KLEHM uhn SOH) of France, and Vittorio Orlando of Italy. Each leader had his own aims for the peace settlement.

Wilson believed that planning for peace was more important than settling boundaries or arranging for *reparations*, payment for war damages. Therefore, he insisted on the creation of a league of nations. The European Allies were determined to punish Germany and demanded reparations. Lloyd George had recently campaigned for Parliament, declaring: "We shall squeeze the orange [Germany] until the pips squeak." Although he might have moderated his views,

Graph Skill   *The costs of the war were staggering. The Allies spent over $100 billion and suffered more than 18 million casualties. According to this graph, which nation had the largest number of casualties?*

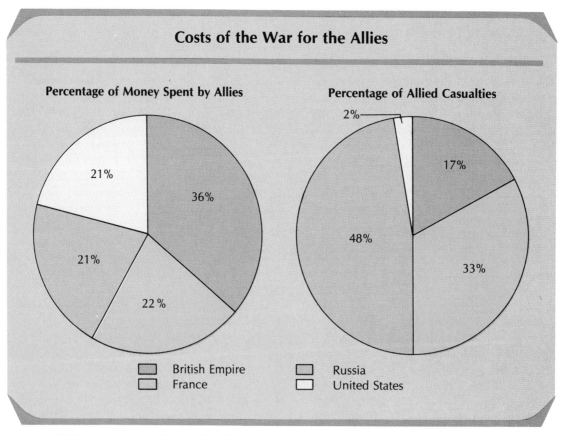

Costs of the War for the Allies

Percentage of Money Spent by Allies

- 36%
- 22%
- 21%
- 21%

Percentage of Allied Casualties

- 48%
- 33%
- 17%
- 2%

British Empire
France
Russia
United States

Source: V.J. Esposito, *A Concise History of World War I.*

British public opinion was fiercely anti-German in 1919. Moreover, Britain wanted control of the former German colonies in Africa.

During the war, fighting on the western front had taken place largely on French soil, and French losses were appalling. At the peace conference, Clemenceau wanted revenge as well as security against any future German attack. He demanded the return of Alsace-Lorraine and the establishment of an independent state, the Rhineland, as a buffer between France and Germany. Clemenceau also sought huge reparations and wanted to annex the coal-rich Saar Basin.

Italy was determined to claim the Austrian territories that it had been promised by its secret treaty with the Allies in 1915. It also demanded the city of Fiume, which it had seized during the war.

Conflicting interests almost brought the peace conference to a standstill. Wilson once packed his bags to leave when the French refused to moderate their demands. After months of bargaining, however, the Allies finally resolved the many conflicting issues.

The Peace Treaties

The victors drafted five separate peace treaties: for Germany; for Austria and Hungary, which had become separate nations; and for Turkey and Bulgaria. The most controversial treaty was the Versailles Treaty with Germany.

The Versailles Treaty. The peace treaty with Germany represented several compromises among the Big Four. France, for example, achieved only some of its aims. It received Alsace-Lorraine but had to give up its demands for the Saar Basin and an independent Rhineland. To calm French fears, however, Germany was forbidden to maintain any military forces in the Rhineland, and the Allies were to occupy the region for 15 years.

A difficult issue was the question of reparations. In the end, the Versailles Treaty required Germany to admit responsibility for the war. On the basis of this "war guilt" clause, the Allies required Germany to pay reparations for the total cost of the war. The "war guilt" clause and reparations would fuel much German bitterness toward the Versailles Treaty in the years ahead.

The Versailles Treaty deprived Germany of its overseas colonies, which were turned over to the newly created League of Nations. The league established these former German colonies as *mandates*, territories that were administered but not owned by league members. Britain and France received German colonies in Africa as mandates. German colonies in Asia and the Pacific were given as mandates to Japan, Australia, and New Zealand.

The treaty also limited the size of the German army and required Germany to turn its fleet over to the Allies. Areas of eastern Germany, mainly inhabited by Poles, were added to a newly created Polish state.

In May 1919, the Allies summoned a German delegation to Versailles and told it to sign the treaty. At first, the Germans refused to sign such a severe treaty. When the Allies threatened to renew hostilities, the Germans signed on June 28, 1919, exactly five years after the assassination of Francis Ferdinand at Sarajevo.

The Germans were not the only ones to criticize the treaty. President Wilson described the Versailles Treaty as "severe." But he agreed to the harsh demands of Britain and France in order to gain their backing for the League of Nations. The league covenant, or constitution, was included as part of the Versailles Treaty.

The other settlements. Peace treaties with the other Central Powers changed boundaries in Europe. (See the map on page 581). The Austro-Hungarian Empire had already ceased to exist. Its place was taken by the independent nations of Austria and Hungary. In addition, two new nations, Czechoslovakia and Yugoslavia, were created in Eastern Europe.

Romania gained territory from the former Austro-Hungarian Empire, as did Italy. However, Italy was unhappy with the peace settlement because it did not receive Fiume. Bulgaria lost its Aegean coastline to Greece.

Like Germany, Austria, Hungary, and Bulgaria had to pay reparations. In addition, Austria, a German-speaking nation, was barred forever from uniting with its neighbor Germany.

The idea of national self-determination, included in Wilson's Fourteen Points, influenced the creation of other new nations in Eastern Europe. Poland was reconstituted as a nation for the first time since 1795. (See page 362.) The Russian lands Germany had acquired by the Treaty of Brest-Litovsk were formed into the independent Baltic nations of Lithuania, Latvia, and Estonia.

In 1919, the peace treaty ending World War I was signed in the Hall of Mirrors at the palace of Versailles. Nearly 50 years earlier, Bismarck had proclaimed the German Empire in this same room after the Franco-Prussian War. The Versailles Treaty humiliated Germany, which was not allowed to participate in the negotiations. This painting shows two German officials on one side of the table. Facing them, in the center, is Georges Clemenceau. David Lloyd George sits on the right. Woodrow Wilson, on the left, holds a copy of the treaty.

The Ottoman Empire was broken up. Turkey kept Asia Minor and the Balkan area around Istanbul. The Dardanelles were placed under international control. Greece was given control of the Aegean islands. In the Middle East, former Ottoman lands became League mandates. Britain acquired mandates in Iraq, Transjordan, and Palestine, while France took Lebanon and Syria.

Problems of the Peace

The peace settlements dealt with momentous issues and involved the lives of millions of people. Sometimes, haste and the need for compromise led to solutions that were unsatisfactory to all parties. As a result, the peace settlements left a legacy of anger and bitterness, especially among the defeated powers.

Germans resented the loss of territory in Europe and of their colonies overseas. They were burdened with billions of dollars in reparations payments. They also felt the Versailles Treaty was unjust in holding Germany alone responsible for the war.

In addition, the principle of national self-determination had not always been followed. Many Germans, for example, lived in western Poland. Several million other German-speaking people lived within the new nation of Czechoslovakia. These people and others felt betrayed by the peace settlements.

The peace settlement reduced Austria to a small landlocked nation that lacked self-sufficiency in agriculture and industry. The newly created nations of Eastern Europe tried to establish democratic governments, but they faced many problems, as you will read.

Even some of the victors were dissatisfied with the peace settlements. France still feared a revival of German power. Both Italy and Japan felt they had been denied rewards due to them. Although Russia had fought with the Allies until 1917, it had been excluded from the peace conference and in fact had lost more territory than Germany. (See the map above.)

Map Skill *The peace treaties that ended World War I redrew the map of Europe. The defeated Central Powers lost land to newly created nations in Eastern Europe. Which of the Central Powers lost the most territory? Which of the Allies also lost much territory?*

Finally, Wilson's great hope for maintaining peace in the postwar world, the League of Nations, was launched without American support. When Wilson returned home after the Paris Peace Conference, he found the American people and Congress preferred isolationism to further involvement in international affairs. The Senate refused to ratify the Versailles Treaty because many senators objected to the League of Nations.

SECTION REVIEW

1. Locate: Rhineland, Saar Basin.
2. Identify: Fourteen Points, League of Nations, Versailles Treaty.
3. Define: reparation, mandate.
4. Describe two of Wilson's main goals for the peace settlements.
5. (a) Who were the Big Four at the Paris Peace Conference? (b) Which nation did each represent?
6. How did the Versailles Treaty punish Germany?
7. What new nations were created in Eastern Europe by the peace settlements?

Chapter 30 Review

In Perspective

By the early 1900s, rivalries among European nations had created dangerous tensions. Increasingly, the major powers sought allies to help them in the event of war. However, the alliance system that emerged only heightened tensions. In June 1914, the assassination of the Austrian archduke Francis Ferdinand in Serbia sparked an international crisis. Austria-Hungary blamed Serbia for the murder and issued an ultimatum. Efforts to resolve the crisis failed, and Europe was plunged into war.

The war lasted from 1914 to 1918 and involved almost every European nation, their overseas colonies, and Japan. Nations on both sides devoted all their efforts to achieving victory. But the war dragged on, inflicting heavy casualties. In April 1917, the United States joined the Allies against the Central Powers. American troops helped the Allies withstand a German offensive in the spring of 1918. Later in 1918, the Central Powers collapsed one by one. The fighting ended in November, when Germany signed an armistice with the Allies.

Restoring peace in a world torn apart by war proved to be difficult. Each of the Allies had its own goals for the peace settlement. Wilson's Fourteen Points had been accepted as the basis for negotiation, but these guidelines were often ignored. In the end, five treaties were drawn up—one for each of the defeated Central Powers. The Versailles Treaty made Germany admit guilt for the war and pay huge reparations. The harsh terms of this treaty created deep resentment among Germans.

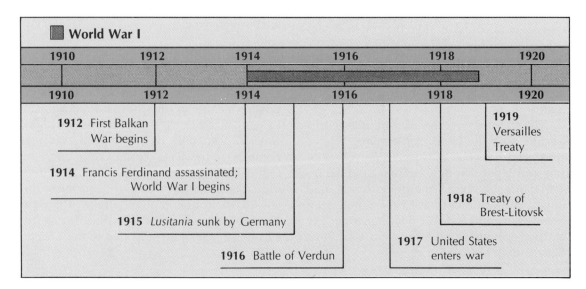

World War I					
1910	1912	1914	1916	1918	1920

1912 First Balkan War begins

1914 Francis Ferdinand assassinated; World War I begins

1915 *Lusitania* sunk by Germany

1916 Battle of Verdun

1917 United States enters war

1918 Treaty of Brest-Litovsk

1919 Versailles Treaty

Recalling Facts

Identify each of the following as a cause or an effect of World War I.

1. The Balkans become the "powder keg" of Europe.
2. Germany pays reparations to other European nations.
3. Britain receives German colonies in Africa.
4. European nations strengthen their armed forces.
5. The Austro-Hungarian Empire is split into several countries.
6. President Wilson issues his Fourteen Points.
7. Francis Ferdinand is assassinated at Sarajevo.
8. European nations compete for overseas colonies.
9. The League of Nations is created.
10. Rival alliance systems are formed in Europe.

Chapter Checkup

1. (a) Describe the rivalries among European powers in the early 1900s. (b) How did each help set the stage for war?
2. (a) Which major European powers were most interested in the Balkans? (b) Why was each interested in this region? (c) How did rivalries among Balkan nations create further problems in this region?
3. (a) What group was responsible for the assassination of the Austrian archduke? (b) What role did Serbia play in the assassination plot? (c) What role did Austria-Hungary believe Serbia had played?
4. (a) Why were other European powers drawn into the crisis over the archduke's assassination? (b) Why did Austria-Hungary refuse to settle the issue at the conference table?
5. (a) Why did Russia withdraw from the war? (b) How did the Russian move affect Germany?
6. (a) What position did the United States take at the beginning of World War I? (b) Why did American public opinion change during the war? (c) How did the entry of the United States into the war help the Allies?
7. (a) Why did Wilson issue the Fourteen Points? (b) Which point did Wilson think would guarantee the peace settlement? (c) How did other European leaders view Wilson's Fourteen Points?

Critical Thinking

1. **Expressing an Opinion** In your opinion, why did the assassination of Francis Ferdinand ignite a world war?
2. **Analyzing a Quotation** On August 3, 1914, British foreign secretary Edward Grey observed to a friend: "The lamps are going out all over Europe; we shall not see them lit again in our lifetime." What do you think Grey meant by this statement?

Relating Past to Present

1. (a) Why were the Balkans known as "the powder keg of Europe"? (b) Do you think there is any region of the world today that might be called a "powder keg"? Explain.

Developing Basic Skills

1. **Map Reading** Study the map on page 581. Then answer the following questions: (a) Which European nations gained territory after the war? (b) Which nations lost territory? (c) How did the peace settlements affect the territory once ruled by Austria-Hungary? (d) Which nation or nations were most likely to resent the territorial changes? Why?
2. **Making a Review Chart** Make a chart with four rows titled United States, Britain, France, and Italy and two columns titled Goals for the Peace and Actual Results. Use what you read about the peace settlements to complete the chart. Then answer the following questions: (a) How were British and French goals for the peace similar? (b) How were they different? (c) What did Italy receive in the peace settlements? (d) In your opinion, which of the Big Four was most likely to be dissatisfied with the peace?

See page 807 for suggested readings.

31 The Aftermath of War

(1919–1939)

Senecio, *by Paul Klee.*

On the night of May 21, 1927, a 25-year-old American pilot, Charles A. Lindbergh, peered out the cockpit of his small plane. Lindbergh later recalled: "Presently, I could make out long lines of hangars, and the roads appeared to be jammed with cars. I flew low over the field once, then circled around into the wind and landed. After the plane stopped rolling, I turned it around and started to taxi back to the lights. The entire field, however, was covered with thousands of people all running towards my ship."

Lindbergh's "ship" was *The Spirit of St. Louis.* After flying more than 3,600 miles (5,760 kilometers) in 33 hours, Lindbergh had landed outside Paris. The crowds had gathered to greet the first man to fly across the Atlantic alone. Lindbergh won worldwide fame for his achievement. He was showered with awards, including the French Legion of Honor, the English Royal Air Cross, and the Belgian Order of Leopold. American President Calvin Coolidge sent a cruiser to bring the young flyer and his plane back to the United States. On his return, Lindbergh received the Distinguished Flying Cross from the President.

A modest and appealing young man, Lindbergh seemed to represent values that all the world could admire: self-reliance, dedication, and bravery. Said one speaker in praising Lindbergh: "We are all better men and women because of this . . . flight of our young friend. Our boys and girls have before them a stirring, inspiring vision of real manhood. What a wonderful thing it is to live in a time when science and character join hands to lift up humanity with a vision of its own dignity."

Lindbergh's flight was not only a daring individual achievement, but it also heralded a new age—the age of air travel. No longer would it take days or weeks of sea travel to journey between continents. Regular air travel between the United States and Europe would soon bring these two continents into close contact.

In the spring of 1927, people gladly celebrated Lindbergh's feat. The world was recovering from the devastation of the Great War. Yet the war had left a legacy of uncertainty and anxiety. It had shattered the lives of so many people. These people felt adrift in the postwar world. In the 1920s and 1930s, people searched for a new sense of security in an uncertain world.

1 Western Europe in the 1920s

Read to Learn
- why postwar Europe faced severe economic problems
- how European nations planned to prevent war

For four years, European nations had devoted their energies to war. Their economies had been focused on producing goods to supply the men at the front. While soldiers celebrated their homecoming, European leaders faced the challenge of returning to a peacetime economy.

Economic Problems in Britain

Britain welcomed returning veterans with the slogan that they deserved "homes fit for heroes." Certainly, the British wanted to honor their fighting men. But when the parades ended, many soldiers found there were no jobs for them. In the early 1920s, Britain faced severe economic problems.

A small island kingdom, Britain depended on trade for prosperity. In the postwar years, however, British commerce was dealt several blows that hurt its export industries—cotton textiles, steel, and coal. First, German submarines had destroyed about 40 percent of the British merchant fleet during the war. Second, other trading nations, especially the United States and Japan, had penetrated many of Britain's overseas markets. Third, many nations imposed high tariffs after the war. These tariffs were aimed at protecting domestic industries from foreign competition. They cut deeply into British exports.

Finally, the decline in trade was due in part to Britain's out-dated technology. As you have read, Britain had been the first nation to industrialize. Even before the war, many of its factories were old, and equipment needed replacing. Coal mines lacked modern machinery. Aged equipment also hurt British steel and shipbuilding industries, which faced stiff competition from newer industrial nations.

Declining trade and loss of foreign markets forced British manufacturers to cut back production and lay off workers. Unemployment, which stood at 700,000 in 1920, jumped to over 2 million, almost a quarter of the work force, in 1921. Although unemployment declined in 1922, some 1 million people were jobless during the rest of the decade.

High unemployment contributed to labor unrest. In 1926, as coal exports fell, mine owners announced wage cuts. In protest, coal miners went on strike and called for a *general strike*, a mass walkout by unionized workers in all industries. The General Strike of 1926 lasted for nine days. Since troops and nonunion workers supplied vital services, the strike failed. It also resulted in anti-labor legislation, which caused widespread bitterness toward the government among workers.

Britain faced another economic problem. During the war, Britain had borrowed billions of dollars from the United States.

On the first day of the British General Strike in May 1926, more than 2 million workers walked off their jobs. Buses, trolleys, and railways stopped. The government proclaimed an emergency. In this photograph, London office workers are shown riding to work on a truck. The General Strike collapsed after nine days, but it left a legacy of bitterness.

Loss of trade made it hard for Britain to repay this debt. At the same time, Germany was unable to make the reparations payments owed to the British. Despite these economic problems, the British government remained a stable democracy.

An Independent Ireland

During the war and afterward, Britain confronted a crisis in Ireland. As you have read, the Irish had for centuries sought freedom from British rule. The British Parliament had passed a home rule bill in 1914, but it delayed taking action when the war broke out. In 1916, nationalist leaders in Ireland organized the Easter Rebellion against British rule. British troops suppressed this uprising, and many rebel leaders were executed.

The executions turned Irish opinion strongly against Britain. Many Irish supported the Irish Republican Army, an underground force that waged guerrilla war against the British.

In 1921, Britain sought an end to the fighting by dividing Ireland into two parts. The southern counties, inhabited by Catho-lics, became an independent nation: the Irish Republic. The northern county of Ulster, which was largely Protestant, remained part of Great Britain. Protestant Irish in Northern Ireland did not want to become part of the Irish Republic. But many Catholics in Northern Ireland demanded a united Ireland. As you will read in Chapter 39, this issue has remained a source of conflict to the present.

Postwar Recovery in France

France had suffered terrible damage from the fighting on the western front. Ten million acres (4 million hectares) of farmland were devastated. About 20,000 factories and 6,000 public buildings had been destroyed. When the war ended, the French embarked on an ambitious program to rebuild their battered land and economy. This reconstruction effort helped keep French unemployment relatively low in the 1920s.

France, like Britain, had borrowed heavily during the war. Government borrowing to pay for reconstruction combined with French war debts caused inflation and undermined confidence in the French currency. In 1926, a government headed by Raymond Poincaré (pwahn kah RAY) reduced government expenses, raised taxes, and stabilized the currency. These reforms helped bring about a strong economic recovery.

France also invested in military preparedness. Two times within recent memory, Germany had invaded France. In the 1920s, the French were determined to prevent this from happening again. Therefore, they constructed the Maginot Line, an elaborate system of fortifications, along the French borders with Germany and Luxembourg.

German Inflation

The Versailles Treaty required Germany to pay stiff reparations. The reparations bill eventually totaled $33 billion. The German government tried to pay these debts by borrowing and by printing more paper money. The result was disastrous inflation. As more money was printed, its value kept dropping.

In 1923, the worst year of German inflation, a housewife had to fill a wheelbarrow with money simply to buy a loaf of bread. A newspaper cost 100 billion marks. Millions of Germans found that their savings had become worthless. The hardships caused by the inflation of the 1920s contributed to political unrest, as you will read in Chapter 32.

When Germany tried to ease the economic crisis by calling a temporary halt to reparations payments, France took matters into its own hands. Early in 1923, French troops occupied the Ruhr, the industrial heartland of Germany. France intended to collect reparations from German steel mills and coal mines. However, Germans in the Ruhr responded with *passive resistance*, nonviolent opposition, and simply refused to work.

German inflation worsened as people in other parts of the country supported Ruhr workers. Eventually, an international committee headed by American banker Charles Dawes resolved the crisis. Under the Dawes Plan of 1924, Germany agreed to resume reparations payments to the Allies, but on a reduced scale. The United States promised to provide loans to help Germany rebuild its economy. France withdrew its troops from the Ruhr in 1925. As the German economy recovered, Germany increased its reparations payments. This allowed France and Britain to repay some of their debts to the United States.

The Diplomacy of Peace

During the 1920s, leaders in Western Europe were hopeful that they would preside over a new era in international relations. They rejected balance-of-power politics and the alliance system, which many people believed had contributed to the war. They looked instead to the League of Nations to keep the peace.

The league was based on the idea of *collective security*, that is, an organized community of nations acting together to preserve peace. In the 1920s, the league helped settle a number of disputes between small powers. It was less successful in resolving crises that involved major powers. Moreover, three major powers—the United States, Germany, and Russia—were not members of the league.

German unhappiness with the Versailles Treaty continued to haunt European diplomacy. In 1925, the Allies met with Germany at the Swiss town of Locarno. France, Britain, and Germany signed a series of agreements known as the Locarno Pact. Western European nations agreed to guarantee existing borders and to seek peaceful solutions to any dispute. In addition, Germany agreed to seek a peaceful settlement of border disputes with its neighbors in Eastern Europe—Poland and Czechoslovakia. Thus, the Locarno Pact improved relations in Western Europe.

In the mid-1920s, Europeans were optimistic about the "spirit of Locarno," which seemed to offer the hope of a stable and lasting peace. In 1926, Germany was permitted to join the League of Nations. Thus, Germany regained its place in the international community.

Postwar inflation ruined many middle class people in Germany. Families often sold treasured family possessions to get money for food. A loaf of bread, if available, cost billions of marks. The value of money decreased so quickly that prices for food items multiplied many times in just a single day. This photograph shows workers picking up the money for one week's payroll from a Berlin bank.

Throughout the 1920s, the great powers discussed plans for disarmament. Their efforts focused on naval disarmament. The United States as well as Japan participated in naval disarmament conferences held in Washington, D.C., and Geneva, Switzerland.

In 1928, efforts to maintain peace resulted in the Kellogg-Briand Pact. American Secretary of State Frank B. Kellogg and French Foreign Minister Aristide Briand were the architects of this pact. Sixty-two nations, including the United States, signed the pact and agreed to "renounce war as an instrument of national policy." The Kellogg-Briand Pact symbolized the optimism of the period. However, although nations gallantly banished war, they established no machinery to enforce peace.

SECTION REVIEW

1. Identify: Irish Republic, Maginot Line, Dawes Plan, Locarno Pact, Kellogg-Briand Pact.
2. Define: general strike, passive resistance, collective security.
3. Describe one economic problem faced by each of the following countries in the postwar period: (a) Britain; (b) France; (c) Germany.
4. What role did the League of Nations play in the 1920s?

2 Changing Patterns of Life

Read to Learn
- about new attitudes after World War I
- how the arts reflected the postwar world

The war had swept away many accepted ideas and practices of the past. During the 1920s, many features of today's world took shape. Most changes were quite slow, but gradually new patterns of life emerged in Europe and the United States.

Expanded Horizons for Women

Before the war, women had won suffrage in only a few countries. After the war, women gained the vote in most of Western Europe, in the United States, in Russia, and in India. In 1924, the Danes elected the first woman to a national cabinet post.

The war had contributed to expanded horizons for women. Many women had helped the war effort by working in factories and offices. But when the war ended, many employers replaced them with men. Other women voluntarily left their jobs after the armistice. However, the number of women in the work force remained higher than it had been in 1914, and it continued to increase during the 1920s.

During the war, some single women had moved into their own apartments instead of living with relatives. Women worked outside the home, earning their own money. During the 1920s, they gained more political and economic rights. Also, European and American families became smaller in the postwar period. With fewer children to raise than in the past, some women had more time to work outside the home or take active roles in their communities.

Women's fashions in the 1920s reflected the new freedom. Short skirts and short hair replaced the styles of the prewar period. Women also wore make-up, a practice that had been unacceptable in 1914.

The Impact of New Technology

Many jobs traditionally performed by women inside the home were made easier by new technology. Stores sold a variety of canned and packaged foods. Labor-saving devices such as electric irons and vacuum cleaners simplified housekeeping.

New technology was not limited to household appliances. As Lindbergh's flight across the Atlantic showed, the air age was beginning. The first international airmail was carried between London and Paris in 1919. Big cities built airports. By the 1930s, passen-

French women demonstrated for the right to vote in the 1920s and 1930s. The French Chamber of Deputies had voted for woman's suffrage in 1919 by an overwhelming majority. But the Senate rejected the measure. The banners in this photograph demand that women receive the right to vote immediately, especially since women paid taxes. However, French women had to wait until 1944 for the right to vote.

ger transport by air was no longer a novelty. At the same time, more people bought automobiles. France, which had only 125,000 registered motor vehicles in 1913, had over 2 million in 1938.

Some postwar technology made people's lives more fun as well as easier. The radio came into wide use, and thousands of movie theaters opened. People danced to tunes coming from hand-cranked phonographs, and the record business boomed.

Postwar Currents of Thought

A revolution in ideas had begun before 1914. After the terrible slaughter of the war, many thinkers rejected the Enlightenment faith in progress and reason. They no longer celebrated the success of science and industry as they had in prewar Europe. In the 1920s, European writers expressed a sense of helplessness and pessimism.

French poet Paul Valéry summed up the postwar mood in these words:

The storm has died away, and still we are restless, uneasy, as if the storm were about to break. Almost all the affairs of men remain in a terrible uncertainty. We think of what has disappeared, and we are almost destroyed by what has been destroyed; we do not know what will be born, and we fear the future, not without reason. . . .

Some writers depicted the futile horror of the war, as German novelist Erich Maria Remarque did in *All Quiet on the Western Front*. (See page 562.) In his long poem *The Waste Land*, T.S. Eliot expressed anguish and disillusionment with an increasingly desolate world. German playwright Bertolt Brecht attacked capitalism in *The Three-Penny Opera*. This play was set in London in the 1700s, but Brecht was actually criticizing the middle class ideals of the 1900s.

Many writers were strongly influenced by the work of Sigmund Freud. As you read in Chapter 24, this Viennese physician taught that irrational, unconscious forces shaped human behavior. At first, Freud's ideas were ridiculed. By the 1920s, however, Freud's theories about human psychology were becoming more accepted.

Many writers used techniques such as stream of consciousness to probe the unconscious minds of their characters. In *Ulysses,* Irish author James Joyce used stream of consciousness to depict a day in the life of a middle class Dubliner. Joyce ignored standard grammar and used bits of thought, foreign words, and unconventional language to suggest the confusion of the unconscious mind. English writer Virginia Woolf gained fame for her novel *To the Lighthouse,* in which characters come to life through complex internal monologues.

Modern Painting

European artists used unconventional means to explore the inner worlds of human emotions. Many artists of the early 1900s had rejected realism and impressionism. Their works were increasingly abstract—that is, they did not represent objects as most people saw them.

Cubists used geometric forms in complex patterns to represent objects such as a guitar, a newspaper headline, or a pipe. The founder of cubism, Pablo Picasso, later painted in many different styles.

Other painters abandoned realism altogether and stressed color, line, and form. In *Composition With Red, Yellow, and Blue,* Dutch artist Piet Mondrian presented a series of brightly colored, boxlike shapes that had no conventional meaning.

An unusual artistic movement that flourished briefly in the 1920s was dada. The word dada, meaning "hobby horse" in French, was chosen because it implied nonsense. Dada painters and writers scorned traditional artistic forms as meaningless in a world turned upside down by the senseless slaughter of the war. Marcel Duchamp, a leading dada artist, ridiculed traditional art by exhibiting shovels as works of art. Followers of dada glorified outrageous behavior. One produced a copy of Leonardo da Vinci's *Mona Lisa* with a mustache and ridiculous grafitti. Dada writers wrote poems by picking words out of a hat.

Pablo Picasso's Portrait of Jacqueline *shows cubist ideas. Cubist painters translated natural shapes into geometrical forms. They often portrayed different sides of a subject, such as front and side, in the same picture.*

SECTION REVIEW

1. Identify: T.S. Eliot, Bertolt Brecht, James Joyce, Virginia Woolf, Pablo Picasso, dada.

2. List three ways in which women's lives changed after the war.

3. Describe three postwar developments in technology that affected the way people lived.

4. How was the mood of postwar Europe different from the mood of the 1800s?

3 From Normalcy to New Deal in the United States

Read to Learn ■ how United States policy reflected a desire for "normalcy"
■ how the United States responded to the Great Depression

The United States was reluctantly drawn into World War I. But Americans were wholehearted in their efforts to win a victory. Wilson's Fourteen Points and the American promise to make the world safe for democracy put the United States in the spotlight at the Paris Peace Conference. After 1919, however, many Americans saw the war as a tragic mistake. They wanted the United States to withdraw from world affairs.

Postwar Isolationism

After World War I, isolationist sentiment swept across the United States. President Wilson campaigned hard to win approval for the Versailles Treaty and American participation in the League of Nations. But the Senate rejected the treaty in November 1919. Senator William E. Borah expressed the fear of many Americans when he predicted the United States would become "a part of . . . European turmoils and conflicts from the time we enter this league."

Events in Europe strengthened isolationist feelings in the United States. During the Russian Revolution, the radical Bolshevik Party under Lenin had seized power and made Russia a communist state. (See page 606.) When bombs exploded in several American cities in 1919 and 1920, many Americans feared that foreign-born radicals were plotting a Bolshevik uprising in the United States. In 1919, Attorney General A. Mitchell Palmer launched a series of raids to round up suspected "Reds." The government arrested and imprisoned thousands of people during this so-called Red Scare.

Isolationism and the Red Scare resulted in pressure to change the nation's immigration policy. The United States had restricted the number of immigrants allowed from China and Japan but had never limited immigration from Europe. After World War I, some people worried that immigrants were changing the character of American society for the worse. As a result, in 1921 and again in 1924, Congress passed acts placing quotas on European immigration.

Yet the United States did not withdraw entirely from world affairs. It participated in naval disarmament negotiations and sponsored the Dawes Plan to ease German reparation payment problems. Its role in drawing up the Kellogg-Briand Pact also indicated American interest in preserving world peace.

Prosperity—On the Surface

During the 1920s, Americans were preoccupied with domestic affairs. Warren G. Harding, who succeeded Wilson as President in 1921, promised a return to "normalcy." The word was a new one, but his audience had no difficulty understanding it. Normalcy meant not only withdrawal from foreign involvement but also a healthy peacetime economy. Indeed, the United States achieved a high level of prosperity during the 1920s.

Unemployment, which stood at 11.7 percent in 1921, dropped to 2.4 percent in 1923. For the rest of the decade, the jobless rate never exceeded 5 percent. Steady employment and good wages turned many American families into eager consumers. Sales of passenger cars more than tripled between 1921 and 1929. Thousands of new homes were built, resulting in a soaring demand for appliances and other home furnishings.

Changing patterns of daily life were more pronounced in the United States than in Europe. Newspapers and magazines featured stories about free-spirited "flappers." These young women shocked their elders with their flashy clothes and use of slang. The average family owned a radio. Some 60 million Americans went to the movies every week to see such stars as Charlie Chaplin and Rudolph Valentino. Jazz swept the

Wall Street, the financial center of the world, captured the imaginations of many Americans. This 1928 cover of a popular magazine shows men and women of all ages and social classes watching the ticker tape that recorded the rise and fall of the stock market. Investors told success stories that made it seem impossible to lose money on the stock market. Millions of Americans who had never before bought stocks invested their savings in the stock market in the 1920s.

country, along with such daring dances as the foxtrot and the Charleston. During the Roaring Twenties, many Americans seemed to spend their time pursuing wealth and pleasure.

Beneath the surface of the Roaring Twenties, however, all was not well. As a group, farmers did not share in the general prosperity. During the war, farmers had found a ready market for their crops and had increased production. After the war, demand slackened because European farms were back in operation. Crop surpluses drove prices down. The price of wheat fell from a wartime high of $2.26 a bushel to less than $1.00 a bushel in 1922. Other groups, such as coal miners and textile workers, were also doing poorly.

The Stock Market Crash and the Great Depression

Americans who had money to invest bought stocks and celebrated their good fortune as stock prices soared in the late 1920s. But stock prices were artificially high. In 1929, the stock market bubble burst. In October, stock prices tumbled, causing panicked investors to sell at a loss. By November, the total market value of stocks traded on the New York Stock Exchange had fallen by about $30 billion. Investors whose stocks had been worth millions suddenly found that their stocks were worthless.

The stock market crash undermined confidence in the economy. It led to the Great Depression, a period of slow business activity, high unemployment, and falling prices and wages. The Great Depression was the worst business slump in American history. It soon triggered a worldwide economic crisis, as you will read.

By 1932, about 85,000 American businesses had failed. Unemployment rocketed from 3.2 percent in 1929 to 23.6 percent in 1932. In the United States, panic-stricken citizens rushed to withdraw their money from banks. But banks had loaned money to European and American businesses and did not have enough cash to honor their customers' deposits. As a result, thousands of banks closed.

The Great Depression caused enormous hardship. The unemployed roamed the country vainly searching for jobs. Families broke up under the pressure of despair. People could not pay their rent and were

During the Great Depression, many small farmers were forced off their farms because they could not pay their debts. In addition, in the 1930s, a severe drought drove many farmers off their land. Families such as this one piled their possessions into old cars and headed west. Known as "Okies" or "Arkies" because so many of them came from Oklahoma or Arkansas, these people hoped to find work in California, Washington, and Oregon.

evicted from their homes. Some moved into tarpaper shacks built in vacant lots and lived as best they could.

The United States had weathered depressions in the past, and the economy had eventually recovered on its own. Herbert Hoover, elected President in 1928, and most other government leaders expected the same thing to happen this time. Hoover did, however, ask Congress to fund public works projects that gave work to the unemployed. He also backed the creation of the Reconstruction Finance Corporation, a government agency that lent money to hard-pressed banks and businesses.

These measures were inadequate to meet the severe economic crisis. Hoover publicly predicted an early end to the depression. He hoped that his optimism would help restore confidence in the economy and encourage business leaders to invest in new ventures, thereby creating more jobs. But the depression dragged on.

The New Deal

In 1932, Americans voted overwhelmingly for the candidate of the Democratic party, Franklin D. Roosevelt. During the presidential campaign, Roosevelt had promised a "new deal for the American people," although he did not say just what this would involve. During Roosevelt's first three months in office, the New Deal took shape. It

---

Daily Life ■ Popular Entertainment in the Twenties and Thirties

In the postwar period, Americans and Europeans clustered around radios to listen to their favorite programs. They also packed into movie houses to watch heros and heroines emerge larger than life on the "silver screen." During the twenties and thirties, radios and movies won a role in popular culture that they have held ever since.

Regularly scheduled radio programming began in the United States on November 2, 1920, when a Pittsburgh station broadcast the presidential election returns. Two years later, there were 550 stations and 1.5 million radios. In Europe, radio experienced a similar boom.

The magic of radio brought the world into people's living rooms. Radio brought live performances of operas and symphonies to families who had never heard classical music. Sports announcers vividly recreated prize fights and ballgames for listeners at home.

Radio shows changed with the onset of the Great Depression. In the thirties, the most popular program in the United States was a variety show hosted by bandleader and singer Rudy Vallee. Each week, Vallee introduced guest comedians, singers, and musicians, as well as authors and celebrities. Comedians Jack Benny and Fred Allen offered humorous programs, a temporary escape from depression worries.

Sound effects added greatly to the excitement and suspense of programs, including westerns such as *The Lone Ranger* and mysteries such as *The Shadow*. The sounds of a storm were created by waving a thin sheet of metal close to the microphone. Crackling tissue paper and breaking matchsticks sounded like fire.

On Halloween night, 1938, radio make-believe terrified many listeners. Actor Orson Welles broadcast *The War of the Worlds* as if it were an actual news broadcast. Announcers grimly reported the landings of invaders from another planet. All over the country, people who had tuned in late and missed the beginning of the show panicked, thinking a real invasion was occurring.

If people's imaginations were captured by the crackling tissue-paper fires of radio, movies could have an even greater impact. During World War I, the United States grabbed the lead in the movie industry. In New York and Hollywood, a small town in California, hundreds of silent films were made.

In 1927, the first sound movie, *The Jazz Singer,* was made in the United States. In the next two years, movie attendance jumped from 60 million a week to 110 million, as audiences rushed to see the latest "talkie."

During the depression, Hollywood became the dream factory for the nation. People escaped from their troubles by watching lavish musicals, gangster films, and romances. Admission to the dream cost only 25 cents.

was a bold program intended to combat the Great Depression. It committed the government to unprecedented intervention in the economy.

The New Deal called for both economic and social programs. Among the first measures passed by Congress were laws to restore confidence in banks. The Emergency Banking Relief Act, for example, provided for the reopening of some banks under federal supervision. The Glass-Steagall Act enabled the government to guarantee deposits of up to $5,000 for each customer.

To reduce unemployment, the Works Progress Administration (WPA) was established. The WPA put millions of people to work on projects such as building bridges, highways, and dams. In addition, the Civilian Conservation Corps provided work for unemployed youths. The federal government also provided relief funds to states so they could give money to the needy.

Along with these measures, the New Deal included social programs. Congress enacted the Social Security Act. It provided old-age benefits and a system of unemployment insurance. The National Labor Relations Act encouraged union organization and collective bargaining. As a result, workers won increased job benefits.

Under the New Deal, the lives of many ordinary people improved. Yet Roosevelt's programs did not restore prosperity to the United States. Unemployment remained high until another world war broke out in Europe in 1939. Whether or not the New Deal was a success is still much debated. However, it resulted in the federal government playing a far larger role than ever before in a peacetime economy.

SECTION REVIEW

1. Identify: Red Scare, Great Depression, Herbert Hoover, Franklin D. Roosevelt, New Deal.
2. Why did Congress restrict immigration from Europe in the 1920s?
3. What evidence showed the prosperity of the United States in the 1920s?
4. How was the Great Depression different from earlier depressions?
5. Describe three measures Roosevelt took to combat the Great Depression.

4 Crises of the 1930s in Europe

Read to Learn ■ how the Great Depression affected Britain and France
■ about the problems postwar Eastern Europe faced

The stock market crash and Great Depression in the United States soon had disastrous effects in Europe and elsewhere. As Americans cut back on their investments in Europe, European trade and manufacturing fell. The number of jobless rose. The European Allies still owed large war debts to the United States but were unable to pay them, in part because Austria and Germany stopped reparations in 1932.

Europeans responded to the Great Depression in different ways, as you will read. In nations still recovering from the impact of the war, the economic collapse increased the sense of desperation. Some people turned to leaders who offered radical solutions to the crises of the 1930s.*

British Response to the Great Depression

In Britain, as elsewhere, the Great Depression inflicted terrible suffering on the unemployed and their families. The government provided relief payments, popularly called "the dole." But these were kept low and bought only the barest necessities. Life on the dole meant a diet based almost entirely

---

* You will read about Italy and Germany during the Great Depression in Chapter 32.

on white bread, margarine, and tea. Shabby clothes and missing teeth became the unwanted badges of Britons who lived on the dole.

The Labour party was in power when the Great Depression struck. To gain broader support for his policies, however, Prime Minister Ramsay MacDonald formed a coalition government in which the Labour and Conservative parties shared power. MacDonald headed the coalition until 1935, when the Conservative leader Stanley Baldwin took power.

Conservatives in Britain opposed widespread government intervention such as Roosevelt had introduced in the United States. However, the coalition government did work to increase exports and passed protective tariffs to help British manufacturing.

Graph Skill *The Great Depression began in the United States in 1929. It quickly spread throughout the world. As businesses failed, millions of people lost jobs. According to this graph, was unemployment worse in the United States or in Britain during most of the Great Depression?*

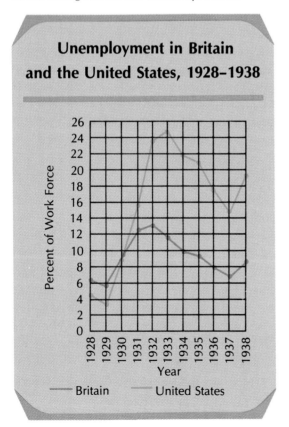

Unemployment in Britain and the United States, 1928–1938

Source: Angus Maddison, *Economic Growth in the West.*

It lowered interest rates, which led to a boom in housing construction. The economy gradually recovered after 1932. In fact, by 1937, the British economy was stronger than it had been in the troubled 1920s.

Deep Divisions in France

France was heavily agricultural and less dependent on foreign trade than Britain. As a result, its economy withstood the early shocks of the Great Depression. By 1932, however, the worldwide economic slump had affected France, too. Exports fell, and unemployment rose.

Although France escaped some of the worst effects of the depression, the economic slump contributed to political instability. As you read in Chapter 25, there were many political parties in the Third Republic, from socialists on the left to monarchists on the right. For a government to remain in power, it had to form a coalition of supporters from several parties. If supporters became dissatisfied with government policies, they withdrew from the coalition, causing the government to fall. In 1933, France had five different coalition governments.

Many people on the far right opposed the parliamentary democracy that existed in France. In February 1934, they rioted against the Third Republic when a scandal linked high-ranking government officials to a swindler, Serge Stavisky. Anti-democratic forces claimed that the Stavisky scandal proved the Third Republic was hopelessly corrupt.

Supporters of the republic feared that groups on the far right wanted to establish a dictatorship in France. This fear prompted groups on the left to set aside their differences and form a coalition government, the Popular Front.

In 1936, the Popular Front, led by Léon Blum, tried to introduce social reforms such as a 40-hour work week and paid vacations. Although these reforms were popular with workers, business leaders objected to them. As opposition grew, the Popular Front collapsed. Thus, by the late 1930s, France was a deeply divided nation.

A Troubled Era in Eastern Europe

The new nations of Eastern Europe shared many problems in the postwar period. Eastern Europe was not highly industrialized. Only about 10 percent of the people worked in industry. Most people worked on small farms. Although land reforms in several countries had given land to the peasants, their small plots and relatively primitive equipment limited farm production.

When Eastern European nations gained independence at the end of the war, they adopted democratic constitutions. Yet the peoples of Eastern Europe did not have strong traditions of democracy. For centuries, they had been ruled by authoritarian regimes. When economic problems worsened, people often turned to strong leaders who rejected democratic forms of government and established dictatorships.

Austria. A small, landlocked country, Austria suffered from a lack of raw materials and foreign trade. During the 1920s, foreign loans helped Austria to expand its industry, but the onset of the Great Depression ended foreign investment in Austria.

Between 1929 and 1932, industrial production fell by 40 percent, and unemployment soared. Many middle and upper class Austrians feared that the economic crisis would help the socialists or communists seize power. In 1933, the Austrian Chancellor, Engelbert Dollfuss, suspended parliament in response to this fear. The next year, he dissolved all opposition political parties, ended the organized labor movement, and had himself officially declared dictator.

Hungary. During the 1920s and 1930s, Hungary had an elected parliament. But the land-owning aristocracy dominated the government. Peasants were denied the right to vote, and Hungarian leaders resisted any attempt to enact land reform. During the economic crisis brought on by the Great Depression, the extreme right gained power in Hungary. The new government had the support of conservatives and nationalists and established a dictatorship in Hungary.

Poland. The Polish constitution of 1921 guaranteed a democratic form of government. It provided for a two-house parliament and universal suffrage. But competition for power among several political parties led to the rise and fall of a series of governments. Political instability prevented the government from dealing effectively with problems facing the country.

Impatient with democracy, some Poles clamored for a strong leader who would guide their country with a firm hand. They turned to General Joseph Pilsudski (peel SOOT skee), who led a revolt in 1926. After a few days of fighting, the government fell. Pilsudski dissolved the parliament, arrested critics of his regime, and set himself up as dictator.

Czechoslovakia. During the postwar period, Czechoslovakia maintained a democratic government in the face of many difficulties. The government introduced land reform and built up industry. One problem facing the government, however, was the diverse ethnic makeup of the country. Czechs made up a majority of the population and controlled much of the nation's wealth and power. This irritated the other ethnic groups, including the Slovaks, Magyars, and Germans.

To reduce tension, the government gave each group some autonomy. For example, Germans were allowed to use German in their schools. Despite such measures, ethnic minorities continued to demand self-rule in the 1930s. Three million Germans lived in the Sudetenland, a region in northern Czechoslovakia. In the late 1930s, the Sudeten Germans would become the focus of an international crisis, as you will read in Chapter 33.

SECTION REVIEW

1. Identify: Ramsay MacDonald, Popular Front, Engelbert Dollfuss, Joseph Pilsudski.
2. Describe one way in which the British government responded to the Great Depression.
3. (a) Why was France spared the worst economic effects of the Great Depression? (b) How did the Great Depression affect France politically?
4. List three problems faced by nations of Eastern Europe in the postwar era.
5. Which Eastern European nation or nations remained democratic into the mid-1930s?

5 Nationalist Struggles Outside Europe

Read to Learn ■ what postwar changes took place in the Middle East
■ how nationalism affected China, Africa, and Latin America

World War I contributed to growing nationalism among the peoples of the Middle East, Asia, Africa, and Latin America. Nationalist leaders had hoped that the principle of self-determination, discussed at the Paris Peace Conference, would apply to European colonies in Asia and Africa. But their hopes for self-government were disappointed.

Revolution in Turkey

As you read, the peace settlement deprived the Ottoman Empire of most of its territory. In 1919, Greece seized land still ruled by the Turks in Asia Minor. The sultan barely responded to the Greek attacks. Outraged Turkish nationalists, led by army officer Mustafa Kemal, resisted the Greeks fiercely. By 1922, Kemal had expelled the Greeks from Asia Minor. During the years 1915 to 1922, the Ottoman Empire also expelled or executed almost all of its native Armenian population. One and a half million Armenians were systematically killed.

In 1922, the Ottoman Empire was abolished. A year later, Kemal became the first president of the Republic of Turkey.

Kemal made sweeping political and social changes designed to make Turkey a strong industrial nation, free from foreign influence. He introduced a constitution and a legal system based on European models. Under the new law code, the power of the Islamic clergy was reduced. Kemal also introduced the western alphabet, a western-style calendar, and the metric system.

To make Turkey look modern, Kemal banned the wearing of the fez, a brimless felt hat worn by men during the Ottoman Empire. Kemal also introduced the use of surnames and himself took the name Atatürk, meaning father of the Turks.

Other changes affected women. Women gained the right to vote and hold office. Laws were passed that discouraged the practice of segregating women in public places.

Unrest in the Middle East

As you have read, formerly Ottoman lands in the Middle East were awarded to France and Britain as mandates. (See page 581.) During the postwar period, Arab nationalists demanded self-government. But the discovery of oil fields in the Middle East made western powers anxious to retain control of this area.

Despite nationalist uprisings, France retained its mandates in Syria and Lebanon. Iraq, a British mandate, gained independence in 1930 and later joined the League of Nations. Egypt, which had been a British protectorate since 1882, was granted independence in 1923. But Britain kept troops in Egypt to protect the Suez Canal. British influence in both Iraq and Egypt remained strong. Britain also kept complete control over its mandate in Transjordan.

Mustafa Kemal was the president of Turkey from 1923 to 1938. Kemal—later called Atatürk, or father of the Turks—changed many traditions.

In the 1920s and 1930s, the British mandate of Palestine was the focus of controversy between Arab and Jewish nationalists. In 1917, Britain had issued the Balfour Declaration, which said that Britain would "view with favor the establishment in Palestine of a national home for the Jewish people." The Balfour Declaration encouraged Zionists, Jewish nationalists who wanted a homeland in Palestine.* However, the population of Palestine was ninety-eight percent Arab. Moreover, during the war, the British had supported the idea of an independent Arab nation that might include Palestine. As more Jews settled in Palestine, tensions between Arabs and Jews increased.

Another focus of concern in the Middle East was Iran. During the Age of Imperialism, Britain and Russia had gained spheres of influence in Iran. After World War I, Iranian nationalists found a leader in army officer Reza Khan. In 1925, Reza Khan seized power and took the name Reza Shah Pahlavi. (Shah is the title meaning king.) Like Atatürk in Turkey, the shah of Iran introduced many reforms to modernize and industrialize his nation. But both Britain and Russia jockeyed for influence over Iranian affairs.

India on the Road to Independence

During World War I, Britain had pledged to loosen its control over the Indian subcontinent some time in the future. This vague promise did not satisfy Indian nationalists, who demanded self-government. To deal with growing unrest, Parliament gave British authorities in India the power to imprison agitators without trial. This move resulted in greater dissatisfaction.

In 1919, a British official, Reginald Dyer, banned all public meetings in Amritsar, a town in northern India. When a crowd defied his order and assembled in a walled garden, Dyer ordered his troops to open fire. When the shooting ended, 379 Indians lay dead. Indians were outraged.

---

* In 1897, an Austrian Jew, Theodor Herzl, had founded the Zionist Organization to work for the establishment of a homeland for Jews in Palestine.

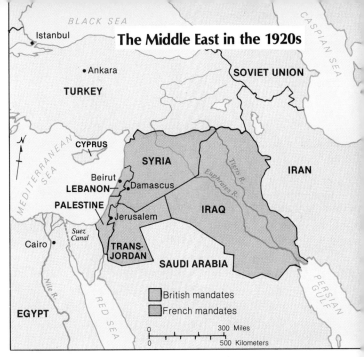

The Middle East in the 1920s

British mandates
French mandates

Map Skill *After World War I, Britain and France received parts of the former Ottoman Empire as mandates. Britain also sought to keep its influence in Egypt and Iran. What mandates did France receive?*

Britain made concessions to Indian nationalists in the Government of India Act of 1919. This law gave Indians control of many local matters. But it left the most important government functions, such as taxation, foreign policy, and justice, in British hands. The nationalist Congress party condemned the Government of India Act because it did not go far enough.

In the postwar period, the Congress party was led by Mohandas Gandhi, a British-educated lawyer who had first emerged as a spokesman for Indians in South Africa. Gandhi advocated a policy of nonviolent resistance to British rule. He urged Indians to boycott British goods and revive cottage industries such as spinning cotton cloth. These industries had declined when Britain had begun selling its own manufactured products in India. Gandhi also led a peaceful "march to the sea" so Indians could make salt in defiance of an unpopular law banning the making of salt from sea water.

Gandhi adopted a simple, austere way of life. He gave up western-style clothing in favor of the dhoti, the homespun garment

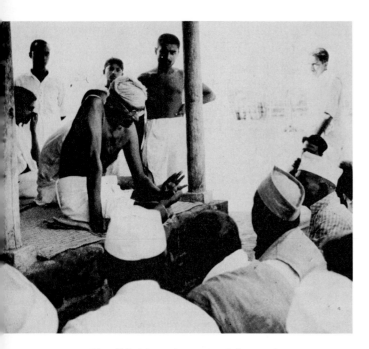

Gandhi's ideas about nonviolent resistance influenced millions of Indians as well as people beyond the borders of India. Despite worldwide fame, Gandhi lived a simple life. He ate very little and dressed in the simple clothing of Indian peasants. In this photograph, Gandhi is shown talking to a group of his followers.

that Hindu men wore. His dedication to Indian independence earned him the title Mahatma, "Great Soul." Gandhi wanted to restore Indians' pride in their traditional culture. Yet he rejected the Hindu caste system, especially the treatment of untouchables as outcasts.

Despite Gandhi's call for nonviolence, there were riots against British rule. In addition, clashes occurred between Hindu and Muslim nationalists. Although Britain granted Indians an even greater role in government in 1935, Gandhi and the Congress party still demanded complete independence.

Turmoil in China

The Manchu dynasty, you will recall, had been overthrown in the Revolution of 1911. However, the revolution did not bring peace.

Sun Yat-sen, leader of the revolution, served as president of China for only a month before he was ousted by a general. Gradually, the country fell into chaos as warlords battled for control across the countryside. They supported their armies by heavy taxation of peasants and merchants.

Sun Yat-sen established a base in Canton and rallied young patriots to the Kuomintang, or Nationalist party. Sun was a popular figure because he spoke so eloquently of a new China. His ideas were summed up in the "Three Principles of the People." (See page 534.)

Sun realized he would need an army to reunite China and put his principles into practice. Therefore, he organized a Kuomintang army under a young officer, Chiang Kai-shek (CHANG kī SHEHK). Sun died in 1925. Two years later, Chiang led his army on a victorious march northward from Canton. By 1928, the Kuomintang was powerful enough to proclaim the Republic of China as the nation's government.

At the same time, Chiang had to deal with a rival political organization, the Chinese Communist party. Leaders of the Chinese Communist party, organized in 1921, had encouraged its members to join the Kuomintang as well. The Communists hoped that they could eventually control the much larger and more powerful Kuomintang. They were outmaneuvered, however, by Chiang, who struck swiftly in 1927. He expelled Communists from the Kuomintang, killing many of them and forcing the survivors into hiding.

Mao Zedong (mow dzoo doong) was one of the Communists who escaped. He began to rebuild his party's fortunes in a remote mountain region in southeastern China. He attracted support by helping poor landless peasants. He also spoke out against western imperialism in China. Mao built an army and soon began winning territory.

Chiang launched four "extermination campaigns" against the Communists. Kuomintang forces finally routed Mao's armies in 1934. About 90,000 Communist troops fled from Kiangsi to begin a 6,000 mile (9,600 kilometer) march toward the desolate Shensi

Province in northwestern China. Only about 7,000 troops survived this "Long March."

In Shensi, Mao became the undisputed leader of the Chinese Communists. But his forces were so small and battered that they seemed to have little future. Yet while the Kuomintang and Communists were fighting, another threat to peace was developing. As you will read in Chapter 32, in the early 1930s, Japan was expanding its attacks on the Asian mainland.

Nationalism in Africa

During World War I, black African troops had fought in both the British and French armies. African leaders believed that their wartime sacrifices would result in a greater measure of political freedom. They were thus bitterly disappointed when the peace settlement awarded the former German colonies in Africa as mandates to Britain, France, and Belgium.

After the war, Europeans tightened their grip on their African colonies. However, Africans continued to oppose colonial rule. In Morocco and Algeria, nationalists fought against French rule. Resistance occurred in British colonies, too. In Nigeria, women who sold their goods in markets protested against high taxes. These protests developed into the Aba Women's Riots. The women's complaints about taxes grew into a demand that "all white men should return to their country." The British suppressed the riots, in which 50 women were killed.

During the 1920s and 1930s, several Africans whose leadership would shape the future of the continent were studying and working in Europe. In England, Jomo Kenyatta of Kenya wrote a book called *Facing Mount Kenya*. In this book, he described how British rule had disrupted the traditional culture of his people. In France, Léopold Senghor gained fame for his poetry and other writings that expressed pride in African culture. Kenyatta and Senghor were part of a growing movement among educated Africans to revive the cultural heritage of Africans. They believed that cultural pride would help unify Africans in the struggle to achieve self-government.

Developments in Latin America

World War I had little political or military impact on Latin America, although the increased wartime demand for raw materials did affect Latin America economically. Between 1910 and 1920, Latin American nations almost tripled their volume of exports. Chile, for example, had stepped up its export of nitrate, a mineral used in the making of explosives. These exports fell sharply when the war ended, however.

After the war, European investments in Latin America also declined. In the 1920s, the United States replaced Britain as the largest investor in the region. The growing economic power of the United States touched off nationalist reactions marked by anti-Americanism in several Latin American nations. Anti-Americanism increased during the Great Depression, when world market prices for raw materials fell sharply. Latin American nations that depended on the export of one or two raw materials were especially hard hit. Between 1929 and 1932, the value of Latin American exports dropped by 65 percent.

In the 1930s, the United States announced its intention to pursue a "Good Neighbor Policy" toward Latin America. It renounced the Roosevelt Corollary, which the United States had used to justify military intervention. (See page 557.) Moreover, to prove its good intentions, the United States cancelled the Platt Amendment limiting Cuban sovereignty. It also withdrew troops it had stationed in Haiti.

Nevertheless, nationalists in many Latin American nations realized their countries could not become truly independent until they reduced their dependence on the export of raw materials. Thus, they urged the building of new industries. Nationalist feeling led Mexico to take a bold step in 1938. It seized oilfields owned by Britain, the United States, and the Netherlands in Mexico and *nationalized* them—that is, it brought them under government control. Foreign owners protested strongly, but the Mexicans stood firm. Eventually, the Mexican government paid the foreign companies for the property it had seized.

SECTION REVIEW

1. Identify: Mustafa Kemal, Balfour Declaration, Zionists, Chiang Kai-shek, Mao Zedong, Long March, Jomo Kenyatta, Léopold Senghor.
2. Define: nationalize.

3. List two of the changes Atatürk introduced in Turkey.
4. What two groups claimed the right to live in Palestine?
5. Describe Gandhi's policy of nonviolent resistance.
6. Why were African nationalists disappointed in the peace settlement?
7. What new policy did the United States follow in Latin America in the 1930s?

Chapter 31 Review

In Perspective

In the aftermath of war, European nations had to rebuild their economies and find jobs for returning soldiers. These tasks proved difficult in Britain, which suffered from aging industries and foreign competition for world trade. Inflation hurt both France and Germany, whose currencies became almost worthless in the early 1920s. Despite economic troubles, diplomats worked to preserve the peace settlement.

The war had greatly changed Europe. Women gained new rights and roles in society. New technology such as cars, radios, and movies influenced people's lives. Yet during the 1920s and 1930s, the works of European writers and artists reflected a sense of despair.

Prosperity in the United States was closely tied to the economies of other nations. The stock market crash in 1929 triggered the Great Depression, which soon affected the rest of the world. The Great Depression contributed to political instability.

In the postwar period, nationalists challenged European rule in many parts of the globe. For example, in India, Gandhi led the Congress party in nonviolent protests against British rule. In China, nationalists sought to reunite their country, but political rivalry between the Kuomintang and Communist parties dimmed that hope.

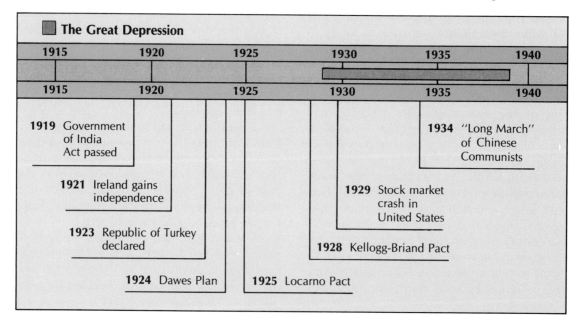

The Great Depression

1915	1920	1925	1930	1935	1940

1919 Government of India Act passed

1921 Ireland gains independence

1923 Republic of Turkey declared

1924 Dawes Plan

1925 Locarno Pact

1928 Kellogg-Briand Pact

1929 Stock market crash in United States

1934 "Long March" of Chinese Communists

Recalling Facts

Choose the word or phrase that best completes each of the following statements.

1. British workers called the General Strike of 1926 to protest (a) the Versailles Treaty; (b) wage cuts; (c) American and Japanese competition.

2. The Easter Rebellion was an uprising of (a) Irish nationalists; (b) Protestants in Northern Ireland; (c) British troops stationed in Ireland.

3. France built the Maginot Line to (a) limit German economic competition; (b) prevent another German invasion; (c) force Germany to pay reparations.

4. Sigmund Freud influenced European thought through his teaching of (a) passive resistance; (b) the horror of war; (c) the role of the unconscious.

5. The United States showed its growing isolationism by (a) signing the Kellogg-Briand Pact; (b) passing quota acts; (c) embarking on the Good Neighbor policy.

6. During the New Deal, the United States government tried to (a) reduce unemployment; (b) end federal supervision of banks; (c) reduce welfare benefits.

7. Indian nationalists objected to the Government of India Act because it (a) kept Gandhi out of office; (b) did not grant independence; (c) made Hindus and Muslims equal.

Chapter Checkup

1. (a) What economic difficulties did Britain face after World War I? (b) How did it meet the crisis caused by the General Strike? (c) How did it respond to the crisis in Ireland?

2. (a) Why did France invade the Ruhr in 1923? (b) How did Germans respond to this invasion? (c) How was this crisis resolved?

3. (a) Why did Americans support isolationism after World War I? (b) Was United States isolationism complete? Explain.

4. (a) How did the Stavisky scandal in France lead to a crisis in the Third Republic? (b) How did supporters of the Third Republic try to save France from a dictatorship? (c) Did they succeed? Explain.

5. Describe what happened to democratic institutions of government in each of the following nations: (a) Austria; (b) Hungary; (c) Poland; (d) Czechoslovakia.

6. (a) What did Arab nationalists in the Middle East want? (b) Why did European nations oppose their demands?

7. (a) How did Sun Yat-sen try to create a new China? (b) What problems did he face in achieving his goals?

8. How did educated Africans such as Jomo Kenyatta and Léopold Senghor try to strengthen African nationalism?

Critical Thinking

1. **Analyzing** (a) Describe the ways in which Europeans and Americans sought to prevent another war after the Great War. (b) Do you think these were likely to succeed? Why or why not?

2. **Comparing** (a) How was the Great Depression similar in the United States and Britain? (b) How was it different?

3. **Understanding Economic Ideas** (a) What effects did the Great Depression have on economies around the world? (b) How did the economic crisis test the strength of the new democracies of Eastern Europe?

Relating Past to Present

1. (a) How did women's horizons expand in the postwar period? (b) How do you think World War I and its aftermath contributed to expanded horizons for women today?

Developing Basic Skills

1. **Graph Reading** Study the graph on page 596. Then answer the following questions: (a) What percentage of Americans was out of work in 1929? In 1933? (b) What percentage of British citizens was out of work in 1929? In 1933? (c) In which year was unemployment at its worst in Britain? In the United States? (d) Why do you think unemployment was such a difficult problem during the Great Depression?

2. **Researching** Choose one of the nationalist leaders you read about in this chapter. Research his background in order to answer the following questions: (a) Where was the person born and raised? (b) What training and experience contributed to his emergence as a nationalist leader? (c) What goals did he have for his country? (d) Why do you think he became a nationalist leader?

See page 807 for suggested readings.

32 The Rise of Totalitarian States

(1922–1936)

German poster of Adolf Hitler holding a Nazi flag.

> **Chapter Outline**
>
> 1 Revolution in Russia
>
> 2 The Soviet Union Under Stalin
>
> 3 Fascism in Italy
>
> 4 The Rise of Nazi Germany
>
> 5 Militarism in Japan

On the night of January 30, 1933, many German towns held festive parades to celebrate the victory at the polls of the National Socialist German Workers' party and its leader, Adolf Hitler. Among those watching the parades was a ten-year-old girl. Years later, she recalled the occasion.

"My parents took us children, my twin brother and myself, into the center of the city. There we witnessed the torchlight procession with which the National Socialists celebrated their victory. Some of the uncanny [strange] feel of that night remains with me even today. The crashing tread of the feet, the somber pomp of the red and black flags, the flickering light from the torches on the faces, and the songs with melodies that were at once aggressive and sentimental."

At the time, the girl was thrilled: "I longed to hurl myself into this current, to be submerged and borne along by it." An enormous joy swept over her. " 'For the flag we are ready to die,' the torch-bearers had sung. . . . I was overcome with a burning desire to belong to these people for whom it [the flag] was a matter of life and death."

The girl eventually joined the youth movement organized by the National Socialists, or Nazis, as party members were called. Like millions of other Germans, she believed in the Nazi promise of strength, struggle, and victory. During the 1920s and 1930s, powerful governments were established in Russia, Italy, and Japan as well as Germany. With promises of a glorious future, leaders in these countries won massive popular support. Many people followed these leaders because of the uncertainties of the times. The growing power of dictators would put an end to the hopes for a more peaceful world.

1 Revolution in Russia

Read to Learn ■ what caused the Russian revolution
■ how Lenin's policies changed Russia

In 1917, Russia was engulfed by revolution, as you read in Chapter 30. The threat of revolution had hung over Russia for decades. But the strains of World War I triggered the downfall of the Romanov dynasty and the emergence of a new Russian society.

Prelude to Revolution

After the Revolution of 1905, some political reforms were introduced in Russia. (See page 499.) But peasants, factory workers, and many middle class intellectuals were not satisfied. Nicholas II believed it was his sacred duty to preserve the absolute power of the czar. He rejected most efforts at reform and distrusted the advice of the Duma, the Russian legislature.

World War I was a disaster for the Russians. Badly led and poorly armed, Russian armies suffered huge casualties. While Nicholas II tried to rally morale at the front, his wife, Czarina Alexandra, preserved his absolute power at home. She, in turn, relied almost totally on the advice of Grigori Rasputin, an uneducated and corrupt monk.

Rasputin acquired his influence over Alexandra because only he seemed able to help Alexis, her only son and the heir to the throne. Alexis suffered from hemophilia, a rare blood disease. Several nobles who were angry at Rasputin's meddling in the government conspired to murder him in December 1916. The death of Rasputin had little effect on the government. But the czarina was haunted by the monk's prophecy: "If I die or you desert me, in six months you will lose your son and your throne." His prophecy came true in three months.

The March Revolution

Early in March 1917, as World War I dragged on, riots broke out in Petrograd. (See page 572.) Mobs roamed the streets demanding "bread and peace." Bakeries were looted by hungry rioters. Many of the troops ordered to quell the revolt mutinied and joined the protesters. On March 12, the Duma formed a provisional government and called for the election of an assembly to draw up a constitution for Russia. Three days later Czar Nicholas II abdicated.

Even while Russians celebrated the overthrow of the czar, the Provisional Government faced many problems. Many Russians wanted to continue fighting in the war against Germany. Others demanded an immediate peace. Peasants expected to receive their own land at once, while city workers expected higher wages and more food.

Faced with conflicting demands, the Provisional Government took a moderate course. Its leaders, Prince George Lvov and, later, Alexander Kerensky, were determined to pursue the war and firmly rejected the demand for peace. They introduced some liberal reforms such as freedom of speech and religion and equality of all people before the law. However, they resisted pressure from peasants for immediate redistribution of land from large estates.

The Provisional Government was not the only political power in Russia. At the outbreak of the revolution, radical revolutionaries who had been living in exile returned to Russia. In Petrograd and other Russian cities, these radical revolutionaries formed *soviets*, councils of workers, soldiers, and intellectuals. The soviets claimed the right to run factories and issue their own orders to soldiers in the army. Their orders undermined the authority of the Provisional Government, especially at the front.

The soviets were strongest in the cities. But in the countryside, peasants conducted their own revolution, seizing land from nobles. By the summer of 1917, the Provisional Government seemed unable to enforce order in Russia.

Bolshevik Takeover

When the revolution broke out in March, Vladimir Ilyich Lenin, a dedicated revolutionary, was in exile in Zurich, Switzerland. With the help of Germany, Lenin returned to Russia in April.* The German government hoped Lenin would contribute to the chaos and disorder in Russia, thereby weakening the Russian war effort. As soon as he reached Petrograd, Lenin set to work to gain control of the soviets in order to achieve his own program for revolution.

Leninism. Lenin had been born into a middle class Russian family. He had become a revolutionary after his brother was executed for plotting to kill the czar. As a student, Lenin read the works of Karl Marx and developed a firm belief in revolutionary socialism. (See page 451.) In other words, he was convinced that the abolition of private property and the establishment of a classless society would be achieved by revolution.

Marx, you will recall, had predicted that oppressed workers would overthrow industrial capitalism and establish a communist party. Lenin knew that Russia was not an industrial society such as Marx had described. However, even though the industrial working class in Russia was very small, Lenin argued that a socialist revolution could take place there. He thought the masses of Russian peasants would help the revolution. But Lenin believed a socialist revolution would succeed only if it were carried out by a small, well-organized, and highly disciplined group of leaders.

Lenin had organized his followers into the Bolshevik party in the early 1900s. The Bolsheviks had relatively few members in April 1917, but Lenin skillfully built up support for the party. He wrote stinging editorials in Bolshevik newspapers criticizing the Provisional Government and calling for an end to the war. He demanded that the peasants be allowed to "take over the *entire* land immediately."

During the summer of 1917, the Bolsheviks won control of the key soviets of Petro-

After the March Revolution, the Bolshevik party began organizing opposition to the Provisional Government. In this photograph, pro-Bolshevik soldiers are shown patrolling the streets of Petrograd in a car taken from the Provisional Government. They have fixed red flags to their bayonets to show their support for a socialist revolution.

grad and Moscow. In October, the Petrograd Soviet chose Leon Trotsky, a close associate of Lenin, as its chairman. A brilliant organizer, Trotsky helped plot a Bolshevik takeover of power.

The November revolution. On the night of November 6, 1917, armed Bolsheviks moved against the headquarters of the Provisional Government in Petrograd. The Provisional Government had lost most of its popular support because it had failed to lead Russia to victory in the war. As a result, the Bolsheviks encountered only light resistance. They seized government buildings, the railway station, telephone exchanges, and electric lighting plants.

Lenin and Trotsky had timed this move to coincide with a meeting of the All-Russian Congress of Soviets. At this meeting, delegates from soviets all over Russia approved the Bolshevik seizure of power and chose Lenin to lead the new government. Lenin immediately announced his intention to take Russia out of the war and redistribute land

---

* German agents had contacted Lenin in Zurich. They arranged for a special sealed train to carry Lenin from Switzerland through Germany to Russia.

to the peasants. As you have read, he quickly negotiated the Treaty of Brest-Litovsk with Germany.* His other goals, however, were delayed by the outbreak of civil war.

Civil War in Russia

Even as Lenin negotiated peace with Germany, anti-Bolshevik forces launched efforts to overthrow the new government. From 1917 to 1921, the Bolsheviks—officially renamed Communists in March 1918—fought a wide range of enemies. Their opponents were unable to unite behind a single leader or accept a single set of goals. Some wanted the czar restored to power. Others supported socialism but opposed Lenin. By 1918, there were 18 rival groups seeking to oust the Communists from power and rule Russia.

During the civil war, the Communists were called "Reds" because the color red had long been associated with revolutionary socialists. Their chief opposition came from the "Whites," various groups that included army officers and nobles as well as peasants and people from the middle class. The Allied Powers sent troops to help the Whites because they did not want war supplies sent to Russia before 1917 to fall into German hands.

Although the Communists were almost defeated in 1919, Trotsky organized an efficient Red Army that turned the tide of the civil war. Disunity among the Whites also helped the Communists. Moreover, the Communists convinced some peasants to support their cause. They claimed a White victory would mean an end to land reform. Finally, Allied intervention aroused Russian nationalism so that many non-Communists fought with the Red Army to defend their homeland.

Lenin followed a policy called "war communism" during the civil war. The government took control of most industries, railroads, and banks. It ordered peasants to turn over surplus grain to the government, but often it simply seized the grain needed to supply the Red Army. The government also re-

---

* The Germans were forced to renounce the Treaty of Brest-Litovsk at the end of World War I.

sorted to terror and censorship to silence critics of the revolution. It ordered the execution of the czar and his family to prevent them from becoming a rallying symbol for opponents to communism. Then, like the czars before them, the Communists created a secret police, the Cheka, whose agents hunted down and executed so-called enemies of the state. In 1921, the efforts of the Communists paid off, and the Whites were defeated.

Lenin's New Economic Policy

The civil war devastated Russia. Peasants cut back on their crops because the government was seizing most of their grain. Then, in 1920 and 1921, crops failed. Millions of Russians died in the resulting famine. Hundreds of thousands of workers fled the cities to search for food in the countryside. Steel production fell far below what it had been in 1914. The economy sputtered to a standstill.

When the civil war ended, Lenin turned his attention to building a new Russian society. His goal was to create a communist state. Communism is a system of government in which the state owns all the means of production, including industry and agriculture. In theory, it calls for a "dictatorship of the people" and promises a classless society. But to achieve his long-term goal, Lenin had to make several compromises with communist theory. His immediate problem was to ease the desperate economic crisis.

In March 1921, Lenin announced the New Economic Policy (NEP), a program designed to rebuild the shattered Russian economy. The NEP eliminated many harsh measures of war communism and permitted some return to capitalist practices. To encourage agricultural production, for example, the government stopped seizing grain from peasants. Peasants were encouraged to sell their surplus grain on the open market. The government kept control of heavy industry, railroads, and banks but allowed small manufacturers to run their own businesses.

Under the NEP, which lasted until 1928, the Russian economy improved. Industry

Under the czars, few Russians learned to read and write. After the Russian Revolution, many schools were set up for adults. The new schools were open to everyone. Basic courses such as reading, writing, and arithmetic were taught along with courses explaining the benefits of socialism.

and farm production returned to prewar levels. Workers enjoyed shorter hours and better conditions. For a time, the government relaxed the terror and censorship it had employed during the civil war.

Lenin introduced political and social changes. Russia was made up of many different nationalities. The Communists recognized this fact by organizing four autonomous, or self-governing, republics. In 1922, Russia was officially renamed the Union of Soviet Socialist Republics (USSR), or Soviet Union.* (See the map on page 613.)

During the revolution and afterwards, the old social structure was swept away. Titles of nobility were eliminated, and soldiers stopped addressing officers as "your excellency." The Eastern Orthodox Church, which had been very powerful under the czars, lost its influence. Laws were passed

that guaranteed equality for men and women. In the early 1920s, many Russians expected that the revolution would give them greater freedom than they had had under the czars.

SECTION REVIEW

1. Identify: Bolshevik party, Leon Trotsky, Reds, Whites, war communism, Cheka, New Economic Policy, USSR.

2. Define: soviet.

3. List two reasons for discontent in Russia before the revolution in March 1917.

4. What problems did the Provisional Government face in the spring of 1917?

5. How did Lenin think a revolution in Russia must be carried out in order to succeed?

6. Why did a civil war break out in Russia after the Bolshevik takeover?

7. Describe two results of Lenin's New Economic Policy.

* Today, the Soviet Union includes 15 soviet socialist republics.

2 The Soviet Union Under Stalin

Read to Learn
- how Stalin implemented his goals for the Soviet Union
- how the Soviet people lived under Stalin

Lenin suffered a series of strokes beginning in 1922. Even before Lenin's death in 1924, a struggle over who would be Lenin's successor was brewing. The chief contenders were Trotsky and Joseph Dzhugashvili, better known as Joseph Stalin. Stalin took this name, which means man of steel, as a young revolutionary. Later, he would more than live up to its meaning.

Stalin's Rise to Power

As a young man, Stalin had studied briefly to become a priest, but in 1903 he joined the Bolsheviks. Along with other Bolsheviks, he conspired against the czar. During the Russian Revolution, he rose within the party. By 1922, Stalin had become secretary-general of the Communist party. He used this position to gain greater influence within the party. He carefully built up support by recruiting and promoting party members loyal to him.

When Lenin died, Stalin used his strong position in the party to outmaneuver his chief rival, Trotsky. Trotsky thought that the Soviet Union should move more quickly toward communism and should increase its efforts to bring about world revolution. Stalin skillfully turned Trotsky's criticisms of government policies against him, accusing Trotsky of undermining the state.

By 1927, Stalin had won the support of the majority of party members. The party expelled Trotsky and his followers and then exiled Trotsky to Siberia. With Trotsky out of the way, Stalin was able to establish himself as dictator. In 1929, Trotsky left the Soviet Union. He settled in Mexico, where he was murdered in 1940 by political enemies.

The Five-Year Plans

Stalin saw the Soviet Union as surrounded by enemies. He thought the nation was weak militarily in part because its economy was not industrialized. "We are 50 or 100 years behind the advanced countries. We must make good this distance in 10 years. Either we do it, or we shall go under." Stalin believed the only way the Soviet Union could survive a foreign attack was to develop its industry.

In 1928, Stalin launched his first five-year plan, an economic program that set specific production goals in industry and agriculture. In 1933 and 1938, he again made five-year plans to strengthen the Soviet economy.

Plans for industry. Stalin's plans concentrated on heavy industry. He poured Russian resources into building steel mills, electric power stations, cement plants, and oil refineries, all industries that were essential to a strong modern nation.

Between 1928 and 1940, the five-year plans appeared to yield impressive results. Steel production more than quadrupled, and oil production tripled. By 1940, the Soviet Union had become the second largest producer of iron and steel in Europe.

The Soviet Union industrialized at great cost, however. The quality of finished goods was often poor. Often, costly projects were built that served no useful purpose. They were simply show pieces meant to impress foreign journalists. In addition, Stalin's economic goals were achieved at a tremendous sacrifice in human terms.

The government launched a massive propaganda campaign to glorify work and encourage worker productivity. Each factory and each worker had production quotas, or goals. If workers failed to meet their quotas, the government punished them for laziness or sabotage.

Collectivized agriculture. Stalin realized the Soviet Union needed to make its agriculture more efficient in order to industrialize. He ordered all peasants to give up their land and farm animals and form *collective farms*, large, government-run enterprises. On the collective farms, peasants were supposed to be paid according to the amount of work they did. A portion of a collective's harvest was paid to the government.

Collectivization had many goals. First, it sought to increase food production by introducing machines on the collective. Second, it was designed to give the government control over farm production. Third, collectivization was intended to free people from farming so they could work in industry. Finally, it was seen as a way to extend socialism to the countryside.

Most peasants opposed collectivization, which began in 1928. The stiffest resistance came from *kulaks*, prosperous peasants who did not want to lose their farms. Protesting kulaks destroyed their livestock and crops. Stalin responded with a brutal crackdown on all opposition. Millions of kulaks were executed or sent to forced-labor camps in Siberia. As a result, farm production fell in the early 1930s, and a terrible famine caused widespread starvation. Stalin later admitted that 10 million people had died during collectivization.

By 1939, most peasants had been placed on collective farms. But even with the use of farm machinery, production increased slowly. Food shortages continued to occur. Eventually, Stalin compromised, allowing peasants on collective farms to maintain their own small garden plots, which helped feed their families.

Under Stalin's program of collectivization, the government took over peasants' land, livestock, and farm tools. Party-appointed managers supervised the collective farms. Stalin tried to mechanize agriculture. But in the 1930s, much work was still done by hand, as this photograph of women farm workers shows.

A Totalitarian State

Stalin harnessed the skill and energy of the Soviet people to make the Soviet Union a strong communist state. But to achieve this goal, he organized a new kind of government, today called a totalitarian state. In a *totalitarian state*, the government is a single-party dictatorship that controls every aspect of the lives of its citizens. Individual rights count for little or nothing. Citizens are expected to obey the government without question. Critics are quickly silenced. Furthermore, the totalitarian state supports extreme nationalism.

Totalitarian states differ from the absolute monarchies you read about in Chapter 18, although both exercise absolute authority. The totalitarian state has much greater power over the people. In the twentieth century, dictators such as Stalin have used new technology to persuade the masses of the people to support their cause. Under Stalin, the government controlled newspapers, the radio, and all other means of communication. He used the press to pour out propaganda praising his policies.

Daily Life Under Stalin

Stalin relied on censorship to bolster support for his regime. Soviet writers and artists were expected to glorify the Soviet Union and praise Stalin. In 1932, for example, the government organized writers into the Union of Soviet Writers. The union monitored the work of all writers and rewarded those who praised the state. Those who refused to praise Stalin and the state were expelled from the union and could not get their work published.

Stalin also used terror to silence opposition to his rule. As you have read, millions of peasants died during collectivization. In the 1930s, Stalin cracked down on his critics within the Communist party. Thousands of party members were purged, or expelled, from the party. A high party official, Serge Kirov, was assassinated in 1934, probably by Stalin's agents. However, Stalin used Kirov's death as an excuse to launch the Great Purge. In the next four years, millions of men and women were arrested. Many of them were tried and executed. The terror inspired by the purges affected everyone in the Soviet Union. No one was safe from government persecution.

During the 1930s, the standard of living in the Soviet Union remained low. People were faced with constant food and housing shortages. Stalin's five-year plans emphasized heavy industry at the expense of consumer goods. Thus, many items such as clothing and household appliances were always

Profiles ■ "Confessions" of an Old Bolshevik

Between 1934 and 1939, Stalin conducted the Great Purge of the Communist party. Dozens of prominent party officials were accused of treason. Many of the accused were "Old Bolsheviks," Lenin's original supporters. In 1936, 1937, and 1938, these Old Bolsheviks appeared as defendants in cleverly staged, public show trials.

Stalin never appeared in the courtroom, but his presence was continually felt. Many defendants made public confessions, admitting their guilt to a variety of crimes against the state. Stalin wanted these confessions so that the defendants would be convicted by their own words and could not be seen as martyrs. While some of the accused were undoubtedly tortured into confessing, others were probably motivated by a lifetime of loyalty and obedience to the party.

Few party leaders escaped the Great Purge. Nikolai Bukharin, once a close associate of Stalin, was among the accused. In August 1936, the prosecutor at the first round of show trials announced that Bukharin was under investigation. But Bukharin's prestige and popularity as an Old Bolshevik saved him for a time. The next year, defendants at the show trials accused Bukharin of sabotage, treason, and murder. At a meeting of the Communist Party Central Committee, Stalin and his supporters demanded the arrest of Bukharin. Bukharin, who was present at the meeting, told a Stalin supporter: "I will not tell lies about myself." Stalin's supporter replied: "We'll arrest you, and you'll confess."

Bukharin was arrested and spent 13 months in jail. He was charged with the attempted murder of Lenin, organizing kulak uprisings, and poisoning livestock. When he refused to confess, his wife and infant son were exiled to a distant city and threatened with death.

Finally, Bukharin made a general confession admitting that he was "politically responsible" for many of the charges against him. At his trial, however, Bukharin turned the tables on the prosecutor. He denied each specific charge. He cross-examined witnesses and revealed contradictions in their testimony. Bukharin knew that his actions would not save his life, but he hoped to reveal the truth.

The prosecutor demanded that Bukharin and the other defendants be "shot like dirty dogs." *Pravda*, the official newspaper of the Communist party, which Bukharin had once edited, declared: "By exterminating [them] the Soviet land will move even more rapidly along the Stalinist route, . . . the life of the Soviet people will become even more joyous." On March 15, 1938, the Soviet government announced that Bukharin had been executed.

expensive and hard to obtain. Despite these drawbacks, the Soviet government managed to keep some support from the masses of people. Although wages were low, there was no unemployment. The government also provided old age pensions and free public education, which had been unknown under the czars.

Many Russians hoped that through education they could improve their position in society. In theory, communism provides a classless society. However, under Stalin, a small group of people enjoyed greater privileges than the rest. These were skilled workers such as engineers, artists, and intellectuals who supported Stalin, as well as high party officials.

After the Russian Revolution of 1917, women won equal rights. During the 1920s and 1930s, many women took jobs outside the home. Because wages were so low, their salaries were needed to help their families survive. Women worked in factories. They also attended schools and universities and entered professions such as medicine in large numbers.

Quest for Foreign Recognition

When the Bolsheviks seized power in 1917, they expected to lead a world revolution. To coordinate this communist revolution, the Russian Communist party created the Communist International, or Comintern, in 1919. The Comintern included representatives from communist parties all over the world who were pledged to revolution. In the chaos following World War I, the Comintern supported several communist revolutions that broke out in Germany and in Eastern Europe. These revolutions were quickly suppressed. However, Soviet support for revolutionary activity made it an outcast among other nations.

During the 1920s, the Soviet Union downplayed its call for world revolution. Soviet leaders sought diplomatic relations and commercial ties with other nations. In 1924, Britain officially recognized the Soviet government. Other nations soon followed. In 1933, when the Soviet Union promised to end its propaganda activities in the United States, the American government gave it diplomatic recognition. The following year, the Soviet Union joined the League of Nations.

Propaganda posters portrayed Stalin as the father of the Soviet people. In this 1936 poster, Stalin towers above the young Soviet athletes. Physical fitness for children was emphasized as one way of building a strong Soviet state.

SECTION REVIEW

1. Identify: five-year plans, Comintern.
2. Define: collective farm, kulak, totalitarian state.
3. How did Stalin become powerful within the Communist party?
4. (a) Why did Stalin launch his five-year plans? (b) List two results of Stalin's five-year plans.
5. What different methods did Stalin use to exercise control over the Soviet people?
6. Which group or groups of people had special privileges in Soviet society?

The Soviet Union
in the 1930s

Map Skill *In the 1930s, the Soviet Union was made up of 11 soviet socialist republics, as this map shows. In theory, each republic was independent. In practice, the Russian Soviet Federated Socialist Republic always dominated the Soviet Union. How does the area ruled by the Soviet Union in the 1930s differ from that ruled by the Russian Empire in 1914?*

3 Fascism in Italy

Read to Learn ■ why Mussolini came to power in Italy
■ how Italians lived under Mussolini

Italy, you will recall, was one of the "Big Four" powers at the Paris Peace Conference of 1919. But Italy did not gain all the territory it wanted. As a result, many Italian nationalists denounced the government as weak. Other dissatisfied groups contributed to growing unrest in Italy.

Postwar Unrest

Like most European nations, Italy faced severe political and economic problems in the years right after World War I. During the war, the Italian government had promised social change and land reform. Its failure to fulfill these promises stirred protests.

In the summer of 1920, dissatisfied workers went on strike and occupied factories. In the countryside, landless peasants seized the property of wealthy landlords. Many Italians, especially middle class property owners, were deeply troubled by these outbreaks of lawlessness.

The growing popularity of socialist parties also worried middle class Italians. In 1919, socialists won more seats in parliament

613

than any other party. When parliament met that year, socialist members shouted "Long live socialism!" instead of offering their greetings to the king, as custom demanded. In 1920, a communist party was formed in Italy, heightening middle class fears of revolution.

The Italian government seemed unable to prevent worker revolts or preserve order in the countryside. An ambitious politician, Benito Mussolini, leader of an anticommunist party, used this turmoil to gain power.

Benito Mussolini

As a young man, Mussolini had been a socialist. When World War I broke out, he abandoned socialism and became an enthusiastic nationalist, fighting for Italy. In 1919, Mussolini organized many war veterans into the Fascist party. The word fascist comes from the ancient Roman word "fasces," meaning a bundle of rods tied around an ax handle. During the Roman Empire, the fasces had symbolized unity and authority. Mussolini set out to bind Italians together. He used reminders of the glory of ancient Rome to inspire patriotism and obedience to authority.

Fascism. At first, Mussolini had no clear goals for his Fascist party. Gradually, however, fascism developed as a political movement. A key element of fascism was glorification of the state. Mussolini expressed this idea in his slogan: "Everything in the state, nothing outside the state, nothing against the state."

Fascists condemned democracy because they believed rival political parties destroyed the unity of the state. They supported a single-party system guided by a single strong ruler. Fascists despised socialism and communism. They defended private property and private enterprise, which they thought should be regulated by the government.

Another element of fascism was aggressive nationalism. A strong state, fascists argued, had every right to overcome a weaker one. They believed aggression represented action, while a desire for peace merely in-

dicated weakness. Fascists also glorified military sacrifice.

Appeal of fascism. Fascism appealed to many Italians. Veterans of World War I appreciated the fascist emphasis on militarism. Italian nationalists applauded the idea of reviving the glories of ancient Rome. Some middle and upper class Italians were impatient with Italy's parliamentary government and yearned for a strong leader who would establish order. They also supported fascist ideas about private property. Mussolini's speeches about "action" and "struggle" stirred the imaginations of many young Italians.

The March on Rome. In the early 1920s, bands of Mussolini's followers, uniformed in black shirts, roamed the streets of Italian cities beating up communists, socialists, and union members. These "Black Shirts" ousted communists and socialists from city governments in Bologna and Milan. With each success, the number of fascists grew.

Sensing a rising tide of support, Mussolini prepared to seize power. In October 1922, he announced he would lead a "March on Rome" to defend the capital from a communist revolution. In fact, there was no threat of a communist revolution, but Mussolini hoped that the approach of his Black Shirts would frighten the government into surrender. And it did. When fascist bands approached Rome from four directions, King Victor Emmanuel III refused to use the army against them. A few days later, the king named Mussolini prime minister.

Italy as a Fascist State

As prime minister, Mussolini was given emergency powers for one year. Before the year was up, however, he pushed a law through parliament that in effect guaranteed a Fascist majority in parliament. In the next few years, Mussolini moved steadily to increase his power.

Outwardly, the form of government did not change drastically. Italy remained a monarchy with an elected parliament. But Mussolini had the right to make laws on his own initiative. The Fascist party controlled elections and outlawed all opposition parties.

Like the Communist party in the Soviet Union, the Fascist party controlled the nation. Party members held important government jobs and leading posts in the army and the police. Mussolini used other methods of the totalitarian state. He imposed government censorship and banned criticism of the government. Fascists bought the leading Italian newspapers and wrote articles full of praise for "Il Duce," meaning the leader, a title Mussolini had adopted.

"Mussolini is always right" was the motto that all Italians were expected to follow. Police rounded up critics, who were held in remote island prisons. In schools, children were taught fascist ideas. They wore black uniforms and learned discipline, duty, and obedience—the virtues Mussolini thought had been a source of strength in ancient Rome.

Fascism differed from communism because it supported private enterprise. However, to improve the Italian economy, Mussolini introduced a new type of economic organization, the corporative system. Employers and employees in each branch of industry joined a government-sponsored "corporation." Independent unions were abolished. The corporation controlled such matters as wages and prices in its industry. The corporations were largely dominated by business interests and the government.

In the 1920s, Italy enjoyed a brief economic recovery. However, Mussolini was unable to prevent the Great Depression from having a severe impact on Italy. Mussolini blamed Italy's troubles on world economic conditions and sought to distract the people by embarking on an aggressive foreign policy.

Foreign Policy

Mussolini dreamed of building an Italian empire. "We have a right to an empire," he claimed, "as a fertile nation which has the

In Italy, as in other totalitarian states, political education and military training began at an early age. Here, Mussolini reviews a military parade of Fascist youth during a celebration on the twentieth anniversary of Italy's entry into World War I. Children were taught the virtue of obedience to Il Duce. They chanted such Fascist slogans as "Believe! Obey! Fight!"

pride and will to propagate its race over the face of the earth." In 1924, he negotiated a treaty with Yugoslavia that gave Italy the city of Fiume. Three years later, Mussolini imposed a protectorate over Albania. But he was not satisfied and, in the 1930s, turned to Africa.

As you read in Chapter 27, Italy had acquired colonies in North Africa in the late 1800s. Italians still deeply resented their defeat in 1896 by Ethiopia. (See page 511.) In 1934, a clash on the border between Ethiopia and the Italian colony of Somaliland gave Mussolini an excuse to make territorial demands on Ethiopia. Ethiopia appealed to the League of Nations for protection against Italy. The league delayed action, and Italy invaded Ethiopia in October 1935.

Eventually, the league called for economic sanctions against Italy. That is, league members agreed not to sell arms or lend money to Italy. But they did not cut off oil supplies to Italy, a move that might have slowed the Italian invasion.

The Ethiopians fought bravely, but their cavalry and ancient rifles were no match for Italian planes, tanks, and artillery. In May 1936, Ethiopia fell to the invaders. The next month, Haile Selassie (HĪ lee suh LAS ee), the exiled emperor of Ethiopia, traveled to the League of Nations headquarters in Geneva. Although he made a moving appeal for help, the league took no steps to rescue Ethiopia. In July, the league voted to end the economic sanctions against Italy.

SECTION REVIEW

1. Identify: Benito Mussolini, Black Shirts, March on Rome, corporative system, Haile Selassie.
2. Why were many Italians dissatisfied with the government in 1919?
3. (a) List three main ideas of fascism. (b) Who supported fascism?
4. How did Mussolini increase his power after 1922?

4 The Rise of Nazi Germany

Read to Learn ■ why Hitler came to power in Germany
■ what the goals of the Third Reich were

At the end of World War I, Germany was shaken by terrible inflation. Although the German economy recovered from inflation in late 1923, the nation faced other problems. As in Italy, a fascist political movement led by a discontented war veteran, Adolf Hitler, gained popular support in the 1920s. In the next decade, Hitler rose to power and established a brutal totalitarian state in Germany.

The Weimar Republic

Two days before World War I ended, Germany became a republic. The new government held its first national assembly in the town of Weimar. Thus, Germany in the 1920s was often called the Weimar Republic. The new government was led by moderate socialists in its early years.

The Weimar Republic faced enormous problems from the start. It had been discredited in the eyes of many Germans when its representatives signed the hated Versailles Treaty. German generals and other war veterans claimed that Germany had not been defeated but had been "stabbed in the back" by communists, Jews, and liberals in the Weimar government. Although these accusations were untrue, many people looked for someone to blame for the German defeat in World War I.

Political extremists caused unrest in postwar Germany. On the far left were communists, who supported the Marxist idea of world revolution. On the far right were fascists and extreme nationalists, who denounced the Versailles Treaty and opposed the democratic constitution of the Weimar

Republic. Revolts by both communists and fascists rocked the Weimar Republic in its early years.

Economic difficulties were exploited by enemies of the Weimar Republic. The inflation of the early 1920s and, later, the Great Depression swelled the ranks of the discontented. Political and economic chaos in Germany created a climate that favored the rise of Adolf Hitler, the fanatical leader of the Nazi party.

Adolf Hitler

Hitler was born in Austria in 1889, the son of a customs official. He dropped out of high school in 1905 and two years later moved to Vienna, where he tried unsuccessfully to become an artist. During his stay in Vienna, Hitler listened to Austrian nationalists who stressed the close ties between German-speaking Austria and Germany. He also picked up the violent anti-Semitism, or hatred of Jews, that many Austrian and German nationalists preached.

When World War I broke out, Hitler enlisted in the German army. He emerged from the war an extreme nationalist and echoed the ideas of those Germans who believed their country had been stabbed in the back. Hitler settled in Munich, Germany. His skill as a public speaker made him popular among extreme nationalists. By 1921, Hitler had gained control of the National Socialists German Workers' party, better known as the Nazi party.

Growth of Nazi Power

Only about 6,000 people belonged to the Nazi party in 1921, but the party grew rapidly. The disastrous inflation of 1922 and 1923 and French occupation of the Ruhr weakened support for the Weimar Republic. In wild, emotional speeches, Hitler attacked the Weimar Republic and denounced the Versailles Treaty. By 1923, Nazi party membership had climbed to 50,000.

Following Mussolini's example, Hitler believed he had enough support to overthrow the Weimar Republic. On November 8, 1923, he led an uprising in Munich. But he failed to ignite a general revolt, and the army quickly crushed the uprising. Hitler was arrested, tried, and found guilty of treason. He was sentenced to five years in prison but was released within a year.

While in prison, Hitler wrote *Mein Kampf*, which means *My Struggle*. In it, he detailed his political ideas for Germany. Many Germans who read *Mein Kampf* and later heard Hitler's speeches came to believe in his ideas. Hitler claimed the German people belonged to a superior "Aryan" race that was destined to control inferior races and rule the world. Hitler considered Jews an inferior race. He blamed Jews for Germany's economic troubles and for conspiring with communists to further the cause of world revolution. In addition to Jews and communists, he attacked the Soviet Union as an obstacle to German expansion.

When Hitler emerged from prison in 1924, he found the Nazi party had lost much of its strength. Hitler worked hard to rebuild the party, promising benefits to peasants, workers, and the middle class. He also won support from some wealthy business leaders. The Great Depression greatly helped the Nazis. As unemployment rose, thousands of desperate people flocked to local Nazi party headquarters in search of a free meal and companionship. (See the graph on page 618.) They also found hope in Hitler's ideas. Between 1928 and 1932, the Nazis won more and more seats in the Reichstag, the German legislature.

By 1932, the Nazis had become the largest single party in the Reichstag. On January 30, 1933, German president Paul von Hindenburg asked Hitler to become chancellor. Because the Nazis did not have a majority of seats in the Reichstag, Hitler had to form a coalition government. However, Hitler moved swiftly to increase his power.

Hitler called for elections in March, hoping to increase Nazi strength in the Reichstag. A week before the elections, a fire, probably set by the Nazis, destroyed the Reichstag building. Hitler accused communists of setting the fire and of planning a revolt. He used the threat of a communist

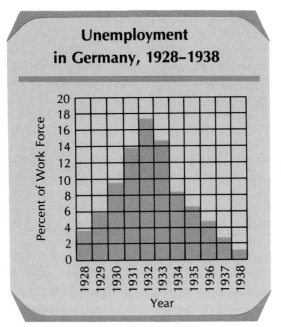

Unemployment in Germany, 1928–1938

Source: Angus Maddison, *Economic Growth in the West.*

Graph Skill *In Germany, as elsewhere around the world, unemployment soared during the Great Depression. In what year did unemployment in Germany begin to drop? How did it compare with unemployment in Britain and the United States? (See the graph on page 596.)*

uprising to convince President von Hindenburg to issue emergency orders abolishing freedom of speech and assembly.

The Nazis did not quite win a majority in the March elections, but Nazi delegates managed to force the Reichstag to pass the Enabling Act. This act gave Hitler dictatorial power for four years. After the passage of this act, Hitler needed less than a year to eliminate all opposition parties and establish a fascist state in Germany.

Establishing the Third Reich

When President von Hindenburg died in August 1934, Hitler combined the offices of president and chancellor. He adopted the title "Führer" (FYOOR uhr), or leader. He also proclaimed the birth of the Third Reich, successor to the Holy Roman Empire and the German Empire, which had lasted from 1871 to 1918. The Third Reich, boasted Hitler, would last a thousand years.

Totalitarian rule. Hitler used many of the methods of Stalin and Mussolini to build a totalitarian state in Germany. In June 1934, he rounded up rivals in the Nazi party and hundreds of political opponents and had many of them murdered. He established a secret police, the Gestapo, to hunt down and arrest anyone suspected of opposing Nazi rule. New laws were passed that made the good of the state more important than individual rights. Hitler also sought and won the loyalty of army officers, who responded eagerly to his plans for German expansion.

The Nazis extended their control to every aspect of life, including the press, schools, and religion. Joseph Goebbels, Hitler's minister of propaganda, made radio stations play military music and speeches glorifying the Nazi state.

Students were encouraged to join the Hitler Youth, an organization that taught military discipline, patriotism, and obedience to the Führer. Many young Germans enthusiastically wore the uniform and badge of the Hitler Youth, which promised excitement and advancement. The Hitler Youth helped Nazis round up "un-German" books, which were burned in spectacular public bonfires.

The government forced most private Roman Catholic schools to close because Hitler wanted all German children to attend public schools controlled by the Nazis. In 1935, the Nazis reorganized the Protestant churches in Germany and tried to force ministers to deliver pro-Nazi sermons on Sundays.

Campaign against the Jews. As he had promised in *Mein Kampf*, Hitler moved ruthlessly against German Jews. In March 1933, Jews were expelled from all government jobs and from teaching positions in the universities. Soon afterward, Jews were forbidden to practice such professions as law and medicine.* The Nuremberg Laws of 1935 deprived German Jews of their citizenship and banned marriages between Jews and non-Jews. Furthermore, all Jews had to register with the government and wear a yellow Star

---

*Many German Jews, including the well-known physicist Albert Einstein, emigrated to the United States.

of David on their clothing so they could be easily identified.

Nazi policy toward the Jews became harsher in 1938 after a Jewish youth murdered a German diplomat in Paris. On November 10, Nazis organized riots in a number of German cities. Many Jews were killed and hundreds of Jewish shops and synagogues were destroyed. Some 20,000 Jews were arrested and sent to concentration, or prison, camps. Persecution of Jews would intensify in the years ahead, as you will read in the next chapter.

Hitler's Programs for Strengthening Germany

Like the Fascists in Italy, the Nazis in Germany preached the need for hard work, sacrifice, and service to the state. Hitler had grand plans for Germany. He promised economic recovery and the acquisition of "living space" beyond the borders of Germany.

Economic recovery. Hitler's major economic goals for Germany were to reduce unemployment and make the country strong and self-sufficient. He launched vast building programs, including housing, highways, and sports arenas. He ignored the Versailles Treaty, which prohibited German rearmament, and set about rebuilding the German military. Thousands of workers were employed by munitions factories that received huge orders for arms from the government.

To pay for his public works programs, Hitler increased taxes and imposed strict controls on wages and prices. He banned strikes and outlawed unions. Workers and employers were organized into the National Labor Front. Because wages were low, the National Labor Front offered workers inexpensive vacations and supported Nazi propaganda efforts to glorify labor.

In the 1930s, economic recovery became a reality. Unemployment dropped from 6 million in 1933 to 1 million in 1936. Moreover, the standard of living rose for the average worker.

Plans for expansion. German rearmament and the quest for economic self-sufficiency were both part of Hitler's plans for expansion. In *Mein Kampf*, Hitler had in-

Book burnings were commonplace in Nazi Germany. Here, Nazis collect books to be destroyed. According to one proclamation, any book was to be burned "which acts subversively on our future or strikes at the root of German thought, the German home, and the driving forces of our people." Works of Jewish artists and intellectuals were burned. In addition, books by such American authors as Jack London, Helen Keller, and Upton Sinclair went up in flames.

sisted that the "Aryan master race" was destined to rule "inferior peoples." He included the Slavs of Eastern Europe among the "inferior peoples." Thus, he claimed, Germany had the right to expand eastward and win the "living space" he felt Germany needed.

To prepare for German expansion, Hitler proclaimed in 1935 that Germany would disregard the Versailles Treaty. He proceeded to increase the German armed forces from the limit of 100,000 imposed in 1919 to more than half a million. He claimed that the growing size of the Soviet army justified this step and made German rearmament necessary.

The League of Nations condemned Hitler's actions but took no steps against Germany. (Hitler had already withdrawn Germany from the league in 1933.) However, France was frightened enough by Hitler's ambitions to form an anti-German military alliance with the Soviet Union. Britain refused to be drawn into this alliance. In fact, the British signed a naval agreement with Germany in June 1935. This agreement recognized Germany's right to build submarines, even though the Versailles Treaty had specifically prohibited Germany from having a submarine fleet.

By the mid-1930s, Hitler had made German strength and determination clear to the world. As you will read in Chapter 33, the democratic nations of Western Europe and the United States were not united in their responses to Hitler's aggressions.

SECTION REVIEW

1. Identify: *Mein Kampf,* Paul von Hindenburg, Führer, Third Reich, Gestapo.
2. List three problems facing the Weimar Republic in the 1920s.
3. What ideas did Hitler develop in his early years?
4. What effect did the Great Depression have on the Nazi party?
5. What steps did Hitler take to ensure his power in the Third Reich?
6. What were the results of Hitler's program for German economic recovery?

5 Militarism in Japan

Read to Learn
- why democracy failed in Japan
- how the military ruled Japan

Japan had joined the Allies in World War I. It emerged from the war with a prosperous economy and the former German colonies in the Pacific. In the 1920s, Japanese manufacturing and commercial strength enabled it to move into many markets once dominated by the British. But as an industrial nation, Japan became increasingly dependent on foreign trade. Thus, when the Great Depression struck, its economy reeled from the effects of shrinking trade.

An Era of Democratic Reform

In the 1920s, industrialization strengthened the Japanese economy and helped produce a well-educated middle class that favored democratic institutions. The victory of the democratic Allies in World War I also added to the prestige of democracy in Japan.

Political parties gained greater power in the 1920s, and the tradition of unquestioned obedience to the emperor weakened. In the past, the emperor's advisors had named the prime minister. During the 1920s, the political party with the most seats in parliament gained this power. Thus, the prime minister needed the support of parliament to stay in office. This made the government responsible to parliament and to the voters.

The Japanese introduced other reforms. In 1925, a law giving suffrage to all men over age 25 increased the number of voters by about 9 million. Other reforms in the 1920s included the creation of a national health insurance plan and the removal of some restraints on labor unions.

Impact of the Depression

Because of its dependence on foreign trade, Japan was hit hard by the Great Depression. From 1929 to 1931, the value of Japanese exports fell by 50 percent. World demand for luxuries such as Japanese silk declined. Many Japanese businesses were ruined. Moreover, industrial nations imposed high tariffs on foreign goods in order to protect their own industries. As a result, Japanese manufacturers lost their foreign markets, and unemployment in Japan climbed.

Like governments elsewhere, the government of Japan seemed unable to solve the economic crisis. Critics denounced the government for its weakness. Many people, especially the military, grew impatient with the parliamentary system.

The government's disarmament policy also came under attack. Japan had participated in the naval disarmament conferences of the 1920s. At the London Naval Conference of 1930, Prime Minister Yuko Hamaguchi agreed to keep the size of the Japanese navy below that of either the British or the American fleet.

This move was extremely unpopular with the military and with extreme nationalists who had ambitions of creating a Japanese empire in Asia. In November 1930, Hamaguchi was shot by a man linked to an extreme nationalist group. Over the next few years, other moderate political leaders were assassinated.

The Military in Power

The military had occupied an important place in Japanese society since the days of the samurai. (See page 257.) In the climate of crisis of the 1930s, the Japanese military began to take matters into its own hands. In September 1930, the army defied the civilian government and attacked Manchuria, a region of northeastern China. The prime minister resigned to protest the army's disobedience. When his successor asked the emperor to place the army under civilian control, he was assassinated by a group of army officers.

By May 1932, the military was in control of Japan. It established a fascist state. Unlike Italy and Germany, however, Japan did not have a single leader or a specific program. Instead, a small group of military leaders dominated the government. They did not abolish the constitution, parliament, or even political parties. Civilian officials continued in their jobs, but they had no control over the generals in the war department, who dictated policy.

In the 1930s, Japan exhibited many features of a totalitarian state. The government arrested critics, imposed censorship, and dismissed liberal professors from the universities. A secret police searched out and punished so-called enemies of the state. The press and the schools taught total obedience to the emperor. Extreme nationalist groups glorified war and the empire.

Aggression in Manchuria

Many Japanese were dissatisfied with their nation's position in the world. As you have read, the high tariffs of other nations limited Japanese exports. A small island nation, Japan lacked important raw materials such as coal and oil. Moreover, the Japanese islands were densely populated. But the United States, Australia, and Canada restricted the immigration of Japanese to their countries. The Japanese strongly resented these policies, which were based on racial prejudice.

The military leaders of Japan offered a solution to these problems—the acquisition of an overseas empire. Japan had already acquired some overseas territory, as you can see from the map below. In 1907, for example, it had established a protectorate over Korea. By adding to these lands, the military promised, Japan could obtain access to raw materials, win new foreign markets, and gain an outlet for its surplus population.

Japan had long been interested in Manchuria, a province of China that bordered on Korea. Manchuria had rich supplies of coal

Map Skills *The Japanese extended their empire onto the Asian mainland in the 1900s, as you can see on this map. In the 1930s, Japan invested heavily in Manchuria, planning to expand deeper into China. What territory had Japan already acquired by 1918?*

and iron. In 1930, the Japanese invaded Manchuria and quickly crushed resistance by local Chinese forces. They then set up the country of Manchukuo, which was a puppet state, totally controlled by Japan.

China went before the League of Nations to protest Japanese aggression in Manchuria. The league condemned the Japanese invasion. But it took no further action, in part because the major powers were distracted by the Great Depression. Japan withdrew from the league in 1933.

In the 1930s, Japan assumed a new role in Asia. It posed as the leader of people who opposed western imperialism. At the same time, Japan sought support from other fascist powers. In 1936, it signed a military agreement with Nazi Germany and prepared to launch new adventures in Asia.

SECTION REVIEW

1. Locate: Korea, Manchuria.
2. What evidence suggests that Japan was becoming more democratic in the 1920s?
3. Give two reasons why Japan was so severely hurt by the Great Depression.
4. What totalitarian measures were used in Japan in the 1930s?
5. Why did Japan want to expand its empire?

Chapter 32 Review

In Perspective

In March 1917, moderate revolutionaries overthrew the czar in Russia. In November, radical revolutionaries led by Lenin seized power. After Lenin's death in 1924, Stalin emerged as dictator. He crushed all rivals and created a totalitarian state.

In the 1920s and 1930s, totalitarian states were established in Italy, Germany, and Japan. Italians turned to Mussolini because he promised a revival of the glory of ancient Rome. Hitler's Nazi party won support from many Germans because of the weakness of the Weimar government and the Great Depression.

After World War I, Japan enjoyed economic prosperity and growing democracy. But it turned away from democratic government during the depression and supported military leaders. These leaders embarked on an aggressive foreign policy in the 1930s.

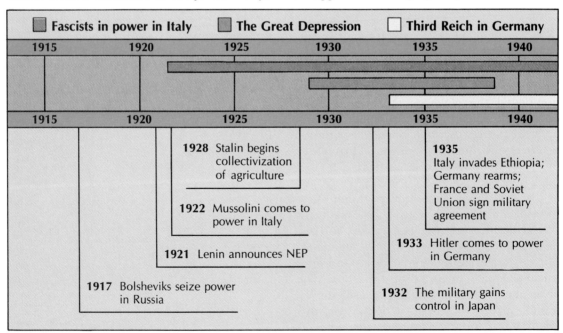

| ■ Fascists in power in Italy | ■ The Great Depression | □ Third Reich in Germany |

| 1915 | 1920 | 1925 | 1930 | 1935 | 1940 |

1928 Stalin begins collectivization of agriculture

1935 Italy invades Ethiopia; Germany rearms; France and Soviet Union sign military agreement

1922 Mussolini comes to power in Italy

1921 Lenin announces NEP

1933 Hitler comes to power in Germany

1917 Bolsheviks seize power in Russia

1932 The military gains control in Japan

Recalling Facts

Identify the country in which each of the following events took place.

1. The Gestapo arrested anyone opposed to the ruling party.
2. The New Economic Policy encouraged agriculture.
3. The government defied the Versailles Treaty and began to rearm.
4. The government sent troops to invade Manchuria.
5. Peasants were moved onto collective farms.
6. Jews were forced to wear a yellow Star of David.
7. Black Shirts attacked socialists.
8. Newspapers praised Il Duce.

Chapter Checkup

1. (a) How did World War I contribute to the outbreak of the Russian Revolution? (b) What rival political power opposed the Provisional Government? (c) How did this rival power undermine the Provisional Government?
2. (a) Describe the Bolshevik takeover in November 1917. (b) Why were the Bolsheviks able to defeat their enemies in the civil war? (c) What were Lenin's chief goals after the civil war ended?
3. (a) What were Stalin's major goals for the Soviet Union? (b) How did he ensure his control over the Soviet Union? (c) How did Stalin's policies affect the Russian people?
4. (a) What conditions in Italy helped Mussolini win power? (b) Why did fascism appeal to many Italians?
5. Explain how each of the following contributed to Hitler's rise to power: (a) Versailles Treaty; (b) Great Depression; (c) *Mein Kampf*.
6. (a) What accusations did Hitler make against Jews? (b) What policies did he follow toward Jews once he was in power?
7. (a) How did the Great Depression affect the Japanese economy? (b) Why was the Japanese military dissatisfied with the civilian government? (c) How did the military want to solve the economic crisis?

Critical Thinking

1. **Comparing** Compare Lenin's New Economic Policy to Stalin's five-year plans. (a) How were they similar? (b) How were they different?
2. **Applying Information** In the 1920s and 1930s, Italy, Germany, and Japan embraced fascism. Why do you think fascism became such a powerful movement in these countries in the postwar period?

Relating Past to Present

1. (a) How does a totalitarian state ensure complete control over the people? (b) Why did totalitarian states of the twentieth century have more power than the absolute monarchs of earlier times? (c) Which recent inventions do you think have increased the power of totalitarian governments the most?

Developing Basic Skills

1. **Graph Reading** Study the graph on page 618. Then answer the following questions: (a) What percentage of Germans was out of work in 1928? (b) When did unemployment reach its peak? (c) Why do you think unemployment declined in the mid-1930s?
2. **Map Reading** Study the map on page 621. Then answer the following questions: (a) What territory did Japan control in 1890? (b) What lands did it acquire between 1918 and 1934? (c) What area or areas might have become the object of Japanese expansion in the late 1930s?
3. **Comparing** Make a chart with four rows and three columns. Title the rows the Soviet Union, Italy, Germany, and Japan. Title the columns Leader, Economic Program, and Foreign Policy. Complete the chart using what you have learned in this chapter about events in the 1930s. Then answer the following questions: (a) Which country or countries had a single strong leader in the 1930s? (b) What similarities do you see in the economic programs of Italy and Germany in the 1930s? (c) How did the economic goals of the Soviet Union and Italy differ? (d) How were the foreign policies of all four countries similar?

See page 807 for suggested readings.

33 The World at War

(1936–1945)

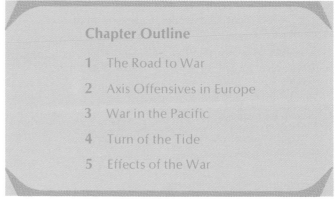

Chapter Outline

1 The Road to War

2 Axis Offensives in Europe

3 War in the Pacific

4 Turn of the Tide

5 Effects of the War

British soldiers resist a German tank attack in Holland, May 1940.

On June 22, 1940, an American reporter waited in the forest of Compiègne, northeast of Paris. In this same clearing, Germany had signed the armistice that ended World War I in November 1918. Now another surrender was to take place, but this time the roles were reversed. Germany was the victor, and France, the vanquished. The German leader, Adolf Hitler, had a keen sense of drama, and he set the stage carefully. The railroad car in which the earlier surrender had been signed was removed from a museum in Paris and transported to Compiègne for the occasion.

Hitler arrived, and the reporter watched him get out of his car. Nazi flags fluttered in the warm June air. The reporter noted: "Then he strode slowly toward us, toward the little clearing in the woods. I observed his face. It was grave, solemn, yet brimming with revenge. There was also in it, as in his springy step, a note of the triumphant conqueror, the defier of the world. There was something else, difficult to describe, in his expression, a sort of scornful, inner joy at being present at this great reversal of fate—a reversal he himself had wrought."

It was time for the ceremony to begin. "It is now 3:23 P.M. and the Germans stride over to the armistice car. For a moment or two, they stand in the sunlight outside the car, chatting. Then Hitler steps up into the car, followed by the others. . . . It is a grave hour in the life of France. The Frenchmen keep their eyes straight ahead. Their faces are solemn, drawn. They are the picture of tragic dignity. . . . The whole ceremony in which Hitler has reached a new pinnacle in his . . . career and Germany avenged the 1918 defeat is over in a quarter of an hour."

The defeat of France was one of many victories for Nazi Germany after 1936. Aggression by Germany, Italy, and Japan in the 1930s threatened world peace, eventually leading to world war. World War II, which lasted from 1939 to 1945, would prove to be the most devastating war in human history.

1 The Road to War

Read to Learn
- how the Spanish Civil War encouraged fascism
- how appeasement policies helped lead to World War II

In 1925, the Locarno conference stimulated a spirt of peaceful cooperation among nations. Ten years later, the international scene had changed. Japan had seized Manchuria. Italy had invaded Ethiopia, and Germany was rearming. The League of Nations appeared powerless in the face of such threats to world peace. Nor had uninvolved nations been willing to take a strong stand. This pattern was repeated in the Spanish Civil War.

The Spanish Civil War

Spain had been politically unstable since the days of Napoleon. In the early 1900s, the country was torn apart by strikes, and groups in the provinces demanded independence. In addition, many Spaniards felt that the Catholic Church had too much power. In 1931, the king was forced to abdicate, and a republican government was established.

The new Spanish government was dominated by liberals and socialists. Under its leadership, the Catholic Church lost its status as the country's official religion, and much of its property was confiscated. Students were no longer required to receive Catholic religious instruction. The government also reduced the size of the army. These moves angered both the church and the military.

Unrest continued under the republican government. Socialist unions staged disruptive strikes, and anticlerical forces set fire to Catholic convents. The clergy denounced the policies of the government, and monarchists called for the return of the king. When parliamentary elections in 1933 resulted in a more conservative government, liberals, socialists, and communists formed a coalition known as the Popular Front.

Beginning of the conflict. The Popular Front defeated the conservative parties in parliamentary elections held in February 1936. The government then released thousands of leftists from prison. It also assigned high-ranking military officers who opposed the republic to remote posts. During the spring of 1936, it confiscated some large estates and gave the land to the peasants. These actions brought a violent response from the right.

In July 1936, a group of generals led by Francisco Franco staged an uprising against the republican government, and civil war began. The generals wanted to restore the power of the church and destroy socialism and communism in Spain. The followers of Franco, called Nationalists, openly called for the creation of a fascist state. Defenders of the government were known as Republicans.

Foreign intervention. The Spanish Civil War soon became an international issue. The League of Nations tried to enforce neutrality. It set up a border patrol in an effort to keep outside supplies from reaching either side, but it was unsuccessful. Mussolini sent Italian troops to reinforce the Nationalist forces. Hitler dispatched the German air force to bomb cities held by the Republicans. Both leaders regarded Spain as a place

625

Pablo Picasso recorded the horrors of the Spanish Civil War in his painting Guernica *(GUHR nee kuh). Guernica is a small town in northern Spain. On April 26, 1937—a Monday, and thus a market day when farmers gathered in the main square—German planes bombed the town and strafed defenseless people in the streets. The center of the town was destroyed, and over 1,500 people died. The bombing of Guernica gave the world a view of a terrifying new kind of warfare.*

to test new weapons and tactics. Cooperation between Italy and Germany in Spain led to the creation in October 1936 of a military alliance known as the Rome-Berlin Axis.

Aid from the Axis powers helped the Nationalists win a succession of military victories. Stalin sent weapons and advisers to the Republicans, but this aid did not match the assistance provided by the Axis. The British opposed Axis aid to the Nationalists but did little to stop it. In France, Léon Blum's government wanted the Spanish republic to survive. But it did not provide military aid for fear of a hostile reaction from the powerful French right. Isolationist feelings in the United States prevented government help for either side.

The Spanish Civil War ended in 1939 with victory for the Nationalists. Franco then imposed a fascist dictatorship on Spain. As a result of the war, Germany and Italy developed contempt for the democratic powers. Since Britain, France, and the United States had done little to prevent Axis intervention in Spain, Hitler and Mussolini felt encouraged to interfere in other countries.

Other Challenges to Peace

Even before the outbreak of the Spanish Civil War, Hitler had begun to put into action his expansionist plans. On March 7, 1936, he sent German troops into the Rhineland. The Treaty of Versailles had barred German troops from this area. But Hitler claimed that the 1935 military alliance between France and Russia justified his action.

Hitler met with little resistance to this violation of the Versailles Treaty. Britain and France condemned his move but took no action. British leaders believed that resistance might lead to an unwanted war. Furthermore, many people in Britain thought that the Germans had a right to occupy the Rhineland since it was German territory. France stood paralyzed during the German occupation of the Rhineland. The French prime minister favored a military response, but France could not act without British support.

Next on Hitler's agenda of expansion was Austria, his native land. Anschluss, union between Austria and Germany, was forbidden by the Versailles Treaty, but this mattered little to Hitler. In March 1938, threats of German military action forced the chancellor of Austria to resign and appoint an Austrian Nazi party official in his place. The new chancellor immediately asked Hitler to send troops to Austria "to help maintain order." German troops marched into Austria on March 12. The next day Austria became part of Germany.

The British prime minister, Neville Chamberlain, refused to be alarmed by the Anschluss. He rejected suggestions that Britain join the anti-German alliance already formed between France and the Soviet Union. Chamberlain warned that an aggressive stance toward Germany would destroy the possibility of future negotiations. In France, a rapid change of governments prevented effective response to the Anschluss.

The Policy of Appeasement

Chamberlain's attitude toward the Anschluss grew out of a policy of appeasement. *Appeasement* means making concessions to an aggressor in order to preserve the peace. Memories of the huge battlefield losses in World War I made British and French leaders reluctant to present a military challenge to Hitler. *Pacifism*, or refusal to fight in a war, was widespread in both countries.

Other factors also contributed to the policy of appeasement. To many people in Britain, crises in the Rhineland and Austria seemed far away and not important enough to risk a war. Some people thought a strong Germany would be a check on Soviet power and the spread of communism. In addition, there was a fairly common feeling in Britain that Germany had been treated too harshly by the Treaty of Versailles.

Some people in France shared these ideas, and the French government also followed a policy of appeasement. In addition, the French were unprepared to stand up to Hitler without British backing. At the same time, political discord in France sapped public morale and determination.

The United States followed a policy of isolationism during the 1930s. Both Congress and President Roosevelt were determined to keep the United States out of any future European conflicts.

Neutrality laws passed in 1935 and 1936 barred the United States from selling arms to any country involved in a war. They also prohibited American ships from carrying arms to a warring nation. Roosevelt condemned Germany's ambitious foreign policy during the 1930s but refused to join an anti-German military alliance.

Crisis Over Czechoslovakia

After the Anschluss, Hitler turned his attention to Czechoslovakia. Three million Germans lived in the Sudetenland, the western border region of Czechoslovakia. Hitler encouraged the Sudeten Germans to demand self-government within Czechoslovakia. In the fall of 1938, after the Czech government rejected these demands, Hitler gave a speech claiming that "the misery of the Sudeten Germans is indescribable." He promised to come to their aid if the Czech government did not grant them self-government.

A German invasion seemed likely, but Chamberlain hoped that appeasement would resolve the crisis. Chamberlain convinced the unhappy Czechs to agree to self-government for the Sudetenland. No sooner was this demand met than Hitler imposed new ones. He insisted that Czechoslovakia give up the region and that Germany be allowed to send troops there immediately.

Chamberlain now asked for a four-power conference to settle the Czech crisis. Hitler agreed and invited the leaders of Britain, France, and Italy to meet with him in Munich on September 29. Neither Czechoslovakia nor its ally, the Soviet Union, was invited to attend the conference.

At the Munich conference, the four powers agreed to allow German troops to occupy the Sudetenland, but they guaranteed the independence of the rest of Czechoslovakia. To Chamberlain's relief, Hitler announced that he had no more territorial claims in Europe. The people of Czechoslovakia mourned the division of their country. But Chamberlain proclaimed that after the agreement there would be "peace for our time." Europeans breathed a sigh of relief as the threat of war passed.

Hitler's easy victory at Munich encouraged him to move boldly. In March 1939, six months after the Munich conference, German troops occupied the rest of Czechoslovakia. Hitler's violation of the Munich agreement shocked Chamberlain. The policy of appeasement had rested on the false assumption that Hitler could be trusted. The events in Czechoslovakia proved that the policy was bankrupt.

Poland

A week after German troops occupied Czechoslovakia, Hitler turned to Poland. He demanded the return of the city of Danzig and the Polish Corridor.* These demands alarmed Britain and France. On March 31, 1939, Chamberlain announced to the House of Commons that Britain would aid Poland if

---

* The Versailles Treaty had made the German city of Danzig an independent, international city and had created the Polish Corridor, a small strip of land between Poland and the Baltic Sea. (See the map below.)

Map Skill   *Between 1935 and 1939, Italy and Germany threatened the peace in Europe on several occasions. As you can see on this map, Hitler's aggression against Germany's neighbors increased the size of the Third Reich. In what order did the invaded countries fall to the Third Reich?*

Poland were attacked. Britain soon established a military draft and voted more money for defense spending. France also vowed support for Poland, and the French government hurried to rearm.

During the tension-filled spring and summer of 1939, both Britain and Germany entered into negotiations with the Soviet Union. Its long border with Poland made the Soviet Union especially concerned by the Polish crisis. Stalin wanted to form a military alliance with Britain and France. But dislike of Soviet communism and doubts about the effectiveness of the Soviet army caused the British and French to hesitate. They also refused to agree to Stalin's demands for dominance in Eastern Europe.

Meanwhile, Hitler moved with great purpose. Although he detested communism and the Russians, he desperately wanted Stalin's assurance that the Soviet Union would not interfere with his planned invasion of Poland. On August 23, the world was astonished by the announcement of what became known as the Nazi-Soviet Pact. In this nonaggression treaty, Germany and the Soviet Union pledged not to attack each other. Secret clauses provided for the future division of Poland and other parts of Eastern Europe between the two powers.

The Nazi-Soviet Pact allowed Germany to move against Poland. At dawn on September 1, 1939, German troops crossed the Polish border. Two days later, Britain and France declared war on Germany. The second world war of the century had begun.

SECTION REVIEW

1. Locate: Rhineland, Sudetenland, Danzig, Polish Corridor.
2. Identify: Francisco Franco, Rome-Berlin Axis, Anschluss, Neville Chamberlain, Nazi-Soviet Pact.
3. Define: appeasement, pacifism.
4. (a) Describe the two sides in the Spanish Civil War. (b) Who aided the Nationalists?
5. (a) How did Britain react to Hitler's occupation of the Rhineland in 1936? (b) How did France react?
6. What was the policy of the United States toward conflicts in Europe during the 1930s?
7. What did the European nations decide at the Munich conference?

---

2 Axis Offensives in Europe

Read to Learn
- how Europe fell to the Nazi blitzkrieg
- how people lived—and died—under Nazi rule

World War II pitted the Axis against the Allies. Germany and Italy were the major Axis powers in 1939. Japan joined the Axis in 1940. Several nations in Eastern Europe also supported the Axis. The Allies eventually included Britain, France, the Soviet Union, the United States, China, and 43 other nations.

Early Months

On September 1, the German army launched a new kind of attack on Poland. It was called *blitzkrieg*, which means lightning war in German. Combined forces of planes, tanks, artillery, and mechanized infantry swiftly pierced Polish defenses. Their aim was to break the Polish forces into small groups and thus overwhelm them.

The Poles fought bravely but were unable to stop the blitzkrieg. German planes prevented an orderly retreat by machine-gunning army units as they withdrew from battle. Terrified civilians clogged the roads, which were subject to enemy strafing. The Germans bombed Polish cities and destroyed the Polish air force before the planes had a chance to take off. Britain and France declared war on Germany. But they could not send aid to Poland in time. On September 27, 1939, Poland surrendered.

While Polish forces were still fighting in the west, Soviet troops moved into Poland from the east. In accordance with the Nazi-Soviet Pact, the Russians seized the eastern half of Poland. The Germans occupied the rest.

Because Stalin feared that Hitler would eventually attack the Soviet Union, he went to work to shore up his defenses. First, he secured fortified bases in Estonia, Latvia, and Lithuania. In 1940, the Soviet Union occupied and then annexed these three countries. When Finland refused to allow Soviet military bases on its territory, the Soviets invaded. The "winter war" between Finland and the Soviet Union began in November 1939 and did not end until the Finns surrendered in March 1940. The Soviet Union did not occupy Finland, but Finland was forced to give up some strategic territories.

Collapse in Western Europe

After conquering Poland, Hitler waited. Nothing much happened for the next seven months, and people began talking about the "phony war." But the sense of security some may have felt was soon shattered.

In April 1940, Hitler unleashed a blitzkrieg against Denmark and Norway. The Danes surrendered immediately, but the Norwegians fought until their resistance was broken at the end of the month. In May, blitzkrieg attacks forced Luxembourg and the Netherlands to surrender after brief fighting. British and French troops tried unsuccessfully to defend Belgium, which surrendered on May 26.

France had massed troops along the Maginot Line in the northeast, hoping to prevent a German invasion. However, in mid-May, the Germans simply bypassed these fortifications and attacked France through Belgium. The Germans penetrated deeply into the country in a few days. By the end of May, they had pushed a combined British and French army across France to Dunkirk on the English Channel. The British rushed every available naval vessel, merchant ship, and pleasure boat across the channel to Dunkirk. They evacuated about 20,000 British and 140,000 French troops to safety in Britain. However, much valuable equipment was left behind. The French soldiers who escaped at Dunkirk became the nucleus of the Free French, a force that took part in many later Allied actions.

France stood on the edge of defeat. On June 10, Italy invaded southern France. On June 16, the German army marched into Paris. The next day France asked for an armistice. As you read at the beginning of the chapter, the French surrender took place at Compiègne on June 22.

Germany occupied the northern two thirds of France and directly took over the government there. In southern France, the Germans oversaw the creation of a puppet state, known as Vichy France because its capital was at Vichy.

The Battle of Britain

After the French surrender, Britain stood alone. A German invasion of the British Isles seemed certain. Neville Chamberlain, unpopular because of his appeasement policy, had been forced to resign. The new prime minister, Winston Churchill, was an inspiring leader. He warned that hard times lay ahead and that he could offer people only "blood, toil, tears, and sweat." Churchill's courage and determination rallied British spirits. On June 4, at the end of the Dunkirk rescue operation, Churchill proclaimed:

> We shall defend our island, whatever the cost may be. We shall fight on the beaches, we shall fight on the landing grounds, we shall fight in the fields and in the streets, we shall fight in the hills. We shall never surrender.

Hitler planned to weaken and demoralize the British before invading. Therefore, in July, he ordered German bombers to attack British cities and defense installations. The punishing bombardment, called the battle of Britain, lasted three months. The city of Coventry was nearly destroyed. London was bombed night after night. Thousands of Londoners slept in subway stations for safety, while firefighters hosed down flaming buildings and rescue teams dug trapped people out of the rubble.

Germany ultimately lost the battle of Britain. Britain's Royal Air Force (RAF) attacked the German planes with skill and daring. British fighter pilots were aided by radar, a recent British invention. With radar, the British could detect the approach of enemy planes. The British downed some 2,300 German planes, losing about 900 of their own.

Churchill expressed the gratitude of the British to the pilots of the RAF when he declared, "Never in the field of human conflict was so much owed by so many to so few." Instead of destroying British morale, the battle of Britain strengthened it. By the end of 1940, Hitler had cancelled plans for an invasion of Britain, although bombings continued off and on for several years.

The Nazi Empire in Europe

Despite Germany's setback in the battle of Britain, the Axis had won an impressive string of victories by the end of 1940. It controlled all of Western Europe except for neutral Sweden and Switzerland. Spain, though technically neutral, was pro-Axis and allowed Germany to use its ports. In the east, Germany held Austria, Czechoslovakia, and western Poland. Hungary and Romania joined the Axis late in 1940, and Bulgaria joined early in 1941.

In several occupied countries, such as Poland and the Netherlands, German officials took direct control of the government. Elsewhere, the Germans set up puppet governments run by local people who followed Nazi orders.

The Nazis exploited occupied Europe for its economic value to Germany. They heavily taxed some people, such as the French. In Eastern Europe, the Germans seized men and women and sent them as slave labor to work in German factories. They also seized manufactured goods and shipped them to Germany. Nazi leaders amassed great art collections by looting the museums of Europe. One of Hitler's top aides said: "Whether nations live in prosperity or starve to death like cattle interests me only in so far as we need them as slaves to our civilization."

Churchill's leadership inspired the British people throughout the war. In radio speeches, he promised: "We have but one aim and one single, irrevocable [unchangeable] purpose. We are resolved to destroy Hitler and every vestige [trace] of his Nazi regime. From this nothing will turn us—nothing." In this photograph, Churchill is shown inspecting the House of Commons after it was bombed in May 1941.

In accordance with Hitler's hatred of Jews, the Nazis persecuted Jews in occupied Europe. Jews had to register with government authorities and wear yellow identification stars. Nazis confiscated their businesses and other property. Jews in Poland were forced to live in ghettos, restricted areas. They were deprived of adequate supplies and forbidden contact with the outside world. Millions of Jews throughout occupied Europe were sent to concentration camps, where many starved or were murdered. Only after the war did the Allies discover the ultimate fate of millions of Jews and other people the Nazis considered unfit to live. (See page 641.)

Economics and History ■ The Ultra Secret

Through the use of radio in World War II, military commanders could issue orders to officers thousands of miles away. Cryptographers, or code writers, developed elaborate codes to disguise messages since messages could be picked up by the enemy as well. Code breakers on both sides tried to decipher the secret codes of the enemy. One spectacular code-breaking success was not revealed publicly until 30 years later.

During the war, the German army used a code machine that the British secret service called Enigma. Enigma used two typewriters and a series of lettered wheels that could be rearranged to produce as many as 22 billion code combinations. Operators of the machine changed the position of the wheels daily, according to instructions in a secret manual.

Enigma was based on a business machine that had been sold in the 1920s. In the early 1930s, the Polish secret service discovered that German diplomats were using an improved version of the machine for communicating with Berlin. The Poles stole one of the German machines, and before the Germans overran their country, the Poles shared the secret with the British and French.

A British team of cryptographers began to monitor German messages. Possession of the machine did not guarantee easy decoding, but as the war progressed, the British became better at decoding German messages. The information they obtained was called "Ultra" and was guarded with the utmost care. The British did not want the Germans to know when they had broken the German codes.

Ultra played an important role in the battle of Britain. Britain's small Royal Air Force was able to deploy its planes effectively because the British knew the flight plans of German bombers in advance. The need to keep Ultra secret from the Germans also led to tragedy. A British cryptographer reported after the war that Churchill knew the Germans planned to bomb Coventry. However, Churchill could not evacuate the city because he feared the Germans would learn that their code had been broken.

The most effective use of Ultra may have been during Allied preparations for the Normandy invasion. By the time this invasion was being planned, the Allies were regularly intercepting and decoding messages sent from Berlin to German commanders in Western Europe. The Allies learned the size and location of German forces and realized that the Germans did not suspect the site of the planned invasion.

Underground movements dedicated to ending Axis rule sprang up throughout Europe and grew in strength throughout the war. Resistance units sabotaged Nazi supply depots, derailed trains, and blew up bridges. They also supplied the Allies with valuable information about Axis troop movements, published secret newspapers, and hid escaped prisoners and downed pilots.

Further Attacks

In the fall of 1940, Axis leaders turned their attention to the Balkans and North Africa. Mussolini invaded Greece in October but was met with stiff resistance. Not until the spring of 1941, after Germany sent troops to aid Mussolini, did the Axis take over Greece and Yugoslavia as well.

Meanwhile, the Italians had also launched a campaign against British possessions in North Africa. They invaded Egypt in September 1940, but the British counterattacked, advancing into Libya and Ethiopia. Fighting in this area seesawed for many months.

All these offensives were overshadowed by another surprise blitzkrieg in June 1941—the German attack on the Soviet Union. The time had come, Hitler felt, to seize rich Soviet farmland and oil fields. He was willing to risk a two-front war, something German generals had feared since World War I.

On June 22, a force of 3 million German soldiers invaded the Soviet Union. The Soviets resisted but were forced to fall back. The effectiveness of Soviet forces was undermined in part by the loss of many top Soviet generals in the purges of the 1930s. As the Soviets withdrew, they destroyed farm equipment and crops, hoping that this "scorched earth" policy would deprive the enemy of supplies. After four months of fighting, the Germans had overrun the Ukraine and were approaching Moscow and Leningrad. Then, at the end of 1941, the German advance was halted.

Soviet resistance stiffened, and a bitterly cold winter came to Russia's aid. The Germans were unprepared for winter. They had to rely on long supply lines, which were often disrupted by Soviet soldiers. Both sides dug in for a long campaign. The German siege of Leningrad lasted for over two years. During this time, the city's population dropped from 4 million to 2.5 million as a result of fighting, starvation, and disease.

American Neutrality

When World War II began, President Roosevelt proclaimed that the United States would remain neutral. Isolationists praised his decision. While most Americans sympathized with the Allies, many feared that aiding them would lead to war with Germany.

Isolationist feeling declined as a result of the fall of France and the battle of Britain.

Americans began to worry about where Hitler would strike next if Britain fell. In September 1940, the United States transferred 50 destroyers to the British navy. Congress then passed the Lend-Lease Act in March 1941. This act authorized the President to furnish military supplies to nations "vital to the defense of the United States."

Under the Lend-Lease Act, the United States shipped tons of supplies to Britain and the Soviet Union. As a result, American merchant vessels came under attack by German submarines. Britain, Canada, and the United States organized convoys to protect supply ships, but many were sunk. It was events in Asia, however, that would bring the United States into the war.

SECTION REVIEW

1. Locate: Estonia, Latvia, Lithuania, Dunkirk, Leningrad.
2. Identify: "phony war," Vichy France, Winston Churchill, Lend-Lease Act.
3. Define: blitzkrieg.
4. What did Stalin do when Germany invaded Poland?
5. What was the outcome of the battle of Britain?
6. What roles did resistance movements play in the war?
7. How did Soviet forces react to the German invasion in 1941?
8. How did American feeling about the war in Europe change after the fall of France and the battle of Britain?

3 War in the Pacific

Read to Learn
■ why the United States entered World War II
■ how the Japanese pursued goals of empire

As you read in Chapter 32, Japan grew increasingly militaristic in the 1930s. The Japanese had taken Manchuria in 1931. This move proved to be only the beginning, and Japan set out to extend its power throughout East Asia.

Japanese Expansion

In 1937, Japan launched a full-scale war against the Chinese. Japanese troops poured into northeastern China and fanned out to the south and west. The Chinese resisted, but their forces were not strong enough to keep the Japanese from advancing. By the end of 1938, Japan controlled northern and central China and the city of Canton.

The seizure of Chinese ports and business centers enabled the Japanese to restrict the activities of foreign investors in China. Late in 1938, Japan announced the establishment of a "new order in East Asia," under which Japan would enjoy commercial supremacy in China.

When World War II broke out in Europe, Japan was openly sympathetic to its fellow fascists powers, Germany and Italy. It signed an alliance with them in the fall of 1940, thus creating the Rome-Berlin-Tokyo Axis. Meanwhile, the Japanese had occupied French Indochina and announced a "protective custody" over the Dutch East Indies after France and the Netherlands fell to Germany.

Attack on Pearl Harbor

Japanese aggression in Asia was of great concern to the United States. Americans had refused to grant recognition to Manchukuo, the puppet state set up in Manchuria. After Japan renewed its attack on China in 1937, the United States cancelled its 30-year-old commercial treaty with Japan. The United States condemned the seizure of French Indochina in 1940 and stopped exporting gasoline and scrap metal to Japan. Early in 1941, it moved the American Pacific fleet from the west coast to Pearl Harbor in Hawaii to demonstrate military readiness.

During most of 1941, Japan concentrated on taking over the rest of Southeast Asia with its rich natural resources. Japanese plans for conquest seemed even more threatening after October 1941, when General Hideki Tojo, an outspoken expansionist, became prime minister of Japan.

In November 1941, Tojo's government sent representatives to Washington, D.C., to negotiate with American officials. The Japanese offered to withdraw their troops from southern Indochina if the Americans would resume economic relations with Japan. Japan insisted, however, that it be allowed to occupy China. The United States rejected these proposals.

Even while these negotiations were going on in Washington, a decision to attack the United States had been made in Tokyo. The Japanese had decided several months earlier that war with the United States was inevitable. Rather than wait for a situation that they might not be able to control, they wanted to set their own timetable. They hoped a surprise attack would cripple the Americans and ensure a Japanese victory. American military leaders knew that trouble was brewing. But they expected an attack on the Philippines or in Southeast Asia.

However, early in the morning on Sunday, December 7, Japanese planes roared out of the sky over the American naval base at Pearl Harbor in Hawaii. During a punishing two-hour raid, the Japanese sank or badly damaged 8 American battleships, damaged 10 other ships, destroyed 188 planes, and killed over 2,500 Americans. The next day a grim President Roosevelt appeared before Congress to ask for a declaration of war. He called December 7 "a date which will live in infamy." Congress quickly complied with the President's request. Three days later, Japan's allies, Germany and Italy, declared war on the United States.

Japanese Victories

The Japanese followed their successful attack on Pearl Harbor with lightning assaults elsewhere in the Pacific. Within three months, they had captured the American islands of Guam and Wake. They took the British colony of Hong Kong on December 25. By early May 1942, they controlled Singapore, the Dutch East Indies, the Malay Peninsula, and Burma.

The Japanese had attacked the Philippines almost immediately after the raid on Pearl Harbor. The United States general Douglas MacArthur led the Allied defense in the Philippines but could not stave off a Japanese victory. In March 1942, when the Japanese had conquered most of the Philip-

After the bombing of Pearl Harbor, Japanese attackers radioed Tokyo with the message, "Tora, tora, tora." Tora, which means tiger, was a code word for: "We have succeeded in the surprise attack." But the Japanese failed to destroy the entire American Pacific fleet. Three aircraft carriers were not in the harbor during the attack. In the naval warfare of World War II, aircraft carriers proved to be valuable floating weapons.

pines, MacArthur left with the promise, "I shall return." He established headquarters in Australia and assumed command of all Allied forces in the Pacific.

Japan enjoyed several advantages in its drive for an empire. Britain was too involved in the war against Germany to mobilize its resources effectively against Japan. France and the Netherlands had been defeated and could not protect their Asian territory. Long supply lines between the United States and Asia also helped Japan.

The Japanese Empire

Its military conquests provided Japan with rich economic resources. It now controlled about three fourths of the world's rubber

and tin, both critical materials in time of war. Oil from the Dutch East Indies fueled Japanese planes and trucks. Indochinese rice fed Japanese soldiers. Japan called its empire the "Greater East Asia Co-Prosperity Sphere." This pleasant-sounding phrase did not hide the fact that the sphere was totally controlled by Japan.

The Japanese tried to gain the support of those they ruled by stressing the slogan "Asia for the Asians." In other words, they claimed to have rescued Asia from the grip of European colonial rule. Thus, the Japanese skillfully played on the bitterness that many Asians felt toward the British, French, Dutch, and Americans.

Although some Asians did initially welcome the Japanese, most soon realized that a new colonial power had merely replaced an old one. Japanese occupation authorities forced laborers to work on construction projects, often treating them cruelly. Their seizure of local rice supplies led to food shortages. They abused religious leaders and violated religious shrines.

Nationalists organized resistance against the Japanese. Resistance fighters blew up railroad lines and provided military information to Allied armies. The military skills they developed aided them in their struggles for independence after the war.

SECTION REVIEW

1. Locate: Pearl Harbor, Philippines.
2. Identify: Douglas MacArthur, Greater East Asia Co-Prosperity Sphere.
3. How did Japan gain control of commerce in China?
4. Why did the Japanese decide to make a surprise attack on Pearl Harbor?
5. What areas did Japan capture in 1942?
6. (a) Why did some Asians welcome the Japanese? (b) Why did their attitude change?

4 Turn of the Tide

Read to Learn
- how the war changed course in favor of the Allies
- how the Allies defeated Japan

The Axis powers enjoyed nearly unbroken military success between September 1939 and the summer of 1942. Then the tide began to turn in favor of the Allies, both in Europe and in the Pacific. By 1944, the end of the war was in sight.

Millions of women entered the work force during World War II. Women helped turn out the airplanes, ships, and ammunition needed in the war effort. In some factories in the United States, up to 90 percent of the workers were women. Here, women install cables in a plane.

The Great Mobilization

Although over 40 nations had joined the Allies by 1945, three—Britain, the Soviet Union, and the United States—played the decisive roles in defeating the Axis. These nations, led by Churchill, Stalin, and Roosevelt, determined most Allied strategy during the war.

The war effort required a total commitment. Britain mobilized fully for war after the German invasion of France in 1940. Production of consumer goods fell as industry converted to war production. Scarce items such as soap and gasoline were rationed. Parliament gave the government the power to assign civilian workers to jobs vital to the war effort.

Women played an important role in the British war effort. They served in even larger numbers than in World War I, both in industry and in the armed services. Women were largely responsible for antiaircraft defenses, and they ran the radar stations that helped win the battle of Britain.

The Soviet Union also transformed its economy to fight the war. Even before the German invasion, the Soviets had begun building industrial plants in the remote east. After the German attack in June 1941, the Soviets dismantled some 1,500 factories in western Russia and reassembled them east of the Ural Mountains. Like people in the other Allied nations, Soviet citizens made great personal sacrifices in support of the war effort. The government appealed to feelings of Russian nationalism to win much support.

After the Japanese attack on Pearl Harbor, the United States also geared up for war. Production of planes, tanks, and weapons increased dramatically. Through rationing and price controls, the government allocated scarce goods.

A special burden was borne by Japanese Americans, however. Because of the attack on Pearl Harbor, many other Americans feared that Japanese Americans living on the west coast might sabotage the war effort. As a result, in 1942, the government moved more than 100,000 Japanese Americans—two thirds of them born in the United States—to huge inland relocation camps. They were detained in the camps for the rest of the war.

Turning Points in North Africa and Europe

After months of Axis triumphs, two Allied victories signaled a change in the course of the war. One occurred in North Africa; the other, in the Soviet Union.

In North Africa, a brilliant German tank commander, General Erwin Rommel, known as the "Desert Fox," had begun a powerful offensive against the Allies in the spring of 1942. After forcing the British out of Libya, his tanks pushed toward the British position at El Alamein in Egypt. If the Germans captured this strategic city, they could seize the Suez Canal and cut the British lifeline to India.

The British, commanded by General Bernard Montgomery, blocked the Nazi thrust at El Alamein and launched a counteroffensive. They drove Rommel back into Tunisia and captured 9,000 German soldiers. In the fall, a combined British-American force under General Dwight Eisenhower landed in Morocco and Algeria. The two Allied forces converged on Tunisia, trapping Rommel's forces.

In mid-May 1943, the Axis forces in North Africa surrendered. Churchill later called the battle of El Alamein "the turning point in British military fortunes" during the war. "Up to Alamein we survived," he said. "After Alamein we conquered."

Allied fortunes also improved on the Russian front. In the fall of 1942, Hitler had launched a massive offensive against the city of Stalingrad. Fierce house-to-house fighting raged for two months, but the defenders held out. This gave Soviet forces time to organize a counteroffensive, which began in November. Over 80,000 Germans were forced to surrender, and over 200,000 Germans lost their lives in the battle. After their victory at Stalingrad, Soviet armies began to drive the Germans westward out of Soviet territory.

Allied Offensives in Europe

For months, Stalin had been urging Britain and the United States to attack the Axis on a second European front in order to relieve some of the pressure on the Soviet Union. He wanted an invasion of France from Britain, but the other Allied leaders decided to strike first in Italy because they considered it a weaker spot.

The invasion of Italy. On July 10, 1943, a combined British-American force landed on Sicily. They subdued Italian forces there in about a month. Meanwhile, Mussolini was forced out of power by other officials within the Fascist party. Pietro Badoglio took control of the government and had Mussolini arrested. But Mussolini was rescued by German parachutists and taken to northern Italy.

Badoglio joined forces with the Allies, but thousands of German troops remained in Italy. From the time the Allies landed on the Italian mainland in early September 1943, they encountered tough resistance. But they pushed northward up the Italian peninsula. On June 4, 1944, Allied troops marched into Rome, the first capital city to be freed from Nazi control. However, parts of Italy remained under German control until the spring of 1945.

The invasion of France. While British and American forces were struggling through Italy, Allied generals were preparing for the invasion of France under the leadership of General Eisenhower. A huge invasion force assembled in Britain. Thousands of ships stood ready to ferry the troops—British, Canadian, American, Free French, and others—across the English Channel.

D-Day, the day of the invasion, was June 6, 1944. Within 24 hours, 120,000 troops were landed at five different beachheads on the Normandy coast. They were joined by over 800,000 more men within three weeks.

Although the invading force was met by heavy German artillery fire, it fought its way through the coastal region of northern France by mid-August. By this time, another Allied force had invaded southern France and was pushing northward. The first Allied troops entered Paris on August 25, with cheering crowds lining the boulevards. Nazi rule of France had finally ended. The Allies were poised for an invasion of Germany itself.

Map Skill   *Axis influence reached its height in Europe and North Africa early in 1942. But then, Allied forces began successful offensives in North Africa, indicated by arrows on this map. The Allies invaded Italy in 1943. In June 1944, the Allies landed in Normandy, France. This invasion was a major step toward Allied victory in Western Europe. When did Soviet forces launch offensives to drive Axis armies out of Eastern Europe?*

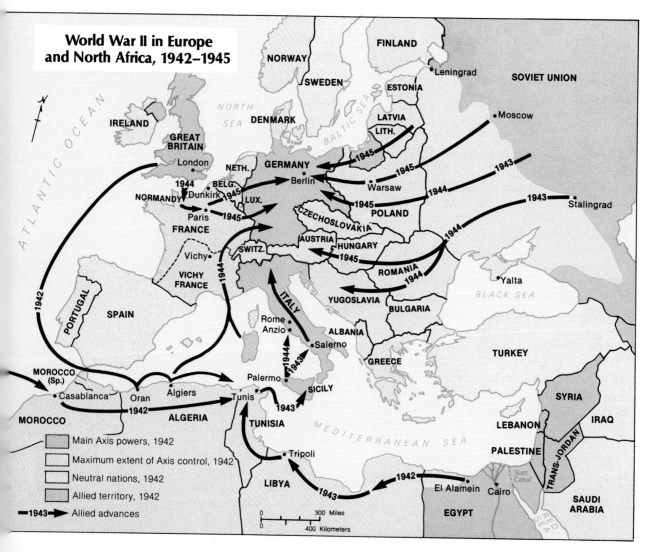

World War II in Europe and North Africa, 1942–1945

Main Axis powers, 1942
Maximum extent of Axis control, 1942
Neutral nations, 1942
Allied territory, 1942
1943 Allied advances

Advance on Berlin

More than a year before the invasion of Normandy, the Allies had begun heavy bombings of Germany. In the summer of 1943, for example, six raids by British and American planes all but wiped out the city of Hamburg. Air attacks on Germany increased in 1944. Berlin and other major cities were hit repeatedly, as were aircraft factories and oil refineries. By the end of 1944, German oil production was down 75 percent.

Allied armies crossed into Germany in mid-September 1944, but the Germans stopped their advance. The Allies were forced to withdraw, but they made plans for another invasion. These plans were disrupted in December 1944 when the Germans launched an attack on American positions in Belgium and Luxembourg near the German border. In the battle of the Bulge, the Allies at first lost ground but regained it by early January 1945.

Now Allied air attacks on Germany became fiercer than ever. In mid-February, British and American bombers attacked the city of Dresden with fire bombs, killing over 100,000 civilians. Factories and railroad lines were pounded into rubble.

In late April, American units approached Berlin from the west, and Soviet units approached from the east. Meanwhile, German resistance in Italy was collapsing. Mussolini tried to escape to Switzerland but was caught and killed by members of the Italian resistance.

As Allied troops approached Berlin, Hitler took refuge in an underground bunker. Realizing that Germany faced certain defeat, he committed suicide on April 30. A week later, on May 7, Germany surrendered unconditionally to the Allies. The war in Europe was over.

Turning Points in the Pacific

For six months after Pearl Harbor, the Japanese won a series of uninterrupted victories in Asia and the Pacific. In the summer of 1942, they were planning an attack on Port Moresby, New Guinea. From there, they planned to move on the Allied nation of Australia. However, in May, a Japanese fleet in the Coral Sea, east of Australia, was attacked by planes launched from American carriers. The planes destroyed several ships and checked the Japanese advance. This was Japan's first major defeat of the war.

A second Japanese defeat occurred a month later at Midway, about 1,000 miles (1,600 kilometers) from Hawaii. A large Japanese fleet on its way to attack the American fleet at Midway was badly damaged by American planes, and the Japanese withdrew. (See the map on page 640.)

After the battle of Midway, the United States took the offensive in the Pacific. Its goal was to recapture the Philippines and invade Japan. The Americans devised an "island hopping" campaign. They decided not to try to take every Japanese-held island but rather to bypass some and occupy others. The captured islands would serve as stepping-stones to their objectives.

The Americans advanced slowly and with heavy casualties. The Japanese fought with tremendous determination, but they had to give up one strategic outpost after another. In October 1944, General MacArthur returned to the Philippines, taking Manila in February 1945.

On the Asian mainland, the Allies supported nationalist forces who resisted the Japanese. In China, the United States aided Chiang Kai-shek. In Indochina, the Allies supplied Ho Chi Minh, leader of a coalition of communists and nationalists known as the Viet Minh. Japan suffered few defeats on the mainland, but resistance there tied up many Japanese troops.

Defeat of Japan

On April 1, 1945, United States forces landed on Okinawa, a small Japanese island about 1,000 miles (1,600 kilometers) from Tokyo. American casualties there were especially heavy. Japanese pilots carried out kamikaze* attacks, suicide missions in which they crashed planes loaded with explosives into

---

* Kamikaze means "divine wind" in Japanese. When the Mongols threatened Japan in the thirteenth century, the Mongol fleet was destroyed by a typhoon, which the Japanese named kamikaze.

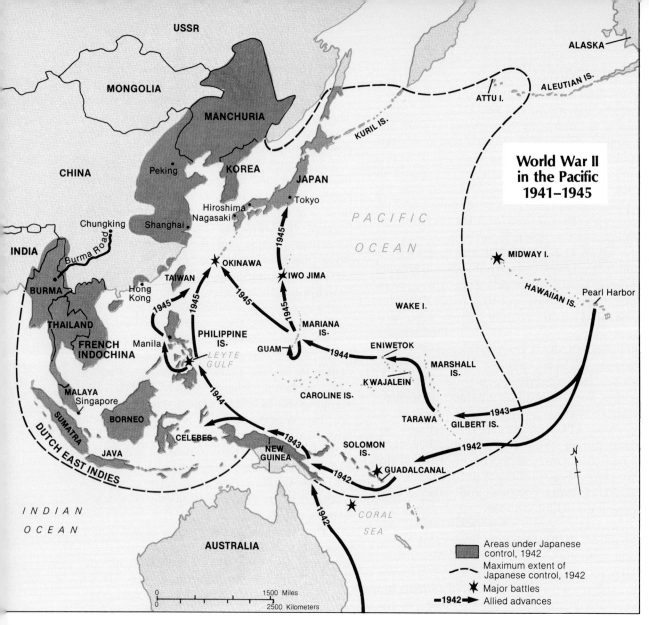

Map Skill *By 1942, the Japanese empire in Asia had reached its height. Japan controlled much of China, Southeast Asia, the Philippines, and a string of islands across the Pacific. After the battle of Midway, however, the United States went on the offensive. By island-hopping, Allied forces regained control of strategic bases. When did they retake the Philippines? What major battles were fought as the Allies prepared to invade Japan?*

American ships. Japanese infantry fought with equal fanaticism. American troops finally captured Okinawa at the end of June.

By this time, Allied planes were bombing Japan with ferocity. In a single raid on Tokyo in March 1945, 100,000 people died and over 60 percent of the commercial buildings were wiped out. By the summer of 1945, most of the Japanese navy and air force had

been destroyed. Yet Japan still had an army of 2 million men. Just as important, the Japanese retained the will to fight. The road to final victory for the Allies appeared long and difficult.

In the United States, Harry S. Truman had succeeded President Roosevelt, who had died in April 1945. In mid-July 1945, the United States successfully tested an atomic bomb in the New Mexico desert. The atomic bomb was much more devastating than conventional bombs. Truman hesitated to use this new weapon. But Truman's military advisers warned that an American invasion of Japan might result in as many as 1 million American casualties. Truman decided to use the atomic bomb on Japan if necessary.

From mid-July to early August, Truman met with Stalin and Churchill at Potsdam, Germany. The three Allied leaders warned the Japanese, without being specific, that if they did not agree to unconditional surrender they would suffer "complete and utter destruction." The Japanese ignored this warning.

On August 6, 1945, the United States dropped an atomic bomb on Hiroshima. The blast leveled 42 square miles (109 square kilometers) of the city and killed at least 80,000 people immediately. Almost 40,000 others were seriously injured, and countless thousands were stricken with radiation sickness.

Despite the destruction at Hiroshima, Japan still refused to surrender. Three days later a second atomic bomb was dropped on Nagasaki, killing 40,000. Japan could hold out no longer. On August 14, the Japanese surrendered, ending World War II.

SECTION REVIEW

1. Locate: El Alamein, Stalingrad, Normandy, Coral Sea, Midway, Okinawa, Hiroshima, Nagasaki.

2. Identify: Erwin Rommel, Bernard Montgomery, Dwight Eisenhower, D-Day.

3. What action did the United States government take against Japanese Americans after the Japanese attack on Pearl Harbor?

4. How was Stalingrad a turning point?

5. Why did the Allies decide to open a second front in Italy?

6. (a) Describe the "island hopping" campaign of the United States. (b) Was it successful?

7. What factors contributed to President Truman's decision to use the atomic bomb in Japan?

5 Effects of the War

Read to Learn   ■ about the human and economic costs of World War II
■ what political, scientific, and social changes resulted from the war

In September 1945, peace had returned. Once again, people surveyed the destruction of war and determined the cost—both human and material. The cost of World War II was greater than that of any other conflict in history. The effects of the war would be felt for generations.

Aftermath of War

World War I was a ground war, fought mainly from trenches. In World War II, planes traveled long distances to drop bombs. As a result, the destruction of the war was widespread. Both military and civilian deaths reached record numbers. More than 12 million soldiers lost their lives. (See the table on page 643.)

Civilians suffered much more in World War II than they had in World War I. In the Soviet Union, for example, 15 million civilians were killed. Throughout much of Europe, millions of "displaced persons" were homeless when the war ended.

The war reduced much of Europe and Japan to rubble. German bombs damaged or destroyed almost 4 million homes in Britain. Allied bombs destroyed 7 million buildings in Germany. The German invasion of the Soviet Union resulted in the destruction of 31,000 factories and 1,700 towns.

The Holocaust Revealed

One effect of the war was not fully discovered until Allied soldiers marched into Germany. This was the result of a policy that Hitler had called the "final solution of the Jewish question"—the total extermination of Jews in Europe.

641

In some areas occupied by Nazis, all the Jews of a town were shot and buried in a mass grave. At Babi Yar in the Ukraine, for example, 33,000 Jews from Kiev were killed in two days. Mass executions by shooting were too slow and too public, however, so the Nazis built huge camps for the express purpose of killing people. The most notorious were Auschwitz, Maidanek, and Treblinka in Poland. Other camps were located in Germany. Trainloads of Jews were shipped to these camps from all over Europe. There, they were stripped, forced into special chambers, and gassed.

Reports of Hitler's death camps reached the Allies throughout the war. But Allied troops were appalled at what they found when they reached these camps. Survivors told of atrocities committed by German guards. Prisoners at this death camp in Evensee, Austria, reported that people were starving to death at the rate of 2,000 a week.

Altogether, some 6 million Jews died in what has come to be called the Holocaust—the systematic murder of Jews carried out by the Nazis. Jews were not the only victims of the Nazi extermination camps. Many others—Slavs, Gypsies, the physically and mentally disabled, and political prisoners—were also killed.

Political Issues in Europe

Before the war, serious differences had divided the Soviet Union and the western powers.* Many people in the West had condemned Stalin's communist dictatorship. The Soviets, for their part, had denounced what they called "western imperialism." The need to fight Nazi Germany had made allies of the Soviet Union, Britain, and the United States. But once the German threat was ended, the old rivalry between East and West quickly reemerged.

The future of Eastern Europe became a crucial issue toward the end of the war. The Axis nations of Bulgaria, Romania, and Hungary surrendered to the Soviets when they were invaded. Soviet troops also drove the Nazis from Poland and Czechoslovakia. Thus, at the war's end, the Soviets occupied most of Eastern Europe. Stalin promised the people there that they would be allowed to determine their own futures through free elections. But the Allies feared that Stalin would impose communist regimes on the region.

Another political issue that loomed large at the end of the war was the treatment of Germany.† Soviet leaders hoped to create a weak German state that would be easily influenced by Moscow. Both Britain and the United States resisted such a plan.

The war transformed the role of Western Europe in world affairs. Enormous casu-

---

* Since World War II, the United States, the nations of Western Europe, and other nations opposed to Soviet expansion have often been referred to as the "West" or the "western powers." The Soviet Union and its allies are often called the "East" or the "eastern powers."

---

† This issue as well as the issue of Eastern Europe were discussed at wartime conferences of the Allies, as you will read in Chapter 34.

Casualties in World War II

	Military Dead	Military Wounded	Civilian Dead
Britain	398,000	475,000	65,000
France	211,000	400,000	108,000
Soviet Union	7,500,000	14,102,000	15,000,000
United States	292,000	671,000	*
Germany	2,850,000	7,250,000	5,000,000
Italy	77,500	120,000	100,000
Japan	1,576,000	500,000	300,000

All figures are estimates.
*Negligible number of civilian dead.

Source: Henri Michel, *The Second World War.*

Chart Skill *World War II resulted in a staggering number of dead and wounded. Systematic aerial bombing of cities, which the Germans had begun during the Spanish Civil War, led to many civilian casualties. The bombings of Hiroshima and Nagasaki resulted in over 150,000 casualties. Which nation bore the greatest burden in both military and civilian casualties?*

alties and physical damage had drained its strength. Leadership in world affairs was now in the hands of two superpowers, the United States and the Soviet Union.

The Postwar World

The world after World War II was very different from what it had been before the war. The conflict set in motion changes that could not be ignored.

Nationalism became a major force throughout the world. In colonies ruled by European nations, demands for independence were stronger than ever. People in some colonies, such as India, had done a good share of the fighting in the war and had been promised greater freedom as a reward. In other colonies, such as French Indochina, nationalists had fought against the Japanese during the war. They were determined to resist a return to European rule.

The war contributed to social changes in many countries. In the United States, for example, black Americans gained job opportunities that had long been denied them. In June 1941, President Roosevelt had issued an order banning racial discrimination in businesses that had government defense contracts. This action raised hopes for further government action against racial discrimination.

The economic role of women also changed. In Britain, about 80 percent of women between the ages of 18 and 40 either held a job or served in the military during the war. Thousands returned to their homes with the coming of peace, but many saw a future of wider opportunities.

The war years were marked by far-reaching developments in science and technology. Scientists developed synthetic materials to replace natural ones that were in short supply. Improvements in airplanes, the invention of radar, and other developments changed the nature of war itself. However, the development of the atomic bomb may have had the most significant impact on the future. Many people have called the years since 1945 the "Atomic Age."

SECTION REVIEW

1. Identify: Holocaust.
2. What contributed to the greater number of civilian deaths in World War II than in World War I?
3. What did Hitler mean by the "final solution of the Jewish question"?
4. Describe one political issue that emerged at the end of the war.
5. How did the war affect nationalism in European colonies?

Chapter 33 Review

In Perspective

Between 1936 and 1939, aggression by Italy and Germany threatened the peace. Germany and Italy met little resistance from other nations. But when Germany invaded Poland in September 1939, Britain and France declared war, and World War II began.

The German army quickly conquered Poland, and by the end of June 1940 Germany controlled most of Western Europe. However, its efforts to defeat Britain through air attacks failed. In June 1941, the Nazis invaded the Soviet Union, driving deep into Soviet territory.

The United States provided aid to the Allies through the Lend-Lease Act, but it remained technically neutral until the Japanese attacked Pearl Harbor. By May 1942, Japan had conquered a large part of East Asia and the Pacific.

In 1942, the Allies began to advance against the Axis powers. Victories in North Africa led to an Allied invasion of Italy, and the Soviet Union began a successful counter-offensive at Stalingrad. In the Pacific, the United States won important battles in the Coral Sea and at Midway. The landing at Normandy in June 1944 led to the final defeat of Germany. In the Pacific, a costly campaign of island hopping ended when the United States dropped atomic bombs on two Japanese cities. With the Japanese surrender, World War II ended.

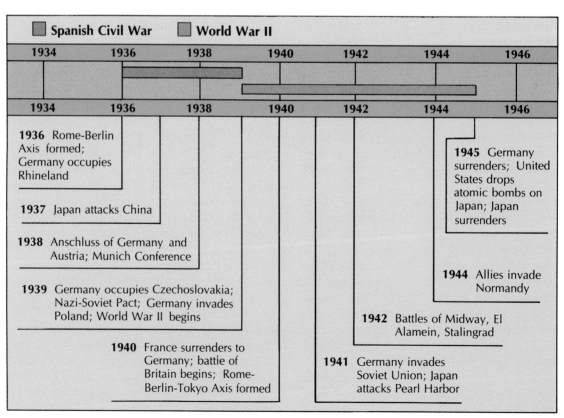

Spanish Civil War	World War II

1934	1936	1938	1940	1942	1944	1946

1936 Rome-Berlin Axis formed; Germany occupies Rhineland

1937 Japan attacks China

1938 Anschluss of Germany and Austria; Munich Conference

1939 Germany occupies Czechoslovakia; Nazi-Soviet Pact; Germany invades Poland; World War II begins

1940 France surrenders to Germany; battle of Britain begins; Rome-Berlin-Tokyo Axis formed

1941 Germany invades Soviet Union; Japan attacks Pearl Harbor

1942 Battles of Midway, El Alamein, Stalingrad

1944 Allies invade Normandy

1945 Germany surrenders; United States drops atomic bombs on Japan; Japan surrenders

Recalling Facts

Review the time line on page 644 and your reading in this chapter. Then choose the letter of the correct time period for each of the following events.

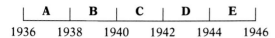

| A | B | C | D | E |

1936   1938   1940   1942   1944   1946

1. France surrenders to Germany.
2. The British defeat the Germans at El Alamein.
3. German troops invade Poland.
4. Atomic bombs are dropped on Hiroshima and Nagasaki.
5. At the Munich conference, European powers agree to German occupation of the Sudetenland.
6. The Japanese attack Pearl Harbor.
7. The Spanish Civil War begins.
8. German troops occupy the Rhineland.
9. The Allied invasion of Normandy begins.
10. United States forces defeat the Japanese at Midway.

Chapter Checkup

1. (a) Why was the Spanish Civil War an international issue? (b) What lesson did Hitler and Mussolini learn from the Spanish Civil War?
2. Describe the policy of appeasement as it was carried out in each of the following events: (a) German occupation of the Rhineland; (b) the Anschluss; (c) the Munich conference.
3. (a) Why did Hitler want to form an alliance with Stalin before he invaded Poland? (b) What did Stalin gain from the Nazi-Soviet Pact?
4. (a) Describe the Nazi conquest of Western Europe. (b) Why was the battle of Britain important?
5. (a) Why did Hitler invade the Soviet Union? (b) How was the German advance halted at the end of 1941?
6. Why was Japan so successful in the months immediately following Pearl Harbor?
7. Describe the effect each of the following battles had on the outcome of the war: (a) El Alamein; (b) Stalingrad; (c) Normandy; (d) Coral Sea; (e) Midway.
8. (a) What were the immediate effects of the war on people's lives? (b) What was its long-range impact?

Critical Thinking

1. **Identifying Immediate and Long-Range Causes** Review Chapter 32 and your reading in this chapter. (a) What was the immediate cause of World War II? (b) What long-range causes can you identify? (c) What relationships do you see between the immediate and long-range causes?
2. **Expressing an Opinion** Many historians argue that Hitler could have been stopped if Great Britain and France had reacted strongly when German troops occupied the Rhineland in 1936. (a) Do you agree? Why or why not? (b) At what other point or points do you think Hitler could have been stopped?

Relating Past to Present

1. What development during World War II do you think still has the greatest impact on the world today? Explain.

Developing Basic Skills

1. **Using Visual Evidence** Study the photographs on pages 624, 631, and 635. Then answer the following questions: (a) What is the subject of each photograph? (b) What can you learn about the nature of World War II from the photographs?
2. **Map Reading** Study the map on page 638 and then answer the following questions: (a) What is the topic of the map? (b) What were the main Axis nations in Europe in 1942? (c) Which nations were not controlled by the Axis in 1942? (d) Which nation do you think would have control of Eastern Europe by the end of the war in 1945? Why?
3. **Comparing** Make a chart with two rows and three columns. Title the rows Bismarck and Hitler, and title the columns Goals, Methods, and Results. Review what you learned in Chapter 26 about Bismarck and the unification of Germany. In the appropriate column, describe the main foreign policy goals of each man, the methods each used to try to achieve his goals, and the results of his efforts. Then answer the following questions: (a) Compare the goals of Bismarck and Hitler. (b) Compare their methods. (c) Which do you think was more successful? Why?

See page 807 for suggested readings.

34 European Recovery and the Cold War

(1945–1968)

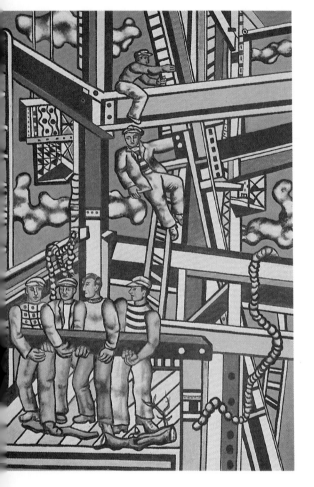

Construction Workers,
by Fernand Léger.

Chapter Outline

1   A Return to Peace

2   Beginning of the Cold War

3   Rebuilding Western Europe

4   The Soviet Union and Eastern Europe

5   Developments in the United States

In March 1946, less than a year after the end of World War II, Winston Churchill made a speech to the graduates of Westminster College in Fulton, Missouri. In his speech, the former prime minister of Britain described postwar Europe: "From Stettin in the Baltic to Trieste in the Adriatic, an iron curtain has descended across the Continent. Behind that line lie all the capitals of the ancient states of Central and Eastern Europe. Warsaw, Berlin, Prague, Vienna, Budapest, Belgrade, Bucharest and Sofia, all these famous cities and populations around them lie in what I must call the Soviet sphere, and all are subject in one form or another, not only to Soviet influence but to a very high and, in many cases, increasing measure of control from Moscow."

The iron curtain Churchill referred to isolated the areas under Soviet influence from the rest of the world. Stalin had clamped strict controls on travel abroad. No "unauthorized" books, newspapers, or magazines were allowed into the Soviet sphere. Foreign radio programs were jammed.

Churchill went on to plead for Anglo-American unity and a strong stand against the expansion of Soviet influence. "From what I have seen of our Russian friends and Allies during the war," he said, "I am convinced that there is nothing for which they have less respect than for weakness, especially military weakness." Churchill urged that the mistakes of the 1930s not be repeated.

Churchill, like many Americans and Western Europeans, worried that the Soviet occupation of Eastern Europe would lead to further Soviet expansion. Tension between the Soviet Union and the western powers was a major problem in the postwar period. This period also witnessed rapid economic recovery from the war, as you will read in this chapter.

1 A Return to Peace

Read to Learn
- what the wartime conferences decided
- how the Allies created the United Nations

When World War II finally ended, the Allied leaders were anxious to avoid the mistakes of the Versailles Treaty of World War I. They did not want the peace settlements to plant the seeds of a future war. But even before the war ended, signs of conflict among the Allies had become evident.

Wartime Conferences

Almost from the beginning of World War II, Allied leaders had met from time to time to plan strategy and discuss postwar policy. The crucial meetings involved the Big Three: Winston Churchill, Franklin D. Roosevelt, and Joseph Stalin.

Even before the United States entered the war, President Roosevelt and Prime Minister Churchill had stated the principles they thought should form the basis of a postwar settlement. In August 1941, they met aboard a British warship in the North Atlantic and issued the Atlantic Charter. This document supported "the right of all peoples to choose the form of government under which they will live." It urged economic cooperation and a "permanent system of general security" to protect nations from "aggression outside of their frontiers."

Churchill, Roosevelt, and Stalin met for the first time in Teheran, Iran, in November 1943. Their main concern was the forthcoming invasion of France. But the three leaders also discussed tentative plans for dealing with Poland and Germany after the war.

The Big Three met again in February 1945 at Yalta, in southern Russia. The war in Europe was near an end, but Allied commanders feared a long, costly campaign in the Pacific. Churchill and Roosevelt wanted

One of the wartime conferences was held at Yalta in the Soviet Union. The Allied leaders posed for the news cameras before or after their meetings each day. In the front row of this photograph, from left to right, are British Prime Minister Winston Churchill, American President Franklin D. Roosevelt, and Soviet Premier Joseph Stalin.

Soviet support in the fight against Japan. Stalin agreed to enter the war against Japan shortly after Germany surrendered. In return, the Soviet Union would receive some territory and other concessions in East Asia.

The future of Eastern Europe was another important topic discussed at Yalta. The Allies agreed that free elections would be held in the Eastern European countries. Eastern Poland was to become part of the Soviet Union, and Poland would receive land in the west as compensation. Germany was to be divided into American, British, French, and Soviet zones of occupation.

The three leaders also agreed to take part in the United Nations, an international peacekeeping organization. Although the meeting at Yalta was a friendly one, its results would cause conflict between the western powers and the Soviet Union.

Conflicts began to appear at the last conference, which was held in Potsdam, Germany, in July 1945. By this time, Harry Truman had succeeded Franklin D. Roosevelt as President. Truman was unhappy with the pro-Soviet governments that had been set up in several countries in Eastern Europe. When he demanded immediate free elections in accordance with the Yalta agreement, Stalin refused. Stalin stated, "A freely elected government in any of these East European countries would be anti-Soviet, and that we cannot allow."

The Occupation of Germany

After Germany surrendered on May 7, 1945, eastern Germany became the Soviet occupation zone, and the rest of the country was divided among Britain, the United States, and France. Berlin, the capital of Germany, lay within the Soviet zone. It was also divided among the four powers. (See the map below.)

Much of Germany had been devastated by the war. Buildings lay in rubble, food was scarce, and epidemics were a threat. Adding to the chaos were millions of refugees who streamed into Germany. Some came from the Sudetenland of Czechoslovakia; others came from German territories that had been given to Poland.

No formal peace treaty ended the war with Germany. Each of the Allies followed its own policy. The Soviet Union punished Germany for the heavy Soviet losses in the war. In their zone, Soviet officials dismantled factories and shipped heavy machinery, trucks, and locomotives east to the Soviet Union.

The United States, Britain, and France took a different approach. They thought that a German nation with a sound economy and a democratic government was the best guarantee against the rise of another Hitler. A strong Germany would also serve as a buffer against the Soviet Union. Therefore, rather than punishing Germany, the western powers helped rebuild the economy in the zones they controlled.

The division of Germany into occupation zones was considered a temporary measure in 1945. However, as time went on, a reunified Germany seemed less and less

Map Skill *During World War II, the Allies drew up plans for the occupation of Germany. Britain, the United States, France, and the Soviet Union each had its own zone of occupation after the war. Berlin, the capital of Nazi Germany, was also divided among the four powers. In which country's zone was Berlin?*

likely. In 1949, Britain, the United States, and France combined their three zones into one nation—the German Federal Republic, or West Germany. Bonn was made the capital of the nation. Konrad Adenauer, leader of the Christian Democratic party, was elected chancellor.

That same year, the Soviet zone became the German Democratic Republic, or East Germany. East Germany was firmly under Soviet control. For the next several years, it continued to suffer from the Soviet policy of economic exploitation. It also suffered from a population drain as thousands of people fled to West Germany.

War Crimes Trials and Denazification

Although the wartime Allies did not agree on overall postwar policy toward Germany, they agreed that Nazism had to be destroyed. One way of achieving this goal was public trials of former Nazi leaders. The Allies chose Nuremberg, the site of many of Hitler's mass rallies, as the location of these trials, known as the Nuremberg trials.

Hitler and Goebbels had committed suicide when the Allies closed in on Berlin. But 20 other former Nazi officials were brought to trial in August 1945. Judges and prosecutors from all four Allied nations took part. The charges included waging aggressive war and "crimes against humanity." Among the crimes were the use of slave labor and the operation of extermination camps. Three Nazi officials were acquitted, seven were sentenced to life imprisonment, and ten were sentenced to death. Trials of other former Nazi officials were held later in Nuremberg and other German cities.

The Allied goal of *denazification* included removing all traces of Nazism in Germany. The occupation powers set up denazification courts to try local Nazi leaders. These trials soon proved to be unmanageable, however, partly because reliable evidence was hard to obtain. They were abandoned after a few months. But other efforts were made to end Nazi influence. Nazi symbols were removed from schools and public places. Nazi textbooks were replaced with ones that taught respect for democracy.

The United Nations

During the war, Allied leaders had planned to create the United Nations (UN), an international organization devoted to world peace. In April 1945, delegates from 50 nations met in San Francisco and adopted the United Nations Charter. The charter committed member nations to submit international disputes to the United Nations for peaceful settlement. Members also agreed to work together to solve the world problems of disease, hunger, and illiteracy.

UN structure. According to the charter, the United Nations has six major bodies. (See the diagram on page 650.) The General Assembly and the Security Council are the two most important bodies. The General Assembly includes representatives from every member nation. It discusses world problems brought before it and recommends action. The Security Council has fifteen members. Ten members serve for two-year terms. Five members are permanent. The charter gave permanent membership to the main Allies of World War II—Great Britain, the United States, the Soviet Union, China, and France.

The Security Council investigates world conflicts and decides on what action the United Nations should take. Among other actions, it can call for economic sanctions or send a peacekeeping force made up of soldiers from member nations. However, the Security Council cannot force member nations to agree to its decisions. Furthermore, any one of the five permanent members can veto Security Council decisions. This power of veto has often paralyzed the Security Council. For example, the Soviet Union cast 77 vetoes between 1945 and 1955. Only 3 other vetoes were cast during this period.

Peacekeeping efforts. Despite the problems, the United Nations has helped bring peace to several unstable areas of the world. In 1947, the UN proposed that the British mandate of Palestine be divided into an Arab and a Jewish state. In 1948, Jewish residents declared their part of the mandate the state of Israel. Shortly afterwards, war broke out between Arabs and Israelis. UN representatives worked for two years to achieve a cease-fire. A shaky peace was monitored by

The United Nations

Security Council
investigates situations that threaten the peace and develops UN policies

Secretariat
is responsible for the administrative work of the UN, headed by the secretary-general

General Assembly
discusses issues and recommends actions

Economic and Social Council
promotes human rights and works for improved economic and social conditions

International Court of Justice
rules on international legal disputes

Trusteeship Council
administers territories that were not self-governing when the UN was established

Chart Skill   *During World War II, Allied leaders agreed on the need to set up an international peacekeeping organization after the war. Thus, in 1945, representatives from 50 nations met in San Francisco and adopted the Charter of the United Nations. Which of the six major UN bodies is responsible for developing UN policies?*

a UN police force, although fighting erupted again in 1956 and 1967. UN mediation also ended fighting between India and Pakistan in 1949. UN forces were sent to Korea in 1950, to the Congo in 1961, and to Cyprus in 1964.

As time passed, the United Nations underwent considerable change. Conflicts between the United States and the Soviet Union weakened the Security Council. The Council was powerless to act in any dispute about which these two superpowers disagreed. When disagreements between the Soviet Union and the United States became common, attention shifted to the General Assembly as a forum. The makeup of the General Assembly also changed. UN member-ship increased, and the balance of power swung away from the superpowers to smaller, developing nations.

SECTION REVIEW

1. Locate: Berlin.
2. Identify: Konrad Adenauer.
3. Define: denazification.
4. What agreement about Poland was reached at Yalta?
5. What was the Soviet policy toward the part of Germany it occupied after the war?
6. Describe the results of the Nuremberg trials.
7. What actions can the United Nations Security Council take in response to world conflict?

2 Beginning of the Cold War

Read to Learn
- how the United States countered Soviet expansion
- how Berlin became a focus of the cold war

In 1946, when Churchill made his iron curtain speech, some people thought his warnings about Soviet expansion were exaggerated. By the end of 1947, however, it was clear that the wartime alliance had fallen apart and that a cold war was beginning. A *cold war* is a state of tension and hostility without armed conflict. Eastern Europe was an early trouble spot in the cold war.

Expansion of Soviet Influence

Toward the end of the war, Soviet troops had moved into Czechoslovakia, Hungary, Romania, and Bulgaria as they forced the Germans westward. After the war, new governments were set up in the countries of Eastern Europe. At first, these governments were coalitions of communists and noncommunists. But gradually, noncommunists were forced out, as were communists who were not loyal to Stalin.

By 1948, the governments of all the countries of Eastern Europe were under communist control. These nations became known as Soviet satellites or Soviet bloc countries. Albania and Yugoslavia, which had not been occupied by Soviet troops during the war, also had communist governments.

Even before the war ended, Stalin had argued that the Soviet Union needed friendly governments in Eastern Europe as a buffer zone against any future German attack. However, to many people in Western Europe and the United States, the Soviet Union seemed bent on world domination. They saw evidence of the expansion of communism in several parts of the world.

In Greece, communists were involved in a civil war against the government. Turkey also felt menaced when the Soviet Union renounced their friendship pact. Furthermore, the Soviet Union demanded the right to fortify the straits between the Black Sea and the Mediterranean. In China, the communist

revolution against Chiang Kai-shek that began in the 1930s took on new force, as you will read in Chapter 37. In Southeast Asia, communist-led forces were battling the French and slowly gaining ground.

The American Response

Before World War II, Britain and France had stood against Soviet ambitions in the Balkans and elsewhere. Now the British and French were too weak to do so. Only the United States had the military and economic strength to counter Soviet power.

In the postwar years, the Soviet Union was the strongest military power in Europe. This French poster expresses the concern felt by many Western European nations and the United States about the Soviet military threat. Stalin is shown in the center with one foot on a white cross.

Containment and the Truman Doctrine. George Kennan, an American diplomat, urged a policy of containment in response to Soviet expansion. The United States, he said, should contain, or hold, the Soviets within their current boundaries by applying political, economic, and, if necessary, military pressure whenever the Soviets tried to expand.

The policy of containment was first applied by President Truman in Greece and Turkey. In February 1947, Britain informed the United States that it could no longer afford to send economic help to the Greek government. Truman was afraid the communists would win the civil war as a result, so he stepped in. In March 1947, he proclaimed the Truman Doctrine. It stated that the United States would support free peoples resisting "attempted subjugation [domination] by armed minorities or by outside pressures." Congress approved $400 million in economic assistance to Greece and Turkey. With this aid, the Greek government defeated the communists, and the Turks were able to withstand Soviet pressure.

The Marshall Plan. The United States also responded to the threat of communist expansion with large-scale economic aid to the war-ravaged nations of Europe. Recovery from the war was proving to be a difficult task. On a trip to Europe in 1947, Secretary of State George Marshall noted that millions of people still faced a daily battle against "hunger, poverty, desperation, and chaos." He feared that nations that could not deal with these problems were in danger of revolution and collapse.

In June 1947, Marshall proposed that the United States organize and fund a program of European recovery. This program became known as the Marshall Plan. All European nations, including those in the Soviet bloc, were invited to participate. Czechoslovakia and Poland seemed interested, but it soon became clear that the Soviet Union would not allow them to participate. The Soviets attacked the plan as "Yankee imperialism," and no communist nation took part.

Between 1948 and 1952, the United States poured $12 billion of aid into Western Europe. The Marshall Plan bolstered the governments and economies of Western Europe and stimulated industrial growth. By improving economic and political conditions, it reduced the danger of communist revolution.

In 1948, the Soviet Union closed all land routes into West Berlin. The United States responded by organizing a massive airlift to bring supplies to the city. Here, Berliners stand on top of a building that was bombed during World War II and watch an American cargo plane bringing in food and other vital supplies. In the 11 months of the airlift, more than 2 million tons of goods were flown into Berlin.

Focus on Berlin

The cold war came close to becoming a "hot" war in 1948 over Berlin. The Soviet Union wanted to prevent the United States, Britain, and France from combining their three German occupation zones into one country. The Soviets were afraid that the combined zone would be the first step toward a strong, reunified Germany, which would threaten Soviet power.

In June 1948, the Soviets stopped all road, rail, and river traffic through East Germany into West Berlin. They hoped to force the western powers to give up Berlin. Truman immediately ordered an American airlift of food and other supplies into West Berlin. When winter came, extra planes were added to bring in coal. The Berlin airlift continued until May 1949, when the Soviets lifted their blockade.

Berlin continued to be a focus of the cold war. Between 1949 and 1961, thousands of East Germans fled into West Berlin. Then, in 1961, the East German government built a wall between East and West Berlin to stop the flow of people. War seemed possible. President John Kennedy called up United States reserves to reinforce West German garrisons. The crisis passed, but the Berlin Wall still stands as a reminder of a divided Germany and a divided Europe.

Military Alliances

By 1949, Europe had clearly split into two opposing camps. One, led by the Soviet Union, championed international communism. The other, led by the United States, favored democracy. This split was reflected in military alliances.

In April 1949, representatives of the United States, Canada, and ten Western European nations signed a mutual defense treaty creating the North Atlantic Treaty Organization (NATO). (See the map on page 654.) Members agreed to go to the aid of any member attacked by an outsider. The United States had clearly committed itself to the defense of Western Europe against Soviet aggression.

Greece and Turkey joined NATO in 1952. When West Germany joined in 1955, the Soviet Union created its own alliance, the Warsaw Pact. In the Warsaw Pact, the Soviet Union and seven Eastern European nations agreed to provide immediate assistance if any of them went to war.

SECTION REVIEW

1. Identify: containment policy, Truman Doctrine, Marshall Plan, NATO, Warsaw Pact.
2. Define: cold war.
3. How did Stalin justify making the nations of Eastern Europe into Soviet satellites?
4. Was the Marshall Plan successful? Explain.
5. How did President Truman react to the Soviet blockade of Berlin?

3 Rebuilding Western Europe

Read to Learn ■ how Germany, France, and Britain recovered from World War II
■ how economic cooperation helped postwar Europe

In postwar Western Europe, the most urgent task was economic recovery. American economic assistance through the Marshall Plan helped a great deal. But the Marshall Plan would not have accomplished as much as it did without the efforts of Europeans to rebuild their industries, transportation systems, and cities.

The German Economic Miracle

Economic recovery was especially notable in West Germany. Between 1950 and 1958, West German industrial production more than doubled. A people facing starvation in 1945 enjoyed one of the highest standards of living in Europe in the late 1950s.

There were several reasons for this "economic miracle." The Marshall Plan provided crucial financial aid to get recovery started. Also, since many plants had been totally destroyed during the war, the Germans rebuilt modern, much more efficient ones. In addition, German political leaders were committed to economic growth. They abolished wartime controls and encouraged private investment.

Christian Democrat Konrad Adenauer led the economic recovery of West Germany. He served as chancellor from 1949 to 1961.

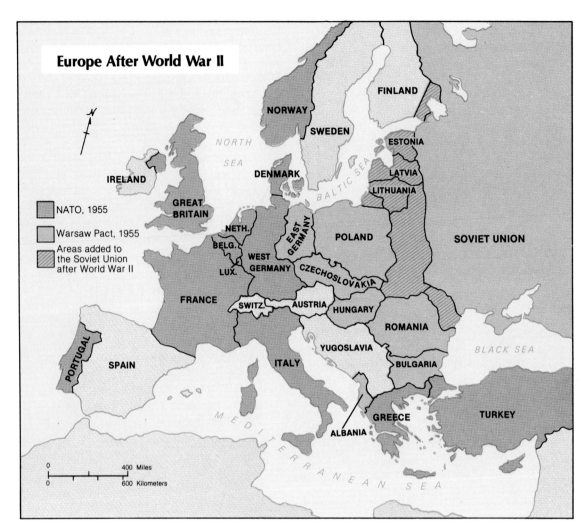

Europe After World War II

NATO, 1955

Warsaw Pact, 1955

Areas added to the Soviet Union after World War II

Map Skill *Concern over Soviet aggression in Eastern Europe led to the creation of NATO in 1949. The United States, Canada, and ten Western European nations pledged troops and money for mutual defense. In 1955, the Soviet Union created the Warsaw Pact. Which nations belonged to this rival alliance?*

Adenauer brought West Germany into NATO in 1955 and helped forge strong alliances with other western powers against the Soviet Union.

The possible reunification of Germany was a frequent political issue during the 1950s. Adenauer insisted that free elections be held throughout the entire country before any unification could take place. Since the East Germans would not agree to free elections, Germany remained divided.

After Adenauer's retirement, German economic growth began to level off. This slowdown helped the main opposition party, the Social Democrats. Under their leader, Willy Brandt, they formed a coalition with the Christian Democrats in 1966. One of Brandt's main goals was to improve relations with East Germany and other Soviet bloc countries.

Postwar France

France experienced its own economic miracle during the 1950s and 1960s. The government nationalized, or took control of, major banks and key industries such as coal and gas. It also encouraged private investment in modern factories. Industrial production increased, but political instability slowed the economic recovery.

Under the Fourth French Republic, set up in 1946, the National Assembly was the most powerful body in French government. Its operation depended on coalitions of several political parties. But coalition governments proved to be unstable.

Algeria. France was burdened with costly colonial wars in Asia and North Africa. These wars weakened public confidence in the government. As you will read in Chapter 37, the French were forced to withdraw from Indochina in 1954. That same year, war erupted in Algeria, where nationalists demanded independence. French settlers in Algeria made up about one fifth of the population. They opposed independence and demanded that France protect them.

The war in Algeria led to the downfall of the Fourth Republic. In May 1958, a group of French colonists led by some military officers seized control of the government in Algiers. Civil war seemed certain. In desperation, the National Assembly turned to the only person in France it believed could unify the country—Charles de Gaulle (duh GAHL). De Gaulle had led the Free French forces in World War II. The National Assembly gave de Gaulle complete power for six months. It also authorized him to supervise the drafting of a new constitution.

De Gaulle created the Fifth French Republic. In contrast to the Fourth Republic, it had a strong executive and a weak National Assembly. Although coalitions were still necessary, the breakup of a coalition did not affect the government as much as under the Fourth Republic. In late 1958, French voters overwhelmingly approved the constitution and elected de Gaulle the first president of the Fifth Republic.

Charles de Gaulle. De Gaulle quickly restored stability in France. In 1962, he formally ended the war in Algeria and recognized Algerian independence. The French economy improved with the end of the colonial wars.

De Gaulle was determined to restore France to a position of world leadership. He believed that neither the United Nations nor the United States could be relied on to come to the aid of Western Europe in time of trouble. Therefore, he insisted on developing French atomic weapons and pursuing an independent course in foreign policy.

In 1966, de Gaulle withdrew French troops from the NATO command. He also tried to improve relations with the Soviet Union. De Gaulle's independent course caused resentment among his western allies, but it pleased French nationalists. However, by 1968, some French were becoming dissatisfied with de Gaulle's authoritarian style of governing.

Postwar Britain

Britain faced an enormous task of rebuilding after six long years of war. Factories had to be rebuilt and modernized. Britain also had to improve its balance of trade—that is, it needed to limit imports and increase exports. To achieve this goal, the British continued wartime rationing. They did without items such as fine woolens that could be sold abroad for foreign currency. The strategy seemed to work. Ten years after the war, the British were more prosperous than they had been in 1938. Agricultural and industrial production increased by 50 percent during that period.

A welfare state. One far-reaching change in postwar Britain was the creation of a *welfare state*, one in which the government assumes responsibility for people's social and economic well-being. In the election campaign of 1945, the Labour party, led by Clement Attlee, promised to increase government services for every man, woman, and child in Britain. The voters elected a Labour majority to Parliament, and Attlee became prime minister.

Once in office, the Labour party carried out its promises. The government nationalized the coal and steel industries. It also introduced a national health service and expanded unemployment insurance and old age pensions. When the Conservative party

In 1940, German bombers destroyed most of the city of Coventry, England, including its cathedral, which was built in the 1300s. The city was rebuilt after the war. In 1962, a newly built cathedral was dedicated. It was a symbol of postwar recovery. However, the ruins of the old cathedral, shown here, were left as a memorial to those who died during World War II.

omy. At the same time, trade unions demanded higher wages. The troubled economy led to the defeat of the Conservatives in 1964. A Labour government, under Harold Wilson, returned to office to try to revive Britain's sagging economy.

From Empire to Commonwealth. Britain also saw the breakup of its empire in the postwar period. As you will read in Chapters 35 and 37, most British possessions became independent between 1947 and 1965.

When they gained their independence, the former British colonies could choose whether or not to join the British Commonwealth of Nations. This association, which was founded in 1931, linked countries that had historical and cultural ties with Britain. Former colonies that joined the Commonwealth remained independent, but they met with each other and with Britain to discuss matters of common interest. They also granted trade advantages to other members.

Canada, Australia, and New Zealand were among the original members of the Commonwealth. As you have read, these nations had won self-government in the 1800s and independence in 1931. Nearly all the nations who won independence from Britain after World War II chose to join the Commonwealth.

Recovery Elsewhere in Western Europe

In Italy, economic recovery from the war was relatively slow. For one thing, Italy had not been as industrialized before the war as other nations in Western Europe. Furthermore, economic development was unequal in northern and southern Italy. The south, poor in resources, lagged behind the more prosperous north. Despite these drawbacks, however, Marshall Plan aid helped the Italian economy. In addition, a program begun in the 1950s broke up large estates and stimulated economic development in the south. As a result, Italy experienced economic growth during the 1950s and early 1960s.

Throughout the 1950s and 1960s, the Christian Democrats dominated Italian poli-

returned to power in 1951, it accepted almost all the Labour party's changes.

Britain faced growing economic competition in international trade in the 1950s. The trade surplus Britain enjoyed in the early 1950s was reversed by the end of the decade. Low productivity, high taxes, and unemployment further hindered the econ-

Changes in European Eating Habits, 1947–1958

	Potatoes		Fresh Fruit		Cheese		Meat	
Britain	253	209	83	94	9	9	100	145
France	326	266	72	92	10	18	117	153
Germany	416	339	65	128	7	15	52	114

☐ Average pounds per person per year, 1947–1950
▨ Average pounds per person per year, 1956–1958

Source: P. Lamartine Yates, *Food, Land and Manpower in Western Europe.*

Chart Skill • *During World War II and for a number of years after it, European governments rationed fruit, dairy products, and meat because of shortages. By the mid-1950s, however, European farming as well as industry had recovered. How did potato consumption per person change in Britain between the two periods shown on this chart? In which European country did meat consumption per person increase the most?*

tics. However, they were challenged by a strong Communist party that had the support of part of the Socialist party. Other socialists supported the Christian Democrats. In the late 1960s, slow economic growth contributed to political instability in Italy.

In Scandinavia, the extent of wartime damage varied from country to country. Sweden, which remained neutral, and Denmark had seen little fighting and recovered quickly. Norway had suffered greater damage, but it rebuilt its cities and merchant fleet in a fairly short time.

All the Scandinavian countries introduced some form of moderate socialism and maintained welfare states. Most business remained in private hands, but the government owned transportation and communication facilities and such vital industries as steel. Comprehensive benefits paid for education, medical care, and pensions. These measures helped redistribute income among more people, but they also resulted in very high taxes.

Economic Cooperation

After World War I, European nations had raised tariff barriers so high that international trade had suffered severely. Leaders in post-World War II Europe did not want to repeat this mistake. They stressed cooperation rather than competition.

A first step toward economic cooperation was the Schuman Plan, adopted in 1951. This plan set up the European Coal and Steel Community, joined by France, West Germany, Italy, Belgium, the Netherlands, and Luxembourg. These nations pooled their coal and steel resources, eliminating tariffs on these vital materials. Each country had equal access to coal and steel at uniform prices. Between 1952 and 1960, iron and steel production rose by 75 percent in these nations.

The success of the European Coal and Steel Community led its members to create the European Economic Community in 1957. The European Economic Community is usually called the Common Market. Members of the Common Market reduced tariffs and made it easier for people to travel from one member country to another. These measures stimulated the economy of Europe during the 1960s. The 1970s, however, brought an economic slowdown.

The success of the Common Market during the 1960s created hopes for greater economic and political cooperation in Europe. Yet one of the most important

European nations, Great Britain, did not belong to the Common Market.

Throughout the 1960s, Britain tried unsuccessfully to join the Common Market. France vetoed its applications for membership, partly because of Britain's special economic relationship with members of the British Commonwealth. In 1959, Britain formed a competing trade group, the European Free Trade Association. Its members included Austria, Denmark, Norway, Portugal, Sweden, and Switzerland. Industrial production in these nations increased during the 1960s but at only about half the rate of that in the Common Market countries.

SECTION REVIEW

1. Identify: Willy Brandt, Charles de Gaulle, Clement Attlee, European Economic Community.
2. Define: welfare state.
3. What was the German economic miracle?
4. How did Charles de Gaulle show France's independence in world affairs?
5. What economic troubles did Britain face in the late 1950s and early 1960s?
6. Why was recovery from the war slower in Italy than in other Western European nations?
7. Describe one action taken by the Common Market to stimulate trade.

4 The Soviet Union and Eastern Europe

Read to Learn
■ about Khrushchev's policies for the Soviet Union
■ about 1950s developments in Yugoslavia, Poland, and Hungary

Nearly 20 million Russians had lost their lives during World War II. After the war, the Soviet Union faced a massive task of reconstruction. Hundreds of thousands of acres of farmland had been laid bare by the Nazi invasion. Entire cities had been destroyed.

Stalin's Last Years

During the war, the Soviet government and people had worked together to defend the homeland. Many of Stalin's controls had been relaxed. Once the war was over, however, Stalin reestablished totalitarian control.

In 1946, Stalin announced a five-year economic plan designed to rebuild Soviet industry to its prewar level. The plan emphasized heavy industry, construction, and armaments. By 1953, Soviet industrial production exceeded its prewar level. But agricultural production lagged far behind, and consumer goods for the Soviet people remained in short supply. Furthermore, people's wages bought 40 percent less than in 1928.

Stalin also cracked down on intellectual freedom. Artists, writers, and musicians who did not follow the official party line were viciously attacked. A new round of purges filled forced-labor camps. Stalin also kindled anti-Semitism as a result of his false claim that Jewish doctors had tried to poison him.

Stalin died in 1953. His death was followed by a power struggle among rival party leaders. Finally a new Communist party boss, Nikita Khrushchev (KROOS chehv), rose to the top.

The Khrushchev Era

In 1956, Khrushchev shocked the world by denouncing Stalin in a speech to a party congress. He accused Stalin of being a murderer, a traitor, and a tyrant responsible for terrible crimes against the Soviet people. Khrushchev went on to criticize the "cult of personality" that had glorified Stalin.

The Soviet Union entered a period of reform after this speech. The reforms became known as de-Stalinization. Conditions in some labor camps were eased, and other camps were closed. Writers and artists gained some freedom, and programs of cultural exchange with the West were launched. The city of Stalingrad was renamed Volgograd. Despite these changes, however, the government remained in control of all aspects of Soviet society. In 1958, for example, it prevented the Russian writer Boris Pasternak from accepting the Nobel prize for his novel *Dr. Zhivago.*

In his economic planning, Khrushchev emphasized agricultural production. He also tried experimenting with less central control of the economy. The government cautiously introduced some incentives to increase production. For example, it gave individual managers more control over how to meet the production goals of their farms and factories.

As a result of such efforts, the Soviet standard of living did improve, but it remained far below the standard of living in the United States and Western Europe. One Soviet achievement of this period that startled the world was the successful 1957 launching of *Sputnik,* the first artificial satellite to orbit the earth.

De-Stalinization also affected the Soviet attitude toward the West. The result was a thaw in the cold war. Instead of speaking of an inevitable clash between communism and capitalism, Khrushchev spoke of a need for "peaceful coexistence" between the world's two superpowers. The new spirit of cooperation favored talks to slow the arms race and ban the testing of nuclear weapons. In 1959, Khrushchev traveled to the United States. He toured factories, inspected an Iowa farm, and visited Hollywood. At the end of his tour, Khrushchev met with President Eisenhower.

The thaw in the cold war was marred by incidents that threatened to lead to conflict between East and West. Early in May 1960, an American spy plane was shot down over Soviet territory. Khrushchev angrily canceled the summit conference that had been planned for later in the month. In the summer of 1961, the building of the Berlin Wall led to another crisis that only gradually died down. (See page 653.)

Khruschev's rule ended in 1964, when party associates forced him to resign from office and retire to a farm in his native village. He was succeeded as party chief by Leonid Brezhnev (BREHZH nehf). As you will read in Chapter 39, Brezhnev would

During his 1959 visit to the United States, Soviet Premier Nikita Khrushchev visited a farm in Coon Rapids, Iowa. He told his host, Roswald Garst, that Iowa corn was superior to corn grown in the Soviet Union. Khrushchev was not always as pleased with his visit to the United States as he appears here. He was not allowed to visit Disneyland because police could not guarantee his safety. A disappointed Khrushchev commented: "Just imagine, I, a Premier, a Soviet representative . . . told that I could not go. . . . Why not? . . . Do you have rocket launching pads there? . . . Or have gangsters taken hold of the place?"

back away from some of Khrushchev's policies.

An Independent Course in Yugoslavia

Yugoslavia, led by Marshall Tito, was one country in Eastern Europe that was not a Soviet satellite. Tito, a communist, had led Yugoslav resistance against the Nazis during World War II. After the Germans were forced out of Yugoslavia, he assumed power as dictator. He nationalized industry and made plans for economic growth.

A strong nationalist, Tito was unwilling to take directions from Stalin. Stalin's

659

response was to expel Yugoslavia from the bloc of Soviet-aligned communist nations in 1948. From that time on, Tito followed an independent course. He granted some measure of economic and individual freedom, but he was quick to crack down on any threats to his dictatorship.

Tito proclaimed Yugoslavia neutral in any East-West conflicts. Yugoslavia did not join NATO or the Warsaw Pact. After Stalin's death, Khrushchev tried to lure Tito into the Soviet bloc. But the Yugoslav leader continued to go his own way.

Unrest in Poland and Hungary

Khrushchev's denunciation of Stalin encouraged two other Eastern European nations, Poland and Hungary, to try to free themselves from Soviet domination. In 1956, Polish workers rioted for higher pay and better working conditions.

In the fall, communist leader Wladyslaw Gomulka (VLAH dee slah guh MOOL kuh) took control of the government. Gomulka was an anti-Stalinist who had served time in prison during Stalin's postwar crackdown. He dissolved the secret police and allowed workers' councils to speak for labor. The Soviets protested and threatened to send troops. In the end, however, Khrushchev accepted the new Polish regime. Poland remained a member of the Warsaw Pact, and Gomulka continued to support Soviet foreign policy.

Encouraged by the Polish example, Hungarian students and workers demonstrated in the fall of 1956. Imre Nagy (NAH djuh), like Tito and Gomulka a nationalist communist leader, became premier. Nagy ended one-party rule and called for free elections. He also pledged to withdraw Hungary from the Warsaw Pact and appealed to western nations for economic aid.

Nagy's plans for western-style democracy and withdrawal from the Soviet alliance displeased the Soviet Union. Khrushchev sent Soviet troops into Hungary. Nagy was removed from power and eventually executed. After bitter fighting, Soviet troops crushed the uprising and thousands of Hungarians fled to the West. Western nations stood by without taking any action. Although the Soviet Union regained control of Hungary in 1956, there would be other challenges to Soviet control of Eastern Europe in the future.

In 1956, strong nationalist feelings in Hungary led to demonstrations against Soviet domination. The anti-Soviet movement within Hungary was spearheaded by students and intellectuals, but it had wide popular support. Here, demonstrators burn pictures of Stalin. The Soviets blamed the Hungarian uprising on foreign intervention. Soviet troops eventually moved in and crushed the uprising.

SECTION REVIEW

1. Identify: Nikita Khrushchev, de-Stalinization, Marshall Tito, Wladyslaw Gomulka, Imre Nagy.
2. Describe one way in which Stalin took control of Soviet society after World War II.
3. What was the result of the thaw in the cold war after Stalin's death?
4. How did Stalin react to Tito's refusal to be dominated by the Soviet Union?
5. Why did Khrushchev accept Gomulka's regime in Poland?

5 Developments in the United States

Read to Learn ■ how the United States responded to domestic problems
■ how the United States handled its foreign affairs

The United States emerged from World War II in a position of world leadership assured by the strength of its military forces and the enormous output of its economy. Furthermore, except at Pearl Harbor, the United States was the only victor that had not been attacked or invaded during the war. After World War I, Americans had favored isolation. Now most Americans assumed that the United States would be leader of what was called the "free world."

A Crisis Over Security

Not long after the defeat of Germany and Japan, many Americans began to fear another enemy: communists at home. This fear was largely a result of tensions caused by the cold war.

Early in 1950, Senator Joseph McCarthy of Wisconsin said that he had a list of 205 State Department employees who were communists. Although this claim was never proven, it won McCarthy nationwide attention. During the next four years, McCarthy's continued charges created an atmosphere of fear and suspicion. The federal government and local governments investigated thousands of employees, looking for "security risks." Businesses, universities, and the entertainment industry carried out similar campaigns. Few communists were found, but many people lost their jobs and their reputations simply because they had been investigated.

Accusations against the army eventually led to McCarthy's downfall. In 1954, Congress televised Senate hearings on McCarthy's charges that there were communists in the army. Many Americans saw the Wisconsin senator as a bully. Soon after these hearings, the Senate censured him for "conduct unbecoming a member." McCarthy lost his popular appeal, and the crisis over security began to fade.

Growing Prosperity

Economic uncertainty plagued the United States after the war. During the war, many goods had been unavailable or had been rationed. When products again became available, consumer demand caused prices to rise rapidly. In two years, the price of food increased by 25 percent.

Labor unions demanded wage increases that had been denied by wartime controls. The result was strikes in many crucial industries, including coal, steel, and railroads. There were over 5,000 strikes in 1946. These strikes led to passage of the Taft-Hartley Act of 1947. This act allowed the government to delay strikes that threatened health or safety. It also outlawed *closed shops*—businesses in which all workers are required to be union members.

Despite the nation's economic problems, Truman won the presidential election of 1948. He then proposed a program called the Fair Deal, which would carry on the traditions of the New Deal. He succeeded with some measures, including one to finance low-income housing and another to extend social security coverage.

In 1952, Americans elected Dwight D. Eisenhower—the general who had led the Allied invasion at Normandy—president. Eisenhower was reelected in 1956. Eisenhower's two terms in office saw an unprecedented growth of the economy. The output of goods and services in the nation increased by 25 percent, and the income of the average family went up 15 percent. Three out of four families drove at least one car, and three out of five owned their own homes.

Demands for Social Change

Many Americans did not share in the prosperity of the 1950s. At least 10 percent of Americans lived in poverty. Furthermore, some Americans had little opportunity to improve their lives. For example, black

Television broadcasting began in the United States and Great Britain in the 1930s, but its development was halted by World War II. In the postwar years, television became a worldwide medium of entertainment and information. The number of sets in the United States rose from 1 million in 1949 to 10 million in 1951. By the end of the 1960s, most countries had some kind of television broadcasting. By 1980, there were over 400 million sets in the world.

Television, which was free and convenient, changed the living habits of millions. People stayed at home more often and stayed up late when television stations extended their schedules late into the night. Television stars became overnight celebrities, and their styles, fashions, and opinions were adopted by many people.

Television provided a wide range of entertainment in its early days. Milton Berle's popular slapstick comedy earned him the title "Mr. Television" in the 1950s. Ed Sullivan, a New York newspaper columnist, became the host of a long-running variety show. He presented a diverse selection of singers, dancers, comedians, and circus acts. He introduced American youth to both Elvis Presley and the Beatles, who are shown here. Westerns such as "Gunsmoke" and situation comedies such as "I Love Lucy" were staples of early television fare.

During the 1950s and 1960s, a growing number of people learned about current events from television rather than from radio or newspapers. Television coverage of the congressional hearings on Senator McCarthy's charges against the army helped end McCarthy's influence, as you read in this chapter.

In the 1960s, satellites made it possible to broadcast events such as the Olympics all over the world. In addition, programs made in one country are often shown in other countries. For example, American television programs are popular in many countries. Thus, television has helped break down barriers between cultures.

Americans faced *segregation*, the practice of separating people according to race. In much of the South, blacks were required by law to attend separate schools and to sit in separate parts of buses and restaurants. In much of the North, segregation existed by custom though not by law. In the North, blacks often had to accept inferior housing, jobs, and education.

During the 1950s and 1960s, there was a growing demand for greater civil rights for black Americans. In 1954, the Supreme Court ruled in the *Brown* v. *Board of Education of Topeka* case that segregated schools were unconstitutional. It ordered school integration to proceed "with all deliberate speed." Many southerners resisted the decision, however.

Black Americans, led by Martin Luther King, Jr., and others, protested continued segregation through boycotts, "sit-ins," and marches. In 1963, more than 200,000 people took part in a march on Washington, D.C., aimed at securing a civil rights law.

President John F. Kennedy, who was elected in 1960, presented Congress with a civil rights bill to ban voting and job discrimination. On November 22, 1963, tragedy struck. President Kennedy was assassinated in Dallas, Texas. Kennedy's Vice President, Lyndon B. Johnson, then became President. Johnson won passage of the civil rights bill in 1964.

Under President Johnson, Congress also passed a large number of social welfare bills. These included medical care for the poor and elderly as well as money for education and low-cost housing.

Groups in addition to black Americans demanded equality during the 1960s. Hispanic Americans and Native Americans organized groups to work for an end to discrimination. Some American women became active in a movement for greater women's rights. Of special concern to many of these women was the demand for economic equality. They wanted equal pay for equal work and the freedom to work at any job.

Relations with the World

The cold war dominated much American foreign policy during the 1950s and 1960s. Preventing the spread of Soviet influence continued to be the main goal of American Presidents. On occasion, such as in Korea and Vietnam, this goal led to armed conflict.

The Korean War. Korea proved to be a severe test of the policy of containment. (See page 652.) After World War II, Korea was divided into two zones. The northern zone was controlled by the Soviet Union, and the southern zone was supervised by the United States. In 1950, Soviet-backed North Korean troops invaded the south. The United States came to the aid of the South Koreans with the approval of the United Nations. After three years of bitter fighting, a cease-fire was signed in July 1953. The invasion of South Korea had been repelled, and the boundary between North and South Korea was restored. (You will read more about the Korean War in Chapter 37.)

The cold war continues. The thaw in the cold war ended in the early 1960s, as you have read. (See page 659.) In 1962, a crisis over Cuba threatened to explode into war between the United States and the Soviet Union. In October of that year, President Kennedy revealed that the Soviet Union was constructing missile launch pads in Cuba.* The United States demanded that the bases be dismantled. It also imposed a naval blockade on Cuba to prevent Soviet ships from bringing missiles to Cuba. Soviet ships ap-

* Fidel Castro led a successful communist revolution in Cuba in the late 1950s.

In 1954, the United States Supreme Court ordered school integration. Three years later, black students tried to enroll in the formerly all-white public schools of Little Rock, Arkansas. The governor of Arkansas called out the National Guard to stop them. President Eisenhower sent federal troops, shown here, to protect black students traveling to and from school.

proached Cuba but turned back just as they approached the blockade. Khrushchev then ordered the missile bases dismantled, and the Cuban missile crisis ended.

At about the same time, the United States was becoming involved in a war in Southeast Asia. President Kennedy sent military advisors and equipment to the government of South Vietnam, which was fighting communist guerillas. Under President Johnson, American involvement in Vietnam developed into a full-fledged war, as you will read.

United States territories and neighbors. The status of several United States territories changed after World War II. The Philippines were granted full independence in 1946. In 1952, Puerto Rico attained commonwealth status. Puerto Ricans wrote their own constitution and elected a governor and legislature, but they continued to be United States citizens. The question of statehood for Puerto Rico has been a controversial one.

Two other territories became states in 1959: Alaska and Hawaii.

Throughout the 1950s and 1960s, the United States maintained friendly relations with Canada. However, many people in Latin America continued to view the United States as a threatening giant.

SECTION REVIEW

1. Identify: Joseph McCarthy, *Brown* v. *The Board of Education of Topeka*, Martin Luther King, Jr.

2. Define: closed shop, segregation.
3. Describe one development that caused many Americans to fear communism at home during the early 1950s.
4. (a) Why did Congress pass the Taft-Hartley Act? (b) What were its major provisions?
5. (a) List three groups that wanted social change in the 1950s and 1960s. (b) What did each group want?
6. Describe one way in which the United States tried to stop Soviet expansion in the 1950s and 1960s.

Chapter 34 Review

In Perspective

The alliance of the Soviet Union, Great Britain, and the United States began to weaken even before World War II ended. After the war, the Soviet Union guaranteed its dominance of Eastern Europe by establishing communist governments there. Through the policy of containment, the United States acted to prevent further Soviet expansion. By the early 1950s, most of Europe was divided into two alliances.

Western European nations recovered rapidly from the war. Economic cooperation through the Common Market contributed to prosperity in the 1950s and 1960s. In the Soviet Union, Stalin restored totalitarian rule, but Khrushchev introduced a period of relaxed controls following Stalin's death.

The United States enjoyed economic prosperity during much of the 1950s and 1960s. In the same period, it witnessed the development of civil rights movements among black Americans and others who demanded equality.

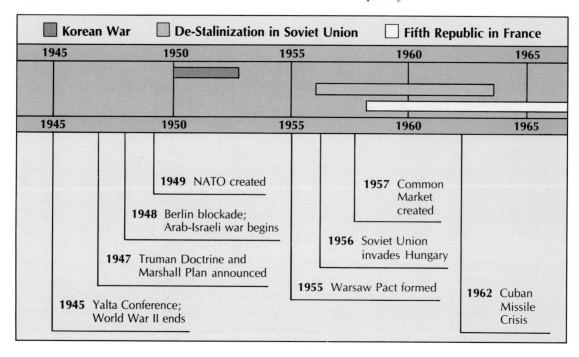

Recalling Facts

Decide if the following statements are true or false. If a statement is false, rewrite the statement to make it true.

1. In February 1945 at Yalta, the Allies believed that victory over Japan would be easy.

2. All members of the United Nations are represented in the General Assembly.

3. The Truman Doctrine was issued in response to a civil war in Greece.

4. Members of the Warsaw Pact agreed to oppose Soviet aggression in Western Europe.

5. Charles de Gaulle was the first president of the Fifth French Republic.

6. New former British colonies joined the Commonwealth after World War II.

7. Stalin conducted new purges after World War II.

8. Under Marshall Tito, Yugoslavia was a member of the Soviet bloc.

9. President Kennedy opposed measures to eliminate voting and job discrimination.

10. The United States came to the aid of South Korea when South Korea was invaded by North Korea in 1950.

Chapter Checkup

1. (a) Why did Churchill and Roosevelt want to cooperate with Stalin at Yalta? (b) Describe the agreements reached at the Yalta Conference. (c) What conflict between the United States and the Soviet Union surfaced at Potsdam?

2. (a) Describe conditions in Germany after the war. (b) How did the policies of the Allies lead to the division of Germany into East and West Germany?

3. (a) How did the Soviet Union establish its control of Eastern Europe after World War II? (b) How did the Truman Doctrine and the Marshall Plan help slow Soviet expansion into other parts of Europe?

4. (a) Why was West Germany able to recover so rapidly from the war? (b) Why was recovery slower in France?

5. (a) What steps did Stalin take to reestablish totalitarian rule after World War II? (b) Describe Khrushchev's attempts to de-Stalinize the Soviet Union.

6. Describe how each of the following affected relations between the Soviet Union and the United States: (a) the Soviet blockade of Berlin in 1948; (b) de-Stalinization; (c) Soviet construction of missile launch pads in Cuba.

7. (a) What economic problems did the United States face after World War II? (b) How was the economic situation different in the late 1950s?

Critical Thinking

1. **Analyzing** (a) How did Khrushchev's policy of de-Stalinization affect developments in Poland and Hungary? (b) Why do you think the outcome of these developments differed?

2. **Comparing** Review what you read about the Red Scare in Chapter 31 and the McCarthy era in this chapter. (a) How were the two periods similar? (b) How were they different?

Relating Past to Present

1. Do you think the cold war continues today? Why or why not? Give specific examples to support your answer.

Developing Basic Skills

1. **Map Reading** Study the map on page 654 and compare it with the map on page 581. Then answer the following questions: (a) What is the subject of the map on page 654? (b) What areas did the Soviet Union gain after World War II? (c) How was Germany after World War II different from Germany after World War I? (d) Which war do you think had the greater impact on political borders in Europe?

2. **Using Visual Evidence** Study the poster on page 651. Then answer the following questions: (a) What is the subject of the poster? (b) Whom do the figures in the background probably represent? (c) What does the large figure probably represent? (d) How might the poster help explain the creation of NATO?

See page 807 for suggested readings.

1949 This Chinese Communist painting glorifies victory over the Nationalists.

1979 Margaret Thatcher was the first woman to become prime minister of Britain.

	1945	1955	1965
POLITICS AND GOVERNMENT	**1947** India divided into India and Pakistan	**1957** Ghana wins independence	**1967** Six-Day War breaks out
ECONOMICS AND TECHNOLOGY	**1947** Invention of transistor opens way for computers	**1958** Great Leap Forward calls on Chinese to increase production	
SOCIETY AND CULTURE	**1948** *Cry, the Beloved Country* describes life under apartheid	**1966** Cultural Revolution disrupts life in China	

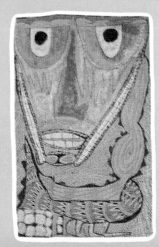

After independence, African nations maintained their traditions, as seen in this tapestry from Nigeria.

This paper mill, built in Japan, is being towed up the Amazon River in Brazil.

Unit Outline

Women in Peru create cloth sculptures such as this one to raise money for the families of political prisoners.

Archbishop Desmond Tutu used peaceful means to fight apartheid in South Africa.

	1975	1985	PRESENT

1971 General Idi Amin becomes dictator of Uganda

1983 Democratic government is established in Argentina

1970 Aswan Dam in Egypt is completed

1986 Nuclear accident occurs at Chernobyl plant in Soviet Union

1973 *Gulag Archipelago* is published

1984 Desmond Tutu receives Nobel Peace Prize

In Japan, as in many nations, traditional culture and high technology coexist.

Lech Walesa led the trade union, Solidarity, as it protested economic and political conditions in Poland.

35 Africa

Independence Day in Nigeria, 1960.

(1945–Present)

At midnight on March 6, 1957, a solemn ceremony took place in Accra, capital of the Gold Coast, a British colony in West Africa. Distinguished Africans and Europeans as well as crowds of local people watched as the Union Jack, the flag of Great Britain, was lowered. In its place, a red, green, and gold flag was raised. At that moment, the colony of the Gold Coast became the independent nation of Ghana.

Among those who proudly witnessed the flag-raising ceremony was Kwame Nkrumah (KWAH mee en KROO muh), Ghana's first prime minister. "There is a new African in the world," Nkrumah told the crowd, "and that new African is ready to fight his own battle. . . . It is the only way in which we can show the world we are masters of our own destiny."

A determined and able leader, Nkrumah had worked for years to liberate his country. He had organized strikes and boycotts against British rule and had been jailed for these activities. Finally, in the early 1950s, Britain granted the Gold Coast limited self-government. While still in prison, Nkrumah was elected prime minister of the Gold Coast. However, limited self-government fell short of Nkrumah's goal. As prime minister, he continued to lead the movement for independence, a goal he achieved that day in March 1957.

Ghana was the first black African nation to win its independence. But even as the people of Ghana celebrated with parades and dancing, Nkrumah declared: "Our independence is meaningless unless it is linked up with the total liberation of the African continent."

Over the next three decades, more than 50 other nations won their independence in Africa. Even as these new nations proudly raised their own flags, however, they were confronted by many political and economic problems. African leaders wanted to establish stable, unified nations and prosperous economies that would give people a better life. In the years after they won their independence, the nations of Africa have experimented with ways to meet these goals.

1 Winning Independence

Read to Learn
- European reactions to African independence movements
- how African nations achieved independence

"We are determined to be free. We want education. We want the right to earn a decent living, the right to express our thoughts and emotions. . . . We demand for Black Africa freedom and independence." In 1945, delegates to a Pan-African Congress cheered these stirring words. The determination of Africans to win freedom from colonial rule transformed the political map of Africa.

Movements for Independence

The people of Africa had long resisted colonial rule. During the Age of Imperialism, independence movements emerged in Egypt, Nigeria, the Gold Coast, and South Africa. After World War I, the demand for self-government in Africa increased.

African nationalism. Independence movements grew out of African nationalism. Although African nationalism was primarily directed against colonial rule, it also included a determination to build societies with strong, stable economies, modern technology, and a high level of education.

Africans educated in Europe and the United States led nationalist movements in different parts of Africa. These leaders admired the democratic institutions of western governments. But they resented western colonial rule, which denied Africans the right to self-government and treated them as second-class citizens.

Educated African leaders organized political parties to work for independence. In the Gold Coast, for example, Kwame Nkrumah rallied mass support behind the Convention People's party. Nkrumah and other leaders used the press to spread their ideas. They gained their greatest followings in the cities. In cities, many Africans learned about these leaders' goals through newspapers and radio broadcasts. Many joined demonstrations and participated in boycotts against colonial rule.

International support. After World War II, movements to end colonial rule multiplied around the world. International political conditions favored independence movements. European nations had been torn apart by World War II. Many Europeans questioned the benefits of overseas empires. Administering colonies was expensive and strained economies already drained by the war. Moreover, most Europeans were not anxious to fight long costly wars to hold onto overseas colonies.

In the United Nations, the United States and the Soviet Union called for an end to European imperialism in Africa. They supported anticolonial movements both for political and economic reasons. The United States hoped independent African nations would become capitalist democracies, while the Soviet Union encouraged socialism in Africa. In addition, the two superpowers wanted to gain access to the vast natural resources of Africa.

European Responses

At first, European nations were reluctant to grant their African colonies independence. Britain and France were willing to make a few concessions to African demands, however. Britain gave some of its African colonies a measure of self-government. For example, it granted the people of the Gold Coast a constitution that gave them the right to elect a legislature. France introduced reforms that allowed its colonies to elect more representatives to the National Assembly in France.

But Africans wanted independence, not limited self-government. When Africans increased their pressure for independence, Britain and France realized that they must grant independence. However, other colonial powers, including Belgium and Portugal, were determined to hold onto their African territories.

As the tide of African nationalism rose, some African leaders resorted to violence to win independence. Yet most African nations achieved independence through peaceful means.

New Nations of Africa

In 1950, there were four independent countries in Africa: Liberia, Ethiopia,* Egypt, and South Africa. During the 1950s and 1960s, a wave of independence swept across the continent. By 1968, 38 new nations had emerged in Africa. The number rose to over 50 in 1982. (See the map on page 671.)

North Africa. Between 1951 and 1956, the North African nations of Libya, Tunisia, and Morocco won independence. Algeria, which included the vast area between Morocco and Tunisia, achieved independence after a bitter eight-year struggle. France considered Algeria part of the French nation

and had encouraged large numbers of French to settle there. These settlers fought against independence even after the French government finally agreed to it. In 1962, Algeria was established as an independent republic.

The peoples of North Africa are largely Muslim and Arabic-speaking. Thus, North African nations have close cultural ties with the Arab nations of the Middle East and often support Arab causes. For example, Colonel Qaddafi (guht DAH fee), who became the leader of Libya in 1969, has strongly supported the Arab nations in the Middle East that oppose Israel.

West and Central Africa. In the late 1950s and 1960s, African nations south of the Sahara Desert won their independence. As you read at the beginning of the chapter, Ghana became the first independent nation of West Africa in March 1957. The next year, Guinea declared its independence from France. In 1960 and 1961, many new nations emerged in West Africa, especially in the region once known as French West Africa.

The British and French had made some efforts to prepare their colonies for independence. They had provided education for Africans and allowed African leaders to gain administrative experience. However, the Belgians had done almost nothing in the Congo. Thus, when the Belgian Congo received its independence in 1960, the region was soon involved in a civil war. Revolts broke out in different regions of the country as rival leaders fought for power. Eventually, the United Nations sent troops to the Congo to help restore order. In 1971, the military leader who had gained control of the Congo renamed his country Zaire. In giving the country an African name, he symbolically rejected its colonial past.

Eastern and southern Africa. Eastern and southern Africa were heavily settled by whites. Like the French settlers in Algeria, British settlers in Kenya, Uganda, Tanganyika, and Rhodesia considered these countries their home. They feared independence because it would give black Africans control of the governments.

---

* Emperor Haile Selassie was returned to the Ethiopian throne when the Italians were defeated in World War II.

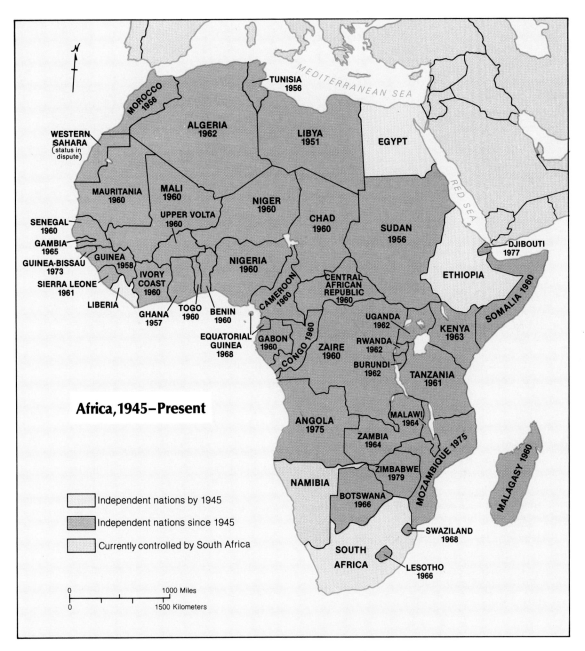

Africa, 1945–Present

Independent nations by 1945

Independent nations since 1945

Currently controlled by South Africa

0   1000 Miles

0   1500 Kilometers

Map Skill   *In 1945, there were only four independent nations in Africa, as this map shows. Since then, many new nations have emerged. What nation was the first to gain independence after World War II? What nation gained independence most recently?*

Black leaders such as Jomo Kenyatta in Kenya organized opposition to colonial rule. Tanganyika, later renamed Tanzania (TAN zuh NEE uh), won its independence in 1961. In the next three years, other East African nations achieved independence, including Uganda in 1962 and Kenya in 1963. (See the map above.)

White settlers in Rhodesia, present-day Zimbabwe (zihm BAH bweh), declared their

The poster shown in this photograph celebrates independence in Kenya. Jomo Kenyatta, first president of Kenya, is shown as the father of the nation. "Harambee" is the motto of Kenya. It is a Swahili expression meaning "a pulling together of all races." In East Africa—especially in Kenya—large numbers of Asians and Europeans live alongside Africans.

independence from Britain in 1965 in order to prevent black Africans from gaining a role in government. Britain refused to recognize the new nation, and many members of the United Nations boycotted Rhodesia. In a long guerrilla war, blacks struggled to oust the white minority government. Finally, in 1979, a compromise was negotiated. The agreement called for black majority rule in Zimbabwe and protection of the rights of the white minority.

In southern Africa, Portugal fought to hold onto its colonies: Angola and Mozambique. Nationalist groups fought a guerrilla war against Portugal. The war became increasingly unpopular in Portugal. In 1975, Portugal agreed to recognize Angola and Mozambique as independent nations.

SECTION REVIEW

1. Locate: Algeria, Libya, Ghana, Guinea, Zaire, Tanzania, Zimbabwe, Angola, Mozambique.
2. List three goals of African nationalists.
3. How did World War II affect the attitude of European nations toward their overseas colonies?
4. (a) What African nations were independent in 1950? (b) How did this situation change in the 1950s and 1960s?
5. Why do the peoples of North Africa often support Arab causes in the Middle East?

2 Challenges Facing African Nations

Read to Learn
- what problems confronted new African nations
- how African leaders proposed to solve these problems

The newly independent nations of Africa faced many challenges. Some problems were unique to Africa. Others were the same as those faced by new nations everywhere. Early in 1965, the president of Zambia summed up these challenges: "Political independence only serves as a key to the door of economic and social progress.... We must open the door ... for all the people.... The big question now is—how do we do this?"

The Colonial Heritage

Several of the problems African nations faced could be traced to their colonial experiences. As you have read, some European nations had done little to prepare their colonies for independence. Thus, the new nations lacked enough experienced leaders during the critical early years.

During the scramble for Africa, European nations grabbed territories and organized them into colonies. They drew boundaries without regard to geography, religion, language, or the ethnic groups living within an area. Thus, many new African nations had no traditions of unity. Rivalries among peoples with different religions, languages, and cultural traditions have made unity extremely hard to achieve in Africa.

The colonial heritage left some positive results, however. Europeans built roads, railroads, schools, and harbors, especially in the last few decades before independence. Although these improvements were made for the financial benefit of Europeans, they gave the new African nations a framework on which to build.

Need for Economic Development

Today, African leaders support the idea of modernization—that is, they want to create stable societies capable of producing a high level of goods and services. They also want to make these goods and services available to all the people of their nations. They see economic development as the key to modernization. Economic development includes improvement of agriculture and development of industry.

Improving agriculture. Eight out of ten Africans depend on agriculture for a living. There are two main types of agriculture in Africa: subsistence farming and growing cash crops. Subsistence farmers usually live in small villages and produce enough for themselves with some left over to sell. Because they have little to sell, they cannot afford to buy much. Better education, equipment, and transportation are needed to help these farmers produce more.

During the colonial period, Europeans encouraged the growing of cash crops, or crops that will be exported. After independence, African nations continued to sell these crops. Cash crops provide Africans with badly needed capital. However, dependence on a cash crop can cause major problems. World demand for a cash crop can fall suddenly, reducing prices and upsetting the economy of a nation. Some African nations have tried to diversify their economies to end dependence on a single cash crop.

The climate makes farming in Africa difficult. (See page 223.) The deserts never get enough rain. Rain forests get too much. In

Graph Skill *Grain production has increased in Africa. However, the demand for food for Africa's growing population has increased more rapidly than grain production. During what period was production of grain closest to demand?*

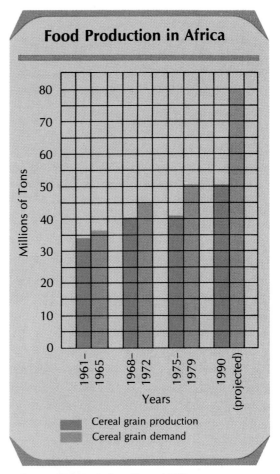

Food Production in Africa

Millions of Tons

Years

- Cereal grain production
- Cereal grain demand

673

Source: FAO, *Agriculture: Toward 2000.*

the savannas, rainfall is unreliable. At the same time, soil in many parts of Africa is less fertile than soil in Europe, Asia, and North America.

In the late 1970s and into the mid-1980s, a drought caused severe problems in the Sahel. Resources in this huge semi-desert region south of the Sahara were not enough to feed the starving population.

Industrial development. In order to industrialize, African nations need capital, skilled technicians, and raw materials. In the past, the capital to build factories and dig mines often came from *multinational corporations.* These large enterprises, which have branches in many countries, established factories in various African nations.

To prevent such powerful foreign corporations from gaining too much influence, some African governments began to insist on owning 51 percent of their key industries. They used foreign aid and investment to back their own efforts. Many nations started to process their own food, minerals, and other raw materials.

However, by the late 1980s, early hopes for rapid industrialization had faded. Foreign debt had soared, and creditors were reluctant to advance more money to African nations. This disappointing lack of economic growth was due in part to unsuccessful government programs. In part it was due to an unstable world economy. Some African governments recognized their role in the economic reverses and devised new policies. They began to put more emphasis on agricultural development and less on industrialization.

Rapid Social Change

After World War II, nations all around the world experienced rapid social change. In African nations, these changes included a tremendous population growth and *urbanization*, the migration of millions of people from rural villages to cities.

Population growth. Between 1950 and 1986, the population of Africa more than doubled, growing from 219 million to 585 million. Improvements in health care, such as new medicines and hospitals, contributed to the skyrocketing numbers of people.

Such rapid population growth posed serious problems. In some countries, natural disasters, such as drought, and lack of fertile farmland resulted in food shortages and sometimes famine. The resources of gov-

Modernization, improved agricultural production, and industrialization are among the chief goals of African nations. African leaders want to strengthen their national economics and reduce dependence on foreign aid and investment. They see education as an important step in achieving these goals. The photograph at left shows graduation ceremonies at the University of Zambia. At right, farmers use modern machinery to bag peanuts, an important cash crop.

Growth of Cities in Africa, 1950–1980

	1950	1960	1970	1980
Accra, Ghana	135,926*	337,828	636,067	840,000*
Dar es Salaam, Tanzania	69,227	128,742	343,911*	870,020*
Kinshasa, Zaire	(not available)	402,492*	1,288,122*	3,000,000*
Lagos, Nigeria	267,407	364,000*	900,169*	4,500,000*

*estimated figures

Sources: US Department of State, *Background Notes*; United Nations, *Demographic Yearbook*; and *Europa Yearbook*.

Chart Skill   *In Africa, as elsewhere, people by the millions have left farms and villages to live in cities. City governments have been strained to provide the new residents with even basic services. In the 30-year time span shown in the table, which city experienced the largest population growth?*

ernments were severely strained to provide basic needs such as education, jobs, and housing.

Urbanization. Rapid urban growth is a feature of industrializing nations everywhere. As you read in Chapter 23, European cities grew rapidly during the Industrial Revolution. African cities experienced a similar surge of growth in the decades after independence.

Cities held many attractions, from high-paying jobs and good schools to housing with running water and electricity. Cities also offered the excitement of crowds and different forms of entertainment, such as movies and sports events. Most important, however, people were lured to cities by the hope of wealth.

Unfortunately, the hopes of many rural people who migrated to the cities were disappointed. In spite of the crowds, people were often lonely and isolated in the cities. They lacked the close personal ties that existed in rural villages. At the same time, there were not enough jobs for the millions of newcomers. Moreover, many did not have the education and skills required for most jobs.

Shantytowns, or makeshift shelters built of scraps of wood and metal, sprang up on the outskirts of many cities. The jobless lived in these crowded slums, providing for their needs as best they could. Yet despite the hardships of city life, they did not want to return to villages.

Emphasis on Education

African leaders have stressed the role of education in helping their nations meet the challenges of today. A large percentage of national budgets goes into education. This has resulted in the building of primary and secondary schools as well as universities and technical schools. In some countries, the number of primary school students has doubled in the last ten years. As a result, the cost of providing education has soared.

The emphasis on education serves different purposes. African leaders see education as a way of encouraging a sense of national unity among the many ethnic and language groups in their countries. Education is also used to provide the skilled workers, managers, teachers, and technicians needed for economic development.

Search for Political Stability

When they became independent, African nations wrote their own constitutions. These constitutions generally established parliamentary democracies and guaranteed individual rights. In the decades since independence, many African nations have struggled —with limited success—to preserve stable, democratic governments.

Some nations turned to one-party systems, outlawing opposition parties. They did this to preserve national unity. They believed that a system with many political parties prevented a nation from working for a common

In the years before and after independence, many young Africans struggled to obtain an education. Legson Kayira was born in the British colony of Nyasaland, present-day Malawi. His family was poor, but they managed to scrape together the 50 cents a year needed to pay Kayira's elementary school fees. The school, Livingstonia, was an eight-mile walk from Kayira's village of Mbale. Its motto was "I Will Try." This motto eventually inspired Kayira to apply to a high school 200 miles from home.

After completing high school, Kayira was expected to return home to teach young people in his village to read and write. But Kayira wanted to continue his studies. There was no college at that time in Nyasaland. However, Kayira had heard about Africans who had gone to the United States to attend college. Although Kayira had no money and no way to get to the United States, he was not discouraged. He decided to walk across Africa to Port Said, Egypt, and take a job on a ship going to the United States.

Kayira told his mother the trip would take him about five days, but he knew it would take much longer. Port Said was more than 3,000 miles from Mbale. The determined young man set out in October 1958 with only a few clothes, a blanket, and a map.

Later, Kayira described part of his long journey: "I walked all the way to Tanganyika. . . . I crossed Tanganyika, worked on the way to get some cents for food. In January [1960] I crossed Lake Victoria and reached Kampala [Uganda]. . . . On September 5th I traveled 50 miles, then got a lift by van to Lira. The next day I traveled to Gulu. At Gulu I stayed with the police for three days, waiting for a bus to Nimule. On September 10th I was at Nimule. On the 13th I walked for 32 miles, then got a lift by van for 50 miles."

Finally, Kayira reached Khartoum in the Sudan. There, he applied for a visa at the United States embassy. Embassy officials told him they could not issue a visa unless he had money for a round-trip plane ticket to the United States. They did, however, write to the college Kayira planned to attend. The people in the small town where the college was located raised the money Kayira needed for his air fare. Finally, in December 1960, Kayira arrived in the United States.

After four years of college, Kayira returned home in 1964. That year, Nyasaland became the independent nation of Malawi. Kayira attended the independence day ceremonies and proudly proclaimed: "A salute to you, Malawi, and Godspeed. We have just begun to try."

cause. Sekou Touré* in Guinea argued that a single party could best represent the interests of the people. He believed that differences of opinion could be worked out within the one-party system.

The military has played a growing role in African politics. Some Africans think the military is the only force strong enough to unify their deeply divided nations. Others support military rule in the hope that a strong leader would stop inflation, end government corruption, and provide enough food for all the people.

In the 1970s and 1980s, military leaders staged *coups d'état*, or revolts, in many countries. General Idi Amin overthrew the president of Uganda in 1971 and established a military dictatorship. To stay in power, Amin murdered his opponents and terrorized the population. Amin was eventually overthrown, but his brutal policies disrupted political, social, and economic life in Uganda.

SECTION REVIEW

1. Define: multinational corporation, urbanization, coup d'état.
2. How did the boundaries established by colonial powers result in problems for independent African nations?
3. (a) List two reasons why improving agriculture in Africa is difficult. (b) What do African nations need in order to industrialize?
4. Why have millions of Africans moved to the cities?
5. Explain why African leaders think education is an important goal.

---

* Touré was a descendant of Samori Touré, who had resisted French rule during the Age of Imperialism. (See page 516.)

676

3 Nigeria and Tanzania: Nations in Transition

Read to Learn
- why civil war took place in Nigeria
- why Nigeria and Tanzania face economic crises

In 1960, Nigeria, which is in West Africa, celebrated its independence. A year later, Tanzania, in East Africa, won its independence. The experiences of these nations since independence illustrate some of the challenges facing all African countries.

Nigeria

About 102 million people live in Nigeria, making it the most populous nation in Africa. Most Nigerians are farmers living in rural areas. Still, large cities such as Lagos and Ibadan are crowded.

Nigeria exports a number of cash crops, ranging from cacao beans, peanuts, and palm oil to timber and tobacco. The country is rich in natural resources, including oil, columbite (used in making stainless steel), tin, and coal. As you will read, wealth from oil has helped the nation to develop economically.

Seeds of conflict. During the Age of Imperialism, Britain ruled the many diverse peoples who lived in what is today Nigeria. When Nigeria became independent in 1960, it included more than 250 ethnic and language groups.

Four ethnic groups are dominant in Nigeria. They make up about three fifths of the Nigerian population. They are the Hausa and Fulani in the north, the Yoruba in the southwest, and the Ibo in the southeast. The Hausa and Fulani are largely Muslim. During the colonial period, they preserved their Islamic traditions. Many Yoruba and Ibo converted to Christianity. Others continued to practice their traditional religions.

Before independence, a number of Ibo received educations in Western Europe. The educated Ibo looked down on the Hausa and Fulani in the Muslim north. At the same time, Muslim Nigerians resented the Ibo, whom they saw as aggressive.

A bitter civil war. Unequal access to Nigeria's wealth created further bitterness within the country. The north had fewer natural resources and had long been deprived of schools and economic development. The southeast had large oil fields that made it a prosperous region.

In the mid-1960s, several military revolts took place in Nigeria. At one point, rioters in the north massacred thousands of Ibo who had settled there. Persecution and a desire to protect their oil wealth led the Ibo to establish the independent Republic of Biafra in southeastern Nigera.

From 1967 to 1970, the central government of Nigeria fought to reunite the nation. The civil war ended in the defeat of Biafra. After the war, efforts were made to build na-

Map Skill *The Nigerian government has sought to develop the country economically. The Niger River, the third largest river in Africa, holds great potential for hydroelectric power. How can railroads contribute to the economic development of Nigeria?*

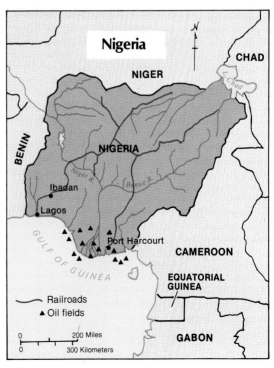

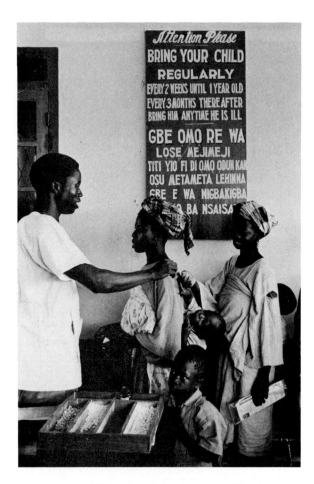

At this public health clinic in western Nigeria, women and children receive vitamin pills and pills to prevent malaria. The Nigerian government has supported public health education. By distributing information about sanitation, nutrition, and disease prevention, the government hopes to stamp out diseases that prevent people from playing an active role in the country's development.

foreign debt. In 1987, western creditor nations agreed to reschedule repayment of some of the 19 billion dollars owed.

Wealth is very unevenly distributed in Nigeria, where less than 1 percent of the population controls 75 percent of the wealth. The wealthy elite live in the cities. But the vast majority of city dwellers remain in poverty. Some economic progress has occurred. However, a major problem in Nigeria, as in other African nations, is the rapidly expanding population. Nigeria's population is expected to almost double in the next 25 years. And food production is not expected to keep pace with the nation's growing numbers.

In an effort to solve this problem, the military regime relocated some city dwellers into the countryside as farmers. And, in 1985, in order to force more people to farm, the government banned imports of rice and maize. Some improved domestic production resulted. But many young people still resist becoming farmers, even though there are not enough other kinds of jobs.

Tanzania

About 24 million people live in Tanzania. As in Nigeria, a wide gap exists between the rich and the poor. Tanzania is poorer than Nigeria. It has few mineral resources and lacks the capital to develop its economy. The chief export is coffee, but Tanzania also exports tea, cotton, and sisal, a plant used in making rope.

Most people in Tanzania are farmers. The population is made up of over 120 ethnic and language groups, but no one group is dominant. Unlike Nigeria and many other African nations, Tanzania has a common language—Swahili—which helps unify the nation. Many East Africans speak Swahili as well as their own local languages.

From colony to statehood. In the Age of Imperialism, first Germany and then Britain ruled the area, then called Tanganyika. In the 1950s, Julius Nyerere (nyuh RAIR aay) led the drive for independence. When the colony became free in 1961, Nyerere became president. In 1964, Tanganyika was united with Zanzibar and given the name Tanzania.

tional unity. Nigeria was reorganized into many small states to eliminate the older regional divisions. The army ran the country until 1979, when national elections were held. Civilian rule, in turn, was overthrown by a military coup in 1983, and all political parties were banned.

Economic progress. During the civil war, the economy had suffered. But with the return of peace, oil production revived economic growth. Then, in the mid-1980s, a drop in demand for oil severely cut this source of income. Nigeria fell deeply into

678

President Nyerere created a government with a one-party system. Every village nominates candidates for public office. The party pays the expenses for all candidates, who campaign together. Thus, when elections are held, voters have a choice. The one-party system has gained popular acceptance in Tanzania.

Economic development. President Nyerere set as his goal an improved living standard for the Tanzanian people. He tried to accomplish this by improving agriculture at the local level. He also stressed the need to develop self-reliance instead of seeking foreign aid. At first Tanzania experimented with agricultural cooperatives. Farmers worked together to grow cash crops such as tea and tobacco.

In the late 1960s, Nyerere announced a program to form "ujamaa" villages. Ujamaa is a Swahili word meaning familyhood. Nyerere's program had three basic ideas: mutual respect, the sharing of production, and the obligation to work. Government assistance included medical care, schools, technical advice, and machinery to the villages. The aim of the program was for each village to become self-reliant.

Nyerere designed a system of education to fit Tanzania's goal of self-reliance. In his book *Education for Self Reliance*, Nyerere described how schools should be built and run. All schools were to help build national unity. And they were to encourage respect for farming as a way of life.

Unfortunately, poor soil and unreliable rainfall make farming in Tanzania difficult at

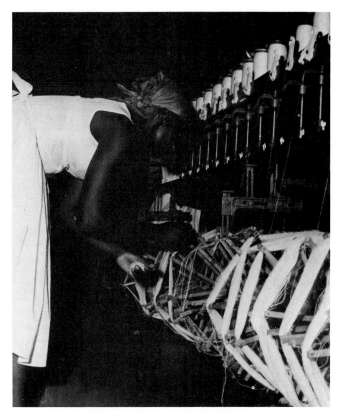

In this photograph, a woman checks spools of sisal in a rope-making factory. Until recently, sisal was the chief export of Tanzania. But the use of synthetic products to make rope has cut into sisal exports. Although former President Nyerere had encouraged self-reliance, Tanzania has had to import agricultural machinery, transportation equipment, fuel, and many manufactured goods. As a result, its imports have exceeded its exports, resulting in an unfavorable balance of trade.

Map Skill *Tanzania has much less potential for hydroelectric power than Nigeria. Much of the interior is arid. How is railroad development related to farming areas?*

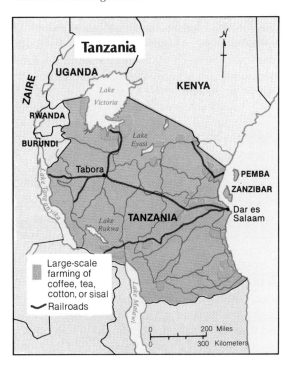

Tanzania

ZAIRE
UGANDA
RWANDA
BURUNDI
KENYA
Lake Victoria
Lake Eyasi
Tabora
PEMBA
ZANZIBAR
Dar es Salaam
TANZANIA
Lake Tanganyika
Lake Rukwa
Lake Malawi

Large-scale farming of coffee, tea, cotton, or sisal
Railroads

0   200 Miles
0   300 Kilometers

best. Severe droughts in 1973–74 and 1983–84 further hindered Nyerere's plans for improving agriculture in the villages. In addition, many farmers resisted the advice of government farm experts. Since agricultural exports were supposed to finance new industries, low crop production also meant low industrial growth. Social services, such as medical and educational programs, also ceased for lack of funds.

Political change. Tanzania remains a poor nation, its development held back by domestic failures and falling world prices for cash crops. In November 1985, President Nyerere was replaced as president by Ali Hassan Mivinyi. It remains to be seen if Mivinyi's policies can stop Tanzania's economic decline.

4 Tensions in Southern Africa

Read to Learn
- how the South African system of apartheid functions
- what resistance to apartheid exists

Most African countries became independent in the 1950s and 1960s. Yet the governments of nations in southern Africa remained largely in the hands of white minorities. As you have read, black Africans in Zimbabwe, Angola, and Mozambique organized guerrilla forces and won power. In the Republic of South Africa, however, the white minority has retained control of the government.

Republic of South Africa

The Republic of South Africa is different from the rest of Africa. It is industrialized and ranks among the world's richest nations. South Africa has extensive fertile farmland, a favorable climate, and vast mineral resources, including gold, diamonds, platinum, manganese, and uranium.

South Africa has a population of 34 million. About 5 million South Africans, roughly 16 percent of the population, are white. Some whites are Afrikaners, descendants of Dutch farmers who settled in South Africa in the late 1600s and 1700s. Other whites are descended from British settlers. The majority of South Africans—over 23 million—are black. The South African government recog- nizes two other racial groups: Asians, who are mostly Indians, and "coloreds," who are people of mixed European, Asian, and African descent.

As you read in Chapter 27, the Union of South Africa obtained self-government in 1910. The British granted South Africa full independence in 1931. At the time of independence, the country was dominated by its white population.

Apartheid. In 1948, the white-controlled government instituted *apartheid* (uh PAHRT hayt), a policy of rigid separation of races. In theory, apartheid allows for separate development for each racial group. In practice, it severely limits the freedom and rights of nonwhites in South Africa. For example, nonwhites are barred from voting in national elections and are restricted to living in certain areas.

Apartheid laws affect what jobs nonwhites hold as well as how much education they receive. Black schools, for example, receive less government support than white schools. Thus, white South Africans have a large supply of cheap labor.

Black homelands. The government has established 11 homelands, called Bantustans, for blacks. It claims that blacks can govern themselves and develop on their own in the Bantustans. It encourages people in these homelands to follow their traditional ways of life. However, much of the land set aside for these homelands has poor soil. More than 85 percent of South Africa is reserved for the white minority. Black men are often forced to get jobs outside their homeland, leaving their families behind.

Opposition to Apartheid

South Africans of all races have struggled to end apartheid. Many black leaders in the fight against apartheid have been imprisoned. For example, when the African National Congress, the major black political party, was banned in 1960, one of its leaders, Nelson Mandela, was put in prison. He has remained in prison to this day.

Albert Luthuli, a Zulu chief, urged passive resistance to apartheid. Like Mahatma Gandhi, Luthuli believed people would win more by peaceful protest than by violence. In 1984, South African Archbishop Desmond Tutu received the Nobel Peace Prize for his efforts to end apartheid peacefully. However, protests against apartheid have often led to violence. For example, blacks protested in 1984 when a new constitution failed to give them any representation in Parliament.

Increased violence. Beginning in 1984, an upsurge in violence spread throughout South Africa. In 1985 the government responded by declaring a state of emergency, which increased the powers of the army and police. These forces clashed frequently with protesting blacks. In six months in 1985, some 1,000 people were killed. Yet the anti-apartheid protests continued.

United States policy. Before 1985, the United States government supported a policy of "constructive engagement" as a way to end apartheid. This policy involved giving financial aid to South Africa's black-ruled neighboring states. Its goal was to make these nations more stable and thus less threatening to South Africa's security. Then the United States would press South Africa for reforms.

As the death toll in South Africa rose in 1986, political pressure against apartheid increased in the United States. To force reforms, many large American corporations began to divest, or withdraw, their holdings in South Africa.

President Ronald Reagan, by Executive Order, banned certain exports to South Africa, such as computer parts and nuclear technology. The United States Congress also voted to impose "punitive sanctions." Other nations have also imposed trade barriers. Many people who do not support these policies argue that black workers will suffer the most from economic sanctions.

South Africa's Neighbors

South Africa's neighbors to the northeast, Zimbabwe and Mozambique, are ruled by black majorities. Mozambique is a one-party state. Its government has accused South Africa of supporting a guerrilla group rebelling within Mozambique. South Africa, on its part, has accused Mozambique of harboring bases of the African National Congress. Seeking mutual security, each nation pledged in a treaty in 1984 that it would not

Map Skill *South Africa has set aside 308 parcels of land to be formed into 11 homelands for black South Africans. Which independent nation is completely surrounded by South Africa?*

support guerrillas fighting the other's government.

The pact was signed by Mozambique's President Samora Machel, himself a former guerrilla. Machel had led Mozambique to freedom from Portugal in 1975. For over 10 years he had served as its powerful president. After Machel died in a plane crash in 1986, his foreign minister, Joaquím Chissano, was named president. Chissano pledged to continue Machel's policies. However, renewed guerrilla action breaking the pact has made Mozambique's future uncertain.

To the northeast of South Africa is mineral-rich Namibia. Once the German colony of South West Africa, it was put under the control of South Africa after World War I. Instead of preparing the region for independence, South Africa invested in and controlled Namibia's economy. It also imposed apartheid on the nation.

In 1966, the United Nations voted to end South Africa's mandate, but South Africa resisted. Since then, black Namibians have fought for independence. The largest guerrilla group within Namibia, the South-West African Peoples Organization (SWAPO), has received support from the Soviet Union, Sweden, and many African nations.

5 Africa in the World Today

Read to Learn
- what part superpower rivalry plays in Africa
- what efforts have been made toward African unity

African nations control valuable mineral resources and export important agricultural products to the rest of the world. The United States and the Soviet Union compete for influence in Africa. Other nations are also anxious to maintain good political and economic relations with Africa. As a result, African nations play an important role in the world today.

Africa and the United Nations

The newly independent African nations wanted recognition as members of the international community. Membership in the United Nations is a symbol of this recognition. Today, African nations have the single largest bloc of votes in the United Nations General Assembly.

However, most African nations have chosen not to side with either the United States or the Soviet Union in the UN. Instead, they join other Third World, or developing, nations that share common economic goals. For example, Third World nations want more opportunities to sell their manufactured goods in western markets and greater access to new technology. Because many Third World nations depend on exports, they work through the UN to find ways to keep prices stable for these exports.

Agencies of the UN have helped African nations in their development. The UN has provided farming experts and engineers to train Africans. It has also provided emergency relief when disaster strikes.

The Horn of Africa

Africa holds a strategic position in the world today. Giant tankers too large to pass through the Suez Canal must carry oil from the Persian Gulf around Africa to Europe. As a result, some African nations have been drawn into superpower rivalries.

The United States and the Soviet Union have taken a keen interest in a region called the horn of Africa. The horn of Africa includes the East African nations of Somalia, Ethiopia, Djibouti, and Kenya. It is not far from the Persian Gulf region, the source of most of the world's oil. The United States has access to air and naval bases in Kenya and Somalia to protect Persian Gulf oil. The Soviet Union has built military bases in the horn of Africa.

Superpower rivalry has complicated local conflicts in the horn of Africa. For example, in the Ogaden, a region ruled by Ethiopia, the local people were fighting for independence. Guerrilla fighting flared into full-scale war in the Ogaden when Somalia, Ethiopia's neighbor and rival, provided aid to the rebels. Fighting in the Ogaden forced many into greatly overcrowded refugee camps. The Soviet Union first supported Somalia in return for a naval base. Then Somalia ousted the Soviets from their naval base and allowed the United States to use the base. The Soviet Union began supplying arms to Ethiopia, leaving the conflict unresolved.

In the 1970s and 1980s, drought and warfare created millions of refugees in East Africa. They flooded temporary refugee camps already crowded with refugees from earlier disasters. Pictures of hungry children, such as this girl from Ethiopia, brought an outpouring of aid from people around the world.

Many African peoples have preserved their traditional cultures. Here, a leader of the Aboure people from the Ivory Coast tells village boys an ancient legend. African legends often combine history and a moral lesson.

Efforts to Achieve African Unity

Africa is a continent with many different nations. Each nation has its own traditions and history. However, many African leaders have worked to establish a sense of African unity.

In 1963, representatives from 30 African nations met in Addis Ababa, capital of Ethiopia. There, they signed a charter establishing the Organization of African Unity (OAU). The goals of the OAU are to promote African unity, encourage economic cooperation, settle issues that arise among members, and support the struggle for the independence of black Africans across the continent. Today, the OAU includes all African nations except the Republic of South Africa.

As a unifying force, however, the OAU has not lived up to its founders' hopes. Most African nations are determined to preserve their independence. Thus, they are not will-

ing to allow outside interference—even by the OAU. As a result, OAU efforts to settle quarrels have had limited success. In addition, the OAU has been unable to prevent civil wars such as the one in Nigeria.

Supporters of African unity also support African culture. In 1977, the World Black African Festival of Arts and Culture met in Nigeria. This festival featured black African music, sculpture, painting, dance, theater, literature, and movies.

Chapter 35 Review

In Perspective

After World War II, Africans stepped up their demands for independence. During the 1950s and 1960s, many new nations emerged in Africa. Many African nations lacked traditions of unity and were divided into different ethnic and language groups. All African nations, however, looked for ways to improve agriculture and develop new industries. To achieve their goals, they needed capital and skilled technicians as well as raw materials.

African nations used different methods in trying to modernize. Nigeria and Tanzania differ in resources but share many of the same problems. Initial progress has suffered setbacks in these nations and elsewhere in Africa.

The Republic of South Africa is unlike other African nations. Its government has imposed a policy of strict racial segregation. Nations around the world have condemned apartheid. Some, including the United States, have imposed sanctions.

The nations of Africa have taken an active role in international affairs, in the UN and through the OAU.

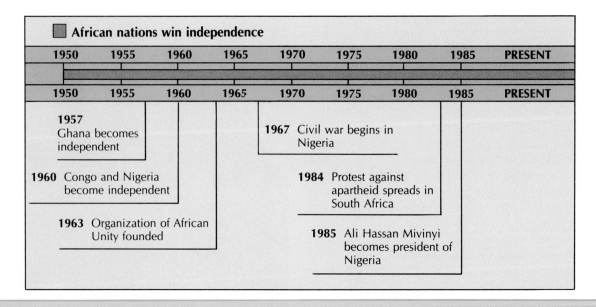

African nations win independence

| 1950 | 1955 | 1960 | 1965 | 1970 | 1975 | 1980 | 1985 | PRESENT |

1957 Ghana becomes independent

1960 Congo and Nigeria become independent

1963 Organization of African Unity founded

1967 Civil war begins in Nigeria

1984 Protest against apartheid spreads in South Africa

1985 Ali Hassan Mivinyi becomes president of Nigeria

Recalling Facts

Choose the word or phrase that best completes each of the following statements.

1. The chief aim of African nationalism was (a) freedom from colonial rule; (b) improved education; (c) African unity.

2. The first nation in West Africa to become independent was (a) the Congo; (b) Nigeria; (c) Ghana.

3. Most people in Africa are (a) herders; (b) farmers; (c) factory workers.

4. **Nigeria achieved early economic progress largely because of its** (a) large population; (b) **program of free education;** (c) oil exports.

5. **The first president of Tanzania was** (a) Julius Nyerere; (b) Kwame Nkrumah; (c) Colonel Qaddafi.

6. The chief goal of apartheid is to (a) preserve black African culture; (b) keep the races separate; (c) improve medical care for nonwhites.

7. The horn of Africa is a part of (a) East Africa; (b) South Africa; (c) West Africa.

Chapter Checkup

1. (a) Describe three ways in which conditions after World War II favored African independence. (b) What role did educated Africans play in the struggle for independence?

2. Explain how each of the following caused problems for the new nations of Africa: (a) the colonial heritage; (b) subsistence farming; (c) rapid population growth; (d) urbanization.

3. (a) What role do multinational corporations play in Africa? (b) How do some African governments try to limit the influence of these corporations?

4. Describe two problems that have restricted or set back economic progress in (a) Nigeria; (b) Tanzania.

5. Compare Nigeria and Tanzania in each of the following areas: (a) population; (b) resources; (c) national unity.

6. (a) Why did South Africa establish apartheid? (b) How does apartheid affect nonwhites in South Africa? (c) How has the South African government responded to efforts to change its racial policy?

7. (a) What role have African nations played in the UN? (b) How has the UN helped African nations?

Critical Thinking

1. **Understanding Economic Ideas** (a) What do African nations mean by economic development? (b) How does economic development enable nations to modernize? (c) List three reasons why you think modernization is difficult to achieve in Africa.

2. **Analyzing a Quotation** In the early 1960s, Tanzanian president Nyerere said: "While other nations are trying to reach the moon, we are trying to reach the village." (a) To what "other nations" do you think Nyerere was referring? (b) How did Nyerere try to reach the villages of Tanzania?

Relating Past to Present

1. (a) Describe two ways in which African nations are still affected by their colonial pasts. (b) Do you think these effects are positive or negative? Explain.

Developing Basic Skills

1. **Researching** Choose one African nation that gained its independence after World War II. Research its history since independence. Then answer the following questions: (a) When did the country win independence? (b) What are its chief economic resources? (c) What problems has it faced in trying to modernize? (d) How successful has it been in solving these problems?

2. **Map Reading** Study the maps on pages 677 and 678. Then answer the following questions: (a) What natural resources are shown on the map of Nigeria? (b) What economic activity is shown on the map of Tanzania? (c) How do you think railroads might affect economic development within each country?

See page 808 for suggested readings.

36 The Middle East

(1945–Present)

A street in Jiddah, Saudi Arabia.

In 1973, Saudi Arabia and a number of other oil-producing nations quadrupled the price of a barrel of oil. Higher oil prices brought a flood of oil wealth to some Middle Eastern countries. In 1975, Sheik Yamani, oil minister from Saudi Arabia, explained why his country still faced many problems despite its vast oil wealth.

"You can't expect to transform a poor and backward country in a day. This wealth is less than two years old, and until cash is transformed into dwellings, highways, hospitals, and schools ... it is senseless to speak of wealth. Wealthy people don't buy gold watches here; for one thing, our tradition forbids us to wear them. As for the powerful cars you see, they're often second-hand ones. Cadillacs bought overseas for the price of a Toyota and brought here because there is no duty, no tax, and fuel costs almost nothing."

The western-educated oil minister maintained that Saudi Arabia was still a poor country. "Not only do we lack industry, agriculture; worse still, we lack manpower. I mean educated and trained manpower. We make our young people study, and we send them to foreign universities, but it takes years to obtain a degree. . . ."

Yamani pointed out that Saudi Arabia had to import foreign experts but had nowhere to house them. "To build hotels, we need contracts, but the contractors themselves need hotels to live in. It's a vicious circle that exhausts us. Among other things, we lack cement. We lack harbors because we lack the cement to build them. Last, but by no means least, we lack water. We haven't a single river, a single lake. We depend on rainfall alone. For 100 years, it has rained less and less frequently, for the last 25 [years] hardly at all."

In Saudi Arabia, as in other Middle Eastern nations, people are facing the challenges of modernization. Since 1945, the Middle East has experienced far-reaching political, economic, and social changes. These changes help make the Middle East a land of marked contrasts. New nations have emerged. But these new nations have traditions going back thousands of years to the earliest civilizations of the ancient Middle East.

1 A Region of Diversity

Read to Learn ■ why religious rivalries affect the Middle East
■ how geography influences Middle Eastern culture

The heartland of the Middle East includes the nations of the Arabian peninsula, Jordan, Israel, Lebanon, Syria, Iraq, Iran, Turkey, and Egypt. (See the map on page 693.) The nations of North Africa, Pakistan, and Afghanistan are sometimes also considered part of the Middle East because of the impact of Islam on their cultures.

The Patchwork Landscape

The Middle East is a region of diverse climates and geography. Mountains, plateaus, deserts, and steppes cover much of the region. A long mountain range stretches from Turkey through Iran to Afghanistan. Another runs along the coast of Lebanon. Vast, high plateaus dominate most of Turkey and large parts of Iran and Afghanistan.

The dominant geographical feature of the Middle East is desert. The largest desert is the Rub al Khali (roob ahl KHAH lee), also known as the Empty Quarter, in southwest Arabia. Some desert land can be made farmland if irrigated. However, without proper care, it quickly becomes desert again.

Bordering the deserts are the steppes, regions that support some scrubby vegetation. There are also several fertile farming regions in the Middle East. The largest of these are the Nile and Tigris-Euphrates valleys.

Adapting to the Environment

As elsewhere, the peoples of the Middle East have adapted their ways of life to the differing geographic conditions. Today, the three most common patterns of life are those of nomadic herders, village farmers, and city dwellers. Nomads make up about 5 percent of the population of the Middle East. The Bedouin (BED oo wihn), for example, roam the deserts of Iraq, Egypt, Jordan, Syria, and Saudi Arabia. They herd camels, goats, and sheep. Some Bedouin cultivate olive and date trees or plant millet around desert oases.

About 60 percent of the people of the Middle East live in farming villages. Farming is difficult in much of the Middle East because of infrequent rain or mountainous terrain. In mountainous regions and river valleys, farmers have developed methods to irrigate the land. Many of them grow cash crops such as cotton, sugar, and tobacco, which they sell to merchants from the cities.

A growing number of people—about 35 percent—live in cities. Since ancient times, cities have played important roles as centers of trade. Damascus, Syria, is one of the oldest cities in the world. In ancient times, it was located on a well-used caravan route. In cities such as Cairo and Baghdad, ancient monuments stand alongside skyscrapers.

Religious and Ethnic Groups

The Middle East is characterized by religious and ethnic diversity. As you have read, this region was the cradle of three major world religions: Judaism, Christianity, and Islam. These religions share some beliefs. For example, each teaches belief in one God and obedience to God's commandments. The city

Every year, thousands of Muslims make a pilgrimage to Mecca in Saudi Arabia. Here, they pray at the Kaaba, which houses the sacred Black Stone. The pilgrimage to Mecca helps unite Muslims from around the world.

of Jerusalem, which is sacred to all three religions, symbolizes this common heritage.

Today, the vast majority of the peoples of the Middle East are Muslim. Nevertheless, millions of Christians and Jews also live in this region. Until recently, Christians outnumbered Muslims in Lebanon. As you will read, the state of Israel was established as a Jewish homeland. Its population is 80 percent Jewish. The rest of the people of Israel are Christian or Muslim.

Different sects, or groups, have developed within each major religion. These groups have further increased religious diversity in the Middle East. Islam, for example, became divided into two branches—Sunnite and Shiite.* Each group developed its own traditions. Rivalries between religious

groups have sometimes erupted into violence.

There are also many ethnic groups in the Middle East. A large number of Muslims are Arabs. But millions of Muslims in the Middle East belong to other ethnic groups. For example, Turks and Iranians are non-Arab Muslims. They speak different languages and have strong feelings of loyalty to their own countries.

The Impact of History

As you read in Chapter 3, the Middle East is the crossroads of the world. It links Europe, Africa, and Asia. Ambitious conquerors and migrating peoples have left their mark on this part of the world. Assyrians, Babylonians, Hittites, Persians, Greeks, and Romans dominated the region in ancient times.

* See page 216 for the early history of these groups.

Later, Arabs and Mongols controlled large parts of the Middle East. As a result, the cultures of this region formed a mosaic in which many different traditions flourished side by side.

By 1500, two great empires had emerged in the Middle East: the Ottoman Empire and the Safavid Empire. The Ottoman Empire was ruled by Turks. At its height, it reached from the Tigris-Euphrates Valley to Morocco. (See the map on page 358.) The Safavid Empire was ruled by Iranians. It included most of what is today Iran. The Safavids pursued an aggressive policy of western expansion, which brought them into frequent conflict with the Ottoman Turks. In addition, religious rivalries fueled centuries of bitter fighting between the two empires.

The religion of the Ottoman Empire was Sunni Islam, whereas the official religion of the Safavid Empire was Shiite Islam. Despite frequent warfare, learning and the arts flourished in both empires. After the 1600s, however, both empires declined.

During the Age of Imperialism, European nations were able to gain influence over much of the Middle East. Before World War I, Germany gained political and military influence over the Ottoman Empire. Thus, when World War I started, the Turks joined the Central Powers. After its defeat in 1918, the Ottoman Empire was divided up by the Allies. As you read in Chapter 31, Turkey became a republic. However, Arab lands that had been part of the Ottoman Empire were made mandates of Great Britain and France.

In the period between World War I and World War II, Arab nationalists demanded independence. But their efforts to achieve this goal were not successful until after World War II. By the late 1940s, all countries in the Middle East had won their independence. (See the map on page 693.)

SECTION REVIEW

1. Locate: Iraq, Iran, Turkey, Egypt, Pakistan, Afghanistan, Damascus, Lebanon, Israel.
2. Identify: Rub al Khali, Safavid Empire.
3. (a) What two important geographical features are found in the Middle East? (b) In what countries or regions are these features found?
4. Describe three ways of life found in the Middle East.
5. (a) What three religions originated in the Middle East? (b) Which religion has the most followers in this region today?

2 Tradition and Change

Read to Learn ■ how Islam influences Middle Eastern cultures
■ how boom and drop in oil prices affect Middle Eastern nations

In the Middle East as elsewhere around the world, the decades after World War II brought great change. Palestine was partitioned, and the nation of Israel was created. The population explosion, urbanization, and new technology had deep effects on Middle Eastern nations. These developments challenged traditional patterns of life.

Islamic Heritage

Islam is a powerful force that unites Muslims around the world. In the Middle East, Islam influences peoples' outlooks and beliefs whether they are nomads, farmers, or city dwellers. Muslims follow the teachings of the Koran. As you have read, after Muhammad's death, Muslim scholars drew up a complete law code based on the Koran.

Islamic law governs all aspects of Muslim life, including worship, daily conduct, and punishments. In some Middle Eastern nations, Islamic law forms the basis for the legal systems. People in the Muslim world believe the law of the Koran came directly from God and therefore cannot be altered. However, Islamic law is subject to interpretation. For example, Sunnites and Shiites differ in the way they interpret the law.

689

Islam supports strong family ties. The Koran gives the father complete authority over the family. Children are taught respect and obedience to their parents. Traditionally, the father arranges the marriages for his children and supervises the activities of the extended family. The Koran protects the property rights of women, but its teachings have been interpreted to support the idea that women are inferior to men.

Patterns of Change

Islamic traditions remain strong in the Middle East. However, since 1945 sweeping economic and social changes have posed a challenge to some of these traditions and have transformed the nations of this region.

Economic development. Middle Eastern governments have supported programs to improve agriculture and expand industry. Some nations have passed land reform programs to break up the estates of large landowners and redistribute the land to peasant farmers. The use of new types of seed and fertilizers, government-sponsored irrigation projects, and the introduction of farm machinery have helped increase agricultural output. At the same time, many nations have encouraged the building of new industries.

Urbanization. The development of industry created a need for skilled workers. Many farmers moved to the cities, seeking work in the factories. As in Africa, people in rural areas of the Middle East were attracted by the glamor, excitement, and increased opportunities of the cities.

Rapid urbanization created the familiar problems of crowded slums and unemployment. Because of inadequate housing in the cities, the families of some workers have remained in their villages to work the land. Today, for example, some Egyptian men take jobs in the factories of Cairo while their families remain to till the soil in Upper Egypt. This division of labor has sometimes weakened traditional family ties.

When entire families moved to the cities, they sometimes found city life lonely and impersonal. However, rural people from the same village tended to settle in the same part of the city. In this way, they reestab-

lished the sense of security they had enjoyed in the country.

Changing Roles for Women

Urbanization and better education are affecting the roles of women in Islamic countries. Traditionally, women remained within the home. They followed their parents' wishes until they were married. After marriage, a woman became a member of her husband's family. Although peasant women worked in the fields, women generally led secluded lives. Women were expected to show modesty in behavior and dress, an idea symbolized by wearing the veil to cover their faces when in public places.

Tradition and change exist side by side in many parts of the Middle East. These women in Riyadh, Saudi Arabia, wear veils that cover most of their faces. When the photographer tried to take their picture, they used their hands to cover their faces completely.

Daily Life ▪ New Roles for Egyptian Women

In recent years, Egyptian women have won new rights and taken a greater role in public affairs. Some people attribute this change to the influence of Jehan Sadat, wife of the late Egyptian president Anwar Sadat. A well-known leader in the women's movement, Jehan Sadat encouraged her husband to take steps to improve the position of Egyptian women.

In 1979, President Sadat announced new laws giving women additional political and legal rights. He added 30 seats to the 360-seat Egyptian parliament. All the new seats were to be reserved for women representatives. At the same time, he decreed that one fifth of the members of local city councils should be women. When the newly elected women entered parliament, Jehan Sadat arranged a series of meetings for them. She encouraged the new members to ask questions and raise issues that concerned them. "I'm very satisfied," Jehan Sadat said after the meetings, "because I fought for many, many years for this."

Jehan Sadat was not the only woman to influence public policy. Women gained important positions in several areas. Sadat appointed another woman, Aminah el-Said, chairman of the board of the largest Egyptian publishing house. Sadat had met Said in the early 1950s when they were both on the staff of the state-run publishing house.

Another woman, Amal Osman, has held the job of Minister for Social Affairs. Formerly a professor at the University of Cairo, Osman has worked to improve education and health care. She has stressed the need for social legislation, especially a social security system for all Egyptians.

The success of Egyptian women has set an example for women in other Arab countries. However, the change has not won universal approval. A visiting Arab leader once told Sadat that he thought it was improper for women engineers to be working in factories along with men. Sadat replied, "Without women, Egypt wouldn't be where she is today."

Educated Egyptian women have moved into leading positions in a number of areas, including medicine, the media, and education. Dr. Haifaa Shanawany has won international recognition for her family-oriented medical services throughout Asia, Africa, and Europe. The example of women leaders in Egypt has helped women in other Middle Eastern nations overcome opposition to their new roles in society.

Today, women in many Islamic countries have stopped wearing the veil. The disappearance of the veil is an outward sign that some basic changes are taking place. In many nations, women are becoming better educated and are taking jobs outside the home. Primary and secondary schools have been opened for girls. Middle Eastern universities now also admit women. And education has allowed women in some countries to assume new roles.

In other Muslim countries, however, a change in the role of women is not considered an advance. Technical and economic development, it is felt, should not affect family life. Some countries have strong Islamic revivalist movements. In these countries, resistance to western views of women's roles is growing.

The kind of work considered acceptable for women varies throughout the Middle East. In Arab societies women traditionally produced crafts, such as clothing, rugs, and pottery. They served in small shops and as midwives. Today in Egypt, Syria, Israel, and Turkey women can follow many careers. But

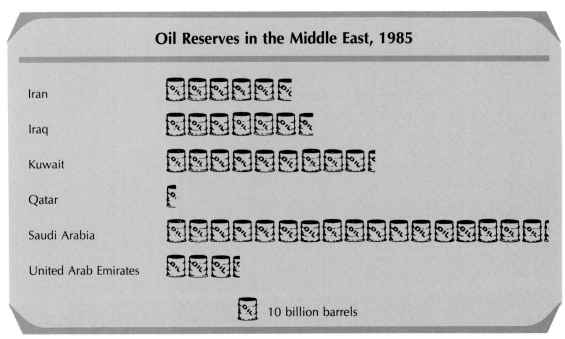

Oil Reserves in the Middle East, 1985

Iran

Iraq

Kuwait

Qatar

Saudi Arabia

United Arab Emirates

10 billion barrels

Source: *OPEC Annual Report, 1985*

Graph Skill *The Middle East is the source of much of the world's oil. In which two nations was warfare affecting oil production in the 1980s?*

even in countries with open opportunities, most women still live at home until they marry. And they strongly support traditional family ties.

The Impact of Oil

The world's largest reserves of oil are found in the Middle East. Since 1945, oil has been the chief export of this region. In the early 1980s, the Middle East was producing one third of the world's oil. Yet only six Middle Eastern nations have large amounts of oil. They are the Persian Gulf states of Iran, Iraq, Kuwait, Qatar, Saudi Arabia, and the United Arab Emirates.

These nations belong to the Organization of Petroleum Exporting Countries (OPEC), which was formed in 1960. OPEC includes 13 oil-exporting nations that meet regularly to set the price of oil. Between 1969 and 1982, the price of crude, or unrefined, oil jumped from $1.20 to $33.80 a barrel. Then, in the mid-1980s, a world oil glut forced prices to drop sharply. Economic recession,

political tensions, and fears for future economic development resulted.

In the meantime, however, oil wealth had already transformed some OPEC nations. For example, only 35 years ago Saudi Arabia was largely a roadless desert. Though the holy cities of Mecca and Medina had long attracted pilgrims from around the world, most Saudis had remained nomadic Bedouin herders.

Today, Saudi Arabia is the world's third largest oil producer, after the Soviet Union and the United States. Thanks to oil, the Saudi government has been able to invest billions of dollars in new industries, from steel mills to ice cream factories. Cities boomed as the government built roads, housing, schools, universities, and hospitals. Free health care and education became available for all citizens.

These economic developments were made largely with western technology. But the Saudi ruling family, the House of Saud led by King Fahd, is determined to keep Saudi culture free of *westernization*—the adoption of western ideas and customs.

Since there is no separation of the state and Islam, Saudi Arabia's constitution is Islam's holy book, the Koran. The Saudis interpret the Koran strictly and do not allow alcohol, dancing, or movies. Most women work only in the home. To the Saudis, western cultural values are destructive to Islamic family and religious traditions. Therefore, all attempts to promote economic development have to agree with traditional values.

3 Emerging Middle Eastern States

Read to Learn
- why modernization caused problems in Turkey and Egypt
- why conflicts developed in Lebanon, Syria, Iraq, and Iran

Like the developing nations of Africa, the nations of the Middle East are seeking ways to advance their economies in order to offer their people a better life. Despite the common Islamic heritage of most Middle Eastern nations, each country has pursued its goals in its own way.

Critical Choices for Turkey

In the 1920s, Kemal Atatürk introduced reforms aimed at modernization and westernization. (See page 598.) Atatürk's policies were accepted mainly in the cities, but religious Turks and people in rural areas opposed many of the changes. Today, Turkey is still caught between these two forces. On the one hand, a full-scale movement presses for the return of Islamic ideals, education, and discipline. On the other hand, successors of Atatürk want to continue westernization. They want to keep religion separate from the state.

Turkey has faced other problems since World War II. In the late 1940s, the Soviet Union threatened to take control of territory in eastern Turkey. Soviet pressure forced Turkey to seek aid from the United States and Western Europe. Under the terms of the Truman Doctrine, which you read about in Chapter 34, the United States supplied Turkey with military and economic aid. Foreign aid allowed Turkey to prevent Soviet aggression and renew its efforts to modernize.

During the 1960s and 1970s, Turkey and Greece clashed over the island of Cyprus. Cyprus is inhabited by both Greeks and Turks and has long been a source of conflict. In 1974, Turkish troops took control of about one third of the island. The United States and other western nations reduced their aid to Turkey in an unsuccessful effort to force Turkish troops to withdraw from Cyprus.

Loss of foreign aid, economic slowdown, and the deep divisions between religious and nonreligious groups led to political unrest in Turkey. In the 1970s, extremists staged many terrorist acts, and the government changed hands many times. Then, in 1980, a military takeover restored order. General Kenan Evren was named president until 1989. Turkey gained some civilian rule in 1983 when elections were held and Turkut Ozal became prime minister.

Nationalism and Reform in Egypt

In the 1950s, Gamal Abdel Nasser raised the banner of Egyptian nationalism. A former army officer, Nasser helped overthrow the Egyptian king in 1952 and became president of Egypt in 1954. Nasser was determined to end British influence in Egypt. Britain had kept troops in Egypt since the Age of Imperialism. Nasser demanded that Britain remove the troops it had guarding the Suez Canal.

Nasser introduced a program of reform to improve the standard of living of Egyptian peasants. A land reform law required all landowners whose property exceeded 200 acres to sell some of their land to the peasants. The government also built schools and health clinics, even in remote Nile villages.

The Aswan High Dam. To improve agriculture in Upper Egypt, Nasser planned to build a huge dam at Aswan. At first, Great Britain and the United States agreed to provide the loans to finance this project. However, when Nasser negotiated with the Soviet Union for aid, the United States and Great Britain withdrew their offers.

In 1956, Nasser responded to this action by announcing that Egypt was taking over the Suez Canal from its British and French owners. Britain and France, with the help of Israel, attempted unsuccessfully to regain control of the canal by force. (See page 699.)

The huge Aswan High Dam was completed in 1970 with Soviet aid. The dam provided hydroelectric power and water for irrigation. It has created thousands of acres of farmland. During the drought years of the 1970s, it provided a reliable source of Nile water to irrigate farmland. It thereby helped prevent widespread famine in Egypt.

Threats to stability. Egypt continued to struggle with many problems. Anwar Sadat, who became president after Nasser's death in 1970, tried to expand the Egyptian economy by attracting foreign investment. Yet foreign investment and the discovery of some oil in Egypt have not greatly helped most Egyptians. They remain extremely poor. The population continues to grow faster than the food supply. Moreover, about 95 percent of the people are crowded into the strip of land along the Nile River. Their dwellings are replacing irrigated farmland.

Map Skill   *Oil has brought some Middle Eastern nations tremendous wealth. OPEC nations have invested profits from oil wealth to build up industry. Which Middle Eastern nations belong to OPEC?*

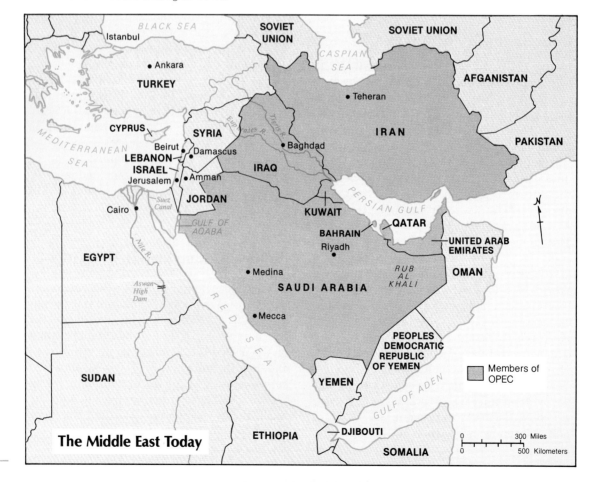

The Middle East Today

The Aswan High Dam has provided a reliable source of water throughout the year for the farms along the Nile River. In addition, generators at the dam harness power from the Nile and have tripled electric output in Egypt. However, the dam also ended the annual flooding that had carried silt and fertilized the farmland along the Nile since ancient times. As a result, farmers have had to buy costly artificial fertilizers for their land.

In Egypt, as elsewhere in the Islamic world, religious revivalists have threatened the nation's political stability. In October 1981, Muslim extremists opposed to President Sadat's policies assassinated him. Hosni Mubarak, successor to the slain president, vowed to use "ruthless measures" to prevent further terrorism.

Civil War in Lebanon

Lebanon became independent in 1945. Its population was about half Christian and half Muslim. The Christians belonged to different sects, including the Maronite Church, the Greek Orthodox Church, and the Armenian Church. Muslims, too, belonged to different sects—Sunni, Shiite, and Druze. At independence, leaders worked out a political system in which each group was represented.

For 30 years after independence, Lebanon enjoyed peace and prosperity. However, economic and political inequalities caused tensions beneath the surface. In addition, Lebanese Muslims and Christians disagreed over the issue of the Palestinians living in refugee camps in Lebanon.

Hundreds of thousands of Palestinians had fled their homeland when it became part of the state of Israel in 1948. Most of the Palestinians were Muslim. They settled in many countries. During the 1960s and 1970s, the number of Palestinians in Lebanon increased. Some Palestinian refugees belonged to the Palestine Liberation Organization (PLO), a group that waged guerrilla war against Israel. After 1970, the PLO used Lebanon as a base for its activities.

PLO activities led to increased tension in Lebanon. Most Lebanese Muslims supported the Palestinians and the PLO. Most Lebanese Christians, on the other hand, feared that the growing number of Palestinians was upsetting the balance of political power.

In 1975, civil war broke out, and Syria invaded Lebanon. This resulted in a power struggle among Syrian, Lebanese Christian, Lebanese Muslim, and PLO forces. At the same time, PLO fighters based in Lebanon launched attacks on Israel, and Israelis attacked their base in return. In 1982, Israel invaded Lebanon, forcing many PLO fighters to leave. An international peacekeeping force, including Americans, arrived in a futile effort to bring peace. American troops left in 1984, and most Israelis withdrew in 1985. Militias of the different Lebanese groups increasingly fought each other through terrorist attacks. But no one group emerged as strong enough to dominate or reunite the nation.

The Military in Syria

Like Lebanon, Syria gained its independence after World War II. During the late 1950s, one political party, the Baath party, gained power. It established a socialist economy in which the government controlled industry and foreign trade.

In 1971, a Baath military officer, Hafez al-Assad, became president. Under Assad, the Syrian economy prospered as both agriculture and industry expanded. The government built a railroad network linking cities, ports, and farming areas.

In the early 1980s, Assad defeated a challenge by the Muslim Brotherhood, a militant Islamic revivalist group. As part of an amnesty, Assad appointed the Brotherhood leader, Isam Attar, to his cabinet. When the Baath party reelected Assad in 1985, Attar also kept his post. Conflict between the two forces was thus kept down.

The military remains powerful in Syria. One-sixth of the country's work force serves in the military. As you will read, the Syrian army has fought several wars with Israel. Syria also remains a powerful influence in Lebanon and Jordan. In 1987, Syrian troops invaded Lebanon to force a cease-fire among warring militias.

Developments in Iraq

Iraq, which includes the ancient region of Mesopotamia, became independent in 1933. Iraq has large oil reserves. Oil wealth has allowed the government to develop agriculture and improve the standard of living of the largely rural population. But Iraq has limited its oil production because it wants to avoid becoming dependent on oil revenue. To produce other revenues, it has made a strong effort to increase food production, hoping to export food to other Middle Eastern nations.

In the 1960s and 1970s, the government was threatened by ethnic divisions. Twenty percent of Iraq's population consists of Kurds, a non-Arab Muslim people who have their own culture and language. For many years, Kurds have demanded a measure of self-government. The government's failure to satisfy these demands has resulted in battles between Kurdish rebels and Iraqi troops.

In the early 1980s, a border dispute between Iraq and Iran led to war between these two countries. Both nations claim control of the Shatt al-Arab, an important waterway at the mouth of the Tigris and Euphrates rivers. During the war, oil fields in both nations were bombed, and the army of each side made temporary advances. The war raged on, with increased intensity, in 1987.

Revolution in Iran

Modernization and oil wealth have caused conflict and turmoil in Iran. In the decades after World War II, the shah of Iran pushed through a series of reforms intended to modernize Iran and encourage westernization. The shah was especially anxious to bring reform to the rural areas. He ordered large estates divided up among landless peasants. Schools, highways, and industries were built. And women were given the right to vote.

The money to finance these reforms came from oil. Iranian oil exports rose steadily in the 1960s and 1970s. Moreover, as a member of OPEC, Iran benefited from the higher prices charged for oil in the 1970s.

Opposition to the shah. Despite the shah's reform programs, Iran's oil wealth did not greatly improve conditions for peasants and poor people in the cities. Instead, the gap between rich and poor widened. Moreover, Shiite Muslims, conservative clergy, and other groups opposed the reforms.

The shah ruled as a virtual dictator for years. As opposition to his reforms grew, he exercised power ruthlessly. He used the Savak, a powerful secret police force, to hunt down and arrest critics. He spent large sums of money to build up the military, which some people feared he might use to enforce his will.

In the late 1970s, tensions in Iran increased. Many Iranian students who had been educated in the West accused the shah of corruption and exercising dictatorial

In the late 1970s, mass rallies, like this one in Teheran, were held to demand the overthrow of the shah. Opposition to the shah came from many groups. Some protested his dictatorial ways. Others denounced his spending so much on weapons. Still others opposed his reform programs, which were moving Iran away from some Islamic traditions. Many Iranian Muslims supported the Ayatollah Khomeini, whose picture is on the poster in the center of this photograph.

power. The Muslim clergy denounced the shah's social policies and western influences on Iranian society. These groups joined forces against the shah. They organized huge strikes and protest rallies in major cities.

An Islamic republic. Opponents of the shah rallied around the Ayatollah* Ruhollah Khomeini (roo HOH luh koh MAY nee), a Muslim leader who lived in exile in France. Khomeini wanted Iranians to return to strict Islamic traditions. He called for the overthrow of the shah and the removal of all foreign influence from Iran.

The shah was unable to silence the growing opposition. In January 1979, he left Iran and went into exile. The next month, Khomeini returned in triumph to Iran. Khomeini and his supporters ended the monarchy and declared Iran an Islamic republic.

The clergy led an Islamic revolution, which affected all aspects of life in Iran. Is-

lamic law and traditions were restored. Western music and dancing were banned. Women, who had gone unveiled for years, started to cover their heads and faces again.

Revolutionaries in Iran were strongly anti-American because the United States had been a strong supporter of the shah. In November 1979, when the exiled shah was admitted to the United States for medical treatment, a group of young Iranians seized the United States embassy in Teheran. They held 59 American citizens hostage and demanded the return of the shah to Iran for trial. Negotiations dragged on until January 1981, when the hostages were finally released.

Although Khomeini remained personally popular, some opposition to the revolution surfaced. But criticism was quickly silenced with force. Ethnic groups such as Kurds living in Iran took advantage of the turmoil to demand self-government. Despite the political unrest, Iranians continued to vote for Khomeini's policies. However, with

Graph Skill *Oil production in Iran climbed steadily in the early 1970s. When did oil production begin to decline? Why did it decline?*

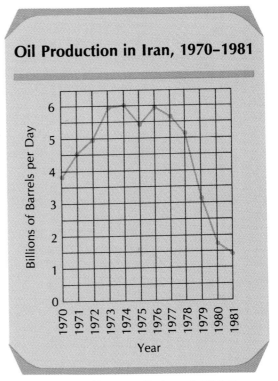

Oil Production in Iran, 1970–1981

(Graph: Billions of Barrels per Day vs. Year 1970–1981)

Sources: *Monthly Energy Review* and *Oil & Gas Journal*.

* Ayatollah (ī uh TOH luh) is a Persian word that means "reflection of Allah." It is the highest title that can be held by a Muslim in the Shiite sect.

Khomeini in his mid-80s and with oil revenues down sharply, Iran's future leadership seems less certain.

SECTION REVIEW

1. Identify: Gamel Adbel Nasser, Aswan High Dam, Anwar Sadat, Palestine Liberation Organization, Hafez al-Assad, Kurds, Ayatollah Ruhollah Khomeini.

2. (a) Why did Nasser seize the Suez canal? (b) How did Britain and France respond to this move?

3. (a) Give one reason why civil war broke out in Lebanon. (b) What four different groups fought in Lebanon in the late 1970s?

4. (a) Why did the Syrian economy flourish in recent years? (b) What strains have offset some economic gains?

4 The Middle East and the World

Read to Learn
- why conflicts took place between Israel and Arab nations
- what efforts were made to resolve Arab-Israeli conflicts

Events in the Middle East have often captured headlines around the world. Because of its strategic location and its oil, the superpowers have competed for influence in this region. The Middle East has also seen an ongoing struggle between Arab countries and the state of Israel.

The Creation of Israel

Throughout their long history, Jews living in different parts of the world kept alive their religious and cultural traditions. Zionists called for a Jewish homeland in Palestine. In the period between the two world wars, Jewish immigration to Palestine increased. Many Jews left Germany for Palestine in the 1930s, when the Nazis launched their vicious anti-Semitic campaign.

After World War II, the number of Jews wanting to settle in Palestine greatly increased. Over 6 million Jews had been killed in Nazi concentration camps. Between 1945 and 1948, many of the survivors of these death camps sought refuge in Palestine. The Arabs, about 70 percent of the population, felt threatened by the sudden arrival of so many Jewish immigrants. Clashes had occurred between Arabs and Jews in the 1920s and 1930s. But after 1945, the fighting escalated as Arabs and Jews fought for control of the towns and villages of Palestine.

Britain, which had administered Palestine since World War I, was unable to impose peace. It turned the problem of Palestine over to the United Nations. In November 1947, a UN commission recommended that Palestine be divided into an Arab state and a Jewish state. The Arabs rejected this plan because they thought it violated their right to self-determination. The Zionists reluctantly accepted the plan.

In May 1948, the British withdrew from Palestine. At the same time, Jewish residents proclaimed one part of Palestine the nation of Israel. The 2,000-year-old dream of the Jewish people to recreate a Jewish state had finally become a reality. Israel gained official recognition from the major world powers. As you will read, Israel faced an immediate threat from Arabs in the rest of Palestine as well as from neighboring Arab states.

Government and Society in Israel

Like the peoples of many other newly created nations, the Israelis adopted a democratic constitution. The constitution established a parliamentary system of government. Israelis also worked to develop their land economically. They set up kibbutzim (KEE boo TSEEM), agricultural and industrial cooperatives. On a *kibbutz*, people live in community housing projects, work together, and share the profits of their labor. Since 1948, Israelis have irrigated desert areas, turning them into fertile farms.

Fifteen percent of the population of Israel is Arab, but Israel is mainly a nation of Jewish immigrants. Settlers arrived in Israel from all over the world. Although these Jewish settlers shared a religious heritage, they

After World War II, many survivors of the Holocaust sought to build a new life in Palestine. This photograph shows the ship Theodore Herzl *arriving in Palestine in 1947 with refugees from Central Europe. Arabs felt threatened by the arrival of so many Jews. As a result, fighting between Arabs and Jews increased.*

brought with them diverse cultures. Cultural differences caused social and political difficulties.

Two major groups in Israel are the Ashkenazic Jews from western countries and the Sephardic Jews from Asia and North Africa. The Ashkenazim are usually better educated than the Sephardic Jews. As a result, they hold the better jobs and the most political power. However, Sephardic Jews outnumber the Ashkenazim. They are beginning to exert greater influence in government and improve their position in society.

The Arab-Israeli Conflict

Since its creation, Israel has been involved in four wars with its Arab neighbors. In 1948, Arab nations supported the demands of Arabs in Palestine for self-determination. They refused to recognize the new nation of Israel. Arab armies from Egypt, Jordan, Lebanon, Syria, and Iraq invaded Israel. The Israelis were outnumbered, but the Arabs failed to unite and suffered a crushing defeat.

The United Nations arranged a ceasefire in 1949. By that time, however, Israel had annexed a large chunk of Arab territory in Palestine and increased its size by about 30 percent. Israel also won control of half of Jerusalem. The other half remained under Arab control. Despite their defeat in the war, Arab nations still refused to recognize Israel and denied it access to the Suez Canal and the Gulf of Aqaba.

After the war, over 700,000 Arabs living in Palestine fled or were expelled from their homes. The United Nations established refugee camps in nearby Arab lands to house these Palestinian Arabs. The suffering of these refugees would remain a controversial issue in the Middle East.

In 1956, a second Arab-Israeli war broke out after Egyptian president Nasser took control of the Suez Canal. As you have read, Britain, France, and Israel attacked Egypt. Israeli forces advanced into the Sinai Peninsula. The UN intervened and ordered the withdrawal of the attacking forces. UN troops were then sent to keep peace on the border between Egypt and Israel.

The Six-Day War. Between 1956 and 1967, Arab nations and Israel spent huge sums to build up their armed forces. Egypt, for example, purchased large amounts of So-

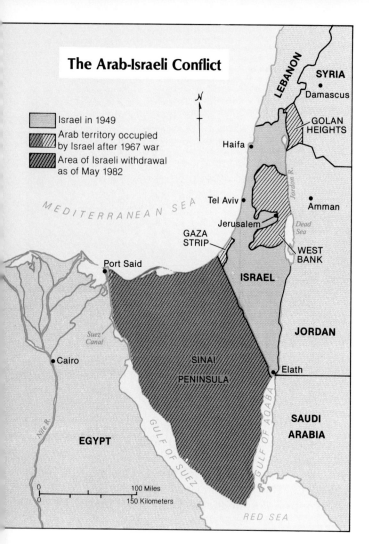

The Arab-Israeli Conflict

- Israel in 1949
- Arab territory occupied by Israel after 1967 war
- Area of Israeli withdrawal as of May 1982

Map Skill *Since 1948, four wars have broken out between Israel and its Arab neighbors. Tension remains high in this part of the Middle East. Syria wants to regain the Golan Heights. The future of the Israeli-occupied West Bank is a controversial subject. In addition, Israeli troops invaded Lebanon in 1982 in order to destroy PLO bases. Which captured area has Israel returned? Which has it kept?*

viet weapons. Israel feared that Egypt and other Arab nations were preparing to attack. In a surprise move, Israel struck first.

In June 1967, the Israeli air force destroyed most of the Egyptian and Syrian air forces on the ground. In six days, the Israelis swept across the Sinai to the Suez Canal. They seized the Golan Heights from Syria as well as the Arab half of Jerusalem and the West Bank from Jordan.

The United Nations again arranged a cease-fire to end the Six-Day War. The Is-

raelis, however, announced their intention to keep all captured territories until a permanent peace settlement had been negotiated. Attempts to reach such a peace settlement failed.

The October War. In October 1973, Egypt and Syria sought revenge for their defeat in the Six-Day War. Egyptian and Syrian troops attacked Israel in an effort to regain Israeli-occupied lands. Egypt wished to regain control of the Suez Canal, lost when Israel took the canal's eastern bank. At first, Egyptian forces pushed the Israelis back across the Sinai. The Syrians advanced towards the Golan Heights. However, the Israelis soon took the offensive. They regained the lands they had lost in the Sinai and in Syria. Once more the UN arranged a cease-five, which ended the October War.

The Arab Oil Embargo

During the October War, the Soviet Union rushed arms and supplies to the Egyptians, while the United States did the same for Israel. As a protest against United States support for Israel, the oil-producing Arab countries imposed an oil embargo. That is, they cut off oil shipments to the United States and the Netherlands, two nations that supported Israel. They also cut back on oil production, creating oil shortages in all the industrial nations. Arab governments then called on these nations to pressure Israel to withdraw from the occupied territories.

The oil embargo was lifted in 1974. Israel still held the occupied territories, but the Arabs had shown they were prepared to use oil as a weapon against Israel and its supporters. The lifting of the embargo coincided with OPEC's decision to quadruple the price of a barrel of oil. Skyrocketing prices for gasoline and other petroleum products contributed to worldwide inflation in the 1970s.

An Uneasy Peace

No peace treaty was ever signed after the wars between the Arabs and the Israelis. In fact, Arab nations saw the period between each war simply as a time when the fighting was suspended. To end this state of constant war, President Sadat of Egypt visited Israel in November 1977. Afterward, representatives of Egypt and Israel met to discuss a possible peace. But negotiations soon reached a stalemate.

In 1978, President Carter of the United States invited Egyptian President Sadat and Israeli Prime Minister Menachem Begin (meh NAH kem BAY gihn) to meet at Camp David, Maryland. At these meetings, the three leaders worked out a framework for a peace settlement. The Camp David agreement set up a timetable for Israeli forces to withdraw from the Sinai, the Gaza Strip, and the West Bank.

The Camp David agreement also called for a formal peace treaty between Egypt and Israel. In March 1979, Sadat and Begin met in Washington, D.C., and signed the peace treaty. The treaty was the first agreement ever signed between an Arab nation and Israel. Other Arab nations condemned Egypt for destroying Arab unity by concluding a separate peace with Israel.

President Sadat hoped that other Arab nations would eventually follow Egypt's lead. However, other Arab nations have maintained their hostile attitude toward Israel. Moreover, although Israel has returned the Sinai to Egypt, other actions called for by the treaty have not been taken.

Unresolved Issues

Two of the major stumbling blocks to peace in the Middle East are the issue of the Palestinian Arabs and the future of Israeli-occupied lands. There are about 3.5 million Palestinian Arabs. Over one third of them live in exile. Some are educated and well-to-do. They live and work in other Arab countries, the United States, or Europe. Most Palestinian Arabs, however, live in miserable poverty in refugee camps. Since 1948, generations of Palestinians have grown up in these camps.

The plight of the Palestinian refugees is closely tied to the Israeli-occupied territory of the West Bank. The West Bank was part of the kingdom of Jordan until Israeli forces occupied it during the Six-Day War. Over 1 million Arabs live in the West Bank and pay taxes to Israel.

Israel has refused to return the West Bank to Jordan because Arab threats against Israel have made the West Bank appear to be a vital buffer for Israel's defense. Moreover, Jewish settlers have built homes and set up businesses there. Today many Israeli settlers commute from suburbs in the West Bank to jobs in Jerusalem and Tel Aviv.

Arabs living in the West Bank see Israeli settlements as part of a long-range plan to drive them out. Their protests have ranged from demonstrations to acts of terrorism.

In fact, within Israel, a small extremist party led by Meir Kahane has called for the expulsion of all Arabs from the West Bank. Yet other Israelis would compromise. Some would accept a Palestinian state west of the Jordan River, excluding Jerusalem. Some think Israel and Jordan should share the job of administering the region.

President Jimmy Carter (center) shakes hands with President Sadat (left) and Prime Minister Begin (right) after the signing of the 1979 peace treaty between Egypt and Israel. The peace treaty marked a first step toward an overall peace settlement in the Middle East. However, other Arab nations have refused to recognize the treaty or participate in direct negotiations with Israel.

Possible solutions arise and then disappear. For example, in 1985, King Hussein of Jordan met with Yasir Arafat (YAH sir AH rah faht), leader of the PLO. They declared their joint willingness to trade territory for peace on the basis of United Nations resolutions. But the plan soon fell apart. Israel, moreover, distrusts the PLO, which has been the source of raids and terrorist attacks in the past. Israel does not want the PLO included in peace talks. Thus, prospects for peaceful settlement remain uncertain.

SECTION REVIEW

1. Locate: Jerusalem, Suez Canal, Gulf of Aqaba, Sinai Peninsula, Golan Heights, West Bank.
2. Identify: Six-Day War, October War, Menachem Begin, Yasir Arafat.
3. Define: kibbutz.
4. Why did many Jews want to settle in Palestine after World War II?
5. Why did oil-producing Arab nations impose an oil embargo on the United States in 1973?

Chapter 36 Review

In Perspective

The Middle East is a land of great diversity. Three world religions originated in this region. Each has influenced the peoples of the Middle East. The majority of people are Muslims, and Islamic traditions are deeply rooted.

Middle Eastern nations have faced the challenges of modernization. In Turkey and Iran, for example, the governments pushed forward with programs for reform. At the same time, traditional forces opposed these reforms. In Iran, the clash of opposing forces resulted in a far-reaching revolution. An Islamic revival movement has appeared in many Middle Eastern nations. Egypt has struggled with the problem of producing enough food for its rapidly growing population.

Since 1948, the Arab-Israeli conflict has created dangerous tensions in the Middle East. Both sides have sought aid from the superpowers. In 1977, Egyptian President Sadat became the first Arab leader to negotiate with Israel. Yet peace remains a distant goal.

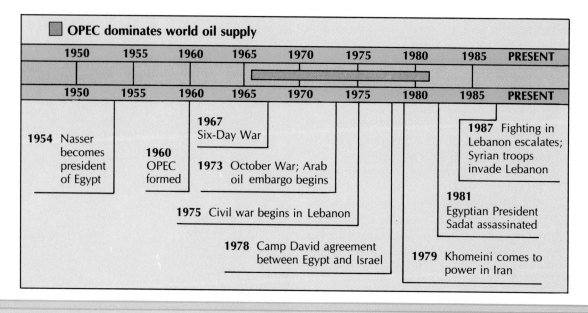

OPEC dominates world oil supply

| 1950 | 1955 | 1960 | 1965 | 1970 | 1975 | 1980 | 1985 | PRESENT |

1954 Nasser becomes president of Egypt

1960 OPEC formed

1967 Six-Day War

1973 October War; Arab oil embargo begins

1975 Civil war begins in Lebanon

1978 Camp David agreement between Egypt and Israel

1979 Khomeini comes to power in Iran

1981 Egyptian President Sadat assassinated

1987 Fighting in Lebanon escalates; Syrian troops invade Lebanon

Recalling Facts

Match each country at left with the statement at right.

1. Saudi Arabia
2. Lebanon
3. Iran
4. Syria
5. Turkey
6. Israel
7. Egypt
8. Iraq

a. Kurds fought for self-government in the 1960s and 1970s.
b. Aswan High Dam was built to irrigate more land.
c. Muslim clergy led a revolution against the shah.
d. Economic problems and terrorism led to a military takeover in 1980.
e. Settlers organized farming and industrial cooperatives.
f. Civil war broke out between Christians and Muslims.
g. Oil wealth allows the government to provide free health care.
h. Military leaders of the **Baath Party** give aid to the PLO.

Chapter Checkup

1. Explain how each of the following contributed to diversity in the Middle East; (a) geography; (b) religion; (c) history.

2. (a) What two empires flourished in the Middle East during the 1500s? (b) What regions were affected by each empire? (c) Why were these empires often at war with each other?

3. (a) How have Middle Eastern nations tried to improve agriculture? (b) How has the growth of industry affected cities?

4. (a) Which people support modernization in Turkey? (b) Which people oppose modernization? (c) How have economic problems contributed to tensions in Turkey?

5. (a) How did Nasser express Egyptian nationalism? (b) What economic reforms did he introduce?

6. (a) How did oil wealth benefit Iran? (b) How did it hurt Iran?

Critical Thinking

1. **Comparing** (a) How are efforts to modernize similar in the Middle East and Africa? (b) What problems do people in both regions face in developing their economies?

2. **Expressing an Opinion** (a) Why did the shah lose support for his reforms in Iran? (b) In your opinion, what steps could have been taken to prevent the revolution in Iran?

Relating Past to Present

1. Review pages 213 to 220 in Chapter 13 and your reading in this chapter. (a) How does the cultural and religious heritage of Islam unite the peoples in the Middle East? (b) How does modernization threaten the traditional ways of life in this region?

Developing Basic Skills

1. **Classifying** Make a chart with four rows and two columns. Title the rows Turkey, Egypt, Iran, and Saudi Arabia. Title the columns Programs for Change and Results. Complete the chart and then answer the following questions: (a) How are programs for change similar in all four countries? (b) How are the results of these programs similar in all four countries? (c) How are they different?

2. **Map Reading** Study the map on page 700. Then answer the following questions: (a) What Arab lands border Israel? (b) What Arab territory did Israel occupy in the Six-Day War in 1967? (c) What territory has Israel returned to Egypt? (d) Why do you think Israel has returned occupied land to Egypt and not to other Arab nations?

See page 808 for suggested readings.

37 Asia

(1945–Present)

A memorial to workers and soldiers in Chengchow, China.

In the Taching oil fields of northwestern China, workers drilled for five days and nights. Finally, their efforts brought success. A tower of crude oil shot into the air. The drilling team had little time to celebrate, however. When they were dismantling the oil derrick, a drill pipe struck the team leader, Wang Chin-hsi, across the legs. Although seriously injured, Wang refused medical attention and kept working. Later he went to a hospital. But he soon returned to work with one leg in a cast.

One night, shortly after Wang's return, an explosion blew off the cement lid that covered a drilling rig. Wang knew that this could cause a blowout that would destroy the entire drilling operation. To prevent such a disaster, he had cement poured into the mud tank of the oil well. Because the drilling team did not have a cement mixer, he then jumped into the waist-deep mud and began trampling the cement into the mud.

For three hours, Wang ignored his injured leg and led the effort to save the well. Finally, no longer able to stand, Wang was helped from the mud tank. Propped on crutches, he finished supervising the operation that saved the oil well. "Team leader Wang," said a fellow worker, "you're a real man of iron!"

This story of Wang's dedication to his job has been told and retold throughout China. It symbolizes the spirit that Chinese leaders encourage as their nation struggles to modernize. China has vast natural resources. But it lacks the modern machinery and technology to develop industry. Thus, it has turned to the energy of its large population to accomplish the task of modernization. After World War II, nations throughout Asia struggled to gain freedom from western control. They then turned to an even greater struggle, transforming their ancient civilizations into modern nations.

1 Independent Nations of South Asia

Read to Learn   ■ how the partition of India reflected ancient differences
■ what problems the nations of South Asia have faced

South Asia is another name for the subcontinent of India. This region was Great Britain's largest, most prized colonial possession. As you read in Chapter 31, Britain made concessions to Indian demands for self-government. But it did not grant outright independence. At the end of World War II, however, Great Britain realized that it could no longer maintain its rule over India.

Partition of India

Under British rule, the subcontinent of India was united under a single government. Yet the people of India were not united. As you read in Chapter 15, deep divisions existed in India between Hindus and Muslims. As the time for independence approached, tension between these two groups increased. Muslims feared that they would be outnumbered by Hindus in an independent India. Therefore, they united behind Muhammad Ali Jinnah, a Muslim nationalist leader. Jinnah demanded the establishment of a separate Muslim state on the Indian subcontinent.

Great Britain became convinced that civil war would break out unless India was partitioned into a Hindu state and a Muslim state. It persuaded Mahatma Gandhi and other Hindu leaders to accept this plan. In August 1947, the British Parliament passed the India Independence Act. This law ended British rule in India. It established two independent nations on the subcontinent: India, which was dominated by Hindus; and Pakistan, which was dominated by Muslims.

The partition of India did not completely separate Hindus and Muslims. Millions of Muslims lived in villages scattered throughout the new country of India. About 10 million Hindus lived in Pakistan. Both groups feared persecution when the British withdrew. Gandhi traveled across India preaching religious toleration. Although his efforts reduced tension for a time, millions of Hindus fled to safety in India. At the same time, Muslims abandoned their homes in India to move to Pakistan.

During this mass movement of peoples, bloody rioting erupted. About 500,000 people were killed. Millions were left homeless. Gandhi, himself, was a victim of this violence. He was killed in 1948 by a Hindu fanatic who opposed Gandhi's efforts to establish peace between Hindus and Muslims.

India Under Nehru

The violence accompanying partition and Gandhi's death were severe blows to the newly independent nation of India. Nevertheless, Indian leaders set about the task of organizing a stable government. In 1950, India adopted a constitution that set up a parliamentary system of government. The first prime minister was Jawaharlal Nehru (juh WAH hur lahl NAY roo).

Nehru strongly supported democratic government in India. He also worked hard to meet India's pressing economic and social needs. Nehru had three well-defined goals for India: developing industry, modernizing agriculture, and uniting the Indian people.

Developing industry. India has many of the natural resources it needs to develop industry. Since independence, it has increased the mining of iron ore, coal, and other minerals. The building of giant dams has resulted in increased hydroelectric power for factories and homes. These dams have also prevented floods and supplied water for irrigation of crops.

Much of the skilled labor and capital needed to develop industry came from within India. However, the Indian government asked foreign engineers to provide technical assistance. The foreign engineers helped build complex modern plants to boost India's industrial output.

As a British colony, India had been dependent on the West for manufactured goods. Twenty years after independence, In-

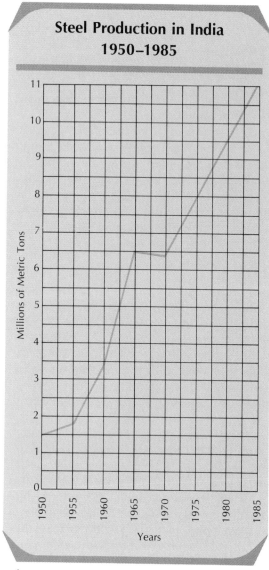

Steel Production in India
1950–1985

Millions of Metric Tons

Years

Sources: United Nations, *Statistical Yearbook*, and United Nations, *Statistical Monthly*.

Graph Skill *The growth of steel production in India reflects economic development. During which period did steel production make the greatest gains?*

dia was producing automobiles, railway locomotives, bicycles, electrical equipment, radios, and aircraft. In the last 30 years, India's industrial output multiplied five-fold. Moreover, high technology such as the computer was introduced, as was nuclear power.

Modernizing agriculture. Along with industrial development, the government has encouraged the modernization of agriculture. About 77 percent of the Indian population lives in rural villages. Most of these people are farmers who use traditional methods of cultivating the land. The Indian government has tried to increase farm production. With foreign assistance, it has provided villagers with better seeds and tools. It has also built agricultural colleges. Graduates of these colleges teach farmers in the villages new, more productive farming methods.

Early increases in crop yields in the 1950s came from expanding the areas under cultivation and using more fertilizers. But rates of growth have slowed. Much farming remains dependent on the monsoon rains. (See page 48.) And too little rainfall can still result in drought and crop failure. To revive agricultural progress, India seeks increased investment in irrigation, electrification, and flood control.

Building national unity. Nehru knew that without popular support, his plans for modernizing India would fail. However, building national unity was not an easy task. Religious conflict between Hindus and Muslims was only one of many divisions in Indian society. Indians spoke dozens of different languages. The caste system preserved social and economic divisions.

The Indian constitution of 1950 was supposed to end these divisions. It established the equality of all people before the law and granted universal suffrage. Discrimination based on caste was made illegal. The government used education as an additional means to further national unity. In schools, for example, students learned the national language, Hindi.

Trials of Indian Democracy

Despite improved industrial and agricultural output and attempts to unify the nation, India faced major problems. Between 1950 and 1986, the population soared from 369 million people to 779 million. Increased food production and new jobs in industry were never enough for this rapidly growing population. Millions of Indians lived in hunger and poverty despite government efforts to improve their standard of living.

Moreover, the political stability that India had enjoyed under Nehru ended after his death in 1964. In 1966, Nehru's daughter, Indira Gandhi, became prime minister. Although she had popular support for a time, economic troubles and student unrest brought her government under attack. In 1975, Indira Gandhi proclaimed a state of emergency. She exercised dictatorial powers and jailed critics of her government.

When Gandhi allowed elections in 1977, she was voted out of office. She again became prime minister in 1980, however. In 1984, Gandhi ordered government troops to storm a temple occupied by armed members of a rebel religious minority, the Sikhs. The same year extremists from the group assassinated her. Indira Gandhi's son, Radjiv, then became prime minister.

Since Indira Gandhi's death, India has become more difficult to govern. In part, this is due to a growing awareness of the power of the ballot. Villagers increasingly vote their own interests rather than as directed by village elites.

In part, India's political unrest reflects a decline in the power of Gandhi's Congress Party. The Congress Party had served to help unite the diverse population. India's contending groups argued within the party framework and resolved most problems there.

Unrest since 1980 has sometimes taken the form of serious riots. For example, late in 1985, the state of Gujarat (gu ja ROT) suffered a riot that started as a dispute between the poor and the middle class. Before it ended, it involved clashes between Hindus and Muslims, Hindus and Sikhs, Shiite and Sunni Muslims, and among different castes within the Hindu community.

Often, the army has been called in to handle such conflicts. Through both force and effective political leadership, Radjiv Gandhi has been able to hold India together. To meet the problem of conflicts in the long run, however, he has taken steps to strengthen India's parliamentary government.

Education has been one of India's priorities. This photograph shows students at a university in northern India attending a botany class. Since winning independence, India has trained many engineers and technical specialists. Today, the number of scientists and engineers in India is exceeded only by the number in the United States and the Soviet Union.

In 1984, Indira Gandhi was assassinated by her Sikh bodyguards. Sikhs are one of several minorities that are discontent with the national government in India.

Pakistan and Bangladesh

Like India, Pakistan faced the problem of establishing national unity. The borders of Pakistan had been drawn around the two areas in which most Muslims lived. As a result, Pakistan was made up of two parts, East Pakistan and West Pakistan. The two parts were separated by 1,000 miles of Indian territory. East Pakistan was more densely populated and poorer than West Pakistan. Differing economic interests, languages, and cultural traditions created divisions within Pakistan. The only real tie between the peoples of East and West Pakistan was their religion, Islam.

Pakistan set out to govern itself as a parliamentary democracy, but the effort failed. A military dictatorship was established in 1958. In the 1960s, public outrage against government corruption resulted in riots and a new military dictatorship. Continuing unrest eventually led to a civil war between East and West Pakistan.

Map Skill *In 1947, the Indian subcontinent was partitioned between India and Pakistan. Pakistan was made up of two widely separated regions, as you can see on this map. What nation did East Pakistan become in 1971?*

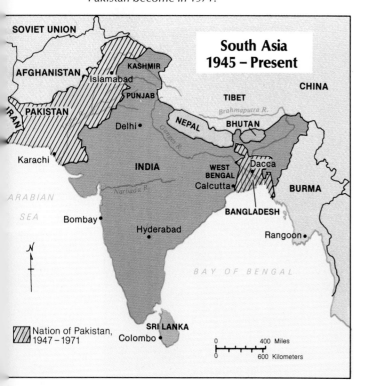

Since independence, leaders from West Pakistan had dominated the government. The people of East Pakistan resented this situation and demanded self-government. Tension increased in 1970 after devastating floods swept over East Pakistan. Government relief supplies were slow to reach the flooded areas. The people of East Pakistan claimed that the delays were deliberate.

In the December 1970 elections, East Pakistan won a majority of seats in the national assembly. But the military dictator in West Pakistan set aside the election results. When riots flared up in East Pakistan, the government sent in troops, who massacred thousands of people. Civil war erupted early in 1971. Millions of refugees fled the fighting in East Pakistan by crossing into India. As a result, India was drawn into the conflict. Indian troops invaded East Pakistan and helped East Pakistan guerrillas defeat the forces of West Pakistan. In December 1971, East Pakistan became the independent nation of Bangladesh.

Problems of Bangladesh. Since its creation, Bangladesh has experienced little economic success. In a measure of annual income per person, only Ethiopia is poorer. Relief supplies from foreign governments helped farmers in their efforts to grow more food; however, most gains were cancelled by population growth. And periodic floods continue to cause famine and destruction.

The limited increases in food production were achieved largely through using locally produced chemical fertilizers. But most farms are too small to take advantage of other advances in technology, such as modern farm machinery.

Prospects of earning money through exports are likewise dim. Jute, once a major export crop, is no longer in demand. To date, both Sri Lanka and India have been more successful than Bangladesh in competing for the world tea market. Industrialization, too, remains a distant goal since natural resources are few.

Prospects for Pakistan. Since 1978, Pakistan has been governed by a military dictatorship. Its leader, Mohammad Zia-ul-Haq, has ruled without democratic processes or institutions. In the mid-1980s, however, Zia began to make some changes. In 1985, a new parliament was elected. Zia brought civilians into important government positions. He also established Islamic courts. As in other Islamic states, a strong religious revival movement, with considerable influence, has developed. In practice, the country is still under martial law.

Meanwhile, Pakistan's economy continues to grow. In recent years, large numbers of Pakistani working in Middle Eastern oil fields spurred development by sending money home. With the collapse of the oil boom, this source of income dried up. However, foreign investments continue to flow into the country, giving Pakistan an increasing potential for growth.

India, Pakistan, and the Cold War

India and Pakistan became independent nations at a time when cold war rivalries divided the world. Both the United States and the Soviet Union sought the friendship of these nations. India remained neutral. But Pakistan allied itself with the United States.

India did accept American military aid when Chinese troops invaded Tibet and crossed into India in the early 1960s. This crisis provoked problems between the United States and Pakistan. Pakistan feared India would use American arms against it, and it turned to China for support.

In the 1980s, superpower politics continued to affect South Asia. In 1979, thousands of Soviet troops invaded Afghanistan, Pakistan's neighbor to the north. Pakistan condemned this Soviet aggression, and the United States offered Pakistan millions of dollars in aid. Both nations wanted to discourage any further possible Soviet advance.

SECTION REVIEW

1. Locate: India, Pakistan, Bangladesh.
2. Identify: Muhammad Ali Jinnah, Jawaharlal Nehru, Indira Gandhi, Mohammad Zia-ul-Haq.
3. Why did Muslims in India want to form a separate state?
4. What were Nehru's three major goals for India?
5. What are some problems of Bangladesh?
6. What political changes were made in Pakistan in the mid-1980s?

---

2 Revolutionary Changes in China

Read to Learn ■ how communism changed China
■ how Chinese revolutionary policy evolved toward cooperation

In September 1945, China celebrated the defeat of Japan. Yet the withdrawal of Japanese armies from China did not bring peace to that troubled land. For the next four years, Chiang Kai-shek's Nationalist forces battled the Chinese Communists led by Mao Zedong.*

---

* In 1979 the Chinese government adopted a new system of spelling, the Pinyin system. In general, this book uses the traditional Wade-Giles system except for personal names and place names that have become common American usage. For example, Mao Tse-tung is now spelled Mao Zedong.

Civil War

The struggle between Chiang Kai-shek and Mao Zedong dated from the late 1920s. (See page 600.) When Japan invaded China, these two leaders agreed to a temporary truce and united against their common enemy. During World War II, the United States supplied Chiang Kai-shek's forces with arms to fight the Japanese. But Chiang's armies suffered from low morale and widespread corruption. Moreover, Chiang seemed to be saving his energies for an all-out campaign against the Communists once Japan was defeated.

During the war, Mao Zedong organized a highly disciplined guerrilla army. His Communist forces won popular support across much of northern China. In the past, Chinese armies had plundered villages in their paths. Mao insisted that his Communist soldiers follow three basic rules when they entered peasant villages: "Do not even take a needle or a thread. Consider the people as your family. All that you have borrowed you must return."

As a result of this policy, Chinese peasants looked on Mao Zedong and his army as their defenders. Moreover, the Chinese Communists stopped landlords from charging rents that were too high. They also prevented local officials from collecting ruinous taxes. In addition, when Japanese forces stormed into northern China, Communist guerrillas protected peasant villages.

By 1945, Mao Zedong's forces occupied northern China and Chiang Kai-shek's armies held the south. The United States tried to convince the two Chinese leaders to form a single government. President Truman sent General George C. Marshall to China to help negotiate a peaceful division of power. But the two leaders refused to share power. The talks stopped, and civil war erupted.

The Communists defeated Chiang Kai-shek's armies in many battles across China. Chiang had once enjoyed the support of the Chinese middle class. But spiraling inflation and official corruption destroyed the people's confidence in his leadership. In 1949, the battle for the Chinese mainland ended with a Communist victory. Chiang Kai-shek and his remaining forces retreated to Taiwan, an island about 100 miles (161 kilometers) off the coast of China.

The People's Republic of China

On October 1, 1949, Mao Zedong proclaimed the People's Republic of China. A new constitution provided for a National People's Congress and a variety of other democratic institutions. In practice, however, the new government was a dictatorship controlled by the Chinese Communist party. As chairman of the Communist party, Mao Zedong was the most powerful person in China. Mao

Map Skill *In 1949, the victorious Chinese Communists proclaimed the People's Republic of China. The defeated Nationalist forces retreated to the island of Taiwan. Since 1949, the government of the People's Republic of China has sought to unite Taiwan with the mainland. In addition, China has been involved in other border disputes. Which areas do both China and Russia claim?*

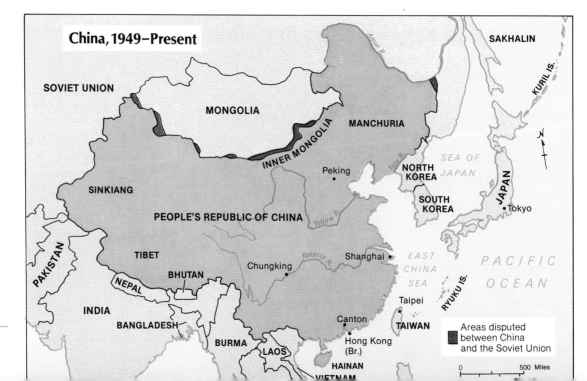

used his power to introduce revolutionary changes.

Land reform. Most Chinese were peasant farmers when the Communists came to power. Since ancient times, they had been exploited by landlords, bandits, and the government. The Chinese Communists won the support of the peasants by introducing land reform.

At first, farmland was taken from "rich landlords." This land was divided among rural families so that each family held about 2.5 acres. In the early 1950s, the Communists launched a much more ambitious land reform program. They ended all private ownership of land and changed traditional ways of farming.

Under the new system, tiny plots owned by individual families were converted into large agricultural cooperatives. Peasants contributed their tools to the cooperative and joined their neighbors to form labor teams. By working together in large units, peasant farmers raised the level of food production. But food shortages still occurred.

The Great Leap Forward. When the cooperatives failed to meet the nation's growing demand for food, Mao Zedong announced the Great Leap Forward in 1958. The Great Leap Forward was an economic program that called on the Chinese people to increase production. As part of this program, China was divided into communes.

A commune averaged about 10,000 acres and 5,000 family households. In each commune, workers from 200 to 300 families were formed into production brigades. Brigades could be moved from job to job. During the growing season, a brigade tended the commune's crops. In the winter, the same brigade might join other brigades in giant projects such as digging irrigation canals.

Industrial development. The Great Leap Forward was supposed to expand Chinese industry as well as agriculture. The government invested heavily in key industries such as iron and steel manufacturing, transportation, and energy. Meanwhile, people in the communes enthusiastically set up hundreds of thousands of small industrial plants. Some plants manufactured farm tools, cloth-

ing, and kitchenware. Others even tried to produce iron in "backyard furnaces."

The government launched an intense propaganda campaign during the Great Leap Forward. If every individual "served the people" with personal sacrifice and hard work, it claimed, China could surpass Great Britain's industrial output in 15 years. At first, production increased. But machines soon broke down because they were used constantly without repairs. Also, workers could not keep up the furious pace of production.

In the early 1960s, Mao Zedong abandoned his hope of leading China into the Industrial Age in a "Great Leap." The government adopted policies that called for long-range industrial development.

A Revolution in Daily Life

The Communists set out to revolutionize daily life. Traditionally, scholars had held the highest position in Chinese society. However, Mao Zedong emphasized the importance of peasants and workers. The government often used harsh methods to destroy the old social class system. For example, landlords who had exploited peasants were identified and punished. At the same time, propaganda campaigns were launched to convince people to support the new ideas.

The government expanded education in order to train people in the technical skills needed in a modern society. People in the communes built thousands of primary schools. For the first time in Chinese history, most young children received a basic education. With limited economic resources, however, middle schools and high schools expanded less rapidly. Only a tiny fraction of the people received a college education.

Schools supported the Communist revolution by teaching patriotism and respect for Mao Zedong's ideas. Education was also extended to older peasants and workers. They learned to read from the *Thoughts of Chairman Mao*, the so-called Little Red Book.

The revolution also affected family life. In 1950, the government adopted a new marriage law that guaranteed women full equal-

The Chinese government uses wall posters to build up public support for government policies. Here, two Chinese study posters that encourage people to support the "four modernizations"—development of science and technology, agriculture, industry, and defense.

ity. The marriage law rejected the traditional idea that men were superior to women. No longer could a man divorce his wife if she did not give birth to sons. By freeing women from the domination of their husbands, Mao expected to mobilize women to work outside their homes.

The Cultural Revolution

In the mid-1960s, Mao Zedong worried that China's revolution was losing momentum. The once-unified Communist party had split into rival factions. Mao Zedong was growing old, and he feared that old class divisions might reemerge in China. To renew the revolution, Mao Zedong launched the "Great Proletarian Cultural Revolution" in 1966. He called on the young to join the struggle. In response, millions of students and young workers formed paramilitary groups called the Red Guards.

All over China, the Red Guards held meetings, parades, and demonstrations. They praised Mao's leadership and pledged

support for his revolutionary ideals. They heaped abuse on Communist party leaders, government officials, factory managers, and teachers. Many of these people were forced out of their jobs because they were accused of lacking the proper enthusiasm for the Cultural Revolution.

The Cultural Revolution disrupted Chinese life. Violence erupted between moderates in the government and the radical Red Guards. Factory production dropped. Schools and universities closed down. Only rural farms escaped the chaos of these years. The Cultural Revolution came to an end in 1969, but its effects were felt into the 1970s.

Chinese Foreign Policy

Mao Zedong sought a major world role for China. He preached world revolution, encouraging the peoples of Asia, Africa, and Latin America to follow China's example and overthrow "bourgeois" governments. As a result, many nations, including the United States, refused to recognize the Communist government in China. Instead, they supported Chiang Kai-shek's Nationalist government on Taiwan.

In 1950, China and the Soviet Union formed an alliance. As an ally of the Soviet Union, China soon became involved in the conflict in Korea.

The Korean War. Since ancient times, China had influenced the neighboring kingdom of Korea. As China weakened in the 1800s, Japan extended its influence into Korea. Japan made Korea a colony in 1911. After the Japanese defeat in World War II, Korea was divided at the 38th parallel into a northern zone and a southern zone. Russian troops entered the northern zone. They established a communist government under Kim Il-sung. In the southern zone, American forces supported a noncommunist government under Syngman Rhee (SIHNG muhn REE).

War broke out between North and South Korea in June 1950. North Korean troops soon pushed into the south. The United States convinced the United Nations to approve a "police action" to stop the North Korean invasion. The United States furnished most of the military forces that fought under the UN banner in Korea.

Early in the war, UN forces launched offensives that carried their troops deep into North Korea. As North Korean forces fell back toward the border between Korea and China, about 200,000 Chinese "volunteers" joined the North Koreans. Thus, Americans and Chinese were soon fighting one another in Korea. During three years of bloody fighting, neither side won a decisive victory. An armistice was finally signed in July 1953. The agreement restored the boundary between North Korea and South Korea at the 38th parallel.

Rivalry between China and Russia. During most of the 1950s, China remained closely allied to the Soviet Union. Soviet loans and technological assistance helped China develop its industry. Yet differences arose between the two allies.

By 1960, the Soviet Union had withdrawn its advisors from China. Soon China and the Soviet Union were competing for influence with developing nations. In the late 1960s, tensions along the Soviet-Chinese border resulted in skirmishes.

New ties with the world. During the Cultural Revolution, China isolated itself from the rest of the world. With the end of the Cultural Revolution, China developed new ties with the world. By 1971, China had received UN recognition. A year later, President Richard M. Nixon of the United States visited Peking and met with Chinese leaders. After more than 20 years of hostility, the United States and the People's Republic of China agreed to establish normal diplomatic relations.

Map Skill *In the first months of the Korean War, North Korean troops conquered most of the peninsula, as the solid red line on this map shows. UN forces soon took the offensive and advanced into North Korea. Which nation gained territory as a result of the armistice?*

The Korean War

Line of farthest North Korean advance, September 1950

Line of farthest UN advance, November 1950

Line of farthest North Korean–Chinese advance, January 1951

Armistice line

USSR

CHINA

Yalu R.

NORTH

KOREA

Pyongyang

38th Parallel

Panmunjom

Inchon   Seoul

YELLOW

SEA

SOUTH

KOREA

Pusan

SEA OF

JAPAN

0   150 Miles

0   200 Kilometers

By the 1980s, China had increased its contacts with Japan and the industrial nations of the West. It purchased American commercial jets and invited Japanese experts to help build a giant steel plant on the Yangtze River. Chinese students and professors went abroad for advanced training. China hoped new relationships with western nations and Japan would bring not only economic benefits but also support for China against the Soviet Union.

Radical Internal Changes

When Mao Zedong died in 1976, a power struggle broke out within the Chinese Communist party. Jiang Qing (JYONG JING), Mao's widow, and radicals in the party wanted to renew the Cultural Revolution. However, moderates won power. They imprisoned Jiang Qing and three of her followers, who became known as the "Gang of Four."

By 1980, Deng Xiaoping (DUHNG syow-PING), a former vice chairman of the Communist party, had become the leader of China. Determined to make China a modern nation, Deng began a series of widespread economic and social changes.

Changes in the economic system. Under the centralized, state-dictated policies of Deng's predecessors, individuals had little reason to excel. Everybody "ate out of one big pot"—that is, they received the same pay for the same job, regardless of effort or quality of work. Many people therefore did not try very hard. In an effort to increase production, Deng introduced a "second revolution." This revolution gave workers the capitalist motives of personal profit and gain.

Eighty percent of China's one-billion population lives in the countryside. For them, Deng devised the agricultural contract responsibility system. Land is still owned collectively, but families farm specific plots. A contract states the amount of a crop that must be turned over to the collective. Fami-

In 1986, China introduced new policies to stimulate economic growth. For example, the government allowed farmers to sell surplus food on the free market.

Large families are a tradition in China, but the government wants to slow the rapid growth of the population. It uses billboards, such as this one, to encourage parents to have only one child.

lies can then keep the excess crops to market as they please. After fulfilling the state's requirement, farmers can grow anything else they wish and sell it for whatever they can get. With profits they earn, they can set up private small businesses or build their own homes.

Relaxing controls in industry has proven to be more complicated. Under the new system, each factory also runs under a contract. Surplus products can be sold on a free market system. Thus, businesses have more freedom to succeed or fail. As part of his program to stimulate industries, Deng has even encouraged foreign investment in some of them.

Whether China can successfully combine communism with the freedoms of even limited capitalism is uncertain. In 1986, student groups demonstrated in China's major cities, demanding more democracy. As a result, Deng dismissed leaders who had supported more liberal political policies.

Changes in the family. After 1950, both the population and the agricultural produc-

tion of China increased 2 to 3 percent every year. Thus, China's farms barely managed to feed the nation. Major economic advances were impossible.

China needed crop surpluses to sell to finance modernization. To accomplish this goal, Deng introduced a one-child-per-family policy. Young married couples are encouraged to pledge to have only one child. In return, they receive special subsidies, bonuses, and other favored treatment. However, China has a high infant-death rate, which limits the program's appeal. Also, traditional desires for a large family remain strong.

Tradition still influences the role of women as well. Equality is written into law but not always practiced. Deng's proposed changes also conflict with traditional attitudes toward the elderly. Children in China take care of their aged parents. If the one-child policy is widely followed, the state or the collective confronts the problem of care of the elderly.

Across China's vast area, the practice of Deng's reforms has been uneven. Deng, who

715

is in his eighties, needs his "revolution" to succeed if it is to be continued by those who come after him.

SECTION REVIEW

1. Identify: George C. Marshall, People's Republic of China, Great Leap Forward, Cultural Revolution, Gang of Four, Deng Xiaoping.

2. How did the marriage law of 1950 affect women in China?
3. Describe two results of the Cultural Revolution.
4. What economic changes were made by Deng Xiaoping's "second revolution"?
5. How might Deng Xiaoping's policies alter the Chinese family?

3 Japan: An Economic Giant in Asia

Read to Learn
- how major social, economic, and political changes dramatically transformed postwar Japan
- how Japan became a world economic leader

In 1945, Japan was a defeated nation. More than 2 million Japanese had been killed in World War II. Japanese cities lay in ruins. Food was so scarce that thousands of Japanese were near starvation. Despite this grim picture, Japan would soon recover its place among the leading industrial powers of the world.

American Occupation of Japan

After the Japanese surrender, American military forces occupied the island nation. President Truman set out two major aims for the American occupation. First, he wanted to destroy Japanese militarism by ending Japan's ability to make war. Second, he wanted to make Japan a strong democratic state.

Defeating Japanese militarism. The Allied powers punished Japan for its part in the war. Japan lost its overseas empire in the Pacific and on the Asian mainland. As in Germany, the Allies held war crimes trials. Japanese military leaders were imprisoned or executed for their wartime activities.

To destroy Japan's ability to make war, the Americans disbanded the Japanese armed forces. They also dissolved over 1,000 military and civilian organizations that had preached aggressive nationalism.

Democratic government. President Truman named General Douglas MacArthur commander of the occupation forces in Japan. Under MacArthur's direction, Japan adopted a new constitution in 1947. The new constitution established Japan as a democracy. The emperor lost his ruling authority and became a figurehead, or national symbol, similar to the monarch of Great Britain.

The constitution set up a Diet, or legislature, with representatives elected by the people. Executive power was held by a prime minister chosen from the majority party in the Diet. The constitution also provided for a court system similar to that of the United States.

The constitution gave women full equality, including the right to vote. A strong bill of rights guaranteed freedom of religion, speech, and the press.

New social and economic patterns. Like many Americans, President Truman believed Japan had been led into war in part because the people had not challenged their military leaders. He hoped that the democratic reforms introduced by the new constitution would not only weaken Japanese militarism but also destroy the authoritarian character of traditional Japanese society.

In the traditional Japanese household, for example, men dominated women. The Americans encouraged women to exercise their new rights. Women were urged to vote and even to run for public office.

The American occupation forces reformed the Japanese education system as well. The school system was expanded, and compulsory attendance laws required students to complete at least nine years of school. Students from every social class were allowed to attend high school and even college. Equally important, textbooks and courses of study were revised. The new books emphasized democratic ideas such as individualism and equality.

Economic reforms also encouraged the new democratic spirit. A massive land reform program allowed Japanese peasants to buy land that they had previously rented. This reduced the power of large landowners and gave peasants greater control over their own lives. Other reforms limited the power of the zaibatsu. These families owned huge industrial businesses and exerted enormous influence over Japanese economic life.

Japanese Independence Restored

By 1948, the Americans had already begun returning responsibility for government and the economy to Japanese leaders. This policy reflected American concern about developments taking place elsewhere in Asia. When China fell into communist hands in 1949, the United States began to see Japan as a possible ally rather than a former enemy.

The outbreak of the Korean War speeded up the process of ending the American occupation. United States troops were sent from bases in Japan to fight in Korea. At the same time, the American government stepped up its efforts to negotiate a peace treaty with Japan. Earlier efforts to arrange a peace treaty had been blocked by the postwar rivalry between the United States and the Soviet Union. Finally, on September 8, 1951, Japan and 48 noncommunist nations signed a treaty. (Communist powers refused to sign the agreement.) Six months later, the United States withdrew its remaining occupation forces.

Japan again emerged as a fully independent nation. But under their new constitution, the Japanese had given up their right to wage war and maintain armed forces. Therefore, after regaining its independence, Japan signed a military agreement with the United States. Under this agreement, the United States pledged to defend Japan against foreign aggression.

Since World War II, the Japanese have adopted many western ideas and customs. However, they have a deep respect for their ancient culture. Here, women dressed in traditional clothing perform dances that have long been part of Japanese theater. The magnificent scenery in the background demonstrates an appreciation for the peace and beauty of nature.

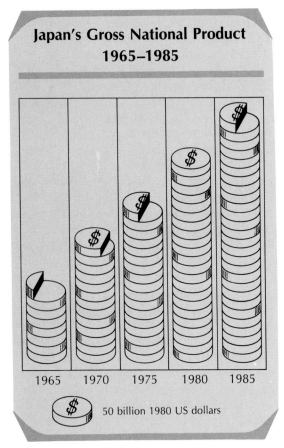

Japan's Gross National Product 1965–1985

1965   1970   1975   1980   1985

$ 50 billion 1980 US dollars

Source: *Handbook of Economic Statistics.*

Graph Skill   *The Japanese GNP has increased dramatically since 1965, as this chart shows. In which five-year period was the increase the largest?*

The Japanese Economic Miracle

Since World War II, the Japanese economy has grown faster than that of any other nation. The United States helped Japan rebuild its shattered industry in the immediate postwar years. However, during the 1950s, the Japanese forged forward on their own.

Since the American occupation ended in 1952, the Japanese *gross national product* (GNP)—the total value of goods and services produced in a year—has grown at a rapid rate. (See the graph above.)

The Japanese economy advanced on several fronts. Foreign trade played a large role in Japan's economic growth. Japanese goods were sold around the world.

The Japanese also developed a strong home market. With increasing prosperity, Japanese workers in large companies earned better wages and enjoyed a higher standard of living than ever before. Families, therefore, could buy more Japanese products. In the late 1950s, the goal of a prosperous Japanese family was a home furnished with a television, refrigerator, and washing machine. In the 1960s, families bought automobiles, color televisions, and air conditioners.

The government was able to help Japanese industry in part because it spent relatively little on defense. Moreover, the Japanese studied and adopted the latest technological and scientific advances. For example, they carved out a major market in the electronics industry by improving an American invention—the transistor.

Not all Japanese shared in the general national prosperity, however. Workers in small businesses seldom earned as much money or enjoyed working conditions as good as workers in large companies. Nevertheless, as Japan entered the 1980s, it was the richest nation in Asia.

Japan in World Affairs

Japan and the United States have maintained close ties since World War II. Yet the Japanese have followed their own course in foreign affairs. In 1970, for example, Japan insisted that the United States return Okinawa, a key American military base, to the Japanese. Foreign policy in the mid-1980s, moreover, placed great stress on strengthening Japanese ties with other western nations. In 1985, for example, Prime Minister Nakasone toured Europe. His goal was to encourage the European community to buy more Japanese exports.

Foreign trade is essential to Japan if it is to continue its economic success. Only about the size of California, Japan has a population half that of the United States. Japan has to import much of its food. It also lacks many raw materials. More than 90 percent of the oil, iron ore, and coal used by Japanese industry must come from abroad.

Thus, the government has tried to maintain friendly relations with the oil-producing nations of the Middle East. At the same time,

Economics and History ■ The Robot Revolution in Japan

At a plant in Nagoya, Japan, a yellow-steel giant heaved a 16-ton load into place with a slow whine. Then it lumbered back, electronic sensors awake to any interference, to carry another load. Nicknamed "Popeye," this steel giant is one of over 15,000 robots operating day and night in Japan.

A robot revolution is well under way in Japan. Robots are at work everywhere. In hospitals, medical students work on robot "patients" equipped with sensitive monitors that respond to treatment. Restaurant robots beckon customers to come in for a meal. On highways, 10-foot tall police robots direct traffic.

Most robots, however, are found in factories. Robots perform tasks ranging from welding, painting, and lifting to packaging and labeling products. Japanese experts predict that in the future robots will find a place in the home doing the laundry and cooking and serving meals.

Robots have mechanical arms and electronic brains. They seldom look like R2D2 of *Star Wars* fame. Instead, they are huge, often cumbersome machines. Most are stationary. They perform routine, repetitive jobs without suffering the boredom of human workers. A Japanese television plant that uses robot workers reports a decline in the number of defective sets produced. On the other hand, robot experts admit these machines will never be able to do work requiring creativity, judgment, and complicated decision-making.

The United States pioneered in robot technology in the early 1960s. But it was the Japanese who discovered ways to apply this technology in industry. In the 1980s, Japan was enjoying soaring sales of robots. Most of the robots produced in Japan were also used there. A small percentage was exported.

The Japanese government has encouraged robot manufacturing. Factory owners and business leaders were eager to put robots to work. Even Japanese workers accepted robots as coworkers. They often greet robots with a cheerful "Good morning." They name their giant coworkers after baseball stars, movie stars, and popular singers. A Japanese worker who spent years in a factory carrying heavy steel plates now does other work while robots carry the heavy loads. "The robots are really honest and obedient workers," he noted cheerfully.

---

it has negotiated agreements to help other nations explore and develop their oil and gas reserves.

Japanese ties with China have also changed. After years of little contact with its mainland neighbor, Japan has become China's largest trading partner. Japan provides China with financial and technical assistance. China, in turn, exports light industrial products and raw materials to Japan. In 1985, ministers from China and Japan began a series of meetings to discuss their growing mutual economic interests.

SECTION REVIEW

1. Define: gross national product.
2. What were the major aims of the American occupation of Japan?
3. List three ways in which the new constitution guaranteed democracy in Japan.
4. Why did Japan form a military alliance with the United States after it regained independence?
5. What factors helped the Japanese develop a strong economy in the postwar period?

4 Nations of Southeast Asia

Read to Learn
- how independence for Southeast Asian countries involved peaceful change for some and bloodshed for others
- how the United States became involved in Vietnam

During the Age of Imperialism, all of Southeast Asia except what is today Thailand became European colonies. Japanese troops overran Southeast Asia early in World War II. But the Japanese faced opposition from nationalist groups. By the end of World War II, nationalist groups had become so strong that they could resist the return of colonial rulers.

The Road to Independence

Thailand regained its independence as soon as Japanese troops withdrew. The road to independence varied, however, for the other nations of Southeast Asia.

The Philippines. The United States had promised independence to the Philippines as early as 1934. After World War II, the United States moved quickly to fulfill this promise. On July 4, 1946, the people of the Philippines celebrated their independence. A constitution set up the framework for a democratic government.

During the 1950s, the demand for land reform in the Philippines grew. The government began to break up large estates and redistribute land to peasants. But some peasants believed the government was moving too slowly. Fighting broke out between government soldiers and peasants who seized the estates of wealthy landowners.

The unrest prompted Philippine president Ferdinand Marcos to declare *martial law*—temporary rule by the military—in 1972. Under martial law, individual rights are limited. Marcos eventually ended military rule. But he issued a new constitution that greatly increased the power of the president.

Marcos' leading political rival, Benigno Aquino (beh NEE nyoh ah KEE noh), lived in self-imposed exile in the United States. When Aquino returned to the Philippines in 1983, he was assassinated as he left his airplane. Followers of Aquino accused the Marcos government of playing a role in the killing.

Marcos had ruled virtually unchallenged for over 20 years. But Aquino's widow, Corazon Aquino (kor ah SOHN ah KEE noh), soon became the crusading leader and presidential candidate of a rapidly growing opposition. When Marcos called for an election in 1986, the political race that developed threatened his power. After an election marred by fraud and violence, Marcos declared himself the winner. The United States refused to rec-

After the assassination of her husband Benigno, Corazon Aquino took up his position as the leading opponent of strongman Ferdinand Marcos in the Philippines. Corazon Aquino was sworn in as president in 1986, and in 1987 the country voted overwhelmingly to support the new constitution she had sponsored.

ognize his victory. With the loss of United States' backing, Marcos went into exile in Hawaii, and Corazon Aquino became president.

In her inaugural address, Corazon Aquino dedicated her government to upholding "truth and justice, morality and decency, freedom and democracy." However, Aquino's "bloodless revolution" faced severe challenges. In an election in 1987, she won an overwhelming victory for herself and her proposed new constitution. But getting former Marcos supporters and the radical left to unite behind her government would require great political skill.

Indonesia. Southeast of the Philippines are the islands once known to Europeans as the Dutch East Indies. The Netherlands had ruled these islands since the 1500s. Led by Achmed Sukarno, nationalists resisted Dutch efforts to reestablish their control after World War II. After four years of fighting, the Dutch agreed to grant independence. In August 1950, the Dutch East Indies officially became the independent nation of Indonesia. General Suharto was named President in 1968 and has ruled since.

Mainland nations. On the mainland, the British had granted Burma limited self-government in 1937. Burma became fully independent in 1948. Another British colony, the Malay States, became the independent nation of Malaysia in 1957.

In 1959, the island of Singapore at the foot of the Malaysian peninsula united with Malaysia. This union lasted until 1965, when Singapore broke away to become an independent nation.

In the French colony of Indochina, serious fighting broke out after World War II. French Indochina included the countries that are today called Laos, Kampuchea, and Vietnam. Fighting in Indochina would last for nearly 30 years and would have worldwide consequences.

War in Vietnam

In 1945, a Vietnamese communist, Ho Chi Minh, gained power in the northern part of Vietnam. When the French returned to Indochina, they recognized this government in the north. But they also set up a separate, noncommunist government in the southern part of Vietnam. Both governments claimed to rule the whole country. Fighting broke out in 1946, when Ho Chi Minh's forces attacked French troops stationed in Vietnam.

Both the Soviet Union and the People's Republic of China announced their willingness to help Ho Chi Minh's communist forces. As part of its containment policy to prevent the spread of communism, the United States sent financial and military aid to the French. Despite this help, French forces lost the battle for Indochina. In May 1954, communist forces surrounded the French army at Dien Bien Phu and forced it to surrender.

The terms for French withdrawal from Indochina were established at an international conference in Geneva, Switzerland. The 1954 Geneva settlement called for the division of Indochina into three independent states: Laos, Cambodia, and Vietnam. Vietnam was temporarily divided into North Vietnam and South Vietnam. Ho Chi Minh's communist forces took North Vietnam, the area north of the 17th parallel. Noncommunist Vietnamese controlled South Vietnam.

According to the Geneva settlement, national elections were to be held in 1956 to reunite Vietnam. These elections were never held, and each government followed its own course. In North Vietnam, Ho Chi Minh built a communist state and received aid from the Soviet Union and the People's Republic of China. In South Vietnam, President Ngo Dinh Diem sought aid from the United States.

American Involvement in Vietnam

At first, the United States assumed that South Vietnam would not require massive aid. President Diem, however, refused to adopt programs to win popular support. Despite American urging, he rejected the idea of land reform to improve the lives of peasants. He did not want to risk losing the support of the landowning class. As a result, some South Vietnamese joined the Vietcong, communist guerrilla forces supported by North Vietnam. The Vietcong grew so strong in the countryside that they threatened to topple the South Vietnamese government.

During the 1960s, the United States increased its role in Vietnam. In 1960, there were only 800 American military advisers in South Vietnam. By 1968, more than 500,000 American troops were fighting alongside South Vietnamese government forces.

The war had spread to North Vietnam in 1964. In July of that year, the North Vietnamese attacked American warships in the Gulf of Tonkin. The United States Congress did not declare war on North Vietnam, but it did adopt the Gulf of Tonkin resolution. By an overwhelming vote, Congress authorized the President "to take all necessary measures to repel any armed attack and to prevent further aggression."

President Lyndon B. Johnson used this resolution to justify American bombing raids over North Vietnam. American planes also bombed the routes used by the North Vietnamese to reach the south.

As the war continued, an increasing number of Americans called for an end to American involvement in Vietnam. In the 1968 presidential campaign, Richard M. Nixon promised that if he were elected he would withdraw American troops from Vietnam. President Nixon ordered a reduction in American forces in Vietnam soon after taking office in 1969. But American troops continued to fight in Vietnam until 1973. In January of that year, American and North Vietnamese officials negotiated a cease-fire in Vietnam, and most American troops were withdrawn.

The fighting in Vietnam did not end when the Americans went home. The armies of North Vietnam and South Vietnam battled for control of the south. By April 1975, the communists had won the war. The next year, the communists united North and South Vietnam. Saigon, the capital of South Vietnam, was renamed Ho Chi Minh City.

The Aftermath of War

During the Vietnam War, the fighting spilled over into neighboring Cambodia. Cambodia had declared its neutrality in the war. However, the North Vietnamese set up supply bases in Cambodia. The United States began bombing these bases in 1969. Early in 1970, American and South Vietnamese forces crossed the Cambodian border to destroy communist supply bases.

Although these forces withdrew, Cambodia was soon plunged into civil war. The United States helped the noncommunist government combat the Khmer Rouge, as Cambodian communists were called. But in

Much of Southeast Asia was a battleground from 1945 to 1975. The 1954 Geneva settlement temporarily divided Vietnam into North Vietnam and South Vietnam. It also called for elections to reunite the country. These elections never took place. North Vietnam supplied arms to communist guerrillas who wanted to overthrow the South Vietnamese government. How might the supply routes from North Vietnam, known as the Ho Chi Minh Trail, have contributed to the widening of the war?

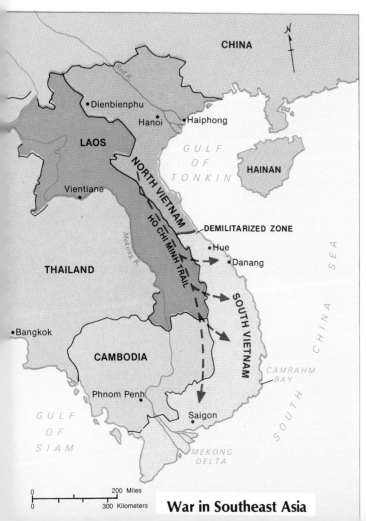

War in Southeast Asia

April 1975, Cambodia fell to communist forces, who renamed the country Kampuchea. Neighboring Laos also became communist in 1975.

In Kampuchea, the Khmer Rouge imposed a brutal reign of terror. The government forced people to leave the cities to work in the fields. An estimated 1 million people were killed. In 1978, Vietnamese communists invaded Kampuchea. They overthrew the Khmer Rouge and established a new communist government in Kampuchea.

Years of warfare in Southeast Asia have resulted in huge numbers of refugees. Upwards of 300,000 refugees from Vietnam and Kampuchea made their way to temporary camps in Thailand, Malaysia, Indonesia, and Hong Kong. Tens of thousands of Vietnamese fled their homeland in whatever boats they could find. A large number of these "boat people" drowned or died of thirst or hunger.

Many nations tried to help these refugees. The United States admitted about 228,000 Vietnamese between 1976 and 1978. European and Asian nations admitted thousands of others. In addition, the United Nations and voluntary relief organizations distributed supplies and provided medical care to the refugees.

Southeast Asia Today

In the years following independence, the Southeast Asian nations that were not involved in the Vietnam War developed rapidly. Despite different colonial backgrounds, they shared many goals. All sought technical advancement and a rise in living standards. Therefore, to strengthen their mutual position in the world, they formed the Association of Southeast Asian Nations (ASEAN) in 1967.

Malaysia, Indonesia, Brunei, and the other ASEAN nations are rich in resources and have productive populations. Together they have been able to achieve an average GNP growth rate of 7 percent a year. (See page 718.) Trade with the rest of the world reached hundreds of billions of dollars in the mid-1980s.

In the late 1960s, the United States followed a policy of "Vietnamization," encouraging the South Vietnamese to take greater responsibility for fighting the war. Here, South Vietnamese soldiers run for cover after helicopters airlifted them to an outpost under communist attack.

However, members of ASEAN recognize the need for assistance from more developed nations. For example, they formed a Center for Technology Exchange with the United States to foster investment and training. They also cooperate politically to help the United Nations and resettlement countries with the flow of refugees from Vietnam, Laos, and Kampuchea.

SECTION REVIEW

1. Locate: Burma, Thailand, Laos, Cambodia, Vietnam.
2. **Identify:** Corazon Aquino, Ho Chi Minh, Dien Bien Phu, Vietcong, Gulf of Tonkin resolution, Khmer Rouge, ASEAN.
3. Define: martial law.
4. Describe the problems each of the following nations faced after independence: (a) Philippines; (b) Vietnam.

723

Chapter 37 Review

In Perspective

Since World War II, vast changes have taken place in Asia. Many independent nations emerged. Each of these nations took its own course toward modernization. The Indian subcontinent was divided into two, and later three, separate nations. However, political instability continued to threaten the area as diverse populations boomed and as agricultural progress began to lag.

The Chinese Communists, led by Mao Zedong, won control of China. The new government transformed traditional patterns of life. Through huge campaigns such as the Cultural Revolution, Mao Zedong tried to keep the revolutionary spirit alive. In recent years, Deng Xiaoping introduced a policy of limited private enterprise to stimulate economic advance. By limiting population growth, Deng hoped to create crop surpluses to finance modernization. Contacts with other nations increased.

American forces occupied Japan from 1945 to 1951. During the American occupation, democratic reforms were introduced in Japan. In the 1950s and 1960s, Japan advanced economically and eventually became the richest nation in Asia. To maintain its position, Japan expanded its trading ties with foreign nations.

In Southeast Asia, some nations won their independence peacefully. In the 1980s in the Philippines, a "bloodless revolution" replaced a strongman government with a democracy. Indochina, however, suffered as a battleground. From 1946 to 1975, war raged in Vietnam. Southeast Asian nations not involved in warfare made strong economic gains.

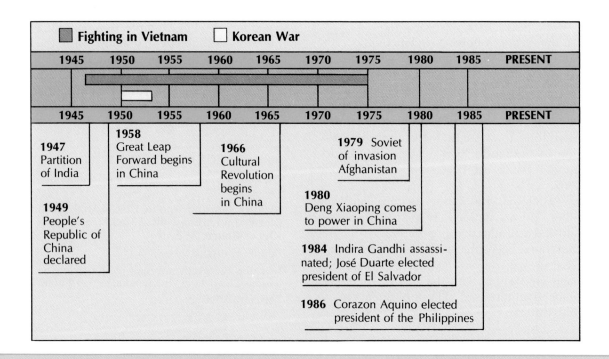

Recalling Facts

Review the time line on page 724 and your reading in this chapter. Then choose the letter of the correct time period for each of the following events.

A	B	C	D	E	F	G

1945 1950 1955 1960 1965 1970 1975 1980

1. President Nixon begins pulling United States troops out of Vietnam.
2. The United States signs a peace treaty with Japan.
3. India and Pakistan become separate nations.
4. The Cultural Revolution begins in China.
5. Communists win control of mainland China.
6. East Pakistan becomes Bangladesh.
7. The People's Republic of China gains UN recognition.
8. The Gulf of Tonkin resolution is passed.
9. Mao Zedong announces the Great Leap Forward.
10. The French army is defeated at Dien Bien Phu.

Chapter Checkup

1. Describe the efforts of India after 1947 to make progress in each of the following areas: (a) industry; (b) agriculture; (c) national unity.
2. (a) Why did civil war break out in Pakistan in 1971? (b) How did India become involved in the fighting? (c) What was the outcome of the civil war?
3. (a) What land reforms were introduced in China in the early 1950s? (b) How did the Great Leap Forward affect Chinese peasants? (c) In what other ways did the Great Leap Forward affect Chinese life?
4. Describe the changes Deng Xiaoping introduced in each of the following areas: (a) economics; (b) family life.
5. (a) How did the Americans try to end militarism in Japan? (b) How did they encourage democracy in Japan?
6. (a) Why does Japan try to maintain friendly relations with Arab nations? (b) How have relations between Japan and China changed in recent years?
7. (a) What problems did the government of the Philippines face after independence? (b) What were the results of the elections of 1986?

8. (a) What different groups were involved in the struggle for power in Vietnam in the late 1940s? (b) How did the 1954 Geneva settlement try to restore peace in Vietnam? (c) Did it succeed? Explain.

Critical Thinking

1. **Analyzing a Quotation** In the *Thoughts of Chairman Mao*, the Chinese Communist leader states: "We must have faith in the masses and we must have faith in the [Communist] Party." Do you think this statement accurately describes what happened in China after 1949?
2. **Analyzing** (a) How might you explain the economic miracle in Japan? (b) What evidence of the economic miracle can you cite?

Relating Past to Present

1. Review the origins of the Hindu-Muslim conflict in India. (See page 244.) (a) How did this conflict affect India at the time of independence? (b) Why do you think hostility between Hindus and Muslims lasted for so many centuries?

Developing Basic Skills

1. **Comparing** Review what you have read about postwar economic developments in India, China, and Japan. Then answer the following questions: (a) How were economic developments similar in each country? (b) How were they different? (c) Which nation do you think has made the greatest progress? Cite evidence to support your answer.
2. **Map Reading** Study the map on page 713. Then answer the following questions: (a) What nations border Korea? (b) What part of South Korea did the North Koreans control in September 1950? (c) Why do you think the Chinese joined the North Koreans late in 1950?
3. **Identifying Immediate and Long-Range Causes** (a) What was the immediate cause of the Gulf of Tonkin resolution? (b) What were the long-range causes? (c) How do you think this resolution led to increased American involvement in Southeast Asia?

See page 808 for suggested readings.

38 Latin America

The School of Medicine
at the University of
Mexico.

In 1934, 14-year-old Eva Duarte packed her few belongings in a cardboard suitcase and left home. She wanted to escape from the poverty of her home town in the Argentine pampas to the exciting city of Buenos Aires. In the glittering capital of Argentina, Eva Duarte hoped to find fame and fortune.

Life in the city shocked the young girl. "There were many more poor than rich in the spot where I spent my childhood," Eva Duarte would say later, "but I imagined that great cities were wonderful places where there were only riches. One day I visited the city and when I got there, I found that it was not what I had imagined." Eva wanted to become an actress, but jobs were scarce and she was not very talented. Nevertheless, she persevered and became a popular radio actress. Soon Eva Duarte was meeting important political personalities. In 1945, she married Juan Perón, an ambitious military officer. A year later, Juan Perón was elected president of Argentina, making Eva "First Lady of Argentina."

During the presidential campaign, Eva had helped her husband win the support of the "descamisados," or shirtless ones, as workers were called because they did not wear starched white shirts. The descamisados adored Evita, their name for the president's wife. They believed it was she who made sure that campaign promises for better wages and working conditions were carried out. Their support for Evita helped Juan Perón against his opponents in the Argentine congress.

Evita defied the all-male tradition in government and took the jobs of Minister of Social Welfare and Secretary of Labor. She used government funds to set up orphanages and homes for young working women. To the women of the descamisados, she promised: "You too will have clothes [as rich as mine]

. . . . Some day you will be able to sit next to any rich woman on the basis of complete equality. What we are fighting for is to destroy the inequality between you and the wives of your bosses."

When Evita died in 1952, millions of descamisados mourned for her. Even when it was discovered that Eva Perón had helped herself to much of the wealth she had collected for the descamisados, her image was not tarnished in the eyes of the poor. To many of them, she still symbolized the rise from poverty to wealth.

The gap between rich and poor is one of the most serious problems facing the nations of Latin America. Since 1945, these nations have pursued the goals of modernization and economic development. They have also moved forcefully to take charge of their own destinies and reduce foreign influence.

1 Challenge of Modernization

Read to Learn
- what problems block economic progress in Latin America
- how modernization has affected Latin American societies

Most Latin American nations had won their independence by 1825, as you read in Chapter 29. Since then, Latin American nations have struggled to establish stable governments and promote economic growth. In recent years, these efforts have met with mixed success.

The Population Explosion

Efforts to achieve economic growth in Latin America have been hindered by another kind of growth: a population explosion. Since 1940, the population of Latin America has more than doubled. Today, the rate of population growth in Latin America is second only to that of Africa.

The results of this population explosion are devastating. Most Latin American economies cannot expand fast enough to meet the basic needs of many of their people. Farmers cannot produce enough food, so malnutrition is widespread. In turn, malnutrition makes people susceptible to diseases that limit their ability to work.

Poverty is a byproduct of the population explosion. Poverty is evident both in the countryside and in the cities. Yet many rural people believe life in the cities is better. They stream into the cities by the millions each year. In Mexico City, for example, officials

The population explosion in Latin America is most evident in the cities. This picture shows a squatter settlement in Rio de Janeiro, Brazil. Hundreds of thousands of poor people live in shanties perched on steep hillsides. Despite the crowded living conditions and lack of services, cities remain a magnet for people from the countryside looking for a better life.

estimate that newcomers arrive at the rate of 1,000 a day.

All too often, newcomers to the cities find no jobs or, at best, poor-paying jobs or no steady work. They crowd into tin shacks and lean-tos, creating vast, crowded urban slums. City governments have made little or no effort to provide sewage and garbage removal in these areas. Thus, the urban poor become easy victims of disease.

Another byproduct of the population explosion is illiteracy. The illiteracy rate in Latin America is high, although conditions vary from country to country. Countries with more developed economies have been able to provide better education for their people. Thus, Argentina and Uruguay, for example, have illiteracy rates of less than 10 percent. In contrast, Haiti has a 50 per-

cent illiteracy rate. Without education, children in poor nations cannot learn the technical skills needed to develop a modern industrial society.

The Landowning System

Another obstacle to modernization in Latin America has been the landowning system. In colonial days, a few wealthy landlords controlled most of the land. This system changed little until the 1950s. About 60 percent of all land in Latin America was in the hands of a few landowners, although the amount varied in each country. In Bolivia, 92 percent of the land was controlled by large landowners.

This landowning system contributed to rural poverty. About 80 percent of the farm

Graph Skill *Unequal distribution of land has been a major problem in many Latin American nations. In the 1960s, most farms were small, as the graph on the left shows. According to the graphs, who owned the largest part of the total land area?*

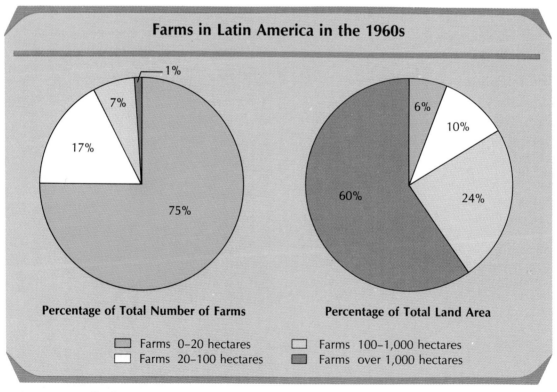

Source: E.R. Wolf and E.C. Hansen, *The Human Condition in Latin America*.

workers in Latin America were landless. They worked on the estates of large landowners, and their pay was generally extremely low. Resentment against the uneven distribution of land has caused unrest among the landless poor.

Land reform programs. Before 1950, only Mexico had introduced large-scale land reform. Since 1950, however, many Latin American governments have put land reform programs into effect. The government of Bolivia, for example, took large amounts of land from owners who did not work the land personally. It then turned the land over to 60,000 families. The government of Venezuela also took over many large estates. It paid the former landowners for the land and redistributed the land to peasant farmers.

Faced with growing unrest, the government of El Salvador announced a sweeping land reform program in 1980. The government broke up all estates larger than 1,235 acres (500 hectares). The owners of these estates were paid for their land. The land was then turned into cooperatives farmed by peasants.

Support for land reform has come from the Catholic Church, itself a large landowner. In 1969, the Latin American Bishops Conference called for land reform throughout Latin America. Church leaders backed up this call by turning over about 250,000 acres (100,000 hectares) of church land to 2,000 families.

Obstacles to increased production. Land reform programs sought to make the land more productive. Many large landowners had left much of their land idle. Small landowners, it was thought, would farm all their land. Moreover, supporters of land reform argued that people would work harder and produce more if they had a personal stake in the product of their labor. However, many of the new landowners lacked knowledge of new farm methods. They also lacked the money to buy tools. As a result, their output often remained low.

Food production has not kept pace with the growing population for other reasons. In some countries, large landowners successfully opposed efforts to break up their hold-ings. Many of these landowners have maintained inefficient farming methods. In addition, the amount of fertile farmland is limited, which has prevented farmers from increasing their output.

Growth of Economic Nationalism

Since colonial days, Latin America has depended on exports. As you read in Chapter 29, foreign investors developed and exported the rich mineral resources of countries such as Brazil and Chile. They also bought large plantations in the West Indies and elsewhere and exported cash crops such as coffee, sugar, and bananas. Foreign companies, rather than the Latin American countries, reaped most of the profits from these exports. Because Latin American rulers often benefited from foreign investments, they did little to develop local manufacturing industries.

During the Great Depression, the world market for many Latin American exports collapsed. The resulting hard times demonstrated how dependent the economies of Latin American nations were on the economies of industrial nations. World War II reinforced this lesson. During the war, Latin American nations suffered from shortages of the foreign manufactured goods they had always imported.

Since 1945, a new spirit of economic nationalism has grown in Latin America. Many Latin American nations have tried to free themselves from dependence on Western Europe and North America for both goods and markets. They have developed local industries to manufacture goods that were once imported. Growing a variety of cash crops has also become a goal of nations that previously depended on the export of just one or two crops.

Most nations have reduced their dependence on foreign investment. Venezuela, for example, took control of its highly profitable oil industry, which was previously run by foreign companies. In Brazil, the government has established an equal partnership with a foreign investor. Together, the government and the investor plan to make part of the Amazon jungle into a vast rice-, lumber-, and paper-producing area.

Economic growth has been uneven in Latin America. Argentina, Brazil, and Mexico, for example, have experienced greater expansion than many other Latin American nations. The largest cities in Latin America are Buenos Aires, São Paulo, and Mexico City. About 30 percent of all goods manufactured in Latin America are produced in these three cities.

Movements for Social Change

Modernization has affected the social structure in Latin America. As industry has grown, a new upper class has emerged. This new class is made up of people who have acquired vast wealth through commercial and industrial enterprises. At the same time, the middle class has also grown. The middle class includes business and industry managers, white-collar office workers, and gov-

Map Skill *Since 1945, Latin American nations have tried to diversify their economies rather than rely on one cash crop. This map shows some of the crops and industries that have developed in Latin America. Which countries probably depend on oil revenues?*

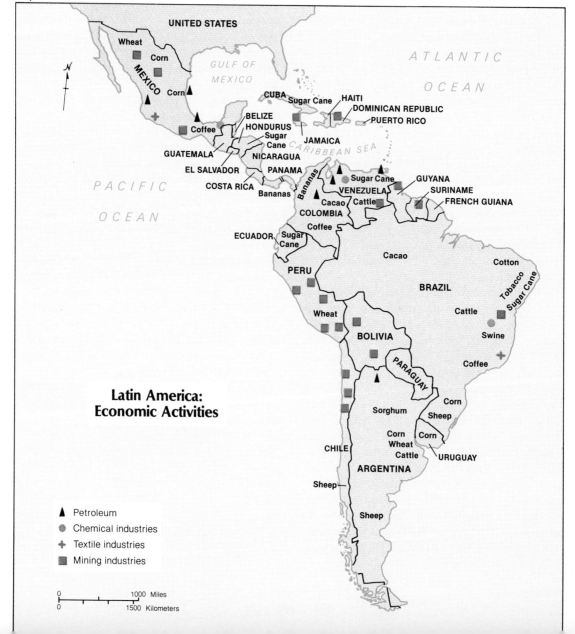

Latin America: Economic Activities

▲ Petroleum
● Chemical industries
✚ Textile industries
■ Mining industries

Gabriela Mistral (mees TRAHL) is the pen name of a well-known Chilean poet. Gabriela Mistral was born Lucila Godoy. Her father, a wandering poet and singer of mixed Spanish and Indian blood, had married a woman from a well-to-do Chilean family. As a girl, Lucila Godoy listened to the songs her father composed for village fiestas. She often sang along with him. But she was painfully aware of the prejudice her mother's family felt towards her and her father because of their Indian blood. Eventually, this prejudice drove her father to abandon his wife and daughter.

A bright student, Lucila Godoy completed school at age 15. She was soon hired to teach at a village school about 12 miles from her town. Each day, she walked or rode to the one-room school where she taught 38 students in grades one through eight. An imaginative teacher, she invented games and used verses to help her students learn arithmetic and spelling.

At age 18, Lucila Godoy fell in love, but her plans for marriage were shattered by the death of her fiancé. She turned to poetry to express her sorrow. She also began writing of the joy she saw in children and the beauty she saw in nature. Eventually, she entered some poems in a poetry contest in Santiago, Chile. A shy person, she used the pen name Gabriela Mistral so no one would know who had written the poems. When she won the contest, she asked a friend to accept the prize for her.

Gabriela Mistral became a successful poet, but she remained a dedicated teacher. She traveled all over Latin America advising governments on education. She also taught in the United States and served as Chilean consul in

several European capitals. Gabriela Mistral was awarded the Nobel Prize for Literature. She was the first Latin American writer to win this honor.

The following poem is entitled "Everything Is a Dance." It is one of Gabriela Mistral's many works celebrating children.

> The stars are children in circling dance,
> At watching the earth they play.
> The wheat-ears are figures of little girls,
> Their sport is to sway—to sway.
>
> The rivers are children in circling dance,
> They meet in the sea, with mirth;
> The waves are dances of little girls,
> They play at embracing the earth!

From *Some Spanish American Poets,* by Alice Stone Blackwell. Reprinted by permission of University of Pennsylvania Press.

ernment officials. The lower classes are divided between rural farmers and urban workers.

Latin American cities show clear signs of economic progress as well as the effects of the population explosion. Rich and poor live side by side. In the business districts, towering new skyscrapers shadow streets clogged with cars. Yet nearby are sprawling slums which house, on average, 25 percent of the population of each city.

Both in the countryside and in the cities, the huge gap between rich and poor has spurred calls for reform. Among the leaders of movements for social change are some clergy of the Catholic Church, middle class intellectuals, and students. These leaders have criticized governments for doing little or nothing to improve the lot of the rural and urban poor. They have called for more extensive land reform programs to help the rural farm workers. In the cities, they have demanded programs to increase employment and provide better living conditions.

Such programs are expensive, however. Many Latin American governments lack the financial resources to fund them. In addition, the wealthy and middle classes have sometimes opposed reforms such as minimum wages. They see these reforms as a limit on their freedom.

Failure to bring about social change has contributed to dangerous tensions. The poor want to escape from their poverty and gain a greater share of the economic pie. Especially in the cities, the unemployed and working poor live in a climate of rising expectations. That is, they see the comforts and luxuries that others enjoy, and they want the same for themselves. Rising expectations have posed yet another challenge to Latin American nations.

SECTION REVIEW

1. Describe two ways in which the population explosion affects Latin American countries.
2. Why did Latin American governments introduce land reform programs?
3. How did Latin American nations try to reduce their dependence on foreign trade after World War II?
4. How do rising expectations affect poor people in Latin America?

---

2 Politics of Change

Read to Learn
- how political conflicts threaten stability in Latin America
- how the United States responded to communism in Cuba

Many Latin American nations have sought to meet their social and economic problems with political solutions. When these political solutions failed, the governments were blamed and the leaders thrown out of office. Sometimes, changes in government occurred peaceably. Often, however, violence was used.

Deep Political Divisions

Political instability results in part from the deep divisions within many Latin American nations. Groups on the political right and left differ over how much reform is needed and what direction reform should take.

On the right are conservative groups, such as wealthy industrialists and landowners. They want to preserve the traditional economic system that is the basis of their wealth and power. Conservative groups often have the support of the military. Although military officers generally come from the middle class, they usually oppose reforms that threaten the traditional order.

On the political left are many urban workers and rural poor, as well as students and intellectuals. They favor swift, sweeping reforms. Their goals include better wages, better working conditions, and better housing. Many leftists support socialism. Thus, they call for nationalization of industries, whether domestic or foreign owned.

Many members of the middle class favor some kind of reform. Without it, they fear an uprising of the poorer classes that would destroy their way of life. However, some want moderate reform carried out over a number of years. Others call for immediate radical change.

High unemployment, overcrowded city slums, and rural poverty have contributed to growing support for leftist groups. Yet the right has traditionally held power in Latin America. Anxious to prevent a socialist revolution, rightist groups have urged governments in many Latin American nations to crack down on opposition political parties.

Experiments with Military Government

Political divisions and the threat of revolution have helped to strengthen the military in Latin America. The military has played a leading role in political affairs since the wars of independence. If efforts to establish a representative democracy led to turmoil in a country, the military often seized power. Military coups d'état, or revolts led by military officers, have been commonplace occurrences in many parts of Latin America. When the military has taken over, the result has usually been dictatorial rule by a military strongman.

Uruguay and Chile. Uruguay and Chile, two nations that had long traditions of democratic rule, experienced military takeovers in the 1970s. In the early 1970s, Uruguay was suffering from a grave economic crisis. At the same time, groups on the extreme left were committing terrorist acts such as kidnappings, assassinations, and bombings. In 1973, eager to halt this disorder, the Uruguayan armed forces revolted against the elected government. The military then used severe repression not only to combat terror-

ist groups but also to quiet any kind of political dissent.

However, the population of Uruguay was used to individual freedoms and democratic processes. Under the military, Uruguay's economic problems remained as severe as ever. Soon public feeling against the military leadership spread throughout the countryside. In response to their growing unpopularity, the military allowed the election of a civilian government in 1985.

In Chile, Salvador Allende (ah YEHN day) was elected president in 1970. Allende, a strong believer in Marxism, campaigned on a platform of socialist reform. Once in office, he began to put his reforms into effect. He nationalized industries and utilities. He also speeded up land reforms that had already been begun.

On the right, industrialists and landowners tried to block Allende's reforms. On the left, some factory and farm workers pro-

Rural poverty has contributed to political turmoil in Latin America. Many of the rural poor are Indians whose way of life has changed little in generations. Here, an Indian woman in Bolivia prepares reeds for weaving. Her ancestors were part of the once-powerful Inca Empire.

tested that the new programs were not being pushed through fast enough. The middle class protested the high inflation rate caused by Allende's reforms.

As different groups challenged Allende, unrest increased. In September 1973, the Chilean military otherthrew the elected government. Allende was killed in the fighting. The military suspended constitutional government and persecuted leftists. Eventually, it issued a new constitution, but the military, headed by General Augusto Pinochet (PEE noh shay), has remained in power.

In November 1984, Pinochet declared a state of siege to check widespread protests against his government. Chileans of different political leanings joined in the rebellions. They opposed economic policies that caused rising unemployment, bank failures, and the weakening of domestic industries. Moreover, they resented the dictatorship's methods of control. The discontent was tempered only by the fear some felt about communism. These fears grew out of what happened in Cuba in the 1950s and 1960s.

Communist Revolution in Cuba

Cuba won its independence from Spain in 1898. (See page 556.) Yet independence gave Cubans little control over their own economic destiny. North American and Western European companies owned many businesses and controlled the major export crop, sugar.

A series of corrupt dictators ruled Cuba. Unemployment was high. People in rural areas lived on the edge of starvation. When Fulgencio Batista seized power in 1961, he did little to improve conditions. He imprisoned critics but could not prevent acts of terrorism against his government.

In the 1950s, Fidel Castro emerged as a leader of revolutionaries opposed to the Batista government. In 1956, Castro and a handful of rebels established their headquarters in the rugged Sierra Maestra mountains of Cuba. The rebels waged guerrilla warfare against Batista's forces. In the next two years, thousands of Cubans joined Castro. Finally, the rebels left their mountain

stronghold and marched on Havana, the Cuban capital. On New Year's Day, 1959, Batista fled Havana. Fidel Castro then proclaimed himself premier.

At first, many Cubans enthusiastically greeted Castro's successful revolution. However, divisions quickly developed between Castro and some of his followers. Soon after he gained power, Castro announced he was a communist and that he intended to make Cuba a "socialist state." Some people who had joined Castro's forces did not approve of this goal. Castro soon forced these opponents into exile.

To achieve his goal, Castro launched a massive land reform program. Large sugar plantations were broken up into plots for small landholders. Later, many of these plots were recombined into large government-run farms. Castro also developed plans to industrialize Cuba. In addition, the government

On January 8, 1959, Fidel Castro entered Havana in triumph. The new Cuban leader won widespread support for his program of land reform and industrialization. A persuasive speaker, Castro used nationally broadcast television speeches to explain his communist revolution to the Cuban people.

offered free education to all Cubans. It also provided free health care and built new public housing.

Castro's government remains unchallenged in the 1980s. However, in a 1986 party conference, Castro himself accused his party of failing to keep to its revolutionary goals. He complained of low productivity, waste, and inefficiency. In an effort to revive the spirit of reform, Castro replaced several of Cuba's top leaders.

Cuba and the United States

The United States had quickly recognized the Castro government in 1959 and offered it aid. But American enthusiasm for Castro soon cooled when the new Cuban leader began denouncing "Yankee imperialism." Support for Castro waned further after he took over some American-owned properties in Cuba without compensation.

Worsening relations between Cuba and the United States led Castro to seek alliances with the Soviet Union and other communist nations. In 1960, Castro concluded an aid and trade pact with the Soviet Union. Soviet planners soon began arriving in Cuba to help Castro carry out his program for industrialization. The United States grew anxious about Soviet influence in Cuba, which is only 90 miles (145 kilometers) off its southeastern coast. When American-owned oil companies in Cuba refused to handle Soviet oil shipments, Castro responded by taking over the oil companies.

Castro created further tension in the Western Hemisphere when he encouraged revolutions in other parts of Latin America. He urged poor rural workers and landless peasants to follow his example and organize guerrilla armies to overthrow the governments. He sent aid to rebels in Venezuela, Guatemala, and Bolivia.

Bay of Pigs invasion. The United States strongly opposed the spread of communism in the Western Hemisphere. In January 1961, it cut off diplomatic relations with Cuba. Many Latin American nations also cut off diplomatic relations with Cuba. Meanwhile, thousands of Cubans had begun seeking ref-

uge in the United States. They were mostly wealthy and middle class people whose property Castro had seized. These Cuban exiles told stories of political repression under Castro.

In April 1961, about 2,000 Cuban exiles trained and armed by the United States launched an attack on their homeland. They landed at the Bay of Pigs on the southern coast of Cuba. They hoped their attack would spark a general uprising against Castro. However, the Bay of Pigs invasion was a disaster. The United States hesitated to give air support, and there was no popular uprising against the government. About 300 attackers were killed. The rest were captured.

The Cuban missile crisis. Soviet leader Nikita Khrushchev had promised to aid Cuba if it were invaded by the United States. Cuba used the Bay of Pigs incident to justify building up its defenses. In October 1962, American reconnaissance planes discovered that the Soviet Union had begun building missile bases in Cuba. The United States asked the Soviet Union to dismantle these bases, which could be used to launch missiles against the United States. When Khrushchev refused, President John F. Kennedy announced a naval blockade of Cuba. American warships were ordered to prevent Soviet ships carrying missiles from reaching Cuba.

A tense waiting game followed as Soviet ships approached the blockaded island. At the last minute, the Soviet Union backed down. Khrushchev agreed to stop constructing the bases and to remove the missiles from Cuba.

Relations have not improved much between the United States and Cuba since the 1960s. On several occasions, Castro has allowed Cubans opposed to his government to leave. Tens of thousands of Cubans have taken these opportunities to flee their homeland. Many have settled in the United States. In 1977, the United States restored limited diplomatic relations with Cuba. But it has maintained a careful watch on Castro's activities inside Cuba as well as on his efforts to export his communist revolution to Latin America.

1. Locate: Uruguay, Chile, Cuba, Havana.
2. Identify: Salvador Allende, Augusto Pinochet, Fulgencio Batista, Fidel Castro, Bay of Pigs, Cuban missile crisis.
3. (a) What goals have groups on the political right supported in Latin America? (b) What goals have groups on the political left supported?
4. (a) Why did the military seize power in Uruguay in 1973? (b) Why did it step down?
5. How did Castro gain power in Cuba?
6. List three reasons why relations became hostile between Castro and the United States.

---

3 Latin America in the Eighties

Read to Learn
- how the economies or conflicts between left and right caused problems in Mexico, Central America, and Venezuela
- why governments in Argentina and Brazil went from military to civilian rule

"Argentina is as different from Paraguay, its next-door neighbor, as the United States is from Tibet or Afghanistan," wrote one observer of Latin America. He continued, "Argentina, Peru, and Haiti are as different from each other as England, India, and the Congo." The differences among Latin American nations are evident in the routes they have taken toward modernization.

Change in Mexico

As you read in Chapter 29, Mexico underwent a major political and social revolution in the early 1900s. Since then, it has achieved a relatively stable government. The Mexican government has taken a strong hand in directing the national economy. A genuine land reform program was carried out in the 1930s. About the same time, the government nationalized British- and American-owned oil companies.

Mexico made progress on several fronts. It built up industry to supply many of its own consumer needs. Thus, it lessened its dependence on imports. Government-sponsored programs brought millions of acres of new farmland under cultivation. Schools in both rural and urban areas helped raise the literacy rate.

Mexico had the fastest growing economy in Latin America. However, its rapidly expanding oil industry was set back by the oil glut of the 1980s, which plunged the nation into debt. Economic growth was also offset by a population explosion. There are now too many farm workers in rural areas and no more land to bring under cultivation. As a result, many rural people migrate to the cities. Mexico cannot yet provide enough jobs for its population of 83 million. Inflation and, in 1985, devastating earthquakes added to Mexico's woes.

Unrest in Central America

Mexico's neighbors in Central America have experienced growing unrest in recent years. Central America is an impoverished region. The capital cities of Guatemala, El Salvador, and Nicaragua have a modern appearance. But most people in these countries live in poverty-stricken rural areas.

The causes of the unrest have been corrupt military rule and unequal distribution of wealth. Military rulers are usually supported by a relatively small group of wealthy landowners and businesspeople. Students and peasants have united to demand reform. When their demands are not met, they have often joined guerrilla armies.

Nicaragua. One revolution took place in 1979, when the Sandinista National Liberation Front overthrew the strongman ruler

736

Anastasio Somoza. At first, the new regime was a coalition of diverse political parties. But it was soon dominated by the left. When moderate and right-wing elements failed to gain in elections held in 1984, some turned to armed attack.

Guerrilla forces opposing the leftist government had begun to take shape as early as 1980. By 1985, the largest group of these anti-Sandinistas, or Contras, was based in Honduras. Sandinista forces were supplied with such equipment as Soviet-built helicopters. The Contras, meanwhile, were extended increasing amounts of United States aid. By 1986, the Reagan administration's support of the Contras had become the focus of heated debate in the United States. While some Americans feared that Nicaragua would become a communist base, others worried about the growing involvement of the United States in Central American affairs.

El Salvador. During the 1980s, revolutionary turmoil developed in other nations, including Guatemala and El Salvador. Terrorist groups on the right and left killed thousands and disrupted daily life in the cities and countryside. Under pressure from the United States, the government of El Salvador introduced land reform. But the civil war in that nation continued.

Cuba and other socialist nations gave aid to left-wing guerrillas to combat right-wing terrorism. Although the United States backed the government of El Salvador, it demanded that the terrorism and power of the extreme right be reduced. Gradually, through elections and domestic reforms, the government of El Salvador became more centrist. In 1984, José Napoleón Duarte (D'WAHR-tay) was elected president. Duarte won support from both business leaders and labor. The United States gave Duarte's government increasing support, and soon guerrillas controlled only about 10 percent of the country.

Costa Rica. The brightest spot in Central America has been Costa Rica. One observer called it "a small democracy with an enlightened citizenry." Costa Rica has enjoyed political stability and achieved a better standard of living than other Central American nations.

In recent years, Central America has been the scene of fierce guerrilla fighting. Leftist guerrillas, often aided by Cuba, have tried to overthrow governments that guerrillas claim represent only wealthy landlords and industrialists. The fighting has taken a large toll among civilians. Here, a guerrilla soldier in the mountains of El Salvador keeps a lookout for government soldiers.

Costa Rica did not suffer from a concentration of land in the hands of a few. More than a century ago, the land was divided into small parcels. In addition, the government has provided public health and education programs to help the poor. Today, the literacy rate in Costa Rica is 93 percent.

Despite a stable, democratic government, Costa Rica has experienced economic problems such as inflation. High food prices have contributed to unrest. As one Costa Rican economist warned, "Unless we resolve our economic problems, Costa Rica could become vulnerable to the troubles of other Central American countries." Recently, leftists and rightists clashed in Costa Rica.

Oil in Venezuela

Like Costa Rica, Venezuela has a stable, democratic government. Thanks largely to its vast petroleum deposits, Venezuela enjoyed rapid economic growth. Oil accounted for almost 70 percent of the nation's revenues. Oil wealth gave Venezuela the highest per capita income of any Latin American nation.

The Venezuelan government nationalized the oil industry in 1976. It paid the foreign companies—mostly American—$1.28 billion for their oil holdings. The government used oil wealth to modernize Venezuela. For example, it vowed to "sow the petroleum revenues back into the soil." Thus, it worked to improve agriculture, teaching farmers new planting methods. At the same time, through land reform, small farmers gained their own land. New roads made it easier to move farm produce to markets. In addition, education and health care were extended into the countryside.

However, the Venezuelan government knows that its oil reserves will eventually run out—possibly by the year 2000. It is trying to build other industries before this happens. But this effort has had limited success. Since oil accounted for 95 percent of the nation's exports, the drastic worldwide drop in demand in the 1980s caused a severe recession. In addition, soaring inflation has widened the gap between rich and poor.

Military and Civilian Rule in Argentina

Since the 1940s, Argentina has experienced frequent political turmoil. Military rulers have regularly overthrown elected governments. The best-known of these military rulers was Juan Perón. An army colonel, he won the backing of the working class. As you read at the beginning of this chapter, Perón was elected president in 1946.

Perón admired the goals of the Italian Fascist leader Benito Mussolini. He wanted to achieve economic self-sufficiency for Argentina and break the control of foreign interests. To carry out his policies, Perón established strict government control over the press, the courts, and the schools.

Despite Perón's program of social reform, Argentina was plagued with economic problems. As economic difficulties multiplied, Perón used more severe methods to quiet his critics. In 1955, the military overthrew him, and he went into exile in Spain.

The army controlled politics for the next 18 years. Yet Perónists, or supporters of Perón, remained strong. In 1973, the aging Perón was invited back to Argentina. He ruled less than a year before he died. Power struggles between groups on the left and right led to constant turmoil and frequent military intervention. The military government arrested thousands of suspected opponents. Most were never heard from again.

In 1982, the military government tried to win popular support by seizing the British-ruled Falkland Islands. Argentina claimed these islands, located 300 miles off its shores. In the brief war that followed, Britain regained control of the Falklands. The next year, partially in reaction to the defeat, the leader of the Radical party, Raúl Alfonsín, was elected president of a new democratic government.

Changing Brazil

As in most Latin American nations, the government in Brazil has played a central role in directing the economy. Its emphasis has been on programs that encourage economic growth and self-sufficiency. In the 1950s, the government decided to build a new capital at Brasilia, 600 miles (965 kilometers) inland from the former capital of Rio de Janeiro. The new capital symbolized the government's determination to develop the vast inland areas of Brazil.

Government funds and private capital have helped Brazilian industry expand. Today, Brazil is the most highly industrialized country in Latin America. New industries have been developed in steel, heavy machinery, electrical equipment, and chemicals. At the same time, older industries such as textile manufacturing remain strong. Service industries have become increasingly important, now accounting for about 60 percent of Brazil's economic output.

Agriculture has not received as much government support as industry. Yet agricultural exports account for much of the na-

During the years of military rule in Argentina, thousands of people suspected of opposing the regime were arrested and never heard from again. In this photograph, relatives of the "disappeared" demonstrate in the Plaza de Mayo in Buenos Aires. The democratic government that replaced the military in 1983 has moved to punish those responsible.

tion's income. Major exports include coffee, cotton, cacao beans, and cattle. Only about 5 percent of Brazil has been brought under cultivation. But the government has begun to exploit agricultural and other resources of inland areas, including the vast Amazon rain forest region.

Ironically, economic growth has contributed to grave economic and social problems in Brazil. Under the military government that ruled Brazil from 1964 to 1985, the middle and upper classes prospered. However, according to the World Bank,* Brazilian economic growth was accompanied by "crushing disparities [differences] of opportunity, for the share of the national income received by the poorest 40 percent of the

---

* The World Bank is an agency of the United Nations that makes loans to countries for economic development.

This modern-looking building is the Catholic cathedral in the heart of Brasilia. Statues of four Apostles stand outside the cathedral. The Catholic Church plays an important role in Latin American nations where the majority of people are Catholic. Members of the Catholic clergy in Brazil and other Latin American nations have spoken out on such issues as poverty and social injustice.

population declined . . . while the share of the richest 5 percent grew."

As in other Latin American nations, the military government failed to solve the problem of a growing population of desperately poor people. Then, in 1985, the military worked out a compromise with civilian party leaders. After over twenty years of controlling Brazil, military domination ended. The task of governing fell to civilians. Ahead was the challenge of building new democratic institutions that would be able to sustain the civilian government. The new regime would need to find ways of developing wealth from the nation's vast untapped resources. Reducing poverty and meeting a huge foreign debt are the major problems facing Brazil as it approaches the 1990s.

SECTION REVIEW

1 Locate: Mexico, Guatemala, El Salvador, Nicaragua, Costa Rica, Venezuela, Argentina, Brazil, Brasilia.

2. Identify: Sandinistas, Contras, José Duarte, Juan Perón, Raúl Alfonsin.

3. (a) Give two reasons for unrest in Central America. (b) How is Costa Rica different from most countries in Central America?

4. Why have military dictatorships been replaced by democracies in (a) Argentina? (b) Brazil?

4 Latin America in World Affairs

Read to Learn
- how Latin American nations cooperate to increase trade and limit conflict
- what role the United States plays in Latin America

Latin America is made up of over 40 nations. The peoples of these nations have set up different political systems. Their economic interests vary, and they pursue diverse foreign policies. Despite their differences, Latin American nations have made efforts to cooperate for mutual benefit.

Regional Cooperation

Some efforts at cooperation have been aimed at forming regional trade organizations. For example, Mexico and ten South American nations formed the Latin American Free Trade Area (LAFTA) in the 1960s. LAFTA was modeled on the European Common Market. (See page 657.) Its goals were to break down trade barriers and thereby increase trade among member nations. Increased trade, LAFTA members hoped, would stimulate greater production and lessen their dependence on the United States and other foreign trading partners.

LAFTA has had limited success, however. Member nations with relatively little industry found it difficult to trade with more industrialized members. They could not produce enough goods to afford the goods of their richer partners. Despite problems, efforts at regional cooperation have continued. Six nations—Colombia, Ecuador, Peru, Bolivia, Chile, and Venezuela—are all in the Andes Mountains and have common regional problems. They have formed the Andean Common Market to work for common economic goals.

Another example of regional cooperation is the aid offered by Mexico and Venezuela to their Latin American neighbors. These two nations are the major oil producers in Latin America. They charge world market prices for their oil. Despite the price drop of the 1980s, many poor Latin American nations have trouble paying for the oil.

To help them, Mexico and Venezuela have agreed to extend credit to Latin American nations that must import oil.

The largest regional organization is the Organization of American States (OAS). This organization was founded in 1948 by 21 American republics, including the United States. The chief OAS aims are to uphold the independence of its members and preserve peace and justice in the Western Hemisphere.

On several occasions, the OAS has successfully put pressure on member nations to end armed conflict with one another. It has also condemned the intervention of one member nation in the affairs of another. For example, in 1962, the government of Peru complained that Cuban Premier Fidel Castro was aiding guerrilla groups inside Peru. The OAS passed trade sanctions against Cuba and excluded it from OAS affairs. When Cuba continued to support leftist guerrillas throughout Latin America, the OAS voted to isolate Cuba. From 1964 to 1975, the OAS maintained a trade embargo against Cuba.

Since the 1970s, the OAS has concentrated on promoting economic development. It has set up programs to ease energy shortages, improve trade and transportation, and provide capital for investment in industry.

The United States and Latin America

The United States has taken a leading role in the OAS. However, some Latin American nations have resented its influence over OAS policy and over Latin American affairs in general. This fear of United States domination dates back to the 1800s. (See pages 555–558.) Today, many Latin Americans feel threatened by the United States because it is the most highly industrialized, powerful nation in the Western Hemisphere.

The United States has firmly opposed the spread of communism in the Western Hemisphere. In 1965, this policy led it to intervene militarily in the Dominican Republic to prevent a communist takeover. The United States also supported anti-Allende groups in Chile in the early 1970s.

In 1984, President Reagan took emergency measures against communism in Grenada, a small island nation in the Caribbean. Grenada had had a Marxist government since 1979. Its prime minister, Maurice Bishop, had established close ties with Cuba. Moreover, rebel leftists supporting more extreme policies took over in 1984 and assassinated Bishop.

Fearing that Grenada would become a center for the spread of revolution, the United States invaded Grenada. Forces from six Caribbean nations joined in the move to restore order. In parliamentary elections held later that year, a centrist coalition government came to power. And in 1985, all United States personnel left the island.

Another concern of the United States has been to protect United States businesses and industries in Latin America. Nationalist feeling in Latin America has often been directed against foreign-owned companies. Many Latin American nations, including Cuba, Chile, and Venezuela, have nationalized foreign-owned businesses.

Alliance for Progress. Since the 1960s, the United States has tried to work with Latin American nations in a spirit of partnership. One such attempt at partnership was the Alliance for Progress, which was begun in 1961. The aim of the Alliance was to bring about a social revolution in Latin America through a massive program of reform. Participating nations pledged to:

> ... accelerate economic and social development, to encourage programs of comprehensive agrarian land reform ... to assure fair wages and satisfactory working conditions, to wipe out illiteracy, to reform tax laws, demanding more from those who have the most, to punish tax evasion severely, and to redistribute the national income to benefit those who are most in need. ...

The United States agreed to contribute $1.3 billion a year over a 10-year period to the Alliance of Progress. The 19 Latin American nations who would receive this aid agreed to get private investors to put billions more into their economies. Private investment was supposed to build new industry and create jobs.

The goals of the Alliance proved to be too far-reaching. Ten years later, in 1971, little progress had been made. But the Alliance for Progress had clearly pinpointed the kinds of reforms needed in Latin America.

Other developments. The United States has made other attempts to improve relations with Latin American nations. For example, many Latin Americans, especially the people of Panama, objected to United States control of the Panama Canal Zone. They saw it as another sign of "Yankee imperialism"— what they considered unjust North American influence over Latin American affairs.

In 1978, after a bitter debate, the United States Senate approved a new treaty with Panama.* By the terms of the treaty, the United States agreed to give Panama complete control of the Canal Zone by the year 2000. Until then, an agency made up of Americans and Panamanians would operate the Canal.

Early in 1982, President Reagan announced plans for a massive aid program for nations of Central America and the Caribbean. The purpose of the program was to enable governments in these regions to strengthen their economies. The President hoped his plan would counter the growing power of leftists and combat the spread of communism in these regions.

Relations between the United States and Mexico have also been the focus of attention. Before the drop in oil prices, Mexico had begun to develop its huge reserves of oil and natural gas. The United States remains interested in the future possibilities of buying these Mexican resources.

Another question at issue has been the large number of Mexican citizens who have crossed illegally into the United States in search of jobs. In 1986, Congress enacted a new immigration law. This law permits mil-

---

* The original treaty with Panama in 1903 gave the United States control of the Canal Zone "in perpetuity," or forever.

The United States has recently proposed a program to aid Caribbean nations. Many Caribbean nations, such as Haiti, are largely rural and poor. This painting by a Haitian artist shows people harvesting corn. Colorful paintings by Haitian artists have become popular throughout the world.

lions of illegal immigrants to stay in the United States legally. But it also makes it a crime for employers to hire workers who do not have proper documents. Thus, the new law aims to discourage future illegal immigration by those who want to come to the United States to find work.

Human Rights in Latin America

As you have read, political turmoil in Latin America has often led to violations of human rights. Human rights include freedom of speech, religion, and the press. They also include the right to a fair trial, to earn a living, and to live in safety from attack. Terrorists and some governments have sometimes shown little regard for human rights. In Latin America, groups on both the right and the left have used kidnappings, assassinations, and bombings to achieve their ends.

In the early 1980s, an estimated 13,000 people a year were killed in El Salvador by terrorist groups and by government forces attempting to restore order. Fearing revolution, some Latin American governments have ended free speech, closed down universities, and thrown political opponents in jail without trial.

For example, Amnesty International, a group that monitors human rights violations, estimated that about 4,000 political prisoners were held without trial in Argentina under the military. Another 6,000 to 15,000 people "disappeared." That is, they were arrested, but the government denied any knowledge of them, and they remain unaccounted for.

743

The democratic government that replaced the military in Argentina has pledged its commitment to human rights. It is seeking punishment for those proven responsible for the torture and death of Argentinians.

Nations around the world, including the United States, have condemned human rights violations. And individuals and organizations continue to work for human rights in Latin America and elsewhere.

SECTION REVIEW

1. Identify: LAFTA, Andean Common Market, OAS, Alliance for Progress.

2. (a) What were two goals of LAFTA? (b) What were the chief goals of the OAS?

3. Describe two aims of United States policy toward Latin American nations.

4. How has political turmoil contributed to human rights violations in Latin America?

Chapter 38 Review

In Perspective

The nations of Latin America face many challenges as they try to achieve modernization. The population explosion has put a severe strain on Latin American governments. Moreover, traditional landholding systems have limited economic development. Nevertheless, most Latin American nations have taken steps to industrialize.

Divisions between groups on the political left and groups on the right have caused turmoil in many nations. To end turmoil, the military has often seized power in Latin American countries. When military governments failed to solve economic problems, some were replaced by democracies.

In the 1950s, Fidel Castro led a revolution in Cuba. Once in power, he made Cuba a communist nation. Relations between Cuba and the United States deteriorated after Castro became an ally of the Soviet Union.

Most Latin American governments have had to struggle to control their economies. Mexico and Venezuela, for example, used oil wealth to modernize and were deeply affected by the oil glut of the 1980s.

In an attempt to encourage mutual cooperation, Latin American nations have formed regional trade organizations. At the same time, the United States has tried to improve relations with Latin American countries by working as a partner with its neighbors in the Western Hemisphere.

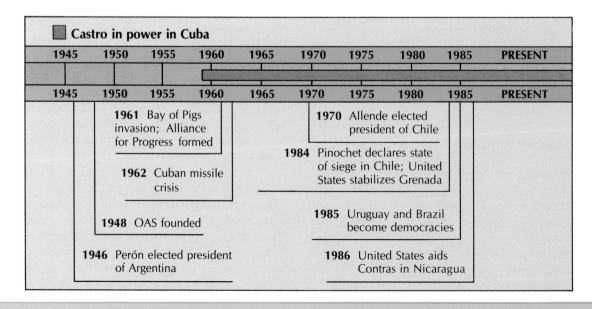

Castro in power in Cuba

1945	1950	1955	1960	1965	1970	1975	1980	1985	PRESENT

1961 Bay of Pigs invasion; Alliance for Progress formed

1962 Cuban missile crisis

1948 OAS founded

1946 Perón elected president of Argentina

1970 Allende elected president of Chile

1984 Pinochet declares state of siege in Chile; United States stabilizes Grenada

1985 Uruguay and Brazil become democracies

1986 United States aids Contras in Nicaragua

Recalling Facts

Choose the word or phrase that best completes each of the following statements.

1. An obstacle to modernization in Latin America has been (a) land reform; (b) the population explosion; (c) the spread of communism.

2. Leftist political groups in Latin America want to (a) preserve the traditional economic system; (b) introduce moderate changes; (c) bring about wide-ranging reform.

3. Salvador Allende was elected president of (a) Cuba; (b) Uruguay; (c) Chile.

4. Fidel Castro angered the United States when he (a) nationalized foreign oil companies; (b) led a revolution against Fulgencio Batista; (c) began industrializing Cuba.

5. A major cause of unrest in Central America is (a) overcrowded cities; (b) the gap between rich and poor; (c) industrialization.

6. Brazil built a new capital at (a) Rio de Janeiro; (b) Havana; (c) Brasilia.

7. The largest organization working for regional cooperation in the Western Hemisphere is (a) LAFTA; (b) the OAS; (c) the Andean Common Market.

Chapter Checkup

1. Explain why each of the following is a problem in Latin America: (a) the population explosion; (b) the landowning system; (c) divisions between the political right and left.

2. (a) Describe the social structure in Latin America. (b) Why do some people demand social change? (c) What kinds of change do they think are necessary?

3. (a) How did the military takeovers in Uruguay and Chile affect these countries? (b) Why was military government replaced in some Latin American countries?

4. (a) How did Castro want to change Cuba after he gained power? (b) How did his actions create problems between the United States and Cuba?

5. Explain what progress each of the following countries has made toward modernization: (a) Mexico; (b) Venezuela; (c) Brazil.

6. (a) What groups supported Juan Perón? (b) How did he win their support? (c) Why was he unable to solve Argentina's problems?

7. (a) What goals did the Alliance for Progress establish? (b) Did it meet its goals? Explain.

Critical Thinking

1. **Comparing** Compare the efforts of Latin American nations to modernize to those of African nations. (a) How are they similar? (b) How are they different?

2. **Evaluating** Some Latin American nations have denounced United States policy toward Latin America as "Yankee imperialism." (a) Why do some Latin American nations see the United States as a threat? (b) How has the United States moved toward greater partnership with Latin American nations?

Relating Past to Present

1. Review the structure of colonial society in Latin America. (See page 545.) (a) How has this structure remained the same? (b) How has it changed? (c) Why do you think it has not changed more?

Developing Basic Skills

1. **Using Statistics** Study the graphs on page 728. Then answer the following questions: (a) What is the subject of the graphs? (b) What percentage of farms were under 20 hectares in size? (c) What percentage of farms were over 1,000 hectares? (d) Which size farm made up the largest percentage of land? (e) Which size farm made up the smallest percentage of land? (f) What conclusion about land ownership can you draw from these graphs?

2. **Researching** Choose one of the nations of Central America. Research its recent history in order to answer the following questions: (a) What is the population of the country? (b) How do most people earn a living? (c) What is the per capita income in the country? (d) Have economic conditions affected political developments in the country? Explain.

See page 808 for suggested readings.

39 Europe and the United States

(1968–Present)

A workers' memorial in Gdansk, Poland.

Chapter Outline

1 Changing Outlooks in Western Europe

2 Conformity and Dissent in the Soviet Bloc

3 Challenge and Change in the United States

On a cold, damp day in December 1980, thousands of Polish workers gathered in the port city of Gdansk. They came to watch the dedication of a monument to 45 workers killed in an antigovernment uprising in 1970. Many of the economic problems that had caused the 1970 uprising still existed in 1980—high prices, shortages of food and other necessities, poor quality goods. An important change had occurred recently, however.

At the base of the monument, along with Catholic Church and Communist party officials, stood Lech Walesa (vah WEHN sah). Walesa was leader of Solidarity, an independent labor union that had been recognized by the Polish government just two months earlier. Solidarity had already won important concessions from the government.

At the dedication ceremony, Walesa lit a memorial flame and proclaimed: "This monument was erected for those who were killed, as an admonition [warning] to those in power. It embodies the right of human beings to their dignity, to order and to justice." At an earlier rally, Walesa had urged workers, "Do not give in, for once you do give in, you will not rise back for a long time. Indeed, we cannot surrender, for those who will follow us will say, 'They were so close, and they failed.' History would not absolve [forgive] us then."

The hopes of the Polish workers were to be dashed in 1981, as you will read in this chapter. However, their struggle for greater freedom and democracy was an important development. It represented a challenge to Soviet control of Eastern Europe and a reaction to severe economic problems. Although less severe than in Poland, economic problems also troubled people in the rest of Europe and in the United States during the 1970s and 1980s.

1 Changing Outlooks in Western Europe

Read to Learn
- what caused unrest in the 1960s and 1970s in Western Europe
- how European nations extended democracy and international cooperation

By the late 1960s, the economic growth of the postwar period was winding down. Many Europeans became less optimistic about the future than they had been during most of the 1950s and 1960s. A symptom of the changing mood was an outbreak of student unrest in 1968.

Student Protests

In 1968, universities in many parts of Europe were the scenes of strikes and demonstrations. Students demanded reforms of the universities and of society. Their actions reflected a deep resentment against the authority of the older generation of leaders in government and business, which they called "the establishment."

Serious student disturbances threatened the government of France. Early in May, students occupied the Sorbonne, a division of the University of Paris. Students built barricades and fought pitched battles with police. Thousands of workers throughout France went on strike to show sympathy for the students. They also demanded changes in work rules and higher wages. Many students and workers called for the resignation of the French president, Charles de Gaulle.

The events of early May caught the French government by surprise. But by the end of the month, de Gaulle was gaining control of the situation. He promised pay raises for workers and reform of the universities. Workers returned to their jobs, and the police put an end to the student occupation of the Sorbonne. De Gaulle also called for new elections to the National Assembly. The elections, which were held in June, were a great victory for de Gaulle.

The outcomes of student uprisings in West Germany, Belgium, Britain, and Italy were similar to the outcome in France. In the end, most governments broadened the participation of students in school adminis-tration and of workers in factories. The student protests of 1968 called people's attention to what came to be called the "quality of life," meaning a clean, humane environment in which to live and work.

A Time of Uncertainty in France and Britain

After the 1968 uprisings, life returned to normal in most of Europe. Yet the future seemed less secure and somehow less promising than it had a decade earlier.

France. De Gaulle, a towering figure in French politics since World War II, retired in 1969 and died the following year. His successor, Georges Pompidou (PAHM pih doo), continued de Gaulle's policy of strengthening France's position in Europe. After Pompidou's death in 1974, Valéry Giscard d'Estaing (duh STANG) became president. Giscard d'Estaing encouraged women to play a more active role in French government and society. He also raised the minimum wage and increased worker benefits. Labor unrest and inflation, however, limited the economic progress of France during the 1970s.

In the spring of 1981, the French held general elections. François Mitterrand, a socialist, defeated Giscard d'Estaing and won the presidency. His government was the first leftist government in France since the Popular Front of the 1930s. Mitterrand announced plans to nationalize more of the French economy and to decentralize political power. French business and commercial leaders were concerned, but Mitterrand assured them that he would proceed slowly.

Britain. Rising inflation and unemployment plagued Britain during the 1960s and 1970s. The Labour government of Prime Minister Harold Wilson tried to halt inflation by imposing a freeze on all wages and prices, but the move failed. A Conservative govern-

On July 29, 1981, Prince Charles, heir to the British throne, married Lady Diana Spencer. The wedding took place in St. Paul's Cathedral, London. The ceremony was staged with pomp and splendor, recalling the traditions of the British monarchy. The magnificent ceremony temporarily distracted the British people from the country's pressing economic problems.

ment led by Edward Heath also had little success in strenghtening the economy. A series of strikes by miners and dockworkers in 1972 only made matters worse.

In January 1973, Britain was admitted to the Common Market. (Ireland and Denmark joined later that year.) The British hoped that membership in the Common Market

would help their lagging economy, but it failed to do so. Between 1974 and 1979, the average annual rate of inflation was 20 percent.

In 1979, the Conservative Margaret Thatcher became Britain's first woman prime minister. Thatcher tried to reduce government spending. As a result, the rate of inflation in Britain began to slow, but unemployment rose dramatically. Many British citizens grew dissatisfied with both the Conservative party and the Labour party because neither had been able to solve the nation's economic problems.

Throughout the 1970s, Britain also had to cope with an explosive situation in Northern Ireland. Since 1921, Northern Ireland had been self-governing. However, it was still part of the United Kingdom of Great Britain and Northern Ireland. The Protestant majority of Northern Ireland firmly controlled the government and economy. Discrimination against the large Catholic minority was widespread. Catholic discontent led to violence beginning in 1969. Britain sent troops to restore order, but unrest continued. Catholic and Protestant extremists carried out terrorist bombings and murders throughout the 1970s. In the 1980s, the area seemed no closer to peace.

New Relations Between West Germany and the Soviet Bloc

In 1969, Willy Brandt became prime minister of West Germany. Brandt was leader of the Social Democrats and a former mayor of West Berlin. One of his goals was to improve relations with the communist countries of Eastern Europe. His policy was called *Ostpolitik*, which is German for "eastern policy."

Step by step over the next five years, Brandt put Ostpolitik into effect. In 1970, West Germany signed a treaty with the Soviet Union. In this treaty, the two nations recognized all existing European boundaries and agreed never to alter them by force. In light of the bitter memories of World War II in both nations, the treaty represented a historic breakthrough. Later that year, West Germany signed a similar treaty with Poland.

In 1972, West Germany signed a treaty with East Germany as a first step toward establishing normal relations. A treaty signed the following year with Czechoslovakia completed Brandt's Ostpolitik. Brandt won the Nobel Prize for Peace for his role in normalizing East-West relations.

The Spread of Democratic Government

During the mid-1970s, three nations of southern Europe ruled by dictators—Greece, Portugal, and Spain—became democracies.

In 1967, a group of right-wing military officers known as "the colonels" had seized power in Greece. They suspended the constitution and imposed a harsh authoritarian regime. The colonels threw thousands of political opponents into jail. Many other opponents went into exile. In 1974, however, the colonels fell from power following an unsuccessful foreign policy adventure. A constitutional government was then restored.

In Portugal, Antonio Salazar had ruled as dictator since the 1930s. After his death, Portugal moved gradually toward democracy. In 1976 it held its first free elections in more than 50 years.

Spain had been ruled by dictator Francisco Franco since the Spanish Civil War. (See page 625.) As he neared the end of his life, Franco chose Prince Juan Carlos as his successor. When Franco died in 1975, Juan Carlos surprised the world by sponsoring parliamentary elections. In 1982, Felipe González, head of the Socialist Workers' party, became prime minister.

Challenges of the 1980s

Economic problems were among the greatest challenges faced by Western Europe in the 1980s. Most European countries suffered from inflation. At the same time, economic growth slowed, and people lost jobs. In Common Market nations, for example, unemployment soared.

Economic problems threatened European cooperation. The Common Market grew to ten members with the admission of Greece in 1981. However, the organization

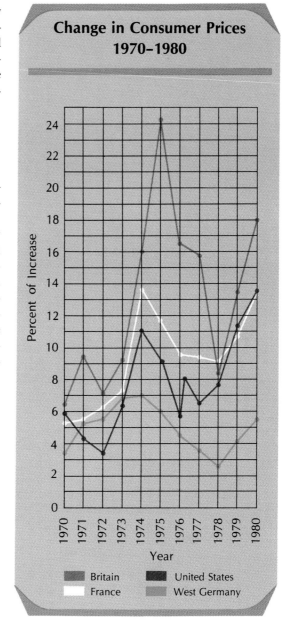

Change in Consumer Prices 1970–1980

Source: Organization for Economic Cooperation and Development, *Economic Outlook*.

Graph Skill *Consumer prices rose throughout the 1970s, as this graph shows. The resulting inflation created severe economic problems for many countries, including the United States and Western Europe. In what years did prices peak in all four nations? What explains this rise?*

was troubled by deep divisions. Conservative governments favored solutions to current problems that were very different from those offered by more liberal governments.

Political parties sprang to life in Spain after King Juan Carlos called for parliamentary elections. This billboard from the 1982 election campaign proclaims that it is "time for a change."

cities, but the majority of people in Western Europe regarded NATO as essential for their security.

Incidents of international terrorism increased throughout the 1970s and 1980s, in Europe as well as in other parts of the world. Hundreds of people were killed and thousands injured. Some terrorists were seeking to overthrow an existing order. Some were separatists trying to win self-determination for their people. Many groups used terrorism as a form of blackmail. They hoped to force nations into releasing their imprisoned members in return for kidnapped hostages. Terrorists also used bombing, arson, and hijacking to publicize their causes.

One of the most prominent victims of terrorism was Pope John Paul II. In the spring of 1981, he was wounded in an assassination attempt by a Turkish radical. Efforts to stem terrorism were frustrated by a few nations that trained or sheltered terrorists.

Another threat to European cooperation involved defense. Since 1949, much of Western Europe had been allied with the United States in the North Atlantic Treaty Organization. Nuclear missiles were an important part of NATO defense. In 1979, NATO decided to deploy, or place, more than 500 more nuclear missiles in Western Europe in 1983 and 1984. Some NATO countries—notably Belgium and the Netherlands—protested that NATO should emphasize arms limitation rather than armaments. As time went by, European opposition to the missiles grew. Demonstrations protesting the deployment of these missiles took place in many

SECTION REVIEW

1. Identify: Valéry Giscard d'Estaing, François Mitterrand, Margaret Thatcher, Willy Brandt, Antonio Salazar.
2. Define: Ostpolitik.
3. How did de Gaulle respond to student demonstrations in Paris in 1968?
4. What conditions contributed to the outbreak of violence in Northern Ireland in 1969?
5. Which European nations became democracies in the 1970s or 1980s?
6. (a) What were some of the goals of terrorists? (b) What methods did they use?

2 Conformity and Dissent in the Soviet Bloc

Read to Learn ■ about life in the Soviet Union
■ how the Soviet Union has tried to control dissent

For the Soviet Union, as for Western Europe, the period that began in the late 1960s brought both uncertainty and challenge. The Soviets remained militarily strong. However, they faced opposition, not only from western nations, but also from their satellite nations and from dissenters within the Soviet Union.

Patterns of Soviet Life

The Soviets had long maintained that central economic planning prevents waste and unemployment. But central planning creates many problems, especially in a large country. A huge bureaucracy is needed to draw up and carry out the plans. When mistakes or bottlenecks deprive an industry of materials, production stops. The quality of products is often poor because workers feel they have no reason to do a good job.

Central planning has not ended shortages of food and consumer goods. Wheat production in the Soviet Union often falls short of projected goals. As a result, the Soviets must buy grain from other countries, including the United States. Consumer goods remain in short supply, although some items have become more readily available. For example, by 1980 over half the population owned television sets. But people still stand in long lines to buy such items as shoes and meat.

In the planned economy of the Soviet Union, all citizens are supposed to be equal. However, the system favors high officials of the party and some professional people. These people are able to obtain luxury housing, automobiles, and vacations abroad. In addition, scarcity of goods has produced an active black market, in which people illegally bargain for goods, services, and privileges. A series of Soviet leaders faced these problems.

Changes in the mid-1980s. In 1985, Mikhail Gorbachev was named General Secretary of the Communist Party and thus head of the Soviet Union. Gorbachev was better educated and, at 54, much younger than his predecessors. Like Deng Xiaoping in China, he set economic reform as his major goal.

Gorbachev was determined to reverse the lagging performance of Soviet industry and agriculture. For example, in one plan to increase production, factories would be judged for their output, number of sales, and fulfillment of contracts on time. In a country where party jobs were usually secure, Gorbachev fired hundreds of managers for incompetence. However, Gorbachev had only a limited ability to change the entrenched Soviet bureaucracy. He had to proceed slowly to overcome resistance of the Soviet people and of party leaders up and down the line.

One of Gorbachev's strategies for economic renewal is summed up by the term *glasnost*. Glasnost means openness, or the

Shortages of fresh fruit and vegetables often occur in Soviet cities. However, families on collective farms grow food on small private plots. They sell these products in marketplaces such as this one in Moscow.

After becoming General Secretary of the Communist Party, Mikhail Gorbachev began a series of reforms to open up Soviet society. He is shown here meeting with President Reagan.

policy of speaking out honestly. One goal of glasnost is more efficient production. As Gorbachev observed, in a society with no opposition, there is no way to monitor progress or events.

With glasnost, the silence surrounding any failure in Soviet society was broken. For the first time, statistics on low grain harvests, infant mortality, disasters, and other happenings were published. However, the basic structure of Soviet society remained the same. How far candor and criticism would be allowed to go remained uncertain.

Voices of Dissent

Throughout the history of the Soviet Union, citizens had been forced to conform. Most Soviet citizens did not question government policy, at least not publicly. Among writers, scientists, and other intellectuals, however, there were a number of *dissidents*, men and

---

Profiles ■ Andrei Sakharov: A Soviet Dissident

Although Andrei Sakharov was one of the leading scientists in the Soviet Union's nuclear research program, he was not well known outside his native land until 1968. In July of that year, *The New York Times* published an English translation of his essay, "Thoughts About Progress, Peaceful Coexistence, and Intellectual Freedom." In this essay, Sakharov expressed opinions that differed from the official Soviet line. In the years that followed, he continued the risky practice of using western news media to denounce human rights violations in the Soviet Union.

As a prominent scientist, Sakharov had received many privileges and material comforts. In 1968, however, the Soviet government withdrew his right to conduct scientific research. His reaction was to become a full-time dissident and human rights activist.

During the 1970s, Sakharov became a pipeline through which news of human rights violations were sent to the West. In 1973, he secretly filmed an interview for Swedish television and held a press conference for western correspondents. He warned the West not to relax its guard against the Soviet Union. The Soviet government accused Sakharov of being "a tool in the enemy's hand" but limited action against him to bureaucratic harassment.

Sakharov visited imprisoned dissidents and tried to visit labor camps in remote areas. His efforts in support of human rights won him the Nobel Prize for Peace in 1975. Sakharov was the first Soviet citizen to receive the prize, but the Soviet government refused to allow him to travel to Norway to accept it.

At the beginning of 1980, after criticizing the Soviet invasion of Afghanistan, Sakharov was banished to the city of Gorky, where westerners could not travel. Despite his banishment, he continued to campaign for human rights.

Then in 1986, the new Soviet head, Mikhail Gorbachev, surprised the world by announcing that Sakharov would no longer be detained. Sakharov returned to his position at Moscow University. The gesture was a symbol of Gorbachev's policy of "openness," or freedom of criticism. (See page 751.) However, many less famous activists remained in prison, mental hospitals, or exile.

women who spoke out against the regime. Some dissidents attacked political repression, especially the use of secret police and censorship. Some wanted greater autonomy for non-Russians, such as Armenians. Soviet Jews were often active in the dissident movement because Jews were subject to much discrimination. During the late 1970s and early 1980s, some Jews were allowed to emigrate from the Soviet Union, but many others were not permitted to leave.

Protest in the Soviet Union sometimes took the form of public demonstrations. But more often, dissidents circulated writings through an undergound press network known as *samizdat* (SAHM ihz DAHT).

Hundreds of dissidents were convicted of distributing "anti-Soviet" literature and sentenced to forced labor camps. Some who disagreed with state policies were labeled mentally ill and sent to mental hospitals. One of the best known Soviet dissidents is Alexander Solzhenitsyn (SOHL zhuh NEET sihn). He wrote of his own prison experience in two novels, *The Cancer Ward* and *The First Circle*. Both novels were circulated in the Soviet Union in samizdat versions. They were then published abroad. The Soviet government attacked Solzhenitsyn for his writings. In 1973, when he published *The Gulag Archipelago*, an account of life in prison camps, the furious Soviet authorities forced Solzhenitsyn to leave the country.

While the glasnost policies introduced by Mikhail Gorbachev in the mid-1980s had primarily economic aims, they offered Soviet citizens other hopes as well. Gorbachev's reforms might provide for a little more freedom of expression in general. Many dissidents still remained in exile or in prison; but others were allowed to return to their homes and normal lives. (See the Profile on page 752.) And more Soviet Jews who wanted to emigrate were given permission to leave.

Challenges in Eastern Europe

Maintaining control over its satellites in Eastern Europe was a continuing concern of the Soviet Union. In two countries especially, Czechoslovakia and Poland, political changes threatened Soviet power and influence.

Czechoslovakia. Early in 1968, Alexander Dubček (DOOB chehk), became the Communist party secretary in Czechoslovakia. Dubček introduced liberal reforms during a period known as the "Prague spring." The government eased restrictions on the press and allowed workers and political groups to meet freely. It restored freedom of expression to intellectuals and educators. Dubček planned to continue Communist party rule in Czechoslovakia. However, he advocated what he called "socialism with a human face."

Soviet leaders watched developments in Czechoslovakia with alarm. Dubček promised that his country would remain a loyal member of the Soviet bloc, but Brezhnev was not convinced. He was afraid that the liberal Czech policies might spread to other satellite nations and lead to a break in the Soviet bloc.

On August 20, 1968, 200,000 troops from the Soviet Union and other Warsaw Pact nations invaded Czechoslovakia. The troops quickly occupied Prague and forced the Dubček government to withdraw the reforms of the "Prague spring." The following year, Dubček was removed from office, and strict party controls were reintroduced. The western powers were shocked by the Soviet invasion but did not take any direct action.

Following the invasion of Czechoslovakia, the Soviet Union issued a declaration that became known as the Brezhnev Doctrine. According to the Brezhnev Doctrine, when socialism was threatened in any country, it was "not only a problem for the country concerned but a common problem and concern of all socialist countries." The doctrine was interpreted as a warning to satellite nations not to become too independent of Moscow.

Poland. On the whole, the nations of Eastern Europe heeded the lesson of Czechoslovakia. In return, the Soviet Union allowed them some flexibility in economic planning and trade with the West. In Hungary, for example, the profit motive was introduced in large state-directed businesses.

As a result of this measure and others, the standard of living in Hungary rose.

In 1980, the Soviet Union faced a new challenge within the Soviet bloc—this time from Poland. Poland suffered from serious economic problems. It was plagued by debt and shortages of basic foods and raw materials.

In the summer of 1980, Polish workers began a series of strikes to protest food shortages, long lines at food stores, and high prices. In October, they won a victory unprecedented in a communist country. The government officially recognized an independent trade union called Solidarity. During the next several months, Solidarity chairman Lech Walesa led workers in several demonstrations. In March 1981, a nationwide protest against police brutality brought millions of Poles into the streets for a peaceful four-hour strike.

In the fall of 1981, Solidarity called for free elections. The Polish government retaliated by demanding that strikes be banned. In December, Solidarity called for a national referendum on whether the Communist party should continue to govern Poland. This was the last straw for the Polish government.

The government declared martial law. It suspended Solidarity and arrested thousands of Poles. Said one bitterly disappointed woman, "We had a year and a half to create something unique and beautiful. This time I thought, there's really a chance to reform socialism. . . . Now I don't believe that can ever happen again. There can't be communism without tanks." Although the Soviet Union did not actively intervene at the time, there was little doubt that the crackdown was endorsed, if not ordered, by Soviet leaders.

As a member of the Warsaw Pact (see the map on page 654), Poland is a satellite nation of the Soviet Union. The Soviet military commands Poland's foreign and military affairs. However, as you have read, governments in Eastern Europe do not receive the full support of the people. Perhaps to appease continuing discontent, the Polish government formally lifted martial law in 1983. A year later it released most of Solidarity's leaders. But many restrictions remain. The threat of new crackdowns hangs over dissidents in the eastern bloc populations.

Relations With Other Nations

A dominant theme of Soviet relations with the West in the early 1970s was *détente* (day TAHNT). Diplomats used the French term meaning relaxation to describe an easing of international tension, especially between the Soviet Union and the United States. In 1972, President Richard Nixon traveled to Moscow. He was the first American President to visit the Soviet Union since World War II. At this time, the two superpowers signed the SALT agreement limiting the number of nuclear warheads and missiles that each country would keep. SALT stands for Strategic Arms Limitation Talks.

The Soviets, however, continued to stockpile conventional weapons and build up their armed forces. They also maintained a military presence in many parts of the world. In Africa, for example, the Soviet Union backed Marxist rebels in struggles against the governments in Mozambique, Angola, and Namibia.

In 1979, the Soviet army intervened directly in Afghanistan. The Soviets feared that an uprising among the Muslims of Afghanistan might spread to Muslims living in nearby regions of the Soviet Union. In December 1979, 40,000 Soviet troops invaded and put down the uprising, supposedly at the request of the Afghanistan government. The invasion brought worldwide protests, but the protests had little effect. Soviet troops gained control of the cities, although armed resistance continued in the countryside.

In general, the international policies of the Soviet Union have meant channeling much of the nation's resources into military spending. The government continues to aid socialist regimes worldwide. However, Gorbachev seems intent on increasing production for domestic consumption. By the mid-1980s, both the United States and the Soviet Union expressed interest in limiting military buildups. But summit meetings between Gorbachev and President Ronald Reagan failed to produce results.

The Soviet occupation of Afghanistan turned into a long, costly war with guerrilla fighters. Tanks helped Soviet soldiers keep control of the cities, but guerrillas continued the struggle in the countryside.

SECTION REVIEW

1. Identify: Mikhail Gorbachev, Alexander Dubček, Brezhnev Doctrine, Solidarity, Lech Walesa, SALT.
2. Define: glasnost, dissident, samizdat, détente.
3. Describe two problems Gorbachev hopes to solve in the Soviet Union.
4. How did the Soviet government react to the writings of Alexander Solzhenitsyn?
5. What reforms were introduced during the "Prague spring?"

3 Challenge and Change in the United States

Read to Learn
- about crucial issues in the United States in the late 1960s and early 1970s.
- what national issues are important as the United States approaches the 1990s.

In the United States, protest and change marked the late 1960s and early 1970s as they did in Western Europe. Americans faced difficult challenges in foreign policy, politics, and the economy. In the 1980s, many people were looking for stability in an increasingly complex world.

The Debate Over the War in Vietnam

The year 1968 was one of student unrest and protest in United States as in Western Europe. Students demonstrated on many college campuses. They demanded a larger part in running the schools and equal treatment

755

In the late 1960s and early 1970s, many Americans protested their nation's involvement in the Vietnam War. Thousands of protestors joined antiwar demonstrations in cities across the United States. Some protestors carried flowers in the barrels of weapons to symbolize their opposition to the war.

for minorities and women. However, the most explosive issue in 1968 was the Vietnam War.

United States involvement in Vietnam had increased dramatically during the 1960s, as you read in Chapter 37. The number of American troops in Vietnam rose from 23,000 in 1965 to over 500,000 in 1968. The number of casualties grew, and there seemed little hope of a successful end to the war. As a result, opposition to the American role in the war increased. Many Americans demanded that the United States withdraw from the war. Others argued that the United States should try to win the war.

President Johnson decided not to seek a second term in 1968 because of the opposi-

tion to his policies in Vietnam. Republican candidate Richard Nixon won the 1968 presidential election. Nixon pledged to "bring the American people together" and to end the war. "America," he said, "cannot . . . undertake all the defense of the free nations of the world."

Nixon introduced the policy of "Vietnamization." South Vietnamese forces were given greater responsibility for the fighting, and American troops were gradually withdrawn. However, to support the South Vietnamese during the American pull out, Nixon resumed American bombing of North Vietnam and authorized an invasion of neighboring Cambodia. These actions intensified antiwar protests.

In May 1970, four students from Kent State University in Ohio and two from Jackson State University in Mississippi were killed during demonstrations against the Cambodian invasion. These deaths jolted the nation and underscored the bitterness and anger the war was causing.

Nixon's secretary of state, Henry Kissinger, began secret negotiations with the North Vietnamese in 1972. Finally, in January 1973, a peace agreement was signed. The last American combat troops were withdrawn by March. The war had taken more than 57,000 American lives and cost the United States over $100 billion.

Continuing Demands for Equality

Demands by women and minorities for equality continued in the 1970s and 1980s. A proposed Equal Rights Amendment to the Constitution caused much debate during the 1970s. It stated in part that "equality of rights under the law shall not be abridged . . . on account of sex." The amendment was passed by Congress in 1972 and was approved by more than 30 states. However, it failed to win approval of three fourths of the states, which is required to add an amendment to the Constitution. Many Americans thought that the amendment threatened traditional values and beliefs. Nevertheless, one important milestone for women occurred in 1981. Sandra Day O'Connor became the first woman to be appointed to the United States Supreme Court.

Another sign that the role of women in American society was changing was their increased enrollment in professional schools. Between 1969 and 1973, the number of women in law schools quadrupled, and the number in medical schools doubled. In 1983, for the first time in United States history, more than half of all women aged twenty and older held jobs outside the home. In 1984, Congresswoman Geraldine Ferraro became the Democratic party's vice-presidential candidate. Her nomination dramatized the increasingly important role of women in government.

Like American women, blacks sought higher education and entered white collar jobs in increasing numbers. Some blacks outside the professional fields, however, suffered greater hardships. As jobs grew scarce in such industries as steel and automobile manufacturing, more blacks had trouble finding work. In general, the wages of blacks also lagged behind those of whites.

In the 1970s and 1980s, other minorities loomed importantly in American society. New immigrants arrived in numbers unequaled since the beginning of the 20th century. Hispanics were the fastest growing minority. Eight million of the nation's 20 million Hispanics were Mexican Americans in the southwestern states. Along the east coast, Hispanics came from Cuba, Puerto Rico, the Dominican Republic, Colombia, and Ecuador. In addition, some four million immigrants from Vietnam, the Philippines, Korea, Taiwan, and India arrived between 1970 and 1980. Many of the immigrants contributed skills in such fields as medicine, engineering, and university teaching. But others, less skilled, found no work or only low-paying jobs. Governments and industries confronted the needs of the new millions who had come in pursuit of a better life.

The Watergate Crisis

The American system of government was tested by events during the presidency of Richard Nixon. Nixon won a second term with a landslide victory in 1972. Almost immediately, however, his administration was rocked by a series of scandals. Vice-President Spiro Agnew was accused of taking bribes when he was governor of Maryland. Agnew eventually resigned from office. President Nixon then chose Gerald Ford, a Michigan congressman, to succeed Agnew.

A much graver matter was the series of events known collectively as Watergate. During the 1972 presidential campaign, a security guard discovered burglars at Democratic party headquarters in Washington's Watergate Hotel. The burglars were traced to Nixon's reelection committee. Further investigation indicated the involvement of some of Nixon's closest aides.

At first, Nixon denied all knowledge of the Watergate break-in. But sworn testimony by members of his staff indicated that the President not only knew of the burglary but also had tried to cover up information about it. Next, it was revealed that tapes had been made of many White House conversations. These tapes were made public as the result of a Supreme Court order. They proved Nixon's role in the cover-up. Faced with possible impeachment on the grounds of obstructing justice, Nixon resigned in August 1974. He was the first President of the United States to resign from office. Vice-President Ford succeeded to the presidency.

The Watergate events shocked the nation. But they showed the strength of the American system of checks and balances. (See page 391.) Congress and the Supreme Court had checked the power of a President who seemed to be abusing his power.

Economic Challenges

The economy of the United States, like that of Europe, suffered from inflation and low economic growth in the 1970s. Low productivity and foreign competition weakened some industries. For example, sales of American cars declined drastically as sales of Japanese cars increased. In addition, the high cost of oil after 1973 contributed to high inflation throughout the decade.

The government tried to lessen dependence on foreign oil by encouraging conservation, the search for new oil fields in the

Television Sets in Selected Countries

Britain
France
Italy
Poland
Soviet Union
United States
West Germany

0 100 200 300 400 500 600 700
sets per 1,000 people

Sources: Organization for Economic Cooperation and Development, *The OECD Member Countries*, and UNESCO.

Graph Skill *The number of television sets per 1,000 people is one indication of the supply of consumer goods in a society. As you can see from this graph, the United States has the largest number of television sets per 1,000 persons. In which nation do people have about the same number of television sets as people in France and West Germany?*

United States, and the development of alternative sources of energy. But during the oil glut of the 1980s, interest in these alternative energy sources again dropped.

Inflation, however, remained a problem throughout the administrations of Richard Nixon, Gerald Ford, and Jimmy Carter. Spiraling prices, as much as any other factor, led to the election of Ronald Reagan as President in 1980.

Reagan promised to curb inflation and balance the budget by cutting government expenses and lowering taxes. The Reagan administration cut some spending and lowered taxes, but it also raised defense spending. Inflation slowed in the 1980s, but Reagan failed to achieve a balanced budget during his first term in office.

In 1984, Reagan was reelected by more electoral votes than any other presidential candidate in the nation's history. His second term brought a promised further decrease in inflation. However, the federal budget deficit

skyrocketed. The deficit, plus resistance to some of Reagan's foreign policies, helped Democrats gain a majority in Congress in 1986.

Foreign Affairs

As you have read, détente characterized American relations with the Soviet Union during the early 1970s. The Nixon administration also tried to improve relations with the People's Republic of China. In February 1972, President Nixon visited China and met with Chinese leaders. An American diplomatic mission was then opened in Beijing. Business leaders from both countries toured each other's facilities and exchanged information. Entertainers from China toured the United States, and American musicians performed in major Chinese cities. Thousands of Americans visited China. The United States extended diplomatic recognition to China in 1979.

Nixon's trip to China was followed in three months by a visit to the Soviet Union, a meeting with Brezhnev, and the SALT treaty. This was the high point of détente between the Soviet Union and the United States. Ford and Carter tried to maintain the spirit of détente, but Soviet actions in various parts of the world made this difficult. Many observers felt that the Russian invasion of Afghanistan late in 1979 ended détente.

In the 1980s, President Reagan stressed strength in American relations with other nations. One hotly debated policy decision involved support for a missile defense system based in space. Congress approved the research aspects of the Strategic Defense Initiative, or SDI—nicknamed Star Wars. But many persons questioned how SDI would be deployed and indeed whether it would work as its supporters predicted.

A more pressing problem confronting the United States and its allies was the increase in terrorism by Middle Eastern extremists. Nations were uncertain whether to respond to violence and hostage-taking with military force or with negotiation. The Reagan administration tried both methods, with some success. Reagan's popularity plunged, however, when an undercover deal with Iran

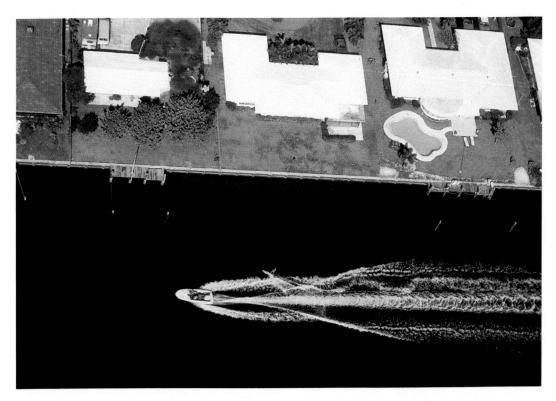

In the past 20 years, millions of Americans have moved to the sunbelt in the south and southwest. This aerial view of homes on the east coast of Florida shows some of the attractions of the sunbelt. Warm temperatures year round and the growth of industry has also attracted people to the sunbelt.

became public knowledge in 1986. In return for military equipment, Iran was supposed to help obtain the release of American hostages held in Lebanon. The arms were delivered as promised, but the hostages were not released. Moreover, profits from the deal were secretly diverted to the Contras in Nicaragua. (See page 737.) The possible illegalities involved in the affair stirred a political scandal that lead to Congressional investigations in 1987, and to dismissals within the Reagan administration.

In the meantime, United States relations with China and the Soviet Union reflected the changes in the administrations of these countries. The Soviet Union and the United States took steps toward limited arms control. And cultural exchanges between the two countries flourished under Gorbachev's "openness" policy. Deng's reforms in China also inspired friendly cultural and economic contacts between East and West.

President Reagan welcomed many leaders of developing nations to the United States. Here, he meets in the White House with President Mobutu of Zaire to explain American policies. President Reagan has encouraged developing nations to become more self-sufficient.

SECTION REVIEW

1. Identify: Vietnamization, Sandra Day O'Connor, Geraldine Ferraro, Strategic Defense Initiative.
2. Why did Lyndon Johnson decide not to run for reelection in 1968?
3. (a) What economic gains did black Americans make during the 1970s and 1980s? (b) In what ways did they continue to lag behind whites?
4. (a) How did President Reagan propose to curb inflation and balance the budget? (b) What were the results of his programs?
5. How did the Reagan administration attempt to free American hostages held by terrorists?

Chapter 39 Review

In Perspective

In 1968, student protests broke out in Western Europe and the United States. This year was also one of unrest in Eastern Europe. The Soviet Union invaded Czechoslovakia to end a move toward greater democracy there. The 1970s and 1980s continued to be a time of change and challenge in Europe and the United States.

In Western Europe, the 1970s and 1980s were years of economic uncertainty for many nations. Unemployment and rising inflation plagued governments. At the same time, the governments in Greece, Portugal, and Spain became democracies. But efforts to make Poland more democratic had mixed results.

The Soviet Union maintained a powerful position in world affairs in the 1970s and 1980s. However, at home the Soviet people were confronted with shortages of many products, especially consumer goods. Mikhail Gorbachev introduced policies of economic reform and glasnost—openness—in an attempt to change Soviet society.

During the late 1960s and the 1970s, the United States faced a war in Vietnam and the scandal of Watergate. Like the countries of Europe, it also suffered from inflation and slowing rates of growth, but these problems subsided under President Reagan. Terrorism increased in the mid-1980s, provoking the Reagan administration into controversial actions. At the same time, United States relations with China and the Soviet Union improved.

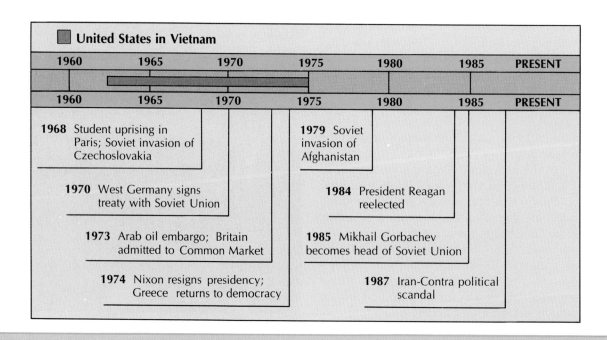

Recalling Facts

Decide if the following statements are true or false. If a statement is false, rewrite the statement to make it true.

1. Charles de Gaulle resigned because of a student uprising in Paris.
2. Britain joined the Common Market in 1973.
3. Willy Brandt opposed the policy of Ostpolitik.
4. Leonid Brezhnev supported the idea of "socialism with a human face."
5. American involvement in Vietnam increased during the 1960s.
6. The Equal Rights Amendment was ratified in the 1970s.
7. One cause of inflation in the United States was the high cost of oil.
8. The federal budget deficit declined under President Reagan.

Chapter Checkup

1. (a) How did inflation during the 1970s affect France and Britain? (b) How did the British government try to improve the British economy? (c) Was it successful? Explain.
2. (a) In which southern European countries did government become democratic during the 1970s? (b) Describe how each became a democracy.
3. (a) Describe the concerns of dissidents in the Soviet Union. (b) How have they expressed their concerns? (c) How has the Soviet government reacted to the activities of dissidents?
4. (a) What did diplomats mean by the term "détente" during the 1970s? (b) What events or developments were part of détente? (c) What contributed to the end of détente?
5. (a) Why did opposition to the American role in Vietnam grow during the 1960s? (b) How did President Nixon try to reduce American involvement? (c) What were the results of his policy?
6. (a) Why did Watergate shock the American people? (b) How did the outcome of the Watergate events show the strength of the American system of government?
7. (a) What were the goals of the new regimes in China and the Soviet Union? (b) How were conditions in these nations similar? (c) How were conditions different?

Critical Thinking

1. **Analyzing** (a) Describe Ostpolitik. (b) Would you consider Ostpolitik an example of détente? Why or why not?
2. **Expressing an Opinion** As the decade of the 1980s began, people in Europe and the United States looked forward with both hope and fear. (a) What events and developments do you think contributed to hope? (b) What events and developments do you think contributed to fear?

Relating Past to Present

1. The origin of the conflict in Northern Ireland is deeply rooted. Review discussions of the relationship between Britain and Ireland on pages 383, 385, 468, and 586. (a) How did bitterness between Catholics and Protestants in Ireland develop? (b) Do you think a solution to the conflict in Northern Ireland is possible? Why or why not?

Developing Basic Skills

1. **Comparing** Review what you read about events in Hungary and Poland in 1956. (See page 660.) Make a chart with four rows titled Poland 1956, Hungary 1956, Czechoslovakia 1968, and Poland 1981 and two columns titled Reforms and Results. in the first column, describe efforts to move toward democracy. In the second column, describe the results. Then answer the following questions: (a) Where and when were efforts to move toward democracy most successful? Why? (b) Where and when were efforts least successful? Why? (c) How might you explain the different results?
2. **Graph Reading** Study the graph on page 749. Then answer the following questions: (a) What was the percentage of increase in consumer prices in Britain in 1971? In France in 1974? In the United States in 1979? (b) In what nation did consumer prices rise the most during the 1970s? (c) In what nation did they rise the least? (d) What happened to consumer prices in the late 1970s?

See page 808 for suggested readings.

40 A New Age of Exploration

(1945–Present)

Liftoff of the space shuttle Columbia.

Before dawn on April 12, 1981, crowds gathered at Cape Canaveral, Florida. As dawn brightened the sky, they watched white clouds of exhaust billowing up from the launch pad, where the space shuttle *Columbia* stood ready for liftoff. At 7 A.M., *Columbia* lifted off with a thunderous roar.

On board the space shuttle, pilots John W. Young and Robert Crippen monitored the successful liftoff. Captain Young had already flown four missions in other spacecraft. He had oribited the moon in 1969 in *Apollo 10*. Three years later, he had landed on the moon. Captain Crippen was on his first space flight. His pulse raced to 130. The pulse of the more experienced Young remained its usual 85.

Six minutes into the flight, the main engines shut down on schedule. "Confirm shutdown," a voice from mission control in Houston, Texas, told the pilots. "*Columbia*, the gem of this new ocean, now in space, not yet in orbit," the voice added.

The voyage of *Columbia* was indeed a historic mission. Astronauts Young and Crippen were testing a new type of spacecraft. Unlike earlier spacecraft, *Columbia* was designed to be reused. Earlier space vehicles had been made for a single flight. They burned up during reentry into the earth's atmosphere. Designers of *Columbia* had equipped it with 31,000 heat-resistant ceramic tiles to shield the vehicle on reentry. The spacecraft was scheduled to glide to a gentle landing in the Mojave Desert, which it did after two days in space.

After its first successful flight, *Columbia* was prepared for another flight seven months later. By 1985, three space shuttles had completed eighteen flights. Scientists hoped these flights would mark the dawn of a new era—the day when space flights would become routine. They saw *Columbia* as the forerunner of space cargo ships. Their job would be to ferry people and equipment to and from orbiting space satellites and laboratories.

In space, medicine, agriculture, and dozens of other fields, many age-old questions have been answered. Often, however, the answers have raised more questions and have provided new worlds for further exploration.

1 The New Scientific Revolution

Read to Learn
- why advances in science and technology are changing lives
- how medical advances improve life and extend lives

Many major advances in science have occurred in the 1900s. Researchers have solved age-old puzzles in chemistry, physics, biochemistry, and medicine. In solving these puzzles, they have made technological advances that have revolutionized people's lives.

Advances in Science and Technology

Before World War II, research scientists usually worked alone. They were generally interested in pure science—that is, developing theories about the causes of events in the natural world. They left *applied science*, or putting their findings to practical use, to engineers and technicians.

During World War II, research scientists such as physicists and chemists worked alongside technicians to develop weapons, medicines, and other technologies needed to win the war. The combination of pure and applied science produced important results. For example, a team of British scientists developed radar, a device that uses radio waves to detect objects. In the United States, a group of scientists working together constructed the first atom bomb.

After the war, experts in science and technology continued to work together to solve complex problems. Most governments have spent large sums to pay for scientific research and development. In addition, industries have invested billions of dollars in scientific research. This research has resulted in thousands of new products and inventions.

Space Exploration

Advances in science and technology have been dramatically evident in the area of space exploration. During World War II, German scientists working with Wernher von Braun developed rockets as weapons. The V-2 rocket, for example, was a guided missile that could be launched against London from bases in Germany.

After the war, some German rocket specialists went to the Soviet Union. Others, including von Braun, went to the United States, where they helped develop an American missile and rocket program. By the 1950s, both the United States and the Soviet Union had built rockets powerful enough to overcome the earth's gravity and leave the earth's atmosphere.

The Space Age begins. In October 1957, the age of space exploration began when the Soviet Union launched the first satellite, *Sputnik I*, into orbit around the earth. The first American spacecraft, *Explorer I*, was sent into orbit in 1958. In 1961, Soviet cosmonaut Yuri Gagarin was the first person sent into orbit. His flight was soon matched by that of John Glenn, the first American to orbit the earth.

After these early successes, scientists set their sights on more distant goals. On July 20, 1969, American astronauts Neil Armstrong and Buzz Aldrin stepped out of their *Apollo 11* spacecraft onto the surface of the moon. "That's one small step for a man," noted Armstrong, "one giant leap for mankind." In five more moon shots, other teams

In the years since the first moon landing in 1969, scientists have learned more about the solar system than they had in thousands of years of human history. In August 1981, Voyager 2 beamed back to earth a series of images of the planet Saturn that were assembled into this picture.

of American astronauts gathered much useful data. In the 1970s, the Soviet Union launched permanent orbiting laboratories. Soviet scientists conducted experiments to determine the effects of prolonged space travel on humans. Two cosmonauts lived aboard one Soviet space platform for 185 days.

The United States and the Soviet Union launched hundreds of unpiloted spacecraft to explore the planets. Soon, scientists were getting clear photographs and accurate information about Venus and Mars as well as about the more distant planets of Jupiter and Saturn.

In 1981, the American *Voyager 2* photographed Saturn and returned data indicating 1,000-mile-per-hour winds on the planet. The spacecraft then flew toward its 1986 destination—Uranus. Eventually, *Voyager 2* will leave the solar system. It carries information about life on earth, including recordings of crickets and Beethoven's Fifth Symphony in case it encounters intelligent life beyond this solar system.

Putting satellites to work. By the early 1980s, the United States and the Soviet Union had launched more than 2,000 spacecraft. India, China, and Japan have each put satellites into orbit. Western European and other nations also cooperate with the United States in the exploration and practical use of space.

Spacecraft have collected a vast amount of information and relayed it back to earth. Some satellites orbit the earth and provide a 24-hour watch on weather. Other satellites are used to transmit signals for radio, television, and telephone communication. Satellites have also provided useful data on crop yields.

Shuttles in space. Space shuttle systems in the United States (see chapter introduction) began to operate regularly in the 1980s. Besides releasing and repairing communication satellites, shuttles acted as space laboratories where scientists performed experiments in biology, medicine, and manufacturing. As planned, costs of operating shuttle flights decreased as other countries and industries paid for research and placement of satellites in space. A shuttle was designed to be used more than 100 times.

In 1986, the National Aeronautics and Space Administration (NASA) and the entire nation experienced a horrifying shock. With seven astronauts aboard—one a social studies teacher—the space shuttle *Challenger* exploded seconds after liftoff. President Ronald Reagan appointed a commission to investigate the reasons for the tragedy. Despite the setback, the American space program, under stricter controls, continued.

The Computer Revolution

Computers have played a major role in space exploration. *Computers* are machines that process information at great speed. Computers on spacecraft, for example, relay information to computers on earth that in turn send data back to the spacecraft.

The development of computers dates back before World War II. Since the 1940s, their use has changed nearly every industry in the world. As faster airplanes were built during World War II, better ways were needed to track them. Engineers turned to a machine invented in 1930 by electrical engineer Vannevar Bush. Bush called his invention a differential analyzer. It was the grandparent of today's computers.

In 1941, Harvard University professor Howard Aiken developed the first workable digital computer. Digital computers solve problems by counting digits, or numbers. Mathematician John von Neumann made the next major advance when he invented a way to store a computer program in the machine. In 1951, engineers at the University of Pennsylvania built UNIVAC, the first large, mass-produced computer. UNIVAC was an enormous machine that filled an entire room.

The invention of the transistor in 1947 led to a revolution in computers. *Transistors* are devices used to control electric currents. Transistors are small, reliable, and relatively inexpensive. With them, scientists could make computers that were smaller, faster, and less expensive than UNIVAC. The invention of the integrated circuit, or chip, in the 1960s further revolutionized computers. Chips are units that contain many transistors. A single chip is very small, often no bigger than a fingernail. These tiny chips made still smaller, faster, and less expensive computers possible. As a result, computers came into use in many fields.

Today, computers are used to handle telephone communications, route airplanes, and store vast amounts of information needed by businesses and governments. In addition, computers are used by engineers and scientists to solve complex problems. The *Apollo 11* moon landing would not have been possible without computers. The development of handheld calculators and personal computers has brought the computer into homes and schools. At the same time, computer-controlled video games have become a popular form of entertainment.

Miracles in Medicine

Like many businesses, hospitals rely heavily on computers as well as on other advanced technology. The postwar era ushered in a "machine age" in medicine.

Medical technology. Some medical technology grew directly out of space research. For example, medical researchers

Computer research and the development of laser technology have led to major advances in communication. Laser disks, such as these, can produce nearly perfect sound for musical recordings. They can also store an immense amount of information. For example, several encyclopedias can be stored on one disk.

wanted to learn the effects of liftoff and prolonged weightlessness on astronauts. As a result, technicians developed tiny sensors to measure the pulse, heartbeat, breathing, and body temperature of astronauts.

Today, similar monitoring devices are used routinely in modern hospitals. In intensive care units, information from sensors is fed into a computer at a central nursing station. Warning bells ring if a patient's pulse falters or breathing stops. Doctors can also get a detailed 24-hour printout on patients' vital signs.

Advances in medical technology have been used in surgery and other fields. In 1952, the first kidney transplant took place. The following year, surgeons performed the first open-heart operation. In the 1960s, heart care was improved by the development of the pacemaker. A pacemaker is a tiny electronic device that is implanted in the body to regulate a patient's heartbeat.

In 1967, Dr. Christiaan Barnard of South Africa performed the first successful human heart transplant. Most of the early heart-transplant patients died within a year. However, by the mid-1980s, about 70 percent survived much longer. Sometimes surgeons implanted artificial, mechanically driven hearts to keep patients alive while awaiting suitable human donors.

More recently, surgeons have pioneered in the field of microsurgery. Using microscopes and tiny instruments, they have operated on tiny areas such as the inner ear. Even more dramatic is the use of *lasers* to remove diseased body tissue. A laser is a device that concentrates light waves into a very intense beam. In laser surgery, a laser beam of light can burn away unwanted tissue in a fraction of a second. Surrounding healthy tissue is barely affected. Lasers are especially important in eye surgery. For example, surgeons can correct a detached, or loose, retina in the eye by "welding" it in place with a laser beam.

Antibiotics. Complicated surgery would be impossible without the medical advances made earlier in this century. These advances included the development of *antibiotics*, chemical substances that destroy bacteria and other microorganisms.

In 1928, British bacteriologist Sir Arthur Fleming accidentally discovered that a mold called penicillin killed bacteria. At first, his discovery was not put to much practical use. During World War II, however, the urgent need to prevent infection of battlefield wounds led to a program to mass-produce penicillin. The discovery of sulfa drugs, which also kill bacteria, was followed by their widespread use as antibiotics. Sulfa drugs and penicillin enabled surgeons to combat infection of wounds.

Vaccines. The first vaccines against viruses were developed in the late 1700s. Then, in the 1800s, Louis Pasteur developed vaccines against the viral diseases rabies and

The machine shown here is a CAT scanner. (CAT stands for Computerized Axial Tomography.) An important tool in medical diagnosis, the CAT scanner provides a three-dimensional, 360° view of the body. It uses x-rays, recorders, and a computer to examine the body for unusual structures or processes.

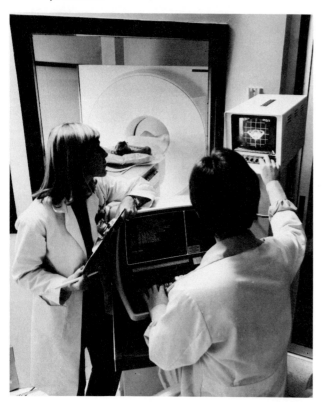

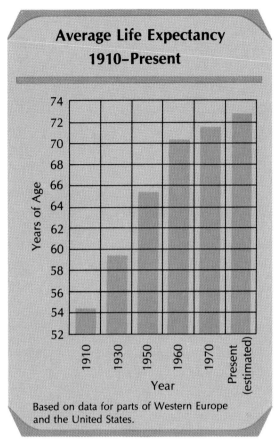

Average Life Expectancy 1910–Present

Years of Age

74
72
70
68
66
64
62
60
58
56
54
52

1910 1930 1950 1960 1970 Present (estimated)

Year

Based on data for parts of Western Europe and the United States.

Sources: *Historical Statistics of the United States*; OECD, *Child and Family*; and United Nations, *Demographic Yearbook*.

Graph Skill *Because of discoveries in medicine, people are living longer than ever before. Compare this graph with the graph on page 455. In what period did life expectancy make the greatest advance?*

programs to vaccinate tens of millions of people. Epidemic diseases that once devastated populations have been wiped out or brought under control. In 1980, the World Health Organization announced that no new cases of smallpox had been reported anywhere in the world. But other problems remain. Research scientists attend study conferences to share information and explore ways of meeting the threat of viruses still spreading out of control.

Genetic engineering. Cures for some now incurable diseases may soon result from genetic engineering. *Genetic engineering* refers to laboratory techniques that alter the hereditary material—the genes—of an organism. Researchers have also found ways to create proteins, such as Interferon, that will aid in fighting some diseases. In industry, scientists have helped with genetically engineered bacteria that improve food production. For example, a hormone derived from these engineering processes causes cows to produce more milk, and some genetically altered plants have increased nutritional value.

Despite such successes, genetic engineering concerns some people who question the morality of changing genetic material, the basic stuff of life. Others fear that harmful bacteria may result from experiments and escape accidentally. To avoid dangers and quell alarm, the National Institutes of Health have set safety guidelines for laboratories working with genes in these new ways.

anthrax. But before the invention of the electron microscope in the 1930s, scientists had not seen viruses. With the electron microscope, scientists were able to study the structure of viruses. They were then able to develop vaccines against many viral diseases, including measles, mumps, diphtheria, typhoid, and cholera. Jonas Salk developed the first polio vaccine in the early 1950s. A few years later, Albert Sabin perfected an oral vaccine for polio.

Since World War II, agencies of the United Nations, national governments, and private health organizations have sponsored

SECTION REVIEW

1. Identify: *Sputnik I*, Yuri Gagarin, John Glenn, Neil Armstrong, *Apollo 11*, *Challenger*, Howard Aiken, Christiaan Barnard, Sir Arthur Fleming, Jonas Salk, Albert Sabin.

2. Define: applied science, computer, transistor, laser, antibiotic, genetic engineering.

3. How does pure science differ from applied science?

4. What kinds of information have satellites in space provided?

5. How have computers affected business and industry?

6. List three medical advances in the 1900s.

2 Resources for the Future

Read to learn
- how nations meet the challenge of the population explosion
- about ways to conserve the earth's resources

Satellites have taken many photographs of the earth from space. Scientists have used some of these photographs to map possible locations of important natural resources. They have found that the earth has abundant supplies of some resources but limited supplies of others.

Graph Skill *The population of the world grew slowly for hundreds of years. When did it begin to grow more rapidly? When did it begin its greatest rise?*

World Population Growth, 1500–2000

Figures for years after 1981 are projections.

Sources: *Atlas of World Population History* and the United Nations.

The World's Population

As you have read, population growth has accelerated in many parts of the world. The conquest of many diseases has contributed to this growth. Today, fewer babies die of disease. In addition, people live much longer than they did in the past. In just over 35 years, the world's population doubled—from 2.5 billion in 1950 to 5 billion in 1986. Recent estimates suggest that the world population will grow to 8 billion in the next 35 years.

The greatest population growth has occurred in developing nations. Between 1950 and 1980, populations in developing nations grew from 1.7 billion to 3.3 billion. (See the map in Reference Section.) The population explosion poses a number of challenges, especially to developing nations. Most governments want to ensure that their people have food, housing, jobs, and the education needed in modern societies. But many developing nations have limited resources to meet these basic needs. Poverty is widespread and increasing in many areas of the world.

In 1985, China had a population of over 1 billion. India had a population of almost 800 million. Together, the Chinese and Indian populations accounted for more than one third of all the people on earth. As you read in Chapter 37, both nations are exploring ways to develop their resources and provide for the expanding numbers of people. For example, to slow the rate of population growth, the Chinese government encourages people to marry later. Deng Xiaoping's policy of one child per family had modernization and an improved way of life as its goals.

Rich Lands, Poor Lands

The population explosion has greatly increased the gap between rich nations and poor nations around the world. Leaders from rich and poor nations have met to discuss ways that rich nations can help poor na-

Throughout this text, you have read, analyzed, and interpreted various kinds of historical evidence. In order to make the best use of evidence, however, you must be able to synthesize it—that is, pull several pieces together to form a whole pattern of a historical event or development.

You will use four pieces of evidence to practice the skill of synthesizing: the graph of world population growth on page 768, the table of large urban areas on page 778, the map of world population density on pages 782–783 in the Reference Section, and the picture on page 727. Use the following steps to study these pieces of evidence and synthesize the information they contain.

1. **Analyze each piece of evidence.** Answer the following questions about the pieces of evidence: (a) According to the graph on page 768, what was the approximate population of the world in 1800? In 1900? In 1980? (b) According to the table on page 778, what was the largest urban area in 1350 B.C.? In 1925? In 1980? (c) According to the map on pages 782–783, what is the population density in most of Europe? In most of North Africa? In most of Mexico? (d) What is the subject of the picture on page 727?

2. **Find relationships among the pieces of evidence.** Answer the following questions: (a) How does the information in the table support the information in the graph? (b) How does the picture illustrate the information in the table? (c) Find the place on the map where you think each of the largest urban areas in 1980 is located. Check your answers on maps in the Reference Section.

3. **Synthesize the evidence in order to draw conclusions.** Answer the following questions: (a) What conclusion can you draw about the change in the total world population since the early 1900s? Cite specific evidence to support your conclusion. (b) Does the evidence support the conclusion that world population is not very evenly distributed over the land surface? Explain. (c) What can you learn about world population from pictures such as the one on page 727 that you cannot learn from graphs, charts, and maps?

tions to develop. However, closing the gap between rich and poor lands poses many difficult challenges.

Rich lands include developed nations such as West Germany, France, Japan, and the United States. These nations have the advantages of well-developed agriculture and industry, advanced technology, and strong education systems. As you have read, poor lands include many developing nations in Africa, the Middle East, Asia, and Latin America.

Developed nations have provided aid such as food and technical assistance to Third World nations. Western investors have made loans of billions of dollars. But it will take time for developing nations to establish modern industrial economies. Moreover, worldwide inflation and natural disasters have upset the plans of many nations in the Third World.

In addition, governments of newly independent nations sometimes over-empha-

Chart Skill   *This chart shows the agricultural gap between developing and developed nations. What percent of the world's people live in developing nations? What percent of the world's farm produce do those nations produce?*

Developing and Developed Nations A Comparison		
	Developing Nations	Developed Nations
Percent of World Population	67	33
Percent of World Farm Production	38	62
Hectares of Farmland per Farm Worker	1.3	8.9
Kilograms of Fertilizer Used per Hectare of Farmland	9	40
Daily Calorie Consumption per Person	2,180	3,315

Source: FAO, *Agriculture: Toward 2000.*

769

sized industrial growth, neglecting farming areas. Thus, food production lagged as population boomed. Even with financial help, most Third World nations failed to juggle their meager resources evenly between infant industries and newly mechanized farms. Machinery broke down and could not be repaired. Sometimes, mismanagement was at fault. But the main problem was the steady stream of people migrating from farms to cities in search of jobs. Some governments tried to stem the tide (see page 678), but for most the trend continued.

Other difficulties further beset developing economies in the 1980s. Many nations suffered from worldwide drops in demand for their products. For example, some oil-producing countries were plunged into debt when the price of oil collapsed. With the failure of oil to create needed income, other industrial progress ceased. By the mid-1980s, many western nations were forced to reschedule payments of the money they had loaned to developing nations.

Developing New Sources of Food

Bad weather in the early 1970s caused disastrous crop failures in India, China, and the Soviet Union. Also, as you read in Chapter 35, drought ruined crops in the Sahel region of Africa. When nations faced with shortages competed to buy food abroad, prices shot up. The resulting food scramble focused attention on the growing problem of hunger around the world. Experts predicted that the food crisis would become worse in the decades ahead.

About 500 million people face hunger and malnutrition daily. In 1979, President Carter's Commission on World Hunger reported that one out of every eight people suffered from malnutrition. There was enough food grown in the 1970s and early 1980s to provide an adequate diet for every human being. The problem was the unequal distribution of food and people.

The United States and Canada produced about 80 percent of the world's grain. Yet these two nations have less than 6 percent of the world's population. While some countries produce surplus food, other countries,

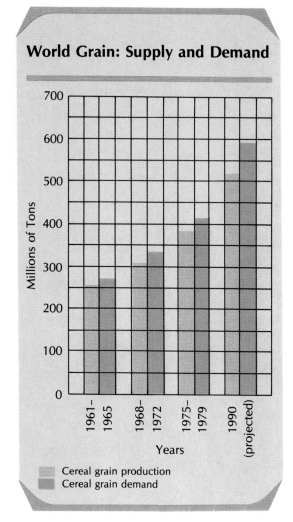

Source: FAO, *Agriculture: Toward 2000.*

Graph Skill   *The production of grain has increased since the 1960s, largely as a result of the Green Revolution. Which has grown faster, supply or demand?*

such as Bangladesh and Ethiopia, have not been able to grow enough to feed their populations. Moreover, some of these countries do not have enough money to buy food year after year on the world market.

Poor nations suffering from famine have received food aid from the governments of developed countries, the United Nations, and private relief organizations. But this type of aid does not solve the long-range problem of increasing food production.

Progress has been made in the area of food production. Efforts to increase food production have resulted in the "Green Revolution." This revolution began in the 1960s, when researchers found ways to double and even triple the amount of food produced on the same amount of land. "Yields which had been almost unchanged for centuries," a UN report noted, "leapt forward."

Experts developed new varieties of high-yield crops and taught farmers in developing nations better soil management methods. Increased use of fertilizers and farm machinery helped boost harvests in India, Mexico, the Philippines, Southeast Asia, and elsewhere.

As often happens with dramatic change, unexpected consequences followed. Many farmers were forced out of business because their small plots could not support the cost of the machinery and chemical fertilizers needed for high yields. And some of the new grain varieties turned out to be more susceptible to insect pests and plant disease.

The Earth's Resources

The Green Revolution has had other undesirable side effects. The large amounts of chemical pesticides and fertilizers used to produce high yields polluted the soil and local water supplies. In 1962, an American writer, Rachel Carson, published a book called *Silent Spring*. In this book, she described the devastating effects that pesticides used on crops have on the land and water, as well as on birds, insects, and fish.

Carson's book raised the issue of the environment. Since the 1960s, people around the world have warned of the dangers in abusing the earth's resources. As a result, scientists began paying more attention to *ecology*, the relationship between living things and their environments. Studies have revealed the delicate balance that exists in nature and how easily pollution can upset this balance.

Third World nations have mixed reactions to environmental issues. They are anxious to industrialize quickly and cannot afford expensive programs to prevent pollution. In addition, many developing nations are willing to risk some pollution from pesticides in order to increase desperately needed food supplies.

Vanishing wildernesses. Around the world, industrial development can also threaten food sources, such as fish, and endanger valuable wilderness areas. Some nations have made efforts to protect undeveloped areas and the resources and wildlife they contain. In Africa, especially, protected wildlife now embraces all manner of wild animals in their natural habitat, a source of interest and knowledge that civilizations today agree should be preserved forever. Former president Julius Nyerere of Tanzania stated that African wildlife is an integral part of his nation's natural resources. As travelers from all over the world come to study and marvel, wildlife becomes an important source of livelihood.

Yet population pressures threaten. When land is cleared and crops are planted,

In the mid-1980s, rock groups performed at huge concerts to raise funds for African nations suffering from famine. Live Aid, a 15-hour world-wide concert, was broadcast by satellite and raised $100 million for famine relief.

For years, people have flocked to zoos around the world to watch the antics of giant pandas. The Chinese have the most pandas in captivity. China is also the only place where giant pandas live in the wild. They inhabit the bamboo forests in a mountainous region of Szechwan (seh chwahn) province in south central China. Good-natured but shy, giant pandas have no natural enemies. They weigh between 200 to 300 pounds. Chinese experts estimate that today fewer than 1,000 giant pandas live in the wild. Only about 50 giant pandas live in zoos.

Nearly every country has made efforts to save its wildlife from extinction. The Chinese government has declared pandas "national treasures" and has sent zoologists to study them in the wild. Zoologists know relatively little about the habits of the giant panda. They want to learn more about these bashful animals in order to protect their way of life.

A team of Chinese and American zoologists has recently traveled into the bamboo forests of Szechwan. There, they captured Long Long, a male panda, and outfitted him with a radio collar. They then released Long Long and listened for radio signals, which told them of his daily travels. The sensitive radio collar often picked up the sound of Long Long munching on bamboo shoots, the panda's chief source of food.

While some zoologists study giant pandas in the wild, others are trying to raise pandas in captivity. At birth, pandas weigh about four ounces and look like hairless white mice.

However, they soon gain weight and their distinctive coat of white and black fur.

The birth of a panda cub in a zoo is a cause for international celebration because so few pandas in captivity have produced offspring. About 12 panda cubs have been born in Chinese zoos over a 20-year period. In August 1981, a panda at the Mexico City Zoo gave birth to a cub named Cancun. Cancun is the first giant panda to be born and survive outside China. He is one indication that the international effort to save the giant panda might succeed.

natural habitats are destroyed. People and animals soon compete for the earth's shrinking living space. In some nations, such as Brazil, jungles are destroyed as people "slash and burn," abandoning the land when planting has depleted the soil.

Desert areas. In some desert areas, efforts to protect the environment are too late. Most desert regions are the result of natural causes such as prevailing winds or mountains that block rainfall. But in the past 50 years, people have contributed to the spread of deserts over land that was once productive.

In some areas, overgrazing has destroyed plants that held dry soil in place.

Wind has blown this soil away, leaving land not suitable for growing plants. In other areas, poor irrigation methods have caused a build-up of salt in soil, creating "salt deserts." Parts of the Tigris-Euphrates Valley, once the "breadbasket" of the ancient Middle East, have become salt deserts. Deserts have spread in northern Africa, India, and the Arabian Peninsula. About 27,000 square miles (70,000 square kilometers) of land has become desert in recent years. (See the map on page 784.)

At the same time, some people have successfully reclaimed desert land. For example, Israeli farmers have developed techniques for farming the desert. They have planted trees to form soil and push back the Negev Desert. They have designed irrigation pipes that carry droplets of water directly to plant roots, preventing evaporation. Other nations have adopted similar techniques to farm arid land.

Other conservation concerns. Environmentalists everywhere are concerned mainly with preventing forms of air and water pollution that threaten health and life. In the mid-1980s, industrial accidents in different parts of the world made millions of people sharply aware of the issue.

In India, a leak from a giant chemical factory spewed deadly fumes, in the worst industrial accident in history. More than 2,000 people died, and at least 200,000 were injured. In Switzerland, a fire at a warehouse sent 30 tons of toxic chemicals into the Rhine River, in Europe's worst industrial spill. The Rhine, Western Europe's most important inland waterway, flows through heavily populated areas of several nations.

When such industrial pollution takes place, scientists often disagree about the extent of environmental damage and how long it will last. Many responsible companies have now taken steps to prevent industrial leaks and spills. And they are developing new techniques to stem the effects of mishaps that may occur.

The Energy Puzzle

Trucks arrive daily at a modern factory in Zurich, Switzerland, to deliver "fuel." The fuel is garbage. The factory burns the garbage to generate the energy it needs to operate. Burning garbage for energy was just one result of the energy crisis of the 1970s.

The energy crisis, brought on by OPEC price increases, focused world attention on several issues. First, it revealed the dependence of industrialized nations on imported oil. For example, like several other European nations, Switzerland had to import all the oil it consumed.

Second, the energy crisis made people aware that world oil reserves would someday be exhausted. Industrialized countries use vast amounts of energy to run factories, heat and light homes, and power cars,

trucks, and airplanes. Since World War II, the chief source of energy has been petroleum.

Third, the energy crisis had vast economic consequences. Oil-importing nations had to pay billions of dollars more for energy when OPEC increased oil prices. In 1970, the United States spent $3 billion to buy imported oil. By 1980, the bill had increased to a staggering $60 billion. At the same time, oil-exporting nations acquired billions of dollars to spend on goods and services. Many OPEC members invested their wealth in the West. Thus, their economies and those of western nations became closely tied.

During the energy crisis of the 1970s, much attention was focused on possible uses of solar energy. Here, solar panels are being installed on the roof of a home in the eastern United States. The panels use energy from the sun to heat the home.

The abrupt, although temporary end of cheap energy created a puzzling problem—how to produce enough energy for the world and how to pay for it. Part of the answer has been to conserve energy. Another part has been to harness energy from new sources, such as power from the sun. Even during the oil glut of the mid-1980s, experts warned that the basic fact had not changed: once natural resources are depleted, they are gone forever.

Chart Skill *Worldwide use of nuclear power is increasing. Despite objections from environmental groups, many nations with limited natural resources have turned to nuclear power. Based on this chart, which nation appears to be the most dependent on nuclear power?*

World Atomic Power, 1987

	No. of Nuclear Reactors	Percent of Electricity Generated by Nuclear Energy
Canada	15	13%
United States	101	17%
Brazil	1	2%
Argentina	2	13%
Britain	37	18%
France	44	65%
Spain	8	22%
Belgium	8	60%
Netherlands	1	5%
East Germany	5	12%
West Germany	20	31%
Switzerland	5	40%
Italy	3	4%
Czechoslovakia	5	15%
Yugoslavia	1	5%
Bulgaria	4	32%
Hungary	2	5%
U.S.S.R.	51	11%
Sweden	12	50%
Finland	4	38%
India	6	4%
Pakistan	1	2%
Japan	32	26%
South Korea	4	18%
Taiwan	6	52%
South Africa	2	4%

New Sources of Energy

Governments in many nations have funded research into alternative sources of energy. Some researchers have explored water power, which was used to power machinery in the early Industrial Revolution. Today, they are trying to find ways to harness the energy of the oceans' tides. In addition, geothermal energy from deep in the earth has been used to produce electricity.

As you have read, industries in some countries are using solid wastes, or garbage, to provide energy. Some states in the United States have also made use of *resource recovery plants*. These are incinerators that burn solid waste and create heat as energy. Disposing of wastes has become a problem in the world's densely populated areas. Garbage-dump landfills are overflowing. Thus, such resource recovery seems to offer a dual solution to energy and disposal needs.

Unfortunately, early resource recovery plants were prone to explosions, and even when operating normally released dioxins—toxic chemicals—into the air. Advances in technology have now reduced these risks. A new plant in Oklahoma operates safely and emits little or no dioxins.

Experiments to find ways of producing inexpensive fuels from a variety of substances have been conducted. For example, in Brazil, researchers have found that a mixture of gasoline and alcohol made from sugar cane can be used to power cars and trucks. Other research has focused on developing equipment for collecting solar energy. This equipment traps energy from the sun's rays, which can then be used to heat homes and factories.

Much research has gone into exploring nuclear power. Nuclear power plants have been built in 26 countries. But breakdowns, accidents, and fears about the safety of nuclear power has raised questions about the future of nuclear plants.

In 1986, the world's first major nuclear accident took place when a reactor exploded and burned at the Chernobyl (chern NOH bul) power station in the Soviet Union. Public health authorities assured an anxious populace that windborne fallout sweeping across nations posed no direct danger. However, many European governments took safety measures. They dumped milk if cows had grazed on contaminated grasses, and they destroyed much produce. The Soviets sought aid from the world's specialists in radiation sickness while struggling to bring the meltdown under control. Eventually, they buried the reactor in sand, boron, and lead. Following the mishap, environmental groups staged protests against the use of nuclear power. But many nations, lacking natural resources, remain committed to its use. (See the table on page 774).

Existing nuclear plants use nuclear fission, the splitting of heavy atoms to produce energy. But nuclear fission also produces radioactive wastes. Safe disposal of these wastes is a problem. As a result, for more than 30 years, researchers have been trying to master nuclear fusion, the joining of two light atoms. Nuclear fusion produces enormous amounts of power but much less radioactive waste than nuclear fission.

In 1981, scientists at Princeton University created the conditions for nuclear fusion—for one tenth of a second. But no one expects a working nuclear fusion plant before the year 2000. Nevertheless, the work of these scientists represents a step toward the development of a safe and unlimited source of energy into the future.

SECTION REVIEW

1. Identify: Green Revolution, Rachel Carson.
2. Define: ecology, resource recovery plant.
3. (a) What advantages do rich lands enjoy? (b) What problems do poor nations face?
4. Why do nations want to preserve their wildlife?
5. (a) How have people helped cause deserts to spread? (b) How have some deserts been reclaimed?
6. List three results of the energy crisis of the 1970s.

3 New Patterns of Culture

Read to Learn
- how mass communication spreads culture
- how technology and art tie nations together

When Prince Charles married Lady Diana Spencer in July 1981 in London, England, the wedding ceremony was beamed via communications satellites to 74 countries. An estimated 750 million people—nearly one out of every five people on earth—watched the wedding on television. This huge audience underscored the impact of mass communication on the world.

Mass Communication

Television, radio, and other forms of mass communication enable people to receive information and entertainment from around the world. When Pope John Paul II was shot in 1981, people rushed to radios and televisions to learn what had happened. In 1985, the world shared the ordeal of Flight 847, when television cameras recorded the drama

of passengers held prisoner in the grounded plane by their skyjackers. In fact, many people believe that television coverage is a major goal of terrorists, to attract attention to their causes.

Other, much happier events such as the Olympics are also seen on televisions worldwide. Such broadcasts enable people from many countries to enjoy a common bond.

In developed nations, especially, television has become an important part of daily life. One survey of American teenagers revealed that they spent 15,000 hours watching television during their high school years. Another survey showed that the average American adult spent nearly 30 hours a week watching television.

Like television, movies often have a worldwide audience. Hollywood movies set new records for movie attendance. Since

World War II, filmmakers in other countries have challenged American dominance in this field. Britain, France, Japan, Italy, India, and Sweden are among the nations that have produced film classics.

Worldwide distribution of films has enabled moviegoers to gain views of life in other lands. For example, Indian filmmaker Satyajit Ray made a series of movies that traced the life of one man from childhood through marriage and parenthood. These movies offered vivid insights into everyday life in India.

The Performing Arts

As movies, television, and radio have captured large audiences, some people have predicted that live performances in theaters would not survive. But the mass media has awakened a new interest in the performing arts. Often, people choose to attend a live

Mikhail Baryshnikov defected from the Soviet Union in 1974. In 1987, as part of his "openness" policy, Soviet leader Gorbachev invited him to appear as a guest performer in the Soviet Union.

performance of an artistic group they have seen on television.

In addition, newspapers and magazines carry frequent articles about trends in art, film, theater, and music. Directors and actors are interviewed on television. Individual performers whose work appeals to the public have become world famous.

The world of ballet. In recent years, audience enthusiasm has led to a major revival of classical dance, or ballet. In the 1950s, there were only a handful of outstanding ballet companies in the world. Two of the leading companies—the Bolshoi and Kirov—were in the Soviet Union. Generally, only people living in major cities could attend the ballet.

In 1961, while the Bolshoi Ballet was on a world tour, its leading male dancer, Rudolf Nureyev, defected to the West. Russian ballerina Natalia Makarova defected in 1970 and joined an American company. In 1974, Mikhail Baryshnikov, one of the greatest male dancers of the century, slipped away from the Kirov Ballet and sought artistic freedom in the West. Intense publicity surrounding the defection of these Russian dancers increased curiosity about ballet and helped build new audiences.

The music of youth. A new musical sound forged a vast youth audience in the postwar period. Fusing traditions of American country and western music and rhythm and blues, American musicians created rock 'n' roll in the 1950s. With its pounding beat, youth-oriented lyrics, and amplified sound, rock became a shared experience among young people around the globe. Today, rock groups throughout the world attract tens of thousands to a single concert.

In 1986, rock stars and organizers joined in a humanitarian effort. In response to devastating famine in Africa, they donated their talents in massive concerts to collect funds for African relief.

New technology also played a part in creating a vast music industry. Lasers that read music from compact disks provided a truer sound than ever before. Electric instruments and electronic synthesizers created new possibilities in music. Transistor radios, cassettes, tape decks, and disk players made music portable.

In the 1970s, Chinese archaeologists discovered the tomb of the emperor Shih Huang Ti. (See page 142.) The emperor, who died in 210 B.C., had ordered the building of the Great Wall of China. He also employed hundreds of workers to prepare his tomb. Archaeologists have just begun to excavate the many life-sized terra cotta figures (left) that were buried in the emperor's tomb. The kneeling archer (right) was supposed to protect the emperor in the afterlife.

Exploring the Past and Present

An information explosion has taken place in the postwar period. For example, as you have read, scientists have gained vast stores of new knowledge in such fields as space and medicine. Mass communication has helped spread this knowledge. Schools and universities have expanded their courses of study to cover massive amounts of new information. In addition, an increasingly literate public is reading about the latest discoveries.

People are also taking a new interest in the past. Many records of the past have been stored in museums. In the postwar period, museums have opened their doors to millions of people. They have mounted well-planned, lively exhibits. Science museums have let people explore complicated space age technology. Museums of art and archaeology have allowed people to learn about other societies.

Proud of their ancient heritages, nations such as Egypt and China have allowed mu-

seums in other countries to display treasured artifacts. In the 1970s, an exhibit of treasures from Tutankhamon's tomb traveled to the United States and Western Europe. A world tour of Chinese artifacts included 3,000-year-old Shang bronzes and terra cotta figures that had guarded the First Emperor's grave. These exhibits have increased people's curiosity about other people's cultures.

Museums have also collected modern works of art. People flock to see the works of twentieth century masters such as Pablo Picasso and Henri Matisse. Competition among museums and private collectors to buy modern works of art has caused prices of these pieces to skyrocket.

In the postwar period, the center of the art world shifted from Paris to New York. In New York, several new schools of painting developed, including abstract expressionism. Jackson Pollock, a leader of this movement, swirled and dripped paint across his canvasses. In another modern art movement, pop art, artists used images from the American mass media. Pop artists based their work

Population of the World's Largest Urban Areas
(in thousands)

1350 B.C.		1000 A.D.		1600 A.D.	
Thebes, Egypt	100	Cordova, Spain	450	Peking, China	706
Memphis, Egypt	74	Constantinople, Turkey	450	Constantinople, Turkey	700
Babylon, Iraq	54	Kaifeng, China	400	Agra, India	500
Chengchow, China	40	Sian, China	300	Cairo, Egypt	400
Khattushas, Turkey	40	Kyoto, Japan	200	Osaka, Japan	400
1925 A.D.		1980 A.D.		2000 A.D. (projected)	
New York, US	7,774	New York, US	20,400	Mexico City, Mexico	31,000
London, England	7,742	Tokyo, Japan	20,000	São Paulo, Brazil	25,800
Tokyo, Japan	5,300	Mexico City, Mexico	15,000	Tokyo, Japan	24,200
Paris, France	4,800	São Paulo, Brazil	13,500	New York, US	22,800
Berlin, Germany	4,013	Shanghai, China	13,400	Shanghai, China	22,700

All figures are estimates.

Chart Skill *The centers of population have changed in the past 3,000 years. This table shows the five largest urban areas at five points in history. It also shows the urban areas projected to be the largest in 2000. Which country appears most often on the chart as having cities with the largest populations?*

on such everyday images as soup cans. American artist Roy Lichtenstein used comic strip characters as subjects for his paintings. The painting "Three Flags" by pop artist Jasper Johns sold for $1 million in 1981. This was the highest price ever paid for a work by a living artist.

Challenges for the Future

The postwar period has brought tremendous changes to people around the globe. As you have read, new nations emerged in Africa, the Middle East, and Asia. Since 1945, these nations and the developing nations of Latin America have taken a prominent role in world affairs. Improved communication and transportation have put people from different parts of the world in closer touch with each other than ever before. In addition, nations have been tied more closely together by economic needs.

In both developed and developing nations, education has contributed to widespread changes. In the United States and Western Europe, college attendance soared in the postwar period. Dozens of new colleges and universities were opened. In the same period, developing nations worked toward increasing literacy rates. Many students from these nations attended universities in the United States and Europe.

Important changes have occurred in the workplace. Working conditions, hours, wages, and fringe benefits have been improved. New inventions have led to the growth of new industries. Computers have begun to revolutionize industry. On farms, new high-yield crops and machinery have changed the way food is produced.

As you have read, the movement of people from rural areas to cities has been a worldwide phenomenon. In cities and their suburbs, people have easier access to education, jobs, and various forms of popular entertainment.

Patterns of change in the postwar era have also affected women. In developed countries, women have entered the workforce in increasing numbers. Women in many countries have expanded their roles in public life.

These patterns of growth and change continue to pose challenges to all nations. As in the past, individual societies are developing their own ways of meeting these challenges.

SECTION REVIEW

1. Identify: Satyajit Ray, Rudolf Nureyev, Jackson Pollock.

2. (a) List three forms of mass communication. (b) What effect has mass communication had on people around the world?
3. How has new technology affected popular music?
4. What subjects did pop artists use in their work?
5. Describe three changes that have taken place in the workplace in recent years.

Chapter 40 Review

In Perspective

Since 1945, vast changes have occurred in many fields. Research scientists working with engineers and technicians have made many advances in technology. Space exploration has offered dramatic evidence of the advances in science and technology. Both the computer revolution and improvements in medicine have transformed the lives of people around the globe.

Scientists have explored ways of meeting the demands of the world's growing population. They have developed new sources of food and are looking for new sources of energy. Even so, world hunger and the need for energy remain among the major challenges for the future. At the same time, nations have made efforts to preserve their wildernesses and wildlife resources.

Mass communication has also had a dramatic effect on peoples' lives. Thanks to satellite communications, millions of people can watch a major event on television. Yet despite radio and television, audiences continue to flock to live artistic performances.

Today, people are taking a new interest in the heritage of the past along with the achievements of the present. Displays of ancient artifacts from different civilizations have drawn huge crowds to museums, while space shots have also attracted thousands of spectators.

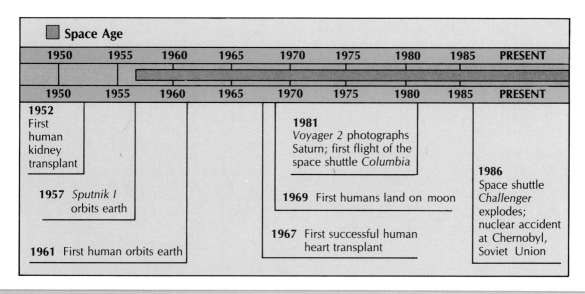

Space Age								
1950	1955	1960	1965	1970	1975	1980	1985	PRESENT
1950	1955	1960	1965	1970	1975	1980	1985	PRESENT

1952 First human kidney transplant

1957 *Sputnik I* orbits earth

1961 First human orbits earth

1981 *Voyager 2* photographs Saturn; first flight of the space shuttle *Columbia*

1969 First humans land on moon

1967 First successful human heart transplant

1986 Space shuttle *Challenger* explodes; nuclear accident at Chernobyl, Soviet Union

Recalling Facts

Decide if the following statements are true or false. If a statement is false, rewrite the statement to make it true.

1. Applied science involves putting science to practical use.

2. The Space Age began during World War II.

3. John Glenn was the first American to orbit the earth.

4. Other nations in addition to the United States and the Soviet Union have launched satellites.

5. The development of radar allowed smaller computers to be built.

6. The use of vaccines has helped wipe out smallpox.

7. Populations are growing fastest in Western Europe.

8. The Green Revolution has helped increase food production.

9. Television and movies have led to reduced interest in live performances of theater and music.

10. The center of the art world today is Paris.

Chapter Checkup

1. (a) How did the need for better weapons during World War II help launch the Space Age? (b) What were the major Soviet achievements in space exploration? (c) What were the major American achievements in space exploration?

2. (a) Describe the development of computers. (b) How are computers used in business and industry? (c) How are they used in medicine?

3. (a) Why was the discovery of penicillin important? (b) How did the electron microscope affect medical research? (c) How have medical advances affected surgery?

4. (a) How widespread is the problem of hunger? (b) What is the major cause of this problem? (c) What steps have been taken to increase food production?

5. Describe how each of the following has influenced people's lives: (a) television and movies; (b) performing arts; (c) museums.

Critical Thinking

1. **Expressing an Opinion** (a) Why do some developing nations ignore warnings about pollution? (b) Do you agree with the position of these developing nations? Explain.

Relating Past to Present

1. Review the description of dawn at Stonehenge on page 2 and the liftoff of *Columbia* at Cape Canaveral on page 762. (a) What similarities do you see in these two events? (b) What differences do you see? (c) How might the builders of Stonehenge have reacted to the *Columbia* liftoff?

Developing Basic Skills

1. **Researching** Choose one of the advances in technology of the postwar period. Research how this advance was achieved. Then answer the following questions: (a) What earlier developments contributed to this advance? (b) Was this advance the work of a single individual or of many people? Explain. (c) What has been the major result of this advance?

2. **Graph Reading** Study the graphs on page 767 and page 455. Then answer the following questions: (a) How did average life expectancy in Western Europe and the United States change between 1910 and 1930? Between 1950 and 1960? (b) During which period between 1910 and the present did life expectancy increase the most? (c) How does average life expectancy in Western Europe and the United States today compare to average life expectancy in these areas in 1850?

3. **Forecasting Future Trends** No one can say exactly what will happen in the future. But people can make forecasts based on trends, or changes taking place in the present. Make a list of five major changes that have taken place since World War II. Next to each, note what aspect of people's lives it has affected. Decide whether this change is likely to continue. Then answer the following questions: (a) Describe a change that has affected political life. (b) Is it likely to continue? Explain. (c) What economic trends have affected people's lives? (d) Which trend do you think will have the greatest impact on future developments?

See page 808 for suggested readings.

Reference Section

World Population

ARCTIC OCEAN

GREENLAND

CANADA

UNITED STATES

ATLANTIC OCEAN

PACIFIC OCEAN

MEXICO

THE BAHAMAS

CUBA

10
38
43 37 26
GUATEMALA
EL SALVADOR
NICARAGUA
COSTA RICA
PANAMA
VENEZUELA
COLOMBIA

4
25
64
65 8
35 77
GUYANA
SURINAME
FRENCH GUIANA

17

ECUADOR

PERU

BRAZIL

WESTERN SAMOA

TONGA

BOLIVIA

58

CHILE

URUGUAY

PACIFIC OCEAN

ARGENTINA

ATLANTIC

Equator

1. AFGHANISTAN
2. ALBANIA
3. ANDORRA
4. ANTIGUA & BARBUʹ
5. AUSTRIA
6. BAHRAIN
7. BANGLADESH
8. BARBADOS
9. BELGIUM
10. BELIZE
11. BENIN
12. BHUTAN
13. BOTSWANA
14. BULGARIA
15. BURUNDI
16. CAMEROON
17. CAPE VERDE
18. CENTRAL AFRICAN REPUBLIC
19. COMOROS
20. CONGO
21. CYPRUS
22. CZECHOSLOVAKIA
23. DENMARK
24. DJIBOUTI
25. DOMINICA
26. DOMINICAN REPUBLIC
27. EAST GERMANY
28. EGYPT
29. EQUATORIAL GUINEA
30. ETHIOPIA
31. FINLAND
32. GAMBIA
33. GHANA
34. GREECE
35. GRENADA
36. GUINEA-BISSAU
37. HAITI

38. HONDURAS
39. HUNGARY
40. IRAQ
41. ISRAEL
42. IVORY COAST
43. JAMAICA
44. JORDAN
45. KAMPUCHEA
46. KUWAIT
47. LAOS
48. LEBANON
49. LIECHTENSTEIN
50. LUXEMBOURG
51. MALAWI
52. MALTA
53. MONACO
54. MOZAMBIQUE
55. NEPAL
56. NETHERLANDS
57. PAKISTAN
58. PARAGUAY
59. P.D.R. YEMEN
60. POLAND

61. QATAR
62. ROMANIA
63. RWANDA
64. SAINT LUCIA
65. SAINT VINCENT & THE GRENADINES
66. SAN MARINO
67. SÃO TOMÉ & PRINCIPE
68. SAUDI ARABIA
69. SENEGAL
70. SIERRA LEONE
71. SINGAPORE
72. SWEDEN
73. SWITZERLAND
74. SYRIA

75. THAILAND
76. TOGO
77. TRINIDAD & TOBAGO
78. TUNISIA
79. TURKEY
80. UGANDA
81. UNITED ARAB EMIRATES
82. UPPER VOLTA (Burkina Faso)
83. WEST GERMANY
84. WESTERN SAHARA
85. YEMEN
86. YUGOSLAVIA
87. ZAMBIA
88. ZIMBABWE

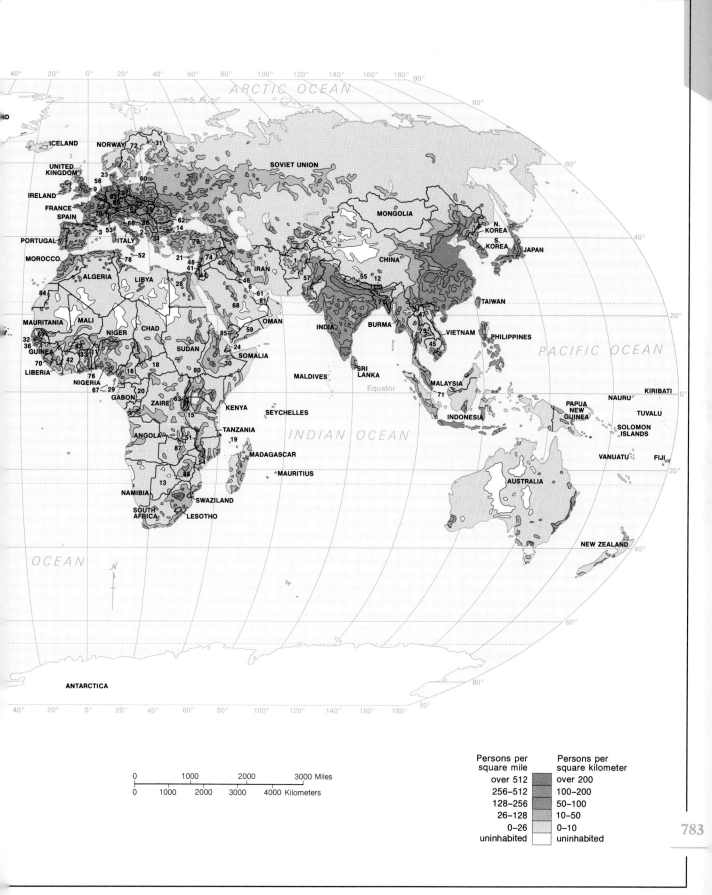

Persons per
square mile

over 512

256–512

128–256

26–128

0–26
uninhabited

Persons per
square kilometer

over 200

100–200

50–100

10–50

0–10
uninhabited

World Climate Zones

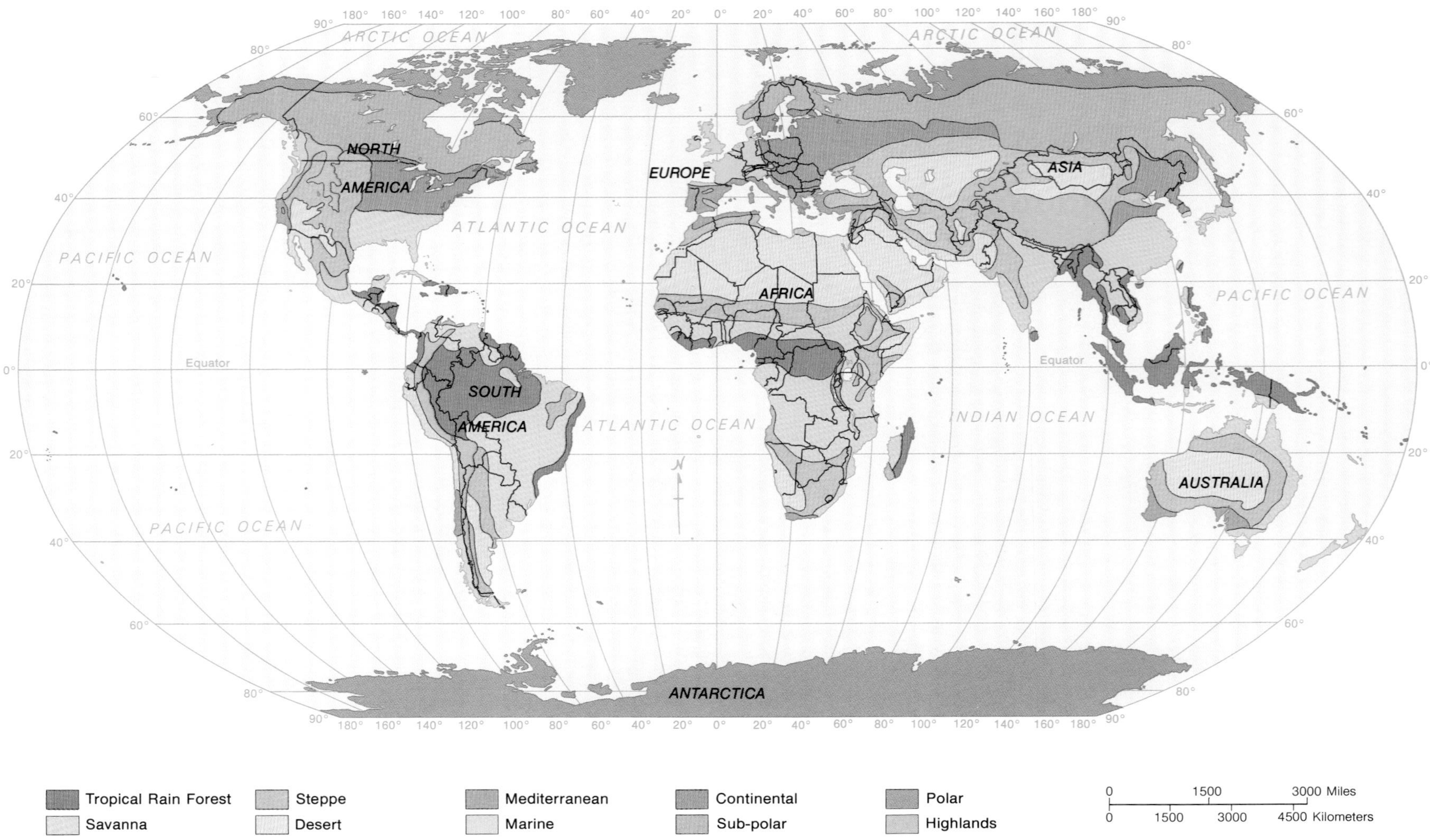

Tropical Rain Forest
Savanna

Steppe
Desert

Mediterranean
Marine

Continental
Sub-polar

Polar
Highlands

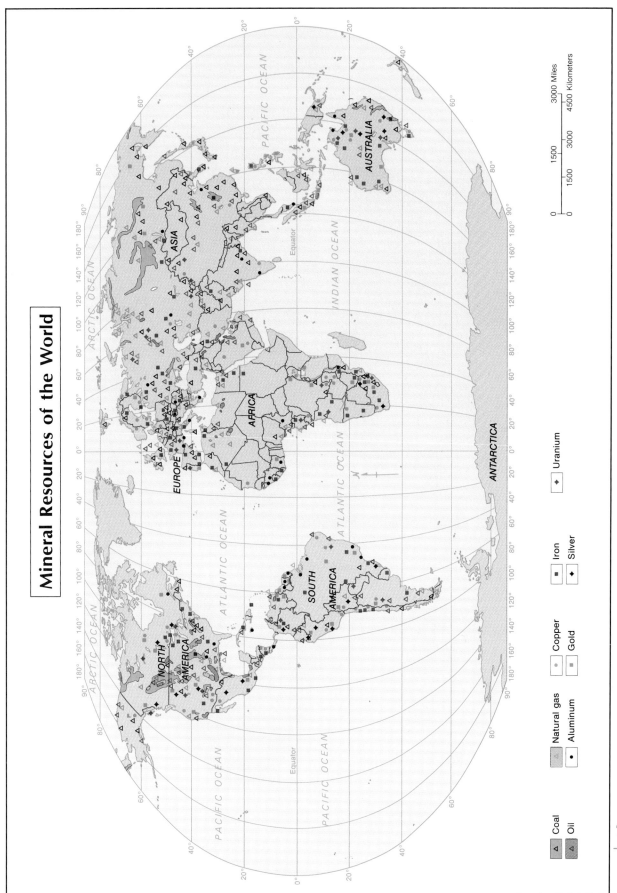

Mineral Resources of the World

ARCTIC OCEAN

PACIFIC OCEAN

ASIA

AUSTRALIA

INDIAN OCEAN

Equator

AFRICA

EUROPE

ATLANTIC OCEAN

ANTARCTICA

NORTH AMERICA

SOUTH AMERICA

ATLANTIC OCEAN

PACIFIC OCEAN

Equator

Coal

Oil

Natural gas

Aluminum

Copper

Gold

Iron

Silver

Uranium

3000 Miles
4500 Kilometers
0   1500   3000
0   1500   3000

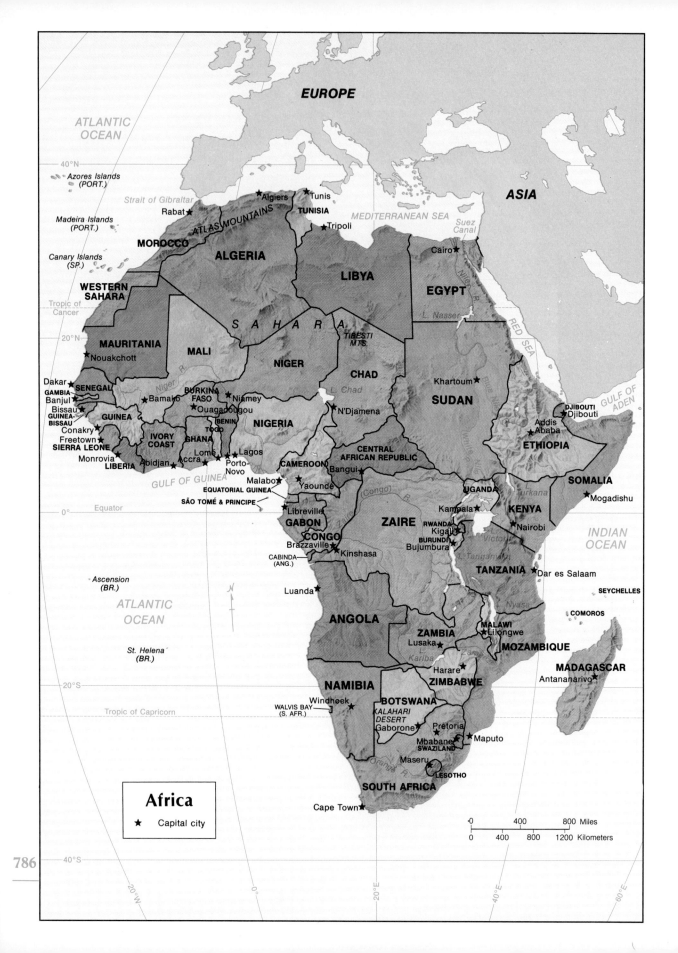

EUROPE

ATLANTIC OCEAN

40°N

Azores Islands (PORT.)

Madeira Islands (PORT.)

Canary Islands (SP.)

Tropic of Cancer

20°N

ASIA

MEDITERRANEAN SEA

Strait of Gibraltar

Rabat ★
★ Algiers   ★ Tunis
TUNISIA
★ Tripoli
Suez Canal

MOROCCO
WESTERN SAHARA

ATLAS MOUNTAINS

ALGERIA

LIBYA

EGYPT

Cairo ★

L. Nasser

S A H A R A

TIBESTI MTS.

RED SEA

MAURITANIA

MALI

NIGER

CHAD

Khartoum ★

SUDAN

GULF OF ADEN

Nouakchott ★

Niger R.

Dakar ★
GAMBIA
Banjul ★
Bissau ★
GUINEA-BISSAU
Conakry ★
Freetown ★
SIERRA LEONE
Monrovia ★
LIBERIA

SENEGAL

Bamako ★
BURKINA FASO
★ Niamey
★ Ouagadougou
BENIN
TOGO
IVORY COAST
GHANA
Abidjan ★
★ Accra
Lomé ★
Porto-Novo ★

★ N'Djamena

NIGERIA

L. Chad

★ Lagos

CAMEROON

Malabo ★
EQUATORIAL GUINEA
SÃO TOMÉ & PRINCIPE

Yaoundé ★

CENTRAL AFRICAN REPUBLIC

Bangui ★

Blue Nile R.

DJIBOUTI
Djibouti ★
Addis Ababa ★

ETHIOPIA

White Nile R.

L. Turkana

SOMALIA

Mogadishu ★

Equator 0°

Libreville ★

GABON

CONGO
Brazzaville ★
★ Kinshasa
CABINDA (ANG.)

ZAIRE

(Congo) R.

Zaire R.

UGANDA
Kampala ★

RWANDA
Kigali ★
BURUNDI
Bujumbura ★

L. Victoria

L. Tanganyika

KENYA

Nairobi ★

INDIAN OCEAN

· *Ascension (BR.)*

ATLANTIC OCEAN

St. Helena (BR.)

Luanda ★

ANGOLA

TANZANIA

Dar es Salaam ★

SEYCHELLES

COMOROS

Nyasa

ZAMBIA
Lusaka ★

MALAWI
Lilongwe ★

MOZAMBIQUE

20°S

Tropic of Capricorn

NAMIBIA

Kariba

Harare ★
ZIMBABWE

MADAGASCAR

Antananarivo ★

Windhoek ★
WALVIS BAY (S. AFR.)

BOTSWANA
KALAHARI DESERT
Gaborone ★

Pretoria ★
Mbabane ★
SWAZILAND

★ Maputo

Orange R.

Maseru ★
LESOTHO

SOUTH AFRICA

Cape Town ★

Africa

★ Capital city

0   400   800 Miles
0   400   800   1200 Kilometers

N

40°S

20°W   0°   20°E   40°E   60°E

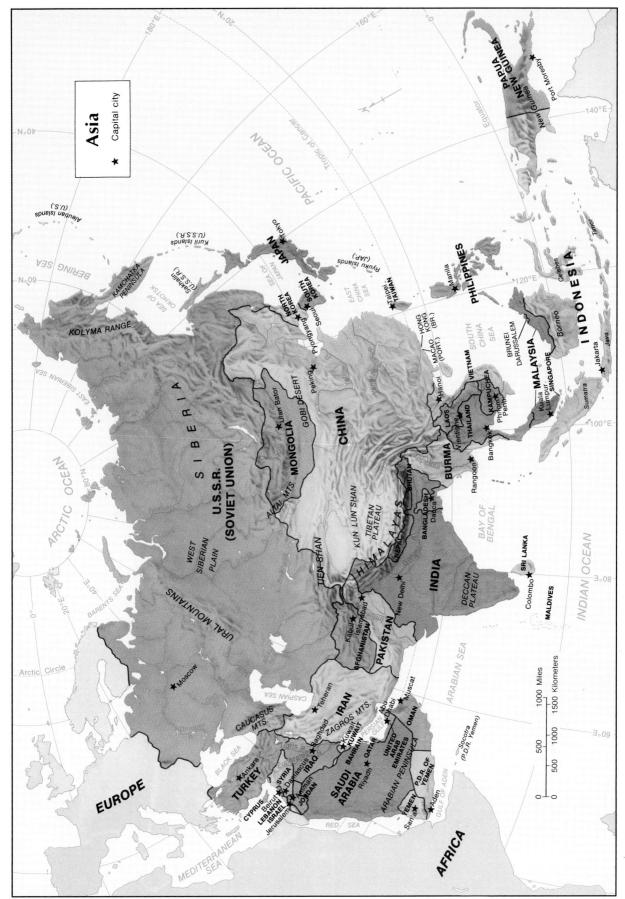

Asia
★ Capital city

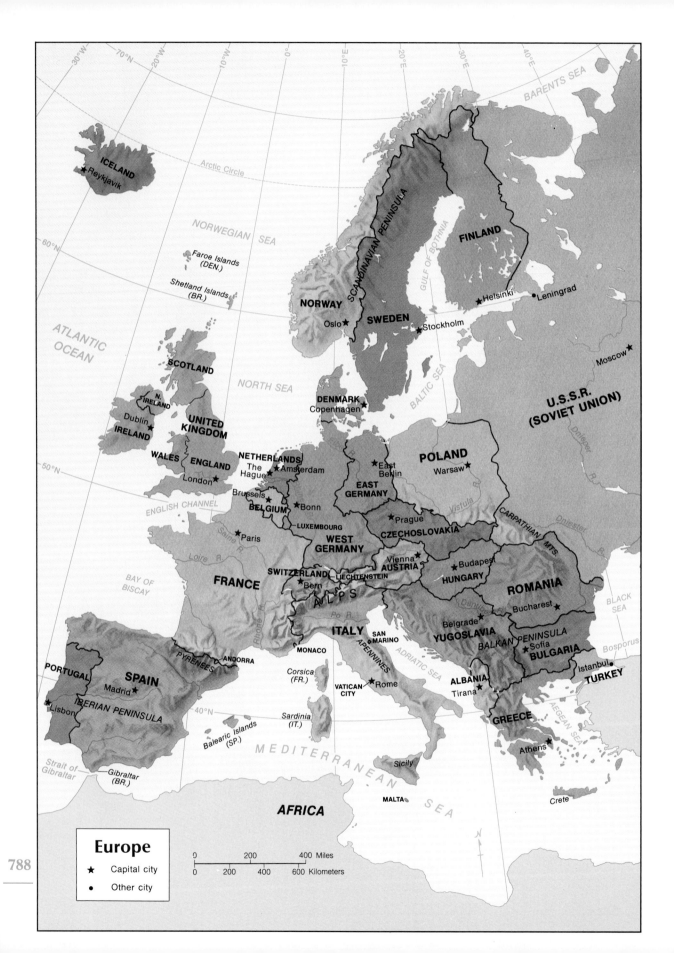

Europe

★ Capital city
• Other city

0   200   400 Miles
0   200   400   600 Kilometers

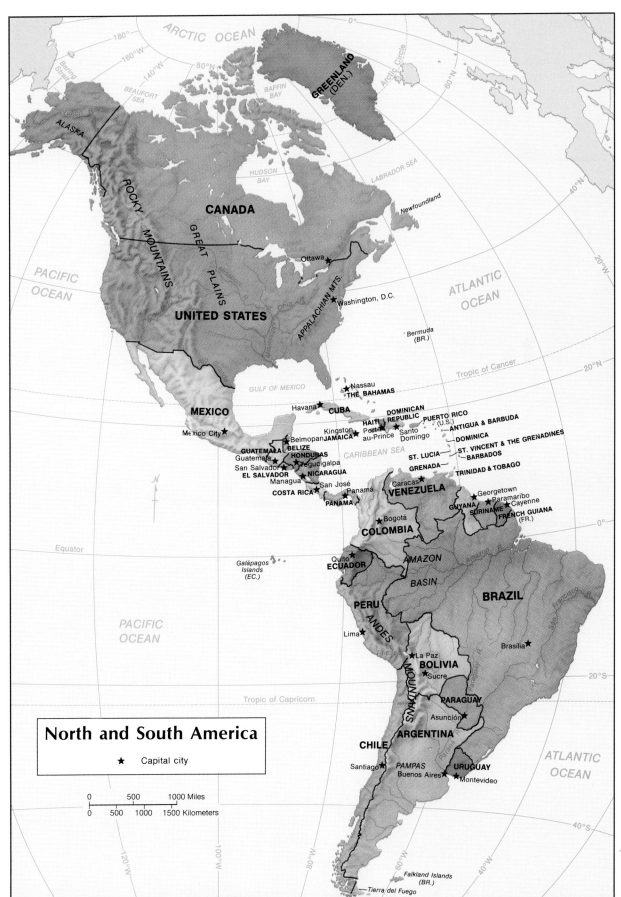

North and South America

★ Capital city

| 0 | 500 | 1000 Miles |
| 0 | 500 | 1000 | 1500 Kilometers |

A Chronology of World History

This chronology includes some of the most important events and developments in world history. It can be used to trace developments in different parts of the world in the areas of government and society, science and technology, the arts and literature, and religion and philosophy. The number next to each entry refers to the chapter in which the event or development is discussed in the text.

	Government and Society	Science and Technology
3000 B.C.– **2501 B.C.**	Civilizations develop in river valleys 1 Old Kingdom in Egypt 2 Sumerian city-states 3	Great Pyramid of Khufu in Egypt 2 Egyptian calendar 2 Sumerian arithmetic 3
2500 B.C.– **2001 B.C.**	Middle Kingdom in Egypt 2 Sargon in Mesopotamia 3 Indus Valley civilization 4	Chinese calendar 4 Irrigation of Nile Delta 2
2000 B.C.– **1501 B.C.**	Minoan civilization 5 Hammurabi's law code 3 Shang dynasty in China 4 New Kingdom in Egypt 2	Indus cities planned 4 Shang mathematics and astronomy 4
1500 B.C.– **1001 B.C.**	Aryans in India 4 Trojan War 5 Tutankhamon in Egypt 2 Dorians invade Peloponnesus 5 Chou dynasty in China 4	Beginning of Iron Age 3
1000 B.C.– **501 B.C.**	Efficient government in Assyria 3 Solomon's rule in Israel 3 Persian Empire 3 Caste system emerges in India 4	Chaldean mathematics and astronomy 3 Great Royal Road in Persian Empire 3 Hippocrates 6
500 B.C.– **1 B.C.**	Persian Wars 5 Athenian democracy 5 Alexander the Great 6 Asoka in India 9 Roman Republic 7	Alexandria in Egypt center of Hellenistic science 6 Colosseum built in Rome 8 Roman aqueducts and roads 8
1 A.D.– **500 A.D.**	Han dynasty in China 9 Roman Empire 7, 8 Maya civilization in Central America 14 Fall of Rome 8 Gupta Empire in India 9	*Natural History* by Pliny the Elder 8 Medical encyclopedia of Galen 8 Decimal system and concept of zero in India 9 Paper invented in China 9 Maya develop calendar and zero 14

The Arts and Literature	Religion and Philosophy	
Gilgamesh Epic 3	Pharaohs as god-kings in Egypt 2 Dumuzi and Inanna in Sumer 3	**3000 B.C.–** **2501 B.C.**
Temples at Luxor and Karnak 2 Egyptian literature 2	Osiris worshipped in Egypt 2 Mother goddess worshipped in Indus Valley 4	**2500 B.C.–** **2001 B.C.**
Chinese bronzes and silk 4 Chinese writing 4 Minoan frescoes 5	Ancestor worship and use of oracle bones in China 4	**2000 B.C.–** **1501 B.C.**
Temple of Hatshepsut in Egypt 2 Obelisks built in Egypt 2	Vedas and Upanishads in India 4 Hinduism develops 4, 9 Akenaton in Egypt 2 Hebrew belief in one God 3	**1500 B.C.–** **1001 B.C.**
Library at Nineveh 3 Phoenician alphabet 3 *Ramayana* in India 4 *Book of Odes* in China 4 *Iliad* by Homer 5	Olympian gods in Greece 6 Buddhism founded 9 Zoroaster in Persian Empire 3 Confucius in China 9	**1000 B.C.–** **501 B.C.**
Parthenon in Greece 5 *Antigone* by Sophocles 6 *Aeneid* by Virgil 7 Stupas built in India 9	Socrates, Plato, and Aristotle in Athens 6 Stoics and Epicureans in Greece 6 Legalism in China 9	**500 B.C.–** **1 B.C.**
The Annals by Tacitus 8 Roman mosaics 8 Kalidasa in India 9 First Chinese dictionary 9 Ajanta cave paintings 9	Christianity founded 8 Christianity becomes official religion of Roman Empire 8 Confucianism influences Chinese government 9	**1 A.D.–** **500 A.D.**

	Government and Society	Science and Technology

501–1000	Charlemagne in Europe 10
	Emergence of feudalism in Europe 10
	Expansion of Islamic Empire 13
	Golden Age of T'ang in China 15
	Kingdom of Ghana in West Africa 14
		Stirrup, heavy plow, three-field system
		  in Europe 10
		Arab advances in science and
		  mathematics 13
		Printing in China 15

1001–1499	Crusades 11 Decline of feudalism in Europe 12 Kublai Khan in China 15 Fall of Constantinople to Turks 13	Flying buttress, clocks, glass in Europe 11 Inca roads and terraces 14 Printing press in Europe 16

1500–1599	Aztec and Inca empires conquered in
	  New World 17
	Magellan rounds Cape Horn 17
	Height of Ottoman Empire 18
	Akbar in India 15
		Scientific Revolution begins in
		  Europe 19
		Copernicus studies planets 19
		Vesalius studies anatomy 19

1600–1699	Emergence of absolute monarchs in
	  Europe 18
	Thirty Years' War 18
	Louis XIV in France 18
	Tokugawa shoguns isolate Japan 15
	English Bill of Rights 20
		Galileo challenges traditional
		  thinking 19
		Invention of microscope 19
		Newton develops mathematical laws 19
		Steam-driven engine developed 23

1700–1799	Enlightened monarchs in Europe 19 American Revolution 20 French Revolution 21	Agricultural Revolution in Europe 23 Industrial Revolution begins in Britain 23 Inventions in textile industry 23
1800–1899	Congress of Vienna 22 Independent nations in Latin America 29 Unification of Italy 26 Unification of Germany 26 American Civil War 25 Age of Imperialism 27, 28, 29	Spread of Industrial Revolution 23 Fulton develops steamship 23 Telephone and electric light invented 23 Advances in physics and chemistry 24 Improvements in medicine 24
1900–Present	World War I 30 Great Depression 31 Rise of totalitarian states 32 World War II 33 Nations of Africa, Middle East, and Asia win independence 35, 36, 37	Assembly-line production 23 Flight at Kitty Hawk 23 Airplanes used in war 30, 33 Space Age begins 40 Invention of computers 40

Glossary

This glossary defines many important historical terms and phrases. Many of the terms are phonetically respelled to aid in pronunciation. See the Pronunciation Key below for an explanation of the respellings. The page number following each definition is the page on which the term or phrase is first discussed in the text. Most of the entries appear in italics the first time they are used in the text.

Pronunciation Key

When difficult terms or names first appear in the text, they are respelled to aid in pronunciation. A syllable in LARGE CAPITAL LETTERS receives the most stress. Syllables with a secondary stress appear in SMALL CAPITAL LETTERS. The key below lists the letters used for respelling. It includes examples of words using each sound and shows how they would be respelled.

Symbol	Example	Respelling
a	hat	(hat)
ay	pay, late	(pay), (layt)
ah	star, hot	(stahr), (haht)
ai	air, dare	(air), (dair)
aw	law, all	(law), (awl)
eh	met	(meht)
ee	bee, eat	(bee), (eet)
er	learn, sir, fur	(lern), (ser), (fer)
ih	fit	(fiht)
ī	mile	(mīl)
ir	ear	(ir)
oh	no	(noh)
oi	soil, boy	(soil), (boi)
oo	root, rule	(root), (rool)
or	born, door	(born), (dor)
ow	plow, out	(plow), (owt)

Symbol	Example	Respelling
u	put, book	(put), (buk)
uh	fun	(fuhn)
yoo	few, use	(fyoo), (yooz)
ch	chill, reach	(chihl), (reech)
g	go, dig	(goh), (dihg)
j	jet, gently, bridge	(jeht), (JEHNT-lee), (brihj)
k	kite, cup	(kīt), (kuhp)
ks	mix	(mihks)
kw	quick	(kwihk)
ng	bring	(brihng)
s	say, cent	(say), (sehnt)
sh	she, crash	(shee), (krash)
th	three	(three)
th	then, breathe	(thehn), (breeth)
y	yet, onion	(yeht), (UHN-yuhn)
z	zip, always	(zihp), (AWL-wayz)
zh	treasure	(TREH-zher)

A

absolute monarch ruler who has complete authority over the government and the lives of the people (page 344)

acropolis (uh KRAHP uhl ihs) hilltop fortress in a city-state of ancient Greece (page 69)

adobe sun-dried brick used for house building by early peoples in the American Southwest (page 235)

agegrade in African family organization, all the boys and girls born in the same year (page 230)

anthropologist (AN thruh PAHL uh jihst) scientist who studies the physical characteristics of people and the way people organize societies (page 3)

antibiotic chemical substance developed during World War II that destroys bacteria (page 766)

apartheid (uh PAHRT hayt) policy of rigid separation of races; practiced in South Africa (page 680)

appeasement (uh PEEZ mehnt) policy of making concessions to an aggressor in order to preserve peace (page 627)

applied science science employed by engineers and technicians putting theoretical pure science to use (page 763)

apprentice (uh PREHN tihs) young person who learns a trade from a master craftsman (page 172)

aqueduct (AK wuh duhkt) in Ancient Rome, canal-like stone structure that carried water to the cities from reservoirs in the country (page 114)

archaeologist (AHR kee AHL uh jihst) scientist who studies the lives of early peoples by analyzing objects they left behind (page 3)

archipelago (AHR kuh PEHL uh GOH) chain of islands (page 253)

archons (AHR kahns) in Ancient Greece, three officials heading the governing council of the aristocracy (page 71)

aristocracy (AR uh STAH kruh see) government headed by a privileged minority or upper class (page 69)

armistice (AHR muh stihs) end to fighting in a war (page 577)

artifact (AHR tuh FAKT) object made by human beings (page 3)

artisan (AHR tuh zuhn) skilled craftsperson (page 10)

assembly line production method that breaks down a complex job into a series of smaller tasks (page 437)

assimilation (uh SIHM uh LAY shuhn) policy whereby an imperial power tries to absorb colonies politically and culturally (page 520)

astrolabe (AS truh LAYB) instrument used to calculate a ship's latitude by measuring the position of the stars (page 321)

atman (AHT muhn) in Hinduism, the universal soul (page 129)

autocracy (aw TAH kruh see) government in which the ruler has unlimited authority (page 496)

autonomy (aw TAHN uh mee) self-government (page 500)

ayatollah (ī uh TOH luh) highest title that can be held by a Muslim in the Shiite sect (page 697)

B

bailiff (BAY lihf) during the Middle Ages, the agent of a lord who managed the lord's smaller estates (page 160)

barter economy system in which one set of goods is exchanged for another (page 10)

Bessemer process procedure developed in the 1850s that made steel production cheaper and easier (page 432)

bill of exchange in the Middle Ages, bank paper allowing merchants to exchange coins for paper in one city, redeem paper for coins in a distant city (page 183)

blitzkrieg (blihts KREEG) lightning warfare; a swift attack (page 629)

bourgeoisie (boor zhwah ZEE) in the Middle Ages, the French word for townspeople; later a term used to describe the middle class (page 171)

bureaucracy (byoo RAH kruh see) system of organizing government by departments or bureaus (page 58)

brahma (BRAH muh) in Hinduism, the single, supreme force uniting everything in the universe (page 129)

bronze hard metal composed of copper combined with tin, developed in the late Neolithic Age (page 8)

bushido (BOO shee DOH) the way of the warrior; during the feudal period in Japan, a code of conduct for samurai stressing obedience to one's lord (page 257)

C

cabildo in sixteenth century Spanish America, city council appointed by the king of Spain (page 330)

caliph (KAY lihf) successor to the prophet Muhammad who acted as both religious and political leader (page 216)

coalition temporary alliance between parties in a government (page 473)

coloni in Ancient Rome, farmers who worked land they had given to nobles in return for protection (page 120)

capital money that can be invested in business (page 337)

capitalist person who invests in business in order to make a profit (page 339)

cash crop crop that can be sold on the world market for money (page 510)

caste social group based on birth; in India, caste determined the jobs people could hold (page 53)

cataract waterfall and rapids posing obstacles to navigation (page 16)

caudillo (kow DEE lyoh) during the 1800s in Latin America, a military dictator (page 450)

censor official in ancient Rome who registered the population for tax and voting purposes and enforced the moral code (page 97)

chivalry (SHIHV 'l ree) code of conduct during the Middle Ages that combined Christian values with the values of a warrior (page 157)

city-state independent town or city and the surrounding countryside (page 32)

clan family group that traces its origin to a common ancestor (page 254)

cold war state of tension and hostility without armed conflict (page 651)

collective farm large government-run farm; created in the Soviet Union in the 1930s (page 609)

collective security group of nations acting together to preserve peace (page 587)

colony territory that an outside power controls directly (page 507)

commercial colonialism practice by which the English East India Company controlled India's foreign trade and kept friendly local rulers in power (page 527)

common law system of law in England based on decisions of royal courts that became accepted legal principles (page 189)

communism form of complete socialism in which there is public ownership of all land and all the means of production (page 451)

conquistador (kohn KEES tah DOHR) conqueror; person given the right by rulers of Spain to establish outposts in the Americas (page 329)

conservatism during the 1800s, a philosophy that supported the traditional order and resisted political and social change (page 415)

consul official from the patrician class who administered the laws of Rome (page 96)

containment policy whereby the United States tried to prevent the Soviet Union from expanding beyond its borders; first applied in the late 1940s (page 652)

corporation business owned by investors who buy shares of stock in the business; investors risk only the amount of their investment (page 437)

coup d'état (koo day TAH) revolt against a government (page 676)

covenant binding agreement (page 43)

creole (KREE ohl) descendant of Spanish settlers born in the Americas (page 545)

Crusades series of wars launched by Christians against Muslims who controlled the Holy Land (page 180)

culture customs, ideas, and way of life of a group of people (page 11)

cuneiform (kyoo NEE uh FORM) term used to describe the wedge-shaped writing of the ancient Sumerians (page 34)

Cyrillic alphabet Slavic alphabet devised in the ninth century by Greek monks Cyril and Methodius (page 210)

czar (zahr) Russian word for Caesar; title of the ruler of the Russian Empire (page 213)

D

daimyo (DĪ myoh) most powerful warrior knights in Japan during the feudal period (page 257)

delta triangular area of marshy flatlands formed by deposits of silt at the mouths of some rivers (page 15)

demesne (dih MAYN) during the Middle Ages, a portion of manor land a lord reserved for his own use (page 159)

democracy government in which citizens have ruling power; first developed in ancient Athens (page 71)

denazification removing all traces of Nazism in Germany after World War II (page 649)

détente (day TAHNT) French word meaning relaxation; easing of international tension, especially between the Soviet Union and the United States (page 754)

devalue to lower the value of items such as coins (page 110)

dictator ruler with absolute power; in ancient Rome, a dictator could only hold power for six months (page 97)

direct democracy system of government in which citizens participate directly rather than through representatives (page 77)

direct primary election in which voters select candidates for office (page 480)

dissident (DIHS uh duhnt) person who speaks out against a government (page 752)

domestic system system in which a merchant paid peasants in the countryside to do work such as spinning and weaving, thus bypassing guild regulations (page 339)

donatario in sixteenth century Brazil, landowner of territory granted by the king of Portugal (page 333)

dynastic cycle rise and fall of Chinese dynasties according to the Mandate of Heaven (page 57)

dynasty (DI nuhs tee) ruling family that passes the right to rule from one member to another (page 19)

E

ecology (ee KAHL uh jee) relationship between living things and their environment (page 771)

émigré (EHM uh gray) person who flees his or her country for political reasons (page 401)

enclosure movement during the 1700s in Britain, the practice of fencing off common lands by individual landowners (page 429)

ecomienda (ehn koh mee EHN dah) right the Spanish government granted settlers in the Americas to demand taxes or labor services from Indians living on land (page 330)

Enlightenment name applied to the 1700s, when philosophers emphasized the use of reason, which they believed would free people from ignorance and perfect society (page 367)

entente cordiale "friendly understanding" between Britain and France in 1904, which preceded the alliance system that helped lead to World War I (page 566)

entrepreneur (AHN truh pruh NER) merchant willing to take financial risks in the hope of making large profits (page 337)

ephor in Sparta, overseer elected by the assembly to direct state affairs and supervise helots (page 73)

excommunication (EHKS kuh MYOO nuh KAY shuhn) exclusion from the sacraments of the Roman Catholic Church (page 164)

extended family large family group usually made up of a husband and wife, their unmarried children, their married sons, and the sons' wives and children (page 52)

extraterritoriality (EHKS truh TEHR uh TAWR ee AL uh tee) the right of foreigners to be protected by the laws of their own nations (page 532)

F

factory system system in which workers and machines are brought together in one place to manufacture goods (page 431)

fascism (FASH ihzm) political philosophy that calls for glorification of the state, a single-party system with a strong ruler, and aggressive nationalism; was advocated by Mussolini (page 614)

Fertile Crescent area of rich soil stretching from the Persian Gulf to the Mediterranean Sea (page 31)

feudal contract in the Middle Ages, rules governing the relationship between lord and vassals, based on traditional practices (page 156)

feudalism (FYOOD 'l ihzm) system of rule by local lords who were bound to a king by ties of loyalty; developed in Western Europe during the Middle Ages (page 155)

fief (feef) during the Middle Ages, an estate that a lord provided a vassal (page 156)

filial piety (FIHL ee uhl PĪ uh tee) respect for one's parents and elders; emphasized by Confucius (page 140)

flying buttress in Gothic cathedrals, stone arm leaning against outside wall to help support weight of roof (page 174)

fossil evidence of plant or animal life preserved in rock (page 3)

franchise (FRAN chiz) the right to vote (page 465)

free market market in which goods are bought and sold without restrictions (page 371)

fresco (FREHS koh) wall painting (page 66)

G

general strike mass walkout by unionized workers in all industries (page 585)

genetic engineering laboratory techniques that alter the genes of an organism (page 767)

glacier thick sheet of ice that spread down from polar regions during the ice ages (page 5)

glasnost policy of "openness" instituted by Soviet leader Mikhail Gorbachev (page 751)

grand jury jury deciding whether enough evidence exists to bring a case to trial (page 189)

guerrilla warfare (guh RIHL uh) from the Spanish word for little war; fighting comprised of hit-and-run attacks (page 411)

guild association of merchants or artisans that governed a town or craft in the Middle Ages (page 171)

H

haiku (HĪ koo) short Japanese poem with 17 syllables that creates a mood or describes a scene (page 259)

hejira (hih JĪ ruh) Muhammad's journey from Mecca to Medina in 622 (page 214)

helot in Sparta, slave who worked the land (page 73)

heretic according to the early Roman Catholic Church, anyone not belonging to the Church (page 152)

hierarchy (HĪ uh RAHR kee) group of persons according to rank (page 119)

hieroglyphics (HĪ er oh GLIHF ihks) system of writing developed by Egyptian priests in which pictures were used to represent words and sounds (page 18)

Holocaust (HAHL uh KAWST) the systematic murder of over 6 million Jews by the Nazis before and during World War II (page 642)

I

ideogram (IHD ee uh gram) picture that symbolizes an idea or action (page 18)

illumination decoration in the margins and on the first letter of paragraphs of Bibles made by monks in the Middle Ages (page 153)

imperator in Ancient Rome, commander-in-chief of the Roman armies (page 106)

imperialism (ihm PIHR ee uhl ihzm) domination by one country of the political, economic, or cultural life of another country or region (page 507)

inflation economic cycle in which an increase in the money supply results in an increase in prices (page 110)

interchangeable parts identical component parts that can be used in place of one another in manufacturing (page 437)

J

joint-stock company private trading company in which shares are sold to investors to finance business ventures (page 337)

journeyman person who completed an apprenticeship and then worked for a master craftsman to perfect his or her skills (page 172)

just price in the Middle Ages, price established by craft guilds, allowing for cost of materials and reasonable profit (page 172)

K

kami (KAH mee) spirits that early Japanese believed controlled the forces of nature (page 254)

karma (KAHR muh) in Hinduism, all the actions in a person's life that affect his or her fate in the next life (page 130)

kibbutz (kih BOOTS) Israeli settlement in which people live in community housing projects, work together, and share the profits of their labor (page 698)

knight in the Middle Ages, lesser noble who served as a mounted warrior for a lord (page 155)

kulak (koo LAHK) prosperous peasant in the Soviet Union who opposed collectivization during the 1930's (page 610)

L

laissez faire (LEHS ay FEHR) French phrase meaning let people do as they choose; used to describe an economic system in which the government does not interfere with the economy (page 449)

latifundia (LAT uh FUHN dee uh) vast estate in ancient Rome (page 103)

latitude (LAT uh TOOD) distance north or south of the Equator; measured in degrees (page 321)

law of gravity mathematic formula devised by Isaac Newton explaining the attraction of objects (page 369)

lay investiture (lay ihn VEHS tuh chuhr) practice during the Middle Ages whereby political rulers appointed many high Church officials (page 192)

legion military formation of ancient Rome made up of about 6,000 soldiers (page 97)

legitimacy (luh JIHT uh muh see) Metternich's principle of restoring to power the royal families that had lost their thrones when Napoleon conquered Europe (page 415)

liberalism during the 1800s, a philosophy that supported guarantees of individual freedom, political change, and social reform (page 415)

limited monarchy government in which a monarch's powers are limited, usually by a constitution and a legislative body (page 190)

loess fine soil distributed by wind and flood waters (page 54)

longitude (LAHN juh TOOD) the distance east or west of a certain point (page 322)

lord in the Middle Ages, powerful noble who maintained his own land but owed allegiance to the king (page 155)

lycée government-run school set up by Napoleon to develop knowledge and patriotism in children of the wealthy (page 408)

lyric poem in Ancient Greece, poem in which the poet's emotions or thoughts are sung by a musician playing a lyre (page 82)

M

mandate after World War I, a territory that was administered but not owned by members of the League of Nations (page 579)

manor during the Middle Ages, the lands, including a village and surrounding lands, administered by a lord (page 159)

martial law (MAHR shul) temporary rule by the military under which individual rights are limited (page 720)

martyr (MAHR ter) person who dies or suffers for his or her beliefs (page 119)

mass production method of manufacturing large quantities of goods in standard sizes (page 437)

matrilineal (MAT ruh LIHN ee uhl) describes a family in which children trace their family line through their mother (page 231)

mercantilism (MER kuhn tihl ihzm) economic philosophy maintaining that a nation's economic strength depends on exporting more goods than it imports (page 338)

messiah savior chosen by God (page 116)

mestizo (mehs TEE zoh) person in Spain's colonies in the Americas who was of mixed European and Indian heritage (page 545)

Middle Ages period of history in Europe following the fall of the Roman Empire and lasting from about 500 to 1350 (page 149)

militarism glorification of the military and a readiness for war (page 489)

mir in Czarist Russia, land granted to village peasants to farm and payoff over a period of 49 years (page 496)

missi dominici during Charlemagne's reign, royal officials who checked on the administrations of local nobles (page 152)

mobilization process of calling troops into active service (page 568)

modernization creation of a stable society capable of producing a high level of goods and services (page 538)

monarchy (MAHN uhr kee) government headed by a king or queen (page 69)

money economy economic system based on the exchange of money rather than on barter (page 41)

monopoly (muh NAHP uh lee) total control by one corporation of the market for a particular product (page 438)

monotheism (MAHN uh thee ihzm) worship of a single god (page 23)

monsoon (mahn SOON) seasonal wind; in India, the summer monsoon brings rain and the winter monsoon brings hot, dry weather (page 48)

multinational corporation large enterprise that operates in many countries (page 674)

N

nationalism feeling of pride for and devotion to one's country (page 411)

nationalize (NASH uh nuh LĪZ) to bring a part of the economy under government control (page 601)

nirvana (nihr VAH nuh) in Hinduism and Buddhism, the ultimate goal of life; the condition of wanting nothing (page 131)

nomad person who travels in search of food (page 5)

nuclear family family made up of parents, children, and occasionally grandparents (page 230)

O

ode in Ancient Greece, poem honoring special people or occasions (page 83)

oracle bones according to religious beliefs of the Shang dynasty in China, bones that could be used to predict the future (page 56)

ostracism (AHS trah sihzm) in ancient Greece, the temporary exile of a citizen from a city-state (page 72)

Ostpolitik policy of improving relations with communist nations of Eastern Europe instituted by Willy Brandt. (page 748)

P

pacifism refusal to fight in a war (page 627)

papyrus (puh PĪ ruhs) reed that grows along marshy shores; used for making paper in ancient Egypt (page 16)

parish rural district first organized by the Roman Catholic Church during Charlemagne's reign (page 152)

passive resistance nonviolent opposition and refusal to cooperate (page 587)

paternalism (puh TER n'l ihzm) system in which an imperial power governs its colonies closely because it believes that the people are not able to govern themselves (page 520)

patriarch in the Byzantine empire, bishop of major city appointed by the emperor (page 208)

patrician (puh TRIHSH uhn) member of the class of wealthy landowners in ancient Rome (page 96)

patrilineal (PAT ruh LIHN ee uh) describes a family in which children trace their family line through their father (page 231)

patroon wealthy landowner in New Netherland, who had much power in governing the estate (page 334)

peninsulare (peh NIHN suh LAHR ay) official sent by Spain to rule Spanish colonies in the Americas (page 545)

phalanx in Ancient Greece, a massive formation of heavily armed foot soldiers (page 70)

pharaoh (FAIR oh) title of the rulers of ancient Egypt who had absolute control over people's lives (page 19)

philosophe (fee loh ZOHF) French word meaning philosopher; person during the Enlightenment who believed that the use of science and reason would lead to human progress (page 370)

philosopher in Ancient Greece, person seeking wisdom and knowledge through systematic study and logic (page 85)

physiocrat (FIHZ ee uh KRAT) philosophe who searched for natural laws to explain the economy (page 371)

pictogram (PIHK tuh gram) picture used to represent an object (page 18)

plantation large estate operated by the owner or an overseer and farmed by workers living on it (page 332)

plebeian (plih BEE uhn) member of the class of common people in ancient Rome, including farmers, artisans, small merchants, and traders (page 96)

pogrom (poh GRAHM) violent raid on a Jewish community, often conducted by government troops (page 497)

polis in Ancient Greece, a city-state consisting of a fortified hilltop and its surrounding fields (page 69)

polytheism (PAHL ih thee ihzm) belief in many gods (page 9)

potlatch (PAHT latch) feast given by wealthy families among Native Americans who lived on the Pacific coast to prove their high social position (page 234)

praetor in Ancient Rome, judge chosen by the assembly to rule on all legal matters (page 97)

predestination (pree DEHS tuh NAY shun) idea that God has chosen who will be saved and who will be condemned (page 315)

prehistory period of time before writing was invented (page 3)

primary source first-hand account written by the person who experienced the event (page 38)

prime minister head of the cabinet in parliamentary governments, usually the leader of the largest party in the legislature (page 386)

proletariat (PROH luh TAIR ee uht) the working class (page 452)

propaganda (PRAHP uh GAN duh) spread of ideas to further a cause or damage an opposing cause (page 475)

proprietary colonies (pruh PRĪ uh TAIR ee) English colonies in North America owned by individuals, usually friends of the king (page 334)

protectorate (pruh TEHK tuhr iht) country with its own government that makes policies under the guidance of an outside power (page 507)

psychology the study of behavior (page 456)

pueblo in the early Southwest, small town with its own elected officials and council of elders (page 235)

purdah (PER duh) practice of secluding women; probably originated in northern India and spread to Islamic lands (page 244)

Q

quipu (KEE poo) cord with many knotted strings that was used by the Inca to record census data, the size of a harvest, and historical events (page 10)

R

rajah (RAH juh) elected chief of an Aryan tribe in ancient India (page 50)

recall vote that allows voters to remove elected officials from office if the officials are incompetent (page 480)

reconquista (REE kahn KEES tah) crusade launched by Christian knights to expel Muslims from Spain (page 195)

regionalism loyalty to a geographic area (page 550)

reincarnation (REE ihn kahr NAY shuhn) rebirth of the soul in another bodily form; a belief of Hinduism and Buddhism (page 51)

Renaissance (REHN uh SAHNS) period from about 1350 to 1600 in which European scholars revived the learning of ancient Greece and Rome (page 298)

reparation (REHP uh RAY shuhn) payment for war damages (page 578)

republic system of government in which citizens who have the right to vote choose their leaders (page 96)

romanticism school of thought in which emotion and imagination were considered more important than reason (page 457)

S

sachem council of Iroquois chiefs who settled disputes among members of tribes belonging to the Iroquois league (page 235)

sacrament (SAK ruh mehnt) one of the seven sacred rites administered by the Roman Catholic Church (page 164)

salon (suh LAHN) informal gathering at which writers, musicians, painters, and philosophers exchanged ideas (page 373)

samizdat (SAHM ihs DAHT) underground network in the Soviet Union through which dissidents circulate their writings (page 753)

samurai (SAM uh RĪ) warrior knights of Japan during the feudal period (page256)

satrapy province in the Persian Empire ruled by a governor responsible to the king (page 39)

savanna (suh VAN uh) grasslands dotted with scattered trees in which rainfall is often unreliable (page 223)

scholasticism (skuh LAS tuh sihzm) school of thought in which reason and logic were used to support Christian belief (page 178)

scientific method an approach to the study of the natural world in which experiments, observation, and mathematics are used to prove scientific theories (page 367)

scribe in ancient times, a person who knew how to read and write (page 10)

secondary source second-hand account based on the writing or evidence not directly experienced (page 38)

segregation (SEHG ruh GAY shuhn) the practice of separating people according to race (page 662)

sepoy (SEE poi) Indian soldier who served in a European army (page 527)

serf peasant who was tied to the lord's land (page 159)

shogun (SHOH guhn) after 1192, the chief general in Japan, who held more political power than the emperor (page 257)

silt a soil rich in minerals deposited by flooding rivers (page 9)

simony in the Middle Ages, buying and selling of religious offices (page 165)

socialism economic and political system in which society as a whole rather than private individuals own all property and operate all businesses (page 420)

sociology the study of society (page 456)

socratic method in Ancient Greece, question-and-answer technique, developed by Socrates, that used reasoning in the search for truth (page 86)

soviet (SOH vee iht) council of workers, soldiers, and intellectuals formed by Russian revolutionaries in 1917 (page 605)

sphere of influence region in which a power claims exclusive investment or trading privileges (page 507)

sputnik first satellite to orbit the earth, launched by the Soviet Union in 1957 (page 763)

status quo (STAYT uhs KWOH) existing state of affairs (page 418)

stupa large dome-like Buddhist structure containing the remains of a saintly monk (page 134)

sultan (SUHL t'n) Muslim ruler (page 243)

survival of the fittest Darwinian theory of natural selection, which states that the best-adapted individuals survive (page 453)

T

tao (DOW) in Taoism, a universal force that can only be felt; also the way a person achieves harmony with that force (page 140)

technology (tehk NAHL uh jee) tools and skills people use (page 7)

theocracy (thee AHK ruh see) form of government in which priests serve as kings (page 9)

tithe (tīth) payment to the Church of 10 percent of a person's income (page 152)

totalitarian state (toh TAL uh TAIR ee uhn) country in which the government is a single-party dictatorship that controls every aspect of citizens' lives (page 610)

tragedy in Ancient Greece, drama focussing on the causes of suffering, usually ending in disaster (page 82)

transistor small device controlling electrical currents, which contributed to the mass production of computers (page 765)

trial jury jury giving verdicts on cases brought to trial (page 189)

tribe group of related families who recognize a common ancestor, speak the same language, and share traditions and beliefs (page 50)

tribune (TRIHB yoon) official in ancient Rome who was elected by plebeians to speak for their interests (page 97)

tribute (TRIHB yoot) payment conquered areas were forced to make to the conquering state (page 103)

troubador (TROO buh dor) wandering poet who entertained at feudal castles (page 158)

tyranny (TIR uh nee) government headed by a single individual who seizes power by force (page 71)

U

ultimatum (UHL tuh MAYT uhm) final set of demands (page 567)

universal male suffrage right of all adult men to vote (page 421)

urbanization the movement of millions of people from rural villages to cities (page 656)

usury (YOO zhoo ree) practice of lending money for interest (page 183)

V

vassal in the Middle Ages, a lesser noble who served a powerful lord (page 155)

vernacular (ver NAK yuh ler) everyday language of people (page 175)

vertical integration form of business in which a corporation controls the industries that contribute to its final product (page 438)

veto power to block the action of another person or government body (page 96)

W

welfare state state in which the government assumes responsibility for people's social and economic well-being (page 655)

westernization adoption of western ideas and customs by nonwestern nations (page 692)

Z

zaibatsu (ZĪ baht SOO) wealthy Japanese families who bought the chief industries of the country in the 1880s and thereby came to dominate the Japanese economy (page 538)

zemstvo (ZEHMST voh) local elected assembly created by the Russian government under Alexander II (page 497)

ziggurat (ZIHG u rat) temple of god of a city-state in ancient Sumer (page 33)

Suggested Readings

Unit One Beginnings of Ancient Civilization

Chapter 1

Barringer, D. Moreau. *And the Waters Prevailed.* Dutton. A fictional account of Stone Age peoples in the Mediterranean region.

Braidwood, R.J. *Archaeologists and What They Do.* Franklin Watts. Informative, readable description of how archaeologists go about their work.

Hamblin, Dora Jane. *The First Cities.* Time-Life. An illustrated account of city life in prehistoric times.

Hawkes, Jacquetta. *The Atlas of Early Man.* St. Martin's Press. A comprehensive discussion of the achievements of early peoples; includes excellent maps, charts, and photographs.

Quennell, Marjorie, and Quennell, Charles B. *Everyday Life in Prehistoric Times.* Putnam. An imaginative account of the daily life of prehistoric peoples.

Chapter 2

Aldred, Cyril. *Tutankhamen's Egypt.* Scribner. A brief narrative of everyday life during Tutankhamen's reign; includes photographs.

Cottrell, Leonard. *Five Queens of Ancient Egypt.* Bobbs-Merrill. Highly readable portraits of five Egyptian queens.

Fairservis, Walter A. *Egypt, Gift of the Nile.* Macmillan. A brief, illustrated survey of ancient Egyptian life, religion, and art.

West, John Anthony. *Serpent in the Sky: The High Wisdom of Ancient Egypt.* Harper. A history of ancient Egyptian culture and achievements.

Waltari, Mika T. *The Egyptian.* Putnam. A lively novel about ancient Egypt as seen through the eyes of Sinuhe, a pharaoh's doctor.

Chapter 3

Edey, Maitland. *The Sea Traders.* Time-Life. A history of the Pheonicians.

Fairservis, Walter A. *Mesopotamia: The Civilization That Rose Out of Clay.* Macmillan. An illustrated discussion of daily life in Mesopotamia.

Goode, Ruth. *People of the First Cities.* Macmillan. A vivid description of the peoples living in the world's earliest known cities.

Renault, Mary. *The Persian Boy.* Bantam. A novel about a young slave boy who serves the Persian emperor Darius.

Chapter 4

Cotterell, Arthur, and Morgan, David. *China's Civilization.* Praeger. A brief survey of Chinese history and culture.

Diez, Ernest. *The Ancient Worlds of Asia.* Putnam. A survey of Asian civilizations.

Fairservis, Walter A. *Before the Buddha Came.* Scribners. A vivid account of the early civilizations of East Asia.

Schulberg, Lucille. *Historic India.* Time-Life. A summary of Indian history from 2500 B.C. to the 1900s; with photographs.

Unit Two Rise of Classical Civilizations

Chapter 5

Barker, D.R. *The Story of Ancient Athens.* St. Martin's Press. A description of life in Athens during its Golden Age.

Bowra, Maurice. *Classical Greece.* Time-Life. Informative account of daily life in Greece; with many pictures.

Coolidge, Olivia. *The Trojan War.* Houghton-Mifflin. A fast-paced story of the siege of Troy.

Renault, Mary. *The King Must Die.* Pantheon. A novel based on the legend of Theseus, a Greek hero.

Chapter 6

Coolidge, Olivia. *Men of Athens.* Houghton-Mifflin. A collection of short stories about prominent Athenians.

Finley, M.I. and Pleket, H.W. *The Olympic Games: The First Thousand Years.* Viking. Fascinating anecdotes about the games that began in ancient Greece.

Hamilton, Edith. *The Greek Way.* Avon. An analysis of Greek philosophy, literature, and art.

Quennell, Marjorie, and Quennell, Charles H. *Everyday Things in Ancient Greece.* Putnam. A survey of ancient Greek culture.

Ruskin, Ariane, and Batterberry, Michael. *Greek and Roman Art.* McGraw Hill. An illustrated history of Mediterranean art.

Chapter 7

Balsdon, J.P.V.D. *Roman Women: Their History and Habits.* John Day. A scholarly account of women of all classes in ancient Rome.

Casson, Lionel. *The Horizon Book of Daily Life in Ancient Rome.* American Heritage. An illustrated survey of Roman life during the second century A.D..

Hadas, Moses. *Imperial Rome*. Time-Life. A comprehensive illustrated history of the Roman Empire.

Lamb, Harold. *Hannibal: One Man Against Rome*. Bantam. An exciting biography of the Carthaginian general.

Wallace, Lew. *Ben-Hur*. Bantam. Fast-paced novel of ancient Rome based on a theme of revenge.

Chapter 8

Chambers, Mortimer, ed. *The Fall of Rome: Can It Be Explained?* Holt. A collection of essays by historians on the fall of Rome.

Grant, Michael. *Saint Paul*. Scribners. A biography of the man who helped spread Christianity.

Hamilton, Edith. *The Roman Way*. Avon. A description of Roman life based on the works of Roman writers.

MacMullen, Ramsay. *Constantine*. Dial. A fascinating biography of Rome's first Christian emperor.

Chapter 9

Kelen, B. *Confucius in Life and Legend*. Nelson. A thorough treatment of the life and times of Confucius.

Kelen, B. *Gautama Buddha*. Avon. An excellent portrait of the Buddha.

Loewe, M. *Everyday Life in Early Imperial China*. Putnam. An illustrated study of daily life in Han China.

Ross, Nancy Wilson. *Three Ways of Asian Wisdom: Hinduism, Buddhism, Zen*. Simon & Schuster. An illustrated analysis of three religious philosophies.

Unit Three Middle Ages in Western Europe

Chapter 10

Harksen, S. *Women in the Middle Ages*. Universe Books. A brief, illustrated discussion of the lives of medieval women.

La Fay, H. *The Vikings*. National Geographic. An illustrated account of Viking exploration, settlement, and conquests between 800 and 1000.

Munz, Peter, and Quennell, Peter, eds. *Life in the Age of Charlemagne*. Putnam. An illustrated description of Charlemagne's empire.

Rowling, M. *Everyday Life in Medieval Times*. Putnam. A vivid description of medieval people from many social and economic backgrounds.

Simons, Gerald. *Barbarian Europe*. Time-Life. A history of Europe in the early Middle Ages.

Chapter 11

Coulton, G.G. *Chaucer and His England*. Barnes & Noble. A vivid description of English life in Chaucer's time.

Duggan, Alfred. *The Story of the Crusades*. Pantheon. A highly readable account of the Crusades.

Fremantle, Anne. *Age of Faith*. Time-Life. An illustrated account of medieval life ranging from religion and politics to art, science, and literature.

Gies, Joseph. *Life in a Medieval City*. Apollo. A portrait of life in Troyes, site of two medieval trade fairs.

Chapter 12

Costain, Thomas B. *The Conquerors*. Doubleday. An interesting account of English kings from William the Conqueror to John.

Fawtier, Robert. *The Capetian Kings of France*. Barnes & Noble. A brief study of the Capetian kings.

Meade, Marion. *Eleanor of Aquitaine*. Hawthorn. An engrossing biography of an intelligent, energetic woman who played a key role in French and English politics.

Seward, Desmond. *The Hundred Years War: The English in France 1377–1453*. Atheneum. An exciting narrative of the Hundred Years' War.

Unit Four Golden Ages Outside Europe

Chapter 13

Glubb, John. *The Life and Times of Mohammed*. Stein and Day. A highly readable biography of Mohammed and the growth of Islam.

Hitti, Philip K. *Islam: A Way of Life*. University of Minnesota Press. A history of Islam from the 700s to the 1100s.

Sherrard, Phillip. *Byzantium*. Time-Life. An illustrated introduction to Byzantine civilization.

Wallace, Robert. *Rise of Russia*. Time-Life. An illustrated survey of Russian history.

Chapter 14

Chu, Daniel, and Skinner, Elliot. *A Glorious Age in Africa*. Doubleday. A fast-reading discussion of the empires of Ghana, Mali, and Songhai.

Courlander, Harold. *A Treasury of African Folklore*. Crown. A fascinating collection of myths, legends, and traditions of different African peoples.

Joseph, Alvin. *Indian Heritage of America*. Knopf. A history of the major Native American cultures.

Leonard, Jonathan Norton. *Ancient America.* Time-Life. An illustrated history of the Maya, Aztec, and Inca.

Chapter 15

Bothwell, Jean. *Dancing Princess.* Harcourt. An exciting novel set in India during the reign of Akbar.

Brent, Peter. *Genghis Khan: The Rise, Authority, and Decline of Mongol Power.* McGraw-Hill. A lively, illustrated narrative of the Mongol Empire.

Busch, Noel F. *The Horizon Concise History of Japan.* American Heritage. A beautifully illustrated history of Japan.

Yutang, Lin. *The Chinese Way of Life.* Collins World. A fictional story of an American-born Chinese boy whose travels in China are compared with those of Marco Polo.

Unit Five **Europe in Transition**

Chapter 16

Bainton, Roland H. *Here I Stand: A Life of Martin Luther.* Mentor. A scholarly, readable biography of Martin Luther, based on Luther's writings.

Chamberlain, E.R. *Everyday Life in Renaissance Times.* Putnam. An illustrated account of the daily life of many different people during the Renaissance.

Hartt, Frederick. *History of Italian Renaissance Art.* Prentice-Hall. An illustrated history of Italian painting, sculpture, and architecture.

Payne, Robert. *Leonardo.* Doubleday. A recent biography of Leonardo da Vinci.

Chapter 17

Hale, John R. *The Age of Exploration.* Time-Life. An illustrated account of the voyages of discovery between 1420 and 1620.

Kingsley, Charles. *Westward Ho!* Dodd, Mead. A fast-paced adventure novel about the competition for empire between Spain and England.

Morison, Samuel Eliot. *The European Discovery of America.* Oxford University Press. An illustrated history of European explorations in North and South America.

Morison, Samuel Eliot. *Christopher Columbus: Mariner.* Little, Brown. An account of the life of Columbus and his voyages of discovery.

Sanderlin, George. *Eastward to India.* Harper & Row. A highly readable account of the Portuguese voyages of exploration.

Chapter 18

Beloff, Max. *Age of Absolutism: 1600–1815.* Harper & Row. A scholarly, readable survey of Europe during the age of absolute monarchs.

Lamb, Harold. *The City and the Tsar: Peter the Great and the Move to the West, 1648–1762.* Doubleday. A fascinating biography of Peter the Great.

Mattingly, Garret. *The Armada.* Houghton-Mifflin. A detailed account of the famous naval battle between Spain and England in 1588.

Mitford, Nancy. *The Sun King: Louis XIV at Versailles.* Harper & Row. An account of the life of Louis XIV and his court at Versailles.

Unit Six **An Age of Revolution**

Chapter 19

Armitage, Angus. *Sun, Stand Thou Still: The Life and Work of Copernicus the Astronomer.* Harry Schuman. A fast-paced biography of Copernicus.

Bruun, Geoffry. *The Enlightened Despots.* Smith. A brief discussion of Enlightenment rulers.

Gay, Peter. *The Age of Enlightenment.* Time-Life. A thorough, illustrated treatment of Enlightment Europe.

Sootin, Harry. *Isaac Newton.* Julian Messner. A fast-moving biography of Newton.

Chapter 20

Cass, Canfield. *Samuel Adams' Revolution 1765–1776.* Harper & Row. An account of the causes, events, and heroes of the American Revolution.

Chidsey, Donald Barr. *The Birth of the Constitution.* Crown. An informal history of the issues and individuals that created the Constitution of the United States.

Howell, Roger. *Cromwell.* Little, Brown. A well-written biography of Oliver Cromwell.

Roberts, Clayton, and Roberts, David. *A History of England.* Prentice-Hall. A comprehensive survey of English history.

Chapter 21

Alderman, Clifford Lindsey. *Liberty, Equality, Fraternity: The Story of the French Revolution.* Julian Messner. A brief, readable account of the French Revolution.

Castelot, André. *Marie Antoinette.* Harper & Row. A profile of the young queen from her marriage at age 15 to her death at age 38.

Dickens, Charles. *A Tale of Two Cities.* Dutton. A classic novel that recreates the excitement and terror of the French Revolution.

Herold, J.C. *The Horizon Book of the Age of Napoleon.* Harper & Row. An illustrated history of the Napoleonic Age.

Chapter 22

Bernard, J. F. *Tallyrand: A Biography.* Putnam. A biography of Talleyrand, the arch rival of Metternich.

May, Arthur. *The Age of Metternich, 1814–1848.* Holt, Rinehart & Winston. A brief treatment of Europe during the time of Metternich.

Nicolson, Harold. *Congress of Vienna: A Study in Allied Unity.* Harcourt. An account of the Congress of Vienna and the problems European leaders faced after the defeat of Napoleon.

Unit Seven   **Dawn of the Industrial Age**

Chapter 23

Aiken, Joan. *Midnight Is a Place.* Viking. A fast-paced novel about children living in a factory town.

Eco, Umberto, and Zorzoli, G.B. *The Picture History of Inventions.* Macmillan. A collection of illustrations of major inventions from the Industrial Revolution to the present.

Hart, Roger. *English Life in the Nineteenth Century.* Putnam. An illustrated discussion of English life in the 1800s.

Zola, Émile. *Germinal.* Dutton. A novel about the lives of French miners.

Chapter 24

Cogniat, Raymond. *The Century of Impressionists.* Crown. An informative discussion of Impressionist painters, with full-color reproductions of paintings and drawings.

Curie, Eve. *Madame Curie.* Doubleday. A biography of Marie Curie written by her daughter.

deKruif, Paul. *Microbe Hunters.* Harcourt. A dramatic account of medical achievements, especially those of the 1800s.

Hugo, Victor. *Les Miserables.* Fawcett. A historical novel that realistically portrays French life in the 1800s.

Talmon, J.L. *Romanticism and Revolt: Europe 1815–1848.* Harcourt. A scholarly survey of currents of thought in the early 1800s.

Chapter 25

Billington, R.A. *Westward Expansion: A History of the American Frontier.* Macmillan. A comprehensive discussion of the westward growth of the United States.

Guérard, Albert. *Napoleon III.* Knopf. An informative biography of Louis Napoleon.

Ketchum, Robert. *The American Heritage Picture History of the Civil War.* American Heritage. A collection of photographs, paintings, drawings, and maps of the Civil War.

Longford, Elizabeth. *Queen Victoria: Born to Succeed.* Harper & Row. An account of the life of Queen Victoria and British society in the 1800s.

Mackenzie, Midge. *Shoulder to Shoulder.* Knopf. An illustrated history of suffragettes in Britain.

Chapter 26

Cowles, Virginia. *The Kaiser.* Harper & Row. An account of William II and his role in the growth of German unity.

Crankshaw, Edward. *The Shadow of the Winter Palace.* Viking. A comprehensive history of Russia under the Romanovs.

Dill, Marshall. *Germany: A Modern History.* University of Michigan. A general history of Germany in the 1800s and 1900s.

McLeon, R.A. *Cavour and Italian Unity.* Exposition. An account of the life of Cavour and his role in unifying Italy.

Unit Eight   **The Age of Imperialism**

Chapter 27

Davidson, Basil. *Black Mother: The Years of the African Slave Trade.* Little, Brown. A thorough treatment of the transatlantic slave trade from the 1500s to 1800s.

Eaton, Jeanette. *David Livingstone: Foe of Darkness.* Morrow. A readable biography of this famous scientist and explorer.

McKown, Robin. *The Colonial Conquest of Africa.* Watts. A readable account of European imperialism in Africa.

Moorehead, Alan. *The White Nile.* Harper. An account of European explorers seeking the source of the Nile River in the late 1800s.

Ulli, Beier. *African Poetry: An Anthology of Traditional African Poems.* Cambridge University. A fascinating collection of poetry from all regions of Africa.

Chapter 28

Buck, Pearl S. *Imperial Woman.* John Day. A fictionalized biography of Tzu-hsi, last empress of the Manchu dynasty.

Collier, Richard. *Great Indian Mutiny.* Dutton. An exciting account of the Sepoy Rebellion.

Edwardes, Michael. *Asia in the European Age, 1498–1953.* Praeger. An account of European imperialism in Asia.

Fleming, Peter. *The Siege at Peking*. Harper & Row. An interesting narrative of the Boxer Rebellion.

Reishauer, Edwin O. *Japan: Past and Present*. Knopf. A comprehensive survey of Japanese history and culture.

Chapter 29

Baily, Bernadine. *Famous Latin-American Liberators*. Dodd. Brief biographies of ten heroes of Latin America independence.

Brown-Baker, Nina. *He Wouldn't Be King: The Story of Simón Bolívar*. Vanguard. A readable biography of the famous South American liberator.

Brown-Baker, Nina. *Juárez: Hero of Mexico*. Vanguard. A biography of Juárez.

Freidel, Frank. *The Splendid Little War*. Little, Brown. A collection of photographs illustrating the Spanish-American War.

Parkinson, Wanda. *The Gilded African: Toussaint L'Ouverture*. Quartet Books. A biography of the leader of Haiti's war of independence.

Shafer, Robert J. *History of Latin Ameria*. Heath. A general survey of Latin American history.

Unit Nine **World War and Peace**

Chapter 30

Baldwin, Hanson. *World War I: An Outline History*. Grove. A brief but comprehensive history of World War I.

Quentin, Reynolds. *They Fought for the Sky*. Holt. An account of the use of airplanes in World War I.

Sellman, R.R. *The First World War*. Criterion. A readable discussion of the political, economic, and social causes of World War I.

Tuchman, Barbara. *The Guns of August*. Macmillan. A dramatic account of the outbreak of World War I and the first month of the war.

Chapter 31

Allen, Frederick Lewis. *Only Yesterday: An Informal History of the Nineteen Twenties*. Harper. An interesting account of the Roaring Twenties in the United States.

Fischer, Louis. *The Life of Mahatma Gandhi*. Harper & Row. A thorough, well-documented biography of Gandhi.

Kinross, Lord. *Attaturk*. Morrow. A biography of Mustafa Kemal, the man who transformed Turkey into a modern state.

Sontag, Raymond J. *A Broken World 1919–1939*. Harper & Row. A scholarly treatment of the years between World War I and World War II.

Steinbeck, John. *The Grapes of Wrath*. Viking. A moving novel about dispossessed farm workers in the United States during the Great Depression.

Chapter 32

Deutscher, Isaac. *Stalin: A Political Biography*. Oxford University. A balanced discussion of Stalin and his programs.

Fermi, Laura. *Mussolini*. University of Chicago. A biography of Mussolini that reveals much about his personality.

Koehn, Ilse. *Mischling, Second Degree*. Greenwillow. An absorbing account of a German girl who became a leader in the Hitler Youth, unaware of her Jewish heritage.

Solzhenitsyn, Alexander. *One Day in the Life of Ivan Denisovich*. Dutton. A devastating portrayal of life in a Stalinist prison camp.

Rubin, Arnold P. *The Evil That Men Do: The Story of the Nazis*. Julian Messner. An account of the Nazi rise to power based on first-hand interviews.

Chapter 33

Frank, Anne. *The Diary of a Young Girl*. Doubleday. Diary of a young Dutch Jewish girl who spent several years hiding from the Nazis.

Hersey, John. *Hiroshima*. Bantam. An account of the bombing of Hiroshima based on interviews with six survivors.

Meltzer, Milton. *Never to Forget: The Jews of the Holocaust*. Harper & Row. A sensitive treatment of the Holocaust.

Mosley, Leonard. *The Battle of Britain*. Time-Life. A fascinating series of photographs with a brief narrative explaining the heroic air battle of Britain.

Sulzberger, C.L. *The American Heritage Picture Story of World War II*. American Heritage. A comprehensive photographic history of World War II.

Chapter 34

Goldman, Eric F. *The Crucial Decade and After: America, 1945–1960*. Random House. A useful discussion of the challenges of the postwar era in the United States.

Fréymond, Jacques. *Western Europe Since the War: A Short Political History*. Praeger. An informative survey of postwar developments in Europe.

Medvedev, Roy A., and Medvedev, Zhores A. *Khrushchev, The Years in Power*. Columbia University. An informative account of Khrushchev and his policies.

Stromberg, Roland N. *Europe in the Twentieth Century*. Prentice-Hall. A survey of European political, social, and economic developments from 1914 to the present.

Unit Ten **The World Today**

Chapter 35

Bernheim, Marc and Evelyne. *In Africa*. Atheneum. A collection of photographs showing the cultures of different African peoples.

Crane, Louise. *Ms. Africa*. Lippincott. Brief biographies of prominent African women.

Jahn, Janheinz. *Muntu: The New African Culture*. Grove Press. A study of the blending of traditional African cultures and western ideas.

Foster, Philip J. *Africa South of the Sahara*. Macmillan. A survey of modern Africa.

Chapter 36

Eban, Abba. *My Country: The Story of Modern Israel*. Random House. An account of Israel since 1948 by a former Israeli prime minister.

Fernea, Elizabeth. *Guests of the Sheikh*. Anchor. A readable account of an American woman's experience in an Iraqi village.

Forbis, William H. *Fall of the Peacock Throne: The Story of Iran*. Harper & Row. An analysis of the revolution in Iran.

Mikhail, Mona. *Images of Arab Women*. A recent discussion of the changing roles of women in the Arab world.

Modern World Problems: Arab-Israeli Conflict. Greenhaven. A balanced treatment of the background and issues in the Arab-Israeli conflict.

Pearson, Robert. *Through Middle Eastern Eyes*. Praeger. A collection of writings that give Middle Eastern views of family, religion, and politics.

Chapter 37

Clyde, Paul H., and Beers, Burton F. *The Far East, A History of Western Impacts and Eastern Responses 1830–1975*. Prentice-Hall. A solid treatment of political developments in East Asia in the 1800s and 1900s.

Edmonds, I.G. *Pakistan: Land of Mystery, Tragedy and Courage*. Holt. An informative description of the creation of Pakistan and the problems it faced after independence.

Fitzgerald, C.P. *Mao Tse-tung and China*. Holmes & Meier. A recent portrait of Mao Tse-tung.

Fitzgerald, Frances. *Fire in the Lake: The Vietnamese and the Americans in Vietnam*. Little, Brown. An analysis of United States involvement in Vietnam.

Schell, Orville. *In the People's Republic: An American's First-Hand View of Living and Working in China*. Vintage. A westerner's view of life in China today.

Chapter 38

Bailey, Helen M., and Nasatir, A.P. *Latin America: The Development of Its Civilization*. Prentice-Hall. A thorough treatment of Latin American history and culture.

Burns, E. Bradford. *Latin America, A Concise Interpretive History*. Prentice-Hall. A sympathetic discussion of modern Latin American history.

Perl, Lila. *Mexico: Crucible of the Americas*. William Morrow. An illustrated, readable survey of Mexican geography, history, and culture.

Walton, Richard J. *The United States and Latin America*. Seabury. A history of United States relations with Latin America.

Chapter 39

Brandt, Willy. *A Peace Policy for Europe*. Holt. A discussion of the political divisions between Western and Eastern Europe.

Hughes, H. Stuart. *Contemporary Europe: A History*. Prentice-Hall. A recent review of Europe in the twentieth century.

Schecter, Leona. *An American Family in Moscow*. Little, Brown. A revealing first-hand account of an American family's experiences in the Soviet Union.

Waldheim, Kurt. *The Challenge of Peace*. Rawson, Wade. A scholarly, readable discussion of United Nations by the former Secretary-General.

White, Theodore. *Breach of Faith: Fall of Richard Nixon*. Atheneum. The Watergate story, written by a distinguished journalist.

Chapter 40

George, Susan. *How the Other Half Dies: The Real Reasons for World Hunger*. Allenheld, Osmun. An examination of famine in developing nations.

Osborne, Adam. *Running Wild: The Next Industrial Revolution*. McGraw-Hill. A survey of the effects of the computer revolution.

Robinson, Donald. *The Miracle Finders: The Stories Behind the Most Important Breakthroughs in Modern Medicine*. David McKay. An informative account of medical advances since 1945, with portraits of the physicians and scientists responsible for the breakthroughs.

Ward, Barbara. *Progress for a Small Planet*. Norton. A discussion of the challenges facing people around the world: energy, food, medicine, and industrialization.

INDEX

Italicized page numbers refer to illustrations. The *m, c,* or *p* preceding the number refers to a map (*m*), chart (*c*), or picture (*p*) on that page. An *n* following a page number refers to a footnote.

World War II, 630–33, 635–37, *m638*, 641–43; after World War II, 655–56; Common Market and, 658, 748; independence of African colonies, 668, 670–72; Suez crisis, 694; in the 1960s and 1970s, 747–48. *See also* Industrial Revolution; World War I.

Great Depression: in US, *p593*, 593–95, 622; in Great Britain, 595–96, *c596*; in France, 596; in Eastern Europe, 597; in Latin America, 601, 729; in Italy, 615; in Germany, 617; in Japan, 620–21

Great Leap Forward, 711

Great Plains Indians, *m234*, 235, 292

Great Royal Road, 39–40, *m40*

Great Schism, 199, 209, 311

Great Trek, 517, *m517*

Great Wall of China, 142, *p142,* ·*143*

Greco-Roman civilization, 113–114, 275; Islamic preservation of, 177, 194, 218; Byzantine preservation of 209–210; Renaissance revival of 301–3, 310–11; Enlightenment and, 371, 375

Greece: Egypt and, 24; geography, 65, *m66*; 271; early civilizations, 65–69; 271–73; Dark Age, 69, 73; city-states 69–74, 271–72; colonies, 69, 70, 95, *m96*, 100; tyrannies, 70–71; democracy in, 64–65; 71–72, 77; 271–72; Persian Wars, 75–76; Athenian Empire, 76–77; Peloponnesian Wars, 77–78, 272; under Philip II, 88; under Alexander the Great, 88–89, *m90*, 273, 688; Roman conquest, 102, 113; independence, 418, 419, 424, 457, 501, 566; First Balkan War and, 567; after World War I, 579, 581, *m581;* war with Turkey, 598; in World War II, 632; civil war, 651, 652; joins NATO, 653, *m654;* Cyprus and, 693; in 1960s and 1970s, 749

Greek civilization: 64–65, 81–92, 271–73; literature, 67–68, 82–83, 92; philosophy, 69, 85–87, 91–92; social classes, 70–71; slavery, 71–73, 77, 451; education; 72, 74; women, 72–74, *p* 73, 77, 83; drama, 80, 81–82; religion, 81; arts, 83–84, *p91*, 92, 272–73; science, 85, 90–91; medicine, *p85*, 85–86, 90; Hellenistic culture, 89–92, 273; influence on Rome, 103, 107, 113, 275

Greek language, 119, 165, 208

Greek Orthodox Church, 695

Green Revolution, 770, *c770*, 771

Greenland, 154, *m789*

Gregory VII, Pope, 192–93, *p193*

Grenada, *m789*

Gross National Product, 718, *c718*

Guam, 541, 556, 634

Guatemala, 548, *m549* 735, 736, *m789*

Guerrilla warfare, 411; in China, 710; in Vietnam, 721 734; in Latin America, 735, 736, 737, 741

Guiana, 416, *m549*, *m789*

Guild, 171–73, 184, 283, 397; decline, 339

Guinea, 670, *m671*, 676, *m786*

Guinea-Bissau, *m671*, *m786*

Guizot, François, 420

Gujarat, 707

Gulf of Aqaba, 699, *m700*

Gulf of Tonkin resolution, 722

Gunpowder, 141, 199, 248

Gupta Empire, 128, 135, *m135*, 136, 137, 277–78

Gustavus Adolphus, king of Sweden, 354

Gutenberg, Johann, 308

Guyana, *m789*

Habeas Corpus Act, 384, *c386*

Hadrian, 107

Haile Selassie, 616, *670n*

Haiti, 546, *p546*, *m549*, 550, 551, *m556*, 601, 736, *p743*, *m789*

Hammurabi, Babylonian ruler, 36–37, 267; law code, 36–38, 43, 267

Handel, George Frederick, 375, 376

Han dynasty, *m142*, 142–146, 279

Han Fei Tzu, 141

Hannibal, 101

Hanoi, *m787*

Hanseatic League, *m170*, 170–71

Hapsburg Empire, 343–44, *m354;* Spanish, 344–347, 353; Austrian, 347, 351–52, 499; Thirty Years' War and, 352–54. *See also* Austrian Empire.

Harappa, 47–49, *m48*, 268

Harding, Warren G., 591

Hargreaves, James, 430

Harold, king of England, *p188*

Harun al-Rashid, 217

Harvey, William, 369

Hastings, battle of, *p188*

Hatshepsut, Egyptian pharaoh, 22, 265

Hausa-Fulani people, 515, 677

Havana, *m789*

Hawaii, 541, *m640*, 664

Haydn, Franz Joseph, 376, 461

Hebrews, 41–44, 267. *See also* Jews.

Heian, *m254*, 255

Hejira, 214

Heliopolis, *m23*, 27

Hellenistic civilization, 89–92, 273; science, 90–91; philosophy, 91–92; arts, *p91*, 92; influence on Rome, 103, 107, 113; in India, 134, 137, 273

Helots, 73

Henry I, king of England, 188–89

Henry II, king of England, 186, 188–89, 199

Henry II, king of France, 311, 347

Henry IV, Holy Roman emperor, 192–93, *p193*

Henry IV, king of France, 347–48

Henry VII, king of England, 201

Henry VIII, king of England, 314, 315–16, 379, *383n*

Henry the Navigator, 323, 338

Heretic, 152, 164, 196, 199

Hermes, 81, *p84*

Herodotus, *m16*, 74, 75, 87

Herophilis, 90

Herzl, Theodor, *599n*

Highlands, climate, *m784*

Hidalgo, Manuel, 548, 550

Hideyoshi, Japanese ruler, 258

Hierarchy, 119

Hieroglyphic writing: Egyptian, 18–19, 22; Olmec, 236, 237

Hildebrand. *See* Gregory VII.

Himalaya Mountains, 63, *m48*, 54, 267, *m787*

Hindenburg, Paul von, 617, 618

Hinduism, 51, *m132*, 243, 276–77, 293; 540; beliefs, 129–30, 244; Buddhism and, 130–31, 135, 243, 276–77; in Southern India, 135–36; Islam and, 244

Hindu Kush Mountains, 47, *m48*, 50, 128, 134, 267–68

Hippocrates, 85–86

Hiroshima, 641

Hispanic Americans, 663

Hispaniola, *m324*, 325, 546, 550

Hitler, Adolf, *p604*, 616, 624, 648; rise of, 617–18; anti-Semitism, 618–19, 633, 642; goals, 619–20; aggressions, 626–28; in World War II, 629–30, *p631*, 632–33, 637; death, 639, 649

Hittite Empire, *m23*, 23, 31, 37, *50n*, 688, 262–63, 267, 688

Ho Chi Minh City, 722

Hobbes, Thomas, 370

Hohenzollern family, 354–55, 490

Holbein, Hans, 305, *p306*

Holocaust, 641–42, *p642*

Holy Alliance, 417–418

Holy Land, 179–82, *m180*, 283

Holy Roman Empire, 150, 285–86, *492n;* early history, 192–94; Protestant Reformation and, 313–14, *m317;* Hapsburg rule, 343; Thirty Years' War and, 352–54, *m354;* dissolved, 409

Homer, 67, *67n*, 68, 69, 83, 175

Honduras, 548, *m549*, 557, *m789*

Hong Kong, 532, *m533*, 634, *m640*, 723, *m787*

Hoover, Herbert, 594

Horace, 113, 115, 275

Horn of Africa, 511, 683

House of Commons, 189–90, 285, 379–80, 382, *p382*, *p631. See also* Parliament.

House of Lords, 189, 285, 379, 382. *See also* Parliament.

House of Representatives, 391

Hudson, Henry, *m324–25*, 326

Hudson River, 326, 333

Hugo, Victor, 458

Huguenots, 315, 334, 347–48, 349

Humanism, 300–1, 306–7, 310

Human rights, 743–44, 753–54

Hundred Years' War, 199–201, *m200*

Hungary: Ottoman control, 343, 358; Hapsburg rule, 354, *m354*, 355, *p356;* revolution of 1848, 422; kingdom, 500, 501; independence, 577, 579; during 1920s and 1930s, 597; in World War II, 631, 642; in Soviet bloc, 651; uprising of 1956, 660, *p660;* in 1970s, 753–54; today, *m788*

Huns, 122–23, *m123*, *c134*, 143, 207, 243, 276

Hunter-gatherers, 5, 6–7, 225, 230, 234

Huss, John, 199, 311–12

Hyksos, 20–21, 34, *42n*

Iberian Peninsula, *m788*

Ibn Battuta, 228

Ibo, 677

Ice Age, 5–6, 231–33

Iceland, 154, *m788*

Icon, 208–9

Ideogram, 18, 54

Ife people, *m227*, 233

Ignatius of Loyola, 317

Iliad (Homer), 67–68, 69, 72, 82, 113

Imam, 214

Illustration Credits (continued from page iv)

UNIT TWO **Page 62** *tl* Giraudon/Art Resource; *tr* Borromeo/Art Resource; *bl* Newsweek Books Picture Collection; *br* Giraudon/Art Resource; **63** *tl, tr, bl* Collection of Laurie Platt Winfrey; *br* The Granger Collection; **64** EPA; **67** EPA/Scala; **68** National Archeological Museum, Athens; **70** EPA/Scala; **73** William Francis Warden Fund, Museum of Fine Arts, Boston; **74** TBM; **75** Newsweek Books Picture Collection; **80** National Archeological Museum, Athens; **82** The Bettmann Archive, Inc.; **83** EPA/Allinari; **84** Scala/Art Resource; **85** National Archeological Museum, Athens; **86** Scala/Art Resource; **89** EPA/Scala; **91** Giraudon/Art Resource; **94, 97** EPA/Scala; **99** Raymond V. Schoder, SJ; **101** The Granger Collection; **105** EPA/Allinari; **109, 112** EPA/Scala; **114** EPA; **115, 117** EPA/Scala; **124** EPA; **128** Freer Gallery, Smithsonian Institution; **130** Collection William Rockhill Nelson Gallery of Art, Atkins Museum of Fine Arts; **137** EPA; **139** Courtesy, Museum of Fine Arts, Boston; **142** EPA/B. Salz; **144** TBM; **145** Bibliothèque Nationale.

UNIT THREE **Page 148** *tl* Collection of Laurie Platt Winfrey; *tr* Giraudon/Art Resource; *bl* The Granger Collection; *br* Collection of Laurie Platt Winfrey; **149** *tl* The Granger Collection; *tr* Giraudon/Art Resource; *bl, br* Collection of Laurie Platt Winfrey; **150** EPA/Scala; **156** The Dean and Chapter Library, Durham Cathedral; **158** The Granger Collection; **161** EPA/Scala; **165** The Pierpont Morgan Library; **168** TBM; **172** Bibliothèque Nationale; **174** EPA/Scala; **177** Staatlich Museum Preussischer Kulturbesitz, Berlin (West); **178** Bibliothèque Nationale; **181** EPA/Scala; **183** The Granger Collection; **186** EPA/Scala; **188** Municipal Museum of Bayeux; **193** EPA/Scala; **195** Rose Fujimoto; **201** *l* EPA/Giraudon; *r* Bibliothèque Nationale.

UNIT FOUR **Page 204** *tl* Lee Boltin; *tr* The Granger Collection; *bl* Collection of Laurie Platt Winfrey; *br* Giraudon/Art Resource; **205** *tl* Art Resource; *tr* Scala/Art Resource; *bl* Lee Boltin; *br* Giraudon/Art Resource; **206** EPA/Scala; **209** Bruno Barbey, Magnum, Inc.; **211** The Bettmann Archive, Inc.; **215** The Metropolitan Museum of Art, Rogers Fund, 1940; **218** The Granger Collection; **219** The Metropolitan Museum of Art, The Cora Timken Burnett Collection of Persian Miniatures and Other Persian Art Objects. Bequest of Cora Timken Burnett, 1957; **222** TBM; **228** Bibliothèque Nationale; **231** Bridgeman Art Library/Art Resource; **232** TBM; **237** Peabody Museum, Harvard; **238** TBM; **242** Bibliothèque Nationale; **246** Victoria and Albert Museum; **248** Eugene Fuller Memorial Collection, Seattle Art Museum; **249** National Gallery of Canada, Ottawa; **250** Museum of Fine Arts, Boston; **259** Kobe Municipal Art Gallery.

UNIT FIVE **Page 296** *tl, tr, bl, br* Scala/Art Resource; **297** *tl* National Maritime Museum, Greenwich, England; *tr, bl* The Granger Collection; *br* Giraudon/Art Resource; **298, 300** EPA/Scala; **302** EPA; **304** *l* EPA/Scala; *r* EPA/Allinari; **305** EPA/Scala; **306** EPA; **308** The Granger Collection; **309** EPA; **310** EPA/Scala; **313** The Granger Collection; **316** National Portrait Gallery, London; **320** The Granger Collection; **321** Museum of the History of Science, Oxford, England; **322** National Maritime Museum, London; **329** AMNH; **332** National Maritime Museum, London; **337, 342, 345** EPA/Scala; **348** The National Gallery, London; **350** Giraudon/Art Resource; **353** EPA; **356** The Granger Collection; **360** The Granger Collection.

UNIT SIX **Page 364** *tl* The Granger Collection; *tr* Giraudon/Art Resource; *bl* Collection of Laurie Platt Winfrey; *br* The Granger Collection; **365** *tl* Giraudon/Art Resource; *tr* Scala/Art Resource; *bl* The Granger Collection; *br* © Yale University Art Gallery; **366, 368** EPA/Scala; **371** Wedgwood; **372** EPA/Snark; **374** TBM; **375** EPA/Giraudon; **378** Historical Society of Pennsylvania; **380** EPA/Scala; **381** TBM; **382** NYPL; **388** American Antiquarian Society; **394** Bibliothèque Nationale; **397** EPA/Giraudon; **399** EPA/Scala; **401** Giraudon/Art Resource; **405** The Granger Collection; **408** EPA/Scala; **414** Lauros/Giraudon; **416** The Granger Collection; **418** Copyright reserved to H.M. the Queen; **420** EPA/Snark.

UNIT SEVEN **Page 426** *tl* JOSSE/Art Resource; *tr, bl* The Granger Collection; *br* TBM; **427** *tl* Chicago Historical Society; *tr, bl* The Granger Collection; *br* Collection of Laurie Platt Winfrey; **428** EPA/Scala; **430** The Granger Collection; **431** EPA; **436** Culver Pictures, Inc.; **437** U.S. Dept. of the Interior, National Park Service, Edison National Historic Site; **438** UPI; **441** NYPL; **442**

The Granger Collection; **444** International Museum of Photography at George Eastman House; **445** Insurance Company of North America; **448** EPA/Scala; **450** NYPL; **451** EPA/Snark; **453** The Granger Collection; **454** Pasteur Institute, Paris; **456** Culver Pictures, Inc.; **458** EPA/Scala; **460** EPA/Scala, Jerry Palubniak; **461** The Granger Collection; **464** The Museum of London; **466** The Bettmann Archive, Inc.; **468** The Mansell Collection; **473** The Phillips Collection, Washington; **474** EPA/Scala; **478** LC; **480** Photograph by Jacob A. Riis, The Jacob A. Riis Collection, Museum of the City of New York; **481** LC; **484** EPA; **486** EPA/Scala; **488** The Granger Collection; **493** NYPL; **494** Courtesy of the Krupp Foundry; **497** NYPL; **498** EPA.

UNIT EIGHT **Page 504** *tl* New Haven Colony Historical Society; *tr* ORION/Art Resource; *bl* Casa Pardo, Buenos Aires; *br* The Granger Collection; **505** *tl* Collection of Laurie Platt Winfrey; *tr* The Bettmann Archive; *b* Scala/Art Resource; **506** Biblioteca Mediceo Laurenziana; **510** Giraudon/Art Resource; **512** AMNH; **513** The Granger Collection; **515** EPA/Scala; **518** EPA/Snark; **522** Royal Geographic Society, London; **523** The Mansell Collection; **526** Bibliothèque Nationale; **529** The Granger Collection; **531** EPA/Scala; **534** LC; **535** UPI; **536, 538, 541** EPA/Scala; **544** EPA; **546** The Granger Collection; **547** Caribbean Tourism Association; **551** TBM; **553** EPA; **557** LC.

UNIT NINE **Page 560** *tl* Indiana University of Art; *tr* Scala/Art Resource; *bl, br* The Granger Collection; **561** *tl* Giraudon/Art Resource; *tr* LC; *bl,* The Granger Collection; *br* LC; **562** The Granger Collection; **564** EPA; **565** EPA/Snark; **567** UPI; **571** Imperial War Museum; **575** Brown Brothers; **576** New Jersey Historical Society; **580** Imperial War Museum; **584** EPA; **586** The Granger Collection; **587** Culver Pictures, Inc.; **589** UPI; **590** EPA; **592, 593** LC; **598** The Granger Collection; **600** Culver Pictures, Inc.; **604** The Pentagon; **606** The Granger Collection; **608** Sovfoto; **610** UPI; **612** Sovfoto; **615** Brown Brothers; **619** Culver Pictures, Inc.; **624, 626** EPA; **631** UPI; **635** National Archives; **636** LC; **642** F.D.R. Library; **646** EPA; **647** Newsweek Books Picture Collection; **651** LC; **652** Culver Pictures, Inc.; **656** Fred Mayer, Woodfin Camp & Assoc.; **659** UPI; **660** Erich Lessing, Magnum Photos, Inc.; **662** Museum of Modern Art/Film Stills Archive; **663** UPI.

UNIT TEN **Page 666** *tl* Rene Burri/Magnum; *tr* Steve Benbow/Woodfin Camp & Assoc.; *bl* Marc & Evelyne Bernheim/Woodfin Camp & Assoc.; *br* Ludwig/Pictorial Parade; **667** *tl* M. Heron; *tr* Tannenbaum/Sygma; *bl* Peter Marlow/Magnum; *br* Rene Burri/Magnum; **668** Marilyn Silverstone, Magnum Photos, Inc.; **672** Marc & Evelyne Bernheim/Woodfin Camp & Assoc.; **674** *l* Marc & Evelyne Bernheim/Woodfin Camp & Assoc.; *r* Campbell/Sigma; **678** Marc & Evelyne Bernheim/Woodfin Camp & Assoc.; **679** Tanganyika Information Services; **683** *t* David Burnett, Mekele Camp, Tigray; *b* Marc & Evelyne Bernheim/Woodfin Camp & Assoc.; **686** Robert Azzi/Woodfin Camp & Assoc.; **688** Abu Hander/Woodfin Camp & Assoc.; **690, 691** Robert Azzi/Woodfin Camp & Assoc.; **695** EPA/Scala; **697** Olivier Rebbot/Woodfin Camp & Assoc.; **699** Keren Hayesod, United Israel Appeal; **701** Susan McElhinney/Woodfin Camp & Assoc.; **704** Bob Davis/Woodfin Camp & Assoc.; **707** *t* Marc & Evelyne Bernheim/Woodfin Camp & Assoc.; *b* Jenhagir Gazdar/Woodfin Camp & Assoc.; **712** Blair Seitz, EPA; **714** William Campbell/Sygma; **715** Alon Reininger, Contact Press; **717** George Fisher, VISCUM, Woodfin Camp & Assoc.; **719** UPI; **720** Charlyn Zlotnik/Woodfin Camp & Assoc.; **726** EPA; **727** UPI; **731** United Nations; **733** Loren McIntyre/Woodfin Camp & Assoc.; **734** UPI; **737** Bob Nickelsberg/Woodfin Camp & Assoc.; **739** Diego Goldberg/Sygma; **740, 743** EPA; **746** Marc Bulka, Gamma; **748** Julian Calder/Woodfin Camp & Assoc.; **750** J. Pavlovsky/Sygma; **751** *t* The Society of Geographical Photography, EPA; *b* A. Nogues/Sygma; **752** Sygma; **755** Henri Bureau/Sygma; **756** Leif Skoogfors/Woodfin Camp & Assoc.; **759** *t* Baron Wolman/Woodfin Camp & Assoc.; *b* John Ficara/Woodfin Camp & Assoc.; **762, 764** NASA; **765** Dan McCoy/Rainbow; **766** John Blaustein/Woodfin Camp & Assoc.; **771** Tom Bytes/Sygma; **772** Wally McNamee/Woodfin Camp & Assoc.; **773** William Hubbell/Woodfin Camp & Assoc.; **776** Ira Wyman/Sygma; **777** *l, r* Marilyn Grayburn.

REFERENCE SECTION **Page 790** *l, r* EPA; **791** *l* The Cleveland Museum of Art, Gift of George P. Bickford; *r* EPA/Scala; **792** *l* TBM; *r* EPA; **793** *l* EPA/Scala; *r* EPA.